The Handbook of Language Teaching

Blackwell Handbooks in Linguistics

This outstanding multi-volume series covers all the major subdisciplines within linguistics today and, when complete, will offer a comprehensive survey of linguistics as a whole.

Already published:

The Handbook of Child Language
Edited by Paul Fletcher and Brian MacWhinney

The Handbook of Phonological Theory
Edited by John A. Goldsmith

The Handbook of Contemporary Semantic Theory
Edited by Shalom Lappin

The Handbook of Sociolinguistics
Edited by Florian Coulmas

The Handbook of Phonetic Sciences
Edited by William J. Hardcastle and John Laver

The Handbook of Morphology
Edited by Andrew Spencer and Arnold Zwicky

The Handbook of Japanese Linguistics
Edited by Natsuko Tsujimura

The Handbook of Linguistics
Edited by Mark Aronoff and Janie Rees-Miller

The Handbook of Contemporary Syntactic Theory
Edited by Mark Baltin and Chris Collins

The Handbook of Discourse Analysis
Edited by Deborah Schiffrin, Deborah Tannen, and Heidi E. Hamilton

The Handbook of Language Variation and Change
Edited by J. K. Chambers, Peter Trudgill, and Natalie Schilling-Estes

The Handbook of Historical Linguistics
Edited by Brian D. Joseph and Richard D. Janda

The Handbook of Language and Gender
Edited by Janet Holmes and Miriam Meyerhoff

The Handbook of Second Language Acquisition
Edited by Catherine J. Doughty and Michael H. Long

The Handbook of Bilingualism
Edited by Tej K. Bhatia and William C. Ritchie

The Handbook of Pragmatics
Edited by Laurence R. Horn and Gregory Ward

The Handbook of Applied Linguistics
Edited by Alan Davies and Catherine Elder

The Handbook of Speech Perception
Edited by David B. Pisoni and Robert E. Remez

The Blackwell Companion to Syntax, Volumes I–V
Edited by Martin Everaert and Henk van Riemsdijk

The Handbook of the History of English
Edited by Ans van Kemenade and Bettelou Los

The Handbook of English Linguistics
Edited by Bas Aarts and April McMahon

The Handbook of World Englishes
Edited by Braj B. Kachru, Yamuna Kachru, and Cecil L. Nelson

The Handbook of Educational Linguistics
Edited by Bernard Spolsky and Francis M. Hult

The Handbook of Clinical Linguistics
Edited by Martin J. Ball, Michael R. Perkins, Nicole Müller, and Sara Howard

The Handbook of Pidgin and Creole Studies
Edited by Silvia Kouwenberg and John Victor Singler

The Handbook of Language Teaching

Edited by

Michael H. Long and Catherine J. Doughty

A John Wiley & Sons, Ltd., Publication

This edition first published 2009

© 2009 Blackwell Publishing Ltd except for editorial material and organization © 2009 Michael H. Long and Catherine J. Doughty

Blackwell Publishing was acquired by John Wiley & Sons in February 2007. Blackwell's publishing program has been merged with Wiley's global Scientific, Technical, and Medical business to form Wiley-Blackwell.

Registered Office
John Wiley & Sons Ltd, The Atrium, Southern Gate, Chichester, West Sussex, PO19 8SQ, United Kingdom

Editorial Offices
350 Main Street, Malden, MA 02148-5020, USA
9600 Garsington Road, Oxford, OX4 2DQ, UK
The Atrium, Southern Gate, Chichester, West Sussex, PO19 8SQ, UK

For details of our global editorial offices, for customer services, and for information about how to apply for permission to reuse the copyright material in this book please see our website at www.wiley.com/wiley-blackwell.

The right of Michael H. Long and Catherine J. Doughty to be identified as the authors of the editorial material in this work has been asserted in accordance with the Copyright, Designs and Patents Act 1988.

Wiley also publishes its books in a variety of electronic formats. Some content that appears in print may not be available in electronic books.

Designations used by companies to distinguish their products are often claimed as trademarks. All brand names and product names used in this book are trade names, service marks, trademarks or registered trademarks of their respective owners. The publisher is not associated with any product or vendor mentioned in this book. This publication is designed to provide accurate and authoritative information in regard to the subject matter covered. It is sold on the understanding that the publisher is not engaged in rendering professional services. If professional advice or other expert assistance is required, the services of a competent professional should be sought.

Library of Congress Cataloging-in-Publication Data
  The handbook of language teaching / edited by Michael H. Long and Catherine J. Doughty.
      p. cm. — (Blackwell handbooks in linguistics)
    ISBN 978-1-4051-5489-5 (hardcover : alk. paper) 1. Language and languages—Study and teaching—Handbooks, manuals, etc. 2. Second language acquisition—Handbooks, manuals, etc. I. Long, Michael H. II. Doughty, Catherine.
    P51.H3265 2009
    418.0071—dc22

                                                                    2009008867

A catalogue record for this book is available from the British Library.

Set in 10/12 Palatino by Graphicraft Ltd, Hong Kong
Printed and bound in Singapore by Fabulous Printers Pte Ltd

1   2009

Craig Chaudron (1946–2006)

Contents

Contributors

Kathleen M. Bailey
Kathleen M. Bailey received her PhD from the University of California at Los Angeles. She is a professor of Applied Linguistics at the Monterey Institute of International Studies, where she has taught since 1981. In 1998–99 she was the President of the international TESOL association.

Alan Beretta
Alan Beretta is Professor of Linguistics at Michigan State University. His research is in neurolinguistics and has been published in such journals as *Brain and Language*, *Cognitive Brain Research*, and *Aphasiology*.

David Brett
David Brett worked in Italy as an ESL teacher for 10 years before becoming a researcher in English Linguistics at the University of Sassari. He has published and presented widely on New Technologies and Second Language Learning, with particular reference to pronunciation teaching. He has also held training workshops for language teachers on various aspects of technology-enhanced teaching, both in Italy and in other countries.

James Dean Brown
James Dean ("JD") Brown is Professor of Second Language Studies at the University of Hawai'i at Manoa. He has authored or co-authored numerous articles and books on topics as diverse as second language testing and quantitative research methods, language curriculum development, using surveys in language programs, teaching connected speech, and heritage language curriculum.

Martin Bygate
Martin Bygate is Professor in Applied Linguistics and Language Education at Lancaster University, UK. He has undertaken funded research and taught courses on oral language teaching and development. Principal publications are *Speaking*

(1987, Oxford University Press), *Grammar and the Language Teacher* (co-edited with A. Tonkyn and E. Williams, 1994, Prentice-Hall), *Researching pedagogic tasks: Second language learning, teaching and testing* (co-edited with P. Skehan & M. Swain, 2001, Pearson Educational Ltd), and, co-authored with Virginia Samuda, *Tasks in second language learning* (2008, Palgrave).

Carol A. Chapelle

Carol A. Chapelle, Professor of TESL/Applied Linguistics at Iowa State University, is Past President of the American Association for Applied Linguistics (2006–7), former editor of TESOL Quarterly (1999–2004), and co-editor of the Cambridge Applied Linguistics Series. Her books include *Computer applications in second language acquisition: Foundations for teaching, testing, and research* (2001, Cambridge University Press), *English language learning and technology: Lectures on applied linguistics in the age of information and communication technology* (2003, John Benjamins), *Assessing language through technology* (with Dan Douglas, 2006, Cambridge University Press), *Building a validity argument for the Test of English as a Foreign Language* (with Mary Enright & Joan Jamieson, 2007, Routledge) and *Tips for teaching with CALL* (2008, Pearson-Longman).

Teresa Chung

Mihwa Chung (Teresa) teaches at Korea University. She has published articles on technical vocabulary, the vocabulary of newspapers, and developing reading speed in a foreign language. Her PhD thesis from Victoria University of Wellington was on the methodology of developing lists of technical vocabulary and the role of technical vocabulary in technical texts.

Joseph Collentine

Joseph Collentine is Professor of Spanish at Northern Arizona University. He has published articles and research about study abroad, the acquisition of grammar, and corpus linguistics. He is currently the director of the Spanish Masters programs at NAU and the coordinator of the Spanish online program.

Graham Crookes

Graham Crookes is Professor, Department of Second Language Studies, University of Hawai'i at Manoa, where he is also Executive Director, ESL Programs. His most recent books are *A Practicum in TESOL* and *Making a Statement: Values, Philosophies, and Professional Beliefs in TESOL* (2003 and 2008, Cambridge University Press).

Jim Cummins

Jim Cummins is Professor and Canada Research Chair in the Curriculum, Teaching and Learning Department at the Ontario Institute for Studies in Education (OISE) at the University of Toronto. His research focuses on literacy development in multilingual school contexts, as well as on the potential roles of technology in promoting language and literacy development.

Robert DeKeyser

Robert DeKeyser (PhD, Stanford University) is Professor of Second Language Acquisition at the University of Maryland. His research is mainly on second language acquisition, with emphasis on cognitive-psychological aspects such as implicit versus explicit learning, automatization of rule knowledge, and individual differences and their interaction with instructional treatments. He has published in a variety of journals, including *Studies in Second Language Acquisition, Language Learning, Language Testing, The Modern Language Journal, TESOL Quarterly*, and *AILA Review*. He has contributed chapters to several highly regarded handbooks, and he recently published an edited volume with Cambridge University Press entitled *Practice in a Second Language: Perspectives from Applied Linguistics and Cognitive Psychology* (2007).

Catherine J. Doughty

Catherine J. Doughty is Senior Research Scientist and SLA Area Director at the Center for the Advanced Study of Language at the University of Maryland, and is an affiliate Professor of SLA at the University of Maryland.

Nick C. Ellis

Nick C. Ellis is Research Scientist at the English Language Institute and Professor of Psychology at the University of Michigan. His research interests include language acquisition, cognition, reading in different languages, corpus linguistics, cognitive linguistics, psycholinguistics, and emergentist accounts of language acquisition.

John Flowerdew

John Flowerdew is Professor of Applied Linguistics, Centre for Language Education Research, School of Education, University of Leeds. For many years he worked at the City University of Hong Kong. He has also worked in South America and the Middle East. As well as writing and editing a number of books, he has published widely in the leading Applied Linguistics, Language Teaching and Discourse Analysis journals, focusing on academic discourse, corpus linguistics, and English for Specific Purposes. His most recent book (with Lindsay Miller) is *Second Language Listening* (2005, Cambridge University Press). His most recent edited book (with Vijay Bhatia and Rodney Jones) is *Advances in Discourse Studies* (2008, Routledge).

Christine Goh

Christine Goh is Associate Professor of applied linguistics in the National Institute of Education, Singapore (Nanyang Technological University). Her interests are in listening and speaking development, and the role of metacognition in L2 learning. She has authored many international journal articles and book chapters on listening research and teaching methodology for listening.

Ewa M. Golonka

Ewa M. Golonka holds a PhD in Russian Linguistics and Second Language Acquisition from Bryn Mawr College. She has taught Russian, linguistics, and SLA at various universities. Currently, she is an Assistant Research Scientist at the University of Maryland Center for Advanced Study of Language.

Marta González-Lloret

Marta González-Lloret has taught at the Spanish division of the LLEA department at the University of Hawai'i for more than a decade. She holds a PhD in Second Language Acquisition from the University of Hawai'i at Manoa and her research interests include second language acquisition, technology for language learning and teaching, and teacher training.

Kira Gor

Kira Gor is Associate Professor of Russian and Second Language Acquisition in the School of Languages, Literatures, and Cultures at the University of Maryland. Her research interests include psycholinguistic mechanisms underlying cross-linguistic and second-language processing of phonology and morphology.

William Grabe

William Grabe is Regents Professor of English at Northern Arizona University, where he teaches in the MATESL and PhD in Applied Linguistics programs. His interests include reading, writing, written discourse analysis, and the disciplinary status of applied linguistics. His most recent book is *Reading in a Second Language: Moving from Theory to Practice* (2009, Cambridge University Press).

Rick de Graaff

Rick de Graaff is a language teaching consultant/researcher at the IVLOS Institute of Education, Utrecht University, the Netherlands. His main fields of interest include: task effectiveness in language teaching, the role of instruction in L2 pedagogy, the role of peer feedback in collaborative writing, and content and language integrated learning. Most recently he has contributed to the *International Journal of Bilingual Education and Bilingualism* and *ITL – International Journal of Applied Linguistics*.

Alex Housen

Alex Housen (MA, UCLA; PhD, University of Brussels) is Senior Lecturer in English, Second Language Acquisition and Bilingualism at the University of Brussels (VUB). His research interests include second/foreign language acquisition, second/foreign language teaching, and bilingualism. His recent publications include *Investigations in Instructed Second Language Acquisition* (with M. Pierrard, 2005, Mouton de Gruyter) and *Bilingualism: Basic Principles and Beyond* (with J. M. Dewaele and L. Wei, 2003, Multilingual Matters).

Ken Hyland

Ken Hyland is Professor of Education and director of the Centre for Academic and Professional Literacies at the Institute of Education, University of London. He has published over 130 articles and 13 books on language teaching and academic writing, most recently *Academic Discourse* (2009, Continuum). He is co-editor of the *Journal of English for Academic Purposes*.

Eunice Eunhee Jang

Eunice Eunhee Jang is Assistant Professor at Ontario Institute for Studies in Education of the University of Toronto. Her research interests include validity and fairness issues in language testing and cognitive diagnostic assessment. Her research has been published in *Journal of Educational Measurement, Language Testing* (in press), *International Journal of Testing, Journal of Mixed Methods Research,* and in the book *New Directions in Psychological Measurement with Model-Based Approaches* (edited by S. Embretson & J. S. Roberts, American Psychological Association).

Scott Jarvis

Scott Jarvis is an Associate Professor of Linguistics at Ohio University, where he teaches courses on second language acquisition, language testing, and other areas of applied linguistics. His main research interests are cross-linguistic influence (or language transfer) and lexical diversity, and his work has appeared in journals such as *Studies in Second Language Acquisition, Language Learning, Applied Linguistics,* and *Language Testing*. He is also co-author with Aneta Pavlenko of *Crosslinguistic Influence in Language and Cognition* (2008, Routledge), and is the Associate Editor for *Language Learning*.

Renée Jourdenais

Renée Jourdenais is an associate professor in the MATESOL/MATFL program at the Monterey Institute of International Studies, where she specializes in second language acquisition and in language teacher education. She also has extensive experience in curriculum development and in language assessment. Her recent research work explores the development of teacher knowledge.

Keiko Koda

Keiko Koda is Professor of Second Language Acquisition and Japanese in the Department of Modern Languages at Carnegie Mellon University. Her major research areas include second language reading, biliteracy development, psycholinguistics, and foreign language pedagogy. Her recent books include *Insights into Second Language Reading* (2005, Cambridge University Press), *Reading and Language Learning* (2007, Blackwell), and *Learning to Read across Languages* (2008, Routledge).

Antony John Kunnan

Antony John Kunnan is Professor of TESOL and Language Education at California State University and the University of Hong Kong respectively. He has published in the *Annual Review of Applied Linguistics, Language Testing,* and *Language*

Assessment Quarterly and in many edited volumes and handbooks. He was the President of the International Language Testing Association in 2004 and is the founding editor of *Language Assessment Quarterly*.

Diane Larsen-Freeman

Diane Larsen-Freeman is Professor of Education, Professor of Linguistics, and Research Scientist at the English Language Institute, University of Michigan. Her most recent book (2008) is *Complex Systems and Applied Linguistics*, co-authored with Lynne Cameron and published by Oxford University Press.

Michael H. Long

Michael H. Long is Professor of SLA in the School of Languages, Literatures, and Cultures at the University of Maryland, College Park, where he teaches courses and seminars in the PhD program in SLA. Mike is the author of over 100 articles and several books, and has served on the editorial boards of *Studies in Second Language Acquisition, TESOL Quarterly, Language Teaching Research*, and other journals. His recent publications include *The Handbook of Second Language Acquisition*, co-edited with Catherine Doughty (2003, Blackwell), *Second Language Needs Analysis* (2005, Cambridge), and *Problems in SLA* (2007, Lawrence Erlbaum).

Sandra Lee McKay

Sandra Lee McKay is Professor of English at San Francisco State University, where she teaches courses in sociolinguistics, as well as methods and materials for graduate students in TESOL. Her books include *Teaching English as an International Language: Rethinking Goals and Approaches* (2002, Oxford University Press, winner of the Ben Warren International Book Award), *Sociolinguistics and Language Teaching* (edited with Nancy Hornberger, 1996, Cambridge University Press) and *Researching Second Language Classrooms* (2006, Lawrence Erlbaum). Her newest book, *International English in Its Sociolinguistic Contexts: Towards a Socially Sensitive Pedagogy* (with Wendy Bokhorst-Heng, 2008, Routledge) is an examination of the social and sociolinguistic context of present-day English teaching and learning.

Rosamond F. Mitchell

Rosamond F. Mitchell is Professor of Education at the University of Southampton. Her research interests are in the area of Second Language Acquisition, especially of French. She is particularly interested in theories of language learning and their empirical implications, and in the interface between linguistic theory and cognitive approaches to the learning of second languages. She is co-editor of *Teaching Grammar: Perspectives in Higher Education* (1996) and co-author of *Second Language Learning Theories* (2004).

Silvina Montrul

Silvina Montrul is Associate Professor of Spanish, Linguistics and Second Language Acquisition at the University of Illinois at Urbana-Champaign. She is author of *The Acquisition of Spanish* (2004, John Benjamins) and *Incomplete*

Acquisition in Bilingualism. Re-examining the Age Factor (2008, John Benjamins). Her research focuses on linguistic and psycholinguistic approaches to adult second language acquisition and bilingualism, in particular syntax, semantics, and morphology. She is also an expert in language loss and retention in minority-language-speaking bilinguals.

Diane Musumeci
Diane Musumeci is Associate Professor and Head in the Department of Spanish, Italian, and Portuguese at the University of Illinois at Urbana-Champaign. She is the author of *Breaking Tradition: An Exploration of the Historical Relationship Between Theory and Practice in Second Language Teaching* (1997, McGraw-Hill).

Paul Nation
Paul Nation is professor of Applied Linguistics in the School of Linguistics and Applied Language Studies at Victoria University of Wellington, New Zealand. His specialist interests are language teaching methodology and vocabulary learning. His latest book on vocabulary is *Teaching Vocabulary: Strategies and Techniques* published by Cengage Learning (2008), and two books, *Teaching ESL/EFL Listening and Speaking* (with Jonathan Newton) and *Teaching ESL/EFL Reading and Writing*, have just appeared from Routledge/Taylor and Francis.

John M. Norris
John M. Norris is associate professor in the Department of Second Language Studies at the University of Hawai'i at Mānoa. His work focuses on assessment, program evaluation, research methods, and task-based language teaching in foreign and second language education. His recent publications include a single-author book *Validity Evaluation in Language Assessment* (2008, Peter Lang) and a co-edited volume with Lourdes Ortega *Synthesizing Research on Language Learning and Teaching* (John Benjamins, 2006).

Lourdes Ortega
Lourdes Ortega is associate professor at the University of Hawai'i, where she teaches graduate courses in second language acquisition and foreign language education. Her most recent book is *Understanding Second Language Acquisition* (2009, Hodder Arnold).

Robert Phillipson
Robert Phillipson is a Professor Emeritus at Copenhagen Business School, Denmark. His *Linguistic Imperialism* (1992, Oxford University Press) has also been published in China and India. Recent publications include *English-Only Europe? Challenging Language Policy* (2003, Routledge) and *Linguistic Imperialism Continued* (Orient Blackswan). Several articles can be downloaded from www.cbs.dk/staff/phillipson.

Charlene Polio
Charlene Polio is an associate professor at Michigan State University, where she directs the MA TESOL program. She has published research on second language

writing, classroom discourse, and second language acquisition and in journals such as the *Journal of Second Language Writing*, the *Modern Language Journal*, and *Studies in Second Language Acquisition*. She is the incoming editor of the *Annual Review of Applied Linguistics* and co-editor of *Multiple Perspectives on Interaction: Second Language Research in Honor of Susan M. Gass* to be published by Routledge.

Håkan Ringbom

Håkan Ringbom is emeritus professor of English at Åbo Akademi University, Turku/Åbo, Finland. Among his previous publications are *The Role of the First Language in Foreign Language Learning* (1987) and *Cross-Linguistic Similarity in Foreign Language Learning* (2007), both with Multilingual Matters.

William P. Rivers

William P. Rivers is Chief Linguist at Integrated Training Solutions, Arlington, VA. His publications include *Language and National Security in the 21st Century* (with Richard D. Brecht, 2001) and *Language and Critical Area Studies after September 11* (with Richard D. Brecht, Ewa Golonka, and Mary E. Hart). His research interests include third language acquisition, computational sociolinguistics, and language policy.

Peter Robinson

Peter Robinson is Professor of Linguistics and SLA in the Department of English, Aoyama Gakuin University, Shibuya, Tokyo, where he teaches and supervises research on second language acquisition, cognitive abilities for language learning, and effects of instruction. Recent publications include Task Complexity, the Cognition Hypothesis and Second Language Instruction, special issue of the *International Review of Applied Linguistics* (co-edited with Roger Gilabert, 2007), *Handbook of Cognitive Linguistics and Second Language Acquisition* (co-edited with Nick Ellis, 2008, Routledge), and *Second Language Task Complexity: Researching the Cognition Hypothesis of Learning and Performance* (in press, John Benjamins).

Carsten Roever

Carsten Roever is a Senior Lecturer in Applied Linguistics in the School of Languages and Linguistics at the University of Melbourne. His research interests include second language acquisition, interlanguage pragmatics, and second language assessment. He has written several book chapters, journal articles, and the book *Testing ESL Pragmatics* (2005, Peter Lang) and has co-authored *Language Testing: The Social Dimension* with Tim McNamara (2006, Blackwell).

Steven J. Ross

Steve Ross teaches at the School of Policy Studies, Kwansei Gakuin University. His research has appeared in *Language Learning, Applied Linguistics, International Journal of Testing, Language Testing, Journal of Pragmatics, Studies in Second Language Acquisition, Second Language Research, System, International Review of Applied Linguistic, TESOL Quarterly*, and in several edited volumes.

Rani Rubdy

Dr Rani Rubdy is Senior Fellow at the National Institute of Education, Nanyang Technological University in Singapore. She is co-editor of two recently published books, *English in the World: Global Rules, Global Roles* (Continuum, 2006) and *Language as Commodity: Global Structures, Local Marketplaces* (Continuum, 2008). Her other recent publications include the book chapters, 'Remaking Singapore for the new age: Official ideology and the realities of practice' in *Decolonization, Globalization: Language-in-education Policy and Practice* (edited by Angel M. Y. Lin & Peter W. Martin, 2005, Multilingual Matters) and 'Language planning ideologies, communicative practices an their consequences' in Springer's *Encyclopedia of Language and Education* (2008).

Tove Skutnabb-Kangas

Tove Skutnabb-Kangas, emerita (University of Roskilde, Denmark and Åbo Akademi University, Finland), bilingual from birth in Finnish and Swedish, has written or edited around 50 monographs and almost 400 articles and book chapters, in 32 languages, about minority education, linguistic human rights, linguistic genocide, subtractive spread of English and the relationship between biodiversity and linguistic diversity. She lives on an ecological farm with husband Robert Phillipson. For publications, see http://akira.ruc.dk/~tovesk/.

Kris Van den Branden

Kris Van den Branden is a professor of linguistics at the Katholieke Universiteit Leuven. He is one of the current directors of the Centre for Language and Education at the same university. His main research interests are in task-based language teaching, the role of interaction in instructed language learning, and the diffusion of innovations in the educational field. He has published in many international journals, and has edited a volume on task-based language teaching in the Cambridge University Press Applied Linguistics Series.

Larry Vandergrift

Larry Vandergrift is Professor at the Official Languages and Bilingualism Institute (OLBI) at the University of Ottawa. His research in the teaching of second/foreign language listening has been published in *Annual Review of Applied Linguistics*, *Applied Linguistics*, *Canadian Modern Language Review*, *Language Learning*, *Language Teaching*, *Modern Language Journal*, and more. He is currently a co-editor of the *Canadian Modern Language Review* and director of the research centre at OLBI.

Karen Vatz

Karen Vatz is a graduate student in the Second Language Acquisition PhD program at the University of Maryland. She is currently working on her dissertation on the representation and processing of grammatical gender in advanced L2 learners. Other areas of interest include bilingual lexical representation and critical period effects.

Alan Waters
Alan Waters is a Senior Lecturer in the Department of Linguistics and English Language, Lancaster University, UK. He has taught EFL and trained teachers in the UK and several other parts of the world. He has published a number of books and articles on a range of ELT topics.

Jessica Williams
Jessica Williams is a Professor of Linguistics at the University of Illinois at Chicago, where she also directs the TESOL program. She has published on variety of topics, including second language writing, lexical acquisition, and the effect of focus on form. Her latest publications include an edited volume (with Bill VanPatten, 2006, Routledge), *Theories in Second Language Acquisition* and the student text, *Academic Encounters: American Studies* (Cambridge University Press, 2007).

Part I Overview

1 Language Teaching

MICHAEL H. LONG

Hundreds of millions of people voluntarily attempt to learn languages each year. They include adults who seek proficiency in a new language for academic, professional, occupational, vocational training, or religious purposes, or because they have become related through marriage to speakers of languages other than their mother tongue. Then, there are (some would argue, "captive") school-age children who experience their education through the medium of a second language, or for whom one or more foreign languages are obligatory subjects in their regular curriculum. In addition to these easily recognizable groups, language teachers around the world are increasingly faced with non-volunteers. These are the tens of millions of people each year forced to learn new languages and dialects, and sometimes new identities, because they have fled traumatic experiences of one kind or another – war, drought, famine, disease, intolerable economic circumstances, ethnic cleansing, and other forms of social conflict – crossing linguistic borders in the process. Since the horror and frequency of such events show no signs of decreasing, language teaching is likely to remain a critical matter for these groups for the foreseeable future, with the scale of forced mass migrations if anything likely to grow in the twenty-first century, due to the potentially disastrous effects of climate change.

For both groups of learners, volunteers and non-volunteers, language teaching is increasingly recognized as important by international organizations, governments, militaries, intelligence agencies, corporations, NGOs, education systems, health systems, immigration and refugee services, migrant workers, bilingual families, and the students themselves. With the growing recognition come greater responsibility and a need for accountability. LT[1] is rarely a matter of life or death, but it often has a significant impact on the educational life chances, economic potential and social wellbeing of individual students and whole societies. Students and entities that sponsor them increasingly want to know not just that the way they are taught works, but that it constitutes optimal use of their time and money.

Demonstrating effectiveness and efficiency is often difficult. Historically, LT has been regarded as an art – or a craft, at least – not a science, with scant regard and little financial support for research. Demand for some languages, notably English and Chinese, has been so great in recent years that, with demand far exceeding supply, few consumers have been in a position to quibble over the quality of their instruction. In the case of some rarely taught languages for which there is a sudden surge in need, e.g., as a by-product of military actions or natural disasters, students and sponsors have no choice but to accept whatever can be found, adequate or not. Even in the case of widely taught languages, like English, Chinese, Arabic, French, German, and Spanish, research that is carried out is sometimes criticized for having been conducted in real classrooms and other "natural" instructional settings, with a resulting lack of control over significant variables that may have influenced the outcomes of interest. Alternatively, when conducted under controlled experimental conditions, studies are sometimes criticized for having produced findings that may not generalize to real classrooms. Series of studies of the same phenomena in both natural and artificial instructional environments, utilizing a variety of research methods, are clearly desirable.

Despite these problems, the situation has gradually improved in recent years, with steady growth in the amount and sophistication of research on LT itself, and in disciplines with much to say about the process LT is designed to facilitate, language learning. Of those feeder disciplines, theory and research in some areas of second language acquisition (SLA) are the most directly relevant, but work in psychology, educational psychology, anthropology, curriculum and instruction, and more, is also valuable. This is not to say that all the answers are known, or even that most of them are, but LT prescriptions and proscriptions that ignore theory and research findings in those fields are gradually and justifiably losing credibility. Where they are kept viable, it is chiefly by commercial interests, which still wield enormous influence, and the continued marketability of whose wares is often best served by ignorance about effectiveness.

The authors of each chapter in this volume were asked wherever possible to draw on research findings when making proposals. This, they have done. Also, while many of them specialize in the teaching of English, on which the greatest number of studies have been carried out, and/or operate in English-speaking countries, they were asked not to focus on the teaching of any one language or any one teaching context – foreign, second, lingua franca, etc. – but to choose examples and synthesize research findings and teaching experience from, and relevant to, a variety of languages and settings. They were asked to provide balanced evaluations of major positions and approaches, but granted scope to advance their own views. This, they have also done.

As is visible in the Table of Contents, in addition to coverage of core foundational issues, *The Handbook of Language Teaching* contains chapters on a few topics seldom found in comparable anthologies and textbooks. These chapters reflect recent developments and changing emphases in the field, or ones we believe deserve more attention. Examples include chapters on the language-learning brain; on programs designed specifically for heritage learners, about whom there is now an explosion of (sometimes rather uninformed) writing; on advanced learners; study abroad; third language, conversion, and cross-training programs; LCTLs (less commonly taught languages), which geopolitics are rapidly making a lot more commonly taught; and (not unrelated) on reading new scripts; as well as on radical language teaching and the diffusion of innovation. In another departure from the norm, instead of one chapter on teaching various skills, and a separate one on testing them, we invited one author to cover both in a single chapter. The idea is to avoid overlap and facilitate greater coherence of treatment. We selected individuals whose prior work showed they can handle both at the required level. While certainly not unique to this volume, there is also expert coverage of the increasingly apparent and important politics and social and political context of language teaching.

One author conspicuously missing from the assembled company is the late Craig Chaudron, a widely respected expert on many aspects of LT, and a valued colleague and close personal friend. Craig had agreed to contribute a chapter to the handbook, but as many readers will know, died unexpectedly in 2006. His untimely passing is a tragic loss for all who knew him, and for the field as a whole. This volume is humbly dedicated to his memory.

NOTES

We are grateful to Danielle Descoteaux, Julia Kirk, and the staff at Wiley-Blackwell for their support at all stages of the development of this volume, and to the reviewers of individual chapters.

1 The following abbreviations are used throughout the volume:

FL – foreign language
L1 – first, or native, language
L2 and SL – second language in the broad sense, including any additional language to the L1
LT – language teaching
SLA – second language acquisition.

Part II Social, Political, and Educational Contexts of Language Teaching

2 The Social and Sociolinguistic Contexts of Language Learning and Teaching

SANDRA LEE MCKAY AND
RANI RUBDY

We live in an age of linguistic diversity increased greatly by globalization, the movement of people across borders, and the widespread acquisition of additional languages by individuals in their own countries. All of these factors have led to an increase in the number of second-language learners and the kinds of contexts in which they are learning languages.

This chapter is about the social and sociolinguistic context of present-day foreign and second-language learning and teaching. In examining the social context of language learning, we focus on how language teaching contexts are affected by the larger social, political, and educational setting in which the teaching takes place. In examining the sociolinguistic context of language teaching, we focus on how the linguistic features of interactions, both inside and outside of the classroom, are affected by the social context in which the interaction takes place.

Our division is in many ways similar to a traditional distinction made in the field of sociolinguistics where one of the major debates is whether to take social or linguistic factors as primary in investigating the relationship between the social context and language variables. As evidence of this debate, Wardaugh (1992) and others make a distinction between *the sociology of language* and *sociolinguistics*. Whereas the sociology of language investigates the manner in which social and political forces influence language use, sociolinguistics takes linguistic factors as primary in its investigations of language and society.

In keeping with this distinction, the first part of the chapter focuses on two areas of investigation typically studied in the sociology of language that influence the social context of language learning: language planning and policy, and societal multilingualism. The second part of the chapter focuses on two areas of investigation typically studied in what Wardaugh terms sociolinguistics: language contact and variation, and ethnographic sociolinguistics. The final section of the chapter uses case studies of second and foreign language teaching to illustrate how the social and sociolinguistic context can influence language pedagogy.

Whereas this chapter will discuss the learning and teaching context of various languages, a good deal of attention will be given to the learning of English. This is because today English is the most widely studied second and foreign language (Crystal, 1997), causing the study of the social and sociolinguistic context of the learning of this language to be of interest to many learners and practitioners.

The Social Context of Language Learning and Teaching

Language planning and policy

The social context of language learning and teaching is greatly impacted by a nation's political decision to give special status to a particular language or languages. This status can be achieved either by making the language an official language of a country or by giving special priority to the language by requiring its study as a foreign language. Today there are over 75 countries in which English has been or continues to be an official language of the country, with many more nations requiring the study of English in the public schools (Crystal, 1997). This situation provides tremendous incentives for the learning of English.

The political choice of designating an official language is fully discussed in Chapter 3. What is important for our purposes is how this choice affects the social context of language learning and teaching. Three ways in which the designation of an official language has consequences for language learning and teaching are (a) the insight the designation provides into prevalent social attitudes toward particular languages, (b) the effect of the language policy on the stated language-in-education policy, and (c) the setting of linguistic standards.

The designation of an official language can foster a great deal of political tension that polarizes social attitudes toward particular languages. Malaysia's decision, for example, to recognize Bahasa Melayu as the country's sole official language was strongly opposed by the ethnic Chinese and Tamil populations, who preferred giving English equal status. The debate in South Africa over which languages to designate as official was also based on ethnic lines. In both cases the decision of whether or not to give special status to a particular language became a rallying point for social and ethnic groups. Such social attitudes obviously can affect an individual's motivation to learn or not learn a particular language.

A second consequence of a language being designated as one of the official languages of the country is that in most cases the country's official language or languages are used, or at least designated to be used, as the medium of instruction in the schools. The National Educational Policy of South Africa is a case in point. In 1997, the former Minister of Education argued that South Africa's national language-in-education policy was integral to the government's strategy of redressing the discrimination of the past and building a non-racial nation in South Africa. He contended that being multilingual should be a defining characteristic of being South African (Chick & McKay, 2001).

While providing for choice from a range of language-in-education policy models, the South African National Educational Policy identified additive bilingualism/multilingualism as the normative orientation of the language-in-education policy. This policy, however, contradicts the beliefs of many South African parents that the best way to acquire English, the dominant ex-colonial language, is to commence studying the language as early as possible; that maintenance of the first language is unnecessary and perhaps undesirable; and that the best way for speakers of other languages to acquire English is submersion, that is, a subtractive approach. Given the strong desire on the part of many parents for their children to learn English, English-medium education is currently the only option offered by South Africa's most sought-after schools. This situation exemplifies the manner in which the stated language-in-education policy is often undermined by prevalent social beliefs as to the value of particular languages.

National language policies can also influence language learning and teaching by the setting of standards. For example, in Singapore today, there is a segment of the population that speaks a localised dialect of English widely known as Singlish or Singapore Colloquial English (SCE). Like many stigmatized varieties, Singlish has begun to gain immense popularity among young professionals, who increasingly use it in domains of friendship and solidarity. Its negative association with the poorly educated and its accelerated usage among the general populace in recent years alarmed the Singapore authorities sufficiently to warrant the mounting of a *Speak Good English Movement*, a campaign that overtly promotes the use of standard English, and whose implicit agenda is to stem the spread of Singlish before it becomes an integral part of the cultural life of the present generation of school-goers in Singapore. As in the case of Singapore, government policies can influence not only which language is promoted but also which variety of that language is preferred.

Societal multilingualism

When a country has more than one official language and the majority of the population is bilingual, there are generally particular domains in which each language is used. Ferguson (1959) coined the term *diglossia* to describe the situation of a community in which most of the population is bilingual and/or bidialectal and the two codes serve different purposes. The term was originally used by Ferguson to describe a context in which two varieties of the same language are used by people of that community for different purposes. Normally one variety, termed the *High*, or *H*, *variety*, is acquired in an educational context and used by the community in more formal domains, such as in churches or universities. The other variety, termed the *Low*, or *L*, *variety*, is acquired in the home and used in informal domains, like the home or social center, to communicate with family and friends.

Later, Fishman (1972) generalized the meaning of diglossia to include the use of two separate languages within one country in which one language is used primarily for formal purposes and the other for more informal purposes. The expansion of the meaning of the term made it applicable to countries in which English is one of the official languages, as in South Africa, Singapore, and India. In these countries, English often assumes the role of what Ferguson calls the High variety, with the other languages of the country, or a different variety of English, being used in informal domains.

The fact that these different languages or varieties serve different purposes has implications for second-language teaching. In many cases the language or dialect that serves the purposes of the Low variety has lower status, so that speakers of this variety are marginalized in society and in the school system. Because of this, speakers of this variety are often given the impression that their home language is inferior; furthermore, their lack of access to the High variety can impede their progress in the educational establishment and, ultimately, in society.

Two additional concepts in the study of societal multilingualism that are important for our purposes are language maintenance and language shift. In the case of language maintenance, members of a language minority group work to promote the maintenance of their first language. This is the case of many language minority groups in the United States who have established after-school first-language maintenance programs, funded print and media programs in their first language, and supported special events in which the first language is used. (See McKay & Wong, 2000.) Language shift, on the other hand, occurs when members of a language minority replace the use of their first language in favor of another one. This is the case for almost all third generation immigrants to the United States.

The concepts of language maintenance and shift are particularly relevant to the topic of linguistic diversity in an era of globalization. Today, many warn of the danger of the spread of English and the threat it poses to the continued existence of indigenous and smaller languages (Nettle & Romaine, 2000; Phillipson, 2003). For such individuals, English is seen as the culprit in the decrease in the number of languages spoken in the world. However, there are others (e.g., Brutt-Griffler, 2002) who maintain that the spread of English is not a step toward a monolingual world of English speakers but rather a step toward a world in which bilingualism is the norm. Indeed the tremendous increase in the number of second-language speakers of English would seem to support this position.

The growth of individuals who are learning another language in their own country in order to partake in regional or global exchanges has important im-plications for second and foreign language learning and teaching. To begin with, such individuals have another language that serves their informal and intimate needs. Hence, they typically have little need to develop informal registers of the regional or global language. Second, in many instances individuals will ac-quire the additional language in order to communicate with other non-native speakers of that language. Because of this, much more attention should be given in language classes to developing strategies that help learners to communicate in exchanges in which neither speaker is fully fluent in the language.

The Sociolinguistic Context of Language Learning and Teaching

Language contact and variation

One common effect of language contact is language change. In such cases, the various languages used within a multilingual context may undergo phonological, lexical, and grammatical changes as bilinguals make use of two or more languages on a regular basis. This situation is occurring in many countries today where English has an official role in the society. In these countries, English is being influenced by the other languages it comes in contact with. In addition, English is often influencing other languages through the borrowing of English terms.

Many studies have been undertaken to determine the types of grammatical changes that are occurring in various multilingual contexts in which English plays a significant role. (See, for example, Kachru, 2005.) Frequently, researchers begin by examining a written corpus of English of a particular multilingual context to determine what kinds of grammatical innovations exist and how acceptable these structures are to both native speakers of English and local speakers of English. In general, when investigations of language change use a written corpus of published English, only very minor grammatical differences are found. (See, for example, Parasher, 1994.)

Often the kinds of grammatical changes that occur tend to be minor differences, such as variation in what is considered to be a countable noun (e.g., the standard use of *luggages* in English in the Philippines and the use of *furnitures* in Nigeria) and the creation of new phrasal verbs (e.g., the use of *dismissing off* in English in India, and *discuss about* in Nigeria). In contexts in which such features become codified and recognized as standard within that social context, there arises what Kachru (1986) has termed a *nativized variety* of English.

What is perhaps most puzzling in the development of alternate grammatical standards in the use of English is the fact that whereas lexical innovation is often accepted as part of language change, this tolerance is generally not extended to grammatical innovation. In Widdowson's (1994) view, the reason for this lack of tolerance for grammatical variation is because grammar takes on another value, namely that of expressing a social identity. Hence, when grammatical standards are challenged, they challenge the security of the community and institutions that support those standards.

Investigations of language contact have also focused on the code-switching behavior of bilinguals. One of the most comprehensive theories of codeswitching is that of Myers-Scotton (1993). She explains code-switching in terms of a theory of rights and obligations. She proposes a markedness model of code-switching which assumes that speakers in a multilingual context have a sense of which code is the one expected to be used in a particular situation. This is termed the *unmarked* code. However, speakers can also choose to use the *marked* code, that is, the language or language variety that is not expected in a particular social context. Using data from multilingual African contexts, Myers-Scotton demonstrates how bilingual speakers make code choices to signal a variety of social relationships. Unfortunately, in many language learning and teaching contexts, the rich linguistic repertoire of bilinguals is not recognized, and policies are often implemented to prohibit the use of any code other than the target language.

Studies in language contact have several implications for the teaching and learning of another language. As mentioned above, language contact will inevitably result in language change. Since today many individuals are using English in contact with other languages on a daily basis, their use of English is changing, and they are in the process of establishing their own standards of English grammar and pronunciation. In general, research on these emerging varieties of English indicates that the codified and accepted standard of English that exists in these communities has few differences from other standard varieties of English. Hence, it is important for L2 teachers to recognize the integrity of the varieties of the language they teach, to realize that they are important sources of personal identity and signs of the current mobility of populations, and to avoid promoting negative attitudes toward such varieties.

Studies on code-switching have illustrated the regularity of code-switching behavior and the purposes that code-switching can serve for bilinguals. Given the many contexts today where English is used as one of the additional languages within a country, more research is needed regarding how individuals make use of English in reference to the other languages they speak. Such research will be valuable in establishing classroom objectives that complement the students' use of English within their own speech community. In addition, in classrooms in multilingual contexts where the teacher shares a first language, more research is needed to determine how students' first language can be used to further their competence in a target language.

Ethnographic sociolinguistics

A good deal of current work in sociolinguistics falls under what is referred to as an ethnomethodologically oriented approach to the field of sociolinguistics, with linguistic interaction as the focal point. One of the central concepts of ethnographic or interactional sociolinguistics is the term *speech community*. Hymes (1972) contends that members of a speech community must share the same rules of speaking and be familiar with at least one common linguistic variety. Individuals are typically members of several speech communities and alter their norms of language use to conform to other members of the same speech community. With growing mobility, individuals today can belong to many different speech communities.

Work in linguistic interaction began as a reaction to Chomsky's (1957) focus on the language of an idealized speaker-listener in a homogeneous speech community with complete knowledge of the language. This notion was challenged by Hymes (1974), who insisted that studies on language use should strive to account for the communicative competence of a native speaker of a language. Gumperz (1982) also challenged Chomsky's notion of an idealized speaker in a homogeneous speech community, arguing instead that language use in a speech community is influenced by social and cultural factors. Gumperz's studies on communication between blacks and whites in the United States and between Indians and British in England demonstrated how differences in language use among speech communities can cause misunderstandings leading to racial and ethnic stereotypes and inequalities in power.

The work of Rampton (1995, 1997) has taken the debate about linguistic diversity one step further. He maintains that globalization, as well as late/postmodernity (a term he prefers to postmodernism), warrants a fresh look at the issues important to sociolinguistics and L2 research. Rampton believes that the time has come for sociolinguists to challenge the notion that societies are compact and systematic entities and instead to recognize the heterogeneity and fluidity of modern states. In keeping with much of the discourse of postmodernism, he argues persuasively that sociolinguistics should give more attention to investigating issues related to fragmentation, marginality, and hybridity and recognize that "being marginal is actually a crucial experience of late modernity. Being neither on the inside nor the outside, being affiliated but not fully belonging, is said to be a normal condition" (Rampton, 1997, p. 330).

The ability to signal identity through surface linguistic features has significant ramifications for language learning and teaching. In many contexts around the world, one of the major goals of teaching a second or foreign language is to promote the acquisition of the standard form of the target language. As a result, those who use an alternate form of the target language as a way of signaling their hybridity and affiliation with a particular speech community are often penalized. They are marginalized in the society and often penalized in a school system that uses one standard to determine proficiency in the language.

In order for current sociolinguistic research to be in touch with issues of late modernity, further research is needed that investigates linguistic diversity without preconceived ideas about native speakers and language standards. Such research should examine how particular varieties of language illustrate the fluidity of modern society. This type of research is presently underway in investigations of English as a lingua franca (ELF), which Firth (1996) defines as a contact language "between persons who share neither a common native tongue nor a common (national) culture, and for whom English is the chosen foreign language of communication" (p. 240). Since it is estimated that today about 80 percent of oral exchanges in English do not involve native speakers of English (Seidlhofer, 2004), more research is needed to determine the characteristics of such exchanges. Most of the current research in this area has taken place in Expanding Circle countries (see below), much of it in Europe. (See Seidlhofer 2004 for a review of ELF research.)

Major Second and Foreign Language Learning and Teaching Contexts

As a way of illustrating how the social and sociolinguistic factors described above have implications for second and foreign language learning and teaching, it is helpful to consider the three major types of learning contexts described by Kachru (1986) in reference to English learning: (a) the Inner Circle, where English is the primary language of the country, such as in Australia, Canada, and the United Kingdom; (b) the Outer Circle, where English serves as a second language in a multilingual country, such as in Singapore, India, and the Philippines; and (c) the Expanding Circle, where English is widely studied as a foreign language, such as in China, Japan, and Korea.

This very broad distinction of learning contexts can be generalized to all second and foreign languages. In doing so, any teaching context in which a learner is learning the major language of the host country would be termed an *Inner Circle learning context*. This is the type of social context faced by many immigrants today, who in an age of globalization often immigrate to other more prosperous countries, typically for better economic opportunities. This is the case of many Turks in Germany, Poles in Ireland, and Indians in Great Britain. The second major type of second and foreign language learning is an *Outer Circle learning context*, in which the learner is acquiring one of the major languages spoken in the country. This would be the case of English speakers learning French in Quebec or Zulu speakers learning English in South Africa. Finally, in *Expanding Circle learning contexts*, learners are learning a language, often a language of regional or global importance, in a country in which the language has no official role. This is the case of American learners studying Mandarin or Japanese learners learning English. The question is, in what way do the social and sociolinguistic constructs described above provide insight into the learning and teaching context? In order to address this, we examine some representative case studies in each context. We begin with Inner Circle learning contexts.

Inner Circle learning contexts

Language maintenance and language shift, as well as language-in-education policy, are particularly relevant to Inner Circle learning contexts. In many instances, government and educational leaders make decisions that can encourage either language maintenance or shift among its minority population. British government policies regarding the acquisition of English among minority language speakers illustrate the effect that government policy can have on language maintenance and shift. During the 1960s and 1970s in the United Kingdom, students with limited English proficiency were placed either in specialist language centers or withdrawn from mainstream classrooms for special ESL instruction. Then, in 1986, the Commission for Racial Equality decided that language centers constituted a form of racial discrimination in that language minority students, typically members of racial minority groups, were being singled out and that such programs were creating further social and racial barriers between groups.

As Rampton (1995) notes, British government policy in general tolerates the use of minority languages only as a transitional measure during the early years of schooling, and there is no encouragement for the development of bilingualism during a child's education. Obviously, such policies are designed to promote language shift, with no encouragement for language maintenance. What are the implications of such policies for language learning and teaching? In general, they promote a view of a language classroom as an English-only environment in which the first-language resources a child has are not recognized. Such policies also do not typically promote favorable attitudes toward bilingualism or code-switching.

These pedagogical policies are in sharp contrast to the linguistic situation many language minority youths encounter outside the classroom. Here, as Rampton (1995) carefully documents in his investigation of British language minority adolescents, code alternation both between Standard English and Stylised Asian English and between English and the students' first language plays an important role in "the organization of interracial adolescent *solidarities*" (p. 141). Whereas the actual interactions of British adolescents with adults and their peers demonstrate the sociolinguistic sophistication of bilingual youths, this is not recognized as an asset or promoted in classrooms which support an English-only model that recognizes and legitimizes only standard English.

The language-in-education policies in countries like the United Kingdom reflect a huge gap between the sociolinguistic reality of language minority groups and prevalent pedagogical approaches to the teaching of English. If pedagogical models are to be sensitive to the social interactions of the local context, much more attention needs to be given in Inner Circle learning contexts to the value of bilingualism, the maintenance of existing linguistic resources, and the sociolinguistic knowledge of language learners.

Presently, Australia is making some attempt to encourage the development of bilingualism among its citizens. As an inducement to encourage the learning of languages other than English (LOTE), some Australian universities are offering bonus points to those university applicants who include the study of LOTE in their required university entrance subjects (Smolicz & Secombe, 2003). Even with this incentive, only 10–20 percent of students take LOTE as a university entrance subject. As Smolicz and Secombe point out, this is "particularly striking for students from the majority English-speaking background, many of whom see no obvious benefits from investing the effort required to learn a new language, in view of the availability of what they perceive as 'easier options', as well as the global dominance of English" (2003, p. 16). Attitudes such as this suggest that the English-speaking populations of Inner Circle countries may be the least likely to become bilingual in an increasingly multilingual and multicultural world.

Outer Circle learning contexts

Diglossia, language change, linguistic standards, and code-switching are particularly relevant to many Outer Circle learning contexts. Not least because many of the Outer Circle countries are inherently characterized by a rich and complex multiethnic, multicultural, and multilingual ethos wherein English was transplanted and taught either as an important official language or a language of higher education, or both.

Partly a legacy of colonial history and partly the effect of post-independence policies, English was introduced as a panacea for solving the economic and educational problems of many newly independent states in the Outer Circle, such as India, the Philippines, Singapore, and those of Africa, and soon became a dominant language of the ruling elite. The study of English was therefore initially restricted to a particular socio-economic class, with a focus on literature and culture. Today, its earlier role in these contexts as an "instrument of science and technology" and a language of "development" and "national unity" is increasingly being replaced by economic and pragmatic motivations, due to the meshing of English with globalization. This has meant a strong demand for communication skills and everyday use of English, in place of the study of literature, for creating a competent workforce for the multinational corporations and outsourcing centers that represent this global trend.

Many "new" and distinct *indigenized* or *nativized* varieties of English (Kachru, 1986) have evolved, due to the processes of change that English has undergone by acquiring new linguistic and cultural features as a result of contact with indigenous languages and cultures. These contact varieties have become institutionalized and are recognized by their speakers as autonomous varieties of English in their own right, notwithstanding the struggle for legitimacy and equivalence with long-established "native" varieties, particularly British and American Englishes, that continue to be looked upon as powerful reference points in the practice of English language instruction in some of those settings.

A crucial consideration for speakers of English in the Outer Circle has been the choice of a pedagogical model for teaching English as a second/foreign language, that is, whether to adopt an external "native speaker" standard or an internal one as the appropriate model in serving the purposes of their local contexts. Governments and education ministries differ sharply in the positions they have taken. For instance, Indian English (English of educated Indians) is taught and learnt in all educational institutions in India and this is the variety also used in the administration, the judiciary, the military, and the media. This rejection of what Phillipson (2001) terms "a debilitating dependence on native speaker models" (p. 195) is in tune with the sociolinguistic realities of the Indian subcontinent, where most Indians use English as a *lingua franca* to communicate with other Indians or Asians from language groups not their own, much less frequently with Inner Circle speakers. This also means that Indian English has "multiple identities" that are markers of distinctive regional variation within it.

India has adopted a policy known as the "three language formula," wherein students in the mainstream typically learn their mother tongue or regional language as their first language, and English and Hindi as their second and third languages, respectively. Of the roughly 200 languages that actively contribute to making India a functionally multilingual country and not just a demographically multilingual one, 41 languages, including its 18 official languages, are available for study in the school curriculum (NCERT, 1999, cited in Annamalai, 2004, p. 177). However, because English is the only language taught in all states as either a first (e.g., in privately run English-medium schools), second, or third language and is taught in the largest number of schools overall, from one point of view it has been argued that making English compulsory in Indian schools has rendered hundreds and thousands of children handicapped. Because it marginalizes vernacular medium students and defeats the policy goal of nation-building with equal educational opportunities for all, free India, it is argued, is free only politically and not educationally (Krishnaswamy & Krishnaswamy, 2006).

Whereas English still remains essentially an urban middle-class phenomenon in India, and as the language of the ruling bureaucracy and higher education it is domain-specific and register-based, English in Singapore occupies a unique position among Asian countries. In Singapore, English has first-language status in the educational curriculum at all levels and is the *de facto* working language of administration, business, and the media. While the more standard variety of English is the one taught in schools, alongside it has developed a variety which has a distinctive phonology, syntax, and lexicon, which shows a high degree of influence from the other local languages such as Hokkien, Cantonese, Malay, and Tamil, a contact variety thought to be pioneered in the classroom and the playground by children (Gupta, 1994). Because English in Singapore and Malaysia was found to display a range, it was initially characterized as a "lectal continuum" within a "post-creole continuum" (Platt & Weber, 1980), extending from the *basilect* at one end, which showed features of creoles, to the *acrolect* at the other, approximating Standard (superstrate) English, with the *mesolect* mediating transitionally between the two. However, since English in these regions was acquired through the formal school system, a description more favored today is one that sees it as a form of diglossia (Gupta, 1994; Foley et al., 1998), with Standard Singapore English (SSE) constituting the High variety, used in public, formal and educational domains and Singapore Colloquial English (SCE), the Low variety used in the home and neighborhood. Members of the Singaporean speech community know well when SCE is or is not appropriate and even where code-mixing between SSE and SCE is commonplace, children do separate the codes at a very early age (Gupta, 1994).

Standards of English have remained a continuing concern at the highest levels of government. Despite the fact that educated Singaporeans have come to enjoy a greater degree of English language proficiency in present-day Singapore, there is currently strong official pressure to promote an exonormative standard – notably British or American English – so as to curb further "decay" of the language through processes of indigenization. Varied measures have been undertaken to bring about targeted change. The Speak Good English Movement, for instance, was mounted in 2000 as a timely check to contain the popularity of the local vernacular "Singlish," considered a non-standard variety with an alluring potential for symbolizing Singaporean identity and solidarity among young Singaporeans. For some, the movement was viewed as a way to help Singapore plug into the English-dominant global economic network, while others saw it as a way to facilitate linguistic homogenization by devaluing and diminishing the existing linguistic resources of the average Singaporean (Chng, 2003; Kramer-Dahl, 2003; Rubdy, 2001).

The dominance of English in Singapore has been enormously boosted by the institutionalization of English as the medium of instruction and first language in schools since 1979, as a measure to create national unity and forge a national identity and consciousness that transcended ethnic boundaries, as well as by the assignation of the local "mother tongue" languages to second-language status, such that all Singaporeans may be described as "English-knowing bilinguals" (Pakir, 1991). Singapore is, in fact, well on its way toward becoming a largely English-speaking country, certainly one that is English dominant (Lim, 2004). Equally, the Speak Mandarin campaign that was put in place as a measure simultaneously to uphold Asian values and counter the influence of "Western decadence," and that is now paying off with the emergence of China as a powerful trading partner, has had an overwhelming success in increasing the widespread use of Mandarin. However, this has happened at the expense of the many Chinese dialects that it has replaced, leading to extensive language shift and language loss, and threatening intergenerational continuity. The language-in-education policy thus causes the language of school and government to displace the language of home and neighborhood (Tickoo, 1996).

Kamwangamalu (2003) reports on a similar trend in South Africa, where English is "spreading like wildfire" and has infiltrated the family domain, particularly in urban black communities, who "see the language as an open sesame by means of which one can achieve unlimited upward social mobility," and prefer English-medium education over an education in their own native languages, such as Sotho, Zulu, or Xosa. Kamwangamalu maintains that if the current trend toward monolingualism in English continues, the African languages will face attrition and death. He points to the anxiety and agony expressed in South Africa by, on the one hand, some purists "who believe that the language is being mutilated through *nativization* by its new users (i.e., non-native speakers); and, on the other hand, African language activists and community leaders, who see the spread of English into the family domain as a threat to the maintenance and a prelude to the demise of the indigenous languages" (Kamwangamalu, 2003, pp. 68–9).

The seemingly people-driven spread of English in South Africa reflects a growing but worrying trend observable also in other Outer Circle countries. The "English advantage" that India has as a key to employment in the global market is appreciated by many Indians. So, "English for all" is the new slogan. The demand that English is also for the masses is gaining ground, and it is estimated that with the introduction of a new policy for English at the primary level, about 150 million children at the primary stage will be learning English in India. This move could bring about a dramatic change in the demographics of the English-speaking population in this country and that of the Anglophone world, as well (Krishnaswamy & Krishnaswamy, 2006).

Expanding Circle learning contexts

Language-in-education policies play an important role in the learning and teaching of foreign languages. Current Chinese language-in-education policies illustrate the manner in which the learning and teaching of English has been strongly influenced by government policies in regard to both the requirements for studying English and the methods promoted in English language classrooms. In 1976, Deng Xiaoping launched a national modernization program in which English education was seen as a key component: "English was recognized as an important tool for engaging in economic, commercial, technological and cultural exchange with the rest of the world and hence for facilitating the modernization process" (Hu, 2005, p. 8).

In 1978, the Ministry of Education issued the first unified primary and secondary curriculum for the era of modernization. This curriculum introduced foreign language learning at Primary 3. The directive also mandated that efforts in promoting English language proficiency were to be aimed at strengthening English language teaching in elite schools, which were expected to produce the English-proficient personnel needed to successfully undertake national modernization. In fact, in 1985, the Ministry of Education exempted poorly resourced schools from providing English instruction. In addition, the Ministry of Education gave several economically developed provinces and municipalities the autonomy to develop their own English curricula, syllabi, and textbooks for primary and secondary education (Hu, 2005). These materials tended to be more innovative, learner-centered, and communicative than earlier classroom texts and materials.

The directives summarized above illustrate the dangers that can arise from state mandated guidelines for language teaching. First, such mandates can determine when foreign language learning begins in the public school system. The Chinese Ministry of Education, like governments in many other Asian countries, is formally promoting the early learning of English, even though the issue of early exposure to foreign language learning is still being debated (see Hyltenstam & Abrahamsson, 2001). Second, state mandates can determine who has access to English language learning. In China, recent policies have tended to support English learning among the Chinese elite, in this way exacerbating educational inequality. Finally, state mandates can determine how a language is taught. In China, as in many other Asian countries, current curriculum developments have tended to promote more learner-centered, communicative methods. The problem, however, has been a lack of teacher education that will ensure the effective implementation of new methods.

Malaysia is a country that historically presents a sharp contrast to China's English teaching policy in that, in its early independence days, Malaysia tried officially to discourage the spread of English. At independence in 1957, the Malays made up close to half the population, the Chinese a little over a third, and the Indians 10 percent (Gill, 2005). In the previous colonial system, English-medium schools were located in urban areas and were primarily attended by non-Malays and a small number of elite Malays. Many Malay nationalists were frustrated by the fact that those who spoke English were non-Malays and that knowing English gave them a social and economic advantage. The Malays believed that designating Bahasa Melayu as the official language would lead to its development as a language of higher status and thus provide Malays with the linguistic capital previously held by the English-speaking Chinese and Indians (Gill, 2005). To promote the status of Bahasa Melayu, the language was established as the language of education, with all universities required to use Bahasa Melayu as the medium of instruction. The resistance of the Chinese and Indian population to this policy led the government to undertake a rapid implementation of the language-in-education policy, so that the status of Malay language could be established.

What is surprising is that this early attempt in Malysia to control the spread of English among its population is currently being re-examined. As evidence of this change in policy, in 2002 the Prime Minister of Malaysia, Tun Dr. Mahathir Mohamad, announced that starting immediately, science and mathematics were to be taught in English in both the primary and tertiary levels. The question is, what led to this change in policy from one of restraining the spread of English to one of encouraging its development as an additional language.

Gill (2005) contends that the change was brought about because the nationalistic language policy had resulted in a generation of university graduates who were fluent in the national language but not in English. The problem is that in an age of globalization, in order to be competitive, Malays need English to access the tremendous amount of scientific and technological knowledge available in English. Without access to this information, the government believes Malaysia can not be competitive in a global market. In this way, current changes in Malaysia's education policy "were largely influenced by the two domains which are important in the growth and status of any language – the domain of business and the domain of science and technology" (Gill, 2005, p. 256).

The case of Malaysia offers a vivid example of how the larger social and political context can affect language-in-education policies. Malaysia, like many countries today, is struggling with an attempt to balance its nationalistic priorities with the need to stay competitive in a global economy. At the present time, Malaysia appears to be replacing its desire to promote its national language with its felt need to establish an English-knowing population that will make it a competitive society in today's global economy.

In contrast to Malaysia, Sweden is struggling with its national language being dominated by English.

> Today Swedish, like many national languages throughout the world, is in an awkward position. It is at the same time a strong national language with the potential to dominate other languages within its borders and a potentially dominated language with respect to English as an international language. (Hult, 2004, p. 182)

According to Hult, the prominence of English in higher domains like education, commerce, and industry threatens Swedish "to the point where there is a risk of a two-tiered society developing, with English used for high status interaction and Swedish for lower status common daily interaction" (Hult, 2004, p. 183). There is also concern within Sweden that the consequence of this situation would be greater social inequality, with those that know English having greater access to high status social positions than those without it. This situation has led the Swedish government to commission the Swedish Language Council, a semi-public Swedish language planning body, to draft a program designed for the promotion and protection of Swedish.

The situation in Sweden is indicative of many European countries today, in which the fear of the growing use of English is in sharp contrast to the prevalent belief that knowledge of English provides access to the global economy. It is this ambivalent attitude that fuels countries to require the study of English while at the same time jealously protecting their own national language.

Conclusion

The social and sociolinguistic context of language learning and teaching has a significant impact on which languages are taught, when they are taught, and how they are taught. This fact has several implications for second and foreign language professionals. First, second and foreign language professionals, no matter which language they are teaching, need to work vigorously to ensure that all individuals be given the opportunity to become multilingual in an increasingly multilingual and multicultural world and to maintain the linguistic resources they have. In order to do this, they need to voice their disapproval of any policies that minimize those opportunities. Second, language professionals need to be sensitive to the local social and sociolinguistic context and to implement language teaching goals and methods that complement the social reality of their language learners. Finally, language professionals need to work to see that all learners have equal opportunities to achieve their language learning goals, so that they can reap the social and economic benefits that come from being a bilingual in the current global culture.

REFERENCES

Annamalai, E. (2004). Medium of power: The question of English in education in India. In J. W. Tollefson & A. Tsui (eds.), *Medium of instruction policies: Which agenda? Whose agenda?* (pp. 117–94). Mahwah, NJ: Lawrence Erlbaum.

Brutt-Griffler, J. (2002). *World English: A study of its development*. Clevedon, UK: Multilingual Matters.

Chick, K. & McKay, S. L. (2001). Teaching English in Multiethnic schools in the Durban area: The promotion of multilingualism or monolingualism. *South African Linguistics and Applied Language Studies* 19, 3–4, 163–78.

Chng, H. H. (2003). "You see me no up": Is Singlish a problem? *Language Problems and Language Planning* 27, 47–62.

Chomsky, N. (1957). *Syntactic structure*. The Hague: Mouton.

Crystal, D. (1997). *English as a global language*. Cambridge: Cambridge University Press.

Ferguson, C. (1959). Diglossia. *Word* 15, 325–40.

Firth, A. (1996). The discursive accomplishments of normality. On "lingual franca" English and conversation analysis. *Journal of Pragmatics* 26, 237–59.

Fishman, J. (1972). *The socoiology of language*. Rowley, MA: Newbury House.

Foley, J. A., Kandiah, T., Bao, Z., Gupta, A. E., Alsagoff, L., Ho, C. L., Wee, L., Talib, I. S., & Bokhorst-Heng, W. (eds.) (1998). *English in new cultural contexts*. Singapore: Oxford University Press.

Gill, S. (2005). Language policy in Malaysia: Reversing direction. *Language Policy* 4, 241–60.

Gumperz, J. J. (1982). *Discourse strategies*. Cambridge: Cambridge University Press.

Gupta, A. (1994). *The step-tongue: Children's English in Singapore*. Clevedon, UK: Multilingual Matters.

Hu, G. (2005). English language education in China: Policies, progress and problems. *Language Policy* 4, 5–24.

Hult, F. M. (2004). Planning for multilingualism and minority language rights in Sweden. *Language Policy* 3, 181–201.

Hyltenstam, K. & Abrahamsson, N. (2001). Age and L2 learning: The hazards of matching practical "implications" with theoretical "facts." *TESOL Quarterly* 35, 151–70.

Hymes, D. (1972). On communicative competence. In J. Pride & J. Holmes (eds.), *Sociolinguistics* (pp. 269–93). Harmondsworth: Penguin.

Hymes, D. (1974). *Foundations of sociolinguistics*. Philadelphia: University of Pennsylvania Press.

Kachru, B. B. (1986). *The alchemy of English*. Oxford: Pergamon Press.

Kachru, B. B. (2005). *Asian Englishes: Beyond the canon*. Hong Kong: Hong Kong University Press.

Kamwangamalu, N. M. (2003). Globalization of English, and language maintenance and shift in South Africa. *International Journal of the Sociology of Language* 164, 65–81.

Kramer-Dahl, A. (2003). Reading the "Singlish Debate": Construction of a crisis of language standards and language teaching in Singapore. *Journal of Language, Identity, and Education* 2, 159–90.

Krishnaswamy, N. & Krishnaswamy, L. (2006). *The story of English in India*. Delhi: Foundation Books.

Lim, L. (ed.) (2004). *Singapore English: A grammatical description*. Philadelphia: John Benjamins.

McKay, S. L. & Wong, S. C. (2000). *Immigrants in the United States*. Cambridge: Cambridge University Press.

Myers-Scotton, C. (1993). *Social motivation for codeswitching*. Oxford: Claredon Press.

Nettle, D. & Romaine, S. (2000). *Vanishing voices: The extinction of the world's languages*. Oxford: Oxford University Press.

Pakir, A. (1991). The range and depth of English-knowing bilinguals in Singapore. *World Englishes* 10, 167–79.

Parasher, S. V. (1994). Indian English: Certain grammatical, lexical and stylistic features. In R. K. Angihotri & A. L. Khanna (eds.), *Second language acquisition: Socio-cultural and linguistic aspects of English in India* (pp. 145–64). New Dehli: Sage.

Phillipson, R. (2001). English for globalization or the world's people? *International Review of Education* 47, 185–200.

Phillipson, R. (2003). *English-only Europe? Challenging language policy*. New York: Routledge.

Platt, J. T. & Weber, H. (1980). *English in Singapore and Malaysia: Status, features, functions.* Kuala Lumpur: Oxford University Press.

Rampton, B. (1995). *Crossing: Language and ethnicity among adolescents*. New York: Longman.

Rampton, B. (1997). Second language research in late modernity. *Modern Language Journal* 15, 3, 329–33.

Rubdy, R. (2001). Creative destruction: Singapore's Speak Good English Movement. *World Englishes* 20, 341–55.

Seidlhofer, B. (2004). Research perspectives on teaching English as a lingua franca. *Annual Review of Applied Linguistics* 24, 209–39.

Smolicz, J. J. & Secombe, M. J. (2003). Assimilation or pluralism? Changing policies for minority languages education in Australia. *Language Policy* 2, 3–25.

Tickoo, M. L. (1996). Fifty years of English in Singapore: All gains, (a) few losses? In J. A. Fishman, A. W. Conrad, & A. Rubel-Lopez (eds.), *Post-imperial English: Status change in former British and American colonies. 1940–1990.* (pp. 431–55). Berlin and New York: Mouton de Gruyter.

Wardhaugh, R. (1992). *An introduction to sociolinguistics*. Cambridge, MA: Blackwell.

Widdowson, H. (1994). The ownership of English. *TESOL Quarterly* 28, 377–88.

3   The Politics and Policies of Language and Language Teaching

ROBERT PHILLIPSON AND TOVE SKUTNABB-KANGAS

As long as we have the language, we have the culture. As long as we have the culture, we can hold on to the land.

Manu Metekingi, *Māori from the Whanganui iwi ("tribe")*[1]

Language and culture cannot be separate from each other – if they are, the language only becomes a tool, a thing . . . Our language and culture are our identity and tell us who we are, where we came from and where we are going.

Task Force on Aboriginal Languages and Cultures, 2005, p. 58

To give millions a knowledge of English is to enslave us. The foundation that Macaulay laid of education has enslaved us.

Gandhi, *barrister-at-law, architect of Indian independence, 1908, quoted in Naik, 2004, p. 255*

It was because we were taught in our own language that our minds quickened . . . If the whole mind is not functioning from the beginning its full powers remain undeveloped to the end. While all around was heard the cry for English teaching, my third brother was brave enough to keep us to our Bengali course.

Rabindranath Tagore, *1913 Nobel Prize Laureate for Literature, 1992, pp. 53–4*

The English language teaching sector directly earns nearly £1.3 billion for the UK in invisible exports and our other education related exports earn up to £10 billion a year more.

Neil Kinnock, *Chair British Council, politician, ex-EU Commission Vice-President, in Graddol, 2006, p. 4*

English in Africa: an imperial language, the language of linguistic Americanization, a language of global capitalism . . . creating and maintaining social divisions serving an economy dominated primarily by foreign economic interests and, secondarily, by a small aspiring African bourgeoisie.

Alamin Mazrui, *PhD Stanford, expert on World Bank language policies, 2004, p. 30*

One feels so handicapped working from here, and also in a language not one's own. The proponents of a worldwide right and duty to learn English will never admit the cost for the non-native speakers on whom the World English is imposed.

Ajit Mohanty, *PhD Edmonton, cutting-edge bilingualism researcher, personal correspondence, June 8, 2004*

English is not enough. We are fortunate to speak a global language but, in a smart and competitive world, exclusive reliance on English leaves the UK vulnerable and dependent on the linguistic competence and the goodwill of others . . . Young people from the UK are at a growing disadvantage in the recruitment market.

Nuffield Languages Enquiry, 2000, *www.nuffield.org*

Unhappily for those who have sought to devise a "science" of Language Policy and Planning there are no protocols for doing or designing LPP that can be induced from practice, abstracted, tested and refined into procedures and then transferred across contexts and applied in diverse settings . . . the field is too dependent on the descriptive traditions of linguistics from which it derives, and insufficiently in communication with policy analysis sciences, with political science, with sociology and with critical schools of thought.

Joseph Lo Bianco, *PhD Melbourne, language policy expert, 2002, pp. 23, 25*

Introduction

These glimpses into the world of language policy demonstrate that educational language policy and its analysis are of major significance for the individual, for group vitality, for national identities, and international relations. They also reveal how language policy interlocks with political decision-making. The intrinsic complexity of language policy, in practice and in theory, is increasingly being addressed in books and journals. Language policy requires a multi-disciplinary approach. The concerns of educationalists and language professionals need to draw on insights from political science, international law, and economics. Even within educational language studies, there is a tendency toward excessive specialization. For instance, books on language policy (e.g., Ricento, 2006; Spolsky, 2004) generally ignore translation studies, a productive field of activity that interlocks with language technology, globalization (Cronin, 2003), and conflict (Baker, 2006). Our review will focus on historical contextualization and conceptual clarification, and build on examples of ongoing language policy issues at the global, regional, and national levels.

Committed scholarship should ensure that language policy experience and analysis contribute to the resolution of complex political problems. This requires that academic, educational, and political discourse interact dialectically. It also presupposes recognition of the value of all the world's languages and their use in addressing life's challenges: in the words of the Kenyan Nobel Peace Prize Laureate, Wangari Maathai, referring to the powerful addressing the population at large: "if you don't speak in their language, you may touch the head, but you may never touch the heart. And that is what a mother tongue does . . . if you lose your language, you lose yourself."[2]

Historical and Global Contextualization

Foreign languages were traditionally learned by the privileged for the social prestige they represented and facilitated, whether the canonical texts of Arabic, Latin, or Sanskrit, or more recent internationally influential languages. The Russian aristocracy was literate and vocal in French but often had little proficiency in Russian, the language of the masses. It is arguable that in African and Asian former colonies, English may now be functioning rather as did French in nineteenth-century Russia. The main difference is that the class of English users worldwide is now connected to a neoliberal economic system ("the new imperialism," Harvey, 2005) and ideological systems, forms of consciousness, consumption, and growthism that cultural globalization is propagating (Seabrook, 2004). The penetration of contemporary English is thus vastly deeper than that of Latin, French, and other dominant languages in earlier times (see Gandhi, Tagore, and Mohanty above). It is also of considerable economic importance in itself (see Kinnock above), though there are risks if one does not know other languages (see Nuffield Foundation above). English is central to corporate globalization spearheaded by economic, political, and military forces in the "English-speaking" countries (Mazrui above).

The incorporation and co-option of local elites follows the pattern by which the privileged in colonies learned the language of the invader. This was already the case in Roman England (Tacitus, [AD 97] 1948). In Europeanized *settler* colonies (the Americas, Australasia, South Africa) educational policies were elaborated ad hoc, often by missionary societies, following or preceding military suppression. Although in some parts of the USA in the early nineteenth century there was a bilingual education policy, "throughout the 19th and much of the 20th centuries, federal Indian education policy was one of almost zero tolerance for linguistic and cultural difference" (McCarty, Romero, & Zepeda, 2006, p. 94). In the *extraction* colonies of the British empire (such as Malaysia or West Africa), the learning of the colonial language was paramount for local elites and intermediaries, as in the French and Portuguese colonies, and has remained a significant legacy in the postcolonial age. In Finland, where 70 percent of the population, mostly Finnish-speakers, were not represented in the parliament during the Russian era (1807–917), the first use of Finnish in the parliament (in 1894, by a representative of the gentry) was called "unbelievably barbaric" and "illegal." The language of parliament was not Russian but Swedish, the language of the former colonial power (1155–1809) and all Finnish-speakers were supposed to know it. Linguistic hierarchization (linguicism) and genocide were the norm in settler colonies, and have also been vigorously pursued by monolingually oriented states elsewhere (Skutnabb-Kangas, 2000).

In the twentieth century, "modern," "living," or "foreign" language learning progressively shifted from a predominantly literary focus to more instrumental purposes. However, departments of English in former colonies generally retain literature as a core concern (on India, see Joshi, 1994; on Sri Lanka, Kandiah, 1999), emulating departments of English as a mother tongue in the major English-using countries. Many "foreign" language departments are similar. Thus the Modern Language Association of the USA (www.mla.org) brings together the study of many languages, but its "divisions" and "discussion groups" are overwhelmingly concerned with literature, and pedagogy is marginal.

The MLA claims leadership in the national education community (i.e., the USA), but also records 30,000 members in 100 countries. In this respect the professional association is comparable to TESOL (a mainly US body that claims to serve "a global group of devoted teachers, educators, researchers, and friends of the profession," www.tesol.org) and its British-based equivalent, IATEFL (whose "mission is to link, develop and support English Language Teaching professionals throughout the world," www.iatefl.org). Even if TESOL and IATEFL generally represent language learning constituencies that are often seen as marginal to mainstream education, their professionalism exercises considerable influence globally on the content of education, teacher training, theoretical paradigms, and methodological innovation, with major cultural consequences. Journals reflect this hegemony: ". . . most of what gets published in the most influential applied linguistics journals is generally a product of what we could term the Anglo-American centre. It is primarily academics from the academic centre, above all in North America, who are funded and encouraged to do research" (Block, 1997, p. 3). Considerable amounts of US funding are also directed toward scholars worldwide, which can result in reciprocal stimulation, as for instance in a recent book on language policy in China (Zhou and Sun, 2004), but always with the risk of inequality reinforcing Western paradigms, orientalism, and academic imperialism (for criticism of these, see Odora Hoppers, 2002; Smith Tuhiwai, 1999). The handbook in your hands, which aims at global relevance, incurs the same risk.

Capitalism deifies the law of the market, and requires continuous expansion that does not respect national borders. English currently oils the wheels of most global finance and commerce. Educational services are increasingly seen as commodities and market opportunities, rather than as a human right and public good that each country is responsible for. Thus Educational Testing Services of New Jersey, a hugely profitable "non-profit" body, announces its global ambitions proudly (www.ets.org):

> As ETS's wholly-owned subsidiary, ETS Global BV is structured to bring ETS's expertise and experience with tests, assessments, and related services to educational and business communities around the world. ETS Global BV now has subsidiaries in Europe and Canada, and it will be expanding into other countries and regions as well . . . Our global mission goes far beyond testing. Our products and services enable opportunity worldwide by measuring knowledge and skills, promoting learning and performance, and supporting education and professional development for all people worldwide.

This linguistic-educational imperial thrust is viscerally connected to corporate-driven globalization. In contrast, human rights, especially economic and social rights, serve, according to human rights lawyer Katarina Tomaševski (1996, p. 104), to act as correctives to the "free" market, instead of giving market forces free range. Tomaševski claims that "The purpose of international human rights law is . . . to overrule the law of supply and demand and remove price-tags from people and from necessities for their survival" (1996, p. 104). The necessities for survival include not only economic and social rights such as basic food and housing, but also basic civil, political, *and cultural* rights necessary for a dignified life. Basic linguistic human rights in education belong to these. Thus all second and foreign-language teaching that promotes the subtractive spread of "big" languages violates basic human rights (see below).

The distribution of European languages worldwide reflects a global European-ization process. Other major languages, such as Arabic and Japanese, are also promoted globally. The learning of Chinese worldwide is being promoted in Confucius Institutes (following the trail of Cervantes, Dante, and Goethe Insti-tutes) and anticipates an increase from 30 million learners to 100 million within a few years (Graddol, 2006, p. 63). Figures for speakers of a first and especially of a second language are notoriously unreliable (see Skutnabb-Kangas, 2000, pp. 30–46), or fraudulent (a French example, Chaudenson, 2003), not least be-cause of imprecise definitions of language (as well as dialect, sociolect, etc.) and proficiency. Migration, urbanization, and technological developments are making the linguistic mosaic ever more complex, and leading to new forms of multilin-gualism, at the same time as oppressive state language policies continue to erode linguistic diversity.

Politics and/or Policy?

There are no quick fixes in language policy (see Lo Bianco above) or politics. In English there are the two lexical items *policy* and *politics*, whereas many languages have a single term for both (Danish *politik*, French *politique*, etc.). This tends to blur the distinction between the two concepts. If a user of English as a second language refers to the "language politics" of an institution, what is intended may be the language policy in force. The "politics of language" often indicates political struggles in which linguistic identity and language rights may be contentious, polarizing factors. Language *policy* can be defined as referring to all the measures, explicit and implicit, which have an impact on the language ecology in a given context, including the rights of speakers of a given language, and the use made of languages for given functions. It is thus a broader term than language planning. The *politics of language* refers to the political domain and its discourses, what politicians do or say, language promotion or suppression, and to struggles for rights or recognition for a given language. A challenge to scholars is to investigate how their (our?) language policy and politics activities relate to political power nationally and internationally, and their/our function in up-holding a globally oppressive system. A good example of failure to do so occurs when it is claimed that "international" English is a neutral language, discon-nected from the power and powers behind it:

> English being disembedded from national cultures can never mean that it floats culture-free (. . . or) is culturally neutral. The point may be simple, but it is often elided; and this elision constitutes a politics of English as a global language which precisely conceals the cultural work which that model of language is in fact performing. (Kayman, 2004, p. 17)

Kayman also makes the intriguing point that the prophets and proponents of English as a global language can be compared to Europeans occupying other continents that were falsely seen as *terra nullius*. Contemporary linguists who proclaim the neutrality of English treat the language as a cultural *terra nullius* (Kayman, 2004, p. 18). The forms and functions of "global" English have been extensively analysed (see the review of three books in Phillipson, 2004), includ-ing whether its present position is unassailable (Graddol, 2006).

Mainstream political science is archetypically represented by Huntington's *The Clash of Civilizations and the Remaking of the World Order* (1996), essentially a blueprint for global US dominance. Language, and the cultural universe and ways of thought it embodies, is a key dimension to this global mission. David Rothkopf, director of Kissinger Associates, wrote an article entitled "In praise of cultural imperialism?" in *Foreign Policy* in 1997 (pp. 45, 48):

> It is in the economic and political interest of the United States to ensure that if the world is moving toward a common language, it be English; that if the world is moving toward common telecommunications, safety, and quality standards, they be American; and that if common values are being developed, they be values with which Americans are comfortable. These are not idle aspirations. English is linking the world . . . Americans should not deny the fact that of all the nations in the history of the world, theirs is the most just, the most tolerant, the most willing to constantly reassess and improve itself, and the best model for the future.

It is false to regard globalization as a new phenomenon. There have been blueprints for US dominance of the two American continents since the Monroe Doctrine of 1823 and for global domination for over a century. The need for new markets due to capital over-accumulation was a primary concern of US foreign policy throughout the twentieth century. The role of scholarship in legitimating the thrust for global dominance is explored in *American Empire: Roosevelt's Geographer and the Prelude to Globalization* (Smith, 2003). Geography is inseparable from economics, politics, and international affairs. The promotion of English globally is part and parcel of this process: it is integral to globalization. In polit-ical discourse the dominant economic system of capitalism has been conflated with "democracy" and "freedom."

Linguistic Human Rights, Linguistic Diversity, and Language Maintenance in and through Education: Issues of Language Policy and Politics

In today's world, it is impossible to imagine linguistic diversity consisting of more or less monolingual groups living in isolation from all others. Most probably this has never been the case. Even groups with very high degrees of self-sufficiency, and little risk of ecological disasters such as drought, have traded with each other, and many in the group have known the neighboring language(s) (see, e.g., Corballis, 2002; Diamond, 1998; Nettle, 1999; Wells, 2002). Many, if not most speakers of numerically small languages are necessarily multilingual as adults, and some degree of individual multilingualism is a prerequisite for them for participation in the wider society. Few are today decisively against *individual* multilingualism, *once it has been achieved*, while many are trying to prevent children from achieving high levels of bi-or multilingualism, for instance through depriving them of mother tongue medium education. In contrast, many are against *societal* multilingualism, and, especially, any linguistic human rights for Indigenous peoples and minorities that would enable them to maintain their languages and reproduce themselves as minorities. And many are against the world's linguistic diversity, claiming it is problematic and not cost-effective (see Skutnabb-Kangas, 2007, for an overview of language policy and language rights).

Many researchers plead directly or indirectly for the elimination of both multilingualism and linguistic diversity. They claim it is unnecessary, messy, costly and inefficient (for some examples, see de Swaan, 2001; Glazer, 1997; Kymlicka, 2001; Ladefoged, 1992; Kymlicka & Patten, 2003). To label linguistic diversity as a complication, obstacle, or problem is to deny and lament not suggestions or dreams, but *facts*. With very few exceptions, the world's countries *are* multilingual, and, with Debi Pattanayak's subtle Indian understatement, "[o]ne language is an impractical proposition for a multilingual country" (1988, p. 382). The teaching profession often legitimates the normalization of English as The Preferable (and Only) Language of the World, partly by overemphasizing its usefulness and importance, partly by invisibilizing other languages (not mentioning them or belittling them). English can also, paradoxically, be invisibilized when it is presented as the self-evident default norm, as in a Peace Corps advertisement where one FAQ (Frequently Asked Question) to USA applicants was: "Do you need to know a language?" The answer was "No." English was obviously not seen as "a language."

Why is linguistic diversity needed? The following list gives a short summary of reasons that have been presented by various researchers:

- Languages have been called the libraries of the intangible heritage of humankind, in terms of both form (diversity of ways of structuring a language, and of the underlying cognitive categories and processes) and content (most of humankind's knowledge is encoded in languages; grammars have been called "fossilized experience").

- For many people, languages are cultural core values, central for their identities (see Metekingi, 2003–6; and Task Force, 2005).
- Creativity precedes innovation, which is followed by investment. Creativity can be one of the results of additive teaching and multilingualism. Creativity and new ideas are the main assets (cultural capital) in a knowledge society and a prerequisite for humankind to adapt to change and to find solutions to the catastrophes of our own making. The more linguistically and culturally diverse the world is, the more new ideas and creativity of various kinds are likely to exist. High levels of multilingualism may enhance creativity; monolingualism and homogenization kill it.
- English is not enough. "Good" English will fairly soon be like literacy yesterday or computer skills today: employers see it as self-evident and necessary but not sufficient for good jobs. Supply and demand theories predict that when many people possess what earlier was a scarce commodity (near-native English), the price goes down (Grin, 2001). The value of "perfect" English skills as a financial incentive decreases substantially when a high proportion of a country's or a region's or the world's population knows English well.
- Linguistic diversity and biodiversity are correlationally and probably also causally related. Knowledge about how to maintain biodiversity is encoded in small languages because it is their speakers who live in the world's biologically (and linguistically) most diverse areas. Through killing these languages (or letting them die), we kill many of the prerequisites for maintaining biodiversity (see Harmon, 2002; Maffi, 2001; Posey, 1999; Skutnabb-Kangas, Maffi, & Harmon, 2003; Skutnabb-Kangas & Phillipson, 2007, for overviews).
- Finally, Colin Baker sums up the importance of ecological diversity in his review of Skutnabb-Kangas 2000 (Baker, 2001, p. 281):

> Ecological diversity is essential for long-term planetary survival. Diversity contains the potential for adaptation. Uniformity can endanger a species by providing inflexibility and unadaptability. As languages and cultures die, the testimony of human intellectual achievement is lessened. In the language of ecology, the strongest ecosystems are those that are the most diverse. Diversity is directly related to stability; variety is important for long-term survival. Our success on this planet has been due to an ability to adapt to different kinds of environment over thousands of years. Such ability is born out of diversity. Thus language and cultural diversity maximises chances of human success and adaptability.

Biocultural diversity (biodiversity + linguistic diversity + cultural diversity) is thus essential for long-term planetary survival because it enhances creativity and adaptability and thus stability. Today we are killing biocultural diversity faster than ever before in human history.

Schools can, even in one generation, make the intergenerational transfer of small Indigenous and minority languages impossible, and thus make the languages seriously endangered (not learned by the next generation of children). The educational system participates in committing linguistic and cultural genocide, according to two of the five definitions of genocide (II(b) and II(e)) in the United Nations International Convention on the Prevention and Punishment of the Crime of Genocide (E793, 1948). Education offered to most Indigenous and many minority children is intentionally "forcibly transferring children of the group to another group" and "causing serious bodily *or mental* harm to members of the group" (emphasis added). This is done through assimilationist subtractive submersion education, using a dominant language – instead of the children's own language – as the teaching language (see Skutnabb-Kangas, 2000; Magga et al., 2005, and references in both, for evidence and further discussion). Without binding educational linguistic human rights, especially a right to mainly mother tongue-medium education in state schools, with good teaching of a dominant language as a second language, given by competent bilingual teachers, most Indigenous peoples and minorities have to accept *subtractive* education through the medium of a dominant/majority language. They learn a dominant language at the cost of the mother tongue(s). These are displaced, and later often replaced by the dominant language. Subtractive teaching subtracts from the child's linguistic repertoire, instead of adding to it. For linguistic genocide to be stopped and for the linguistic diversity of the world to be maintained, basic linguistic human rights (LHRs) are necessary, especially in education.

The most important LHR with these aims is the right to use one's own language as the main teaching language, together with the right to learn a dominant official language and thus to become high-level bilingual or multilingual. There is today no universal right guaranteeing this. Language is seen in most human rights documents as one of the important "characteristics" on the basis of which people are supposed not to be discriminated against, a negative right. But when one moves from the prefaces of the documents to educational rights, language is often not mentioned, and if it is, the provisions are extremely vague or conditional and there are so many modifications and "claw-backs" that the rights are virtually meaningless (see Skutnabb-Kangas, 2000, for thorough exemplification). Two recent European HRs instruments[3] offer some possibilities, not so much because of their formulations, which are often weak,[4] but mainly because the monitoring committees, which examine the reports that participating states have to write, have tried to prompt states to action. The Organization for Security and Cooperation in Europe and some other organizations (including UNESCO) have issued recommendations and/or guidelines that are steps in the right direction, but these are in no way binding.

Even if they were binding, it is doubtful to what extent they would be implemented. This is an example of how policy in education (a decision to use the mother tongue as the teaching language) interlocks with the politics of the economy (free or for-fee education). Most education of Indigenous and minority children is not even starting to fulfill the requirements posed by Katarina Tomaševski in terms of "the four a's": education has to be available, accessible, acceptable, and adaptable. Tomaševski, the former United Nations Special Rapporteur on the Right to Education, examines 170 countries in her last report *The State of the Right to Education Worldwide. Free or Fee: 2006 Global Report* (www.katarinatomasevski. com) to see to what extent education is free or for-fee. Even primary education is fee-paying in more than half of the countries (see her Table 25); thus education is not available to children. The pattern of economic (poverty-based) exclusion from primary school is part of a global strategy for "no poverty reduction." Education is often priced out of the reach of the poor. The trend has been a transition from free-and-compulsory to market-based education where the costs of even primary education have been transferred from governmental to family budgets. But even if children could afford primary education, being forced to accept teaching in a language that is not the (Indigenous or minority) language makes the teaching non-accessible, except in the most trivial sense of children possibly understanding a few contextualized issues and learning some aspects of concrete everyday language. This kind of education often fits well with the conclusions of a study from Zambia: "There is a clear risk that the policy of using English as a vehicular language may contribute to stunting, rather than promoting, academic and cognitive growth" (Williams, 1998). There has to be a major change in the politics of education before we can even start to discuss meaningful language policies in education for Indigenous and (autochthonous or immigrant) minority children, or, for that matter, many other children from subordinated groups/ peoples.

Some changes are on their way. The pessimistic prognoses state that minimally 50 percent, maybe up to 90–95 percent, of today's spoken languages may be extinct or very seriously endangered (not learned by children) around 2100. Language revitalization movements are growing all over the world. The Māori language nests (pre-schools where fluent elders are teaching language and culture to children, parents, and even pre-school teachers) have spread from Aotearoa to Hawai'i, to the Saami areas in Norway and Finland, to Canada, etc. Indigenous immersion programs for revitalization are likewise spreading to many Indigenous peoples, for instance in Canada and the USA, where the languages have been partially lost (on concepts, see Skutnabb-Kangas & McCarty, 2008). There are discussions about redefining mother tongues so that Indigenous individuals whose parent or grandparent generation has experienced linguistic genocide through education could both claim a mother tongue on the basis of identification only, without knowing this mother tongue, and demand compensation for the language lost. In Papua New Guinea, in India, especially Orissa, in Nepal, in Vietnam, in many African countries, and several other places where the languages are still alive, Indigenous/tribal children are starting to have their own languages as teaching/learning languages while at the same time learning official languages. The United Nations Permanent Forum on Indigenous Issues (UNPFII, http://www.un.org/esa/socdev/unpfii/) is making language regenesis, reclamation, revival, revitalization, maintenance, and further development one of the focal program points.

Language Policy, Exemplified by the European Region

Language policies are necessary for the European Union, which is undergoing an intensive process of integrating 27 member states. Policies in education, culture, and language have traditionally been the prerogative of each state. Since 1992 the EU has had a mandate to "supplement" this through a considerable number of programs, such as student and staff mobility, language learning, and awareness raising, as well as funding for minority languages (http://ec.europa.eu/education/policies/lang/languages_en.html). Currently the EU advocates the learning of two foreign languages by all schoolchildren, building on curriculum development work by the Council of Europe over several decades, such as the Common European Framework of Reference for Languages (www.coe.int/T/DG4/Linguistic/Default_en.asp). Levels of foreign-language competence vary greatly between the different member states. The supra-statal initiatives show innovation being promoted by bureaucratic elites rather than a profession's internal dynamics. Reform in foreign-language learning is very slow globally, despite some imaginative initiatives, for instance, Content and Language Integrated Learning (CLIL), one of the EU's mantras for achieving more success in foreign-language learning, or the Cultures and Languages Across the Curriculum (CLAC) Movement in the USA (www.clas.pdx.edu/clac/). Another EU language mantra is an early start to foreign-language learning, a notion that is intuitively appealing, hence easy for politicians to latch on to and promote. Experience shows, however, that considerable educational changes need to be in place before the age factor can influence outcomes decisively (see Phillipson, 2003, pp. 95–104). Persuading Europeans to learn two foreign languages represents an attempt to diversify the languages learned.

The EU has commissioned studies of a range of language pedagogy issues, e.g., of foreign-language teacher training in 32 European countries, including case studies of good practice, bilingual education, and a profile of the language teacher of the future (Grenfell, Kelly, & Jones, 2003). Other studies argue persuasively for a paradigm shift in foreign-language education (Dendrinos and Mitsikopoulou, 2004). Unlike the bland, technocratic discourse of many EU policy statements, such authors see it as axiomatic that discourses on language policy and foreign-language education are neither ideologically nor politically neutral.

Among multiple market forces strengthening English is the Bologna process, the integration of higher education and research across 45 countries. The 1999 Bologna objectives declare the intention "within the framework of our institutional competences and taking full respect of the diversity of cultures, languages, national education systems and of University autonomy," to consolidate a European Higher Education Area at the latest by 2010. The ministerial meeting at Bergen, Norway on 19–20 May 2005 (www.bologna-bergen2005.no) focused on the coordination of structural uniformity (a standardized degree structure in 45 countries), quality assurance, the recognition of degrees and study periods, attractiveness, and competitiveness. What is striking is that not once in the communiqué is there any reference to languages, to bilingual degrees or multilingualism. What emerges unambiguously is that in the Bologna process, "internationalization" means "English-medium higher education" (Phillipson, 2006).

This clearly entails the risk of what political discourse in several European countries refers to as "domain loss." This is a seemingly innocuous but deceptive term. Like the language policy term "language spread," or "language death," it seems to imply a natural, agent-less process (see Skutnabb-Kangas & McCarty, 2008, for conceptual clarification). Clearly there are agents involved in domains being lost or gained, in languages "disappearing" and in any diglossic division of academic labor. The process of domain loss can be seen as linguistic capital accumulation by dispossession. As in the commercial world in its global pursuit of markets and profit (Harvey, 2005), some combination of internal motivation and external pressure contributes to this trend.

Users of English benefit from these processes, just like speakers of all killer languages that are learned at the expense of small disappearing languages. These benefits are exemplified in a study of foreign languages as public policy in education, commissioned by the Haut Conseil de l'évaluation de l'école, Paris (Grin, 2005). The study calculated that the current dominance of English in continental European education systems results in quantifiable privileged market effects, communication savings effects, language learning savings effects, alternative human capital investment effects, and legitimacy and rhetorical effects. Continental European countries are transferring to the UK and Ireland at least €10 billion per annum, and more probably about €16–17 billion. The UK and Ireland benefit since they invest so little in foreign-language learning as compared with their EU partners. If this European study in the economics of language were to be extrapolated globally, it would show a massive global transfer of not only linguistic but economic capital from the rest of the world to the few English-dominant countries. Voices are being raised that demand more equality in sharing the communication burden: some kind of compensation is due to those who go to the expense of learning the languages of more powerful people. Exposing this aspect of the politics of language teaching is an urgent task for applied linguists and economists of language.

Grin has assessed what the costs and benefits are of a language policy which maintains and promotes minority languages, and what the costs (and benefits) are if they are not. Some of his encouraging conclusions, which we endorse, are as follows (Grin, 2003, p. 26):

- diversity seems to be positively, rather than negatively, correlated with welfare;
- the available evidence indicates that the monetary costs of maintaining diversity are remarkably modest;
- devoting resources to the protection and promotion of minority cultures [and this includes languages] may help to stave off political crises whose costs would be considerably higher than that of the policies considered;

- therefore, there are strong grounds to suppose that protecting and promoting regional and minority languages is a sound idea from a welfare standpoint, not even taking into consideration any moral argument.

NOTES

1 The quote from Manu Metekingi comes from a film shown at the Whanganui Iwi Exhibition, at Te Papa Tongarewa Museum of New Zealand, Wellington, 29 November, 2003 – May, 2006. The Exhibition tells about "our heartland, the Whanganui River, and our place within it." The Whanganui iwi write: "The well-being of our river is intertwined with its people's well-being" (from the brochure describing the exhibition, with the theme: "Ko au te awa, ko te awa ko au. I am the river, the river is me"). Thanks to the staff at Te Papa for identifying the person for us – neither the quote nor his name is in the brochure, only in the film.
2 Talk at University of California, Irvine, 20 March 2006, see http://humanities.uci.edu/faultline/.
3 The *Framework Convention for the Protection of National Minorities* (http://conventions. coe.int/treaty/en/Treaties/Html/157.htm) and the *European Charter for Regional or Minority Languages* (http://conventions.coe.int/treaty/en/Treaties/Html/148.htm).
4 An example is the *Framework Convention's* Article covering medium of education. It is so heavily qualified that the minority is completely at the mercy of the state (emphases added): "In areas inhabited by persons belonging to national minorities traditionally or in *substantial* numbers, *if there is sufficient demand*, the parties shall *endeavour* to ensure, *as far as possible* and *within the framework of their education systems*, that persons belonging to those minorities have *adequate* opportunities for being taught in the minority language *or* for receiving instruction in this language."

REFERENCES

Baker, C. (2001). Review of Tove Skutnabb-Kangas *Linguistic Genocide in Education – or Worldwide Diversity and Human Rights? Journal of Sociolinguistics* 5, 2, 279–83.

Baker, M. (2006). *Translation and conflict: A narrative account.* London: Routledge.

Block, D. (1997). Publishing patterns and McDonaldization. *IATEFL Newsletter* (April/May), 12–15.

Chaudenson, R. (2003). Geolinguistics, geopolitics, geostrategy: The case for French. In J. Maurais and M. A. Morris (eds.), *Languages in a globalising world* (pp. 291–7). Cambridge: Cambridge University Press.

Corballis, M. C. (2002). *From hand to mouth: The origins of language.* Princeton/Oxford: Princeton University Press.

Cronin, M. (2003). *Translation and globalization.* London: Routledge.

Dendrinos, B. & Mitsikopoulou, B. (eds.) (2004). *Policies of linguistic pluralism and the teaching of languages in Europe.* Athens: Metaixmio, and the National and Kapodistrian University of Athens.

de Swaan, A. (2001). *Words of the world: The global language system.* Cambridge: Polity.

Diamond, J. (1998). *Guns, germs and steel: A short history of everybody for the last 13,000 years.* London: Random House.

Glazer, N. (1998). *We are all multiculturalists now.* Cambridge, MA: Harvard University Press.

Graddol, D. (2006). *English next? Why Global English may mean the end of "English as a Foreign Language."* London: The British Council. (downloadable at www.britishcouncil.org/learning-research)

Grenfell, M., Kelly, M., & Jones, D. (2003). *The European language teacher: Recent trends and future developments in teacher education.* Bern: Peter Lang.

Grin, F. (2001). English as economic value: Facts and fallacies. *World Englishes* 20, 2, 65–78.

Grin, F. (2003). Language planning and economics. *Current Issues in Language Planning* 4, 11, 1–66.

Grin, F. (2005). *L'enseignement des Langues Étrangères comme Politique Publique.* Paris: Haut Conseil de l'Évaluation de l'École.

Harmon, D. (2002). *In light of our differences: How diversity in nature and culture makes us human.* Washington, DC: The Smithsonian Institute Press.

Harvey, D. (2005). *The new imperialism.* Oxford: Oxford University Press. (First edition published 2003.)

Huntington, S. (1996). *The clash of civilizations and the remaking of the world order.* New York: Simon and Schuster.

Joshi, S. (ed.) (1994). *Rethinking English: Essays in literature, language, history.* Delhi: Oxford University Press.

Kandiah, T. (1999). Re-visioning, revolution, revisionism: English and the ambiguities of post-colonial practice. *The Sri Lanka Journal of the Humanities* 24 & 25, 31–64.

Kayman, M. A. (2004). The state of English as a global language: Communicating culture. *Textual Practice* 18, 1, 1–22.

Kymlicka, W. (2001). *Politics in the vernacular: Nationalism, multiculturalism and citizenship.* Oxford: Oxford University Press.

Kymlicka, W. & Patten, A. (eds.) (2003). *Language rights and political theory.* Oxford: Oxford University Press.

Ladefoged, P. (1992). Another view of endangered languages. *Language* 68, 4, 809–11.

Lo Bianco, J. (2002). Real world language politics and policy. In S. J. Baker (ed.), *Language policy: Lessons from global models* (pp. 8–27). Monterey, CA: Monterey Institute of International Studies.

Maffi, L. (ed.) (2001). *On biocultural diversity: Linking language, knowledge and the environment.* Washington, DC: The Smithsonian Institute Press.

Magga, O. H., Nicolaisen, I., Trask, M., Dunbar, R., & Skutnabb-Kangas, T. (2005). *Indigenous children's education and indigenous languages.* Expert paper written for the United Nations Permanent Forum on Indigenous Issues. New York: United Nations.

Mazrui, A. A. (2004). *English in Africa: After the Cold War.* Clevedon, UK: Multilingual Matters.

McCarty, T. L., Romero, M. E., & Zepeda, O. (2006). Reimagining multilingual America: Lessons from Native American youth. In O. García, T. Skutnabb-Kangas, & M. E. Torres-Guzmán (eds.), *Imagining multilingual schools: Languages in education and glocalization* (pp. 91–110). Clevedon, UK: Multilingual Matters.

Metekingi, M. (2003–6). Film shown at the Whanganui Iwi Exhibition, at Te Papa Tongarewa Museum of New Zealand, Wellington, 29 November, 2003 – May, 2006.

Naik, C. (2004). India's language policy in an uncertain century. In P. Dias (ed.), *Multiple languages, literacies and technologies: Mapping out concepts, analysing practices and defining positions* (pp. 246–63). New Delhi: Books for Change.

Nettle, D. (1999). *Linguistic diversity*. Oxford: Oxford University Press.

Nuffield Foundation, The (2000). *Languages: The next generation. The final report and recommendations of the Nuffield Languages Inquiry*. London: The Nuffield Foundation.

Odora Hoppers, C. A. (ed.) (2002). *Indigenous knowledge and the integration of knowledge systems: Towards a philosophy of articulation*. Claremont: New Africa Books.

Pattanayak, D. P. (1988). Monolingual myopia and the petals of the Indian lotus: Do many languages divide or unite a nation? In T. Skutnabb-Kangas & J. Cummins (eds.), *Minority education: From shame to struggle* (pp. 379–89). Clevedon, UK: Multilingual Matters.

Patten, A. & Kymlicka, W. (2003). Introduction: Language rights and political theory: Context, issues, and approaches. In W. Kymlicka & A. Patten (eds.), *Language rights and political theory* (pp. 1–51). Oxford: Oxford University Press.

Phillipson, R. (2003). *English-only Europe? Challenging language policy*. London: Routledge.

Phillipson, R. (2004). Review article, English in globalization: Three approaches (books by de Swaan, Block and Cameron, and Brutt-Griffler). *Journal of Language, Identity, and Education* 3, 1, 73–84.

Phillipson, R. (2006). English, a cuckoo in the European higher education nest of languages? *European Journal of English Studies* 10, 1, 13–32.

Posey, D. A. (ed.) (1999). *Cultural and spiritual values of biodiversity: A complementary contribution to the Global Biodiversity Assessment*. London: Intermediate Technology Publications, for and on behalf of the/United Nations Environmental Programme.

Ricento, T. (ed.) (2006). *An introduction to language policy: Theory and method*. Oxford: Blackwell.

Rothkopf, D. (1997). In praise of cultural imperialism?' *Foreign Policy* 53, 38–53.

Seabrook, J. (2004). *Consuming cultures: Globalization and local lives*. London: New Internationalist.

Skutnabb-Kangas, T. (2000). *Linguistic genocide in education – or worldwide diversity and human rights?* Mahwah, NJ: Lawrence Erlbaum.

Skutnabb-Kangas, T. (2007). Language planning and language rights. In M. Hellinger & A. Pauwels (eds.), *Linguistic diversity and language change* (pp. 365–97), Handbooks of Applied Linguistics 9. Berlin: Mouton de Gruyter.

Skutnabb-Kangas, T., Maffi, L., & Harmon, D. (2003). *Sharing a world of difference: The earth's linguistic, cultural, and biological diversity*. Paris: UNESCO Publishing. UNESCO, Terralingua, and World Wide Fund for Nature (ISBN UNESCO 92-3-103917-2; also in Catalan, French, Korean and Spanish).

Skutnabb-Kangas, T. & McCarty, T. (2008). Clarification, ideological/epistemological underpinnings and implications of some concepts in bilingual education. In J. Cummins & N. Hornberger (eds.), *Bilingual education*, vol. 5 of *Encyclopedia of Language and Education* (2nd edn., pp. 3–17). Kluwer Academic.

Skutnabb-Kangas, T. & Phillipson, R. (2007). Language and ecology. In J.-O. Östman & J. Verschueren (eds.), in collaboration with Eline Versluys, *Handbook of pragmatics*. Amsterdam: Benjamins.

Smith, N. (2003). *American empire: Roosevelt's geographer and the prelude to globalization*. Berkeley and Los Angeles, CA: University of California Press.

Smith Tuhiwai, L. (1999). *Deconstructing methodologies: Research and Indigenous peoples*. Dunedin/New York: University of Otago Press/Zed Books.

Spolsky, B. (2004). *Language policy*. Cambridge: Cambridge University Press.

Tacitus (1948). *Tacitus on Britain and Germany*. A new translation of the 'Agricola' and the 'Germania', by H. Mattingly. Harmondsworth: Penguin.

Tagore, R. (1992). *My reminiscences*. New Delhi: Rupa.

Task Force on Aboriginal Languages and Cultures (2005). *Towards a new beginning: A foundational report for a strategy to revitalize First Nation, Inuit and Métis languages and cultures. Report to the Minister of Canadian Heritage, June 2005*. Ottawa: Aboriginal Languages Directorate. www.aboriginallanguagestaskforce.ca

Tomaševski, K. (1996). International prospects for the future of the welfare state. In *Reconceptualizing the welfare state* (pp. 100–17). Copenhagen: The Danish Centre for Human Rights.

Wells, S. (2002). *The journey of man: A genetic odyssey*. Princeton & Oxford: Princeton University Press.

Williams, E. (1998). *Investigating bilingual literacy: Evidence from Malawi and Zambia*. Education Research no. 24. London: Department For International Development.

Zhou, M. & Sun, H. (eds.) (2004). *Language policy in the People's Republic of China: Theory and practice since 1949*. Boston, MA: Kluwer Academic.

FURTHER READING

Dunbar, R. & Skutnabb-Kangas, T. (2008). *Forms of education of indigenous children as crimes against humanity?* Expert paper written for the United Nations Permanent Forum on Indigenous Issues (PFII). New York: PFII. [In PFII' system: "Presented by Lars-Anders Baer, in collaboration with Robert Dunbar, Tove Skutnabb-Kangas and Ole Henrik Magga".] www.un.org/esa/socdev/unpfii/documents/E_C19_2008_7.pdf

García, O., Skutnabb-Kangas, T., & Torres Guzmán, M. (eds.) (2006). *Imagining multilingual schools: Languages in education and glocalization*, Linguistic Diversity and Language Rights series. Clevedon, UK: Multilingual Matters.

Phillipson, R. (2009). *Linguistic imperialism continued*. New Delhi: Orient BlackSwan.

Tomaševski, K. (2001). *Human rights obligations: Making education available, accessible, acceptable and adaptable*. Right to Education Primers 3. Lund/Stockholm: Raoul Wallenberg Institute of Human Rights and Humanitarian Law/Sida (Swedish International Development Cooperation Agency).

Many useful articles can be found in the following journals: *Journal of Language, Identity and Education*; *Language Policy*; *Language Problems and Language Planning*; *Critical Inquiry in Language Studies*.

4 History of Language Teaching

DIANE MUSUMECI

What is the relevance of the history of language teaching for a volume that contains state-of-the-art perspectives on issues facing the profession? Cutting edge research does not require it. Modern theories need not consider it. Yet none of the topics addressed in this volume is novel. Each has been considered at an earlier – sometimes much earlier – point in the history of language teaching. Most have been part of the disciplinary discourse for centuries. Notwithstanding, the field of applied linguistics devotes scant attention to its history. In his 1983 volume entitled *Fundamental Concepts of Language Teaching*, H. H. Stern lamented the fact that "language teaching theory has a short memory" and lacks "historical depth" (pp. 76–7). Brumfit and Mitchell (1990), Musumeci (1997), as well as Thomas (2004), also argue for an historical perspective. Mitchell and Myles (2004) address the problem of ahistoricity by grounding their excellent introduction to current second-language learning theories within the "recent history" of the post-WWII period. Aside from the intrinsic merit of historical research, even a passing acquaintance with the people, philosophies, and events that have shaped the history of second-language teaching provides the possibility of contextualizing current trends, practices, and debates.

Given the long and varied history of second-language teaching, a strictly chronological account of that tradition would be necessarily superficial at best in the space of a single essay. Instead, this chapter will outline the teaching of one particular language over the course of several centuries. In doing so, the topics presented in their contemporary context elsewhere in this volume will be treated here within a broader historical perspective. It is hoped that in this manner the reader may be exposed to the complexity that has characterized the history of language teaching and to the recurring issues that form the core of that tradition, as well as encountering relevant, at times perhaps surprising, insights that such a perspective offers.

The Context of Second-Language Teaching

Whereas systematic research on second-language acquisition is a relatively recent phenomenon, the practice of language teaching enjoys a long tradition, one that is linked to theories of mind and thought, philosophy, culture, economics, and education. One can easily imagine that second-language learning has been going on since peoples with different language systems first encountered one another on the savannahs of Africa, in the Mesopotamian valley, and on the plains of northern Europe. However, despite a history of second-language learning that certainly predates writing, formal accounts of second-language teaching typically begin in the Western tradition with the teaching of Latin, and to a lesser extent, Greek, in the centuries following the decline of the Roman Empire in the fifth century of the Common Era. The reason for this starting point is simple: Latin was the language of wider communication, the language of education, scholarship, and commerce, the lingua franca for almost two millennia. It was very much the equivalent of English in the globalized world today *even though, for the vast majority of that time, it was not the first language of anyone who used it.*

For centuries, the acquisition of second-language literacy skills; i.e., learning to read and write in Latin, constituted the foundation of all formal education. Erudite people also spoke it. That the historical tradition is based almost exclusively on the model of teaching Latin (and its subsequent influence on the teaching of other Western European languages) reflects a distinct disciplinary and cultural bias: First, because it investigates primarily formal instruction, despite the fact that until late in that history such instruction rarely included anyone but the most elite males of society; and second because the Western written tradition is certainly not the only one, and there is much that one could undoubtedly learn from other, oral, and more ancient traditions (Reagan, 1996).

In addition to a disciplinary bias, concise histories of second-language teaching necessarily have a narrow focus. Although the variety of approaches to language teaching that date from the mid-twentieth century (audiolingualism, the Direct Method, the Silent Way, Suggestopedia, the Natural Approach, communicative language teaching, content-based instruction, and task-based instruction to name the most salient) are well documented, histories typically cite the grammar-translation method used to teach Latin as the predominant instructional approach to the teaching of all languages until that point (Mackey, 1965; Richards & Rogers, 2001; Titone, 1968). It is generally understood that this method consisted of the study of grammatical rules, followed by translation from the second language into the first and back again. In an attempt to provide evidence for a much less hegemonic history of pedagogical practice, Kelly (1969) instead provides a compendium of materials and techniques that have formed a legacy of 25 centuries of language teaching, his eponymous work. More recently, Howatt and Widdowson (2004) present a richly detailed and fascinating account of the history of English language teaching over several centuries in an updated version of Howatt's classic 1984 text. Other historical accounts that examine the highly contextualized teaching of one language include Kibbee's (1991) examination of the early practice of teaching of French in England.

Taking a decidedly different approach to the historical record, Thomas (2004) offers an impressive scholarly volume that traces over two millennia key philosophical concepts underlying the notion of Universal Grammar, that is, the principles deemed to be part of the innate human capacity to learn language. In a much less exhaustive, but similarly thematic, approach based primarily upon evidence from the fifteenth through the seventeenth centuries – a span which marked the apex of the teaching of Latin as a universal language and the inception of its subsequent demise – Musumeci (1997) explores the disparity between theory and practice in language teaching and argues that language teaching as rule-governed practice may not have been nearly as widely prescribed as the historical summaries suggest. Instead, the rote teaching of forms and rules has consistently coexisted with a concomitant insistence on language as communication and the privileged status of attention to meaning in the acquisition process. The tension between treating the second language as the object of instruction versus a system of communication has persisted throughout the history of language teaching, with the former often a by-product of external, pragmatic forces rather than an instantiation of theoretical stance.

Within either historical approach, broadly diachronic or thematic, two problems immediately arise in any attempt to characterize second-language teaching. First, one cannot presume that actual teaching practice at any given time was monolithic. Even today with the academy's emphasis on experimentation and data-driven research, the contemporary literature contains few detailed and systematic accounts of actual classroom behavior, let alone the numerous samples across a broad range of contexts that would be necessary to provide an informed characterization of current practice. The body of research on instructed second-language acquisition, as Doughty (2003) points out, has been complicated by the fact that "any particular implementation [of a method] by an individual teacher is subject to variation" (p. 263). How much more difficult it is, then, to accurately reconstruct that practice in past centuries when the norms governing scientific discovery, let alone educational practice, were quite different. To further complicate matters, the philosophical treatises, letters to princes and nobles, and sermons which constitute much of the historical record focus largely on reform, with the consequence that, where observations and accounts do exist, they are typically presented for the purpose of demonstrating ineffective practice leading to unsatisfactory outcomes. As an example, the following quote from the seventeenth-century educational reformer and renowned author of language textbooks Johannes Comenius foreshadows the rationale of those who have recently proposed the elimination of foreign language programs from universities in favor of outsourcing to study-abroad providers:

> Camp followers and military attendants, engaged in the kitchen and in other menial occupations, learn a tongue that differs from their own, sometimes two or three,

quicker than the children in schools learn Latin only, though children have an abundance of time, and devote all their energies to it. And with what unequal progress! The former gabble their languages after a few months, while the latter, after fifteen or twenty years, can only put a few sentences into Latin with the aid of grammars and of dictionaries, and cannot do even this without mistakes and hesitation. (p. 69)

Not surprisingly, proponents of educational reform select worst-case scenarios to provide evidence for their argument, that is, what needs to change, rather than what is effective or beneficial. In other words, a change of practice is advocated because the current system is reported not to produce the desired results. It is noteworthy that the rhetoric of reform does not require proof that this is indeed the case. Instead it relies on the readers' conviction that the author speaks from authority and experience.

Just as the reformer need only convince the reader of the inadequacy of the current state of affairs, to be effective his or her argument need not necessarily provide evidence that the new system will guarantee success. To that end, a different strategy may be employed: namely, that the advocated change is actually not a new practice at all, rather a "tried and true," albeit little-known, component of the long-standing tradition. As a case in point, the US in the 1960s experienced a sudden interest in the history of language teaching precisely for this reason: the introduction of what was purported to be a "scientific" approach to language learning, the "New Key," as audiolingualism was called. Based on principles of behaviorism in psychology, it was a language teaching method that advocated carefully constructed pattern practice that would result in the forma-tion of good linguistic habits deemed necessary for successful language learning. By arguing that the "new" method, while supported by the latest thinking in psychology and offering a radical departure from grammar-translation, was in fact seeded throughout centuries of second-language teaching, proponents of the approach provided empirical evidence to justify its adoption. Indeed, Kelly's tome, which remains the gold standard as an archive of language teaching tech-niques, is rife with references to historical exemplars of audiolingual tenets. Mackey and Titone reflect similar interpretive biases.

Spikes in historical interest appear to coincide with the advent of approaches to second-language learning that challenge the explicit teaching of grammar rules as the primary, or even sole, method of instruction. In this way, proponents of the innovation situate the new approach within a broader historical framework and seek validation in past experience. Thomas and Musumeci may well provide further testament to this phenomenon, with regard to Universal Grammar and meaning-based instruction, respectively.

On the other hand, advocates for language teaching methodologies that ex-pound an explicit grammatical focus from the very beginning may not feel com-pelled to look for historical evidence to support their position. Such lack may reflect an underlying assumption that theirs is the historically supported stance, the norm. Certainly, a prevailing belief that all language teaching prior to the mid-twentieth century entailed a grammar-translation approach would support such a notion. Blanket references to "traditional" methods of language teaching favor such interpretation. One would be surprised to read of a second-language curriculum characterized as "traditional" that advocated an experiential, multi-sensory, or immersion-type approach. Upon examination, however, language teaching history demonstrates a broad range of approaches, methods, and techniques dependent upon prevailing notions about how language is acquired, the context in which it occurred – which, in turn, affected the perceived purpose in learning the second language – the resources that were available, and the role of the participants. In light of the historical record, the definition of what is "traditional" language teaching becomes impossibly difficult to establish. The next section provides an account of how the first three factors – beliefs about language learning, methodologies, and the historical context – intertwined in the history of second-language teaching. A brief historical perspective on the perceived roles of the teacher and learner concludes this chapter.

Beliefs about Language Learning, Methodologies and Historical Context

The questions that present-day research in second-language acquisition addresses derive from theoretical frameworks that posit a set of underlying beliefs, assumptions, or principles. Doughty and Long (2003) provide an authoritative and comprehensive account of the key issues surrounding current research. Is language an innate ability unique to human beings? Is it a skill that is acquired through exposure and interaction? To what extent does learning a second language resemble first-language acquisition? To what extent is explicit versus implicit attention to linguistic rules a condition for successful acquisition? What is the nature of errors: Are they part of a developmental process that will eventually dissipate with increasing exposure and experience or are they something pernicious to be avoided or immediately corrected before they become a permanent part of the underlying grammar? What is the role of the learners' first language in the learning of the second? These are only a few of the questions surrounding second-language acquisition that have intrigued educators for centuries. The most fundamental question, the extent to which language is the result of an innate ability or learned behavior, forms the basis of early philosophical thought. In turn, the answer to that question intimately informs the construction of language teaching methodology.

At its most extreme, the innatist position holds that language acquisition results from an essential human ability specific to language that resides in the mind. A pedagogical corollary of this position is that language acquisition manifests itself according to a predestined route that instructional intervention serves at best to accelerate. Although the research evidence that substantiates this position dates to the second half of the twentieth century, one can trace the earliest roots for an innatist stance to an ancient philosophical position originating with the Greek philosopher, Plato (427–347 BCE). Stated in the simplest of terms, Plato proposed that human beings possess knowledge intrinsically. Such knowledge need simply be activated and drawn out. As a result, the teacher's role is to educate, from the Latin *educere*, which means literally 'to lead forth'. It is from Plato that we learn of the Socratic method, an instructional technique in which the teacher asks a series of carefully constructed questions each based on the student's previous response, leading students to arrive at the answer from what they already know. The basic premise of another ancient Greek philosopher, Aristotle (384–322 BCE), is radically different. Aristotle proposed that a human being comes into the world as a blank slate, *tabula rasa*, upon which knowledge is inscribed either by experience or by rule. The teacher's role in the Aristotelian tradition was to provide that knowledge, to instruct; from the Latin *instruere*, meaning 'to build'. Those who believe that language is largely a learned behavior may be more concerned with the environmental features surrounding language acquisition and with explicit instruction in rules. For example, they may fear the consequences of exposing learners to poor examples and leaving errors unchecked, and thus the possibility of acquiring inexpungeable mistakes or bad habits. Quintilian, a Roman educator in the first century CE whose twelve-volume text *Institutio oratoria* [Education of an orator] is a foundational contribution to Western educational theory, warns that children must be presented only with the best models, such that "Care must be taken that tender minds, which will imbibe deeply whatever has entered them while rude and ignorant of everything, may learn not only what is eloquent, but, still more, what is morally good" (*Institutio oratoria* I.8.4, in Murphy, 1987, p. 64).

From the very beginning, the Western tradition has struggled with the question of nature versus nurture, the innatist versus environmentalist position, a biological as opposed to a behavioral explanation for language acquisition. Mitchell and Myles (2004) provide a highly readable account of the continuing nature versus nurture debate and its influence on the most recent theories of second-language acquisition. Their discussion reiterates the diversity of frameworks that guide contemporary research on second-language learning.

Clearly, it would be absurd to reduce our current understanding of second-language acquisition to a simple dichotomy. In dealing with a complex knowledge system like language, one would expect that certain theories better explain some aspects of the phenomenon than others. On the one hand, proponents of connectionism address several issues – the contribution of repetition, frequency of stimuli, and automaticity – that find their genesis in an Aristotelean model of learned behaviors. On the other hand, proponents of Universal Grammar have established a rigorous research paradigm in which to investigate the extent to which innate abilities can be reactivated and with what success. What is particularly interesting from an historical perspective is the vantage point that it affords one to examine these basic philosophical questions as they permeate the history of second-language teaching from the earliest records to the present day, receding and reemerging in response to intellectual shifts, as well as external pressures, as that tradition unfolds.

Among the external factors that contribute to underlying beliefs and consequently prescriptions for practice, it is nearly impossible to overestimate the enormous influence of organized religion on education, including the teaching of language. The Aristotelian philosophy as interpreted by the early Church Fathers was the one adopted by the Christian Church, itself the major source and foundation of institutionalized education from the early Middle Ages onward. As a social institution, the Church possessed the infrastructure and the authority necessary for the provision of such education. One must keep in mind, however, that during this time mass public education did not exist. Although purportedly obligatory in the Aztec empire, in Europe the notion of compulsory education of children was unheard of from the fall of the Roman empire until the Protestant Reformation, when the theologian and church reformer Martin Luther (1483–1547) proposed in 1524 that all children acquire basic literacy in order to read the Bible. Strasbourg passed an edict to that effect in 1598, but it wasn't until the late eighteenth century that similar legislation began to spread slowly across the continent, first arriving in the United States in Massachusetts in 1852 and in England still later in 1870.

Until almost the twelfth century, formal education in Western Europe took place in monasteries that offered instruction in liturgy and prayer. Cathedral schools trained clergy in Canon law, preaching, and disputation, that is, the ability to defend a position through logical argumentation orally. Until the seventeenth century, other than religious schools that trained boys for the clergy, monastery, or choir – in descending order of required proficiency in Latin – education of children was limited to instruction of the elite by private tutors. The foundation of the earliest universities in the late eleventh and twelfth centuries (Bologna in 1088, Paris in 1150, and Oxford in 1167) allowed students the opportunity to build upon that early education. In this way, a student at age 14 or so, having mastered basic literacy in Latin under a tutor's guidance, could study the seven liberal arts – the trivium of grammar, logic, and rhetoric, followed by the quadrivium of arithmetic, geometry, music theory, and astronomy – before proceeding to advanced study in law, medicine, or theology. At the university, Latin was both the initial core subject as well as the medium of instruction. All lectures, readings, and discussion took place in Latin.

From their letters, we learn that university students in the twelfth century shared many of the same concerns of students today: they ask their parents for money and clothes; they complain about the cost of books and supplies; and they request more time to finish their degrees (Haskins, 1958). *The Manuale Scholarium*, a student guide to the university, provides a lively account of student life in the medieval period. In it we learn of the explicit requirement that Latin be used at all times as the ordinary means of communication in class and outside it, on penalty of a fine should a student be caught using the vernacular. The "wolves" were students appointed to surreptitiously record and report infractions of the rule. That students found the rule difficult to keep is recorded in one of the manual's dialogues:

Cam.   May the minions of hell destroy him. If I ever find out his name, he won't
　　　 get away.
Bar.   What ails you?
Cam.   Listen to me; I've been up against the wolf twelve times . . . I'll see to it, I'll
　　　 find him. Later, I'll avenge this injustice.
Bar.   It isn't an injustice, but rather the rule. Don't be surprised that you've been
　　　 reported so often; he could have reported you a hundred times. To tell the
　　　 truth, I haven't heard a single word from you in Latin for a whole week.
(The Manuale Scholarium, ch. 11, in Seybolt, p. 73)

Clearly, although Latin was the fulcrum upon which the entire curriculum balanced, already in the twelfth century it was neither the students' first nor preferred language for everyday communication even at the university. The need to establish strict rules enforcing its use among the students provides compelling evidence of its contrived status as their lingua franca. However, such rules also underscore a prevailing conviction that oral proficiency was best acquired by using the language for meaningful communication.

Given the dependence on Latin texts to provide the bulk of one's formal education, the rediscovery of original classical texts during the Renaissance fostered an explosion of academic interest. This interest inflamed the desire among certain scholars not only to correct the errors of spelling, grammar, and syntax that had multiplied in medieval manuscripts, but also to recreate, to the greatest extent possible, the best of the classical world, including the widespread diffusion of the Latin language as a means to imitate that experience. To that purpose, they proposed a revision of the medieval curriculum: namely, the *studia humanitatis* (literally, the study of humanity) designed to make students wise and moral, ideal citizens of the world, and universally proficient in Latin.

The new program of learning is described in great detail in a treatise entitled *De ingenuis moribus et liberalibus studiis* [On the Conduct and Education of Young People], written around 1400 by the Latin scholar, Vergerius. Taught entirely in Latin, the curriculum was based on early exposure to classical texts and included the study of history, eloquence (persuasive speaking), grammar (writing), rhetoric (public speaking, including oration), poetry, music, arithmetic, geometry, and science. One of the most celebrated humanists, as proponents of the new curriculum were called, was Guarino Guarini (1374–1460), also known as Guarino da Verona, a fifteenth-century scholar of Latin and Greek and tutor to Lionello d'Este, prince of Ferrara, where Guarino eventually opened his own school. Guarino was convinced that the new program of learning provided the essential formative education for all citizens, especially those in positions of power and civil authority, not just the future teacher-scholar. Moreover, he insisted that one of the strengths of the *studia humanitatis* lay in the fact that it sought to develop high levels of speaking ability in Latin:

To be admired for fluency, to be appreciated for speaking good Latin, is beginning to be true of the period, not just of individuals, so that today one is less likely to be praised for speaking well than to be criticized for speaking badly; today we are expected to speak good Latin, more so than in the past when we were criticized for speaking a barbarous language. (Guarino Guarini, *Letter to Cristoforo Sabbion, Chancellor of Verona*, in Garin, 1958, p. 420, translation mine)

The humanists contended that second-language literacy skills alone were necessary but insufficient training for a citizen of the Renaissance world. Instead, the educated person would also be able to speak Latin fluently, confidently, and persuasively. The means to attain such fluency was being immersed in the study of humanities in the second language, Latin.

Like Guarino, other Latin (and Greek) tutors became famous during the Renaissance for the small schools that they operated, often limited to a select group of children who attended lessons along with the patron's children. Vittorino da Feltre (1378–1446) was one of these. His *Casa Giocosa* (Joyful House) was where he taught the Duke of Gonzaga's children along with others. (Guarino insisted, as a condition of employment, that he be allowed to enroll additional pupils whom he selected based on their intellectual ability rather than their families' social position.) The school is included in histories of education as one of the first boarding schools. It boasted a total immersion experience, with instruction geared to the ability and needs of each child. His curriculum included games and recreation, physical education, and music, in addition to the humanistic subjects of Latin and Greek. Associates of Vittorino attested to his extraordinary success.

Unfortunately, it is impossible to determine from the historical record to what extent the success of Vittorino's school was a result of the teacher's expertise, the methodology (early full immersion to the extreme), specific learner characteristics (aptitude, age, motivation), and the second language itself (highly prestigious, structurally similar to the students' first language). One might suspect that the last factor – shared structural features between Latin and the Italian vernaculars – must certainly have influenced at least the rate of acquisition among Vittorino's pupils. Would the same hold true for structurally more disparate languages? Given students' success in acquiring Greek, as well as Latin, apparently so.

One might argue that the linguistic proficiency expected of a five-year-old is quite different from what one might demand from an educated adult. Nevertheless, it appears that a talented and expert teacher along with a motivated group of pupils given unlimited time and resources to enjoy total immersion in the second language offered the ideal conditions for rapid and successful acquisition. Many of the most learned men of the day were trained in Guarino's and Vittorino Da Feltre's schools.

But despite success stories like those of Guarino and Vittorino Da Feltre, the humanists' campaign to resurrect Latin as the universal language ultimately failed. While their introduction of the *studia humanitatis* would have lasting effects on the curriculum, the case for spoken Latin could not turn the rising tide of the vernacular languages, which constituted the common system of communication among the burgeoning and increasingly influential middle class. Even parents of university students began to complain about the waste of time and money spent on learning a language that served no practical purpose. In his *Letters to the Majors and Aldermen*, in which he makes the case for basic literacy for everyone, Luther warns against an overzealously pragmatic approach that would lead to the abandonment of the content of the humanities along with Latin, a tossing of the baby with the bathwater. He specifies that even in the vernacular, basic literacy is not a sufficient outcome of instruction:

> And pay no attention to the contempt which the ordinary devotee of Mammon manifests for culture, so that he says: "Well, if my son can read, write, and cipher, that is enough; for I am going to make a merchant out of him." Without scholars it would not be long till business men in their perplexity would be ready to dig a learned man out of the ground ten yards deep with their fingers; for the merchant will not long remain a merchant, if preaching and the administration of justice cease. (Luther, *Letters to the Mayors and Aldermen*, in Boyd, 1966, p. 247)

Pragmatic concerns are not so easily set aside, and tensions between Mammon and the Academy reverberate still. The fading utility of Latin for anything but the most scholarly pursuits would eventually be extinguished with the availability of vernacular translations of the Bible made possible by the invention of the printing press in 1440. For the first time, literacy in one's first language could both ensure success in the affairs of this world and guarantee one's salvation in the next. Before that would happen on a wide scale, however, another century would pass. In the meantime, a sophisticated and prestigious program of education that would set the academic standard for foreign language instruction emerged.

The influence of the Catholic Church on education reached its pinnacle with the system of education developed by the Jesuits, a religious order founded in the 1500s by Ignatius of Loyola, and still influential to this day. Known for their intellectual rigor and strict discipline, the Jesuits accepted only the brightest students into their schools, suggesting a suspected link between intelligence and foreign language aptitude, at least in so far as the method by which Latin appears to have been taught. The Jesuits were also instrumental in solidifying the tradition of presenting the whole of the grammar in the first year or even in only half a year. Although a few students, who must have possessed an extraordinary aptitude for language learning, appeared to benefit from this practice and were able to proceed immediately to the study of content in the second year, the majority advanced at a much slower rate. Consequently, the second year consisted of a review of the grammar, with continued review each year until the material had been mastered.

The Jesuits' *Ratio studiorum* [Plan of Study] offers one of the most detailed extant manuals for school administration and teaching practice, surpassing even that of Quintilian. In it one can find rules covering everything from the responsibilities of the rector to those of the janitor and everyone in between. It also provides an exquisitely clear description of a language teaching method that later came to be characterized as "grammar-translation."

The general format of the language classes consisted of recitation of memorized passages (from Cicero and a grammar book), a review of the previous lesson, a lecture, and a dictation, followed by the presentation of a new grammar point. Directives for how the lectures in the first-year grammar class were to be conducted are provided in almost excruciating detail:

> The prelection [lecture] in Cicero which shall not exceed four lines will be in this form: First, let him [the teacher] read the entire passage continuously, and state its topic very briefly in the vernacular. Second, let him express the sentence in words of the vernacular. Third, starting from the beginning, let him indicate the structure and explain the sentence, telling which words govern which cases; let him go over many things pertaining to the laws of the grammar already explained; let him offer some observations or other of the Latin language, but as simple as possible; let him explain the metaphors by well-known examples, but let him not dictate anything, except perhaps the topic. Fourth, let him again go through the words of the author in the vernacular. (*Ratio, Rules to the Professor of Lower Grammar Classes*, in Fitzpatrick, 1933, p. 233)

Lectures in the second- and third-year classes followed the same format, changing only the number of lines to be read (from four to seven), with the inclusion of more dictation in the second year and emphasis on word derivations in the third. Outside of lectures, students prepared written translations of sentences (later, passages), to and from the vernacular. Teachers were exhorted to devote scrupulous attention to error correction. Either the teacher himself would correct the translations or a particular type of activity, the *concertatio*, would serve the same purpose. This activity consisted of students identifying errors in each other's written work and demanding a repetition of the rule that had been broken. For example, if a student had written an incorrect ending on a word, the one who found it would ask for a recitation of "the whole declension or conjugation in order or in broken order, alone or with an adjective or noun or pronoun" (*Ratio*, in Fitzpatrick, 1933, p. 234). Interestingly, this was one of the rare activities that the *Ratio* recommended be conducted as an oral exercise entirely in Latin without recourse to the vernacular, limited as it was to the use of fixed expressions and the repetition of grammatical rules.

A comparison with the teaching methods advocated by the humanists of the previous century immediately reveals a glaring difference: namely, the enormous reliance in the *Ratio* on the use of the students' first language in order to teach the second. The directives of the *Ratio* indicate clearly that Latin was no longer the medium of instruction, or at least not the sole medium of instruction, in the Jesuit system. Instead, the teacher was explicitly advised to provide learners with a first-language translation of the Latin words and sentences, not just once, but several times over the course of a single lecture, and not only in the first-year course, but in the second and third years as well. The use of the vernacular undoubtedly ensured comprehension on the part of the students. However, it also obviated the function of Latin as the primary route to access meaning. Whereas the humanists had recommended that, in order for students to achieve both literacy and functional oral proficiency, Latin be the medium of instruction in interesting subject matter, in the grammar-translation method advocated by the *Ratio studiorum*, it became, instead, the object of study, in what today we might recognize as a "focus on forms" approach (Doughty & Williams, 1998; Long, 1991). Moreover, by separating the study of language and the study of content for a period that could last as long as three years, a divide was created within the curriculum that exists to the present day.

The use of the vernacular languages for instruction of the elite students in the Jesuit schools reflected their rising cachet in society at large. What precipitated their transformation from "barbarous" tongues to such elevated status? The seventeenth century witnessed a combination of social and religious forces that solidified the status and power of the vernacular languages of Europe. Intense religious antagonism, not only between Roman Catholics and Protestants but within the sects themselves, could not allow an international language associated with the Roman Church on the one hand, and classical (pagan) culture on the other. Economic factors, too, favored the vernacular languages of France, Holland, and England as they displaced Catholic Spain as the dominant commercial power.

The nationalistic objectives of seventeenth-century Europe were decidedly at odds with the notion of global communication. The formation of nation states was aided by linguistic, in addition to geographical, boundaries. National languages served to strengthen national identities. During this period, academies were formed to promote, regulate, and preserve the linguistic integrity of the vernacular languages. The Accademia della Crusca in Florence was established in 1582, the Académie Française in 1635, and the Real Academia Española in Madrid in 1713. The Accademia della Crusca published the first dictionary of Italian in 1612, which served in turn as the model for the first dictionaries published in French (1694) and in Spanish (1726–39).

The elevated prestige of the vernacular languages affected more than the status of spoken Latin, already in jeopardy in the Middle Ages; it compromised even the utility of developing reading proficiency in Latin. No longer dependent on ecclesiastic authority and Latin, individuals could interpret Scripture for themselves in their first languages, thanks to the proliferation of translations of the Bible (Luther's translation of the New Testament into German in 1522 and of the Old Testament in 1534; Tyndale's translation into English in 1526, with the authorized King James version in 1611; Czech in 1568; Welsh in 1588; and the London Polyglot Bible in ten languages in 1653). By this time, the printing press had advanced to the point that, not only did students likely have individual copies of texts, even of the same edition, but new versions of books appeared on the market that offered interlinear translations. In this way, students could view synoptically on the same page a line of text in Latin and its vernacular translation. One can imagine how such texts must have facilitated the conduct of the lessons, ensuring comprehension and easing the lives of teachers and students alike! "Reading between the lines" literally gave instant access to meaning. Such a welcome innovation did not come without cost, however, as it also allowed students to bypass the second language entirely, much like watching a film with subtitles or listening to a simultaneous translation. No longer the necessary vehicle by which to access interesting subject matter, Latin was reduced at best to a linguistic puzzle or a challenging mental exercise, and at worst to a dull catalogue of abstract, nonsensical rules.

Interestingly, the most celebrated educational reformer of the seventeenth century Johannes Amos Comenius was known primarily not for his curricula (which he structured from infancy through university), nor for his interest in the invention of a new universal language to replace Latin, nor for his many philosophical and theological treatises, nor even for his *Didactica Magna* [*The Great Didactic*] of 1657, in which he outlined his plan for a universal system of education. Comenius is famous above all for his textbooks: the *Janua Linguarum Reserata* [The Gate of Tongues, Unlocked] of 1631, the *Vestibulum* [*The Vestibule*] of 1633, and perhaps most famous of all, the *Orbis Sensualium Pictus* [*The World of Things in Pictures*] of 1658. The acclaim for Comenius' textbooks cannot be overstated. Their popularity was such that they were translated into twelve European languages and several Asian ones, as well; they continued to be published for almost two centuries after the author's death.

Comenius' passion for educational reform stemmed from his frustration with what he perceived to be the appalling inefficiency of the schools, those "slaughter-houses of the mind," a problem that he blames on the instructional methods employed: "Latin grammar was taught us with all the exceptions and irregularities; Greek grammar with all its dialects, and we, poor wretches, were so confused that we scarcely understood what it was all about" (*Didactica Magna*, ch. 16, p. 122). Schools, he argues, fail for two reasons: First and foremost because they lack appropriate materials and, second, because they do not follow the "natural order," that is, "that the matter come first and the form follow" (*Didactica Magna*, ch. 16, p. 115). With regard to language teaching, this meant that instruction erroneously begins with the grammar (the form) rather than authors or examples (the matter). Instead, three principles guided Comenius' proposed reform: "that no language be learned from a grammar, but from suitable authors," "that the understanding be first instructed in things, and then taught to express them in language," and finally, "that examples come before rules" (p. 116). In some sense, Comenius' insistence on meaning ("things") before form and a reliance on "authors" to supply that content of that meaning echoes that of the early humanists. However, the intellectual milieu of the seventeenth century – a period of dramatic scientific discovery that challenged long-standing beliefs and established a new science of observation and experimentation – along with the consequences of the Reformation and Comenius' own religious convictions, had undermined the authority of the ancient authors. The suspicion that such authors might not constitute either trustworthy or appropriate material served as an impetus for the design of textbooks whose content and structure were more suitable for children in school.

The first of Comenius' textbooks, the *Janua Linguarum Reserata*, presents 8,000 of the most common Latin words arranged to form 1,000 sentences in a progression from the shortest, most simple constructions in the early chapters to increasingly more complex constructions in the latter. Congruent with his notion that instruction in content and language proceed simultaneously, each of the 100 chapters deals with one class of phenomena; for example, fire, diseases, trade, arithmetic, angels. Despite the inclusion of a vernacular translation for each Latin sentence, teachers complained that the book was too difficult. In response, Comenius created a preparatory text, the *Vestibulum*, in which 1,000 of the most common words are arranged into 427 simple sentences. However, subsequent editions of the *Vestibulum* became simpler still, until they were finally reduced to Latin-vernacular word lists.

Despite an apparent shift in his methodological stance, as evidenced in the later versions of the *Vestibulum*, as well as related incongruencies in his much less widely known methods book, *Didactica Magna*, Comenius' acclaim as a textbook author increased. Around 1650 he began to sketch out his third and most significant historical contribution, the *Orbis Sensualium Pictus*, a true breakthrough in educational practice. Designed as a preschool text, the *Orbis* was meant to teach the vocabulary of real-world objects and events. Its innovation lies in the use of illustrations, not as decorative elements or as supplements, but as an integral part of the text itself. Typeset as columns of Latin sentences with side-by-side vernacular translations, words in both languages are numerically keyed to the corresponding elements in the accompanying illustration. According to a biographer, the success of the *Orbis* was "even more extraordinary" than that of the *Janua*, such that two books, the *Orbis* and the Bible, formed the essential home library for generations of children (Keatinge, 1910, p. 78).

The creation of the first illustrated "picture book" for children is accomplishment enough to rate permanent inclusion in every history of education. However, despite their popularity, Comenius' language textbooks did not ensure the easy and successful acquisition of Latin any more than the "grammar-translation" approach of the Jesuits. Moreover, another of Comenius' recognized contributions to the history of Western education is the legitimacy that his textbooks gave to the use of the vernacular as the language of instruction (Cole, 1950).

Although his *Janua* was a bilingual textbook, Comenius championed the notion of primary instruction in the students' first language. His school plan began with the Vernacular School. Only upon its successful completion would those boys whose professional aspirations required a more sophisticated program of study advance to the Latin School. With regard to modern foreign languages, he advised that, once having attained first-language literacy, boys between the ages of 10 and 12 could profitably study foreign languages in the period between the Vernacular and the Latin Schools. In Comenius' opinion, the best means for that study "is to send them to the place where the language that they wish to learn is spoken, and in the new language to make them read, write, and learn the class books of the Vernacular School" (*Didactica Magna*, p. 273). In other words, he advocated study abroad within an immersion or content-based model. In this way, Comenius did not disagree with the humanists: he agreed that 10-year-olds could learn second languages without difficulty and that an effective way to ensure successful acquisition was to immerse students in the second-language environment, where the language was also the medium of instruction. The reason that Latin could not be taught like any modern language was that the goal of that instruction had changed. The need for functional proficiency in Latin no longer existed.

No longer the language of wider communication, having been displaced by the vernaculars as the language of commerce, diplomacy, science, and scholarship, Latin's only remaining communicative function had existed solely within the instructional setting, and shared even that with a predomination of the learners' first language, a context so circumscribed and artificial that it probably could not have been sustained by any means on the wide scale demanded by the impending imperative of mass public education. Although it continued to enjoy esteem in the academy, until the early twentieth century the place of Latin in the general curriculum was settled: for the vast majority of students it was a prestigious but arcane academic exercise that served to enrich the learner's lexicon through derivation and word-formation skills, to teach abstract grammatical categories, and perhaps to allow for rudimentary translation of a few lines of Vergil's *Aeneid* or Julius Caesar's *De Bello Gallico*. It is difficult to imagine that Latin was once the historical equivalent of World English today, just as it is equally unfathomable that English could be replaced by yet another language, perhaps one that is currently spoken by a relatively small group of people in some remote part of the world. And, yet, this is precisely what happened to a prestigious world language, despite an educational system that was predicated entirely on its preservation and transmission.

The Role and Status of the Language Teacher

Histories of education are commonly organized around the identification of the great philosophers and famous educators (Cole, 1950; Boyd, 1966; Smith & Smith, 1994). Yet another benefit that the student of applied linguistics might derive from the study of the history of second-language teaching is an appreciation of its intellectual legacy. Such illustrious figures to the contrary, however, the historical record suggests that the average language teacher was seldom held in such high esteem. Grammar may have been the cornerstone of the entire curriculum, but the grammar teacher himself was often disparaged. By definition, a grammarian is one versed in the knowledge of grammar, a philologist, and/or a teacher of grammar. It has also come to be used as a term of reproach: a "mere grammarian" or a "dry, plodding grammarian." The pedagogue (from the Greek *pedagogos*) was originally the slave who accompanied boys to and from school and who supervised their behavior; later the Romans extended the meaning of the term to signify the teacher. It, too, has acquired a decidedly negative connotation. Like the grammarian and the pedagogue, the pedant also refers to a teacher, schoolmaster or tutor, and consequently to someone who is "excessively concerned with accuracy over trifling details of knowledge or who insists on adherence to formal rules." The Commedia dell'Arte, the Italian improvisational comic theater begun in the mid-1500s and popular through eighteenth century, included as one of the stock characters il Dottore, a pompous, ridiculous figure immediately recognizable by his pedantry. How did the profession arrive at this point?

From the earliest days of language teaching in ancient Rome, educated Greek slaves provided instruction in Greek language and the arts to interested members of the household. Itinerant teachers offered instruction for a fee to whomever they could recruit as students. Some of the greatest educators were tutors, but few were teachers in classrooms with many learners, let alone students of diverse preparation, motivations, and abilities.

That language teaching in the schools was held in lowest regard is evident in the following excerpt from a Jesuit who proposed for himself the severest of penances:

> Relieve me of the care of others, take away my preaching and my study, leaving me only my breviary, and bid me come to Rome, begging my way, and there put me to work in the kitchen, or serving table, or in the garden, or at anything else. *And when I am no longer good for any of this, put me in the lowest class of grammar and that until death, without any more care for me . . . than you have for an old broom. (Letter to Ignatius from Lainez*, 1552, in Young, 1959, p. 273, emphasis mine)

As if to further underscore the marginal status of the language teacher, the Jesuits invented a two-tiered system of instruction that forms the basis of second-language programs at many universities to this day: the use of advanced students to instruct the language classes, freeing professors to teach the more prestigious "subject matter" courses. Musumeci (1997) argues that this distinct separation of subject matter (content) and language (skill) further fueled the demise of Latin as a meaningful subject in the curriculum. By reducing language to a mere skill, the esteem in which the teacher was held diminished proportionally.

The introduction of mass public education in northern Europe in the seventeenth century created a demand for teachers that must have outstripped the supply. Rather than raise the status of the teacher according to the usual rules of modern economics, however, it appeared to have had an opposite effect: increasing supply by lowering the acceptable standards. Comenius lamented the fact that good teachers were few and far between, the best having been snatched up by the wealthy to serve as tutors for their children, depriving the state of an important resource.

In Comenius' instructional framework, the teacher is the single source of knowledge that is poured into the students, like water from a fountain or the warmth of the sun (*Didactica Magna*, pp. 163, 165, 166, 250). Given the student's status as a blank tablet on which the teacher wrote or painted knowledge, Comenius held the teacher entirely responsible for a student's failure to learn: "If the result be not successful, it is more than certain that this is not the fault of the tablet (unless it have some inherent defect), but arises from ignorance on the part of the writer or painter" (p. 44). Despite the enormous instructional burden that he placed on the teacher's shoulders, Comenius minimized the instructor's relative merits as follows:

> An organist can read any piece of music from his notes, though he might not be able to compose it or to sing or play it from memory; and a schoolmaster, in the same way, should be able to teach anything, if he have before his eyes the subject matter and the method by which it should be taught. (*Didactica Magna*, p. 288)

Comenius' passionate belief in the foremost importance of sound materials and methodology reduces the teacher to a technician who simply puts the plan into action, but has no role in its design. He is a musician who cannot compose or sing or even play from memory. The adage "those who can, do; those who can't, teach" comes painfully to mind.

Finally, despite the ongoing admonition of the importance of supplying learners with good language models from the very beginning of the language learning process, for most of its history the profession had little to say about whether those models need be native speakers. This, too, is an artifact of Latin, a language that for centuries of its instruction was the first language of no one; all teachers were de facto non-native speakers. Howatt and Widdowson (2004) point out that the tradition of the non-native teacher persisted throughout the early days of teaching English as a second language. In fact, the highly proficient non-native speaker who shared the learners' first language and culture and who could predict the difficulties that students would encounter enjoyed a unique advantage over the native-speaker instructor.

Potential effects of the instructor's status as a native or non-native speaker of the second language continue to be investigated in present-day research. Nevertheless, it would be naive to believe that the factors that decide who should teach a language revolve solely around linguistic concerns. When language is understood to be a cultural commodity or a lucrative national product, the native speaker becomes part of the linguistic economy, and the economic reality can be significant. As an example, recent calculations report that English language teaching contributed over £10 billion to the United Kingdom's economy in 2001–2, with the prediction that the market was poised to undergo yet another major expansion (Johnes, 2004). Given such high stakes, one can well understand the motivation to portray native-speaker teachers as highly desirable and valuable resources.

The Role and Status of the Learner

The teacher is only part of the equation; what about the learner? Is the student an active participant in his or her learning or a blank tablet upon which to write? The underlying philosophy in conjunction with the current technology supply the metaphors for learning. Not surprisingly, Quintilian likens the student to a container, "we are by nature most tenacious of childish impressions, just as the flavour first absorbed by vessels when new persists, and the colour imparted by dyes to the primitive whiteness of wool is indelible. Further it is the worst impressions that are most durable" (*Institutio oratoria* I, in Ulich, 1954, p. 104). Using almost identical words, one of the early Church doctors, Jerome (347–420), offers advice on the proper education of a daughter when he warns, "Early impressions are hard to eradicate from the mind. When once wool has been dyed purple who can restore it to its previous whiteness? An unused jar long retains the taste and smell of that with which it is first filled" (*Letter to Laeta*, in Ulich, 1954, pp. 165–6) Such expressions reflect a fear that exposure to poor models and allowing errors to go uncorrected will have lasting detrimental effects for the learner.

Although they reappear with some regularity throughout the history of second-language teaching, these concerns do not reflect the only response to learner error. For example, such metaphors are conspicuously absent in the language of some early humanists. Guarino insisted, as well, on the importance of excellent language models, warning that teachers should refrain from obscene language that students might later imitate. Unlike the *tabula rasa* models, his metaphors for students, instead, emphasize their active role in a discovery process of learning. He offers the following advice to students who struggle to interpret the meaning of a text:

> If, instead, it [the meaning] escapes you and "remains hidden to you" go back, knock so to speak on the door, until even if it takes time, it opens just a crack to your understanding. Here you should imitate your hunting dogs that, if rummaging through bush and shrubs they don't find the bird on the first try, receive the order to repeat the procedure, because that which doesn't emerge at the first attempt might be flushed at the next. (*Letter to Lionello d'Este*, in Garin, 1958, p. 380, translation mine)

In the expressive skills, as well, Guarino concentrates on the creative rather than the mechanical aspects of the task, comparing the learner to a sculptor or artist who from a heap of raw materials (ideas) creates a polished piece of work.

To support his argument for the importance of early education, Comenius, instead, builds his case by enumerating the classical metaphors for care in the early stages: the initial pliancy of wax, the vessel that retains the essence of what it first held, the sapling that conforms to the shape of its early environment. However, in an interesting twist, he combines these with new metaphors, peculiar to his time; namely, the specialization of labor and mass production. He suggests that just as one goes to the cobbler for shoes and the locksmith for a key, children go to school for instruction. The implication is that the teacher supplies a commodity (knowledge), and the school is the place where scholars are produced, like shoes or keys. Mass education is likened to fish hatcheries or the cultivation of fruit orchards. Moreover, he argues that, given the proper tools and method, instruction can proceed almost effortlessly:

> It will be no harder to teach schoolboys, in any number desired, than with the help of the printing press to cover a thousand sheets daily with the neatest writing . . . The whole process, too, will be as free from friction as is the movement of a clock whose motive power is supplied by weights. It will be as pleasant to see education carried out on my plan as to look at an automatic machine of this kind, and the process will be as free from failure as are these mechanical contrivances, when skilfully made. (*Didactica Magna*, pp. 96–7)

With the appropriate materials and method, instruction will proceed with the efficiency of the printing press and the precision of clockwork. In reaction against the elitist system of the Jesuits, Comenius insisted that all children benefit from education regardless of their natural ability, arguing that "a sieve, if you continually pour water through it, grows cleaner and cleaner, although it cannot retain liquid" (*Didactica Magna*, p. 67).

At first glance, an examination of the metaphors that were used in the past to describe language teachers and learners may appear antiquated or quaint. However, even a brief overview of the historical panorama reveals the extent to which the existent technology influences the ways in which second-language learning and teaching are construed. It is not surprising that the modern equivalent of the printing press, the computer, serves the same function today. Most of the literature in second-language acquisition research would be impossible to interpret without the metaphors from twentieth-century information technology that allow the profession to refer to language learners as bilingual processors and the pathways and products of that learning in terms of input, intake, output, working memory, and processing capacity.

Conclusion

In historical accounts of second-language teaching, clichés abound: there is nothing new under the sun and the pendulum swings widely from one approach to its apparent counterpart. Indeed, anyone who has been teaching language for more than 20 years or so has experienced such shifts first hand. A familiarity with the history of language teaching reveals a complex constellation of factors that affect those changes. It can also serve to identify some underlying trends with regard to language education reform. When the primary goal of second-language teaching is the development of functional oral skills, the prescribed method employs the second language as the medium of instruction; that is, as a vehicle to convey meaning. The goal of developing second-language literacy requires at least a reliance on the reading of authentic texts and extensive writing practice. On the one hand, it appears that the successful implementation of total immersion requires a combination of features that may be impossibly difficult to control in a large, institutionalized setting, where the expertise of the teacher, the motivations and abilities of the students, the prestige of the second language, and the economic resources are not guaranteed. On the other hand, language teaching methods that are easier to implement in a large, institutionalized setting with a wide range of teachers and learners, in which the second language is the focus rather than the medium of instruction, and students rely heavily on their first language, result in limited functional skills for the majority of students. The historical record implies that, directives aside, attempts to force students to use a language that is not necessary for the acquisition of subject matter knowledge in the classroom or that serves no practical purpose outside it have small hope of success.

REFERENCES

Boyd, W. (1966). *The history of western education.* New York: Barnes and Noble.

Brumfit, C. & Mitchell, R. (1990). *Research in the language classroom.* London: Modern English Publications in Association with The British Council.

Cole, L. (1950). *A history of education: Socrates to Montessori.* New York: Holt, Rinehart, and Winston.

Comenius, J. A. (1657). *Didactica Magna* [The Great Didactic]. In M. W. Keatinge, (trans. and ed.), 1907: *The Great Didactic of John Amos Comenius*, vol. 2. London: Adam and Charles Black.

Doughty, C. J. (2003). Instructed SLA: Constraints, compensation, and enhancement. In C. J. Doughty & M. H. Long (eds.), *The handbook of second language research* (pp. 256–310). Oxford: Blackwell Publishing.

Doughty, C. J. & Long, M. H. (eds.) (2003). *The handbook of second language research.* Oxford: Blackwell Publishing.

Doughty, C. J. & Williams, J. (eds.) (1998). *Focus on form in classroom second language acquisition.* New York: Cambridge University Press.

Fitzpatrick, E. A. (ed.) (1933). *St Ignatius and the Ratio Studiorum.* New York: McGraw-Hill.

Garin, E. (ed.) (1958). *Il Pensiero Pedagogico dello Umanesimo.* Florence: Giuntine & Sansoni.

Guarini, G. Le Epistole di Guarino da Verona. [The Letters of Guarino da Verona.] In Garin, E. (ed.) (1958), *Il Pensiero Pedagogico dello Umanesimo.* Florence: Giuntine and Sansoni.

Haskins, C. H. (1958). *Studies in mediaeval culture.* New York: Frederick Ungar Publishing Company.

Howatt, A. P. R. & Widdowson, H. G. (2004). *A history of English language teaching.* Oxford: Oxford University Press.

Johnes, G. (2004). The global value of education and training exports to the UK economy. *UK Trade and Investment*, April. London: The British Council.

Keatinge, M. W. (trans. and ed.) (1907). *The Great Didactic of John Amos Comenius*, vol. 2. London: Adam and Charles Black.

Keatinge, M. W. (trans. and ed.) (1910). *The Great Didactic of John Amos Comenius*, vol. 1. London: Adam and Charles Black.

Kelly, L. G. (1969). *25 centuries of language teaching.* Rowley, MA: Newbury House.

Kibbee, D. (1991). *For to speke Frenche trewely: The French language in England, 1000–1600: Its status, description and instruction.* Amsterdam: Johns Benjamin.

Long, M. H. (1991). Focus on form: A design feature in language teaching methodology. In K. de Bot, R. B. Ginsberg, & C. Kramsch (eds.), *Foreign language research in cross-cultural perspective* (pp. 39–52). Amsterdam: John Benjamins.

Luther, M. (1524). Letter to the mayors and aldermen of all of cities of Germany in behalf of Christian schools. In R. Ulich (ed.) (1954), *Three thousand years of educational wisdom* (pp. 218–38). Cambridge, MA: Harvard University Press.

Mackey, W. F. (1965). *Language teaching analysis.* London: Longman.

Mitchell, R. & Myles, F. (2004). *Second language learning theories.* London: Hodder Arnold.

Murphy, James J. (ed.) (1987). *Quintilian on the teaching of speaking and writing.* Carbondale: Southern Illinois University Press.

Musumeci, D. (1997). *Breaking tradition: An exploration of the historical relationship between theory and practice in second language teaching.* New York: McGraw-Hill.

Reagan, T. (1996). *Non-western educational traditions.* Mahwah, NJ: Lawrence Erlbaum.

Richards, J. C. & Rogers, T. S. (2001). *Approaches and methods in language teaching.* Cambridge: Cambridge University Press.

Seybolt, T. (trans.) (1921). *The Manuale Scholarium: An original account of life in a mediaeval university.* Cambridge, MA: Harvard University Press.

Smith, L. G. & Smith, J. K. (eds.) (1994). *Lives in education: A narrative of people and ideas.* New York: St Martin's Press.

Stern, H. H. (1983). *Fundamental concepts of language teaching.* Oxford: Oxford University Press.

Thomas, M. (2004). *Universal grammar in second-language acquisition: A history.* London: Routledge.

Titone, R. (1968). *Teaching foreign languages: An historical sketch.* Washington, DC: Georgetown University Press.

Ulich, R. (ed.) (1954). *Three thousand years of educational wisdom.* Cambridge, MA: Harvard University Press.

Vergerius, P. P. (1403). De ingenuis moribus et liberalis studiis. [On the conduct and education of young people]. In W. H. Woodward (trans. and ed.) (1921), *Vittorino da Feltre and Other Humanist Educators* (pp. 96–118). Cambridge: Cambridge University Press.

Woodward, W. H. (trans. and ed.) (1921). *Vittorino da Feltre and other humanist educators.* Cambridge: Cambridge University Press.

Young, W. J. (trans. and ed.) (1959). *Letters of St Ignatius of Loyola.* Chicago: Loyola University Press.

Part III Psycholinguistic Underpinnings of Language Learning

5 The Language-Learning Brain

ALAN BERETTA

In second language learning and teaching, there seem to be two principal ways in which neurolinguistics is of interest: as a source of evidence to support a particular approach to SLA, usually via the critical period issue; and as a source of evidence to promote some supposedly "brain-compatible" classroom teaching technique and to dismiss other techniques that fail on this criterion. The latter use of language–brain research is, to say the least, premature. Even the neuroimaging work on the critical period issue appears to entertain higher expectations than can reasonably be sustained in view of the uncontroversial fact that far less complex problems in language–brain research remain to be solved. This chapter attempts to provide a more realistic perspective.

In an attempt to anchor debate to reality, the question that first needs to be considered is what the enterprise of neurolinguistics could possibly be. After all, there is nothing obvious about what is meant by grafting *linguistics* onto *neuro*. Once this question is confronted, the answer that it yields may serve as a basis for judging what claims are warranted and what expectations might reasonably be entertained with respect to brains and second language teaching and learning.

What is Neurolinguistics?

Someone wishing to find out what neurolinguistics is might turn to the Linguistic Society of America's website (www.lsa.org), as it contains sketches of the various sub-disciplines of linguistics. Here is what it says about *neurolinguistics*:

> What is neurolinguistics about? Where in your brain is a word that you've learned? If you know two languages, are they stored in two different parts of your brain? Is the left side of your brain really the language side? If you lose the ability to talk because of a stroke, can you learn to talk again? Do people who read languages written from left to right (like English) think differently from people who read languages written from right to left (like Hebrew and Arabic)? What about if you

read a language that is written using some other kind of symbols, like Chinese or Japanese? If you're dyslexic, is your brain different from the brain of someone who has no trouble reading? All of these questions and more are what neurolinguistics is about.

You and I may be interested in some of these questions or not. You and I may find some of them quite bizarre. But you and I would be none the wiser after reading this passage as to what neurolinguistics could possibly be. The problem is not that the passage fails to demarcate neurolinguistics, to specify what counts as neurolinguistic and what does not. Let us be quite clear about that: boundary-setting for domains of interest is never at issue in any kind of scientific inquiry, as is plain from the slightest acquaintance with the history of science. The problem is this, that the term *neurolinguistics* links together two areas of inquiry, which begs the question of what sort of relationship they could have, given current levels of understanding, and what sort of insight the relationship might ever yield such that anyone could care. A random series of questions, clinical, Whorfian, whatever, does not begin to offer any idea what is at stake, that is, what is at stake *theoretically*.

Having broached the notion of theory, a caution is in order. Theory certainly matters, but whatever theory is at issue, it cannot be *neurolinguistic theory*. The term make no sense at all at present. It is true that one constantly hears about political theory, feminist theory, social theory, educational theory, queer theory, critical theory, framing theory, and border theory, but in these sorts of cases, it is difficult to see why common sense and experience of the world could not arrive at the same conclusions as are given by the theories. If the term *theory* is to be used in the way it is normally understood in the sciences, that is, an idea that yields genuine insight and which agrees with solid and publicly demonstrable evidence, then it is pointless to talk about *neurolinguistic theory*.

A criticism that the LSA description of neurolinguistics is atheoretical coupled with a statement that the very idea of *neurolinguistic theory* is at present entirely senseless appears to be paradoxical. Even more so, since it will be maintained in what follows that neurolinguistic inquiry had better be guided by theory or it is worthless. In order to resolve these apparent contradictions, and to give some idea of what combining the *neuro* and the *linguistic* might yield, discussion will start from a position of common sense, which is the starting point for many when they contemplate the relationship between language and brain, and which unfortunately remains the apparent guiding principle for many seasoned language–brain researchers. It will be argued that common sense needs to be abandoned, which prepares the ground for a notion of theoretically-guided neurolinguistic inquiry.

The commonsense approach is to wonder how something mental, like language, can interact with a physical brain, and yet know that it must. Thus, starting from common sense, it is possible to approach the language–brain relation as mind–body dualists, no better off than Descartes was more than 300 years ago when he formulated the problem, similarly confronted with a mystery and similarly left with no way to move forward. Descartes really did have no option but to posit two distinct substances because in his mechanical universe, everything was constrained by the laws of mechanism, everything physical; that is, everything except mind. Researchers today, on the other hand, have the advantage of hindsight, not smarter, as they say, just later. With hindsight, it is known that the idea of a mechanical universe crumbled later in the seventeeth century, when Newton proposed a notion of gravity, but the consequences for the mind–body problem do not seem to have been immediately apparent. However, by the eighteenth century, the chemist Joseph Priestley was able to see that the inevitable consequence was the total rejection of the commonsense mind–body problem and a radical re-conception of the relationship between the mental and the physical. Priestley, too, started out as a mind–body dualist, so what better than to follow his progress from that belief to the standard materialism that is considered normal in cognitive science today.

Priestley initially assumed "the soul to be a substance so entirely distinct from matter as to have no property in common with it" (1777, p. xi). The "soul," or "spirit," or "mind" consisted of something airy and insubstantial, while the "body," or "matter," or the "physical" was solid, inert, and occupied space. He began to wonder whether "either the material or the immaterial part of the universal system was superfluous" but "relapsed into the general hypothesis of two entirely distinct and independent principles in man" (p. xii). Having idly wondered about the issue, Priestley thought it through in earnest in *Disquisitions relating to matter and spirit* (1777). Mindful of gravitational force and also of more recent insight into electromagnetic forces, he concluded that the commonsense notion of body was dead to science; matter with properties such as inertness, solidity, and so forth, he reasoned, does not exist. Matter instead possesses "powers," forces of attraction and repulsion which lack solidity, do not occupy space, are not inert. "Matter is not the inert substance it has been supposed to be" since "powers of attraction and repulsion are necessary to its very being" (p. xxxviii); without the power of attraction, "there cannot be any such thing as matter . . . for when we suppose bodies to be divested of it, they come to be nothing at all" (p. 5); take away attraction and "solidity itself vanishes" and particles would just fall apart and "be dispersed" (p. 6).

The mind–body problem, in Priestley's argument, was based on a notion of body that science had shown not to exist. Since the mind–body problem was how something lacking solidity and not occupying space could interact with bodies that had solidity and did occupy space, the problem has disappeared because physical properties, in a new conception of matter, also lack solidity and do not occupy space. For Priestley, it made better sense to think of an enlarged conception of matter "especially as we know nothing more of the nature of substance than that it is something which supports properties" (p. 17); "powers of sensation or perception, and thought" (p. 22) could belong to the same substance as supports properties of attraction and repulsion. As he observed, "powers of sensation and thought . . . have never been found except in conjunction with a certain organized system of matter" (p. 26) which comprises both mind and brain. "Thought is a property of the nervous system, or rather of the brain" (p. 27); whatever matter supports a brain, supports a mind too.

In the same vein as Priestley, it has been argued more recently that the notion of body turns out to be a useless concept which has no more meaning in effect than whatever "finds a place in intelligible explanatory theory" and theory can contain within it anything, "however offensive to common sense" (Chomsky, 1995, p. 5). With the loss of any meaningful notion of *body* 300 years ago, the mind–body problem no longer had any coherent formulation. The challenge for language–brain research is of a more familiar kind in the sciences: a unification problem, how to unify two bodies of theoretical knowledge (Chomsky, 1995). There is linguistic theory and there is brain theory, but at present neither theory constrains the other. For centuries, physics and chemistry were in the same position and unification only became possible a couple of generations ago (Brock, 1992; Chomsky, 1995). Within physics today, a major question is to how to unify the different forces (gravitational, electromagnetic, strong and weak nuclear). So, when the term *neurolinguistics* is used, reasonably, all that can be meant is an area of inquiry whose ultimate goal is theory unification, but with a full recognition that unless substantial progress is made in that direction, the term *neurolinguistic theory* is without content since it presupposes that unification has already occurred.

How can progress toward eventual unification be made? The most obvious answer is for linguists and brain scientists to continue doing what they are already doing, namely, developing ever more explanatory theories of language and of brains, with the hope that with increased understanding, it will one day be possible to perceive how unification is possible. This answer, of course, prescribes no particular role for neurolinguistics at all. Neurolinguistics has a purpose only to the extent that examining language in brains can be informative about either brains or about language. Does examining language in brains tell us anything about language? That is, is it possible to think of a problem in linguistics such that something about brains provides an answer? The question is rhetorical because the only answer, until more is known about brains perhaps, is silence. Let us ask the converse question: Does examining language in brains tell us anything about brains? The answer to this question, one suspects, is not quite so debilitating because it may be reasoned that if something worthwhile is known about language, then at least it is possible to ask the brain something coherent. Of course, no one knows how a brain computes language – that is what it is like to be non-unified – but to the extent that the brain makes such distinctions that agree with the distinctions made in a theory of language, it might, not irrationally, be hoped that something is being learned about how brains care about language. What is learned, however, will have the character of *peculiar facts* because we do not have a relevant understanding of brains. Again, such is the nature of inquiry when two bodies of knowledge are not unified. The best prospect is to ask the brain a linguistically coherent question and look for an answer that matters to current brain theory. Then the inquiry is coherent in the only ways currently available, and the hope is that it becomes possible to build bridges that will provide eventual insight.

There is an alternative: experiment that treats language as a mere commonsense notion and brains only in terms of location. That description covers much of the vast literature on language and brain, including most of the work that seems closest to the interests of L2 researchers and teachers, the work on differences and similarities between L1 and L2 in brain territory. It is the kind of inquiry that Poeppel and Embick (2005) refer to, without approval, as the *standard program* in neurolinguistics.

Before discussing this further, a few more comments on common sense and theory. In the early days of modern science, the mechanical philosophy was based on a commonsense apprehension of Nature. Expectations were very high. Think of Bacon's hope that, if a natural and experimental history such as he proposed was provided, "the investigation of nature and of all sciences will be the work of a few years" (1620). From hopes for imminent and comprehensive understanding amenable to common sense, very soon afterwards, with the advent of Newton's gravitational force which defied the prevailing commonsense assumption of mechanism that physical objects could only move through direct contact with other physical objects, expectations changed. From that time on, it would be necessary to resign ourselves to a far more limited access to Nature's secrets, namely, access via the proxy of theory entirely unconstrained by the dictates of common sense (Chomsky, 2000). Centuries later, this has become familiar. The physicist Richard Feynman comments that, "one had to lose one's common sense in order to perceive what was happening at the atomic level" (1985, p. 5). Quantum theory, he notes, is "absurd from the point of view of common sense. And it agrees fully with experiment" (p. 10). Quantum theory tortures common sense, but Feynman observes that physicists have learned not to care if common sense is tortured. What matters is insight-giving theory that agrees with experiment.

Although the shift from common sense to theory must have been hard to take during the early days of modern science, it is rather surprising to find that, so many years later, a great deal of neuroimaging work on language anachronistically prefers commonsense notions of language to theoretical principles. In an attempt to draw attention to this atheoretical tendency, Poeppel (1996) criticized several high-profile researchers for their imaging studies of phonological processing which concerned themselves little with what was known about phonological processing or even about phonology. The criticism was not appreciated (Démonet et al., 1996). I recall a discussion a couple of years ago with a well-known scholar who has published many imaging studies of language. I was informed that it was premature in neuroscience for experiment to worry about theoretical issues. What was needed, he explained, was a long period of description, so informal notions of language were appropriate. Venturing dissent, I was asked to explain why so many highly intelligent people were doing descriptive research. I could not answer then and I am unable to answer now. However, imagine physicists, faced with some tough problem, and deciding that what was called for was a period in which theoretical concepts would be put on ice and replaced with informal notions of, say, *work* or *energy* or *light*. Everyone would scoff at such a suggestion, and yet, when it comes to language, that is precisely the approach that is so often adopted. It amounts to what Chomsky has called methodological dualism, more ruinous than mind–body dualism.

It is not just linguistic theory that is ignored, but theory of brain also seems very thin on the ground in the standard research program in neurolinguistics. Since most neuroscience studies of language use positron emission tomography (PET) or functional magnetic resonance imaging (fMRI), the focus is heavily on location. Although there is by now a vast literature describing locations of this informal notion of language or that, it is far from obvious that neural location does any theoretical work. Function has to occur somewhere, and to some extent we can already navigate a brain in terms of different functions, and certainly these are useful facts to know. But that does not mean that location is doing explanatory work; it may instead be merely epiphenomenal, just as linearity is epiphenomenal in linguistic theory – every sentence has to be heard or produced in a linear string, but that observation has no theoretical status.

Electrophysiological tools, by contrast, record aspects of brain that are theoretically more obviously interesting. Electroencephalography (EEG) and magnetoencephalography (MEG) record brain activity directly, and the signal they pick up is the synchronous firing of a large number of neurons. Synchronous firing has long been considered a central explanation of how neurons form assemblies for particular computational tasks (Abeles, 1991; Gray et al., 1989; Singer, 2000). Also, as Phillips (2005, p. 81) has pointed out, there are substantial hypotheses regarding timing of language function but no detailed hypotheses regarding location. In neural studies of second language processing, however, EEG studies are few and far between and MEG studies, so far as I know, are non-existent.

Some Promising Neurolinguistic Research

The above characterization of neurolinguistics may serve (or not) to keep expectations in perspective, but hopefully not to curb interest. That is far from the intention. So long as we devise experiments that ask the brain theoretically coherent questions, we are doing the only reasonable thing we can do, which at least holds out the possibility of building bridges between language and brain.

For example, some rather intriguing work has been carried out which finds a neural response to phonological categories. This is unusual, as most neurolinguistic studies have focused on acoustic and phonetic features, but have not addressed phenomena relevant to the phonological level of analysis. Phonetic categories, of course, group together a number of similar sounds, and neural responses have been established for within-category discrimination of these sounds. For example, Dehaene-Lambertz et al. (1997) found that within-category contrasts produced a Mismatch Response, a particular neural response to a sequence of standards (identical sounds) interrupted by a deviant (different sound). The deviant elicits the mismatch response at ~150–250 ms in auditory cortex.

But does the auditory cortex register phonological categories? Since phonological categories are abstract symbolic representations that have an all-or-none character, within-category variation is irrelevant; the same rules apply across the board to all members of a category. One body of research was able to use the mismatch response to get at phonological categories. It is a well-known fact that the perceptual cue for voicing in stop consonants (e.g., /t/ and /d/) is voice onset time (VOT) – the amount of time that elapses between the release of a consonant and the onset of voicing. Stop consonants that have shorter VOTs are perceived as voiced, while those with longer VOTs are perceived as unvoiced. The perceptual boundary is quite sharply drawn at ~30 ms. Phillips et al. (2001; see also Aulanko et al., 1993) used a range of different VOT values of /dae/ and /tae/. With VOT varying both within and between /dae/ and /tae/, there was no many-to-one ratio of standards and deviants at acoustic or phonetic levels; all sounds were different in terms of VOT. There could only be a many-to-one ratio if all of the different realizations of each category were treated as the same thing, that is to say, at the phonological level. In the event, different VOT values of one category /tae/ interrupted by a single value of /dae/ elicited the characteristic mismatch response in auditory cortex, indicating that the brain does care about phonological categories.

In addition to the impressive body of work taking us, in Poeppel's phrase, from vibration in the ear to abstraction in the head, thoughtful work has been pursued that investigates lexical access. Embick et al. (2001), in a MEG study of lexical frequency, found that the first peak in the magnetic waveform to vary as a function of frequency occurred at ~350 ms after stimulus presentation. In a lexical decision task, the M350 peak for frequent words was earlier than the peak for non-frequent words. The M350 also occurred earlier for repeated words than for non-repeated words (Pylkkänen et al., 2000). In a further study, Pylkkänen, Stringfellow, & Marantz (2002) observed that the M350 responded to phonotactic probability, but not to density similarity neighborhoods. That is, it is sensitive to the frequencies of sounds and their sequences in words, but not to the extent with which a word sounds like lots of other words. This is interesting because in behavioral studies, it had been shown that phonotactic probability and neighborhood density had opposite effects: phonotactics facilitated sublexical processing, while density had an inhibitory effect, slowing word recognition. What Pylkkänen et al. did was to use stimuli that possessed both properties. The fact that the M350 responded to phonotactics and not density argues that the peak indexes an early stage of (sub)lexical processing rather than a later recognition stage when competition from like-sounding words would obtain.

Further sharpening our grasp of the M350, Fiorentino & Poeppel (2007) showed that it is not an index simply of lexical access but of root access, a rather more precise concept because roots and what is contained in them are important theoretical entities (see, e.g., Halle & Marantz, 1993). Another important theoretical issue is polysemy, the different senses of a word. Syntactic principles operate on identity in sentences such as *The newspaper decided to change its format* (Chomsky, 1970): *newspaper* and *its* have identical reference and yet they have two different senses (*newspaper* refers to the publisher and *its* to the publication). Of interest, then, is whether polysemous senses share the same root, and are thus identical at that level, or whether they have separate roots, as is widely agreed to be the case with homonymy. Both positions have their adherents but evidence one way or the other has been difficult to obtain. Two recent MEG studies have investigated polysemy and homonymy (Beretta, Fiorentino, & Poeppel, 2005; Pylkkänen, Llinas, & Murphy, 2006). Without going into detail, the findings of these studies can be explained if the M350 accesses roots and if polysemous senses, but not homonymous meanings, share the same root.

Neurolinguistic Research and L2 Learning and Teaching

One strand of research that is often discussed in the second language literature asks the question: Is L1 like L2 in the brain? There are many reviews of this literature (e.g., Fabbro, 2001; Perani, 2005; Perani & Abutalebi, 2005), so a cursory summary will suffice before it is asked in what ways the body of work is informative.

Starting with PET and fMRI studies, the general picture that seems to be emerging is twofold. First, acquisition of L2 engages very much the same neural regions as L1. Second, these relatively stable common patterns can be mediated by age of acquisition and the level of proficiency attained. Basically, with respect to tasks that are claimed to tap grammatical resources, subjects who acquired their L2 early show the same regional activation, whereas those who acquired their L2 late use the same areas as L1 but also show some additional activation. With respect to tasks that are considered to access lexical-semantic processing, in early or late acquisition of L2, if proficiency is high, the same neural areas are activated.

Why ask a brain if L1 is like L2 with regard to location? For Kim et al. (1997), as for many others, this is self-explanatory: "Here we investigate the fundamental question of how multiple languages are represented in the human brain" (p. 171). No further motivation is offered. Leaving aside, for the moment, the fact that the term *fundamental* is misplaced given that far simpler questions have barely been addressed (as mentioned earlier), the lack of any clearly stated theoretical focus reflects the descriptive nature of much of the work. The main issue stated in a number of reports concerns critical periods in language acquisition, but unlike much of the behavioral work in this domain of inquiry (such as Johnson & Newport, 1989; White & Genesee, 1996), there is little or no concern for questions that are driven by some aspect of linguistic theory. The result is that the behavioral work is often capable of fairly precise interpretation whereas the neurolinguistic work is not.

As in the behavioral literature, independent variables that are frequently manipulated in the neuroimaging literature are age of first exposure to a language and level of attainment. What distinguishes the two literatures is the content of the dependent variables. Dependent variables in at least some of the behavioral studies attempt to isolate some linguistically relevant element or other, while the dependent variables in typical PET and fMRI studies bear no obvious relation to what is known about the nature of language. Some studies (e.g., Chee, Tan, & Thiel, 1999) ask subjects to take letter strings like *cou* and think of a word that begins with those letters, perhaps *coulomb* or *courtesy*; or to think of words that end in a letter string like *ter*, maybe *banter*. Others ask subjects to think of a word that begins with a single letter that is called out to them (Perani et al., 2003). Still others have subjects listen to stories (Perani et al., 1996), or silently describe events that happened during the previous day (Kim et al., 1997), or listen to (unspecified) sentences in different languages (Pallier et al., 2003), or translate and read words (Price, Green, & von Studnitz, 1999), listen to dialogues (Nakai et al., 1999), and so forth. Language, in some sense, is plainly involved in all of these tasks, but in none of the reports is there any indication as to which theoretical element is being tapped into, and it is hard to imagine candidates. Perani et al. (1998) start out by discussing parameter setting, something behavioral studies have pursued, but in the event they end up using a story-telling task, a task that does not pick out any particular parameter at all.

Part of the problem of relating L2 to L1 in brain space is that we know precious little about L1 in brain space. Even the rare experiment that contrasts sentences that differ only in respects that have relevance in the linguistic literature, such as subject vs. object movement in relative clauses in L1, has found it difficult to nail down anything solid and reliable. For example, Caplan and his colleagues have carried out a series of experiments looking only at relative clauses. In the first study, Stromswold et al.'s (1996) PET study of relative clauses, syntactic processing showed increased activation, not only in Broca's area, but in a specific portion of that area, the pars opercularis. A follow-up study (Caplan, Alpert, & Waters, 1998) with the same materials, but with female instead of male subjects, found increased activation in one part of the pars opercularis, higher and more anterior than for males. This difference was not predicted, but after the fact, it was speculated that this might indicate a male–female difference. A separate experiment in the same report looked at relative clauses with two propositions vs. relative clauses with one proposition. No increased activation was found in the traditional language areas, but in visual cortex. Clearly, this was not predicted, but it was considered that it was "most likely due to differences in some aspect of post-interpretive processing . . . visual mental imagery processes" (p. 548). A later study found increased regional cerebral blood flow for one kind of relative clause in a part of Broca's area not implicated in the earlier studies, the pars triangularis (Caplan et al., 2000). Why should that be? Apparently, "both these areas can be activated by syntactic processing" (p. 70). Undeterred, Caplan et al. (2001) proceed to examine relative clauses with and without padding. They find no difference for the critical part of the sentence (immediately following the padding). Perhaps this was because relative clauses involved movement out of subject or object position, perhaps different task demands, possibilities that "can only be answered by further detailed studies" (2001, p. 37). A further detailed study (Caplan, Waters, & Alpert, 2003) used the same materials and tasks as

Stromswold et al. (1996) and Caplan et al. (1998), but this time with subjects aged 70–79. Unlike the earlier studies, increased blood flow was found in the left inferior parietal, which must be "related to sentence processing . . . and syntactic comprehension" (p. 118). There was also increased activation in left superior frontal cortex, near the midline, an area which, it is surmised, "may be involved in syntactic processing" (p. 118). Why might older subjects apparently use totally different parts of the brain from the younger subjects? One possibility mooted is that they had received two years less education. This was explored in a second experiment in Caplan et al. (2003). Younger subjects with less education were tested. Now, increased activation was observed in superior frontal, but a part of it quite distinct from any previously seen. Increases were also reported in the motor planning region, which might be due to different eye movements, or "could reflect greater deployment of attention" (p. 122). An increase in the precuneal parietal, not the parietal area observed in the older subjects, showed increased activation too, and it was considered that this could be due to subtle aspects of language processing. But, perhaps the older subjects' different neural activation was not due to their lower education, but to their less accurate task performance, a possibility also examined by Caplan et al. (2003). Older subjects whose performance matched the younger subjects were tested. Increased regional blood flow was found in one more area of prefrontal cortex not implicated in the earlier studies, an area normally considered to be involved in executive functioning. Caplan et al. note that it would appear also to be involved in syntactic processing.

This series of studies is of interest because of the persistent attention to a quite well-circumscribed range of sentence types. In the end, we know that if you place subjects in a PET or fMRI scanner, then something is going to happen, but it is very hard to say in advance what that will be, and after the fact, very difficult to narrow candidate explanations. This is not just a problem for Caplan and his colleagues, but a problem for everyone at a time when theories of language and brain seem far away from each other. If one asks subjects to listen to stories in L1 or L2, for example, then surely prediction and explanation are rendered all the more indeterminate.

Turning to the EEG studies, the picture that emerges from the relatively fewer studies that have been carried out is, roughly speaking, that as proficiency increases ERPs (event-related potentials) for L2 processing become more like those in L1. Research by Friederici and her colleagues has suggested that semantic violations modulate the N400, while phrase structure violations have an effect on early anterior negativity and afterwards on late positivity (the P600). An early study by Weber-Fox and Neville (1996) found qualitatively different ERPs between L2 and L1 for syntactic processes, but quantitative differences for semantic processes (such as a delayed N400 for those who acquired the L2 at a later age). Isel, Hahne, and Friederici (2000) and Hahne and Friederici (2001), using similar stimuli but for different L2s, found N400 modulation for semantic violations, along with a lack of the expected early anterior negativity modulation for phrase structure violations and no P600. Hahne (2001), again using similar stimuli, found an N400 effect for both L1 and L2 groups, while for phrase structure violations there was no modulation of early anterior negativity for the L2 group, in contrast to the L1 group, suggesting that automaticity of processing was reduced. The P600 was similar for both L1 and L2. Reflecting on these findings across different studies, Hahne (2001) notes that the subjects in her study were more proficient in L2 than the subjects in Isel et al. (2000) and Hahne and Friederici (2001), and while the main difference between her study and the other two is that the more proficient subjects showed a P600 effect, all three studies revealed N400 modulation, as does an experiment by McLoughlin, Osterhout, and Kim (2004). She infers from these facts that semantic processes are the first to become L1-like, and syntactic processes become so with greater proficiency. This does not address the difference in anterior negativities, but a recent study (Ojima, Nakata, & Kakigi, 2005) finds that high-proficiency L2 subjects do show anterior negativities for syntactic processing whereas low-proficiency L2 subjects do not. In addition, a study by Friederici, Steinhauer, and Pfeifer (2002) finds that training on an artificial language called BRICANTO that reportedly has UG-like constraints yields the same early automatic negativities and P600 effects as seen in normal L1 processing. Age does not seem to be a contributory factor in these experiments, but level of proficiency does. These considerations are used to argue against a very strong form of the critical period hypothesis.

The EEG studies of critical period issue are conducted against a background of increasingly well-understood electrophysiological responses in the time course of linguistic processing, namely the N400, LAN (left anterior negativity), and the P600. As such, the program is seeking to construct language–brain relations in a way that has some neural justification (timing matters in proposals regarding neuronal population coding), and also in a way that is not incoherent linguistically, though rather blunt. Blunt, because the contrasts are relatively coarse and there is no attention to the very fine computations that linguistic theory cares about.

Some Confusions

The above treatment of the L1/L2 neuroimaging studies is perhaps slightly less sanguine than is to be found in some reviews, but if reservations have been expressed about research that is plainly serious, it is hard to know what to say about some of the views that have been advanced in sections of the second language literature regarding what claims neuroscience entitles us to make about second language acquisition and teaching.

It transpires there is such a literature whose concern is for brain-compatible language teaching (Bimonte, 1998; Dhority & Jensen, 1998; Genesee, 2000; Lombardi, 2004). Apparently, the brain is complex and adaptive, and varies across individuals, so language teaching should be approached with a variety of techniques, such as group work, and so forth. The brain is social, so teaching should involve cooperative learning strategies. The brain is emotional, so it is critical to lower the "affective filter." Left brain and right brain are respectively associated with rational and artistic orientations, so one can deploy art or music to teach math, physics, or language; though some of the authors regard teaching based on left-brain/right-brain considerations to be outmoded. The brain links language to other parts of the brain, so good teaching practice should, for example, not present phonics independently of meaning. To do so would be misguided. Brain connections are shaped by the environment, so teaching makes a difference and one should not give up on older learners. And so on.

The blandest comment that presents itself is that the conclusions do not follow from the premises. However, even this is tantamount to saying that the authors have abandoned the most rudimentary notions of rationality. So, lacking any understanding of what counts as argument in this literature, I will not, indeed cannot, criticize it any further.

With regard to SLA, the picture is not much clearer. A typical account might, for example, seek to promote a language socialization paradigm and jettison cognitive science models, and claim that brain research provides the impetus (e.g., Watson-Gegeo, 2004). The appeal to neuroscience is littered with misconceptions, such as that it is a problem for cognitive science approaches that "research has discovered no structure in the brain that corresponds to a Language Acquisition Device as argued by Chomsky" (p. 333). Chomsky argued no such thing, of course, but profound confusions of this sort will not be pursued here (however, see Gregg, 2006 for a thorough critique).

Conclusion

Neurolinguistics is an area of inquiry whose ultimate goal is theory unification. To engage in neurolinguistic work is to attempt to integrate what is known about language, which I have been referring to as '"linguistic theory," with what is known about brains, which I have been informally calling "brain theory." Given that at present neither theory constrains the other, it is obvious that neurolinguistics is at a very preliminary stage of development. The challenge facing neurolinguistics is awe-inspiring, and there are those who have concluded (prematurely, since we simply do not know) that the relationship of mind to brain will forever remain a mystery (e.g., McGinn, 1993, 1999; Uttal, 2005). It is unfortunate, then, that much of language–brain research is conducted without reference to either linguistic or brain theory, because it suggests that there is some other way of finding out about nature than via theory. Indeed, as noted earlier, the standard research program in neurolinguistics largely proceeds as if what is called for is description. The prospects for theory unification are remote indeed if most current work is atheoretical.

Commenting on an earlier research program that favored theory-free description, the biologist Ernst Mayr (cited in Hull, 1988) offered a cautionary tale. In the nineteenth century, in an attempt to solve the mysteries of inheritance, one scientist, Carl Friedrich von Gärtner, judged that the best approach was theory-free Stakhanovite data collection, relentless unbiased description. He carried out literally 10,000 cross-breeding experiments. Unfortunately no one was ever able to make use of his work; they were always forced to conduct their own experiments because, even in as many as 10,000 experiments, the contrasts demanded by one hypothesis or another were never found. Not surprising when we consider that theories contain within them exotic elements that torture common sense. The relevant contrasts would not occur to anyone absent a theory. Von Gärtner's data collections now lie "buried in the stacks of a few libraries around the world, as sterile as the day that they were conceived" (Hull, 1988, p. 489). It is not unreasonable to wonder if today's mass accumulation of descriptive neuroimaging data on language and the brain can have much more hope of chancing upon the right contrasts that might permit insightful language–brain connections than von Gärtner's work contributed to an understanding of inheritance.

Given the preliminary nature of neurolinguistic inquiry and the descriptive bent of much of the work currently conducted, the upshot is that brain research can at present provide evidence that is little more than suggestive to a model of L2 acquisition and less than that to the practice of language teaching. The neuroimaging studies on the critical period question can be seen, at best, as to be taken under advisement. It may seem compelling to use brain data to make a point, but there is little justification for privileging brain data over other kinds of data. The same goes for teaching research. If there was some reason to support group work or dispense with it before, there is no better reason to be found in the neurolinguistic literature. Practical applications, such as to teaching, are remote, beyond remote.

REFERENCES

Abeles, M. (1991). *Corticonics: Neural circuits of the cerebral cortex.* Cambridge: Cambridge University Press.

Aulanko, R., Hari, R., Lounasmaa, O. V., Näätänen, R., & Sams, M. (1993). Phonetic invariance in the human auditory cortex. *NeuroReport* 4, 1356–8.

Bacon, F. (1620). *Preparative toward a natural and experimental history.* http://etext.library. adelaide.edu.au/b/bacon/francis/preparative/complete.html.

Beretta, A., Fiorentino, R., & Poeppel, D. (2005). The effects of homonymy and polysemy on lexical access: An MEG study. *Cognitive Brain Research* 24, 57–65.

Bimonte, R. (1998). Mysteries of the brain: Students thrive in a brain-compatible learning environment. *Momentum* 16–18.

Brock, W. H. (1992). *The Norton history of Chemistry.* New York: Norton.

Caplan, D., Alpert, N., & Waters, G. (1998). Effects of syntactic structure and propositional number on patterns of regional cerebral blood flow. *Journal of Cognitive Neuroscience* 10, 541–52.

Caplan, D., Alpert, N., Waters, G., & Olivieri, A. (2000). Activation of Broca's area by syntactic processing under conditions of concurrent articulation. *Human Brain Mapping* 9, 65–71.

Caplan, D., Vijayan, S., Kuperberg, G., et al. (2001). Vascular responses to syntactic processing: Event-related fMRI study of relative clauses. *Human Brain Mapping* 15, 26–38.

Caplan, D., Waters, G., & Alpert, N. (2003). Effects of age and speed of processing on rCBF correlates of syntactic processing in sentence comprehension. *Human Brain Mapping* 19, 112–31.

Chee, M. L. W., Tan, E. W. L., & Thiel, T. (1999). Mandarin and English single word processing studied with functional magnetic resonance imaging. *The Journal of Neuroscience* 19, 3050–6.

Chomsky, N. (1970). Remarks on nominalism. In R. A. Jacobs & P. S. Rosenbaum (eds.), *Readings in English transformational grammar* (pp. 184–221). Waltham, MA: Ginn & Co.

Chomsky, N. (1995). Language and nature. *Mind* 104, 1–61.

Chomsky, N. (2000). Linguistics and brain science. In A. Marantz, Y. Miyashitu, & W. O'Neil (eds.), *Image, Language, Brain* (pp. 13–23). Cambridge, MA: MIT Press.

Dehaene-Lambertz, S., Dupoux, E., Mehler, J., et al. (1997). Anatomical variability in the cortical representation of first and second languages. *NeuroReport* 8, 3809–15.

Démonet, J. F., Fiez, J. A., Paulesu, E., et al. (1996). PET studies of phonological processing: Critical reply to Poeppel. *Brain and Language* 55, 352–79.

Dhority, L. & Jensen, E. (1998). *Joyful fluency: Brain-compatible second language acquisition*. San Diego: Brain Store.

Embick, D., Hackl, M., Schaeffer, J., et al. (2001). A magnetoencephalographic component whose latency reflects lexical frequency. *Cognitive Brain Research* 10, 345–8.

Fabbro, F. (2001). The bilingual brain: Cerebral representation of languages. *Brain and Language* 79, 211–22.

Feynman, R. P. (1985). *QED: The strange theory of light and matter*. Princeton, NJ: Princeton University Press.

Fiorentino, R. & Poeppel, D. (2007). Compound words and structure in the lexicon. *Language and Cognitive Processes* 12, 953–1000.

Friederici, A., Steinhauer, K., & Pfeifer, E. (2002). Brain signatures of artificial language processing: Evidence challenging the critical period hypothesis. *Proceedings of the National Academy of Sciences USA* 99, 529–34.

Genesee, F. (2000). *Brain research: Implications for second language learning*. Center for Research on Education, Diversity & Excellence, Occasional Report, ERIC_00_12_brain. ERIC Clearinghouse on Language and Linguistics: Washington, DC.

Gray, C. M., König, P., Engel, A. K., & Singer, W. (1989). Oscillatory responses in cat visual cortex exhibit inter-columnular synchronization which reflects global stimulus properties. *Nature* 338, 334–7.

Gregg, K. (2006). Taking a social turn for the worse: The language socialization paradigm for second language acquisition. *Second Language Research* 22, 1–30.

Hahne, A. (2001). What's different in second-language processing? Evidence from event-related brain potentials. *Journal of Psycholinguistic Research* 30, 251–66.

Hahne, A. & Friederici, A. (2001). Processing a second language: Late learners' comprehension mechanisms as revealed by event-related potentials. *Bilingualism: Language and Cognition* 4, 123–41.

Halle, M. & Marantz, A. (1993). Distributed morphology. In K. Hale & S. J. Keyser (eds.), *The view from Building 20* (pp. 111–76). Cambridge, MA: MIT Press.

Hull, D. (1988). *Science as a process: An evolutionary account of the social and conceptual development of science*. Chicago: University of Chicago Press.

Isel, F., Hahne, A., & Friederici, A. (2000). *Auditory processing of German sentences by French late bilinguals*. Poster presented at the Conference of Architectures and Mechanisms of Language Processing (Amlap). Leiden, The Netherlands, September.

Johnson, J. S. & Newport, E. L. (1989). Critical period effects in second language learning: The influence of maturational state on the acquisition of English as a second language. *Cognitive Psychology* 21, 60–99.

Kim, K. H., Relkin, N. R., Lee, K. M., & Hirsch, J. (1997). Distinct cortical areas associated with native and second languages. *Nature* 388, 171–4.

Lombardi, J. (2004). Practical ways brain-based research applies to ESL learners. *Internet TESL Journal* 10, 8.

McGinn, C. (1993). *Problems in philosophy: The limits of inquiry.* Oxford: Blackwell.

McGinn, C. (1999). *The mysterious flame: Conscious minds in a material world.* New York: Basic Books.

McLoughlin, J., Osterhout, L., & Kim, A. (2004). Neural correlates of second-language word learning: Minimal instruction produces rapid change. *Nature Neuroscience* 7, 703–4.

Nakai, T., Matsuo, K., Kato, C., et al. (1999). A functional magnetic resonance imaging study of listening comprehension of language in human at 3-tesla comprehension level and activation of the language areas. *Neuroscience Letters* 263, 33–6.

Ojima, S., Nakata, H., & Kakigi, R. (2005). An ERP study of second language learning after childhood: Effects of proficiency. *Journal of Cognitive Neuroscience* 17, 1212–28.

Pallier, C., Dehaene, S., Poline, J.-B., et al. (2003). Brain imaging of language plasticity in adopted adults: Can a second language replace a first? *Cerebral Cortex* 13, 155–61.

Perani, D. (2005). The neural basis of language talent in bilinguals. *Trends in Cognitive Sciences* 9, 211–13.

Perani, D. & Abutalebi, J. (2005). The neural basis of first and second language processing. *Current Opinion in Neurobiology* 15, 202–6.

Perani, D., Abutalebi, J., Paulesu, E., et al. (2003). The role of age of acquisition and language usage in early, high-proficient bilinguals: An fMRI study during verbal fluency. *Human Brain Mapping* 19, 170–82.

Perani, D., Dehaene, S., Grassi, F., et al. (1996). Brain processing of native and foreign languages. *NeuroReport* 7, 2439–44.

Perani, D., Paulesu, E., Sebastian-Galles, N., et al. (1998). The bilingual brain: Proficiency and age of acquisition of the second language. *Brain* 121, 1841–52.

Phillips, C. (2005). Electrophysiology in the study of developmental language impairments: Prospects and challenges for a top-down approach. *Applied Psycholinguistics* 26, 79–96.

Phillips, C., Pellathy, T., Marantz, A., et al. (2001). Auditory cortex accesses phonological categories: An MEG mismatch study. *Journal of Cognitive Neuroscience* 12, 1038–55.

Poeppel, D. (1996). A critical review of PET studies of phonological processing. *Brain and Language* 55, 317–51.

Poeppel, D. & Embick, D. (2005). The relation between linguistics and neuroscience. In A. Cutler (ed.), *Twenty-first century psycholinguistics: Four cornerstones* (pp. 1–16). Mahwah, NJ: Lawrence Erlbaum.

Price, C. J., Green, D. W., & von Studnitz, R. (1999). A functional imaging study of translation and language switching. *Brain* 122, 2221–35.

Priestley, J. (1777). *Disquisitions relating to matter and spirit.* Kila, MT: Kessinger.

Pylkkänen, L., Llinas, R., & Murphy, G. (2006). Representation of polysemy: MEG evidence. *Journal of Cognitive Neuroscience* 18, 1–13.

Pylkkänen, L., Stringfellow, A., Flagg, E., & Marantz, A. (2000). A neural response sensitive to repetition and phonotactic probability: MEG investigations of lexical access.

Proceedings of the Twelfth International Conference on Biomagnetism (pp. 363–7). Helsinki University of Technology.

Pylkkänen, L., Stringfellow, A., & Marantz, A. (2002). Neuromagnetic evidence for the timing of lexical activation: An MEG component sensitive to phonotactic probability but not to neighborhood density. *Brain and Language* 81, 666–78.

Singer, W. (2000). Response synchronization: A universal coding strategy for the definition of relations. In M. Gazzaniga (ed.), *The new cognitive neurosciences*, (2nd edn., pp. 325–38). Cambridge, MA: MIT Press.

Stromswold, K., Caplan, D., Alpert, N., & Rausch, S. (1996). Localization of syntactic comprehension by positron emission tomography. *Brain and Language* 52, 452–73.

Uttal, W. R. (2005). *Neural theories of mind: Why the mind-brain problem may never be solved.* Mahwah, NJ: Lawrence Erlbaum.

Watson-Gegeo, K. A. (2004). Mind, language, and epistemology: Toward a language socialization paradigm for SLA. *Modern Language Journal* 88, 331–50.

Weber-Fox, C. M. & Neville, H. J. (1996). Maturational constraints on functional specializations for language processing. *Journal of Cognitive Neuroscience* 8, 231–56.

White, L. & Genesee, F. (1996). How native is near-native? The issue of ultimate attainment in second language acquisition. *Second Language Research* 12, 233–65.

6 Sequences and Processes in Language Learning

LOURDES ORTEGA

In this chapter I review major findings concerning the sequences and processes associated with the development of a second language. I begin by characterizing the nature of interlanguage. The bulk of the chapter is then devoted to an overview of sequences, or systematic patterns uncovered in the development of various areas of the L2 grammar. Next, I examine some central processes by which learners attend selectively to aspects of the L2 input, reorganize their mental representations in light of new evidence as this becomes available to them, and then move (or not) along the sequences. I conclude the chapter with five generalizations that summarize the implications of knowledge about sequences and processes for second and foreign language teaching.

Learner Language or Interlanguage

During the 1950s and 1960s, researchers interested in understanding language teaching and learning set out to compare external differences between a given first language (L1) and a given target language (L2). The hope was that such a Contrastive Analysis approach would help them uncover areas of difficulties for L2 learners (e.g., Stockwell, Bowen, & Martin, 1965). However, beginning in the 1970s, and influenced by seminal findings that had begun to accumulate about child L1 acquisition, researchers turned to a different strategy and began analyzing the actual language samples that learners produced when they attempted to use their L2 in speaking. (Writing and signing data have also been examined, although less extensively; see, e.g., Bardovi-Harlig, 1995, for L2 writing; and Mayberry, in press, for L2 signing.) A central concept that emerged with the study of actual learner language was interlanguage (Selinker, 1972), or the language system that each learner constructs at any given point in development. Interlanguage reflects an interim competence that contains elements from both the L1 and the L2 grammar, but also elements that go beyond both. The new associated methodologies of Error Analysis and later Performance Analysis (Long & Sato, 1984) led to an

unprecedented wealth of findings about interlanguages. More recent developments in the last 20 years have added detail and explanatory power to the older
findings.

Interlanguages are natural languages

Interlanguages are believed to be systematic, natural languages in their own
right. In other words, learners are constrained in their development of a second
language by the same natural principles that constrain the development of any
human language. An unresolved question among second language acquisition
researchers is whether these constraints and natural limits are provided by a
genetic endowment specific to the human language faculty, as proponents of
Universal Grammar posit (e.g., White, 2003), or by the same general cognitive
learning mechanisms that help humans process and learn any other kind of
information, as language psychologists argue (e.g., DeKeyser, this volume; Ellis,
this volume). In this chapter, I adopt the latter position. I assume that general
cognition principles can help us understand how L2 learners develop grammar
knowledge and the ability to use it in order to communicate, at least for the great
majority of interlanguage phenomena that are of relevance and interest for language teaching.

Interlanguages are more than the sum of input and first language

The nature of interlanguage is delimited by three well-known but nevertheless
striking facts. First, learners build mental representations that are rather different
from what the input in their surrounding environment looks like. For example,
consider the following sentence from Oshita (2000, p. 313), who identified it in an
L2 English essay written by an L1 Spanish speaker:

(1)   It [a wall] was falled down in order to get a bigger greenhouse.

We can see that the English morpheme *-ed* has been added to a verb whose past
and past participle forms are irregular in English (*fall, fell, fallen*) and furthermore
that a verb that is intransitive in English (*fall*) has been made into a causative
verb with a transitive meaning ('make to fall' or 'tear down'). When L2 English
learners produce such interlanguage solutions, they have most certainly not picked
them up from their surrounding input. These are not forms or meanings that can
be learned from, say, English-speaking friends or textbooks.

Second, although knowledge of the first language definitely influences interlanguages in various ways (see Ringbom & Jarvis, this volume), many so-called
errors cannot be explained by recourse to the L1 alone, including example (1)
above. Spanish has regular and irregular verbal morphology and uses it to
mark past tense and past participles, and it also has a verb for the intransitive
meaning 'fall' (*caer*) and another for the transitive meaning 'make to fall' (*derribar*).
Moreover, even when the L1 appears logically to explain an interlanguage

solution, other explanations may in fact be needed. To illustrate, if we hear *How I do this?* from an L1 Spanish learner and an L1 Punjabi learner, whose languages do not have inversion, we may conclude it is their respective L1s that are inducing this choice. However, if we sampled learners from a wide enough range of L1 backgrounds, including languages where inversion does exist (e.g., Dutch and German), we would find that they, too, use un-inverted questions in their English interlanguage at an early stage of L2 development. In the presence of this additional evidence, we must then conclude that the L1 cannot be the correct explanation for lack of inversion. In fact, we will later see that the utterance *How I do this?* results from a universally attested interlanguage solution to the problem of question formation in English, called fronting (cf. stage 3 in Table 6.5).

A third, striking fact is that many interlanguage solutions are also attested in the production of children acquiring their first language (who, therefore, do not have any other L1 knowledge on which to rely, for better or worse). Thus, the solutions in (1) have been also amply documented in data from children learning L1 English. How can we explain interlanguage solutions that are neither directly attributable to the input nor to the L1, and that are shared by first and second language acquirers?

The unavoidable conclusion is that these forms are interim systematic innovations that learners independently create when they are trying to figure out the workings of the new language system they are learning. As will become clear, these interlanguage inventions are motivated by the complex interaction of multiple forces. Those include the evidence available or absent in the input (White, 2003) and knowledge of the L1 and other known languages (Ringbom & Jarvis, this volume). But additional forces stem from the interaction between the universal shape of languages and the conceptual apparatus of the human mind. They include syntactic, semantic-discoursal (Anderson & Shirai, 1994; Hyltenstam, 1987), and statistical, as well as conceptual and sensorimotor, processing influences (N. Ellis, 2006; this volume), on the one hand, and communicative pressures and social incentives learners experience as they use the language to make meaning (Klein & Perdue, 1997; von Stutterheim & Klein, 1987), on the other.

Sequences in Language Learning

Interlanguage development is systematic, not haphazard. For a substantial number of language areas, learners are seen to traverse several stages, each consisting of predictable solutions, on their way to developing the various full-fledged subsystems of the target language. Patterned development through stages should not be equated with linear progression from inaccurate to accurate use of the L2 in a form-by-form or function-by-function, piecemeal fashion. For all the phenomena described in this section, learners undergo non-linear and unevenly paced increases and decreases in accuracy. For all phenomena, as well, some learners may never progress all the way to a full targetlike system represented in their mental grammars. In order to illustrate L2 sequences, we will examine findings for five interlanguage domains.

Systematicity in the development of accuracy: Morpheme orders

A robust case of systematicity in interlanguage, well known since the 1970s, pertains to a set of English inflectional morphemes found to be mastered by L2 English users in a certain order, shown in Table 6.1. This order represents the point at which learners across studies reached a conventional level of 80 or 90 percent accurate suppliance for each of the forms (see Krashen, 1977).

In Table 6.1, I have grouped morphemes into four sets to acknowledge the fact that, on occasion, some studies have reported slightly different ranks for structures within a given grouping. For example, Jia and Fuse (2007) reported that ten Mandarin Chinese-speaking children, who had arrived in the United States between the ages of 5 and 16 and whose L2 development was followed by the researchers for five years, found regular past tense *-ed* more challenging than third-person *-s* (possessive *-'s* was not investigated). Three of them were seen to master third-person *-s* to 80 percent accuracy after a year and a half or later in the United States, but none had yet mastered *-ed* at the end of the five-year study period. However, the rank of structures is never violated across the groups in Table 6.1 (see Goldschneider & DeKeyser, 2001, Appendix A). The accuracy order has been shown to be similar for both young and adult L2 learners, for both naturalistic and instructed learners, regardless of L1 background or whether the data are oral or written.

Table 6.1   Morpheme accuracy order, from earliest to latest mastery

Morpheme	Illustration
-ing Plural *-s* *Be* copula	*the girl is watch**ing** shop window with the food* *Chaplin give away a lot of cigar**s** and chocolate to the kid**s*** *she **is** the one*
Be auxiliary *a/the*	*the girl **is** watching shop window with the food* *she steals **a** bread . . . he took **the** bread*
Irregular past	*the police **misunderstood***
Regular past *-ed* third-person *-s* Possessive *-'s*	*she crash**ed** with a man* *she steal**s** a bread* *the bread shop'**s** owner*

Note. Illustrations are from L2 oral narratives produced by college-level learners of English in Japan after watching *Alone and Hungry*, a short video clip from Charlie Chaplin's *Modern Times*; unpublished author data © Ortega, Iwashita, Rabie, & Norris.

Larsen-Freeman (1976) identified the frequency and salience of these forms in the input as possible powerful determinants of the order, but it was not until 25 years later that Goldschneider and DeKeyser (2001) were finally able to garner concrete empirical evidence about this possibility. They established frequency benchmarks and operationalized salience via a scoring of four formal and functional dimensions. They then pooled the data for twelve morpheme studies and entered them into a regression analysis to see whether frequency plus the four dimensions of salience would shed light on the previously speculative explanations for the accuracy order shown in Table 6.1. They found that, indeed, each of the five factors on its own correlated reasonably well with the pooled morpheme data (in the range of $r = 0.40$ to 0.60), and that, when combined, they explained 71 percent of the variance in the data. Thus, we can conclude that the systematicity found in interlanguage development, at least for many aspects of morphology, reflects properties in the language input related to statistical distribution (frequency) and perceptual and functional cues (salience) as they interact with human cognitive capacities to learn from the linguistic evidence (N. Ellis, 2006, this volume).

Focus on complex form–function mappings: Sequenced development of temporal expression

Researchers have also uncovered systematicity in how learners come to express a given function in the L2 through the range of forms available. The expression of temporality has been well studied from this functional perspective, leading to the robust conclusion that learners of a second language (as well as children learning their first language) undergo three phases, each characterized by reliance on a different set of resources that help them express temporality: pragmatic, lexical, and grammatical.

In the initial phase, learners can mark tense only by means of pragmatic devices. For example, they stick to the chronological order in which things occur and use the sequential order of discourse to convey temporal relations among events, as illustrated in the following two contrasting examples from von Stutterheim and Klein (1987, p. 198):

(2)   Schule fertig, Deutschland komm
      'school finish, Germany come'

(3)   Deutschland komm, Schule fertig
      'Germany come, school finish'

Most interlocutors would naturally interpret (2) as meaning 'after finishing school I came to Germany' and (3) 'after I came to Germany I finished school.'

At a second stage, L2 learners begin expanding their repertoire and are able to recruit lexical devices in order to mark temporal relations more explicitly, as shown in example (4) from Schumann (1987, p. 25):

(4)   and me come in '47
      'and I came in 1947'

Lexical resources at this stage can help express a variety of temporal and aspectual meanings, such as calendric reference (*in '47*), anaphoric time (*after, before*), duration (*two hours*), frequency (*always*), and even two-point temporality (*again*) (Klein & Perdue, 1997).

It is only after this lexical stage that morphological forms may emerge in interlanguage to express grammatical notions related to time and temporality, such as grammatical tense and aspect. Not all forms emerge at once, and only one function or meaning is expressed by a given form initially (something to which we will return when we examine processes). Some grammatical meanings appear to be more basic or earlier acquired than others, for example, aspect before tense (Andersen, 1991), progressive before past (cf. Table 6.1), and perfective before imperfective (Andersen, 1991; cf. Table 6.2).

The patterned development of tense and aspect during this third phase, moreover, is guided by the inherent aspect or lexical semantics of each verb to which morphology is attached, reflecting an initial trajectory that relies on prototypical pairings of verb morphology with verb semantics. This is the prediction, in a nutshell, of the Aspect Hypothesis (see Andersen & Shirai, 1994). For example, the English imperfective marking *-ing*, which carries a prototypical durative meaning, emerges in interlanguage in combination with verbs depicting situations that imply duration, such as *run, walk*, or *sing* (such situations are called "activities" in linguistic theories of tense and aspect) and then spreads to other verbs with less prototypically durative meaning. Conversely, the English simple past marker *-ed* emerges first in combination with verbs that imply an action with duration and also a beginning and end, such as *meet someone, catch something, see someone/ something* (called "achievements"), and only later appears in combination with other verb semantics.

Table 6.2 summarizes the stages of development of perfective and imperfective aspect in L2 Spanish (expressed by the morphology of *pretérito* and *imperfecto*). As can be seen, development unfolds in a gradual form–function mapping process guided by prototypical pairings of verbal morphology with verb semantics. Similar stages of development have been found for other L2s that have the perfective/imperfective distinction, as well (e.g., French *passé composé* and *imparfait*; Italian *passato prossimo* and *imperfetto*; see review in Bardovi-Harlig, 2000). Although the tense/aspect systems of other languages may be rather different, similar prototype influences have been shown to shape the development of grammatical expression of temporality in those different cases too, such as L2 Japanese (Sugaya & Shirai, 2007) and L2 Korean (Lee & Kim, 2007).

More systematicity: Developmental sequences of negation

Not only morphology, but also syntax unfolds in predictable sequences in the production of L2 learners. One case is negation, which has been studied in L2

Table 6.2 Stages in the development of perfective (*pretérito*) and imperfective (*imperfecto*) aspect in L2 Spanish

Form–function development	Stages	Verb semantics (inherent lexical aspect)			
		Achievements +Punctuality +Telicity +Dynamicity	*Accomplishments* −Punctuality +Telicity +Dynamicity	*Activities* −Punctuality −Telicity +Dynamicity	*States* −Punctuality −Telicity −Dynamicity
Emergence of one form in one context	1	PRETERIT			
	Preterit in achievements: *por fin los dos líderes de la parroquia cambiaron su actitud hacia mí* ('finally, the two leaders of the parish changed their attitudes towards me')				
	2	Preterit			IMPERFECT
	Imperfect in states: *cuando era pequeña* ('when I was young')				
Spread to additional contexts	3	Preterit	PRETERIT	IMPERFECT	Imperfect
	Imperfect in activities: *me dolía la cabeza mucho por la altitud* ('my head hurt a lot because of the altitude') Preterit in accomplishments: *en las navidades pasadas vení a casa de mis padres* ('last Christmas I comed to my parents' house')				
	4	Preterit	Preterit IMPERFECT	Imperfect	Imperfect
	Imperfect in accomplishments: *cada navidad venía a casa de mis padres* ('every Christmas I would come to my parents' house')				
	5	Preterit	Preterit Imperfect	Imperfect PRETERIT	Imperfect
	Preterit in activities: *no sé por qué, pero ayer me dolió la cabeza toda la tarde* ('I don't know why, but my head hurt all afternoon yesterday')				
Full form–function mapping	6	Preterit IMPERFECT	Preterit Imperfect	Imperfect Preterit	Imperfect PRETERIT
	Preterit in states: *aquel día . . . fue fatal* ('that day . . . was terrible') Imperfect in achievements: *se fue . . . porque no encontraba trabajo aquí en Dinamarca* ('he left . . . because he couldn't find a job here in Denmark')				

Note. Capitalized labels indicate first emergence of a form with a given semantic verb type. Illustrations show cutting edge of interlanguage (i.e., new attested form–function pairings) at each successive stage. All illustrations are from Cadierno (2000) and were produced in essays by ten advanced college-level learners of Spanish in Denmark, except for illustrations for stages 4 and 5, which are invented examples that have been added here.

English (Cancino, Rosansky, & Schumann, 1978; Stauble, 1978), as well as several other target languages. The four stages found for L2 English negation are summarized in Table 6.3.

These negation stages reflect internal grammar representations that learners build and gradually revise as they are better able to approximate the target system. Learners "outgrow" each stage as they develop. However, it is important to emphasize that each new stage represents a more advanced solution to the problem of how to negate in English, even though only the last stage results in a solution that converges with the target system. It is also important to appreciate that pre-verbal negation is the first stage not only for L1 Spanish learners whose L1 is consistent with that solution (*no* + verb) but also for other L2 learners whose L1, just like English, only allows post-verbal negation. Hyltenstam (1987) suggests that this first stage may be related to the fact that, across languages of the world, pre-verbal negation is a more common grammar configuration than post-verbal negation. This is not to say, however, that the L1 does not play any role in sequenced development. Speakers of languages (e.g., Italian, Greek, Russian, and Spanish) where pre-verbal negation is the grammatical norm will remain in the first pre-verbal negation stage in English longer than, for example, L1 Norwegian or L1 Japanese speakers, whose L1s, just like the L2 in this case, require post-verbal negation (Schumann, 1979; Zobl, 1982). In other words, L2 development may be slowed down by the influence of the L1, but not altered.

Table 6.3   Developmental stages for negation in L2 English

Stage	Pattern	Illustration
1	Pre-verbal negation with *no/not* *No/Not* + verb	*No saw him.* 'I didn't see him.'
2	Pre-verbal negation with *don't* *Don't* + verb	*I don't saw him.* 'I didn't see him.'
3	Postverbal negation in restricted contexts *AUX* + *not/don't*	*I will don't see you tomorrow.* 'I will not see you tomorrow.'
4	Postverbal negation in all contexts	*They didn't see nobody.* 'They didn't see anybody.'

Note. Illustrations are all reported in Stauble (1978), collected over a 10-month period in interviews with the same L2 speaker, 12-year-old Jorge from Colombia (who was one of the informants in Cancino et al., 1978). The verb which the negating functor modifies is underlined in each example.

Development of word order and questions

In the late 1970s, Meisel, Clahsen, and Pienemann (1981) uncovered another pattern in L2 development, this time for word order in L2 German, based on data from 45 migrant workers from Romance language backgrounds who were living in Germany. The stages are summarized in Table 6.4. Unlike the negation sequence in Table 6.3, which represents successive stages that learners gradually outgrow, the word order stages are cumulative. This means that each stage adds an important piece to the increasingly more complete repertoire of syntactic options, until the interlanguage system matches the full complexity of the repertoire available in the target grammar. Only stage 2 happens to lead to a solution that is inconsistent with the target input, i.e., that results in an ungrammatical word order, due to lack of inversion. This is because, while the context that calls for inversion emerges in stage 2, the actual syntactic operation of inversion will not be acquired (at stage 4) until learners also acquire the ability to handle verb separation in production, at stage 3. Learners who develop high levels of accuracy may eventually be able to shed the ungrammatical solution represented by stage 2, but not all learners will.

Table 6.4 The emergence of word order in L2 German according to Meisel, Clahsen, & Pienemann (1981)

Stage	Description	Illustration
1	Canonical word order *Subject-Verb-X*	*die Kinder spielen mim Ball* 'the children play with the ball'
2	Adverb preposing *X-Subject-Verb*	*<u>da</u> Kinder spielen* 'there children play'
3	Particle separation *Verb . . . AUX/COMP or Particle*	*alle Kinder <u>muß</u> die Pause <u>machen</u>* 'all children must the break have'
4	Inversion *X-Verb-Subject*	*dann <u>hat sie</u> wieder die Knoch gebringt* 'then has she again the bone bringed'
5	Verb-end *Final position for verbs in subordinate clauses*	*er sagte, <u>daß</u> er nach House <u>kommt</u>* 'he said that he home comes'

Note. All illustrations are from Pienemann (1985) and were produced by elementary school children in Germany from L1 Italian background (except for the example in stage 5, which is invented by Pienemann). Close English translations, also taken from Pienemann, reflect German word order.

It should be remembered, moreover, that developmental sequences are about emergence and not accuracy. Thus, for example, a learner could apply the inversion rule to only one relevant case and miss its application to another 10 cases, and we would still consider him or her to be at stage 4, not 2. Indeed, learners may make use of the full repertoire of German word order once they reach stage 5, but they will do so with varying levels of accuracy in their production.

Initially, the developmental sequence for German word order was explained by Meisel et al. via two processing strategies hypothesized to be relevant: A canonical word order strategy (COS) and an initialization/finalization strategy (IFS). The COS strategy posited that producing canonical subject-verb-object word order (stage 1) is easier than producing more varied word orders. The IFS strategy was predicated on the assumption that initial and final components of strings are perceptually more salient to learners. Therefore, moving material to the initial (stage 2) or final (stage 3) position of a syntactic string is easier than moving material to (stage 4) or from (stage 5) positions inside the same string. The same COS and IFS rationale was later applied by Pienemann and colleagues in Australia to explain the developmental order of emergence of English question formation (Pienemann, Johntson, & Brindley, 1988). The stages are summarized in Table 6.5.

In the mid-1990s, Pienemann reconceptualized the explanations for the COS and IFS as part of a more precise and complex Processability Theory (Pienemann, 1998), which combined the linguistic framework of Lexical-Functional Grammar with an assumed corresponding psycholinguistic processing architecture in the mind of the learner. In a nutshell, the newly theorized explanation was that at beginning proficiencies, L2 learners are limited in their capacity for what syntactic information they can hold in memory during processing (hence the term "processability" in the name of the theory). They need gradually to develop the psycholinguistic capacity to match grammatical information contained within and across units in the linguistic material they encounter, and they are capable of doing so gradually with more distant elements in linguistic units. The Processability rationale has been successfully applied to a range of sequences across many target languages besides German and English (Pienemann, 2005).

Implicational, hierarchical acquisition of relative clauses

The final area of interlanguage systematicity we will examine is relativization. The L2 patterns uncovered to date in this aspect of grammar are related to wider patterns found across human languages affecting not only how different types of relative clauses emerge in L1 acquisition (Diessel & Tomasello, 2005), but also how frequent the various types are in L1 natural use, and the ease with which they are processed and comprehended by adult L1 users in experimental studies (e.g., Fox and Thompson, 2007; Reali & Christiansen, 2007). The explanations for these universal patterns are likely to include a number of syntactic, semantic-discoursal, cognitive, and statistical influences.

Table 6.5 The emergence of questions in L2 English according to Pienemann, Johnston, & Brindley (1988)

Stage	Description	Illustration
1	Words and fragments with rising intonation	*One astronaut outside the space ship?* *A ball or a shoe?*
2	Canonical word order with rising intonation	*He have two house in the front?* *Two children ride a bicycle?* *The boy threw a shoes?* *The dog don't have a spot?*
3	Fronting of a questioning element (*wh*-word, *do*, something else)	*Where the little children are?* *What the boy is throwing?* *What the boy with the black short throw?* *Do the boy is beside the bus?* *Do you have a shoes on your picture?* *Is the boy is beside the bus?*
4	Inversion in two restricted contexts: (1) in *wh*-questions with copula, (2) in *yes/no* questions with auxiliaries other than *do*	*Where is the sun?* *Where is the space ship?* *The ball is it in the grass or in the sky?* *Is there a dog on the house?* *Garbage, is it full?*
5	Inversion expands to the full range of targetlike contexts	*How many astronauts do you have?* *What is the boy throwing?*
6	Negative questions Question tags Questions in embedded clauses	*Doesn't your wife speak English?* *You live here, don't you?* *Can you tell me where the station is?*

Note. All illustrations are from Spada and Lightbown (1993 and 1999); questions for stages 1 through 5 were produced by francophone 10- to 12-year-olds in intensive English programs in Canadian schools during task-based oral interactions with a researcher. Questions for stage 6 are examples invented by the researchers.

In the L2, the most widely investigated influence stems from the typological concept of markedness (see Batistella, 1996, for a broad discussion), which was applied to relative clauses by Keenan and Comrie (1977) and resulted in their proposal of a Noun Phrase Accessibility Hierarchy that describes relativization options across all human languages. The hierarchy is illustrated with L2 data in Table 6.6. At the highest position of the hierarchy (that is to say, the most frequent and least marked) are subject relative clauses; at the lowest (i.e., the least frequent and most marked) are object of comparison relative clauses.

Table 6.6   Relative clauses in L2 German following Keenan & Comrie's (1977) Noun Phrase Accessibility Hierarchy

Clause type	L2 illustration	English equivalent
Subject	*Ich bin auf einen Baum geklettert, <u>der neben das Ufer stand.</u>*	I climbed up a tree <u>that stood next to the bank.</u>
Direct object	*Du bist der Jungen, <u>der ich in dem Sturm sah.</u>* [targetlike relativizer: *den*]	You are the boy <u>that I saw in the storm.</u>
Indirect object	*Ein funktionierender Rechtsstaat, offene Gesellschaft und die Achtung der menschenrechte sind die Anforderungen, <u>den die Beitrittskandidaten entsprechen müssen.</u>* [targetlike relativizer: *denen*]	A functioning constitutional state, an open society, and attention to human rights are the requirements <u>that the candidate countries for accession to the European Union must meet.</u> [German *meet = entsprechen +* dative]
Object of preposition	*Es war ein fremdes Land, <u>in dem die Leute eine fremde Sprache sprachen.</u>*	It was a foreign land, <u>in which people spoke a foreign language.</u>
Genitive	*Und die Bäume hatten nur ein bisschen Blätte, <u>deren Schatten am Boden spielten.</u>*	And the trees had only a few leaves, <u>whose shadows played on the ground.</u>
Object of comparison	na	The job went to the driver <u>who Peter is more qualified than.</u>

Note. All L2 illustrations are from the longitudinal corpus of L2 writing produced by college-level German learners in the United States investigated by Byrnes & Sinicrope (2008); they appear here by courtesy of the authors. The English example for object of comparison is invented. na = not attested in the L2 data and not allowed in German L1.

   Cross-linguistically, these six possible types of relative clauses are in a markedness relationship which is hierarchical and implicational. That is, each lower (more marked) type is possible in a given language only if all other preceding (less marked) types are also possible. Some languages have only the simplest type of subject relativization at the top of the hierarchy (e.g., Maori and Tagalog) and, at the other extreme, some languages allow the full range of six types (e.g., Classical Arabic and English). Many languages have five of the six types (e.g., Indo-European languages, such as French, German, Italian, and Spanish, but also genetically unrelated languages, such as Korean), missing the extremely rare object of a comparison type. However few or many possibilities for relativization a given language allows, it will do so following the pattern from highest to lowest in the hierarchy, without gaps.

The same implicationally related markedness hierarchy has been observed within learner grammars in studies that have examined not only L2 English (e.g., Pavesi, 1986), but target languages as varied as Chinese (Hu & Liu, 2007), German (Byrnes & Sinicrope, 2008), Italian (Croteau, 1995), Swedish (Hyltenstam, 1984), and several other L2s (Shirai & Ozeki, 2007; Tarallo & Myhill, 1983). The evidence is particularly robust for subject, object, and object of preposition types (evidence on the other three types is scarcer and more difficult to interpret, as noted by Tarallo & Myhill, 1983). Specifically, the ability to relativize in an L2 appears to unfold in the same order proposed in Keenan and Comrie's hierarchy and depicted in Table 6.6, based on the fact that when a given learner is able to produce more marked types (particularly the, in English, conspicuous object of a preposition), he or she will also likely be able to produce the highest (least marked) positions of subject and direct object, and not the other way around. As in all empirical research, of course, observations are never perfect, and most studies report a few learners whose production showed some gaps, particularly around the overall infrequent types of indirect object, genitive, and object of comparison. These gaps typically affect as low as 9–13 percent of the samples obtained with experimental elicitation procedures (e.g., Hyltenstam, 1984; Pavesi, 1986) or as high as 20 or 30 percent of learners in corpus data made up of extended discourse (Byrnes & Sinicrope, 2008). Not only the ability to produce a given type, but also the frequency and accuracy with which a given type is used, conform to observations in the L1 studies. Thus, types in the higher positions of the hierarchy are more frequent in L2 production, and also tend to contain fewer errors, whereas lower, more marked, types tend to induce more solutions that may be non-targetlike in the L2, such as resumptive pronouns (*The teacher who you introduced me to her works for me now*) (see Hu & Liu, 2007; and Hyltenstam, 1984, for further discussion).

Processes

Processes are the manifestation of putative mechanisms by which learners develop (or fail to develop) their internal grammars. They help characterize changes in accuracy levels and refinements in scope and degree of systematicity, as representations of the L2 grammar are assembled, expanded, revised, and elaborated. These processes attest to the importance of variability (both systematic and random) as a property of all natural languages that helps explain cycles of stability and instability in the dynamic self-organization of the language system as development proceeds (de Bot, Lowie, & Verspoor, 2007). For reasons of space, only a few central processes will be covered here: simplification, overgeneralization, restructuring, U-shaped behavior, and fossilization.

Simplification reflects a strategy that is called upon when messages, however simple or complex, must be conveyed with little language. But as Corder (1981) noted, "you cannot simplify what you do not possess" (p. 110). Thus, simplification may be a misnomer, as it results from incipient or incomplete learning of items (language forms or low-scope rules), or isolated instances that have not yet been fully represented and integrated into a broader system by the internal grammar.

Massive simplification (sometimes compared to pidginization, see Seigel, 2006) is seen during very early stages of L2 development, particularly among naturalistic learners who begin using vocabulary and discourse with little syntax and no morphology, drawing on only the most basic meaning-making principles, or what Klein and Perdue (1997) have called the Basic Variety. Later on, when (and if) complex syntax and some morphology emerge, simplification is also seen across all subsystems. Thus, even though a full range of formal choices is available in the morphology of the target language, a base (invariant) form tends to be chosen by learners at first; and even though multiple form–meaning mappings exist in the target language, a one-meaning-one-form mapping is initially represented in the learner grammar (Andersen, 1984a). For example, Anthony, a 12-year old L1 English learner of Spanish investigated by Andersen (1984b), used two invariant forms of the Spanish article, one devoted to mark definiteness (*la*, 'the' in feminine singular form) and one to mark indefiniteness (*un*, 'a' in masculine singular form), despite the full choice of eight forms that are available in the Spanish input. Which one meaning or form will be chosen out of those available may depend on the same input properties that explain other L2 phenomena: frequency and (perceptual and functional) salience. As an illustration, Sugaya and Shirai (2007) showed that even though the Japanese marker *te i-ru* can have a progressive (*Ken-ga utat-te i-ru*, "Ken is singing") and a resultative meaning (e.g., *Booru-ga oti-te i-ru*, "The ball has fallen"), L2 Japanese learners at first use it for the progressive meaning only. They argued that the progressive meaning is preferred because *te i-ru* is the only form that can convey action in progress in Japanese, whereas the resultative meaning (which in fact is more frequent in the input) can be also conveyed by several additional forms, such as *ta* and *te-a-(ru)*. In this area of L2 Japanese, functional salience rather than frequency initially affects learners' developing grammars.

Overgeneralization involves the application of a form or rule not only to contexts where it applies in the target language, but also to others where it does not apply. Random or unsystematic overgeneralization, also called oversuppliance, does not appear to correspond to the systematic application of any pattern or logic. For example, naturalistic as well as instructed learners begin using *-ing* from very early on, but they also overgeneralize it to many nontargetlike contexts, sometimes for substantial periods, and even when simultaneously they may fail to supply it in other contexts. This is shown in the following two contrasting cases attested by Pica (1985, p. 143) with L1 Spanish learners of English as a foreign language:

(5)　I like to studying English.

(6)　I was study languages last year.

However, even in cases of apparently random oversuppliance, an underlying systematicity may eventually be discovered if the analyst has rich enough data and searches deep enough. Certainly, it is the case that oversuppliance tends to be congruent with developmental constraints. For example, Camps (2002) found that second-semester college-level learners of L2 Spanish overgeneralized both the preterit and the imperfect. However, 39 percent of the time they overused the more stable preterit in contexts where the less consolidated, later emerging imperfect was required, whereas cases involving overgeneralization of the more recently acquired imperfect to preterit contexts were rare (only 4.5 percent).

Overgeneralization can also be systematic. An important case of systematic overgeneralization in morphology involves overregularization, or the attempt to make irregular forms fit regular patterns. It typically emerges after a certain level of development has been reached, in that it presupposes that learners have at least partially figured out some form or rule. The overuse of *-ed* with irregular verbs (as in *falled, comed, goed*, or even *wented*) is a well-known case of over-regularization (cf. example (1) at the beginning of this chapter, and Table 1.1; and see discussion in Clahsen, 2006, and Marslen-Wilson & Tyler, 1998, for L1; and in Leung, 2006, for L2). After systematically overgeneralizing, the learning task is to retreat from the overgeneralization and to adjust the application of the form or rule to increasingly more relevant contexts. This task calls upon the related processes of restructuring and U-shaped behavior, to which we turn.

Restructuring is the process of self-reorganization of grammar knowledge representations. During periods when restructuring of internal representations is happening, learners may seem to "backslide" and produce "errors" they did not seem to produce earlier, producing a pattern known as *U-shaped behavior*. Sharwood Smith and Kellerman (1989) define it as "the appearance of correct, or nativelike, forms at an early stage of development which then undergo a process of attrition, only to be reestablished at a later stage" (p. 220).

An oft-cited L2 illustration of successive restructuring accompanied by U-shaped behavior can be found in Huebner's (1983) study of Ge, a naturalistic learner of English as an L3 (he spoke Hmong as L1 and Lao as L2). Ge's development of the definite English article underwent several restructuring phases. Initially, he mostly marked nouns either with no articles or with *da* (his rendition of *the*) in what appears to have been a one-form-one meaning purpose for it: to encode the meaning of "assumed known to hearer" (which only partially overlaps with the notion of definiteness). Given that Ge's other languages did not have an article system, the internal grammar representation at this point may have simply been a unique rule that could be expressed as "in English, nouns must be marked as $-/+$ 'assumed known to hearer' with $-/+$ *da*." A month and a half into the study, this representation was destabilized, and Ge began using *da* to mark between

80 and 90 percent of all noun contexts he produced. Huebner called this extremely pervasive overgeneralization "flooding." This interlanguage solution may have been random, or it may have been motivated by a restructured rule like "nouns must always be marked by an article in English." In fact, this new "rule" can be considered a better (albeit overly general) approximation to the target rule, which says "all nouns must be marked by a three-way choice: *zero article/the/a*." Be that as it may, the flooding of *da* to a majority of contexts naturally resulted in much higher levels of non-targetlike use of the definite article, leading to an appearance of regression or backsliding to Ge's English (the U-shaped behavior). A little over five months into the study, oversuppliance of *da* retreated from first-mention contexts (which are – 'assumed known to hearer' but specific; as in *a woman is walking down the street*), and shortly before reaching the seventh month, *da* began to retreat from even more non-targetlike indefinite contexts, giving way to a restructured rule that yielded stable targetlike suppliance for *da* at 80–90 percent levels for the rest of the observation period. Ge's development of the article *da* (*the*) shows that an item sometimes has to get worse before it can get better in language development. Or, as Kellerman (1985) put it, learners must go "beyond success" (an expression he borrowed from Annette Karmiloff-Smith) and restructure in what may appear to be a non-targetlike direction, before they can refine their representations of the L2.

Simplification, overgeneralization, restructuring, and other fundamental processes help learners move along the sequences. But there is no guarantee that the outcomes of these processes will keep propelling all learners toward convergence with the target system. Despite apparently favorable conditions for learning, many L2 users may stop anywhere along a given sequence of development, perhaps permanently. The term *fossilization* was coined by Selinker (1972) to refer to such cases of "premature cessation of development in defiance of optimal learning conditions" (Han, 2004, p. 23).

In a study that spanned seven years and focused on grammaticality judgments, as well as free writing, Han (2000, 2006) investigated whether the ability to use passives in English had fossilized in the grammar of Geng and Fong, two advanced users of English from Chinese L1 backgrounds. Over the seven-year period, both Geng and Fong consistently failed to supply passive in some cases where English requires it, as illustrated in (7), and sometimes oversupplied it in other contexts where the active voice would be pragmatically and discoursally preferred in English but where the passive voice was not ungrammatical, as shown in (8):

(7) I do not know whether these problems have solved in the newest release.
     (written by Fong in 1996; Han, 2000, p. 89)

(8) What I can do for you is to give you a list of professors . . . The list will be sent to you later.
     (written by Fong in 1996; Han, 2000, p. 94)

In addition, both L2 users showed indeterminacy in their knowledge of English unaccusativity, on occasion ungrammatically overgeneralizing the passive voice to unaccusative verbs, as illustrated in (9), and other times using unaccusatives grammatically, as shown in (10):

(9) Thanks to John's blocking the event were stopped after 3/7/03.
(written by Geng in 2003; Han, 2006, p. 69)

(10) The action already stopped on 1/6 probably after receiving our mail.
(written by Geng in 2003; Han, 2006, p. 69)

The persistence of both the nativelike and non-nativelike solutions over the seven years is indeed suggestive of permanent cessation of learning in this one area of the L2. Surprisingly, Geng and Fong were otherwise extremely advanced learners under optimal learning circumstances. They had had formal English instruction for six years in their home country, China, and had scored over 600 on the TOEFL before moving to the United Kingdom to obtain their doctoral degrees. Upon receipt of their degrees each continued living in English-speaking environments, and both actively published in English in international journals in their fields. Han suggested Gong and Feng's apparent case of fossilization was caused by the subtle influence of the L1, which unlike English lacks passive morphology and is a topic-prominent language. On the other hand, reviewing this and other studies, Long (2003) proposed that sensitivity to the input (or lack thereof) may be a better explanation for fossilization in general.

In the end, the notion of fossilization, despite its immense popularity, has proved to be extremely problematic. Long (2003) critically examined the reasons for this, only some of which can be mentioned here. First, complete and permanent cessation of learning is difficult to demonstrate empirically, unless learners are followed longitudinally and over their life time, or at least over a very long period. Yet, most fossilization studies have only documented "lack of" learning for short periods of time, rarely more than two or three years. Notable exceptions are multi-year longitudinal studies of Patty by Lardiere (2007), Ayako by Long (2003), and the one just discussed of Fong and Geng by Han (2006). Second, many so-called fossilized learners investigated in the literature may not have enjoyed optimal learning conditions, missing out in one or more of three areas: sufficient exposure and practice, positive attitudes toward the target language and society, and the aid of (high quality) instruction. Third, there is conceptual lack of clarity with regard to at least two questions: (1) Is fossilization meant to denote a process or mechanism that causes cessation of learning, or is it simply being used to denote lack of success in ultimate attainment, that is, the product or consequence of some other mechanism? (2) Where should the evidence for cessation of learning be sought? In the absence of any change (measuring stability versus systematic change), or in what Long calls volatility, or a stable mixture of systematic plus random variability that never restructures into any systematic new representation?

Another issue that muddies the waters of fossilization can be added here. Namely, some researchers discuss fossilization as a universal process (or product) that allegedly characterizes all L2 learners by definition, be it as part of the discussion of the availability of Universal Grammar (Lardiere, 2007) or as related to the entrenchment of L1 knowledge (Han, 2006). From either research perspective, *all* learners will inevitably fossilize sooner or later, and fossilization may ultimately mean that so-called nativeness is unattainable in an L2 (a tautology of doubtful value for researchers who have begun to examine L2 learning through a bilingual prism; see Ortega, 2007). Other times, however, fossilization is discussed as a process or product that helps explain individual differences in ultimate attainment, as a unique tendency for some particularly unsuccessful learners to "stop" learning much sooner than others, as was the oft-discussed case of Alberto, reported by Schumann (1978). This is perhaps the notion of fossilization that concerns most language teachers, but it seems to be the one gradually being dispreferred by most contemporary research on fossilization. In fact, we may want to avoid speaking of "fossilized learners" or even fossilized grammars. Until our understanding of cessation of learning phenomena is clearer, it may be better to speak of stabilization and to consider this process as affecting only local areas of grammar (Han, 2004; Long, 2003).

Sequences, Processes, and Instruction: Five Generalizations and a Coda

I conclude this chapter with five generalizations about the relationship between interlanguage development and instruction that summarize the implications of the developmental sequences and processes for second and foreign language teaching.

1 Instruction cannot affect the route of L2 development in any fundamental way. Several studies have shown that students in classrooms proceed along the developmental sequences regardless of the order in which they are taught. For example, German textbooks typically introduce the inversion rule before they feature the verb separation rule (cf. Table 6.4), perhaps on the basis of a data-free intuition of most textbook writers that verb separation is logically more "complex" than subject-verb inversion. Yet, R. Ellis (1989) found that the order in which 39 students of German in the United Kingdom learned the word order fitted the developmental sequence in Table 6.4 and was unaffected by the textbook order followed by their teachers. Likewise, Bardovi-Harlig (1995) reported no relationship between when the past perfect (*John entered college in 1980. He had graduated from high school five years earlier*) was taught to 16 college learners of English by their teachers and when it emerged in these students' L2 writing. Rather than instruction, two developmental prerequisites were the predictors of emergence of past perfect: (1) learners first had to reach stable accuracy of about 80 percent in the suppliance of *-ed*; and (2) they then had to begin creating contexts involving reverse-order reports (cf. the example above) that semantically call for the use of the past perfect. Over a period of 15 months, 10 of the 16 learners met these two prerequisites and, regardless of instruction, began using the new form.

2 *Instruction can have some effect on processes, fostering some and inhibiting others.* It has been shown that overgeneralization is fostered and, conversely, simplification inhibited, by instruction. Among the earliest studies to document this are Lightbown (1983) and Pica (1985). Particularly in classrooms where teachers teach grammar explicitly and have students practice the language in mechanical drills, oversuppliance of morphology is to be expected. For example, Camps (2002) reported that the 15 second-semester Spanish students he investigated suddenly oversupplied subjunctive in about 20–30 percent of contexts that required preterit and imperfect, coinciding with the point toward the end of the semester at which teachers taught this form to their students. Temporary overgeneralization, however, does not need to be interpreted negatively. As Long (1988) suggested, high levels of overgeneralization coupled with low levels of simplification may be indicative of "healthier error profiles" (p. 120), in that overgeneralization (particularly if aided by development-sensitive instruction) may give way to restructuring and, ultimately, to more development.

3 *Instruction can be ineffective and even counterproductive when it ignores developmental readiness.* In two different studies involving ten 7- to 9-year-old children and three adult classroom learners, respectively, Pienemann (1984, 1989) discovered that the teaching of stage 4 (inversion) benefited only those learners who were developmentally ready, that is, at stage 3 of verb separation. For some of the learners who were not ready, nothing was gained and, moreover, an undesirable effect of instruction was that they began avoiding the use of adverb preposing (stage 2), presumably to avoid making errors. Other findings by Mackey (1999) and Spada and Lightbown (1999) have suggested that some developmentally unready learners may accrue benefits from instruction and advance to the next stage prior to the one taught, but that they will not skip stages. Thus, teachers cannot teach everything they want and instead should carefully consider what their students are developmentally ready to learn. Premature instruction may be counterproductive if it discourages learners from taking risks, which may delay development.

4 *Not all sequences present equal challenges for instruction.* On the other hand, it is important to recognize that the systematicity of interlanguage development is of different kinds for different areas of language. More specifically, not all developmental sequences are equally open or impervious to instruction in similar ways. For areas of language where accuracy improvements have been shown to pose differential difficulty for learners (such as the morpheme order in Table 6.1), instruction may be possible at any level. For areas where development through stages means that an increasingly more complex option in a repertoire is cumulatively added (such as the sequences in Tables 6.2, 6.4, and 6.5), learners may not skip stages and teachers will do well to consider developmental readiness. Finally, for areas of the grammar that exhibit cross-linguistic markedness relations (such as the hierarchy in Table 6.6), instruction of a more marked case

can help learners get the less marked cases for free, as it were. This has been shown in a good number of studies that successfully targeted the teaching of object-of-preposition relative clauses to students who were already able to handle relativization, but only of the subject type, and who after instruction showed gains not only in the taught type, but also all the intervening types in the hierarchy (e.g., Doughty, 1991).

5 *Instruction has large positive effects on rate of development and level of ultimate attainment.* It would be mistaken to conclude that instruction does not matter, just because it cannot override development. Instructed learners progress at a faster rate, they are likely to progress further along the sequences, and they typically become more accurate overall than uninstructed learners. For example, after daily use of English, but without specific instruction, many naturalistic learners do not produce *-ed*, or produce it with extremely low levels of accuracy (cf. Table 6.1). This has been shown even with learners who had the advantage of a relatively early start when they were first surrounded by the L2, as was the case for the two 10- and 12-year-old boys studied by Sato (1990) for ten months or the ten young children and adolescents studied by Jia and Fuse (2007) for five years. By comparison, Bardovi-Harlig (1995) found that 135 instructed English learners in a college-level intensive English program exhibited levels of accuracy in the use of *-ed* that averaged about 70 percent for the lowest curricular level and 90 percent for the highest. Likewise, many naturalistic L2 German learners may not reach the particle-separation stage (cf. stage 3 in Table 6.4) even after several years of living in the L2 environment (Meisel et al., 1981). By contrast, in the foreign language classroom, findings by R. Ellis (1989) and Jansen (2008) suggest that most students will have reached that stage (and some may even have traversed the entire developmental sequence!) by the end of the second semester. For relativization, too, Pavesi (1986) found that only about a fourth of 38 naturalistic learners with six years on average of living in the L2 environment had reached object of preposition (cf. Table 6.6), whereas the same stage had been reached by about 40 percent of 48 high school students in Italy with an average of four years of instruction in English as a foreign language. Byrnes and Sinicrope (2008) found evidence of the object of preposition stage at just the end of the second year of study for about a fourth of 23 college students of German in the United States.

In light of these five generalizations, language teachers may ask themselves whether they should teach to the sequences and processes. It would be unadvisable to develop instructional curricula around the known sequences and processes of L2 development, for several reasons. First, we do not have sufficient descriptions of all aspects of the grammar of any target language to do so. Furthermore, the holistic question of how different sequences relate to each other in the grammar of individual learners has rarely been examined, giving textbook writers and curriculum developers little guidance as to how to sequence grammatical targets according to developmental learner readiness principles. More importantly, language learning amounts to much more than the learning of syntax and morphology. It also involves the learning of vocabulary, pragmatics, phonology, and so on. Although much is also known about how these areas are learned by L2 users, it would be difficult to exploit all this knowledge in a syllabus or curricular plan. The most fundamental objection, however, is that learning an L2 calls for a much more encompassing approach than a focus on bits and pieces of language could possibly afford us. Rather than trying to organize instruction around grammar in what Wilkins (1976) called a synthetic syllabus, we have a wide range of options more attuned to what we know about psycholinguistic, cognitive, and socioeducational principles for good language teaching. Many of these options are discussed in sections IV through VI in this handbook.

Nevertheless, knowledge about the sequences and processes of interlanguage development can inform good teaching by helping teachers (and their students) cultivate a different attitude toward "errors," and more enlightened expectations for "progress." It can help them recognize that many so-called errors are a healthy sign of learning, that timing is hugely important in language teaching, and that not all that can be logically taught can be learned if learners are not developmentally ready. Knowledge about sequences and processes can also help counter the deficit view that interlanguages are defective surrogates of the target language by making it clear that interlanguages are shaped by the same systematicity and variability that shape all other forms of human language.

NOTE

This chapter draws on material from Ortega (2009).

REFERENCES

Andersen, R. W. (1984a). The one-to-one principle of interlanguage construction. *Language Learning* 34, 77–95.

Andersen, R. W. (1984b). Whats gender good for, anyway? In R. W. Andersen (ed.), *Second languages: A cross-linguistic perspective* (pp. 77–100). Rowley, MA: Newbury House.

Andersen, R. W. (1991). Developmental sequences: The emergence of aspect marking in second language acquisition. In T. Huebner & C. A. Ferguson (eds.), *Crosscurrents in language acquisition research and linguistic theories* (pp. 305–23). Amsterdam: John Bejamins.

Andersen, R. W. & Shirai, Y. (1994). Discourse motivations for some cognitive acquisition principles. *Studies in Second Language Acquisition* 16, 133–56.

Bardovi-Harlig, K. (1995). The interaction of pedagogy and natural sequences in the acquisition of tense and aspect. In F. Eckman, D. Highland, P. Lee, J. Mileham, & R. Weber (eds.), *Second language acquisition theory and pedagogy* (pp. 151–68). Mahwah, NJ: Lawrence Erlbaum.

Bardovi-Harlig, K. (2000). *Tense and aspect in second language acquisition: Form, meaning, and use.* Malden, MA: Blackwell.

Batistella, E. L. (1996). *The logic of markedness*. New York: Oxford University Press.

Byrnes, H. & Sinicrope, C. (2008). Advancedness and the development of relativization in L2 German: A curriculum-based longitudinal study. In L. Ortega & H. Byrnes (eds.), *The longitudinal study of advanced L2 capacities* (pp. 109–38). New York: Lawrence Erlbaum Taylor & Francis.

Cadierno, T. (2000). The acquisition of Spanish grammatical aspect by Danish advanced language learners. *Spanish Applied Linguistics* 4, 1–53.

Camps, J. (2002). Aspectual distinctions in Spanish as a foreign language: The early stages of oral production. *International Review of Applied Linguistics* 40, 179–210.

Cancino, H., Rosansky, E., & Schumann, J. (1978). The acquisition of English negatives and interrogatives by native Spanish speakers. In E. Hatch (ed.), *Second language acquisition: A book of readings* (pp. 207–30). Rowley, MA: Newbury House.

Clahsen, H. (2006). Dual-mechanism morphology. In Keith Brown (ed.), *Encyclopedia of language and linguistics*, vol. 4. Oxford: Elsevier.

Corder, P. (1981). *Error analysis and interlanguage*. Oxford: Oxford University Press.

Croteau, K. C. (1995). Second language acquisition of relative clause structures by learners of Italian. In F. R. Eckman, D. Highland, P. W. Lee, J. Mileham, & R. R. Weber (eds.), *Second language acquisition theory and pedagogy* (pp. 115–28). Mahwah, NJ: Erlbaum.

de Bot, K., Lowie, W., & Verspoor, M. (2007). A Dynamic Systems Theory approach to second language acquisition. *Bilingualism: Language and Cognition* 10, 7–21.

Diessel, H. & Tomasello, M. (2005). A new look at the acquisition of relative clauses. *Language* 81, 882–906.

Doughty, C. (1991). Second language instruction does make a difference: Evidence from an empirical study of ESL relativization. *Studies in Second Language Acquisition* 13, 431–69.

Ellis, N. C. (2006). Language acquisition as rational contingency learning. *Applied Linguistics* 27, 1–24.

Ellis, R. (1989). Are classroom and naturalistic acquisition the same? A study of the classroom acquisition of German word order rules. *Studies in Second Language Acquisition* 11, 305–28.

Fox, B. A. & Thompson, S. A. (2007). Relative clauses in English conversation: Relativizers, frequency, and the notion of construction. *Studies in Language* 31, 293–326.

Goldschneider, J. & DeKeyser, R. M. (2001). Explaining the "natural order of L2 morpheme acquisition" in English: A meta-analysis of multiple determinants. *Language Learning* 51, 1–50.

Han, Z. (2000). Persistence of the implicit influence of NL: The case of the pseudo-passive. *Applied Linguistics* 21, 78–105.

Han, Z. (2004). *Fossilization in adult second language acquisition*. Clevedon, UK: Multilingual Matters.

Han, Z. (2006). Fossilization: Can grammaticality judgment be a reliable source of evidence? In Z. Han & T. Odlin (eds.), *Studies of fossilization in second language acquisition* (pp. 56–82). Clevedon, UK: Multilingual Matters.

Hu, X. & Liu, C. (2007). Restrictive relative clauses in English and Korean learners' second language Chinese. *Second Language Research* 23, 263–87.

Huebner, T. (1983). *A longitudinal analysis of the acquisition of English*. Ann Arbor, MI: Karoma.

Hyltenstam, K. (1984). The use of typological markedness conditions as predictors in second language acquisition: The case of pronominal copies in relative clauses. In R. W. Andersen (ed.), *Second languages: A cross-linguistic perspective* (pp. 39–58). Rowley, MA: Newbury House.

Hyltenstam, K. (1987). Markedness, language universals, language typology, and second language acquisition. In C. Pfaff (ed.), *First and second language acquisition processes* (pp. 55–78). Cambridge, MA: Newbury House.

Jansen, L. (2008). Acquisition of German word order in tutored learners: A cross-sectional study in a wider theoretical context. *Language Learning* 58, 185–231.

Jia, G. & Fuse, A. (2007). Acquisition of English grammatical morphology by native Mandarin-speaking Children and adolescents: Age-related differences. *Journal of Speech, Language & Hearing Research* 50, 1280–99.

Keenan, E. & Comrie, B. (1977). Noun phrase acessibility and universal grammar. *Linguistic Inquiry* 8, 63–99.

Kellerman, E. (1985). If at first you do succeed. In S. M. Gass & C. Madden (eds.), *Input in second language acquisition* (pp. 345–53). Rowley, MA: Newbury House.

Klein, W. & Perdue, C. (1997). The basic variety (or: Couldn't natural languages be much simpler?). *Second Language Research* 14, 301–47.

Krashen, D. (1977). Some issues relating to the Monitor Model. In H. D. Brown, C. A. Yorio, & R. H. Crymes (eds.), *On TESOL '77. Teaching and learning English as a second language: Trends in research and practice* (pp. 144–58). Washington, DC: TESOL.

Lardiere, D. (2007). *Ultimate attainment in second language acquisition: A case study.* Mahwah, NJ: Lawrence Erlbaum.

Larsen-Freeman, D. (1976). An explanation for the morpheme acquisition order of second language learners. *Language Learning* 26, 125–34.

Lee, E. & Kim, H.-Y. (2007). On crosslinguistic variations in imperfective aspect: The case of L2 Korean. *Language Learning* 57, 651–85.

Leung, Y.-K. I. (2006). Verb morphology in L2A vs. L3A: The representation of regular and irregular past participles in English-Spanish and Chinese-English-Spanish interlanguages. In S. Foster-Cohen, M. M. Krajnovic, & J. M. Djigunovic (eds.), *EUROSLA Yearbook 6* (pp. 27–56). Amsterdam: John Benjamins.

Lightbown, P. M. (1983). Exploring the relationships between developmental and instructional sequences in L2 acquisition. In H. W. Seliger & M. H. Long (eds.), *Classroom oriented research in second language acquisition* (pp. 217–45). Rowley, MA: Newbury House.

Long, M. H. (1988). Instructed interlanguage development. In L. Beebe (ed.), *Issues in second language acquisition: Multiple perspectives* (pp. 115–41). Rowley, MA: Newbury House.

Long, M. H. (2003). Stabilization and fossilization in interlanguage development. In C. J. Doughty & M. H. Long (eds.), *Handbook of second language acquisition* (pp. 487–535). Malden, MA: Blackwell.

Long, M. H. & Sato, C. J. (1984). Methodological issues in interlanguage studies: An interactionist perspective. In A. Davies, C. Criper, & A. Howatt (eds.), *Interlanguage* (pp. 253–79). Edinburgh: Edinburgh University Press.

Mackey, A. (1999). Input, interaction, and second language development: An empirical study of question formation in ESL. *Studies in Second Language Acquisition* 21, 557–87.

Marslen-Wilson, W. & Tyler, L. K. (1998). Rules, representations, and the English past tense. *TRENDS in Cognitive Sciences* 2, 428–35.

Mayberry, R. I. (in press). Second language learning of sign languages. In Keith Brown (ed.), *Encyclopedia of language and linguistics*, 2nd edn., vol. 10. Oxford: Elsevier.

Meisel, J., Clahsen, H., & Pienemann, M. (1981). On determining developmental stages in natural second language acquisition. *Studies in Second Language Acquisition* 3, 109–35.

Ortega, L. (2007). Second language learning explained? SLA across nine contemporary theories. In B. VanPatten & J. Williams (eds.), *Theories in second language acquisition: An introduction* (pp. 221–46). Mahwah, NJ: Lawrence Erlbaum.

Ortega, L. (2009). *Understanding second language acquisition*. London: Hodder Arnold.

Oshita, H. (2000). What is happened may not be what appears to be happening: A corpus study of "passive" unaccusatives in L2 English. *Second Language Research* 16, 293–324.

Pavesi, M. (1986). Markedness, discoursal modes, and relative clause formation in a formal and an informal context. *Studies in Second Language Acquisition* 8, 38–55.

Pica, T. (1985). Linguistic simplicity and learnability: Implications for language syllabus design. In K. Hyltenstam & M. Pienemann (eds.), *Modelling and assessing second language acquisition* (pp. 137–51). Philadelphia: Multilingual Matters.

Pienemann, M. (1984). Psychological constraints on the teachability of languages. *Studies in Second Language Acquisition* 6, 186–214.

Pienemann, M. (1985). Learnability and syllabus construction. In K. Hyltenstam & M. Pienemann (eds.), *Modelling and assessing second language acquisition* (pp. 23–76). Philadelphia: Multilingual Matters.

Pienemann, M. (1989). Is language teachable? Psycholinguistic experiments and hypotheses. *Applied Linguistics* 10, 52–79.

Pienemann, M. (1998). *Language processing and second language development: Processability Theory*. Amsterdam/Philadelphia: John Benjamins.

Pienemann, M. (ed.) (2005). *Cross-linguistic aspects of Processability Theory*. Amsterdam: John Benjamins.

Pienemann, M., Johnston, M., & Brindley, G. (1988). Constructing an acquisition-based procedure for second language assessment. *Studies in Second Language Acquisition* 10, 217–43.

Reali, F. & Christiansen, M. H. (2007). Processing of relative clauses is made easier by frequency of occurrence. *Journal of Memory and Language* 57, 1–23.

Sato, C. (1990). *The syntax of conversation in interlanguage development*. Tübingen: Gunter Narr.

Schachter, J. (1974). An error in error analysis. *Language Learning* 24, 205–14.

Schumann, J. (1978). Second language acquisition: The pidginization hypothesis. In E. Hatch (ed.), *Second language acquisition: A book of readings* (pp. 256–71). Rowley, MA: Newbury House.

Schumann, J. (1979). The acquisition of English negation by speakers of Spanish: A review of the literature. In R. W. Andersen (ed.), *The acquisition and use of Spanish and English as first and second languages* (pp. 3–32). Washington, DC: TESOL.

Schumann, J. (1987). The expression of temporality in basilang speech. *Studies in Second Language Acquisition* 9, 21–41.

Selinker, L. (1972). Interlanguage. *International Review of Applied Linguistics* 10, 219–31.

Sharwood Smith, M. & Kellerman, E. (1989). The interpretation of second language output. In H. W. Dechert & M. Raupach (eds.), *Transfer in language production* (pp. 217–36). Norwood, NJ: Ablex.

Shirai, Y. & Ozeki, H. (2007). The L2 acquisition of relative clauses in East Asian languages. Special issue of *Studies in Second Language Acquisition* 29, 155–374.

Siegel, J. (2006). Links between SLA and Creole studies: Past and present. In C. Lefebvre, L. White, & C. Jourdan (eds.), *L2 acquisition and creole genesis* (pp. 15–46). Amsterdam: John Benjamins.

Spada, N. & Lightbown, P. M. (1993). Instruction and the development of questions in the L2 classroom. *Studies in Second Language Acquisition* 15, 205–21.

Spada, N. & Lightbown, P. M. (1999). Instruction, first language influence, and developmental readiness in second language acquisition. *The Modern Language Journal* 83, 1–22.

Stauble, A. E. (1978). The process of decreolization: A model for second language development. *Language Learning* 28, 29–54.

Stockwell, R., Bowen, J., & Martin, J. (1965). *The grammatical structures of English and Spanish*. Chicago: University of Chicago Press.

Sugaya, N. & Shirai, Y. (2007). The acquisition of progressive and resultative meanings of the imperfective aspect marker by L2 learners of Japanese: Trasfer, universals, or multiple factors. *Studies in Second Language Acquisition* 29, 1–38.

Tarallo, F. & Myhill, J. (1983). Interference and natural language processing in second language acquisition. *Language Learning* 33, 55–73.

von Stutterheim, C. & Klein, W. (1987). A concept-oriented approach to second language studies. In C. W. Pfaff (ed.), *First and second language acquisition* (pp. 191–205). Rowley, MA: Newbury House.

White, L. (2003). *Second language acquisition and Universal Grammar*. New York: Cambridge University Press.

Wilkins, D. A. (1976). *Notional syllabuses*. Oxford: Oxford University Press.

Zobl, H. (1982). A direction for contrastive analysis: The comparative study of developmental sequences. *TESOL Quarterly* 16, 169–83.

7 The Importance of Cross-Linguistic Similarity in Foreign Language Learning

HÅKAN RINGBOM AND SCOTT JARVIS

Second language research has tended to concentrate on differences, as they are manifested in linguistic variation of numerous kinds, rather than on similarities. To the learner, however, similarities have a much more direct effect on language learning and performance than differences do. Learners are constantly trying to establish links between the TL (target language) and whatever prior linguistic knowledge they have. Instead of seeking out differences, they tend to look for similarities wherever they can find them. They make use of intra-lingual similarities, which are perceived from what they have already learnt of the target language. However, at early stages of learning, when their TL knowledge is limited, the L1 is generally the main source for perceiving linguistic similarities, though other known languages, especially if they are related to the target language, and if they have been acquired to a high level of proficiency, may also have an important part to play. Perceiving and making use of cross-linguistic similarities to prior knowledge is important in the learner's striving to facilitate the learning task, and these are processes central to transfer. Some of the most influential work in this area includes, in chronological order, Selinker (1969), Kellerman (1977), Gass and Selinker (1983), Kellerman and Sharwood Smith (1986), Ringbom (1987), Dechert and Raupach (1989), Odlin (1989), Kellerman (1995), Jarvis (2000), and recently Odlin (2003). Jarvis and Pavlenko (2008) is a survey of cross-linguistic influence, especially of the work that has been done in the last 20 years.

Actual, Perceived, and Assumed Similarities

Perceiving cross-linguistic similarities is of course a subjective process that often results in an inaccurate or incomplete awareness of the actual similarities that exist across languages. Accordingly, it is important to distinguish between *actual similarities* and *assumed similarities*. These two types of similarity, in fact, relate to different levels. Actual similarities or differences belong to the domain of linguistics and can accordingly be analyzed linguistically, whereas what the learner does with or assumes about the TL relates to the processes taking place in the learner's mind. Actual and assumed similarities can hypothetically be fully congruous if the learner accurately perceives the objective similarities between two languages, but this appears to be relatively rare. Indeed, in the foreign-language learning setting, the disparity between actual and assumed similarities can be great, and this results from (1) learners' failure to notice a number of the actual similarities that exist across languages, (2) learners' misperception of the nature of many of the similarities that they do notice, and (3) learners' assumptions that there exist certain similarities between the languages that actually do not exist and which the learners have correspondingly never previously encountered (see Jarvis & Pavlenko, 2008; Ringbom, 2006; 2007).

Attempts have been made to establish criteria for actual similarities. These attempts include the work of Ellegård (1978) and Ard and Homburg (1992). There is also an ongoing project in the Research Institute at the University of Groningen that involves the use of computational methods for determining cross-linguistic similarity (see www.rug.nl/let/onderzoek/). So far, however, there is still little agreement in the field concerning how to define or measure the actual, objective similarities existing across languages.

Even if there were complete agreement concerning how to measure the degree of actual similarity between languages, the literature on foreign and second language learning, as well as the literature on cross-linguistic influence, make it clear that assumed similarities have a greater and more direct effect on language learning and performance than actual similarities do (Kellerman, 1978; Odlin, 1989, p. 142; 2006, pp. 23–4). Although actual similarities do seem to account quite well for learners' rate of acquisition and the amount of time they need to achieve certain levels of proficiency in the target language (Ard & Homburg, 1992; Odlin, 1989; Ringbom, 1987, p. 66), there are a number of constraints on the effects that actual similarities have on foreign-language learning, and these constraints appear to be related primarily to learners' perceptions and assumptions. For example, Kellerman (1978) has shown that learners rely on only certain types of actual similarities and not on others, depending on how language-specific they consider the language features in question to be. Ringbom (2007) has additionally explained that actual similarities are symmetrical across languages (applying equally from Language A to Language B and vice versa), whereas assumed similarities may have a stronger effect in one direction than in the other. Finally, actual similarities are constant over time, whereas the perception of similarities changes as the learner's TL experience and proficiency increase (Kellerman, 1979).

Although assumed similarities have the strongest and most direct impact on language learning and performance, there are different types of assumed similarities, and they work differently in comprehension and production. In comprehension, especially of a related language, learners directly *perceive* similarities, by which we mean that learners encounter and become aware of features of the

TL that they recognize as bearing resemblances to a language they already know. These similarities are normally *formal* similarities – i.e., similarities pertaining to the spelling, pronunciation, and/or morphological make-up of words or multi-word structures. When producing the new language, on the other hand, learners are not engaged in perceiving similarities but rather in encoding their ideas into language structures they have previously learned or into language structures that they create in the absence of learned knowledge, which tend to be based heavily on the similarities they *assume* to exist between the two languages. These assumed similarities may be formed on the basis of previously perceived similarities in comprehension, but if such similarities have not been perceived, as is usually the case across wholly unrelated languages, where few formal similar-ities can be established, learners only assume that the new language works in the same way as their L1, and this tends to lead to errors. In cases where learners are learning a third or fourth language, their assumption tends to be that the TL is semantically and pragmatically similar to the L1 but formally similar to the language (the L1, L2, L3, etc.) that they perceive as being typologically closest to the TL (Ringbom, 1987; 2007). (Note: Several studies have noted a foreign-language effect in L3 acquisition, whereby under certain circumstances the L2 may exert a greater influence on L3 production than the L1 does. This is espe-cially true if the L2 is typologically similar to the L3, and factors such as profi-ciency and order of acquisition also appear to have an effect. See De Angelis, 2005; Dewaele, 1998; Singleton, 2006, pp. 136–8; Williams & Hammarberg, 1998.)

Learners have a strong tendency to assume semantic and pragmatic similar-ities between the L1 and TL without having ever perceived those similarities, and this is true regardless of how typologically distant the two languages are (e.g., Biskup, 1992; Eisenstein & Bodman, 1993; Jarvis, 1998; Ringbom, 1987). Concerning formal similarities, on the other hand, learners tend not to assume that the formal properties of words and multi-word structures are similar until they have actually perceived those similarities, although, crucially, this depends largely on the typological distance between the two languages and also on the learners' levels of proficiency. In typologically similar languages, there are more similarities to perceive, and when learners have crossed a certain threshold of perceived similarities, they often assume additional formal similarities that they have never perceived.

Learners of English in Finland have been found to cross this threshold in relation to the similarities between Swedish and English, related languages, whereas they do not cross this threshold in relation to the similarities between Finnish and English, which are typologically unrelated languages. The actual formal similarities between Swedish and English are numerous and cut across all word classes (e.g., Sw. *arm* = 'arm'; Sw. *fot* = 'foot'; Sw. *tänka* = 'think'; Sw. *äta* = 'eat', Sw. *röd* = 'red'; Sw. *blå* = 'blue'; Sw. *vad* = 'what'; Sw. *från* = 'from'; Sw. *vi* = 'we') and they also cut across numerous inflectional and syntactic patterns (Sw. *den blå bilen* = 'the blue car'; Sw. *Henriks hus är litet* = 'Henrik's house is little'). Concerning the similarities between Finnish and English, a number of actual formal similarities can be found here, as well, but most of these involve only medium- to low-frequency loanword nouns that represent entities and notions that Finnish has adopted from other languages, primarily from Swedish and English (e.g., Fi. *auto* = 'automobile'; Fi. *radio* = 'radio'; Fi. *televisio* = 'television'; Fi. *filmi* = 'film'; Fi. *presidentti* = 'president'). Aside from words of this type, Finnish shares very few grammaticalization and lexicalization patterns with English. (See, however, Seppänen, 1998, who lists seven grammatical correspondences between Finnish and English, many of which also occur between Finnish and other Germanic languages. Cf. Ringbom, 2007.)

As mentioned, learners' perceptions of the similarities between Swedish and English cross a crucial similarity threshold (cf. Eckman, 2004; Wode, 1976), whereas their perceptions of the similarities between Finnish and English do not. The consequences of this threshold are clearest in the English production of learners who know both Swedish and Finnish. Learners whose L1 is Finnish and L2 is Swedish, and who are at a low level of English proficiency, have been found to be especially prone to over-assuming the similarities between Swedish and English, producing errors such as the following (errors in the Finnish National Matriculation Exam): *A teacher is a forebild for pupils* (Sw. *förebild* = 'model', 'good example'); *He is good at mathematics but he success at other amnys, too* (Sw. *ämne* = 'subject'). They rarely produce corresponding errors based on an over-assumption of formal similarities between Finnish and English. (Note: Anglophone learners of Greek have likewise been found to disregard the similarities between English and Greek due to the perceived distance between the languages. See Singleton, 2006, p. 139.) Like the Finns, Swedes also sometimes over-rely on assumed similarities between Swedish and English, even on chance similarities: *A crucial problem is the drinking of alcohol before sitting behind the rat* (Sw. *ratt* = 'steering wheel'). Mostly, however, Swedish learners at the intermediate and advanced levels of English proficiency tend to over-assume formal similarity in low-frequency words, which may often result in the use of an existing Swedish word instead of a formally similar English one: *I am not an eremit* (Sw. *eremit* = 'hermit'; *A new house made of marmor* (Sw. *marmor* = 'marble'). (For statistics and examples, see Ringbom, 1987.)

Types of Cross-Linguistic Similarity Relationships

In the continuum of cross-linguistic similarity relationships, three distinct types can be discerned: *similarity*, *contrast*, and *zero relations*. The similarity relation means that an item or pattern in the TL is perceived as formally and/or functionally similar to a form in the L1 (or other previously learned language). Full-scale cross-linguistic similarity of both form and function is rare, except in closely related languages that are mutually comprehensible, such as Norwegian and Swedish.

In a contrast relation, the learner perceives a TL pattern as in important ways differing from an L1 form or pattern, though there is also an underlying similarity between them. An English-speaking learner of German, who is used to a specific third-person suffix used with the present tense of verbs, will notice that German has a host of other personal endings for the verb as well. This means that there will be problems for the learner in producing the correct verb forms, but the learner is basically aware of the existence of a system and does not have to expend great effort to learn to understand the types of functions expressed by verbal suffixes. An example of a contrast relation is native speakers of English learning a Germanic or Romance target language: They will encounter similarities and differences in varying proportions, and the foundation of similarities will allow them to contrast what is different. As James (1980) says, "it is only against the background of sameness that differences are significant" (p. 169).

The zero relation does not mean that the learner finds nothing at all that is relevant to his L1 as the learning progresses. There are, after all, some linguistic universals common to all languages. But the level of abstraction in these is so high that an average learner cannot easily notice features that a totally different TL has in common with the L1. A zero relation simply means that items and patterns in the TL at early stages of learning are seen to have little or no perceptible relation to the L1 or any other language the learner knows. A learner who knows only Indo-European languages and starts learning Chinese will find it difficult to relate anything in the TL to his previous linguistic knowledge. The zero, or near-zero relation between Chinese and English poses great difficulties at early stages of learning, since the learner has to spend considerable time figuring out how the new language really works. As the learner's proficiency develops, he or she may become aware of an increasing number of points of contrast between the two languages. Thus, what represents a zero or near-zero relation for a beginning learner may in many respects eventually come to be seen as a contrast relation by that learner.

Item Transfer and System Transfer in Comprehension, Learning, and Production

Learners' reliance on perceived and assumed cross-linguistic similarities – i.e., transfer – can be manifested at three different levels: (1) *item transfer*, (2) *system transfer* or *procedural transfer*, and (3) *overall transfer*. These different levels of transfer can best be understood against the backdrop of the distinction between item learning and system learning, where the term *item* is defined as an individual form (e.g., sound, letter, morpheme, word, phrase, syntactic unit), and *system* is defined as a set of principles for organizing forms paradigmatically (e.g., assigning different functions to different forms of a word, as in *go, goes, going, gone, went*) and syntagmatically (e.g., rules for forming compound words, word order rules), and for mapping meanings onto those forms. Probably the first scholar to refer to the distinction between item learning and system learning as it pertains to language acquisition (L1 in this case) was Cruttenden (1981), who said that item learning "involves a form which is uniquely bonded with some other form or with a unique referent, whereas system-learning involves the possibility of the commutation of forms or referents while some (other) form is held constant" (p. 79).

The distinction between item learning and system learning sheds light on one of the basic questions in transfer research: What is actually transferred? Item transfer means that a one-to-one relationship is established in the learner's mind between an item in the TL and either an item or a concept in the L1. Especially in the early stages of acquiring a new language, the unique bondage characteristic of item learning is predominantly cross-linguistic, since the (adult) language learner already has a full system of linguistic and conceptual representations, even if the structure and substance of those representations are not identical across languages. Initially, learning takes place on an item-by-item basis in all areas of language: phonological, morphological, syntactic, lexical, and phraseological.

The cross-linguistic similarities that underlie item transfer are a concretely perceived similarity of form usually combined with an associated assumed similarity of function or meaning. Being grounded in perceived (not just assumed) formal similarities between languages, item learning has a predominantly positive effect on learning, notably on learning for comprehension. When they are able to perceive similarities between L1 and L2 items, learners make use of an oversimplified L2 = L1 equivalence hypothesis, mapping the functions or meanings of L2 items directly onto existing L1 items during comprehension, and mapping the functions or meanings of L1 items onto L2 items during production. This is the case particularly at early stages of learning, when the learner's linguistic resources in the L2 are insufficient to make much use of intra-lingual similarities. The learner establishes oversimplified cross-linguistic one-to-one relationships to reduce the workload. At these early stages of learning, learners tend to focus on form rather than meaning or function, as meaning and function are more abstract and less accessible to direct observation and analysis. Perceived formal similarities aid learners in establishing cross-linguistic relations (also known as *interlingual identifications*, Odlin, 1989) in long-term memory.

Perceived similarity of form combined with an assumed similarity of meaning/function provide the basis for establishing simplified one-to-one relations between L2 items and L1 items, which come to be represented as "primary counterparts" (a term used by Arabski, 1979) in the learner's mind. In system transfer – which might be better termed *procedural transfer* – abstract principles of organizing information are transferred. Positive procedural transfer lies behind the easy comprehension of a related TL, although it is not easy to point to concrete evidence for it. In this type of transfer, the learner assumes that there is cross-linguistic functional equivalence, but does not necessarily assume any formal item similarity between languages. Procedural transfer in the foreign-language learning context is predominantly transfer from L1, or possibly from another language the learner knows very well; by contrast, a language the learner knows only superficially generally serves as the source of only item transfer but not procedural transfer. Apparently, grammatical rules and semantic properties must be well internalized, or even fully automatized, in order to be transferred. Since functional and semantic systems in two languages are hardly ever fully congruent, procedural transfer tends to lead to error, a negative effect, though the difficulty of recognizing positive effects of transfer must be acknowledged. What has been called interference or negative transfer in L2 production, might, in fact, be better described as the absence of relevant concrete (positive) transfer, leading to subsequent wrong assumptions about cross-linguistic similarities between L1 and L2. Positive transfer could then be described as "the application of at least partially correct perceptions or assumptions of cross-linguistic similarity."

Inevitable oversimplifications that occur during item learning will be modified as learning progresses. The learning of systems is always preceded by the learning of items, and, in fact, system learning involves a gradual modification of the oversimplified one-to-one relations that have been formed during item learning. The procedural transfer that occurs in learners' TL production is of three kinds: *intrusive, inhibitive,* and *facilitative* (see Hammerly, 1991). Intrusive transfer leads to the inappropriate use of L1-based items and structures. Inhibitive transfer prevents or inhibits the learner from learning how to use new words and structures appropriately. For example, TL words and structures that have no parallel in the L1 provide the learner with no concrete basis for positive item transfer and are therefore often avoided (cf. Sjöholm, 1995). Facilitative (positive) procedural transfer boosts learners' ability to access, process, and organize TL information due to similarities between the L1 and TL systems. Facilitative procedural transfer is often difficult to recognize, but it clearly constitutes an important factor affecting the learner's ease of comprehending a language perceived to be close. In language production, facilitative procedural transfer is especially hard to pin down because it coincides with successful acquisition of the TL. Nevertheless, the fact that learners of a related language regularly outperform learners of an unrelated language in their TL production attests to its presence (see, e.g., Ringbom, 1987).

Overall transfer is an umbrella term referring to the learner's reliance on conceptions of both formal similarities across individual items and functional equivalences between the underlying systems. The amount of overall transfer that will be present in a learner's language performance (both comprehension and production) depends on how much cross-linguistic similarity the learner can generally perceive between items and systems in the two languages, beginning from a common alphabet, phonemes in common and similar phonotactics, and extending to similarities in grammatical categories (case, gender, word classes), as well as to the number of cognates and other lexical similarities that exist across both languages. Quick and effective item learning for comprehension is what above all distinguishes the learning of a related TL from the learning of an unrelated language. As for procedural transfer, the matter is more complex. Learners normally assume that L1 procedures work also for L2 comprehension. The extent to which these assumptions actually work determines whether the effect is positive or negative. If inappropriate L1 procedures are applied to L2 comprehension, misinterpretations are likely to arise. Syntactic congruence plays a key role: if the L2 has categories that are absent in the L1, the functions of these have to be learnt for full comprehension to occur. Across closely related languages this does not pose much of a problem: L1 procedures are fairly appropriate and tend to work well for comprehension. When learners have reached a stage of knowing a sufficient number of items (words), approximate comprehension can easily occur.

The two distinctions between item learning and system learning and between comprehension and production can be joined together to provide a simplistic model of the development of foreign-language learning. In SLA research, the concept of learning has been used in two different ways. It has referred to the learner's gradual achievement of an ability to use the target language productively, and in doing so has neglected the prior ability of being able to understand the language. In SLA research, the term *learning* has also been applied to both receptive and productive aspects of language proficiency, but then the very different mechanisms of comprehension and production are ignored.

We should, in fact, distinguish four different types of learning: (1) item learning for comprehension; (2a) item learning for production; (2b) system learning for comprehension; and (3) system learning for production. Cross-linguistic similarity is relevant to all of these stages but influences them somewhat differently. The starting point for the learner is item learning for comprehension. Across related languages, a fair receptive knowledge can be attained quite quickly. When learners can make use of positive item transfer to facilitate their acquisition of the ability to understand a new language, they can free many cognitive resources for other aspects of receptive learning. If, on the other hand, there is a zero or near-zero similarity relation between the languages, the normal gap between receptive and productive vocabulary will be reduced, in that the acquisition of receptive competence takes a long time for such learners. This can be seen quite clearly in a study by Takala (1984), who found similar-sized "active" and "passive" vocabularies in Finnish-speaking learners of English in a formal foreign-language learning situation.

Item learning for production and system learning for comprehension are stages following the initial stage of item learning for comprehension. They usually develop in parallel, but the learner can, of course, focus more on either of these, depending on the aims, the learning situation, individual learner characteristics, and so forth. In vocabulary production, formal similarity between words such as cognates may help the learner locate the intended L2 word in his or her mental lexicon for the TL (De Groot, 1993). But errors are more likely to occur in production than in comprehension, partly because of the absence of a context in production that would rule out the wrong interpretations that formal similarities can induce.

System learning for comprehension means that oversimplified one-to-one relations are gradually modified. The learner learns, for example, that one L2 word can have several meanings, that the past tense of verbs can be expressed by different morphemes, and, in general, that pragmatic aspects of the target language are also relevant for learning. Gradually the learner develops an improved understanding of how different L2 units correspond to L1 units and how they relate to the underlying concepts. Cross-linguistic relations are not as easy to establish in system learning as they are in item learning since the functional and semantic systems in two languages are reasonably congruent only in very closely related languages. In system learning, the relevant cross-linguistic similarities are functional or semantic, and formal similarity plays a subordinate role, if any. This corresponds to what several studies of the organization of the learner's mental lexicon have found: that as learning progresses, learners rely less on phonological similarity and more and more on semantic similarity (Singleton, 1994, p. 54; 1999, p. 189; Kroll & De Groot, 1997, p. 174).

The message of L2 texts can be at least approximately comprehended if inflectional affixes and function words are left unnoticed or unanalyzed. For production, on the other hand, accuracy is more vital, and if grammatical morphemes are omitted, the result is errors causing misunderstanding or at least irritation in the listener. The learner has to recognize and appropriately make use of the many linguistic means of expressing the same meaning and also become able to use the same linguistic form for several purposes. This applies to both grammar and vocabulary. As system learning progresses, learners gradually learn to expand their lexical network in many dimensions. In this process, the importance of cross-linguistic similarity decreases at the same time as intra-lingual similarities within the TL become more and more important.

Implications for Teaching

Finally, concerning the relationship between learning and teaching, it is necessary to point out that much more knowledge is needed about the mechanisms through which language learning proceeds before the field is justified in pronouncing definitive statements about how languages can be taught most effectively. Nevertheless, we can point to some implications that are relatively clear. First, given the important role that cross-linguistic similarities play in language learning, a natural question to follow is whether and to what extent they could be put to effective use in teaching. In general terms, a good strategy would be to make use of, and even overuse, actual similarities at early stages of learning.

A project that has a didactic aim along these lines is EuroCom, where textbooks and other materials are being produced to make use of the facilitative potential for reading comprehension inherent in speakers of languages that are related, but not as close as to be mutually comprehensible. The project's main focus has been on the Romance languages, and the initiative has come from speakers of German. So far, German has been the main L1 used in the project. For an account in English of the EuroComRom project, see McCann, Klein, and Stegmann (2003). The basic idea of EuroComRom is simple. If you know one Romance language, you already have a lot of relevant knowledge that can be used for understanding all others. The learner is helped on the way by descriptions of what are called "The Seven Sieves," where systematic correspondences between all Romance languages are set out. The seven sieves are (1) international vocabulary, (2) pan-Romance vocabulary, (3) sound correspondences, (4) spelling and pronunciation, (5) syntactic structures, (6) morphosyntax, and (7) affixes. A project led by Britta Hufeisen applying the same principles on Germanic languages has also begun (see Duke, Hufeisen, & Lutjeharms, 2004; Hufeisen, 2005).

Another clear implication is that learners of a closely related language have a far smaller learning burden than learners of a distant language. This means that there is less that they need to learn, that what they do need to learn is likely to be incorporated more easily into their existing knowledge, and that it will take them less time to arrive at a criterion level of language proficiency (see Ingram, 1975, p. 272; Odlin, 1989). Depending on the relative absence of cross-linguistic similarities, learners of a distant language will take considerably longer to reach that criterion level of proficiency in the TL (e.g., Ard & Homburg, 1992), they may need to pass through more stages of acquisition (e.g., Master, 1997), and they will tend to produce a higher proportion of errors (e.g., Schumann, 1986). Nevertheless, even though they have a larger learning burden, learners of a distant language can be ultimately as successful as learners of a closely related language when learning conditions are favorable (cf. Palmer, 1917/1968, p. 33; Sweet, 1899/1964, p. 54).

As in any concrete teaching situation, making use of cross-linguistic similarities requires that a number of both contextual and learner variables be considered. At least the following are particularly relevant:

The actual relation between the L1 and L2. If the two languages are closely related, the teacher certainly needs to briefly outline the systematic recurring correspondences. But the closer the relation, the more teaching can concentrate on the actual differences that exist. Thus the teaching of Scandinavians learning another Scandinavian language would naturally focus on differences in pronunciation and the most common false friends. Where the languages are very distant, such as Japanese and English, the existence of mid- and high-frequency loanwords may facilitate learning. It is true that the loanwords from English into Japanese have been considerably modified, and the similarities have been obscured particularly by the differences in scripts and phonological systems. Even so, according to recent views (Daulton, 2007; Uchida & Scholfield, 2000), this built-in lexicon, *gairaigo*, provides a powerful tool for more effective learning. Developing strategies for maximally efficient use of high-frequency English loanwords provides a challenge for teachers and researchers in Japan.

Comprehension vs. production. If the learner is already able to comprehend the TL, at least approximately, teaching spoken and written production of that language may be necessary only for learners having a strong need to integrate with the TL community. This is the case when their job situation requires writing proficiency in the TL. For most purposes in the inter-Scandinavian context, however, Swedes, Norwegians, and Danes can count on generally being understood if they speak or write their own standard L1. Teaching a language not immediately comprehensible should acknowledge that cross-linguistic similarities are particularly important for comprehension.

Language proficiency. When a non-native language is closer to the TL than to the L1, comprehension can be facilitated by focusing on the similarities between the L2 and L3. For the productive aspects of L3 learning, however, it seems very likely that only a high level of proficiency in a similar L2 is really useful. The inherent risks of confusion between related languages are more easily actualized if the learner has not successfully internalized grammatical rules and semantic properties in the L2.

Individual learner characteristics. While some learners appear to have blinders on, in that they do not take notice of even obvious cross-linguistic similarities, others are too prone to assuming similarities where they do not exist. Teaching needs to strike a balance between encouraging learners to make use of actual similarities and preventing exaggerated reliance on merely assumed similarities (cf. Haastrup, 1991, p. 341).

REFERENCES

Arabski, J. (1979). *Errors as indications of the development of interlanguage.* Katowice, Poland: Uniwersytet Slasky.

Ard, J. & Homburg, T. (1992). Verification of language transfer. In S. Gass & L. Selinker (eds.), *Language transfer in language learning* (pp. 47–70). Amsterdam: Benjamins.

Biskup, D. (1992). L1 influence on learners' rendering of English collocations: A Polish/German empirical study. In P. Arnaud & H. Béjoint (eds.), *Vocabulary and applied linguistics* (pp. 85–93). London: Macmillan.

Cruttenden, A. (1981). Item-learning and system-learning. *Journal of Psycholinguistic Research* 10, 79–88.

Daulton, F. E. (2007). *Japan's built-in lexicon of English-based loanwords.* Clevedon, UK: Multilingual Matters.

De Angelis, G. (2005). Interlanguage transfer of function words. *Language Learning* 55, 379–414.

Dechert, H. & Raupach, M. (eds.) (1989). *Transfer in language production.* Norwood, NJ: Ablex.

De Groot, A. M. B. (1993). Word-type effects in bilingual processing tasks: Support for a mixed-representational system. In R. Schreuder & B. Weltens (eds.), *The bilingual lexicon* (pp. 27–51). Amsterdam: Benjamins.

Dewaele, J.-M. (1998). Lexical inventions: French interlanguage as L2 versus L3. *Applied Linguistics* 19, 471–90.

Duke, J., Hufeisen, B., & Lutjeharms, M. (2004). Die sieben Siebe des EuroCom für den multilingualen Einstieg in die Welt der germanischen Sprachen. In H. G. Klein & D. Rutke (eds.), *Neuere Forschungen zur Europäischen Interkomprehension* (pp. 109–34). Aachen: Shaker.

Eckman, F. R. (2004). From phonemic differences to constraint rankings. *Studies in Second Language Acquisition* 26, 513–49.

Eisenstein, M. & Bodman, J. (1993). Expressing gratitude in American English. In G. Kasper & S. Blum-Kulka (eds.), *Interlanguage pragmatics* (pp. 64–81). Oxford: Oxford University Press.

Ellegård, A. (1978). On measuring language similarity. In J. Weinstock (ed.), *Nordic languages and linguistics* (pp. 195–216). Austin, TX: University of Texas.

Gass, S. & Selinker, L. (eds.) (1983). *Language transfer in language learning.* Rowley, MA: Newbury House.

Haastrup, K. (1991). *Lexical inferencing procedures or talking about words: A book about receptive procedures in foreign language learning with special reference to English.* Tübingen: Gunter Narr.

Hammerly, H. (1991). *Fluency and accuracy.* Clevedon, UK: Multilingual Matters.

Hufeisen, B. (2005). Mehrsprachigkeit: Fit für Babel. *Gehirn & Geist: Das Magazin für Psychologie und Hirnforschung* 6, 28–33.

Ingram, E. (1975). Psychology and language learning. In J. B. P. Allen & S. P. Corder (eds.), *Papers in applied linguistics: The Edinburgh Course in Applied Linguistics,* vol. 2, Language Learning Series (pp. 218–90). London: Oxford University Press.

James, C. (1980). *Contrastive analysis.* London: Longman.

Jarvis, S. (1998). *Conceptual transfer in the interlingual lexicon.* Bloomington, IN: Indiana University Linguistics Club Publications.

Jarvis, S. (2000). Methodological rigor in the study of transfer: Identifying L1 influence in the interlanguage lexicon. *Language Learning* 50, 245–309.

Jarvis, S. & Pavlenko, A. (2008). *Crosslinguistic influence in language and cognition.* Mahwah, NJ: Lawrence Erlbaum.

Kellerman, E. (1977). Towards a characterization of the strategy of transfer in second language learning. *Interlanguage Studies Bulletin* 2, 58–145.

Kellerman, E. (1978). Giving learners a break: Native language intuitions as a source of predictions about transferability. *Working Papers on Bilingualism* 15, 59–92.

Kellerman, E. (1979). Transfer and non-transfer: Where are we now? *Studies in Second Language Acquisition* 2, 37–57.

Kellerman, E. (1995). Crosslinguistic influence: Transfer to nowhere? *Annual Review of Applied Linguistics* 15, 125–50.

Kellerman, E. & Sharwood Smith, M. (eds.) (1986). *Crosslinguistic influence in* Second Language Acquisition. Oxford: Pergamon.

Kroll, J. & De Groot, A. M. B. (1997). Lexical and conceptual memory in the bilingual: Mapping form to meaning in two languages. In A. M. B. De Groot & J. Kroll (eds.), *Tutorials in bilingualism: Psycholinguistic perspectives* (pp. 169–99). Mahwah, NJ: Lawrence Erlbaum.

Master, P. (1997). The English article system: Acquisition, function, and pedagogy. *System* 25, 215–32.

McCann, W. J., Klein, H. G., & Stegmann, T. D. (2003). *EuroComRom – the seven sieves: How to read all the Romance languages right away,* 2nd revised edn. Aachen: Shaker.

Odlin, T. (1989). *Language transfer: Cross-linguistic influence in language learning.* Cambridge: Cambridge University Press.

Odlin, T. (2003). Crosslinguistic influence. In C. Doughty & M. Long (eds.), *The handbook of second language acquisition* (pp. 436–86). Oxford: Blackwell.

Odlin, T. (2006). Could a contrastive analysis ever be complete. In J. Arabski (ed.), *Cross-linguistic influences in the second language lexicon* (pp. 22–35). Clevedon, UK: Multilingual Matters.

Palmer, H. (1917/1968). *The scientific study and teaching of language,* Language and Language Learning Series. London: Oxford University Press.

Ringbom, H. (1987). *The role of the first language in foreign language learning.* Clevedon, UK: Multilingual Matters.

Ringbom, H. (2006). The importance of different types of similarity in transfer studies. In J. Arabski (ed.), *Cross-linguistic influences in the second language lexicon* (pp. 36–45). Clevedon, UK: Multilingual Matters.

Ringbom, H. (2007). *Cross-linguistic similarity in foreign language learning.* Clevedon, UK: Multilingual Matters.

Schumann, J. (1986). Locative and directional expressions in basilang speech. *Language Learning* 36, 277–94.

Selinker, L. (1969). Language transfer. *General Linguistics* 9, 67–92.

Seppänen, A. (1998). Finnish and English from a comparative perspective. In R. W. Cooper (ed.), *Compare or contrast: Current issues in cross-language research.* Tampere English Studies 6 (pp. 15–51). Tampere, Finland: Tampere University.

Singleton, D. (1994). Learning L2 lexis: A matter of form? In G. Bartelt (ed.), *The dynamics of language processes: Essays in honor of Hans W. Dechert* (pp. 45–57). Tübingen: Gunter Narr.

Singleton, D. (1999). *Exploring the second language mental lexicon.* Cambridge: Cambridge University Press.

Singleton, D. (2006). Lexical transfer: Interlexical or intralexical? In J. Arabski (ed.), *Cross-linguistic influences in the second language lexicon* (pp. 130–43). Clevedon, UK: Multilingual Matters.

Sjöholm, K. (1995). *The influence of crosslinguistic, semantic, and input factors on the acquisition of English phrasal verbs: A comparison between Finnish and Swedish learners at an intermediate and advanced level.* Åbo, Finland: Åbo Akademi University Press.

Sweet, H. (1899/1964). *The practical study of languages,* Language and Language Learning Series. London: Oxford University Press.

Takala, S. (1984). Evaluation of the students' knowledge of English vocabulary in the Finnish comprehensive school. *Reports from the Institute for Educational Research* 350. Jyväskylä, Finland: University of Jyväskylä.

Uchida, E. & Scholfield, P. (2000). *Why words differ in difficulty: The learnability of English-Japanese cognates for Japanese learners of English.* Last accessed: July 18, 2006. http://privatewww.essex.ac.uk/~scholp/emimart2.htm.

Williams, S. & Hammarberg, B. (1998). Language switches in L3 production: Implications for a polyglot speaking model. *Applied Linguistics* 19 (pp. 295–333).

Wode, H. (1976). Developmental sequences in naturalistic second language acquisition. *Working Papers on Bilingualism* 11, 1–13.

FURTHER READING

Cenoz, J., Hufeisen, B., & Jessner, U. (eds.) (2001). *Cross-linguistic influence in third language acquisition: Psycholinguistic perspectives.* Clevedon, UK: Multilingual Matters.

Cook, V. (ed.) (2002). *Portraits of the L2 user.* Clevedon, UK: Multilingual Matters.

Ellis, R. (2008). *The study of second language acquisition,* 2nd edn. Oxford: Oxford University Press.

Jarvis, S. & Pavlenko, A. (2008). *Crosslinguistic influence in language and cognition.* New York/ London: Routledge.

Nation, I. S. P. (1990). *Teaching and learning vocabulary.* New York: Newbury House.

Odlin, T. (ed.) (1994). *Perspectives on pedagogical grammar.* Cambridge: Cambridge University Press.

Ringbom, H. (2007). *Cross-linguistic similarity in foreign language learning.* Clevedon, UK: Multilingual Matters.

Schmitt, N. & McCarthy, M. (eds.) (1997). *Vocabulary: Description, acquisition and pedagogy.* Cambridge: Cambridge University Press.

8 Cognitive-Psychological Processes in Second Language Learning

ROBERT M. DEKEYSER

This chapter discusses core concepts in the cognitive psychology of second language learning: what are the various components of L2 knowledge? how are these components used? and most importantly, how are they learned or acquired, monitored, practiced, and consolidated?

The Components of Second Language Knowledge

The competence–performance distinction

While this is the oldest and most widely known of the distinctions we are discussing in this chapter, having been formulated by Chomsky (1965, p. 4), and having been the subject of countless books and articles, both in the L1 and L2 domains (e.g., Chipere, 2003; Hymes, 1972; McNamara, 1995; Sorace, 2003; Tarone, 1983; Taylor, 1988), it is probably the least useful for our purposes. It leaves out the whole area of processing, explicitly so (see, e.g., Chomsky, 1965, p. 9), and gives the impression that whatever is not part of competence is not systematic and not of linguistic interest. At the same time, of course, it presupposes that the rules of grammar are indeed rules of the mind (cf. e.g., Pinker, 1999; Pinker & Prince, 1988; Pinker & Ullman, 2002a, 2002b; Ullman, 2004), and not just a convenient summary of probabilistic behaviors, as the connectionists would have it (cf. e.g., Elman et al., 1996; McClelland & Patterson, 2002a, 2002b; Rumelhart & McClelland, 1986), and that competence is not merely an emergent property of performance (as Hall, Cheng, & Carlson, 2006, propose).

On the other hand, the terms are often used in a much broader sense, coinciding more or less with the knowledge–use distinction discussed below. This terminological vagueness is a source of great confusion and tends to sweep a variety of phenomena under the carpet, whether they be entirely cognitive in nature, such as syntactic processing mechanisms (e.g., Boland, 2005; Gibson, 1998; Pritchett, 1992), or more socially determined, such as accommodation of the interlocutor (e.g., Bell, 1984), or both (e.g., Tarone, 1983). It could even be argued that neither competence nor performance is of much interest to the applied linguist, the former being a highly abstract, almost philosophical concept, and the latter an uninteresting collection of anomalies and restrictions, while the whole area in between, stretching from representation in a wider sense to processing and to socially variable use, is at the core of second language acquisition research and of applied linguistics more broadly.

The representation–processing distinction

A more useful distinction for the second language acquisition researcher than competence versus performance is representation versus processing. A large body of psycholinguistic literature has accumulated that deals with phonological, morphological, syntactic, and lexical processing, both in L1 and L2. It aims to find out what goes through the mind, in real time, of somebody who listens to, speaks, reads, or writes in a native or near-native language: what are the processes that bridge the gap between the form in which knowledge is stored in the mind and the form in which it is audible or visible in perception and production? This literature draws both on symbolist (e.g., Boland, 1995; Gibson, 1998; Pritchett, 1992) and connectionist (e.g., Elman et al., 1996) accounts of the representations that underlie processing, with symbolist accounts predominating. Clearly, the nature of processing depends on the nature of representation. It could be argued, therefore, that the study of processing should wait for more agreement on what representation looks like; others would argue, however, that the study of real-time processes gives unique insights into what representations processing draws on. As both the nature of representation and the nature of processing are not fully understood, it can even be hard to determine whether certain behavioral phenomena are due to the nature of representation or the nature of processing. Well-known foci of this debate in L1 are the discussion of whether subjacency restrictions are an issue of representation or of processing (see e.g., Huang, 1982; Pesetsky, 1987; Rizzi, 1982) and the research on the extent to which prepositional phrase attachment is influenced by discourse context or an issue of autonomous syntax (see e.g., Altmann, 1998; Frazier, 1987).

In L2 research, the representation–processing dichotomy has become prominent in the area of syntax recently through the work of Juffs (1998, 2004; Juffs & Harrington, 1995) on relative clauses, *wh*-questions, and various types of garden path effects, that of Lieberman, Aoshima, and Phillips (2006) and Williams, Möbius, and Kim (2001) on *wh*-questions, and of Jiang (2004, 2007) on plural -*s*, and of Trenkic (2007) on third-person -*s*. There is also recent work in the areas of L2 phonological processing (e.g., Escudero & Boersma, 2004; Sebastián-Gallés & Soto-Faraco, 1999) and L2 lexical processing (e.g., Hernandez & Meschyan, 2006; Sunderman & Kroll, 2006).

The declarative–procedural distinction

This distinction is well known in cognitive psychology – even though it came out of computer science – and is increasingly used by SLA researchers. Declarative knowledge is knowledge THAT something is, and can further be divided into semantic memory (knowledge of concepts, words, facts) and episodic memory (knowledge of events experienced). Procedural knowledge is knowledge HOW to do something, whether this involves psychomotor skills (knowing how to swim, ride a bicycle, or play tennis) or cognitive skills (knowing how to solve an equation, write a computer program, conjugate a verb, or read a text). The declarative–procedural distinction is central to models of skill acquisition, such as ACT-R (Anderson & Lebiere, 1998), has neurological support (e.g., Eichenbaum, 2000, 2002; Squire, 1992; Squire & Kandel, 1999; Squire & Knowlton, 2000; Squire & Zola, 1996), and has recently been brought to bear on issues of L1 processing (e.g., Pinker & Ullman, 2002a, 2002b) and of L1–L2 differences (e.g., Ullman, 2001, 2004, 2005).

This distinction is often equated with the explicit–implicit dichotomy, and the two pairs of concepts do overlap greatly, and can often be equated in certain contexts, but explicit is not exactly the same as declarative, and implicit not exactly the same as procedural. Declarative knowledge is not necessarily explicit, because it is not necessarily accessible to awareness (linguistic competence in the Chomskyan sense being a good example). On the other hand, procedural knowledge is not necessarily implicit, because it can be the result of proceduralization (and partial) automatization of declarative knowledge, and still allow or even require a certain degree of conscious access when being used. Nor is implicit knowledge necessarily procedural: knowledge of category prototypes, even including the knowledge of chunk strength involved in artificial grammar learning, may be implicit, but this implicit knowledge is neither declarative nor procedural (Squire & Knowlton, 2000); similarly, priming in amnesic patients seems to draw on knowledge that is implicit (no conscious access) but declarative (Kihlstrom, Dorfman, & Park, 2007).

In the second language domain, the declarative–procedural distinction has been used both in behavioral experiments (e.g., DeKeyser, 1997) and in neurophysiological studies (ERP, e.g., Morgan-Short, Steinhauer, Sanz, & Ullman, 2007; Mueller, Hahne, Fujii, & Friederici, 2005; Tokowicz & MacWhinney, 2005). Both lines of inquiry suggest a shift from reliance on declarative to reliance on procedural knowledge during the learning process within an individual. Such a shift has also been demonstrated, of course, in neurological studies of other forms of skill learning (e.g., Poldrack et al., 2001). Furthermore, the much more obvious difficulty of adult learners with grammar than with vocabulary suggests that the grammatical/procedural system is less available to them than lexical/declarative memory (Ullman, 2001, 2005).

The explicit–implicit distinction

Explicit knowledge is knowledge that one is aware of, that one has conscious access to. As a result in can be verbalized, at least in principle; not everybody has the cognitive and linguistic wherewithal to articulate that knowledge clearly and completely. Implicit knowledge is outside awareness, and therefore cannot be verbalized, only inferred indirectly from behavior, whether it be, for example, semantic priming showing implicit declarative knowledge (faster than usual reaction to the word *cat* because one has recently seen a related word such as *dog*, even though one may not be aware of having seen this word), or apparently rule-governed behaviors, such as complex mental calculation or the production of a complex sentence both showing implicit procedural knowledge, i.e., knowledge of the rules underlying these behaviors, without being able to conceptualize those rules, let alone verbalize them. Most of us have long forgotten the steps involved in various forms of mental arithmetic that we were taught in grade school, and most of us have never even known, in the explicit sense, the basic rules of grammar of our native language (just ask the average American undergraduate when one puts an -*s* on the verb in English!).

In the second language domain, the extent to which L2 speakers are aware of the grammar knowledge they have – whatever the extent of this knowledge may be – depends, of course, on how they have learned the language. Furthermore, given the problems involved in operationalizing concepts such as awareness and verbalization (see, e.g., R. Ellis, 2004, 2005), it is virtually impossible to design "pure" measures of implicit or explicit knowledge of L2. Perhaps such "pure" measures should not even be a goal anyway, given that at least some psychologists see the implicit–explicit distinction as a matter of degree, as a continuum whose extremes may be rarely represented (e.g., Dienes & Perner, 1999).

The distinction is very important, however, for determining how L2 learners acquire and use L2 knowledge (see below), and therefore researchers have used a variety of imperfect measures (such as metalinguistic tests for explicit knowledge and timed grammaticality judgments for implicit knowledge). R. Ellis has taken the issue a step further by carrying out a factor analysis in order to determine to what extent two factors, implicit and explicit knowledge, can be identified as underlying a variety of L2 tests. While the methodological specifics are very tricky (Isemonger, 2007), this approach does seem promising (depending on the results of the factor analysis, one could put different weights on different tests for subsequent investigations of implicit and explicit knowledge), and further refinement seems to be leading to increasingly clear-cut results (Ellis & Loewen, 2007).

A special note is in order here about the term "metalinguistic (awareness)." This term is used with at least three different meanings in our field, which further obscures the debate. One can distinguish three layers of "metalinguistic knowledge": the first one is simply the awareness of what is right or wrong in a given sentence, without necessarily knowing why. This is the layer that Gombert (1992, p. 10) has called epilinguistic and that Karmiloff-Smith (1992, p. 52) refers to as "the E1 representational format," which "involves a redescription of information into a format that is accessible to certain tasks outside normal input–output relations but not yet to metalinguistic explanation." Clearly, this kind of knowledge can be entirely implicit, and therefore the term "metalinguistic" in this context is very confusing, because many equate "metalinguistic" with explicit. A second layer is "metalinguistic" in the sense of metacognition about language.

Just as one can have metacognitive knowledge about how one types, drives, or does mental arithmetic (and perhaps even of how one's typical behavior deviates from what one was taught!), one can have the same metacognitive knowledge about one's linguistic behavior. This is the sense of "metalinguistic" that corresponds to "explicit." The third layer is "metalinguistic" in the sense of language about language; this is the ability to verbalize, for which explicit knowledge is a necessary but not a sufficient condition.

The item–rule distinction

The use of rules can be laborious, even when they are proceduralized and even partially automatized. Therefore, under conditions of time pressure, it is very useful to have a shortcut available, and for those situations where a certain input is frequently processed by a rule and therefore frequently yields the same output, an associative learning process for that input-output pair may be more efficient. To take an example from math again, we all learned early on that instead of laboriously calculating 7×5 as being $7 + 7 + 7 + 7 + 7$, going from 7 to 14 to 21 to 28 to 35, it is easier to just memorize the item from the table of multiplication that tells us $7 \times 5 = 35$ (note that the same distinction can be made at the lower level of addition in the sense that $7 + 7 = 14$ is itself a shortcut for $7 + 1 + 1 + 1 + 1 + 1 + 1 + 1 = 14$).

In the same way, for verb forms we often produce, it becomes more economical to store them as an "item" rather than having to put them together on the basis of a rule; for seldom used combinations, storage of all the items would be too cumbersome, and rule use is more economical. It is not surprising, therefore, that irregular forms are almost always high-frequency forms: as they are high-frequency, they tend to be retrieved as items, hence there is no analogical pressure, i.e., no pressure to make them conform to a rule; for low-frequency items, people tend to fall back on the rule, even if the prescriptive grammar requires an irregular, which over time leads to regularization. According to some, this need to combine rapid reaction with flexible knowledge that can be used under changing circumstances constitutes the evolutionary pressure that led to the declarative–procedural distinction (see e.g., Poldrack et al., 2001). (Note that the item–rule distinction is yet another one that often overlaps with the declarative–procedural distinction (cf., e.g., Pinker & Ullman, 2001), but cannot be equated with it: rules can be stored in declarative form before being proceduralized and automatized, as is traditionally held by skill acquisition theory).

Not only inflectional morphology can be produced this way; entire strings of words that are often used together may be stored and retrieved as "chunks," saving even more mental resources. Hence the well-known phenomenon of formulaic knowledge, both in L1 and L2 (see, e.g., Myles, 2004; Myles, Hooper, & Mitchell, 1998; Schmitt, 2004; Wray, 2001): L2 speakers, in particular, can often produce whole strings very rapidly and without errors, even if in other contexts they would have to slow down in order to produce some of the same morphological forms, and L2 learners can often produce such strings long before they can use the constitutive elements productively. Even what appear to be subtle grammar errors may in fact be due to the use of certain lexemes with the grammatical morphemes they are most frequently used with, regardless of the appropriateness of those morphemes to express the specific meaning intended; this is especially likely to happen for structures where the form–meaning mapping is already obscure, as is the case for the Spanish "reflexive" pronoun *se* (Zyzik, 2006).

Neurological data confirm differences in storage for items and rules, and a shift from one to the other over time (e.g., Doeller et al., 2006; Fletcher et al., 1999; Opitz & Friederici, 2003, 2004).

Conclusion: Multiple sources of knowledge

As should be clear from the above, all L2 speakers have L2 knowledge of many kinds. On top of universal grammar (assuming it exists and is still accessible in L2 learning) and of elements transferred from L1, all learners have both declarative and procedural knowledge, implicit and explicit knowledge, knowledge of items and rules, and knowledge of how to process language in real time for production or comprehension. The good language learner will acquire as much knowledge of as many kinds as possible, and perhaps more importantly, will be able to draw on these various kinds of knowledge effectively and efficiently during language use, as we will see in the two sections that follow.

How the Components of Second Language Knowledge Are Used

The knowledge–use distinction

As mentioned above, this distinction is not to be confused with the narrower competence–performance dichotomy. Knowledge, as the previous section illustrates, includes much more than competence in the Chomskyan sense, the latter being necessarily implicit. Often students will have considerable amounts of explicit knowledge about parts of the L2, but little or no competence, i.e., implicit, intuitive knowledge, of the same elements in the same L2. Nor is use the same as performance. Many systematic differences in use that depend on both social and cognitive constraints are outside the scope of grammatical competence, while being more than moment-to-moment, more or less random, deviations from competence. Grammatical competence is only part of communicative competence, which is only part of knowledge, and performance is only part of use (cf. Canale & Swain, 1980; McNamara, 1995; Taylor, 1988). The age-old problem, then, of students who know all the rules but can't speak is *not* one of a gap between competence and performance but one of a gap between insufficiently proceduralized/automatized explicit knowledge, on the one hand, and very limited implicit and/or automatized knowledge on the other hand (see DeKeyser, 2007b).

Using implicit and explicit knowledge

A number of authors tried to document the extent to which students draw on implicit and explicit knowledge in language use (e.g., Bialystok, 1979; R. Ellis, 2004, 2005, 2006; Ellis & Loewen, 2007; Golonka, 2006; Green & Hecht, 1992; Hernandez & Meschyan, 2006; Hu, 2002; Hulstijn & Hulstijn, 1984; Jiang, 2004, 2007; Macrory & Stone, 2000; Renou, 2000; Schulz, 2002; Trenkic, 2007). While these authors define use in different ways, and while methodological problems abound in this area of research (see especially DeKeyser, 2003; and Isemonger, 2007), three points are fairly generalizable:

1 different tasks draw on the two kinds of knowledge to different extents;
2 just about all tasks draw on both explicit and implicit or automatized knowledge to some extent;
3 the gap between explicit and implicit or fully automatized knowledge is particularly wide for some elements of grammar.

R. Ellis (2006), in particular, shows that among the 17 ESL/EFL structures he examined, the rank order was quite different depending on whether a test was used that drew predominantly on implicit or explicit knowledge. No structures elicited significantly better scores for implicit than for explicit tests, but some were descriptively better. Several structures, however, yielded significantly higher scores on the explicit than on the implicit test; the biggest difference was found for the indefinite article, question tags, plural *-s*, and regular past *-ed*. Ellis also shows how, for some structures, explicit knowledge was a predictor of overall proficiency scores on tests of listening, speaking, reading and writing (especially for relative clauses and indefinite articles), whereas for other structures, it was implicit knowledge rather than explicit knowledge that predicted proficiency (especially for comparatives, unreal conditionals, *since/for*). These two kinds of data clearly suggest that different kinds of knowledge are accessed depending on the structure and the test, assuming, of course, that implicit and explicit are the best labels for the different kinds of tests involved; the factor analyses in R. Ellis (2005, 2006) and Ellis and Loewen (2007) can only show that two different components of knowledge are involved, not that the implicit–explicit distinction is the best label, rather than some correlated dichotomy.

As a case in point, Hu (2002) argues strongly, on the basis of ESL learners' differential performance on prototypical versus peripheral items, and their differential sensitivity to different factors conducive to monitoring (focus on form, sufficient time, knowledge of rule), that the phenomenon of differential knowledge access is not so much an issue of retrieval of explicit versus implicit knowledge, but of differentially automatized structures, i.e., various levels of explicit knowledge. Similarly, Jiang (2004, 2007) and Trenkic (2007) argue convincingly, the former for plural *-s*, and the latter for third-person *-s*, that, while the difficulty in using these structures spontaneously may be very sensitive to processing constraints, the processing constraints involved are a matter of general cognition in the absence of implicit knowledge (and hence are evidence of a representational rather than a processing deficit in the psycholinguistic sense described above).

Using declarative, procedural, and automatized knowledge

While the implicit–explicit distinction may be the most useful for assessment at a given point in time, the declarative–procedural–automatized distinction is the most useful from a developmental perspective. To what extent is the learner's L2 knowledge represented in these three forms at various stages of the learning process, and to what extent can one form of knowledge be instrumental in developing a different form of knowledge? This question has been the subject of a decades-long debate in applied linguistics and has often been referred to as the interface issue, the acquisition–learning distinction or even the implicit–explicit distinction. Again, while in many cases these terms can be used interchangeably, it is most useful to use the distinction from skill acquisition theory to investigate to what extent second language learning (in adults) can develop along this path. Krashen has stated that "learning cannot turn into acquisition" (1985, pp. 42–3) and that automatization of explicitly learned rules only appears to be the case, because explicit knowledge of a given rule often far precedes its automatized form, but this temporal ordering does not imply causation (1985, p. 41), only that acquisition takes longer than learning (in other words, the two processes happen in parallel; one is not conducive to the other).

More recently Hulstijn (2002, p. 211) has argued that explicit knowledge of second language grammar cannot turn into implicit knowledge through automatization, and that, strictly speaking, there is no "automatization *of* rules" (emphasis in the original), because automatization implies a qualitative change, not mere speeding-up. This may appear to be another clear "no" answer to DeKeyser's question as to "whether the declarative knowledge that results from explicit learning processes can be turned into a form of procedural knowledge that is accessible in the same way as implicitly acquired knowledge" (2003, p. 328). It is important, however, not to misinterpret the word "turn into" in this context. The interface hypothesis, of which DeKeyser is a proponent, does *not* imply that one kind of knowledge turns into another in the sense that the more there is of one kind (procedural, automatized, or implicit), the less there is of the other (declarative, explicit) (*pace* Segalowitz & Hulstijn, 2005, p. 378). What it means is that the presence of one is conducive to, or plays a causal role in the development of the other, and on that point the literature is quite clear, in the sense that, while explicit learning certainly does not necessarily lead to eventual automatized, let alone implicit, knowledge, the likelihood of learners achieving a fairly high degree of automaticity in their use of a structure keeps evolving in parallel with their declarative knowledge about that structure, even in the latter years of foreign language instruction. (This position is a variant of the strong, not the weak interface position as these two are described, e.g., in R. Ellis (1993, 1994), because the weak interface position implies that explicit knowledge is merely helpful in triggering or speeding up implicit learning processes, whereas the strong interface hypothesis implies a more direct causality in the sense that explicit declarative knowledge, given practice of sufficient quantity and quality, leads to proceduralization, (at least partial) automatization, and only in some cases, eventually, after proceduralization and automatization have taken place, to implicit representation.)

Schulz (2002), for instance, showed that declarative knowledge (even metalinguistic in the sense of verbalization) among learners of German L2 in college was a better predictor of their grammatical proficiency on a written test (r = 0.52) than experience abroad was. Other studies that demonstrate a link between students' declarative knowledge of a structure and their ability to use it, even fairly rapidly and correctly, which implies proceduralization and a certain degree of automatization as a function of the initial declarative knowledge, are de Jong (2005) and DeKeyser (1997). Both of these studies show that a certain degree of automaticity can be reached in learners who have solid declarative knowledge (whereas DeKeyser (1995) showed that no procedural, let alone automatized or implicit, knowledge developed in the absence of declarative knowledge, even after thousands of exposures, for the rather straightforward morphosyntactic form–meaning mappings investigated there). Both studies also demonstrate the skill specificity of the procedural knowledge documented (in the sense of little transfer between receptive and productive skills). As stated above, procedural knowledge is highly specific and therefore very limited in its transfer potential; only the more abstract declarative knowledge transfers relatively easily to new tasks.

Even for vocabulary, and even in the rather advanced learner, automatization may not be complete, and a certain degree of attention shifting (Segalowitz & Frenkiel-Fishman, 2005) or executive control (Hernandez & Meschyan, 2006) may be necessary; this does not prevent the learner (or indeed the bilingual) from being highly fluent.

In conclusion, then, while it may be the case that declarative knowledge does not turn into procedural or automatized knowledge in the sense that the more there is of the latter, the less there is of the former, and while it may also be the case that highly automatized knowledge is still not necessarily qualitatively the same as implicit knowledge, there is no reason to doubt the causal effect of declarative knowledge on the development of automatized knowledge.

How the Components of Second Language Knowledge Are Learned, Acquired, Practiced, Monitored, and Consolidated

The previous section describes how learners draw on their various sources of L2 knowledge for (communicative) use. This ability to use their knowledge is, of course, the result of an often very long process of learning, practicing, monitoring, receiving feedback, modifying hypotheses, and practicing again. This section goes into some detail about each of these processes.

Learning and acquisition

The distinction between explicit and implicit learning, usually referred to in the SLA literature as learning versus acquisition, is a huge topic in cognitive psychology, where it is the subject of hundreds of empirical studies. The part of that literature that is most directly relevant to language learning, especially the research on artificial grammar learning, was covered in quite some detail in DeKeyser (2003), who came to the conclusion that "a thorough reading of the literature on implicit learning . . . must leave one very skeptical about the possibility of implicit learning of abstract structure, at least by adults" (p. 321). This is not only a vast, but highly controversial literature, leading some to draw more tentative conclusions at that time: "while there can be no doubt that both spontaneous and more deliberate L2 performance exist, what type of knowledge underlies each, and whether there is any connection between the two during SLA and L2 use, are contentious issues that are from settled in SLA, let alone any other domain of human cognition" (Doughty, 2003, p. 258).

The debate in experimental psychology has gone on since then, through empirical laboratory studies, literature reviews in journals and edited volumes, and conference panels. Space does not permit going into much detail here, so only some key references will be discussed. On the one hand, Pothos (2007), on the basis of his literature review and conceptual analysis of implicit and explicit *knowledge* of artificial grammars, comes to the conclusion that both forms of knowledge exist in parallel, or at least that different task demands lead to implicit versus explicit retrieval of the same kind of knowledge. He stresses, however, that there "has been no evidence that such rules [a rule-based representation of the artificial grammar, corresponding 'to the view of rules postulated in language (Chomsky, 1965)'] are developed in AGL [artificial grammar learning], nor a proposal for a corresponding learning mechanism" (2007, p. 239).

On the other hand, Sallas, Mathews, Lane, and Sun (2007) conclude from their experiments on implicit and explicit *learning*, also with artificial grammars, that it is important to draw learners' attention to structure, at exactly the right stage of the learning process; participants "achieved both fast and accurate string generation only if they were aided by structural (diagram) information during training and relevant information was highlighted just when it was needed" (p. 2130). These results contrast with those of Domangue et al. (2004), who managed to elicit either fast or accurate performance, but not both, depending on whether the instruction had focused on structural information (explicit knowledge) or memorization of lower-level information (implicit learning of structure). Crucial to the Sallas et al. findings were the facts that they did not quantify accuracy as the number of correct chunks in a string, but rather the number of perfect strings; that the learning of the model was facilitated through computer animation, enhancing both salience and attention; and that ample practice was provided to allow proceduralization and automatization. Similar results were found by Bitan and Karni (2004) for letter decoding and word recognition in an artificial script.

Thus, explicit learning followed by practice for proceduralization and automatization can be superior to implicit learning, even in this artificial grammar domain, which has been a favorite paradigm for demonstrating the importance of implicit learning. Sallas et al. (2007) suggest that their results have practical implications for learning in a variety of domains taught in school: "Although our artificial grammar may seem different from topics normally taught in the classroom, such findings appear consistent with research suggesting that even topics whose underlying structure is relatively explicit and salient are typically learned better with guided instruction than relatively unguided discovery learning" (p. 2132). Here, of course, the attention is shifting to the distinction between inductive versus deductive explicit learning, and the educational psychology literature on this point is increasingly in favor of deductive presentation, in spite of many attempts over the decades, with a variety of conceptual variants and different terminologies, to show advantages of inductive learning. For a particularly interesting overview on this point, see Kirschner, Sweller, and Clark (2006).

The psychological literature on artificial grammar learning and other forms of implicit learning remains hard to interpret, however, in part because of the difficulty of distinguishing a number of overlapping dichotomies used as more or less equivalent in different studies. For a very good discussion of the relationship between these dichotomies as they apply to that literature, however, see Kihlstrom et al. (2007).

Meanwhile, in the domain of second language learning, the debate about implicit and explicit learning continues as well, and there too, a consensus is gradually developing that a synergy may be at play. Contrary to the development in cognitive psychology, however, where the synergy is seen as operating on the same specific element, synergy in SLA is often conceived of as implicit learning for some elements and explicit learning for others. In John Williams' work, for instance, there are indications that form–meaning mappings are learned explicitly, while form–form mappings may be learned implicitly (see especially Williams & Lovatt, 2003); other studies by the same author, however, suggest that both have to be learned explicitly (Williams, 2003) or that even abstract form-meaning mappings can be learned implicitly (Williams, 2005). The particularly rich discussion in Williams (2005) makes it clear that much more work is needed to try to isolate the role of various potential confounding variables, such as implicit–explicit knowledge of agreement patterns (in particular gender) in other languages and the degree of "abstractness" of the meaning involved (e.g., animacy vs. proximity). Furthermore, the 2005 study used an artificial pattern learned in the context of English sentences, which may also have influenced the nature or the degree of attention that subjects paid to the form–meaning mappings in question (articles agreeing with the noun for animacy and proximity).

Williams' research, even though conducted with a "natural language" in the sense of form–meaning mappings as in any existing human language, is still based on a miniature artificial language in the sense that learners are only exposed to a very small system, with words and rules created for the experiment. In an experiment with Samoan as L2, Robinson (2005) too found evidence for different learning processes depending on the structure involved, in the sense that the relationship between the percentage correct for old items, new grammatical items, and new ungrammatical items was very different, depending on the structure involved (ergative, locative, incorporation).

Like Williams' research, Robinson's was carried out in a laboratory context. Most research on the development of implicit and explicit knowledge with classroom learners in recent years has involved different kinds of feedback, rather than the presentation aspect of instruction. Studies such as Egi (2007), R. Ellis, Loewen, and Erlam (2006), Lyster (1998a, 1988b, 2004), Mackey (2006), Mackey, Gass, and McDonough (2000), Nassaji (2007), and Sheen (2006) all point to the importance of the explicitness of feedback, along with other aspects of feedback that make it easier to notice and learn explicitly. For more information on learning from L2 feedback, see especially Leeman (2007), Mackey and Goo (2007), Nicholas, Lightbown, and Spada (2001), and Russell and Spada (2006).

Given the difficulty of defining, and especially of operationalizing implicit and explicit knowledge (see above), the issue of the relationship between implicit and explicit learning is likely to remain controversial for some time to come (R. Ellis, 2006), in the field of SLA as in cognitive psychology (see above). In the meantime, however, the preponderance of the evidence justifies N. Ellis' statement: "Many aspects of a second language are unlearnable – or at best are acquired very slowly – from implicit processes alone" (2005, p. 307).

The debate about the interface of, or overlap between, implicit and explicit knowledge extends into discussions of practice and monitoring, two areas to which we turn next.

Practice

If practice is understood as "specific activities in the second language, engaged in systematically, deliberately, with the goal of developing knowledge of and skills in the second language" (DeKeyser, 2007a, p. 8), then it is immediately clear that no discussion of practice can avoid the distinctions between implicit and explicit learning and between declarative and procedural knowledge. While there can be no doubt that the ultimate goal is to have (highly automatized) procedural L2 knowledge, this does not mean that declarative knowledge is not useful: it is a handy crutch to lean on whenever our procedural knowledge is insufficient, as is the case for early stages of learning, as well as for advanced learners who need to extend their performance into new domains or registers, or who are having occasional trouble retrieving their procedural knowledge.

Nor does the importance of procedural knowledge mean that initial learning activities should always be aimed at procedural knowledge or at implicit learning processes. It does mean, however, that extensive practice is necessary, and that this practice has to bridge the gap between the initial presentation of the L2 knowledge (in traditional deductive learning from the teacher's presentation) or the initial hypotheses formed on the basis of the input (in more inductive learning, be it implicit or explicit) and the desirable end stage of fully proceduralized grammar. It follows that this practice will take different forms, from repeated use of the same formulae in cases where little declarative knowledge is available in analyzed form (cf. e.g., Gatbonton & Segalowitz, 1988), to processing instruction (see esp. VanPatten, 2004; cf. also DeKeyser, 2007c, 2007d) where explicit rule knowledge is available but not proceduralized (especially not in comprehension), to communicative drills in cases where this knowledge needs to be proceduralized in production, and eventually to large amounts of real-life or real-life-like two-way communicative practice for automatization and integration of this know-ledge. "Slot-and-frame patterns, drills, mnemonics, and declarative statements of pedagogical grammar . . . all contribute to the conscious creation of utterances that then partake in subsequent implicit learning and proceduralization" (N. Ellis, 2005, p. 308). It is important that learners receive practice both in comprehension and production, as several laboratory studies (e.g., DeKeyser, 1997; de Jong, 2005) have shown that fluent and accurate performance in both modes for a given structure requires practice of that very structure in both modes. Besides the laboratory research by DeKeyser and de Jong, classroom research (e.g., Toth, 2006, in press) also shows the importance of production practice (and the teacher's role in bringing about procedural knowledge), and research on study abroad shows the long-term consequences of the lack of such production practice: failure to proceduralize in the classroom, which prevents automatization from the ample practice received during study abroad (DeKeyser, 2007b). (For a broader account of the importance of deliberate practice in learning advanced skills in a variety of domains, see especially Ericsson, 2006.)

Monitoring

Monitoring one's speech production is comparing one's output (or imminent output) to one's knowledge. This can be done on the basis of either explicit or implicit knowledge; Krashen referred to the former as "Monitoring" and the latter as "monitoring" or "monitoring by feel."

If monitoring is a resource-consuming process in L1 (Oomen & Postma, 2001, 2002), it is even more so in L2, especially at early stages, when much knowledge is only available in declarative form – or not at all. As long as no solid implicit knowledge has been acquired, monitoring on the basis of explicit knowledge is the only realistic possibility for the second language learner. This process takes not only knowledge, but also time and motivation, as Krashen has pointed out many times (e.g., 1982, 1985). Kormos (1999, 2000, 2006) acknowledges this, but also points out that learners are better able to monitor both form and meaning of their L2 production at the same time than much of the literature would suggest, especially learners who have received substantial explicit teaching.

Moreover, monitoring plays an essential role both in the detection of gaps in one's competence or knowledge and in the process of proceduralization and automatization, and hence, somewhat paradoxically, plays an important role in bringing about practically useful forms of knowledge, which may eventually become implicit (DeKeyser, 2007b; Izumi, 2003; Kormos, 1999; Swain, 1985, 2005; Swain & Lapkin, 1995). The importance of monitoring for the development of L2 knowledge and skill is, given its reliance on explicit knowledge, yet another argument for not minimizing the importance of explicit knowledge in the adult learner.

Knowledge consolidation: Toward robust L2 knowledge

Monitoring, whether self-induced or prompted by corrective feedback, and the ensuing proceduralization and automatization, lead to a form of knowledge where the declarative and the procedural, the implicit and the explicit, rules and items, are all interlinked in a way that is maximally efficient: highly specific procedural knowledge is drawn on for the most familiar uses of language in the most familiar circumstances; more abstract and more flexible declarative knowledge is drawn on, often seamlessly, to fill in the rest. Such integrated knowledge is not only maximally efficient at a given point in time; it is also robust over time because a certain degree of redundancy between the various components of knowledge guarantees smooth retrieval and use of the knowledge required for fluent and accurate performance, in one way or another, even if some components or subcomponents deteriorate over time because of forgetting or interference. Such robust knowledge is only possible, however, if the various components exist *and* have been used often enough in varied enough circumstances for this process of integrative use to have been solidly established.

REFERENCES

Altmann, G. T. M. (1998). Ambiguity in sentence processing. *Trends in Cognitive Sciences* 2, 4, 146–52.

Anderson, J. R. & Lebiere, C. (1998). *The atomic components of thought*. Mahwah, NJ: Lawrence Erlbaum.

Bell, A. (1984). Language style as audience design. *Language in Society* 13, 145–204.

Bialystok, E. (1979). Explicit and implicit judgements of L2 grammaticality. *Language Learning* 29, 81–103.

Bitan, T. & Karni, A. (2004). Procedural and declarative knowledge of word recognition and letter decoding in reading an artificial script. *Cognitive Brain Research* 19, 229–43.

Boland, J. (2005). Cognitive mechanisms and syntactic theory. In A. Cutler (ed.), *Twenty-first century psycholinguistics: Four cornerstones* (pp. 23–42). Mahwah, NJ: Lawrence Erlbaum.

Canale, M. & Swain, M. (1980). Theoretical bases of communicative approaches to second language teaching and testing. *Applied Linguistics* 1, 1, 8–24.

Chipere, N. (2003). *Understanding complex sentences: Native speaker variation in syntactic competence*. New York: Palgrave.

Chomsky, N. (1965). *Aspects of the theory of syntax*. Cambridge, MA: MIT Press.

de Jong, N. (2005). Can second language grammar be learned through listening? An experimental study. *Studies in Second Language Acquisition* 27, 2, 205–34.

DeKeyser, R. M. (1995). Learning second language grammar rules: An experiment with a miniature linguistic system. *Studies in Second Language Acquisition* 17(3), 379–410.

DeKeyser, R. M. (1997). Beyond explicit rule learning: Automatizing second language morphosyntax. *Studies in Second Language Acquisition* 19, 2, 195–221.

DeKeyser, R. M. (2003). Implicit and explicit learning. In C. J. Doughty & M. H. Long (eds.), *The handbook of second language acquisition* (pp. 313–48). Oxford: Blackwell.

DeKeyser, R. M. (2007a). Situating the concept of practice. In R. M. DeKeyser (ed.), *Practice in a second language: Perspectives from applied linguistics and cognitive psychology* (pp. 1–18). New York: Cambridge University Press.

DeKeyser, R. M. (2007b). Study abroad as foreign language practice. In R. M. DeKeyser (ed.), *Practice in a second language: Perspectives from applied linguistics and cognitive psychology* (pp. 208–26). New York: Cambridge University Press.

DeKeyser, R. M. (2007c). The future of practice. In R. M. DeKeyser (ed.), *Practice in a second language: Perspectives from applied linguistics and cognitive psychology* (pp. 287–304). New York, Cambridge University Press.

DeKeyser, R. M. (2007d). Skill acquisition theory. In B. VanPatten & J. Williams (eds.), *Theories in second language acquisition: An introduction* (pp. 97–112). Mahwah, NJ: Lawrence Erlbaum.

Dienes, Z. & Perner, J. (1999). A theory of implicit and explicit knowledge. *Behavioral and Brain Sciences* 22, 5, 735–55.

Doeller, C. F., Opitz, B., Krick, C., Mecklinger, A., & Reith, W. (2006). Differential hippocampal and prefrontal-striatal contributions to instance-based and rule-based learning. *NeuroImage* 31, 1802–16.

Dörnyei, Z. (2005). *The psychology of the language learner: Individual differences in second language acquisition*. Mahwah, NJ: Lawrence Erlbaum.

Domangue, T. J., Mathews, R. C., Sun, R., Roussel, L. G., & Guidry, C. E. (2004). Effects of model-based and memory-based processing on speed and accuracy of grammar string generation. *Journal of Experimental Psychology: Learning, Memory, and Cognition* 30, 1002–11.

Doughty, C. J. (2003). Instructed SLA: Constraints, compensation, and enhancement. In C. J. Doughty & M. H. Long (eds.), *The handbook of second language acquisition* (pp. 256–310). Oxford: Blackwell.

Egi, T. (2007). Interpreting recasts as linguistic evidence: The roles of linguistic target, length, and degree of change. *Studies in Second Language Acquisition* 29, 4, 511–37.

Eichenbaum, H. (2000). A cortico-hippocampal system for declarative memory. *Nature Reviews Neuroscience* 1, 41–50.

Eichenbaum, H. (2002). *The cognitive neuroscience of memory: An introduction*. New York: Oxford University Press.

Ellis, N. (2005). At the interface: Dynamic interactions of explicit and implicit language knowledge. *Studies in Second Language Acquisition* 27, 2, 305–52.

Ellis, R. (1993). The structural syllabus and second language acquisition. *TESOL Quarterly* 27, 1, 91–113.

Ellis, R. (1994). *The study of second language acquisition*. Oxford: Oxford University Press.

Ellis, R. (2004). The definition and measurement of L2 explicit knowledge. *Language Learning* 54, 2, 227–75.

Ellis, R. (2005). Measuring implicit and explicit knowledge of a second language: A psychometric study. *Studies in second language acquisition* 27, 2, 141–72.

Ellis, R. (2006). Modelling learning difficulty and second language proficiency: The differential contributions of implicit and explicit knowledge. *Applied Linguistics* 27, 3, 431–63.

Ellis, R. & Loewen, S. (2007). Confirming the operational definitions of explicit and implicit knowledge in Ellis (2005): Responding to Isemonger. *Studies in Second Language Acquisition* 29, 1, 119–26.

Ellis, R., Loewen, S., & Erlam, R. (2006). Implicit and explicit corrective feedback and the acquisition of L2 grammar. *Studies in Second Language Acquisition* 28, 2, 339–68.

Elman, J. L., Bates, E. A., Johnson, M., Karmiloff-Smith, A., Parisi, D., & Plunkett, K. (1996). *Rethinking innateness: A connectionist perspective on development*. Cambridge, MA: MIT Press.

Ericsson, K. A. (2006). The influence of experience and deliberate practice on the development of superior expert performance. In K. A. Ericsson et al. (eds.), *The Cambridge handbook of expertise and expert performance* (pp. 683–703). New York: Cambridge University Press.

Escudero, P. & Boersma, P. (2004). Bridging the gap between L2 speech perception research and phonological theory. *Studies in Second Language Acquisition* 26, 4, 551–85.

Fletcher, P., Büchel, C., Josephs, O., Friston, K., & Dolan, R. J. (1999). Learning-related neuronal responses in preferontal cortex studies with functional neuroimaging. *Cerebral Cortex* 9, 168–78.

Frazier, L. (1987). Sentence processing: A tutorial review. In M. Coltheart (ed.), *Attention and performance 12: The psychology of reading* (pp. 559–86). Mahwah, NJ: Lawrence Erlbaum.

Gatbonton, E. & Segalowitz, N. (1988). Creative automatization: Principles for promoting fluency within a communicative framework. *TESOL Quarterly* 22, 3, 473–92.

Gibson, E. (1998). Linguistic complexity: Locality of syntactic dependencies. *Cognition* 68, 1–76.

Golonka, E. M. (2006). Predictors revisited: Linguistic knowledge and metalinguistic awareness in second language gain in Russian. *The Modern Language Journal* 90, 4, 496–505.

Gombert, J.-E. (1992). *Metalinguistic development*. Chicago, IL, Chicago University Press.

Green, P. & Hecht, K. (1992). Implicit and explicit grammar: An empirical study. *Applied Linguistics* 13, 168–84.

Hall, J. K., Cheng, A., & Carlson, M. (2006). Reconceptualizing multicompetence as a theory of language knowledge. *Applied Linguistics* 27, 2, 220–40.

Hernandez, A. E. & Meschyan, G. (2006). Executive function is necessary to enhance lexical processing in a less proficient L2: Evidence from fMRI during picture naming. *Bilingualism: Language and cognition* 9, 2, 177–88.

Hu, G. (2002). Psychological constraints on the utility of metalinguistic knowledge in second language production. *Studies in Second Language Acquisition* 24, 3, 347–86.

Huang, C.-T. (1982). *Logical relations in Chinese and the theory of grammar*. Cambridge, MA: MIT Press.

Hulstijn, J. (2002). Towards a unified account of the representation, acquisition, and automatization of second-language knowledge. *Second Language Research* 18, 3, 193–223.

Hulstijn, J. & Hulstijn, W. (1984). Grammatical errors as a function of processing constraints and explicit knowledge. *Language Learning* 34, 23–43.

Hymes, D. (1972). On communicative competence. In J. B. Pride & J. Holmes (eds.), *Sociolinguistics* (pp. 269–93). Harmondsworth, UK: Penguin.

Isemonger, I. M. (2007). Operational definitions of explicit and implicit knowledge: Response to R. Ellis (2005) and some recommendations for future research in this area. *Studies in Second Language Acquisition* 29, 1, 101–18.

Izumi, S. (2003). Comprehension and production processes in second language learning: In search of the psycholinguistic rationale of the output hypothesis. *Applied Linguistics* 24, 2, 168–96.

Jiang, N. (2004). Morphological insensitivity in second language processing. *Applied Psycholinguistics* 25, 4, 603–34.

Jiang, N. (2007). Selective integration of linguistic knowledge in adult second language learning. *Language Learning* 57, 1, 1–33.

Juffs, A. (1998). The acquisition of semantics-syntax correspondences and verb frequencies in EL materials. *Language Teaching Research* 2, 2, 93–123.

Juffs, A. (2004). Representation, processing and working memory in a second language. *Transactions of the Philological Society* 102, 2, 199–225.

Juffs, A. & Harrington, M. (1995). Parsing effects in second language sentence processing: Subject and object asymmetries in wh-extraction. *Studies in Second Language Acquisition* 17, 4, 483–516.

Karmiloff-Smith, A. (1992). *Beyond modularity: A developmental perspective on cognitive science.* Cambridge, MA: MIT Press.

Kihlstrom, J. F., Dorfman, J., & Park, L. (2007). Implicit and explicit memory and learning. In M. Velmans & S. Schneider (eds.), *The Blackwell companion to consciousness* (pp. 525–39). Oxford: Blackwell.

Kirschner, P. A., Sweller, J., & Clark, R. E. (2006). Why minimal guidance during instruction does not work: An analysis of the failure of constructivist, discovery, problem-based, experiential, and inquiry-based teaching. *Educational Psychologist* 41, 2, 75–86.

Kormos, J. (1999). Monitoring and self-repair in L2. *Language Learning* 49, 2, 303–42.

Kormos, J. (2000). The role of attention in monitoring second language speech production. *Language Learning* 50, 2, 343–84.

Kormos, J. (2006). *Speech production and second language acquisition.* Mahwah, N: Lawrence Erlbaum.

Krashen, S. D. (1982). *Principles and practice in second language acquisition.* Englewood Cliffs, NJ: Prentice-Hall.

Krashen, S. D. (1985). *The input hypothesis.* London/New York: Longman.

Leeman, J. (2007). Feedback in L2 learning: Responding to errors during practice. In R. DeKeyser (ed.), *Practice in a second language: Perspectives from applied linguistics and cognitive psychology* (pp. 111–37). New York: Cambridge University Press.

Lieberman, M., Aoshima, S., & Phillips, C. (2006). Nativelike biases in generation of wh-questions by nonnative speakers of Japanese. *Studies in Second Language Acquisition* 28, 3, 423–48.

Lyster, R. (1998a). Negotiation of form, recasts, and explicit correction in relation to error types and learner repair in immersion classrooms. *Language Learning* 48, 2, 183–218.

Lyster, R. (1998b). Recasts, repetition, and ambiguity in L2 classroom discourse. *Studies in Second Language Acquisition* 20, 1, 51–81.

Lyster, R. (2004). Differential effects of prompts and recasts in form-focused instruction. *Studies in Second Language Acquisition* 26, 3, 399–432.

Mackey, A. (2006). Feedback, noticing, and instructed second language learning. *Applied Linguistics* 27, 3, 405–30.

Mackey, A., Gass, S., & McDonough, K. (2000). How do learners perceive interactional feedback? *Studies in Second Language Acquisition* 22, 4, 471–99.

Mackey, A. & Goo, J. (2007). Interaction research in SLA: A meta-analysis and research synthesis. In A. Mackey (ed.), *Conversational interaction in second language acquisition* (pp. 407–52). New York: Oxford University Press.

Macrory, G. & Stone, V. (2000). Pupil progress in the acquisition of the perfect tense in French: The relationship between knowledge and use. *Language Teaching Research* 4, 1, 55–82.

McClelland, J. L. & Patterson, K. (2002a). "Words OR rules" cannot exploit the regularity in exceptions. *Trends in Cognitive Sciences* 6, 11, 464–5.

McClelland, J. L. & Patterson, K. (2002b). Rules or connections in past-tense inflections: What does the evidence rule out? *Trends in Cognitive Sciences* 6, 11, 465–72.

McNamara, T. F. (1995). Modelling performance: Opening Pandora's box. *Applied Linguistics* 16, 2, 159–79.

Morgan-Short, K., Steinhauer, K., Sanz, C., & Ullman, M. T. (2007). An ERP investigation of second language processing: Effects of proficiency and explicit and implicit training. *Journal of Cognitive Neuroscience* (Supplement), 164.

Mueller, J. L., Hahne, A., Fujii, Y., & Friederici, A. G. (2005). Native and nonnative speakers' processing of a miniature version of Japanese as revealed by ERPs. *Journal of Cognitive Neuroscience* 17, 8, 1229–44.

Myles, F. (2004). From data to theory: The over-representation of linguistic knowledge in SLA. *Proceedings of the National Academy of Sciences, USA* 102, 2, 139–68.

Myles, F., Hooper, J., & Mitchell, R. (1998). Rote or rule? Exploring the role of formulaic language in classroom foreign language learning. *Language Learning* 48, 3, 323–63.

Nassaji, H. (2007). Elicitation and reformulation and their relationship with learner repair in student-teacher dyadic interaction. *Language Learning* 57, 4, 511–48.

Nicholas, H., Lightbown, P. M., & Spada, N. (2001). Recasts as feedback to language learners. *Language Learning* 51, 4, 719–58.

Oomen, C. C. E. & Postma, A. (2001). Effects of time pressure on mechanisms of speech production and self-monitoring. *Journal of Psycholinguistic Research* 30, 2, 163–84.

Oomen, C. C. E. & Postma, A. (2002). Limitations in processing resources and speech monitoring. *Language and Cognitive Processes* 17, 2, 163–84.

Opitz, B. & Friederici, A. D. (2003). Interactions of the hippocampal system and the prefrontal cortex in learning language-like rules. *NeuroImage* 19, 1730–7.

Opitz, B. & Friederici, A. D. (2004). Brain correlates of language learning: The neural dissociation of rule-based vs. similarity-based learning. *Journal of Neuroscience* 24, 8436–40.

Pesetsky, D. (1987). Wh-in-situ: Movement and unselective binding. In E. Reuland & A. G. B. ter Meulen (eds.), *The representation of indefiniteness* (pp. 98–129). Cambridge, MA: MIT Press.

Pinker, S. (1999). *Words and rules: The ingredients of language.* New York: Basic Books.

Pinker, S. & Prince, A. (1988). On language and connectionism: Analysis of a parallel distributed processing model of language acquisition. In S. Pinker & J. Mehler (eds.), *Connections and symbols* (pp. 73–193). Cambridge, MA: MIT Press.

Pinker, S. & Ullman, M. T. (2002a). The past and future of the past tense. *Trends in Cognitive Sciences* 6, 11, 456–63.

Pinker, S. & Ullman, M. T. (2002b). Combination and structure, not gradedness, is the issue. *Trends in Cognitive Sciences* 6, 11, 472–4.

Poldrack, R. A., Clark, J., Paré-Blagoev, E. J., et al. (2001). Interactive memory systems in the human brain. *Nature* 414, 546–9.

Poldrack, R. A. & Gabrieli, J. D. E. (2001). Characterizing the neural mechanisms of skill learning and repetition priming: Evidence from mirror reading. *Brain* 124, 67–82.

Pothos, E. M. (2007). Theories of artificial grammar learning. *Psychological Bulletin* 133, 2, 227–44.

Pritchett, B. L. (1992). *Grammatical competence and parsing performance*. Chicago, IL: University of Chicago Press.

Renou, J. M. (2000). Learner accuracy and learner performance: The quest for a link. *Foreign Language Annals* 33, 168–80.

Rizzi, L. (1982). *Issues in Italian syntax*. Dordrecht: Foris.

Robinson, P. (2005). Cognitive abilities, chunk-strength and frequency effects in implicit artificial grammar and incidental L2 learning: replications of Reber, Walkenfield and Hernstadt (1991) and Knowlton and Squire (1996) and their Relevance for SLA. *Studies in Second Language Acquisition* 27, 2, 235–68.

Rumelhart, D. & McClelland, J. (1986). On learning the past tenses of English verbs. In J. McClelland, D. Rumelhart, & PDP Research Group (eds.), *Parallel distributed processing*, vol. 2: *Psychological and biological models* (pp. 217–71). Cambridge, MA: MIT Press.

Russell, J. & Spada, N. (2006). The effectiveness of corrective feedback for the acquisition of L2 grammar: A meta-analysis of the research. In J. Norris & L. Ortega (eds.), *Synthesizing research on language learning and teaching* (pp. 133–64). Philadelphia/Amsterdam: John Benjamins.

Sallas, B., Mathews, R. C., Lane, S., & Sun, R. (2007). Developing rich and quickly accessed knowledge of an artificial grammar. *Memory and Cognition* 35, 8, 2118–33.

Schmitt, N. (ed.) (2004). *Formulaic sequences*. Philadelphia. Benjamins.

Schulz, R. A. (2002). Hilft es die Regel zu wissen um sie anzuwenden? Das Verhältnis von metalinguistischem Bewusstsein und grammatischer Kompetenz in DaF. *Die Unterrichtspraxis* 35, 1, 15–24.

Sebastián-Gallés, N. & Soto-Faraco, S. (1999). On-line processing of native and non-native contrasts in early bilinguals. *Cognition* 72, 111–23.

Segalowitz, N. & Frenkiel-Fishman, S. (2005). Attention control and ability level in a complex cognitive skill: Attention shifting and second-language proficiency. *Memory and cognition* 33, 644–53.

Segalowitz, N. & Hulstijn, J. (2005). Automaticity in bilingualism and second language learning. In J. F. Kroll & A. M. B. de Groot (eds.), *Handbook of bilingualism: Psycholinguistic perspectives* (pp. 371–88). Oxford: Oxford University Press.

Sheen, Y. (2006). Exploring the relationship between characteristics of recasts and learner uptake. *Language Teaching Research* 10, 4, 361–92.

Sorace, A. (2003). Near-nativeness. In C. J. Doughty & M. H. Long (eds.), *The handbook of second language acquisition* (pp. 130–51). Oxford: Blackwell.

Squire, L. (1992). Memory and the hippocampus: A synthesis from findings with rats, monkeys, and humans. *Psychological Review* 99, 2, 195–231.

Squire, L. R. & Kandel, E. R. (1999). *Memory: From mind to molecules*. New York: Scientific American.

Squire, L. R. & Knowlton, B. J. (2000). The medial temporal lobe, the hippocampus, and the memory systems of the brain. In M. S. Gazzaniga (ed.), *The new cognitive neurosciences* (pp. 765–79). Cambridge, MA: MIT Press.

Squire, L. R. & Zola, S. M. (1996). Structure and function of declarative and nondeclarative memory systems. *Proceedings of the National Academy of Sciences, USA* 93, 13515–22.

Sunderman, G. & Kroll, J. F. (2006). First language activation during second language lexical processing: An investigation of lexical form, meaning, and grammatical class. *Studies in Second Language Acquisition* 28, 3, 387–422.

Swain, M. (1985). Communicative competence: some roles of comprehensible input and comprehensible output in its development. In S. M. Gass & C. G. Madden (eds.), *Input in second language acquisition* (pp. 235–53). Rowley, MA: Newbury House.

Swain, M. (2005). The output hypothesis: Theory and research. In E. Hinkel (ed.), *Handbook of research in second language teaching and learning* (pp. 471–83). Mahwah, NJ: Lawrence Erlbaum.

Swain, M. & Lapkin, S. (1995). Problems in output and the cognitive processes they generate: A step towards second language learning. *Applied Linguistics* 16, 3, 371–91.

Tarone, E. (1983). On the variability of interlanguage systems. *Applied Linguistics* 4, 2, 143–63.

Taylor, D. S. (1988). The meaning and use of the term "competence" in linguistics and applied linguistics. *Applied Linguistics* 9, 2, 148–68.

Tokowicz, N. & MacWhinney, B. (2005). Implicit and explicit measures of sensitivity to violations in second language grammar: An event-related potential investigation. *Studies in Second Language Acquisition* 27, 2, 173–204.

Toth, P. (2006). Processing instruction and a role for output in second language acquisition. *Language Learning* 56, 2, 319–85.

Toth, P. (in press). Teacher- and learner-led discourse in task-based grammar instruction: Providing procedural assistance for L2 morphosyntactic development. *Language Learning*.

Trenkic, D. (2007). Variability in second language article production: Beyond the representational deficit vs. processing constraints debate. *Second Language Research* 23, 3, 289–327.

Ullman, M. T. (2001). A neurocognitive perspective on language: The declarative/procedural model. *Nature Reviews: Neuroscience* 2, 717–26.

Ullman, M. T. (2004). Contributions of memory circuits to language: The declarative/procedural model. *Cognition* 92, 231–70.

Ullman, M. (2005). A cognitive neuroscience perspective on second language acquisition: The declarative/procedural model. In C. Sanz (ed.), *Mind and context in adult second language acquisition* (pp. 141–78). Washington, DC: Georgetown University Press.

VanPatten, B. (ed.) (2004). *Processing instruction: Theory, research, and commentary*. Mahwah, NJ: Lawrence Earlbaum.

Williams, J. N. (2003). Inducing abstract linguistic representations: Human and connectionist learning of noun classes. In R. van Hout, A. Hulk, F. Kuiken, & R. Towell (eds.), *The interface between syntax and the lexicon in second language acquisition* (pp. 151–74). Amsterdam: Benjamins.

Williams, J. N. (2005). Learning without awareness. *Studies in Second Language Acquisition* 27, 2, 269–304.

Williams, J. N. & Lovatt, P. (2003). Phonological memory and rule learning. *Language Learning* 53, 1, 67–121.

Williams, J. N., Möbius, P., & Kim, C. (2001). Native and non-native processing of English wh-questions: Parsing strategies and plausibility constraints. *Applied Psycholinguistics* 22, 4, 509–40.

Wray, A. (2001). *Formulaic language and the lexicon*. New York: Cambridge University Press.

Zyzik, E. (2006). Transitivity alternations and sequence learning: Insights from L2 Spanish production data. *Studies in Second Language Acquisition* 28, 3, 449–85.

9 Optimizing the Input: Frequency and Sampling in Usage-Based and Form-Focused Learning

NICK C. ELLIS

Estimating How Language Works: From Tokens to Types to System

Learners' understanding of language and of how it works is based upon their experience of language. They have to estimate the system from a sample. This chapter considers the effects of input sample, construction frequency, and processing orientation on learning. It draws out implications for usage-based acquisition and form-focused instruction for second (L2) and foreign (FL) language learners.

A language is not a fixed system. It varies in usage over speakers, places, and time. Yet despite the fact that no two speakers own an identical language, communication is possible to the degree that they share constructions (form–meaning correspondences) relevant to their discourse.[1] Language learners have to acquire these constructions from usage, and beginners don't have much to go on in building the foundations for basic interpersonal communication. They have to induce the types of construction from experience of a limited number of tokens. Their very limited exposure poses them the task of *estimating* how linguistic constructions work from an input sample that is incomplete, uncertain, and noisy. How do they achieve this, and what types of experience can best support the process?

Nativelike fluency, idiomaticity, and selection are another level of difficulty again. For a good fit, every utterance has to be chosen, from a wide range of possible expressions, to be appropriate for that idea, for that speaker, for that place, and for that time. And again, learners can only *estimate* this from their finite experience. What are the best usage histories to support these abilities?

Language, a moving target, can neither be described nor experienced comprehensively, and so, in essence, *language learning is estimation from sample*. Like other estimation problems, successful determination of the population characteristics is a matter of statistical sampling, description, and inference. For language learning the estimations include: What is the range of constructions in the language? What are their major types? Which are the really useful ones? What is their relative frequency distribution? How do they map function and form, and how reliably? How can this information best be organized to allow its appropriate and fluent access in recognition and production? Are there variable ways of expressing similar meanings? How are they distributed across different contexts? And so on. Et cetera. And so forth. Like.

Frequency of usage, in various guises, determines acquisition (Ellis, 2002a, 2002b). There are three fundamental aspects of this conception of language learning as statistical sampling and estimation:

- The first and foremost concerns *sample size*: As in all surveys, the bigger the sample, the more accurate the estimates, but also the greater the costs. Native speakers estimate their language over a lifespan of usage. L2 and FL learners just don't have that much time or resource. Thus, both of these *additional language* (AL) learner groups are faced with a task of optimizing their estimates of language from a limited sample of exposure. Broadly, power analysis dictates that attaining nativelike fluency and idiomaticity requires much larger usage samples than does basic interpersonal communicative competence in predictable contexts. But for the particulars, what sort of sample is needed adequately to assess the workings of constructions of, respectively, high, medium, and low base occurrence rates, of more categorical versus more fuzzy patterns, of regular versus irregular systems, of simple versus complex "rules," of dense versus sparse neighbourhoods, et cetera?

- The second concerns *sample selection*: Principles of survey design dictate that a sample must properly represent the strata of the population of greatest concern. Thus, *Needs Analysis* (Brown, this volume) is relevant to all AL learners. Thus, too, the truism that FL learners, who have much more limited access to the authentic natural source language than L2 learners, are going to have greater problems of adequate description. But what about learning particular constructions? What is the best sample of experience to support this? How many examples do we need? In what proportion of types and tokens? Are there better sequences of experience to optimize estimation? What learning increment comes from each experience? Is this a constant or does it diminish over time as dictated by the power law of practice? And so forth.

- A final implication of language acquisition as estimation concerns *sampling history*: How does knowledge of some cues and constructions affect estimation of the function of others? What is the best sequence of language to promote learning new constructions? And what is the best processing orientation to make this sample of language the appropriate sample of usage? Like.

This chapter first describes the units of language acquisition – linguistic constructions – and then considers how sample size and sample selection affect the development of constructions (their consolidation, generalization, and probabilistic tuning) from naturalistic input. There are established effects of input token frequency, type frequency, Zipfian frequency distribution[2] of the construction-family, and neighborhood homogeneity.

Next, it describes how sample size and sample selection affect usage-based language acquisition across the board – native and AL both. It reviews how learners' models of language broadly reflect the constructions in their sample of experience and how they unconsciously tally and collate a rich knowledge of the relative frequencies of these constructions in their input history. Because language learning is less an issue of the collection of linguistic constructions than of their cataloguing, organization, and marshalling for efficient appropriate use, this *implicit* knowledge is essential to fluent processing. In order for the estimation procedures rationally to produce a model of the language that optimizes the probabilistic knowledge of constructions and their mappings, learners must be exposed to a representative sample of authentic input that is appropriate to their needs. The chapter also considers the implications of modularity and transfer-appropriate processing for tuning the full range of necessary representative modalities and functions of usage.

Finally it nods at analyses of transfer in AL acquisition, how prior estimation of L1 biases the usage-based estimation of an AL, and why form-focused instruction may be necessary to reset some counters to tally the L2 more appropriately.

The Units of Language Acquisition

Construction Grammar (Goldberg, 1995, 2003, 2006; Tomasello, 2003) and other *Cognitive Linguistic* theories of first (Croft & Cruise, 2004; Langacker, 1987; Taylor, 2002; Tomasello, 1998) and second language (Robinson & Ellis, 2008b) acquisition hold that the basic units of language representation are *constructions*. These are form–meaning mappings, conventionalized in the speech community, and entrenched as language knowledge in the learner's mind. Constructions vary in specificity and in complexity, including morphemes (*anti-, -ing,* N-*s*), words (*aardvark, and*), complex words (*antediluvian, multimorphemic*), idioms (*hit the jackpot*), semi-productive patterns (*Good <time of day>*), and syntactic patterns [Subj [V Obj$_1$ Obj$_2$]]; [Subj *be-* Tns V -*en by* Ob$_1$]. Hence morphology, lexicon, and syntax are uniformly represented in Construction Grammar. Constructions are symbolic, in that their defining properties of morphological, lexical, and syntactic form are associated with particular semantic, pragmatic, and discourse functions. Constructions form a structured inventory of a speaker's knowledge of the conventions of their language, where schematic constructions can be abstracted over the less schematic ones, which are inferred inductively by the speaker in acquisition. A construction may provide a partial specification of the structure of an utterance; hence, an utterance's structure is specified by a number of distinct constructions. Constructions are independently represented units in a speaker's mind. Any construction with unique, idiosyncratic formal or functional properties must be represented independently in order to capture a speaker's knowledge of their language. However, absence of any unique property of a construction does not entail that it is not represented independently and simply derived from other, more general or schematic constructions. Frequency of occurrence may lead to independent representation of even "regular" constructional patterns.

Acquiring Constructions

Usage-based theories of naturalistic language acquisition hold that we learn language through using language. Creative linguistic competence emerges from learners' piecemeal acquisition of the many thousands of constructions experienced in communication, and from their frequency-biased abstraction of the regularities in this history of usage. Competence and performance both *emerge* from the conspiracy of memorized exemplars of construction usage, with competence being the integrated sum of prior usage and performance its dynamic contextualized activation (Ellis, 1998, 2003, 2006a, 2007; Ellis & Larsen Freeman, 2006).

Many of the constructions we know are quite specific, formulaic utterances based on particular lexical items, ranging, for example, from a simple "Wonderful!" to increasingly complex phrases like "One, two, three," "Once upon a time," or "Won the battle, lost the war." These sequential patterns of sound, like words, are acquired as a result of chunking from repeated usage (Ellis, 1996; Pawley & Syder, 1983; Wray, 2002). In building up these sequences, learners bind together the chunks that they already know, with high-frequency sequences being more strongly bound than lower-frequency ones (Ellis, 2002a). In analyzing these sequences, the highest-frequency chunks stand out as the most likely constituents of the parse. The constructions already acquired by the learner constitute the sample of evidence from which they implicitly and explicitly identify regularities, so generalizing their knowledge by inducing unconscious schemata and prototypes that map meaning and form, and by abducing conscious metalinguistic hypotheses about language, too. These are the foundations, then, of new expressions and new understandings.

Constructionist approaches to language acquisition (Bybee & Hopper, 2001; Goldberg, 2003; Robinson & Ellis, 2008b; Tomasello, 1998, 2003) thus emphasize piecemeal learning from concrete exemplars. A high proportion of children's early multi-word speech is produced from a developing set of slot-and-frame patterns. These patterns are often based around chunks of one or two words or phrases, and they have "slots" into which the child can place a variety of words, for instance subgroups of nouns or verbs (e.g., *I can't* + VERB; *where's* + NOUN + *gone?*). Children are very productive with these patterns, and both the number of patterns and their structure develop over time. But initially, they are lexically specific. For example, if a child has two patterns, *I can't* + X and *I don't* + X, the verbs used in these two X slots typically show little or no overlap, suggesting (1) that the patterns are not yet related through an underlying grammar (the child doesn't "know" that *can't* and *don't* are both auxiliaries or that the words that appear in the patterns all belong to a category of Verb), and (2) that learners are picking up frequent patterns from what they hear around them and only slowly making more abstract generalizations as the database of related utterances grows (Pine & Lieven, 1993; Pine, Lieven, & Rowland, 1998; Tomasello, 1992). Tomasello's (1992) *Verb Island* hypothesis holds that it is verbs and relational terms that are the individual islands of organization in young children's otherwise unorganized grammatical system: the child initially learns about arguments and syntactic markings on a verb-by-verb basis, and ordering patterns and morphological markers learned for one verb do not immediately generalize to other verbs. Positional analysis of each verb island requires memories of the verb's usage, the exemplars of its collocations, and the constructions it commonly inhabits. Over experience, syntagmatic categories emerge from the regularities in this data set, the learner's sample of language.

The chapters in Robinson and Ellis (2008b) extend these cognitive linguistic/construction grammar theories of child language acquisition to the naturalistic acquisition of ALs in adulthood, so developing a usage-based approach to SLA. Some of the key features are as follows.

Frequency and the Roles of Input

AL Learners' knowledge of a linguistic construction depends, too, on their experience of its use, the sample of its manifestations of usage. Different frequencies of exemplification, and different types of repetition of a linguistic pattern, have different effects upon acquisition – the consolidation, generalization, and productive use of constructions. A key separation is between type and token frequency.

Type and token frequency

The token frequency of a construction is how often in the input that particular word or specific phrase appears; we can count in a sample corpus the token frequency of any specific form (e.g., the syllable [ka], the trigram *aze*, the word *frog*, the phrase *on the whole*, the sentence *I love you*). Type frequency, on the other hand, is the calculation of how many different lexical items a certain pattern, paradigm, or construction applies to, i.e., the number of distinct lexical items that can be substituted in a given slot in a construction, whether it is a word-level construction for inflection or a syntactic construction specifying the relation among words. For example, the "regular" English past tense *-ed* has a very high type frequency because it applies to thousands of different types of verbs, whereas the vowel change exemplified in *swam* and *rang* has much lower type frequency. Similarly the prepositional transfer construction [Subj [V ObjDir *to* ObjInd]] has a high type frequency (*give, read, pass, donate, display, explain . . .*) because many different verbs can be used in this way, whereas the ditransitive alternative [Subj [V ObjInd ObjDir]] is only used with a small set of verbs like *give, read,* and *pass* and not others (**donate, *display, *explain*).

Consolidating a particular formulaic construction: The role of token frequency

Like other concrete constructions, a word *can* be sketchily learned from a single exposure, as a *fast mapping* (Carey & Bartlett, 1978), a relation between an approximation of its sound and its likely meaning, forged as an explicit episodic memory relating its form and the perception of its likely referent (Ellis, 2005). The hippocampus and limbic structures in the brain allow us such unitary bindings from single experiences, rapid explicit memory, one-off learning, the establishment of new conjunctions of arbitrarily different elements (Ellis, 2002b; Squire, 1992), the learning of separate discrete episodes – what you saw across the field as your friend said *gavagai* or the particular color of tray that accompanied hearing *chromium* for the first time. There is benefit in being able to keep such episodic records distinct. But fast mappings are rough, ready, fragile, and, without reiteration, often transient. Repetition strengthens memories (Ebbinghaus, 1885), and there are clearly defined effects of frequency, spacing, and distribution of practice in the consolidation, elaboration, and explicit learning of foreign-language vocabulary, both naturalistically and from flash-cards, CALL programs, and the like (Ellis, 1995).

Repeated processing of a particular construction facilitates its fluency of subsequent processing, too, and these effects occur whether the learner is conscious of this processing or not. Your reading of the various occurrences of the word *chunk* in this chapter so far has primed the subsequent reading of this word and contributed to your lifetime usage practice of it, despite the fact that you cannot remember where in the text these occurrences fell. Although you are conscious of words in your visual focus, you definitely did not just now consciously label the word *focus* as a noun. On reading it, you were surely unaware of its nine alternative meanings, though in a different sentence you would instantly have brought a different meaning to mind. What happens to the other meanings? Psycholinguistic evidence demonstrates that some of them exist unconsciously for a few tenths of a second before your brain decides on the right one. Most words (over 80 percent in English) have multiple meanings, but only one of these can become conscious at a time. So your reading of *focus* has primed subsequent reading of that letter string (whatever its interpretation), and your interpretation of *focus* as a noun has primed that particular subsequent interpretation of it. In this way, particular constructions (e.g., [ba], *ave, kept, man, dead boring, on the whole, I love you*, [wʌn] = 'one') with high token frequency are remembered better, recognized faster, produced more readily and otherwise processed with greater facility than low token frequency constructions (e.g., [za], *aze, leapt, artichoke, sublimely boring, on the organelle, I venerate you*, [wʌn] = won) (see Ellis, 2002a for review). Each token of use thus strengthens the memory traces of a construction, priming its subsequent use and accessibility following the power law of practice relationship, whereby the increase in strength afforded by early increments of experience is greater than that from later additional practice. In these ways, language learning involves considerable unconscious "tallying" (Ellis, 2002a) of construction frequencies, and language use requires exploitation of this implicit statistical knowledge (Bod, Hay, & Jannedy, 2003; Bybee & Hopper, 2001; Chater & Manning, 2006).

High token repetition is said to *entrench* constructions (Langacker, 1987), protecting them from change. Thus it is that it is the high frequency past tenses in English that are irregular (*went, was, kept*), their ready accessibility holding off the forces of regularization from the default paradigm (**goed, *beed, *keeped*), whereas neighbors of lower frequency eventually succumb (with *leaped* starting to rival *leapt* in usage). Bybee (2008) calls this the *conserving* function of high token frequency. High token frequency also leads to *autonomy*, whereby creative constructions learned by rote may never be analyzed into their constituent units, e.g., learners may never have considered that *gimme* consists of *give* + *me*, nor the literal roots of a *dicey situation*. Finally, considerable practice with a particular token also results in automaticity of production and processes of reduction, assimilation, and lenition involving loss and overlap of gestures. A maxim of Bybee (2003, p. 112), on a variant of Hebb's "Cells that fire together wire together," is that "Items that are used together fuse together." The phenomenon is entirely graded – the degree of reduction is a continuous function of the frequency of the target word and the conditional probability of the target given the previous word and that of the target given the next word (Bybee & Hopper, 2001; Ellis, 2002a; Jurafsky et al., 2001). Such changes underpin grammaticalization in language change (Bybee, 2000; Croft, 2000).

In sum, although a particular construction *can* be roughly learned from a single exposure, multiple repetitions of that same token in different contexts are needed to enmesh and elaborate it into the meaning system – to turn it from a fast-mapped, tentative working hypothesis to a more complete, rich representation of the full connotations of a word (Carey & Bartlett, 1978). For example, it has been estimated that between 8 and 12 encounters are needed of a novel word in text before its meaning will be adequately comprehended from inference and its form and meaning retained (Horst, Cobb, & Meara, 1998; Saragi, Nation, & Meister, 1978). Multiple repetitions are also necessary for entrenched representation, ready accessibility, automatized processing, idiomatic autonomy, and fast, fluent, and phonetically reduced production.

Generalizing a construction from formula to limited scope pattern to productive abstract schema: The role of type frequency

The productivity of phonological, morphological, and syntactic patterns is a function of their type rather than token frequency (Bybee, 1995; Bybee & Hopper, 2001). Type frequency determines productivity because: (1) The more lexical items that are heard in a certain position in a construction, the less likely it is that the construction is associated with a particular lexical item and the more likely it is that a general category is formed over the items that occur in that position. As novel exemplars are added in memory, they affect the category too, their features resonate with the whole population, adding their weight to the prototype, and stretching the bounds slightly in their direction. (2) The more items the category must cover, the more general are its criterial features and the more likely it is to extend to new items. (3) High type frequency ensures that a construction is used frequently, thus strengthening its representational schema and making it more accessible for further use with new items (Bybee & Thompson, 2000).

When a construction is variously experienced with different items occupying a position, it allows the parsing of its schematic structure. Having an initial formulaic exemplar of the Caused-Motion construction [Subj V Obj Prep Obl$_{path/loc}$], perhaps *she pushed it down the road*, subsequent experience of *she pushed it ((up) the hill)*, *she pushed it ((to) the service station)*, *she pushed it ((to) the gas pump)* allows identification of the common components, their structural commonalities, and their regularities of reference. Common items (pronouns like *she, he, I*, rather than complex noun phrases *Mrs Struthers, the miraculous moose, the distressed driver*, etc.; high frequency prepositions like *to, up, down*, etc., rather than complex locatives *Alabama-way, paralleling the path of flight*, etc.) repeat more in these slots and thus help to bring out the commonalities of the adjacent slot-fillers. Braine (1987) showed in experiments involving the learning of artificial languages that it was relatively easy to learn "categories" and rules for combining them, providing the "words" exemplifying these categories were either preceded or followed by a fixed item. Otherwise, the categories were difficult or impossible to learn. In natural language, it is the grammatical words that often serve as anchors like this. It is the closed class "little words," the grammatical functors, that have both the highest frequency in the language and the highest connectivity or *degree*. When the sequential co-occurrences of words in discourse are described in terms of graphs of word connections, mapping the interactions like social networks, the world wide web, or other complex systems, these graphs show so-called small-world properties of being highly clustered and richly interconnected (Ferrer i Cancho & Solé, 2001; Ferrer i Cancho, Solé, & Köhler, 2004). Despite having many thousands of nodes (the > 450,000 words populating a language), the average number of jumps in the path needed to get from any word to any other in this graph is remarkably small, at less than three. A small number of highly connected words allows these properties. And it is the function words, the prepositions, pronouns, determiners, etc., that do this, having *both* high token frequency and high degree of connectivity.[3]

So, these highest frequency components and chunks are the recurrent constituents of the construction that anchor its parse: as sub-unit constructions with high token frequency, they are recognized faster, produced more readily and otherwise processed with greater facility than low token frequency constructions, and, thus, they outline and bracket the schematic structure of the construction more readily. In 11-month-old infants, it is these frequently occurring functor forms that serve as a framework against which potential candidates for vocabulary membership may be identified and extracted from the speech stream (Shi et al.,

2006). In these ways, although verb islands predominate in seeding generalizations, patterns based on other high frequency lexical types, such as bound
morphemes, auxiliary verbs and case-marking pronouns ("pronoun islands"),
are also important in the parsing and identification of the schematic structure of
constructions (Childers & Tomasello, 2001; McClure, Lieven, & Pine, in press;
Pine, Lieven, & Rowland, 1998; Wilson, 2003).[4] In growth, too, these are the
high-degree nodes of the kernel lexicon of the language network, to which new
sub-unit constructions are preferentially attached, allowing scale-free growth
distribution according to the so-called Barbarási-Albert model (Barbarási & Albert,
1999; Ferrer i Cancho & Solé, 2001).

Chunking is a ubiquitous feature of human learning and memory. Chunking
affords the ability to build up structures recursively, with the embedding of small
chunks within larger ones leading to a hierarchical organization in nature (Simon,
1962, see particularly his parable of the two watchmakers, Hora and Tempus), in
memory (Newell, 1990), and in the hierarchies and tree structures of grammar
(Bybee, 2003; Ellis, 1996, 2003). In these ways, constituent structure is emergent,
with constructions as grammatical schemata at all levels of specificity (from very
specific (*my chapter*), through limited scope (*my* + NOUN), more general (POS-
SESSIVE + NOUN), to fully general (DETERMINER + NOUN)) emerging from
the conspiracy of component constructions whose commonalities, in turn, are defined by their inclusion in the networks of other constructions (Bybee, 2003, 2008).

Functional motivations

Constructions are useful because of the symbolic functions that they serve. It is
their communicative functions, semantic, pragmatic, or discursive, that motivate
their learning. Goldberg (1995) claims that verb-centered constructions are more
likely to be salient in the input because they relate to certain fundamental perceptual primitives, and, thus, that this construction of grammar involves in parallel
the distributional analysis of the language stream and the analysis of contingent
perceptual activity. It has been argued that basic level categories (e.g., hammer,
dog) are acquired earlier and are more frequently used than superordinate (tools,
canines) or subordinate (ball pein hammer, weimaraner) terms because, besides
their frequency of use, this is the level at which the world is optimally split for
function, the level where objects within the class share the same broad visual
shape and motoric function, and, thus, where the categories of language most
directly map onto perceptual form and motoric function (Lakoff, 1987; Rosch
et al., 1976; Rosch, Varela, & Thompson, 1991). Goldberg extends this notion to
argument structure more generally:

> Constructions which correspond to basic sentence types encode as their central
> senses event types that are basic to human experience . . . that of someone causing
> something, something moving, something being in a state, someone possessing some-
> thing, something causing a change of state or location, something undergoing a
> change of state or location, and something having an effect on someone. (Goldberg,
> 1995, p. 39)

Ninio (1999) and Goldberg, Casenhiser, and Sethuraman (2004) show for child language acquisition that individual "pathbreaking" semantically prototypic verbs form the seeds of verb-centered argument-structure patterns, with generalizations of the verb-centered instances emerging gradually as the verb-centered categories themselves are analyzed into more abstract argument structure constructions. The verb is a better predictor of sentence meaning than any other word in the sentence and plays the central role in determining the syntactic structure of a sentence. Since the same functional concerns motivate AL and L1 both, we should expect the same pattern for L2 and FL acquisition.

Learning categories and prototypes: From tokens to types

Because constructions are linguistic categories, we need to consider the psychology of concept and category learning (Ashby & Maddox, 2005; Cohen & Lefebvre, 2005): Humans can readily induce a category from experience of exemplars. Categories have graded structures (Rosch & Mervis, 1975). Rather than all instances of a category being "equal," certain instances are better exemplars than others. The prototype is the best example among the members of a category and serves as the benchmark against which the surrounding "poorer," more borderline instances are categorized; it combines the most representative attributes of that category in the conspiracy of its memorized exemplars. People have memory for the tokens they have seen before – previously experienced patterns are better judged than novel ones of equal distortion from the prototype. Although we don't go around consciously counting types and tokens, we nevertheless have very accurate implicit knowledge of the underlying distributions and their most usual settings. Similarity and frequency are, thus, important determinants of learning and generalization:

The more *similar* an instance is to the other members of its category and the less similar it is to members of contrast categories, the easier it is to classify (e.g., we better classify sparrows (or other average-sized, average-colored, average-beaked, average-featured specimens) as birds than we do birds with less common features or feature combinations, like geese or albatrosses) (Tversky, 1977). The greater the token *frequency* of an exemplar, the more it contributes to defining the category, and the greater the likelihood it will be considered the prototype of the category (e.g., sparrows are rated as highly typical birds because they are frequently experienced examples of the category birds). The unmarked forms of linguistic oppositions are more frequent than their marked forms (Greenberg, 1966). Token frequency is particularly important in this way in early and intermediate levels of learning, less so as learning approaches asymptote (Homa, Dunbar, & Nohre, 1991; Nosofsky, 1988).

There are important effects of presentation order in the implicit tallying that underlies category formation. In learning, the greater the variability of exemplars, the lower the rate of acquisition but the more robust the categorization/the less variability of distortion, the faster the category is learned (Posner & Keele, 1968, 1970). But it looks like there's an optimal balance to be had here. When people try to teach a category to someone else *explicitly*, there is high agreement on the teaching sequences that are naturally adopted: The typical sequence starts with several ideal positive cases, followed by an ideal negative case and then borderline cases (Avrahami et al., 1997). Avrahami et al. tested to see whether this is indeed an optimal instruction sequence by comparing it with other orders that emphasized the full breadth of category from the outset. Exemplifying category breadth from the outset, borderline cases and central cases all, produced slower and less accurate explicit learning. For *implicit* learning of categories from exemplars, so, too, acquisition is optimized by the introduction of an initial, low-variance sample centered upon prototypical exemplars (Elio & Anderson, 1981, 1984). This low variance sample allows learners to get a "fix" on what will account for most of the category members. Then the bounds of the category can later be defined by experience of the full breadth of exemplars.

Form, function, and frequency: Zipfian family profiles

Goldberg, Casenhiser & Sethuraman (2004) tested the applicability of these generalizations to the particular case of children acquiring constructions. Phrasal form–meaning correspondences (e.g., X causes Y to move $Z_{path/loc}$ [Subj V Obj $Obl_{path/loc}$]) do exist independently of particular verbs, but there is a close relationship between the types of verb that appear therein (in this case *put, get, take, push,* etc.). Furthermore, in natural language, the frequency profile of the verbs in the family follows a Zipfian profile (Zipf, 1935) whereby the highest frequency words accounted for the most linguistic tokens. Goldberg et al. demonstrated that in samples of child language acquisition, for a variety of constructions, there is a strong tendency for one single verb to occur with very high frequency in comparison to other verbs used (e.g., the [Subj V Obj $Obl_{path/loc}$] construction is exemplified in the children's speech by *put* 31% of the time, *get* 16%, *take* 10%, and *do/pick* 6%). This profile closely mirrored that of the mothers' speech to these children (with, e.g., *put* appearing 38% of the time in this construction that was otherwise exemplified by 43 different verbs). Ellis and Ferreira-Junior (Ellis & Ferreira-Junior, in press a, b) have replicated the Zipfian family profiles of these same constructions for the speech of naturalistic adult learners of English as a second language in the ESF project (Perdue, 1993).

The same can be seen in the constructions for compliments. Manes and Wolfson (1989) examined a corpus of 700 examples of compliments uttered in day-to-day interactions. Just three constructions accounted for 85% of these: [NP <*is/looks*> *(really)* ADJ] (53%), [*I (really)* <*like/love*> NP] (16%), and [PRO *is (really) (a)* ADJ NP] (15%). Eighty percent of these depended on an adjective to carry the positive semantic load. While the number of positive adjectives that could be used is virtually unlimited, in fact two-thirds of all adjectival compliments in the corpus used only five adjectives: *nice* (23%), *good* (20%), *pretty* (9%), *beautiful* (9%), and *great* (6%). Non-adjectival compliments were focused on a handful of semantically positive verbs, with *like* and *love* accounting for 86%.

Thus, it appears that in natural language, at least for the constructions considered in this way so far, tokens of one particular verb account for the lion's share of instances of argument frames, and that the pathbreaking verb for each is the one with the prototypical meaning from which that construction is derived. How about that? As Morales and Taylor (2007) put it: "Language is exquisitely adaptive to the learning capabilities of its users." The natural structure of natural language seems to provide exactly the familial type:token frequency distribution to ensure optimized acquisition of linguistic constructions as categories.

Optimizing instruction samples for construction learning

What are the implications for instruction using curriculum-driven input samples? What we know about category formation suggests that these type:token frequency considerations should apply here too. *Optimal acquisition should occur when the central members of the category are presented early and often.*

For syntactic constructions, Goldberg, Casenhiser, and Sethuraman (2004) tested whether, when training novel patterns (a construction of the form [Subj Obj V-*o*] signaling the appearance of the subject in a particular location, for example, *the king the ball moopo-ed*) exemplified by five different novel verbs, it is better to train with relatively balanced token frequencies (4-4-4-2-2) or with a family frequency profile where one exemplar had a particularly high token frequency (8-2-2-2-2). Undergraduate native speakers of English learned this novel construction from three minutes of training using videos. They were then tested for the generalization of the semantics of this construction to novel verbs and new scenes. Learners in the high token frequency condition showed significantly better learning than those in the balanced condition, a finding Goldberg (Goldberg, 2006; 2008) has now observed in studies of child acquisition too.

For morphological constructions, Bybee (2008) analyzed the ways that natural frequency skewing affects the acquisition of verbal inflexions. The most frequent forms of a paradigm (third person/first person singular) either have no affix or a short affix, and the other forms of the paradigm can typically be derived from them. Thus, she argues, the high token frequency forms of the paradigm are the anchoring points of the other forms. Lower frequency forms are analyzed and learned in terms of these more robust forms creating a relationship of dependency.

Frequency variation is ubiquitous across natural languages. Morales and Taylor (2007) present connectionist simulations evidencing how learning can be enhanced through frequency variation: training samples where there were variable numbers of tokens per type produced more accurate and more economical learning than did training with more uniform frequency profiles.

There is clearly a need to extend these initial studies to explore more thoroughly the sampling of exemplars of a wide range of second language constructions for optimal acquisition, but in the interim, the best informed practice is to introduce a new construction using an initial, low-variance sample centered upon prototypical exemplars to allow learners to get a "fix" on the central tendency that will account for most of the category members. Tokens that are more frequent have stronger representations in memory and serve as the analogical basis for forming novel instances of the category.

Corpus and cognitive linguistic analyses are essential to the determination of which constructions of differing degrees of schematicity are worthy of instruction, their relative frequency, and their best (= central and most frequent) examples for instruction and assessment (Biber, Conrad, & Reppen, 1998; Biber et al., 1999). Gries (2008) describes how the three basic methods of corpus linguistics (frequency lists, concordances, and collocations) inform the instruction of second language constructions. Achard (2008), Tyler (2008), Robinson and Ellis (2008a) and other readings in Robinson and Ellis (2008b) show how an understanding of the item-based nature of construction learning inspires the creation and evaluation of instructional tasks, materials, and syllabi, and how cognitive linguistic analyses can be used to inform learners how constructions are conventionalized ways of matching certain expressions to specific situations and to guide instructors in precisely isolating and clearly presenting the various conditions that motivate speaker choice.

Tuning the System: Frequency and the Attainment of Nativelike Fluency and Selection

Language is fundamentally probabilistic: every piece is ambiguous. Each of these example formulas ("One, two, three," "Once upon a time," "Wonderful!," "Won the battle, lost the war") begins with the sound "wʌn". At this point, what should the appropriate interpretation be? A general property of human perception is that when a sensation is associated with more than one reality, unconscious processes weigh the odds, and we perceive the most probable thing. *Psycholinguistic* analyses demonstrate that fluent language users are sensitive to the relative probabilities of occurrence of different constructions in the speech stream (Bod, Hay, & Jannedy, 2003; Bybee & Hopper, 2001; Chater & Manning, 2006; Ellis, 2002a, 2002b; Jurafsky & Martin, 2000). Since learners have experienced many more tokens of "one" than they have "won," in the absence of any further information, they typically favor the unitary interpretation over that involving gain or advantage. But they need to be able to suppress this interpretation in a context of "Alice in wʌn . . ." Learners have to figure language out: their task is, in essence, to learn the probability distribution P(*interpretation|cue, context*), the probability of an interpretation given a formal cue, a mapping from form to meaning conditioned by context. This figuring is achieved, and communication optimized, by implicit tallying of the *frequency*, *recency*, and *context* of constructions.

This incidental learning from usage allows language users to be *rational* in the sense that their mental models of the way language works are optimal given their linguistic experience to date (Ellis, 2006b). The words that they are likely to hear next, the most likely senses of these words, the linguistic constructions they are most likely to utter next, the syllables they are likely to hear next, the graphemes they are likely to read next, the interpretations that are most relevant, and the rest of what's coming next across all levels of language representation, are made more readily available to fluent speakers by their language processing systems. Their unconscious language representations are adaptively probability-tuned to predict the linguistic constructions that are most likely to be relevant in the ongoing discourse context, optimally preparing them for comprehension and production. With practice comes modularization too, the development of autonomous specialist systems for different aspects of language processing. These "zombie agents" are independent – experience of reading a word facili-tates subsequent reading of that word, experience of speaking a word facilitates subsequent speaking of that word, but cross-modal priming effects are null or slight in fluent speakers. So reading practice tallies the reading system, speaking practice tunes the speaking system, etc. Fluency in each separate module requires its own usage practice (see Gatbonton & Segalowitz, 2005 for communicative approaches designed to engender this). This specificity of practice gain from different forms of processing underlies many failures of learning and generaliza-tion as summarized in the Transfer-Appropriate Processing (TAP) framework (Morris, Bransford, & Franks, 1977). Lightbown (2007) reviews the implica-tions of TAP for L2 instruction, how there is a need to increase the number of settings and processing types in which learners encounter the material they need to learn.

Just as extensive sampling is required for nativelike fluency, so it is, too, for nativelike selection. Many of the forms required for idiomatic use are, neverthe-less, of relatively low frequency, and the learner thus needs a large input sample just to encounter them. More usage still is required to allow the tunings under-pinning nativelike use of collocation – something which even advanced learners have particular difficulty with. Hence the emphasis on the representative samples necessary for English for Academic and Specific Purposes (EAP/ESP) (e.g., Swales, 1990). Linguists interested in the description of language (e.g., British National Corpus, 2006) have come to realize that really large corpora are necessary to describe it adequately – 100 million words is just a start, and each genre, dialect, and type requires its own properly targeted sampling. Child language researchers have also begun the relevant power analyses to explore the relations between construction frequency and sample size for accurate description, reaching the conclusion that for many constructions of interest, *dense* corpora are an absolute necessity (Tomasello & Stahl, 2004). So, too, in learners' attainment of fluent language processing, whether in L1 or AL, there is no substitute for usage, lots of appropriate usage.

Becoming fluent requires a sufficient sample of needs-relevant authentic input for the necessary implicit tunings to take place. The "two puzzles for linguistic theory," nativelike selection and nativelike fluency (Pawley & Syder, 1983), are less perplexing when considered in these terms of frequency and probability. There's a lot of tallying to be done here. The necessary sample is certainly to be counted in terms of thousands of hours on task.

The Language Calculator Has No "Clear" Button

A final implication of language acquisition as estimation relates again to *sampling history*, this time in terms of the difference between first langauge (L1) and adult language (AL) acquisition. AL learners are distinguished from infant L1 acquirers by the fact that they have previously devoted considerable resources to the estimation of the characteristics of another language – the native tongue in which they have considerable fluency (and any others subsequently acquired). Since they are using the same apparatus to survey their additional language too, their computations and induction are often affected by transfer, with L1-tuned expectations and selective attention (Ellis, 2006c) blinding the computational system to aspects of the AL sample, thus rendering biased estimates from naturalistic usage and the limited endstate typical of L2A. These effects have been explored within the traditions of contrastive analysis (James, 1980), language transfer (Odlin, 1989), and more recently within cognitive linguistics (Robinson & Ellis, 2008b). From our L1 we learn how language frames the world and how to use it to describe action therein, focusing our listeners' attention appropriately. Cognitive linguistics is the analysis of these mechanisms and processes that underpin what Slobin (1996) called "thinking for speaking." But learning an AL requires "rethinking for speaking" (Robinson & Ellis, 2008a). In order to counteract the L1 biases to allow estimation procedures to optimize induction, all of the AL input needs to be made to count (as it does in L1A), not just the restricted sample typical of the biased intake of L2A. Certain types of form-focused instruction can help to achieve this by recruiting learners' explicit, conscious processing to allow them to consolidate unitized form–function bindings of novel AL constructions (Ellis, 2005). Once a construction has been represented in this way, so its use in subsequent processing can update the statistical tallying of its frequency of usage and probabilities of form–function mapping.

Language is its dynamic usage. It ever changes. For learners and linguists alike, its sum can only ever be estimated from limited samples of experience. Understanding the units and the processes of their estimation helps guide theory and application, learning and instruction.

NOTES

I thank Patsy Lightbown for constructive comments on a previous draft of this chapter.
1   Depending as well, of course, upon degree of shared context, embodiment, attention, cultural understandings, communicative intent, etc.
2   Whereby the frequency of the tokens of verbs seeding a construction type decays as a power function of their rank (Zipf, 1935).
3   The high token frequency of these items, though, means that in the course of language use, they have become phonetically eroded. These items lack perceptual salience and are consequently difficult to perceive from bottom-up, data-driven sources alone, a

factor which makes their second language acquisition difficult (Ellis, 2006c, 2008). They are also semantically light, abstract, and often homonymous, factors also making them difficult to acquire (Ellis, 2008). So it is the semantically rich and basic verbs which seed the constructions, these other grammatical functors making their contribution by marking the commonalities of the parse pattern.

4   Again, emphasizing the proviso concerning their low salience, low contingency, and abstractness.

REFERENCES

Achard, M. (2008). Cognitive pedagogical grammar. In P. Robinson & N. C. Ellis (eds.), *Handbook of cognitive linguistics and second language acquisition* (pp. 432–55). London: Routledge.

Ashby, E. G. & Maddox, W. T. (2005). Human category learning. *Annual Review of Psychology* 56, 149–78.

Avrahami, J., Kareev, Y., Bogot, Y., Caspi, R., Dunaevsky, S., & Lerner, S. (1997). Teaching by examples: Implications for the process of category acquisition. *The Quarterly Journal of Experimental Psychology: Section A* 50, 3, 586–606.

Barbarási, A.-L. & Albert, R. (1999). Emergence of scaling in random networks. *Science* 286, 509–11.

Biber, D., Conrad, S., & Reppen, R. (1998). *Corpus linguistics: Investigating language structure and use.* New York: Cambridge University Press.

Biber, D., Johansson, S., Leech, G., Conrad, S., & Finegan, E. (1999). *Longman grammar of spoken and written English.* Harlow, UK: Pearson Education.

Bod, R., Hay, J., & Jannedy, S. (eds.) (2003). *Probabilistic linguistics.* Cambridge, MA: MIT Press.

Braine, M. D. (1987). What is learned in acquiring word classes – a step towards acquisition theory. In B. MacWhinney (ed.), *Mechanisms of language acquisition* (pp. 65–87). Hillsdale, NJ: Lawrence Erlbaum Associates.

British National Corpus (2006). http://www.natcorp.ox.ac.uk/

Bybee, J. (1995). Regular morphology and the lexicon. *Language and Cognitive Processes* 10, 425–55.

Bybee, J. (2000). Mechanisms of change in grammaticalization: The role of frequency. Unpublished manuscript.

Bybee, J. (2003). Sequentiality as the basis of constituent structure. In T. Givón & B. F. Malle (eds.), *The evolution of language out of pre-language* (pp. 109–32). Amsterdam: John Benjamins.

Bybee, J. (2008). Usage-based grammar and second language acquisition. In P. Robinson & N. C. Ellis (eds.), *Handbook of cognitive linguistics and second language acquisition* (216–36). London: Routledge.

Bybee, J. & Hopper, P. (eds.) (2001). *Frequency and the emergence of linguistic structure.* Amsterdam: Benjamins.

Bybee, J. & Thompson, S. (2000). Three frequency effects in syntax. *Berkeley Linguistic Society* 23, 65–85.

Carey, S. & Bartlett, E. (1978). Acquiring a single new word. *Proceedings of the Stanford Child Language Conference / Papers and Reports on Child Language Development* 15, 17–29.

Chater, N. & Manning, C. (2006). Probabilistic models of language processing and acquisition. *Trends in Cognitive Science* 10, 335–44.

Childers, J. B. & Tomasello, M. (2001). The role of pronouns in young children's acquisition of the English transitive construction. *Developmental Psychology* 37, 739–48.

Cohen, H. & Lefebvre, C. (eds.) (2005). *Handbook of categorization in cognitive science.* Amsterdam: Elsevier.

Croft, W. (2000). *Explaining language change: An evolutionary approach.* London: Longman.

Croft, W. & Cruise, A. (2004). *Cognitive linguistics.* Cambridge: Cambridge University Press.

Ebbinghaus, H. (1885/1913). *Memory: A contribution to experimental psychology,* trans. H. A. Ruger & C. E. Bussenius. New York: Teachers College, Columbia.

Elio, R. & Anderson, J. R. (1981). The effects of category generalizations and instance similarity on schema abstraction. *Journal of Experimental Psychology: Human Learning & Memory* 7, 6, 397–417.

Elio, R. & Anderson, J. R. (1984). The effects of information order and learning mode on schema abstraction. *Memory & Cognition* 12, 1, 20–30.

Ellis, N. C. (1995). The psychology of foreign language vocabulary acquisition: Implications for CALL. *Computer Assisted Language Learning* 8, 2–3.

Ellis, N. C. (1996). Sequencing in SLA: Phonological memory, chunking, and points of order. *Studies in Second Language Acquisition* 18, 1, 91–126.

Ellis, N. C. (1998). Emergentism, connectionism and language learning. *Language Learning* 48, 4, 631–64.

Ellis, N. C. (2002a). Frequency effects in language processing: A review with implications for theories of implicit and explicit language acquisition. *Studies in Second Language Acquisition* 24, 2, 143–88.

Ellis, N. C. (2002b). Reflections on frequency effects in language processing. *Studies in Second Language Acquisition* 24, 2, 297–339.

Ellis, N. C. (2003). Constructions, chunking, and connectionism: The emergence of second language structure. In C. J. Doughty & M. H. Long (eds.), *The handbook of second language acquisition* (pp. 33–68). Oxford: Blackwell.

Ellis, N. C. (2005). At the interface: Dynamic interactions of explicit and implicit language knowledge. *Studies in Second Language Acquisition* 27, 305–52.

Ellis, N. C. (2006a). Cognitive perspectives on SLA: The Associative Cognitive CREED. *AILA Review* 19, 100–21.

Ellis, N. C. (2006b). Language acquisition as rational contingency learning. *Applied Linguistics* 27, 1, 1–24.

Ellis, N. C. (2006c). Selective attention and transfer phenomena in SLA: Contingency, cue competition, salience, interference, overshadowing, blocking, and perceptual learning. *Applied Linguistics* 27, 2, 1–31.

Ellis, N. C. (2007). Dynamic Systems and SLA: The wood and the trees. *Bilingualism: Language & Cognition* 10, 23–5.

Ellis, N. C. (2008). The dynamics of second language emergence: Cycles of language use, language change, and language acquisition. *Modern Language Journal* 92, 2, 232–49.

Ellis, N. C. & Ferreira-Junior, F. (in press, a). Construction learning as a function of frequency, frequency distribution, and function. *Modern Language Journal.*

Ellis, N. C. & Ferreira-Junior, F. (in press, b). Constructions and their acquisition: Islands and the distinctiveness of their occupancy. *Annual Review of Cognitive Linguistics.*

Ellis, N. C. & Larsen Freeman, D. (2006). Language emergence: Implications for Applied Linguistics (Introduction to the Special Issue). *Applied Linguistics* 27, 4, 558–89.

Ferrer i Cancho, R. & Solé, R. V. (2001). The small world of human language. *Proceedings of the Royal Society of London, B* 268, 2261–5.

Ferrer i Cancho, R., Solé, R. V., & Köhler, R. (2004). Patterns in syntactic dependency networks. *Physical Review* E69, 0519151–8.

Gatbonton, E. & Segalowitz, N. (2005). Rethinking communicative language teaching: A focus on ACCESS to fluency. *Canadian Modern Language Review* 61, 325–53.

Goldberg, A. E. (1995). *Constructions: A construction grammar approach to argument structure.* Chicago: University of Chicago Press.

Goldberg, A. E. (2003). Constructions: a new theoretical approach to language. *Trends in Cognitive Science* 7, 219–24.

Goldberg, A. E. (2006). *Constructions at work: The nature of generalization in language.* Oxford: Oxford University Press.

Goldberg, A. E. (2008). The language of constructions. In P. Robinson & N. C. Ellis (eds.), *A handbook of cognitive linguistics and SLA* (pp. 197–215). Mahwah, NJ: Lawrence Erlbaum.

Goldberg, A. E., Casenhiser, D. M., & Sethuraman, N. (2004). Learning argument structure generalizations. *Cognitive Linguistics* 15, 289–316.

Greenberg, J. (1966). *Language universals.* The Hague: Mouton.

Gries, S. T. (2008). Corpus-based methods in analyses of SLA data. In P. Robinson & N. C. Ellis (eds.), *A handbook of cognitive linguistics and SLA* (pp. 406–31). Mahwah, NJ: Erlbaum.

Homa, D., Dunbar, S., & Nohre, L. (1991). Instance frequency, categorization, and the modulating effect of experience. *Journal of Experimental Psychology: Learning, Memory, and Cognition* 17, 444–58.

Horst, M., Cobb, T., & Meara, P. (1998). Beyond A Clockwork Orange: Acquiring second-language vocabulary through reading. *Reading in a Foreign Language* 11, 207–23.

James, C. (1980). *Contrastive analysis.* London: Longman.

Jurafsky, D., Bell, A., Gregory, M., & Raymond, W. D. (2001). Probabilistic relations between words: Evidence from reduction in lexical production. In J. Bybee & P. Hopper (eds.), *Frequency and the emergence of linguistic structure* (pp. 229–54). Amsterdam: Benjamins.

Jurafsky, D. & Martin, J. H. (2000). *Speech and language processing: An introduction to natural language processing, speech recognition, and computational linguistics.* Englewood Cliffs, NJ: Prentice-Hall.

Lakoff, G. (1987). *Women, fire, and dangerous things: What categories reveal about the mind.* Chicago: University of Chicago Press.

Langacker, R. W. (1987). *Foundations of cognitive grammar*, vol. 1: *Theoretical prerequisites.* Stanford, CA: Stanford University Press.

Lightbown, P. M. (2007). Transfer appropriate processing in classroom second language acquisition. In Z.-H. Han & E. S. Park (eds.), *Understanding second language process* (pp. 27–44). Clevedon, UK: Multilingual Matters.

Manes, J. & Wolfson, N. (1989). The compliment formula. In F. Coulmas (ed.), *Conversational routine* (pp. 116–32). The Hague: Mouton.

McClure, C., Lieven, E., & Pine, J. M. (in press). Investigating the abstractness of children's early knowledge of argument structure. *Journal of Child Language.*

Morales, F. & Taylor, J. R. (2007). *Learning from relative frequency.* Available as LAUD (Linguistic Agency, University of Duisburg) preprint, paper no. 690.

Morris, C. D., Bransford, J. D., & Franks, J. J. (1977). Levels of processing versus transfer appropriate processing. *Journal of Verbal Learning & Verbal Behavior* 16, 519–33.

Newell, A. (1990). *Unified theories of cognition*. Cambridge, MA: Harvard University Press.

Ninio, A. (1999). Pathbreaking verbs in syntactic development and the question of proto-typical transitivity. *Journal of Child Language* 26, 619–53.

Nosofsky, R. M. (1988). Similarity, frequency, and category representations. *Journal of Experimental Psychology: Learning, Memory, and Cognition* 14, 54–65.

Odlin, T. (1989). *Language transfer*. New York: Cambridge University Press.

Pawley, A. & Syder, F. H. (1983). Two puzzles for linguistic theory: Nativelike selection and nativelike fluency. In J. C. Richards & R. W. Schmidt (eds.), *Language and communication* (pp. 191–225). London: Longman.

Perdue, C. (ed.) (1993). *Adult language acquisition: Crosslinguistic perspectives*. Cambridge: Cambridge University Press.

Pine, J. M. & Lieven, E. V. (1993). Reanalyzing rote-learned phrases: Individual differences in the transition to multi-word speech. *Journal of Child Language* 20, 551–71.

Pine, J. M., Lieven, E. V., & Rowland, C. F. (1998). Comparing different models of the development of the English verb category. *Linguistics* 36, 807–30.

Posner, M. I. & Keele, S. W. (1968). On the genesis of abstract ideas. *Journal of Experimental Psychology* 77, 353–63.

Posner, M. I. & Keele, S. W. (1970). Retention of abstract ideas. *Journal of Experimental Psychology* 83, 304–8.

Robinson, P. & Ellis, N. C. (2008a). Conclusion: Cognitive linguistics, second language acquisition and L2 instruction: Issues for research. In P. Robinson & N. C. Ellis (eds.), *Handbook of cognitive linguistics and second language acquisition* (pp. 489–545). London: Routledge.

Robinson, P. & Ellis, N. C. (eds.) (2008b). *A handbook of cognitive linguistics and second language acquisition*. London: Routledge.

Rosch, E. & Mervis, C. B. (1975). Cognitive representations of semantic categories. *Journal of Experimental Psychology: General* 104, 192–233.

Rosch, E., Mervis, C. B., Gray, W. D., Johnson, D. M., & Boyes-Braem, P. (1976). Basic objects in natural categories. *Cognitive Psychology* 8, 382–439.

Rosch, E., Varela, F., & Thompson, E. (1991). *The embodied mind*. Boston, MA: MIT Press.

Saragi, T., Nation, I. S. P., & Meister, G. F. (1978). Vocabulary learning and reading. *System* 6, 72–128.

Shi, R., Cutler, A., Werker, J. E., & Cruikshank, M. (2006). Frequency and form as determinants of functor sensitivity in English-acquiring infants. *Journal of the Acoustic Society of America* 119, EL61–EL67.

Simon, H. A. (1962). *The sciences of the artificial*. Cambridge, MA: MIT Press.

Slobin, D. I. (1996). From "thought and language" to "thinking for speaking." In J. J. Gumperz & S. C. Levinson (eds.), *Rethinking linguistic relativity* (pp. 70–96). Cambridge: Cambridge University Press.

Squire, L. R. (1992). Memory and the hippocampus: A synthesis from findings with rats, monkeys, and humans. *Psychological Review* 99, 195–231.

Swales, J. M. (1990). *Genre analysis: English in academic and research settings*. Cambridge: Cambridge University Press.

Taylor, J. R. (2002). *Cognitive grammar*. Oxford: Oxford University Press.

Tomasello, M. (ed.) (1998). *The new psychology of language: Cognitive and functional approaches to language structure*. Mahwah, NJ: Lawrence Erlbaum.

Tomasello, M. (1992). *First verbs: A case study of early grammatical development*. New York: Cambridge University Press.

Tomasello, M. (2003). *Constructing a language*. Boston, MA: Harvard University Press.

Tomasello, M. & Stahl, D. (2004). Sampling children's spontaneous speech: How much is enough? *Journal of Child Language* 31, 101–21.

Tversky, A. (1977). Features of similarity. *Psychological Review* 84, 327–52.

Tyler, A. (2008). Cognitive linguistics and second language instruction. In P. Robinson & N. C. Ellis (eds.), *Handbook of cognitive linguistics and second language acquisition* (pp. 456–88). London: Routledge.

Wilson, S. (2003). Lexically specific constructions in the acquisition of inflection in English. *Journal of Child Language* 30, 75–115.

Wray, A. (2002). *Formulaic language and the lexicon*. Cambridge: Cambridge University Press.

Zipf, G. K. (1935). *The psycho-biology of language: An introduction to dynamic philology*. Cambridge, MA: MIT Press.

Part IV Program Design

10 Bilingual and Immersion Programs

JIM CUMMINS

Introduction

The term *bilingual education* refers to an organized and planned program that uses two (or more) languages of instruction. The central defining feature of bilingual programs is that the languages are used to teach subject matter content rather than just the languages themselves. Bilingual instruction can be implemented at any grade or age level, ranging from pre-school through university or college. Bilingual education can be traced back to Greek and Roman times and currently a large majority of countries throughout the world offer some form of bilingual education either in public or private school settings (Cummins & Hornberger, 2008).

The goals of bilingual programs vary widely across contexts. Some programs aim to develop proficiency in two languages; others do not. For example, the most common form of bilingual education for linguistic minority students in the United States during the past 40 years, *transitional bilingual education*, aims only to promote students' proficiency in English. When it is assumed that students have attained sufficient proficiency in the school language to follow instruction in that language, home language instruction is discontinued and students are transitioned into mainstream classes taught exclusively in English.

The term "immersion" is used in two very different ways in educational discourse. In the first sense, immersion programs are organized and planned forms of bilingual education in which students are "immersed" in a second-language instructional environment with the goal of developing proficiency in two languages. First-language instruction is typically introduced within a year or two of the start of the program and forms an integral part of the overall plan. In its second sense, the term "immersion" refers to the immersion of immigrant or minority language children in a classroom environment where instruction is conducted exclusively through their second (or third) language (frequently the dominant language of the society or a global language of wider communication). The intent is to develop proficiency in the language of instruction. Such programs vary in the amount of support they provide to enable students to acquire proficiency in the language of instruction – in some cases extensive support is provided by specialist language teachers, but in other cases students are left to "sink or swim." This second sense of the term "immersion" reflects popular usage but, as described below, is diametrically opposed to the conceptualization of immersion education within the educational research community. In the remainder of this paper, "immersion education" will be used to describe the first sense of the term – a planned program aimed at bilingual development – while "immersion" or "submersion" will be used to refer to the exclusive use of students' second language (L2) as a medium of instruction with the goal of developing proficiency only in the language of instruction.

The term "immersion education" came to prominence in Canada during the 1960s to describe innovative programs in which the French language was used as an initial medium of instruction for elementary school students whose home language was English. Immersion programs explicitly aim to promote fluency and literacy in students' first and second languages (L1 and L2). These programs were originally implemented at the Kindergarten level (age 5 – termed *early immersion*) but were later also implemented in Grades 4 or 5 (termed *middle immersion*) and Grades 7 or 8 (termed *late immersion*). About 300,000 Canadian students currently participate in immersion programs. This represents about 6 percent of the national school population. In early immersion programs, students whose L1 is English are initially "immersed" in a French language school environment for two to three years prior to the introduction of formal teaching of English. Instruction through French is designed specifically to enable students to gain access to academic content despite their initially low levels of French proficiency. English language arts are typically introduced in Grade 2 and English is used as a medium for teaching other subject matter (e.g., science, math, social studies) by Grades 3 or 4. Generally, by Grade 4, 50 percent of the instructional time is spent through each language.

Johnson and Swain (1997) point out that there is nothing new in the phenomenon of teaching students through the medium of a second language. In fact, throughout the history of formal education, the use of an L2 as a medium of instruction has been the rule rather than the exception. The Canadian French immersion programs, however, were the first to articulate a set of pedagogical principles underlying immersion education (Lambert & Tucker, 1972). They were also the first to be subjected to intensive long-term research evaluation, although some large-scale research had been undertaken in other contexts prior to the Canadian experience (e.g., Macnamara, 1966 in Ireland, and Malherbe, 1946 in South Africa).

Johnson and Swain (1997) summarize eight core features of immersion programs:

- The L2 is a medium of instruction.
- The immersion curriculum parallels the local L1 curriculum.
- Overt support exists for the L1.
- The program aims for additive bilingualism where students "add" L2 proficiency while continuing to develop their L1.

- Exposure to the L2 is largely confined to the classroom.
- Students enter with similar (and limited) levels of L2 proficiency.
- The teachers are bilingual.
- The classroom culture is that of the local L1 community.

It is clear that immersion education represents a carefully planned program that goes far beyond simply instructing students through a second language. In practice, however, when applied to immigrant and minority language students, the term "immersion" is frequently used to refer to programs that fall far short of the conditions specified by Johnson and Swain.

The Sociopolitical Context of Bilingual Education

There are an estimated 5,000 languages spoken in the world's 200 or so sovereign states. Thus, the majority of states encompass multiple languages within their boundaries. About two-thirds of all children in the world grow up in a bilingual or multilingual environment. To illustrate, 90 million of China's more than one billion population belong to a national minority and most of these minority groups speak languages other than Mandarin, the official language of the country. Linguistic diversity also exists among the Han majority group as a result of multiple "dialects" that represent mutually unintelligible spoken languages, even though all share the same writing system. Singapore, Switzerland, India, and most African countries are just a few other examples of countries that recognize multiple national languages and which regulate the status and use of these languages in education, government, and other social arenas.

In the current era of globalization, with unprecedented human mobility and social interchange across cultural and linguistic boundaries, processes of language learning (and language loss) are apparent in societies around the world. Government policies attempt to influence these processes by supporting the teaching of certain languages in schools and, in some cases, by actively discouraging the maintenance of other languages, usually the languages of subordinated groups within the society. Bilingual programs have emerged in recent years as a viable option for governments and communities interested in promoting more effective learning of socially valued languages and/or maintaining languages that are endangered, such as many indigenous languages in North America.

Despite their utility as a tool for language planning, bilingual programs have also aroused considerable controversy in some countries. Opposition to bilingual education tends to be highly selective. It focuses only on the provision of L1 instruction to students from minority or socially subordinated groups (e.g., Spanish-speakers in the United States, Turkish-speakers in Germany, etc.). There is virtually no controversy about the provision of bilingual programs or second-language immersion programs to children of the dominant group(s) in society. For example, French immersion programs for anglophone students in Canada have been minimally controversial during the past 40 years because they serve the interests of the dominant group. Similarly in Europe and the United States, when the target students are from the dominant group, instruction through the medium of a second language is seen as educational enrichment – a more efficient way of teaching additional languages and adding to the cultural capital of the student.

Thus, opposition to bilingual education is fueled primarily by ideological concerns relating to diversity and power. Use of a language as a medium of instruction confers recognition, status, and often economic benefits (e.g., teaching positions) on speakers of that language. Consequently, bilingual education is not simply a politically-neutral instructional innovation. It is also a sociopolitical phenomenon that is implicated in the ongoing competition between social groups for material and symbolic resources.

Types, Goals, and Participants

Typologies of bilingual education focus on characteristics of students in the program, the goals of the program, and organizational structures. The more important distinctions are outlined below:

- *Majority/minority languages or students.* These terms refer to whether a language is the language of the numerically dominant group in a society or that of a numerically non-dominant group.
- *Dominant/subordinated students or groups.* These terms are often used interchangeably with *majority/minority* but they refer explicitly to power and status relations between societal groups rather than to the numerical size of the groups. *Minoritized* is sometimes used interchangeably with *subordinated* (Skutnabb-Kangas & McCarty, 2008).
- *Enrichment/remedial programs.* The term *enrichment bilingual education* refers to programs that aim to enrich students' educational experience by strongly promoting bilingualism and biliteracy. French immersion programs in Canada and dual language programs involving both majority and minority language students in the United States are examples of enrichment programs. Dual language programs are also termed *two-way immersion* programs. *Remedial programs*, by contrast, aim to remediate or compensate for presumed linguistic deficits that bilingual children bring to school.
- *Maintenance/transitional programs. Maintenance programs* aim to help language minority students maintain and develop their proficiency in their home language while *transitional programs* are designed as a temporary bridge to instruction exclusively through the dominant language of the school and society.
- *Late-exit/Early-exit programs.* Transitional bilingual programs are often distinguished according to the grade level at which students transition from the bilingual program into mainstream monolingual classes. Early-exit programs are typically motivated by the assumption that students will benefit by transitioning from the bilingual program into the mainstream program as

rapidly as possible. The transition usually occurs by Grade 2 or 3. By contrast, late-exit programs, also known as *developmental programs* in the United States, transition students close to the end of elementary school (Grade 5 or 6). The assumption is that academic outcomes in both the majority language and students' L1 will benefit from strong promotion of both languages.

- *Immersion/submersion programs.* Immersion programs, as conceptualized within the educational research community, are a form of bilingual education that immerse students in a second-language instructional environment for between 50 and 100 percent of instructional time with the goal of developing fluency and literacy in both languages. Students may be either from the dominant linguistic group or members of an ethnocultural or indigenous community whose heritage language is one of the languages of instruction. In this latter case, the goal is usually to maintain or revitalize an endangered language. Submersion programs, by contrast, provide 100 percent of instruction through the dominant language (students' L2); teachers typically do not understand students' L1, and few instructional supports are available to help students understand instruction or express themselves through either L1 or L2. These programs are also termed *sink-or-swim* programs. The term "structured immersion" has been used in the United States (e.g., by Rossell & Baker, 1996) to refer to English instructional programs that provide comprehension supports (including the possibility of some very limited use of students' L1) to enable English language learners to understand instruction. These programs are dismissed by advocates of bilingual education as simply another form of submersion (e.g., Skutnabb-Kangas & McCarty, 2008).

Bilingual programs can also be categorized according to who participates in the program. Four broad overlapping categories can be distinguished. The first category involves programs intended for indigenous students (e.g., Maori students in New Zealand) and those from nationally recognized minority groups (e.g., students of Breton heritage in France or of Basque heritage in the Basque Autonomous Community in Spain). Typically these programs are intended to either maintain or revitalize the minority language.

The second category involves students from the dominant or majority group. The goal is to develop bilingual and biliteracy skills among these students. Examples are the Canadian French immersion programs and dual language programs in the United States that enroll both majority and minority language students.

The third category involves students who come from immigrant communities. Most of these programs are transitional and remedial in nature with the primary goal of supporting students' academic development in the majority language.

The final category of bilingual education programs involves children who are deaf or hard-of-hearing. These programs use a natural sign language, such as American Sign Language (ASL), as a medium of instruction together with the dominant language of the society, frequently with a focus on the written form of this language. Bilingual-bicultural programs are common and well accepted in Scandinavian countries such as Sweden and Denmark (Mahshie, 1995) but are still struggling to gain acceptance in North America and many other parts of the world (Small & Mason, 2008).

General Outcomes of Bilingual Education Programs

Formal academic research has been conducted on bilingualism and bilingual education since the 1920s and a voluminous literature has accumulated on these topics (e.g., August & Shanahan, 2006; Cummins, 2001; García & Baker, 2007; Genesee et al., 2006; May, 2008). At this point, considerable confidence can be placed in some general conclusions about the outcomes of bilingual education; specifically, the research evidence is clear that for both minority and majority language students, well-implemented bilingual programs are an effective way of promoting proficiency in two languages (e.g., August & Shanahan, 2006).

A finding common to all forms of bilingual education is that spending instructional time through two languages entails no long-term adverse effects on students' academic development in the majority language. This pattern emerges among both majority and minority language students, across widely varying sociolinguistic and sociopolitical contexts, and in programs with very different organizational structures. Three additional outcomes of bilingual programs can be highlighted.

1 Significant positive relationships exist between the development of academic skills in first and second languages

In order to account for these findings and the fact that instruction through a minority language entailed no adverse consequences for students' academic development in the majority language, Cummins (1979, 1981) proposed the "interdependence hypothesis." This hypothesis was formally expressed in the following way:

> To the extent that instruction in Lx is effective in promoting proficiency in Lx, transfer of this proficiency to Ly will occur provided there is adequate exposure to Ly (either in school or environment) and adequate motivation to learn Ly. (1981, p. 29)

In concrete terms, what this hypothesis means is that in, for example, a Basque-Spanish bilingual program in the Basque Country in Spain, Basque instruction that develops Basque reading and writing skills is not just developing Basque skills, it is also developing a deeper conceptual and linguistic proficiency that is strongly related to the development of literacy in the majority language (Spanish). In other words, although the surface aspects (e.g., pronunciation, fluency, etc.) of different languages are clearly separate, there is an underlying conceptual proficiency, or knowledge base, that is common across languages. This common underlying proficiency (or what Genesee et al. (2006) call a cross-linguistic *reservoir of abilities*) makes possible the transfer of concepts, literacy skills, and learning strategies from one language to another. This is true even for languages that are dissimilar (e.g., American Sign Language and English, Spanish and Basque; Dutch and Turkish). The transfer of skills, strategies, and knowledge explains why spending instructional time through a minority language entails no adverse consequences for the development of the majority language.

There is extensive empirical research that supports the interdependence hypothesis (see reviews by Dressler & Kamil, 2006; Baker, 2001; Cummins, 2001; Genesee et al., 2006). The most comprehensive review was conducted by Dressler and Kamil as part of the Report of the National Literacy Panel on Language-Minority Children and Youth (August & Shanahan, 2006). They conclude:

> In summary, all these studies provide evidence for the cross-language transfer of reading comprehension ability in bilinguals. This relationship holds (a) across typologically different languages . . . (b) for children in elementary, middle, and high school; (c) for learners of English as a foreign language and English as a second language; (d) over time; (e) from both first to second language and second to first language; (p. 222)

Cummins (2008) has suggested that, depending on the sociolinguistic situation, five types of cross-linguistic transfer are possible:

- transfer of conceptual elements (e.g., understanding the concept of photosynthesis);
- transfer of metacognitive and metalinguistic strategies (e.g., strategies of visualizing, use of visuals or graphic organizers, mnemonic devices, vocabulary acquisition strategies, etc.);
- transfer of pragmatic aspects of language use (willingness to take risks in communication through L2, ability to use paralinguistic features such as gestures to aid communication, etc.);
- transfer of specific linguistic elements (e.g., knowledge of the meaning of *photo* in *photosynthesis*);
- transfer of phonological awareness – the knowledge that words are composed of distinct sounds.

The documentation of multiple forms of cross-linguistic transfer (e.g., Dressler & Kamil, 2006) raises the pedagogical issue (to be considered in more detail in a later section) of whether teachers should actively aim to promote transfer across languages among bilingual or emergent bilingual students. A number of researchers have argued for the adoption of bilingual instructional strategies (e.g., Cummins, 2008; Jessner, 2006), but this orientation contravenes the long-term assumption that bilingualism is best developed within bilingual programs through the implementation of monolingual instructional strategies (e.g., Lambert, 1984).

2 *The most successful bilingual programs are those that aim to develop bilingualism and biliteracy*

Short-term transitional programs are less successful in developing both L2 and L1 literacy than programs such as dual language or maintenance programs that continue to promote both L1 and L2 literacy throughout elementary school. Lindholm-Leary and Borsato (2006) express this pattern of findings as follows:

> There is strong convergent evidence that the educational success of ELLs [English language learners] is positively related to sustained instruction through the student's first language . . . most long-term studies report that the longer the students stayed in the program, the more positive were the outcomes. (p. 201)

This pattern of results refutes the assumption underlying many transitional bilingual programs that students should be transferred out of the bilingual program as rapidly as possible.

3 *Bilingual education for minority students is, in many situations, more effective in developing L2 literacy skills than monolingual education in the dominant language, but it is not, by itself, a panacea for underachievement*

The National Literacy Panel on Language-Minority Children and Youth (August & Shanahan, 2006) concluded that bilingual instruction exerts a moderate but significant effect on minority students' English academic achievement.

> In summary, there is no indication that bilingual instruction impedes academic achievement in either the native language or English, whether for language-minority students, students receiving heritage language instruction, or those enrolled in French immersion programs. Where differences were observed, on average they favored the students in a bilingual program. The meta-analytic results clearly suggest a positive effect for bilingual instruction that is moderate in size. This conclusion held up across the entire collection of studies and within the subset of studies that used random assignment of students to conditions. (Francis, Lesaux, & August, 2006, p. 397)

This finding concurs with the results of other recent comprehensive reviews (e.g., Genesee et al., 2006; Rolstad, Mahoney, & Glass, 2005). However, it is important to emphasize that underachievement among subordinated group students derives from many sources (e.g., socioeconomic status, inferior schools, low teacher expectations, etc.) and simply providing some L1 instruction will not, by itself, transform students' educational experience nor reverse the effects of social discrimination and poverty.

Dissenting Perspectives

As noted above, opposition to bilingual education for linguistic minority students derives primarily from ideological concerns related to immigration and national identity in societies that are increasingly diverse. However, two groups of researchers in the United States and Germany respectively have disputed the general pattern of findings presented above regarding the outcomes of bilingual education (Esser, 2006; Rossell & Baker, 1996; Rossell & Kuder, 2005). Rossell and Baker carried out a literature review of studies, which (they claimed) compared bilingual education with "structured immersion" in the dominant language of the school. In a detailed review, Cummins (1999) argued that the Rossell and Baker review is "characterized by inaccurate and arbitrary labeling of programs, inconsistent application of criteria for 'methodological acceptability', and highly inaccurate interpretation of the results of early French immersion programs" (p. 30). The credibility of their review can be gauged from the fact that 90 percent of the studies they claimed as support for "structured immersion" (English-medium programs) are interpreted by the authors of these studies as supporting the effectiveness of bilingual and even trilingual education. Similar problems characterize the more recent review written by Rossell and Kuder (2005).

Esser's (2006) arguments against bilingual education for immigrant and minority students in the German context are based on an uncritical acceptance of the claims made by Rossell and her colleagues (Rossell & Baker, 1996; Rossell & Kuder, 2005) together with inferences drawn from analysis of large-scale international studies such as the Programme for International Student Assessment (PISA) conducted by the Organisation for Economic Cooperation and Development (OECD) (Stanat & Christensen, 2006). His general argument against bilingual education is based on the claim that lack of proficiency in the school language is a major cause of academic difficulties among immigrant students and, consequently, language assimilation through immersion in the school language is a necessary condition for both academic success and social integration. Esser's analysis of the PISA data suggests that knowledge and use of the school language in the home is strongly related to academic success whereas knowledge of the home language either makes no contribution or is negatively related to school success (depending on whether L1 knowledge is accompanied by strong L2 knowledge). He finds no evidence that bilingual education promotes academic development for minority students and suggests that "retention of the first language usually takes place at the cost of second language acquisition (and vice-versa)" (pp. 97–8).

Esser's (2006) argument is unconvincing because he interprets correlational data as causal and fails to take account of the fact that the relationship within PISA between home language and achievement disappeared for a large majority (10 out of 14) of OECD-member countries when socioeconomic status and other background variables were controlled (Stanat & Christensen, 2006, table 3.5, pp. 200–2). The disappearance of the relationship in a large majority of countries suggests that language spoken at home does not exert any independent effect on achievement but is rather a proxy for variables such as socioeconomic status and length of residence in the host country. Furthermore, any relationship between home language use and achievement is tangential to the issue of whether bilingual education is a legitimate and potentially useful policy option for teaching immigrant and linguistic minority students. The research data (summarized above) overwhelmingly demonstrate the legitimacy of bilingual education and neither Esser nor Rossell and her colleagues provide any credible evidence to the contrary.

Outcomes of Immersion Programs

The outcomes of second-language immersion programs are consistent with the more general findings from bilingual education. The immersion data derive primarily from the Canadian French immersion programs, which have been researched extensively, but also from studies in countries such as Spain (Huguet, Lasagabaster, & Vila, 2008), Japan (Bostwick, 1999), Ireland (Harris, 2007), Singapore (Pakir, 2008), South America (de Mejía, 2008), Sweden (Buss & Laurén, 1995), and the United States (Genesee & Lindholm-Leary, 2008). Note that "immersion" in these contexts is a form of bilingual education that aims to develop fluency and literacy in two languages. The Canadian findings are summarized below as illustrative of the more general trends.

In early immersion programs, students gain fluency and literacy in French at no apparent cost to their English academic skills. Within a year of the introduction of formal English language arts, students catch up in most aspects of English standardized test performance. Usually students require additional time to catch up in English spelling, but by Grade 5 there are normally no differences in English test performance between immersion students and comparison groups whose instruction has been totally through English. One potential limitation of these findings is that standardized tests do not assess all aspects of English academic skills; in particular, writing development is usually not assessed in such tests. However, the few studies that have examined English writing development specifically show no evidence of problems among immersion students in this regard (e.g., Swain, 1975). There is also no evidence of any long-term lag in mastery of subject matter taught through French in early, middle, or late immersion programs.

With respect to French skills, students' receptive skills in French are better developed (in relation to native speaker norms) than are their expressive skills. By the end of elementary school (Grade 6) students are close to the level of native speakers in understanding and reading of French but there are significant gaps between them and native speakers in spoken and written French. The gap is particularly evident with respect to accuracy of grammar and range of vocabulary knowledge and use. These gaps are clearly related to the restricted input that students receive in French. There is typically minimal contact or interaction with French speakers outside the school context and very few students read for pleasure in French. After the initial grades, reading in French tends to be primarily textbook reading, which is typically not particularly engaging for students. Thus, there are few opportunities for students to extend their exposure to French and expand their knowledge of vocabulary and grammar.

Writing also tends to be carried out only within the school context and applied to academic tasks that are often not highly engaging for students. Students seldom write for authentic purposes where they are encouraged to invest their identities in creative writing projects. As discussed later, a change in pedagogical approach that would emphasize extensive reading and writing across a wide range of genres might significantly improve students' range of vocabulary and grammatical accuracy in their expressive French.

The overall outcomes of French immersion programs can be summarized as follows:

- Students acquire good receptive skills (listening and reading) in French but their productive skills (speaking and writing) are limited with respect to grammatical accuracy and range of vocabulary.
- Teaching through L2 entails no adverse effects on L1 literacy development.
- In early immersion programs, students are able to develop decoding skills in French despite the fact that their French proficiency in the early grades is very limited.
- A large majority of students spontaneously develop English decoding skills in Grades 1 and 2 with no formal instruction in English reading.
- Immersion appears appropriate for a wide variety of students – not just an academic elite. Students with special needs, as well as those who speak a language other than English or French at home, can succeed in immersion programs.

In short, while immersion programs by themselves typically do not result in nativelike French proficiency, they do provide an excellent foundation for students to later "re-immerse" themselves in a genuine French language context, if they so desire, and develop their L2 skills closer to native speaker norms.

In the next section, I briefly sketch bilingual and immersion programs in different parts of the world in order to illustrate the range of sociolinguistic and sociopolitical contexts within which these programs have been implemented.

Illustrative Sketches of Bilingual and Immersion Programs

Malawi

Williams (1996) examined the impact of language of instruction on reading ability in L1 and L2 in Malawi and Zambia. In Malawi, Chichewa is the language of instruction for years 1–4 of primary school, with English taught as a subject. In

Zambia, English is the medium of instruction, with one of seven local languages taught as a subject. Williams administered an English reading test and a local language reading test (Chichewa in Malawi and the almost identical Nyanja in Zambia) to year 5 learners in six schools in each country. He reported no significant difference in English reading ability between students in each country, despite the huge difference in amount of English instruction. However, there were large differences in favor of Malawi in local language reading ability. Williams concluded that these results "are consistent with research on minority groups suggesting that instruction in L1 reading leads to improved results in L1 with no retardation in L2 reading" (p. 183).

Singapore

Pakir (2008) points out that the complexity of the language situation in Singapore does not fit neatly into dichotomous majority/minority language categorizations. English is one of the four official languages of Singapore together with Mandarin, Malay, and Tamil. English, the language of the former colonial power, was initially seen as a "neutral" language and was adopted as the major medium of instruction in school and the "first school language." The other languages were labeled "ethnic mother tongues" and given status as "second school languages." Thus, the bilingual education policy privileges English but also places strong emphasis on the Asian languages of the population. These languages are taught as subjects within the English-medium system. The Singapore educational system appears to be working effectively, as judged by international comparisons. Students from the major language backgrounds have performed well in international comparisons, not only in mathematics and science but also on measures of English literacy, where their scores are at similar levels to several countries where English is the first language of students (e.g., New Zealand, Scotland).

Mexico

Hamel (2008) notes that in 2005, approximately 55,000 indigenous teachers instructed over 1.2 million primary school students who were speakers of one of the 62 indigenous languages still spoken in Mexico. About half of the total indigenous primary school population are now taught by indigenous teachers. Unfortunately, however, the predominant focus in schools serving indigenous students has been on assimilation. Hamel points out that reading primers in indigenous languages funded and produced by the Mexican state are not extensively or effectively used. Reading is typically taught in Spanish from Grade 1. According to Hamel, "the attempt to teach literacy in a second language without sufficient acquisition of the necessary oral skills leads the teachers to underexploit the communicative potential of the primers, and to return to traditional practices of synthetic methods and structural pattern drill" (p. 317).

However, in recent years, new experimental projects have been implemented based on a pluralist conception of the state and full respect for indigenous peoples and their ethnic rights. These projects aim to maintain or revitalize indigenous cultures and languages. As one example, Hamel described how, in 1995, the P'urhepecha (Tarascan) teachers from two bilingual elementary schools in Michoacán, in the central Highlands of Mexico, changed the curriculum so that all subject matter including literacy and mathematics was taught in P'urhepecha, the children's L1. Teachers had to create their own materials and develop a writing system. Comparative research several years later reported that students who had acquired literacy in their L1 achieved significantly higher scores in both languages than those who were taught reading and writing in Spanish.

Pedagogical Issues within Bilingual and Immersion Programs

A number of pedagogical and organizational issues have been debated in the context of bilingual and immersion programs. One of these concerns the allocation of languages with respect to both instructional time and academic content to be taught through each language. A related issue concerns the appropriate language for initial reading instruction – should students be introduced to reading in their L1, the L2, or both languages more or less simultaneously? A third issue concerns the extent to which the two languages within a bilingual or immersion program should be kept separate or, alternatively, brought into contact, with the goal of encouraging transfer across languages and developing awareness of language.

Language allocation

It is generally accepted that within bilingual and immersion programs strong emphasis should be put on development of conversational and academic skills in the minority language. For dominant group students (e.g., in a second-language immersion program), exposure to the minority language is usually minimal outside of the school context; therefore, the development of proficiency in that language depends almost exclusively on input within the school. Students from language minority groups, on the other hand, are typically exposed to the minority language within the home. However, the status of this language is often low in comparison to the status of the dominant language. Students frequently internalize the status differential between the languages and, in the absence of L1 instruction, adopt the majority language as their language of choice with consequent loss of their L1 proficiency. Thus, within bilingual programs for minority students, strong emphasis on the minority language is intended to counteract the status imbalance between the languages and enable students to feel proud of their bilingual skills and develop literacy in both languages.

These considerations have led some policy makers and researchers to recommend maximizing instructional time through the minority language, particularly in the early stages of bilingual and immersion programs. However, reinforcement of the minority language is not just a matter of quantity of instruction. Some of the most successful bilingual and dual language programs in the United States have divided instructional time equally between Spanish and English (e.g., Freeman, 1998). Programs that have initially emphasized the minority language over the majority language (e.g., 90 percent Spanish, 10 percent English in the early grades) have also demonstrated a high level of success (e.g., Lindholm-Leary, 2001). Thus, a variety of options are possible and the research does not point to the superiority of any particular model of language allocation. There is consensus, however, that at least 50 percent of the instructional time should be spent through the minority language for as long as possible throughout the elementary school years.

In the context of language revitalization efforts, immersion programs often maximize instruction through the minority language as a means of extending the domains in which the language is used and the functions served by the language. Most Maori immersion programs in Aoteroa/New Zealand, for example, use Maori exclusively from pre-school through Grade 4 (and sometimes longer), with English introduced only at Grade 5. Typically, English is taught in a classroom separate from the rest of the school so that the school functions essentially as an "English-free zone." The rationale for this policy is that the school is one of the very few places where Maori is normalized as a legitimate language of communication, and academic skills developed through Maori will transfer to English, which is the home language of most of the students. Although debate continues in the Aoteroa/New Zealand context about when and how English should be introduced (e.g., May, Hill, & Tiakiwai, 2003), the decision is essentially a local one, since the broader research suggests that a range of options are feasible and consistent with successful bilingual development.

Similar considerations apply to the issue of which subjects should be taught through each language. This is essentially a decision that should be taken at the local level, taking account of issues such as parent preferences, textbook availability, teacher expertise in particular subject matter, and assessment regime in the wider educational context. For example, in the United States, high-stakes tests are typically administered in Grade 3 through the majority language (English). This reality may lead some policy makers to adopt a 50/50 rather than a 90/10 model and ensure that subjects that will be tested (e.g., reading and mathematics) are taught through English for a sufficient period of time to ensure that students will be successful on the tests.

Language of initial reading instruction

Most immersion programs provide initial reading instruction through students' L2 (e.g., French immersion programs). However, this practice is not based on any research suggesting that introducing reading in L2 is superior to teaching children to read in their L1. It is simply consistent with the philosophy of immersion and the fact that countless evaluations have demonstrated that students can acquire decoding skills through a language that is still inadequately developed.

Immersion and dual language programs that teach reading through students' L1 have also demonstrated success. Similarly, teaching literacy in both languages simultaneously or in quick succession appears to be quite feasible (e.g., Freeman, 1998). As in the case of language allocation, the decision regarding initial language of reading instruction is best viewed as a local option.

There is considerable consensus among researchers, however, that for minority students in bilingual programs, reading should normally be introduced in L1. In some cases, the home language has a more regular sound–symbol relationship than is the case with the dominant language (e.g., Spanish and English in the United States). There is also the consideration that many minority students from low-income backgrounds may come to school with relatively little exposure to literacy in the home; under these circumstances, it makes sense to introduce reading through the language the student already knows. Literacy instruction through minority students' L1 also facilitates the involvement of parents in their children's literacy development and reinforces the status of students' L1.

However, there is also extensive research that demonstrates that many language minority students acquire L2 decoding skills under conditions of initial L2 literacy instruction (Geva, 2006). Thus, the issue of initial literacy instruction remains a local option even though most bilingual programs serving language minority students introduce reading to students through their L1 for the reasons outlined above.

Monolingual or bilingual instructional strategies?

Lambert (1984) clearly expressed the monolingual instructional philosophy under-lying French immersion programs:

> No bilingual skills are required of the teacher, who plays the role of a monolingual in the target language . . . and who never switches languages, reviews materials in the other language, or otherwise uses the child's native language in teacher-pupil interactions. In immersion programs, therefore, bilingualism is developed through two separate monolingual instructional routes. (p. 13)

Adoption of monolingual instructional strategies within immersion programs reflects what Howatt (1984), in his history of English language teaching, referred to as the "monolingual principle." This principle emphasizes instructional use of the target language (TL) to the exclusion of students' L1, with the goal of enabling students to think in the TL with minimal interference from L1. This principle initially gained widespread acceptance more than 100 years ago in the context of the *direct method* and has continued to exert a strong influence on various language teaching approaches since that time (Howatt, 1984). According to Yu (2000), "the direct method imitated the way that children learn their first language, emphasizing the avoidance of translation and the direct use of the foreign language as the medium of instruction in all situations" (p. 176). Con-sistent with direct method principles, translation across languages is seen as unacceptable within immersion (and many bilingual) programs.

There is certainly a rationale for creating largely separate spaces for each language within a bilingual or immersion program. However, there are also compelling arguments to be made for teaching for transfer across languages. The reality is that students are making cross-linguistic connections throughout the course of their learning in a bilingual or immersion program (Jessner, 2006), so why not nurture this learning strategy and help students to apply it more efficiently?

Teaching for cross-linguistic transfer is consistent with both the interdependence hypothesis and the extensive research supporting the crucial role that prior knowledge plays in all learning (e.g., Bransford, Brown, & Cocking, 2000). The interdependence hypothesis has drawn attention to the reality of cross-linguistic transfer in virtually all second-language learning situations. It is reasonable to argue that learning efficiencies can be achieved if teachers explicitly draw students' attention to similarities and differences between their languages and reinforce effective learning strategies in a coordinated way across languages. For example, if the teacher is explaining the meaning of the term *predict* in science (taught in English) within a French immersion program, it makes sense to explain the meaning of the root (from the Latin *dicere* meaning 'to say') and the prefix (meaning 'before'), as well as drawing students' attention to the fact that the root and prefix operate in exactly the same way in the French word *prédire*.

Similarly, the centrality of prior knowledge in the learning process implies that instruction should explicitly attempt to activate students' prior knowledge and build relevant background knowledge as necessary. This holds true regardless of whether students are being instructed through L1 or L2. However, monolingual instructional approaches appear at variance with this fundamental principle of learning because they regard students' L1 (and, by implication, the knowledge encoded therein) as potentially an impediment to the learning of L2. As a result, these approaches are unlikely to focus on activation of students' prior knowledge. In cases where monolingual approaches do acknowledge the role of prior knowledge, they are likely to limit its expression to what students can articulate through their L2.

Among the bilingual instructional strategies that can be employed to promote literacy engagement in both L1 and L2 are the following (Cummins, 2008):

- focus on cognates in contexts where the languages share common linguistic origins;
- creation and web-publication of dual language multimedia books and projects (see, for example, www.multiliteracies.ca and http://thornwood.peelschools. org/Dual/); the creation of dual language books clearly involves translation across languages, a practice that has hitherto been viewed as pedagogically unacceptable in immersion and bilingual programs;
- sister class exchanges in which students use the Internet to connect with other bilingual students and use both L1 and L2 to create literature and art and/or to explore issues of social relevance to them and their communities.

Immersion researchers are beginning to acknowledge that students' use of their L1 serves some legitimate and useful learning functions within the L2-medium classroom (Swain & Lapkin, 2000, 2005). According to Swain and Lapkin (2005), students' use of the L1 enables them to develop strategies to carry out tasks in the target language and to work through complex problems more efficiently than they might be able to do through their L2. They also point to the changing demographic realities of immersion education in Canada and in other contexts – an increasing number of students from language backgrounds other then English and French are now in immersion programs. They argue that it is important to support the home language development of these students within the immersion program, in addition to the teaching of French and English.

In short, although most bilingual and immersion programs continue to rely almost exclusively on monolingual instructional strategies, there is emerging recognition that students' L1 *can* function as a cognitive and linguistic resource to scaffold more accomplished performance in the L2.

Conclusion

Research during the past 40 years has clearly established bilingual and immersion programs as a legitimate educational option for both majority and minority language students. For majority language students, bilingual/immersion education provides an effective means of developing proficiency in a target language at no cost to students' fluency or literacy in their L1. For minority students, bilingual education similarly promotes development of fluency and literacy in two languages; furthermore, in the case of minority students who are at risk of school failure, bilingual education has demonstrated its potential to support students' overall academic development more effectively than programs conducted exclusively through the majority language.

In the current era of unprecedented population mobility, the economic and personal utility of bilingual and multilingual skills has become increasingly obvious, and this phenomenon has propelled awareness of, and interest in, bilingual and immersion education. Population mobility also increases the number of children from linguistically diverse groups in countries around the world. Although it is clearly not feasible to implement bilingual programs on a large scale in school situations that are highly multilingual, there is increasing recognition among educators in many contexts that minority students' home languages represent (1) a significant intellectual and personal resource for the students themselves, (2) an important communicative tool within families, and, (3) in an interdependent world, an economic and diplomatic resource for the nation as a whole. In Ontario, Canada, for example, Ministry of Education documents now highlight the importance of students' home languages and provide concrete strategies to enable educators to support students' languages within the mainstream (English-medium) classroom (Ontario Ministry of Education, 2006).

Although there is no longer serious debate about the scientific legitimacy of bilingual education for linguistic minorities, the ideological debate is likely to continue for the foreseeable future, partly because it has very little directly to do with education. The issues concern the extent to which societies should adopt a pluralist approach that encourages children and communities to maintain and develop their languages and culture, in addition to acquiring the majority language, or alternatively, whether schools should promote the assimilation of immigrants and encourage minority students to abandon their home languages and cultures. In contexts where this debate is raging, bilingual programs are frequently seen as valuable and worthy of public funding when they are directed toward the acquisition of additional languages by dominant group students, but highly problematic when the beneficiary of bilingual education is a minority or subordinated group.

REFERENCES

August, D. & Shanahan, T. (eds.) (2006). *Developing literacy in second-language learners.* Mahwah, NJ: Lawrence Erlbaum.

Baker, C. (2001). *Foundations of bilingual education and bilingualism,* 3rd edn. Clevedon, UK: Multilingual Matters.

Bostwick, R. M. (1999). A study of an elementary English language immersion school in Japan. Unpublished Doctoral dissertation, Temple University, Philadelphia.

Bransford, J. D., Brown, A. L., & Cocking, R. R. (2000). *How people learn: Brain, mind, experience, and school.* Washington, DC: National Academy Press.

Buss, M. & Laurén, C. (1995). Language immersion: Teaching and second language acquisition: From Canada to Europe. *Proceedings of the University of Vaasa Research Papers. Tutkimuksia No. 192.* Vaasa: University of Vaasa.

Cummins, J. (1979). Linguistic interdependence and the educational development of bilingual children. *Review of Educational Research* 49, 222–51.

Cummins, J. (1981). The role of primary language development in promoting educational success for language minority students. In California State Department of Education (ed.), *Schooling and language minority students: A theoretical framework.* Evaluation, Dissemination and Assessment Center, California State University, Los Angeles.

Cummins, J. (1999). Alternative paradigms in bilingual education research: Does theory have a place? *Educational Researcher* 28, 26–41.

Cummins, J. (2001). *Negotiating identities: Education for empowerment in a diverse society,* 2nd edn. Los Angeles: California Association for Bilingual Education.

Cummins, J. (2008). Teaching for transfer: Challenging the two solitudes assumption in bilingual education. In J. Cummins & N. H. Hornberger (eds.), *Encyclopedia of language and education,* 2nd edn., vol. 5: *Bilingual education* (pp. 65–75). New York: Springer Science/Business Media LLC.

Cummins, J. & Hornberger, N. H. (eds.) (2008). *Encyclopedia of language and education,* 2nd edn., vol. 5: *Bilingual education.* New York: Springer Science/Business Media LLC.

de Mejía, A. M. (2008). Enrichment bilingual education in South America. In J. Cummins & N. H. Hornberger (eds.), *Encyclopedia of language and education,* 2nd edn., vol. 5: *Bilingual education* (pp. 323–31). New York: Springer Science/Business Media LLC.

Dressler, C. & Kamil, M. (2006). First- and second-language literacy. In D. August & T. Shanahan (eds.), *Developing literacy in second-language learners: Report of the National Literacy Panel on Language-Minority Children and Youth* (pp. 197–238). Mahwah, NJ: Lawrence Erlbaum.

Esser, H. (2006). *Migration, language, and integration.* AKI Research Review 4. Berlin: Programme on Intercultural Conflicts and Societal Integration (AKI), Social Science Research Center. Retrieved 21 December 2007 from http://www.wzb.eu/zkd/aki/files/aki_research_review_4.pdf.

Francis, D., Lesaux, N., & August, D. (2006). Language of instruction. In D. August & T. Shanahan (eds.), *Developing literacy in second-language learners: Report of the National Literacy Panel on Language-Minority Children and Youth* (pp. 365–413). Mahwah, NJ: Lawrence Erlbaum.

Freeman, R. D. (1998). *Bilingual education and social change.* Clevedon, UK: Multilingual Matters.

García, O. & Baker, C. (2007). *Bilingual education: An introductory reader.* Clevedon, UK: Multilingual Matters.

Genesee, F. & Lindholm-Leary, K. (2008). Dual language education in Canada and the USA. In J. Cummins & N. H. Hornberger (eds.), *Encyclopedia of language and education,* 2nd edn., vol. 5: *Bilingual education* (pp. 253–63). New York: Springer Science/Business Media LLC.

Genesee, F., Lindholm-Leary, K., Saunders, W. M., & Christian, D. (eds.) (2006). *Educating English language learners: A synthesis of research evidence.* New York: Cambridge University Press.

Geva, E. (2006). Second-language oral proficiency and second-language literacy. In D. August & T. Shanahan (eds.), *Developing literacy in second-language learners: Report of the National Literacy Panel on Language-Minority Children and Youth* (pp. 123–39). Mahwah, NJ: Lawrence Erlbaum.

Hamel, R. E. (2008). Bilingual education for indigenous communities in Mexico. In J. Cummins & N. H. Hornberger (eds.), *Encyclopedia of language and education,* 2nd edn., vol. 5: *Bilingual education* (pp. 311–21). New York: Springer Science/Business Media LLC.

Harris, J. (2007). Bilingual education and bilingualism in Ireland North and South. *International Journal of Bilingual Education and Bilingualism* 10, 359–68.

Howatt, A. (1984). *A history of English language teaching.* Oxford: Oxford University Press.

Huguet, A., Lasagabaster, D., & Vila, I. (2008). Bilingual education in Spain: Present realities and future challenges. In J. Cummins & N. H. Hornberger (eds.), *Encyclopedia of language and education,* 2nd edn., vol. 5: *Bilingual education* (pp. 225–37). New York: Springer Science/Business Media LLC.

Jessner, U. (2006). *Linguistic awareness in multilinguals: English as a third language.* Edinburgh: Edinburgh University Press.

Johnson, R. K. & Swain, M. (1997). *Immersion education: International perspectives.* Cambridge: Cambridge University Press.

Lambert, W. E. (1984). An overview of issues in immersion education. In California State Department of Education (ed.), *Studies on immersion education: A collection for United States educators* (pp. 8–30). Sacramento: California State Department of Education.

Lambert, W. E. & Tucker, G. R. (1972). *Bilingual education of children: The St. Lambert experiment.* Rowley, MA: Newbury House.

Lindholm-Leary, K. (2001). *Dual language education*. Clevedon, UK: Multilingual Matters.

Lindholm-Leary, K. J. & Borsato, G. (2006). Academic achievement. In F. Genesee, K. Lindholm-Leary, W. Saunders, & D. Christian (eds.), *Educating English language learners* (pp. 176–222). New York: Cambridge University Press.

Macnamara, J. (1966). *Bilingualism and primary education*. Edinburgh: Edinburgh University Press.

Mahshie, S. N. (1995). *Educating Deaf children bilingually: With insights and applications from Sweden and Denmark*. Washington, DC: Gallaudat University.

Malherbe, E. G. (1946). *The bilingual school*. Johannesburg: The Bilingual School Association.

May, S. (2008). Bilingual/immersion education: What the research tells us. In J. Cummins & N. H. Hornberger (eds.), *Encyclopedia of language and education*, 2nd edn., vol. 5: *Bilingual education* (pp. 19–33). New York: Springer Science/Business Media LLC.

May, S., Hill, R., and Tiakiwai, S. (2003). *Bilingual/immersion education: Indicators of good practice*. Final Report for New Zealand Ministry of Education. Hamilton: Wilf Malcolm Institute of Educational Research.

Ontario Ministry of Education (2006). *Many roots, many voices*. Toronto: Ministry of Education. Available at: http://www.edu.gov.on.ca/eng/document/manyroots/.

Pakir, A. (2008). Bilingual education in Singapore. In J. Cummins & N. H. Hornberger (eds.), *Encyclopedia of language and education*, 2nd edn., vol. 5: *Bilingual education* (pp. 191–203). New York: Springer Science/Business Media LLC.

Rolstad, K., Mahoney, K., & Glass, G. V. (2005). The big picture: A meta-analysis of program effectiveness research on English language learners. *Education Policy* 10, 572–94.

Rossell, C. H. & Baker, K. (1996). The effectiveness of bilingual education. *Research in the Teaching of English* 30, 7–74.

Rossell, C. H. & Kuder, J. (2005). Meta-murky: A rebuttal to recent meta-analyses of bilingual education. In J. Söhn (ed.), *The effectiveness of bilingual school programs for immigrant children*, AKI Research Review 2 (pp. 43–76). Berlin: Programme on Intercultural Conflicts and Societal Integration (AKI), Social Science Research Center. Retrieved 21 December 2007 from http://www.wzb.eu/zkd/aki/files/aki_bilingual_school_programs.pdf.

Skutnabb-Kangas, T. (2000). *Linguistic genocide in education – or worldwide diversity and human rights*. Mawah, NJ: Lawrence Erlbaum.

Skutnabb-Kangas, T. & McCarty, T. L. (2008). Key concepts in bilingual education: Ideological, historical, epistemological and empirical foundations. In J. Cummins & N. H. Hornberger (eds.), *Encyclopedia of language and education*, 2nd edn., vol. 5: *Bilingual education* (pp. 3–17). New York: Springer Science/Business Media LLC.

Small, A. & Mason, D. (2008). American Sign Language (ASL) bilingual bicultural education. In J. Cummins & N. H. Hornberger (eds.), *Encyclopedia of language and education*, 2nd edn., vol. 5: *Bilingual education* (pp. 133–5). New York: Springer Science/Business Media LLC.

Stanat, P. & Christensen, G. (2006). *Where immigrant students succeed: A comparative review of performance and engagement in PISA 2003*. Paris: Organisation for Economic Cooperation and Development.

Swain, M. (1975). Writing skills of grade three French immersion pupils. *Working Papers on Bilingualism* 7, 1–38.

Swain, M. & Lapkin, S. (2000). Task-based second language learning: The uses of the first language. *Language Teaching Research* 4, 253–76.

Swain, M. & Lapkin, S. (2005). The evolving sociopolitical context of immersion education in Canada: Some implications for program development. *International Journal of Applied Linguistics* 15, 169–86.

Thomas, W. P. & Collier, V. P. (2002). *A national study of school effectiveness for language minority students' long-term academic achievement*. Santa Cruz, CA: Center for Research on Education, Diversity and Excellence, University of California-Santa Cruz. Available at: http//www.crede.ucsc.edu.

Williams, E. (1996). Reading in two languages at Year 5 in African primary schools. *Applied Linguistics* 17, 2, 183–209.

Yu, W. (2000). Direct method. In M. Byram (ed.), *Routledge encyclopedia of language teaching and learning* (pp. 176–8). New York: Routledge.

11   Heritage Language Programs

SILVINA MONTRUL

Introduction

The last decade has seen an important change in second language classrooms as a result of recent immigration patterns all over the world, especially in Western Europe, Australia, and North America. Partly due to these demographic changes and to the impact of globalization on international relations, today more than ever before, an increasing number of bilingual speakers of minority languages wish to maintain and/or (re)learn their family language. As a consequence, post-secondary foreign/second language classes typically geared to students who have little to no background in the target language (L2 learners) have had to accommodate speakers who were exposed to the language at home early in childhood (henceforth, heritage language learners or HL learners) and whose levels of oral proficiency in the language range from minimal to advanced.[1] While many institutions place HL learners in foreign/second language classrooms that follow a traditional L2 curriculum, in the 1970s other institutions started to create special courses to address the specific linguistic and cultural needs of HL learners. These are heritage language programs.

With this increasing trend, there is growing recognition that heritage language programs should be informed by a theory of HL acquisition and teaching (Kondo-Brown, 2003; Lynch, 2003; Valdés, 1997, 2005). To date, there is very little systematic research on HL learners and HL acquisition, although the situation is rapidly changing.

My purpose in this chapter is to show how a combination of the linguistic and cognitive views of first and second language acquisition can be extended to make predictions about the heritage language learning process that teaching is designed to bring about. I will then discuss what most recent research has so far uncovered about heritage speakers of different languages and their language learning process. Finally, I will evaluate how existing programs and models for heritage language teaching are consistent with the predictions of the theoretical position I advance here.

Heritage Languages and Speakers

Although originally coined in Canada, the term *heritage language* began to be used in the United States in the 1990s to refer to minority languages (Cummins, 2005). Commonly used terms in different parts of the world are *international, community, immigrant, ethnic, indigenous, minority, ancestral, third*, and *non-official language*. In the United States, a *heritage language* is a language other than English spoken by immigrants and their children (Valdés, 2001).[2] One problem with this definition is that immigrant languages may have dual or multiple statuses. For example, in the United States, Spanish is the most widely studied foreign language in elementary and high schools. It is also a second language, since the United States ranks fifth in the world for the number of Spanish speakers. And because Spanish is spoken by Latino immigrants, it is also a heritage language. Polish, on the other hand, is a heritage language whose distribution is highly restricted.

Like the term heritage language, *heritage speaker* is not easy to define. From an ethnolinguistic perspective, what defines a heritage speaker is cultural and linguistic identity (Carreira, 2004; Wiley, 2001). A heritage speaker is a member of an ethnolinguistically minority culture, that is, an individual who may or may not have knowledge of the language. From this perspective, individuals who have one grandparent or great-grandparent from the minority language culture are considered heritage speakers, even if the person was not exposed to the language at home and does not speak the language. Similarly, African Americans wishing to learn Swahili to understand their origins may be considered heritage speakers, as may third- or fourth-generation Italians, with no knowledge of the language, living in Argentina or the United States. Two main reasons motivating these individuals to learn the heritage language are familiarity with the culture and/or a desire to reconnect with their ancestral roots.

While linguistic and cultural identity is certainly a feature that characterizes heritage speakers, researchers approaching the issue from linguistics and education take linguistic proficiency in the heritage language as a defining factor. In the US context, Valdés (2001) defines a heritage speaker as a *bilingual* individual "raised in a home where a non-English language is spoken, who speaks or merely understands the heritage language, and who is to some degree bilingual in English and the heritage language" (p. 1). The term *bilingual*, like the term *speaker* in *heritage speaker*, implies that the individual must have some oral command of the heritage language. But what makes matters even more complicated is that the profiles of these speakers vary greatly. Sociolinguists often relate generation of immigration and degree of bilingualism as a result of acculturation patterns (Silva-Corvalán, 1994). Table 11.1 illustrates some characteristics of heritage speakers based on generation and degree of bilingualism.

First generation immigrants immigrate to the host country as adults. They are typically monolingual speakers of the heritage language, and most of them learn the majority language late in life (and imperfectly). Command of the heritage

Table 11.1 Linguistic characteristics of heritage speakers

Generation	*Possible language characteristics*	
First generation (parents)	Monolingual in the heritage language	Incipient L2 learner of the majority language
Second generation (children)	Dominant in the heritage language	Dominant in the majority language
Third generation (grandchildren)	Dominant in the majority language	Monolingual in the majority language

language is strong in this immigrant group, although there can be some attrition after more than 10 years of intense exposure to the majority language (Köpke and Schmid, 2003).

The children of the first generation are the second generation immigrants. This group may include the children of first generation immigrants born in the host country to at least one first generation parent. It also includes immigrant children who come to the host country before the age of 5. In terms of types of bilingual profile, this group may include: (1) simultaneous bilinguals, those exposed to the heritage and the majority language before the age of 5; (2) sequential bilinguals or child L2 learners, those exposed to the heritage language at home until age 4–5, and to the majority language once they start pre-school; and (3) late child L2 learners, children monolingual in the heritage language, who received some elementary schooling in their home country and immigrated around age 7–8.

It is in the second generation when language shift in the home typically occurs, due to the fact that children are schooled in the majority language and have a strong desire to fit in with the new society. With language shift, there are concomitant changes in the bilingual balance of second generation children until adulthood. As the majority language begins to be used more than the home language, the heritage language may be either incompletely acquired or undergo attrition.[3] In early childhood, many of these children are either monolingual or dominant in the heritage language. As bilingualism progresses during the elementary school period, the children can be balanced in the two languages (typically at age 10–11, according to Kohnert, Bates, & Hernández, 1999) and eventually become dominant in the majority language. When they reach adolescence, they are already dominant in the majority language, and by the time they are adults the majority language is both stronger and dominant in proficiency and domains of use. Due to this rapid shift, which is very common in the United States as a result of its covert English-only language policies, by the third generation (the grandchildren of the first generation immigrants) heritage speakers are native speakers of the majority language. Some may have partial knowledge of the heritage language (if a grandparent or other relative lives in the home), while most do not. By the fourth and subsequent generations, the language is no longer used in the family. This pattern of declining bilingualism shows how heritage languages do not survive intergenerational transmission in many countries even when they are supported by continuous immigration.

The Acquisition of Heritage Languages

From an acquisition perspective, heritage speakers are bilinguals who were exposed to the heritage language early in childhood. Thus, age of onset of bilingualism and type of linguistic support throughout the lifetime are key factors in understanding different heritage speaker profiles. Adult heritage speakers may have failed to develop full linguistic competence as they began using the majority language intensively at different ages in childhood and did not receive schooling in the heritage language. Heritage speakers are a case of incomplete acquisition (Montrul, 2002; Polinsky, 1997). As a result, many of these individuals want to acquire, reacquire, or expand their knowledge of the heritage language in a classroom setting in early adulthood. Currently, there are two main models to instruct such HL learners: L2 programs or HL programs. Ignoring for the moment practical issues affecting the implementation of one model over the other, important theoretical assumptions underlie the two models, even if these assumptions are not spelled out explicitly.

The L2 program model assumes that HL and L2 learners with little or no previous knowledge of the language are linguistically alike, while the HL model assumes that there are important cultural and linguistic differences between heritage and non-heritage learners. Two questions remain unanswered: first, how are HL learners similar to or different from L1 and L2 learners? And second, what theoretical approach(es) can account for the type of knowledge HL learners have or lack? These questions are crucial for understanding the linguistic needs of these learners and identifying the best way to address their needs in the classroom.

L1 and L2 acquisition

Early L1 acquisition happens through the aural medium and takes place in a naturalistic setting by means of interaction with caregivers and with limited access to correction and feedback on grammatical form. L1 acquisition is *universal, uniform,* and *complete.* It is universal because by 3–4 years of age all normally developing monolingual children master the basic structure of their native language, including its phonology, morphosyntax, semantics, and some aspects of pragmatics and sociolinguistic conventions. It is uniform because children exposed to the same language or dialect reach the same level of linguistic development (and competence) despite variations in input. In effect, children converge on the grammar of other members of the speech community. It is complete because the outcome of the acquisition process is successful, although this does not mean it is entirely error free. While basic acquisition of the structure and conventions of the language is relatively rapid, children make errors along the way. In all languages there are well-documented developmental stages in different areas of linguistic knowledge, such that some structures and sounds are controlled earlier than others. However, the phenomenon of fossilization (Lardiere, 2006; Long, 2003; Selinker, 1972), or arrested development, so typical of adult L2 acquisition, does not occur.

With the linguistic foundations of the language and the essentials of native-speaker competence in place by age 3–4, language acquisition continues beyond this early period. Around age 4, children's metalinguistic ability develops through emergent literacy and continues at school, where children learn to read and write, expand their vocabulary, and acquire more complex structures. Exposure to rich oral and written input allows children to learn to communicate in different registers and styles, both orally and in writing. At the end of the process, children become educated adult native speakers capable of functioning in many social and professional contexts.

Postpuberty L2 acquisition, on the other hand, typically occurs in a classroom setting, with heavy emphasis on reading and writing, and grammatical explanations, practice, feedback, and assessment of the developing L2 skills. Unlike L1 acquisition by children, adult L2 acquisition is *not universal* – not everybody learns a second language. L2 acquisition is *variable* rather than uniform – not all L2 learners attain the same level of linguistic competence in the second language. In terms of outcome, L2 acquisition is typically *incomplete* – most learners never reach the competence of a native speaker. Throughout the process of acquisition, L2 learners make both developmental errors, like L1 learners, and transfer errors due to influence from their L1, especially at early stages. A key difference between L1 and L2 acquisition, however, is that while child L1 learners overcome developmental errors without need for instruction, L2 learners continue to make many errors even after receiving instruction, practice, and correction. Although some researchers argue that attainment of full linguistic competence in the L2 is in principle possible, it is by no means guaranteed. Fossilization can occur at any point in L2 development.

Due to these characteristics, it has been hypothesized that L1 and L2 acquisition utilize very different learning mechanisms, as spelled out in Bley-Vroman's (1989) Fundamental Difference Hypothesis (FDH). According to Bley-Vroman (and other generative linguists), child L1 acquisition happens so rapidly and efficiently because the process is guided largely by innate mechanisms, which are assumed to be part of Universal Grammar (Chomsky, 1981). That is, at the outset of language acquisition, children are guided by the inventory of principles and constraints subsumed under Universal Grammar. To explain the apparent differences between L1 and L2 acquisition in terms of outcome, the main claim of the FDH is that access to Universal Grammar is subject to a critical period, such that when learning a second language, postpuberty L2 learners can only rely on their L1 knowledge (a particular instantiation of Universal Grammar, but not the full spectrum of linguistic options) and the principles and parameters active in their language. Unable to utilize domain-specific (i.e., purely linguistic) mechanisms as L1 learners, L2 learners resort to domain-general problem-solving skills, like analogy or pattern matching, instead.[4]

This particular position within generative linguistics is echoed within cognitive and neurolinguistic perspectives on L2 acquisition, which do not necessarily view language and language learning as innate, but take into account the distinction between procedural and declarative knowledge and implicit and explicit language learning (DeKeyser, 2003; Paradis, 2004). Implicit knowledge refers to that learned without awareness of what is being learned, and is learned incidentally or not (depending on the researcher). Implicit knowledge is stored in procedural memory, and when this knowledge is accessed or recalled, it is executed automatically and quickly. By contrast, explicit knowledge is acquired with awareness of what is being learned, and with conscious effort. Because explicit knowledge is learned explicitly, individuals can verbalize this knowledge on demand. It is stored in declarative or episodic memory, where our world knowledge is stored.

Adult educated native speakers have both systems of learning available and use them as needed. According to Paradis (2004), when young children speak or comprehend language, they use implicit competence (or knowledge) only. This is also true of adults who are illiterate. By contrast, incipient L2 learners use explicit knowledge of the L2 when producing or understanding the L2, and steadily and in tandem develop implicit competence of it. In agreement with Bley-Vroman's position, De Keyser (2000, 2003) also contends that adult L2 learners use a different cognitive system to learn an L2 because maturational constraints apply to implicit linguistic competence acquired early in childhood. The decline of procedural memory and loss of implicit cognitive mechanisms for language somewhere in childhood – what Bley-Vroman takes to be Universal Grammar and domain-specific mechanisms – force late L2 learners to rely on explicit learning. Where does HL acquisition fit in this model?

Heritage language acquisition

Descriptively, HL acquisition has characteristics of both L1 and L2 acquisition. It is incomplete L1 acquisition that takes place in a bilingual environment rather than in a monolingual one. As such, HL acquisition shares the development path (or lack thereof) and characteristics of L2 grammars as well. Table 11.2 summarizes the characteristics of these three types of acquisition: L1, L2, and HL. Bold type represents the intersecting subset between L1 and L2 acquisition which characterizes HLA.

As can be seen, HL and L1 learners are both exposed to the language in early childhood through the aural medium, and before the emergence of literacy. Recall that this is the period during which the essence of native-speaker competence develops. HL learners may command basic structures of the language if they received abundant input, or only a subset of those structures, if the input was less abundant. Because HL acquisition takes place in a bilingual environment,

Table 11.2   Characteristics of L1, L2, and HL acquisition

L1 Acquisition	*L2 Acquisition*
Early exposure to the language	Late exposure to the language
Naturalistic setting (aural input)	Instructed and/or naturalistic setting (aural and written input)
Abundant input	**Varying amount of input**
Control of features of language acquired very early in life (phonology, some vocabulary, some linguistic structures)	Grammar may be incomplete (no chance to develop other structures and vocabulary)
Developmental errors	**Developmental and transfer errors**
Outcome is successful and complete	**Outcome is variable proficiency. It is typically incomplete**
Fossilization does not occur	**Fossilization is typical**
No clear role for motivation and affective factors to develop linguistic competence	**Motivation and affective factors play a role in language development**
More complex structures and vocabulary developed at school after age 5, when metalinguistic skills develop.	Experience with literacy and formal instruction

Bold type = HL acquisition

as a HL learner develops command of the majority language, he or she also makes transfer errors. The outcome of HL acquisition is also variable and often incomplete, as in L2 acquisition, due to reduction of input and use of language in restricted contexts. Fossilization, so typical of L2 acquisition but unheard of in L1 acquisition, is also frequent in incomplete HL acquisition. Notice that the last row of Table 11.2 is not bold. This is because HL learners do not typically receive schooling in their HL like monolingual children after age 4–5, unless they attend a bilingual or dual immersion program that teaches the HL. Because they do not experience literacy training or formal instruction in their HL, whatever skills they possess are probably transferred from their metalinguistic and literacy development in the majority language.

   If some cases of HL acquisition are incomplete or interrupted L1 acquisition in a bilingual environment, then one theoretical prediction is that HL learner's knowledge of the language (prior to instruction) has been acquired implicitly and through access to Universal Grammar in childhood, before the closure of the critical period. That is, HL learners should have implicit knowledge of aspects of phonology and morphosyntax (basic word order, Pro-drop parameter, binding principles), which emerge very early in childhood and that are not overly dependent on a heavy amount of continuous input. In turn, aspects of language that are context-dependent, acquired after age 5, and reinforced through reading and formal instruction at school – such as specific vocabulary, forms of address and honorifics, complex structures like relative clauses, and semantically and pragmatically conditioned uses of the subjunctive in Spanish and Russian, for example – should either be missing or remain imperfectly acquired, depending on the amount of input received. Table 11.3 lists six predictions this cognitive-linguistic perspective makes for HL acquisition.

In summary, if HL learners are interrupted L1 learners who received some crucial input during the critical period, instruction should be able to turn incomplete native speakers into complete educated native speakers, given optimal amounts of input and time to develop the underdeveloped skills. Timing and amount of input will vary as a function of the HL learner's competence in the language. In principle, it should be faster for HL learners to reach certain linguistic milestones than for L2 learners. By contrast, regardless of amount of input and experience with the target language, L2 learners are not necessarily guaranteed to attain native-speaker competence in the L2. Thus, the theory of language learning just discussed predicts that HL learners have the potential to reach nativelike competence in the HL. With this background, the next section presents recent research findings that bear on this theory.

Research Findings

Comparing L2 and HL learners

The first prediction listed in Table 11.3 – that heritage speakers should be better than L2 learners in basic aspects of phonology and morphosyntax – is confirmed by a series of recent findings. Au et al. (2002) and Oh et al. (2003) compared accent ratings and the production of stop consonants in Spanish (voiceless [p, t, k], voiced [b, d, g]) and Korean (aspirated [p, t, k], lax [p, t, k] and tense [p, t, k]) by very low-proficiency HL and L2 learners. Both studies found that HL learners outperformed L2 learners in both accent ratings and VOT measures. While Au et al. also claimed there was no advantage for HL learners in morphosyntax, this conclusion is premature. Montrul (2005) looked at the syntactic distribution of intransitive verbs in Spanish, and Montrul et al. (2006) focused on the acquisition of object clitic placement and word order in Spanish. Both studies showed that low-proficiency HL learners were more accurate than proficiency-matched L2 learners in a grammaticality judgment task and an online processing task. These advantages for HL learners over L2 learners in basic grammatical areas was also supported by Montrul's (2006) study of subject pronouns, agreement, and word

Table 11.3   Some predictions of a cognitive and linguistic approach to HL acquisition

1   HL learners should be better than L2 learners with aspects of grammar that are acquired early in childhood (phonology; basic aspects of syntax, like word order; basic aspects of morphosyntax, like nominal and verbal agreement), even when their proficiency in the language is low to intermediate.

2   Transfer errors from the stronger language (L2 in HL learners and L1 in L2 learners) should occur in grammatical areas where the two languages differ parametrically.

3   HL learners should be more accurate and faster than L2 learners in oral than in written production and comprehension tasks.

4   HL learners should be more accurate and faster than L2 learners in written tasks that require less metalinguistic awareness.

5   If adults are left with their explicit learning skills for learning language beyond childhood, explicitly learned knowledge may mask implicit linguistic competence in L2 learners, especially if the tasks used to tap that knowledge are metalinguistic.

6   For many researchers, it is not clear that L2 learners eventually develop implicit competence of their L2, although this remains controversial. If L2 learners have lost access to implicit linguistic competence, then they should not be able to perform like native speakers, even after several years of instruction and immersion. By contrast, if HL learners have some implicit knowledge of the HL acquired in childhood, they should eventually catch up with the missing explicit and metalinguistic knowledge that they did not get at school through reading and writing instruction.

order in Spanish. Results showed that while intermediate HL learners had the pro-drop parameter in place, the L2 learners had not yet reset the parameter to the Spanish value, since they did not produce sentences with post-verbal subjects like the HL learners.

Although HL learners may have an advantage over L2 learners in many grammatical domains, both groups make similar types of transfer errors, as prediction 2 states. Montrul (2004) documented striking similarities between L2 and HL learners, where the two groups displayed statistically comparable patterns in their errors with aspectual interpretations in Spanish. Similarly, Kim, Montrul, and Yoon (in press) studied anaphor interpretations in Korean and found that, like L2 learners, Korean HL learners tended to reject long-distance binding interpretations of the anaphor *caki*, for instance, when this anaphor appeared in structural configurations not allowed in English.

Prediction 3 states that, due to gaps in their acquisition of literacy skills in their heritage language, HL learners should be better and faster than L2 learners in tests of oral production (this is also due to the mode of acquisition). Matsunaga

(2003) offers confirming evidence for this prediction. Matsunaga tested Japanese heritage speakers' oral and reading skills against those of L2 learners (some of whom were Chinese and knew kanji, while others did not know any kanji, like the Japanese heritage speakers). Results revealed that the Japanese HL learners had significantly higher oral proficiency than the Japanese L2 learners, but their reading proficiency was about the same. In support of prediction 4, Montrul, Foote, & Perpiñán (2008) tested knowledge of gender agreement in nouns in Spanish heritage speakers and L2 learners using two written tasks and an oral task. Results showed that the L2 learners were statistically more accurate on gender marking than the HL learners in the two written tasks, while the HL learners were significantly better and faster than the L2 learners in the spontaneous oral picture-naming task.

A large part of prediction 5, that some near-natives can pass as natives on metalinguistic tasks, has been addressed by several critical period studies over the years. Some of these studies have documented that even when advanced L2 learners can pass for native speakers impressionistically, they turn out to be nonnative when examined in a controlled experimental situation (Coppieters, 1987; Sorace, 1993).

Prediction 6 refers to outcome differences between L2 and HL learners. What is needed to address this prediction are studies of very advanced heritage speakers who are also extremely fluent in the majority language. The question is whether advanced HL learners will behave like L2 learners or like native speakers. The findings from Guillelmon and Grosjean's (2001) study of English-French early and late bilinguals may be relevant here, although it is not entirely clear whether the early bilinguals in this study are heritage speakers (i.e., can English be considered an immigrant language in France?). Results of a psycholinguistic task showed that the early bilinguals performed like monolingual controls in the processing of grammatical and ungrammatical sentences testing gender agreement in French. By contrast, the late learners were insensitive to gender errors.

Finally, prediction 6 also refers to the positive effects of instruction on advanced L2 and HL learners. There is virtually no research that directly addresses these issues. One exception is the study of Song et al. (1997) on the effects of instruction on child HL learners of Korean attending a Korean community school. They tested knowledge of case markers, word order, and reflexive pronouns. The children who were initially found not to control these aspects of Korean grammar improved significantly on a post-test after receiving explicit instruction on these topics. Although these results with children are encouraging, similar experiments with young adults are sorely needed to assess the effectiveness of this type of instruction for HL development at the postsecondary level.

Differences among HL learners

Empirical evidence showing differences and similarities between HL and L2 learners is important for understanding whether these two groups need similar or different types of language instruction. However, the pedagogical challenges for HL educators do not stop there. The other reality is that it is also difficult, if not impossible, to generalize about the HL learner population, since there are considerable individual differences in linguistic skills in the target HL. As discussed above, most of the variation occurs in second generation speakers, but is not restricted to those immigrants (see Carreira, 2004, for some other complex profiles). Those with only one parent who is a full speaker of the HL will probably speak less fluently than those with both parents who speak the HL. If only the mother speaks the HL, the child is more likely to be proficient in the HL than if only the father speaks the HL. Furthermore, age of onset of bilingualism is a crucial factor in determining proficiency. Montrul's (2002) study of tense-aspect distinctions in Spanish included three groups of heritage speakers: simultaneous bilinguals, sequential bilinguals or child L2 learners of English, and late child L2 learners. Results showed that those bilinguals who received the most exposure at home during childhood before they started learning English after age 5 (the child L2 learners or sequential bilinguals) had more knowledge of Spanish tense-aspect than the simultaneous bilinguals who were exposed to English from birth. The late child L2 learners, who received some schooling in the HL in their countries of origin before moving to the United States, were the closest to the adult native-speaker control group.

Further research including HL learners with different linguistic profiles is Kondo-Brown (2005), a study of Japanese HL learners in Hawai'i. Kondo-Brown looked at the degree of connection to the heritage language (from a merely ethnic connection to having actually been exposed to the language). Kondo-Brown used a locally developed proficiency test and self-assessment measures to investigate differences in listening, speaking, reading, and writing in L2 learners with no previous exposure to Japanese and in HL learners. HL learners were defined in a very broad sense and included individuals with some ethnic connection to Japan (some relative or grandparent), but no active knowledge of the language, as well as HL learners born to Japanese-speaking parents, who were exposed to and used Japanese at home from an early age. Results of tests showed that HL learners with no previous knowledge of Japanese patterned with the L2 learners, whereas HL learners who were bilingual to some degree were significantly different and superior on all measures. This study clearly shows that exposure to the language early in childhood brings advantages to heritage speakers (consistent with prediction 1 in Table 11.3), and that HL learners with just an ethnic connection to the language are like L2 learners.

Also focusing on Japanese learners, Kanno et al. (2008) examined how the linguistic profiles of 15 ACTFL-defined advanced HL and L2 learners correlated with several measures of linguistic proficiency. (See Lee et al., 2008 for a replication of this study with Korean heritage and L2 learners.) All learners completed a guided oral narrative, a written test, and a free conversation. L2 learners were divided into two groups based on learning environment (naturalistic or instructed), while the HL learners were divided into three different bilingual subgroups based on degree of experience and exposure to Japanese beyond the home (those who attended Saturday school, those who received exposure in other contexts, and those whose exposure was limited to the home environment). Results indicated that the oral test provided a good measure of the students' advanced proficiency, but the written test allowed the researchers to identify structural areas that are already controlled by this level of learner, together with systematic gaps in their linguistic knowledge. Overall, the HL learners who were exposed to Japanese from birth and attended Japanese Saturday school outperformed all other L2 and HL learner groups in grammar and vocabulary. In conclusion, research so far supports both important similarities and fundamental differences between HL and L2 learners. Let us now examine the two most current teaching models in light of these findings.

(Re)Learning the Heritage Language in a Formal Setting

Why do heritage speakers come to the classroom to learn the heritage language in a formal setting? At the postsecondary level, two main reasons why heritage speakers turn to language classes are to fulfill linguistic and identity needs (in addition to, perhaps, a foreign language requirement). Languages that are well represented in the community also offer career incentives. Despite these general goals, particular challenges arise in the teaching of heritage languages, challenges that have to do with the number of HL and L2 learners interested in learning the target language (i.e., enrollments), the size of the heritage speaker population in the community, and whether or not the target language has a dual status as a foreign, a second, or a heritage language. Two common models currently in place for teaching HL learners are to place both HL and L2 learners in foreign language classes, or to develop dual tracks for L2 learners and heritage speakers if the enrollments and institutional resources warrant it. For example, in areas where Chinese and Japanese have a significant number of community members, they may be taught as dual tracks. French, German, and Italian are typically taught as foreign languages, and where the heritage speaking community is small, HL learners are placed in the same classes. Russian, which has been undergoing declining enrollments as a foreign language, today mostly serves HL learners, especially in urban areas with a high concentration of Russian speakers. South Asian languages and Arabic classes may also combine heritage and non-heritage learners. An additional challenge that arises with these two less commonly taught languages is that many HL learners may be speakers of a different dialect or a cognate language, such as Gujurati speakers learning Hindi.

The FL/L2 model

Typical foreign language classes in North America serve college students whose primary (and very often only) language is English and who may or may not have received some instruction in the target language in high school. Some of the goals of a foreign language program at the postsecondary level are to introduce students to the language and culture, to help them develop an intermediate to high-intermediate level of communicative competence in the language, to promote critical thinking about their own culture and the culture of the language they are learning, and to develop skills to allow them to continue advanced study in the language, literature, or culture. Some L2 programs also offer language for specific purposes (business, health professions, law, etc.) to promote use of the target language in professional contexts. Informed by research on the nature of language acquisition and the effectiveness of formal instruction, many foreign language programs today adopt a communicative, content-based, and task-based methodology, where students work on listening, speaking, reading, and writing by means of individual, pair, and small-group activities whose main focus is negotiating meaning. Students are introduced to the culture of the language as outsiders, and while the topics covered in class are appropriate for college students, the vocabulary and structures presented are very elementary at first, increasing in level of difficulty in a two- to four-year period. Although the teaching and practice of grammar does not take center stage, it is not completely ignored either, since the linguistic objectives of the course must be met as well.

Until now, HL learners have individually enrolled or have been formally placed in the available FL classes, especially when the number of HL learners is very small, or the institution does not offer another option. But how suitable are FL programs for HL learners? This question only becomes significant if student demand is high and if the educational institution has the means to make changes accordingly. Assuming the number of HL learners is substantial, the answer depends on the particular linguistic profile of the HL learners and their level of proficiency in the language. Unlike L2 learners, who typically have similar proficiency in the four skills, HL learners tend to have uneven proficiency in different areas: oral vs. written skills, vocabulary, idiomatic expressions, and some aspects of grammar. Those speakers who have some command of the language are usually bored in classes that start teaching the language from zero. Furthermore, mixing the two types of students raises other affective issues, and this has been investigated by Potowski (2002). L2 learners who have poor oral skills feel intimidated by the advanced oral and pronunciation skills of HL learners. Similarly, HL learners, who may feel that they have a good command of the language, are surprised when they do poorly on written tests requiring them to know the labels for grammatical structures that they can use without reflection. Therefore, HL learners who have a certain command of the language might not be well served by the same approach and curriculum designed for L2 learners. Furthermore, there is the issue of available materials and resources. Textbooks for FL/L2 learners may be cognitively and age-appropriate for HL learners in terms of content, but are not linguistically challenging when they focus on basic pronunciation, grammar, and vocabulary.

This does not mean that a FL/L2 curriculum is always unsuitable. HL learners with no command, or close to minimal command, of the language might be better served by an FL program, since, as Kondo-Brown (2005) showed, HL learners who are not speakers of the language pattern with L2 learners on a number of proficiency measures. Because these particular HL learners will not have any linguistic advantage or disadvantage as compared to L2 learners, the affective issues that arise in mixed classrooms due to disparate proficiency levels may not be relevant in this case. The underlying theoretical assumption behind this practice is that L2 and HL learners are very similar in the types of linguistic knowledge they lack and, being adults, in the way they learn the target language. Therefore, they can benefit from the same instructional approach. Nevertheless, while this model may fulfill the linguistic proficiency goals of students with minimal previous knowledge of the language, it may do little to fulfill the identity goal.

Dual tracks for L2 learners and HL learners

HL practitioners who recognize that HL learners are very different from typical L2 learners advocate different classes and curricula for the two types of learners (Carreira, 2004; Kagan & Dillon, 2003; Potowski, 2005; Potowski & Carreira, 2004; Valdés, 1997, 2001), and a considerable number of postsecondary institutions offer separate classes, or dual tracks, for L2 and HL learners.[5] This tendency is growing. Specialized classes for heritage speakers are typically offered at the elementary and intermediate levels of instruction for languages like Spanish, Chinese, and Japanese. An underlying assumption of this model is that bilingual HL learners are different from L2 learners and more similar to L1 learners (due to their linguistic and cultural past). As such, they are able to learn the target HL at a faster pace than L2 learners, even if their initial proficiency in the language is quite low. This assumption has not yet been empirically verified, however.

There appears to be agreement that the communicative and content-based approach currently in vogue for L2 programs is also ideal for HL classes (Krashen, 2000; Lynch, 2003). A key difference between FL and HL classes is the cultural content, with HL classes focusing on the cultural issues, interests, and social problems affecting the HL community (poverty, discrimination, immigration, separation, diaspora, social, political and educational consequences of bilingualism, clash of cultures, etc.). Moreover, the communicative activities implemented in the classroom (through literature, music, videos) aim to reaffirm the learners' cultural identity. As for fulfilling the linguistic content, Potowski (2005) argues that specialized classes for HL learners should more closely follow the language arts curriculum taught to monolingual elementary school children. That is, strong emphasis should be placed on vocabulary expansion and enrichment, reading, writing, and spelling, in addition to basic grammatical concepts. Furthermore, the sociolinguistic dimension of language, including a discussion of regional dialects and registers and the linguistic diversity in the target language-speaking world, is crucial for promoting linguistic awareness in both HL teachers and learners.

While this model offers specialized instruction for HL learners and seeks to meet both identity and linguistic needs, it faces practical challenges, especially with regard to instructional materials. Language arts textbooks designed for elementary school children learning their first language may be appropriate from the point of view of linguistic coverage, but are unsuitable because the content is not age-appropriate or challenging for college level students. Although some textbooks already exist for Spanish as a heritage language, little is available for other heritage languages.

Another problem is that the dual track program is currently implemented only at the basic level of language instruction (elementary and intermediate). In many language departments that offer a major in the language, HL learners who elect to continue advanced study are once again placed in the same classes as L2 learner majors. As the research discussed above showed, advanced HL learners have gaps in their linguistic knowledge, especially when it comes to knowledge of registers and dialectal variation. HL learners who possess advanced proficiency in informal, non-standard language varieties (what they acquired at home) exhibit low proficiency in formal, standard, and academic language varieties in oral and written discourse (Valdés & Geoffrion-Vinci, 1998). This is especially manifested in languages that use a complex system of honorifics and forms of address (Japanese, Korean, the formal and informal second-person difference in Spanish). HL learners of these languages either do not know these forms or use them randomly. Thus, ideally, more linguistic support for HL learners at the advanced level should be provided.

A third possibility discussed by Carreira (2004), and which heritage languages with fewer L2 and HL learners than others may already be implementing, is to create a hybrid model. This hybrid model takes a HL approach for all courses that enroll HL learners, without making the distinction between L2 and HL classes. All language classes ranging from beginner to advanced would incorporate cultural topics of interest to the two groups of learners, together with more specialized instruction on problem areas for the two groups (e.g., pronunciation for L2 learners and spelling for HL learners). This solution might be pedagogically and administratively ideal for serving the two types of learners, but it would also necessitate reconceptualizing teaching materials and resources.

Placement and proficiency tests

Once a program offers distinct courses and curricula for students with different linguistic and cultural profiles, questions arise over the specific criteria that should be used to place students in those classes. It is common for L2 learners to take a locally developed placement test (Kondo-Brown, 2005), or an ACTFL interview, specifically designed to place L2 learners. Unfortunately, placement procedures for identifying different levels of heritage speaker ability are anything but straightforward. In extending the ACTFL proficiency guidelines to heritage students, Valdés (1997) was able to identify 14 possible proficiency outcomes, clearly showing that heritage speakers do not fit neatly in the guidelines developed for L2 learners. The least proficient HL learners (in a written task) have the intermediate or high intermediate skills of a foreign language learner. And while virtually all HL learners pass the criteria of comprehensibility (their phonology is typically very good), they may lack proficiency in vocabulary and in a range of grammatical areas that go undetected by this measure. Kagan and Dillon (2003) advocate using the linguistic assessment offered by the Foreign Language Standards, instead, which takes into account different communicative modes (or registers): interpersonal, interpretive, and presentational. HL learners may demonstrate command of the interpersonal mode, but lack experience with the interpretive and presentational domains, since they have not had experience using the language in an academic setting.

Finally, HL practitioners and researchers have found it useful to develop extensive language background questionnaires to understand the linguistic past of heritage speakers and their family circumstances. This information also becomes important for assessing the degree of linguistic ability in the HL acquired in the home. Combined with a proficiency test, this information helps identify both linguistic gaps and professional goals of HL learners, and helps HL practitioners decide on the best placement for each learner.

Conclusion

I have discussed two main models for the teaching of heritage languages, and the underlying theoretical assumptions behind them. Due to the infancy of the field of heritage language acquisition and teaching, there is ample room for other teaching models. While the current models are consistent with what research findings have so far uncovered about the nature of heritage language competence and its potential for acquisition and development, more theoretically informed psycholinguistic studies as well as classroom-oriented research on HL learners are needed to test their true pedagogical effectiveness and to learn more about the HL (re)acquisition process in general.

NOTES

I thank Melissa Bowles, Mike Long, Diane Musumeci, Kim Potowski, Marc Thompson, and Gabriela Zapata for invaluable feedback. All remaining errors are my own.

1   For the purposes of this chapter, a HL learner is a heritage speaker relearning the HL in a language class.
2   The term is also used to refer to indigenous languages in the US, even though aboriginals and immigrants vary significantly in their historical, social, linguistic, and demographic characteristics (Fishman, 2001; Wiley, 2001). In this chapter, I will only focus on the acquisition and learning of immigrant languages. For issues related to learning and revitalization of indigenous languages, see Hornberger (2005).
3   Attrition is the process by which aspects of language that were fully acquired at an earlier age are now eroded and eventually lost.
4   Other researchers consider that L2 learners have full access to Universal Grammar, like L1 learners, and deny the implication of maturational constraints (see White, 2003). An elaboration of this position is not relevant for this chapter.
5   This is almost 20 percent of all US universities for Spanish (Ingold et al., 2002).

REFERENCES

Au, T., Knightly, L., Jun, S., & Oh, J. (2002). Overhearing a language during childhood. *Psychological Science* 13, 238–43.

Bley-Vroman, R. (1989). The logical problem of second language learning. In S. Gass & J. Schachter (eds.), *Linguistic perspectives on second language acquisition* (pp. 41–68). Cambridge: Cambridge University Press.

Carreira, M. (2004). Seeking explanatory adequacy: A dual approach to understanding the term "Heritage Language Learner." *Heritage Language Journal* 2, 1. www.heritagelanguages.org.

Chomsky, N. (1981). *Lectures on government and binding*. Dordrecht: Foris.

Coppieters, R. (1987). Competence differences between native and near-native speakers. *Language* 63, 544–73.

Cummins, J. (2005). A proposal for action: Strategies for recognizing language competence as a learning resource within the mainstream classroom. *Modern Language Journal* 89, 585–91.

DeKeyser, R. (2000). The robustness of critical period effects in second language acquisition. *Studies in Second Language Acquisition* 22, 499–534.

DeKeyser, R. (2003). Implicit and explicit learning. In C. J. Doughty & M. H. Long (eds.), *The handbook of second language acquisition* (pp. 313–48). Malden, MA: Blackwell.

Fishman, J. (2001). 300-plus years of heritage language education in the United States. In J. Peyton, D. Ranard, & S. McGinnis (eds.), *Heritage languages in America* (pp. 81–99). McHenry, IL: Center for Applied Linguistics.

Guillelmon, D. & Grosjean, F. (2001). The gender marking effect in spoken word recognition: The case of bilinguals. *Memory and Cognition* 29, 3, 503–11.

Hornberger, N. (ed.) (2005). Heritage/community language education: US and Australian perspectives. Special issue of *International Journal of Bilingual Education and Bilingualism* 8, 2 & 3.

Ingold, C., Rivers, W., Tesser, C., & Ashby, E. (2002). Report on the NFLC/AATP Survey of Spanish Language Programs for Native Speakers. *Hispania* 85, 2, 324–9.

Kagan, O. & Dillon, K. (2003). A new perspective on teaching Russian: Focus on the heritage learner. *Heritage Language Journal* 1, 1. www.heritagelanguages.org.

Kanno, K., Hasegawa, T., Ikeda, K., Ito, Y., & Long, M. H. (2008). Relationships between prior language-learning experience and variation in the linguistic profiles of advanced English-speaking learners of Japanese. In D. Brinton, O. Kagan, & S. Bauckus (eds.), *Heritage language education: A new field emerging*. New York: Routledge.

Kim, J.-H., Montrul, S., & Yoon, J. (in press). Dominant language influence in acquisition and attrition of binding: Interpretation of the Korean reflexive *caki*. *Bilingualism: Language and Cognition*.

Kohnert, J., Bates, E., & Hernández, A. (1999). Balancing bilinguals: Lexical-semantic production and cognitive processing in children learning Spanish and English. *Journal of Speech, Language and Hearing Research* 42, 1400–13.

Kondo-Brown, K. (2003). Heritage language instruction for post-secondary students from immigrant backgrounds. *Heritage Language Journal* 1, 1. www.heritagelanguages.org.

Kondo-Brown, K. (2005). Differences in language skills: Heritage language learner subgroups and foreign language learners. *Modern Language Journal* 89, 563–81.

Köpke, B. & Schmid, M. (2003). Language attrition. The next phase. In M. Schmid, B. Köpke, M. Keijzer, & L. Weilemar (eds.), *First language attrition* (pp. 1–43). Amsterdam: John Benjamins.

Krashen, S. (2000). Bilingual education, the acquisition of English and the retention and loss of Spanish. In A. Roca (ed.), *Research on Spanish in the United States: Linguistic issues and challenges* (pp. 432–44). Sommerville, MA: Cascadilla Press.

Lardiere, D. (2006). *Ultimate attainment in second language acquisition: A case study.* Mahwah, NJ: Lawrence Earlbaum.

Lee, Y.-G., Kim, H.-S., Kong, H., Hong, J.-M., & Long, M. (2008). Variation in the linguistic profiles of advanced English-speaking learners of Korean. In D. Brinton, O. Kagan, & S. Bauckus (eds.), *Heritage language education: A new field emerging* (pp. 165–80). New York: Routledge.

Long, M. H. (2003). Stabilization and fossilization in interlanguage development. In C. J. Doughty & M. H. Long (eds.), *The handbook of second language acquisition* (pp. 487–536). Malden, MA: Blackwell.

Lynch, A. (2003). The relationship between second and heritage language acquisition: Notes on research and theory building. *Heritage Language Journal* 1, 1. www.heritagelanguages.org.

Matsunaga, S. (2003). Instructional needs of college-level learners of Japanese as a heritage language: Performance based analysis. *Heritage Language Journal* 1, 1. www.heritagelanguages.org.

Montrul, S. (2002). Incomplete acquisition and attrition of Spanish tense/aspect distinctions in adult bilinguals. *Bilingualism: Language and Cognition* 5, 1, 39–68.

Montrul, S. (2004). Convergent outcomes in second language acquisition and first language loss. In M. Schmid, B. Köpke, M. Keijzer, & L. Weilemar (eds.), *First language attrition* (pp. 259–80). Amsterdam: John Benjamins.

Montrul, S. (2005). Second language acquisition and first language loss in adult early bilinguals: Exploring some differences and similarities. *Second Language Research* 21, 3, 199–249.

Montrul, S. (2006). Incomplete acquisition as a feature of L2 and bilingual grammars. In R. Slabakova, S. Montrul, & P. Prévost (eds.), *Inquiries in language development* (pp. 335–59). Amsterdam: John Benjamins.

Montrul, S., Foote, R., & Perpiñán (2008). Gender agreement in adult second language learners and Spanish heritage speakers: The effects of age and context of acquisition. *Language Learning* 58, 3, 503–53.

Montrul, S., Foote, R., Perpiñán, S., Thornhill, D., & Vidal, S. (2006). Full access and age effects in adult bilingualism: An investigation of accusative clitics and word order. In N. Sagarra & J. Toribio (eds.), *Selected papers from the Hispanic Linguistics Symposium* (pp. 217–28). Sommerville, MA: Cascadilla Press.

Oh, J., Jun, S., Knightly, L., & Au, T. (2003). Holding on to childhood language memory. *Cognition* 86, B53–B64.

Paradis, M. (2004). *A neurolinguistic theory of bilingualism.* Amsterdam: John Benjamins.

Polinsky, M. (1997). American Russian: Language loss meets language acquisition. In W. Browne, E. Dornisch, N. Kondrashova, & D. Zec (eds.), *Proceedings of the Annual Workshop on Formal Approaches to Slavic Linguistics* (pp. 370–406). Ann Arbor: Michigan Slavic Publications.

Potowski, K. (2002). Experiences of Spanish heritage speakers in university foreign language courses and implications for teacher training. *ADFL Bulletin* 33, 3, 35–42.

Potowski, K. (2005). *Fundamentos de la enseñanza del español a hispanohablantes en los EE. UU.* Madrid: Arco Libros.

Potowski, K. & Carreira, M. (2004). Towards teacher development and national standards for Spanish as a heritage language. *Foreign Language Annals* 37, 3, 427–37.

Selinker, L. (1972). Interlanguage. *IRAL* 10, 3, 209–31.

Silva-Corvalán, C. (1994). *Language contact and change: Spanish in Los Angeles.* Oxford: Oxford University Press.

Song, M., O'Grady, W., Cho, S., & Lee, M. (1997). The learning and teaching of Korean in Community Schools. *Korean Language in America* 111–27. American Association of Teachers of Korean.

Sorace, A. (1993). Incomplete vs. divergent representations of unaccusativity in native and non-native Italian grammars of Italian. *Second Language Research* 9, 22–47.

Valdés, G. (1997). The teaching of Spanish to bilingual Spanish-speaking students: Outstanding issues and unanswered questions. In M. C. Colombi & F. Alarcón (eds.), *La enseñanza del español a hispanoahablantes* (pp. 8–44). Boston, MA: Houghton Mifflin.

Valdés, G. (2001). Introduction. *Spanish for native speakers,* vol. 1. AATSP Professional Development Series Handbook for teachers K-16. New York: Harcourt College.

Valdés, G. (2005). Bilingualism, heritage language learners, and SLA research: Opportunities lost or seized? *Modern Language Journal* 89, 410–26.

Valdés, G. & Geoffrion-Vinci, M. (1998). Chicano Spanish: The problem of the "underdeveloped" code in bilingual repertoires. *Modern Language Journal* 82, 4, 473–501.

White, L. (2003). *Second language acquisition and universal grammar.* Cambridge: Cambridge University Press.

Wiley, T. (2001). On defining heritage languages and their speakers. In J. Peyton, D. Ranard, & S. McGinnis (eds.), *Heritage languages in America* (pp. 29–36). McHenry, IL: Center for Applied Linguistics.

FURTHER READING

Brinton, D., Kagan, O., & Bauckus, S. (eds.) (2008). *Heritage language education: A new field emerging.* New York: Routledge.

Gambhir, V. (ed.) (1995). *The teaching and acquisition of South Asian languages.* Philadelphia: University of Pennsylvania Press.

Kondo-Brown, K. (ed.) (2006). *Heritage language development: Focus on East Asian immigrants.* Amsterdam: John Benjamins.

Krashen, S., Tse, L., & McQuillan, J. (eds.) (1998). *Heritage language development.* Culver City, CA: Language Education Associates.

Montrul, S. (2008). *Incomplete acquisition in bilingualism: Re-examining the age factor.* Amsterdam: John Benjamins.

Peyton, J., Ranard, D., & McGinnis, S. (eds.) (2001). *Heritage languages in America.* McHenry, IL: Center for Applied Linguistics.

Valdés, G., Fishman, J., Chávez, R., & Pérez, W. (2006). *Developing minority language resources: The case of Spanish in California.* Clevedon, UK: Multilingual Matters.

12 Specific Purpose Programs

KEN HYLAND

Specific purposes teaching refers to a distinctive approach to language education based on identification of the specific language features, discourse practices, and communicative skills of target groups, and on teaching practices that recognize the particular subject-matter needs and expertise of learners (Hyland, 2006).

Although somewhat marginal in the US, the growth of such programs world-wide over the past 30 years has been enormous. While Language for Specific Purposes (LSP) programs now exist for learners in a range of languages and contexts, the major growth and developments have been in English. Driven principally by the global spread of money, markets, labor, and technology, English has become central to international capitalism in the early twenty-first century. The dominance of English used as a lingua franca in international business contexts, for instance, is now seemingly beyond dispute, with various studies confirming that English is an intrinsic part of communication in multinational settings and a fact of life for many business people (Nickerson, 2005). Increased demands from employer groups and professional bodies for work-ready graduates equipped with technical and interpersonal communication skills has been accompanied by greater internationalization of higher education and student mobility. As a result, countless students, professionals, migrants, and academics around the world must now gain fluency in the conventions of specific varieties of English to navigate their learning, gain employment, and establish their careers.

Such an expansion has, inevitably, been at the expense of other languages, but while English has been both the main force and beneficiary of this movement, there are already signs that global English may be a transitory phenomenon as other languages, particularly Mandarin and Spanish, begin to challenge English in some domains. Irrespective of the language of instruction, specific purposes programs are now a vibrant and flourishing feature of language learning in many countries around the world. In this chapter I intend to look at some of the features which underpin and inform these programs, focusing in particular on conceptions of specificity, needs assessment, analyses of texts and contexts, and instructional approaches. First, however, it is worth providing some background to specific programs and briefly looking at the justifications for them.

The Concept of Specific Purposes

Conceptions of "specific purpose" actually divide into two very different areas. The first is a traditional European field with a strong Scandinavian and German presence focusing on the translation of documents in various languages, lexical categorization, and international cooperation on common terminology. The second is an Anglo-American English for Specific Purposes (ESP) tradition with an interest in the description of argumentative and rhetorical patterns in academic and workplace discourses. Pedagogy, however, now converges toward an ESP model, distinguished by the goal of identifying the demands placed by academic or workplace contexts on communicative behaviors and developing pedagogic practices by which these behaviors can be taught. Far from such communication demands being a matter of control of general lexis and grammar, there is now a quite considerable body of international research, experience, and practice which evidences the heightened, complex, and highly diversified nature of such demands.

Assisted by an explosion of ethnographic and discourse analytic research, practitioners, have gradually learnt more about the different teaching contexts in which students find themselves and about the particular communicative demands placed on them by their studies. Originally LSP was a materials and teaching-led movement focusing on texts and responding to the growing numbers of L2 students beginning to appear in university courses. Since then a developing research base has emphasized the rich diversity of texts, contexts, and practices in which students operate in the modern university and workplace. We now recognize the kinds of challenges that disciplinary and occupationally specific communication practices present to students and, as these fields change, so in turn does their associated communication.

Informed both by research and a healthy orientation to real-world applications, LSP has sought to bring these considerations to the classroom and encourage universities in the view that responsibility for meeting these challenges lies collectively with the student and institution rather than students alone. Underlying this goal is the view that difficulties cannot be addressed by some piecemeal remediation of individual error or a simple topping up of "deficiencies" in their existing language skills. On the contrary, LSP argues that what is needed is a solution-oriented approach focusing on the specific communicative competencies needed by learners. The issue of specificity challenges all teachers to take a stance on how they view language and learning and to examine their courses in the light of this stance. It forces us to ask questions about what we think students should learn and how we think they learn best.

The Case for Specific Purposes Programs

Specific purposes programs emphasize the view that language teaching is not simply concerned with teaching words, structures, lexical phrases, and so on divorced from any real context of use. Instead, it forces us to explore language as a carrier of disciplinary and professional values as a result of the frequency and importance of such structures and phrases to the communities that employ them. A key justification for specific purposes programs is, therefore, that learning is an induction into a new culture rather than an extension of existing skills. The language competencies required by the disciplines may grow out of those which students practice in school, but require students to understand the ways language forms and strategies work to construct and represent knowledge in particular areas. In the classroom this has taken the form of a shift from how language is used in isolated written or spoken texts toward contextualized communicative genres and an increasing preoccupation with identifying strategies suitable for both native and non-native speakers of the target language.

Specificity also receives some support from research in second language acquisition (SLA) which undermines the often heard idea that low-proficiency students need to control core forms before getting on to specific, and presumably more difficult, features of language. In fact, SLA has shown that students do not learn in a step-by-step fashion according to some externally imposed sequence, but acquire features of the language as they need them, rather than in the order that teachers present them. So while students may need to attend more to sentence-level features at lower proficiencies, there is no need to ignore specific language uses at any stage as students are likely to notice, understand, and use particular features in the course of communicating in their field.

Theoretical endorsement for specific purpose programs also comes from the philosophical perspective of social constructionism which stresses that disciplines and professions are largely created and maintained through the distinctive ways that members construct a view of the world through their discourses. What counts as convincing argument, appropriate tone, persuasive interaction, and so on, is managed for a particular audience (Hyland, 2000). There is also a growing body of evidence that professional and academic discourses represent a variety of specific literacies, so that even attempts to create a common "Academic Word List," for instance, fail to identify potential meaning variations across disciplines (Hyland & Tse, 2007). This, as Bhatia (2002, p. 27) observes, supports specific purposes pedagogies:

> students interacting with different disciplines need to develop communication skills that may not be an extension of general literacy to handle academic discourse, but a range of literacies to handle disciplinary variation in academic discourse.

This is not to say that there are *no* generalizable skills or language features of professional discourses. We tend to find, for instance, more nominalization, more lexical density, and more impersonality in academic and many professional texts, imparting a greater formality than is common in many everyday registers. But adopting specificity offers more efficient, motivating, and justifiable ways to teach. This response, as we shall see, is not without its problems and critics, and many teachers are concerned about how far they are able to model the expertise of subject specialists and control the subject-knowledge their students have to engage with. However, the fact that the complexity and prestige of certain professional and academic literacies works to exclude many individuals, preventing their access to academic success or membership of valued communities, means that language teachers have a responsibility to expand this access by making communicative conventions transparent to learners.

Needs, Contexts, and Genres

LSP is perhaps most widely associated with the emphasis practitioners give to needs analysis as a systematic way of identifying the specific sets of skills, texts, linguistic forms, and communicative practices that a particular group of learners want to acquire (e.g., Dudley-Evans & St John, 1998). Needs assessment is the foundation on which all teaching decisions are based in specific purposes programs and refers to the techniques for collecting and assessing information relevant to course design: it is the means of establishing the *how* and *what* of a course and replaces the teachers' intuitions, which often perform the same role in general language courses. It is a continuous process, since input from needs analyses helps modify teaching and so shades into *evaluation* – the means of establishing the effectiveness of a course.

Needs analysis is sometimes seen as a kind of educational technology designed to identify goals with precision and accountability, but this actually gives the process a misleading impartiality, suggesting that teachers can simply read off a course from an objective situation. But needs are not always easy to determine and, because they mean different things to different participants, carry marked political implications. Essentially, needs analyses construct a picture of learning goals which bring to bear the teacher's values, beliefs, and philosophies of teaching and learning, often together with the input of learners, subject tutors, employers, and other stakeholders.

Needs is, in fact, an umbrella term that embraces a range of elements, incorporating learners' goals and backgrounds, their language proficiencies, their reasons for taking the course, their teaching and learning preferences, the situations they will need to communicate in, and the genres most often employed in them. Needs can involve what learners know, don't know, or want to know, and can be collected and analyzed in a variety of ways (e.g., Brown, 1995). Needs, therefore, embraces both a consideration of the *present situation*, "starting where the students are" and looking at what they can do now, and what they want to do, and of the *target situation*, considering their future roles and the linguistic skills and knowledge they need to perform competently in those roles (Dudley-Evans & St John, 1998). There is, in other words, a high degree of learner centeredness in specific purposes programs as teachers attempt to tap into the subjective needs of learners and their expectations. But there is also a strong desire to understand the communicative resources they will need in their target discourse communities, and these needs are often significantly prioritized.

So while information about learners is important, and efforts are made to assemble information on their proficiencies, subject-knowledge awareness, life goals, and institutional expectations, needs are largely seen as communication needs rather than learning needs. This principally involves collecting objective and product-oriented data: identifying the contexts of language use, observing the language events in these contexts, and collecting and analyzing target genres.

Analysis of the spoken and written genres commonly used in the target context is perhaps the most widely used way of establishing what students need to do with language as a basis for specific purposes courses. Genre analysis, involving whole text analyses with exemplar texts taken from the learners' fields of study or work, is now widely employed in LSP. Essentially, *genre* is a term for grouping texts according to their similarities, representing how writers typically use language to respond to recurring situations and indexing their context (Hyland, 2004). This is because writing and speaking are based on the expectations participants bring to any situation as a result of their prior communicative experiences. Genres offer participants "frames for social action" (Bazerman, 1997, p. 19), providing them with effective ways of getting things done using language. Thus genres help structure and construct a social context for community members in an increasingly genrefied academic and professional world.

To gain insights into actors' genre-using behaviors and perceptions, LSP teachers frequently seek out the views of subject area specialists through a range of qualitative data-gathering techniques. Research has therefore moved beyond texts to include their sites of use, and this has involved employing methods which are interpretive, contextualized, and respectful of participants' views, such as ethnographic case studies, reader responses, and interviews with insiders. Such *emic* perspectives seek to show how social contexts are constructed and understood by participants and to reveal what people actually do when using language by locating acts of communication as they occur in the behavior of groups. These participatory explorations of discourse domains, moreover, not only reveal insights into target practices, but immerse LSP practitioners themselves into the discoursal worlds of their students.

Such complex conceptualizations of genre provide a fuller and more multi-faceted picture of the requirements which operate in students' target contexts, but identification of the key rhetorical resources of genres remains one of the major LSP needs analysts' jobs. Teachers are assisted here by a growing literature on a range of professional and student genres, such as direct mail letters, business faxes, student textbooks, and PhD dissertations. Such analyses not only provide insights into target texts, but also highlight the different kinds of argument and writing/speaking tasks valued by different fields. Coffin et al. (2003), for instance, identify three genres as being pivotal to each of three main domains of knowledge: project proposals in the sciences, essays in the humanities, and reports and case studies in the social sciences.

These contextually grounded, socio-rhetorical understandings of specific genres have been increasingly supported in recent years by corpus-based studies which add a lexico-grammatical dimension to structural understandings of professional genres. Despite complaints that corpus data are merely samples of language divorced from their communicative contexts, such studies have offered insights into the ways specific features, such as self-mention, directives, conditionals, or images, are used in different domains. In fact, small, specialized corpora of whole expert and learner texts have a lot to offer needs analysts, especially if they are compiled and analyzed by ESP specialists familiar with the context and with access to specialist informants in the area. The compiler-cum-analyst can act as a kind of mediating ethnographic specialist informant to shed light on the corpus data and move special purpose programs even further toward empirically based understandings of academic and professional genres.

Finally, it would also be true to say that LSP has moved to a greater sensitivity to the learning context. Deliberation on the kinds of pedagogies and goals that the learning context offers is sometimes called *means analysis*, and it refers to what can be realistically achieved within a course, given institutional constraints and resources of time, materials, technological support, teacher expertise, motivation, and the attitudes which teachers have toward the teaching–learning philosophy the course represents. A key consideration here is the relationship of the course to its immediate environment, as institutions differ considerably in the priority they give to language programs and their attitudes to LSP-subject tutor collaboration, pedagogic innovation, and teacher autonomy. More broadly, local socio-cultural attitudes and practices also need to be considered to avoid imposing unwelcome methods or course content onto learners. Canagarajah (1999), for instance, cautions against the imposition of unfamiliar pedagogic models, such as the kinds of task-based, collaborative methods valued by Western teachers, into situations where they may conflict with students' cultural backgrounds and prior learning experiences.

Rights and Identities in LSP

Needs analysis may be at the heart of LSP, but it also raises serious questions about practice. Analyses are necessarily limited to particular questions or issues, and as a result of this, the framing of those issues will have an impact on the data collected and the conclusions drawn. As Dudley-Evans and St John (1998) point out, "what we ask and how we interpret are dependent on a particular view of the world, on attitudes and value." Ethnographically oriented needs analyses have revealed that different actors in a social setting have different perceptions of similar tasks and situations, which leads them to different objective and felt needs. Using a combination of participant observation, unstructured interviews, and questionnaires, for example, Jasso-Aguilar (1999) found that the language actually needed by maids to perform everyday duties in a Waikiki hotel was very different from the "aloha" language that supervisors and management wanted them to learn to converse with guests. That such an institutional need can be translated into the driving force for a course shows how power can be exercised in decision-making.

Needs, in other words, are in the eye of the beholder and, as a result, will be defined differently by different stakeholders who might initially approach course design with divergent agendas. Are subject tutors, for instance, likely to hold the same views on "needs" as LSP teachers? Do employers have a say? Will students buy in to an independent characterization of their needs? For these reasons it is important to consult students as participants in any needs analysis if the course is to be useful to them. In addition to such participatory needs analysis, the use of soft systems methodology has been suggested as a way of involving different stakeholders (Tajino, James, & Kijima, 2005). This is an action research methodology, borrowed from business contexts, which recognizes explicitly that different individuals and groups have different interpretations of the world and which seeks to provide a framework to accommodate these in course design.

Decisions about what to teach and how to teach it are therefore not neutral professional questions but involve issues of authority in decision-making, with important consequences for learners. In fact, treating *need* as something existing and measurable is itself an ideological stance, and we need to reflect on whether students' needs are best served by adopting exclusively pragmatic and instrumental goals, or whether we should assist them to a more participatory and critical stance. LSP practitioners often see themselves as pragmatists doing their best to help learners succeed in unfamiliar and challenging worlds by providing them with the skills and resources to join established and often exclusionary communities. In this perspective meeting learners' needs is seen as empowering them to take on new roles and to improve their life chances.

Pennycook (1997) offers the term *critical pragmatism* as a means of directing LSP toward a stance which is less service-oriented and more ideologically aware, recognizing a variety of locally effective ways to help students demystify the academic worlds in which they find themselves. Benesch (2001) takes up the ways that ideology pervades needs analysis and suggests that it should include an examination of "who sets the goals, why they were formulated, whose interests are served by them, and whether they should be challenged" (Benesch, 2001, p. 43). Benesch argues that English for Academic Purposes (EAP) teachers should not subordinate their instruction unquestioningly to the demands of subject disciplines, as this reduces language teachers to a service role and subjects students to the domination of their disciplines and fields. To show that teaching is more than initiating students unquestioningly into particular discourse communities, she advocates supplementing traditional needs analysis with *rights analysis*. This goes beyond a reactive determination of institutionally determined target requirements to "search for alternatives to strict adherence to those requirements" (Benesch, 2001, p. 45).

Rights analysis therefore involves evaluating the findings of needs analysis and interrogating the results to create more democratic and participatory involvement by students in decision-making. Her argument is that rights are not pre-established entitlements worked out for the benefit of students by LSP teachers, but have to be discovered in each particular setting, seeing what is possible and beneficial for a particular group of students. While teachers often recognize that students typically take a pragmatic view toward their studies and are sceptical of politics, they often hear them complain about the apparently arbitrary conventions of academic writing, of the vagueness of course assignments, of the obscurity of their readings, and of the lack of fit between their home and academic experiences. Effective teachers therefore look at the implications of their work, attempting to avoid unexamined, socially reproductive practices to best assist students to acquire the kind of education that they desire. The notion of rights therefore encourages students to assess their options and prioritize what they need for themselves.

The idea that LSP teachers should support students in taking an active responsibility for their learning strongly resonates with the literature on autonomy in language learning. This argues that developing reflective, critical, and procedural skills encourages greater engagement and commitment to learning and willingness to question teaching practices. It also bears a strong resemblance to a *negotiated syllabus* which has a long history in English language teaching and is widespread in postgraduate education in the UK. A negotiated syllabus means that the content of a particular course is a matter of discussion between teacher and students, according to the wishes and needs of the learners in conjunction with the expertise, judgment, and advice of the teacher.

Closely related to the conception of needs in LSP is the view that communication is not simply a set of discrete skills but a social practice carrying particular values and opportunities which can influence students' participation in education and their subsequent life chances. Of importance here is that academic and professional discourses privilege certain identities which may conflict with the habits of meaning the student brings to the class from his or her home experiences. This has been seen as a powerful coercive force which compels students to make a "cultural shift" in order to take on alien identities as members of those communities. Gee (1990, p. 155), for instance, stresses the importance of this shift:

> someone cannot engage in a discourse in a less than fluent manner. You are either in it or you're not. Discourses are connected with displays of identity – failing to display an identity fully is tantamount to announcing you do not have that identity – at best you are a pretender or a beginner.

In other words, academic and professional success means representing yourself in a way valued by your discipline, adopting the values, beliefs, and identities which academic discourses embody, and suppressing what is familiar and more "natural." This can mean that students often feel uncomfortable with the "me" they portray in their academic writing, finding a conflict between the identities required to write successfully and those they bring with them (Ivanic, 1998). Lillis (2001) refers to an *essayist literacy* which is privileged in formal schooling and so advantages certain social groups while restricting the access of many minorities. A fundamentally monologic context of needs assessment can thus be carried over into classroom practices where the LSP tutor accepts the conventions of the discipline as a single voice which determines what a task is and how it should be carried out, without negotiating the expectations surrounding it or the voice the student writer wishes to portray in engaging in it. In other words, treating communicative conventions as unproblematic can position LSP students in similar ways to treating needs as unproblematic, and requires from the LSP teacher an explicit recognition of both student wants and target needs.

Organizing Specific Language Instruction

Many of these considerations are implemented in specific purposes programs by focusing on both the purposes for which people are learning a language and the kinds of language performance that are necessary to meet those purposes. For some this means adopting a *process syllabus*, which is a way of organizing instruction that is essentially learning focused and relatively learner-led so that teaching and learning are negotiated between teachers and students (Breen & Littlejohn, 2000). Process syllabuses provide a decision-making framework for student–teacher collaboration in the purposes, content, and ways of working in a course and offer students a voice in the management of their learning. In the innovative *TalkBase* program at the Asian Institute of Technology in Bangkok, for instance, teachers coordinate and take part in activities, but the content is supplied by students through group interaction and outcomes are not determined in advance. Process syllabuses are therefore central to LSP philosophies as they can help guide students toward a relevant professional expertise through authentic opportunities to develop their knowledge and engage more meaningfully in the learning process.

More generally, however, LSP practitioners have attempted to emphasize what is to be learned and have tended to employ *text-based* and *content-based* syllabuses. *Text-based syllabuses* organize instruction around the genres that learners need and the social contexts in which they will operate (Hyland, 2004). Following this approach involves adopting a scaffolded pedagogy to guide learners toward control of key genres based on whole texts selected in relation to learner needs. Based on sociocultural learning theory (Vygotsky, 1978), scaffolding is a metaphor of learning which refers to those supportive behaviors by which an expert can help a novice learner to gradually achieve higher, independent levels of performance. In LSP classrooms it involves active and sustained support by a teacher who models appropriate strategies for meeting particular purposes, guides students in their use of the strategies, and provides a meaningful and relevant context for using the strategies. Texts and tasks are therefore selected according to learners' needs and sequenced according to one of a number of principles:

- by following their use in a real-world series of interactions (such as taking notes, assembling data, and drafting a research report);
- by perceived increasing levels of difficulty, from easiest to most complex (such as moving from a recount genre through an exposition to an explanation, each involving more complex cognitive and rhetorical demands on students);

- by determining the key skills or functions relevant to students' most immediate short-term needs.

The planning of classroom activities in a text-based syllabus is informed by a view of learning as a series of linked stages which provide the support needed to move learners toward a critical understanding of texts. It is informed by the constructivist perspective that learning is not a linear process but a result of activating learners' prior experience and the first-hand knowledge gained from new explorations aided by more knowledgeable others. This is represented in the teaching–learning cycle shown in Figure 12.1, which is organized to achieve different purposes:

1   setting the context – to reveal the main purposes of the selected genre and the settings in which it is used;
2   modeling – to analyze the genre to reveal its stages and key features;
3   joint construction – to provide guided, teacher-supported practice in the genre;
4   independent construction – to give learners opportunities for independent use of the language monitored by the teacher;
5   comparing – to assist learners to relate what has been learnt to other genres and contexts.

The cycle is intended to be used flexibly, allowing students to enter at any stage, depending on their existing knowledge of the genre, and to enable teachers to return to earlier stages for revision. A key purpose of the cycle is, therefore, to ensure repeated opportunities for students to reflect on and critique their learning by developing understandings of texts, acting on these through writing or speaking, reviewing their performance, and using feedback to improve their work. The model allows the vocabulary and literacy skills gained in previous cycles to be further developed by working through a new cycle at a more advanced level of expression of the genre. The cycle also encourages different teacher and learner roles and different pedagogic tasks at different stages, as teachers are more actively interventionist in early stages and gradually withdraw this support at later stages to give students increasing independence in using the genre.

A third main approach employed in LSP programs is to organize instruction through a *content-based syllabus*. There are various interpretations of what Content Based Instruction (CBI) actually means, although all share a focus on subject content as a carrier of language rather than a focus on language itself. For some practitioners, CBI simply means adopting any relevant themes from the students' field as a way of providing sheltered assistance toward their transition into a new community. Miller's (2001) course for engineering undergraduates in Hong Kong, for instance, follows a general LSP approach approach by adapting material from popular engineering periodicals rather than the texts the students are actually using in their subject course. In this way he feels able to "maintain my

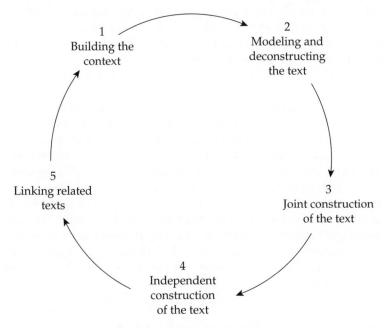

Figure 12.1 The teaching–learning cycle

own and my students' confidence in my ability as their language teacher to handle the material well." Such a perspective offers a way of providing learners with some of the more general strategies they need to participate in their academic studies, but also reflects the anxieties of many LSP teachers concerning their ability to engage adequately with the disciplines.

Other CBI approaches take a more immersion-like approach with scaffolding for both instructor and students provided by a subject-area specialist. The types of possible cooperative relationships with subject departments can be seen as a continuum of involvement with increasing degrees of subject-language integration (Dudley-Evans & St John, 1998):

- *Cooperation*: the use of subject teachers as specialist informants who simply provide information about texts, course assignments, and the discoursal framework of the discipline.
- *Collaboration*: where language and subject teacher work together outside the class with the subject tutor offering advice or providing input into teaching materials or directly linking two courses.
- *Team teaching*: the closest engagement between subject tutor and EAP teacher with both working together in the same classroom.

Perhaps the most widely discussed approach is the adjunct model where the language course is linked with a content course which shares the same content base; the rationale being that students will develop strategies and skills which will transfer from one course to the other.

Essentially, there is a recognition here that language teachers are outsiders, who can only approximate the knowledge and skills of subject-area insiders. This kind of collaboration can be fraught, however, as participants may be suspicious and even openly critical of each other. Conflicts may be even more fundamental and result from divergent philosophies of knowledge and learning between the fields of language and science (Barron, 2003). Clearly, respect for learner knowledge and some engagement with the subject discipline are essential to the development of an effective LSP course. In practice, many LSP syllabuses are hybrid, drawing on aspects of two or three different syllabus types and introducing the professional interactive competence of individuals from various sources. Most generally, it is worth emphasizing the longitudinal nature of much CBI and the fact that students can only develop the rhetorical and argumentative skills associated with particular subject disciplines through sustained, incremental practice over a period of time.

Research-Informed Pedagogy in LSP

Finally, I should mention some of the current instructional practices found in specific purposes programs. In general, considerable efforts have been made by practitioners in recent years to steer learners away from simplistic and formulaic approaches to specialist discourses and to avoid the prescriptive teaching of target genres. In particular, they have sought to harness and build on students' understandings of their fields to develop their discourse awareness by placing greater emphasis on exploratory, context-sensitive, and research-informed understandings of learning and language which promote both learner awareness and learner autonomy.

One approach, pioneered by John Swales and adopted more widely in LSP, is to ask students, often in small groups, to analyze, compare, and manipulate representative samples of a target discourse in a process known as *rhetorical consciousness-raising*. Consciousness-raising is a "top-down" approach to understanding language which encourages learners to see grammatical features as "the on-line processing component of discourse and not the set of syntactic building blocks with which discourse is constructed" (Rutherford, 1987, p. 104). Focusing on language is not therefore an end in itself but a means of teaching learners to use language effectively by encouraging them to experience for themselves the effect that grammatical choices have on creating meanings. For Swales (1999) the approach is:

> more concerned with producing better academic writers than with simply producing better academic texts. In other words we aim to provide our participants with

skills and strategies that will generalize beyond the narrow temporal domains of our actual courses.

Consciousness-raising takes various forms, but all address the ways meaning is constructed, so that while this may mean highlighting particular text elements, these are not isolated from the overall purpose of the text. The literature review jigsaw task Swales and Lindemann (2002) give their dissertation students, for instance, involves no single right answer, but encourages students to reach their own rhetorically motivated, discipline-based patterns. Consciousness-raising approaches to do not only focus on genre moves, however, but on interpersonal aspects of language use, such as hedges, stance, and evaluation, to encourage students to reflect on their identities as writers, the impact they have on readers, and their participation in their target communities (Hyland, 2006).

Swales and Feak's (2000) academic writing textbook *English in Today's Research World*, for instance, draws on an EAP research tradition to develop in novice research writers both a sensitivity to the language used in different academic genres and insights into the conventions and expectations of their target communities. This is principally accomplished by encouraging students to analyze text extracts, often through comparison with other genres or with aspects of academic writing in English with their native language. This kind of contrastive reflection helps to show how practices are specific to particular groups and to identify how little is actually universal. The approach therefore moves users toward a descriptive understanding of research language and encourages them to question a monolithic, asocial view of writing while developing both their writing skills and awareness of effective rhetorical patterns.

Another path to consciousness-raising is discussed by Johns (1997) as a "socioliterate approach," where learners acquire academic literacies via "exposure to discourses from a variety of social contexts" and inquiry into their own literate lives and the literacy practices of others. Johns argues for the need to "destablize" undergraduates' notions of academic writing by moving them away from school genres which encourage them to pour content into familiar templates. Instead, she recommends introducing students to the concepts of genre and context through familiar "homely" genres, such as wedding invitations, then moving on to explore pedagogic genres like textbooks and exam prompts, and then less familiar academic genres. This helps students to gain an understanding of the ways register features interact with social purposes and cultural forces in known genres before they study academic genres. A key element is for students to become ethnographic researchers themselves, not only exploring texts, but interviewing subject tutors and more advanced students about specific classes and assignments or their own use of genres. In addition, Johns advocates the use of *literacy portfolios* to link reading and writing activities and to help learners understand connections between the genres they write and encounter at university.

A complementary methodology used to build students' discourse competence in LSP classes gives considerable recognition to the importance of *collaboration*, or peer interaction, and *scaffolding*, or teacher-supported learning. Together, these concepts assist learners through two notions of learning:

- shared consciousness – the idea that learners working together learn more effectively than individuals working separately;
- borrowed consciousness – the idea that learners working with knowledgeable others develop greater understanding of tasks and ideas.

As discussed above, scaffolding emphasizes interaction with experienced others in moving learners from their existing level of performance to a level of "potential performance," or what they are able to do without assistance. Vygotsky argued that progress through this "zone of proximal development" is not achieved only through input, but rather through social interaction and the assistance of more skilled and experienced others. Teachers, therefore, assist this process by modeling, by opportunities for practice, and by providing students with an explicit grammar, but this is not the decontextualized, disembodied grammar of traditional language classes. Instead of seeing texts as constructed from isolated building blocks, this starts with how grammatical features represent the speaker's or writer's choices for achieving certain purposes, expressing certain relationships, and conveying certain information.

Accounts of practice in occupationally specific programs are relatively rare, but cooperation with subject-area specialists seems to be a more common feature than in academic courses, particularly in practice-oriented programs like nursing and business, and where instruction takes place at workplace sites. Where such collaboration is not possible, practitioners often strive to draw on the subject knowledge of learners themselves by creating mixed-expertise classes or by using videos of experienced professionals performing and talking their way through tasks. Planken, van Hooft, and Korzilius (2004) describe a number of awareness-raising tasks incorporated into foreign language courses for learners of Business French, German, Spanish, and English, in which students observe and analyze authentic business interactions as a precursor to their own proficiency practice. Students are asked to identify the rhetorical strategies they observe, for instance in a video recording of a business negotiation, and to comment on how that strategy is realized linguistically. Other teachers move closer to target contexts by taking their students to various field-related environments as participant-observers of the communicative practices employed there.

Finally, technology plays an increasingly important role in LSP instruction by providing access to authentic contexts. It does not, however, just furnish practitioners with opportunities to record, collect, and analyze real-world interactions and language data; but it also facilitates the creation of materials from these previously hidden interactions, bringing business meetings, doctor–patient discussions, and lawyer–client interviews into specific purposes classrooms. More generally, technology has given students access to a massive supply of authentic language data tailored to their needs rather than simply a standard set of examples. Access to language corpora has allowed many teachers to supplement instruction with discovery and refocus attention on accuracy as an appropriate aspect of learning. Encouraging learners to actively understand target discourses by systematically interrogating corpora has its dangers, however, and not all students respond well to this, but as a student research tool it can promote a learner-centered, inductive approach and encourage an awareness of conventional patterns which cannot be achieved in any other way.

Conclusions

I hope to have shown in this brief chapter that specific purpose programs play a full and active part in applied linguistics and language teaching today. Drawing their strength from a variety of theories and a commitment to research-based language education, such programs are now situated at the front line of both theory development and innovative practice in teaching. The richness of the field, however, prevents a full account here, and I have omitted many of the influences, practices, and directions which characterize it. In particular, I have not been able to give space to the importance of computer-mediated communication between learners and experts in LSP contexts, nor to the current state of the art with regard to materials, nor to the ways that the visual structure of academic and professional texts have been explored in research and exploited in courses. Neither has it been possible to consider the downside: the weaknesses in institutional recognition and professional training; the relatively paucity of research on spoken discourses; the gulf between much discourse analytic research and its practical application in classrooms; and a tendency to accept institutional imperatives in defining needs too readily, particularly in occupational contexts.

Overall, however, LSP seems to be in good health and moving forward. Its international diversity and scope, its varied practices and approaches, its sensitivity to local contexts and the subject-matter needs and expertise of learners, its solid research base in target discourses, and its grounding in sociocultural theories of learning and communication provide a strong basis for a future in which both first and second language speakers will require specific strategic competencies.

REFERENCES

Barron, C. (2003). Problem-solving and EAP: Themes and issues in a collaborative teaching venture. *English for Specific Purposes* 22, 3, 297–314.

Bazerman, C. (1997). The life of genre, the life in the classroom. In W. Bishop & H. Ostram (eds.), *Genre and writing* (pp. 19–26). Portsmouth, NH: Boynton/Cook.

Benesch, S. (2001). *Critical English for academic purposes*. Mahwah, NJ: Lawrence Erlbaum.

Bhatia, V. (2002). A generic view of academic discourse. In J. Flowerdew (ed.), *Academic discourse* (pp. 21–39). Harlow: Longman.

Breen, M. & Littlejohn, A. (eds.) (2000). *Classroom decision-making: Negotiation and process syllabuses in practice.* Cambridge: Cambridge University Press.

Brown, J. D. (1995). *The elements of language curriculum.* Boston, MA: Heinle & Heinle.

Canagarajah, A. S. (1999). *Resisting linguistic imperialism in English teaching.* Oxford: Oxford University Press.

Coffin, C., Curry, M., Goodman, S., Hewings, A., Lillis, T., & Swann, J. (2003). *Teaching academic writing: A toolkit for higher education.* London: Routledge.

Dudley-Evans, T. & St John, M.-J. (1998). *Developments in English for Specific Purposes.* Cambridge: Cambridge University Press.

Gee, J. (1990). *Social linguistics and literacies: Ideology in discourse.* Brighton, UK: Falmer Press.

Hyland, K. (2000). *Disciplinary discourses: Social interactions in academic writing.* London: Longman. (Reprinted in 2004 by University of Michigan Press.)

Hyland, K. (2004). *Genre and second language writing.* Ann Arbor, MI: University of Michigan Press.

Hyland, K. (2006). *English for academic purposes: An advanced resource book.* London: Routledge.

Hyland, K. & Tse, P. (2007). Is there an academic vocabulary? *TESOL Quarterly* 41, 2, 235–54.

Ivanic, R. (1998). *Writing and identity: The discoursal construction of identity in academic writing.* Amsterdam: John Benjamins.

Jasso-Aguilar, R. (1999). Sources, methods and triangulation in needs analysis: A critical perspective in a case study of a Waikiki hotel maids. *English for Specific Purposes* 18, 27–46.

Johns, A. M. (1997). *Text, role and context: Developing academic literacies.* Cambridge, Cambridge University Press.

Lillis, T. (2001). *Student writing: Access, regulation, desire.* London: Routledge.

Miller, L. (2001). English for engineers in Hong Kong. In J. Purphy & P. Byrd (eds.), *Understanding the courses we teach* (pp. 236–55). Ann Arbor: University of Michigan Press.

Nickerson, C. (2005). English as a *lingua franca* in international business contexts. *English for Specific Purposes* 24, 4, 367–80.

Pennycook, A. (1997). Vulgar pragmatism, critical pragmatism, and EAP. *English for Specific Purposes* 16, 4, 253–69.

Planken, B., van Hooft, A., & Korzilius, H. (2004). Promoting intercultural communicative competence through foreign language courses. *Business Communication Quarterly* 67, 308–15.

Rutherford, W. (1987). *Second language grammar: Learning and teaching.* London, Longman.

Swales, J. (1999). How to be brave in EAP: Teaching writing in today's research world. Paper presented at the LSP Forum held in Prague, September 17–19.

Swales, J. & Feak, C. (2000). *English in today's research world: A writing guide.* Ann Arbor: University of Michigan Press.

Swales, J. & Lindemann, S. (2002). Teaching the literature review to international graduate students. In A. Johns (ed.) *Genre in the classroom: Multiple perspectives* (pp. 105–19). Mahwah, NJ: Lawrence Erlbaum.

Tajino, A., James, R., & Kijima, K. (2005). Beyond needs analysis: Soft systems methodology for meaningful collaboration in EAP course design. *Journal of English for Academic Purposes* 4, 1, 43–66.

Vygotsky, L. (1978). *Mind in society: The development of higher psychological processes*, ed. M. Cole, V. John-Steiner, S. Scribner, & E. Souberman. Harvard, MA: Harvard University Press.

FURTHER READING

Benesch, S. (2001). *Critical English for academic purposes*. Mahwah, NJ: Lawrence Erlbaum.

Candlin, C. N. (ed.) (2002). *Research and practice in professional discourse*. Hong Kong. City University of Hong Kong Press.

Hyland, K. (2006). *English for academic purposes: An advanced resource book*. London: Routledge.

Johns, A. M. (1997). *Text, role and context: Developing academic literacies*. Cambridge: Cambridge University Press.

Swales, J. (2004). *Research genres*. Cambridge: Cambridge University Press.

13 Study Abroad Research: Findings, Implications, and Future Directions

JOSEPH COLLENTINE

One of the most important variables that affects the nature and the extent to which learners acquire a second language (L2) is the context of learning, that is, whether the learning takes place within the society in which the L2 is productive or where the first language (L1) is productive. Second language acquisition (SLA) research takes place in three primary contexts, which differ in sociological and functional terms. The *foreign-language* (FL) classroom exists in the domestic setting of the L1, and learners tend to use the L2 within the classroom and as it relates to academic purposes. The *intensive domestic immersion* setting is different from the FL context in that students dedicate the majority (if not all) of their academic term to studying the L2, and this context often entails an increase in the functional purposes of the L2 when learners sign a "contract" not to use the L1. The *study abroad* (SA) context takes place in countries where the L2 enjoys an important sociological and functional status, entailing a combination of planned curriculum and a host family. This chapter provides an overview of the state of the art of SA research. This review uncovers a pattern not clearly articulated to date: specifically, the most salient domains of interest (e.g., cognitive, pragmatic, sociolinguistic factors) that arise out of the SA literature are quite different from the salient domains in other contexts of learning. Informed by this literature, I conclude with recommendations as to the ideal design of SA programs in a modern FL curriculum.

It is extremely challenging for researchers to isolate the effects of the learning context on acquisition because one must be aware that, within any of these situations, learners acquire the L2 in two sub-contexts: *communicative contexts* as well as *learning contexts* (Batstone, 2002). Communicative contexts require that the learner use the L2 to exchange information and engage in essential social and interpersonal functions. Learning contexts manage input and output so that learners will attend to form and take intentional steps toward improving their linguistic expertise. The influence of these covariates complicates the assessment of a learning context since the FL classroom heavily favors learning contexts, intensive domestic immersion settings attempt to provide both communicative and learning contexts, and SA presumably provides more opportunities for processing and using the L2 in communicative contexts. SA learners must determine the relationship between the L1, the L2, and their identities as social individuals and language learners. For researchers, the complication then becomes which theoretical frameworks can capture the cognitive and social developments through which learners pass in the SA setting. As Collentine and Freed (2004) note, research in a SA context provides an important contextualization for understanding the interaction between cognitive, sociolinguistic, and socio-cultural factors in the construction of a comprehensive theory of SLA. This chapter attempts to delineate the contribution of SA research to SLA theory by exploring its (brief) history as a sub-discipline. The chapter also details the types of populations that researchers have studied, the efficacy of this learning context, how researchers operationalize "efficacy" (and the effects on the interpretation of results), the roles of input and interaction, the cognitive changes (e.g., phonological memory) that occur abroad, important issues identified in the research relating to learner identity, and the role of pedagogy in SA contexts on acquisition.

A Brief History of Study Abroad Research

SA research can be seen as having two periods. The first attempted to understand the overall efficacy of SA programs. These studies concentrated on measuring the gains learners make abroad largely from broad measurement instruments. This period extends from the 1960s to Barbara Freed's publication of her seminal volume *Second language acquisition in a study abroad context* in 1995 (Freed, 1995b). Freed succeeds in framing SA research within the SLA theory-building enterprise, challenging researchers to view SA research as a means of studying the effects of "learning context" on acquisition.

The first period examined gains (or simply post-treatment abilities) with instruments that sought to assess learners' overall L2 abilities.[1] Carroll's (1967) widely-cited study looked at the language skills of 2,782 college seniors on tests that measured linguistic skills in the L2 (i.e., their metalinguistic knowledge), finding that even a short duration abroad (touring or summer) predicted higher levels of proficiency. Willis et al. (1977) summarized a series of studies on British students, concluding that these studies lacked an overall systematic assessment of learners gains. Willis et al.'s (1977) own study on British students in France and Germany showed general support for residency abroad. The strongest gains were in listening and speaking and less in reading abilities. Dyson (1988) conducted another macro study on 229 British students in France, Germany, and Spain, showing that the learning context improved listening and speaking skills. Opper, Teichler, and Carlson (1990) conducted a large-scale study on the efficacy of SA on students in more than 80 programs in Britain, France, Germany, and Sweden. The study is limited in its validity because it relies on self-reported assessments of general language skills (listening, reading, speaking, and writing) whereby the learners generally reported important gains. It provided nonetheless an important clue to a key factor that has been identified in the SA research: SA appeared to be particularly powerful for learners with lower levels of proficiency.

Perhaps the key observation to be gleaned from this study is the notion that there are threshold levels of development at which SA will be optimally beneficial (discussed further below). Another key study of this period that laid the foundation for current SA research was Möhle and Raupach (1983), who found SA not to have an important effect on improving morphosyntactic abilities but to have a positive effect on fluency, a factor in SLA research that has become an important focus of late since it helps us to understand the interaction between online processing mechanisms and linguistic competence such as working and phonological memory (see Segalowitz, 2003). The final noteworthy studies of this period are Brecht and Davidson (1991) and Brecht, Davidson, and Ginsburg (1995), who examined 668 American learners' acquisition of Russian in a SA context. The data reinforced a growing hunch that individual differences (e.g., reading aptitude) are exceptionally evident in this learning context and that preprogram explicit grammar instruction predicts gains abroad.

Freed (1995a) is the first effort to synthesize SA research. She identifies a number of issues that researchers in her volume and others have addressed since its publication. She notes a growing suspicion that the linguistic benefits of the SA context were not the same as those of the traditional classroom (Regan, 1995), and there were surprisingly few empirical studies that actually compared these two learning contexts. She also recognizes the hypothesis that there might be a proficiency threshold at which learners most benefit from SA (Brecht & Davidson, 1991; Brecht, Davidson, & Ginsburg, 1995; Regan, 1995). Additionally, there was almost no research that examined SA gains within current theoretical frameworks that dealt with how new linguistic information becomes internalized in the learner's competence (e.g., interactionist, input-oriented, and socio-cultural models). Freed (1995b) presents studies addressing two issues in her volume, providing important SA–AH (at home) studies comparing orders of acquisition abroad to orders documented in FL contexts (Guntermann, 1995; Lafford, 1995). Freed (1995a) also provides studies on the acquisition of pragmatic competence within a sociolinguistic framework (Regan, 1995; Siegal, 1995).

Since Freed (1995b), noteworthy collections of SA experiments have been published. And, while these collections have concentrated on Americans going abroad (Collentine & Freed, 2004; DuFon & Churchill, 2006; Gore, 2005; Pellegrino-Aveni, 2005), Murphy-Lejeune (2002) examines SA in the European context. What follows delineates the key topics that SA research is currently addressing. The research addresses a variety of issues that relate to the internal cognitive mechanisms affecting acquisition and the external sociolinguistic mechanisms, as well as the socio-cultural issues of SLA in a SA context of learning.

Populations of Study and the Threshold Hypothesis

Kinginger (2007), as well as Coleman (1997), characterizes the existing body of SA research as falling into two categories, with each focusing on different populations and distinct levels of development. Research on American, university-level learners tends to examine acquisition at the beginning stages of development, with study participants sampled from first- and second-year language programs. While there is a good amount of research on learners at the beginning levels of development, Lafford and Collentine (2006) report that SA research on American students of Spanish has sampled participants whose preprogram proficiency ranged from the novice to the advanced high levels. It is true that there exists little information about American learners' success in advanced-level, direct-enrollment programs (i.e., where students sit in classes with otherwise proficient/native speakers of the L2). American, university-level L2 programs – and so SA curricula – concentrate on fostering acquisition at the financially lucrative early stages of acquisition (where FL enrollments in general are highest). Kinginger (2007) asserts that SA research such as Murphy-Lejeune (2002) has focused on European learners at more advanced levels, stemming from the European Commission's inter-university programs, such as the ERASMUS program, which allows students to complete part of their university studies in another EU country and university (41 percent of such students study language or philology; http://www.erasmus.ac.uk/statistics/contents_04_05.htm).

There is a growing interest in SA SLA issues along the Pacific Rim, and these learners – Japanese, Chinese, Korean, and Taiwanese university-level adults slightly beyond the initial stages of development – tend to target English as their L2, either in North America or the South Pacific (Churchill, 2006; Tanaka & Ellis, 2003). If current estimates that 80 percent of foreign students in the world are from Asian countries are correct (Altbach & Bassett, 2004), these populations will become an increasingly important source of data.

There are important pockets of SA contexts and learner profiles that have yet to be studied. Students are attending so-called language camps with increasing frequency. Korean.net, for instance, reports that nearly 40,000 Korean students enrolled in domestic EFL immersion programs in 2005.[2] The *New York Times* recently reported that nearly 75 percent of American summer camps have foreign nationals attending their activities, and many camps provide some EFL instruction (Bick, 2007). To this researcher's knowledge, there is no existing literature either documenting these experiences or providing data on their value, although the usual unsubstantiated and anecdotal claims of efficacy are not hard to uncover.

Learners of all levels of development (who are largely self-selecting) have been studied in the SA literature. However, Lafford and Collentine (2006) discuss the growing consensus amongst researchers that there is a *threshold* which learners must reach to benefit fully from the SA context of learning. And, while the general notion of a threshold level is important for program designers to keep in mind, from a linguistic competence perspective it is probably too broad in scope. There are most likely specific domains that require a particular developmental threshold for overall gains to occur. Golonka (2006) – refining the Brecht, Davidson, and Ginsberg (1995) analysis – presents evidence suggesting that preprogram linguistic (grammar, vocabulary, accuracy) and metalinguistic (self-corrected errors and sentence repair) levels predicted which SA learners of Russian would attain the Advanced level on the ACTFL proficiency scale. Segalowitz and Freed (2004) found that, amongst Spanish L2 learners, an initial threshold level of basic word recognition and lexical access processing abilities may be necessary for oral proficiency and fluency to develop abroad significantly. Lafford (2004) surmises that advanced learners bring more formulaic expressions to SA communicative contexts and can therefore spend more attention resources on form, whereas novices must attend primarily to meaning. Finally, Segalowitz and Freed (2004) report that the most important gains that SA learners of Spanish make abroad are in the domain of fluency (as measured by temporal/hesitation phenomena), and O'Brien et al. (2007) report that these fluency gains abroad are a function of students' potential for phonological memory storage, which varies from adult to adult. While this last factor is not controllable from a preprogram perspective, it argues that a student's cognitive and linguistic abilities will mediate developmental gains in the program.

The Issue of Study Abroad Efficacy

Many researchers and educators have surmised that the SA context is the *sine qua non* for achieving global L2 competence (Rivers, 1998). Freed (1995a) acknowledged that, while some empirical studies conducted up until 1995 provided evidence that SA facilitates acquisition (e.g., DeKeyser, 1991; Teichler & Steube, 1991), a sizable amount of evidence challenged researchers to consider whether the study abroad context might impede acquisition at the beginning stages (e.g., Freed, 1990; Spada, 1985, 1986), which, again, points to a threshold effect. Cohen and Shively (2007) summarize the research to date, asserting: "An intriguing finding in the study abroad research literature that prompted the current study was that study-abroad students do not necessarily achieve greater language gains than their peers who stay home and study the target language" (p. 189). Clearly, overall efficacy is difficult to assess in the absence of data stemming from large-scale studies such as those reported by Brecht and Davidson (1991) and Segalowitz et al. (2005). Yet, SA studies tend to be longitudinal in nature, as opposed to much SLA research that examines short-term effects. These studies support Carroll's (1967) initial assertion about the advantages of SA, but they require a great deal of qualification: whereas SA affects gains in certain language-specific domains, it does not affect development in all aspects of a learner's competence. Interestingly, linguistic aspects that do indeed seem to benefit from SA, such as fluency and discursive abilities, are often not those in which AH FL program directors hope to see improvements, such as those grammatical aspects around which the AH, focus-on-forms syllabus is designed. The following two sections summarize what we know to date about the important cognitive and linguistic aspects of L2 development with which SA interacts.

Important Cognitive Constructs in the Study Abroad Literature

One consistent theme in the SA literature is individual differences and individual variation (variation is addressed in the next section). An area of SLA research that is making important contributions to our understanding of individual differences – or, between-subject variation – examines the interaction of short-term memory stores (e.g., working memory, phonological memory), speed of information access, attention control, and acquisition (see DeKeyser, 2001).

Segalowitz and Freed (2004) are interested in the cognitive processing abilities that underlie "expert abilities." They present data indicating that cognitive abilities interact with development abroad in complex ways. They found lexical access to be related to overall proficiency gains amongst SA learners of Spanish, such that learners who access lexical items faster show greater gains. They also present data suggesting that learners exhibiting greater attention control at the completion of their SA program spoke less fluently. Segalowitz and Freed (2004) speculate that the increased attention control in the SA context may reflect increased monitoring of output. O'Brien oversees two studies examining the interaction of phonological memory and SA gains in learners of Spanish, both of which indicate that phonological memory assists not only children (in vocabulary gains) but also adults in an L2 context. O'Brien et al. (2006) showed that phonological memory abilities have a positive effect on one's abilities to produce multi-propositional utterances at the early stages of Spanish learners' development (i.e., narrative abilities) in addition to a positive effect on the acquisition of particular grammatical functors at later stages. O'Brien et al. (2007) add to our understanding of the cognitive mechanisms underlying the general fluency gains associated with SA experiences, showing that phonological memory also predicts fluency gains. Finally, Tokowicz, Michael, and Kroll (2004) examine working memory capacity and single-word translation errors, presenting data that suggest that SA learners engage in more approximate than precise translations but that this tendency is limited to those with higher working memory capacities.

This literature suggests that learners' predisposed cognitive abilities determine how much one can produce (and how fast) as a result of SA, and may impact the ways that learners approach attention-demanding processes (such as translations and story-telling). It also indicates that researchers ought to consider carefully how they interpret observable behaviors, such as fluency. The Segalowitz and Freed (2004) study provides some evidence that where there is a lack of fluency, there may be more monitoring occurring (due to greater attention control), which is not an unreasonable conclusion, since Golonka (2006) shows a strong relationship between metalinguistic abilities and overall proficiency gains.

Important Linguistic Constructs in the Study Abroad Literature

As mentioned above, there has been a growing concern about the overall lack of efficacy of SA on acquisition (cf. Cohen & Shively, 2007). In the following I show that, while it is not accurate to claim a superiority for SA on fostering acquisition, it is likewise erroneous to conclude that important, positive changes (toward native-speaker norms) do not occur as a result of the SA context of learning. The developmental growth one finds in this learning context appears not to be what one finds in the AH setting (although the field admittedly has a dearth of comparative AH–SA studies) nor what learners and their AH teachers expect (e.g., dramatically improved grammatical and phonological accuracy). The linguistic-specific growth that occurs is in the domain of global discursive abilities, the expansion of knowledge of verb paradigms, and in the domain of pragmatics. A review of this research reveals much about the communicative needs and demands placed on learners in the SA context.

One of the consistent conclusions that researchers have drawn from the SA literature has been that the development of grammatical abilities does not seem to outpace that of the AH context. DeKeyser (1990, 1991) found that residence abroad had little impact on the development of overall grammatical abilities and that SA learners were equal to or inferior to their AH counterparts in their use of grammar. Collentine (2004) gauged SA learners' acquisition of a variety of morphosyntactic features, showing that they do not make as much progress as AH learners on precisely those grammatical aspects that many FL teachers emphasize, namely, verbs and subordinate conjunctions.

These studies, in sum, indicate that the appreciable development of morphosyntax and general grammatical abilities is not to be expected, at least within the timeframe of a semester to a year abroad. Indeed, two of these studies (Collentine, 2004; DeKeyser, 1990) suggest that the AH experience affords certain advantages as regards overall grammatical development for intermediate learners. A notable exception is Isabelli and Nishida (2005), who reveal that SA has an advantage with respect to subjunctive development when learners are at more advanced stages, thus supporting the threshold hypothesis.

A further complication to this scenario arises out a comparison of Golonka (2006), who found preprogram metalinguistic knowledge to predict proficiency gains, and Izumi and Iwasaki (2004). The latter examined the effects of amount of SA experience on a grammaticality judgment test by Japanese-speaking English FL learners, where the participants were asked to give reasons for their evaluations. The purely classroom EFL learners used intuitive, analyzed, and metalinguistic knowledge more or less equally, while the learners who experienced living abroad for several years used intuitive knowledge and very little metalinguistic knowledge. It may be that preprogram metalinguistic knowledge is an important prerequisite, but that not all learners depend on that knowledge in communicative situations to process grammar. It may also be that, as the Segalowitz and Freed (2004) data suggest, some processes become more automatized abroad, so that metalinguistic awareness is converted into implicit grammatical knowledge. Clearly, more research is needed in this area.

Research is starting to suggest that the organizing principles around which SA learners develop their grammatical abilities stem from the discursive demands they face in communicative contexts. This ought not to be surprising, given what we have known for a while about uninstructed SLA. The *Second Language Acquisition by Adult Immigrants* study was conducted from 1981 to 1988 in five

European countries by the *Max Planck Institut für Psycholinguistik*, mostly on L2 learners of German (Perdue & Klein, 1992), showing that L2 grammaticalization arises out of functional pressures to achieve discursive coherence. Collentine (2004) used corpus-based techniques (see Biber, 1988) to compare the development of narrative abilities, as well as growth in the semantic density, of AH and SA learners of Spanish, revealing that the SA context afforded a significant advantage. Similarly, Cheng and Mojica-Díaz (2006) compared SA learners of Spanish on their subjunctive abilities (using a native-speaker baseline), finding no significant improvement after a two-month period, although they report some learners started producing more tightly structured argumentation over time.

Fine-grained analyses of SA learners' grammatical performance over time suggest another plausible explanation for why researchers in the past have not found an appreciable quantifiable advantage for SA context in grammatical development: the SA context fosters grammatical variation. Regan (1995) examined SA learners of French and their use of the *ne* negation particle, showing that AH learners tended to adopt a single, standardized construct for negation whereas their SA counterparts varied between the inclusion and omission of the *ne* particle as a function of sociolinguistic factors. Howard (2002, 2006), who has examined SA Irish learners of French, has presented convincing evidence that SA learners spend much time varying within and accommodating the individual elements of a paradigm (e.g., present-tense French inflections). His data also suggest that L2 phonological development interacts with the increased inflectional variability (or perhaps inflectional confusion) in the SA context, which is not surprising given that inflectional morphology tends to comprise short phonemic segments (and suffers neutralization in modern French; cf., Howard, Lemée, & Regan, 2006).

Some researchers suspect that one of the reasons for a weak SA grammar effect is that learners have much less access to the L2 than one might suspect, especially as it relates to its pragmatic features. Native speakers find it difficult to abandon certain mentor–apprentice modes of interaction with learners (Pellegrino-Aveni, 2005; Wilkinson, 2002). Barron (2003), examining Irish SA learners of German, argues that learners form social networks with other speakers of their L1, limiting their access to native speakers. Others suggest that learners are not adequately aware of the rules of pragmatics within the target culture (Wilkinson, 2002). Cohen and Shively (2007) present data from a controlled experiment suggesting that preprogram efforts to raise French and Spanish learners' awareness of speech acts had only a marginal effect on their ability to mitigate the intensity of requests and no significant effect on their ability to recognize the appropriateness of other acts, such as apologies.

Some recent research on SA pragmatics reinforces O'Brien et al.'s (2006) position that SA has differential effects on learners depending on their preprogram level of development.[3] Shardakova (2005) reports that SA learners of Russian with low preprogram proficiency adopt culturally appropriate apologies, while more advanced candidates develop their own strategies, which are not consistent with cultural prescriptions, reflecting the extent to which linguistic behaviors in a SA environment can be a function of identity as much as input and types of interaction (see below for more on the notion of identity). This pattern of tension between pragmatic appropriateness and rejection of target cultural (linguistic) practices in terms of routines and speech acts is a recurring theme in the SA literature (DuFon & Churchill, 2006). This may account for the general consensus amongst researchers of SA pragmatics that, while SA learners outpace their AH counterparts in pragmatic development, they may spend years attaining native-speaker behaviors, if they so choose. All told, pragmatic competence seems to develop quite slowly in the SA context (Hoffman-Hicks, 1999; Rodríguez, 2001). Protracted pragmatic development is not surprising since learning new scripts/ discourse grammar (i.e., in the case of speech acts) and illocutive meanings along-side locutive ones (i.e., double meanings for certain phrases and constructs, such interrogatives that represent imperatives) represents a considerable task.

This review indicates that grammatical and pragmatic development abroad becomes complicated by the sociocognitive and socio-cultural pressures that learn-ers face in the SA context, a situation that sends many more messages to learners than does the AH context as to the complete repertoire of skills and behaviors one needs to be communicatively functional. Communicative demands at the discursive, as opposed to the sentential, level may well force the learner to make adjustments to his or her preprogram, personal or internal syllabus (Lafford, 2004). If linguistic variation is more prevalent in the SA context than the AH context, SA learners may need to incorporate non-standard forms into their development competence. This greater variability in the SA input may force the SA learner to accommodate the L2 forms with which AH learners may only need to (re)familiarize themselves at test time. Finally, pragmatic development seems to be slow in the SA context, yet important gains are made in the SA context. However, issues of (self-) identify may well interact with the extent to which pragmatic norms become adopted by the learner.

The (Assumed) Roles of Input and Interaction

One of the most undisputed assumptions about the SA context is that learners receive vast amounts of input and have numerous opportunities for commun-icative interaction. There is a tendency in the field to attribute gains that learners make to the enormous amount of available input. However, there has been no attempt independently to document in a fully quantified manner the types of input and interaction that learners have abroad. The assumptions that exist in the literature may be too strong. Pellegrino-Aveni (2005) documents from a qualit-ative perspective the types of interactions SA learners of Russian have, arguing that self-preservation (e.g., face-saving) needs effectively impede learners' contact with native speakers. There have been attempts to document the types of input and interaction learners have in a SA context, such as the Language Contact Profile (LCP) employed by Segalowitz and Freed (2004). This sort of assessment tool is helpful, in that it has built-in redundancies, so as to triangulate the reported contact for any given subject. However, it is a self-report, and its validity is limited in the same way all self-reports are (such as in clinical research), where data sets represent self-perceptions and require objective, third-party validation, such as by host families and professors abroad.

The lack of primary data on the amount of input learners receive abroad is, in fact, symptomatic of a larger problem in SA research and in the enterprise as a whole. Large-scale studies of how much input and interaction learners have in AH contexts really do not exist either. Yet, the field of SLA knows a good deal about the effects of input and interaction on acquisition because we have almost three decades of controlled treatment data (Mackey & Goo, 2007; Norris & Ortega, 2001). No concerted research agenda exists either in theory or practice to control the amounts and types of input and interaction learners receive in the SA context. Taking this observation a step further, we are confronted with the conclusion that we do not know how input differs in the SA context, comprehensible or otherwise. Barron (2003), for instance, notes that learners often misinterpret important aural cues and draw erroneous conclusions about the L2, since negative evidence is not available. Additionally, Magnan and Back (2007), using a modified version of the LCP, present data suggesting that the living situation and access to authentic aural media do not predict oral proficiency gains abroad. The field of L1 acquisition has developed a number of tools for documenting what learners are exposed to in naturalistic settings, and SA researchers could use these methods and instruments as a starting point.

McGeeking (2006), studying SA students of Japanese, is one of the few studies to document how learners negotiate for meaning in the home-stay environment, reporting that numerous opportunities exist (see also Dings & Jobe, 2003, as well as Smartt & Scudder, 2004). Yet the opportunities to negotiate appear to be mitigated in the SA context by personal and interpersonal factors. Wilkinson (2002) reports that home-stay families find it difficult to use naturalistic language with their SA learners of French, preferring to use teacher-talk, denying the learners opportunities for authentic input via interaction. Churchill (2006) documents that SA learners of English from Japan vary in the amount of authentic interactions they have depending on length of stay, which in turn is a function of the extent to which the learners are fully integrated into the target learning community, which is difficult in five-week programs.

What is unclear is whether there are more reports that have made it to press in the SA literature than in the AH literature about the interpersonal mitigating factors that impede opportunities for negotiating for meaning. Much research purporting to comment on negotiation opportunities is conducted within a sociocultural framework (cf. Kinginger, 2007; DuFon & Churchill, 2006), and so the epistemology is not the same as that from which SLA has traditionally examined interaction (i.e., from a largely cognitive perspective; McGeeking (2006) is a notable exception). Until these two epistemologies can achieve a common terminological interface, our understanding of negotiation in SA contexts relative to the existing SLA literature will remain weak.

Identity

Researchers approaching the SA context from a socio-cultural perspective have focused on the individual histories of students and the tension that exists between maintaining individuality, issues of self esteem, worldviews (e.g., social hierarchies), and the need to advance their own development through native-speaker interactions (Wilkinson, 1998). Churchill (2006) documents how the manner in which learners are received (or not) affects the amount of interaction they have. Kinginger (in press) provides an exhaustive summary of the socio-cultural literature relating to SA. She concludes that the most important theme is that, in those moments when learners' personal sense of identity with the target culture (or with the representatives that they know, such as the home-stay family) is distant, or when learners sense that they have too many obstacles to attaining higher levels of proficiency (either through negative interactions or from a sense of linguistic inadequacy), SA learners abandon their role as "language learners," thus impeding the development process.

Programmatic Considerations

There are a number of programmatic implications to be gleaned from the research presented to date. From an administrative perspective, it is difficult for a home institution to have a strong effect on a host institution's syllabi and methodological approaches. SA instructors are often employees of other institutions and adjunct faculty who have less of a stake in the long-term needs of the learner or program. Programs such as the University of Delaware's, where there is a tight integration between the home and abroad curricula and a faculty development program, can serve as models for ensuring greater quality control over pedagogy (cf. Chieffo & Zipser, 2001). The last ten years have seen a noticeable interest in, and research on, the role of tasks and authentic interactions within an L2 curriculum. For instance, Doughty and Long (2003) suggest that Task-Based Language Teaching provides one such curricular framework that, based on SLA research, details the types of interactions in which learners can engage according to developmental level. An exploration of the plausibility and the outcomes of this sort of language program within a SA curriculum might at least provide a principled starting point from which to study the "missing SA methodology" (Lafford & Collentine, 2006).

It is unclear what the ideal duration of a SA program might be, although a consideration of this question raises intriguing questions for SLA researchers. Programs tend to range from about five weeks to a year in length. Expectations about (1) how much development occurs and, more importantly, (2) which aspects of a learner's competence develop must be measured against the observations made above that exponential growth will not occur within such a time frame. In the absence of a solid base of SA–AH comparative studies, it is possible (naively) to look at SA research solely as a set of longitudinal SLA investigations. This would lead SLA researchers to the conclusion that L2 acquisition is a protracted process. If the field were to imagine (again, naively) that AH research represents the possible effects of pedagogical interventions in a laboratory setting, SA research indicates that sociopragmatic variables and the inherent linguistic variation existing outside this laboratory will essentially increase the "content" that learners must acquire. The SA learner is confronted with functional demands that invite us to view the AH student as one who learns the language for so-called special purposes. As Freed (1995b) notes, it is no longer tenable to consider a student who enrolls in a SA program as a FL learner, since the SA converts him/her into the learner of a L2. Thus, the end goal of the SA student (whether or not the learner completely abandons his/her role as a language learner; cf. Kinginger, in press) is often different from the AH learner's, and the amount of time needed to complete the L2 agenda becomes longer than that needed for the FL agenda.

If there is a consensus, it is that a student may begin a SA program too early in his/her development. The research considered above indicates that a certain level of metalinguistic knowledge (we do not know yet how much) is a prerequisite for developing the L2 abroad (Brecht & Davidson, 1991; Magnan & Back, 2007). At the very least, SA outcomes are sensitive to learners' preprogram competence levels (Golonka, 2006; O'Brien et al., 2006). At this point, it is possible to suggest: (1) the amount and type of preprogram preparation should be studied in greater depth; (2) these preprogram considerations should inform the types of L2 knowledge and levels of development in programs.

The research does not control for the effects of the homestay with host families. A review of the literature indicates that most students stay with a host family. Lazar (2004), however, reports that the actual amount of time that learners spend with their host families varies both in quantity and quality, and these interactions have an appreciable effect on acquisition in general. Lafford (2004) found a significant negative correlation between the amount of time spent talking with host families and the use of communication strategies to bridge communication gaps. The literature reported here indicates that issues of (1) identity and (2) the host family's perceived role as a mentor may determine how much one learns (Wilkinson, 2002).

Concluding Remarks

Most research conducted to date on SA has concentrated on the American university experience, as seen by the above literature review. As Kinginger (2007) notes, other parts of the world such as Europe have a different relationship with the SA experience, depending on their proximity to other languages and the value they place on bilingualism. Perhaps because the field of SLA is still in the early stages of building a theory of acquisition, it may not be surprising that very little research exists on the effects of SA on learners such as those in the ERASMUS programs that explicitly purport to promote learners' proficiency. We need to learn much more about the effects of SA on advanced learners, especially given that we suspect there is a developmental threshold at which it starts to be generally effective.

Researchers also need to consider the effects of particular teaching strategies and syllabus design on learner development. The knowledge base reviewed above indicates that this area of SA research is still in its descriptive phase. There are good models of curricular design whose impact we should start to investigate.

NOTES

1 See Freed (1995a) for an extensive, historical overview of the research on SA up to 1995.
2 www.kois.go.kr/news/News/newsprint.asp?serial_no=20050725004.
3 See DuFon and Churchill (2006) for an extensive overview of the research to date on pragmatic research in the SA context.

REFERENCES

Altbach, P. & Bassett, R. (2004). The brain trade. *Foreign Policy* 44, 30–1.

Barron, A. (2003). *Acquisition in interlanguage pragmatics: Learning how to do things with words in a study abroad context*. Amsterdam: John Benjamins.

Batstone, R. (2002). Contexts of engagement: A discourse perspective on "intake" and "pushed output." *System* 30, 1–14.

Biber, D. (1988). *Variation across speech and writing*. Cambridge: Cambridge University Press.

Bick, J. (2007). Around the campfire, global ghost stories. *New York Times*, June 21.

Brecht, R. & Davidson, D. (1991). Language acquisition gains in study abroad: Program assessment and modification. Paper presented at the NFLC Conference on Language Testing, Washington DC.

Brecht, R., Davidson, D., & Ginsberg, R. (1995). Predictors of foreign language gain during study abroad. In B. Freed (ed.), *Second language acquisition in a study abroad context* (pp. 37–66). Philadelphia: John Benjamins.

Carroll, J. (1967). Foreign language proficiency levels attained by language majors near graduation from college. *Foreign Language Annals* 1, 131–51.

Cheng, A. & Mojica-Díaz, C. (2006). The effects of formal instruction and study abroad on improving proficiency: The case of the Spanish subjunctive. *Applied Language Learning* 16, 17–36.

Chieffo, L. & Zipser, R. (2001). Integrating study abroad into the foreign language curriculum. *ADFL Bulletin* 32, 79–85.

Churchill, E. (2006). Variability in the study abroad classroom and learner competence. In M. DuFon & E. Churchill (eds.), *Language learners in study abroad contexts* (pp. 203–27). Clevedon, UK: Multilingual Matters.

Cohen, A. & Shively, R. (2007). Acquisition of requests and apologies in Spanish and French: Impact of study abroad and strategy-building intervention. *Modern Language Journal* 91, 189–21.

Coleman, J. (1997). Residence abroad within language study. *Language Teaching* 30, 1–20.

Collentine, J. (2004). The effects of learning contexts on morphosyntactic and lexical development. *Studies in Second Language Acquisition* 26, 227–48.

Collentine, J. & Freed, B. (2004). Introduction: Learning context and its effects on second language acquisition. *Studies in Second Language Acquisition* 26, 153–72.

DeKeyser, R. (1990). From learning to acquisition? Monitoring in the classroom and abroad. *Hispania* 73, 238–47.

DeKeyser, R. (1991). Foreign language development during a semester abroad. In B. Freed (ed.), *Foreign language acquisition: Research and the classroom* (pp. 104–19). Lexington, MA: D. C. Heath.

DeKeyser, R. M. (2001). Automaticity and automatization. In P. Robinson (ed.), *Cognition and second language instruction* (pp. 125–51). Cambridge, MA: Cambridge University Press.

Dings, A. & Jobe, T. (2003). Negotiating obstacles: Extended repair sequences in native/ non native interaction. In P. Kempchinsky & C. Piñeros (eds.), *Theory, practice, and acquisition: Papers from the sixth Hispanic Linguistics Symposium and the fifth Conference on the Acquisition of Spanish and Portuguese* (pp. 371–81). Somerville, MA: Cascadilla.

Doughty, C. & Long, M. (2003). Optimal psycholinguistic environments for distance foreign language learning. *Language Learning and Technology* 7, 50–80.

DuFon, M. & Churchill, E. (2006). *Language learners in study abroad contexts*. Clevedon, UK: Multilingual Matters.

Dyson, P. (1988). *The year abroad: Report for the Central Bureau for Educational Visits and Exchanges*. Oxford: Oxford University Language Teaching Centre.

Freed, B. (1990). Language learning in a study abroad context: The effects of interactive and non interactive out-of-class contact on grammatical achievement and oral proficiency. In J. Alatis (ed.), *Linguistics, language teaching and language acquisition: The interdependence of theory, practice, and research* (pp. 459–77), Georgetown University round table on languages and linguistics. Washington, DC: Georgetown University Press.

Freed, B. (1995a). Introduction. In B. Freed (ed.), *Second language acquisition in a study abroad context* (pp. 3–34). John Benjamins: Philadelphia.

Freed, B. (1995b). *Second language acquisition in a study abroad context*. John Benjamins: Philadelphia.

Golonka, E. (2006). Predictors revised: Linguistic knowledge and metalinguistic awareness in second language gain in Russian. *Modern Language Journal* 90, 496–505.

Gore, J. (2005). *Dominant beliefs and alternative voices: Discourse, belief, and gender in american study abroad*. New York: Routledge.

Guntermann, G. (1995). The peace corps experience: Language learning in training and in the field. In B. Freed (ed.), *Second language acquisition in a study abroad context* (pp. 149– 70). John Benjamins: Philadelphia.

Hoffman-Hicks, S. (1999). The longitudinal development of French foreign language pragmatic competence: Evidence from study abroad participants. Unpublished doctoral dissertation, Indiana University.

Howard, M. (2002). Prototypical and non-prototypical marking in the advanced learner's aspectuo-temporal system. *EuroSLA Yearbook* 2, 87–114.

Howard, M. (2006). Variation in advanced French interlanguage: A comparison of three (socio)linguistic variables. *Canadian Modern Language Review* 62, 379–400.

Howard, M., Lemée, I., & Regan, V. (2006). The L2 acquisition of a socio-phonetic variable: The case of /l/ deletion in French. *Journal of French Language Studies* 16, 1–24.

Isabelli, C. & Nishida, C. (2005). Development of the Spanish subjunctive in a nine-month study-abroad setting. In D. Eddington (ed.), *Selected proceedings of the sixth Conference on the Acquisition of Spanish and Portuguese As First and Second Languages* (pp. 78–91). Sommerville, MA: Cascadilla Press.

Izumi, S. & Iwasaki, M. (2004). Development of explicit and implicit knowledge of different grammatical forms by learners with different ESL learning backgrounds. *Sophia Linguistica* 52, 1–33.

Kinginger, C. (2007). Research on language education through programmes of study and residence abroad: Recent publications. *International Journal of Bilingual Education and Bilingualism* 10, 104–12.

Kinginger, C. (in press). Language learning in study abroad: Case studies of Americans in France. *Modern Language Journal*.

Lafford, B. (1995). Getting into, through, and out of a survival situation: A comparison of communicative strategies used by students studying Spanish-abroad and "at home." In B. Freed (ed.), *Second language acquisition in a study abroad context* (pp. 97–122). John Benjamins: Philadelphia.

Lafford, B. (2004). The effect of context of learning on the use of communication strategies by learners of Spanish as a second language. *Studies in Second Language Acquisition* 26, 201–26.

Lafford, B. & Collentine, J. (2006). The effects of study abroad and classroom contexts on the acquisition of Spanish as a second language: From research to application. In B. Lafford & R. Salaberry (eds.), *Spanish second language acquisition: From research findings to teaching applications* (pp. 103–26). Washington, DC: Georgetown University Press.

Lazar, N. (2004). A short survey on causal inference, with implications for context of learning studies of second language acquisition. *Studies in Second Language Acquisition* 26, 329–48.

Mackey, A. & Goo, J. (2007). Interaction research in SLA: A meta-analysis and research synthesis. In A. Mackey (ed.), *Conversational interaction in second language acquisition* (pp. 407–52). Oxford: Oxford University Press.

Magnan, S. & Back, M. (2007). Social interaction and linguistic gain during study abroad. *Foreign Language Annals* 40, 43–61.

McGeeking, A. (2006). Negotiation in a Japanese study abroad setting. In M. DuFon & E. Churchill (eds.), *Language learners in study abroad contexts* (pp. 177–202). Clevedon, UK: Multilingual Matters.

Möhle, D. & Raupach, M. (1983). *Planen in der Fremdsprach.* Frankfurt: Peter Lang.

Murphy-Lejeune, E. (2002). *Student mobility and narrative in Europe: The new strangers.* New York: Routledge.

Norris, J. & Ortega, L. (2001). Does type of instruction make a difference? Substantive findings from a meta-analytic review. *Language Learning* 51, 157–213.

O'Brien, I., Segalowitz, N., Collentine, J., & Freed, B. (2006). Phonological memory and lexical, narrative, and grammatical skills in second-language oral production by adult learners. *Applied Psycholinguistics* 27, 377–402.

O'Brien, I., Segalowitz, N., Freed, B., & Collentine, J. (2007). Phonological memory predicts second language oral fluency gains in adults. *Studies in Second Language Acquisition* 29, 557–81.

Opper, S., Teichler, U., & Carlson, J. (eds.) (1990). *Impact of study abroad programmes on students and graduates.* London: Jessica Kingsley.

Pellegrino-Aveni, V. (2005). *Study abroad and second language use: Constructing the self.* Cambridge: Cambridge University Press.

Perdue, C. & Klein, W. (1992). Why does the production of some learners not grammaticalize? *Studies in Second Language Acquisition* 14, 259–72.

Regan, V. (1995). The acquisition of sociolinguistic native speech norms: Effects of a year abroad on second language learners of French. In B. Freed (ed.), *Second language acquisition in a study abroad context* (pp. 245–68). John Benjamins: Philadelphia.

Rivers, W. (1998). Is being there enough? The effects of home stay placements on language gain during study abroad. *Foreign Language Annals* 31, 492–500.

Rodríguez, S. (2001). The perception of requests in Spanish by instructed learners of Spanish in second- and foreign-language contexts: A longitudinal study of acquisition patterns. Unpublished doctoral dissertation, Indiana University.

Segalowitz, N. (2003). Automaticity and second languages. In C. J. Doughty and M. H. Long (eds.), *Handbook of second language acquisition* (pp. 382–408). Malden, MA: Blackwell.

Segalowitz, N. & Freed, B. (2004). Context, contact, and cognition in oral fluency acquisition. *Studies in Second Language Acquisition* 26, 173–99.

Segalowitz, N., Freed, B., Collentine, J., Lafford, B., Lazar, N., & Díaz-Campos, M. (2005). A comparison of acquisition of Spanish as a second language in two different contexts of learning: Study Abroad and the versus regular academic classroom. *Frontiers* 10, 1–18.

Shardakova, M. (2005). Intercultural pragmatics in the speech of American L2 learners of Russian: Apologies offered by Americans in Russian. *Intercultural Pragmatics* 2, 423–51.

Siegal, M. (1995). Individual differences and study abroad: Women learning Japanese in Japan. In B. Freed (ed.), *Second language acquisition in a study abroad context* (pp. 225–44). John Benjamins: Philadelphia.

Smartt, J. & Scudder, R. (2004). Immersion study abroad in Mexico: Using repair behaviors to assess proficiency change. *Foreign Language Annals* 37, 592–607.

Spada, N. (1985). Effects of informal contact on classroom learners' proficiency: A review of five studies. *TESL Canada Journal* 2, 51–62.

Spada, N. (1986). The interaction between types of contact and types of instruction: Some effects on the second language proficiency of adult learners. *Studies in Second Language Acquisition* 8, 181–99.

Tanaka, K. & Ellis, R. (2003). Study-abroad, language proficiency, and learner beliefs about language learning. *JALT Journal* 25, 63–85.

Tiechler, U. & Steube, W. (1991). The logics of study abroad programs and the impacts. *Higher Education* 21, 325–49.

Tokowicz, N., Michael, E., & Kroll, J. (2004). The roles of study-abroad experience and working-memory capacity in the types of errors made during translation. *Bilingualism: Language and Cognition* 7, 255–72.

Wilkinson, S. (1998). On the nature of immersion during study abroad: Some participants' perspectives. *Frontiers* 4, 121–38.

Wilkinson, S. (2002). The omnipresent classroom during summer study abroad: American students in conversation with their French hosts. *Modern Language Journal* 86, 157–73.

Willis, F., Doble, G., Sankarayya, U., & Smithers, A. (1977). *Residence abroad and the student of modern languages: A preliminary survey.* Bradford, UK: Modern Languages Centre, University of Bradford.

14 Less Commonly Taught Languages: Issues in Learning and Teaching

KIRA GOR AND KAREN VATZ

Introduction

A "Less Commonly Taught Language" (LCTL), a definition stemming out of educational policy, is a language considered important by the government, but unsustainable by the market. Political priorities drive a nation's linguistic need, although developing the educational infrastructure to support this need presents serious challenges. While "LCTL" is predominantly a US term referring to languages other than French, German, and Spanish (Brecht & Walton, 1997), the concept exists globally and it is a nation's current educational policy and political situation that determine what languages are classified as less commonly taught (LCT). For instance, in the US, languages such as Persian and Japanese have only recently become thought of as LCT, not because of the number of speakers of those languages, which has not changed significantly, but because those countries have come to play an increasingly important role in the global political arena and economy, whereas a language such as Dutch, which is equally, if not more, uncommon in foreign language curricula, is not classified as LCT. Furthermore, LCTLs are not universal, that is, a language classified as LCT in one country may be the predominant foreign language in another country. For example, Chinese is a LCTL in the US, but in many Asian countries it is offered, and often required, as part of the standard foreign language curriculum.

Brecht and Walton (1997) outline political, economic, social, and communication factors as playing a crucial role in determining a nation's foreign language needs. Specifically, language is a political tool for people to assert their identity in territorial and cultural conflicts. For example, Kazakhstan has recently replaced Russian as a lingua franca with its own language, making Kazakh important not only in Russia, but also in countries with a political or economic stake in that part of the world. International trade drives economic relationships, which also has consequences as to what languages are considered important to a nation. Social issues such as humanitarian aid and environmental protection require international cooperation that relies on communication among more people from different language backgrounds. And finally, ease of international travel and advances in communication technology facilitate direct interaction between people of different countries, necessitating extensive language skills.

However, identifying a language as critical does not automatically result in that language achieving popular status in a country's foreign language curriculum, either from a financial or learner perspective. Often, the reason for teaching a language originates from historical circumstances, as is the case for colonial languages (e.g., French in North Africa) and autochthonous languages (e.g., Gaelic in Ireland). A language may also be considered "classical," (e.g., Latin in the US) and remain prevalent despite its lack of political value. Therefore, because a country's current language needs are not always addressed, government intervention is frequently necessary to support LCTLs and incorporate them into existing educational policy, which is met by challenges. First, developing the infrastructure necessary to support the teaching of LCTLs is challenged by the shortage of programs, materials, trained teachers, and access to immersion opportunities. Within the US, LCTLs are typically only offered at the under-graduate and graduate levels at major universities and elite liberal arts colleges, and even within these institutions they are largely supported by federal funding from Title VI of the Higher Education Act (Brecht & Walton, 2000), and more recently, the National Security Language Initiative. Second, developing programs for all the potential LCTLs is in many cases unfeasible. For instance, some 50 languages have been identified as relevant to worldwide security interests (The National Language Conference, 2004). It is not practical for any one country to invest in developing language programs to support this breadth of language capability. Finally, LCTLs are often genetically, typologically, and culturally distant from the native language of the learner, decreasing the language's learnability and making it difficult for learners to achieve functional proficiency without a considerable time investment and often an extended immersion experi-ence (Brecht & Walton, 2000). While this challenge attracts highly motivated language learners, it also results in low enrollments, making it difficult to justify maintaining the program financially. This chapter will look at LCTLs through the prism of research and theories in second language acquisition (SLA) and identify cognitive and linguistic difficulties inherently associated with learning a LCTL. It will then adopt a teaching perspective and address general problems and possible solutions to building a curriculum for teaching LCTLs.

Are LCTLs Difficult?

The reasons for languages being "less commonly taught" are many, as we note above. However, there is a prevalent attitude among educators in the United States that a major factor discouraging students from studying certain languages is their inherent difficulty. While this statement is generally correct, not every-thing about learning a given LCTL is problematic, and insights from SLA and several other disciplines are needed to develop a coherent framework to account for the level of difficulty of various linguistic and cultural phenomena. Identification of these areas of difficulty is a first step in elaborating an efficient pedagogical approach.

On the one hand, the term Less Commonly Taught Language does not imply in its definition that a language is inherently more difficult. It is, instead, a cultural and political statement referring to the status of a given language's position within a country's foreign language curriculum. Therefore, the term LCTL, which encompasses the status of Norwegian, Japanese, and Avestan, refers to a politically motivated definition and makes no reference to the language's difficulty. On the other hand, there is a general belief that were Norwegian, Japanese, and Avestan taught to a group of American students, those studying Japanese and Avestan would surely show a slower rate of acquisition than those studying Norwegian, all other factors being equal (i.e., teachers and resource availability). Indeed, the notion that some languages are more difficult than others has been supported by a National Foreign Language Center (NFLC) study assessing the impact of in-country study on language proficiency (Frank, 2000). Proficiency gains were measured for National Security Education Program (NSEP) study abroad fellows in China, Russia, and Spain. Entering the program at the intermediate–low to intermediate–mid proficiency levels on the oral proficiency scale adopted by the American Council of Teachers of Foreign Languages (ACTFL), learners of Spanish were most likely to achieve advanced proficiency, followed by learners of Mandarin Chinese, and finally learners of Russian. While the differences were not significant, due to a limited sample size, it appears that despite equivalent pre-program proficiency scores and comparable program duration, rates of advanced level attainment are higher in Spanish than in Mandarin Chinese and Russian.

The notion of language difficulty has been addressed by US government language training institutions in terms of "the inherent difficulty posed to native speakers of American English in learning the target language" (Frank, 2000). In this approach, languages are categorized into three levels of difficulty according to the number of hours of study typically required to achieve ILR (Interagency Language Roundtable) level 3 proficiency, corresponding to Superior on the ACTFL scale. For example, Spanish, requiring relatively few hours of study (approximately 575–600) to achieve ILR level 3, is a Category 1 language, whereas Korean, requiring approximately 2,200 class hours, is classified as a Category 3 language (Languages of the World, 2007). Therefore, it appears that some LCTLs may be inherently more difficult for American learners. The question, then, is, why are certain languages more difficult? More specifically, what cognitive factors contribute to one language being more difficult to acquire than another?

A major factor that is likely to contribute to the difficulty of a LCTL is its non-cognate status to the learner's native language. Traditionally, cognate languages are defined as related in origin, having descended from the same ancestral root. Accordingly, the term non-cognate language refers to those that are not genetically related and implies typological distance, primarily relating to the languages' differing structures and lexicon. However, the term non-cognate may also be applied to different writing systems, and, perhaps more significantly, cultural distance. While structural distance between languages is an attractive candidate for explaining language-learning difficulty, research shows that, first, typological distance does not translate directly into the level of difficulty, and second, there are other powerful factors at work in the acquisition of LCTLs, such as the lexicon, phonological system, writing system, and cultural distance. Thus, the level of difficulty of a particular LCTL is defined by a combination of factors, and while there is a practice of assigning levels of difficulty to particular LCTLs for American learners, which is driven by the needs of curricular planning, more research is needed to provide a sound theoretical and empirical foundation to this global, holistic scale. At the same time, SLA research provides insights into the operation of individual factors, or components, contributing to the overall level of difficulty. The following sections will, first, address the general approaches to language difficulty arising from theoretical perspectives on SLA, and then focus on individual aspects of language acquisition, which constitute sources of difficulty.

Theoretical and Empirical Approaches to LCTLs in SLA: Sources of Difficulty

Language typology, influence of the native language, and universal constraints

Second language acquisition research identifies two major factors shaping interlanguage (IL, language of L2 learners): the influence of the native language, or transfer from the native language to the target language (L1 transfer); and universal constraints on language perception and production. In addition to these major forces, whose interplay shapes the course of SLA, processing constraints and properties of the input to the learner, in particular, input frequencies and the effects of practice, interact with working and long-term memory as the learner gradually achieves automaticity in speech perception and production. This section will briefly review the main claims and findings from these fields of inquiry, and draw implications for LCTLs.

L1 transfer implies that certain linguistic structures, patterns, or rules from L1 are transposed and applied to L2, which may lead to two possible outcomes: a facilitative effect when both L1 and L2 indeed share the structure (positive transfer, see Ringbom & Jarvis, this volume); and a negative effect, resulting in errors in L2, when L1 and L2 do not share the structure (negative transfer). Whether L1 transfer of either kind takes place depends on a set of conditions. First, there should be certain proximity between the two phenomena in L1 and L2 in order for this transfer to be possible. For example, when acquiring the Russian case system with numerous inflectional markers, native speakers of English have nothing to transfer from their native language, or in other words, there are no conditions for L1 transfer. Native speakers of Czech, another Slavic language with a similar inflectional system, however, have been observed to substitute Czech case inflections for Russian ones (Duskova, 1984, cited by Gass & Selinker, 2001, p. 74). This constraint on L1 transfer has received the name of "crucial similarity measure" (Wode, 1983), and is especially operative in L2 phonological acquisition (see below). Second, "perceived similarity measure," a subjective assessment of similarity between L1 and L2 phenomena (Kellerman, 1978), appears to determine whether L1 transfer will be used as a strategy when L2 processing involves meaning and reaches the conscious level, as in the use of lexical items or idioms. And finally, there are factors external to the linguistic properties of L1 and L2 per se, which pertain to task and learner characteristics. For example, a study of L2 acquisition of Japanese progressive and resultative meanings of the imperfective aspect marker by L1 speakers of English, German, and Slavic languages demonstrated that both the task type, or rather, modality, production, and perception, as well as proficiency level, determined whether L1 transfer would take place (Sugaya & Shirai, 2007). In particular, lower proficiency was more conducive to L1 transfer, while higher proficiency relied more on universals in creating form–meaning associations. Considering what is known about L1 transfer, what role is it expected to play in the acquisition of LCTLs? Given that LCTLS are often typologically distant from learners' native language, or are non-cognate languages, the role of L1 transfer should be rather limited, both on the level of linguistic structure and vocabulary. This applies to both positive and negative transfer. At the same time, lower-proficiency learners are more likely to apply L1 transfer as a strategy, especially, under communicative pressure, as this may be the only available resource for them in an attempt to repair a communication breakdown. The most "extreme" case of L1 transfer in such a case would be code-switching.

Universal constraints are defined in different terms depending on the theoretical framework, and they can either pertain to linguistic structures or to cognitive processing and memory. Several assumptions and empirical findings in cross-linguistic and SLA research underlie the notion of universal constraints. First of all, Universal Grammar (UG) (Chomsky, 1986), research on typological universals (Greenberg, 1976), and markedness theory (Jakobson, 1936/1972), while differing in scope and theoretical underpinnings, all point to the fact that languages share some general universal properties. At the same time, UG emphasizes innateness and specificity of language, while typological studies focus on how certain linguistic properties are distributed across all the languages, which ones are common, and which are rare. Typological universals may take the shape of implicational universals, when the presence of feature A in a certain language also implies the presence of feature B, but the presence of feature B does not imply the presence of feature A. For example, the presence of voiced consonants /b, d, g/, either in the individual language in general, or in a particular position in the word, word-initial, medial or final, implies the presence of voiceless consonants /p, t, k/, but the presence of voiceless consonants does not imply the presence of voiced ones.

Markedness theory assigns the marked status to one member of a binary opposition, as in voiced and voiceless consonants mentioned above, or organizes a set of structures in a certain hierarchical order, as in the most researched implicational universal concerning relative clause formation, Noun Phrase Accessibility Hierarchy (Keenan & Comrie, 1977). Markedness is usually associated with a cluster of properties, thus a marked item requires more effort, is more difficult, more complex structurally, less frequent, and less productive than its unmarked counterpart. It is not obvious what kind of causal relationship applies to this cluster of properties, but it appears that difficulty and complexity are at the core of the factors underlying markedness. If this is indeed the case, then it is to be expected that more complex or difficult linguistic structures occur less frequently across languages, but also that less frequent structures are inherently more complex and difficult.

Second, while typologically distant languages are likely to exhibit more differences than typologically proximate languages, some linguistic features are "scattered" across languages and do not follow a predictable pattern. For example, agglutination, a typological feature whereby words are formed of long strings of mostly unmodified affixes, occurs in genetically unrelated languages, such as Hungarian, Turkish, Korean, and Bantu languages. Third, universal constraints, whether they come in the form of UG, observations from typological studies, or markedness, imply that not every imaginable structure or combination of structures is possible in human languages. The question arises whether interlanguages are constrained in the same way, and researchers coming from different theoretical backgrounds espouse this view (Eckman, 2004; O'Grady, 2003; White, 2004). Eckman proposed the Structural Conformity Hypothesis (SCH), according to which "All universals that are true for primary languages are also true for ILs" (1996, p. 204). If this is the case, then markedness and universal constraints determine different patterns in SLA, as they do in native languages. Under the SCH, it is not the learner's native language that affects the acquisition of certain L2 structures, but rather the universal markedness of the L2 structures. In other words, a learner may have difficulty learning a marked structure in the L2, even if that same structure exists in the learner's L1. Conversely, a learner may not have difficulty in learning an unmarked L2 structure, even if that structure does not exist in the learner's L1. Since LCTLs, at least in the American context, represent typologically distant and highly diverse languages, many features found in them are typologically marked, and likely to be problematic for L2 learners. Therefore, acquisition of many aspects of LCTLs can be predicted to pose difficulties for L2 learners. In psycholinguistic terms, acquisition of typologically distant or non-cognate languages requires control of numerous new concepts, structures, etc. This novelty effect leads to depletion of attentional resources and overload on working memory, which ultimately delays automatization of L2 processing.

Four likely candidates that contribute to the difficulty in acquiring a non-cognate language, in addition to linguistic structure, are the lexicon, the phonological system, the writing system and script, and cultural distance. The lexicon, if no part of it is shared with the L2, will create an additional burden on processing and make attention to and processing of new aspects of the language all the more difficult. The phonological system, if it contains novel sounds, features, or contrasts, may involve difficulties at the level of production and/or perception. The writing system and script may also add to difficulty in acquisition if they are different from that of the native language. For one thing, they will limit the opportunity for input, and in addition, they may contain ambiguities that lead to unpredictability in word recognition. Finally, a language of a non-cognate culture will likely consist of complex pragmatic and cultural references that are closely linked to linguistic performance. The following sections will address these four aspects of learning LCTLs.

The lexicon

The role of the lexicon in SLA has been thoroughly examined in the SLA literature, and specifically in the context of positive transfer between proximate and distant languages. Nation (2001) proposes that different words will have different "learning burdens" according to how much effort is required to learn the word. Specifically, Nation proposes that patterns and knowledge of an L2 word may be available to the learner from the learner's L1, previous knowledge of the L2, or even other L2s. For example, similarities between the L1 and L2 in sounds and spelling patterns, the pairing of certain words together (e.g., collocations), and grammatical patterns will reduce the learning burden and thus facilitate acquisition of a particular word(s). The learning burden is likely to be less for vocabulary of a closely related, or cognate, language, than for a non-cognate language.

Ringbom (1992; Ringbom & Jarvis, this volume) examined this phenomenon in Finnish and Swedish learners of English pointing out that Swedish learners achieve higher scores, even with fewer years of study, than Finnish learners. Ringbom attributes the Swedes' advantage to positive lexical transfer, which facilitates reading and listening comprehension (although more so for reading than listening). Ringbom argues that a learner of a related language can easily convert the L1-based lexical knowledge to the L2, "because the procedures for comprehending and using identical or very similar L1 words in L2 are already automatized" (1992, p. 102). For a learner of an unrelated language, however, the L1 knowledge is not accessible for automatized use in the L2, thus resulting in a heavier learning burden.

Furthermore, learning a non-cognate lexicon will impede learning other aspects of the language, in that a heavier learning burden requires cognitive resources that would otherwise be allocated elsewhere. Odlin (2003) summarizes the advantage of learning a linguistically proximate language: "the advantage that cognate vocabulary confers can allow learners to take advantage of positive transfer to increase their comprehension of the target language with far greater ease, thereby freeing many cognitive resources for other language learning tasks" (p. 441). Therefore, learners of an L2 that is lexically related to their L1, such as Swedish learners of English, will have more resources available, facilitating, and even speeding up, lexical, and subsequently, general L2 acquisition. Acquisition of LCTLs will show the opposite inhibitory tendency.

Phonological system

Phonology is always a major issue for adult learners, and few, if any, are able to overcome a foreign accent. Phonemic discrimination studies have shown that infants lose their ability to discriminate between non-native contrasts as early as 10–12 months (Werker & Tees, 1984), and SLA researchers have placed the close of the critical period for acquiring a nativelike accent around age 6 (Long, 1993).

The mechanisms underlying production and perception are asymmetrical, with some sounds being more difficult to hear, and others to pronounce. It is true, however, that perceptual difficulties usually constitute the core with articulatory difficulties superimposed on them, hence the focus on perception in the major models of phonological acquisition (see below). A rare exception is the /r/–/l/ distinction in English, which is difficult for Japanese learners to hear, yet Sheldon and Strange (1982) found that learners were able to accurately produce both sounds despite an inability to perceive the difference. LCTLs often have difficult sounds and sound contrasts (e.g., murmured consonants in Hindi/Urdu; clicks in Bantu languages; plain, tense, and aspirated consonants in Korean, etc.), making accurate perception and production challenging for learners of non-cognate languages.

Kuhl (1993), Flege (1995), and Best (1994) propose three separate models of language perception that attempt to explain non-native phonemic representation within the context of a learner's native speech system. Kuhl's Native Language Magnet model, focusing mainly on vowel perception, posits that native speakers develop acoustic prototypes for phonemic categories, which act as perceptual magnets. A non-native phoneme that is perceptually close to a native prototype will be drawn to and represented by that prototype, whereas a non-native phoneme that is perceptually distant from native prototypes will not be influenced by the magnet and will exist independently in its own space. Therefore, a non-native phonemic contrast that is drawn to a native prototype will be more difficult for learners to discriminate than a non-native contrast that is represented independently of native prototypes.

Flege's (1995) Speech Learning Model also proposes that the distance between native and non-native sounds determines ease of acquisition. He argues that non-native categories will develop if there is no native equivalent, which will facilitate perception and production. Non-native sounds that are similar to native sounds, however, will be incorporated into existing native categories, making perception and production inaccurate.

Finally, Best's (1994; Best, McRoberts, & Goodell, 2001) Perceptual Assimilation Model claims that non-native phonemes may be assimilated into the native system as a categorized exemplar of a native phoneme, an uncategorized phoneme, or a nonassimilable nonspeech sound. How a non-native phoneme is assimilated determines its perceptual difficulty. Sounds that are assimilated into a native exemplar may pose no problem for the learner if there is a good fit between the non-native sound and the native exemplar; however, a poor fit will result in perceptual difficulty. In the case of the uncategorized phoneme, the native system will have less of an impact on perception, and difficulty will depend on perceived proximity to nearby phonemes. Finally, nonassimilable nonspeech sounds are not processed linguistically, and will, therefore, not pose a problem.

All three models have one point in common: non-native sounds that are easily assimilated into the native language phonological system are problematic (compare this conclusion to the concept of the "crucial similarity measure" discussed above). How do these theories apply to acquisition of LCTLs, which often contain sounds and sound contrasts not found in most common Indo-European languages, and do they account for the level of difficulty they present? First, phonological difficulties in SLA almost never involve only the perceptual level, which is the focus of all three models. Typically, phonological difficulties arise either both in perception and production or in production only. Second, while it is uncontroversial that similar sounds easily pass through the "phonological sieve" and are perceived as their native counterparts (often leading to a perceptual error), there are types of sounds that are difficult to perceive and/or produce, in the typological markedness sense. And third, the most challenging task in phonological acquisition is differentiation of sound contrasts when neither member of the contrast is found in L1, and they belong to a typologically marked domain. For example, tones found in Mandarin, Cantonese, Thai, and Vietnamese are difficult, as the learner needs to learn to perceive and produce four or more phonological tones accurately and be aware of the distinctions. To illustrate, consider the different facets of phonological difficulties involved in the acquisition of Arabic consonants. There are pharyngeal and laryngeal consonants in Arabic, and these sounds are difficult to differentiate both in perception and production, since pharyngeal and laryngeal articulations, typologically rare and marked, are notoriously problematic. Furthermore, Arabic has a phonological distinction between plain and emphatic consonants with additional pharyngeal articulation, the latter being difficult to perceive, but especially to pronounce. To summarize, the phonology of LCTLs is likely to present problems for L2 learners at the level of perception, production, or both. These problems will mostly be due to universal constraints, as learners are dealing with new and marked phonological units, features, and contrasts, and to a lesser degree to L1 transfer resulting from perceptual assimilation of L2 sounds (see Nguyen & Macken, 2008).

Writing system and script

The L2 writing system and script can also provide strategic support if similar to the L1 and, conversely, can create an obstacle if different from the L1 (see Koda, this volume). The writing system refers to the most general distinction between alphabetic, syllabic, and logographic languages, while script refers to the actual graphic symbols (e.g., Roman and Cyrillic scripts). Orthography, or the rules of graphic–phonological conversion, will have less impact when the writing system and script already differ, as is often the case with LCTLs. MacWhinney (2006) discusses recoding, a compensatory strategy strongly affected by the L1, that L2 learners may use to enhance language learning. Recoding, according to

MacWhinney, "involves the construction of alternative images of new words and phrases...the easiest way to do this is to represent the new word orthographically" (p. 151). He argues that orthographic learning provides learners with a "solid recoding of transient auditory input" (p. 151) and allows them access to input from additional sources, such as books, signs, and product labels. Recoding will be relatively easy for a learner whose writing system and script are the same in the L1 and L2 (for example, French–English), however, it will be quite difficult for a learner who has to learn a new script, and especially, a writing system. An English speaker learning Russian must map the Roman script onto the Cyrillic script. Because both of these scripts are alphabetic and rely on a grapheme–phoneme correspondence, this task can be accomplished with some difficulty. However, learning a logographic writing system (e.g., Chinese Hanzi characters) will create a major obstacle for older learners and may prevent them from taking advantage of the recoding strategy, making the language-learning process all the more difficult for learners of a language with a different writing system.

An additional complexity is present in languages with wide gaps between the written and spoken varieties, such as the numerous dialects of Arabic compared to written Modern Standard Arabic. A student learning Moroccan Arabic must not only learn the spoken variety, but also the written variety, which is significantly different structurally, as well as phonologically. In this case, access to written input requires substantially more work than if the student were learning Spanish, where the spoken language is closely represented by the writing system. Therefore, a student learning Arabic not only has to learn an L2 script that is different from the L1, but also an L2 writing system that is different from the spoken L2 system.

However, the importance of the writing system as a language acquisition tool may be debated in light of recent findings on the acquisition of Chinese. NSEP studies on the acquisition of Mandarin Chinese by American learners (Frank, 2000) have suggested that Chinese is a Category 2 language in speaking, despite its difficult writing system. That is, it seems that speaking can be acquired successfully independent of the writing system in an immersion-type learning environment with heavy emphasis on oral communication. Nonetheless, access to written media can be a rich and important source of both linguistic and socio-cultural input for language learners. An L2 with a different writing system may prevent a learner from taking advantage of written input, especially in the early stages of acquisition, and thereby slow the rate of acquisition.

Pragmatics and cross-cultural communication

Languages of non-cognate cultures are often characterized by very different pragmatic rules than those of the native language. While there is limited research on L2 pragmatics, these often subtle and complex linguistic aspects of basic communication, such as the speech acts of giving and receiving compliments, accepting and declining an offer or invitation, and apologizing or adhering to an honorifics hierarchy, contribute to the difficulty of acquiring a typologically distant language. For example, the pragmatic strategies involved in Japanese honorifics are closely linked to linguistic performance; while the linguistic forms themselves are not necessarily difficult, knowing when and to whom to apply the proper address form is culturally foreign to native English speakers and, therefore, difficult to acquire.

Another component of pragmatics that is necessary for successful communication is what Kramsch (1991) identifies as sociolinguistic knowledge: "Background knowledge and shared assumptions have been shown to be a crucial element in understanding oral and written forms of discourse" (p. 217). For example, the ability to understand and employ literary references in languages such as Arabic and Chinese, whose literary culture dating back 1,500 years is incorporated into daily speech, presents a challenge for L2 learners. In other languages, such as Persian, there is an equivalent depth in the oral tradition that is still present in the language today. Again, these skills are not necessarily linguistic in nature, but rather require cognitive skills and cultural sensitivity that develop from cultural experience and education. Because they are manifested in language comprehension and production, they contribute to the practical difficulty of the language. It would be difficult to acquire this type of knowledge from studying LCTL in a foreign language classroom outside its broader context; a cultural immersion is most likely the only route to acquiring what Kramsch (2006) has termed symbolic competence.

To conclude, structural (typological) differences between non-cognate languages, as well as L2 lexicon, phonological system, writing system and script, and cultural distance are major inhibiting factors in the acquisition of certain LCTLs.

Teaching Less Commonly Taught Languages

Teaching LCTLs in the US presents numerous challenges, and while some of them are related to the inherent linguistic difficulty of many of the languages discussed above, others transcend the realm of linguistic debates and are grounded in the social and educational context. Despite fundamental differences between the principles underlying the grouping of LCTLs in the US and lesser-used languages in the European Union, some of these challenges are shared by both educational communities. This section will address the issues in teaching LCTLs, and for lack of space will be restricted to adult L2 learners, which will leave two major educational issues outside the scope of the present discussion: child L2 acquisition and K-12 instruction in LCTLs (see Brecht, 2007), and the special instructional needs of heritage speakers (see Montrul, this volume).

It is true that non-cognate status and typological distance of LCTLs from English create an additional level of difficulty in the acquisition of their linguistic structure, sound systems, writing systems and scripts, vocabulary, including idiomatic use, and socio-cultural and linguo-pragmatic aspects. What are the implications of these additional learning problems for teaching LCTLs? They increase the need for appropriate pedagogical approaches and instructional techniques aimed at developing metalinguistic awareness and structural knowledge in L2 learners. Two aspects of instruction play a key role in addressing these problems: the type and amount of input (Gor & Long, forthcoming) and practice (DeKeyser, 2007). And indeed, developing metalinguistic awareness when dealing with novel linguistic concepts may require explicit input, while high quantities of structured input will ensure internalization of high-frequency items and structures. Koda (this volume) claims that both quality and quantity of L2 print are to a large extent responsible for the development of the metalinguistic awareness necessary for reading new writing systems and scripts (as well as orthography). Intensive practice in LCTLs will promote control and automaticity in the use of linguistic structures, and decrease overload on working memory, thus releasing L2 processing resources.

Automaticity refers to the way psychological mechanisms operate, with automatic processing often characterized as being fast, unstoppable, load independent, effortless, and unconscious (Segalowitz, 2003, p. 384). In other words, automatic processing is not affected by the load of information to be processed, nor does it require effort, leaving attentional resources free for other tasks. Research to date on automaticity in the field of SLA has focused mainly on word recognition and grammatical structure acquisition, where speed of processing is linked to fluency. According to Nation (1993), a certain degree of automaticity in basic vocabulary must be achieved before new vocabulary can be acquired. Considering LCTLs' non-cognate status, developing automaticity for novel vocabulary and typologically distant grammatical structures will take time, delaying fluency and reducing the attentional resources, such as working memory, available for processing and subsequently acquiring additional aspects of the language.

What kind of teaching method would be most appropriate for LCTLs? In the last two decades, foreign language teaching in many countries has been dominated by the communicative approach, stemming from the construct of communicative competence (Hymes, 1974), which came to replace grammar–translation and audio–lingual methods. Communicative language teaching (CLT), closely associated with the influential proficiency movement, emphasizes the development of learners' ability to communicate, express themselves, get their meaning across, and engage in social interactions. Pedagogical practices developed to accomplish this mission produce relatively quick results, empowering the student with a sense of gains made, and not just effort invested. This agenda, a welcome change from the teaching methods it replaced, is heavily geared toward speaking, even at the early stages of L2 learning. In recent years, communicative language teaching has become the target of criticism summarized below by Magnan:

> Following most textbooks used in the United States, CLT encourages personalized activities through which students talk about themselves with their classmates (Magnan, 2006). This practice introduces three problems for language learning: (a) talk about self generally does not elicit the analytical language that collegiate language departments consider pertinent to their intellectual missions; (b) too much

talk about self perpetuates self-referential notions of language and culture, preparing students to present an egocentric view when abroad; (c) talk with U.S. classmates fosters a U.S. frame of reference and discourse, although the words to express them are foreign. (2007, p. 250)

In a discussion devoted to the future of CLT in *The Modern Language Journal* (volume 90(2), 2006), Kramsch advocated an alternative approach promoting the development of symbolic competence (Kramsch, 2006). The proposed shift of focus to the study of texts and culturally bound meanings (Larson, 2006) highlights the challenge of reading authentic texts in LCTLs, which provides a window into the target culture, but often stumbles at different writing systems and scripts, while understanding a new culture through language increases in importance with the greater distance between the native and target culture. The arguments raised against CLT mostly target lower-level instruction and as such are not in conflict with the core principles underlying this approach. Teaching and learning LCTLs need to address several goals: to provide explicit and abundant input and opportunities for focused practice required for learning language structure, to pay attention both to oral and written communicative competence, and to complement functional language ability with the development of cultural sensitivity.

Since the distance between L1 and LCTLs, linguistic and cultural, is often greater than for commonly taught languages, their teaching (as learning) requires additional effort and resources. Ironically, educational policy and practices, which were shaped by an interaction of academic and socio-political circumstances, led to the opposite outcome, with the lack of available resources exacerbating inherent difficulties in developing efficient curricula for teaching LCTLs. Indeed, academic programs offering instruction in LCTLs are plagued by the lack of a trained cadre of instructors, adequate and rich pedagogical materials for different learner levels, institutional support, and national and international infrastructure (see Al-Batal, 2007, about the teaching of Arabic). As mentioned above, based on the estimates of the number of contact hours needed to reach ILR level 3 proficiency by the State Department, all of the languages falling into Category 3 (exceptionally difficult, most time required), Arabic, Cantonese, Mandarin, Japanese, and Korean, are LCTLs critical for US national interests. Consequently, in order to achieve the same level of proficiency in one of these LCTLs as in a language belonging to Categories 1 or 2, smaller classes and/or more coursework will be necessary. However, requests for limiting the number of seats per class may meet resistance from the administration of academic institutions, as small classes are often perceived as a sign that a certain language has low enrollments due to low demand or, conversely, they will be in conflict with the need to accommodate very high enrollments in some of these languages. One of the inevitable consequences of the fact that LCTLs typically require more time and effort to learn is decreasing learners' motivation when immediate results and rapid gains in proficiency are lacking. Thus, to build successful academic programs, LCTL curricula need to stimulate student motivation. The ability to communicate from the very start fostered within the paradigm of CLT is one of the means to boost learner motivation, engaging students in a new fascinating cultural experience being another one.

The critical role a number of LCTLs play in US national security has generated an enormous momentum, with an increasing demand for highly proficient speakers of these languages and public interest in learning them. Several organizations and research centers in the US focus on providing resources and teaching support for LCTLs: The National Council of Less Commonly Taught Languages (NCOLCTL), the hub of the web-based network CouncilNet, The National Foreign Language Center (NFLC), whose LangNet offers support for several dozen LCTLs, and The Center for Applied Linguistics (CAL), as well as university-affiliated research centers, such as The Center for Advanced Study of Language (CASL) at the University of Maryland and The Center for Advanced Research on Language Acquisition (CARLA) at the University of Minnesota. The European Bureau for Lesser-Used Languages (EBLUL) performs a similar mission in the European Union. Only joint efforts of SLA researchers, instructors, and experts in language pedagogy and cross-cultural communication, administrators, and language policy makers will win a brighter future for LCTLs.

REFERENCES

Al-Batal, M. (2007). Arabic and national language educational policy. *The Modern Language Journal* 91, 2, 268–71.

Best, C. T. (1994). The emergence of native-language phonological influences in infants: A perceptual assimilation model. In J. C. Goodman & H. C. Nusbaum (eds.), *The development of speech perception: The transition from speech sounds to spoken words* (pp. 167–224). Cambridge, MA: MIT Press.

Best, C. T., McRoberts, G. W., & Goodell, E. (2001). Discrimination of non-native consonant contrasts varying in perceptual assimilation to the listener's native phonological system. *Journal of the Acoustical Society of America* 109, 2, 775–94.

Brecht, R. D. (2007). National language educational policy in the nation's interest: Why? How? Who is responsible for what? *The Modern Language Journal* 91, 2, 264–5.

Brecht, R. D. & Walton, A. R. (1997). National language needs and capacities: A recommendation for action. In J. Hawkins et al. (eds.), *International education in the new global era: Proceeding of a national policy conference on the Higher Education Act, Title VI, and Fulbright-Hays programs* (pp. 92–102). Los Angeles: UCLA International Studies and Overseas Programs.

Brecht, R. D. & Walton, A. R. (2000). System III: The future of language learning in the United States. In R. Lambert & E. Shohamy (eds.), *Language policy and pedagogy: Essays in honor of A. Ronald Walton* (pp. 111–27). Amsterdam: John Benjamins.

Chomsky, N. (1986). *Knowledge of language: Its nature, origin and use*. New York: Praeger.

DeKeyser, R. (2000). The robustness of critical period effects in second language acquisition. *Studies in Second Language Acquisition* 22, 499–533.

DeKeyser, R. (ed.) (2007). *Practice in a second language: Perspectives from applied linguistics and cognitive psychology*. Cambridge: Cambridge University Press.

Duskova, L. (1984). Similarity: An aid or hindrance in foreign language learning? *Folia Linguistica* 18, 103–15.

Eckman, F. R. (1996). A functional-typological approach to second language acquisition theory. In W. C. Ritchie & T. K. Bhatia (eds.), *Handbook of second language acquisition* (pp. 195–211). San Diego: Academic Press.

Eckman, F. R. (2004). Universals, innateness, and explanation in second language acquisition. *Studies in Language* 28, 3, 682–703.

Flege, J. E. (1995). Second language speech learning: Theory, findings and problems. In W. Strange (ed.), *Speech perception and linguistic experience: Theoretical and methodological issues in cross-language speech research* (pp. 233–72). Timonium, MD: York.

Frank, V. (2000). Impact of in-country study on language ability: National Security Education Program undergraduate scholarship and graduate fellowship recipients. Technical Report, The National Foreign Language Center.

Gass, S. M. & Selinker, L. (2001). *Second language acquisition: An introductory course.* London: Lawrence Erlbaum.

Gor, K. & Long, M. H. (forthcoming). Input and second language processing. In W. C. Ritchie & T. K. Bhatia (eds.), *Handbook of second language acquisition.* New York: Academic Press.

Greenberg, J. (1976). *Language universals.* The Hague: Mouton.

Hymes, D. (1974). *Foundations in sociolinguistics: An ethnographic approach.* Philadelphia: University of Pennsylvania Press.

Jakobson, R. (1936/1972). *Child language, aphasia, and phonological universals*, 2nd edn. The Hague: Mouton.

Keenan, E. & Comrie, B. (1977). Noun phrase accessibility and Universal Grammar. *Linguistic Inquiry* 8, 63–99.

Kellerman, E. (1978). Giving learners a break: Native language intuitions as a source of predictions about transferability. *Working Papers on Bilingualism* 15, 59–92.

Kramsch, C. (1991). Culture in language learning: A view from the United States. In K. De Bot, R. Ginsberg, & C. Kramsch (eds.), *Foreign language research in cross-cultural perspective* (pp. 217–40). Philadelphia: John Benjamins.

Kramsch, C. (2006). From communicative competence to symbolic competence. *The Modern Language Journal* 90, 2, 249–52.

Kuhl, P. K. (1993). Innate predispositions and the effects of experience in speech perception: The native language magnet theory. In B. de Boysson-Bardies, S. de Schonen, P. Jusczyk, P. McNeilage, & J. Morton (eds.), *Developmental neurocognition: Speech and face processing in the first year of life* (pp. 259–74). Dordrecht: Kluwer Academic.

Languages of the World (2007). Retrieved February 24, 2008, from www.nvtc.gov/lotw/index.html.

Larson, P. (2006). The return of the text: A welcome challenge for less commonly taught languages. *The Modern Language Journal* 90, 2, 255–8.

Long, M. H. (1993). Second language acquisition as a function of age: Research findings and methodological issues. In K. Hyltenstam & A. Viberg (eds.), *Progression and regression in language* (pp. 196–221). Cambridge: Cambridge University Press.

MacWhinney, B. (2006). Emergent fossilization. In Z. Han & T. Odlin (eds.), *Studies of fossilization in second language acquisition* (pp. 134–56). Clevedon, UK: Multilingual Matters.

Magnan, S. (2006). Enjeux et défis de l'enseignement du français langue étrangère en France et aux Etats-Unis. *French Review* 80, 332–52.

Magnan, S. (2007). Reconsidering communicative language teaching for national goals. *The Modern Language Journal* 91, 2, 249–52.

Nation, I. S. P. (1993). Using dictionaries to estimate vocabulary size: Essential, but rarely followed, procedures. *Language Testing* 10, 27–40.

Nation, I. S. P. (2001). *Learning vocabulary in another language.* Cambridge: Cambridge University Press.

The National Language Conference: A call for action (2004, June 22). Retrieved February 28, 2008, from http://www.nlconference.org.

Nguyen, N. & Macken, M. A. (2008). Factors affecting the production of Vietnamese tones. *Studies in Second Language Acquisition* 30, 49–77.

Odlin, T. (2003). Cross-linguistic influence. In C. J. Doughty & M. H. Long (eds.), *The handbook of second language acquisition* (pp. 436–86). Oxford: Blackwell.

O'Grady, W. (2003). The radical middle: Nativism without Universal Grammar. In C. J. Doughty & M. H. Long (eds.), *The handbook of second language acquisition* (pp. 19–42). Oxford: Blackwell.

Ringbom, H. (1992). On L1 transfer in L2 comprehension and L2 production. *Language Learning* 42, 1, 85–112.

Segalowitz, N. (2003). Automaticity and second languages. In C. J. Doughty & M. H. Long (eds.), *The handbook of second language acquisition* (pp. 382–408). Oxford: Blackwell.

Sheldon, A. & Strange, W. (1982). The acquisition of /r/ and /l/ by Japanese learners of English: Evidence that speech production can precede speech perception. *Applied Psycholinguistics* 3, 243–61.

Sugaya, N. & Shirai, Y. (2007). The acquisition of progressive and resultative meanings of the imperfective aspect marker by L2 learners of Japanese: Transfer, universals, or multiple factors? *Studies in Second Language Acquisition* 29, 1–38.

Werker, J. F. & Tees, R. C. (1984). Cross-language speech perception: Evidence for perceptual reorganization during the first year of life. *Infant Behaviour and Development* 7, 49–63.

White, L. (2004). "Internal" versus "external" universals. *Studies in Language* 28, 3, 704–7.

Wode, H. (1983). Contrastive analysis and language learning. In H. Wode (ed.), *Papers on language acquisition, language learning and language teaching* (pp. 202–12). Heidelberg: Groos.

15 Third Language Acquisition Theory and Practice

WILLIAM P. RIVERS AND EWA M. GOLONKA

Introduction

The popular belief that bilinguals or multilinguals learn a subsequent language more easily than monolinguals has received substantial attention from researchers in recent years, as minority language communities in the European Union achieve greater educational autonomy and as United States government (USG) language training programs seek to respond to rapidly changing requirements for global expertise. In the European context, researchers have paid significant attention to the acquisition of a third language (L3) by childhood bilinguals, such as Basque-Spanish or Catalan-Spanish bilingual secondary school students learning English in Spain, or Swedish-Finnish bilingual children learning English in Finland. These acquisition paradigms have sparked recent research on transfer in L3 acquisition (Cenoz, 2001; Ringbom, 2001, 2007), metalinguistic awareness in L3 acquisition (Cenoz & Valencia, 1994), and parameter setting within the Universal Grammar (UG) paradigm (Klein, 1995; Zobl, 1992).

In this chapter, we present the current state of the theory and practice of adult L3 acquisition in instructional settings. We label this deliberately, in that we are concerned with the theoretical issues arising when adults who know more than one language learn another, as well as the practical issues arising in organized, formal programs for such adult learners. We will show from the literature and from our work that this type of language acquisition differs substantially from adult L2 acquisition.

We begin with a discussion of the state of the research literature in L3 acquisition, and then turn to the praxis, based on our own qualitative research on directed adult L3 acquisition programs in the United States. Throughout, we seek to address the following questions: Why should L3 acquisition differ from L2 acquisition? What are the theoretical implications of the evidence?

Review of the Literature

In examining the research basis for L3 acquisition, we draw upon a number of areas of inquiry in SLA and psycholinguistics. Some of these areas, such as transfer, do at times address L3 acquisition specifically. Others, such as metacognition in adult language learners, may find that L3 acquisition is a factor in one or another result, at times an unexpected factor. We examine, in turn, findings from work on linguistic transfer, typology and "linguistic distance"; UG and the Interlanguage Structural Conformity Hypothesis (ISCH), which can be seen as outgrowths of the parameter-setting school of the late 1980s and early 1990s; metacognition and metalinguistic awareness; learner autonomy; and last, the small body of work on directed L3 acquisition for adults.

Transfer

From a psycholinguistic perspective, the main focus of research in L3 acquisition is the concept of cross-linguistic influence (see Ringbom & Jarvis, this volume), which includes some aspects of phonetic, morphological, lexical, syntactic, and pragmatic transfer, as well as interference and language attrition related to L3 acquisition. Earlier studies of transfer in L3 sought to identify error as an effect of prior linguistic experience; Ahukanna, Lund, and Gentile (1981), for example, identified semantic errors in learners of French in Nigeria for whom Igbo was L1 and English L2. They found that more advanced students made fewer errors and were thus presumably less susceptible to interference effects, that L2 caused more interference than L1, and that semantic errors were more frequent than other types. The majority of studies on L3 acquisition that have focused on cross-linguistic influence have revealed that it is generally productive and that it facilitates L3 learning. Two related issues arise in these studies: typological distance/phylogenetic relatedness and transfer. Typological distance has been shown to play an important role in transfer (Cenoz, 2001; Fouser, 1995; Kellerman, 1983; Singleton, 1987). The results of Cenoz's (2001) study indicated that Spanish-Basque bilinguals learning English demonstrated a stronger influence from Spanish, typologically a closer language to English, than from Basque, a non-Indo-European language.[1] In his recent book, Ringbom (2007) argued that prior cross-linguistic knowledge is very important to the language learner and that the extent to which it may influence the learning of a new language depends on language proximity, i.e., similarities, not language distance, i.e., differences. When discussing language proximity, researchers often refer to the concept of psychotypology (Kellerman, 1983), that is, the way the learner perceives differences between the languages based on previously acquired knowledge, noting that perception of language distance might not correspond to the actual distance between the languages.

Few extant measures are designed to quantify language proximity and thereby determine the distance between languages. Studies of the measurement of language distance usually address specific pairs of languages and specific aspects of languages, and are not framed in terms of the relative learnability of one or another language. An exception is Chiswick and Miller's (2004) study, in which the researchers discussed and tested the Foreign Service Institute's (FSI) quantitative measure of the distance between English and a number of other languages. Their study, based on US Census data, examined the English proficiency of immigrants in the 1990 US and Canadian Censuses, and is worth some consideration, as it is the first (and thus far, only) attempt to validate a scale of language difficulty in the general population. They impute the titular language of the country of origin as L1, and use the Census question on "how well is English spoken at home" as the outcome variable, assigning null if "not at all" or "not well" and unity if "well" or "very well." From the perspective of SLA research, both the imputation of L1 and the use of self-assessed global proficiency ratings are cause for caution in interpreting the results, but they do find a linear correlation between the FSI difficulty scale and learnability of English for speakers of some 43 languages. Moreover, they test the scale in a way that FSI did not intend when it was developed, in that the FSI scale measures the learnability of a range of foreign languages for English speakers (and more precisely, English-speaking students at the Foreign Service Institute), whereas Chiswick and Miller test the scale against a range of foreign language speakers learning English. In other words, they assume that the scale is reciprocal.[2]

Recent computational work has led to promising text-based approaches for estimating the relative distance among languages by applying computational measures of entropy between samples in parallel corpora (Juola, 2003), or by estimating genetic drift between related languages, again using parallel texts (Nakhleh, Ringe, & Warnow, 2005). Juola applies the Kullback-Liebler distance, which measures the degree of similarity between two samples of text, providing an "entropy number" which indicates the information loss between two samples, to parallel texts of the Bodleian Oath in more than 30 languages. He thus derives a scalar measure of the degree to which the transliterated sound symbols in each translated version of the oath differ from the English version. Nakhleh et al. apply methods from genetic analysis to estimate the degree of drift among related languages, using primarily Bible corpora from a mother language (such as Latin) and the same texts in daughter languages to estimate the degree of drift. Again, they obtain scalar measures of relatedness among the languages. However, neither method has been used to test learnability, and as with scales such as the FSI and DLI learnability scales, these two methods depend on fixing one language (e.g., English) as the starting point against which difficulty or distance is measured. This brings up two other issues: first, even assuming English as L1, there are a large number of L1–L2–L3 triads possible – tens of thousands. Thus, developing relatedness measures among L1–L2–L3 triads would be impractical. Second, any measure of difficulty must be relative – there are no abstract models to which one might appeal to create an absolute difficulty or learnability measure. Clearly, the linguistic distance between languages cannot easily be measured or quantified.

Besides the distance between the languages, the researchers also have cited the activation of source languages and the order in which they were acquired as interacting with transfer. In the reviewed studies, the source of transfer can be either the learner's L1 (Ringbom, 2001), or a second language or other non-native language (De Angelis & Selinker, 2001; Hammarberg, 2001; Sikogukira, 1993; Leung, 1998). Several factors determine conditions in which transfer occurs and conditions for choosing the source language. Ringbom (2001), for example, argued that transfer can be either L1-based or L2-based, and that the choice of the donor language can depend on typological distance or degree of L2 proficiency. However, what is most important is that the source of transfer depends on the type of transfer investigated, whether lexical, morphological, or syntactic. Ringbom concluded that although lexical transfer is usually L2-based, grammatical and semantic transfers are nearly always L1-based. De Angelis and Selinker (2001) described interlanguage transfer as the influence of one non-native language on another non-native language. They analyzed the language production of two adult multilinguals and concluded that the learners' interlanguages, not the learners' previously learned languages, needed to be taken into consideration while analyzing lexical and morphological transfer. De Angelis and Selinker found evidence for lexical and morphological transfer and noted that this evidence is restricted to the transfer of form only. They argued that transfer of meaning, as well as multilingual language processing, are in need of further research. Leung (1998) also investigated transfer between interlanguages on three grammatical tasks given to Chinese (L1) speakers with a background in English (L2) who were learning French (L3). Leung concluded that two of these tasks revealed L2 transfer to L3 and one reflected more universal factors than transfer from L2.

Another factor discussed in the literature as influencing transfer is L2 status (Hammarberg, 2001). Hammarberg described the different roles that L2 (German) played in speech production of L3 (Swedish) in the speech of his polyglot subject, Sarah Williams. Hammarberg observed that Sarah Williams' lexicon was most often influenced by her L2 German, and that German, not her native English, provided the most supply for her L3 Swedish. After ruling out all other possibilities, he concluded that the reason for L2 being a donor language was L2 status, in other words, the fact that German and Swedish were "foreign languages" for his subject. Hammarberg also referred to the notion of "recency" of the language; that is, the use of the most recently acquired language by the learner as the source of transfer.

In general, researchers agree that transfer from L2 to L3 is most salient in the lexicon, and that lexical transfer has the most facilitative effects on L3 learning. Lexical transfer can help in successful comprehension of texts because learners can rely on a large number of cognates in related languages. Clearly, the existence of false cognates between L2 and L3 may sidetrack learners, but usually the number of true cognates is much larger than the number of *faux amis* (Ringbom, 2001). Semantic transfer or meaning-based transfer is very often L1-based, even if the L2 and L3 are typologically closely related (Ringbom, 2001). De Angelis and Selinker (2001) analyzed transfer between interlanguages and concluded that the evidence of lexical and morphological transfer in their study is restricted only to transfer of form. They argued that transfer of meaning, as well as multilingual language processing, was in need of further research.

UG and parameter setting

Zobl (1992) and Klein (1995) examined the effect of prior linguistic experience on UG and parameter setting and concluded that certain qualities, such as less conservative TL grammars, metalinguistic skills, and enhanced lexical knowledge, play a role in facilitating the setting of UG parameters. Zobl (1992), for example, on the basis of trends found in his empirical study, claimed that multilinguals create less conservative interlanguage grammars because of over-generalizations of grammars that enable them to learn TL at a faster rate.

Klein (1995) presented empirical evidence to support the argument that L2 acquisition and L3 acquisition are indeed different. She tested for differences between groups of monolinguals and multilinguals in the acquisition of lexical items and certain syntactic constructions. Specifically, two grammaticality judgment tests were administered to both groups of participants, one on the acquisition of preposition stranding, that is, syntactic constructions, and the other on the acquisition of specific verbs and their prepositional compliments, that is, lexical items. Klein hypothesized that, according to the parameter-setting model of language acquisition, there should be no difference between L2 and L3 learners in terms of parameter setting alone.[3] In other words, L3 learners should not have advantages over L2 learners because the parameters had been set in L1, and it should not matter whether it is the learner's L2, L3, or L4. However, the results of Klein's study showed differences between the two groups, with multilinguals outperforming monolinguals on the two types of tests (grammaticality judgments of preposition stranding and verb subcategorization); however, the difference between the groups on a third test (grammaticality judgments of null-prep) was not statistically significant.[4] Klein concluded that heightened metalinguistic skills, enhanced lexicon, and less conservative learning helped multilinguals in re-setting of UG parameters.

Metacognition and metalinguistic awareness

The facilitative role of previous linguistic experience in L3 learning can be found in the area of metacognition, in that the experience of learning another language may later employ the learner's metacognitive self-assessment and metacognitive self-management, in addition to providing the learner with explicit, declarative metalinguistic knowledge about how languages work. Ramsay (1980) discovered that multilinguals tended to perform far better than monolinguals on an achievement test. Successful learners in Ramsay's study tended to use more cognitive and metacognitive strategies, including substantially more verbalization and vocal practice, use of mnemonic devices, a more positive attitude toward the learning process (an affective strategy), use of positive affect reinforcement, use of more sources of information, and more risk taking and less fear of errors. Ramsay noted that metacognitive strategies can be distinguished as the primary difference between novice and expert learners across a broad set of abstract systems of knowledge, specifically in language, at both a very discrete level (the processing of specific constituent units) and a discourse level. Wenden (1999) reviewed literature on metacognition in language learning and drew a similar conclusion: Good language learners as well as self-directed language learners exhibit metacognitive behaviors. Möhle (1989) examined learning strategies in German multilingual university students taking a variety of Indo-European languages (French, Spanish, and English), hypothesizing that the narration of a film with no overt linguistic information would be influenced by cognitive processing. She found evidence of controlled lexical transfer, again a metacognitive strategy.

Metalinguistic awareness is believed to play an important role in L3 acquisition and in the investigation of the differences between L2 and L3 acquisition (Bartlet, 1989; Jessner, 1999; Klein, 1995; Thomas, 1988; Zobl, 1992). Bartlet (1989) examined the influence of L3 on procedural (metalinguistic) knowledge in a case study on interference in L3 (English) from L2 (Spanish) among multilingual Yaqui Indians in Arizona. Bartlet found evidence of broad use of metacognitive and communicative strategies in oral discourse and oral narrative. Jessner (1999) investigated the role of metalinguistic awareness in multilinguals within the framework of the Dynamic Model of Multilingualism. She analyzed qualitative data collected from trilingual adults via think-aloud protocol sessions to illustrate different strategies learners use in searching for a word in L3. All of the cited examples relate to metalinguistic thinking that involves three languages, all of which are typologically related. For instance, Jessner provided examples of code-switching involving either two or three languages, along with learners' attempts to look for equivalents or cognates in the three languages. Basing her conclusions on the relevant literature and this study alone, Jessner argued that metalinguistic awareness is desirable and can be increased through teaching similarities between languages and through activating students' prior linguistic knowledge. Two other studies, Zobl (1992) and Klein (1995), attributed better performance of multilinguals than monolinguals on grammaticality judgment tests to metalinguistic awareness.

Learner autonomy

Learner autonomy has also surfaced as an area of interest in the study of L3 acquisition. We define learner autonomy here as the active, independent management of learning by the learner (rather than independent study outside the classroom), where the learner sets or attempts to control the goals, curriculum, pedagogical method, or content of the learning program. A qualitative method was applied by Rivers (1996, 2001), who used a variety of data-collection techniques, including questionnaires, focus groups, classroom observation, and interviews, to investigate the characteristics and behaviors of college students learning a third language. Rivers (1996) compared proficiency outcomes of L3 learners from three programs: a program in languages of the former Soviet Union at the University of Maryland, a cross-training program at the Defense Language Institute (DLI), and a DLI study of immersion training with learners enrolled in L2 courses. He found that L3 learners were more successful than L2 learners of the same target language; that is, they learned more of the language and in a shorter time than L2 learners, based on end-of-course proficiency tests administered by DLI and other USG agencies. In another study, Rivers (2001) analyzed self-directed language learning behaviors of 11 adult learners of Georgian and Kazakh as a third language. All subjects' L1 was English and all had advanced (Interagency Language Roundtable (ILR) 3/3/3 or better) proficiency in L2 Russian. Rivers found that all learners accurately assess their progress, learning styles, and learning strategy preferences, as well as conflicts with teaching styles and behaviors of other learners within the class. Next, based upon these self-assessments of learner styles and preferences, all learners revealed a high tendency toward controlling their learning process, the tendency toward learner autonomy being demonstrated by their requesting and demanding changes to course content and structure. Finally, the majority of learners made attempts to modify the learning environment by using self-directed language learning strategies that referred to different aspects of course structure, for example, type and mode of input, workload, and classroom activities.

Praxis: Research on Adult L3 Instruction

In an effort to promote Portuguese language courses in American colleges and universities, Holton (1954) provided an overview of similarities between Spanish and Portuguese, claiming that learners with a good command of Spanish could acquire a reading facility in Portuguese in a very short time and with minimum effort. As he put it, "It would seem to be a valuable piece of intellectual merchandise obtained at a wonderful bargain price" (p. 447). Jensen (1989) and Jordan (1991) suggested that the high degree of mutual intelligibility between Portuguese and Spanish could be used in teaching Portuguese to students who had Spanish as a second language. Jensen (1989) administered a series of listening proficiency tests in Spanish to Portuguese speakers, and tests in Portuguese to Spanish speakers, and found that Portuguese was 60 percent intelligible to Spanish speakers and that Spanish was 50 percent intelligible to Portuguese speakers. Jordan (1991) argued for the use of contrastive analysis techniques in teaching Portuguese to speakers of Spanish, and listed the pedagogical benefits and risks of using this technique for teaching closely related languages. Based on the principle that there is a high degree of mutual intelligibility between closely related languages, such as Spanish and Portuguese, Gribble (1987) created a Bulgarian course for Russian speakers and Townsend (1995) a Czech course for Russian speakers. The efficacy of these courses, which are highly contrastive in nature, has not been measured; we note them here as they do, at least implicitly, draw upon the assumption of mutual intelligibility and lexical and linguistic transfer between closely related languages.

A notably different view was offered by Teixeira-Leal Tarquinio (1977), who recommended that, for English-speaking students at American universities, it is unsound to take both Spanish and Portuguese concurrently, pointing to the inter-ference of Spanish, especially in beginning Portuguese classes. She warned that this practice could lead to a hybrid product of "espanguês." Teixeira-Leal Tarquinio provided a list of specific phonological, morphological, and syntactical items whose transfer may cause difficulties for these students, claiming that one of the two languages must be mastered before beginning to learn the other. It needs to be noted that the author based her view on observations of students in American universities learning Portuguese and Spanish concurrently. This view seems to support claims about the importance of L2 proficiency in L3 acquisition. What needs to be determined in future research is the effect of the proximity of Spanish and Portuguese, or any other closely related languages, on proficiency level and order of acquisition.

In the US, the primary locus of deliberate L3 instruction has been the lan-guage training institutes of the USG. Over the past 15 years, rapidly changing and emerging government language requirements, coupled with the assumption that significant time savings could be achieved in L3 training courses, have led to courses in Serbian/Croatian for Russian, Polish, and Czech second language learners; Tausug for Tagalog speakers; Malaysian for Bahasa Indonesian speakers; Portuguese for Spanish speakers; Kazakh, Kyrgyz, and Georgian for Russian speakers; Haitian Creole for French Speakers; and several courses in one or another Arabic vernacular for speakers of Modern Standard Arabic.

Several courses at the Defense Language Institute Foreign Language Center (DLI) have retrained speakers of one language in another closely related lan-guage: Czech L2 speakers in Serbian/Croatian (Corin, 1994), French speakers in Haitian Creole, and Russian, Polish, and Czech speakers in Serbian/Croatian. This type of instruction, in which the target language and the learners' previously known languages are closely related, is called conversion. Corin (1994) reported on a Serbian/Croatian conversion course at the DLI that retrained 40 Czech linguists in Serbian/Croatian in a 3-month period. Based on the outcomes of the three-month course reported on the ILR scale (median oral proficiency score = Level 2; mode = Level 1+), Corin concluded that conversion works, that L2 profi-ciency may influence L3 gains, and that learner style interacted with the teaching materials and methods (global learners performed better). There were no tradi-tional grammars; the learners had to derive rules for the target language from their L2s. Kulman and Tetrault (1993) reviewed USG L3 courses and proposed Rapid Survey courses for closely related languages, for example, a Ukrainian course for Russian speakers. According to Kulman and Tetrault, such courses would make use of the phonologies, morphologies, and syntaxes of the L2 and TL, as well as contrastive analysis, to enable L3 learners to predict parallel and divergent structures in languages.

Current best practices in USG conversion training were summarized in Brecht et al. (1998). The authors claimed that best practices in conversion training concentrate on attempts to capitalize upon the students' prior knowledge and prior language learning experience. Brecht et al. list three advantages that individuals with previous language learning background possess over persons without such experience: (1) prior knowledge of the donor language (L2), (2) greater metalinguistic awareness, and (3) general language-learning skills. The authors also explain two models of USG cross-training and conversion programs: the Quick Response Short-Term Demand Model and the Long-Term Programmed Career-Based Model. In the former, also called the "crisis model," cross-training/conversion is a method for responding to changing requirements as a result of rapidly developing geopolitical events that can unfold much faster than the time normally required to train a linguist. However, such courses are often organized on short notice, with little time to develop curricula, methods, and materials, select students, and to train teachers. The latter, also called the "programmed career" model, is based on the idea of expanding the language background of USG personnel with language qualifications as part of their career development. Brecht et al. argued that very often the "crisis model" is applied rather than the more desirable "programmed career" model.

For closely related languages, the potential programmatic benefits of this training are immediately clear for the rate of acquisition. This advantage is vital: faster rate of acquisition leads to shorter courses; shorter courses require less investment and are more responsive to rapidly emerging language requirements, such as those that arose during the US interventions in Bosnia and Kosovo. In fact, Rivers (2001) reported that cross-training courses in Kazakh and Kyrgyz (with Russian as L2) were one third the length of basic courses in these Category 3 languages. Corin (1994) and Brecht, et al. (1998) reported that Serbian/Croatian conversion courses were between one half and two thirds the length of the basic course.

Regarding the putative benefit of L3 acquisition, and the use of cross-training and conversion courses by USG training schools, we return to the hypothesis initially stated: For the learner, the acquisition of a third language is aided by knowledge of a second language. The literature is in broad agreement that L3 learners are at an advantage, be they adults who, having acquired a second language as adults, turn to a third, as is the case in most USG cross-training and conversion programs, as well as much of higher education when L3 learning occurs, or children in multilingual societies learning a foreign language in addition to their native language (typically a minority language) and the titular language. The advantages such learners enjoy in comparison to *ab initio* adult second language learners include:

- the use of more metacognitive behaviors, particularly metacognitive self-management, in the learning process used by the learner to direct the learner's in-class learning behaviors, as well as language use behaviors outside of the formal instructed environment;

- the use of a wider variety of cognitive learning strategies;
- more demonstration of autonomous learning;
- better affective behaviors and, in particular, a more positive attitude toward the learning process;
- higher proficiency outcomes for a given course length.

However, these advantages do not accrue equally for all adult L3 learners. Rivers (1996, 2001) noted distinct differences in affective behaviors with respect to adjusting to varying learning styles among the students and between the students and instructors. Some learners were able to negotiate these differences with little adverse effect on themselves or the classroom environment, while others were not. Rivers attributed this to poor metacognitive self-assessment. Other studies on linguistic transfer have noted that the advantages often afforded by transfer can be mitigated by inaccurate transfer: false cognates (lexical), overgeneralization of morphological and syntactic constructions, and so forth. However, overall, the second language learner with reasonably high L2 proficiency is a prime candidate for L3 training. The findings from studies on linguistic transfer also point to the typological distance between languages as an important factor in positive transfer – the more closely related the languages, the more linguistic transfer is possible. There is still not enough research conducted on typologically unrelated languages to provide evidence on the role of linguistic knowledge during L3 learning.

Summary of current research and praxis

Our rather cursory review reveals several areas where one might well posit that L3 acquisition is qualitatively and quantitatively different from SLA. We would argue that L3 acquisition then requires either a new theoretical framework unique to L3 acquisition (such as proposed by Flynn, Foley, & Vinnitskaya, 2004; Herdina & Jessner, 2002; and Hufeisen, 2000) or an extended SLA framework (such as argued by Marx & Hufeisen, 2003) to account for L3 acquisition within a broader framework of adult language acquisition. Such an extended framework would likely focus on the psycholinguistic and neurolinguistic changes wrought by acquiring a second language to some significant level of competence. One might further argue that such a framework would necessarily focus on metacognitive and metalinguistic traits to a significant degree, in that these areas are rather less well investigated than typology or relatedness, for example, and would tend to be independent of the particular L1–L2–L3 triads in question for a given learner.

Insofar as the applications and results of L3 acquisition differ from SLA – we know from established practice in L3 acquisition that the programs and outcomes can differ significantly, and that learner processes may differ considerably at the psycholinguistic, sociolinguistic, neurolinguistic, cognitive, and metacognitive levels – one might well argue that programming in L3 acquisition ought to capitalize on these factors. We turn next to a case study of the state of the art for directed L3 acquisition programs for adults in the US.

A Case Study of USG L3 Programs

The authors recently conducted a study of practices in USG L3 training with the goal of enhancing instruction in third language courses. We collected retrospective survey data from program managers and instructors of current and past L3 courses in:

- Tagalog to Tausug
- Bahasa Indonesian to Malaysian
- Spanish to Portuguese
- Russian to Serbian/Croatian
- Russian to Ukrainian
- Ukrainian to Russian
- Multiple languages to Uzbek
- Mandarin to Cantonese
- Modern Standard Arabic (MSA) to Egyptian Arabic
- MSA to Levantine Arabic
- Hindi to Urdu

Most courses met for 16 weeks, 6 hours per day, 5 days per week, with the exception of Russian to Serbian/Croatian courses that met for 12 or 16 weeks and the Bahasa Indonesian to Malaysian course that met for 34 weeks. A total of 39 people were interviewed: 18 language instructors, 5 program managers, and 16 students. Students in these courses were adult learners of the target language and may or may not have been native speakers of the language from which they were retrained. In some courses proficiency in L2 was measured, and in some, attainment of a certain proficiency level was required.

Analytical methodology

The authors took a qualitative, grounded theory approach to analyze a corpus of ethnographic data collected from classroom observations and learner, instructor, and course manager focus groups at six language schools. The focus groups were semi-structured face-to-face interviews with small groups of informants. The team also observed two basic MSA classes (six and eight students in each) for comparison purposes. All observed classes were one hour long. Two or three researchers were present in each of the classes; they sat in the back and took notes. The notes included: a running list of classroom activities, notes on classroom behaviors, direct quotes of the learners and teachers.

Results and discussion

The courses we examined differed on external factors related to learning environment, such as course goals, methods and materials used, and teacher characteristics. For the most part, they were intended as L3 courses, with the exception of the Uzbek course, which was initially designed as a basic course. However, because of the presence of students with backgrounds in typologically close languages, such as Azeri and Turkish, as well as languages that have donated substantial lexis to Uzbek, such as Arabic and Persian, the Uzbek course evolved into an L3 course. L3 goals were not always explicitly set and communicated to students. In Serbian/Croatian courses, for example, L3 goals were not explicitly included in the course description, but students were told that they were taking an L3 course.

Beyond confirming that the primary perceived benefit for L3 courses in the language training institutes of the USG is the more rapid acquisition of the target language, the signal result of this preliminary case study of L3 acquisition course structure and goals is that the courses themselves differed greatly in terms of which putative advantages of L3 acquisition were exploited. The courses we examined differed significantly in relation to factors external to the learners themselves, particularly with respect to course goals (whether the course was explicitly an L3 course and whether that goal was expressed in course design, pedagogical methodology, or course materials); transfer (whether transfer was explicit in course design and materials and whether contrastive analysis was used); instructor background (some instructors had a background in the learners' second language, while others did not); and materials used (materials were typically adopted from basic language courses with little or no modification for the L3 course, although there were notable exceptions).

On the other hand, in our interviews, instructors, program managers, and students indicated striking similarities in their reports of learner behavior. We summarize these perceptions in Figure 15.1. Learners accessed transfer phenomena, typically but not exclusively doing so in an overt fashion, comparing their L2 to L3, regardless of course design or instructor input. Learners clearly noticed and took advantage of differences and similarities between the two languages, but whether the phenomenon was noticing (without awareness) or metalinguistic awareness, remains unanswered. L3 learners also demonstrated a high degree of autonomy in language learning processes and usage of metacognitive learning strategies, such as organization, planning, and evaluation. All in all, they were taking advantage of their previous learning experience. Most courses proceed from an assumption that the greatest benefit is derived from retraining highly proficient learners into a closely related language. This may confound some of the putative benefits. That is, by screening for such advanced, experienced learners, USG L3 programs tend to select learners who might enjoy these and other advantages due to aptitude, verbal skills, maturity, or general intelligence, rather than their experience with a second language.

Directions for further research

This study, and the larger project to which it belongs, raises interesting questions about L3 learning in general. First, the best evidence we have thus far is that L3

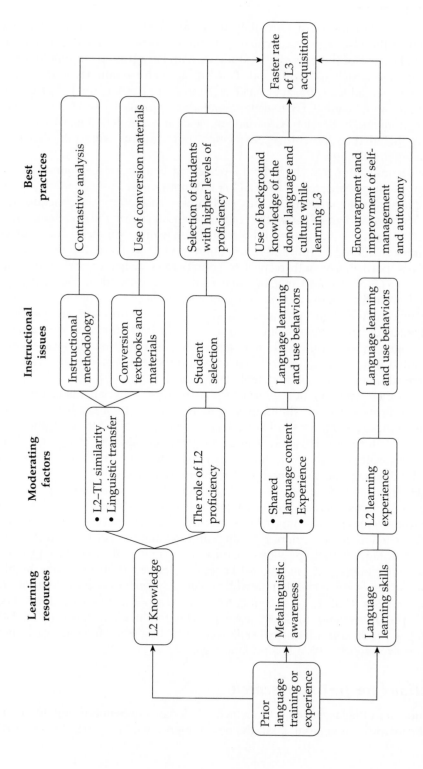

Figure 15.1 Maximizing prior language learning and experience in conversion training

courses in the USG tend to succeed – that is, the goal of reaching a specified proficiency in one half to two thirds of the time required for attainment of comparable proficiency via an L2 course is achieved – in a remarkably uniform and consistent way, regardless of the specifics of course design, instructional methods, or materials. We intend over the next several years to test this assumption by a careful ethnographic examination of diverse L3 training courses, coupled with a correlational study of learner factors predictive of success in L3 training courses. It may be that the chief influence on the rate of acquisition is some construct of typological and genetic distance between the learners' second and third languages. The metalinguistic and metacognitive effects noted in the research literature and echoed in our interviews hold some significant promise for SLA, in particular in advanced and independent learning situations, such as extended immersion abroad or daily professional use of the language.

We would advance a brief set of research questions for L3 acquisition, in hopes of sparking a discussion of the kinds of research reviewed in our chapter, as well as some of the initial results from studies of L3 acquisition. In other words, we would advance a set of questions unified around L3 acquisition as a theme, given the interest in L3 acquisition in the US for adults and the prevalence of L3 acquisition in other countries with complex multilingual societies.

- Does bilingualism – of any type – bring about changes in language acquisition in general?
- Does bilingualism – of any type – bring about changes in general cognition and/or the cognitive processes associated with adult language acquisition?
- Does bilingualism – of any type – bring about changes in general metacognition and/or the metacognitive processes associated with adult language acquisition?
- Does bilingualism – of any type – bring about changes in neurophysiology? How do such changes affect adult SLA?

We believe that these approximate a research agenda for the L3 acquisition field, one that would greatly enrich our understanding of the processes underlying all adult language acquisition.

NOTES

1 By linguistic distance, Cenoz means phylogenetic relationship. See Nakhleh, Ringe, and Warnow (2005) for a detailed assay at defining and measuring the relative distance among Indo-European languages and Juola (2003) for an attempt to create scalar measures for relative distances among unrelated languages. Distance has also been defined in terms of learnability; the difficulty scales employed by the Foreign Service Institute (FSI) and the Defense Language Institute (DLI) are examples.

2 One should note that other attempts to assay the learnability of specific features in L1–L2 dyads, such as the Interlanguage Structural Conformity Hypothesis (see, for example, Carlisle, 1998), do not assume reciprocity for learnability of specific features.

3   In broad terms, the Principles and Parameters model holds that linguistic structures – syntactic, lexical, phonological – are governed by a set of parameters, the setting of which allows or disallows phenomena such as trace movement in question formation or obligatory devoicing of final stops. These settings are fixed during first language acquisition, and if they should vary in the second (or third) language, then the corresponding parameter must also be "reset" for that language, to allow proper production of the particular structure.

4   Preposition stranding may occur in question formation when the trace noun is found in a prepositional phrase: "The students worried about the test," can become "About which test did the students worry?" (so-called Pied-Piping) or "Which test did the students worry about?" (preposition stranding) (Klein, 1995, p. 432). The incorrect response "Which tests did the student worry" occurs among learners of English whose L1 does not have prepositions which govern and mark case. In Klein's study, verb subcategorization refers to the complements taken by the allowable prepositions governed by the verb; and null-prep refers to incorrect stimuli without the required preposition.

REFERENCES

Ahukanna, J., Lund, N., & Gentile, J. (1981). Acquisition of problem solving skills. In J. Anderson (ed.), *Cognitive skills and their acquisition* (pp. 191–230). Hillsdale, NJ: Lawrence Erlbaum.

Bartlet, G. (1989). The interaction of multilingual constraints. In H. Dechert & M. Raupach (eds.), *Interlingual process* (pp. 5–16). Tübingen: Gunter Narr.

Brecht, R., Frank, V., Rivers, W., & Walton, A. (1998). *A guide for foreign language cross-training*. Research Report No. 98-01. Monterrey, CA: Defense Language Institute Foreign Language Center.

Carlisle, R. (1998). The acquisition of onsets in a markedness relationship: An empirical study. *Studies in Second Language Acquisition* 20, 245–60.

Cenoz, J. (2001). The effect of linguistic distance, L2 status and age on cross-linguistic influence in third language acquisition. In J. Cenoz, B. Hufeisen, & U. Jessner (eds.), *Cross-linguistic influence in third language acquisition: Psycholinguistic perspectives* (pp. 8–20). Clevedon, UK/Buffalo: Multilingual Matters.

Cenoz, J. & Valencia, J. F. (1994). Additive trilingualism: Evidence from the Basque Country. *Applied Psycholinguistics* 15, 195–207.

Chiswick, B. & Miller, P. (2004). Linguistic distance: A quantitative measure of the distance between English and other languages. *Journal of Multilingual and Multicultural Development* 26, 1, 1–18.

Corin, A. (1994). Teaching for proficiency: The conversion principle. A Czech to Serbo-Croatian conversion course at the Defense Language Institute. *ACTR Letter: Newsletter of the American Council of Teachers of Russian* 20, 1, 1–5.

De Angelis, G. & Selinker, L. (2001). Interlanguage transfer and competing linguistic systems in the multilingual mind. In J. Cenoz, B. Hufeisen, & U. Jessner (eds.), *Cross-linguistic influence in third language acquisition: Psycholinguistic perspectives* (pp. 42–58). Clevedon, UK/Buffalo: Multilingual Matters.

Flynn, S., Foley, C., & Vinnitskaya, I. (2004). The Cumulative-Enhancement Model for language acquisition: Comparing adults' and children's patterns of development in first, second and third language acquisition of relative clauses. *International Journal of Multilingualism* 1, 1, 3–16.

Fouser, R. (1995). Problems and prospects in third language acquisition research. *Language Research* 31, 2, 387–415.

Gribble, C. (1987). *Reading Bulgarian through Russian.* Columbus, OH: Slavica.

Hammarberg, B. (2001). Roles in L1 and L2 in L3 production and acquisition. In J. Cenoz, B. Hufeisen, & U. Jessner (eds.), *Cross-linguistic influence in third language acquisition: Psycholinguistic perspectives* (pp. 21–41). Clevedon, UK/Buffalo: Multilingual Matters.

Herdina, P. & Jessner, U. (2002). *A dynamic model of multilingualism: Perspectives of change in psycholinguistics.* Clevedon, UK: Multilingual Matters.

Higgs, T. & Clifford, R. (1982). The push toward communication. In T. Higgs (ed.), *Curriculum, competence, and the foreign language teacher.* Skokie, IL: NTC & ACTFL.

Holton, J. (1954). Portuguese for Spanish Speakers. *Hispania* 37, 4, 446–52.

Hufeisen, B. (2000). A European perspective: Tertiary languages with a focus on German as L3. In J. Rosenthal (ed.), *Handbook of undergraduate second language education: English as a second language, bilingual, and foreign language instruction for a multilingual world* (pp. 209–29). Mahwah, NJ: Lawrence Erlbaum.

Jensen, J. (1989). On the mutual intelligibility of Spanish and Portuguese. *Hispania* 72, 848–52.

Jessner, U. (1999). Metalinguistic awareness in multilinguals: Cognitive aspects of third language learning. *Language Awareness* 8, 201–9.

Jordan, I. (1991). Portuguese for Spanish speakers: A case for contrastive analysis. *Hispania* 74, 788–92.

Juola, P. (2003). The time course of language change. *Computers and the Humanities* 37, 1, 77–96.

Kellerman, E. (1983). Now you see it, now you don't. In S. Gass & L. Selinker (eds.), *Language transfer and language learning* (pp. 112–34). Rowley, MA: Newbury House.

Klein, E. (1995). Second versus third language acquisition: Is there a difference? *Language Learning* 45, 419–65.

Kulman, A. & Tetrault, E. (1993). Language cross training: Alternatives and permutations. *Cryptologic Quarterly.*

Leung, Y.-K. I. (1998). Transfer between interlanguages. In A. Greenhill, M. Hughes, H. Littlefield, & H. Walsh (eds.), *Twenty-Second Boston University Conference on Language Development* (pp. 477–87). Medford, MA: Cascadilla Press.

Marx, N. & Hufeisen, B. (2003). Multilingualism: Theory, research methods and didactics. In G. Brauer & K. Sanders (eds.), *New vision in foreign and second language education* (pp. 178–203). San Diego: LARC Press.

Möhle, D. (1989). Multilingual interaction in foreign language production. In H. Dechert & M. Raupach (eds.), *Interlingual process* (pp. 179–94). Tübingen: Gunter Narr.

Nakhleh, L., Ringe, D., & Warnow, T. (2005). Perfect phylogenetic networks: A new methodology for reconstructing the evolutionary history of natural languages. *Language* 81, 2, 381–420.

Ramsay, R. (1980). Language-learning approach styles of adult multilinguals and successful language learners. In V. Teller & S. White (eds.), *Studies in child language and multilingualism* (pp. 73–96). New York: New York Academy of Sciences.

Ringbom, H. (2001). Lexical transfer in L3 production. In J. Cenoz, B. Hufeisen, & U. Jessner (eds.), *Cross-linguistic influence in third language acquisition: Psycholinguistic perspectives* (pp. 59–68). Clevedon, UK/Buffalo: Multilingual Matters.

Ringbom, H. (2007). *Cross-linguistic similarity in foreign language learning.* Clevedon, UK: Multilingual Matters.

Rivers, W. (1996). *Self-directed language learning and third-language learners.* ERIC Document ED411679.

Rivers, W. (2001). Autonomy at all costs: An ethnography of metacognitive self-assessment and self-management among experienced language learners. *Modern Language Journal* 85, 279–90.

Sikogukira, M. (1993). Influence of languages other than the L1 on a foreign language: A case of transfer from L2 to L3. *Edinburgh Working Papers in Applied Linguistics* 4, 110–32.

Singleton, D. (1987). Mother and other tongue influence on learner French. *Studies in Second Language Acquisition* 9, 327–46.

Teixeira-Leal Tarquinio, L. (1977). The interference of Spanish in beginning Portuguese class. *Hispania* 60, 1, 82–7.

Thomas, J. (1988). The role played by metalinguistic awareness in second and third language learning. *Journal of Multilingual and Multicultural Development* 9, 235–46.

Townsend, C. (1995). *Teaching the Czech language through Russian: Преподавание ческого языка посредством русского (Prepodavanije češkogo jazyka posredstvom russkogo).* Columbus, OH: Slavica.

Wenden, A. (1999). Metacognitive knowledge and language learning. *Applied Linguistics* 19, 515–37.

Zobl, H. (1992). Prior linguistic knowledge and the conservatism of the learning procedure: Grammaticality judgments of unilingual and multilingual learners. In S. Gass & L. Selinker (eds.), *Language transfer in language learning* (pp. 176–96). Amsterdam/Philadelphia: John Benjamins.

Part V Course Design and Materials Writing

16 Foreign and Second Language Needs Analysis

JAMES DEAN BROWN

Introduction

To start this chapter, I will address the three most basic questions about needs analysis: What is needs analysis? What literature is available on language needs analyses? And, what are the steps in needs analyses? The rest of the chapter will then provide more details about each step.

What is needs analysis?

The concept of *needs analysis* (also known as *needs assessment*) commonly refers to the processes involved in gathering information about the needs of a particular client group in industry or education. Naturally, in educational programs, needs analyses focus on the learning needs of students, and then, once they are identified, needs are translated into learning objectives, which in turn serve as the basis for further development of teaching materials, learning activities, tests, program evaluation strategies, etc. Thus needs analysis is the first step in curriculum development.

In Brown (1995, p. 36), I provided a more formal definition which combined a number of other definitions I had found in the literature. Unfortunately, the resulting definition was a rather ponderous one: "the systematic collection and analysis of all subjective and objective information necessary to define and validate defensible curriculum purposes that satisfy the language learning requirements of students within the context of particular institutions that influence the learning and teaching situation."

I will simplify that definition here by breaking it into several pieces. *Needs analysis* (NA) is the systematic collection and analysis of all information necessary for defining a defensible curriculum. A *defensible curriculum* is one that satisfies the language learning and teaching requirements of the students and teachers within the context of particular institution(s) involved. (I will necessarily return to this issue below.) Naturally, the *information necessary* to achieve this

Table 16.1 Steps in the NA process

Schutz and Derwing (1981, p. 35)	Jordan (1997, p. 23)	Graves (2000, p. 100):	Stages (steps combined)
1 Define the purpose	1 Define the purpose of analysis	1 Decide what information to gather and why	**A Get ready to do NA**
2 Delimit the target population	2 Delimit student population		1 Define the purpose of the NA
3 Delimit the parameters of investigation	3 Decide upon approach(es)	2 Decide the best way to gather it: when, how and from whom	2 Delimit the student population
			3 Decide upon approach(es) and syllabus(es)
4 Select the information-gathering instrument	4 Acknowledge constraints/limitations	3 Gather the information	4 Recognize constraints
	5 Select methods of collecting data	4 Interpret the information	5 Select data collection procedures
5 Collect the data	6 Collect data	5 Act on the information	**B Do the NA research**
6 Analyze the results	7 Analyze and interpret results		6 Collect data
7 Interpret the results			7 Analyze data
			8 Interpret results
8 Critique the project	8 Determine objectives	6 Evaluate the effect and effectiveness of the action	**C Use the NA results**
	9 Implement decisions (i.e., decide upon syllabus, content, materials, methods, etc.)	7 Decide on further or new information to gather	9 Determine objectives
			[Implement decisions (assessments, materials, teaching strategies, etc.)]
	10 Evaluate procedures and results		10 Evaluate and report on the NA project
			[Decide on further information to gather (for ongoing curriculum evaluation)]

defensible curriculum includes all subjective and objective information, and any other types of information that turn out to be appropriate in the particular NA.

What literature is available on language NA?

Over the years, a few books have been devoted to the specific notion of language NA, including Richterich and Chancerel (1977, 1987), Munby (1978), Trim (1980), Buckingham (1981), Richterich (1983), and most recently Long (2005b). In addition, a number of papers have been published that review the literature on NA, most recently those by West (1994, 1997) and Long (2005a). Generic language curriculum books have also included increasingly large sections on NA over the years: Dubin and Olshtain (1986, pp. 13–14); Nunan (1988, pp. 43–53; 1991, pp. 13–24, 75–84), Clark (1987, pp. 35–7), Yalden (1987, pp. 131–8), White (1988, pp. 83–93), Brown (1995, pp. 37–70), Graves (2000, pp. 97–121), and Richards (2001, pp. 51–111).

What are the steps in a NA?

Schutz and Derwing (1981) advocated using eight steps in a NA, "which would seem to constitute an absolute minimum for any needs assessment effort worthy of the name" (p. 35); Jordan (1997, p. 23) argued for ten steps, while Graves (2000, p. 100) listed seven steps. Notice that all three sets of steps have been combined in the last column of Table 16.1 into what I consider three general stages of NA (Get ready to do NA; Do the NA research; and Use the NA results), with ten secondary steps listed under those stages.[1] The rest of this chapter will be organized around the ten steps shown in the last column of Table 16.1 followed by a conclusion section.

Get Ready to Do NA

Define the purpose of the NA

A number of perspectives have been proposed for thinking about the purposes of NA. These perspectives generally take the form of frameworks within which NAs can be conducted or types of information that can serve as the basis of a NA.

Frameworks

Stufflebeam et al. (1985, cited in Brown, 1995, pp. 38–9) identified the following four philosophies that can underlie NA (with language-related definitions supplied by me):

1 *Discrepancy philosophy* – needs are any differences between future desired student language performances and what they can currently do.
2 *Democratic philosophy* – needs are any learning goals that are preferred by a majority of the stakeholders involved.

3 *Analytic philosophy* – needs are whatever the students would naturally learn next based on what is known about them and the learning processes involved.
4 *Diagnostic philosophy* – needs are any language elements or skills that would be harmful if missing.

Similarly, three different types of needs were discussed by Hutchinson and Waters (1987):

1 *Necessities* are "objective needs," or what learners need to know to successfully function in the target L2.
2 *Lacks* are differences between target L2 proficiency and what learners currently know (see the discrepancy philosophy above).
3 *Wants* are "subjective needs," or what and how the learners would like to learn.

Brindley (1984, p. 28) pointed to even more types of needs including *wants, desires, demands, expectations, motivations, lacks, constraints,* and *requirements.*

West (1994, pp. 8–12; 1997, pp. 71–4) and Jordan (1997, pp. 23–8) provided lists of different types of NA that overlap considerably with each other. A combination of the three lists would include the following nine types of language NA:

1 *Target-situation analysis* seeks information on the language requirements learners face in learning a specific type of language.
2 *Deficiency analysis* accounts for learners' current wants and needs *and* their target situation deficiencies or lacks.
3 *Present-situation analysis* focuses on the students' proficiencies at the outset of instruction.
4 *Learning-oriented analysis* takes the view that needs (in terms of syllabus, content, teaching methods, materials, etc.) should be negotiated between students and other stakeholders.
5 *Strategy analysis* focuses on learners' preferences in terms of learning strategies, error correction, group sizes, amount of homework, etc.
6 *Means analysis* focuses on the learning situation, with as few preconceptions as possible in terms of practicality, logistics, cultural appropriateness, etc.
7 *Language audits* take a large-scale view of NA in terms of strategic language policies for companies, professional sectors, governmental departments, countries, etc.
8 *Set menu analysis* sets out to create a menu of main courses from which the sponsors or learners can select.
9 *Computer-based analysis* is done by computer to match perceived needs to a database of materials ". . . from which the course content can be negotiated between students and teacher . . ." (West, 1997, p. 74).

Types of information

Berwick (1989, pp. 49–51) listed six planning orientations for the types of information in educational systems:

1 Organized body of knowledge
2 Specific competencies
3 Social activities and problems
4 Cognitive or learning processes
5 Feelings and attitudes
6 Needs and interests of the learner

A variety of other different types of information can serve as the basis of a NA, for example:

1 Goal-oriented vs. process-oriented language needs (Widdowson, 1981, p. 2)
2 Language content vs. learning content (Brindley, 1984, pp. 31–2)
3 Content vs. methodology parameters (Nunan, 1985)
4 Linguistic content vs. learning process (Brown, 1995, p. 41)
5 Language needs vs. situation needs (Brown, 1995, p. 40; Richards, 2001, pp. 90–1)

Some combination of all these alternative frameworks and types of information will probably serve best in most present day NAs.

Delimit the student population

There are at least two ways in which the student population should be delimited. One is in terms of the scale of the project and the other is in terms of the focus of the NA.

Scale of the NA

The scale of a NA has to do with how broadly it is aimed. Some NAs have been large-scale indeed. For example, the international, multi-language NA efforts of the Council of Europe were designed to identify the needs of adult foreign language learners (e.g., Conseil de la Coopération Culturelle, 2000; Council of Europe, 2001; Richterich, 1983, 1985; Richterich & Chancerel, 1977, 1987; Trim, 1973, 1980). Somewhat more modestly scaled NAs have been described for the societal level in the United States (Brecht & Rivers, 2005), for the US military (Lett, 2005), and for large organizations like universities (Coleman, 1988).

In theory, a NA could be conducted on international, national, state or provincial, county or school district, multi-program, program, or classroom levels, all of which represent quite different scales. However, most commonly, NAs are conducted at a local level. Indeed, Purpura et al. (2003, p. 9) go so far as to argue that "All needs assessments are *situation-specific*" (italics in original). The questions of how specific the *situation* should be and, by extension, how specific a NA should be are crucial ones that must be addressed in the early stages of any such efforts (for more on this issue, see Hyland, 2002; Dovey, in press).

Focus of the NA

Seedhouse (1995) discusses NA for the general-English classroom. However, by and large, NAs have been conducted for much more specific purposes. As a result, in teacher-training texts on English for specific purposes (ESP), NA usually figures prominently. For example, there are 11 pages on NA in Hutchinson and Waters (1987, pp. 53–64), 22 pages in Jordan (1997, pp. 20–42), and 12 pages in Dudley-Evans and St John (1998, pp. 25–6, 57–9, 121–7). Typically, ESP is further divided into two categories, one for *occupational purposes* (EOP) and the other for *academic purposes* (EAP).

EOP includes many subcategories in which NAs have been conducted: *business and workplace* (e.g., Chew, 2005; Crosling & Ward, 2002; Edwards, 2000; Holliday, 1995; Holmes, 2005; So-mui & Mead, 2000; Tanaka, 2001; van Hest & Oud-De Glas, 1990; Vandermeeren, 2005), *healthcare* (e.g., Bosher & Smalkoski, 2002; Cameron, 1998; Chia et al., 1999; Lepetit & Cichocki, 2002; Uvin, 1996), *hotel workers* (Jasso-Aguilar, 1999, 2005), *journalists* (Gilabert, 2005), *footballers* (Kellerman, Koonen, & van der Haagen, 2005), and *coffee shop workers* (Downey Bartlett, 2005).

EAP has also been the focus of many NAs including *general EAP needs* (e.g., Braine, 2001; Chan, 2001; Jordan, 1997; Kim et al., 2003; Waters, 1996), *writing needs* (Casanave & Hubbard, 1992; Hale et al., 1996; Leki, 1995), *oral/aural needs* (Ferris, 1998; Ferris & Tagg, 1996a, 1996b; Kim, in press; Teng, 1999), and *heritage learner needs* (see discussion and references in Kondo-Brown, 2007).

Outside the traditional EOP/EAP distinction, other NAs have focused on survival English for *immigrants* (e.g., Nunan, 1990; Winn, 2005) and *computer assisted language learning* (e.g., Decamps & Bauvois, 2001; González-Lloret, 2003).

NA for languages other than English

So far the discussion of NA appears to be all about English, in ESL settings. However, a number of NAs have been conducted in non-English-speaking countries for English as a foreign language (EFL) (e.g., Bacha, 2003; Kormos, Kontra, & Csolle, 2002; and Moreno, 2003 to cite three among many). Other NAs have been conducted for languages other than English. Some of these have been the multi-country efforts in Europe discussed above. Others have included a large number of languages by addressing *foreign languages* (e.g., Oukada, 2001; Porcher, 1983; and Purpura et al., 2003), or focused a bit more narrowly on three languages like Spanish, French, and German (Alalou, 2001; Alalou & Chamberlain, 1999; and Horwitz, 1988). NAs have also been conducted for specific languages like *French* (Dalgalian, 1983; Harlow, Smith, & Garfinkel, 1980; Licari, Londei, & Mandolini, 1983; Sapin-Lignieres, 1983), *German* (von der Handt, 1983), *Japanese* (Iwai et al., 1999), and *Korean* (Chaudron et al., 2005; Kim et al., 2003).

Decide upon approach(es) and syllabus(es)

Approaches

Brown (1995, p. 5) described *approaches* as "ways of defining what and how the students need to learn" and listed the following approaches:

1   Classical
2   Grammar-translation
3   Direct
4   Audiolingual
5   Communicative

Naturally, other belief systems that could be called approaches may exist (the cognitive approach comes immediately to mind).

Syllabuses

Curriculum design has often been discussed in terms of *types of syllabuses*. Wilkins (1976, pp. 2–14) distinguished between *synthetic syllabuses* ("organized in terms of tasks derived from the description of the language," p. 3) and *analytic syllabuses* ("organized in terms of the purposes for which people are learning language and the kinds of language performance that are necessary to meet those purposes," p. 13). White (1988, pp. 44–61) discussed two types of syllabuses from a somewhat different perspective: *Type A syllabuses* ("What is to be learnt?", p. 44) are distinguished from *Type B syllabuses* ("How is it to be learnt?", p. 44).

Brown (1995, pp. 6–14) defined *syllabuses* as "ways of organizing the course and materials" and listed the following seven:

1   Structural
2   Situational
3   Topical
4   Functional
5   Notional
6   Skills-based
7   Task-based

In recent years, other syllabuses have also gained prominence (lexical and problem-solving syllabuses come immediately to mind).

Given the above ways that teachers, students, and administrators may vary in their belief systems about what and how students should learn languages (approaches), it is not surprising that those same stakeholders may often disagree about how language courses and materials should be organized (syllabuses).

Recognize constraints

The constraints that are faced in NAs tend to be situation related rather than language related. For instance, in his article focusing on ESP communication constraints, Singh (1983) listed constraints, all of which *focus on the situation* and could impinge on the conduct of a NA: adequacy of syllabuses, administrative attitudes toward second/foreign language teaching and learning, availability of audio-video aids, class size, government language policies, availability of time for NA, departmental organization, relevance of foreign/second language learning to other subjects, scheduling, society's general attitudes toward second/foreign language learning, status of teachers, as well as teaching/learning traditions.

Singh's list provides a good starting point, but there are many other possible constraints, which will differ widely from situation to situation. Some may *focus on the teachers* in terms of their: training, qualifications, language proficiency, skills, expertise, experience, language, morale, motivation, styles, beliefs, and principles (list of factors from Richards, 2001, p. 99). More crucially, the teachers' willingness to cooperate in a NA project can determine whether it lives or dies, and their readiness to relinquish sovereignty over their classrooms could also be a factor, as could how satisfied they are with their working conditions, or how well they get along with their administrators, etc.

Consider also the overall effects of factors like money or religion. There are rare settings where money to support language education is plentiful as in Saudi Arabia – during my time working there (1982–5), I found the quality of the buildings, amount of classroom space, quality and amount of equipment, numbers of teachers, numbers and adequacy of textbooks were all excellent. Earlier, when I was teaching in China in (1980–2), all of the same factors were in short supply because money was in short supply. In constrast, the reverse was true with regard to religion. In Saudi Arabia, the students had the right to leave the classroom any time they wanted to pray. That is a constraint that was unthinkable where I was teaching in China.

Many other constraints may unexpectedly rear their heads in a particular NA. For example, the overall amount of time available for studying a language and the intensity of that time may be important constraints. Other constraints may have to do with the degree to which classrooms are homogeneous or heterogeneous with regard to their language background, age, academic status, proficiency level, etc. Such differences could clearly impose constraints on what a NA can find or accomplish.

Some scholars make a distinction labeled *means analysis*. According to Purpura and Graziano-King (2004, pp. 4–5), "a *means analysis* examines those factors that impede or facilitate curriculum implementation or change. A means analysis is not so much concerned with the language or the learner per se, but with the contextual variables of the learning/teaching environment (Jordan, 1997; Richterich, 1983)." Indeed, some researchers might consider the constraints listed above more relevant to *means analysis* than to *needs analysis*. However, as Dudley-Evans and St John (1998, p. 124) point out, "means analysis is suggested (Holliday and Cooke, 1982, p. 133) as an adjunct to needs analysis." I would go even further and say that needs analysts ignore such constraints at their peril.

In addition, given the large number of potential constraints, needs analysts may be tempted to just give up. However, most constraints can be overcome by simply setting realistic goals for the NA with an eye to attaining a "balance between 'what is needed' and 'what is possible'" (Singh, 1983, p. 156).

Select data collection procedures

According to Purpura et al. (2003, pp. 9–11), a NA should be situation specific, learner centered, pragmatic, and systematic. These characteristics are particularly important for planning the data collection procedures that will be used in a NA because those procedures must be appropriate for the specific situation, should be learner centered (though all other stakeholders must also be involved), must be practical (within the constraints imposed by the situation), and must be systematic in the sense that they will function well together and lead to defensible results.

Therefore, at some relatively early stage, needs analysts must carefully plan what procedures they will use for gathering their information. Stufflebeam et al. (1985, pp. 90–1) suggest five *factors that affect choices* of information-gathering procedures:

1 Characteristics of the information source
2 Situational characteristics
3 Type of information needed
4 Technical measurement criteria
5 Level of accuracy desired

Buckingham (1981) noted early on that "a great variety of assessment instruments and processes are available, and the use of more than one means of assessment is desirable" (p. 15). Hutchinson and Waters (1987) provide a few suggestions for the types of NA data gathering procedures: questionnaires, interviews, observations, data collection (e.g., gathering texts), informal consultations with sponsors, learners, etc. (p. 58). Jordan (1997) provided a bit longer list of data gathering procedures: "documentation, tests, questionnaires, forms/checklists, interviews, record-keeping and observation," with special emphasis on advance documentation, language test at home, language test on entry, self-assessment, observation and monitoring, class progress tests, surveys, structured interview, learner diaries, case studies, final tests, evaluation/feedback, follow-up investigations (pp. 30–8).

Perhaps the most complete lists of NA procedures are provided by Brown (1995, 2001) and Long (2005a), as shown in Table 16.2. In Brown (1995), I listed 26 different procedures and described each in turn (pp. 45–55). Long (2005a) provided what turns out to be a list that is in almost complementary distribution to my list. However, Long provided more information about each by describing each procedure, but also by citing examples of studies that used each procedure along with references for additional information about each. All the procedures in Table 16.2 taken together give a broad perspective on the many options available for gathering information in NA (including well over 40 different procedures). Clearly, trying to use all of them in any given NA would be impractical. So selecting among them will prove important. Naturally, needs analysts should select those procedures that best fit the purpose, scale, focus, approaches, syllabuses, and constraints of the particular NA.

I should make one last point about Table 16.2. Notice that, by far, the majority of the procedures listed in the table have an asterisk after them. These are the ones that lend themselves to qualitative research methods rather than quantitative methods. I will expand on this below.

Do the NA Research

Collect data

What questions should be addressed? In NA, we are in the business of gathering information, and gathering information inevitably leads to asking questions. I have found at the beginning of a NA that I often have no idea what the appropriate questions are, much less which of those questions are the most important. So the first task a needs analyst faces is often to figure out what types of questions are relevant.

I find it useful to refer to the question categories suggested by Patton (1987) and Rossett (1982) in trying to think of useful questions. These question types are all shown in Table 16.3 along with some ideas for what each question type might ask about.

The profile of communicative needs provided by Munby (1978) can also serve as nine aspects of communication about which needs analysts might want to ask questions:

Table 16.2   Procedures for NA

Types	Listed in Brown (1995, 2001)	Listed in Long (2005a)
Existing information	Records analysis* Systems analysis* Literature review* Email, letter writing, phone calls*	
Tests	Aptitude Proficiency Placement Diagnostic Achievement	
		Task-based CR performance tests
Intuitions		Non-expert intuitions* Expert practitioner intuitions*

Table 16.2 *(cont'd)*

Types	Listed in Brown (1995, 2001)	Listed in Long (2005a)
Observations	Case studies* Diary studies* Behavior observation* Interactional analysis Inventories*	Diaries, journals, logs* Participant observations* Non-participant observations* Classroom observations*
Interviews	Individual (in person, telephone, Internet)* Group*	Unstructured interviews* Structured interviews* Interview schedules*
Meetings	Delphi technique* Advisory* Focus group* Interest group* Review*	
Questionnaires	Biodata surveys Opinion surveys (closed-response) Opinion surveys (open-response)* Self-ratings (closed-response) Self-ratings (open-response)* Judgmental ratings (closed-response) Judgmental ratings (open-response)* Q sort (closed-response)	Surveys and questionnaires
Target language	Text analysis* Discourse analysis*	Discourse analysis* Role plays, simulations* Content analysis* Register/rhetorical analysis* Computer-aided corpus analysis* Genre analysis*

Table 16.3 Ideas for types of questions to address in NA

Author	Question type	Ask about
Patton (1987)	*Behaviors/experiences*	Encounters or experiences in certain language learning settings, what they do when those things happen, how they behave or act in those settings, etc.
	Opinions/values	Thoughts, impressions, attitudes, values, opinions, etc. on various aspects of their language or language learning processes
	Feelings	Sentiments and emotional reactions about particular topics, issues, and components of the learning and teaching processes
	Knowledge	Facts, information, and knowledge about the language learning and teaching processes in a particular context
	Sensory	Visual, auditory, tactile, and/or olfactory aspects of the language learning and teaching processes
	Demographic/background	Biographical, descriptive, or historical information that has bearing on the language learning teaching processes
Rossett (1982)	*Problems*	Difficulties and problems participants perceive in a particular language learning and teaching context
	Priorities	Topics, functions, skills, activities, grammar points, etc. that participants feel are most important, second most important, third most important, etc.
	Abilities	Language aptitudes, proficiencies of participants, especially with regard to reading, writing, speaking, listening, pragmatics, etc.
	Attitudes	Wants, wishes, and attitudes (e.g., toward the language being studied, toward native speakers of the language and their culture, toward course objectives, etc.)
	Solutions	Answers or solutions to whatever problems or quandaries are uncovered in the above question types

1   Personal (important background information)
2   Purpose (reason for communicating)
3   Setting (place where communication happens)
4   Interaction variables (power, gender, psychological, etc. relationships)
5   Medium, mode, and channel (means of communicating)
6   Dialects (variations that will be encountered)
7   Target level (level of proficiency needed)
8   Anticipated communicative events (different levels of functions or tasks that will be required)
9   Key (particular way communication is accomplished)

How should data collection proceed?

This is a tricky part of any NA because needs analysts inevitably find themselves encroaching on the territory of other people. The first goal should therefore be to get all pertinent stakeholders to cooperate in the data-gathering process. Winn (2005, pp. 293–4) listed some useful strategies to use, *if possible*, when doing NA data collection:

1   Use inside connections in trying to gain entrée.
2   Be sure to go through channels in seeking permission in early stages.
3   Gradually get to know the participants.
4   Situate yourself as a learner, not an expert.
5   Observe a relatively large number of participants.
6   Use pre-interview conversations and follow-up interviews.
7   Use a variety of information sources to allow for comparisons of the data.
8   Be creative and flexible.
9   Volunteer and work in organizations where you are gathering data.

Analyze data

Quantitative or qualitative?

Research can vary from quantitative to qualitative on a number of dimensions: the *quantative research approach* tends to use quantitative (data) and be experimental, statistical, highly intervening, highly selective, variable operationalizing, hypothesis testing, deductive, controlled, cross-sectional, large sample, and etic, while the *qualitative research approach* tends to use qualitative (data) and be non-experimental, interpretive, non-intervening, non-selective, variable defining, hypothesis forming, inductive, natural, longitudinal, small sample, and emic (see Brown, 2004a for definitions of all this terminology). Clearly, these are at least two very different approaches that can be used in NA research.

Concerns with consistency, fidelity, verifiability, and meaningfulness

Long (2005a) argued that "... *all* approaches to NA, new or old, could benefit from some serious work on issues of reliability and validity" (p. 22). I agree, but I would argue that we must first be clear about how we think and talk about

Table 16.4   Standards for judging of quantitative and qualitative research reports (summarized from Brown, 2004a)

Quantitative	*RESEARCH STANDARDS*	*Qualitative*
Reliability	CONSISTENCY	Dependability
Validity	FIDELITY	Credibility
Replicability	VERIFIABILITY	Confirmability
Generalizability	MEANINGFULNESS	Transferability

issues like reliability and validity. Table 16.4 (based on Brown, 2004a) shows the standards that are used for judging the worth of research, especially in quantitative and qualitative research reports. Note that all researchers must concern themselves with research standards related to consistency, fidelity, verifiability, and meaningfulness (shown down the middle of the table). However, quantitative researchers will do so by focusing on the concepts of reliability, validity, replicability, and generalizability, while qualitative researchers will zero in on dependability, credibility, confirmability, and transferability.

In discussing Table 16.2, I pointed out that the vast majority of the potential NA procedures lend themselves to qualitative rather than quantitative research methods. While much has been written about quantitative research methods in applied linguistics (see Brown, 2004b for a review of the available books on this topic), fewer resources are available specifically focused on doing qualitative research in second language settings. Four books offer at least a chapter-length treatment of qualitative language research methods (Brown, 2001; Freeman, 1998; Johnson, 1992; and Nunan, 1992), and a number of articles have appeared in the *TESOL Quarterly* on qualitative language research methods (e.g., Davis, 1992, 1995; Lazaraton, 1995).

In addition, some NAs have openly applied qualitative approaches (e.g., Holliday, 1995; Sawyer, 2001). Many other NAs have applied qualitative methods without realizing it. Indeed, most of the NAs cited earlier in this chapter took what I would call at least a *predominantly* qualitative research approach. Certainly, questionnaires with Likert scales were often involved, but careful scrutiny will reveal that most of the interpretations were actually qualitative in nature.

What I am suggesting here is that we should probably admit that NAs are usually at least predominantly qualitative in methodology, and that, therefore, we should frame our NAs, not in quantitative terms, but rather in qualitative terms. Notice that, while the qualitative terminology defined in Table 16.5 can be said to be analogous to the quantitative research concepts of reliability, validity, replicability, and generalizability, each is defined quite differently (see second column) from the quantitative analogs. Note also that the strategies used to enhance dependability, confirmability, credibility, and transferability (listed in the last column) are quite different from the strategies used to enhance the analogous concepts in quantitative research. All of this is discussed in much more depth elsewhere (e.g., Brown, 2001, 2004a; Davis, 1992, 1995).

Table 16.5 Key concepts in qualitative research methods (summarized from Brown, 2001)

Key Concepts in Qualitative Research	Definition	Enhanced by
Dependability	Consistency of observations, effects of changing conditions in the objects of study, etc. to help better understand the context being studied	Overlapping methods Stepwise replications Inquiry audits
Credibility	Fidelity of identifying and describing the object(s) of study especially as judged by the various parties being studied	Prolonged engagement Persistent observation Triangulation Peer debriefing Negative case analysis Referential analysis Member checking
Confirmability	Verifiability of the data upon which all interpretations in a study are based.	Audit trails Data records
Transferability	Meaningfulness of the results of a study and their applicability in other settings	Thick description

Triangulation

One concept that has been surfacing with increasing frequency in the NA literature is that of *triangulation*. Triangulation is not really a specific procedure, but rather is a research strategy that has been applied in a number of NAs (e.g., Bosher & Smalkoski, 2002; Gilabert, 2005; Jasso-Aiguilar, 1999, 2005; Kikuchi, 2004; Long, 2005a). As Long (2005a, p. 28) puts it, "*Triangulation* is a procedure used by researchers . . . to increase the credibility of their data and thereby, eventually, to increase the credibility of their interpretations of those data." He adds that it ". . . involves the researchers comparing different sets and sources of data with one another . . ." In Brown (2001, p. 229), I took a slightly larger view of triangulation when I identified seven potential types of triangulation: *data triangulation* (using multiple types of procdures), *investigator triangulation* (using multiple needs analysts), *theory triangulation* (using multiple conceptual frameworks), *methodological triangulation* (using multiple data gathering procedures), *interdisciplinary triangulation* (using the perspectives of multiple disciplines), *time triangulation* (using multiple data gathering occasions), and *location triangulation* (using multiple locations).

However, simply using multiple measures and triangulation does not guarantee that a qualitative NA will be dependable and credible. As Fielding and Fielding (1986, p. 31) put it, "using several different methods can actually increase the chance of error. We should recognize that the multi-operational approach implies a good deal more than merely piling on of instruments." Instead, the combinations of different perspectives, sources, data types, etc. must be carefully thought through and planned so that they cross-validate each other. As Huberman and Miles (1994, p. 438) suggested, "A general prescription has been to pick triangulation sources that have different biases, different strengths, so they can complement one another."

In addition, if appropriate, the combinations should be sequenced in such a way that each builds on what was learned from previous procedures. As Long (2005a, p. 33) put it, "In particular, carefully sequenced use of two or more procedures can be expected to produce better quality information."

For an example of how multiple procedures can be combined and sequenced effectively, see the "Participatory appraisal" NA reported in Holme and Chalauisaeng (in press), which used a number of procedures and combined them in such a way that the total information gathered was much greater in quality than the sum of the information collected with each individual procedure.

Interpret results

Given that NAs are generally qualitative in nature, what can needs analysts do to make sure their interpretations are sound? First, it is crucial that the NA data be gathered and analyzed in such a way that the interpretions will be seen as dependable, confirmable, credible, and transferable. Second, the interpretations should be done very carefully following the three suggestions I made in Brown (2001, p. 230) for minimizing researcher bias: (1) carefully arrange your triangulation so it minimizes the biases of different data sources and maximizes their strong points, (2) carefully examine how your preconceptions may be affecting your data choices, and (3) study how you may be attracted to unusual or salient data. Third, the results should be examined not only for how various data sources cross-validate each other, but also for any differences that occur among data sources. For instance, if there is a mismatch between the views of teachers and students on preferred classroom activities (as found in Spratt, 1999), that may be important information.

Use the NA Results

Determine objectives

One natural outcome for any language NA will be the specification of objectives for specific language courses. Put another way, objectives are the link that connects the NA to the rest of the curriculum (i.e., to the materials, testing, teaching, and program evaluation). Indeed, specifying objectives is a way of fitting what was learned in the NA to the actual instruction that will be delivered.

In addition, the act of fleshing out objectives based on the NA will help needs analysts begin to understand everything that is involved in meeting the students' perceived needs. Aspects of the students' needs that were overlooked during the NA will tend to surface at this point. Thus, specifying objectives is a natural and important next step in a NA.

A number of benefits can be gained from using objectives (for a list of ten such benefits, see Brown, 1995, p. 96), but there are also some potential pitfalls involved. To avoid these pitfalls, Brown (1995, pp. 96–7) provides six guidelines to remember:

1 Objectives can range in type and level of specificity.
2 Objectives are not permanent. They must remain flexible enough to respond to changes in perceptions of students' needs *and* changes in the types of students served.
3 Objectives must be developed by consensus among all of the teachers involved.
4 Objectives must not be prescriptive in terms of restricting what the teacher does in the classroom to enable students to perform well by the end of the course.
5 Because of all of the above, objectives will necessarily be specific to a particular program.
6 Above all else, the objectives must be designed to help the teachers, not hinder their already considerable efforts.

Evaluate and report on the NA project

What a report might contain

Overall, an effective NA report will explain the results with an eye to evaluating the effectiveness of the NA itself. Such a report might contain a description of the theoretical and practical context of the project. It should also include a clear description of the research methodology employed, including descriptions of the participants (administrators, teachers, students, future employers, etc.), materials (observation forms, interview schedules, questionnaires, tests, etc.), procedures (step-by-step, how was the NA information gathered?), and analyses (including explanation of the ways credibility, confirmability, and transferability were enhanced). Naturally, such a report would also usefully supply a discussion (of what the results of the NA mean in terms of the needs of the various participants in the program) and a set of conclusions drawn from the results and discussion. It is also useful to end such a NA report by supplying all the objectives that were derived from the NA.

Audiences and dissemination

While the report is being written, it is also vital to consider who the *audiences* will be. Will the audience for the report be just the teachers in the program? Or would it also be useful and politically wise to create shorter and simpler reports for students, administrators, higher authorities, politicians, or even for the general public?

Thinking about *dissemination* is also important. After all, if you have gone to all the trouble of doing a NA, you probably want key groups of people to know about it. Some options for disseminating NA results include oral presentations at faculty meetings, public meetings, and professional conferences, or written reports distributed through institutional curriculum documents, newsletters, journals, and books.

Conclusion

In this chapter, I have attempted to show the stages and steps that can be included in a sound NA. I hope that this discussion of the many alternatives available to needs analysts will help them do a better job in the future. However, in looking back over the chapter, I cannot help feeling that there is still something crucial missing.

I think the missing component has something to do with our overemphasis on language needs. The many articles about NA and the dozens of actual NA reports cited in this chapter tended to focus almost entirely on the language needs of the students. The problem with this approach is that it is not going far enough. It ignores the fact that language teachers, students, administrators, parents, etc. often have quite different views about what constitutes good language teaching and learning.

Once we accept that the various participants in a program may have quite differing views, it should be clear that we need to know what the various groups of stakeholders are thinking. NA is the perfect means for finding out what people are thinking and for exploring how the views of various groups are similar and different. That does not mean that everybody is right, nor does it mean that everybody should get what they think they want. It does mean that we need to know what everybody is thinking so we can deal politically with the similarities and differences in their views. Naturally, we must also use the best available knowledge and theory about language learning and teaching. If we can then combine all of these elements into a sound NA, we stand a good chance of creating a *defensible curriculum*.

In short, an obsessive focus on language needs that seeks the "truth" is probably destined to fail. A NA designed to investigate what bits of language the students "really need" to learn is doomed to collapse from the weight of its own single-minded focus. In contrast, a needs analysis that balances information about what options are available (approaches and syllabuses) with information about what various groups of stakeholders think about those options necessarily recognizes that there is no single truth, that NA is a political process, and therefore, that the goal of a NA is a *defensible curriculum*.

To actually do such a NA, I think we should indeed be gathering data about the students' language needs, but we should also be assembling information on the views of different groups of stakeholders and use that information to:

1 discover what the options (in perceived student needs with regard to approaches, syllabuses, objectives, etc.) are and what people think about those options;

2 decide which options are most likely to serve as a defensible basis for curriculum (i.e., options that might lead to a sort of average or consensus "truth");

3 marshall information and formulate arguments (sometimes alternative arguments) for the most viable options in perceived student needs with regard to approaches, syllabuses, objectives, etc.;

4 work to get all stakeholders to come to agreement, to form a consensus, or to at least compromise on those perceived needs;

5 work to accommodate the views of those who disagree with perceived needs, if possible;

6 try to change the views of those stakeholders who disagree with the perceived needs, when necessary;

7 show respect for all participants by listening and taking their views seriously (even if we ultimately have no intention of doing what they want).

Above all else, it is crucial to involve the teachers in all aspects of the NA processes. They are the people who will have to deliver the curriculum and live with it long after the current students (and perhaps the needs analysts) have moved on. More than any other group of stakeholders, the teachers will need to feel respected. To ignore the teachers in a NA is to doom the resulting curriculum to failure. To include the teachers is crucial because, in one way or another, any curriculum project will require them to make changes in their working habits, to do extra work, and, more importantly, to relinquish some portion of their classroom sovereignty. Needs analyses rightly focus on the needs of students, but we must never forget that teachers have needs, too.

NOTE

1 Note that two of the steps in the last column of Table 16.1 are shown in brackets. I bracketed them and exclude them as NA steps because I view assessment, materials, teaching, and program evaluation as separate curriculum elements (see Brown, 1995).

REFERENCES

Alalou, A. (2001). Reevaluating curricular objectives using students' perceived needs: The case of three language programs. *Foreign Language Annals* 34, 453–69.

Alalou, A. & Chamberlain, E. (1999). Using student expectations and perceived needs to rethink pedagogy and curriculum: A case study. *Foreign Language Annals* 32, 27–44.

Bacha, N. (2003). English across academic and professional communities: A study of EFL learners' needs at the Lebanese American University. *AAICU Journal* 2, 29 pp. Retrieved August 3, 2006 from: www.anatolia.edu.gr/act/aaicu2/pdf/nahla_bacha.pdf.

Berwick, R. (1989). Needs assessment in language programming: From theory to practice. In R. K. Johnson (ed.), *The second language curriculum* (pp. 48–62). New York: Cambridge University Press.

Bosher, S. & Smalkoski, K. (2002). From needs analysis to curriculum development: Designing a course in health-care communication for immigrant students in the USA. *English for Specific Purposes* 21, 1, 59–79.

Braine, G. (2001). Twenty years of needs analysis: Reflections on a personal journey. In J. Flowerdew & M. Peacock (eds.), *Research perspectives on English for Academic Purposes* (pp. 195–207). Cambridge: Cambridge University Press.

Brecht, R. D. & Rivers, W. P. (2005). Language needs analysis at the societal level. In M. H. Long (ed.), *Second language needs analysis* (pp. 79–104). Cambridge: Cambridge University Press.

Brindley, G. (1984). *Needs analysis and objective setting in the Adult Migrant Education Program.* Sydney: Adult Migrant Education Service.

Brown, J. D. (1995). *The elements of language curriculum: A systematic approach to program development.* Boston: Heinle and Heinle.

Brown, J. D. (2001). *Using surveys in language programs.* Cambridge: Cambridge University Press.

Brown, J. D. (2004a). Research methods for Applied Linguistics: Scope, characteristics, and standards. In A. Davies & C. Elder (eds.), *The handbook of applied linguistics* (pp. 476–500). Oxford: Blackwell.

Brown, J. D. (2004b). Resources on quantitative/statistical research for applied linguistics. *Second Language Research* 20, 4, 408–29.

Buckingham, T. (1981). *Needs assessment in ESL.* Washington, DC: Center for Applied Linguistics.

Cameron, R. (1998). A language-focused needs analysis for ESL-speaking nursing students in class and clinic. *Foreign Language Annals* 31, 2, 203–18.

Casanave, C. & Hubbard, P. (1992). The writing assignments and writing problems of doctoral students: Faculty perceptions, pedagogical issues, and needed research. *English for Specific Purposes* 11, 33–49.

Chambers, F. (1980). A re-evaluation of needs analysis in ESP. *ESP Journal* 1, 1, 25–33.

Chan, V. (2001). Determining students' language needs in a tertiary setting. *English Teaching Forum* 39, 3, 16–27.

Chaudron, C., Doughty, C. J., Kim, Y., et al. (2005). A task-based needs analysis of a tertiary Korean as a foreign language program. In M. H. Long (ed.), *Second language needs analysis* (pp. 225–61). Cambridge: Cambridge University Press.

Chew, K.-S. (2005). An investigation of the English language skills used by new entrants in banks in Hong Kong. *English for Specific Purposes* 24, 4, 423–35.

Chia, H. U., Johnson, R., Chia, H. L., & Olive, R. (1999). English for college students in Taiwan: A study of perceptions of English needs in a medical context. *English for Specific Purposes* 18, 2, 107–19.

Clark, J. L. (1987). *Curriculum renewal in school foreign language learning.* Oxford: Oxford University Press.

Coleman, H. (1988). Analyzing language needs in large organizations. *English for Specific Purposes* 7, 155–69.

Conseil de la Coopération Culturelle (2000). *Un cadre Européen commun de reference pour les langues: Apprendre, enseigner, évaluer.* Strasbourg, France: Conseil de la Coopération

Culturelle, Comité de l'Éducation, Division des Langues Vivantes. Also viewed August 23, 2006 at www.coe.int/t/dg4/linguistic/Source/Framework_FR.pdf.

Council of Europe (2001). *Common European Framework of Reference for Languages: Learning, teaching, assessment.* Cambridge: Cambridge University Press. Also viewed August 23, 2006 at: www.coe.int/t/dg4/linguistic/Source/Framework_EN.pdf.

Crosling, G. & Ward, I. (2002). Oral communication: The workplace needs and uses of business graduate employees. *English for Specific Purposes* 21, 1, 41–57.

Dalgalian, G. (1983). Identifying needs in a production-training project. In R. Richterich (ed.), *Case studies in identifying language needs* (pp. 117–26). Oxford: Pergamon.

Davis, K. A. (1992). Validity and reliability in qualitative research on second language acquisition and teaching: Another researcher comments. . . . *TESOL Quarterly* 26, 605–8.

Davis, K. A. (1995). Qualitative theory and methods in applied linguistics research. *TESOL Quarterly* 29, 427–53.

Decamps, S. & Bauvois, C. (2001). A method of computer-assisted language learning: The elaboration of a tool designed for an "un-schoolable" public. *Computer Assisted Language Learning* 14, 1, 69–96.

Dovey, T. (in press). What purposes, specifically? Re-thinking purposes and specificity in the context of the "new vocationalism." *English for Specific Purposes.*

Downey Bartlett, N. J. (2005). A double shot 2% mocha latte, please, with whip: Service encounters in two coffee shops and at a coffee cart. In M. H. Long (ed.), *Second language needs analysis* (pp. 305–43). Cambridge: Cambridge University Press.

Dubin, F. & Olshtain, E. (1986). *Course design.* Cambridge: Cambridge University Press.

Dudley-Evans, T. & St John, M. J. (1998). *Developments in English for Specific Purposes: A multidisciplinary approach.* Cambridge: Cambridge University Press.

Edwards, N. (2000). Language for business: Effective needs assessment, syllabus design and materials preparation in a practical ESP case study. *English for Specific Purposes* 19, 291–6.

Ferris, D. (1998). Students' views of academic aural/oral skills: A comparative needs analysis. *TESOL Quarterly* 32, 289–318.

Ferris, D. & Tagg, T. (1996a). Academic listening/speaking tasks for ESL students: Problems, suggestions, and implications. *TESOL Quarterly* 30, 2, 297–320.

Ferris, D. & Tagg, T. (1996b). Academic oral communication needs of EAP learners: What subject-matter instructors actually require. *TESOL Quarterly* 30, 1, 31–58.

Fielding, N. G. & Fielding, J. L. (1986). *Linking data.* Beverly Hills, CA: Sage.

Freeman, D. (1998). *Doing teacher research: From inquiry to understanding.* Boston, MA: Heinle & Heinle.

Gilabert, R. (2005). Evaluating the use of multiple sources and methods in needs analysis: A case study of journalists in the Autonomous Community of Catalonia (Spain). In M. H. Long (ed.), *Second language needs analysis* (pp. 182–99). Cambridge: Cambridge University Press.

González-Lloret, M. (2003). Designing task-based CALL to promote interaction: En busca de esperaldas. *Language Learning and Technology* 7, 1, 86–104.

Graves, K. (2000). *Designing language courses: A guide for teachers.* Boston, MA: Newbury House.

Hale, G., Taylor, C., Bridgeman, B., Carson, J., Kroll, B., & Kantor, R. (1996). *A study of writing tasks assigned in academic degree programs.* Princeton, NJ: Educational Testing Service.

Harlow, L. L., Smith, W. F., & Garfinkel, A. (1980). Student-perceived communication needs: Infrastructure of the functional/notional syllabus. *Foreign Language Annals* 13, 11–22.

Holliday, A. (1995). Assessing Language needs within an institutional context: An ethnographic approach. *English for Specific Purposes* 14, 2, 115–26.

Holliday, A. & Cooke, T. (1982). An ecological approach to ESP. *Lancaster Practical Papers in English Language Education* (Issues in ESP) 5, 123–43.

Holme, R. & Chalauisaeng, B. (in press). The learner as needs analyst: The use of participatory appraisal in the EAP reading classroom. *English for Specific Purposes.*

Holmes, J. (2005). When small talk is a big deal: Sociolinguistics challenges in the workplace. In M. H. Long (ed.), *Second language needs analysis* (pp. 344–71). Cambridge: Cambridge University Press.

Horwitz, E. K. (1988). The beliefs about language learning of beginning university foreign language students. *The Modern Language Journal* 72, 283–94.

Huberman, A. M. & Miles, M. B. (1994). Data management and analysis methods. In N. K. Denzin & Y. S. Lincoln (eds.), *Handbook of qualitative research* (pp. 428–44). Thousand Oaks, CA: Sage.

Hutchinson, T. & Waters, A. (1987). *English for Specific Purposes.* Cambridge: Cambridge University Press.

Hyland, K. (2002). Specificity revisited: How far should we go now? *English for Specific Purposes* 21, 385–95.

Iwai, T., Kondo, K., Lim, D. S. J., Ray, G., Shimizu, H., & Brown, J. D. (1999). *Japanese language needs assessment 1998–1999* (NFLRC NetWork #13) [HTML document]. Honolulu: University of Hawai'i, Second Language Teaching and Curriculum Center. Retrieved from: www.lll.hawaii.edu/nflrc/NetWorks/NW13.

Jasso-Aguilar, R. (1999). Sources, methods, and triangulation in needs analysis: A critical perspective in a case study of Waikiki hotel maids. *English for Specific Purposes* 18, 1, 27–46.

Jasso-Aguilar, R. (2005). Sources, methods, and triangulation in needs analysis: A critical perspective in a case study of Waikiki hotel maids. In M. H. Long (ed.), *Second language needs analysis* (pp. 127–58). Cambridge: Cambridge University Press.

Johnson, D. M. (1992). *Approaches to research in second language learning.* New York: Longman.

Jordan, R. R. (1997). *English for Academic Purposes.* Cambridge: Cambridge University Press.

Kellerman, E., Koonen, H., & van der Haagen, M. (2005). "Feet speak louder than the tongue": A preliminary analysis of language provisions for foreign professional footballers in the Netherlands. In M. H. Long (ed.), *Second language needs analysis* (pp. 200–22). Cambridge: Cambridge University Press.

Kikuchi, K. (2004). Triangulating perceptions of learners' needs: An alternate way of conducting needs analysis. *2004 JALT Pan-SIG Proceedings.* Tokyo: JALT.

Kim, S. (in press). Academic oral communication needs of East Asian international graduate students in non-science and non-engineering fields. *English for Specific Purposes.*

Kim, Y., Kong, D.-K., Lee, Y.-G., Silva, A., & Urano, K. (2003). A task-based needs analysis for the English Language Institute at the University of Hawaii at Manoa. *Korean Journal of Applied Linguistics* 19, 2, 93–114.

Kondo-Brown, K. (2007). Issues and future agendas for teaching Chinese, Japanese, and Korean heritage students. In K. Kondo-Brown & J. D. Brown (eds.), *Teaching Chinese, Japanese and Korean heritage language students: Curriculum needs, materials, and assessment* (pp. 17–43). Mahwah, NJ: Lawrence Erlbaum.

Kormos, J., Kontra, E. H., & Csolle, A. (2002). Language wants of English majors in a nonnative context. *System* 30, 517–42.

Lazaraton, A. (1995). Qualitative research in applied linguistics: A progress report. *TESOL Quarterly* 29, 3, 455–72.

Leki, I. (1995). Coping strategies of ESL students in writing tasks across the curriculum. *TESOL Quarterly* 29, 2, 235–60.

Lepetit, D. & Cichocki, W. (2002). Teaching languages to future health professionals: A needs assessment study. *Modern Language Journal* 86, 3, 384–96.

Lett, J. A. (2005). Foreign language needs assessment in the US military. In M. H. Long (ed.), *Second language needs analysis* (pp. 105–24). Cambridge: Cambridge University Press.

Licari, C., Londei, D., & Mandolini, M. (1983). Notes on a questionnaire for identifying the language needs of French in Bologna. In R. Richterich (ed.), *Case studies in identifying language needs* (pp. 88–96). Oxford: Pergamon.

Long, M. H. (2005a). Methodological issues in learner needs analysis. In M. H. Long (ed.), *Second language needs analysis* (pp. 19–76). Cambridge: Cambridge University Press.

Long, M. H. (2005b). *Second language needs analysis.* Cambridge: Cambridge University Press.

Moreno, A. I. (2003). Análisis de necesidades para el aula de lengua inglesa en filología inglesa: Un estudio de caso. *Barcelona English Language and Literature Studies* 12 (no page numbers). Accessed August 25, 2006 from: www.publicacions.ub.es/revistes/bells12/PDF/art10.pdf.

Munby, J. (1978). *Communicative syllabus design: A sociolinguistic model for defining the content of purpose-specific language programs.* Cambridge: Cambridge University Press.

Nunan, D. (1985). *Language teaching course design: Trends and issues.* Adelaide: National Curriculum Resource Centre.

Nunan, D. (1988). *The learner-centered curriculum.* Cambridge: Cambridge University Press.

Nunan, D. (1990). Using learner data in curriculum development. *English for Specific Purposes* 9, 17–32.

Nunan, D. (1992). *Research methods in language learning.* Cambridge: Cambridge University Press.

Oukada, L. (2001). Toward responsive beginning language curricula. *Foreign Language Annals* 34, 107–17.

Patton, M. Q. (1987). *How to use qualitative methods in evaluation.* Newbury Park, CA: Sage.

Porcher, L. (1983). Reflections on language needs in the school. In R. Richterich (ed.), *Case studies in identifying language needs* (pp. 127–49). Oxford: Pergamon.

Purpura, J. E. & Graziano-King, J. (2004). Investigating the foreign language needs of professional school students in international affairs: A case study. *Teachers College, Columbia University Working Papers in TESOL and Applied Linguistics* 4, 1, 1–33.

Purpura, J. E., Graziano-King, J., Chang, J., et al. (2003). An analysis of the foreign language needs of SIPA students at Columbia University. Unpublished Technical Report submitted to the Mellon Foundation through the Arts and Sciences at Columbia University, New York.

Richards, J. C. (2001). *Curriculum development in language teaching.* Cambridge: Cambridge University Press.

Richterich, R. (ed.) (1983). *Case studies in identifying language needs.* Oxford: Pergamon.

Richterich, R. (1985). *Besoins langagiers et objectifs d'apprentissage.* Paris: Hachette.

Richterich, R. & Chancerel, J.-L. (1977). *L'Identication des besoins des adultes apprenant une langue étrangère.* Strasbourg: Conseil de l'Europe.

Richterich, R. & Chancerel, J.-L. (1987). *Idenifying the needs of adults learning a foreign language.* Englewood Cliffs, NJ: Prentice-Hall International.

Rossett, A. (1982). A typology for generating needs assessments. *Journal of Instructional Development* 6, 1, 28–33.

Sapin-Lignieres, B. (1983). A method of research into needs applied to teachers of French in northern Greece. In R. Richterich (ed.), *Case studies in identifying language needs* (pp. 97–105). Oxford: Pergamon.

Sawyer, R. (2001). An ethnographic approach to needs analysis for international graduate students of science in Japan. In E. F. Churchill & J. W. McLaughlin (eds.), *Temple University Japan Working Papers in Applied Linguistics: Qualitative research in applied linguistics: Japanese learners and contexts* (pp. 102–17). Tokyo: Temple University Japan.

Schutz, N. W. & Derwing, B. L. (1981). The problem of needs assessment in English for specific purposes: Some theoretical and practical considerations. In R. Mackay & J. D. Palmer (eds.), *Languages for specific purposes: Program design and evaluation* (pp. 40–5). Rowley, MA: Newbury House.

Seedhouse, P. (1995). Needs analysis and the general English classroom. *ELTJournal* 49, 1, 59–65.

Singh, R. K. (1983). ESP: Communication constraints. *System* 11, 2, 155–8.

So-mui, F. L. & Mead, K. (2000). An analysis of English in the workplace: The communication needs of textile and clothing merchandisers. *English for Specific Purposes* 19, 351–67.

Spratt, M. (1999). How good are we at knowing what learners like? *System* 27, 141–55.

Stufflebeam, D. L., McCormick, C. H., Brinkerhoff, R. O., & Nelson, C. O. (1985). *Conducting educational needs assessments*. Hingham, MA: Kluwer-Nijhoff.

Tanaka, H. (2001). English communication needs of an international advertising company: An ethnographic appraisal. In E. F. Churchill & J. W. McLaughlin (eds.), *Temple University Japan Working Papers in Applied Linguistics: Qualitative research in applied linguistics: Japanese learners and contexts* (pp. 143–63). Tokyo: Temple University Japan.

Teng, H. (1999). Needs analysis of EFL listening by Taiwanese college students. *KOTESOL Proceedings of PAC2* (pp. 169–77). The Second Pan Asian Conference, Seoul, Korea.

Trim, J. L. M. (1973). *Système d'apprentissage des langues vivantes par les adultes: Un système Européen d'unités capitalisables*. Strasbourg: Conseil de la Coopération Culturelle du Conseil Européen.

Trim, J. L. M. (1980). *The place of needs analysis in the Council of Europe Modern Language Project: Foreign language teaching: Meeting individual needs*. Oxford: Pergamon.

Uvin, J. (1996). Designing workplace ESOL courses for Chinese health-care workers at a Boston nursing home. In K. Graves (ed.), *Teachers as course developers* (pp. 39–62). Cambridge: Cambridge University Press.

van Hest, E. & Oud-De Glas, M. (1990). *A survey of techniques used in the diagnosis and analysis of foreign language needs in industry*. Brussels: Lingua.

Vandermeeren, S. (2005). Foreign language needs of business firms. In M. H. Long (ed.), *Second language needs analysis* (pp. 159–81). Cambridge: Cambridge University Press.

von der Handt, G. (1983). Needs identification and curricula with particular reference to German for migrant workers. In R. Richterich (ed.), *Case studies in identifying language needs* (pp. 24–38). Oxford: Pergamon.

Waters, A. (1996). *A review of research into needs in English for Academic Purposes of relevance to the North American higher education context*. TOEFL monograph series #6. Princeton, NJ: Educational Testing Service.

West, R. (1994). Needs analysis in language teaching. *Language Teaching* 27, 1–19.

West, R. (1997). Needs analysis: State of the art. In R. Howard & G. Brown (eds.), *Teacher education for LSP* (pp. 68–79). Clevedon, UK: Multilingual Matters.

White, R. V. (1988). *The ELT curriculum: Design, innovation and management*. Oxford: Blackwell.

Widdowson, H. G. (1981). English for specific purposes: Criteria for course design. In M. Selinker, E. Tarone, & V. Hanzeli (eds.), *English for Academic Purposes: Studies in Honor of Louis Trimble* (pp. 1–11). Rowley, MA: Newbury House.

Wilkins, D. (1976). *Notional syllabuses.* Oxford: Oxford University Press.

Winn, M. (2005). Collecting target discourse: The case of the US naturalization interview. In M. H. Long (ed.), *Second language needs analysis* (pp. 265–304). Cambridge: Cambridge University Pres.

Yalden, J. (1987). *Principles of course design for language teaching.* Cambridge: Cambridge University Press.

17 Syllabus Design

PETER ROBINSON

Introduction: Two Basic Distinctions

Units and sequence

Syllabus design is based essentially on a decision about the "units" of classroom activity, and the "sequence" in which they are to be performed. The syllabus thus formalizes the content to be learned in a domain of knowledge or behavior, and "arranges this content in a succession of interim objectives" (Widdowson, 1990, p. 127). As in other areas of instruction (see Reigeluth, 1999) there are options in, and differing theoretical rationales for, the units to be adopted in specifying and sequencing pedagogic content for second language (L2) learners, and a number of these will be described in this chapter. Theoretical rationales, of course, should be concerned with issues of how the L2 is internalized and learned, and also accessed and acted upon, since it is the cognitive processes leading to learning and successful performance, as they take place in specific pedagogic contexts, that the syllabus is intended to promote. Individual differences between learners in the cognitive and other abilities contributing to their "aptitudes" for learning and performing in the L2 will also modulate, and contribute to variance in, the effectiveness of specific pedagogic contexts and sequencing decisions at the group or program level (Robinson, 2002, 2005a, 2007a). These are theoretical and empirical issues for research into instructed second language acquisition (SLA) to address, in order to establish an optimally effective, learner-sensitive approach to syllabus design. Experimental and classroom-based research into a number of psycholinguistic issues in instructed SLA has begun with this prospect in view.

Perhaps the most fundamental issue for syllabus design addressed by this research so far is the following: Is the L2 best learned explicitly, by understanding and practicing a series of formal units of language, however characterized, or is it best learned incidentally from exposure to the L2 during communicative activities and tasks (see, e.g., Doughty, 2001; Doughty & Williams, 1998; N. Ellis, 2005, this volume; Ortega, this volume; Robinson, 1996a, 1997, 2001)? Commitment to one or the other of these broad pedagogic orientations and psycholinguistic positions underlies a number of proposals that have been made for units of syllabus design. Units have been based on an analysis of the *language* to be learned, in terms of a series of grammatical structures, graded in difficulty, as in Ellis (1993, 1997), or of lexical items and collocations, graded in frequency, as in Willis (1990). Units have also been based on an analysis of the components of simple versus complex *skilled behavior* in the second language, e.g., the reading microskills described by Richards (1990) or the communicative skills forming part of Munby's (1978) communicative needs profiler, and Johnson's (1996) work. Units have also been based on observed real-world *performative acts* involving the L2, or "target tasks" for a population of learners identified during a needs analysis (see Brown, this volume). Target tasks involve varied real-world activities, such as greeting passengers and serving meals on an airplane (Long, 1985, 2005) or finding a journal article in a library with the aid of library technology and then using it to find needed answers to questions (Robinson & Ross, 1996). Target task L2 performance is gradually approximated during classroom performance of simpler pedagogic versions of these tasks. Examples of these, and other units, that have been proposed will be given below.

Along with choices in the units to be adopted, there are choices in the "sequence" in which they can be presented. Some sequencing criteria are specific to a particular unit, or units, as will be described below – such as more to less "frequent" in the case of lexical items. However, the relative merits of broader sequencing options, and educational philosophies supporting them, have been discussed in the literature on L2 syllabus design. A syllabus can consist of a *prospective* and fixed decision about what to teach, and in what order. In this case the syllabus will be a definition of the contents of classroom activity. This is largely the approach to syllabus design discussed in this chapter. However, sequencing decision can also be made *online*, during classroom activity as in the "process" syllabus (Breen, 1984) or the "negotiated" syllabus (Clarke, 1991). In this case the initial syllabus will only guide, but not constrain, the classroom activities. Finally, Candlin (1984) has proposed that a syllabus can be *retrospective*, in which case no syllabus will emerge until after the course of instruction. In this case, the syllabus functions only as a record of what was done, imposing no controlling constraint on the classroom negotiation of content.

The role of the learner in approaches to syllabus design

Another distinction which is useful in conceptualizing options in syllabus design was made initially by Wilkins (1976) and refers to the learner's role in assimilating the content provided during group instruction and applying it individually to real-world language performance and interlanguage development. *Synthetic* syllabi involve a focus on specific elements of the language system (such as grammatical structures, or language functions), often serially and in a linear sequence. The easiest, most learnable, most frequent, or most communicatively important (sequencing decisions can be based on each of these often non-complementary criteria, and on others) are presented before their harder, later learned, less frequent, and more communicatively redundant counterparts. These syllabi assume the learner will be able to put together, or synthesize in real-world performance, the parts of the language system they have been exposed to separately. In contrast, *analytic* syllabi do not divide up the language to be presented in classrooms, but involve holistic use of language to perform communicative activities. The learner's role in these syllabi is to analyze or attend to aspects of language use and structure as the communicative activities require them to, in line with: (1) their developing *interlanguage systems*; (2) their preferred *learning style* and *aptitude profile*; and (3) to the extent that they are *motivated* to develop to an accuracy level which may not be required by the communicative demands of the task. For these reasons analytic approaches to syllabus design have been argued to be more sensitive to SLA processes and learner variables than their synthetic counterparts. This distinction will also be related to the following description of syllabi that have been proposed.

Traditional Approaches to Syllabus Design

Grammatical syllabi

Since the 1920s, and the work of Harold Palmer and others in the Reform Movement (see Howatt & Widdowson, 2004) who emphasized the controlled presentation of grammatical structures and oral practice following classroom presentation, grammatical syllabi have featured prominently in programs for second and foreign language learners. Intuitive criteria of relative usefulness, and simplicity were used as a basis of selection and grading: "The grammatical material must be graded. Certain moods and tenses are more useful than others; let us therefore concentrate on the useful ones first . . . we will not learn off the whole set of prepositions, their uses and requirements, but we will select them in accordance with their degree of importance" (Palmer, 1922, p. 68). These intuitive criteria, reflected in the decisions about selection and grading in basic structure lists for language teaching (e.g., Hornby, 1959) continue to be influential (see the discussion of R. Ellis, 1993, 1997 below). While SLA research into learnability, teachability, and developmental sequences (e.g., Pienemann, 1989) has had little influence on grading, more recent developments in corpus analysis (see Flowerdew, this volume; Gries, 2008; Sinclair, 2004) which identify central patterns of use in specific discourse domains attempt to put at least the "useful" criterion on an empirical footing. SLA research has shown that the additive "accumulation" of increasingly complex and accurate grammatical structures in a linear sequence is not what happens during second language development, but this is what a structural syllabus would seem to predicate as evidence of learning in classrooms that employ it. Nonetheless, Wilkins comments; "The use of a grammatical syllabus can be regarded as the conventional approach to language teaching since the majority of syllabi and published courses have as their core an ordered list of grammatical structures" (1976, p. 7). A concern to develop syllabi which attempted to at least supplement structural criteria for grading teaching sequences by emphasizing the "uses" to which structures could be put during communicative activities led to alternative proposals in the 1970s that also continue to be influential.

Notional-functional syllabi

In the 1970s, the Council of Europe initiated a project (see Richterich, 1972; Van Ek, 1976; Wilkins, 1976) which aimed to specify a common framework for teaching and assessing "communicative competence" in foreign language education. The aim was to specify syllabi in terms of three categories of meaning common across languages: semantico-grammatical meaning, or notions, such "time" and "quantity"; modal meanings, such as degree of certainty and scale of commitment; and communicative functions, such as agreeing, requesting, complimenting. These provided a way of going from specified types of meaning, or universal communicative and conceptual categories, to their realization in specific languages. This is an unordered inventory: what provides sequencing constraints on these notional categories, and their realizations in language, is the idea of a common core of notions/functions, useful for all communicative goals and purposes, which must be mastered before those particular to specific communicative purposes. Brockett (2000) is a contemporary example of the use of this approach to syllabus design which aims to sets standards for Japanese instruction across various state and private sector institutions in the United States. Core communicative functions are grouped into superordinate categories, which include, socializing, getting things done, communicating factual information. These are themselves subcategorized and the functions matched to essential patterns and phrases. For example, "leave taking" within the superordinate "socializing" category, is specified in terms of formal parting (*ja, shitsurei shimasu*); at night (*oyasumi nasai*); and inviting to come again (*mata kite kudasai*). Concepts or notions are also listed in this way, so the notional category of "existential concepts" is divided into subcategories, such as "possibility and impossibility," and matched with an essential pattern such as . . . *koto ga dekiru*. At a level beyond mastery of the core functions and notions, lesson content or topics appropriate to learners with specific occupational needs (such as nurses) also provide a constraint on which further functions/notions, and their linguistic exponents are to be taught, and these too can be sequenced using criteria such as going from concrete to more abstract (e.g., from "giving a patient an injection," to " taking care of the elderly," to "illness"), or more to less common, or more to less useful, however defined. The Notional-Functional Syllabus, then, is little more than an inventory of notions and functions to be covered at different levels of a language teaching program. As many have noted (e.g., White, 1988, p. 76), functions can be realized with any number of forms or structures (How about going to see/Would you like to see/ Have you seen the new Woody Allen film?). Consequently, Brockett comments, "It is probable that curricula can be most successfully organized around the principle of introducing students to structural patterns in the context of their communicative functions, and concepts within the specific topic areas" (2000, p. 19). Grammatical criteria for grading and sequencing the formal exponents of functions are therefore as important to this approach to syllabus design as they are in the structural syllabus described above.

A further problem with the functional syllabus is that, in almost all cases, the functional value of an utterance in extended discourse is a binary relation between two contributions (Widdowson, 1978). Simply listing grammatical exponents of functions misrepresents the fact that B's contribution in the following has a different speech act value depending on A's contribution:

A: Where are you?/John is on the phone.
B: I'm busy on the computer.

Crombie (1985a) is an exhaustive attempt to list all the possible inter- and intra-propositional semantic relations, and exemplify how they can be linguistically coded and signaled in English. The general semantic relations described in the "Relational Approach" to syllabus design (Crombie, 1985b) include temporal relations (e.g., chronological sequence); matching relations (e.g., simple comparison/contrast); cause–effect relations (reason–result/means–result), and so on. Once again, however, while such inter- and intra-propositional relations can be called "units," it is not clear on what principled basis they are to be sequenced for presentation. Further, the taxonomy given is not definitive, but rather "one which I hope will prove useful in the design of language teaching programs" (Crombie, 1985a, p. 17).

Contemporary Rationales for Syllabus Design

The structural syllabus

Like other contemporary rationales for syllabus design, Ellis (1993, 1997) draws extensively on SLA research and theory to motivate his arguments for a role for a structural syllabus. Ellis' argument rests on two distinctions: between explicit conscious knowledge and implicit tacit knowledge, and between declarative knowledge of facts and procedural knowledge of how to do things (see Anderson, 1992; DeKeyser, 2001; Robinson, 1996a). He argues that explicit, declarative knowledge of L2 grammar can influence the development of implicit declarative knowledge, and through communicative activity, implicit declarative knowledge can be proceduralized and used in spontaneous skilled performance. This is a "weak interface" model, which allows explicit knowledge, under some conditions, to influence the development of tacit representations or competence. The main condition is that the learner must be developmentally ready to incorporate the explicit grammar instruction into their interlanguage. Ellis cites research by himself (1989), Pienemann (1989) and others showing that learners pass through stages of development in the acquisition of, amongst other things, word order rules, question forms, and negation. Unless grammatical instruction is timed to the learner's point of development it will not influence the developing implicit knowledge base. Since stages of development are learner internal and hidden from the teacher, timing is difficult to manage. However, Ellis argues explicit grammatical knowledge serves a number of other functions: it can be used to monitor production; it can help learners notice features in the input; and it can help learners compare their own production with a target model, and in some cases notice the gap between between them. Knowing about grammar, Ellis argues, is therefore useful. Tasks promote consciousness-raising, and noticing of target grammar rules. Tasks are therefore pedagogic devices for teaching units of grammar (examples are described in Ellis, 2003; Ellis & Noboyushi, 1993; Fotos & Ellis, 1991), and are used to implement a prospective synthetic structural syllabus.

The lexical syllabus

Drawing on a different type of empirical evidence – large-scale corpora of spoken and written language use – Willis also argues for a synthetic syllabus, where word and collocation are the units of analysis. Willis nowhere draws on SLA research to the extent Ellis does to motivate his proposal, but does conclude that SLA research findings show "input does not equal intake" and that "the assumption that language can be broken down into a series of patterns which can then be presented to learners and assimilated by them in a predictable sequence" is wrong (Willis, 1990, p. iii). Arguing against "a methodology which presents learners with a series of patterns" in a presentation, practice, production sequence, Willis proposes taking "meaningful exposure as a starting point" (1990, p. iv). Exposure should be organized in three ways: (1) language is *graded* in difficulty; (2) language exemplifying the commonest patterns is *selected*; and (3) the language syllabus is *itemized* to highlight important features. Exposure is thus tightly controlled. Rather than *linguistically* grading the content of the syllabus, Willis argues for lexically grading it, using corpora of language use to identify word frequency at the 700-word, the 1,500-word, and the 2,500-word levels. Words in the corpora are itemized as collocations exemplifying each word's typical patterns of use. In effect, though, lexical grading leads to linguistic grading since, as Willis notes, by identifying the commonest words, "inevitably it focuses on the commonest patterns too . . . the lexical syllabus not only subsumes a structural syllabus, it also indicates how the structures which make up the syllabus should be identified" (1990, p. vi). In the lexical syllabus these three corpora are the bases of exposure at three levels of learner development. Willis claims that exposure is not sequenced or controlled within these levels, and the lexical syllabus "does not dictate what will be learned and in what order"; rather "it offers the learner experience of a tiny but balanced corpus from which it is possible to make generalizations about the language as a whole" (1990, p. vii). In other words, the learner corpus which forms the basis of exposure at each level is carefully itemized, but these items are not presented individually and serially.

Willis describes the development of the COBUILD Course (an exemplar of the lexical syllabus) as a process of first intuitively deciding on interesting topics, then developing tasks and choosing texts to complement them, and then highlighting lexical items within, e.g., the first 700-word level, as they occurred in the texts. This series of highlighted items constitutes syllabus content, but items are sequenced according to no criteria that are discussed, apart from teacher intuition (see Willis, 1990, pp. 74–90). The methodology accompanying the syllabus (described in Willis, 1990, and in more detail by Jane Willis, 1996) involves a *pre-task* introduction to a topic, and exposure to texts; a *task cycle* where a task is planned, drafted and rehearsed; and a final *language focus* where learners consciously focus on forms used during the task. Course planning and content, hence the syllabus, is thus largely determined by the choices of texts and tasks – topics about which the lexical syllabus says nothing. This is, then, a language-focused synthetic syllabus, but with some control given to the learner about which forms to attend to and focus on, since the itemized corpora at each level function as a guide, rather than as a prospective plan, allowing more online negotiation of content than Ellis allows.

The skill syllabus

Drawing on the work of Anderson (1992) and the declarative, procedural distinction referred to by Ellis (1997), Johnson argues that SLA and general skill learning draw on the same general cognitive mechanisms. Traditionally, skill acquisition has been viewed as a speed-up in the use of initially attention-demanding declarative knowledge. With practice, attentional demands diminish and declarative knowledge is proceduralized. Johnson argues that many aspects of L2 learning can be viewed as the reverse process, from initially fast, unattended and unanalyzed use, drawing on procedural knowledge alone, to declarative knowledge. This occurs when formulaic language is used fluently at first, without any knowledge of its internal structure. As this becomes attended to and analyzed, declarative knowledge emerges. Declarative knowledge is valuable because it allows greater generalizability of language use, and is not context-dependent, in contrast to procedural knowledge. Johnson concludes that his proposals support a skills syllabus, similar to, but going beyond, the earlier attempts of Munby (1978) and Wilkins (1976) to specify the units of communicative syllabus design. In essence, Johnson proposes a four-tier model of syllabus design. Occupying the first tier are what Johnson, following Munby, calls language-specific skills, such as "identifying the present perfect," or correctly contrasting /i/ and /iː/: "In our attempts to break language behavior down into subskills, the general areas of phonetics/phonology and syntax would, then, follow traditional lines and would not pose any new difficulties for syllabus designers" (Johnson, 1996, p. 164). But the old difficulties are surely difficulties enough. Are separate subskills to be identified for each phonetic contrast, for example? And how does "learning difficulty" affect decisions about selecting and sequencing subskills? Another tier would contain semantic categories, such as notions and functions, "but only those about which pedagogically accessible generalizations can be made" (1996, p. 165), that is, notions and functions which can be generalized to many contexts. An example given is *inviting* versus *being polite*. Johnson claims inviting need not be taught, and so need not be part of the syllabus, since it is largely phrasal and situation-specific, whereas in being polite, "useful generalizations . . . can be made about such things as 'being circumspect and indirect in approach'" (1996, pp. 165–6). A third tier would involve skills often referred to in "process" approaches to teaching writing skills, such as *generating* new ideas, *drafting* essays, *structuring* and *evaluating* them. It seems then that skill is being used as a term to cover three different types of unit: language item, semantic category, and writing strategy. This is because Johnson is concerned with the transition from knowledge states – procedural to declarative and vice versa – that learning all these units has in common. The fourth and final tier of Johnson's skills syllabus concerns processing demands; the level of complexity of the classroom task should also be specified and enter into sequencing decisions. In summary, Johnson also favors a synthetic syllabus, prospectively organized, based on subskills at a number of levels, linguistic, semantic and pragmatic, and strategic. The role of the syllabus designer is to draw up an inventory of the subskills at each of these levels (as Munby, 1978 attempted to do), then sequence them, and weave them together in a principled way.

The task syllabus

While in practice still not a common choice of unit, tasks have been increasingly researched and theorized as a basis for syllabus design in recent years (see Bygate, Skehan, & Swain, 2001; R. Ellis, 2003, 2005; Long, 1985, 2007; Garcia-Mayo, 2007; Nunan, 2004; Robinson, 1995, 1996b, 2001, 2005b, 2007b; Robinson, Ting, & Urwin, 1995; Skehan & Foster, 2001). Target tasks (see Long & Crookes, 1993) are units of real-world activity involving language use identified on the basis of a needs analysis (see Long, 2005), subsequently broken down into simpler versions, which are presented in order of increasing complexity, so as eventually to approximate the full complexity of the target task demands. In this view, the features of tasks contributing to their relative complexity are the basis of sequencing decisions. However, in many discussions of tasks, and examples of what claim to be task-based materials, tasks are used to force attention to, or to practice a particular structure, function, or subskill. Skehan (1998) refers to these as "structure-trapping" tasks. These include the tasks advocated by Ellis (1997, 2003), and Loschky and Bley-Vroman (1993), where the use of tasks to direct attention to grammatical form is theoretically motivated and an explicit part of the rationale for their use, as well as those in commercially available task-based courses, such as Richards, Gordon, and Harper (1995) and Nunan (1996). In these latter cases, what were typically called exercises or activities in older course books are now called tasks, but there is no difference between them. The organizing principle of these course books, apparent from the syllabus descriptions at the front, are grammatical structures, listening microskills, functions, topics, and often more.

In contrast to structure-trapping tasks, and in contrast to course books using task as a synonym for language exercise, Skehan and Long view tasks as purely meaningful activities. Tasks do not implement a covert grammatical or lexical syllabus; tasks alone are the units of syllabus design.

Long (2000, 2007; Long & Crookes, 1993; Long & Robinson, 1998) and Skehan (1996, 1998; Skehan & Foster, 2001) are in broad agreement about the SLA motivation for analytic syllabi, and task-based syllabi in particular, citing research showing: (1) little resemblance between acquisitional sequences and instructional sequences based on linguistic forms (e.g., Ellis, 1989; Lightbown, 1983); (2) evidence that learning is non-linear and cumulative, rather than linear and additive, as synthetic language syllabi imply (see Selinker & Lakshmanan, 1992 on backsliding, and Kellerman, 1985, on U-shaped behavior); and (3) research showing the influence of learnability on the order in which items can be learned (e.g., Mackey, 1999; Pienemann, 1989). Even if a structural syllabus could be sequenced based on what is known of learnability and language development, it would be impossible to time and target instruction at the stage learners are ready to progress to accurately, since there is variation in rate of acquisition, meaning groups of learners do not progress in lockstep, homogeneously through acquisition sequences. Additionally, as Long (2000) points out, linguistic grading, as required by many synthetic structural approaches, at least in the early stages, results in classroom language and texts which are artificial, and functionally and linguistically impoverished, prohibiting exposure to language that learners may be ready to learn. Given their broad agreement over the motivation for choice of task-based syllabi, there are some differences of scope and focus in their proposals.

Long (1985, 2000; Long & Crookes, 1993) describes a number of steps to be taken in implementing task-based language teaching. First, conduct a needs analysis to identify the target, real-world tasks learners need to perform in the L2, then classify the target tasks into types or superordinate categories such as "making/ changing reservations." From the target tasks, derive pedagogic tasks: "Adjusted to such factors as learners' age and proficiency level, these are a series of initially simple, progressively more complex approximations to the target task" (Long, 2000, p. 185). These tasks are then sequenced to form a syllabus, and the program is implemented with appropriate methodology and pedagogy. One methodological principle Long advocates is "focus on form." That is, where individuals or groups of learners are heard repeatedly producing non-target like forms, teacher intervention to provide corrective feedback is recommended. This can take several forms, such as implicit negative feedback, or recasts of learner forms, brief written illustration of the correct form, brief rule explanations, input enhancement of forms in aural and written texts used on task, and a variety of other techniques (see Doughty & Williams, 1998 for an extended summary). Like Long, Skehan rejects linguistic grading as a criterion for task and syllabus design, defining a task as an activity in which, "Meaning is primary; There is a goal which needs to be worked on; the activity is outcome-evaluated; There is a real world relationship" (Skehan, 1998). Skehan concludes that this definition rules out "an activity that focuses on language itself" such as a transformation drill, or the consciousness-raising tasks described by Ellis (1997), and many of the tasks in Nunan (1996, 2004).

Grading and sequencing tasks

Researched proposals for grading and sequencing tasks in terms of their information-processing and interactional demands have begun to be developed in recent years. One position, taken by Skehan (1998; Skehan & Foster, 2001), is that more demanding tasks "consume more attentional resources . . . with the result that less attention is available for focus on form" (1998, p. 97), therefore sequencing tasks from less cognitively demanding to more demanding optimizes opportunities for attention allocation to language form. Task design is also seen as a means to promote "balanced language development" in the areas of accuracy, fluency, and complexity of production. This can be done because certain task characteristics "predispose learners to channel their attention in predictable ways, such as clear macrostructure towards accuracy, the need to impose order on ideas towards complexity, and so on" (1998, p. 112). However, due to scarcity of attentional resources, tasks can lead either to increased complexity, or accuracy of production, but not to both. Tasks should therefore be sequenced by choosing those with characteristics that lead to each, at an appropriate level of difficulty, as determined by three factors. (1) *Code complexity* is described in "fairly traditional ways," as in descriptions of structural syllabi, or developmental sequences (1998, p. 99). (2) Cognitive *complexity* is the result of the *familiarity* of the task, topic or genre, and the *processing* requirements, information type, clarity and organization, and amount of computation required. (3) *Communicative stress* involves six characteristics, including time pressure, number of participants, and opportunities to control interaction. Unlike Johnson, Willis, or Ellis, Skehan does not argue that tasks should be used to deliver and practice a linguistic syllabus. Tasks are sequenced from less to more difficult to minimize what he argues are the negative effects, given limited attentional capacity, of increased cognitive and attentional demands on linguistic performance. The goals of task-based instruction are to promote language development in the areas of accuracy, fluency, and complexity of speech, as well as comprehension, and task selection and classification are not constrained by the need to articulate pedagogic tasks with target tasks identified in a needs analysis.

In contrast, Robinson (2005b, 2007b, 2007c) assumes behavior descriptions of target tasks for populations of learners are the starting point for pedagogic task design. Based on behavior descriptions, *task conditions* (i.e., the *interactional* demands of target tasks) are classified using task characteristics, distinguishing them in terms of participation and participant variables (see Table 17.1). *Participation* variables include: (1) whether the solution to the task is optional (open) or fixed (closed); (2) whether information exchange goes from A to B (one-way), or is reciprocal (two-way); (3) whether agreement is required (convergent) or the opposite (divergent), etc. *Participant* variables concern interlocutors' relative status, familiarity with each other, and the extent of shared cultural background, etc.

Table 17.1　Characteristics for pedagogic task design and sequencing decisions

Task complexity *(Cognitive factors)*	*Task condition* *(Interactive factors)*
(Classification criteria: cognitive demands)	(Classification criteria: interactional demands)
(Classification procedure: information-theoretic analyses)	(Classification procedure: behavior descriptive analyses)
Subcategories: 　(a) cognitive variables making 　cognitive/conceptual demands	Subcategories: 　(a) participation variables making 　interactional demands
+/− here and now +/− few elements −/+ spatial reasoning −/+ causal reasoning −/+ intentional reasoning −/+ perspective-taking	+/− open solution +/− one-way flow +/− convergent solution +/− few participants +/− few contributions needed +/− negotiation not needed
(b) cognitive variables making performative/procedural demands	(b) participant variables making interactant demands
+/− planning time +/− prior knowledge +/− single task +/− task structure +/− few steps +/− independency of steps	+/− same proficiency +/− same gender +/− familiar +/− shared content knowledge +/− equal status and role +/− shared cultural knowledge

Similarly, following behavior descriptions of target tasks, *task complexity* (i.e., the cognitive demands of target tasks) is classified using task characteristics, distinguishing them in terms of cognitive/conceptual, and performative/procedural demands. The cognitive/conceptual demands include: (1) whether the task requires reference to events happening now, in a mutually shared context (Here-and-Now) versus events that occurred in the past, elsewhere (There-and-Then); (2) reference to few, easily distinguished, versus many similar elements; (3) reference to spatial location, where easily identifiable and mutually known landmarks can be used, versus reference to location without this support, etc. (see Table 17.1). The Cognition Hypothesis (Robinson, 2001, 2003a, 2003b, 2005b; Robinson & Gilabert, 2007) argues that sequencing pedagogic tasks from simple to complex in terms of cognitive/conceptual demands leads to interlanguage *development* and L2 learning. This is because expending the mental effort needed to make more demanding *cognitive/conceptual* distinctions in language should prime learners – and direct their attentional and memory resources – to aspects of the L2 system required to understand and convey them accurately, thereby facilitating "noticing" of these, and so speeding up L2 grammaticization in conceptual domains, as well as promoting the use of more complex syntax. In contrast, *performative/procedural* demands of tasks (see Table 17.1) concern variables such as planning time, or whether the task requires one versus multiple simultaneous outcomes to be accomplished. Increasing complexity along these dimensions of cognitive demand (e.g., from tasks with planning time to tasks without) requires increasingly skilled *access* to and *control* over current interlanguage L2 resources.

In this proposal, the criteria for grading and sequencing tasks, using these characteristics, are explicit. *Interactional demands* of pedagogic tasks *are not graded and sequenced*. The task conditions, e.g., +/– one-way flow of information, +/– equal status and role, are replicated each time pedagogic task versions are performed. A rationale for this, offered only briefly here, is that holding task conditions constant is important to ensuring transfer of training to real-world contexts. The more task conditions are practiced in pedagogic versions, the more elaborate and consolidated the scripts become for real-world performance (Schank & Abelson, 1977), on which successful transfer will draw, outside the classroom (Broad, 1997). *Cognitive demands* of pedagogic tasks, however, *are graded and sequenced*. Simpler versions with respect to all relevant cognitive demand characteristics are performed first, and then task complexity (i.e., cognitive demands) is gradually increased on subsequent versions to target task levels. Task complexity is, therefore, the *sole* basis for pedagogic task sequencing.

There are two stages in which task complexity is increased, and which are decision points for task and syllabus design. In each sequence of pedagogic tasks, relevant performative/procedural variables are first increased in complexity (so if the target task requires dual task performance, without planning time, then planning time is first provided, and the dual task characteristics are first performed separately). The rationale for this is to promote access to and consolidate the learner's current L2 interlanguage system during pedagogic task performance. Subsequently increasing performative and procedural demands to target task levels thereby promotes increased automatic access to, and learner "control" over, the current system in responding to pedagogic task demands.

In the second stage, once the performative/procedural demands have reached targetlike levels, cognitive/conceptual demands are gradually increased to targetlike levels. As described above, these can direct learners' attentional and memory resources to aspects of the L2 system needed to encode increasingly complex concepts, and to meet increasingly complex functional demands requiring their expression in language. This promotes analysis and development of the current interlanguage system. Increasing these demands should lead to more *accurate* and *complex* learner production, more *noticing* of task relevant input, and heightened memory for it, and so lead to more *uptake* of forms made salient in the input through various focus on form interventions.

Conclusion

The proposal for grading and sequencing tasks made above, and for task characteristics that can be manipulated by materials and syllabus designers for this purpose, has been, in large part, motivated by theories of cognitive processing in cognitive psychology and by findings from SLA research. Only in the later stages of the twentieth century did it become possible to motivate pedagogic design and decision-making in this way. Very similar cognitive-processing approaches to task analysis, grading, and sequencing are now currently widespread in many other areas of instructional design (see e.g., Hollnagel, 2003; Schraagen, Chipman, & Shalin, 2000). Very similar philosophies and broad principles of instructed learning, too, also underlie the proposals that have been made for learn-by-doing simulations, and the use of tasks, in other areas of education: "... children are learning in a decontextualised fashion. Lessons are taught in a way in which use of knowledge or skills is divorced from how they would be used in real life ... When students learn how, they inevitably learn content knowledge in the service of accomplishing their task" (Schank, Berman, & MacPherson, 1999, pp. 165–6). The shift from synthetic to analytic approaches to syllabus design, reflected in the sequencing of sections in this chapter, is one that can be expected to continue. Future research, theory, and practice in L2 syllabus design would do well to look to these other areas of instructional theory and curriculum development for the insights they can offer, while continuing to integrate them with what is known of the processes constraining and promoting L2 acquisition.

REFERENCES

Anderson, J. R. (1992). Automaticity and the ACT* theory. *American Journal of Psychology* 105, 165–80.

Breen, M. (1984). Process syllabuses for the language classroom. In C. J. Brumfit (ed.), *General English syllabus design* (pp. 47–60). Oxford: Pergamon.

Broad, M. (1997). Overview of transfer of training: From learning to performance. *Performance Improvement Quarterly* 10, 2, 7–21.

Brockett, C. (2000). *A communicative framework for introductory Japanese language curricula.* Washington State Japanese Language Curriculum Guidelines Committee: Second Language Teaching and Curriculum Center, Technical Report # 20. Honolulu: University of Hawai'i Press.

Bygate, M., Skehan, P., & Swain, M. (eds.) (2001). *Researching pedagogic tasks: Second language learning, teaching and testing.* London: Longman.

Candlin, C. (1984). Syllabus design as a critical process. In C. J. Brumfit (ed.), *General English syllabus design* (pp. 29–46). Oxford: Pergamon.

Clarke, D. (1991). The negotiated syllabus: What is it and is it likely to work? *Applied Linguistics* 12, 13–28.

Crombie, W. (1985a). *Process and relation in discourse and language learning.* Oxford: Oxford University Press.

Crombie, W. (1985b). *Discourse and language learning: A relational approach to syllabus design.* Oxford: Oxford Uniiversity Press.

DeKeyser, R. M. (2001). Automaticity and automatization. In P. Robinson (ed.), *Cognition and second language instruction* (pp. 125–51). Cambridge: Cambridge University Press.

Doughty, C. J. (2001). Cognitive underpinnings of focus on form. In P. Robinson (ed.), *Cognition and second language instruction* (pp. 206–57). Cambridge: Cambridge University Press.

Doughty, C. J. & Williams, J. (1998). Pedagogical choices in focus on form. In C. J. Doughty & J. Williams (eds.), *Focus on form in classroom second language acquisition* (pp. 197–262). New York: Cambridge University Press.

Ellis, N. (2005). At the interface: Dynamic interactions of implicit and explicit knowledge. *Studies in Second Language Acquisition 27*, 305–52.

Ellis, R. (1989). Are classroom and naturalistic acquisition the same? A study of the classroom acquisition of German word order rules. *Studies in Second Language Acquisition 11*, 305–28.

Ellis, R. (1993). The structural syllabus and second language acquisition. *TESOL Quarterly 27*, 91–113.

Ellis, R. (1997). *SLA research and language teaching.* Oxford: Oxford University Press.

Ellis, R. (2003). *Task-based language learning and teaching.* Oxford: Oxford University Press.

Ellis, R. (ed.) (2005). *Planning and task performance in a second language.* Amsterdam: John Benjamins.

Ellis, R. & Noboyushi, J. (1993). Focused communication tasks. *ELT Journal 47*, 203–10.

Fotos, S. & Ellis, R. (1991). Communicating about grammar: A task-based approach. *TESOL Quarterly 25*, 87–112.

Garcia-Mayo, M. P. (ed.) (2007). *Investigating tasks in formal language learning.* Clevedon, UK: Multilingual Matters.

Gries, S. Th. (2008). Corpus analysis and second language acquisition data. In P. Robinson & N. C. Ellis (eds.), *Handbook of cognitive linguistics and second language acquisition* (pp. 406–31) London: Routledge.

Hollnagel, E. (ed.) (2003). *Handbook of cognitive task design.* Mahwah, NJ: Lawrence Erlbaum.

Hornby, A. S. (1959). *The teaching of structural words and sentence patterns.* Oxford: Oxford University Press.

Howatt, A. P. & Widdowson, H. G. (2004). *A history of English language teachng*, 2nd edn. Oxford: Oxford University Press.

Johnson, K. (1996). *Language teaching and skill learning.* Oxford: Blackwell.

Kellerman, E. (1985). Input and second language acquisition theory. In S. Gass & C. Madden (eds.), *Input in second language acquisition* (pp. 345–53). Rowley, MA: Newbury House.

Lightbown, P. (1983). Exploring relationships between developmental and instructional sequences. In H. G. Seliger & M. H. Long (eds.), *Classroom oriented research in second language acquisition* (pp. 217–43). Rowley, MA: Newbury House.

Long, M. H. (1985). A role for instruction in second language acquisition. In K. Hyltenstam & M. Pienemann (eds.), *Modeling and assessing second language acquisition* (pp. 77–99). Clevedon, UK: Multilingual Matters.

Long, M. H. (2000). Focus on form in task-based language teaching. In R. Lambert & E. Shohamy (eds.), *Language policy and pedagogy: Essays in honor of Ronald Walton* (pp. 181–96). Amsterdam: John Benjamins.

Long, M. H. (ed.) (2005). *Second language needs analysis.* New York: Cambridge University Press.

Long, M. H. (2007). *Problems in SLA*. Mahwah, NJ: Lwrence Erlbaum.

Long, M. H. & Crookes, G. (1993). Units of analysis in syllabus design: The case for task. In G. Crookes & S. Gass (eds.), *Tasks in a pedagogical context* (pp. 9–54). Clevedon, UK: Multilingual Matters.

Long, M. H. & Robinson, P. (1998). Focus on form: Theory, research, and practice. In C. J. Doughty & J. Williams (eds.), *Focus on form in classroom SLA* (pp. 15–41). New York: Cambridge University Press.

Loschky, L. & Bley-Vroman, R. (1993). Grammar and task-based methodology. In G. Crookes & S. Gass (eds.), *Tasks and language learning: Integrating theory and practice* (pp. 123–67). Clevedon, UK: Mulitilingual Matters.

Mackey, A. (1999). Input, interaction and second language development. *Studies in Second Language Acquisition* 21, 557–87.

Munby, J. (1978). *Communicative syllabus design*. Cambridge: Cambridge University Press.

Nunan, D. (1996). *Atlas*. Boston, MA: Heinle and Heinle.

Nunan, D. (2004). *Task-based language teaching*. Cambridge: Cambridge University Press.

Palmer, H. (1922). *The scientific study and teaching of languages*. London: Harrap.

Pienemann, M. (1989). Is language teachable? *Applied Linguistics* 10, 52–79.

Reigeluth, C. M. (ed.) (1999). *Instructional-design theories and models: A new paradigm of instructional theory*, vol. 2. Mahwah, NJ: Lawrence Erlbaum.

Richards, J. (1990). *The language teaching matrix*. Cambridge: Cambridge University Press.

Richards, J., Gordon, D., & Harper, A. (1995). *Listen for it: A task-based listening course*. Oxford: Oxford University Press.

Richterich, R. (1972). *A model for the definition of language needs of adults learning a modern language*. Strasbourg: Council of Europe.

Robinson, P. (1995). Task complexity and second language narrative discourse. *Language Learning* 45, 99–140.

Robinson, P. (1996a). *Consciousness, rules and instructed second language acquisition*. New York: Peter Lang.

Robinson, P. (ed.) (1996b). *Task complexity and second language syllabus design: Data-based studies and speculations*. Special issue of *University of Queensland Working papers in Language and Linguistics*. Brisbane: CLTR.

Robinson, P. (1997). Individual differences and the fundamental similarity of implicit and explicit adult second language learning. *Language Learning* 47, 45–99.

Robinson, P. (2001). Task complexity, task difficulty and task production: Exploring interactions in a componential framework. *Applied Linguistics* 22, 27–58.

Robinson, P. (2002). Learning conditions, aptitude complexes and SLA: A framework for research and pedagogy. In P. Robinson (ed.), *Individual differences and instructed language learning* (pp. 110–33). Amsterdam: John Benjamins.

Robinson, P. (2003a). Attention and memory during SLA. In C. J. Doughty & M. H. Long (eds.), *Handbok of second language acquisition* (pp. 630–78). Oxford: Blackwell.

Robinson, P. (2003b). The Cognition Hypothesis of adult, task-based language learning. *Second Language Studies* 21, 45–107. www.hawaii.edu/sls/uhwpesl/21(2)/Robinson.pdf.

Robinson, P. (2005a). Aptitude and second language acquisition. *Annual Review of Applied Linguistics* 25, 46–73.

Robinson, P. (2005b). Cognitive complexity and task sequencing: A review of studies in a componential framework for second language task design. *International Review of Applied Linguistics* 43, 1–32.

Robinson, P. (2007a). Aptitude, abilities, contexts and practice. In R. M. DeKeyser (ed.), *Practice in second language learning: Perspectives from applied linguistics and cognitive psychology* (pp. 256–86). Cambridge: Cambridge University Press.

Robinson, P. (2007b). Criteria for classifying and sequencing pedagogic tasks. In M. P. Garcia-Mayo (ed.), *Investigating tasks in formal language learning* (pp. 7–27). Clevedon, UK: Multilingual Matters.

Robinson, P. (2007c). Task complexity, theory of mind and intentional reasoning: Effects on L2 production, interaction, uptake and perceptions of task difficulty. In P. Robinson & R. Gilabert (eds.), *Task complexity, the Cognition Hypothesis and second language instruction*. Special issue of *International Review of Applied Linguistics* 45, 195–215.

Robinson, P. & Gilabert, R. (2007). Task complexity,the Cognition Hypothesis and second language learning and performance. In P. Robinson & R. Gilabert (eds.), *Task complexity, the Cognition Hypothesis and second language*. Special issue of *International Review of Applied Linguistics* 45, 161–76.

Robinson, P. & Ross, S. (1996). The development of task-based testing in EAP programs. *Applied Linguistics* 17, 455–76.

Robinson, P., Ting, S., & Urwin, J. (1995). Investigating second language task complexity. *RELC Journal* 25, 62–79.

Schank, R. & Abelson, R. (1977). *Scripts, plans, goals and understanding*. Hillsdale, NJ: Lawrence Erlbaum.

Schank, R., Berman, T., & Macpherson, K. (1999). Learning by doing. In C. M. Reigeluth (ed.), *Instructional-design theories and models: A new paradigm of instructional theory*, vol. 2. (pp. 161–82). Mahwah, NJ: Lawrence Erlbaum.

Schraagen, J. M., Chipman, S. F., & Shalin, V. L. (eds.) (2000). *Cognitive task analysis*. Mahwah, NJ: Lawrence Erlbaum.

Selinker, L. & Lakshmanan, U. (1992). Language transfer and fossilization. In S. Gass & L. Selinker (eds.), *Language transfer in language learning* (pp. 196–215). Amsterdam: John Benjamins.

Sinclair, J. McH. (2004). *Trust the text*. London: Collins.

Skehan, P. (1996). A framework for task-based approaches to instruction. *Applied Linguistics* 17, 34–59.

Skehan, P. (1998). *A cognitive approach to language learning.* Oxford: Oxford University Press.

Skehan, P. & Foster, P. (2001). Cognition and tasks. In P. Robinson (ed.), *Cognition and second language instruction* (pp. 183–205). Cambridge: Cambridge University Press.

Van Ek, J. (1976). *The threshold level for modern language learning in schools*. London: Longman.

White, R. (1988). *The ELT curriculum: Design, management, innovation*. Oxford: Blackwell.

Widdowson, H. G. (1978). *Teaching language as communication*. Oxford: Oxford University Press.

Widdowson, H. G. (1990). *Aspects of language teaching*. Oxford: Oxford University Press.

Wilkins, D. (1976). *Notional syllabuses*. Oxford: Oxford University Press.

Willis, D. (1990). *The lexical syllabus: A new approach to language teaching*. London: Collins.

Willis, J. (1996). *A framework for task-based learning*. Oxford: Longman.

FURTHER READING

Council of Europe (2001). *Common European Framework of Reference for Languages: Learning, teaching, assessment*. Cambridge: Cambridge University Press.

Long, M. H. & Crookes, G. (1992). Three approaches to task-based syllabus design. *TESOL Quarterly* 26, 27–56.

Nunan, D. (1988). *Syllabus design*. Oxford: Oxford University Press.

Prabhu, N. S. (1987). *Second language pedagogy.* Oxford: Oxford University Press.

Richards, J. (2001). *The second language curriculum.* Cambridge: Cambridge University Press.

Robinson, P. (2001). Task complexity, cognitive resources, and second language syllabus design: A triadic framework for examining task influences on SLA In P. Robinson (ed.), *Cognition and second language instruction* (pp. 285–317). Cambridge: Cambridge University Press.

Robinson, P. & Gilabert, R. (eds.) (2007). *Task complexity, the Cognition Hypothesis and second language instruction.* Special issue of *International Review of Applied Linguistics* 45, 161–289.

18 Advances in Materials Design

ALAN WATERS

To derive the design of an object from its natural functions and conditions.
Walter Gropius

Introduction

Any discussion of the topic of this chapter must begin with a clarification of the central terms involved. "Materials" can, of course, mean any or all of the very wide range of resources capable of aiding language learning. Here, however, it refers to major international language teaching textbooks, such as the *Headway* (e.g., Soars & Soars, 2003), *Interchange* (e.g., Richards, Hull, & Proctor, 2004) and other series. This is partly for reasons of space – the field is vast, and only a small part of it can therefore be covered here (and even then, not comprehensively) – but primarily in order to connect what follows with previous and ongoing discussions on the topic of developments in materials design, many of which have focused on the same type of resource. Also, because of the relative ubiquity of materials of this kind, such a focus makes it more likely that readers will already be familiar with and/or able to refer personally to the examples cited.

This leaves much out of account, particularly as the majority of language teaching materials used around the world, especially in state educational systems, are probably locally produced. Although unavoidable in this context, this is obviously an important omission, and one of a number of aspects of materials design (as will be seen) where a good deal more research might be undertaken. It should also be mentioned that all the samples of materials referred to are concerned with the teaching of English as a foreign language. Nevertheless, the underlying principles and issues involved should be of relevance to all areas of foreign language teaching.

It is also important to attempt to define the sense in which the term "advances" is being used. At least two major perspectives exist regarding the matter. The first of these is an applied linguistics point of view, as expressed in, e.g., Littlejohn (1992), Tomlinson (1998, 2003), and others. In a nutshell, this perspective argues that the design of teaching materials should, as far as possible, reflect advances in academic theorizing and research concerning language, language learning, and education. The second view is what might be termed an "audience-based" one – that is, a perspective about materials design which makes primary reference to perceptions of the needs of end users of teaching materials. Though present in the literature on materials design to a limited extent (see, e.g., Bell & Gower, 1998; Mares, 2003; Richards, 2001), this view has been expressed mainly in the form of concrete developments in various aspects of materials design, as prompted by authors' and publishers' "readings" of audience feedback, i.e., their under-standing of what design features are seen to work best in order to facilitate language learning and teaching in the situations where the materials will be used.

In practice, these two trends have often intermingled, with many sets of teaching materials attempting to reflect, to varying degrees, insights from applied linguistics, as well as those based on perceptions of audience need. Nevertheless, in academic discussions of the topic, it is the applied linguistics perspective which has tended to predominate. "Advances" in materials design have therefore usually been interpreted rather one-sidedly, as a reflection of the extent to which textbooks have succeeded in incorporating features which have been seen as desirable from an academic point of view.

It has been recognized for some time, however, that the general relationship between applied linguistics and language teaching should be a dialectical one, thereby granting due cognizance to issues of practice as the starting point (though not the only end) for "applied" intellectual enquiry (see, e.g., Widdowson, 2000). In what follows, therefore, the term "advances" has been conceived of in the first instance as a function of those developments in materials design that can be seen as likely to contribute to making classroom language learning, in the type of situations the materials are intended for, a more positive experience than would otherwise be the case. In other words, the overall criterion being used is one of "fitness for purpose," regardless of "theoretical 'correctness'." As a corollary, a realigned and expanded research agenda in this area is delineated, with a view to creating the means for the two main materials design perspectives identified to develop a more productive symbiosis than has occurred hitherto.

The remainder of this chapter consists, first of all, of a brief reprise of the findings of two "benchmark" reviews of developments in materials design from the late 1980s. This serves as a "baseline" for the subsequent sections, which are concerned with investigating how a number of the main features of materials analyzed in the two reviews, as well as other aspects, have developed sub-sequently, via an examination of a range of contemporary textbooks. The final section attempts to draw the main threads together and to consider the implica-tions for further development in this area.

Departure

The two earlier textbook surveys in question are Rossner (1988) and Clarke (1989). In Rossner, given the general acceptance at the time, as now, of the view that the goal of language learning is communication, the point of departure is "to examine what materials-writers have understood to be the role of their work in the communicative classroom" (Rossner, 1988, p. 140). On the basis of an analysis of a representative cross-section of coursebooks (e.g., Swan & Walter, 1984), supplementary materials (e.g., Frank, Beres, & Rinvolucri, 1989) and "resource books" (e.g., Sion, 1985) of the time, Rossner concludes that:

> materials . . . have not suddenly become "communicative" . . . ; rather, materials have become more and more varied as the drive for more and more interesting, and less and less constraining, ways of carrying out language "practice" in the classroom has gathered pace. (p. 142)

In other words, a more "traditional" focus is perceived to have remained intact, despite the addition of a communicative "overlay."

The following main criticisms of the materials are also made. First, they are seen to suffer from an "embarras de richesses." Getting to know, selecting appropriately, and using them judiciously are therefore viewed as more complex and time-consuming tasks than was the case in the pre-communicative era. Second, most of their communication activities are not regarded as providing "true communication with a real purpose" (Rossner, 1988, p. 160), because of their frequent artificiality and lack of relevance to learners' lives. Third, the predominance of UK and US publishers is seen as "dangerous," since, in general, they are "unable to avoid projecting through their topics and their approaches to them, through the language they select, and through the very ethos of the activities they craft, values and educational attitudes which are intrinsically Western and mainly 'Anglo-Saxon'" (p. 160). The review as a whole concludes by saying that "In the communicative era, more than ever before, materials should not seek to mold teachers and learners but should be available for molding by them" (p. 161). As a whole, thus, the materials in question are seen as insufficiently suited to the needs of their intended audiences because of their logistical complexity, lack of personalization, and the cultural bias of their content and methodology. How subsequent sets of materials have fared with respect to all these features will also be explored in due course.

Like Rossner, the purpose of Clarke (1989) was to "indicate some of the ways in which the now established principles of communicative language learning have been translated into actual teaching materials" (p. 73). In doing so, the first part of the paper (i.e., sections 2–8) focuses mainly on the "authenticity debate," in order to prepare the way, in the second part, for an analysis of the extent to which various concepts concerned with the notion of "authenticity" – of text, text use, and learner response – can be seen to have influenced the design of a range of then contemporary textbooks (e.g., Abbs & Freebairn, 1980; Soars & Soars, 1986; Swan & Walter, 1985).

With respect to authenticity of text, many of the materials are seen as having gone "to considerable lengths to stimulate [sic] real materials and to reflect 'real life' in order to create an aura of authenticity" (Rossner, 1988, p. 79). However, at the same time, some of these features, such as photographs, are seen as having "very little or no direct pedagogical value," and there is a "widespread phenomenon of 'simulated realia'," i.e., graphics, which "do not involve reproduction of the actual text but seek to suggest an identity with some authentic original by devices such as drawing book shapes round lists of appointments to suggest diaries" (p. 79). The latter is also seen to be a feature of many of the listening texts used in the materials, most of which are "scripted or semi-scripted," despite claims to authenticity (p. 80).

In terms of the authenticity of tasks to texts, traditional *wh-* comprehension questions continue to dominate: "the authentic input data provide little more than pretexts for traditional 'reading comprehension' activities based, for the most part, on irrelevant details being excavated for no particular reason, with no further use proposed for this information" (Clarke, 1989, p. 81). "Authentic materials (which are by definition user-specific)" are thereby seen as being used "for the development of 'general' reading and 'comprehension' skills" (p. 81). Similarly, authentic texts are also reported as being frequently used as vehicles for traditional language focus exercises, such as substitution tables, and the texts themselves are often modified, e.g., by having gaps inserted in them. As a result "the focus of those materials tends to remain on the forms or functions of the language rather than the use to which the language can be put" (p. 82).

Authenticity of context (i.e., the building up of a realistic context of use around the language being focused on) is also seen as underdeveloped in most of the materials in question, with the language practice factor remaining dominant. Similarly, the development in the materials of authenticity of the task to the learner is seen as circumscribed by the difficulties of creating sufficient individuation and personalization at the same time as attempting to cater to a mass market: "Commercial requirements to sell as widely as possible necessarily vitiate the authenticity of much of this material insofar as the discourse types, situations and roles proposed can by no means be guaranteed to evoke learner authentication" (p. 83).

In overall terms, thus, the most obvious feature of Clarke's analysis, like Rossner's, is the identification of a number of fundamental ways – principally to do with issues of "realism" – in which the majority of the teaching materials reviewed were seen to have failed to live up to the theoretical ideals of the communicative approach. However, Clarke concludes by pointing out that the theoretical basis for advocating authenticity in teaching materials is characterized by contradictory stances, even though there is a tendency for this to be overlooked, and for the pro-authenticity view to predominate regardless. He feels it is therefore important to note that "the use of authentic materials does not inevitably result in performance-based activity, while such activity *can* be generated without the use of authentic materials" (1989, p. 84, original emphasis). He characterizes the teaching materials of the time in overall terms as follows:

> While most modern textbooks work hard at achieving at least the aura of authenticity, it should be noted that much of their content still focuses on knowledge of the

language rather than its use . . . it is quite apparent that there is no escaping from the production of pedagogical materials and no need to conceal the fact that there will always be a need for transitional materials, which, while not in themselves authentic, can be authenticated by the learner. The extent to which modern materials tend not to exemplify the communicative principles they purport to embody seems to support this assertion. (p. 84)

The implication here – that materials have to address needs that extend beyond or in contradistinction to the incorporation of "authentic data" – echoes the flavor of the discussion in the second part of the introduction to this chapter. Clarke appears to argue that the reason why the materials in question have the characteristics identified is not so much because of shortcomings on the part of the authors and publishers, but because the goal of authenticity in its conventional formulation is inappropriate, since what counts as "authentic" from the learner's perspective may well be a different matter.

In other words, a fundamental dichotomy of tendencies is perceived to exist. On the one hand, the main thrust of applied linguistics was (and has continued to be) toward accounting for the factors involved in "natural" language *use*, and advocating that these should form the basis of teaching materials. On the other hand, however, we have teaching materials which, while decked out in the trappings of target situation authenticity, remain, at root, fundamentally language *learning* oriented, i.e., based on the view that the kind of authenticity most required for foreign language learning should relate first and foremost to the learner as a current interim acquirer rather than as a potential future user of the language. As will be seen, a similar tension underlies most subsequent developments in language teaching textbook design.

Analysis

Authenticity

Authenticity of text

In the *New Headway Intermediate* Teacher's Book (Soars, Soars, & Sayer, 2003), the authors state that the Student's Book reading and listening texts "come from authentic sources with the necessary adaptations to suit the level" (p. 4). This is confirmed by an examination of the texts in the Student's Book itself, which have many of the attributes of authentic texts in terms of layout, subject-matter, cohesion, and so on, but, in most cases, the language, while natural-sounding, lacks the idiomaticity and complexity of normal native-speaker discourse. They are thus "simple accounts" (Widdowson, 1979, p. 184). Much the same appears to hold true for a wide range of other recent coursebooks, e.g., *New Hotline Elementary* (Hutchinson, 1998), *Cutting Edge Intermediate* (Cunningham & Moor, 1999), *Language to go Intermediate* (Crace & Wileman, 2002), *In English Elementary* (Viney & Viney, 2004a), *Interchange Student's Book 1* (Richards, Hull, & Proctor, 2005), and so on. In other words, rather than a move toward greater use of genuinely authentic texts, there seems to have been a consolidation of the status ante quo, i.e., the use of pseudo-authentic or specially-constructed texts has become something of a norm in modern textbook design.

Authenticity of text use

The way in which such texts are used in most modern textbooks tends to be mainly for comprehension or language work purposes, although there are also often pre- and/or post-comprehension or language work activities which involve the learners in relating the information content of the texts to their own lives. Thus, in *Language to go Intermediate* (Crace & Wileman, 2002, p. 69), the "Listening" section begins by getting the students to look at pictures of a number of possible future electronic communication inventions and describe them. They then listen to four short texts about the inventions and match each of them to the relevant picture. After this, they listen again in order to match a list of the inventions with the year when it is predicted they will be available. This is followed by a "Grammar focus" section containing a number of exercises concerned with the main language point (*will* and *will have done*) in the texts. The page ends with a "Get talking" section in which students make predictions about their futures.

Although there is variety in terms of whether the main focus is more or completely on the comprehension or language development side, and as to whether there are also activities which relate the language and/or ideas to the students' own lives, many other recent textbooks follow the same basic pattern in terms of listening and reading text exploitation (see, e.g., *Cutting Edge Intermediate* (Cunningham & Moor, 1999, pp. 104–5); *Interchange Student's Book* 1 (Richards et al., 2005, p. 111); *New Hotline Elementary* (Hutchinson, 1998, pp. 58–9); *In English Elementary* (Viney & Viney, 2004a, pp. 142–8); *New Headway Intermediate Student's Book* (Soars & Soars, 2003, pp. 84–5), and so on). Thus, in overall terms, as with the type of text used, most contemporary textbooks, while allowing for a measure of authentic text use via activities which encourage the learners to relate the content to their own lives, tend to focus primarily on exploiting them for comprehension and language development work.

Authenticity of task to learner

As with trends in terms of text type and text use, communication tasks in many modern textbooks appear to have become more closely based on the likely knowledge and interests of the typical learner rather than involving communication situations taken more directly from real life. They are therefore mostly of a kind that might also occur outside the classroom, but appear to have been constructed primarily in order to provide an opportunity to use the language being studied in conjunction with the students' existing world. Thus, for example, in *Cutting Edge Intermediate*, Module 7, the main task (Cunningham & Moor, 1999, pp. 74–5) is concerned with getting the learners to make a list of "dos and don'ts" about everyday behavior for visitors to their countries; in *New Headway Intermediate*,

Unit 11, one of the main tasks (Soars & Soars, 2003, pp. 90–1) involves the students in making a poster concerned with asking and answering a question about an area of world knowledge; in *Language to go Intermediate*, the main task in Unit 29 (Crace & Wileman, 2002, pp. 60–1) consists of having the learners discuss what they will or might do if a variety of everyday situations were to occur; in *In English Elementary*, Unit 27 culminates in a task (Viney & Viney, 2004a, p. 141) in which the learners give their views about the likelihood of a variety of predictions about the future of the world; in *New Hotline Elementary*, Unit 7 ends by getting the learners to stage a class fashion show (Hutchinson, 1998, p. 62); and so on. The primary concern of such tasks appears to be one of authenticity to the learning situation, i.e., the provision of tasks that have the potential to enable the learners to put the language knowledge in question into practice in a lifelike way, by being geared sufficiently closely to their level, interests, and so on – a matter of attempting to simulate rather than replicate real-life use.

In overall terms, thus, many major textbooks have evolved to reinforce and develop further the tendencies noted by Rossner and Clarke at the end of the 1980s, namely, on the one hand, to deploy pseudo-authentic texts and exploit them in inauthentic ways, and, on the other, to move away from (more authentic) "target" tasks and closer toward (less authentic) "pedagogical" ones (Nunan, 2004, pp. 1–4). This has occurred despite a continuing growth of interest in and belief in the pedagogical value of "real language data" and real-world tasks in applied linguistics (see, e.g., Carter, Hughes, & McCarthy, 1998; Skehan, 1998).

This trend appears to have occurred because of the important pragmatic advantages which can thereby accrue to textbook writers in their attempts to make their materials fit for their primary purposes. In reflecting on their experiences in writing a major international textbook series, Bell and Gower (1998) say, "our original intention to draw target language out of authentic texts failed at the intermediate level, partly because of the difficulty of finding texts which contained clear examples of the focus language together with interesting content" (p. 127). They also go on to add that, as the writing process progressed:

> it was clear there were going to be problems with unadapted authentic texts. Finding texts with a generative topic of the right length and the right level of comprehensibility for the level . . . as well as an accessible degree of cultural reference and humour was not easy. So we compromised on this ambition and wonder now whether we should have compromised more and simply gone for texts which were interesting. (p. 128)

In other words, texts for learning purposes clearly need to satisfy a number of needs, primarily related to fitness for the learning purpose, and "authentic" texts may often be inappropriate in this respect. It therefore seems plausible to regard the long-term trend away from "authenticity" and toward "artificiality" in textbooks as concerned with increasing their potential to cater more adequately to the full range of students' learning needs. Artificial but life-like texts make it possible to provide a much greater variety of texts that are likely to be accessible to most learners than would otherwise be the case; their use as vehicles for comprehension and/or language work is not inauthentic to the purposes for which they were constructed; and the use of "pedagogic" tasks can increase relevance to the learners' world, while still providing a meaningful simulation of real-life language use.

Language practice

Despite the addition of various elements giving the textbooks they reviewed a more communicative "gloss," both Rossner (1988) and Clarke (1989), as has already been pointed out, saw them as nevertheless retaining an overall focus on "language practice." Since those reviews were written, academic ideas in this area have, in general, continued to move further and further away from viewing a direct focus on the conscious study of language forms as being a desirable pedagogical strategy, with various more "indirect" alternatives being favored instead, such as "consciousness-raising" (Ellis, 1993). However, while many textbooks have for some time incorporated activities of this kind, a language practice element has also remained prominent and, over the years, rather than declined, appears to have actually increased.

Thus, for example, in Unit 7 of the original, 1986 version of *Headway Intermediate* (Soars & Soars, 1986), the language work element comprises two Presentation and Practice sections, the first consisting of two consciousness-raising (C-R) exercises concerning the meaning of the main language structure in focus (the present perfect) and two related "practice" exercises, the second a further C-R activity and related practice exercise, plus a "language review" section (i.e., overall explanation of the rules), a translation exercise, and an "analysis" exercise. In the subsequent Skills Development section, there is a further analysis activity and related practice exercise, and a focused role-play. So all in all, the unit contains three C-R and five language practice activities. In the equivalent unit in the latest edition of the same textbook (Soars & Soars, 2003), the language work concerning the main language focus (once again, the present perfect) is as follows. In the first two pages (pp. 54–5) there is a practice exercise (Test your grammar) in which the students show their existing ability to use the form under focus, as well as to analyze it. This is followed by two fill-in-the-gap practice exercises and a C-R exercise. In the next two pages (pp. 56–7) there is one C-R activity, three analysis ones, and seven language practice exercises. The Listening and Speaking section on p. 61 contains two further practice exercises. There are, thus, altogether, two C-R and twelve language practice exercises concerned with the main language focus of the unit in this edition.[1] Similarly, in Unit 6 of the original edition of *Hotline Elementary* (Hutchinson, 1991), which focuses on the past continuous, there were three C-R and seven language practice exercises. In the later edition, *New Hotline Elementary* (Hutchinson, 1998), the equivalent unit contains three C-R and thirteen language practice exercises. Thus, while the number of CR exercises in the two textbooks has remained reasonably similar, the language practice ones have increased substantially.

Many other modern textbooks also contain a substantial proportion of exercises of both kinds. On the basis of their survey of nine sets of materials published between 1991 and 2000 (with the majority having been issued in the latter half of this period), Nitta and Gardner (2005) show that approximately equal numbers of C-R and language practice exercises were used. As they conclude, "While recent SLA research continues to provide arguments against the efficacy of practising tasks, the evidence from our analysis suggests that they still occupy an essential place in general ELT materials . . . moreover, many suggest using workbooks for further practice" (p. 9). However, as they also go on to say:

> Notwithstanding this continued emphasis on practice, our findings have revealed that contemporary coursebooks usually juxtapose C-R tasks with practising tasks. Rather than exclusively selecting one approach, material writers tactfully design grammar syllabuses building on both C-R and practice. Accordingly, though researchers insist on the effectiveness of C-R rather than practice in theory – and rationally their arguments are convincing – ELT practitioners may not be prepared to abandon the familiar, tried and true "practice" exercises. (p. 10)

In other words, it appears that the pragmatic experience of classroom teaching – as it feeds into materials writing via data obtained from practitioners by publishers' agents (Donovan, 1998) – has added a dimension to textbook design in this area which is generally lacking in the academic paradigm, based, as much of it is, mainly on a model of "natural" language use not redolent of the circumstances pertaining in the average school-level or adult language learning situation. As Widdowson (2003) points out (cf. Prabhu, 1992):

> a moment's reflection makes it clear that what is taught in classrooms in certain crucial respects *cannot* be in accordance with actual language use. Actual language use occurs naturally within the continuities of social life, appropriately activated by context, and motivated by the needs of communication and the expression of communal and individual identity. The language subject does not occur naturally at all: it appears, like other subjects, discontinuously on the timetable, fitted into a schedule as suited to administrative convenience. Usually, there is no natural communal or individual impetus to use the language: contexts have to be contrived and motivation created. And this is done within restricted units of time called periods and units of activity called lessons, which are organized into such things as exercises, tasks, tests, group work, and so on. Furthermore, these events are, for the most part, controlled and orchestrated by teacher authority, and directed at an eventual measurable outcome. On the face of it, it is hard to see any resemblance to the natural conditions of actual language use at all. (p. 112, original emphasis)

Thus, rather than perceiving the continued or increased provision for so much practice work in textbooks as regrettable (as in, e.g., Tomlinson et al., 2001), it can be viewed more positively as evidence of a need for re-thinking research and theorizing in this area. In other words, as Swan (2006) argues, the policy adopted by textbooks in this matter can be regarded as helping to avoid the perils of a "subtractive" approach:

> Changes in theoretical or pedagogic fashion often come about because of dis-illusionment: our teaching doesn't seem to be getting very good results, and the temptation is to drop what we are doing and look for alternatives. But this may not bring about any net gain. If we are doing too much formal input and not enough communicative output, the solution is to balance things up, not to move to a position where we are doing too much communicative output and not enough formal input . . . Such approaches [i.e., the latter] are nearly always subtractive as well as additive, putting a great deal of emphasis on one or other ingredient of language teaching while neglecting others. (pp. 53–4)

The implications of this policy for the further development of a materials design research agenda within applied linguistics will be considered in the final part of this chapter.

Syllabus/Unit structure

An additive approach is also evident in the way that contemporary textbooks tend to be structured in terms of their "horizontal" (syllabus) and "vertical" (unit) dimensions. In terms of the former, the "multi-syllabus" (Swan & Walter, 1990) is nowadays the norm. Thus, the Contents of each unit in *In English Elementary* include "Language Focus," "Communication Skills/Functions/Formulas," "Topic/Vocabulary," and "Extension" (additional language work, etc.) (Viney & Viney, 2004b, pp. 3–7); in *New Headway Intermediate* (Soars & Soars, 2003), in addition to the Unit Topic (e.g., "It's a wonderful world!"), the categories are "Grammar," "Vocabulary," "Everyday English," "Reading," "Speaking," "Listening," and "Writing"; in *Cutting Edge Intermediate* (Cunningham & Moor, 1999), in addition to the overall Module topic, (e.g., "About you"), the main contents headings are "Language focus," "Vocabulary," "Speaking," "Reading/Listening," "Task," and "After the task." Other books also include additional elements, such as a "learning to learn" syllabus (see, e.g., *New Hotline Elementary* (Hutchinson, 1998)). Such multi-stranded forms of organization typify nearly all modern international textbooks.

Such a trend can be interpreted as a "cover all bases" approach, aimed at ensuring that no "market need" is overlooked, or, more positively, as an implicit recognition of the complex, multi-layered nature of the language learning "task." It can be argued that the earlier type of textbook syllabus, in which only a single aspect tended to predominate (e.g., structures, functions, situations, etc.), probably lessened the extent to which other elements were properly developed. The more explicit acknowledgment of a wider range of syllabus components in modern materials has the potential to reduce this problem, and is more in keeping with (some) contemporary views about language and language learning.

It might be argued, however, that a more appropriate textbook design response to a growing recognition of the complex nature of language learning would have been to *reduce*, rather than increase, the degree of explicit segmentation and specification of the ingredients in the language learning "cake." As Skehan (1996, p. 19) states:

SLA research . . . has established that teaching does not and cannot determine the way the learner's language will develop. The processes by which the learner operates are "natural" processes. Teachers and learners cannot simply "choose" what is to be learned. To a large extent the syllabus is "built in" to the learner.

The development of the multi-syllabus as a mainstay of the modern textbook is therefore noteworthy in terms of the way that, in this respect also, theorizing and research appear to have gone in one direction, and textbook design in another.

In addition to "syntagmatic" textbook structuring of this kind, something of a consensus also seems to have emerged over the last two decades regarding textbook unit structure. The mold appears to have been established in this respect by the appearance of the first *Headway* series (Soars & Soars, 1986) in the 1980s, and boils down to an initial section in which the main area(s) of language being focused on are presented, analyzed, and practiced, and the main subject-matter theme of the unit is introduced; this is followed by a series of skills-based sections in which the same and, often, additional, related language points are cycled through a series of reading, listening, speaking, and, sometimes, writing texts and related activities, most or all of them linked thematically to the subject matter introduced in the first section (see, e.g., Cunningham & Moor, 1999, pp. 48–57; Hutchinson, 2000, pp. 14–21; Soars & Soars, 1998, pp. 38–46). There are, of course, variations on this theme. Some textbooks contain extra sections on matters such as everyday expressions, (see, e.g., Soars & Soars, 2003, p. 93), "learner training" (see, e.g., Hutchinson, 1998, pp. 43 & 52), or include a more integrated, macro task section (see, e.g., Cunningham & Moor, 1999, pp. 96–9), and so on, but it appears that most modern textbooks use a unit structure along the lines indicated.

It can be argued that such a framework is, at root, a development and refinement of the traditional "PPP" (Presentation-Practice-Production) paradigm (Tomlinson, 2001, p. 69), the main differences being a greater focus on communicative practice and production work and the more consistent development of "carrier" content throughout the unit. Thus, the widespread use of a structure of this kind shows that, once again, in this respect as well, the evolution of the textbook since the late 1980s has continued to be not so much a process of wholesale "communicativization," but, rather, the grafting of a communicative "veneer" on to what has remained a basically language-focused stock. It seems likely that this has also occurred for reasons similar to those already discussed, i.e., primarily as a response to the wishes of end users, for whom an overall focus on language work, with a communicative gloss, appears to have remained the priority, despite the widespread criticisms of all forms of PPP in the professional literature in recent years.

However, it is also important to note the existence of exceptions to some aspects of a unit structure of this kind. For example, Crace & Wileman (2002) has a unit length which is much shorter than is typical. Likewise, the *Interchange* series (Richards et al., 2004), although also typically centering around a structural (or, in later parts, functional) area of language, and also possessing a common overall content theme, has a unit structure consisting of 10–12 "mini"-sections (vs. the 4–5 longer sections typical of other textbooks), each of which usually occupies only half a page or less (vs. the whole page or more typical of many other textbooks). Each unit contains two "cycles," each comprising four core sections (three concerned with language presentation and practice, and one with language use), plus additional sections on, e.g., pronunciation, reading, speaking, etc. As a result, there is a proportionally greater amount of language focus than skills work in each unit.

In addition, each of the sections is relatively self-contained, in contrast to the way interconnections will often occur across sections in other textbooks, e.g., in the cases of Activity 4 on p. 56 and Language Focus 2 on p. 62 in Cunningham and Moor (1999), pp. 46–8 and pp. 80–1 in Soars & Soars (2003), and so on. The former also consist of only one, two, or sometimes three activities, none of which is subdivided, once again in contrast to the layout of many other textbooks, in which there are usually 4–5 activities, often subdivided, in each section. Furthermore, texts are relatively short, even at higher levels, as are activity rubrics, giving only the main instructions (once again, in contradistinction to many other coursebooks).

The primary difference between the *Interchange* unit structure and the more typical one described earlier is that the former has a much less "all-embracing" feel to it. Because sections are relatively shorter and less complex, and more self-contained, it seems reasonable to assume that the learning focus is likely to be clearer and the teaching–learning process easier to manage, with both learners and teachers having greater potential freedom to use their preferred modus operandi, since they do not have to engage in so much detail and at such length with texts and activities of the kind used in many other textbooks. The very comprehensiveness of the more typical textbook unit model – with its extensive program of interlinked texts and activities – can thus also be seen as its main potential inherent weakness. Such a structure commits teachers and learners to adopting a particular type of learning–teaching methodology – one that appears to be less widespread and less well suited than other models, among non-native speaker teachers, in particular (see, e.g., Medgyes, 1994: ch. 3) – or requires them to modify or reject it and attempt to use the book in a way to which it may not readily lend itself.

There are also other grounds for asking whether the current predominant textbook unit structure serves the best interests of teachers and learners as well as it might. An important concern in both earlier, as well as more recent, critiques of textbooks (e.g., Atlan, 1995; Tomlinson et al., 2001) is the extent to which, on the one hand, the content of texts and the setting of activities tend to promote an Anglo-Saxon worldview, and on the other, restrict the opportunities for learners to learn by using the context of their own lives. Shorter texts with fewer activities directly related to their content, in the manner of books such as *Interchange*, can, on the face of it, lessen the amount of "investment" learners (and teachers) are required to make before reaching a point where the language can be used meaningfully for their own purposes. This would seem especially important to take into account in view of the increasing recognition in recent years that English is nowadays most often learned for the purpose of communication with other non-native speakers, rather than with native speakers (see, e.g., McKay, 2002).

In other words, just as the communicative approach has gradually come to be seen as a culture-specific rather than context-free methodology, so, perhaps, it is time for some of the design principles underpinning many modern international textbooks to be similarly reappraised, so that they become more attuned to building on the potential that exists within the main styles of language learning and teaching that exist around the world, and cater better to the communication needs of an English as an International Language situation, rather than reflecting so strongly so much in terms of learning methods and content that can be regarded as specific to Western/Anglo-Saxon culture. Rossner's stricture in this respect (see above) can, therefore, still be seen as applying to the majority of cases.

Conclusion

The earlier parts of this chapter have attempted to document a number of the main developments in language teaching materials design over recent years. An historical perspective was adopted, in order to clarify the extent to which the current situation can be seen as a reflection of previous trends. The findings indicate that, first, by and large, in terms of the aspects analyzed, earlier tendencies have been reinforced, with something of an orthodoxy in textbook design having now emerged. Nevertheless, as has also been adduced, other well-established and widely used publications exist which serve to provide something of an alternative to, and potential critique of, the more prevalent model. In addition, in both cases, the analysis indicated that the ontogenesis of the majority of the developments appeared to be related to perceptions of audience need, and were largely in contradistinction to concurrent trends in academic conceptualization.

In terms of the prevailing academic viewpoint, thus, the extent to which the current situation can be seen as representing a set of "advances" in materials design is, of course, problematic. As was noted at the outset, there has been a tendency in academic circles to view advances in textbook design as a function of the extent to which materials reflect succeeding developments in applied linguistics. However, in addition to its "applied science" orientation, such a stance assumes that writers and publishers, in taking the opposite tack, would willingly pursue a course that is against their best interests. It also implies that teachers' and learners' views, when they differ from academic perspectives, are to be discounted (cf. Widdowson, 2003, pp. 130–1).

A sounder stance would, therefore, appear to be one which views academic ideas more as means of illuminating and critiquing textbook design features, rather than being regarded as their prime determiner. Equally, a more humane attitude to the perceptions of textbook users and the efforts of writers and publishers seems called for. As accounts such as Bell and Gower (1998), Richards (2001, ch. 7), and Mares (2003) indicate, arriving at what might constitute a satisfactory textbook design is a difficult, complex, and highly skilled process, involving, in particular, the notion of a *compromise* between what might be theoretically desirable and what is practicable and appropriate in audience terms.

Alternative perspectives of this kind might involve, for example, viewing the notion of authenticity less as a wholesale prescription and more as a safeguard against too much artificiality in texts and activities. Similarly, the less linear, more process-oriented focus on form approach to the teaching of language structures, rather than being seen as a replacement for the PPP paradigm used in many current textbooks, can instead be viewed more productively as a way of raising awareness of the limitations of a language teaching approach which is too segmentary and deterministic; and so on.

Such a realignment of attitudes might also desirably underpin a far larger program of empirical enquiry in applied linguistics into textbook design than has occurred hitherto. For example, very little academic research appears to have been done on attempting to establish what learners and teachers in various situations actually think about competing textbook designs, in terms of the various features which have formed the main focus of the analysis in earlier parts of this chapter. Equally, a larger number of studies of the kind conducted by Hutchinson (1996), into actual textbook use, would be a very useful source of further data for informing optimization of their design. And, of course, third-person accounts of the textbook design process itself would be likely to increase understanding in the area. In such ways, it is to be hoped, both a better basis for determining what might constitute advances in materials design, as well as enhanced means of enabling them to occur, might be achieved.

NOTE

1　At the same time, the later C-R exercises adopt an inductive approach, a trend which has become widespread in other modern textbooks as well.

REFERENCES

Abbs, B. & Freebairn, I. (1980). *Developing strategies: Student's book.* London: Longman.

Atlan, M. (1995). Culture in EFL contexts: Classroom and coursebooks. *Modern English Teacher* 4, 2, 58–60.

Bell, J. & Gower, R. (1998). Writing course materials for the world: A great compromise. In B. Tomlinson (ed.), *Materials development in language teaching* (pp. 116–29). Cambridge: Cambridge University Press.

Carter, R., Hughes, R., & McCarthy, M. (1998). Telling tails: Grammar, the spoken language and materials development. In B. Tomlinson (ed.), *Materials development in language teaching* (pp. 67–86). Cambridge: Cambridge University Press.

Clarke, D. (1989). Communicative theory and its influence on materials production: State-of-the-art article. *Language Teaching* 22, 2, 73–86.

Crace, A. & Wileman, R. (2002). *Language to go intermediate student's book.* Harlow, UK: Pearson Education.

Cunningham, S. & Moor, P. (1999). *Cutting edge intermediate student's book.* Harlow, UK: Pearson Education.

Donovan, P. (1998). Piloting: A publisher's view. In B. Tomlinson (ed.), *Materials development in language teaching* (pp. 149–89). Cambridge: Cambridge University Press.

Ellis, R. (1993). Talking shop: Second language acquisition research: How does it help teachers? *ELT Journal* 47, 1, 3–11.

Frank, C., Beres, M., & Rinvolucri, M. (1989). *Challenge to think.* Oxford: Oxford University Press.

Hutchinson, E. G. (1996). What do teachers and learners actually do with textbooks? Teacher and learner use of a fisheries-based ELT textbook in the Philippines. Unpublished PhD thesis, Lancaster University.

Hutchinson, T. (1991). *Hotline starter student's book.* Oxford: Oxford University Press.

Hutchinson, T. (1998). *New hotline elementary student's book.* Oxford: Oxford University Press.

Hutchinson, T. (2000). *Project 3 student's book.* Oxford: Oxford University Press.

Littlejohn, A. (1992). Why are English language teaching materials the way they are? Unpublished PhD thesis, Lancaster University.

Mares, C. (2003). Writing a coursebook. In B. Tomlinson (ed.), *Developing materials for language teaching* (pp. 130–40). London: Continuum.

McKay, S. L. (2002). *Teaching English as an International Language: Rethinking goals and approaches.* Oxford: Oxford University Press.

Medgyes, P. (1994). *The non-native teacher.* London: Macmillan.

Nitta, R. & Gardner, S. (2005). Consciousness-raising and practice in ELT coursebooks. *ELT Journal* 59, 1, 3–13.

Nunan, D. (2004). *Task-based language teaching.* Cambridge: Cambridge University Press.

Prabhu, N. S. (1992). The dynamics of the language lesson. *TESOL Quarterly* 26, 2, 161–76.

Richards, J. C. (2001). *Curriculum development in language teaching.* New York: Cambridge University Press.

Richards, J. C., Hull, J., & Proctor, S. (2004). *Interchange: Student book 2.* Cambridge: Cambridge University Press.

Richards, J. C., Hull, J., & Proctor, S. (2005). *Interchange: Student book 1.* Cambridge: Cambridge University Press.

Rossner, R. (1988). Materials for communicative language teaching and learning. *Annual Review of Applied Linguistics* 8, 140–63.

Sion, C. (ed.) (1985). *Recipes for tired teachers.* Reading, MA: Addison-Wesley.

Skehan, P. (1996). Second language acquisition research and task-based instruction. In D. Willis & J. Willis (eds.), *Challenge and change in language teaching* (pp. 17–30). Oxford: Macmillan Heinemann.

Skehan, P. (1998). *A cognitive approach to language Learning.* Oxford: Oxford University Press.

Soars, J. & Soars, L. (1986). *Headway intermediate student's book.* Oxford: Oxford University Press.

Soars, J. & Soars, L. (1998). *New headway English course upper-intermediate.* Oxford: Oxford University Press.

Soars, L. & Soars, J. (2003). *New headway intermediate student's book.* Oxford: Oxford University Press.

Soars, L., Soars, J., & Sayer, M. (2003). *New headway intermediate: Teacher's book.* Oxford: Oxford University Press.

Swan, M. (2006). Two out of three ain't enough: The essential ingredients of a language course. In B. Beaven (ed.), *IATEFL Selections 2006* (pp. 45–54). Canterbury: IATEFL.

Swan, M. & Walter, C. (1984). *The Cambridge English course 1*. Cambridge: Cambridge University Press.

Swan, M. & Walter, C. (1985). *The Cambridge English course 2*. Cambridge: Cambridge University Press.

Swan, M. & Walter, C. (1990). *The new Cambridge English course 2: Teacher's book*. Cambridge: Cambridge University Press.

Tomlinson, B. (ed.) (1998). *Materials development in language teaching*. Cambridge: Cambridge University Press.

Tomlinson, B. (2001). Materials development. In R. Carter & D. Nunan (eds.), *Teaching English to speakers of other languages* (pp. 66–71). Cambridge: Cambridge University Press.

Tomlinson, B. (ed.) (2003). *Developing materials for language teaching*. London: Continuum.

Tomlinson, B., Dat, B., Masuhara, H., & Rubdy, R. (2001). Survey review: EFL courses for adults. *ELT Journal* 55, 1, 80–101.

Viney, P. & Viney, K. (2004a). *In English elementary student's book*. Oxford: Oxford University Press.

Viney, P. & Viney, K. (2004b). *In English elementary teacher's book*. Oxford: Oxford University Press.

Widdowson, H. G. (1979). *Explorations in applied linguistics*. Oxford: Oxford University Press.

Widdowson, H. G. (2000). On the limitations of linguistics applied. *Applied Linguistics* 21, 1, 3–25.

Widdowson, H. G. (2003). *Defining issues in English language teaching*. Oxford: Oxford University Press.

FURTHER READING

Byrd, P. (ed.) (1995). *Material writers guide*. Boston, MA, Heinle and Heinle.

Cunningsworth, A. (1995). *Choosing your coursebook*. Oxford: Heinemann.

Hall, D., Hidalgo, A. C., & Jacobs, G. M. (eds.) (1995). *Getting started: Materials writers on materials writing*. Singapore: SEAMEO Regional Language Centre.

Mishan, F. (2005). *Designing authenticity into language learning materials*. Bristol: Intellect.

Renandya, W. A. (ed.) (2003). *Methodology and materials design in language teaching*, Anthology Series 44. Singapore: SEAMEO RELC.

19 Corpora in Language Teaching

JOHN FLOWERDEW

Introduction

Applications of corpus linguistics to language teaching began in the late eighties and early nineties. Examples of early work are Higgins and Johns (1984), Higgins (1988), Johns (1988, 1991), Tribble and Jones (1990), Stevens (1991), and J. Flowerdew (1993a). Most work in this area, as in other areas of applied linguistics and language teaching, has focused on English. However, some examples on other languages are Wichmann (1995), Ahmed and Davies (1997), Dodd (1997), King (1997), Kennedy and Miceli (2001), Rule et al. (2003), Belz (2004), Rule (2004), and Bolly (2005). Previous overviews of the field are Leech (1997), Aston (2001), Biber and Conrad (2001), Bernardini (2004), and Stubbs (2004).

Interest in corpus-based approaches to language teaching has developed quite rapidly in recent years, so that now there is a wealth of literature and, although less, still considerable application in this area. Application at the level of primary and secondary schools, however, has not kept pace with the considerable developments that are now going on at the tertiary level, especially in languages for specific purposes (LSP). Gavioli (2005), for example, is only able to cite one project at primary level (Sealey & Thompson, 2004).

One of the reasons for the relatively slow rate of classroom application has been the limitations of the technology. However, as Leech stated already in 1997, "computers have grown smaller, cheaper, and massively more powerful" (1997, p. 2). Since that statement, this trend has continued. In addition, more and more corpora have become available and it is easier to create personalized corpora. Furthermore, people are becoming increasingly computer literate and are therefore more easily introduced to the new approach. But if the start has been rather slow, this has a positive side, in that corpus applications to pedagogy have avoided, to quote Leech (1997, p. 4) again, the "bandwagon" effect. In developing more slowly, the risk of corpus-based approaches to language teaching following the path of the language laboratory, for example, with its its meteoric rise and ultimate demise, may be avoided.

What are the Principles in Corpus Linguistics that Can Be Applied to Language Teaching?

A corpus is a large database of language. Although the first corpora were relatively small – the Brown corpus (developed at Brown University, USA in the early 1960s) consisted of one million words – there now exist corpora consisting of hundreds of millions of words (e.g., the British National Corpus (BNC), 100 million words; and the Bank of English (COBUILD at Birmingham University, UK), over 500 million words). At the same time, however, much smaller corpora with as few as 100,000 words or less are being created all the time for specialist applications. It should be borne in mind, however, that, as pointed out by Gavioli and Aston (2001, p. 238), even the very large corpora contain less language than the average user will have experienced in their daily life.[1] In addition, the linguistic content of corpora is different from what is experienced by individuals in real life, many of them consisting largely of written language. Furthermore, while each text is given equal weighting in a corpus, in real life some texts will hold more value and be experienced more times than others (poetry and religious texts, for example, might be highly valued and heard or read many times). While some corpora are kept in a "raw" state (e.g., Bank of English), many are "tagged" (i.e., coded, according to parts of speech) and "parsed" (i.e., analyzed for grammatical structure) (e.g., BNC).

The potential of corpus techniques for investigating patterns of lexis, grammar, semantics, pragmatics, and textual features is well established (e.g., Sinclair, 1991; McEnery & Wilson, 1996; Biber et al., 1998; Kennedy, 1998; Hunston, 2002; Stubbs, 2004). Most work in corpus linguistics to date has relied on word frequency lists, which provide criteria upon which to base a search, and keyword in context (KWIC) concordances, the presentation of every instance of a selected word, phrase, or particle in the corpus down the middle of the page, with a limited amount of cotext on either side. Figure 19.1 provides part of a concordance for the word *meaning*.

The power of the corpus approach lies in the combination of frequency data regarding all the words in a corpus and the verbal environment in which these words occur. This combination permits the detailed investigation of typical patterns of use of lexis and grammar – information which can be obtained at the click of a mouse. A concordance output may appear to be a reified object, but this is not the case, because it may be ordered in various ways from left and right of the keyword or phrase and these changes reveal different collocational and grammatical patterns. Some critics have complained that concordance lines provide no information about situational context. This is also indeed accepted by proponents (e.g., Sinclair, 1991, p. 34; McEnery & Wilson, 1996, p. 79). However, it may be pointed out that situational information can be built into or accompany a corpus and that there is no reason why corpus evidence may not be supported by ethnographic investigation (L. Flowerdew, 2005, 2008). On the other hand, as Stubbs (2004, p. 108) notes, practice has demonstrated that the meaning of a

dictionary like we all do and the first meaning in the dictionary is all to do with #
a proper Italian pronunciation for that meaning leaf or sheet and so really in its basi
heet and so really in its basic basic # meaning portfolio means a case for carrying loo
ussed before she'd also assessed orally meaning they want to check if her teeth are oka
ather different it has a very different meaning and that is that you can't override
tes   following a step input   oscillates meaning it it goes backwards and forwards and that
o push out the   residual   demand curve meaning it would   comm   not only command a
e static properties of the equilibrium meaning we shifted one of the curves and look
kets i'm going to use the word bundles meaning a collection of or a combination of tw
y're falling apart   i think what you're meaning is that you've got an i # an interfacia
and it fits the syntax   and it fits the meaning that's it i'll # i'll go for that hy
defined concepts which we all know the meaning of but don't need or not even able to d
pecies   and   i take you understand the meaning of those numbers here minus-two m
index   and a little label at the top N meaning the time index so that's the times th
en out # and that's the same   same meaning the reason the word's choosed in this
holism   bec   # for our intentionality meaning our human concepts our human understan
e that it has managed to   bleed all the meaning out of maternity we don't have matria
but you under what you understand the meaning of what i'm saying here no i don't
but in economics it has a very specific meaning input-output models were invented by
er goods   yeah   but this is the literal meaning of this if you increase final demand
e in one country and have   very little meaning in another but it has # been a key i
gn so we must talk about the government meaning the legislature and the executive the
u're part of what this   can be taken as meaning is that you can consent to be under the
solution but it's a compromise solution meaning that each party will have to give up q
ed of snakes   that's F-L-plus S-N-minus meaning this model monkey was afraid of flow
nitive   case   possessive case of a word meaning kind a kind of something right a nou
about three-thousand years ago # word meaning exactly the same thing is like this

Figure 19.1   Concordance of the word *meaning* from a corpus of academic lectures

search word or phrase is often identifiable within a short span of cotext, enough
to fit into one line on the computer screen. Furthermore, most concordancers
allow the user to inspect the wider cotext of a selected instance, so the analyst is
not limited to the single corpus line.

As already mentioned, corpus techniques have created new knowledge about
the behaviour of lexis, grammar, semantics, pragmatics, and textual features.
Because corpus linguistics is based on the theory that language varies according
to context – across space and time – the potential for finding out new facts about
language is infinite. If this theoretical insight is applied to pedagogy, then the
case for the use of corpora in teaching becomes very powerful. Because no dictionary or grammar is able to fully describe the language, the educationist, whether
materials designer or classroom practitioner – or indeed learners themselves –
may play an important role in identifying regularities in the language which are
not to be found in such texts.

Another proven benefit of corpus-based approaches to the study of language
is that analysis is based on empirical, as opposed to introspected or elicited, data,
"real" language as many proponents refer to it.[2] As Aston (2001, pp. 7–8) has
pointed out (see also J. Flowerdew, 1996), native-speaker intuition about language
is often wrong – on the one hand, many uses included in traditional descriptions

do not occur with any frequency in large general corpora and, on the other hand, many uses which occur in corpus data are not recognized in traditional descriptions. This means that teachers and learners have been being given inaccurate and incomplete descriptions of the language.

What Information Can the Corpus Provide?

A corpus can yield various types of information which can be of potential use in language pedagogy. It can provide information about the behavior of words, multi-word phrases, grammatical patterns, semantic and pragmatic features, and textual properties. Knowledge of these features and their relative frequencies can be helpful to language practitioners in deciding what items to teach and when to teach them, as well as, importantly, providing input for reference materials. In this section various concepts regarding different aspects of language behavior will be presented, each followed by an indication of how the concept might be applied in language pedagogy.

Word frequency

Concept
At the most basic level, the corpus can provide word lists organized either according to frequency or alphabetically. Used in conjunction with the concordancer, frequency is not limited to the word forms, but may extend to the different meanings of a given word or phrase; the editing function of the concordancer can be used to group the items according to the different meanings. Frequency data can also be obtained for recurrent sequences (variously referred to as n-grams, pre-fabs, and lexical bundles) e.g., *I don't know, all of a sudden, all over the place, don't have a clue*. Furthermore, relative frequencies between two or more corpora can be calculated, those words occurring significantly more frequently in one corpus than another being referred to as keywords (Scott & Tribble, 2006).

Application
Frequency information is immensely useful in helping to prioritze what to teach. Aston (2001, p. 8) quite rightly mentions other relevant criteria: range, availability, coverage, learnability, and prototypicality (see also Widdowson, 2004, p. 87; Kaltenböck & Mehlmauer-Larcher, 2005, p. 77), but, other things being equal, frequency of occurrence is an important criterion for syllabus design and teaching. A considerable time ago Nattinger and de Carrico (1992) recommended the application of lexical phrases to language teaching. If one takes the view that all language teaching is LSP teaching, insofar as learners need to acquire a range of registers and genres, then comparative data, as provided by keyword analysis, will provide information regarding what to teach and when to teach in relation to specific genres and registers (see Scott & Tribble, 2006).

Collocation

Concept

Collocation is concerned with how words typically occur (or do not occur) together. Recurrent patterns highlighted by the concordancer will indicate typical collocations, although programs can provide lists of collocates. Hunston (2002, p. 12) gives the example of *shed*, which collocates with *light, tears, garden, jobs, blood, cents, image, pounds, staff, skin,* and *clothes*. Typically different collocates will affect the precise meaning of the word, e.g., *shed blood* means to suffer, *shed pounds* means to lose weight, and *shed image* means a deliberate changing of how one is perceived (Hunston, 2002, p. 12).

Application

How does one correct the learner who says "I will open the air-conditioner," where the collocates are not appropriate? One way, of course is to explain that in standard English one says "switch on" rather than "open" when referring to an air-conditioner or other electrical appliance. However, this lesson is likely to be more powerful and therefore more effective if, instead, the learner can look at concordances of the word *open* + noun phrase and see that while *open* collocates with other concrete nouns such as *gate, door,* and *window,* there are no instances of *open* + *air-conditioner*. On the other hand, a concordance of *air-conditioner* will probably yield numerous examples with *switch on* and *switch off.* In addition to this use with students, the concordancer can also give confidence to teachers, especially to less proficient non-native speakers, where they are unsure of their intuitions (J. Flowerdew, 1996).

Colligation

Concept

A distinction can be made between collocation, which is the combination of individual words, and colligation, which refers to how lexical words are associated with particular grammatical words or categories. Hunston (2002, p. 13), again, gives the example of the word *head* which has the following colligations: *of, over, on, back,* and *off.* Again the colligations affect the meaning of the word, thus Hunston gives examples such as *head of department, hit someone over the head, throw one's head back.*

Application

Kaltenböck and Mehlmauer-Larcher (2005, pp. 73–4) give some examples of pedagogical activities designed to develop colligational awareness. For example, in one simple task students are given a set of sentences where deleted prepositions have to be inserted after searching a corpus:

The building is adjacent . . . the train station.
It is usually a good idea to abide . . . the law.
You should give clear indication . . . your intentions.
He was aghast . . . the violence he witnessed.

In another example task (with the International Corpus of English (ICE) GB corpus, which is tagged for parts of speech), students consider verb complementation with the gerund and the infinitive:

TASK: What can the corpus tell us about the difference in meaning/use between *remember doing something* and *remember to do something?*) (Try [searching for]: "re-member to" and "remember" <V> = *remember* followed by a verb.

Kaltenböck and Mehlmauer-Larcher (2005) make the important point that corpus queries such as those required for these tasks require less "expert knowledge" than would be needed if a reference grammar were used, with the knowledge of grammatical metalanguage that would be implied for the latter task.

Semantic preference

Concept

Here we are concerned with how a word or phrase relates to a group of collocating words that (1) share an element of meaning, (2) are related to particular genres or registers, or (3) belong to lexical sets in terms of synonymy, meronymy, antonymy, etc. Semantic preference is arrived at by sorting collocates into groups based on semantic relations such as those just mentioned. The specific semantic preference is labelled by a gloss, such as "words or phrases relating to measurement," "words or phrases belonging to the register of production engineering," or "words or phrases relating to history."

Application

Semantic field theory, which can be seen as an introspective precursor of semantic preference, has been applied (mostly intuitively) in language teaching for a very long time (Corder, 1973, p. 316). Indeed it can be seen as closely related to situational ("at the post office," "at the airport," "in the supermarket," "in the office," etc.) and topical ("travel," "shopping," "family," etc.) syllabuses. It is also implicitly applied in notional syllabuses (Wilkins, 1972). The assumption here is that certain lexical (and grammatical) items belonging typically in given fields are likely to co-occur and can be learned together in semantic sets. However, a corpus approach takes us beyond introspection to identify empirically established relationships. The choice of corpus here is crucial, larger corpora being more reliable, because smaller corpora will not be likely to provide enough data to determine general preferences. On the other hand, specialist corpora consisting of specific genres or registers have great potential for application to LSP.

Semantic prosody

Concept

If semantic preference can tell us about the semantics of a word or phrase, "semantic prosody" (Sinclair, 1991; Louw, 1993), or for Stubbs (2001) "discourse prosody," can tell us about typical pragmatic values – the attitude or evaluation a speaker or writer attaches to what they are saying. Semantic prosody is similar to connotation. However, it does not just apply to a single word, but to the word and its association with its collocates. Thus, to take an example from Stubbs (1996), the word *cause* typically collocates with negatively loaded words – e.g., *accident, concern, damage, death, trouble* – and thereby takes on a negative semantic prosody; *provide*, on the other hand, is typically used with positive collocates – e.g., *aid, care, food, opportunities, relief, support* – and thus takes on a positive semantic prosody. Most studies of semantic prosody describe examples in simple terms of positive or negative evaluation. However, it seems that finer grained analysis is possible. Thus Hunston (2002, p. 141) gives the example of *sit through*, which is often used with lexical items which indicate boring or lengthy things.

Application

The analysis of the semantic prosodies associated with the lexical items in a corpus is a way to acquire context knowledge which is important for writers trying to master tasks within a specific genre (Tribble, 2000). This sort of information is now starting to be incorporated into dictionaries, but a learning activity in the form of analyzing words in context and identifying their semantic prosodies might be a more effective learning strategy, insofar as learners are more likely to remember what they themselves have discovered.[3]

Register and genre

Concept

Research in corpus linguistics has done much to show how patterns may vary across various registers or genres. As Biber and Conrad (2001, p. 332) put it, "strong patterns of use in one register often represent only weak patterns in other registers." To illustrate this, Biber and Conrad show, for example, how the 12 most frequent lexical verbs (*say, get, go, know, think, see, make, come, take, want, give,* and *mean*) in a corpus of 20 million words drawn from four registers (conversation, fiction, newspaper language, and academic prose) are very unequally distributed across the four registers. These verbs, for example, represent 45 percent of all verbs in conversation versus only 11 percent for academic prose.

Application

Biber and Conrad (2001) argue that the verbs referred to above should be given priority in pedagogy. In practice, however, they note that low-level ESL grammar books tend not to use these verbs, preferring activity verbs such as *eat, play, work, run*, *travel*, and *study*, which, as they concede in a footnote, are easier to learn. Nevertheless, Biber and Conrad argue that just because they are more difficult to learn does not mean that the high-frequency verbs should be neglected, "as these are the ones students will most often hear in their day-to-day interactions with native speakers" (p. 333).[4]

At a more micro level, working with small corpora composed of specific text types, Gavioli (2001) has shown how particular recurrent patterns tend to occur within such corpora. Comparing two corpora, one composed of lonely hearts ads and the other of letters to a newspaper agony aunt, for example, she (or, in fact, her students, because in her paper Gavioli is showing how corpus analysis can be done by learners (see below)) shows certain similarities and differences. Taking the adjectives *pretty*, *attractive*, and *beautiful*, for example, she shows that *pretty* and *attractive* always refer to people's physical appearance in both corpora. *Beautiful*, in the letters, however, also refers to music and the home. In addition, neither *pretty* nor *attractive* occurs in a series of adjectives. However, *beautiful* occurs in a co-ordinate pattern with another positive adjective, in phrases such as *mature and beautiful*; *beautiful and well-behaved*; *beautiful and wonderful*; *sweet and beautiful*. This is not the sort of information that can be found in reference grammars or dictionaries and it provides a strong argument for a corpus-based approach to the development of genre awareness (J. Flowerdew, 1993b).

What Corpora?

One of the problems with applying corpora to language teaching is deciding which the most appropriate corpora are. As Leech (1997, p. 18) has pointed out, "the corpora which are easiest to compile are not necessarily those which are most useful for language learning purposes." Not all corpora will be suitable for all learners.

Until recently, the most pressing problem in this area was the dearth of spoken corpora, most corpora being wholly or primarily made up of written language. The reason for this is simple. It is difficult and expensive to collect spoken language, which then has to be recorded and transcribed. It is true that spoken corpora are starting to be created – for example the CANCODE corpus of spoken English developed jointly by the University of Nottingham and Cambridge University Press – but there is still an emphasis on the written word (not to mention problems of accessibility). The BNC, for example, has 90 million written words compared to 10 million of speech). Given the emphasis in modern-day language pedagogy on the spoken word, this is a serious problem.

Another problem is that most corpora are based on native-speaker models. In a climate where there is much discussion of the role of world Englishes in language pedagogy, the use of native-speaker models may be questioned (Hunston, 2002). This does not just concern lexico-grammar. As Carter (1998b, p. 49) has demonstrated, colloquial speech is deeply embedded in cultural understandings. The simplest of phrases may require knowledge of the culture for understanding.

Among many examples, Carter provides the following service encounter from CANCODE:

[In a fish and chip shop]
A: Can I have chips, beans, and a sausage?
B: Chips, beans, and a sausage.
A: Yeah.
B: Wrapped up?
A: Open please.

Carter points out how in this extract the word "open" in this particular context is used as an antonym of "wrapped up" and "carries a specific cultural meaning of food being served in paper so that it can be eaten immediately, even perhaps while walking home" (p. 48). Carter asks to what extent such cultural allusions should be removed. Furthermore, he asks how relevant it is to be able to make observations such as that fish and chip shops in Britain serve not only fish and chips, but also other food, such as sausages, burgers, and curry.

The foregoing suggests that corpora made up of different language varieties might be needed. Hong Kong learners or Filipino learners, it might be argued, should have as their target educated Hong Kong or educated Filipino English, not British English. Similarly, it would seem sensible that learners of French in Canada might want a standard and hence a corpus based on Canadian French rather than the metropolitan variety. The problem is being addressed to a degree, for English, with the ICE corpora, referred to earlier, a suite of corpora of 15 different national/regional varieties, such as Australian English, British English, East African English, Filipino English, Indian English, etc. Given the complexity of coordinating and collecting such a range of corpora, however, it is perhaps understandable that these corpora are relatively small, at one million words each. Of course, the question of what standard to adopt is itself controversial. To take the example of Canadian French, many learners want to acquire the metropolitan standard, even though they will be using their French in Canada. To take another example, at a recent corpus conference an Indian member of the audience was asked if Indians would want to learn Indian English. His answer was that they would definitely not want to be associated with such a variety which they did not even acknowledge as such, preferring so-called "standard" English. This raises the question of language rights, in this case the rights of the learners (or their parents) to have the target variety that they want. In addition, where regional or local varieties have developed, in a globalizing world, with all that goes with it – mass migration, mass tourism, international business travel, the internationalization of (especially tertiary) education, use of the Internet and other electronic communication devices, and the internationalization of popular culture and mass media – learners may need not only the local variety, but also some standard for international intelligibility.

An alternative solution in terms of appropriate models might lie in lingua franca corpora, corpora composed of language produced by proficient non-native speakers who are interacting with each other or with native speakers. In English, it is said that more English is spoken in the world among non-natives than natives, so lingua franca corpora might seem a logical way to go. However, research to date has not come up with systematic descriptions of such language and it is questionable whether – certainly at the level of phraseology and the grammatical code – such systematic patterns are discernible. Interestingly Anna Mauranen (2006; personal communication June 2006) has identified in her ELFA (English as a Lingua Franca for Academic Purposes) corpus certain pragmatic regularities, such as greater use of grammatical rephrasing and a greater toler-ance for ambiguity. But she has not identified any new lexico-grammatical or phraseological regularities.

Further confusing the picture as regards suitable corpora, there are other learner differences that need to be taken into account. For example, a model for young learners might be child language, teenagers may want a teenage model, women and men might want models of the speech of either gender; then again, learners may want specific academic or professional language (see below on corpora and LSP). It is true that there are different types of corpora or sub-corpora (for exam-ple, the CHILDES corpus of children's speech (MacWhinney & Snow, 1991) and the British National Corpus has a section on young people's spoken language, referred to separately as the COLT corpus (Stenström et al., 2002)). However, these corpora or sub-corpora have not been designed with language teaching specifically in mind and their suitability, certainly in terms of their size and representativeness, might be questioned.[5]

Finally, the authenticity of corpus data may mean that it is difficult for less advanced learners to process. Perhaps corpora of simplified language might be needed for such learners, or some sort of filter which removes concordances which contain vocabulary items which do not occur in a pre-established list (Kuo et al., 2001).

Applications

Applications of corpus linguistics to language teaching may be direct or indirect (Stubbs, 2004). A direct application would be advanced users of academic English using a corpus of the language of their speciality to assist them in writing academic papers (see Lee and Swales, 2006 for an account of such a procedure). Indirect applications would be the application of corpus findings to the creation or refinement of dictionaries, reference grammars, and pedagogic materials.

Indirect applications

Use in developing reference material
One of the first applications in this area was *Collins COBUILD English Language Dictionary* (1987) edited by John Sinclair; Other dictionaries have made use of

corpora to a greater or lesser extent, e.g., *Longman Dictionary of Contemporary English*, *Oxford Advanced Learner's Dictionary*, *Macmillan English Dictionary for Advanced Learners*. As Leech (1997, p. 14) points out, some of the advantages of corpus-based lexicography are that corpus data:

- can be searched quickly and exhaustively,
- can provide frequency data,
- can be easily processed to produce updated lists of words,
- can provide authentic examples for citation,
- can readily be used by lexicographical teams for updating and verifying other levels of descriptions such as dictionary definitions.

A precursor of grammars totally based on corpus data was *A Comphrehensive Grammar of the English* Language (Quirk et al., 1985), which relied on manually collected examples of use that were stored in a giant database. This might be called a *corpus-informed* grammar. The first grammar to be fully based on a corpus, what might be called a *corpus-driven grammar*, was *Collins COBUILD English Grammar* (Sinclair, 1990). This has been followed by the *Longman Grammar of Spoken and Written English* (Biber et al., 1999), and, more recently, by the *Cambridge Grammar of English* (Carter & McCarthy, 2006). At this point, it might be noted that, while the *Longman Grammar* is no doubt a great achievement, especially in the great advance achieved in the incorporation of frequency data according to four different domains of use, the corpus-driven grammars, especially COBUILD and Cambridge tend to be inconsistent in their coverage of the basic features of the language. In terms of comprehensiveness, Quirk et al. (1985) cannot be beaten. No doubt with further work the comprehensiveness of corpus-driven grammars will improve.

Pedagogic materials

Again, Collins (now HarperCollins), with John Sinclair as editor in chief, were the first here, with an extensive series called *Collins COBUILD English Guides*. Titles focused on such linguistic features as *Determiners* (Berry, 1996) *Linking Words* (Chalker, 1996), and *Reporting* (Thompson, 1993). Coming again out of the work at Birmingham was the first proposal for syllabus design to be based on corpora – *The Lexical Syllabus: A New Approach to Language Teaching* (D. Willis, 1990), and also *Collins COBUILD English Course* (Willis & Willis, 1989).

Direct Applications

Corpora and syllabus design

If one accepts a corpus view of language, i.e., that it consists to a great extent of recurrent patterns (what Sinclair, 1991 refers to as the "idiom principle"), then important implications apply for syllabus design. Instead of being organized in terms of grammatical forms, the syllabus can be designed around the most important recurrent patterns (see Sinclair & Renouf, 1988; Willis, 1990; Willis & Willis, 1989). This type of syllabus is referred to as a lexical syllabus, although this is somewhat misleading, as it is designed around lexical patterns, not single words. The idea of basing a syllabus on patterns of use was, in fact, put forward as early as 1980 by Nattinger:

> Perhaps we should base our teaching on the assumption that, for a great deal of the time anyway, language production consists of piecing together the ready-made units appropriate for a particular situation and that comprehension relies on knowing which of these patterns to predict in these situations. Our teaching, therefore, would center on these patterns and the ways they can be pieced together, along with the ways they vary and the situations in which they occur. (cited in Richards & Rogers, 2001, pp. 133–4)

Although the emphasis is on lexical patterning in the lexical syllabus, grammar is not neglected, it can be argued, as the main lexical patterns will incorporate the main grammatical forms. Willis (1990, p. vi) takes this a stage further, claiming that "the lexical syllabus not only subsumes a structural syllabus, it also indicates how the structures which make up the syllabus should be exemplified." For the COBUILD course, for the first level, the most frequent 700 words were selected from the COBUILD corpus, these words accounting, according to Willis (1990, p. vi), for around 70 percent of all English text.

The underlying principle of the lexical syllabus is frequency. Sinclair and Renouf (1988) argue that the most frequent words typically have a range of uses and that many of these uses are typically not covered in beginners' courses. They give the example of the word *make*. This word most typically occurs in patterns such as *make decisions, make discoveries, make arrangements*. These abstract uses are more frequent than the concrete use, as in *make a cake*. Sinclair and Renouf thus argue that the abstract forms should be taught to beginners, as well as the concrete ones. It should be noted, however, that this is a very strong argument, which neglects the counter-argument of "teachability," the fact that the concrete meaning is more easily taught. Widdowson (2004, p. 87) puts forward the teachability argument, as follows: "Words and structures might be identified as 'pedagogically' core or nuclear, and preferred as a prototype at a particular learning stage because of their coverage or their generative value, because they are catalysts which activated the learning process, whatever their status might be in respect to their actual occurrence in contexts of use." This is the same argument as noted with the examples given by Biber and Conrad of the most frequent verbs. On the other hand, it might be argued that the teachability of the concrete forms should imply that they are taught first, but then the other abstract uses immediately follow. This seems to have been the principle adopted in the COBUILD dictionary, where concrete meanings still come before abstract ones. Thus the concrete meaning of "lifebelt," for example, comes before the metaphorical ones.

Data-driven learning

The beginning of classroom concordancing is generally attributed to Tim Johns and his work with non-native speaking postgraduate science students at the University of Birmingham. Johns referred to this approach as "data-driven learning" (DDL). In this form of learning, learners are seen as "language detectives" (Johns, 1997, p. 101), seeking answers to questions that can be found by means of corpus queries and/or concordance lines. Learners are detectives because concordances do not offer explanations; they simply provide (patterned) data for analysis. Learners are required to identify and analyze the recurrent patterns to be found in the concordance lines and make their own generalizations. They may do this by working on the concordance print-outs (Johns' preferred method) or directly with the computer and the corpus. Johns (cited in Ma, 1994, p. 197) sees this approach as falling between "the highly-organized, graded and idealized language of the typical coursebook" and the "potentially confusing but far richer and more revealing 'full flood' of authentic communication."

The DDL approach has alternatively been described as one of "authenticity and discovery" (Ma, 1994, p. 197). Leech (1997, p. 3) comments how "it often happens that a student working on a relatively small corpus assignment comes up with original observations and discoveries which have probably never been brought to notice before, even in the most detailed dictionaries and grammars of language." Indeed, an example of such a discovery has already been presented in this chapter with Gavioli's example of the genre-specific use of particular adjectives in letters to agony aunts and lonely hearts ads. A number of writers provide examples of the sort of activities that can be exploited in DDL (e.g., Aston, 2001; Dodd, 1997; Gavioli, 2001; Hunston, 2002) A commercially produced workbook based on concordance print-outs is Thurston and Candlin (1993). Here is just one simple activity from Gavioli (2001, p. 125):

WORKSHEET

1. In groups of two or three use the corpus of Lonely hearts ads to identify 4 or 5 patterns which are typically used to do each of the following
   - introduce the seeker
   - add descriptions of the seeker
   - introduce the sought
   - add descriptions of the sought

You can generate concordances to get suggestions.

2. Use the patterns you have identified to produce at least two new lonely hearts ads. Complete any missing parts of the text as necessary.

This activity is interesting because it requires the learners to go beyond just analyzing concordance lines, i.e., working out possible functions for patterns which are presented to them. Here they first have to come up with their own corpus queries and then find patterns which typically realize the functions which are embodied in their queries. This is, therefore, the reverse procedure to the more typical one.

This activity takes us on to ones used with more advanced learners, where they use specialist corpora for real-world writing tasks. In probably the first example of such an application, Ma (1994) created a corpus of computer user manuals for his students, who had to write a chapter of such a manual, using the corpus and a concordancing program as a writing resource. In a similar approach, Bianchi and Pazzaglia (2007) created a corpus for psychology students consisting of experimental articles in that discipline, the task being for students to write a research article of their own, using the corpus as a resource. Interestingly, this corpus was divided into sub-corpora of the different "moves" (Swales, 1990) in the articles. Taking this sort of procedure a stage even further, Lee and Swales (2006) had a heterogeneous group of graduate students who created their own corpora specific to their particular discipline. These corpora were used as a resource for working on the writing required on their higher degree programs. One issue that has to be confronted with this type of application is where to draw the borderline between reusing typical phraseological patterns, on the one hand, and copying longer sections of texts extracted from the corpus – a case of plagiarism – on the other (see Pecorari, 2003, 2006; J. Flowerdew & Li, 2009). This issue needs to be handled carefully by the teacher, although it could also be seen as an opportunity to alert students to issues of plagiarism.

Corpora and LSP

The three studies reported in the preceding paragraph are all concerned with LSP and they are very recent. This section will step back from these studies and consider corpora and LSP since its beginning, because LSP (primarily English for specific purposes (ESP)) has been one of the major fields of development for corpus application to language teaching (see Gavioli, 2005 for a complete monograph on this topic, and L. Flowerdew, 2002 for an overview paper for English for academic purposes (EAP) – here we cannot do full justice to this area, merely citing a number of key examples). The earliest known concordances, which, of course, were compiled by hand, were based on biblical texts. The first complete concordance of the Latin Bible was created by the Benedictine Hugo de San Charo in the thirteenth century (Tribble & Jones, 1990, p. 7). Early concordances, in their focus on one register (biblical texts) can, in fact be seen as a form of LSP. In the modern era, a precursor of modern corpus work is an influential article by Barber (1962). Barber's study, carried out by hand, and with a view of pedagogic application, is based on three scientific research articles, making a "corpus" of about 23,000 words (tiny by today's standards). Barber studied various syntactic features of this corpus, one of the most striking findings being the very low occurrence of progressive aspect. This finding, as Swales (1988, p. 1) reports, was influential in the teaching of English for Science and Technology (EST), suggesting that attention should be given to the other aspects rather than the progressive.

Probably the earliest application of corpus analysis to syllabus and materials design in ESP was conducted by J. Flowerdew (1993a), where a corpus was created from transcriptions of lectures that biology students concurrently taking an ESP course attend during their biology course, along with the assigned readings. This corpus was used as the basis for selecting key vocabulary (about 1,000 items, chosen on the basis that they occur more than 10 times in the corpus). This lexis formed the core vocabulary of the ESP course. With the use of concordances, the most typical recurrent phraseological patterns in which this vocabulary occur were identified and incorporated into materials. In addition, based on a close reading of the text and examination of the word list and concordancing lines, important notions and functions were identified, along with their typical realization patterns. These were also incorporated into the syllabus and course materials. This same database was used when it came to assessing the performance of students during and after the course.

Contemporary work in ESP is very much influenced by genre theory (Swales, 1990; Bhatia, 1993) and ESP corpora are typically compiled from texts belonging to the same genre. The emphasis on genre has meant a move away from a simple focus on the frequency of syntactic structures to a consideration of form–function relations and how linguistic features correlate with generic moves and other pragmatic aspects of particular genres. A good example of the genre approach is Gledhill's (2000) study of research articles in the field of cancer (also summarized in Gavioli, 2005, p. 57). The corpus for this work is divided into sub-corpora according to the generic moves of research articles (introduction, method, results, discussion, conclusion). This allows Gledhill to identify salient lexis in the various moves. This is done using key-word analysis, key-words being those words which are statistically more frequent in one move than in the rest of the corpus.[6] Having identified the key-words, Gledhill then uses concordances to identify their particular rhetorical functions e.g., "such" is often used to reformulate biochemical processes (e.g., *antitumour agents such as NMY; use of hormonal enzymes such as dismutase*), "can" is used to express potential clinical processes (e.g., *methods can be considered; alterations can be prepared*). Finally Gledhill shows how the key-words often form part of recurrent phraseological patterns. So, for example, "to" is found in constructions which take the following pattern [biomedical process] (possessive) <ability to> [biochemical process], as in expressions such as:

[the reactant] Its	*ability to*	*alter tolerance to self*
we extended its [tumor]	*ability to*	*differentiate*
calibrating their [leukocytes]	*ability to*	*modify factor specific DNA*

In another example of genre-based corpus work, Swales et al. (1998) focused on the use of the imperative in research articles. Using a corpus of 50 articles (5 from each of 10 disciplines), computer-assisted analysis provided data on all instances of imperatives in both the main texts and footnotes of these articles. In those disciplines where imperatives occurred in the main text (only five out of the ten selected), they tend to occur in the more argumentative sections of articles, but are very unevenly distributed across disciplines, being most preval-ent in fields where mathematical reasoning occurs. In addition, there are a range of field-specific usages. In terms of function, based on interviews with some of the writers, Swales et al. argue that the decision to use imperatives may be part of a bundle of grammatical features that promote irony, closer collegiality, or playfulness, which they hypothesize is a contemporary trend of scholarly writing in the post-modern age.[7] Imperatives are not used in the research article as face-threatening devices, as suggested in standard grammars, but as one of the resources available to writers which allows them to maintain a harmonious relationship with their readers.

The use of computers is also helpful for taxonomic research into the various functional categories which a given linguistic form is used to realize. In order to develop a taxonomy of the functions of reporting verbs in academic articles, for example, Hyland (2002) used the following procedure. First, he computer-searched his corpus for canonical citation forms, such as a date in brackets, a number in squared brackets, and Latinate references to other citations. In addition, a con-cordance was made of all of the names in the bibliographies of the articles which made up the corpus, and of second person pronouns. This search yielded all of the citations in the corpus, from which Hyland was able to extract the reporting verbs and classify them according to the specific type of activity they refer to: research acts (which contain verbs which represent experimental activities or actions carried out in the real world (e.g., *observe, discover, notice, show*)), cognition acts (which contain verbs which are concerned with the researcher's mental pro-cesses (e.g., *believe, conceptualize, suspect, assume, view*)), and discourse acts (which contain verbs which involve linguistic activities and focus on the verbal expression of cognitive or research activities (e.g., *ascribe, discuss, hypothesize, report, state*)).

The sort of analyses described here might seem very fine-grained, but in ESP situations they have the potential to provide teachers with very specific informa-tion which can be incorporated into teaching. At the level of the classroom, an interesting teaching procedure is reported by Weber (2001). Weber took "a concordance- and genre-based" (Weber, 2001, p. 14) approach to teaching law students to write academic essays. Students first of all had to analyze a corpus of essays written by native-speaker law students, either individually or in small groups, and identify, through consensus, elements which seemed essential to the structure of the essays (they identified four: identifying and/or delimiting the legal principle; referring to the authorities; applying these judicial precedents and/or reasoning on the basis of these precedents; moving toward a conclusion and/or giving advice to the parties concerned). The students then had to search for language that seemed to correlate with the structural elements they had identified. In groups, they selected the most significant examples. They then were given the opportunity to work with different corpora of non-legal genres, searching for the language they had identified in the legal genre and seeing how different the uses were in the other genres. Next, they were given case studies and asked to write very short essays, incorporating the four structural elements they had identified and using the language they had identified in the concordances. The essays were then subjected to peer review and group discussion and finally a short conference was held with each student. Weber (2001, p. 19) describes the activity as giving the students "a firm foundation both in essay writing and in legal reasoning." It is also a very good example of how data-driven learning can be applied using a communicative, task-based format.

While the examples cited thus far in the field of ESP have been quite specific, mention should be made of more generic EAP (English for Academic Purposes) work. One example here would be Coxhead's Academic Word List (Coxhead, 2000; Coxhead & Nation, 2001). This is a list of 2,000 words which are identified on the basis of their frequency and range in academic English. The list is derived from a comparison between a 3.5 million-word corpus of academic English (from different disciplines and genres) and a reference corpus consisting of the same amount of fictional writing. The words included in the list are neither the typically very high frequency words of everyday English nor the technical language of specific disciplines. Also worthy of mention are large-scale academic corpora which are being made available in the public domain. The best-known of these is the MICASE corpus of American spoken academic language developed at the University of Michigan (www.lsa.umich.edu/eli/micase/index.htm), but there is also the counterpart BASE corpus of spoken British academic language developed by the universities of Reading and Warwick (www.rdg.ac.uk/AcaDepts/ ll/base_corpus/) and its companion written BAWE corpus (www.coventry.ac.uk/ researchnet/d/505/a/2850).

Learner Corpora

A learner corpus is a collection of texts which have been produced by learners of a language. Learner corpora allow for the comparison of learner language with native-speakers of the target language (L2 vs. L1) or with other groups of learners (L2 vs. L2) (see Granger, 2004a for an overview). The best-known work in this area has been conducted by Sylviane Granger and her colleagues at the University of Louvain in Belgium. This work has resulted in the creation of a suite of different, but comparable, learner corpora of argumentative essays from a whole range of different L1 learners. Corpora such as those contained in ICLE can be used as a tool for contrastive interlanguage analysis and for error analysis (Granger, 2004b). As well as identifying discrepancies between different stages of interlanguage and between L2 and L1 users on the basis of "errors," frequency data drawn from learner corpora can show how learners may over- or under-use certain patterns of the target language, features which have been identified as the reason for LS speakers from sounding "non-nativelike."[8] In terms of the quantity of work being done with learner corpora, this is very popular. At the time of writing. the online bibliography for learner corpora at the Centre for English Corpus Linguistics, Université catholique de Louvain (Belgium) (http:// cecl.fltr.ucl.ac.be/learner%20corpus%20bibliography.html) had over 330 entries.

In terms of application, the contribution of learner corpora to language teaching is primarily "indirect," to use Stubbs' (2004) term; learner corpora have primarily been used to assist in the production of reference tools. Granger (2004a, 2004b) cites a number of dictionaries which have made use of learner corpus findings. Two examples of these are the *Longman Dictionary of Contemporary English* (using a 10 million-word learner corpus), and the *Cambridge Advanced Learner's Dictionary* (using a 16 million-word corpus), both of which contain notes drawn from analysis of their respective corpora advising users on how to avoid common errors. Granger (2004b, p. 3) notes that information is generic in nature (i.e., not specific to any particular L1), due to the limited space available in paper dictionaries. With the greater use of online dictionaries it is likely that information for specific L1 groups will be made available.

Concerning more "direct" uses, Granger (2004a, 2004b) cites a number of computer programs that are designed to help learners with the types of errors which have been identified in learner corpora. One well-known example of these is Milton's (1998) *Word Pilot*, a program which allows students and teachers to explore lexical patterns in any text type, using lists of problematic words and phrases identified by analysis of a large corpus of Cantonese mother tongue users of English. Target lexis extracted by analysis of other learner corpora can be loaded into the program as well. Milton (2006) has since extended this development to a suite of programs that assist second language writers to improve their written fluency and proofread for common errors. These programs include online vocabulary databases, an Internet-based grammar, various lookup resources, and a tool that assists teachers to insert feedback in students' electronic documents (Milton, 2006). This suite of programs can be accessed at http://mywords.ust.hk.

Another example of the application of learner corpora is *IWiLL* (Wible et al., 2001), an interactive web-based tool which allows students and teachers to create and use an online database of Taiwanese learners' essays and teachers' error annotations. Granger (2004b) also cites an application by Hewings (2000), who used a learner corpus and an ESP corpus to compare a range of linguistic features with his students. One example Hewings gives is of the personal pronoun *I*. It was found that where students tend to use *I* to express their own opinion (*I believe, I think, I suppose*), in the ESP corpus *I* was mainly used as a text-organizing device or for reporting a procedure (*As I have already pointed out, The survey I conducted among my students*).

Conclusion

In this review, an attempt has been made to cover as much ground as possible. Inevitably, however, in a chapter of this type, there remain some gaps. This is due partly to limitations of space, partly the ignorance of the author, and partly because certain issues have not been dealt with in the literature very thoroughly, if at all. This review has taken an overall positive view of corpora and language pedagogy. Perhaps some caveats are in order in this conclusion. Cook (1998) claims that some corpus linguists "overreach" themselves and that "they talk as though the entire study of language can be replaced by the study of their collections" (p. 57). While this may or may not be true (and if it is, it probably only applies to a very few applied linguists), it *is* true to say that corpus applications to language teaching have been promoted by enthusiasts. However, as indicated already, many more applications are taking place in tertiary institutions (where teachers are better resourced and more research-oriented) than in schools. Ways need to be found to encourage corpus-based work at this level. While, as has been seen, a lot has been written extolling the virtues of corpora in language pedagogy, less has been written about some of the problems, for example some of the difficulties novice corpus users encounter. More needs to be written up on this (although see, e.g., Bernardini, 2000; Frankenberg-Garcia, 2005; Kennedy & Miceli, 2001). Another issue worthy of consideration is the question of the need to keep corpora up to date. Language is changing very quickly, but data for some of the major corpora currently in use were collected a considerable time ago. One can wonder to what extent, for example, the teenage language sub-component of the BNC (the COLT corpus) can still be said to represent the way English is spoken by British teenagers today, given that the data were collected in the mid-1990s. There is a need for new corpora or an updating of existing ones. Other issues worthy of consideration are the relative paucity of literature on teacher education (but see, e.g., Hunston, 1995; Farr, 2008; O'Keeffe & Farr, 2003; Tsui, 2004) and evaluation of pedagogic applications (but see, e.g., Cobb, 1997, 1999; Farr, 2008; Kennedy & Micheli, 2001; Yoon & Hirvela, 2004). Overall, however, the outlook for corpora and language teaching looks healthy. The prognosis, if not perfect, is very good.

NOTES

I should like to acknowledge feedback from David Lee on an earlier draft of this paper.

1 Although, looked at in another way, corpora may contain language which individuals are unlikely to be familiar with, in so far as they may contain language from genres or registers outside a given individual's experience.

2 The term "real" in this context has been critiqued (see e.g., Carter, 1998a and Cook, 1998).

3 This process is known as data-driven learning (see below).

4 The same caveats regarding frequency, as noted above, apply here.

5 It should be noted that CANCODE, which is not available publicly, was developed "with an eye to [the data's] potential relevance to ELT" (Carter, 1998a, p. 43).

6 This represents an advance on the approach adopted by J. Flowerdew (1993a), who used raw frequency data, software not being available at the time to perform key-word analysis. See Scott and Tribble (2006) for a book-length treatment of the application of key-word analysis to language teaching.

7 Swales et al. are not the only corpus-oriented ESP practitioners to make use of specialist informants (e.g., Hyland, 2000; L. Flowerdew, 2005, 2008).

8 Users of learner corpora are open to the criticism that native speakers will be the target norm (Hunston, 2002, pp. 211–12). This may not necessarily be the case, however. It is up to the users of learner corpora to select the norm as they see fit. It is quite possible

to conceive of a lingua franca corpus as the norm, or a corpus of educated Hong Kong or Filipino English, although none have been used as such to date.

REFERENCES

Ahmed, K. & Davies, A. (1997). The role of corpora in studying and promoting Welsh. In A. Wichmann, S. Fligelstone, T. McEnery, & G. Knowles (eds.), *Teaching and language corpora* (pp. 157–72). London: Longman.

Aston, G. (2001). Learning with corpora: An overview. In G. Aston (ed.), *Learning with corpora* (pp. 7–45). Houston: Athelstan.

Barber, C. L. (1962/1988). Some measurable characteristics of modern scientific prose. In J. Swales (ed.), *Episodes in ESP* (pp. 3–14). London: Prentice-Hall.

Belz, J. A. (2004). Learner corpus analysis and the development of foreign language proficiency. *System* 32, 4, 577–91.

Bernardini, S. (2000). Systematising serendipity: Proposals for concordancing large corpora with language learners. In L. Burnard & T. McEnery (eds.), *Rethinking language pedagogy from a corpus perspective* (pp. 225–34). Frankfurt: Peter Lang.

Bernardini, S. (2004). Corpora in the classroom. An overview and some reflections on future developments. In J. M. Sinclair (ed.), *How to use corpora in language teaching* (pp. 15–36). Amsterdam/Philadelphia: John Benjamins.

Berry, R. (1996). *Determiners*. London: Collins.

Bhatia, V. K. (1993). *Analysing genre: Language use in professional settings*. Harlow, UK: Longman.

Bianchi, F. & Pazzaglia, R. (2007). Student writing of research articles in a foreign language: Metacognition and corpora. In R. Facchinetti (ed.), *Corpus Linguistics 25 Years on* (pp. 259–87). Amsterdam/New York: Rodopi.

Biber, D. & Conrad, S. (2001). Quantitative corpus-based research in TESOL: Much more than bean counting. *TESOL Quarterly* 35, 2, 331–5.

Biber, D., Conrad, S., & Reppen, R. (1998). *Corpus linguistics: Investigating grammar of spoken and written English*. London: Longman.

Biber, D., Johansson, S., Leech, G., Conrad, S., & Finegan, E. (eds.) (1999). *Longman grammar of spoken and written English*. London: Longman.

Bolly, C. (2005). *Constructions récurrentes, collocations et séquences figées avec le verbe à haute fréquence "prendre": Pour une méthode "mixte" d'analyse de corpus (FL1 et FL2)*. In C. Cosme, C. Gouverneur, F. Meunier, & M. Paquot (eds.), *Proceedings of the Phraseology 2005 Conference* (pp. 57–60), Louvain-la-Neuve, October 13–15.

Carter, R. (1998a). Orders of reality: CANCODE, communication and culture, and Reply to Guy Cook. *ELT Journal* 52, 1, 43–56; 64.

Carter, R. (1998b). Telling tails: Grammar, the spoken language and materials development. In B. Tomlinson (ed.), *Materials development in language teaching* (pp. 67–86). Cambridge: Cambridge University Press.

Carter, R. & McCarthy, M. (eds.) (2006). *The Cambridge Grammar of English*. Cambridge: Cambridge University Press.

Chalker, S. (1996). *Linking words*. London: Collins.

Cobb, T. (1997). Is there any measurable learning from hands on concordancing? *System* 25, 3, 301–15.

Cobb, T. (1999). Breadth and depth of lexical acquisition with hands-on concordancing. *Computer Assisted Language Learning* 12, 345–60.

Cook, G. (1998). The uses of reality: A reply to Ronald Carter. *ELT Journal* 52, 1, 57–63.

Corder, S. P. (1973). *Introducing applied linguistics*. Harmondsworth, UK: Penguin.

Coxhead, A. (2000). A new academic word list. *Tesol Quarterly* 34, 2, 213–38.

Coxhead, A. & Nation, P. (2001). The specialised vocabulary of English for Academic Purposes. In J. Flowerdew & M. Peacock (eds.), *Research perspectives on English for Academic Purposes* (pp. 252–67). Cambridge: Cambridge University Press.

Dodd, B. (1997). Exploiting a corpus of written German for advanced language learning. In A. Wichmann, S. Fligelstone, T. McEnery, & G. Knowles (eds.), *Teaching and language corpora* (pp. 131–45). London: Longman.

Farr, F. (2008). Evaluating the use of corpus-based instruction in a language teacher education context: Perspectives from the users. *Language Awareness* 17, 1, 25–43.

Flowerdew, J. (1993a). Concordancing as a tool in course design. *System* 21, 2, 231–44.

Flowerdew, J. (1993b). A process, or educational, approach to the teaching of professional genres. *ELT Journal* 47, 4, 305–16.

Flowerdew, J. (1996). Concordancing in language learning. In M. Pennington (ed.), *The power of CALL* (pp. 97–113). Houston: Athelstan.

Flowerdew, J. & Li, Y.-Y. (2009). Plagiarism and second language writing in an electronic age. *Annual Review of Applied Linguistics* 27, 161–83.

Flowerdew, L. (2002). Corpus-based Analyses in EAP. In J. Flowerdew (ed.), *Academic discourse* (pp. 95–114). London: Longman.

Flowerdew, L. (2005). An integration of corpus-based and genre-based approaches to text analysis in EAP/ESP: Countering criticisms against corpus-based methodologies. *English for Specific Purposes* 24, 321–32.

Flowerdew, L. (2008). Corpora and context in professional writing. In V. Bhatia, J. Flowerdew, & R. Jones (eds.), *Advances in discourse studies* (pp. 115–27). London: Longman.

Frankenberg-Garcia, A. (2005). A Peek into what today's language learners as researchers actually do. *International Journal of Lexicography* 18, 3, 335–55.

Gavioli, L. (2001). The learner as researcher: Introducing corpus concordancing in the classroom. In G. Aston (ed.), *Learning with corpora* (pp. 108–37). Houston: Athelstan.

Gavioli, L. (2005). *Exploring corpora for ESP learning*. Amsterdam/Philadelphia: John Benjamins.

Gavioli, L. & Aston, G. (2001). Enriching reality: Language corpora in language pedagogy. *ELT Journal* 55, 3, 238–46.

Gledhill, C. (2000). The discourse function of collocation in research article introductions. *English for Specific Purposes* 19, 115–35.

Granger, S. (2004a). Computer learner corpus research: Current status and future prospects. In U. Connor & T. A. Upton (eds.), *Applied corpus linguistics: A multidimensional perspective* (pp. 123–45). Amsterdam: Rodopi.

Granger, S. (2004b). Practical applications of learner corpora. In B. Lewandowska-Tomaszczyk (ed.), *Practical applications in language and computers (PALC 2003)* (pp. 291–301). Frankfurt: Peter Lang.

Hewings, M. (2000). *Using computer-based corpora as a teaching resource*. Available from www.realenglish.tm.fr.

Higgins, J. (1988). *Language, learners and computers*. London: Longman.

Higgins, J. & Johns, T. (1984). *Computers in language learning*. London: Collins.

Hunston, S. (1995). Grammar in teacher education: The role of a corpus. *Language Awareness* 4, 1, 15–31.

Hunston, S. (2002). *Corpora in applied linguistics*. Cambridge: Cambridge University Press.

Hyland, K. (2000). *Disciplinary discourses: Social interactions in academic writing*. Harlow, UK: Pearson Education.

Hyland, K. (2002). Activity and evaluation: Reporting practices in academic writing. In J. Flowerdew (ed.) *Academic discourse* (pp. 115–30). London: Longman.

Johns, T. (1988). Whence and whither classroom concordancing. In T. Bongaerts, P. De Haan, S. Lobbe, & H. Wekker (eds.), *Computer applications in language learning* (pp. 9–27). Dordrecht: Foris.

Kaltenböck, G. & Mehlmauer-Larcher, B. (2005). Computer corpora and the language classroom: On the potential and limitations of computer corpora in language teaching. *ReCALL* 17, 1, 65–84.

Kennedy, C. & Miceli, T. (2001). An evaluation of intermediate students' approaches to corpus investigation. *Language Learning & Technology* 5, 3, 77–90.

Kennedy, G. (1998). *An introduction to corpus linguistics*. London: Addison Wesley Longman.

King, P. (1997). Creating and processing corpora in Greek and Cyrillic alphabets on the personal computer. In A. Wichmann, S. Fligelstone, T. McEnery, & G. Knowles (eds.), *Teaching and language corpora* (pp. 277–91). London: Longman.

Kuo, C.-H., Wible, D., Wang, C.-C., & Chien, F.-Y. (2001). The design of a lexical difficulty filter for language learning on the Internet. In T. Okamoto, R. Hartley, J. Kinshuk, & Klus, J. (eds.), *Advanced learning technology: Issues, achievements and challenges* (pp. 53–4). Los Alamitos, CA: IEEE Computer Society.

Lee, D. & Swales, J. (2006). A corpus-based EAP course for NNS doctoral students: Moving from available specialized corpora to self-compiled corpora. *English for Specific Purposes* 25, 1, 56–75.

Leech, G. (1997). Teaching and language corpora: A convergence. In A. Wichmann, S. Fligelstone, T. McEnery, & G. Knowles (eds.), *Teaching and language corpora* (pp. 1–23). London: Longman.

Louw, B. (1993). Irony in the text or insincerity in the writer? The diagnostic potential of semantic prosodies. In M. Baker et al. (eds.), *Text and technology* (pp. 157–76). Amsterdam/Philadelphia: John Benjamins.

Ma, B. (1994). Learning strategies in classroom concordancing. In L. Flowerdew & K. Tong (eds.), *Entering text* (pp. 197–226). Hong Kong: Hong Kong University of Science and Technology and Guangzhou Institute of Foreign Languages.

MacWhinney, B. & Snow, C. (1991). The *CHILDES project: Tools for analyzing talk*. Hillsdale, NJ: Lawrence Erlbaum.

Mauranen, A. (2006). English in the hands of non-natives: What's going on? Plenary address presented at ICAME 27, Helsinki, May.

McEnery, T. & Wilson, A. (1997). Teaching and language corpora. *ReCALL* 9, 1, 5–14.

McEnery, T. & Wilson, H. (1996). *Corpus Linguistics*. Edinburgh: Edinburgh University Press.

Milton, J. (1998). Exploiting L1 and interlanguage corpora in the design of an electronic language learning and production environment. In S. Granger (ed.), *Learner English on computer* (pp. 186–98). London/New York: Addison Wesley Longman.

Milton, J. (2006). Resource-rich web-based feedback: Helping learners become independent writers. In K. Hyland & F. Hyland (eds.), *Feedback in second language writing: Contexts and issues* (pp. 123–39). Cambridge: Cambridge University Press.

Nattinger, J. (1980). A lexical phrase grammar for ESL. *TESOL Quarterly* 14, 337–44.

Nattinger, J. & de Carrico, J. (1992). *Lexical phrases and language teaching*. Oxford: Oxford University Press.

O'Keeffe, A. & Farr, F. (2003). Using language corpora in initial teacher education: Pedagogic issues and practical applications. *TESOL Quarterly* 37, 3, 389–418.

Pecorari, D. (2003). Good and original: Plagiarism and patchwriting in academic second-language writing. *Journal of Second Language Writing* 12, 317–45.

Pecorari, D. (2006). Visible and occluded citation features in postgraduate second-language writing. *English for Specific Purposes* 25, 4–29.

Quirk, R., Greenbaum, S., Leech, G., & Svartvik, J. (1985). *A comprehensive grammar of the English Language*. London/New York: Longman.

Richards, J. C. & Rogers, T. (2001). *Approaches and methods in language teaching*. Cambridge: Cambridge University Press.

Rule, S. (2004). French interlanguage oral corpora: Recent developments. In F. Myles & R. Towell (eds.), *The acquisition of French as a second language*. Special issue of *Journal of French Language Studies* 14, 3, 343–56.

Rule, S., Marsden, E., Myles, F., & Mitchell, R. (2003). Constructing a database of French interlanguage oral corpora. In D. Archer, P. Rayson, E. Wilson, & T. McEnery (eds.), *Proceedings of the Corpus Linguistics 2003 Conference*, UCREL Technical Papers no. 16 (pp. 669–77). University of Lancaster.

Scott, M. & Tribble, C. (2006). *Textual patterns: Key words and corpus analysis in language teaching*. Amsterdam/Philadelphia: John Benjamins.

Sealey, A. & Thompson, P. (2004). "What do you call the dull words?" Primary school children using corpus-based approaches to learn about language. *English in Education* 38, 1, 80–91.

Sinclair, J. M. (1990). *Collins COBUILD English grammar*. London: HarperCollins.

Sinclair, J. M. (1991). *Corpus, concordance collocation*. Oxford: Oxford University Press.

Sinclair, J. M. & Renouf, A. (1988). A lexical syllabus for language learning. In R. Carter & M. McCarthy (eds.), *Vocabulary and language teaching* (pp. 140–60). London: Longman.

Stenström, A., Andersen, G., & Hasund, K. (2002). *Trends in teenage talk: Corpus compilation, analysis and findings*. Amsterdam/Philadelphia: John Benjamins.

Stevens, B. (1991). Concordance-based vocabulary exercises: A viable alternative to gap-fillers. In T. Johns & P. King (eds.), Classroom concordancing. Special issue of *English Language Research Journal* 4, 47–61.

Stubbs, M. (1996). *Text and corpus analysis*. Oxford: Blackwell.

Stubbs, M. (2001). *Words and phrases: Corpus studies of lexical semantics*. Oxford: Blackwell.

Stubbs, M. (2004). Language corpora. In A. Davies & C. Elder (eds.), *The handbook of applied linguistics* (pp. 106–32). Oxford: Blackwell.

Swales, J. M. (ed.) (1988). *Episodes in ESP*. London: Prentice-Hall.

Swales, J. M. (1990). *Genre analysis: English in academic and research settings*. Cambridge: Cambridge University Press.

Swales, J. M., Ahmad, U. K., Chang, Y.-Y., Chavez, D., Dressen, D. F., & Seymour, R. (1998). Consider this: The role of imperatives in scholarly writing. *Applied Linguistics* 19, 1, 97–121.

Thompson, G. (1993). *Reporting*. London: Collins.

Thurston, J. & Candlin, C. (1993). *Exploring academic English: A workbook for student essay writing*. Sydney: National Centre for English Language Teaching and Research.

Tribble, C. (2000). Genres, keywords, teaching: Towards a pedagogic account of the language of project proposals. In L. Burnard & T. McEnery (eds.), *Rethinking language pedagogy from a corpus perspective* (pp. 75–90). Frankfurt am Main: Peter Lang.

Tribble, C. & Jones, G. (1990). *Concordances in the classroom*. London: Longman.

Tsui, A. (2004). ESL teachers' questions and corpus evidence. *International Journal of Corpus Linguistics* 10, 335–56.

Weber, J. J. (2001). A concordance- and genre-informed approach to ESP essay writing. *ELT Journal* 55, 1, 14–20.

Wible, D., Kuo, C.-H., Chien, F.-Y., Liu, A., & Tsao, N.-L. (2001). A web-based EFL writing environment: Integrating information for learners, teachers, and researchers. *Computers and Education* 37, 297–315.

Wichmann, A. (1995). Using concordances for the teaching of modern languages in higher education. *Language Learning Journal* 11, 61–3.

Widdowson, H. G. (2004). *Text, context, and pretext: Critical issues in discourse analysis*. Oxford: Blackwell.

Wilkins, D. A. (1972). *Notional syllabuses*. London: Longman.

Willis, D. (1990). *The lexical syllabus: A new approach to language teaching*. London: HarperCollins.

Willis, J. & Willis, D. (1989). *Collins COBUILD English course*. London: Collins.

Yoon, H. & Hirvela, A. (2004). ESL student attitudes towards corpus use in L2 writing. *Journal of Second Language Writing* 13, 257–83.

FURTHER READING

Conrad, S. (2000). Will corpus linguistics revolutionize grammar teaching in the 21st century? *TESOL Quarterly* 34, 438–60.

Fox, G. (1998). Using corpus data in the classroom. In B. Tomlinson (ed.), *Materials development in language teaching* (pp. 25–43). Cambridge: Cambridge University Press.

Swales, J. M. (2002). Integrated and fragmented worlds: EAP materials and corpus linguistics. In J. Flowerdew (ed.), *Academic discourse* (pp. 150–64). London: Longman.

20 Technology-Enhanced Materials

DAVID BRETT AND MARTA GONZÁLEZ-LLORET

Introduction

Newspapers, magazines, leaflets, pens, scissors, glue, and a clean working surface – these were the tools used 20-odd years ago by the second or foreign language teacher when creating materials for use in the classroom and elsewhere. Today the setting has changed considerably as the "clean working surface" has become the computer desktop, newspaper articles are found online, suitable images can be found effortlessly using a search engine, additional text is typed in, and the whole exercise is assembled and "glued together" using a mouse rather than one's own hands. If we were to include this scenario in our definition of "technology-enhanced materials," we could conclude that technology has indeed permeated the profession deeply and materials creation almost invariably implies the use of these new tools. We will instead adopt a slightly narrower perspective in the forthcoming pages, and focus not so much on ways in which technology has facilitated the creation of materials and ameliorated the presentation thereof, as attention will instead be directed toward tools and related strategies that simply did not exist before the unprecedented revolution in the field of communications that took place at the end of the last century.

There is no doubt that technology can help enhance the quality of input, and the authenticity of resources, provide relevant and useful feedback, connect students with remote audiences, and train them in the use of technological advances that are fundamental skills in everyday life. Technology is, however, no more and no less that the use practitioners and learners make of it. Nowadays, technological advances have made computer-assisted language learning (CALL) a wide field that includes the use of the Internet (multimedia sources, online dictionaries); communication tools such as MOOs,[1] email, chat rooms, and audio/videoconferencing; software and applications designed specifically for language learning, the authoring and publication of web, digital audio and video materials, etc., all of which seek to enhance and promote language learning. In this chapter, we will explore some of the possible scenarios and most relevant sources of technological advances that teachers or materials designers can encounter when implementing technology in the classroom, addressing their potential for language teaching and learning. The resources presented here were selected for their methodological and pedagogical possibilities as second language teaching and learning tools. However, they are but a small sample of the resources currently available in the technological world.

The Pedagogical Evolution of CALL

As historians have noted, the field of language learning has suffered strong pendulum swings of fashion over the years, due mainly to the lack of a commonly accepted theory of how foreign or second languages are acquired (Long, 1997). CALL, as a field of study, has evolved following the gravitational pull of these pedagogic shifts in SLA.

On one side of the pendulum, second language methodology was initially influenced by structural linguistics (Bloomfield, 1933), and consequently favored structural and lexical syllabi and the teaching of explicit grammar rules, repetition of models, transformation exercises, and the memorization of short dialogues and phrases. At this time, the implementation of technology for language learning was reduced to grammatical drills, lexical games, transformation exercises, and language-learning software designed mainly for autonomous student–computer interaction.

In a shift away from the structural synthetic approach, language-learning methodology moved to a communicative approach, where the main focus was on meaning and the student, rather than on the language itself. Reflecting this variation, in the field of CALL, computers evolved from being a tool for individual learning to a vehicle facilitative of human-to-human communication. Computers evolved from containers of individualized input to tools for engagement in authentic discourse with other users of the language. The Internet and the World Wide Web became the main tools for language learning in the classroom, and networked-based language teaching (Kern & Warschauer, 2000), or e-tandem learning projects, proliferated. Today, this area of CALL is still a vast field of study, with research that is both descriptive and empirical in nature, and focuses mainly on the applications and effects of asynchronous (email, bulletin boards) and synchronous (chat rooms, audio and video conferencing) computer-mediated communication (CMC). The issues examined range from studies of the characteristics specific to CMC language that promote interaction and language acquisition (e.g., Pellettieri, 1999; Smith, 2003), to issues of identity (e.g., Freiermuth, 2002), and cross-cultural studies on the effects of CMC on language, and communicative and cultural competence (e.g., Belz, 2002, 2003; Belz & Kinginger, 2003; Chun, 1994; Kramsch & Thorne, 2002). In contrast with the previous period, the relationship between the student and the computer is not limited to individual human–machine interaction. Students are encouraged to become competent users of the medium, developing *computer-mediated literacy* (Warschauer, 2003b).

Technology is not just a tool for individual language learning, but a skill for independent language use and effective daily communication in an increasingly digital world.

To pursue the analogy of the pendulum swing in pedagogical approaches to language teaching, language professionals' views are now moving back toward the vertical, from purely communicative practices to focusing on accuracy without neglecting the communicative intention, or what is known as Focus on Form (Doughty & Williams, 1998; Long, 1991). Technology offers numerous possibilities for enhancing accuracy in the different skills and, at the same time, presenting meaningful, interesting, and communicative activities. Blogs and Wikies are examples of new Internet tools that can be employed to foster language accuracy and focus on form while engaging learners in collaborative, creative, and constructive writing activities (see review below).

The provision of feedback, one of the great challenges faced by CALL today, is being addressed by new technologies and views on learning. (See Nagata, 1993, and Ware & Warschauer, 2006, on electronic feedback.) As technology evolves, it is in the language teachers' hands to select those tools that are most appropriate for implementing their pedagogical approach and/or to help develop those skills that best fit their teaching philosophy. As Warschauer stated in an interview with Ancker (2002):

> if you start with teachers who have a very good approach to project-based curriculum, they will be able to very easily integrate computers into that. But if you start with computers without a good curriculum or a good pedagogy, the computer itself won't help very much. (p. 5)

As technology develops and diffuses, and applications in the field of language learning increase, CALL is becoming a broad field of study, with multiple sub-areas, where research is rapidly proliferating. Some researchers advocate a unified field with a consensus on empirical research that would allow a growing evaluation of the impact of technology on language learning (Zhao, 2004). Others, on the contrary, propose the integration of technology in all fields of language learning rather than viewing CALL as a separate small subfield in applied linguistics (Chapelle, 2005). We agree with Chapelle's idea of full integration of technology as part of all fields of language learning. An empirical study of the effectiveness of computerized feedback on essays may be closer in design, application, and conclusions to SLA research on the different forms of feedback on writing than a study on identity shifts in cross-cultural electronic-tandem learning, although both may employ computers as tools for language engagement. Rather than trying to integrate all forms of technology under the umbrella of language-learning tools, research should focus on exploring what forms of technology match which pedagogical and methodological approaches, and how these can be integrated into the language classroom. The use of technology should be approached in much the same way as any other technique or tool, i.e., for its effectiveness for language learning. (See for example Doughty & Long, 2003, for technological resources that are compatible with task-based language teaching (TBLT) as a methodological approach.) It has been suggested that when we achieve full integration of technology into the language learning environment, rather than seeing it as a separate CALL component, we will see technology as something transparent, part of any curriculum development, pedagogical, or methodological choice we make, or materials we create. As Warschauer stated (1999):

> The truly powerful technologies are so integrated as to be invisible. We have no "BALL" (book-assisted language learning), no "PALL" (pen-assisted language learning), and no "LALL" (library-assisted language learning). When we have no "CALL," computers will have taken their place as a natural and powerful part of the language learning process. (n.p.)

Technology and Materials Creation

The role played by the individual teacher in the creation of materials is one of fundamental importance and stances on this issue have changed considerably over the years. Weible's (1983) position, at the dawn of the IT revolution, was that "teachers must not become too remote from the actual programming effort" (p. 64) and, therefore, should learn to script their own exercises. This view is today seen as being overly optimistic: as the creators of the highly successful Hot Potatoes program note, "few working teachers have the time to do formal programming courses, and most would think that any kind of programming is therefore beyond them" (Arneil & Holmes, 2004). It is often difficult to obtain a general picture of how much technology has permeated the profession, as surveys of technical skills often draw answers from subjects who have already expressed an interest in this aspect of language teaching (for example Hegelheimer et al., 2004), whereas technophobes, by definition, shy away from technology-based workshops and are loath to fill in questionnaires on the topic. One study addressing such topics (Gillespie & Barr, 2002) conducted a survey in three tertiary institutions that reported telling data: "17% of colleagues at Cambridge and 15% at Ulster use the Web for publishing course notes or other class material, compared to 62% in Toronto" and "more staff in Toronto have used the Web to design language-learning exercises and material: 31% in Toronto, compared with 14% and 8% in Cambridge and Ulster respectively." Motivation, facilities, computer literacy, and work pressure were mentioned as being among the influential factors, as was the presence of support staff, the latter pointing an admonitory finger at the oft-reported tendency for administrators to prefer investment in "tangible" (i.e., machinery), rather than human, resources.

However, it may also be argued that, on the whole, technology has not been rendered particularly accessible to those in the language teaching profession. Many of the tools and functions that are availed of have been developed elsewhere and with different criteria in mind. Tailoring these to the specific task at hand requires considerable knowledge and expertise, as Laurillard (2003, p. ix) states:

Technological innovation is driven by many factors, but not one of them concerns a pedagogical imperative. There is no dialogue between teachers and technologists about what kind of technological innovation learners need: neither side knows how to begin the dialogue.

Hence, due to incomplete knowledge of the potential, teachers may not be ambitious enough in their demands; likewise, while possessing the technical know-how, technologists may not provide optimum solutions, due to a lack of awareness of specific needs. Furthermore, in the near future, we are unlikely to see a repetition of the fundamental changes to the potential for the creation and diffusion of materials that took place in the last decade (Brett, 2006a). Indeed, developments which have taken place in recent years have concerned relatively minor improvements to technology that emerged in the 1990s; for example, in web technology, greater emphasis is placed on the rationalization of data transfer, e.g., Cascading Style Sheets (CSS) and Ajax (see Godwin-Jones, 2005a for the latter) and security (e.g., the blocking of active content). The latter, in fact, represents a step backward, as interactive quizzes and multimedia content may be blocked by default on the user's computer.

Hence, the adaptation of existing technology to the field of second language learning is a process that is far from complete, and "the dizzying array of technologically feasible options in distance learning" (Doughty & Long, 2003) remains vastly underexploited. For example, given the very nature of the field, the insertion of audio in materials to be viewed on- and off-line, is highly desirable, yet near-optimum solutions have only recently started to emerge and are far from being widely adopted (Brett, 2005b). Similarly, there is much room for improvement in the creation of authoring tools, both regarding existing and innovative exercise typologies. Regarding the former, a move must be made toward the provision of intrinsic feedback (Bangs, 2008), which has been defined as that which should "mimic a good teacher offering helpful advice and encouragement" (Bangs, 2008). An example of such feedback may be constituted by a text-entry exercise in which input is not compared with the correct answer(s) on a Boolean right/wrong basis, but, rather, is parsed character by character, word by word, in order to highlight non-corresponding items in the input (Brett, 2006b). The expansion of exercise typologies to provide more varied and stimulating input will invariably involve drag'n'drop activities (Brett, 2004). For instance, little use has yet been made of the possibility of creating exercises that entail the movement of audio clips to match, order, or group phrases – activities that constitute a fundamental step forward with regard to the linear listening exercises presented in the traditional tape-and-textbook scenario.

Of fundamental importance in the design phase of materials creation for language learning, or any other discipline for that matter, is the division between content and functionality (Bangs, 2008). As Ward (2002) notes "often the language content is inextricably linked with the code and the two cannot be separated." As a result, it is difficult to make small alterations to materials in successive phases to adopt them to specific learning contexts; similarly, it is hard to rectify materials after having noticed mistakes, ambiguities, misleading items, and so forth. Furthermore, if content is inseparable from processing, the whole system becomes liable to redundancy as licenses for proprietary software may expire, or the developers may decide not to update the software to new standards. Ward (2002) and Cushion (2004) discuss these factors and propose storage of materials content in XML (eXtensible Markup Language) as a viable solution. The latter author also discusses the possibility of pooling materials by designing data storage so that content is readable by multiple applications; a concrete example is given in the form of interoperability between material created with the Hot Potatoes and GISMO tools (see Review of Resources, below). In addition, a complete separation of content from functionality also facilitates the translation of material from one language to another (Bangs, 2008). For example, the considerable investment entailed in creating activities that are rich in graphics and interactivity can be made to pay off if such material can be easily adopted for use with multiple languages.

Finally, it is important to note that authoring tools are no more than a necessary go-between to mediate interaction between users and the complex scripting and processing that underlie the creation of even the simplest of exercises. While, on the one hand, materials creation is facilitated, so that even those with little or no technical knowledge can swiftly become productive, templates do entail a compromise, in that it can be somewhat difficult to tailor output so as to incorporate specific interactions. As Bangs (2008, section 5) observes:

> On the one hand, many more teachers have been able to create the routines they require with minimal training; but on the other, very many items of courseware do not seem to offer a structured approach to the learning process, mainly through the inability to use the tools in a sophisticated way without considerable programming expertise being acquired.

Hence, these tools may be deemed inappropriate for the creation of materials foreseeing sophisticated levels of interaction, such as those required by task-like activities, desirable characteristics of which are outlined in Doughty and Long (2003). This dilemma is unlikely to disappear in the foreseeable future, as all computer languages require strict adherence to the use of set terms and syntax and are unanimous in their failure to proffer forgiveness if these criteria are not met. Furthermore, sophisticated interaction involves provision for myriad "what if?" scenarios, resulting in scripts which run into four-figure lengths. Therefore, a line must be drawn: on one side lie the features and functions that can be included using authoring tools or templates, the nether side being the realm of the experts, i.e., programmers working in close collaboration with instructional designers, graphic artists and, of course the Subject Matter Experts (SMEs). On the basis of the considerations outlined throughout this section, particular and continuous attention must be paid to the former area, so as to ensure that the potential for the creation of material by non-experts is exploited fully and that tools are updated regularly to incorporate new technological solutions as they emerge.

Teachers as Authors: What Can Be Expected

With an unlimited budget and a team of expert graphic designers, programmers, and technicians, teachers could make their "teaching with technology" dreams come true. However, reality is very different and most projects are the result of small collaborations, fostered by grants, between teams of teachers or institutions. In this section, we shall illustrate a few examples that range from materials created with a large budget and a substantial pool of human resources to modest projects created by individual language teachers interested in employing technology in their language classrooms.

Large projects/Commercial enterprises

Vcom3D, Inc. and the Defense Language Institute have created several web-based prototypes for the teaching of language and "cultural familiarization" to military personnel through simulations which incorporate realistic, lifelike 3D animated characters to teach verbal and non-verbal behavior (www.vcom3d.com). These highly sophisticated simulations constitute an enthralling glimpse into a possible future for language teaching; however, the resources currently required for the production of such material prove to be prohibitive for most language teachers.

Several other examples of large corporations or commercial enterprises that develop and provide tools for language learning will be examined later in the Review of Resources section. Some of these enterprises, i.e., most messenger services, such as Yahoo Messenger, AOL, and MSN, were not developed specifically as language teaching tools; however, they have become central to CALL. Others, like Hot Potatoes, were developed for educational purposes, but not exclusively for language learning. There are tools, however, like LexiKAN Software (www.lexikan.com), designed specifically to teach languages, in this case Japanese kanji, hiragana, and katakana.

Collaborative projects

An excellent example of a collaborative project is a program developed for L2 Spanish at the University of Montreal by Asencio and Desnoyers (2004), "Viaje al pasado: los aztecas" (www.ccdmd.qc.ca/ri/aztecas), by a team of designers, programmers, and two language teachers. The project is available through CD-ROM, and can also be accessed through their web page. It includes activities, exercises, and two adventures wherein the students take on simulated roles to try to accomplish a specific goal (through the target language). During the activity, the students are presented with rich texts, and are provided with tools to help them deal with difficult vocabulary items: dictionaries, books, graphics, explanations, etc., designed as elaborated, not simplified, forms of input (Doughty & Long, 2003). The activities include different forms of multimedia input, a strategy which has been proposed as beneficial for language learning (Al-Seghayer, 2001; Chun & Plass, 1996; Jones & Plass, 2002), and the students engage in several skills.

Individual-teacher projects

Like many other language teachers, we have produced examples of technology to be integrated in our language classrooms created with neither an additional budget, nor specific training in matters technological. González-Lloret (2003, 2007) provides examples of technology in the service of language teaching. "En busca de Esmeraldas" is a virtual reality simulation for the teaching of directions in L2 Spanish, based on Long's Methodological Principles of TBLT (Doughty, 2001; Doughty & Long, 2003) to promote collaborative work among students. "Crítica Poética" is a task-based unit to help advanced Spanish learners improve their literary criticism skills in the target language. Brett (2005a) has created a web site called "English phonetics and phonology for non-native speakers" (http://davidbrett.uniss.it), in which numerous examples of connected speech are presented, and phenomena such as weak forms, yod coalescence, elision, etc., are highlighted and explained. In creating this site, the author has attempted to incorporate a number of innovative features, such as Flash MP3 players for optimum delivery of sound for language-learning purposes, and a series of drag'n'drop exercise templates. These solutions have been created in such a way that they can be easily re-used by others in the field, even in other languages, as whole interfaces can be translated. Authoring tools have been developed for some tasks, e.g., the insertion of audio into web pages.

Another interesting example of technology used to enhance language materials is an advanced Indonesian distance course at the University of Hawai'i, developed by Dr Uli Kozok, using Hot Potatoes (reviewed below), WebSequitor, and Flash material, all integrated in WebCT as the class environment (http://bahasa.net/online/305.html). This is the first distance learning course for the Indonesian language to be offered by a university to a worldwide audience, and in this course, technology is an essential part of the course implementation.

Review of Resources

Courseware

- *Hot Potatoes* (http://hotpot.uvic.ca) – "Hot Pot," as it is known to aficionados, is certainly one of the most user-friendly and widely adopted authoring tools available. This program, which is free of charge for workers in publicly-funded, non-profit-making, educational institutions, produces JavaScript-based exercises to be read by browsers, that are, hence, suitable for on- and off-line use. The types of exercises that can be created include multiple-choice, jumbled sentences, crosswords, matching/ordering, and gap-fill. A feature called the "Masher" can be used to group exercises into modules. Source files are XML-based, hence enhancing interoperability. An associated Yahoo users group (http://groups.yahoo.com/group/hotpotatoesusers/) deals not only with bugs, but also explores ways to reach optimum multimedia solutions.

- *GISMO* (http://languages.londonmet.ac.uk/CALL/call/home.htm) – The GISMO (Guildhall Interactive Software for Multimedia Online) authoring tool, which is free of charge for education institutions, permits the creation of 12 different types of browser-based exercises. Exercises can be organized into articulated learning modules. Of particular interest are high levels of support for non-Roman scripts and an online voice recording facility. The system stores data in XML and the creator is a strong advocate of interoperability and the pooling of CALL resources (Cushion, 2004).
- *CLIC* – This freeware program by Francesc Busquets allows the development of multimedia activities for language learning. Several different types of activities can be created: puzzles, associations, crosswords, identification activities, exploration activities, open-ended answers and multiple choice. (http://clic.xtec.net/en/index.htm)
- *MaxAuthor* – The freely distributed MaxAuthor program was developed at the University of Arizona under the auspices of the Critical Languages Series project. The program produces material for distribution on CD-ROMs and also over the web. A feature of particular interest is the great stress placed on the inclusion of audio. Exercise typologies offered include listening dictation, pronunciation, multiple choice, vocabulary completion, and audio flashcards. (http://cali.arizona.edu/docs/wmaxa)
- *MALTED* – The MALTED authoring system was developed by a team, including educators and programmers in the UK, Spain, France, and Ireland, under the auspices of the EU Telematics Applications programs: Socrates and Leonardo da Vinci. The content created can be delivered in two different ways: using a stand-alone Runtime System (RTS) involving local installation; and a web version, by way of the MALTED Applet. A wide range of learning activities can be created, involving pervasive use of multimedia, yielding a result that is both pedagogically sound and professionally sophisticated. The system is offered as free software under the terms of the GNU agreement. (http://malted.cnice.mec.es/ingles/whatMalted.htm)
- *Adobe Authorware*[2] – Authorware is an upmarket commercial tool for the creation of e-learning packages to be distributed on CD-ROMs or over the web. It allows the inclusion in learning modules of a vast array of media and file types and the creation of high levels of interactivity. Nevertheless, this tool has not been widely adopted within the CALL community. Some authors make reference to the tool's intricacy: "despite its emphasis on usability, first-time users should beware that they face a significant learning curve" (Potter, 2003). (www.adobe.com/products/authorware)
- *Flash and Director* – This short review of authoring tools for the creation of language learning materials would not be complete without reference to Flash and Director, both marketed by Adobe. These two programs were not developed with education in mind, as their main applications are in the fields of advertising, graphics, games, and the creation of state-of-the-art websites and e-commerce kiosks. Nevertheless, their marriage of excellent handling of

multimedia with powerful scripting languages (actionScript for Flash, and Lingo for Director) has made them a first choice for developers of language learning materials wishing to create tailor-made interfaces and interactivity. The versatility of these programs' output is such that they can be used to create both authoring tools and finished exercises. In some aspects, the two programs are similar; however, Flash is more suitable for web-based material, as the player needed to view Flash content approaches 100 percent diffusion amongst web-users' computers (diffusion of the Shockwave player needed to view Director's output is little more than 50 percent). On the other hand, Director is more suitable for the creation of materials to be viewed locally, and/or applications which require access to the local hard disk. Two functions of interest that can be carried out using Director and not Flash are: rendering 3D environments, and accessing the local microphone for "listen-and-repeat" type activities in offline environments. Given the versatility and power of these programs, it is implicit that their use requires considerable expertise; they are, therefore, unsuitable for those approaching the field of materials creation for the first time. (www.adobe.com/products/flash/flashpro; www.adobe.com/products/director)

Learning management systems

Creating technology-enhanced materials for local or online use only partially harnesses the potential available if learners' interactions are not recorded in some way that makes them available for subsequent viewing. Instructors may want to know who has completed such exercises, obtaining such a grade, etc.; similarly, learners may desire to know what stage they are at in a course and how they have fared. These necessities have led to the development of Learning Management Systems (LMSs)[3] that, besides permitting the tracking and statistical elaboration of user behavior, offer other features, such as chat rooms and discussion boards that enhance the notion of "community" amongst the otherwise frequently isolated users of the materials by facilitating not only learner–instructor communication but also that between learners. LMSs come in different packages: institutions may choose to establish their own, in-house, platforms using PHP, Perl, or other technologies, or choose to adopt ready-made solutions, such as the commercially available Blackboard (www.blackboard.com) and WebCT (www.webct.com).[4] Moodle (www.moodle.org) is an option that has attracted considerable attention in recent years; while being free and open-source, it is far from a "poor man's" alternative, and does not compare unfavorably to similar products that bear conspicuous price tags.

Internet tools

CMC

Synchronous (text, audio, and video conferencing) and asynchronous (email, bulletin boards) computer-mediated communication Internet tools are some of the most widely employed for language learning. Ways of communicating with others over the Internet are becoming increasingly available to the public free of cost. The most popular commercially available tools for conferencing (text, audio and video) are the Messengers by AOL, MSN and Yahoo. CMC is probably one of the Internet tools most employed in language classrooms for the capacity that it has to connect geographically dispersed audiences, especially students, with other speakers of the language they are learning. The main advantage of CMC for language learning lies in the potential it has for collaborative learning and for allowing learners to interact, modify, and elaborate their input (Doughty & Long, 2003), while engaging in meaningful "conversation." A great deal of research on CALL in recent years has focused on some aspect of CMC that potentially makes it an optimal tool for language learning, concentrating mainly on text interactions or "chats." (See Chapelle, this volume, and Kern, 2006, for discussions of the effectiveness of CMC for language learning.) Recently, with faster connecting capability among learners and schools, research has started to explore the capability of audio and videoconferencing for language learning, and how this may differ from text-only interaction. This also entails exploring and comparing several audio and voice tools, such as Wimba (www.wimba.com); Skype (www.skype.com); and PalTalk (www.paltalk.com/) (e.g., Compton et al., 2006; Wang, 2004a, 2004b).

Blogs and wikies

Blogs are the new generation of bulletin boards. They are hosted on the Internet, rather than a web environment, and are generally freely accessible. Users can include not only text but also multimedia (pictures, video, and sound), as well as hypertext (links to other pages on the Internet). Blogs are chronologically organized, with the most recent posting first, followed by previous postings, and it is not necessary to have any web-authoring knowledge, since most blogging software presents the writer with an interface that is similar to that of a word-processing program, and is, therefore, intuitive and easy to use. Blogs allow students not only to practice L2 reading and writing skills, but also to collaborate, persuade, contend, and develop ideas as individuals and as part of a group in a public arena, rather than in the closed environment of a classroom forum, a factor which gives them a sense of agency (Kramsch, Van Ness, & Lam, 2000). Blogs can also be used as tools for peer reviewing, providing feedback, and as spaces for collaborative project-writing. To cater for the growing interest in blogs as an alternative to forums and bulletin boards, numerous sites now offer simple, ready-to-use blog services (Blogger, www.blogger.com; WordPress, http://wordpress.com, or Moveable Type, www.movabletype.org), including blogs for educational purposes (elearnspace, www.elearnspace.org; edublogs, htpp://edublogs.org.uk/cs/blogs/mfle; The modern languages blog, www.ltscotland.org.uk/cs/blogs/mfle; eslblogs, http://eslblogs.org; China blog list, www.chinabloglist.org; L2 Spanish blog http://principiantes.wordpress.com). Blogs are without doubt a fast growing CALL tool. However, their potential for language learning is still an area to be explored empirically.

Although blogs can be used for collaborative writing, the chronological order of the postings limits the interactivity of the users. Wikies, on the other hand, encourage truly collaborative writing efforts. The term "wiki" (Hawaiian meaning 'quick' or 'fast') is short for WikiWikiWeb, a open-editing system in which anybody can edit, add, or delete content (although the process of deleting must be corroborated to take effect, and logs of the changes are kept). The most popular wiki is certainly Wikipedia (www.wikipedia.com), a publicly created encyclopedia that has swiftly reached mammoth proportions (see LeLoup & Ponterio, 2006, for an evaluation of its use for language learning). Wikispaces (www.wikispaces.com) is an environment in which wikies can be created easily (e.g., a wiki dedicated to CALL by Daniel Craig, http://danielcraig.wikispaces.com/CALL+Class+Resources).

Similar to blogs, the potential of wikies for language learning lies in their collaborative nature and the potential that this has for L2 writing acquisition. Godwin-Jones (2003) provides an excellent review of blogs and wikies as language tools, and in this era of electronic information, wikies and blogs are tools that stimulate new conceptions of literacy, in which texts are perceived to be non-linear and interspersed with multimedia, where the frontier between writing and reading is blurred.

WebQuests (http://webquest.org/index.php)

WebQuests are inquiry-oriented activities based on information on the Internet created originally at San Diego State University by Bernie Dodge. They are designed to maximize the use of students' time spent surfing the web while promoting thinking skills, such as comparing, classifying, inducing, deducing, analyzing, abstracting, and constructing support. WebQuests are particularly popular for use with primary and secondary school learners and are typically created by teachers or groups of teachers for one or more curriculum subjects, including second languages, always following a fixed structure that identifies them as WebQuests. The main advantage of WebQuests as CALL activities lies in the fact that they utilize authentic resources on the Internet to engage students in collaborative tasks that result in a tangible product (poster, class presentation, web page, etc.). The creation of a WebQuest requires no knowledge of web page creation, since the initial input given to the students can be presented on paper. However, most WebQuest instructions are created as simple web pages which incorporate links to the relevant pages the students must visit. The main disadvantage of these activities is that they are time-consuming to create, although once created, they may be reused with small changes and updates. In addition, many teachers render such output available to colleagues over the Internet.

Associations

* *CALICO* – The Computer Assisted Language Instruction Consortium is a professional organization dedicated to the world of education and technology, with emphasis on modern language teaching and learning. It provides access

to special interest groups and Calico's annual conference, as well as the *Calico Journal*, all of which are excellent sources of research on new technologies applied to language learning. (www.calico.org)

- *IALLT* – The International Association for Language Learning Technology is dedicated to promoting effective uses of media centers for language teaching, learning, and research. It holds a biennial conference and The *Journal of Language Learning Technologies*, a refereed journal, is published twice a year. (www/iallt.org)

- *APACALL* – The Asia-Pacific Association for Computer-Assisted Language Learning. Its membership is free. Members can subscribe to the APACALL E-list, join one APACALL SIG (special interest group), and submit chapters/articles to the *APACALL Book Series/APACALL Journal*. (www.apacall.org)

- *WorldCALL* – With headquarters at Griffith University, Australia, and with Mike Levy as Executive Director, this organization promotes opportunities for those nations currently underserved in the areas of CALL and TELL for participation and collaboration in the development of materials, research, and technological capabilities. (www.upv.es/worldcall)

- *Eurocall* – Although this association for teachers and researchers interested in CALL is based in Europe, presenters from all over the world are attracted to its annual conference. The proceedings thereof are published in *ReCall* (Cambridge University Press). (www.eurocall-languages.org)

- *IATEFL Learning technologies SIG* – This special interest group for members of the worldwide ESL association IATEFL hosts frequent events and a discussion forum. Thrice yearly it publishes *Call Review*, which is available online to SIG members. (www.iatefl.org)

Journals

In addition to articles about technology and language learning in journals devoted to all issues on language teaching and learning, there are a few journals devoted to new technologies and language learning.

- *LL&T* – *Language Learning and Technology*. A refereed online journal sponsored and funded by the University of Hawai'i National Foreign Language Resource Center (NFLRC) and the Michigan State University Center for Language Education and Research (CLEAR), and co-sponsored by the Center for Applied Linguistics (CAL). (http://llt.msu.edu)

- *System* – A journal devoted to the applications of educational technology and applied linguistics to problems of foreign language teaching and learning of a variety of languages. (www.elsevier.com/wps/find/journaldescription.cws_home/335/description#description)

- *CALL* – Computer Assisted Language Learning Journal, published by Taylor & Francis, is dedicated to the use of computers and L1 and L2 learning, teaching and testing. It also provides a discussion forum. (www.tandf.co.uk/journals/titles/09588221.asp)

Other online resources

In addition, it is possible to find online publications, some of which are accessible free of charge, relating to organizations, conferences, universities, and individuals:

- *CALL4All* – A collection of websites related to language learning and teaching, compiled by Jean Paul Loucky. (www.call4all.us)
- *Foreign Language and Culture* – A large site compiling links to language and culture all around the world. (http://www.speakeasy.org/~dbrick/Hot/foreign.html)
- *Graham Davies' Favorite Websites* – A site of alphabetically-ordered annotated links related to foreign language learning and teaching. (www.camsoftpartners.co.uk/websites.htm)
- *ICT4LT* – Originally funded by the European Commission, this extensive series of modules on ICT for language teachers is continuously revised, offering analysis and "hands-on" advice by top practitioners. The Questionnaire and "can do" lists are a good starting point for newcomers to the field. (www.ict4lt.org)
- *Instituto Cervantes* – Centro Virtual Cervantes. A very comprehensive website, with many useful links for teachers and learners of Spanish. (http://cvc.cervantes.es)
- *Japanese Online* – A useful site for learners of Japanese. It provides free learning services to study the Japanese language. It includes a popular forum/bulletin board service. (www.japanese-online.com)
- *Journal of Computer-Mediated Communication* – A web-based, peer-reviewed interdisciplinary journal. Its focus is on social science research into computer-mediated communication via the Internet, the World Wide Web, and wireless technologies. (http://jcmc.indiana.edu)
- *Language Guide* – Free resources for language learners and teachers provided by Language Revolution. (www.languageguide.org)
- *NFLRC* – Selected papers from the Distance Education, Distributed Learning & Language Instruction 2004 Symposium. (www.nflrc.hawaii.edu/networks/nw44)
- *The PGCE MFL Webpages* – Several web pages, collected by Dr Norbert Pachler at the Institute of Education, University of London. They include web-based resources for French, German, Spanish and Italian. (www.ioe.ac.uk/schools/clc/pachler/pgcemfl/indexnew.html)
- *Wikipedia on CALL* – Includes a history section as well as multiple links to professional associations, journals and other sites. (http://en.wikipedia.org/wiki/Computer-assisted_language_learning)

Non-computer resources

While computers are certainly the technology that has had most impact on second and foreign language learning in recent years, it is important not to neglect other tools that can and have been incorporated into courses and curricula. Video has recently taken a quantum leap forward, as DVD, rather than the video-cassette, has become the standard format. The new format offers a series of advantages that can all be exploited for activities in the classroom or elsewhere: the possibility to change the audio language, to view subtitles or not, and to divide scenes into bite-sized pieces. Satellite television, and the more recent development of digital television both allow learners to access authentic materials from all over the world (see Sherman, 2003, for an excellent introduction to the use of such resources). Digital acquisition of televised material, a feature already available to home users, represents a more convenient solution to that of the video cassette, as video clips can be presented in a single format, together with transcriptions, comprehension questions, stills, and other items. This procedure is likely to become the norm in the near future, as current trends display a tendency for all media equipment to merge with a PC to form a single "media centre." These new tools offer authors and instructors a range of possibilities of presenting rich input that can be manipulated at will.

Handheld devices are another recent technological phenomenon, and their vast diffusion, particularly among the younger generations, has prompted several studies to evaluate their potential as language-learning tools. Kiernan and Aizawa (2004) describe a study of the use of cell phones in freshmen classes in Japan. Chinnery (2006) conducted a survey of studies concerning cell phones and other handheld devices, such as personal digital assistants (PDAs) and MP3 players (the most popular example of which is the iPod). While concluding in favor of the use of these technologies, he notes that "while cell phone ownership may be almost universal for college-aged individuals, this is not true for other populations or media"; needless to say, ownership of PDAs is low even amongst those in tertiary education. To the contrary, the MP3 player is a modestly priced item and constitutes an innovative solution for accessing both didactic and authentic materials. Regarding the former, teachers can create their own MP3 files with great ease and subsequently distribute them by whatever means are deemed suitable (via the Web, CD-Rom, etc.); authentic materials can be obtained in the form of podcasts, "a portmanteau which combines iPod and broadcasting" (Chinnery, 2006). Although the term was originally used to describe a form of audio blog, most major radio stations now offer "podcasts" of their programs, some for free, some on a subscription-only basis, which can be downloaded and transferred to a media player. Research is barely starting to produce results on the impact of this technology on language acquisition (Godwin-Jones, 2005b), and it is almost exclusively focused on English as the target language. See, for example, English as a Second Language Podcast (www.eslpod.com) and Technology for Language Learning hosted by Gary Cziko of the University of Illinois at Urbana-Champaign (tllpodcast.blogspot.com) for examples related to the field of CALL.

In this chapter, we have not included a special section on technology and testing, due to the large amount of specific software that can be found for this purpose. Some of the resources reviewed above, e.g., Hot Potatoes, are being used by language teachers to develop tests, and most learning management systems incorporate an assessment component in their online environments.

Tests such as DIALANG, a language system based on the Council of Europe's "Common European Framework of reference," which allows free diagnosis of language level in 5 skills for 14 European languages, are available through the Internet (www.dialang.org/english/index.htm). (See Roever, 2001, for a discussion of web-based language testing and the differences between this and computer-based testing, and Chapelle, this volume, for research findings on CALT (Computer-Assisted Language Testing).)

Conclusion

No discussion of the applications of new technologies to language learning would be complete without making reference to scenarios in which access to these means are lacking. As in many other fields, there is growing concern in the profession about the "Digital divide" – how adoption of new technologies may contribute to the development of a two-tiered system in which those with access to technology are given an unfair advantage over those without (Warschauer, 2003a, 2003b). Egbert and Yang (2004) discuss strategies that can be adopted in contexts where access to technological resources is low (e.g., lack of Internet access/low connection speeds; the absence of, or insufficient numbers of, computers; or outdated hardware, systems, and software), and argue that CALL materials can be used effectively even in the absence of "cutting-edge" technologies.

An analogous consideration regards the suitability of CALL materials for rendering different scripts. Due to their historical roots, computers, the Web and associated technologies and scripting languages all bear a distinct bias toward the Roman character set, in particular, the diacritic-free version used by the English language. Scripts using other symbol sets, and/or writing conventions, are therefore somewhat penalized, as they are technically more difficult to render. The major software developers pay varying degrees of attention to these necessities, and while the advent of UNICODE has resolved most of the problems relating to character rendering, right-to-left scripts (such as Arabic, Farsi, and Hebrew) still cannot be rendered by such major tools as Adobe Flash and Director without tiresome workarounds. Hence, authors desiring to create materials for such languages cannot avail themselves of these otherwise excellent programs that are used to create a large proportion of interactive materials in the commercial field.

We would like to conclude this chapter by underlining the concept that computers are not a miracle tool to solve problems in curriculum development or to fill gaps in the pedagogic design of language classrooms. Computers are tools, and the use that we make of them must invariably be related to the language classroom syllabus, the methodological and pedagogical principles adopted, and student needs. The value of technology in the classroom resides not only in the content provided by or through the technology, but also in the use of the technology itself, as a vital life skill and as a connector of speakers of a language all over the world.

NOTES

1 MOOs (MUD object oriented) are text-based, online, virtual reality systems to allow multiple users to connect at the same time.
2 Authorware, Flash, and Director were previously marketed by Macromedia.
3 LMSs are also known as Virtual Learning Environments (VLEs) and Course Management Systems (CMSs).
4 In October 2005, Blackboard and WebCT announced their intention to merge.

REFERENCES

Al-Seghayer, K. (2001). The effect of multimedia annotation modes on L2 vocabulary acquisition: A comparative study. *Language Learning & Technology* 5, 1, 202–32.

Ancker, W. P. (2002). The challenge and opportunity of technology: An interview with Mark Warschauer. *English Teaching Forum* 40, 4, 1–8. Available online at http://exchanges.state.gov/forum/vols/vol40/no4/p2.pdf.

Arneil, S. & Holmes, M. (2004). Hacking in Hot Potatoes: A little knowledge brings a lot of power. *TEL&CAL* 2, 45–9.

Asencio, M. & Desnoyers, A. (2004). *Viaje al Pasado: los Aztecas*. Montreal: Cégep du Vieux-Montréal. Available at www.ccdmd.qc.ca/ri/aztecas.

Bangs, P. (2008). Introduction to CALL authoring programs. In G. Davies (ed.) *Information and communications technology for language teachers (ICT4LT)* (module 2.5). Slough, Thames Valley University [Online]. Available from: www.ict4lt.org/en/en_mod2-5.htm [Accessed December 5, 2008.]

Belz, J. (2002). Social dimensions of telecollaborative foreign language study. *Language Learning & Technology* 6, 1, 60–81.

Belz, J. A. (2003). Linguistic perspectives on the development of intercultural competence in telecollaboration. *Language Learning & Technology* 7, 2, 68–117.

Belz, J. A. & Kinginger, C. (2003). Discourse options and the development of pragmatic competence by classroom learners of German: The case of address forms. *Language Learning* 53, 4, 591–647.

Bloomfield, L. (1933). *Language*. New York: Henry Holt.

Brett, D. (2004). Drag'n'drop exercises made easy. Presentation at Eurocall conference, Vienna, September.

Brett, D. (2005a). Creating interactive material for teaching phonetics using Macromedia Flash MX, *Proceedings of Phonetics Teaching Learning Conference 2005*, July 26–8, University College London.

Brett, D. (2005b). Why is the web such a silent place? *Proceedings of the eighth CercleS Conference*. Bratislava: University of Bratislava.

Brett, D. (2006a). Keeping up with technological development: Should we stride or should we stroll? *Proceedings of the Dada International Workshop, "Modi Mode Mezzi"* Bolzano, Italy, March 30–31.

Brett, D. (2006b). *Conductor*: a Flash-based tool for the creation of rich and varied CALL material. Presentation at Eurocall 2006 conference, Granada, Spain, September 4–7.

Chapelle, C. (2005). Interactionist SLA theory in CALL research. In J. L. Egbert & G. M. Petrie (eds.), *CALL research perspectives* (pp. 53–64). Mahwah, NJ: Lawrence Erlbaum.

Chinnery, G. M. (2006). Going to the MALL: Mobile-assisted language learning. *Language Learning & Technology* 10, 1, 9–16.

Chun, D. (1994). Using computer networking to facilitate the acquisition of interactive competence. *System* 22, 1, 17–31.

Chun, D. M. & Plass, J. L. (1996). Facilitating reading comprehension with multimedia. *System* 24, 503–19.

Compton, L., Grgurovic, M., O'Bryan, A., Bekrieva-Grannis, D., & Cotos, E. (2006). Review of conferencing applications and their potential use for language learning. Paper presented at CALICO Conference. Honolulu, Hawai'i.

Cushion, S. (2004). Increasing accessibility by pooling digital resources, *ReCALL* 16, 1, 41–50.

Doughty, C. J. (2001). Principles for CALL pedagogy. Plenary address at Hawai'i Association of Language Teachers, Honolulu.

Doughty, C. J. & Long, M. H. (2003). Optimal psycholinguistic environments for distance foreign language learning. *Language Learning & Technology* 7, 3, 50–80.

Doughty, C. J. & Williams, J. (1998). *Focus on form in classroom second language acquisition.* Cambridge: Cambridge University Press.

Egbert, J. & Yang, Y. F. (2004). Mediating the digital divide in CALL classrooms: Promoting effective language tasks in limited technology contexts. *ReCall* 16, 2, 280–91.

Freiermuth, M. R. (2002). Online chatting: An alternative approach to simulations. *Simulation & Gaming* 32, 2, 187–95.

Gillespie, J. H. & Barr, J. D. (2002). Reluctance, resistance and radicalism: A study of staff reaction to the adoption of CALL/C & IT in modern languages departments. *ReCall* 14, 1, 120–32.

Godwin-Jones, R. (2003). Blogs and Wikies: Environments for on-line collaboration. *Language Learning & Technology* 7, 2, 12–16.

Godwin-Jones, R. (2005a). Ajax and Firefox: New Web applications and browsers. *Language Learning & Technology* 9, 2, 8–12.

Godwin-Jones, R. (2005b). Skype and Podcasting: Disruptive technologies for language learning. *Language Learning & Technology* 9, 3, 9–12.

González-Lloret, M. (2003). Designing task-based CALL to promote interaction: En Busca de Esmeraldas. *Language Learning & Technology* 7, 1, 86–104.

González-Lloret, M. (2007). Implementing task-based language teaching on the Web. In K. Van den Branden, M. Verhelst, & K. Van Gorp (eds.), *Task-based language education.* Cambridge: Scholars Press.

Hegelheimer, V., Reppert, K., Borberg, M., Daisy, B., Grgurovic, M., Middlebrooks, K., & Liu, S. (2004). Preparing the new generation of CALL researchers and practitioners: What nine months in an MA program can (or cannot) do. *ReCALL* 16, 2, 432–47.

Jones, L. C. & Plass, J. L. (2002). Supporting listening comprehension and vocabulary acquisition in French with multimedia annotations. *Modern Language Journal* 86, 546–61.

Kern, R. (2006). Perspectives on technology in learning and teaching languages. *TESOL Quarterly* 40, 1, 183–210.

Kern, R. & Warschauer, M. (eds.) (2000). Introduction. In *Theory and practice of network-based language teaching* (pp. 1–19). Cambridge: Cambridge University Press.

Kiernan, P. J. & Aizawa, K. (2004). Cell phones in task based learning: Are cell phones useful language learning tools? *ReCALL* 16, 1, 71–84.

Kramsch, C. & Thorne, S. (2002). Foreign language learning as global communicative practice. In D. Block & D. Cameron (eds.), *Language learning and teaching in the age of globalization* (pp. 83–100). London: Routledge. Retrieved February 2005 from http://language.la.psu.edu/~thorne/KramschThorne.html.

Kramsch, C., Van Ness, F., & Lam, E. W. S. (2000). Authenticity and authorship in the computer-mediated acquisition of L2 literacy. *Language Learning & Technology* 4, 4, 78–104.

Laurillard, D. (2003). Foreword. In U. Felix (ed.), *Language learning online: Towards best practice*. Lisse, Netherlands: Swets and Zeitlinger.

LeLoup, J. W. & Ponterio, R. (2006). Wikipedia: A multilingual treasure trove. *Language Learning & Technology* 10, 2, 4–7.

Long, M. H. (1991). Focus on form: A design feature in language teaching methodology. In de Bot, K., Ginsberg, R. B., & Kramsch, C. (eds.), *Foreign language research in cross-cultural perspective* (pp. 39–52). Amsterdam: John Benjamins.

Long, M. H. (1997). Focus on form in task-based language teaching [electronic version]. *Fourth Annual McGraw-Hill Satellite Teleconference*. Available online at www.mhhe.com/socscience/foreignlang/conf/first.htm.

Nagata, N. (1993). Intelligent computer feedback for second language instruction. *The Modern Language Journal* 77, 3, 330–9.

Pellettieri, J. (1999). Why talk? Investigating the role of task-based interaction through synchronous network-based communication among classroom learners of Spanish. Unpublished doctoral dissertation, University of California at Davis.

Potter, A. (2003). A product review of Macromedia Authorware 6.5. *Internet and Higher Education* 6, 211–13.

Roever, C. (2001). Web-based language testing. *Language Learning & Technology* 5, 2, 84–94.

Sherman, J. (2003). *Using authentic video in the language classroom*. Cambridge: Cambridge University Press.

Smith, B. (2003). Computer-mediated negotiated interaction: An expanded model. *The Modern Language Journal* 87, 1, 38–57.

Thorne, S. (1999). An activity theoretical analysis of foreign language electronic discourse. Unpublished doctoral dissertation. University of California, Berkeley.

Wang, Y. (2004a). Distance language learning: Interactivity and fourth-generation Internet-based videoconferencing. *CALICO Journal* 21, 2, 373–95.

Wang, Y. (2004b). Supporting Synchronous distance language learning with desktop videoconferencing. *Language Learning & Technology* 8, 3, 90–121.

Ward, M. (2002). Reusable XML technologies and the development of language learning materials. *ReCALL* 14, 285–94.

Ware, P. & Warschauer, M. (2006). Electronic feedback and second language writing. In K. Hyland & F. Hyland (eds.), *Feedback and second language writing*. Cambridge: Cambridge University Press. Available online at www.gse.uci.edu/faculty/markw/feedback.pdf.

Warschauer, M. (1999). CALL vs. electronic literacy: Reconceiving technology in the language classroom. Available online at www.cilt.org.uk/research/resfor2/warsum1.htm.

Warschauer, M. (2003a). Demystifying the digital divide. *Scientific American* 289, 2, 42–7.

Warschauer, M. (2003b). *Technology and social inclusion: Rethinking the digital divide*. Cambridge, MA: MIT Press.

Weible, D. (1983). The foreign language teacher as courseware author, *CALICO Journal* 1, 1, 62–4.

Zhao, Y. (2004). Recent developments in technology and language learning: A literature review and meta-analysis. *CALICO Journal* 21, 1, 7–27.

Part VI Teaching and Testing

21 Methodological Principles for Language Teaching

MICHAEL H. LONG

The Methodological Pendulum

Historians of language teaching have documented considerable fluctuation in methodological preferences over the decades (see, e.g., Musumeci, 1997, this volume). Lacking much by way of an empirical base until recently, the field has experienced major swings back and forth in the advocacy of what may be described as "interventionist" approaches, on the one hand, e.g., grammatical syllabuses, grammar translation, and audiolingualism, and "laissez faire" approaches, on the other, e.g., the process syllabus, immersion, and the Natural Approach. In terms of the important distinction made by Wilkins (1976, and elsewhere), the former tend to be *synthetic*, focusing on the target language itself, presenting small pieces (structures, notions, functions, lexical items, collocations) one at a time, and requiring learners to synthesize them for communication. *Analytic* approaches do the reverse, starting with the learner, respecting internal learner syllabuses, presenting gestalt samples of the L2, and helping students to analyze the input and induce underlying rules and the meanings and functions of words. Research findings, summarized below, on processes in interlanguage development and on learnability and teachability are inconsistent with synthetic approaches, and consistent with analytic ones, but also suggest that something more than pure implicit learning, specifically, what I call *focus on form* (Long, 1991, 2000a; Long & Robinson, 1998), makes adult SLA more efficient, and is required if near-native proficiency is the goal.

Pendulum swings notwithstanding, and while very different approaches have been advocated on university courses, at conferences, and in the pages of methodology textbooks over the years, observational studies of real lessons, as opposed to one-off demonstrations, have found that what goes on in classrooms has varied less than might have been expected. Brand name "methods" (Grammar-Translation, Direct Method, Audio-Lingual, Audio-Visual, Silent Way, Total Physical Response, Counseling Learning – Community Language Learning, Suggestopedia, Natural Approach, etc.) differ in some respects, but tend to countenance many of the same activities and procedures. On the classroom floor, rather abstract strategic prescriptions and proscriptions take a back seat to the 101 tactical decisions teachers must make as even the slowest-paced lesson unfolds. The results over time tend to look very similar and, it is often noted, uncannily like lessons those teachers themselves experienced as school-aged pupils, a decades-long cyclical pattern captured in the phrase "the persistence of the recitation" (Hoetker & Ahlbrand, 1967). This fundamental commonality could account for the failure of the so-called "comparative methods" studies of the 1960s and 1970s to find sustained differences in student achievement; it is not that what goes on in classrooms does not matter, but that what goes on in classrooms is often rather similar, regardless of the methods labels attached to them.

Data-based studies of LT that have looked closely at real lessons, as opposed to treating classrooms like black boxes (Long, 1980) where this or that "method" has supposedly been implemented, have found considerable differences between what advocates of the methods prescribe or proscribe and what teachers actually do over time, between how teachers were trained to teach and how they actually teach, and even between what teachers believe they have been doing and what they have actually been doing (see, e.g., Dinsmore, 1985; Long et al., 1976; Long & Sato, 1983; Nunan, 1987; Swaffer, Arens, & Morgan, 1982). It turns out that "method" is an inappropriate, even irrelevant, way of conceptualizing or evaluating LT. Like materials writers, teachers in all areas of education, including language teaching, tend to plan, implement, and recall lessons in terms of less abstract units, such as activities or tasks (Shavelson & Stern, 1981).

On What Basis Advice, Then?

Articles in pedagogy journals and commercially published textbook materials both reveal what most language teachers already know: recipes for language teaching are two a penny. Some are based on years of classroom experience, precious few on theory or research findings in SLA or education, and many on little more than chutzpah and the pundit's or publisher's desire for a healthier bank balance. Arguments back and forth, moreover, even when not influenced by base commercial interests, often concern prescriptions or proscriptions of different scope. "It is/is not permissible to use the learner's L1," for example, may be more or less defensible in foreign, second, and lingua franca language situations, among others, with homogeneous or heterogeneous groups of students, at different proficiency levels, and/or when stipulated for any, for particular sub-classes of, comprehension problems. Other arguments may occur at cross-purposes. Instructions from some pedagogies to correct errors, and from others not to so so, for instance, can often turn out to mean different things to different people, ranging from heavy-handed, on-record interventions the instant errors arise to unobtrusive, implicit negative feedback without interfering with students' efforts to communicate, i.e., a matter of how, not whether, to "correct."[1]

Given the historical record, the wide range of settings and situations in which languages are taught, and the variance in players and learning purposes, it may seem unreasonable, therefore, if not downright arrogant, for anyone to propose universally applicable methodological principles for LT. Are research findings robust enough for the field to be confident about *any* proposals for LT? Are not second, foreign, and other language settings, or local situations within each, so different as to preclude recommendations that would apply in all contexts? Two considerations are relevant here.

First, the fact is, LT is no different from most professions. The state of knowledge in language learning and teaching is developing all the time, just as it is in medicine or engineering; it is just (much) less developed. The responsibility of professionals in any field is not to know the right answer, but to be able to defend recommendations in light of what is thought to be the right answer or the likeliest right answer (best practice), given what is known or thought to be known at the time. What is irresponsible is to throw up one's hands and declare that no proposals should be made and defended until everything is known for sure (which will never happen), and use that as implicit or explicit justification for whatever proposal follows, or for no proposal, or to recommend that, meanwhile, teachers should use a pinch of this, a dash of that, i.e., the so-called "eclectic method" (an oxymoron).[2]

Second, language learning is a cognitive process, albeit one that occurs in a social setting. While some individual differences, e.g., in language aptitude, are important enough, and measurable reliably enough, to warrant differentiated classroom treatment where student numbers and resources permit, the architecture of human brains varies very little among adults or among children (although there are differences across the lifespan as a function of age, of course), and certainly not as a function of *where* learning and teaching are carried out. The same cognitive architecture and processing options pertain, for example, when a Chinese learner of English boards a plane in the PRC, a foreign language setting, as when he or she disembarks a few hours later in a country where English is spoken, a second language setting. The reasons why students learn English in the PRC or the UK, i.e., needs and goals, may differ, as may attitudes, motivation, and opportunities for L2 exposure on the street, but although what should be taught (L2 varieties, which genres or skills, etc.) will vary, the way learners process linguistic input in each place does not, and so should presumably be targeted by teaching in the same optimal ways in Beijing or Birmingham.

In that light, proposing that LT take into account a minimal set of currently defensible methodological principles, varying the way they are instantiated in the classroom in accord with local circumstances, makes sense – indeed, is professionally responsible. There is often more than one reasonable way for a physician to treat an illness, for a civil engineer to design a bridge, or for an instructor to teach English or Chinese, but that is not to say that one proposal is no better or worse than the next. Such an approach would never be tolerated in the practice of medicine or any other profession and should not be in LT. LT is rarely a life or death issue, but rapid achievement of foreign or second language proficiency can have a critical effect on marriages, cultural integration, and the educational life chances and job opportunities of countless children and adults, most obviously, but by no means only, involuntary learners, such as refugees. It is clearly the case that far less is known about SLA and LT than about anatomy, physiology, and medicine, but that is a question of degree, not kind, and does not justify an "anything goes" attitude. The published literature of the past few decades shows that quite a lot is known about language acquisition and teaching, and it would be irresponsible to ignore it. That said, it behooves anyone adding to the methodological or pedagogic stew to describe recommendations explicitly, in order both to avoid ambiguity and to make claims testable, and to provide a clear rationale, plus supporting evidence. Ideally, too, proposals should be accompanied by criteria by which they can be evaluated.

Methodological Principles, Pedagogic Procedures, and Evaluation Criteria

In discussions of how to teach second and foreign languages, it is useful to distinguish between methodological principles and pedagogical procedures. While first introduced as part of proposals for Task-Based Language Teaching (TBLT; see, e.g., Doughty & Long, 2003a; Long, 1985, to appear), the distinction is helpful when describing any approach to language teaching. Evaluation criteria are the standards by which proposals can be judged.

Methodological principles

Methodological principles (MPs) are universally desirable instructional design features, motivated by theory and research findings in SLA, educational psychology, general educational curriculum design, and elsewhere, which show them either to be necessary for SLA or facilitative of it. *Facilitative* effects are important because the goal of a theory of language teaching is a maximally *efficient* approach, not, as in the case of a theory of SLA, one which is primarily concerned with what is *necessary* and *sufficient* for learning to occur (for further discussion, see Long, 2000b, pp. 4–5, 2007a, pp. 16–20). Negative feedback, for example, may or may not turn out to be necessary for language development, but numerous studies have shown it to be facilitative, justifying MP7: "Provide negative feedback" (see below, and Table 21.1). The theoretical and empirical support means that MPs are candidates for any approach to language teaching, task-based or otherwise.

Pedagogic procedures

Whereas MPs are putative language teaching universals, *Pedagogic procedures* (PPs) comprise the potentially infinite range of options for instantiating the principles at the classroom level. MPs specify *what* should be done; PPs suggest *how* it can be done. Variation in how is often appropriate for learners of different ages, aptitude, cognitive style, proficiency, or L1 and L2 literacy level, for more salient and less salient target forms, and so on, and is handled at the level of PPs. Given that variations in implementation are designed to respond precisely to particular needs and conditions at the local level, often moment by moment as a lesson unfolds, choices among PPs are usually best left to the classroom teacher, typically the expert on local conditions, and will not be dealt with here. Whereas MPs are founded upon, and can be evaluated against, current theory and research findings, choice among PPs is mostly a matter of teacher judgment, with different choices potentially justified at different times with the same learners or at the same time with different learners. Consequently, choice among the wide range of PPs for providing negative feedback, for example, from the overt and explicit end of the spectrum, such as use of a rule or explanation, to the covert and implicit end, such as corrective recasts, and many points in between, cannot be judged well- or ill-founded without knowing the context. For instance, the former might be appropriate for a less salient target feature and educated adult learners (e.g., an error with an unstressed prefix, such as *undecisive*, which does not result in miscommunication), but unnecessary for the same learners with a more salient target (e.g., a stressed, meaning-bearing, free morpheme, such as *did*), and wholly inappropriate for either type of target feature with young children.[3]

Evaluation criteria

Evaluation criteria (EC) for MPs are the standards by which proposals can be judged, the ways in which their likely validity may be assessed. EC could take many forms, including, most obviously, EC1: "Theoretical motivation," EC2: "Empirical support," and EC3: "Logical argumentation." To illustrate, in the case of MP7: "Provide negative feedback," EC1 is met by the predictions of theories of or in (S)LA as disparate as Skill Acquisition Theory (DeKeyser, 2001, 2007), Emergentism (N. Ellis, 2007; Larsen-Freeman & Ellis, 2006), Cognitive Interactionism (Gass, 1997; Long, 1996b; Gass & Mackey, 2007), Universal Grammar (White, 1991, 2003), and Sociocultural Theory (Aljaafreh & Lantolf, 1994; Lantolf & Thorne, 2006). EC2 is met by the findings of numerous empirical studies, and meta-analyses of studies, of the positive influence of both implicit and explicit corrective feedback on L2 development (e.g., Long, 2007b; Mackey & Goo, 2007; Russell & Spada, 2006). EC3 is met by arguments such as that of White (1987, 1991) concerning the logical impossibility of unlearning L1 options on the basis of positive evidence alone when the input gives no indication of their impossibility in the L2, a situation that potentially occurs whenever options in the L2 are a subset of those in the L1 in a given domain, e.g., those for adverb placement for L1 speakers of French or Spanish learning L2 English (see below).

EC1 and EC3 will often be important, given the paucity of controlled studies in some areas. A lack of research is usually due to the difficulty of conducting studies of some issues in real educational settings, the shortage of people with sufficient training in research methods and sufficient time to invest in the effort, and the lack of adequate funding for the purpose.[4] Since language teaching is not simply something that can be put off for a few years while the research is carried out, alternative criteria are needed. Additional potential EC include those employed in other fields, some of them widely discussed in the philosophy of science literature. An example of a criterion of that type (see below) is EC4: "Consistency with accepted theories in other fields." To illustrate, MP7: "Provide negative feedback" receives independent support, and meets EC4, because of the well-established importance of negative feedback in almost every other type of human learning and performance (see, e.g., Annett, 1969), not just language learning. Conversely, MP5: "Encourage inductive ('chunk') learning" would be hard to justify if it were accepted in cognitive psychology (it is not) that adults are only capable of learning explicitly.

Some Relevant SLA Research Findings

While language teaching still lacks a firm research base in several critical areas, 40 years of work in SLA on the teaching and learning of a variety of languages has produced a considerable amount of detailed information useful for teachers and materials writers, and potentially for some educated adult learners, themselves. Several textbook-length reviews of the findings have been published (see chapters in, e.g., Doughty & Long, 2003b; R. Ellis, 1994; Gass & Selinker, 2004; Larsen-Freeman & Long, 1991; Lightbown & Spada, 2006; Ritchie & Bhatia, 1996). Of crucial importance for discussions of teaching methodology is the unavoidable conclusion that *learners, not teachers, have most control over their language development*. Students do not – in fact, cannot – learn (as opposed to learn about) target forms and structures on demand, when and how a teacher or a textbook decree that they should, but only when they are developmentally ready to do so. Instruction can facilitate development, but needs to be provided with respect for, and in harmony with, the learner's powerful cognitive contribution to the acquisition process.

A major source of evidence for the strength of the learner's role in SLA, and simultaneously, about the limits of instruction, is work on processes in interlanguage development. *Interlanguages* (ILs), individual learners' transitional versions of the L2, are the psycholinguistic equivalent of idiolects. While ILs exhibit systematic and free variation, and no two ILs are exactly alike, studies have shown that they exhibit common patterns and features across differences in learners' age and L1, acquisition context, and instructional approach. For example, independent of those and other factors, learners pass through well-attested *developmental sequences* on their way to mastery of target-language structures, or, as is often the case, to an end-state short of mastery (Johnston, 1985, 1997; Ortega, this volume). Developmental sequences are fixed series of stages in the evolution of grammatical (as well as phonological and semantic) systems and sub-systems, such as the four-stage sequence – *No V, don't V, aux-neg,* and *analyzed don't* – for negation in ESL (for a review of early findings on ESL negation by Spanish speakers, see Schumann, 1979), the six-stage sequence for German SL word order (Meisel, Clahsen, & Pienemann, 1981), and sequences for relative clauses (Doughty, 1991; Eckman, Bell, & Nelson, 1988; Gass, 1982; Hyltenstam, 1984) and past time reference (Meisel, 1987; Sato, 1986, 1990). The transitional structures are often not attested in the L1 or the L2 input, but created by the learners themselves. Some appear to be universal. For instance, an initial pre-verbal (*Neg V*) negation stage appears in the ILs of L1 speakers of languages, such as Japanese or Turkish, that have post-verbal negation, even when the target language, e.g., Swedish, also has post-verbal negation (Hyltenstam, 1977). L1 effects on the sequences can be observed, but are constrained. For example, speakers of L1s, such as Spanish, which have pre-verbal negation tend to spend longer in the *No V* stage in ESL than speakers of L1s that do not (Zobl, 1982), but L1 influences do not lead to omission of the stage or to alteration of the order of stages.

Another indication of what Corder (1967, and elsewhere) referred to as the powerful internal "learner syllabus" is the occurrence of common errors and error types in the ILs of learners of different ages and L1 backgrounds, and across formal, informal, and mixed learning contexts. The most often noted of these, perhaps because they are salient and seem easily interpretable as reflecting underlying "hypothesis-testing" learning processes, are morphological errors, such as *goed*, or *sheeps*. While striking, such so-called overgeneralization errors are relatively infrequent (perhaps 2 percent of all errors), and just one of four pervasive error types documented in a study of native-Spanish-speaking naturalistic, instructed, and mixed learners of English by Pica (1983). Pica found that whether learning in FL classrooms only, on the street in an L2 environment, or in the L2 environment while also receiving classroom instruction (so-called "mixed" learners), although the relative frequencies differed, all three groups made (1) overgeneralization errors, where regularized irregular morphemes are supplied in obligatory contexts, e.g., *She eated the apple*; (2) overuse errors, where morphemes are supplied in non-obligatory contexts, e.g., *Mary liking movies*, or *The boys like soccer*, when the referent is a single boy; (3) omission errors in obligatory contexts, e.g., *He go shopping yesterday*; and (4) substitution errors in obligatory contexts, e.g., *He goes shopping last year*. As with many transitional structures seen at various stages within developmental sequences, neither L1 transfer nor habit formation can explain the appearance of many of the errors. For example, resumptive pronouns are observed in the relative clauses of Italian learners of English (Pavesi, 1986), as in *That is the man who he stole the car*, or *She is the woman who he loves her*, yet resumptive pronouns are found in neither language. All these error types are hard to account for, either in SLA theory or in classroom practice, if, as is the case in most classrooms the world over, students experience and are drilled in exclusively standard target-language forms. While practice has a role in automatizing what has been learned, i.e., in *control* of an acquired form or structure, common developmental stages and errors like those documented by Hyltenstam, Pica, Pavesi, and many others show that L2 acquisition is not simply a process of forming new habits to override the effects of L1 transfer; powerful creative processes are at work.

Even when presented with, and drilled in, exclusively target-language forms and structures, and even when errors are routinely "corrected," instructed learners' acquisition of a "structure of the day" is rarely either sudden and categorical or complete, as is assumed by most synthetic materials and methodology. On the contrary, while sudden changes in performance suggest occasional fundamental restructuring of the underlying IL grammar (McLaughlin, 1990), acquisition of grammatical structures and sub-systems like negation or relative clause formation is typically gradual, incremental, sometimes taking months or even years to accomplish. Nor is development always target oriented. An increase in error rate may precede, and even be an inevitable precursor of, acquisition of a new rule or constraint, e.g., when learners attempt application of an existing one in a more complex linguistic environment (Meisel et al., 1981). Development of individual structures over time, and often of the L2 as a whole, exhibits plateaus, occasional movement away from, not toward, the L2, and "backsliding," resulting in U-shaped or zigzag trajectories rather than smooth, linear contours (Huebner, 1983; Kellerman, 1985; Selinker, 1972). ILs often stabilize far short of the target variety, moreover, with learners persistently using non-targetlike forms and structures for communication that they were never taught, and targetlike forms and structures with non-targetlike functions (Sato, 1990). The stabilization is sometimes for such long periods that the non-targetlike state is claimed to be permanent, i.e., indicating not just stabilization, but fossilization (Han & Odlin, 2005; Lardiere, 2006; Sorace, 2003), although unambiguous evidence for fossilization is, at best, scarce (Long, 2003).

No matter the L1 or the order or manner in which target-language structures are presented to them by teachers or textbook writers, learners analyze the input and come up with their own interim grammars, the product broadly conforming to developmental sequences observed in naturalistic settings (see, e.g., Eckman et al., 1988; R. Ellis, 1989; Fathman, 1978; Gass, 1982; Krashen, 1977; Lightbown, 1983). They master the structures in roughly the same manner and order whether learning in classrooms, on the street, or both (Pica, 1983). Studies show that attempts to make them skip a stage fail (as they must if "developmental sequence" is to retain its meaning and predictive utility), leading Pienemann to formulate his *learnability hypothesis* and *teachability hypothesis*: what is processable by students at any time determines what is learnable, and, thereby, what is teachable (Pienemann, 1984, 1989). The effectiveness of negative feedback on error has been shown to be constrained in the same way (see, e.g., Mackey, 1999).

None of this is to say that instruction is irrelevant or unhelpful. Some of the very studies that suggested developmental sequences are impervious to instruction simultaneously demonstrated its positive effects elsewhere, provided the timing is right. A study by Pienemann (1984), for instance, found that young learners developmentally ready for a stage in German L2 word order targeted during two weeks of instruction benefited from that instruction and advanced to that stage, whereas learners in the same class who were at an earlier stage than their classmates did not improve. Reviews of studies comparing L2 development with and without instruction, and/or with different quantities of each, have found that instruction has little or no effect on the course of development, e.g., error types or passage through developmental sequences, but can be effective in other ways with both children and adults, first by speeding up learning, and second by improving the prognosis for forms and functions made difficult by their low saliency, rarity in the input, low communicative valency, and other factors (De Graaf & Housen, this volume; Doughty, 2003; R. Ellis, 1994; Long, 1983, 1988).

Type of instruction makes a difference, too. A statistical meta-analysis by Norris and Ortega (2000) of some 40 studies found clear effects for different kinds of teaching, with explicit treatments outperforming implicit ones, focus on form and focus on forms performing comparably, and both statistically better than simple exposure. Those results are especially encouraging for advocates of focus on form. Most implicit learning takes time, and while generally appropriate at all proficiency levels (especially when something other than the linguistic code is a learning goal, as is the case in content-based and task-based instruction, and immersion education, for instance), it comes into its own as learning targets become harder, require far more exposure, and are difficult or impossible to handle explicitly at all because too subtle, too complex, or too hard to reduce to a form digestible by non-linguists (most students). The majority of studies of the effects of instruction or of different types of instruction are short-term, in order to help researchers avoid threats to internal validity that tend to occur more frequently the longer studies continue. Acquisition of even moderately complex linguistic structures takes time. Because researchers need to see measurable results in a short period if they are to test hypotheses, they typically target relatively easy grammar points already known to be learnable by the students who will be serving as subjects. Explicit instruction is known to work best in all fields, when it works at all, with simple learning targets. When combined with focus on forms, with which it usually goes hand in hand, and applied to simple linguistic targets in short-term studies of language teaching, there is an intrinsic research bias in favor of explicit over implicit instruction, and focus on forms over focus on form. In this light, the fact that implicit instruction and focus on form do so well suggests they are viable even with easy targets, not just required with hard ones at more advanced levels. Positive findings for implicit negative feedback (corrective recasts) and for language learning during task-based L2 conversation have been obtained in two other recent statistical meta-analyses (Mackey & Goo, 2007; Russell & Spada, 2006).

Implications for Approaches to LT

The findings briefly summarized above (a tiny percentage of those produced by SLA researchers in recent years) dispel any notions that learners learn what teachers teach when they teach it, yet whether recognized or not, this is an implicit assumption underlying synthetic approaches to LT. The results are simply incompatible with use of a synthetic syllabus and teaching methodology, the combination I refer to as "focus on forms," where syllabus content consists of a pre-set list of linguistic (phonological, morphological, syntactic, lexical, or collocational) forms and functions, as opposed to some other area subject matter, such as mathematics, art, or physical education, or from target tasks for the learners concerned. As distinct from one-off uses in demonstration lessons or controlled experiments with simple structures carefully selected for specific groups of learners, a synthetic syllabus and the pedagogic materials that embody it will almost always have been written without reference to students' present or future communicative needs, as identified via a thorough needs analysis, and so are inefficient. They risk teaching more – skills, vocabulary, genres, etc. – than students can use, but also less, through not teaching language abilities they do or will need. They will also almost always have been prepared in ignorance of any particular group of students' current developmental stages, especially if enshrined in industrial strength, commercially published textbook materials. Moreover, as any experienced teacher knows, and as shown, e.g., by the Pienemann (1984) study described earlier, learners within a group will often be at different developmental stages, even when labeled as having attained X or Y level of proficiency or having scored within a specified range on a placement test. Learners can achieve roughly similar overall proficiency and test scores despite strengths and weaknesses in different areas of their IL repertoires.

The research clearly shows that attempting to impose a pre-set series of linguistic forms (pronunciation contrasts, grammatical structures, notions, functions, lexical items, collocations, etc.) is largely futile and counter-productive. It is largely futile because it only works if a form coincidentally happens to be learnable (by some students in a class), and so teachable, at the time it is presented. It is counter-productive for two reasons. First, attempts to teach forms that are unlearnable when introduced lead to frustration and failure on the part of teachers and students, alike. Second, the inappropriate focus, typically instantiated through presentation of isolated model sentences intended to provide minimal contexts for the target forms, results in impoverished input and output opportunities and means that richer input that would have been appropriate is not provided. So-called spiral, or cyclical, grammatical syllabi, which systematically revisit previously presented forms increase the chances of "hits,'" but are still inefficient because they attempt to work independently of the internal learner syllabus. By focusing on full native forms, typically with early forced production, followed by "correction" of the inevitable errors, as in ALM and the Silent Way, for example, synthetic approaches also implicitly assume that learners can move from no knowledge of a form to nativelike mastery in one step, which the research shows almost never happens. They also assume that discrete forms and structures can be learned in isolation from one another, whereas the reality is far more complex. Nativelike (stage 4) command of English negation, for example, requires control of verbal auxiliaries, tense, person, number, and word order.

It is worth noting that not just traditional linguistically based syllabi, but also most thematic, topic-based, and content-based approaches sit uneasily with the same research findings. With a few notable exceptions, e.g., work in the Vancouver

School Board project (Early, 1991; Early, Mohan, & Hooper, 1989), most content-based teaching, for example, is largely synthetic. Instead of starting with the structure of the day, learners are typically presented with texts – static models of L2 use, but above the sentence level – whose content is (ideally) relevant to some other area of their studies, e.g., social studies through French for anglophone children in Canadian French immersion programs, maths for US elementary school children taught through Chinese, or art history and other film or "culture" courses for college foreign language students. The texts are sometimes *genuine*, i.e., originally written for native speaker readers. Sometimes, they are *simplified* – either genuine texts modified by removal of complex syntax, substitution of higher- for lower-frequency lexical items, etc., or texts written for non-native speakers with the same linguistic constraints in mind. Although often resulting in rather stilted examples of target-language use, such texts are more likely to be of interest to teachers and students than a tedious diet of tightly linguistically controlled input consisting largely of model sentences (*The clock is on the wall. Is the clock on the wall? Where is the clock?*), preceded or followed by equally unnatural "dialogues" or short "reading passages" designed to practice the same structure(s). Either text type is likely to suffer, however, from the same weaknesses as the more minimally contextualized structures in a traditional grammatical syllabus, for once again, much of the linguistic content will inevitably be developmentally inappropriate input for the current IL stage of all but the most advanced group of students, or for some students within a group.[5] Once heard or read, moreover, the texts tend to become found objects, to be analyzed for their linguistic content (structures, vocabulary, etc.) using the same focus on forms methodology employed with overtly synthetic syllabi.

Whereas synthetic approaches have obvious problems from an acquisitional perspective, some analytical approaches are broadly consistent with the research findings, although themselves in need of supplementing. Offered gestalt samples of language use as part of an analytic approach, learners are freed from the unnatural, and often impossible, task of trying to learn a language one developmentally inappropriate piece at a time. Analytic approaches provide richer input, encountered in typically less contrived, more realistic, models of target-language use. They allow learners to use their cognitive abilities to segment that input and induce rules and patterns they are capable of processing on a given day. If preceded by a well-conducted learner needs analysis, the texts can be guaranteed to be relevant to learners' interests and communicative needs (see MP10: "Individualize instruction"), an option available to content-based teaching, too, of course, but seemingly rarely taken up. If part of a genuinely task-based syllabus, moreover, the texts will be encountered by learners not as ends in themselves, but as a natural part of performing dynamic pedagogic tasks, and so authentic in a way worthy of the designation.

Simply exposing learners to rich input, as is possible with some analytic approaches, e.g., the Natural Approach, sheltered subject-matter teaching, and some forms of immersion education, even in the context of authentic tasks, is insufficient, however. Research findings on the results of such hands-off approaches, plus those on the effects of instruction, indicate the utility of MP6: "Focus on form."

As demonstrated by the results of evaluations of French immersion programs in Canada (see, e.g., Lapkin, Hart, & Swain, 1991; Lightbown, Spada, & White, 1993; Swain, 1991) and by case studies of individuals (e.g., Ioup et al., 1984), high-level communicative abilities are achievable through systematic experience of communicative target-language use over extended periods of time. Except in the cases of the most talented learners, however, such accomplishments take an inordinate amount of time and generally fall far short of nativelike proficiency. The best graduates of the Canadian programs, for example, may have listening and reading skills statistically comparable to those of monolingual French age peers after 15 years, yet frequently continue to make quite basic grammatical errors in such areas as gender marking and article usage in their speaking and writing (Swain, 1991). One potential solution may simply be additional exposure to comprehensible input, as Krashen (1985, and elsewhere) suggested, but unless there are good reasons for not providing instruction, or unless instruction is simply unavailable, numerous studies show that acquisition can be speeded up by teaching of certain kinds, with the prognosis especially improved for forms made difficult for adults by their low saliency (DeKeyser, 2005).

To avoid a return to lessons full of grammar rules, overt error "correction" and pattern drills, with all their nasty side-effects, as many of the problem areas as possible should be handled within otherwise communicative lessons by briefly drawing learners' attention to some items as and when problems arise, i.e., by *focus on form*. In this *reactive* mode (part of the definition, not an optional feature, of focus on form), the learner's underlying psychological state is more likely to be optimal, and so the treatment, whatever PPs are employed, more effective. For example, while comparing car production in Japan and the USA as part of a *pedagogic task* designed to help students develop the ability to prepare and deliver a sales report, the *target task*, a learner might say something like "Production of SUV in the US fell by 30% from 2000 to 2004." If the very next utterance from the teacher or another student is a partial recast in the form of a confirmation check, e.g., "Production of SUVs fell by 30%?", as proposed in Long (1996b), the likelihood of the learner noticing the plural -*s* is increased by the fact that he or she is *vested* in the exchange, so is *motivated* to learn what is needed and *attending* to the response, already knows the meaning he or she was trying to express, so has freed up *attentional resources* to devote to the form of the response, and hears the correct form in close juxtaposition to his or her own, facilitating *cognitive comparison*. These are all reasons why implicit corrective recasts are believed to work as well as they do (for reviews of findings, see Long, 2007b; Mackey & Goo, 2007; Russell & Spada, 2006), without disturbing the fundamental communicative focus of a lesson, and why negative feedback is believed to work better than provision of the same numbers of models of a target form and/or tokens in ambient input (positive evidence). In contrast, with *focus on forms*, the teacher or the textbook, not the student, has selected a form for treatment. The learner is less likely to feel a need to acquire the new item, so will likely be less motivated, and less attentive. If the form is new, moreover, so, typically, will be its meaning and use, requiring the learner to process all three simultaneously.

If a problematic form is considered tricky, perhaps because of L1 influence or low saliency, a more explicit brief switch of pedagogic focus by the teacher to the language itself, sometimes just a matter of seconds, may be beneficial, e.g., "Car or cars?" In either case, and however overt the PP the teacher employs to induce student focus on form, this reactive approach to treating (in this example of plural -s) a simple grammar point is operating in tandem with the learner's internal syllabus, in that the focus on form was triggered by a problem that occurred in the student's performance, not by a pre-set syllabus having prescribed it for that day's lesson. A student's attempt to produce a form is not always but often an indication of his or her developmental readiness to acquire it.

MPs such as these, MP 6: "Focus on form, not forms," and MP7: "Provide negative feedback," implicitly where this will suffice, are ways in which a wholly analytic approach relying purely on incidental learning (learning language while doing something else) needs to be supplemented. Learning is speeded up that way. Also, certain specifiable problems can be dealt with that may not be treatable at all through provision of positive evidence alone. To take a simple example, White (1987, 1991, and elsewhere) has drawn attention to cases where an L1 and L2 are in a superset – subset relationship in a particular domain. Native speakers of languages like French and Spanish learning English, for instance, can say the equivalent of "I drink coffee every day" and "I drink every day coffee" in their L1, whereas the latter is ungrammatical in English since it violates the constraint against separating verbs and direct objects. Since they will encounter the first in the L2 input, and since their production of either will be readily understood by English speakers, they may never notice that the second is wrong unless someone or something draws their attention to the problem, e.g., by providing some form of negative evidence.

Ten MPs

SLA research should obviously feature prominently in proposals for LT. SLA researchers study the very process LT is designed to facilitate, after all, and ignoring relevant findings, as synthetic approaches do, would be akin to medical practitioners paying no attention to the results of research on human anatomy, physiology, or the relative effectiveness of various treatments for specific ailments. SLA is not the only source of relevant information, of course. Work in the psychology of learning and cognition, educational psychology, curriculum and instruction, linguistics, anthropology, and the history and philosophy of education, among other sources, provides valuable insights and motivates some of the proposals. Some MPs derive convergent validation from work in two or more fields.

Motivated by these and other sources, ten MPs that currently constitute the methodological component of TBLT have been described and justified at some length elsewhere (Doughty & Long, 2003a; Long, to appear).[6] Table 21.1 lists the MPs, followed in the "sources" column by a few of what are often numerous potential references to original sources and/or reviews of a large supporting literature, and in the rightmost column by an indication of EC that are met in each case.

MP1: "Use task, not text, as the unit of analysis" MP3: "Elaborate input," and MP6: "Focus on form" are original to TBLT. Others, e.g., MP2: "Promote learning by doing," MP7: "Provide negative feedback," and MP10: "Individualize instruction," are based on long traditions in philosophy, SLA, psycholinguistics, language teaching, curriculum theory, the history of education, and educational psychology. While originally developed as part of TBLT (see, e.g., Doughty & Long, 2003a; Long, 2000a; Long & Norris, 2000), all but MP1: "Use task, not text, as the unit of analysis," could, and perhaps already do, operate in some non-task-based analytic approaches, such as "sheltered" instruction, process syllabus-based courses, a few varieties of content-based LT, and some types of bilingual and immersion education. Few approaches embody all ten MPs, however. Contra both MP1 and MP3: "Elaborate input," for example, much immersion education and most content-based approaches organize instruction around either genuine or simplified texts, not tasks. In addition to the well-documented psycholinguistic problems with both text types (see Long, 1996a, 2007c; Long & Ross, 1993), part of the rationale for MP3 is that the use of static, "found" models of language use, albeit at the supra-sentential level, in the form of texts typically leads to other undesirable classroom behaviors, such as a focus on forms.

To conclude, it is worth reiterating that, as in most fields of human activity, the state of knowledge in second and foreign language learning and teaching is developing all the time. Given the history of SLA and other sciences, it is unlikely that the cognitive-interactionist theory of SLA implicit in the MPs and underlying TBLT as a whole will turn out to be correct, although it is to be hoped that at least some parts of it will be. To say that further research is needed is an understatement, however, and the findings may well show that some of the current ten MPs are unfounded, that others require modification, and that new ones need to be formulated. Meanwhile, proposing a theoretically coherent set of MPs, prima

Table 21.1   MPs, sources, and EC

	MP	*Sources*	*EC*
Activities			
MP1	Use task, not text, as the unit of analysis.	Long (1985, 2007c); Long & Crookes (1992, 1993); Robinson (2001a, 2001b, this volume); Skehan (1998), Van den Branden (2006)	EC1, EC2, EC3, EC4
MP2	Promote learning by doing.	Avrich (1980); Doughty & Long (2003a); Shotton (1993); Smith (1983)	EC1, EC3, EC4

Table 21.1 *(cont'd)*

	MP	*Sources*	*EC*
Input			
MP3	Elaborate input (do not simplify; do not rely solely on "authentic" texts).	Long (1996b, 2007c); Long & Ross (1993); Oh (2001); Yano, Long, & Ross (1994)	EC2, EC3
MP4	Provide rich (not impoverished) input.	N. Ellis & Larsen-Freeman (2006); Gass (1997); Krashen (1985); Long (1996b); Pica et al. (1996)	EC1, EC2, EC3
Learning processes			
MP5	Encourage inductive ("chunk") learning.	N. Ellis (2002a, 2002b, 2006, 2007); N. Ellis & Larsen-Freeman (2006); Schmitt (2004); Wray (2000, 2002)	EC1, EC4
MP6	Focus on form.	Doughty (1991); N. Ellis (2005); Hulstijn (2005); Long (1991, 2000a); Long & Robinson (1998); Norris & Ortega (2000); Schmidt (2001); Williams (2005)	EC1, EC2, EC3, EC4
MP7	Provide negative feedback.	Annett (1969); DeKeyser (1993); Long (2007b); Mackey & Goo (2007); Russell & Spada (2006)	EC1, EC2, EC3, EC4
MP8	Respect "learner syllabuses"/ developmental processes.	R. Ellis (1989); Lightbown (1983); Mackey (1999); Pienemann (1984, 1989)	EC1, EC2
MP9	Promote cooperative/ collaborative learning.	Barnes (1976); Gass (1997, 2003); Gass & Mackey (2007); Hatch (1978); Jacobs (1998); Liang, Mohan, & Early (1998); Long (1996b); Long & Porter (1985); Mackey & Goo (2007); McCafferty, Jacobs, & DaSilva Iddings (2006); Oxford (1997); Pica et al. (1996); Russell & Spada (2006); Sato (1986, 1988, 1990); Webb (1991)	EC1, EC2, EC3, EC4
Learners			
MP10	Individualize instruction (psycholinguistically, and according to communicative needs).	Altman & James (1980); Logan (1973); Long (2005); Robinson (2003); Sawyer & Ranta (2001); Wesche (1981)	EC1, EC2, EC4

facie defensible given what is known or thought to be known about the processes involved, responds to an immediate need; learning and teaching new languages are too important for too many people to do otherwise.

NOTES

1   "Correct" appears in scare quotes because it wrongly implies that correction is a perlocutionary speech act. In practice, the best a teacher can do is to provide some kind of *negative feedback* on learner error. It is the learner who then modifies ("corrects"), or not, his or her developing L2 knowledge system.
2   Coherent theoretically motivated proposals may well turn out to be wrong, wholly or in part, but at least have a chance of being right, whereas "eclectic methods" are certain to be wrong, given that different methods reflect different underlying theories about language learning, however implicit or unclearly articulated, and since no more than one theory, at best, can logically be correct.
3   To say that teachers are best suited to make decisions on PPs does not imply that methodologists abdicate responsibility at the classroom level. Choices should be rational, based on teaching experience and, where available, research findings. Doughty and Williams (1998), for example, provide detailed rationales and discuss research findings for a continuum of choices, from unobtrusive to obtrusive, among the many PPs available for providing negative feedback. Research-based rationales for principled, non-arbitrary choices among PPs in other language teaching domains are much needed.
4   Vast amounts of time and money are invested around the world each year in training language teachers, but minimal amounts of either on developing the knowledge base that should form the major component in such training. Compare the established facts and validated procedures to be understood and assimilated by trainee physicians, architects, lawyers, engineers, and future members of other professions with those available to language teachers.
5   *Elaborated* texts (including some films used with advanced learners) avoid most of these problems – hence, MP3: "Elaborate input." See Long (1997, 2007c, pp. 119–38), Oh (2001), Vatz (2007), and Yano, Long, and Ross (1994) for examples, data, and discussion of the psycholinguistic problems and merits of genuine, simplified, elaborated, and modified elaborated text types.
6   Doughty and Long (2003b), which can be accessed on line at the *Language Learning and Technology* website, also outlines how the MPs could be instantiated in distance language courses.

REFERENCES

Aljaafreh, A. & Lantolf, J. P. (1994). Negative feedback as regulation and second language learning in the zone of proximal development. *Modern Language Journal* 78, 465–83.
Altman, H. B. & James, C. V. (eds.) (1980). *Foreign language teaching: Meeting individual needs.* Oxford: Pergamon.

Annett, J. (1969). *Feedback and human behaviour.* Baltimore: Penguin Books.

Avrich, P. (1980). *The modern school movement. Anarchism and education in the United States.* Princeton, NJ: Princeton University Press.

Barnes, D. (1976). *From communication to curriculum.* Harmondsworth, UK: Penguin Books.

Corder, S. P. (1967). The significance of learners' errors. *International Review of Applied Linguistics* 5, 2, 161–70.

DeKeyser, R. (1993). The effect of error correction on L2 grammar knowledge and oral proficiency. *Modern Language Journal* 77, 4, 501–14.

DeKeyser, R. (2001). Automaticity and automatization. In P. Robinson (ed.), *Cognition and second language instruction* (pp. 125–51). New York: Cambridge University Press.

DeKeyser, R. (2005). What makes second-language grammar difficult? A review of issues. *Language Learning* 55, Supplement 1, 1–25.

DeKeyser, R. (2007). Skill acquisition theory. In B. VanPatten & J. Williams (eds.), *Theories in second language acquisition* (pp. 97–113). Mahwah, NJ: Lawrence Erlbaum.

Dinsmore, D. (1985). Waiting for Godot in the EFL classroom. *ELT Journal* 39, 225–34.

Doughty, C. J. (1991). Second language acquisition does make a difference: Evidence from an empirical study of SL relativization. *Studies in Second Language Acquisition* 13, 3, 431–69.

Doughty, C. J. (2003). Instructed SLA: Constraints, compensation, and enhancement. In C. J. Doughty & M. H. Long (eds.), *Handbook of second language acquisition* (pp. 256–310). New York: Basil Blackwell.

Doughty, C. J. & Long, M. H. (2003a). Optimal psycholinguistic environments for distance foreign language learning. *Language Learning and Technology* 7, 3, 50–80. (http://llt.msu.edu)

Doughty, C. J. & Long, M. H. (eds.) (2003b). *Handbook of second language acquisition.* New York: Basil Blackwell.

Doughty, C. J. & Williams, J. (1998). Pedagogical choices in focus on form. acquisition. In C. J. Doughty & J. Williams (eds.), *Focus on form in classroom second language acquisition* (pp. 197–262). Cambridge: Cambridge University Press.

Early, M. (1991). Language and content learning K through 12: The Vancouver School Board Project. *Cross Currents* 18, 2, 183–9.

Early, M., Mohan, B. A., & Hooper, H. R. (1989). The Vancouver School Board Language and Content Project. In J. H. Esling (ed.), *Multicultural education and policy: ESL in the 1990s. A tribute to Mary Ashworth* (pp. 107–22). Toronto: Ontario Institute for Studies in Education.

Eckman, F. R., Bell, L., & Nelson, D. (1988). On the generalization of relative clause instruction in the acquisition of English as a second language. *Applied Linguistics* 9, 1, 1–20.

Ellis, N. (2002a). Frequency effects in language processing: A review with implications for theories of implicit and explicit language acquisition. *Studies in Second Language Acquisition* 24, 2, 143–88.

Ellis, N. (2002b). Reflections on frequency effects in language processing. *Studies in Second Language Acquisition* 24, 2, 297–339.

Ellis, N. (2005). At the interface: Dynamic interactions of explicit and implicit language knowledge. *Studies in Second Language Acquisition* 27, 2, 305–52.

Ellis, N. (2006). Sequencing in SLA: Phonological memory, chunking, and points of order. *Studies in Second Language Acquisition* 18, 1, 91–126.

Ellis, N. (2007). The associative-cognitive CREED. In B. VanPatten & J. Williams (eds.), *Theories in second language acquisition* (pp. 77–95). Mahwah, NJ: Lawrence Erlbaum.

Ellis, N. C. & Larsen-Freeman, D. (2006). Language emergence: Implications for applied linguistics – Introduction to the special issue. *Applied Linguistics* 27, 4, 558–89.

Ellis, R. (1989). Are classroom and naturalistic acquisition the same? A study of the classroom acquisition of German word order rules. *Studies in Second Language Acquisition* 11, 3, 305–28.

Ellis, R. (1994). *The study of second language acquisition.* Oxford: Oxford University Press.

Fathman, A. (1978). ESL and EFL learning: similar or dissimilar? In C. Blatchford & J. Schachter (eds.), *On TESOL '78* (pp. 213–23). Washington, DC: TESOL.

Gass, S. M. (1982). From theory to practice. In M. Hines & W. Rutherford (eds.), *On TESOL '81* (pp. 129–39). Washington, DC: TESOL.

Gass, S. M. (1997). *Input, interaction, and the second language learner.* Mahwah, NJ: Lawrence Erlbaum.

Gass, S. M. (2003). Input and interaction. In C. J. Doughty & M. H. Long (eds.), *Handbook of second language acquisition* (pp. 224–55). New York: Basil Blackwell.

Gass, S. M. & Mackey, A. (2007). Input, interaction, and output in second language acquisition. In B. VanPatten & J. Williams (eds.), *Theories in second language acquisition* (pp. 175–99). Mahwah, NJ: Lawrence Erlbaum.

Gass, S. M. & Selinker, L. (2004). *Second language acquisition: An introductory course,* 2nd edn. Hillsdale, NJ: Lawrence Erlbaum.

Han, Z. & Odlin, T. (eds.) (2005). *Studies of fossilization in second language acquisition.* Clevedon, UK: Multilingual Matters.

Hatch, E. M. (1978). Discourse analysis and second language acquisition. In E. M. Hatch (ed.), *Second language acquisition: A book of readings* (pp. 402–35). Rowley, MA: Newbury House.

Hoetker, J. & Ahlbrand, W. P., Jr. (1967). The persistence of the recitation. *American Educational Research Journal* 6, 2, 145–67.

Huebner, T. (1983). Linguistic system and linguistic change in an interlanguage. *Studies in Second Language Acquisition* 6, 1, 33–53.

Hulstijn, J. (2005). Theoretical and empirical issues in the study of implicit and explicit and implicit second language learning: Introduction. *Studies in Second Language Acquisition* 27, 2, 129–40.

Hyltenstam, K. (1977). Implicational patterns in interlanguage syntax variation. *Language Learning* 27, 2, 383–411.

Hyltenstam, K. (1984). The use of typological markedness conditions as predictors in second language acquisition: The case of pronominal copies in relative clauses. In R. W. Andersen (ed.), *Second language: A cross-linguistic perspective* (pp. 39–58). Rowley, MA: Newbury House.

Ioup, G., Boustagui, E., El Tigi, M., & Moselle, M. (1994). Reexamining the critical period hypothesis: A case study of successful adult SLA in a naturalistic environment. *Studies in Second Language Acquisition* 16, 1, 73–98.

Jacobs, G. M. (1998). Cooperative learning or just grouping students: The difference makes a difference. In W. A. Renandya & G. M. Jacobs (eds.), *Learners and language learning* (pp. 172–93). Singapore: SEAMEO Regional Language Centre.

Johnston, M. (1985). *Syntactic and morphological progressions in learner English.* Canberra: Commonwealth Department of Immigration and Ethnic Affairs.

Johnston, M. (1997). Development and variation in learner language. Unpublished doctoral dissertation. Canberra: Australian National University.

Kellerman, E. (1985). If at first you do succeed . . . In S. M. Gass & C. Madden (eds.), *Input and second language acquisition* (pp. 345–53). Rowley, MA: Newbury House.

Krashen, S. D. (1977). Some issues relating to the Monitor Model. In H. D. Brown, C. Yorio, & R. Crymes (eds.), *On TESOL '77* (pp. 144–58). Washington, DC: TESOL.

Krashen, S. D. (1985). *The input hypothesis: Issues and implications.* New York: Longman.

Lantolf, J. P. & Thorne, S. L. (2006). *Sociocultural theory and the genesis of second language development.* Oxford: Oxford University Press.

Lapkin, S., Hart, D., & Swain, M. (1991). Early and middle French immersion programs: French language outcomes. *The Canadian Modern Language Review* 48, 1, 11–44.

Lardiere, D. (2006). *Ultimate attainment in second language acquisition: A case study.* Mahwah, NJ: Lawrence Erlbaum.

Larsen-Freeman, D. & Ellis, N. (2006). Language emergence: Implications for applied linguistics. *Applied Linguistics* 27, 4, 558–89.

Larsen-Freeman, D. & Long, M. H. (1991). *An introduction to second language acquisition research.* London: Longman.

Liang, X., Mohan, B. A., & Early, M. (1998). Issues of cooperative learning in ESL classes: A literature review. *TESL Canada Journal* 15, 2, 13–23.

Lightbown, P. M. (1983). Exploring relationships between developmental and instructional sequences. In H. W. Seliger & M. H. Long (eds.), *Classroom-oriented research on second language acquisition* (pp. 217–43). Rowley, MA: Newbury House.

Lightbown, P. M. & Spada, N. (2006). *How languages are learned*, 2nd edn. Oxford: Oxford University Press.

Lightbown, P. M., Spada, N., & White, L. (1993). The role of instruction in second language acquisition. *Studies in Second Language Acquisition* 15, 2, 143–63.

Logan, G. E. (1973). *Individualizing foreign language learning: An organic process.* Rowley, MA: Newbury House.

Long, M. H. (1980). Inside the "black box": Methodological issues in classroom research on language learning. *Language Learning* 30, 1, 1–42. Reprinted in 1983 in H. W. Seliger & M. H. Long (eds.), *Classroom-oriented research on second language acquisition* (pp. 3–41). Rowley, MA: Newbury House.

Long, M. H. (1983). Does second language instruction make a difference? A review of research. *TESOL Quarterly* 17, 3, 359–82.

Long, M. H. (1985). A role for instruction in second language acquisition: Task-based language teaching. In K. Hyltenstam & M. Pienemann (eds.), *Modeling and assessing second language development* (pp. 77–99). Clevedon, UK: Multilingual Matters.

Long, M. H. (1988). Instructed interlanguage development. In L. M. Beebe (ed.), *Issues in second language acquisition: Multiple perspectives* (pp. 115–41). Cambridge, MA: Newbury House/Harper and Row.

Long, M. H. (1991). Focus on form: A design feature in language teaching methodology. In K. de Bot, R. B. Ginsberg, & C. Kramsch (eds.), *Foreign language research in cross-cultural perspective* (pp. 39–52). Amsterdam: John Benjamins.

Long, M. H. (1996a). Authenticity and learning potential in L2 classroom discourse. In G. M. Jacobs (ed.), *Language classrooms of tomorrow: Issues and responses* (pp. 148–69). Singapore: SEAMEO Regional Language Centre.

Long, M. H. (1996b). The role of the linguistic environment in second language acquisition. In W. C. Ritchie & T. K. Bahtia (eds.), *Handbook of second language acquisition* (pp. 413–68). New York: Academic Press.

Long, M. H. (1997). Authenticity and learning potential in L2 classroom discourse. In G. M. Jacobs (ed.), *Language classrooms of tomorrow: Issues and responses* (pp. 148–69). Singapore: SEAMEO Regional Language Centre.

Long, M. H. (2000a). Focus on form in task-based language teaching. In R. L. Lambert & E. Shohamy (eds.), *Language policy and pedagogy* (pp. 179–92). Philadelphia: John Benjamins.

Long, M. H. (2000b). Acquisition and teaching. In M. Byram (ed.), *Encyclopedia of language teaching* (pp. 4–5). London: Routledge.

Long, M. H. (2003). Stabilization and fossilization in interlanguage development. In C. J. Doughty & M. H. Long (eds.), *Handbook of second language acquisition* (pp. 487–535). Oxford: Blackwell.

Long, M. H. (ed.) (2005). *Second language needs analysis.* Cambridge: Cambridge University Press.

Long, M. H. (2007a). Second language acquisition theories. In M. H. Long, *Problems in SLA* (pp. 3–20). Mahwah, NJ: Lawrence Erlbaum.

Long, M. H. (2007b). Recasts in SLA: The story so far. In M. H. Long, *Problems in SLA* (pp. 75–116). Mahwah, NJ: Lawrence Erlbaum.

Long, M. H. (2007c). Texts, tasks, and the advanced learner. In M. H. Long, *Problems in SLA* (pp. 119–38). Mahwah, NJ: Lawrence Erlbaum.

Long, M. H. (to appear). SLA and TBLT. Manuscript. College Park: University of Maryland.

Long, M. H., Adams, L., McLean, M., & Castanos, F. (1976). Doing things with words: Verbal interaction in lockstep and small group classroom situations. In J. Fanselow & R. Crymes (eds.), *On TESOL '76* (pp. 137–53). Washington, DC: TESOL. Reprinted in 1988 in D. Allwright, *Observation in the language classroom* (pp. 153–71). Harlow, UK: Longman.

Long, M. H. & Crookes, G. (1992). Three approaches to task-based language teaching. *TESOL Quarterly* 26, 1, 27–56.

Long, M. H. & Crookes, G. (1993). Units of analysis in syllabus design: The case for task. In G. Crookes & S. M. Gass (eds.), *Tasks in pedagogical context: Integrating theory and practice* (pp. 9–54). Clevedon, UK: Multilingual Matters.

Long, M. H. & Norris, J. M. (2000). Task-based teaching and assessment. In M. Byram (ed.), *Encyclopedia of language teaching* (pp. 597–603). London: Routledge.

Long, M. H. & Porter, P. (1985). Group work, interlanguage talk, and second language acquisition. *TESOL Quarterly* 19, 2, 207–27.

Long, M. H. & Robinson, P. (1998). Focus on form: Theory, research and practice. In C. J. Doughty & J. Williams (eds.), *Focus on form in second language acquisition* (pp. 15–41). Cambridge: Cambridge University Press.

Long, M. H. & Ross, S. (1993). Modifications that preserve language and content. In M. Tickoo (ed.), *Simplification: Theory and application* (pp. 29–52). Singapore: SEAMEO Regional Language Centre.

Long, M. H. & Sato, C. J. (1983). Classroom foreigner talk discourse: Forms and functions of teachers' questions. In H. W. Seliger & M. H. Long (eds.), *Classroom-oriented research on second language acquisition* (pp. 268–85). Rowley, MA: Newbury House.

Mackey, A. (1999). Input, interaction and second language development. *Studies in Second Language Acquisition* 21, 4, 557–87.

Mackey, A. & Goo, J. (2007). Interaction research in SLA: A meta-analysis and research synthesis. In A. Mackey (ed.), *Conversational interaction in second language acquisition* (pp. 407–52). Oxford: Oxford University Press.

McCafferty, S. G., Jacobs, G. M., & DaSilva Iddings, A. C. (eds.) (2006). *Cooperative learning and second language teaching.* Cambridge: Cambridge University Press.

McLaughlin, B. (1990). Restructuring. *Applied Linguistics* 11, 2, 1–16.

Meisel, J. M. (1987). Reference to past events and actions in the development of natural second language acquisition. In C. Pfaff (ed.), *First and second language acquisition processes* (pp. 206–24). Cambridge, MA: Newbury House.

Meisel, J. M., Clahsen, H., & Pienemann, M. (1981). On determining developmental stages in natural second language acquisition. *Studies in Second Language Acquisition* 3, 2, 109–35.

Musumeci, D. (1997). *An exploration of the historical relationship between theory and practice in second language teaching.* New York: McGraw-Hill.

Norris, J. M. & Ortega, L. (2000). Effectiveness of L2 instruction: A research synthesis and quantitative meta-analysis. *Language Learning* 5, 3, 417–528.

Nunan, D. (1987). Communicative language teaching: Making it work. *ELT Journal* 41, 2, 136–45.

Oh, S-Y. (2001). Two types of input modification and EFL reading comprehension: Simplification versus elaboration. *TESOL Quarterly* 35, 1, 69–96.

Oxford, R. L. (1997). Cooperative learning; collaborative learning; and interaction: Three communicative strands in the language classroom. *Modern Language Journal* 81, 4, 443–56.

Pavesi, M. (1986). Markedness, discoursal modes, and relative clause formation in a formal and an informal context. *Studies in Second Language Acquisition* 81, 1, 38–55.

Pica, T. (1983). Adult acquisition of English as a second language under different conditions of exposure. *Language Learning* 33, 4, 465–97.

Pica, T., Lincoln-Porter, F., Paninos, D., & Linnell, J. (1996). Language learners' interaction: How does it address the input, output, and feedback needs of language learners? *TESOL Quarterly* 30, 1, 59–84.

Pienemann, M. (1984). Psychological constraints on the teachability of languages. *Studies in Second Language Acquisition* 6, 2, 186–214.

Pienemann, M. (1989). Is language teachable? Psycholinguistic experiments and hypotheses. *Applied Linguistics* 10, 1, 52–79.

Ritchie, W. C. & Bhatia, T. J. (1996). *Handbook of second language acquisition.* New York: Academic Press.

Robinson, P. (2001a). Task complexity, cognitive resources and second language syllabus design: A triadic theory of task influences on SLA. In P. Robinson (ed.), *Cognition and second language instruction* (pp. 285–317). Cambridge: Cambridge University Press.

Robinson, P. (2001b). Task complexity, task difficulty and task production: Exploring interactions in a componential framework. *Applied Linguistics* 22, 1, 27–57.

Robinson, P. (ed.) (2003). *Individual differences and instructed language learning.* Amsterdam/Philadelphia: John Benjamin.

Russell, J. & Spada, N. (2006). The effectiveness of corrective feedback for the acquisition of L2 grammar. In J. M. Norris & L. Ortega (eds.), *Synthesizing research on language learning and teaching* (pp. 133–64). Amsterdam/Philadelphia: John Benjamins.

Sato, C. J. (1986). Conversation and interlanguage development: Rethinking the connection. In R. R. Day (ed.), *Talking to learn: Conversation and second language acquisition* (pp. 23–45). Rowley, MA: Newbury House.

Sato, C. J. (1988). Origins of complex syntax in interlanguage development. *Studies in Second Language Acquisition* 10, 3, 371–95.

Sato, C. J. (1990). *The syntax of conversation in interlanguage development.* Tübingen: Gunter Narr.

Sawyer, M. & Ranta, L. (2001). Aptitude, individual differences, and instructional design. In P. Robinson (ed.), *Cognition and second language instruction* (pp. 310–53). Cambridge: Cambridge University Press.

Schmidt, R. (2001). Attention. In P. Robinson (ed.), *Cognition and second language instruction* (pp. 3–32). Cambridge: Cambridge University Press.

Schmitt, N. (ed.) (2004). *Formulaic sequences: Acquisition, processing and use*. Amsterdam/ Philadelphia: John Benjamins.

Schumann, J. H. (1979). The acquisition of English negation by speakers of Spanish: A review of the literature. In R. W. Andersen (ed.), *The acquisition and use of Spanish and English as first and second languages* (pp. 3–32). Washington, DC: TESOL.

Selinker, L. (1972). Interlanguage. *International Review of Applied Linguistics* 10, 209–31.

Shavelson, R. J. & Stern, P. (1981). Research on teachers' pedagogical thoughts, judgments and behavior. *Review of Educational Research* 51, 455–98.

Shotton, J. (1993). *No master high or low: Libertarian education and schooling in Britain, 1890– 1990*. Bristol: Libertarian Education.

Skehan, P. (1998). *A cognitive approach to language learning*. Oxford: Oxford University Press.

Smith, M. P. (1983). *The libertarians and education*. London: George Allen & Unwin.

Sorace, A. (2003). Near-nativeness. In C. J. Doughty & M. H. Long (eds.), *Handbook of second language acquisition* (pp. 130–51). New York: Basil Blackwell.

Swaffer, J. K., Arens, K., & Morgan, M. (1982). Teacher classroom practices: Redefining method as task hierarchy. *Modern Language Journal* 66, 1, 24–33.

Swain, M. (1991). French immersion and its off-shoots: getting two for one. In B. F. Freed (ed.), *Foreign language acquisition research and the classroom* (pp. 91–103). Lexington, MA: D. C. Heath.

Van den Branden, K. (ed.) (2006). *Task-based language education: From theory to practice*. Cambridge: Cambridge University Press.

Vatz, K. (2007). The effects of modified elaborated texts on ESL reading comprehension. Paper presented at TBLT 2007, University of Hawai'i, Honolulu.

Webb, N. M. (1991). Task-related verbal interaction and mathematics learning in small groups. *Journal for Research in Mathematics Education* 22, 5, 366–89.

Wesche, M. (1981). Language aptitude measures in streaming, matching students with methods, and diagnosis of learning problems. In K. C. Diller (ed.), *Individual differences and universals in language learning aptitude* (pp. 119–54). Rowley, MA: Newbury House.

White, L. (1987). Against comprehensible input: The Input Hypothesis and the development of L2 competence. *Applied Linguistics* 8, 1, 95–110.

White, L. (1991). Adverb placement in second language acquisition: Some effects of positive and negative evidence in the classroom. *Second Language Research* 7, 133–61.

White, L. (2003). *Second language acquisition and Universal Grammar*. Cambridge: Cambridge University Press.

Wilkins, D. (1976). *Notional syllabuses*. Oxford: Oxford University Press.

Williams, J. N. (2005). Learning without awareness. *Studies in Second Language Acquisition* 27, 2, 269–304.

Wray, A. (2000). Formulaic sequences in second language teaching: Principle and practice. *Applied Linguistics* 21, 4, 463–89.

Wray, A. (2002). *Formulaic language and the lexicon*. Cambridge: Cambridge University Press.

Yano, Y., Long, M. H., & Ross, S. (1994). The effects of simplified and elaborated texts on foreign language reading comprehension. *Language Learning* 44, 2, 189–219.

Zobl, H. (1982). A direction for contrastive analysis: The comparative study of developmental sequences. *TESOL Quarterly* 16, 2, 169–83.

22 Teaching and Testing Listening Comprehension

LARRY VANDERGRIFT AND CHRISTINE GOH

For years, the role of listening in language acquisition and communication was undervalued and neglected. Second and foreign language (SL/FL) listening was often developed incidentally through language exercises where oral language was used. It eventually earned its rightful place during the communicative language teaching era. Language was taught for face-to-face communication, and listening was an important skill in this regard. It was also a channel for comprehensible input (Krashen, 1985) and an important aspect of interlanguage communication necessary for language acquisition (Swain, 1985). With these changing perceptions of SL/FL listening, there was a concerted effort to describe its characteristics and how to teach it (e.g., Anderson & Lynch, 1988). These positive developments were sustained by theoretical insights from disciplines such as psychology, education, communication studies, and linguistics. More significantly, theories about human cognition have introduced language teachers to the exciting possibilities of language development through active learner involvement and control. These cognitive theories provided an important framework for describing SL/FL listening (e.g., Goh, 2002a, 2005; Vandergrift, 2003a) and instructional methods and techniques (Flowerdew & Miller, 2005; Goh, 2002b; Mendelsohn & Rubin, 1995; Vandergrift, 2003b, 2004).

This review of teaching listening is organized around three main topics: (1) cognitive and social dimensions of listening, (2) approaches to teaching listening, and (3) assessment of listening.

Cognitive and Social Dimensions of Listening

In the process of text comprehension, meaning is not simply extracted from the input; it is constructed by listeners based on their knowledge of the language system, their prior knowledge, and the context of the interaction. This process is constrained by the limitations of memory, as noted by Graesser and Britton (1996): "Text understanding is the dynamic process of constructing coherent representations and inferences at multiple levels of text and context, within the bottleneck of a limited-capacity working memory" (p. 349). Furthermore, in conversational listening, comprehension is an outcome of joint action, where listeners and speakers carry out individual acts of communication in a coordinated manner (Clark, 1996). This pragmatic view of listening is echoed by Rost (2002), who asserts that "listening is an intention to complete a communication," and high-level inferences during listening require listeners to make assumptions about speakers' intentions, amongst other things (p. 40).

Cognitive dimensions of listening

One of the first cognitive models to be applied in SL/FL listening research was Anderson's model of perceptual processing, parsing, and utilization (Anderson, 1995). It accounts for the interactive processing that takes place in short-term memory and has been used in the discussion of listening strategies (O'Malley, Chamot & Küpper, 1989; Vandergrift, 1997) and listening problems (Goh, 2000). The connectionist model, which proposes processing through a spreading activation of interconnected or associative neural networks in the brain (Bechtel & Abrahamsen, 1991), has also been applied. Researchers have argued for the need to help learners build these networks, so that fast parallel processing of language is possible (Buck, 1995; Hulstijn, 2003). Recent discussions on the brain's capacity for processing and temporary storage of information have focused on working memory. A dominant model of working memory includes:

- the phonological loop and the visuo-spatial sketchpad, which are responsible for short-term processing;
- the central executive, which directs attention to the input and coordinates various cognitive processes; and
- the episodic buffer, which integrates information processed through the above-mentioned processing systems into a single mental representation (Baddeley, 2000).

This model accounts for the integration of audio and visual information, and the connection between working memory and long-term memory. It can therefore bring a new perspective into the discussion of SL/FL listening comprehension processes where multiple modalities of input are increasingly typical of both in-class and out-of-class listening experiences (e.g., Gruba, 2004).

Although there are different models for the intricate workings of cognitive processing systems, the approaches mentioned above share some fundamental principles concerning cognition and have common implications for SL/FL listening:

1 For processing of information to take place, attention must be directed at the input and some amount of decoding and analysis of the signals must occur. Listeners must perceive and recognize words in a stream of speech and at the same time parse it into meaningful units or "chunks." While these processes are automatized in competent language users, lower-proficiency listeners still depend a great deal on controlled processing of the linguistic information. One of the key objectives of listening instruction, therefore, is to help learners recognize and parse linguistic input quickly. When visual input (e.g., facial expressions, gestures, illustrations, videos, slides) is present, it is often an integral part of the message, so the information will have to be processed simultaneously with auditory input (Gruba, 2004). For example, gestures and facial cues can facilitate the comprehension of videotaped lectures; however, the degree to which these cues are used will vary as a function of listening proficiency (Sueyoshi & Hardison, 2005).

2 *As new information is being processed, it is acted upon by existing knowledge or schemata retrieved from long-term memory.* Known commonly as top-down processing, the use of prior knowledge assists listeners in constructing interpretations that are complete and meaningful. Top-down processing can help SL/FL listeners bridge gaps in comprehension and construct a reasonable interpretation without depending too much on linguistic features (Izumi, 2003). Prior knowledge can be generated from "parallel activities" (e.g., reading, viewing) that accompany a listening event, such as attending a lecture. Flowerdew and Miller (2005, p. 90) refer to this as the "intertextual dimension" of comprehension. Prior knowledge facilitates quicker processing. Tyler (2001) found that when listeners had access to the topic, differences in working memory consumption between native and "experienced" non-native listeners were not statistically significant. Top-down processing is clearly important; however, learners sometimes miss opportunities to apply prior knowledge because their attention is focused entirely on trying to decode and parse the speech stream.

3 *The ability to process speech successfully depends on how much linguistic information is processed quickly.* During listening, information is processed under severe time pressure, so processing that demands fewer attentional resources would clearly be advantageous. This is often referred to as automatic processing. In listening, automatization can occur at the phonological and grammatical levels. Automatic lexical recognition can have a significant effect on listeners' understanding and recall (Jefferies, Ralph, & Baddeley, 2004). As Segalowitz (2003) explains, automaticity can vary both quantitatively (e.g., speed of processing) and qualitatively (e.g., restructuring of information). In the case of non-proficient listeners, many comprehension processes are controlled; that is, they take place under the learners' conscious attention. On hearing the input, listeners try to match sounds to the contents in their mental lexicon. This they do by applying top-down and bottom-up strategies, along with metacognitive strategies to direct their attention, monitor their interpretation, and problem-solve. In general, skilled SL/FL listeners combine various strategies in an orchestrated and harmonious manner (Goh, 2002b; Vandergrift, 2003a).

Social dimensions of listening

Listening does not take place in a vacuum; texts and utterances need to be interpreted in their wider communicative context. In face-to-face communication, this may involve the comprehension of gesture and other non-verbal or culturally bound cues that can add to (or change) the literal meaning of an utterance (Harris, 2003). SL/FL listeners need to be conscious of the status relationships between interlocutors, and of how these relationships can affect comprehension and the freedom to negotiate meaning, particularly in contexts where listeners are in an unequal power relationship (Carrier, 1999). In order to signal a comprehension problem in communicative interaction, listeners need to use efficient clarification strategies appropriate to the setting and the interlocutor. The social dimension also encompasses pragmatic and psychological aspects of listening comprehension.

Pragmatic comprehension involves the rapid and accurate application of pragmatic knowledge; i.e., knowledge about a speaker's intention in a given context that goes beyond the literal meaning of an utterance (Rose & Kasper, 2001). Listeners use this knowledge, which is often culture-specific, to make inferences and determine implied meaning. The ability to process both contextual and linguistic information successfully appears to be a function of language proficiency. Cook and Liddicoat (2002) found that lower-proficiency SL/FL listeners experienced greater difficulty in interpreting different types of requests because they were not able to free up enough processing capacity to attend to both linguistic and other information sources at the same time. Results of a more recent study by Garcia (2004) corroborate these findings and also provide evidence for better comprehension of conversational implicatures (understanding the attitude and intentions of a speaker) by higher-proficiency listeners. In a similar vein, Taguchi (2005) found a strong proficiency effect for accuracy, but not for speed, in comprehension of implicatures, leading her to conclude that the ability to understand implied information and the ability to process this information rapidly may be two different dimensions of pragmatic comprehension.

The psychological dimension of listening is often related to the language classroom. Learners frequently comment on the anxiety associated with listening and its effect on listening performance. Elkhafaifi (2005) found significant negative correlations between listening anxiety and the listening comprehension scores of learners of Arabic. As discussed later, this may be due to the emphasis on product rather than process in the teaching of SL/FL listening. Not surprisingly, success in SL/FL listening also appears to be related to motivation. Vandergrift (2005) found a positive relationship among SL/FL listening proficiency, use of metacognitive strategies (integral to self-regulated learning), and reported levels of intrinsic and extrinsic motivation (fundamental to self-determined behavior). Listeners who scored low on the motivation measure, perhaps because of lack of self-confidence and self-efficacy, reported using fewer effective listening strategies.

Approaches to Teaching SL/FL Listening

For most of its history, the teaching of SL/FL listening emphasized the extraction of meaning from texts and overlooked the need to teach learners how to listen. Instruction focused mainly on verifying the outcomes of listening rather than developing the learning processes integral to successful comprehension. Even when pre-listening activities were used to activate prior knowledge, the focus was limited to prior knowledge about the contents. In light of the importance of learner awareness and control in learning, listening instruction should offer scaffolded learning experiences to help listeners discover and rehearse listening processes. If students are not taught *how to listen*, listening activities become nothing more than disguised forms of testing learners' existing listening abilities, which only serves to increase anxiety about listening.

In this section, we will discuss recent research in teaching SL/FL listening within the broad framework of bottom-up (lexical segmentation and word recognition skills) and top-down (metacognitive awareness-raising) approaches. We will then present an integrated pedagogical model for developing skilled listeners who can automatically self-regulate comprehension processes. Due to space constraints, this section will not deal with instruction in the social dimension of listening, which involves the use of communication strategies for meaning negotiation.

Bottom-up approaches

Bottom-up processing in listening entails the perception of sounds and words in a speech stream. When there is adequate perception of lexical information, listeners can use their background knowledge to interpret the input. The bottom-up approach to teaching listening acknowledges the primacy of the acoustic signal and focuses on helping learners develop critical perception skills.

A major challenge faced by SL/FL listeners is word segmentation. Listeners, unlike readers, do not have the luxury of regular spaces that signal the beginnings or ends of words. They must parse the stream of sound into meaningful units, and word boundaries are often hard to determine. Even if they know a word, SL/FL listeners may not always recognize it in concatenated speech. Word-segmentation skills are language-specific and acquired early in life. These procedures are so solidly engrained in the listener's processing system that they are involuntarily applied when listening to a new language, making listening to a rhythmically different language particularly difficult (Cutler, 2001). This problem is particularly heightened for lower-proficiency listeners (Goh, 2000; Graham, 2006). Listening instruction must help learners cope with these difficulties, so that they can identify words in the stream of sound, and there is research evidence that this is possible.

In her review of the literature on speech segmentation, Cutler (2001) concludes that SL/FL listeners can inhibit the natural compulsion to apply native language segmentation procedures when listening to a new language that is rhythmically different. Prosodic features such as stress and intonation are important cues for determining word boundaries, and there is some evidence that calling attention to these features is helpful to SL/FL listeners. Attending to pause-bounded units rather than syntactic cues can be fruitful in comprehending English, regardless of the listeners' age and language background (Harley, 2000). Inserting word boundaries before stressed syllables can help to identify words in a stream of speech (Field, 2005). Use of word-onset (initial phonemes of a word) also proves to be a reliable word-recognition strategy, likely due to the prosodic information accompanying the word (Lindfield, Wingfield, & Goodglass, 1999). Finally, Sanders, Neville, and Woldorff (2002) found that "late" learners can use lexical information and stress cues to segment concatenated speech; however, the extent to which these SL/FL listeners can use stress cues will depend on their native language. In sum, knowing that listeners can learn to use segmentation cues different from those of their native language suggests that these processes are amenable to instruction.

Word-segmentation skills can be acquired by giving SL/FL listeners opportunities to "accumulate and categorize acoustic, phonemic, syllabic, morphological and lexical information" (Hulstijn, 2003, p. 422). Hulstijn outlines a six-step procedure: (1) listen to the oral text without reading the written version; (2) determine your level of comprehension; (3) replay the recording as often as necessary; (4) check the written text; (5) recognize what you should have understood; and, finally, (6) replay the recording until you understand it without written support. This procedure can help the SL/FL listener to note other important phenomena in connected speech, such as reduced forms, assimilation, elision and resyllabification. In order to develop word-segmentation skills, learners need to be made aware of these phenomena, pay attention to them, and, during listening practice, replay them so they can puzzle them out for themselves (Field, 2003).

Word-recognition training can take many forms. Some possibilities include: analysis of parts of the text transcription, dictation, and analogy exercises (see Goh, 2002b and Field, 2005). Listening to "i-1 level" texts, i.e., aural texts where most words are known, can develop automaticity in word recognition when SL/FL listeners note the slight discrepancies between the aural form and written form of the text (Hulstijn, 2001). Approaching bottom-up processing at the prosodic level, Cauldwell (2002) presents activities to help learners perceive "prominence" (i.e., word stress in the context of discourse). One of his techniques models the way in which words between prominent syllables are "crushed" so as to enable learners to perceive how words and syllables are weakened in authentic speech. Early research had indicated that phonological modifications (e.g., elision, assimilation, liaison) affected the comprehension of ESL learners of both low and high proficiency (Henrichsen, 1984).

Wilson (2003) proposes the use of the dictogloss technique as a tool. After listening, SL/FL listeners are guided to notice the differences between their reconstructed text and a written transcription of the original. This technique has the potential to improve perceptual processing because it forces learners to focus on their listening problems, consider the reasons for their errors, and evaluate the importance of those errors (Wilson, 2003).

Exact repetition and reduced speech rate have also been examined as techniques for teaching SL/FL listening (Jensen & Vinther, 2003). When exposed to verbatim repetitions of videotaped dialogues in different modes, Fast (F) or Slow (S), all three experimental groups (F-S-S, F-S-F, and F-F-F) outperformed a control group in detailed comprehension and acquisition of phonological decoding strategies. Furthermore, the F-F-F group outperformed the other two groups, demonstrating that reduction in speed of a text will not necessarily improve comprehension. The researchers concluded that listening perception training should be integrated with regular listening activities that allow students to "indulge in hypothesis work regarding all the linguistic features" (p. 419), an approach also advocated by others (e.g., Goh, 2002b; Hulstijn, 2001; Wilson, 2003).

The advent of digital technology has further enhanced the use of audio and video texts for individual listening practice and classroom instruction (e.g., Gruba, 2004; Hoeflaak, 2004). Learners can listen to any chunk of text they choose and save texts on the computer for future review (copyright notwithstanding). With the latest podcasting technology, learners can also listen to a wide selection of media broadcasts in and out of class, and save them for future review (Robin, 2007).

Top-down approaches

The top-down dimension of SL/FL listening instruction involves teaching learners to reflect on the nature of listening and to self-regulate their comprehension processes. Its aim is to develop learners' metacognitive knowledge about listening (Goh, 2008).

Metacognitive knowledge refers to an individual's understanding of the ways different factors act and interact to affect the course and outcome of learning (Flavell, 1979). It can contribute to effective self-direction and can have positive effects on the outcome of learning (Boekaerts, Pintrich, & Zeidner, 2000; Eilam & Aharon, 2003). This knowledge can be further divided into person knowledge, task knowledge, and strategy knowledge (see Figure 22.1).

Learners' metacognitive knowledge about listening can be developed in several ways. One method that is easy for both teachers and learners to use is

---

Person knowledge
Knowledge concerning the personal factors that might support or hinder one's listening, e.g., anxiety or problems during listening.

Task knowledge
Knowledge concerning the purpose of a listening task, its demands, text organization and structure, factors that could hinder the task, and type of listening skills required to achieve the listening purpose (e.g., listening for details, listening for gist).

Strategy knowledge
Strategies useful for enhancing listening comprehension, e.g., strategies for dealing with listening problems and checking one's interpretation.

Figure 22.1 Metacognitive knowledge about listening (adapted from Goh, 2002b)

listening diaries (Goh, 1997). Diaries with selected prompts can direct learners' reflections on specific listening events so that they can evaluate their performance and take positive steps to improve their listening skills. Teachers can also plan process-oriented activities as part of their listening lessons (Liu & Goh, 2006; Vandergrift, 2002; Zeng, 2007), a method which has also proved to be effective even with young learners (Goh & Taib, 2006). In small groups and teacher-led discussions, learners share personal observations recorded in their listening diaries. They can learn about new listening strategies through these collaborative dialogues.

Metacognitive awareness-raising tasks can also be incorporated into various stages of a listening lesson. Vandergrift (2003b) used several listening tasks to guide French learners in using prediction. Not only did the learners successfully use the strategy, but they also reported increased motivation and heightened metacognitive awareness about the role of strategies in listening comprehension. Liu and Goh (2006) asked learners to use a metacognitive guide when listening on their own. The learners answered prompt questions before and after listening tasks to aid in pre-listening preparation, evaluate their performance, and plan their strategy use for future listening. These studies demonstrated the usefulness of top-down teaching approaches where teachers can promote metacognitive processes and strategy use through scaffolded listening tasks.

Individual metacognitive reflections can be further enhanced through the use of introspective instruments, such as questionnaires. There are indications that the use of such questionnaires may encourage listeners to apply strategies they consider to be useful (Zhang & Goh, 2006). A recently developed instrument, the Metacognitive Awareness Listening Questionnaire (MALQ), is grounded in research and theory about SL/FL listening, and scores are significantly related to listening success (Vandergrift et al., 2006). The MALQ can be used by (1) SL/FL listeners to evaluate their own understanding of the listening process; (2) teachers to diagnose student awareness of those processes; and (3) researchers to track the development of metacognitive knowledge about listening as a result of instruction in listening processes.

Raising metacognitive awareness through listening diaries, process-oriented discussions, and questionnaires are indirect methods for improving listening performance. Learners step back from real-time listening, examine their listening processes and develop their own thinking about what it takes to be an effective listener.

Integrated model for teaching SL/FL listening

An effective listening curriculum recognizes listening comprehension as an active, strategic and constructive process. Although listening is an individual mental operation, the teaching and learning of how to listen need not be so. While it is true that teachers are unable to manipulate learners' mental processes during listening, there are tasks and activities that can strengthen their ability to control those processes for themselves (Buck, 1995; Goh, 2002b; Mendelsohn, 1998;

Vandergrift, 2002, 2003a). Individual listening can be supported by collaborative activities where students focus on the nature and demands of a listening task. Activities that include the application of strategies during listening lessons enable learners to experience these processes themselves. One way is to incorporate strategies in a lesson sequence (Field, 2001; Liu & Goh, 2006; Vandergrift, 2002, 2003b). Listeners are guided at specific stages to use the metacognitive processes underlying successful listening to regulate their comprehension (see Figure 22.2).

This pedagogical cycle develops both top-down and bottom-up dimensions of listening, and metacognitive awareness of the processes underlying successful SL/FL listening. By orchestrating hypothesis formation and verification, and judiciously applying prior knowledge to compensate for gaps in understanding, the listener acquires implicit knowledge of listening processes. In addition, by matching all or parts of the aural and written forms of the text, the listener becomes aware of form–meaning relationships and gains word-recognition skills. It is important, however, that the exposure to the written form take place only after listeners have engaged in the cognitive processes that underlie real-life listening. If listeners are allowed access to the written form too early in the cycle, they risk developing an inefficient online translation approach to listening (Eastman, 1991).

Guiding learners through the process of aural comprehension as part of regular listening activities can help them to improve overall as listeners (Field, 2001; Goh, 2002a; Vandergrift, 2002, 2003a; Wilson, 2003) and to develop "playful media literacy" (Gruba, 2006). Students need repeated and systematic practice with a variety of listening tasks that activate the metacognitive processes used by skilled listeners; however, all tasks should be grounded in the same metacognitive cycle. While the teacher will initially play a greater role, scaffolding should be gradually removed, so that students do the work themselves and the process becomes automatic. Initially, students may be asked to devise a plan for their listening before they embark on the task.

This pedagogical cycle has strong theoretical support, in that it closely parallels the research findings demonstrating implicit learning through task performance (Johnston & Doughty, 2006). It also has empirical support. In a carefully controlled study conducted over the period of one semester, intermediate-level learners of French who were guided through this process approach to listening significantly outperformed learners in the control group (Vandergrift & Tafaghodtari, in press). To control for the mitigating effects of the teacher variable, both groups were taught by the same teacher using the same texts. The hypothesis that the less skilled listeners in the experimental group would make greater gains than their more skilled peers was also verified, demonstrating that less skilled listeners, in particular, can benefit from this kind of guided listening practice.

Advanced-level SL/FL listeners can also benefit from this kind of listening practice. Mareschal (2007) found that a low-proficiency and a high-proficiency group of learners of French exposed to this listening pedagogy during intensive eight-week language training were better able to regulate listening processes. Analyzing data from a completed listening questionnaire (MALQ), stimulated

Stages of listening instruction	Related metacognitive processes
Planning/predicting stage 1 Once students know the topic and text type, they predict types of information and possible words they may hear.	1 Planning and directed attention
First listen/verification stage 2 Students listen to verify initial hypotheses, correct as required and note additional information understood.	2 Monitoring
3 Students compare what they have written with peers, modify as required, establish what needs resolution and decide on the important details that still need special attention.	3 Monitoring, planning and selective attention
Second listen/verification stage 4 Students selectively attend to points of disagreement, make corrections and write down additional details understood.	4 Monitoring and problem-solving
5 Class discussion in which all class members contribute to the reconstruction of the text's main points and most pertinent details, interspersed with reflections on how students arrived at the meaning of certain words or parts of the text.	5 Monitoring and evaluation
Final listen/verification stage 6 Students listen for the information revealed in the class discussion which they were not able to decipher earlier and/or compare all or selected sections of the aural form of the text with a transcription of the text.	6 Selective attention and monitoring
Reflection stage 7 Based on the earlier discussion of strategies used to compensate for what was not understood, students write goals for the next listening activity. A discussion of discrepancies between the aural and written forms of the text could also take place at this stage.	7 Evaluation

Figure 22.2 Stages of listening instruction and related metacognitive processes (adapted from Vandergrift, 2004)

recalls, diaries, and a final summative report, she was able to document how the listening training impacted the listeners' self-regulatory ability, strategy use, metacognitive knowledge, and listening success, particularly for the low-proficiency group. The aural–written verification stage proved to be particularly valuable to the low-proficiency group for developing auditory discrimination skills and to the high-proficiency group for more refined word recognition skills.

Listening Assessment

The most comprehensive treatment of the assessment of SL/FL listening is the seminal work by Buck (2001). Since space limitations preclude a full treatment of the issues related to listening assessment, readers are encouraged to consult this excellent resource for an accessible, yet research-based coverage of the topic. We will focus on what appear to be the major challenges in the assessment of SL/FL listening in the most recent research literature.[1] These include questions related to construct validity, task type, item type, and input mode.

Construct validity is important for assessment because it entails defining the construct, operationalizing the behaviors that need to be assessed, and then creating tasks (appropriate texts and response items) to elicit these behaviors. Construct validity is a particular challenge for listening, given its covert nature. Listening processes are difficult to verify empirically and, as noted above, these processes interact in complex ways with different types of knowledge and, in the end, comprehension can only be inferred on the basis of task completion. More introspective studies are required to reveal, admittedly to a limited degree, what motivates listener response to task requirements, and how the listener variables, task-types, knowledge-types, and listening processes interact in determining listener response.

Generally, the purpose of the listening test and the context of language use will guide construct definition (Buck, 2001). However, in contexts where the target language use situation is not clearly defined (which is often the case for general proficiency tests and SL/FL classroom assessment), Buck proposes a default listening construct that defines listening as

> the ability to 1) process extended samples of realistic spoken language, automatically and in real time; 2) understand the linguistic information that is unequivocally included in the text; and, 3) make whatever inferences are unambiguously implicated by the content of the passage. (p. 114)

This definition is sufficiently flexible and broad to fit most contexts of language use and allows listeners to demonstrate their comprehension ability.

In an attempt to find empirical evidence for some of the competencies underlying academic listening (from theorized listening taxonomies), Wagner (2002) examined the construct validity of a video-based test, guided by a model of six competencies and two factors (bottom-up and top-down processing). Some evidence for the validity of a two-factor model emerged; however, instead of generating the bottom-up and top-down factors, the two factors that emerged related to the processing of (1) explicitly stated information, and (2) implicit information. Wagner attributes the lack of definitive results to the difficulty of differentiating between listening processes that appear to occur simultaneously. Furthermore, he suggests that the implicit and explicit distinction may be artificial, since listeners need to understand the explicit to infer the implicit. Research by Wagner, important in attempting to define the listening construct empirically, demonstrates the enormous difficulty of the task.

In their investigation of differences in task characteristics and task conditions, Brindley and Slayter (2002) found that speech rate and response mode influenced task and item difficulty. They found that the complex interaction among various components of a task made it hard to identify the difficulty level of an item. Adjusting one task variable did not necessarily make the task easier or more difficult, since task difficulty proved to be a function of the interaction of listener characteristics and task characteristics. The speech rate variable, for example, is difficult to operationalize when rates may vary throughout a text. They also highlight issues related to construct validity and reliable assessment in classroom contexts. Speaker accent and dialect, for example, can bias tests against ESL listeners (Major et al., 2005).

Notetaking during a computer-based listening test may help SL/FL listeners, depending on the length of the lecture, the topic, and listener proficiency (Carrell, Dunkel, & Mollaun, 2004). Furthermore, jotting down notes can compensate for memory constraints and enhance face validity of the test.

The issue of item difficulty was investigated by Rupp, Garcia, and Jamieson (2001) using multiple regression analysis (MRA) and classification and regression tree (CART). While MRA pointed to text characteristics and text–item interaction as contributors to item difficulty, CART showed how these overlapped in different combinations in easy versus difficult items. Although increased item difficulty was commensurate with increased sentence length, word count. and type–token ratio, these variables were influenced by information density, lexical overlap with distracters, item type, and type of match. Furthermore, Cheng (2004) determined that response format has a significant effect on listening test performance. Students completing multiple-choice cloze items outperformed students completing traditional multiple-choice items who, in turn, outperformed students completing open-ended questions.

The question of mode of input in assessing listening is receiving more research attention with the increased availability of multimedia and digital technologies. Test developers are interested in determining the relevance and usefulness of visual support in the assessment of SL/FL listening. Coniam (2001) found that students listening to an audio version of an educational discussion obtained higher comprehension scores than a group listening to the video version. Furthermore, over 80 percent of the video group felt that the video had not facilitated comprehension and they expressed preference for audio. Ginther (2002) investigated the relative effect of two kinds of visuals on the comprehension of mini-talks in the computerized TOEFL test. Content visuals (pictures related to the actual content of the verbal exchange) slightly enhanced comprehension; however, context visuals (pictures that set the scene for the upcoming verbal exchange) were less useful.

Given that this visual support appears to be only marginally useful, do test-takers actually watch the video monitor? Wagner (2006) found that listeners do pay attention to the video monitor (on average 69 percent of test time) instead of the test materials only, although there was a wide range in duration of listener viewing time. Listener attention did not vary at any point during the test; however, a greater percentage of time was given to watching dialogues than lecturettes. In contrast to the listeners in the Coniam study, these listeners supported the use of videotexts in listening assessment and did not find video distracting. Similar findings were reported by Feak and Salehzadeh (2001) on the development and validation of a listening placement test using video. Mutiple speaker interactions, where the visual complemented the spoken element, were judged by both students and instructors to be a valid test of language use in diverse academic environments.

Acknowledging that audio will continue to play a prominent role in SL/FL listening assessment, Read (2002) investigated the effects of different types of audio-taped input for assessment in an academic setting. Students listening to a scripted monologue outperformed those listening to an unscripted discussion of the same content. These results conflict with earlier findings that oral texts incorporating unscripted dialogue were easier to understand. Read attributes this discrepancy to the complexity of the text variables and concludes that listening tests should include a variety of input reflecting a range of genres. Given the complexity of SL/FL listening, assessment will involve compromises. Therefore, in evaluating listening tests, one must keep in mind the constructs measured and the limitations of what is humanly possible (Alderson, 2005).

Conclusion

The teaching of listening in SL/FL programs has come a long way since the days when listening was developed incidentally or was merely a handmaiden to the learning of other language skills. One positive development has been the use of pre-listening activities to enable learners to apply their prior knowledge during listening. There remains, however, a need to teach learners better perception skills, particularly within the context of listening input and class activities. In addition, teachers should focus more on the listening process, rather than just the outcome of listening activities. A focus on the cognitive and metacognitive aspects of learning to listen can help learners to self-regulate their comprehension. With these two priorities in mind, we have offered a pedagogical model through which teachers can incorporate both bottom-up and top-down dimensions in listening instruction.

In spite of some recent advances, listening remains the least understood of the four language skills (listening, speaking, reading, and writing), making teaching and assessment complex and challenging. More research on the knowledge, skills, and processes involved in listening, and how these interact, will further inform our teaching and assessment of this essential communication skill. Nevertheless, there is much existing knowledge about language processing and metacognition in learning on which teachers can draw to guide their instructional practices.

NOTE

1   Based on Vandergrift (2007).

REFERENCES

Alderson, J. C. (2005). *Diagnosing foreign language proficiency: The interface between learning and assessment*. New York: Continuum.

Anderson, A. & Lynch, T. (1988). *Listening*. Oxford: Oxford University Press.

Anderson, J. R. (1995). *Cognitive psychology and its implications*, 4th edn. New York: Freeman.

Baddeley, A. D. (2000). The episodic buffer: a new component of working memory? *Trends in Cognitive Sciences* 4, 417–23.

Bechtel, W. & Abrahamsen, A. (1991). *Connectionism and the mind: An introduction to parallel processing in networks*. Oxford: Blackwell.

Boekaerts, M., Pintrich, P., & Zeidner, M. (2000). *Handbook of self-regulation*. San Diego: Academic Press.

Brindley, G. & Slayter, H. (2002). Exploring task difficulty in ESL listening assessment. *Language Testing* 19, 369–94.

Buck, G. (1995). How to become a good listening teacher. In D. Mendelsohn & J. Rubin (eds.), *A guide for the teaching of second language listening* (pp. 113–28). San Diego: Dominie Press.

Buck, G. (2001). *Assessing listening*. Cambridge: Cambridge University Press.

Carrell, P., Dunkel, P., & Mollaun, P. (2004). The effects of notetaking, lecture length, and topic on a computer-based test of EFL listening comprehension. *Applied Language Learning* 14, 83–105.

Carrier, K. (1999). The social environment of second language listening: Does status play a role in comprehension? *Modern Language Journal* 83, 65–79.

Cauldwell, R. (2002). Phonology for listening: Relishing the messy. Retrieved August 25, 2006, from www.speechinaction.com/Phonology for listening: relishing the messy.

Cheng, H. (2004). A comparison of multiple-choice and open-ended response formats for the assessment of listening proficiency in English. *Foreign Language Annals* 37, 544–55.

Clark, H. H. (1996). *Using language*. Cambridge: Cambridge University Press.

Coniam, D. (2001). The use of audio or video comprehension as an assessment instrument in the certification of English language teachers: A case study. *System* 29, 1–14.

Cook, M. & Liddicoat, A. J. (2002). The development of comprehension in interlanguage pragmatics: The case of request strategies in English. *Australian Review of Applied Linguistics* 25, 19–39.

Cutler, A. (2001). Listening to a second language through the ears of a first. *Interpreting 5,* 1–23.

Eastman, J. K. (1991). Learning to listen and comprehend: The beginning stages. *System 19,* 179–88.

Eilam, B. & Aharon, I. (2003). Students' planning in the process of self-regulated learning. *Contemporary Educational Psychology 28,* 304–34.

Elkhafaifi, H. (2005). Listening comprehension and anxiety in the Arabic language classroom. *Modern Language Journal 89,* 206–20.

Feak, C. B. & Salehzadeh, J. (2001). Challenges and issues in developing an EAP video listening placement assessment: A view from one program. *English for Specific Purposes 20,* 477–93.

Field, J. (2001). Finding one's way in the fog: Listening strategies and second-language learners. *Modern English Teacher 9,* 1, 29–34.

Field, J. (2003). Promoting perception: Lexical segmentation in second language listening. *ELT Journal 57,* 325–34.

Field, J. (2005). Intelligibility and the listener: The role of lexical stress. *TESOL Quarterly 39,* 3, 399–423.

Flavell, J. (1979). Metacognition and cognitive monitoring: A new area of cognitive development enquiry. *American Psychologist 34,* 906–11.

Flowerdew, J. & Miller, L. (2005). *Second language listening: Theory and practice.* New York: Cambridge University Press.

Garcia, P. (2004). Pragmatic comprehension of high and low level language learners. *TESL-EJ, 8.* Retrieved May 13, 2006 from www-writing.berkeley.edu/TESL-EJ/ej30/a1.html.

Ginther, A. (2002). Context and content visuals and performance on listening comprehension stimuli. *Language Testing 19,* 133–67.

Goh, C. (1997). Metacognitive awareness and second language listeners. *ELT Journal 51,* 361–9.

Goh, C. (2000). A cognitive perspective on language learners' listening comprehension problems. *System 28,* 55–75.

Goh, C. (2002a). Exploring listening comprehension tactics and their interaction patterns. *System 30,* 185–206.

Goh, C. (2002b). *Teaching listening in the language classroom.* Singapore: SEAMEO Regional Language Centre.

Goh, C. (2005). Second language listening expertise. In K. Johnson (ed.), *Expertise in second language learning and teaching* (pp. 64–84). Basingstoke, UK: Palgrave Macmillan.

Goh, C. (2008). Metacognitive instruction for second language listening development: Theory, practice and research implications. *Regional English Language Centre Journal 39,* 2, 188–213.

Goh, C. & Taib, Y. (2006). Metacognitive instruction in listening for young learners. *ELT Journal 60,* 222–32.

Graesser, A. C. & Britton, B. K. (1996). Five metaphors for text understanding. In B. K. Britton & A. C. Graesser (eds.), *Models of understanding text* (pp. 341–51). Hillsdale, NJ: Lawrence Erlbaum.

Graham, S. (2006). Listening comprehension: The learners' perspective. *System 34,* 165–82.

Gruba, P. (2004). Understanding digitized second language videotext. *Computer Assisted Language Learning 17,* 15–82.

Gruba, P. (2006). Playing the videotext: Media literacy perspectives on L2 listening comprehension. *Language Learning & Technology 10,* 77–92.

Harley, B. (2000). Listening strategies in ESL: Do age and L1 make a difference? *TESOL Quarterly 34,* 769–76.

Harris, T. (2003). Listening with your eyes: The importance of speech-related gestures in the language classroom. *Foreign Language Annals* 36, 180–7.

Henrichsen, L. E. (1984). Sandhi-variation: A filter of input for learners of ESL. *Language Learning* 34, 103–26.

Hoeflaak, A. (2004). Computer-assisted training in the comprehension of authentic French speech: A closer view. *Computer Assisted Language Learning* 17, 315–37.

Hulstijn, J. H. (2001). Intentional and incidental second language vocabulary learning: A reappraisal of elaboration, rehearsal and automaticity. In P. Robinson (ed.), *Cognition and second language instruction* (pp. 258–86). Cambridge: Cambridge University Press.

Hulstijn, J. H. (2003). Connectionist models of language processing and the training of listening skills with the aid of multimedia software. *Computer Assisted Language Learning* 16, 413–25.

Izumi, S. (2003). Comprehension and production processes in second language learning: In search of the psycholinguistic rationale of the output hypothesis. *Applied Linguistics* 24, 168–96.

Jefferies, E., Ralph, M., & Baddeley, A. D. (2004). Automatic and controlled processing in sentence recall: The role of long-term and working memory. *Journal of Memory and Language* 51, 623–43.

Jensen, E. D. & Vinther, T. (2003). Exact repetition as input enhancement in second language acquisition. *Language Learning* 53, 373–428.

Johnston, J. D. & Doughty, C. J. (2006). *L2 listening sub-skills*. Center for Advanced Study of Language Technical Report, University of Maryland, College Park.

Krashen, S. (1985). *The input hypothesis: Issues and implications*. London: Longman.

Lindfield, K. C., Wingfield, A., & Goodglass, H. (1999). The contribution of prosody to spoken word recognition. *Applied Psycholinguistics* 20, 395–405.

Liu, X. L. & Goh, C. (2006). Improving second language listening: Awareness and involvement. In T. S. C. Farrell (ed.), *Language teacher research in Asia* (pp. 91–106). Alexandria, VA: TESOL.

Major, R. C., Fitzmaurice, S. F., Bunta, F., & Balasubramanian, C. (2005). Testing the effects of regional, ethnic and international dialects of English on listening comprehension. *Language Learning* 55, 37–69.

Mareschal, C. (2007). Student perceptions of a self-regulatory approach to second language listening comprehension development. Unpublished doctoral dissertation. University of Ottawa.

Mendelsohn, D. (1998). Teaching listening. *Annual Review of Applied Linguistics* 18, 81–101.

Mendelsohn, D. & Rubin, J. (eds.) (1995). *A guide for the teaching of second language listening.* San Diego: Dominie Press.

O'Malley, J. M., Chamot, A. U., & Küpper, L. (1989). Listening comprehension strategies in second language acquisition. *Applied Linguistics* 10, 4, 418–37.

Read, J. (2002). The use of interactive input in EAP listening assessment. *Journal of English for Academic Purposes* 1, 105–19.

Robin, R. (2007). Learner-based listening and technological authenticity. *Language Learning & Technology* 11, 109–15.

Rose, K. R. & Kasper, G. (eds.) (2001). *Pragmatics in language teaching*. Cambridge: Cambridge University Press.

Rost, M. (2002). *Teaching and researching listening*. London: Longman.

Rupp, A., Garcia, P., & Jamieson, J. (2001). Combining multiple regression and CART to understand difficulty in second language reading and listening comprehension test items. *International Journal of Testing* 1, 185–216.

Sanders, L. D., Neville, H. J., & Woldorff, M. G. (2002). Speech segmentation by native and non-native speakers: The use of lexical, syntactic, and stress-pattern cues. *Journal of Speech, Language and Hearing Research* 45, 519–30.

Segalowitz, N. (2003). Automaticity and second language. In C. J. Doughty & M. H. Long (eds.), *The handbook of second language acquisition* (pp. 382–408). Malden, MA: Blackwell Publishing.

Sueyoshi, A. & Hardison, D. M. (2005). The role of gestures and facial cues in second-language listening comprehension. *Language Learning* 55, 661–99.

Swain, M. (1985). Communicative competence: Some roles of comprehensible input and comprehensible output in its development. In S. Gass & C. Madden (eds.), *Input in second language acquisition* (pp. 235–53). Rowley, MA: Newbury House.

Taguchi, N. (2005). Comprehending implied meaning in English as a foreign language. *Modern Language Journal* 89, 543–62.

Tyler, M. (2001). Resource consumption as a function of topic knowledge in nonnative and native comprehension. *Language Learning* 51, 257–80.

Vandergrift, L. (1997). The strategies of second language (French) listeners: A descriptive study. *Foreign Language Annals* 30(1), 387–409.

Vandergrift, L. (2002). It was nice to see that our predictions were right: Developing metacognition in L2 listening comprehension. *Canadian Modern Language Review* 58, 555–75.

Vandergrift, L. (2003a). From prediction through reflection: Guiding students through the process of L2 listening. *Canadian Modern Language Review* 59, 425–40.

Vandergrift, L. (2003b). Orchestrating strategy use: Toward a model of the skilled second language listener. *Language Learning* 53, 463–96.

Vandergrift, L. (2004). Learning to listen or listening to learn? *Annual Review of Applied Linguistics* 24, 3–25.

Vandergrift, L. (2005). Relationships among motivation orientations, metacognitive awareness and proficiency in L2 listening. *Applied Linguistics* 26, 70–89.

Vandergrift, L. (2007). Recent developments in second and foreign language listening comprehension research. *Language Teaching* 40, 191–210.

Vandergrift, L., Goh, C., Mareschal, C., & Tafaghodatari, M. H. (2006). The Metacognitive Awareness Listening Questionnaire (MALQ): Development and validation. *Language Learning* 56, 431–62.

Vandergrift, L. & Tafaghodtari, M. H. (in press). Teaching L2 learners how to listen does make a difference: An empirical study. *Language Learning* 60.

Wagner, E. (2002). Video listening tests: A pilot study. Working papers in TESOL & applied linguistics, Teachers College, Columbia University, 2/1. Retrieved April 19, 2006 from www.tc.edu/tesolalwebjournal/wagner.pdf.

Wagner, E. (2006). L2 video listening tests: An investigation of test-taker behavior. Paper presented at the meeting of the American Association of Applied Linguistics, Montreal, QC, June.

Wilson, M. (2003). Discovery listening: Improving perceptual processing. *ELT Journal* 57, 335–43.

Zeng, Y. (2007). Metacognitive instruction in listening: A study of Chinese non-English major undergraduates. Unpublished MA dissertation, National Institute of Education, Nanyang Technological University, Singapore.

Zhang, D. & Goh, C. (2006). Strategy knowledge and perceived strategy use: Singaporean students' awareness of listening and speaking strategies. *Language Awareness* 15, 199–219.

23 Teaching and Testing Speaking

MARTIN BYGATE

Introduction

Historically, the teaching and testing of speaking have tended to suffer an uneasy relationship with the major dominant approaches to language teaching methodology. Prototypically, speaking was not acknowledged at all as worthy of attention in the grammar-translation approach. While the audio-lingual approach famously highlighted the oral fluency and accuracy of phonology and grammar – giving a refracted perspective on oral second language ability – many contemporary standard tests continued to assess language through written skills (a situation still very common today in many parts of the world). Lack of congruence of a different kind can be found in the more recent communicative language teaching (CLT) paradigm. This has commonly highlighted speaking as central ("communicative" is often taken to mean "oral" and to imply the use of group work) (Thompson, 1996: 11–12). Yet CLT has tended to see speaking largely either as the prime medium for creativity in language development (Brumfit, 1984; van Lier, 1996) or as the site for interactive learning (whether in terms of the interaction hypothesis (Gass, 1997, 2003; Long, 1996), or of socio-cultural theory (Lantolf & Thorne, 2006), or of conversational approaches to language teaching (e.g., Thornbury & Slade, 2006)). In all these various "communicative" developments, speech tends to be viewed as medium rather than as target skill to be fostered. In contrast, this last period has begun to see the testing of speaking concentrate more precisely on the nature of the construct, and on operationalizing its assessment. In so doing it has sharpened the focus on four arguably central professional issues: the construct of speaking, the construct of task, the criteria of performance, and the construct of oral development. As we will see, language teaching has by no means ignored these matters. However the analytical approach adopted by testers may suggest ways forward for pedagogy. In exploring the teaching and testing of second language speaking, this chapter first of all considers how the four dimensions contribute to defining the problem space, and then discusses each of the four areas from a pedagogical perspective, before finally reviewing key recent themes in testing.

The Problem Space

It is uncontroversial to state that the constructs, terminology, and purposes of teaching and testing should be congruent (Alderson, 2005; Bachman & Palmer, 1996; Lantolf & Thorne, 2006: 327ff.; McNamara, 1996). It is not possible knowingly to test or teach speaking, without having at least a partial understanding of what second language speaking involves, of how more and less proficient speakers differ, of how less proficient speakers become more proficient, of what activities are relevant for developing or for showing the development of learners' proficiency, and of what concepts and terminology to use to appraise their performances. So two central questions are:

1 What is it about a stretch of speech which provides evidence of a speaker's proficiency?
2 What does a speaker need to do in order to go beyond that level of proficiency?

These apparently simple questions are not always easily answered. Some years ago a large mixed experience conference audience was shown a transcript of a sample of spoken language taken from a group of learners doing an information gap task, and asked to estimate the speakers' levels of proficiency. The overwhelming majority of the audience judged the speakers to be elementary to low intermediate. As it happened, three of the four students had passed the UCLES Certificate of Proficiency in English, and one was about to take it, so in fact the students would generally have been described as "very advanced." Now admittedly transcripts do not provide the full picture of people's speech, but given that the audience included a large number of experienced, and some very experienced professionals, the discrepancy was thought-provoking and raises a number of interesting questions. These derive from the issue of what would be required for an assessor (whether teacher or tester) to be able to correctly attribute a proficiency judgment on the basis of a small transcribed sample.

Clearly, a key starting point is the quality of the language repertoire used by the speakers. This immediately opens up the issue of the aspects of language that need to be mobilized to complete a task, since a transcript by definition includes phonological (for current purposes including pausal phenomena), morpho-syntactic, lexical, collocational, discoursal, and pragmatic evidence. The notion of "spoken language repertoire" provides, then, a starting point for an appraisal. However, our ability to use the data to estimate speakers' capacities will depend on our capacity to detect differences in constellations of features, and to relate them to gradations of proficiency. It also depends on how we construe differences in levels of proficiency. Our ability to do this depends on a further level of awareness – that of the demands of the task. Certain aspects of a given performance may lead to the assessment that students are elementary because those aspects are simply consistent with a low level of proficiency. This interpretation may arise because the grammar and vocabulary needed, and the pragmatic and discourse routines required, by the task are indeed normally available to relatively elementary students.

Three points emerge from this. First, we can only make such an assessment from our own data-based experience of the tasks. In the example being discussed, the majority of the audience were certainly familiar with the task type (a picture differences task), yet presumably they assumed that if the students had been highly proficient, they would have used samples of language reflecting more advanced features of morpho-syntax, lexis, collocation, discourse, or pragmatics. To be able to make this assumption, the audience cannot have had the necessary experience of scrutinizing the language students used to complete such tasks – tasks influence the language used, and so to appraise students' language we first need to understand the linguistic demands of our tasks.

The second point to be made is that it is not enough to understand the demands of the task: once we have gauged the ranges of language that a task is likely to elicit, it is then possible to return to the speech sample and scrutinize it at a finer level of detail, to seek out features that might offer discriminating evidence. So, for example, it is quite possible that some members of the audience had noted the nature of the task, and had turned their attention to features of pausing, incidence of editing features (such as false starts and self corrections), features of collocational phrasing, length of turn, turn-taking patterns, and overall efficiency, and concluded that these were by no means elementary students. This suggests that a robust appraisal of a particular performance also depends on the ability to identify the presence of features likely to correlate with a given level of proficiency. That is, we need a sense of the likely configurations of features of oral language as proficiency develops (including possible trade-offs between features competing for attention).

Any appraisal made so far, however, is bound to be based on certain other assumptions that have so far not been made explicit. Especially, we don't know the circumstances of performance. This is another crucial area of concern to teachers and to testers alike. For example, we don't know if the students have already performed a similar task, or the same task with the same features but configured differently; we don't know whether the students have planned what they are going to say about their individual picture, or whether they have talked through their individual pictures with a colleague before pairing up with the owner of the partly matching picture to find the differences; we don't know if the recording was undertaken during a high stakes test, with a tight time limit, or made publicly in front of an audience, or privately. Conditions such as planning, rehearsal, examination (or exercise), and public (or private) performance may affect the processes of speaking, and therefore the language produced. By implication, the conditions need to be factored into any eventual appraisal since they relate partly to our understanding of how proficiency develops as a function of learning conditions.

To summarize, appraising a transcript raises questions about the construct of spoken language itself (the performance repertoire); the processes of speech; the construct of oral language development. In what follows, we consider these in turn, and then against this background, consider current major approaches to teaching spoken language, followed by an account of some recent developments in testing.

The Construct of Spoken Language

To define the construct of "second language speaking," we need to be able to describe any given stretch of speech in terms of at least two main parameters (Bygate, 2005a): (1) the repertoire, that is, the range of features and combinations of features that it manifests, along with their respective probabilities; and (2) the range of conditions which explain the occurrence of these features. A description of the features of speech implies a need to categorize. An account of the range of conditions of speech will consist principally of the nature of the processing involved, and the socio-psychological conditions under which the processing takes place.

The spoken repertoire

Although in principle any stretch of language can be spoken, as with all human activity, the conditions of its enactment can be expected to affect its shape. That is, however much speaking – like any use of language – can be related to an underlying (phonological, or lexico-grammatical) norm, both process and product are shaped by the material conditions of their occurrence. This is true as much for such activities as swimming, sailing, or running, as for domains such as architecture (consider the distinction between "vernacular" architecture, found in buildings constructed with limited time and resources, and creative architectural design, which benefits from more planning time and a much wider range of materials). The validity of the construct of spoken language depends on evidence of patterning that is distinct from that of written language, and which can be meaningfully related to the circumstances of its production.

Linguistic features form three main subgroups: phonological features, both segmental and supra-segmental; lexico-grammatical features, including not only morphological and syntactic resources, and a lexical store, but also formulaic (e.g., Wray, 2002) and pragmalinguistic (e.g., Kasper, 2001) units; and discourse features, including socio-pragmatic features (cf. Kasper, 2001) and pragmatic discourse structures (see, for instance, McCarthy, 1998; Richards & Schmidt, 1983). The use of these constellations of features in talk is driven by macro socio-pragmatic purposes (Bachman & Palmer, 1996; Kasper, 2001; Levelt, 1989) (uttering words such as "so are you going to work today?" and "yes" is motivated by the need to fulfill a particular local social and informational purpose). This account brings together various linguistic abilities at different levels of hierarchy: the micro level (where phonemes serve the purpose of instantiating lexico-grammatical items), the mezzo level (where lexico-grammatical items in turn serve the purpose of conveying meanings), and the overarching macro level (that of achieving human convergence). The integration of the macro-pragmatic and the micro-behavioral within a single domain of operation is not unique to language: it is found in any field of human activity, whether artistic, artisanal, recreational, or professional.

Thanks to the development of corpus technology, it is now possible to document the occurrence of a vast range of linguistic features in speech, so as to chart their frequency, whether lexical, formulaic, or morpho-syntactic, and to analyze their pragmatic/functional status. This has resulted in an increasingly comprehensive empirical linguistic account of the characteristics of spoken language (Biber, Conrad, & Leech, 2002a; Biber et al., 2002b; Carter & McCarthy, 1997; Chafe, 1985; Cullen & Kuo, 2007), broadly confirming the importance of two of Chafe's (1985) dimensions – fragmentation/integration and involvement/ detachment. "Fragmentation" refers to the relative lack of group modification and subordination, the relative frequency of sub-clause level units or fragments, and the occurrence of overt "editing" features (Bygate, 1987). Occurrence of these characteristics implies relatively low density information content, low complexity language, and more parataxis, which in moderation are hypothesized to facilitate both speech production and reception. Note that, in contrast, readers and writers tend to prefer integration (increased noun group modification, increased subordination, fewer unintegrated sub-clause units, with overt editing in writing being experienced as "noise").

"Involvement" covers features which signal personal identity and group membership (e.g., generational, cultural, class, or regional group membership), and those which convey personal feelings and attitudes to the interlocutor or the content of discourse (such as disjunctive adverbs or adjectives, including intensifiers and mitigators). It is possible that the use of fragmentation and involvement correlates with proficiency, although to date this has not been demonstrated.

The social dimensions of fragmentation and involvement clearly relate to phonological and lexico-grammatical patterning. However, they can also be implicated in discourse structure. High levels of integration and low levels of personal involvement are also congruent with relatively decontextualized discourse, a kind of discourse that is commonly associated with the use of long, relatively non-interactive, turns, since to sustain long turns generally requires greater use of integrated syntax, and greater control over the degree of involvement. Whereas long turns are relatively free-standing, with interlocutors not bound to respond, in contrast, short turns tend to be relatively dependent on other turns. In this sense, utterances within short turns are themselves fragments, requiring other turns to be rendered complete, or discursively well formed. At the same time, shorter turns and more frequent turn-taking are likely to be more closely associated with high levels of personal involvement. A health warning needs issuing at this point, however: this schematization reflects propensity, rather than rigid incompatibility (long turns, such as political speeches, eulogies, perorations, and personal narratives, can allow significant personal involvement).

Features can be classified (see, for instance, Cullen & Kuo, 2007) in terms of whether they are purely speech derived, such as pausing (see, for instance, papers in Riggenbach, 2000) or turn-taking (McCarthy, 1998), or whether they are just relatively common in speech, such as deictic pronouns, including first- and second-person pronouns, and indeed pronouns in general, ellipsis, interrogatives and negatives, or disjuncts (McCarthy, 1998). The picture that emerges from corpus analyses (for instance, Biber et al., 2002a) suggests that talk is characterized by a range of phonological, lexico-grammatical, and discourse patterns, few of which are unique to speech, but many of which are significantly more common in speech (such as here-and-now deictics, first- and second-person pronouns, question forms, and present progressive aspect), or cluster distinctively in speech (such as parataxis, or particular formulaic expressions clustering with complement constructions). The implications for teaching and for testing are that to be competent at talk, learners need to have access to the kinds of markers of involvement and fragmentation, and engage in activities under conditions in which those markers play their part.

Given that effective teaching and testing depend on constructing appropriate conditions for language use, it is essential to consider how fragmentation and involvement are enabled and constrained by the conditions of speech, and we turn to this in the next section.

The conditions of speech

As with all language use, the construct of spoken language must be grounded in the users' pragmatic purposes and reflect the kinds of conditions under which those purposes are fulfilled. The spoken language construct, which includes the characteristics noted in the previous section, derives from one fundamental if obvious condition, namely the "presence" condition: that is, the fact that speech is prototypically used in the presence of an interlocutor. The fact that an interlocutor is typically present brings with it two further conditions, a *reciprocity* condition, and a *time-pressure* condition. The reciprocity condition primarily reflects the interlocutor's speaking rights, which means that the speaker needs to adjust her talk in light of her knowledge of the interlocutor's own knowledge, interests, expectations. At the same time she needs to facilitate her interlocutor's understanding and participation so that he is able to use his speaking rights (Clark & Krych, 2004). The time-pressure condition also derives from the presence condition, in that the immediacy of the interlocutor brings with it a relative lack of planning time, and the need to allow the interlocutor the time to speak. Both time pressure and reciprocity conditions lead to the need for speech editing, and the presence condition more generally results in the fact that much of the editing is overt (Laver, 1970). It is probably uncontroversial to state that both the reciprocity and time-pressure conditions operate simultaneously.

Reciprocity and time pressure can be seen as the conditions that give rise to the two multi-level linguistic phenomena of "fragmentation" and "involvement." Time pressure can be seen as related to the occurrence of indices of fragmentation, such as editing features (pauses, self-corrections, false starts, reformulations), and lexico-grammatical features, such as the use of parataxis, formulaic hypotaxis (e.g., "I think that . . . ," "I guess . . . ," "it is obvious that . . ."), lack of lexical modification, information staging (McCarthy, 1998, pp. 60–1), front- and end-placing (or "heads" and "tails," McCarthy, 1998, pp. 76–7; Thornbury & Slade, 2006, pp. 80–3), lone noun groups, and verb groups with elided subject or complement noun groups (together labelled "satellite units" in Bygate, 1988).

But we also find *reciprocity* pressures seeping into the occurrence of these features. For instance, editing features, such as reformulations, are not only generated in terms of the speaker's own plans, but also in light of the listener's likely interpretation. Pausing has been interpreted not only in terms of speaker processing load (Pawley & Syder, 1983), but also in terms of the listener's perception (Clark & Fox Tree, 2002). And by using stereotyped phrasings (Pawley & Syder, 1983; Wray, 2000, 2002), formulaic hypotaxis facilitates decoding, and not just encoding. Likewise, information staging, and front- and end-placing, can help make information accessible to the listener, as does ellipsis, while frequent use of pronouns helps clear clutter and make prominent the new target information (Levelt, 1989, ch. 3). Whereas in writing, editing features nearly always remain covert, and fragments become integrated, in speech, editing features remain overt, and fragments remain fragments.

The reciprocity condition can also be seen as having an impact on *involvement*. For instance, face-to-face interaction implies the need to attend to negative face, encouraging the use of mitigation (such as modals, hedges, and vague words); but it also leads to cases of intensification (such as adverbial and adjectival intensifiers, often via the use of slang), as well as metacomments (via disjuncts such as "honestly," "frankly," "surprisingly," "hopefully," "interestingly," or "unbelievably"). However, reciprocity conditions also underpin discourse-pragmatic dimensions. For instance, they motivate the occurrence of discourse structures, such jointly constructed structures involving turn-taking as "transactions," "exchanges," "adjacency units" (McCarthy, 1998), and question-answer sequences. They also give rise to phases of interactional structures, such as openings and closings (e.g., Thornbury & Slade, 2006: 130–1), to various types of 'troubleshooting' (Aston, 1988), such as repairs (Thornbury & Slade, 2006, pp. 28–9), negotiation for meaning sequences, and communication strategies (Yule & Tarone, 1991), as well as the particular types of moves that exchange sequences depend on, such as backchannels (Thornbury & Slade, 2006, pp. 131–3), or clarification requests and confirmation checks (Long, 1996), topic or turn management, and the management of speech acts, including their "sequencing" (Kasper, 2001, p. 52), often undertaken to minimize the likelihood of face-threatening moves. Whereas in writing, recipients are covert, in speech, their participation is overt. Hence, the concerns of "moment" and "presence" often give rise to patterns of language that differ from those of writing.

In teaching and testing, time pressure is a relatively easy condition to create. Reciprocity is rather harder if confined to the asymmetrical contexts of teacher–pupil or tester–candidate interaction (Kasper & Ross, 2007; Young & Milanovic, 1992). The conditions, though, are crucial for motivating the development of appropriate speech production skills, and the use of convergent patterns of language.

Hence, while the dimensions of fragmentation and involvement effectively characterize the surface features of language, they also relate to two key aspects of the psychological circumstances of speech, "improvisation," and "reciprocity." Improvisation refers to the management of speech without specific planning.

Processes of oral language production

Speech, like written language, needs to be processed. Most processing models (de Bot, 1992; Kormos, 2006; Levelt, 1989) agree on the need for four main phases of processing: conceptualization (including access of long-term memory, tracking of the discourse, tracking of interlocutor knowledge and expectations, overall pragmatic purpose, and specific pragmatic-conceptual content of utterances); formulation (involving principally lexico-grammatical selection, sequencing, phonological priming); articulation (the physical process of segmental and suprasegmental processing); and, throughout the different phases, both covert and overt monitoring (Laver, 1970). Models of this kind are sometimes described as "intrapersonal" (Luoma, 2004), and "information-oriented" (Hughes, 2003), implying that they conceive of speaking as an individual, non-interpersonal phenomenon. However, this misses the fact that such models include attention to the interlocutor, including interlocutor feedback, and to the pragmatic purpose of the discourse in general, and of utterances in particular.

Two aspects of this model are important within the construct of second language speaking. The first is the dimension of automated versus controlled modes of processing (e.g., Bialystok, 1990; Bialystok & Sharwood Smith, 1985). Controlled processing is typically associated with conceptual and to some extent formulation phases of processing. Automated processing is associated particularly with articulation, but also to some extent with formulation. This is important, since it opens up the possibility of different types of practice (and conceivably of testing) activities, according to the aspect of the process being targeted by teacher or tester. Clearly, automation is likely to be associated with markers of fluency and complexity (as a function of ease of lexico-grammatical access and articulation), and accuracy, to the extent that automated performance is resistant to interference from task pressures (Segalowitz, 2003). Controlled processing must be crucial for conceptualization, and to some extent for formulation processes, and most especially for effective speech monitoring.

The second aspect of this model that needs consideration is whether control and automation are gradable or categorical conditions. Segalowitz, for instance, quotes Newell (1990: 136) as defining automaticity as follows: "it is fast; unstoppable . . . ; it is independent of the amount of information being processed; it involves exhaustive or complete search of all elements in the display, it involves no awareness of processing . . ." (2003, p. 384). However, as Segalowitz points out, both automaticity and control may be gradable. On the one hand, as Levelt (1978) argued, it seems likely that automated processes (such as those involved in articulation, by definition the most open to automation) can be made accessible to conscious control (for instance, when speaking after a local dental anaesthetic). Indeed, some commentators (e.g., Celce-Murcia, Dornyei, & Thurrell, 1996; Thornbury, 1993) have pointed out that learning second language pronunciation is itself not just a physical but also, at least to some extent, a cognitive process. Hence, automated abilities are to a degree controllable. At the other end of the spectrum, it is likely that processes that are generally controlled, such as topic or message selection (for instance, Fillmore, 1979, famously associated two types of fluency with speed of thought, so as to generate semantically dense or pragmatically appropriate fluent talk), can be automated at least partially, particularly when occurring in familiar discourse contexts (such as at the beginning, ending, and transition points in interviews, talks, or routine events, such as lessons). Intuitively, in proficient speakers, formulation processes, parts of which are concerned with the processes of lexico-morphological selection and syntactic structuring, are likely to need a certain level of automatization, while remaining susceptible to a degree of control. In sum, it is possible to define the constructs of automation and control either as categorical and basically incompatible conditions, or in terms of some kind of gradience. How the construct is defined could make a difference both to teaching and testing.

To summarize, then, "presence" conditions – that is, time pressure and reciprocity – correlate with a greater degree of fragmentation and involvement in speech than in writing. Fragmentation takes the form of overt editing, paratactic utterance construction, formulaic hypotaxis, and "satellite" units. Involvement gives rise to interactive features of talk which can be "schematized." These include turn-taking, adjacency pairs, exchanges, including backchannels, meaning negotiation through "staging," communication strategies, and repairs; and at the lexico-grammatical level, features such as hedging, intensification, disjunctive elements, jargon, and slang. Presence conditions can also be seen as associated with a range of discourse types, such as "talking about self" (Carter & McCarthy, 1997), "small talk" (Coupland, 2000), interviews, "on-task" talk (Carter & McCarthy, 1997), instructions, jokes and personal narratives, and a range of pragmatic routines. It is assumed that these features are stored (as formulaic units, or as routines or schemata) both cognitively and behaviorally. In speech they are processed with degrees of control and automaticity, processing being typically unscripted, and sensitive to interlocutor responses. The next issue is how this capacity is developed.

The Construct of Oral Language Development

As noted above, most approaches to oral language development adopt a perspective whereby acquisition is seen as essentially "medium neutral" (*pace* Bachman & Palmer, 1984). Speaking enters the picture as a medium for acquisition, with acquisitional states not differentiated according to skill. That is, researchers do not assume differential patterns of acquisition or different skills and subskills according to the medium of assessment. As a result, they do not bring the changing shape of oral proficiency per se into the picture, which is an issue that needs posing. As de Bot (1992) points out, this is the case even for accounts of oral proficiency, such as that of Levelt, which, as he says, although helpful, is still only a "steady-state" model of processing. What is needed is an account of the developmental dynamics of oral language proficiency.

In order to move toward a teaching approach, a construct of development is needed. Johnson (1996), drawing on work in cognitive psychology (Anderson, 1983; Shiffrin & Schneider, 1977; Schneider & Shiffrin, 1977), and in the cognition of language (e.g., Bialystok, 1990; Ellis, 1996), argues the utility of the distinction between declarative and procedural knowledge in language teaching methodology. Declarative knowledge is commonly defined as factual knowledge ("knowing that"), of which cognitive psychologists distinguish semantic memory (memory for concepts) and episodic memory (memory of events). Much, if not all, of conceptual memory is likely to arise out of episodic memory, with exemplars encountered on particular occasions gradually serving to define and populate categories. Apart from accumulating the conceptual categories of language, which are, of course, essential to all uses of language, irrespective of medium, speaking is likely to develop declarative knowledge partly, at least, from memories of a wide range of speech events (presumably a type of episodic memory). Speech events are constituted along at least two major dimensions, first in terms of the pragmatic relationships projected between language features and the goals they are used for (e.g., Rose & Kasper, 2001), and second, in terms of discourse structures (the ways in which talk patterns, both within and across turns). People's capacities will reflect the range of learning experiences they have encountered (see Hulstijn, 2007, for a helpful framing of this issue). It is worth noting that the account of declarative knowledge presented here makes clear that much of it will not – indeed, in some cases, probably cannot – be derived explicitly, though it is beyond the scope of this chapter to explore this issue further.

In contrast to declarative knowledge, the term "procedural knowledge" refers to the knowledge of how to do something ("knowing how"). It is one thing to have mapped – say, by observation – the range of types of declarative knowledge needed in order to function orally within a community. Speakers also need to activate their own use of those resources. That is, declarative knowledge needs to be complemented by procedural knowledge. This perspective implies a (probably artificial, but for now useful working) distinction between a repertoire (declarative knowledge), and a person's capacity to use it (procedural knowledge).

In the terms of this account, there are three major issues to unpick in developing our approaches to teaching oral language. The first concerns the range of types of knowledge (declarative and procedural), defined in terms of linguistic, pragmatic, and discourse patterns, that can usefully be targeted for given groups of learners. Authors have identified phonological and articulatory schemata (Celce-Murcia et al., 1996), emerging fluency (Kormos, 2006), referential skills (Yule, 1997), informational patterns (Bygate, 1987), interactive patterns (Bygate, 1987; Carter & McCarthy, 1997; McCarthy, 1998), and pragmatic patterns (Kasper, 2001). This pedagogical focus fundamentally entails research into task or activity design, to assess the ways in which given designs can map onto target areas (see, for instance, Bygate, 1987; Samuda & Bygate, 2008; Yule, 1997). The second issue centers on the ways in which procedural abilities can be developed in classroom contexts. Here, there are two main questions. The first is how best to distribute pedagogical activities (particularly by selecting and sequencing them) so as to stimulate the development of particular procedural capacities (see, particularly, Robinson, 2001, 2007). The second question is how best to *use* particular activities, for example, by adjusting the conditions of implementation, say by varying planning time (Ellis, 2005; Skehan & Foster, 1997, 2001), exploiting task repetition (e.g., Bygate, 2006), or adjusting time pressure (Johnson, 1996). This also entails the question of how to appraise learners' development in particular domains.

The third issue arises from the second and centers on the place of declarative work in managing oral language development, and within this, the role of explicit instruction. Challenges here include: (1) improving understanding of which types of declarative knowledge need to be deliberately highlighted via instruction (for instance certain oral discourse structures may be acquired simply via recurring exposure to certain types of speech event), and where instruction is needed, how to implement it; and (2) of those aspects of declarative knowledge that do merit deliberate instructional targeting, clarifying which can best benefit from the support of explicit instruction, and how to do this (see, for example, Samuda, 2001).

While it remains to be seen which accounts of learning apply most robustly to the development of spoken language, what is needed is an account which combines the range of repertoires (from macro to micro), the processing (both online and reciprocity) capacities appropriate for that range, and a perspective on the dynamic which includes both procedural and declarative modes of processing. Combining the PRO/DEC model with the interactive and task-driven processes described here allows for a range of pedagogical procedures, to which we now turn.

Researching Approaches to Spoken Language Pedagogy

From the 1970s, teacher educators and materials writers increasingly confronted the problem of how to engage learners with language in the context of pragmatically driven oral activities. Byrne (1976), in perhaps the earliest monograph on the teaching of oral language, advocated the use of a PPP (Presentation-Practice-Production) approach, in which drills and short four- to six-line dialogues were a staple ingredient. Morrow and Johnson (1979) developed teaching materials focusing on language reflecting aspects of interpersonal pragmatics, such as apologizing, inviting, and requesting. However, in spite of the specifically oral character of the language focus, the activity types used in the materials involved drill-like procedures, exploiting either a stimulus-response-feedback dynamic, or else the use of dialogues, for instance, embedding a drill-like structure within a four- to six-line dialogue. Hence, although the categorical focus was on the features of spoken language, the activities themselves did not engage learners in the actual pragmatic dimensions of interpersonal talk, but merely in the manipulation and production of alternative pragmatic formulations. That is, the pragmatics of spoken language were mapped into the categorical content, but not into the procedures.

A major change in this aspect of the dynamic structure of oral activities was perhaps first charted explicitly by Abbott (1981), where he reviewed a series of exercises he himself had devised during the previous 20 years. Starting from a broadly audio-lingual approach, each of his subsequent publications modified the design, so as gradually to increase the focus on meaningful discourse. Abbott's endpoint was information-gap activities, in which pragmatic oral discourse was a consistent element: a pedagogical focus on proceduralization had become firmly rooted.

Input-focused approaches

As the preceding account of speaking suggests, there are two kinds of development that can be targeted. One is the oral repertoire, and the other is its processing. As noted above, the term "repertoire" ranges from the level of pragmatic discourse structures, down to that of pragmalinguistic, grammatical, and phonological features. Repertoire can be developed in two main ways, firstly through perceptual input-based activities, and secondly through the careful selection of output-processing tasks. The argument for input-based approaches first emerged in the late 1970s in the guise of the "delayed output" hypothesis (e.g., Asher, 1982; Krashen & Terrell, 1983). However, this approach was based on the assumption of incidental learning in the wake of learners achieving global comprehension (see Hulstijn, 2003), an assumption that was largely discredited through the Canadian immersion studies (e.g., Swain, 1985).

However, the argument against incidental learning through input leaves intact the potential viability of an approach, such as that of VanPatten (1996), based on the use of redundancy reduction to focus input-based activities on particular language features (Loschky & Bley-Vroman, 1993). Research into the use of input-processing activities suggests that carefully targeted perception training can impact directly on acquisition, although the effects on speech production are unclear (e.g., Benati, 2001; Marsden, 2006; VanPatten, 1996).

Likewise, in the domain of the teaching of pronunciation (the "formulation" and "articulation" phases of the speech production process), there is experimental evidence that performance can be altered by concentrating on students' awareness of the phonological repertoire through perceptual processing, rather than by focusing on production skills. For instance, Derwing & Munro (2005) report work by Bradlow et al. (1997) with Japanese learners' use of the /l/–/r/ distinction that demonstrated that pronunciation can be improved simply by focusing on perception, without any production practice. Derwing, Munro, & Wiebe (1998) showed that suprasegmental and segmental practice were both effective, but in different ways: while segmental practice seemed to enable learners to repair in cases of miscommunication, suprasegmental practice seemed more effective in improving comprehensibility of extemporaneous talk. Further, a little guided perceptual instruction could even quite easily override earlier misleading explicit instruction on phonemic distinctions.

Approaches to production-focused activities

Production-focused activities are also claimed to effect repertoire changes. At the level of pragmatic discourse structures, Skehan and Foster (2001) distinguish between problem-solving/discussion/debate tasks, personal tasks (involving direction-giving or recounting of experiences), and narrative tasks (based variously on video extracts and strip cartoons), although discourse structures are not their focus of attention. Others have shown that activities can be designed and used to develop different turn-taking patterns, such as question-answer in picture differences tasks versus more monologic structures of direction-giving tasks (Bygate, 1988; Pinter, 2005), or in picture-sequencing story-reconstructing tasks, phases of long descriptive turns, followed by interactive negotiated turns, followed in turn by monologic collaborative narratives (Bygate, 2007).

Repertoires can also be activated at other levels of operation. This has been shown, for instance, in studies of first language strategies (e.g., Bongaerts & Poulisse, 1989; Wilkes-Gibbs, 1997). In second language teaching, Pinter (2005, pp. 119–20, 123) found that students' production of meaning negotiation devices and communication strategies can be impacted by the use of task repetition. Dobao (2005) and Dobao & Palacios (2007), building on the work of Yule & Tarone (1991), show that the interactive generation of communication strategies by pairs of students can be promoted by the use of carefully structured tasks, working within a taught program. Coulson (2005) also reports the use of tasks to stimulate increases in the collaborative use of communication strategies via what he calls "team talking." Leedham (2005) reports using a cycle of task activity, transcript analysis, and task reiteration to promote the use of backchannelling, and Poupore (2005) reports the impact of problem-solving and jigsaw tasks on promoting a wide range of types of negotiation.

At the level of specific linguistic features, there is an enduring controversy over whether procedurally focused tasks can be used effectively to target particular language while conserving the procedural nature of task talk, or whether attempting to do this (negatively termed "structure-trapping" by Skehan, 1998) undermines learner creativity. However, there is evidence that tasks can selectively activate domains of language. Newton and Kennedy (1996), for instance, demonstrated how task design can be used to target prepositional usage. Mackey (1999) employed tasks to engage learners in active use of interrogative structures. Bygate (1999) used evidence of linguistic patterning in student performances of tasks to argue the need to work from empirical student data, rather than rely on predictions of materials designers, teachers, or testers, a view supported by studies showing differential incidence of lexical phrases by Hobbs (2005) and Baigent (2005), and by Cox (2005) showing differences between the predictions of teachers and the results of analyses of student transcripts. That this dimension of tasks can be used proactively by teachers is demonstrated by Lynch (1997) and Samuda (2001). Samuda reports a teacher's use of a task to highlight conceptual domains which learners have difficulty in formulating, and as a site for their subsequent application of a range of target exponents. This kind of approach exploits the potential noted above for behavioral changes to derive at least in part from engagement with, and awareness of, the relevant repertoire. However, in spite of this research, studies of tasks have tended to focus on the "how" (how fluent, how accurate, how complex?) rather than "what" (what language is being engaged?).

Studies have also explored the use of tasks to promote changes in the *manner* of processing. Lynch and Maclean (2000, 2001), working with adult ESP learners, and Pinter (2005) with 10-year old Hungarian children, show how the repetition of tasks, the repetition occurring either with different interlocutors (Lynch & Maclean, 2000, 2001; Essig, 2005), or combined with additional planning (Essig, 2005; D'Ely, 2006), or else by altering the configuration of a given array (Pinter, 2005), can all be used in pedagogical contexts to improve accuracy, complexity, lexical range, and fluency. Pinter also suggests that success in task completion can be increased through judicious use of task repetition. Foster (1996) reports that provision of unguided planning time promoted increased accuracy. Following on the work of Foster and Skehan (1996) and Skehan and Foster (1997), Yuan and Ellis (2003) report that pre-task planning heightened complexity and fluency, while on-task planning was associated with reduced fluency and complexity, but with increased accuracy. Plough and Gass (1993) report an impact of task familiarity on performance. Finally, Skehan and Foster (2001) propose that the degree of the internal structure of a task can affect the quality of talk. Assuming that degree of internal structure is a function of the cognitive structures of the learners involved, and that this is another facet of familiarity, the various studies severally suggest that altering the familiarity of tasks affects performance in terms of fluency, accuracy, complexity, range, and discourse structuring.

Planning is, of course, a pre-task procedure aimed at drawing attention to form. It is unusual to associate planning with most types of speech, yet pedagogically there are clear grounds for exploiting it. Feedback is functionally the equivalent post-task procedure, and like planning, also sits uneasily with normal conditions of speech. One main issue is whether provision of feedback is more valuable when immediate or delayed. Delayed feedback is rarely considered an option, most attention being focused on the effectiveness of different types of immediate feedback (Doughty & Varella, 1998; Doughty & Williams, 1998; Long, 1977; Lyster, 2004; Mackey & Philp, 1998). Immediate feedback has been studied principally in terms of the impact of different types of delivery. Here research suggests that feedback which focuses on forms that are key to a speaker's current concerns for meaning are most likely to be attended to. However, Lynch (2001, 2007) reports positive results from students transcribing and then correcting recordings of their own productions. This suggests both that delayed feedback can be effective, and that learners can benefit from focusing their attention more broadly than on successful communication of online messages. It would be interesting to know whether transcribing could also lead learners to attend to higher-level discourse structures, an area relatively ignored within the field.

Overall, the evidence is that tasks can be designed and used to target both declarative and procedural knowledge in a range of aspects of oral language performance. This research, however, concerns the parameters of classroom practice. The question remains how the oral language curriculum might be structured to promote development, and this is the focus of the next section.

Organizing the Oral Language Curriculum

The advent of procedurally focused activities (noted above) has made it possible to marshall a procedural and declarative focus at curriculum level. One response was Celce-Murcia et al.'s (1996) proposal to develop a systematic approach to the teaching of oral language, by extending a broad communicative approach to include a more detailed level of attention to "a) specific language input (formulaic language in particular) to communicative tasks, b) raising learners' awareness of the organizational principles of language use within and beyond the sentence level, and c) sequencing communicative tasks more systematically in accordance with a theory of discourse-level grammar" (1997, p. 148). It is clear that all contemporary approaches to the teaching of spoken language endorse the need for the more holistic procedurally focused activities, while at the same time agreeing that a focus on declarative knowledge is also needed. This makes possible two main types of approach to the speaking curriculum. The first could be called a "global" approach. This can take the form of a project-based (Legutke & Thomas, 1991) approach, a topic-/theme-based approach (Burns, 2006; Burns, Joyce, & Gollin, 1996; Feez, 1998), or a task-based approach (e.g., Prabhu, 1987; Robinson, 2007; Skehan, 1998; Willis, 1996, among others). A second is more like a skills-based approach following on from the account sketched out by Littlewood (2004). We consider these briefly in turn.

As Celce-Murcia et al. (1996) point out, a global approach needs some kind of macro-level organization. Task-based approaches all start from the holistic task, using this as a basis for subsequently attending to particular language features, many then having a key concern for sequencing the tasks in a coherent way. For instance, Prabhu claims to remove all specification of language features from his syllabus, and for sequencing purposes adopts the assumption that information-gap tasks are easier than reasoning-gap activities, which he suggests are in turn easier than opinion-gap tasks. Having adopted this syllabus structure, his intention was for any specific linguistic focus to arise purely in response to the particular learners' needs in completing a given task. Skehan generally argues similarly for a non-linguistic syllabus, with attention to language features again coming as a response to actual problems in relation to specific task-driven needs, although he occasionally admits to the possibility of discrete selection and targeting of features likely to be useful (1998, pp. 271, 288).

Robinson's position seems slightly different in that one of the organizing dimensions of his model (e.g., 2007) is that tasks can be "resource-directing," meaning that they can be designed, selected, and sequenced "on the basis of the concepts that the task requires to be expressed and understood (e.g., relative time, spatial location, causal relationship, and intentionality)" (2007, p. 17). This seems to imply that tasks can be sequenced according to the conceptual domains that the syllabus aims to cover. Within the domains, Robinson hypothesizes grades of difficulty as follows: here-and-now > there-and-then; reference to few distinctive elements > reference to many less differentiated elements; reference to mutually known spatial reference points > reference to mutually unknown spatial reference points; information transmission > reasoning about causal events and their relationships; simple information transmission > reasoning about people's intentions and attitudes; use of simple first-person perspective > use of multiple and third-person participant perspectives. Although the terminology is not linguistically specified, this type of mapping, with its proposed gradations of difficulty, suggests the covert presence of some kind of language agenda, something that is not, however, addressed.

Bygate (2005b, 2006), following a series of laboratory studies (e.g., Bygate, 2001), proposes the pedagogical use of meaningful task repetition as a way of helping the construction of oral abilities across different repertoires and conditions. For this, tasks might be used in which repetition is an internal feature of the design, or else which repeat elements of earlier tasks (such as their ideational structure, their conceptual material, or their interactional structure). Finally Willis (1996) argues for the use of teaching cycles in which, although a target task forms the centerpiece for each cycle, the use of native-speaker models prior to learners' own attempts to perform the task suggests the potential for teachers and learners to identify particular linguistic features as targets for attention. It is not clear, however, how the cycles of teaching are themselves sequenced.

One of the problems that a task-based approach has to resolve, then, is how to sequence the tasks in a way that offers a coherent approach to the development of proficiency. Thornbury suggests that "a task-based approach [is thought to favor] an implicit approach to instruction, when in fact learners need clear and explicit models of the language behaviours they are going to encounter" (2005, p. 121). Thornbury may be right for some learners (see for instance Skehan's conformist learners (1998, pp. 279–81)), but more generally, even for those who prefer implicit learning, the sequencing of tasks in part implies some kind of coherence between tasks. Yet parameters for classifying tasks, such as those proposed by Pica, Kanagy, and Falodun (1993) and Skehan (2001), are essentially "content-neutral." There are alternative approaches to the problem.

Legutke and Thomas (1991), for example, report the use of a project-based approach in which a sequence of thematic projects is used to provide an overarching linear structure to a course, while enabling a top-down hierarchical structure within each unit of work. Burns (2006) also proposes a linear and hierarchical structuring. She takes discourse as the macro-structuring device, either in terms of themes which are used to sequence series of thematically linked speech events (such as planning a holiday), or in terms of topics, which can generate sequences of topically related texts. The themes could be expected to function as logically as Legutke and Thomas' projects. In contrast, the principled basis for sequencing the various texts is not made clear. Thornbury (2005) hedges his bets by suggesting a range of possible structures for speaking syllabi, including conversation skills, conversation topics, linguistic features (phonological, grammatical, and discourse), task types (such as surveys, design tasks, research tasks, and imaginative tasks) and genres (2005, pp. 117–22). Acknowledgment of the multiple levels involved does not resolve the problem. For this, more empirical investigations are needed of the various options in action – clearly a necessary step in developing a researched oral language curriculum.

In contrast to this, in terms of a procedural or declarative orientation, Littlewood (2004) adopts a more neutral perspective, arguing that pedagogy has generated a range of types of learning activity, some more procedurally oriented, and others more declaratively focused, which teachers can exploit as they wish. Hence, teachers might work with drills and "pre-communicative" activities to activate lexico-grammatical (e.g., Ur, 1988), pragmalinguistic (e.g., Morrow & Johnson, 1979), or phonological (e.g., Dalton & Seidlhofer, 1994) processing skills before moving to the procedurally oriented use of language features. Alternatively, teachers might use procedurally oriented activities earlier in the study cycle. The issue is whether teachers and learners wish to practice the features without having to attend to the conceptualization and formulation of their own meanings, subsequently leading progressively into more and more procedurally oriented activities, or whether other sequences are more productive. However, to date, the impact and operation of the alternative approaches have not been researched at syllabus or curriculum level.

Behind all this lies the fundamental problem noted above of specifying the constellations of features of speech which can be used to discriminate levels of speaker proficiency on given tasks. It is one thing to construct a range of activity types, and to be able to rank them in order of complexity; it is another to be able to bring together the features of speech in ways that act as indices of speaker proficiency. Here, teaching approaches are still somewhat awash with a complex range of features of speech, to date largely unrelated to discourse structures and strategies.

The instructed development of oral second language proficiency then is an area in need of empirical study, to shed light on the relevant domains of proficiency (both in terms of repertoire and processing capacities), on their development, and on instructional efficacy. For this, particularly valuable insights can be derived from the field of testing, in particular in terms of its concern for construct validity, its interest in the design of test tasks, and its sensitivity to the range of levels of proficiency. We survey and reflect on some key developments in this area in the final section of this chapter.

Testing

For some time, testers have seen their work as related both theoretically and practically to pedagogy. For instance, testers often draw their own models of proficiency from pedagogically motivated research (for instance, Bachman, 1990, the model of which originally drew substantially from Canale & Swain, 1980). Some of the task designs and assessment criteria (e.g., the Common European Framework; see for instance, Morrow, 2004) developed by testers are elaborated through teacher or teacher-tester informants (e.g., North, 1995, 2000) and are hence grounded in teachers' or assessors' craft knowledge. Some test material and test design guides are developed in consort with teachers and then made directly available to teachers (e.g., British Council, 2005).

Yet of all the various connections between teaching and testing, probably best known is the argument that testing can have a direct washback effect on curriculum and classroom procedures. Ur (1996, p. 135), for instance, reports that the introduction of oral testing in Israel resulted in more attention being paid to speaking within schools, and Fulcher comments that it is often claimed that the Foreign Service Institute (FSI) became "the basis for curriculum design in modern foreign language teaching in the United States" (2003, p. 173). Yet tests do not necessarily wash back at all (Luxia, 2005), and if they do, at the very least any washback effects are complex, and open to being either positive or negative (Wall, 1996, 2000). More importantly perhaps, as Fulcher himself comments, tests only wash back into classroom teaching to the extent that they provide "adequate informative feedback" (2003, p. 177). The question of concern here is the extent to which testing practices can illuminate the teaching enterprise, and vice versa.

There are three main aspects in which this seems possible. One is in the development of task content, and their formats – whether interviews, pair or group role plays, pair or group problem-solving tasks, or monologue tasks. This aspect of testing is also capable of helping to shed light on the nature of specific-purpose or domain-specific dimensions of tasks. The second area of potential contribution concerns the ways in which testing research can shed light on our understanding of the variables that can influence performance. These cover such factors as task type and interlocutor, planning time, and gender. The third area of potential contribution is in the development of rating scales. An informative set of rating scales would improve the capacity of teachers to offer students formative feedback, while also providing insights into the nature of proficiency and its development. In what follows, we consider these issues.

The issue of task design raises questions about the kinds of stimulus material to provide candidates, the kinds of interaction formats they should experience, and the kinds of internal variations within the different formats that they should be tested with. As we have seen, spoken language is not simply language spoken. It is reshaped by the "presence" parameter, along the dimension of personal involvement, that can include mitigation (including the use of modality), intensification, reference (including reference to the here-and-now) and temporal and spatial reference, self- and other-repairs (including communication strategies and negotiation for meaning sequences), turn-taking, and sequences of turn types, such as more or less routine question-answer exchanges, collaborative exchanges, or more or less preferred adversarial exchanges. The presence parameter also gives rise to the time pressures associated with online processing that underlie the dimension of fragmentation, and the ways in which it is compensated for by patterns of pausing and the use of formulaic utterances.

Tests that are intended to be sensitive to these features would need to contain tasks and task conditions designed with these characteristics in mind, deliberately bringing into play the relevant kinds and roles of interlocutor. For example, they would need to involve topics and interlocutors that constitute appropriate contexts for speakers to express types and degrees of personal involvement, such as hedges or intensifiers. They would also need to have built-in opportunities for repairs, for turn-taking, and for different types of turn sequences. Following this logic, testers have been scrutinizing test task design (e.g., Van Moere, 2006; Weir & Milanovic, 2003).

In particular, Weir and Milanovic (2003) report on the extensive processes of re-design undertaken by UCLES, which led among other things to the introduction of tasks covering a range of types and content of talk. They also sought to achieve a balanced range of pair and group assessment. This is not unproblematic. Van Moere (2006) reports a low correlation (0.64) across different test occasions, arguing a problematic variation arising from interlocutor or group dynamic. This interlocutor effect can, of course, also arise from examiner variability. Brown (2004), Kasper and Ross (2007), and Ross and Berwick (1992) have all shown examiner effects, whether by over- or under-accommodating to the apparent capacities of the candidate (Ross & Berwick, 1992), or by individual variation in the use of question types (Kasper & Ross, 2007). In a case study, Brown (2004) demonstrates significant differences in a candidate's ratings, that she traces to the interaction styles of the two examiners – a more interview-like style allowing more space for the candidate to develop his turns. However, examiner effects may sometimes be more complex. For instance, although Lorenzo-Dus and Meara (2005) find correlations between the lexical richness of both candidate and examiner performance, on the one hand, and ratings awarded on the other, neither lexical performance nor examiner support entirely account for the grades awarded. Clearly examiner effects need continued investigation.

In addition to tasks and task conditions, we also need rating scales that reflect the criterial features of talk, so as to be able to discriminate between levels of oral proficiency, as distinct from levels of general language proficiency. A second area of activity has been the development of descriptors and ratings scales (Byrnes, 2007; Little, 2006; North & Schneider, 1998, 2007; Salaberry, 2000; Weir & Milanovic, 2003). As various writers (e.g., Hulstijn, 2007; Shohamy, 2000) note, the parameters, conceptual categories (such as those used in assessment descriptors and scales), and findings of SLA and testing should be congruent. Similarly the findings of SLA and language pedagogy should also converge (cf. Byrnes, 2007; Fulcher, 2003), as, of course, should those of language pedagogy and testing (Alderson,

2007a; Fulcher, 2003; Hulstijn, 2007). Unfortunately, currently, none of these congruences have been shown. Discussing the current state of diagnostic testing, Alderson (2007b) remarks that issues like the relevance of what is known of language development to diagnosis of language level or progression are "neither discussed nor researched" (p. 11):

> What we appear to lack, in short, is any theory of what abilities or components of abilities are thought to contribute to language development, or whose absence or underdevelopment might "cause weakness."

Or as Colpin and Gysen put it, also considering the ways in which tests can usefully highlight learners' weaknesses, "with regard to pupils scoring low on the TAL [the Belgian Dutch language proficiency test for 6-year olds], the primary school teacher's ambition should be to falsify the prediction made by the test by skilfully catering to the pupils' language learning needs" (2006, p. 156). If tests such as the TAL can contribute to this aim, it will be by developing an empirical basis for relating test tasks to language performance via proficiency-sensitive descriptors and rating scales.

However, the problem with many of the rating scales is that they are often derived either from teaching tradition (for instance the FSI scale, Fulcher, 2003, pp. 92–7), or from teacher informants (such as the Common European Framework of Reference (CEFR) rating scale, Fulcher, 2003, pp. 107–13). Such scales of course may have the advantage of making sense to the informants themselves, and the reliability derived from careful winnowing of descriptors to identify the most robust. But it is quite possible that descriptors of these kinds are derived from intuitive or traditional models of speech, and potentially quite heavily influenced by models of written language (Hughes, 2003).

So there is an impasse: on the one hand, rating scales can be based on tradition or on teacher intuition, and gain professional credibility; on the other hand, such scales can be criticized for a lack of validity. Salaberry (2000), for example, argues for a further round of revisions on the American Council on the Teaching of Foreign Languages (ACTFL) Oral Proficiency Interview (OPI) scales, while Byrnes (2007) claims that for all their inadequacies, the scales do seem to resonate with – and contribute to – teachers' intuitions about the nature of language development. In somewhat similar vein, Little (2006) argues that the structure of the CEFR global scales, reflecting levels, and the scales of linguistic competence/ language quality and strategic scales reflect the "importance of recognising horizontal [i.e., across skills and through an increasingly wider range of types of communicative activity], as well as vertical progress [through the levels]" (2006, p. 172). Furthermore, if, as Little suggests, "the checklists quickly become the curriculum," and "checklists [are constructed] by translating an existing curriculum into an inventory of communicative tasks" (2006, p. 183), then the point of the triangle of "task-curriculum-exam" may well be gradually harmonized through the mediation of the descriptors and scales. It is noteworthy that little in the literature on the teaching of speaking in a second language has got anywhere close to offering a comparable network of levels and capacities.

Yet, as both Alderson (2007b) and Hulstijn (2007) remark, there is a substantial gap between the practices of systematic sifting of the descriptors and scales on the one hand (North, 1998, 2007), and the principled empirical study of learner corpora, the nature of the underlying constructs that they represent, and their relations – in terms of matches and mismatches – with such frameworks such as the CEFR or ACTFL. Iwashita et al. (2008) note that only a limited number of features correlate significantly with test bands, and with, at best, modest effect sizes. Considering particular features, Little himself (2006, 2007) points out that presence or absence of pausing (a feature discussed in some detail by Fulcher (2003)) is not an indicator of proficiency, since native speakers also pause. As Fulcher says, though, pausing may function differently at different levels of proficiency: in order to understand pausing as a possible indicator, we need to track its incidence (frequency and distribution) across levels and domains of competence (see, also, Towell, Hawkins, & Bazergui, 1996). Yet Kormos and Denes (2004) point out that if the purpose is to assess fluency, it may be that other markers, such as stress patterns, need to be taken into account. In other words, it is likely that the changes in any single marker across proficiency are more complex than one might expect. But not only that, any single marker needs to be considered along with related indices. The same is likely to be true of other features of talk – such as the emergence of formulaic language (Foster, 2001; Taguchi, 2007; Wray, 2002), of communication strategies (as explored by Dobao, 2005), of discourse markers (for instance as enumerated in Carter & McCarthy, 1997), or of higher level categories such as information routines (Bygate, 1987). If we are able to do this, we might begin to map the patterns of oral language development in ways that would make sense both to teachers and to testers. What directions, then, does this suggest for teaching and testing the development of L2 speech?

Conclusion

We noted at the start of this chapter that the problem space implicated in a researched approach to the teaching and testing of oral proficiency implies the study of the language of both pedagogic and test tasks, the relationship between aspects of performance and levels of proficiency, and the development of relevant criteria of appraisal (whether for teaching or assessment). For the development of a systematic pedagogy – in terms of range of materials (both their content and the kinds of interaction they stimulate), the ways in which they can be used, and the ways in which schemes or programs of study can be structured – research in the areas of both teaching and testing, while starting to identify key parameters of the field, nonetheless suggest a need for substantially more conceptually driven empirical research.

Hulstijn (2007) suggests that the construct of proficiency can be usefully operationalized in terms of quantity (the range of language routines) and quality (the ways in which they are mastered, in terms of accuracy and fluency). This, of course, is not a new metaphor for conceptualizing language ability. However, it does help to shed light on how oral language capacities might be understood. For instance, it might suggest the value of shifting away from the endless search for the underlying patterns of "real" language acquisition, and instead lead us to see language acquisition as refracted through development across its distinct modalities, each with its own core, and each with its own more variable peripheries. By posing questions of this kind for speaking, we might come closer to understanding the nature of language acquisition, and to teaching and testing its development more inclusively.

REFERENCES

Abbott, G. (1981). Oral fluency. In G. Abbott & P. Wingard (eds.), *The teaching of English as an international language* (pp. 111–38). Glasgow: Collins.

Alderson, J. (2005). *Diagnosing foreign language proficiency: The interface between learning and assessment*. London: Continuum.

Alderson, J. (2007a). The challenge of (diagnostic) testing: Do we know what we are measuring? In J. Fox et al. (eds.), *Language testing reconsidered* (pp. 21–39). Ottawa: University of Ottawa Press.

Alderson, J. C. (2007b). The CEFR and the need for more research. *The Modern Language Journal* 91, 659–63.

Alexander, R. (2006). *Towards dialogic teaching*, 3rd edn. Thirsk, UK: Dialogos.

Anderson, J. (1983). *The architecture of cognition*. Cambridge, MA: Harvard University Press.

Asher, J. (1982). *Learning another language through actions: The complete teacher's guidebook*. Los Gatos, CA: Sky Oaks Productions.

Aston, G. (1986). Trouble-shooting in interaction with learners: The more the merrier? *Applied Linguistics* 7, 2, 128–43.

Bachman, L. (1990). *Fundamental considerations in language testing*. Oxford: Oxford University Press.

Bachman, L. F. & Palmer, A. S. (1984). Some comments on the terminology of language testing. In C. Rivera (ed.), *Communicative competence approaches to language proficiency assessment: Research and application* (pp. 34–43). Clevedon, UK: Multilingual Matters.

Bachman, L. F. & Palmer, A. S. (1996). *Language testing in practice*. Oxford: Oxford University Press.

Baigent, M. (2005). Multi-word chunks in oral tasks. In C. Edwards & J. Willis (eds.), *Teachings exploring tasks in English language teaching* (pp. 157–70). Basingstoke: Palgrave Macmillan.

Benati, A. (2001). A comparative study of the effects of processing instruction and output-based instruction on the acquisition of the Italian future tense. *Language Teaching Research* 5, 95–127.

Bialystok, E. (1990). Metalinguistic dimensions of bilingual language proficiency. In E. Bialystok (ed.), *Communication strategies: A psychological analysis of second-language use* (pp. 113–40). Oxford: Basil Blackwell.

Bialytsok, E. & Sharwood Smith, M. (1985). Interlanguage is not a state of mind: An evaluation of the construct for second language acquisition. *Applied Linguistics* 6, 2, 101–17.

Biber, D., Conrad, S., & Leech, G. (2002a). *Longman student grammar of spoken and written English.* Harlow: Pearson Education.

Biber, D., Conrad, S., Reppen, R., Byrd, P., & Helt, M. (2002b). Speaking and writing in the university: A multidimensional comparison. *TESOL Quarterly* 36, 1, 9–48.

Bongaerts, T. & Poulisse, N. (1989). Communication strategies in L1 and L2: Same or different? *Applied Linguistics* 10, 253–68.

Bradlow, A. R., Pisoni, D. B., Akahane-Yamada, R., & Tohkura, Y. (1997). Training Japanese listeners to identify English /r/ and /l/: IV. Some effects of perceptual learning on speech production. *Journal of the Acoustical Society of America* 101, 2299–310.

British Council (2005). Examinations reform teacher support project. British Council Hungary (www.examsreform.hu).

Brown, A. (2004). Discourse analysis and the oral interview: Competence or performance. In D. Boxer & A. D. Cohen (eds.), *Studying speaking to inform language learning* (pp. 263–82). Clevedon, UK: Multilingual Matters.

Brown, G. & Yule, G. (1983). *Teaching the spoken language.* Cambridge: Cambridge University Press.

Brumfit, C. J. (1984). *Communicative methodology in language teaching.* Cambridge: Cambridge University Press.

Burns, A. (2006). Teaching speaking: A text-based syllabus approach. In E. Uso-Juan & A. Martinez-Flor (eds.), *Current trends in the development and teaching of the four language skills* (pp. 235–58). Berlin: Mouton de Gruyter.

Burns, A., Joyce, H., & Gollin, S. (1996). *"I see what you mean": Using spoken discourse in the classroom.* Macquarie University: NCELTR.

Bygate, M. (1987). *Speaking.* Oxford: Oxford University Press.

Bygate, M. (1988). Linguistic and strategic features in the language of learners in oral communication exercises. Unpublished PhD dissertation, Institute of Education, University of London.

Bygate, M. (1999). Quality of language and purpose of task: Pattern of learners' language on two oral communication tasks. *Language Teaching Research* 3, 3, 185–214.

Bygate, M. (2001). Effects of task repetition on the structure and control of oral language. In M. Bygate, P. Skehan, & M. Swain (eds.), *Researching pedagogic tasks: Second language learning, teaching and testing* (pp. 23–48). Harlow: Pearson Education.

Bygate, M. (2005a). Oral second language abilities as expertise. In K. Johnson (ed.), *Expertise in second language learning and teaching* (pp. 104–27). London: Palgrave.

Bygate, M. (2005b). Structuring learning within the flux of communication: A role for constructive repetition in oral language pedagogy. In J. A. Foley (ed.), *New dimensions in the teaching of oral communication* (pp. 70–90). Singapore: SEAMEO RELC.

Bygate, M. (2006). Areas of research that influence L2 speaking instruction. In E. Uso-Juan & A. Martinez-Flor (eds.), *Current trends in the development and teaching of the four language skills* (pp. 159–86). Berlin: Mouton de Gruyter.

Bygate, M. (2007). Understanding task demands: The whole as a sum of its parts. (Paper presented at the second International TBLT Conference, Hawaii).

Bygate, M. & Samuda, V. (2005). Integrative planning through the use of task repetition. In R. Ellis (ed.), *Planning and task performance in a second language* (pp. 37–74). Amsterdam: John Benjamins.

Byrne, D. (1976). *Teaching oral English.* Harlow: Longman.

Byrnes, H. (2007). Second and foreign language pedagogy. Paper presented at the Language Learning Roundtable Colloquium: Language Learning celebrates 30 years of AAAL.

Canale, M. & Swain, M. (1980). Theoretical bases of communicative approaches to teaching and testing. *Applied Linguistics* 1, 1–47.

Carter, R. & McCarthy, M. (1997). *Exploring spoken English*. Cambridge: Cambridge University Press.

Celce-Murcia, M., Dornyei, Z., & Thurrell, S. (1996). Direct approaches in L2 instruction: A turning point in communicative language teaching? *TESOL Quarterly* 31, 1, 141–52.

Chafe, Wallace L. (1985). Linguistic differences produced by differences between speaking and writing. In D. R. Olson, N. Torrance, & A. Hildyard (eds.), *Literacy, language and learning* (pp. 105–23). Cambridge: Cambridge University Press.

Clark, H. H. & Fox Tree, J. E. (2002). Using *uh* and *um* in spontaneous speaking. *Cognition* 84, 73–111.

Clark, H. H. & Krych, M. A. (2004). Speaking while monitoring addressees for understanding. *Journal of memory and language* 50, 1, 62–81.

Colpin, M. & Gysen, S. (2006). Developing and introducing task-based language tests. In K. van den Branden (ed.), *Task-based language education: From theory to practice* (pp. 151–74). Cambridge: Cambridge University Press.

Coulson, D. (2005). Collaborative tasks for cross-cultural communication. In C. Edwards & J. Willis (eds.), *Teachings exploring tasks in English language teaching* (pp. 127–38). Basingstoke: Palgrave Macmillan.

Coupland, J. (2000). Introduction: Sociolinguistic perspectives on small talk. In J. Coupland (ed.), *Small talk* (pp. 1–26). London: Pearson Education.

Cox, D. (2005). Can we predict language items for open tasks? In C. Edwards & J. Willis (eds.), *Teachings exploring tasks in English language teaching* (pp. 171–86). Basingstoke: Palgrave Macmillan.

Cullen, R. & Kuo, I.-C. (2007). Spoken grammar and ELT course materials: A missing link? *TESOL Quarterly* 41, 2, 361–86.

Dalton, C. & Seidlhofer, B. (1994). *Pronunciation*. Oxford: Oxford University Press.

de Bot, K. (1992). A bilingual production model: Levelt's "speaking" model adapted. *Applied Linguistics* 13, 1–24.

D'Ely, R. C. S. F. (2006). A focus on learners' metacognitive processes: The impact of strategic planning, repetition, strategic planning plus repetition, and strategic planning for repetition on L2 oral performance. Unpublished doctoral dissertation, Florianopolis, Universidade Federal de Santa Catarina.

Derwing, T. M. & Munro, M. J. (2005). Second language accent and pronunciation teaching: A research-based approach. *TESOL Quarterly* 39, 3, 379–98.

Derwing, T. M., Munro, M. J., & Wiebe, G. (1998). Evidence in favor of a broad framework for pronunciation instruction. *Language Learning* 48, 393–410.

Dobao, A. M. Fernandez (2005). The use of communication strategies by Spanish learners of English: A study of the collaborative creation of meaning, language and linguistic knowledge. Unpublished Doctoral dissertation, University of Santiago de Compostela.

Dobao, A. M. Fernandez & Palacios Martinez, I. M. (2007). Negotiating meaning in interaction between English and Spanish speakers via communicative strategies. *Atlantis* 29, 1, 87–105.

Doughty, C. J. & Varela, E. (1998). Communicative focus on form. In C. J. Doughty & J. Williams (eds.), *Focus on form in classroom second language acquisition* (pp. 114–38), Cambridge: Cambridge University Press.

Doughty, C. J. & Williams, J. (1998). Pedagogical choices in focus on form. In C. J. Doughty & J. Williams (eds.), *Focus on form in classroom second language acquisition* (pp. 197–261). Cambridge: Cambridge University Press.

Ellis, N. (1996). Sequencing in SLA: Phonological memory, chunking and points of order. *Studies in Second Language Acquisition* 18, 91–126.

Ellis, R. (ed.) (2005). *Planning and task performance in a second language.* Amsterdam: John Benjamins.

Essig, W. (2005). Story telling: Effects of planning, repetition and context. In C. Edwards & J. Willis (eds.), *Teachings exploring tasks in English language teaching* (pp. 201–13). Basingstoke: Palgrave Macmillan.

Feez, S. (1998). *Text-based syllabus design.* Macquarie, Sydney: AMES, NCELTR.

Fillmore, C. J. (1979). Fluency. Reprinted in H. Riggenbach (ed.), *Perspectives on fluency* (pp. 43–60). Ann Arbor: The University of Michigan Press.

Foster, P. (1996). Doing the task better: How planning time influences students' performance. In J. Willis & D. Willis (eds.), *Challenge and change in language teaching* (pp. 126–35). Oxford: Heinemann.

Foster, P. (2001). Rules and routines: A consideration of their role in the task-based language production of native and non-native speakers. In M. Bygate, P. Skehan, & M. Swain (eds.), *Researching pedagogic tasks: Second language learning, teaching and testing* (pp. 75–94). Harlow: Pearson Education.

Foster, P. & Skehan, P. (1996). The influence of planning and task type on second language performance. *Studies in Second Language Acquisition* 18, 299–323.

Fulcher, G. (2003). *Testing second language speaking.* Harlow: Pearson.

Gass, S. M. (1997). *Input, interaction and the second language learner.* Mahwah, NJ: Lawrence Erlbaum.

Gass, S. M. (2003). Input and interaction. In C. J. Doughty & M. H. Long (eds.), *The handbook of second language acquisition* (pp. 224–55). Oxford: Blackwell.

Hobbs, J. (2005). Interactive lexical phrases in pair interview tasks. In C. Edwards & J. Willis (eds.), *Teachings exploring tasks in English language teaching* (pp. 143–56). Basingstoke: Palgrave Macmillan.

Hughes, R. (2003). *Teaching and researching speaking.* Harlow: Pearson.

Hulstijn, J. (2003). Incidental and intentional learning. In C. J. Doughty & M. H. Long (eds.), *The handbook of second language acquisition* (pp. 349–81). Oxford: Blackwell.

Hulstijn, J. (2007). The shaky ground beneath the CEFR: Quantitative and qualitative dimensions of language proficiency. *The Modern Language Journal* 91, 663–7.

Iwashita, N., Brown, A., McNamara, T., & O'Hagan, S. (2008). Assessed levels of second language speaking proficiency: How distinct? *Applied Linguistics* 29, 1, 24–49.

Johnson, K. (1996). *Language teaching and skill learning.* Oxford: Blackwell.

Kasper, G. (2001). Classroom research on interlanguage pragmatics. In K. Rose & G. Kasper (eds.), *Pragmatics in language teaching* (pp. 33–60). Cambridge: Cambridge University Press.

Kasper, G. & Ross, S. J. (2007). Multiple questions in oral proficiency interviews. *Journal of Pragmatics* 39, 2045–70.

Kormos, J. (2006). *Speech production and second language acquisition.* Mahwah, NJ: Lawrence Erlbaum.

Kormos, J. & Denes, M. (2004). Exploring measures and perceptions of fluency in the speech of second language learners. *System* 32, 2, 145–64.

Krashen, S. & Terrell, T. (1983). *The natural approach: Language acquisition in the classroom.* Hayward, CA: Alemany Press.

Lantolf, J. P. & Thorne, S. L. (2006). *Sociocultural theory and the genesis of second language development.* Oxford: Oxford University Press.

Laver, J. (1970). The production of speech. In J. Lyons (ed.), *New horizons in linguistics* (pp. 53–75). Harmondsworth: Penguin.

Leedham, M. (2005). Exam-oriented tasks: Transcripts, turn-taking and backchannelling. In C. Edwards & J. Willis (eds.), *Teachings exploring tasks in English language teaching* (pp. 93–102). Basingstoke: Palgrave Macmillan.

Legutke, M. & Thomas, H. (1991). *Process and experience in the language classroom*. Harlow: Longman.

Levelt, W. J. M. (1978). Skill theory and language teaching. *Studies in Second Language Acquisition* 1, 1, 53–70.

Levelt, W. J. M. (1989). *Speaking: From intention to articulation*. Cambridge, MA: MIT Press.

Little, D. (2006). The Common European framework of Reference for Languages: Contents, purpose, origin, reception and impact. *Language Teaching* 39, 3.

Little, D. (2007). The Common European Framework of Reference for Languages: Perspectives on the making of supranational language education policy. *The Modern Language Journal* 91, 4, 645–53.

Littlewood, W. (2004). The task-based approach: some questions and suggestions. *ELT Journal* 58, 4, 319–26.

Long, M. H. (1977). Teacher feedback on learner error: Mapping cognitions. In H. D. Brown, C. A. Yorio, & R. H. Crymes (eds.), *On TESOL '77* (pp. 278–93). Washington, DC: TESOL.

Long, M. H. (1996). The role of the linguistic environment in second language acquisition. In W. C. Ritchie & T. K. Bhatia (eds.), *Handbook of research on language acquisition* (vol. 2, pp. 413–68). New York: Academic Press.

Lorenzo-Dus, N. & Meara, P. (2005). Examiner support strategies and test-taker vocabulary. *IRAL* 43, 239–58.

Loschky, L. & Bley-Vroman, R. (1993). Grammar and task-based methodology. In G. Crookes & S. M. Gass (eds.), *Tasks and language learning: Integrating theory and practice* (pp. 136–27). Clevedon, UK: Multilingual Matters.

Luoma, S. (2004). *Assessing speaking*. Cambridge: Cambridge University Press.

Luxia, Q. (2005). Stakeholders' conflicting aims undermine the washback function of a high-stakes test. *Language Testing* 22, 142–73.

Lynch, T. (1997). Nudge, nudge: Teacher interventions in task-based learner talk. *ELT Journal* 51, 4, 317–25.

Lynch, T. (2001). Seeing what they meant: Transcribing as a route to noticing. *ELT Journal* 55, 2, 124–32.

Lynch, T. (2007). Learning from the transcripts of an oral communication task. *ELT Journal* 61, 4, 311–20.

Lynch, T. & Maclean, J. (2000). Exploring the benefits of task repetition and recycling for classroom language learning. In *Tasks in Language Pedagogy*, special issue of *Language Teaching Research* 4, 3, 221–50.

Lynch, T. & Maclean, J. (2001). "A case of exercising": Effects of immediate task repetition on learners' performance. In M. Bygate, P. Skehan, & M. Swain (eds.), *Researching pedagogic tasks: Second language learning, teaching and testing* (pp. 141–62). Harlow: Pearson Education.

Lyster, R. (2004). Differential effects of prompts and recasts in form-focused instruction. *Studies in Second Language Acquisition* 26, 399–432.

Mackey, A. (1999). Input, interaction and second language development: an empirical study of question formation in ESL. *SSLA*, 21/4: 557–89.

Mackey, A. & Philp, J. (1998). Conversational interaction and second language development: Recasts, responses, and red herrings. *Modern Language Journal* 82, 338–56.

Marsden, E. (2006). Exploring Input Processing in the classroom: An experimental comparison of Processing Instruction and Enriched Input. *Language Learning* 56, 3, 507–66.

McCarthy, M. (1998). *Spoken language and applied linguistics*. Cambridge: Cambridge University Press.

McNamara, T. (1996). *Measuring second language performance*. London: Longman.

Morrow, K. (ed.) (2004). *Insights from the Common European Framework*. Oxford: Oxford University Press.

Morrow, K. & Johnson, K. (1979). *Communicate 1*. Harlow: Longman.

Newell, A. (1990). *Unified theories of cognition*. Cambridge, MA: Harvard University Press.

Newton, J. & Kennedy, G. (1996). Effects of communicative tasks on the grammatical relations marked by second language learners. *System* 24, 3, 309–22.

North, B. (1995). The development of a common framework scale of descriptors of language proficiency based on a theory of measurement. *System* 23, 4, 445–65.

North, B. (2000). *The development of a common framework scale of language proficiency*. New York: Peter Lang.

North, B. (2007). The CEFR Illustrative Descriptor Scales. *The Modern Language Journal* 91, 4, 656–9.

North, B. & Schneider, G. (1998). Scaling descriptors for language proficiency scales. *Language Testing* 15, 217–62.

Pawley, A. & Syder, F. H. (1983). Two puzzles for linguistic theory: Nativelike selection and nativelike fluency. In J. C. Richards & R. W. Schmidt (eds.), *Language and communication* (pp. 191–226). London: Longman.

Pica, T., Kanagy, R., & Falodun, J. (1993). Choosing and using communication tasks for second language instruction. In G. Crookes & S. M. Gass (eds.), *Tasks and language learning: Integrating theory and practice* (pp. 9–34). Clevedon, UK: Multilingual Matters.

Pinter, A. (2005). Task repetition with 10-year old children. In C. Edwards & J. Willis (eds.), *Teachings exploring tasks in English language teaching* (pp. 113–26). Basingstoke: Palgrave Macmillan.

Plough, I. & Gass, S. M. (1993). Interlocutor and task familiarity effects on interactional structure. In G. Crookes & S. M. Gass (eds.), *Tasks and language learning: Integrating theory and practice* (pp. 35–56). Clevedon, UK: Multilingual Matters.

Poupore, G. (2005). Quality of interaction and types of negotiation in problem-solving and jigsaw tasks. In C. Edwards & J. Willis (eds.), *Teachings exploring tasks in English language teaching* (pp. 242–55). Basingstoke: Palgrave Macmillan.

Prabhu, N. S. (1987). *Second language pedagogy*. Oxford: Oxford University Press.

Richards, J. C. & Schmidt, R. W. (1983). Conversation analysis. In J. C. Richards & R. W. Schmidt (eds.), *Language as communication* (pp. 117–55). Harlow: Longman.

Riggenbach, H. (ed.) (2000). *Perspectives on fluency*. Ann Arbor: The University of Michigan Press.

Robinson, P. (2001). Task complexity, task difficulty and task production: Exploring interactions in a componential framework. *Applied Linguistics* 22, 1, 27–57.

Robinson, P. (2007). Criteria for classifying and sequencing pedagogic tasks. In M. del P. Garcia Mayo (ed.), *Investigating tasks in formal language learning* (pp. 7–26). Clevedon, UK: Multilingual Matters.

Rose, K. & Kasper, G. (eds.) (2001). *Pragmatics in language teaching*. Cambridge: Cambridge University Press.

Ross, S. & Berwick, R. (1992). The discourse of accommodation inn oral proficiency interviews. *Studies in Second Language Acquisition* 14, 2, 159–76.

Salaberry, R. (2000). Revising the revised format of the ACTFL Oral Proficiency Interview. *Language Testing* 17, 3, 289.

Samuda, V. (2001). Guiding relationships between form and meaning during task performance: The role of the teacher. In M. Bygate, P. Skehan, & M. Swain (eds.),

Researching pedagogic tasks: Second language learning, teaching and testing (pp. 119–40). Harlow: Pearson Education.

Samuda, V. & Bygate, M. (2008). *Tasks in second language learning.* Basingstoke: Palgrave.

Schneider, W. & Shiffrin, R. (1977). Controlled and automatic human information processing: Part 1. Detection, search and attention. *Psychological Review* 84, 1–66.

Segalowitz, N. (2003). Automaticity and second languages. In C. J. Doughty & M. H. Long (eds.), *The handbook of Second Language Acquisition* (pp. 382–408). Oxford: Blackwell.

Shiffrin, R. & Schneider, W. (1977). Controlled and automatic human information processing: Part 2. Perceptual learning, automatic attending, and a general theory. *Psychological Review* 84, 127–90.

Shohamy, E. (2000). The relationship between language testing and second language acquisition, revisited. *Language Testing* 28, 4, 541–53.

Skehan, P. (1998). *A cognitive approach to language learning.* Oxford: Oxford University Press.

Skehan, P. (2001). Tasks and language performance assessment. In M. Bygate, P. Skehan, & M. Swain (eds.), *Researching pedagogic tasks: Second language learning, teaching and testing* (pp. 167–85). Harlow: Pearson Education.

Skehan, P. & Foster, P. (1997). The influence of planning and post-task activities on accuracy and complexity in task-based learning. *Language Teaching Research* 1, 3, 185–211.

Skehan, P. & Foster, P. (2001). The influence of task structure and processing conditions on narrative retellings. *Language Learning* 49, 1, 93–120.

Swain, M. (1985). Communicative competence: Some roles of comprehensible input and comprehensible output in its development. In S. M. Gass & C. Madden (eds.), *Input in second language acquisition* (pp. 235–53). Rowley, MA.: Newbury House.

Taguchi, N. (2007). Chunk learning and the development of spoken discourse in a Japanese as a foreign language classroom. *Language Teaching Research* 11, 4, 433–57.

Thompson, G. (1996). Some misconceptions about communicative language teaching. *ELT Journal* 50, 1, 9–15.

Thornbury, S. (1993). Having a good jaw: Voice-setting phonology. *ELT Journal* 47, 126–31.

Thornbury, S. (2005). *How to teach speaking.* Harlow: Pearson.

Thornbury, S. & Slade, D. (2006). *Conversation: From description to pedagogy.* Cambridge: Cambridge University Press.

Towell, R., Hawkins, R., & Bazergui, N. (1996). The development of fluency in advanced learners of French. *Applied Linguistics* 17, 1, 84–119.

Ur, P. (1988). *Grammar practice activities.* Cambridge: Cambridge University Press.

Ur, P. (1996). *A course in language teaching: Practice and theory.* Cambridge: Cambridge University Press.

van Lier, L. (1996). *Interaction in the language curriculum: Awareness, autonomy and authenticity.* Harlow: Longman.

Van Moere A. (2006). Validity evidence in a university group oral test. *Language Testing* 23, 4, 411–40.

VanPatten, B. (1996). *Input processing.* Norwood, NJ.: Ablex.

Wall, D. (1996). Introducing new tests into traditional systems: iInsights from general education and from innovation theory. *Language Testing* 13, 334–54.

Wall, D. (2000). The impact of high stakes testing on teaching and learning: Can this be predicted or controlled? *System* 28, 4, 499–510.

Weir, C. J. & Milanovic, M. (eds.) (2003). *Continuity and innovation: The history of the CPE 1913–2002.* Cambridge: Cambridge University Press.

Wilkes-Gibbs, D. (1997). Studying language use as collaboration. In G. Kasper & E. Kellerman (eds.), *Communication strategies* (pp. 238–51). Harlow: Longman.

Willis, J. (1996). *A framework for task-based learning.* Harlow: Addison Wesley Longman.

Wray, A. (2000). Formulaic sequences in second language teaching: Principles and practice. *Applied Linguistics* 21, 4, 463–89.

Wray, A. (2002). *Formulaic language and the lexicon.* Cambridge: Cambridge University Press.

Young, R. & Milanovic, M. (1992). Discourse variation in oral proficiency interviews. *Studies in Second Language Acquisition* 14, 403–24.

Yuan, F. & Ellis, R. (2003). The effects of pre-task planning and on-line planning on fluency, complexity and accuracy in L2 monologic oral production. *Applied Linguistics* 24, 1, 1–27.

Yule, G. (1997). *Referential communication tasks.* Mahwah, NJ: Lawrence Erlbaum.

Yule, G. & Tarone, E. (1991). The other side of the page: Integrating the communication strategies and negotiated input in SLA. In R. Phillipson, E. Kellerman, L. Selinker, M. Sharwood Smith, & M. Swain (eds.), *Foreign/second language pedagogy research* (pp. 162–77). Clevedon, UK: Multilingual Matters.

24   Teaching and Testing Reading

WILLIAM GRABE

The teaching and testing of reading has a history of research effort that goes back for decades. While L2 reading research has a more limited history (as opposed to the L1 research base), there is also a very large database to draw on. This chapter will outline briefly major themes from research that, in combination, form the construct of reading abilities (for both L1 and L2 reading). Determining the construct then provides rationales for various instructional and assessment practices. The focus of this chapter will not be an extensive review of the reading construct. That has been developed in more detail in other sources (e.g., Bowey, 2005; Koda, 2005, 2007; Perfetti, Landi, & Oakhill, 2005). Instead, the goal is to draw connections from the reading construct to effective ways to teach reading and test reading. The chapter will then briefly outline guidelines that should be effective for teaching L2 reading abilities across a range of curricular settings. It will also outline testing tasks that can be effective means for assessing L2 reading abilities.

Research Foundations

Fluent reading comprehension requires a number of processing subskills and linguistic knowledge bases. These processes and knowledge resources allow the reader to comprehend texts to the level required. The identification of these skills and resources has been the outcome of many research studies, and it remains the source of much ongoing research. In this section, research is reviewed that supports the relationship between reading skills and reading comprehension. Much of the research has been conducted in English L1 reading contexts, though increasing amounts of L1 reading research in other languages have also emerged in the past 15 years (Cook & Bassetti, 2005b; Frost, 2005; Joshi & Aaron, 2006; Koda, 2005).

Letter–sound correspondences

Research in beginning reading has shown that beginning readers need to establish strong linkages between orthographic forms and the sounds of the language

(Bowey, 2005; Ehri et al., 2001; Perfetti et al., 2005; Tunmer & Chapman, 2006). Extensive research on L1 contexts across languages has demonstrated that training in phonological awareness and letter–sound correspondences predicts later reading development among children and beginning readers (Ehri, 2006; Ehri et al., 2001; Wagner, Piasta, & Torgesen, 2006). While L1 reading in other languages may not require that same intensity of instructional effort as does English for phonological awareness, all young learners benefit significantly from explicit instruction in letter–sound correspondences (Lundberg, 1999). The automatization of letter–sound relations is the foundation of all alphabetic reading and supports syllabic reading systems, as well. Even Chinese, as a morpho-syllabic system, incorporates some information from the phonetic radical within characters as an aid to word recognition and uses phonological information at the point of lexical access (Chow, McBride-Chang, & Burgess, 2005; He, Wang, & Anderson, 2005; Perfetti & Liu, 2005).

L2 research on letter–sound correspondences has indicated that it is important to establish such correspondences early in L2 reading. For example, Nicholson and Ng (2006) have shown that teaching phonemic awareness and letter–sound correspondences improves ESL preschool children's (ages 3:6 to 4:5) phonological awareness, word reading, short text reading, and pseudoword reading significantly above a comparison group of ESL children being read to. Geva and Yaghoub-Zadeh (2006) demonstrated that there is a strong relationship between phonological awareness and text reading efficiency (accuracy and fluency) with second grade ESL students (see also Gottardo et al., 2001). If letter–sound correspondences are established in the L1, these particular abilities seem to transfer reasonably easily (Durgunoglu, Nagy, & Hancin-Bhatt, 1993; Lesaux, Lipka, & Seigal, 2006; Gottardo et al., 2001).

Word recognition efficiency

English L1 research on eye-movement tracking has shown that good readers recognize words on average in about 200–250 milliseconds, they move their eyes ahead approximately eight letter spaces per focus, they make regressive eye-movements about 12 percent of the time (often for slight adjustments), and they actively focus on more than 80 percent of the content words and about 35 percent of function words. In short, reading is a process of very rapid word recognition carried out through fairly consistent eye behaviors. Automaticity is a key to this rapid word recognition process. The observable eye-movement processes of fluent readers are quite similar in all languages, with variation due to differing amounts of linguistic information provided by individual graphic forms (see Rayner, Juhasz, & Pollatsek, 2005). Word reading efficiency is going to vary somewhat among different orthographic systems (Frost et al., 2005; McBride-Chang et al., 2005). L2 word reading efficiency, in some situations, can be a strong predictor of L2 reading comprehension abilities (Kahn-Horwitz, Shimron, & Sparks, 2005); in other settings, it will not be predictive for multiple complex reasons.

Vocabulary knowledge

Research on English L1 vocabulary knowledge has demonstrated that fluent readers have very large recognition-vocabulary knowledge resources and that vocabulary knowledge is highly correlated with reading ability (see Bowey, 2005; Stahl & Nagy, 2006; Tannenbaum, Torgesen, & Wagner, 2006). While estimates of word knowledge vary greatly (from 19,000 to 200,000 words; Anglin, 1993; Nation, 2001), the most widely accepted figure is that high school graduates know on average 40,000 words as fluent L1 readers (Nagy & Anderson, 1984; Stahl & Nagy, 2006). This is a very large number of words to learn and most accounts suggest that many of these words are learned by exposure to new words through continual reading practice. Stanovich (2000) has argued that extended exposure to print over years leads to major differences not only in vocabulary knowledge but also in increasing comprehension and a range of measures of conceptual knowledge.

Research on L2 vocabulary knowledge has also shown that vocabulary is correlated with L2 reading comprehension. Droop and Verhoeven (2003) reported a strong relationship between third and fourth grade L2 students' vocabulary knowledge and their reading abilities. Schoonen, Hulstijn, and Bossers (1998) also reported very strong relationships between vocabulary and reading, reporting an r^2 of 0.71 for eighth grade EFL students in Holland. This relationship has also been clearly demonstrated in research involving L2 reading assessment studies (Pike, 1979; Qian, 2002).

Early experimental studies on vocabulary instruction have demonstrated that vocabulary learning can lead to reading comprehension improvement (Beck, Perfetti, & McKeown, 1982; McKeown et al., 1985), though the impact of vocabulary on comprehension improvement is complex and requires intensive instructional effort (Nagy, 2005). In the past 20 years, there have been relatively few studies of efforts to teach vocabulary explicitly and then compare the experimental group to a control group for reading comprehension gains. However, Carlo et al. (2004) have demonstrated that intense explicit vocabulary instruction with L2 English fourth graders leads to significant improvement over control groups, not only in greater vocabulary knowledge but also on a measure of reading comprehension abilities.

Morphology, syntax, and discourse knowledge

Research on L1 morphological, syntactic, and discourse knowledge shows that they all have an impact on reading comprehension. A number of studies have shown that morphological knowledge contributes to reading comprehension: research by Anglin (1993), Carlisle (2003), and Nagy et al. (2003) all argue that morphological knowledge (knowledge of word parts) is very important to more advanced word recognition and reading development (see Stahl & Nagy, 2006). The contribution of syntax to reading is less well examined in L1 reading contexts because L1 students develop implicit knowledge of most grammatical structures.

(For this reason, L1 students are not commonly assessed for their grammar knowledge.) However, there is evidence that grammatical knowledge (syntactic parsing) plays a role in L1 reading comprehension (and it is intuitively obvious on reflection) (Bowey, 2005; Lesaux, Lipka, & Siegal, 2006; Perfetti et al., 2005). There is extensive evidence that discourse knowledge contributes in important ways to reading comprehension. Syntheses by Duke and Pearson (2002) and Trabasso and Bouchard (2002) point to the importance of discourse signaling mechanisms, organization patterns in texts, logical relations across clauses and sentences, and text structures that can be recognized and learned (see also Hudson, 2007; Koda, 2005).

Research on L2 syntax and discourse knowledge have both shown that there are strong relationships between these language knowledge bases and reading comprehension. This relationship also appears in reading assessment research. Research studies with Dutch students have shown that syntax is a powerful predictor of reading comprehension abilities. Schoonen et al. (1998) showed that syntax was a very strong predictor of reading ability in a multiple regression study. More recently, Van Gelderen et al. (2004) reported a very strong relationship between syntactic knowledge and reading comprehension. In reading assessment research, both Alderson (2000) and ETS researchers (Enright et al., 2002) have presented very high correlations showing that syntactic knowledge is strongly related to reading comprehension. In research on the role of discourse knowledge, Carrell (1984, 1985) has shown that discourse structure knowledge is strongly related to reading comprehension. Similarly, Horiba (1993) reported that Japanese L2 students at different proficiency levels used discourse knowledge differently in their recall of text information. Focusing more specifically on the role of discourse-based graphic organizers, Tang (1992) showed that students trained to recognize the discourse structure of a text, performed better on a comprehension measure.

Strategic processing

L1 research on strategic processing during reading (e.g., inferencing, comprehension monitoring, and goal setting) demonstrates that strategic processes and metacognition influence reading comprehension. Discourse comprehension researchers have shown that inferencing that arises from "learning from texts" has an important impact on comprehension (Goldman & Rakestraw, 2000; Nation, 2005; Perfetti et al., 2005). Similarly, comprehension monitoring (as in monitoring for problems in text comprehension) appears to be a predictor of comprehension abilities (Cain, Oakhill, & Bryant, 2004). At the same time, these abilities, being metacognitive in nature, are not simple reading strategies. Rather, they constitute a range of skills and abilities, and represent a range of strategic responses to text difficulties.

Experimental research on comprehension instruction and strategy training is extensive (see Pressley, 2006; Trabasso & Bouchard, 2002). Many studies demonstrate a causal impact of instructional skills and strategies on reading comprehension. Important evidence supports answering main idea questions as a post-reading task, using semantic mapping of ideas from a text, previewing specific information from the text, asking student to formulate questions about a text, filling in and generating graphic organizers that reflect the organization of the text, visualizing information from the text, raising awareness of discourse organization of the text, among others. Overall, a number of reasonably effective strategies have been identified in instructional research, though *combinations of strategic responses to texts* appear to be more effective in supporting comprehension development (Trabasso & Bouchard, 2002; see Grabe, 2004). The best strategic approaches to reading instruction involve reciprocal teaching, transactional strategies instruction, and concept-oriented reading instruction (Block & Pressley, 2002; Guthrie, Wigfield, & Perencevich, 2004; Pressley, 2006).

Research on L2 strategic processing is far more limited. There are relatively few studies that demonstrate a relationship between reading strategies and reading comprehension. Chen and Graves (1995) showed that previewing a text was a pre-reading strategy that improved student comprehension. Klingner and Vaughn (2000) drew on reciprocal teaching concepts and developed a four-strategy program for teaching strategic reading, Cooperative Strategic Reading. Results showed some improvements in reading strategy use and in vocabulary growth based on the approach. In a recent meta-analysis of L2 reading strategy research, Taylor, Stevens, and Asher (2006) reviewed the existing empirical research in L2 reading strategy training (10 published studies and 12 dissertations) and concluded that a low to moderate effect exists between strategy training and L2 reading comprehension improvement. The analysis is encouraging, but it should be treated cautiously due to the limited database available for the analysis.

Extended exposure to print

L1 research on extended exposure to print has demonstrated a strong relationship between amount of reading (over long periods of time) and improved reading comprehension (Guthrie, Wigfield, & Von Secker, 2000; Guthrie, Wigfield, & Perencevich, 2004; Stanovich, 2000). Stanovich and colleagues, in a series of studies, showed that exposure to print (amount of reading) was an important independent predictor of reading ability (see Stanovich, 2000 for overview). Sénéchal (2006) also showed that reading exposure was a significant predictor of reading comprehension among 90 fourth grade French-speaking students. Interestingly, despite many claims about Sustained Silent Reading (SSR) and Free Voluntary Reading (FVR), there are no rigorously controlled experimental studies that show a strong relationship between either of these instructional approaches and reading comprehension abilities.

Research on extensive reading is relatively unexplored in L2 reading. The one set of studies that has indicated the positive effects of extensive reading on reading comprehension was that carried out by Elley over a period of 20 years (Elley, 2000). In these studies, he has shown that getting students to read extensively over a long period of time consistently improved reading comprehension abilities, as well as a number of other language skills. In most other studies on extensive reading, there is little controlled empirical evidence that reading extensively has a significant influence on reading comprehension development.

Fluency

L1 research on reading fluency has demonstrated that the reading fluency, or relative non-fluency, of readers with reading difficulties, and especially children, is strongly correlated with reading comprehension (Samuels, 2006). Sabatini (2002) showed that fluency was correlated with reading ability for people with reading difficulties across a wide age range, including adults with reading difficulties. Levy (2001) has shown that there is a moderate correlation between word reading fluency and reading comprehension. Fuchs et al. (2001) and Jenkins et al. (2003) have shown that oral passage reading fluency – orally reading a text for one minute – is strongly related to reading comprehension abilities for L1 children. Walczyk et al. (1999) has shown that increasing reading rate moderately among readers leads to improved comprehension. Breznitz (2006) has also demonstrated this relationship between increased reading rate and improved comprehension among second grade children with reading difficulties. Research using Rapid Automatic Naming (RAN) tasks is somewhat more controversial (Bowey, 2005), but a number of researchers have shown a relationship between RAN measures and reading comprehension for children, both with and without reading disabilities (Georgiou, Parrila, & Kirby, 2006; Geva & Yaghoub-Zadeh, 2006). RAN appears to be a strong predictor of reading difficulties for languages with shallow orthographies (unlike English) (Landerl & Thaler, 2006).

Experimental research focused on reading fluency in L1 settings is fairly well established. A number of studies have shown that training to recognize words faster will lead to faster word recognition on other words if the training is sufficiently extensive (Martin-Chang & Levy, 2006). However, this type of training appears to have only limited direct benefits for reading comprehension. Levy, Abello, and Lysynchuk (1997) showed that training on word recognition for most of the words in a given text led to better text comprehension for that text. Tan and Nicholson (1997) achieved similar results but also demonstrated that word recognition training (through flash card practice) led to better reading comprehension on other texts, as well. However, in other studies, Levy and her colleagues have not demonstrated that learning to recognize words more fluently will lead directly to improved reading comprehension (see Levy, 2001). In the area of passage fluency training, primarily by rereading passages multiple times (sometimes aloud and sometimes silently), there is good evidence that passage rereading leads to both improved reading fluency and improved reading comprehension (Stahl & Heubach, 2005; National Reading Panel, 2000; Samuels & Farstrup, 2006).

There is little research that demonstrates a relationship between reading fluency and reading comprehension development in L2 contexts. However, a series of recent studies carried out by Sawaki and Sabatini (2007; Jiang, Sabatini, & Sawaki,

2007) has reported a strong relationship between oral passage reading fluency and reading comprehension ($r^2 = 0.36$). Also, Geva and Yaghoub-Zadeh (2006) have demonstrated that RAN tasks are related to L2 text reading efficiency and word reading fluency. In a series of L2 training studies by Taguchi, Takayasu-Maass, and Gorsuch (2004) and by Lems (2005), there is clear evidence that fluency practice leads to increased L2 reading fluency and to some improvement in L2 reading comprehension. Improved word-reading fluency through training has also been reported by Fukkink, Hulstijn, and Simis (2005).

Motivation

L1 reading motivation is an area with only limited research focused explicitly on reading abilities. However, a few studies have shown that more motivated readers both read more and have better reading comprehension abilities. Guthrie et al. (2000) showed that third grade and fifth grade readers who were more motivated read more and that eighth and tenth grade readers who were more motivated also were better at reading comprehension. Guthrie, Wigfield, and Perencevich (2004) also showed that specific instructional contexts can improve reading motivation and, as a consequence, improve reading comprehension. There is very little research on L2 reading motivation, a construct that is quite different from general L2 language learning motivation (cf. Mori, 2002).

All of the above components contribute directly to reading comprehension and represent aspects of the construct of reading comprehension. (There are additional components not covered in this review that also impact L2 reading comprehension – e.g., working memory, background knowledge – though these components require more complex descriptions and evaluations.) In almost all cases, L1 research demonstrates that training in these components leads to improved reading comprehension. In addition, the experimental training studies indicate that these component skills are likely to be useful components of a curriculum designed to improve students' L2 reading abilities. Comparable L2 research on training impacts of component skills on reading comprehension is still needed (see Grabe, 2004).

L1 and L2 Reading Differences

The above section developed the concept that L1 and L2 reading abilities share many of the same component skills and that the reading construct is very similar in terms of underlying cognitive and linguistic components. In most respects, this is a reasonable position to take (see Geva & Siegal, 2000; Koda, 2007). At the same time, any consideration of L2 reading abilities has to recognize that there are specific aspects of reading in a second language that distinguish it from L1 reading abilities. Among these differences, six stand out as potentially important for discussions of skills and abilities that support L2 reading comprehension (and that might impact L2 teaching and testing).

1   In the L2, learners have a much smaller linguistic knowledge base of the L2 when they begin reading. Their knowledge of vocabulary is much more limited; their knowledge of syntax is similarly limited and there are no native intuitions about structure; their knowledge of markers of discourse structure and their awareness with text organization in the L2 will also be limited.

2   L2 students, overall, will have much less experience with reading exposure in the L2. They simply will have had much less practice in L2 reading.

3   L2 students will experience L2 reading differently because they have experiences reading in two different languages and because cognitive processing will involve two language systems (e.g., accessing the bilingual lexicon, using a joint strategy system – Garcia, 1998; Kern, 1994) (see also Cook & Bassetti, 2005a: Multi-competence Hypothesis).

4   Aside from the possibilities of developing somewhat distinct cognitive processing, students engaged in L2 reading will also experience a range of transfer effects (cognitive skills, strategies, and goals and expectations). Some transfer effects will involve interference from the L1; others will facilitate L2 reading processes. (See Dressler & Kamil, 2006; Geva & Siegal, 2000; Koda, 2005 on the Interdependence Hypothesis and the Underlying Cognitive Abilities, or Central Processing Hypothesis.) Specific issues related to transfer include the Linguistic Threshold Hypothesis and unique aspects of L2 reading. The Linguistic Threshold Hypothesis argues persuasively that a certain level of L2 linguistic knowledge is needed to support more fluent reading comprehension processes. Unique aspects of L2 reading include the extensive use of glosses while reading, the effort to carry out mental translations while reading, and the extensive use of bilingual dictionaries and guessing word meanings.

5   L2 reading is also distinct in that readers rely on a different combination of general background knowledge. Drawing on information about "how the world works" sometimes varies between L1 and L2 reading experiences.

6   Moreover, L2 readers will encounter distinct social and cultural assumptions in L2 texts that they may not be familiar with or find somewhat hard to accept. Certain types of inferencing that might be routine in L1 reading may not support comprehension processing in the L2, particularly in cases of engaging in reading for purposes of "reading to learn."

There has been a growing debate on the extent of the differences between L1 and L2 readers. Drawing on the arguments made by Bernhardt (2003, 2005), Koda (2005), Genesee et al. (2006), and Geva and Siegal (2000), a number of statements can be developed. First, beginning and intermediate L2 reading abilities are more distinct from L1 reading than advanced L2 reading abilities will be. As an L2 reader becomes fluent and highly skilled in reading comprehension, the reading processes involved become more similar (though perhaps never the same). Second, the linguistic differences between L1 and L2 (e.g., the linguistic differences between Spanish and English vs. the linguistic differences between Chinese and English) will have an impact on L2 reading. This impact of L1/L2 differences will diminish with increasing L2 reading proficiency (but will not disappear). Third, the extent of linguistic differences between L1 and L2 readers will be distinct for children learning to read in the L2 (emerging bilingual learners) and older L2 learners (adolescents and adults). The differences found between L1 and L2 reading will be larger for older learners. Fourth, L2 reading will require a foundation in L2 language skills and knowledge bases in order for higher-level L1 reading skills and strategies to transfer easily.

Finally, the underlying cognitive processes involved in L1 and L2 reading are generally the same. While there are clear and demonstrable differences between L1 and L2 reading among various groups of learners, overall patterns suggest that the underlying component skills are essentially the same (Geva & Siegal, 2000; Koda, 2007). Moreover, as L2 reading proficiency increases, the reading comprehension process looks increasingly similar. This increasing similarity is likely to be true for numerous reasons, including the following: greater amounts of reading practice and exposure to L2 print, more efficient combinations of strategic approaches to L2 reading in line with goals for reading, greater resource knowledge of the L2 and the social/cultural world of the L2, greater fluency and automaticity of L2 reading skills, recognition of successes in L2 reading, and an increasing willingness to read in the L2 for various purposes. One conclusion to be taken from this discussion of L1/L2 differences is that many if not most of the results of research on component skills that support reading comprehension will likely apply across L1 and L2 learner groups (except perhaps for beginning to low-intermediate readers).

L2 Reading Assessment

Discussions of language assessment of all types start with considerations about test validity. This chapter will assume that the concept of validity, or construct validity, is available for review through other sources. It is sufficient to note that validity is an extended argument from multiple perspectives (construct representation, reliability, comparative assessment, consequential impact, and usability) that persuasively argues for the appropriate and fair use of a test in a given context. In this section, I will assume that these principles should guide assessment activities.

In discussing reading assessment, one must decide if the discussion is to focus primarily on classroom assessment, informal assessment, and alternative assessment practices, or on standardized assessments. Classroom assessment of reading development has a much wider scope than standardized assessment options. In situations of formal comprehension assessment in the classroom, often as an achievement test, comprehension gains are assessed on a specific text or set of texts that has been recently taught. Classroom settings for reading assessment also include informal reading inventories or miscue analysis (reading aloud one-on-one with an evaluator who notes errors on a record sheet and then determines what progress a student has made or what instructional support is needed by the student).

The classroom context also allows for various types of alternative assessment options for determining student progress. In the classroom, one has the option of continuous ongoing assessment (quizzes, observations, record keeping of homework, interviews, progress charts, amount of reading, etc.). In such settings, almost any language task that is a teaching task can also be used as an assessment task. What might be lost in the way of relatively weak validity or consistency for any given reading task or measurement in the classroom setting is countered by the continual nature of assessment practices of all types. At the same time, teachers and administrators have a responsibility to develop appropriate tasks and appropriate interpretations of task outcomes so that students are not evaluated unfairly. For this reason, it is important to look at the types of tasks developed for more standardized reading tests and consider how these major tests incorporate and reflect the reading construct, and how they engage L2 learners in fair and appropriate assessment tasks (see Appendix).

Unfortunately, there are not many relevant, easily accessible, and useful classroom-based tests of English L2 reading abilities. This problem is clearly demonstrated by a recent review of L2 literacy development in US K-12 settings (August & Shanahan, 2006a). As the editors state, "The assessments cited in the research to gauge language-minority students' language proficiency and to make placement decisions are inadequate in most respects" (August & Shanahan, 2006b, p. 17). There is certainly a need for good, well-developed low- to medium-stakes reading tests that can be used in a variety of classroom contexts, that are graded for multiple proficiency levels, that are affordable, and that can support instructional decision-making.

In contrast to the more open classroom settings, standardized assessment practices are far more constrained by concerns of validity, reliability, time, cost, useability, and consequence. Most standardized tests attempt to establish a student's level of reading comprehension ability, either in relation to some set of criteria or in relation to a wider population. The time available for such an assessment is limited and the test must be fair and useful. These concerns strongly limit the types of reading assessment tasks that can be used. Until fairly recently, standardized L2 reading assessment has not been overly concerned with the development of reading assessment in terms of an evidence-based construct of reading abilities tied to the group of students being assessed. However, efforts to develop standardized reading tests in the past 15 years have focused much more explicitly on the construct of reading and claims that can be made for reading proficiency based on evidence from the test. There are a number of good examples of standardized assessments being developed from an initial set of claims about the nature of L2 reading ability and a set of tasks that would measure the relevant component skills.

The development of the IELTS (International English Language Testing System) represents one example of building a standardized test from construct assumptions and the gathering of appropriate evidence (Clapham, 1996). Similarly, the efforts to redesign the TOEFL have only recently (since 1995) been driven by the prior establishment of an appropriate L2 reading construct and evidence to support assessment tasks that would measure this construct (see Chapelle, Jamieson, & Enright, 2008). Additional approaches to L2 standardized assessment that are built from claims about reading abilities include the suite of Cambridge English proficiency exams (Weir & Milanovich, 2003) and the Advanced English Reading Test in China (Weir, Huizhong, & Yan, 2000). These approaches to L2 reading assessment strongly document arguments for an L2 reading construct, the importance of specific components of reading ability, the types of tasks that can assess these component abilities, and the creation of overall tests that generate evidence for the claims made (thus building a validity argument for the appropriateness of the test that has been developed).

Drawing on evidence from research on reading abilities to argue for a reading construct is one way in which reading assessment practices have improved. However, the relationship is reciprocal; it is also the case that careful reading assessment research has helped provide evidence for the component abilities central to L2 reading, as well. That is, the evidence provided from assessment research has influenced conceptualizations of component abilities underlying L2 reading comprehension.

For example, it is now clear from assessment research that L2 vocabulary knowledge is a powerful component of L2 reading abilities (Pike, 1979; Qian, 2002). Similarly, and perhaps more surprisingly for some, L2 grammar knowledge is a major component ability for L2 reading comprehension (Alderson, 2000; Enright et al., 2002; Pike, 1979). Appropriate reading strategies (as opposed to test-taking strategies) used in testing contexts also appear to be an important component of L2 reading abilities. While there is other compelling evidence for these components of L2 reading ability (as well as other components of reading ability), it is important to recognize that these component skills have also emerged from research on L2 reading tests.

L2 Implications for Reading Instruction and Assessment

Overall, the combination of research on L1 and L2 reading abilities suggests that there is a reasonably good set of implications for L2 reading instruction and assessment suggested by research results. Reading comprehension requires the following skills and knowledge resources:

1 The ability to decode graphic forms for efficient word recognition
2 The ability to access the meaning of a large number of words automatically
3 The ability to draw meaning from phrase- and clause-level grammatical information
4 The ability to combine clause-level meanings to build a larger network of meaning relations (comprehend the text)
5 The ability to recognize discourse-level relationships and use this information to build and support comprehension

6   The ability to use reading strategies with more difficult text and for a range of academic reading tasks
7   The ability to set goals for reading and adjust them as needed
8   The ability to use inferences of various types and to monitor comprehension in line with reading goals
9   The ability to draw on prior knowledge, as appropriate
10 Abilities to evaluate, integrate, and synthesize information from a text to form a situation model of comprehension (essentially what the reader learns from the text)
11 The ability to maintain these processes fluently for an extended period of time
12 The motivation to persist in reading and to use the text information appropriately in line with reader goals

In an ideal world, each of these implications from research would be subject to a set of instructional training studies and longitudinal development studies to determine the potential for turning implications into effective applications in the classroom. Once interesting applications are developed, it is important to determine the effectiveness of those applications more generally for the development of L2 reading abilities. Of course, we cannot wait for this ideal to be carried out because we need to improve L2 students' reading abilities at the present moment as best we can. Instructional practices, based on current evidence, need to be used in classrooms while additional evidence is gathered. The best that we can offer are practices that have been examined and found useful, and then teachers should draw on their expertise and experience to build the larger curriculum framework for effective teaching.

Teaching L2 Reading

The major argument of the chapter to this point is that a number of key reading subskills can be taught successfully, and further, that the learning of these subskills will contribute to a learner's reading comprehension abilities. How these skills should be taught most effectively is indicated to some extent by the research reviewed above. However, there are many instructional approaches that can potentially contribute to the development of reading abilities. While there is not yet extensive empirical research on the effectiveness of many practices, there is teaching expertise and experience which support these approaches until controlled evidence is collected and assessed. Quite a lot is already known about promising instructional practices. In some cases, we know that instructional activities carried out consistently have been useful with some groups of students and should be useful with a number of other student groups. We know that instructional activities which receive enough instructional time, intensity of effort, and priority in the curriculum can lead to significantly improved reading skills development. We know that students respond well to a number of instructional activities that improve reading skills. We can build on these starting points while additional research is being carried out.

The goal for reading instruction, at a general level, is to incorporate key component skills and knowledge into a reading curriculum. Specific instructional activities included in the curriculum follow from the major themes developed earlier in the article and the resulting implications. To describe how to carry out each suggestion would amount to multiple teaching-instruction handbooks, a task that goes far beyond the scope of the present chapter. More generally, good suggestions and examples for many of the issues described here can be found in a number of good reading textbook sets (e.g., Anderson, 2003; Blanchard & Root, 2007; Silberstein, Dobson, & Clarke, 2002; for many good instructional examples). What can be offered in this chapter is a set of more general curricular principles when building a reading curriculum and rethinking instructional practices. These principles include:

1   A curricular framework for conceptualizing L2 reading instruction that should integrate major skills instruction with extensive practice and exposure to print (building upon a needs analysis, goals and objectives for teaching and testing, attractive and plentiful resources, appropriate curriculum framework, effective teacher support, effective teaching materials and resources).
2   Reading materials and resources that need to be interesting, varied, good-looking, abundant, accessible, and well-used.
3   Some degree of student choice along the way in selecting major reading sources.
4   Reading skills that are introduced and taught by examining the primary texts used in the reading course. There should not be a need for special materials to introduce reading skills (though additional activities for further practice are necessary). If skills are meant to help comprehension, they should help with comprehension of the major texts being read in a class. This link between skills and instructional texts also raises metalinguistic awareness of how texts are put together linguistically.
5   Lessons that are structured around pre-reading, during-reading, and post-reading activities, and these activities should be varied from one major reading to the next.
6   Instruction that is built on an integrated curriculum framework and can support the following developmental goals:
    (a)   Promote word-recognition skills
    (b)   Build a large recognition vocabulary
    (c)   Practice comprehension skills that combine awareness of grammar, main idea identification, and comprehension strategies: strategy instruction is not separate from text comprehension instruction
    (d)   Build awareness of discourse structure (recognize main ideas, recognize major organizing patterns, recognize how the information is organized in parts of the text, recognize overt signals of text structure, recognize anaphoric relations in texts, recognize other cohesive markers in texts)
    (e)   Promote strategic reading
    (f)   Practice reading fluency (build reading rate, build text passage reading fluency, read and reread at home with parent or tape or self)

   (g)   Develop extensive reading
   (h)   Develop motivation
   (i)   Combine language learning with content learning
7   Opportunities for students to experience comprehension success while reading.
8   Expectations that reading occurs in class every day and that many extended
    reading opportunities are provided on a regular basis.

Testing L2 Reading

Carrying out appropriate reading assessments also requires a translation from
"implications from research," as well as an effort to consider useful applications
directly from assessment research to realistic classroom situations. Again, a thorough set of practical recommendations and associated example activities is beyond the scope of this chapter. However, a number of good examples of reading
assessment tasks can be found in Alderson (2000), Hughes (2004), and Weir and
Milanovic (2003). It is also important to highlight two key concepts for reading
assessment. First, reading assessment tasks are a restricted purpose for reading.
The context for assessment itself precludes any strong assumption of a match to
authentic reading in the "real world." One consequence is that assessment tasks
do not need to be avoided or radically distorted because they are not the same as
reading in the real world. Realistic reading assessment tasks, as opposed to real
reading tasks, may be the better benchmark (see Alderson, 2000). Second, reading assessments need to take into account both students' proficiency levels and
students' ages. Tasks need to change to fit a given proficiency range and student
maturity level as part of an appropriate reading assessment battery.
   In closing the discussion of reading assessment, 10 recommendations for
good assessment practices are offered (though the list could easily include 20
recommendations):

1   Students should be tested on a range of relevant skills.
2   Students should be encouraged to read longer texts (for advanced assess-
    ment, 700–1,200 words, assuming 120–150 wpm).
3   Background knowledge influences all comprehension and needs to be ac-
    counted for in a positive way (multiple topics, multiple tasks, general topics,
    limited interdependence of items within some subset of tasks).
4   Group tasks might be used to engage discussions of reader interpretations of
    texts.
5   Extensive reading should not be discouraged by assessment procedures.
6   The importance of identification and fluency skills needs to be explored
    (reading word lists, oral reading for one minute, silent reading on computer,
    timed reading, assessment of rereading).
7   Tests might explore ways to assess synthesis skills, evaluation skills, strateg-
    ies, metacognitive knowledge, and skills monitoring (text monitoring while
    reading).

8   Reading might be tested within a content-focused battery (but item inter-dependence has to be a concern).

9   Tests might consider item types that take advantage of computer interfaces (e.g., allow a text to disappear after reading, use a few hypertext links in a test passage, combine information from multiple texts to complete a task).

10 Many skills might be measured usefully through informal assessment options in classroom contexts. What one loses in reliability and objective controls could be countered by the many formal and informal assessments that can be made in the classroom. (But informal assessment is not a substitute for more formal testing.)

Concluding Comments

There are a number of additional recommendations that can be made for building L2 reading instruction, planning effective multi-level reading curricula, developing appropriate assessment practices, and providing feedback on learning progress (assessment for learning). This article has sought to develop the foundation that leads to useful implications for reading instruction and assessment. It has also outlined a simple array of curricular guidelines for reading instruction and assessment practices that can be developed or adapted to a fairly wide range of L2 reading contexts. At the same time, a short article of this type can only begin to scratch the surface of the potential instructional and assessment options and variations that can help make a difference in reading success with L2 students. The key to these ongoing efforts is to continue exploring effective practices for reading instruction and tasks for reading assessment that are based on important and relevant reading research and persuasive instructional research.

Appendix: Reading Test Item Types (see Alderson, 2000; Hughes, 2004, and others)

The primary purpose of assessment is to collect information to make inferences about students' reading abilities.

1   Cloze formats
2   Gap-filling formats (a rational reason for selecting blanks)
3   Multiple-choice formats
4   Sentence completions
5   Matching (and multiple matching) techniques
6   Classification into groups
7   Text segment ordering
8   Dichotomous items (T/F, Y/N)
9   Editing formats
10 C-tests

11   Cloze elide formats (remove extra word)
12   Text gap formats (place a sentence in the appropriate text gap)
13   Short answer formats
14   Free recall formats
15   Summary formats (1 sentence, 2 sentences, 5–6 sentences)
16   Information transfer formats (graphs, tables, flowcharts, outlines, maps, etc.)
17   Choosing from a "heading bank" to label identified paragraphs
18   Portfolios
19   Project performance
20   Informal assessment methods
    (a)   Have students read aloud for the teacher/tester and make notes/ observations or use of checklist/note miscues on the text
    (b)   Have students read aloud in class
    (c)   Have a student read and then have a discussion on the text (one-on-one)
    (d)   Keep a record of student responses to questions in class after a reading
    (e)   Keep notes on student participation in class discussions on a reading
    (f)   Have students do think-alouds while reading (one-on-one)
    (g)   Have student keep diaries or reading journals
    (h)   Have students do book reports
    (i)   Have students recommend books
    (j)   Have students enact a scene/episode/event
    (k)   Keep charts of student readings
    (l)   Keep charts of reading rate growth
    (m)   Have students list words they want to know after reading and why
    (n)   Record how far a student gets on an extended reading task
    (o)   Observe what reading material is read during free reading or SSR
    (p)   Observe how much students spend time on task during free reading or SSR
    (q)   Note the uses of texts in a multi-step project and discuss
    (r)   Ask students about their reading progress
    (s)   Ask students about their goals for reading with various texts and tasks
    (t)   Have student do paired readings and observe
    (u)   Observe students reading with an audio tape
    (v)   Have students list strategies they have used while reading
    (w)   Have students explain why they gave their answers after or during a task

REFERENCES

Alderson, C. (2000). *Reading assessment*. New York: Cambridge University Press.
Anderson, N. (1999). *Exploring second language reading*. Boston: Heinle & Heinle.
Anderson, N. (2003). *Active skills for reading*, 4 vols. New York: Heinle & Heinle.

Anglin, J. (1993). *Vocabulary development: A morphological analysis.* Monographs of the Society for Research in Child Development 58, 10. Chicago: University of Chicago Press.

August, D. & Shanahan, T. (eds.) (2006a). *Developing literacy in second language learners.* Mahwah, NJ: Lawrence Erlbaum.

August, D. & Shanahan, T. (2006b). Introduction and methodology. In D. August & T. Shanahan (eds.), *Developing literacy in second language learners* (pp. 1–42). Mahwah, NJ: Lawrence Erlbaum.

Beck, I., Perfetti, C., & McKeown, M. (1982). Effects of long-term vocabulary instruction on lexical access and reading comprehension. *Journal of Educational Psychology* 74, 506–21.

Bernhardt, E. (2003). Challenges to reading research from a multilingual world. *Reading Research Quarterly* 38, 112–17.

Bernhardt, E. (2005). Progress and procrastination in second language reading. *Annual Review of Applied Linguistics* 25, 133–50.

Blanchard, K. & Root, C. (2007). *For your information: Reading and vocabulary skills,* 4 vols. New York: Pearson Longman.

Block, C. & Pressley, M. (eds.) (2002). *Comprehension instruction: Research-based best practices.* New York: Guilford Press.

Bowey, J. (2005). Predicting individual differences in learning to read. In M. Snowling & C. Hulme (eds.), *The science of reading: A handbook* (pp. 155–72). Malden, MA: Blackwell.

Breznitz, Z. (2006). *Fluency in reading.* Mahwah, NJ: Lawrence Erlbaum.

Cain, K., Oakhill, J., & Bryant, P. (2004). Children's reading comprehension ability: Concurrent prediction by working memory, verbal ability, and component skills. *Journal of Educational Psychology* 96, 31–42.

Carlisle, J. (2003). Morphology matters in learning to read: A commentary. *Reading Psychology* 24, 291–322.

Carlo, M., August, D., McLaughlin, B., Snow, C., Dressler, C., Lippman, D., Lively, T., & White, C. (2004). Closing the gap: Addressing the vocabulary needs of English-language learners in bilingual and mainstream classrooms. *Reading Research Quarterly* 39, 188–215.

Carrell, P. (1984). The effects of rhetorical organization on ESL readers. *TESOL Quarterly* 18, 441–69.

Carrell, P. (1985). Facilitating ESL reading by teaching text structure. *TESOL Quarterly* 19, 7272–752.

Chapelle, C., Jamieson, J., & Enright, M. (eds.) (2008). *Building a validity argument for the Test of English as Foreign Language.* Mahwah, NJ: Lawrence Erlbaum.

Chen, H.-C. & Graves, M. (1995). Effects of previewing and providing background knowledge on Taiwanese college students' comprehension of American short stories. *TESOL Quarterly* 29, 663–86.

Chow, B., McBride-Chang, C., & Burgess, S. (2005). Phonological processing skills and early reading abilities in Hong Kong Chinese kindergartners learning to read English as a second language. *Journal of Educational Psychology* 97, 81–7.

Clapham, C. (1996). *The development of IELTS: A study of the effects of background knowledge on reading comprehension.* Cambridge: Cambridge University Press.

Cook, V. & Bassetti, B. (2005a). An introduction to researching second language writing systems. In V. Cook & B. Bassetti (eds.), *Second language writing systems* (pp. 1–67). Buffalo, NY: Multilingual Matters.

Cook, V. & Bassetti, B. (eds.) (2005b). *Second language writing systems.* Buffalo, NY: Multilingual Matters.

Dressler, C. & Kamil, M. (2006). First- and second-language literacy. In D. August & T. Shanahan (eds.), *Developing literacy in second-language learners* (pp. 197–238). Mahwah, NJ: Lawrence Erlbaum.

Droop, M. & Verhoeven, L. (2003). Language proficiency and reading ability in first and second language learners. *Reading Research Quarterly* 38, 78–103.

Duke, N. & Pearson, P. D. (2002). Effective practices for developing reading comprehension. In A. Farstrup & S. Samuels (eds.), *What research has to say about reading instruction* (3rd edn., pp. 205–42). Newark, DE: International Reading Association.

Durgunoglu, A., Nagy, W., & Hancin-Bhatt, B. (1993). Cross-language transfer of phonological awareness. *Journal of Educational Psychology* 85, 453–65.

Ehri, L. (2006). Alphabetics instruction helps students learn to read. In R. M. Joshi & P. Aaron (eds.), *Handbook of orthography and literacy* (pp. 649–77). Mahwah, NJ: Lawrence Erlbaum.

Ehri, L., Nunes, S., Willows, D., Schuster, B., Yaghoub-Zadeh, Z., & Shanahan, T. (2001). Phonemic awareness instruction helps children learn to read: Evidence from the National Reading panel's meta-analysis. *Reading Research Quarterly* 36, 250–87.

Elley, W. (2000). The potential of book flooding for raising literacy levels. *International Review of Education* 46, 233–55.

Enright, M., Bridgeman, B., Cline, M., Eignor, D., Lee, Y. W., & Powers, D. (2002). Evaluating measures of communicative language abilities. Paper presented at annual TESOL Convention. Salt Lake City, UT, April.

Frost, R. (2005). Orthographic systems and skilled word recognition processes in reading. In M. Snowling & C. Hulme (eds.), *The science of reading: A handbook.* (pp. 272–95). Malden, MA: Blackwell.

Frost, R., Kugler, T., Deutsch, A., & Forster, K. (2005). Orthographic structure versus morphological structure: Principles of lexical organization in a given language. *Journal of Experimental Psychology: Learning, Memory, and Cognition* 31, 1293–1326.

Fuchs, L., Fuchs, D., Hosp, M., & Jenkins, J. (2001). Oral reading fluency as an indicator of reading competence: A theoretical, empirical, and historical analysis. *Scientific Studies of Reading* 5, 239–56.

Fukkink, R., Hulstijn, J., & Simis, A. (2005). Does training in second-language word recognition skills affect reading comprehension? An experimental study. *Modern Language Journal* 89, 54–75.

Garcia, G. (1998). Mexican-American bilingual students' metacognitive reading strategies: What's transferred, unique, problematic. *National Reading Conference Yearbook* 47, 253–63.

Genesee, F., Geva, E., Dressler, C., & Kamil, M. (2006). Synthesis: Cross-linguistic relationships. In D. August & T. Shanahan (eds.), *Developing literacy in second language learners* (pp. 153–74). Mahwah, NJ: Lawrence Erlbaum.

Georgiou, G., Parilla, R., & Kirby, J. (2006). Rapid naming speed components and early reading acquisition. *Scientific Studies of Reading* 10, 199–220.

Geva, E. & Siegal, L. (2000). Orthographic and cognitive factors in the concurrent development of basic reading skills in two languages. *Reading and Writing* 12, 1–30.

Geva, E. & Yaghoub Zadeh, Z. (2006). Reading efficiency in native English-speaking and English-as-a-second-language children: The role of oral proficiency and underlying cognitive-linguistic processes. *Scientific Studies of Reading* 10, 31–57.

Goldman, S. & Rakestraw, J. (2000). Structural aspects of constructing learning from text. In M. Kamil, P. Mosenthal, P. D. Pearson, & R. Barr (eds.), *Handbook of reading research*, vol. 3 (pp. 285–310). New York: Longman.

Gottardo, A., Yan, B., Siegal, L., & Wade-Woolley, L. (2001). Factors related to English reading performance in children with Chinese as a first language: More evidence of cross-language transfer of phonological processing. *Journal of Educational Psychology* 93, 530–42.

Grabe, W. (2004). Research on teaching reading. *Annual Review of Applied Linguistics* 24, 44–69.

Guthrie, J., Wigfield, A., Barbosa, P., Perencevich, K., Taboada, A., Davis, M., Scafiddi, N., & Tonks, S. (2004). Increasing reading comprehension and engagement through Concept-Oriented Reading Instruction. *Journal of Educational Psychology* 96, 403–23.

Guthrie, J., Wigfield, A., Metsala, J., & Cox, K. (1999). Motivational and cognitive predictors of text comprehension and reading amount. *Scientific Studies of Reading* 3, 231–56.

Guthrie, J., Wigfield, A., & Perencevich, K. (eds.) (2004). *Motivating reading comprehension: Concept-Oriented reading Instruction*. Mahwah, NJ: Lawrence Erlbaum.

Guthrie, J., Wigfield, A., & Von Secker, C. (2000). Effects of integrated instruction on motivation and strategy use in reading. *Journal of Educational Psychology* 92, 331–41.

He, Y., Wang, Q., & Anderson, R. (2005). Chinese children's use of subcharacter information about pronunciation. *Journal of Educational Psychology* 97, 572–79.

Horiba, Y. (1993). The role of causal reasoning and language competence in narrative comprehension. *Studies in Second Language Acquisition* 15, 49–81.

Hudson, T. (2007). *Teaching second language reading*. New York: Oxford University Press.

Hughes, A. (2004). *Testing for language teachers*, 2nd edn. New York: Cambridge University Press.

Jenkins, J., Fuchs, L., van den Broek, P., Espin, C., & Deno, S. (2003). Sources of individual differences in reading comprehension and reading fluency. *Journal of Educational Psychology* 95, 719–29.

Jiang, X., Sabatini, J., & Sawaki, Y. (2007). Efficiency and fluency in ELL reading comprehension. AERA annual conference, Chicago, IL. April.

Joshi, R. M. & Aaron, P. (eds.) (2006). *Handbook of orthography and literacy*. Mahwah, NJ: Lawrence Erlbaum.

Kahn-Horwitz, J., Shimron, J., & Sparks, R. (2005). Predicting foreign language reading achievement in elementary school students. *Reading and Writing* 18, 527–58.

Kern, R. G. (1994). The role of mental translation in second language reading. *Studies in Second Language Acquisition* 16, 441–61.

Klingner, J. & Vaughn, S. (2000). The helping behaviors of fifth graders while using collaborative strategic reading during ESL content classes. *TESOL Quarterly* 34, 69–98.

Koda, K. (2005). *Insights into second language reading*. New York: Cambridge University Press.

Koda, K. (2007). Reading and language learning: Crosslinguistic constraints on second language reading development. *Language Learning Supplement* 57, 1, 1–44.

Kroll, J., Michael, E., Tokowicz, N., & Dufour, R. (2002). The development of lexical fluency in a second language. *Second Language Research* 18, 137–71.

Landerl, K. & Thaler, V. (2006). Reading and spelling acquisition and dyslexia in German. In R. M. Joshi & P. G. Aaron (eds.), *Handbook of orthography and literacy* (pp. 121–34). Mahwah, NJ: Lawrence Erlbaum.

Lems, K. (2005). A study of adult ESL oral reading fluency and silent reading comprehension. In B. Maloch et al. (eds.), *54th Yearbook of the National Reading Conference* (pp. 240–56). Chicago, IL: National Reading Conference.

Lesaux, N., Koda, K., Siegal, L., & Shanahan, T. (2006). Development of literacy. In D. August & T. Shanahan (eds.), *Developing literacy in second-language learners* (pp. 75–122). Mahwah, NJ: Lawrence Erlbaum.

Lesaux, N., Lipka, O., & Siegal, L. (2006). Investigating cognitive and linguistics abilities that influence the reading comprehension skills of children from diverse linguistic backgrounds. *Reading and Writing* 19, 99–131.

Levy, B. (2001). Moving the bottom: Improving reading fluency. In M. Wolf (ed.), *Dyslexia, fluency, and the brain* (pp. 357–79). Timonium, MD: York Press.

Levy, B., Abello, B., & Lysynchuk, L. (1997). Transfer from word training to reading in context: Gains in reading fluency and comprehension. *Learning Disability Quarterly* 20, 173–88.

Lundberg, I. (1999). Learning to read in Scandinavia. In M. Harris & G. Hatano (eds.), *Learning to read and write: A cross-linguistic perspective* (pp. 157–72). New York: Cambridge University Press.

Martin-Chang, S. & Levy, B. (2006). Word reading fluency: A transfer appropriate processing account of fluency transfer. *Reading and Writing* 19, 517–42.

McBride-Chang, C., Cho, J.-R., Liu, H., et al. (2005). Changing models across cultures: Associations of phonological awareness and morphological structure awareness with vocabulary and word recognition in second graders from Beijing, Hong Kong, Korea, and the United States. *Journal of Experimental Child Psychology* 92, 140–60.

McKeown, M., Beck, I., Omanson, R., & Pople, M. (1985). Some effects of the nature and frequency of vocabulary instruction on the knowledge and use of words. *Reading Research Quarterly* 20, 522–35.

Mori, S. (2002). Redefining motivation to read in a foreign language. *Reading in a Foreign Language* 14, 91–110.

Nagy, W. (2005). Why vocabulary instruction needs to be long-term and comprehensive. In E. Hiebert & M. Kamil (eds.), *Teaching and learning vocabulary: Bringing research to practice* (pp. 27–44). Mahwah, NJ: Lawrence Erlbaum.

Nagy, W. & Anderson, C. R. (1984). How many words are there in printed school English? *Reading Research Quarterly* 19, 304–30.

Nagy, W., Berninger, V., Abbott, R., Vaughn, K., & Vermeulen, K. (2003). Relationship of morphology and other language skills to literacy skills in at-risk second-grade readers and at-risk fourth-grade writers. *Journal of Educational Psychology* 95, 730–42.

Nation, I. S. P. (2001). *Learning vocabulary in another language*. New York: Cambridge University Press.

Nation, K. (2005). Children's reading comprehension difficulties. In M. Snowling & C. Hulme (eds.), *The science of reading* (pp. 248–65). Malden, MA: Blackwell.

National Reading Panel (NRP) (2000). *Teaching children to read: An evidence based assessment of the scientific research literature on reading and its implications for reading instruction*. Washington, DC: National Institute of Child Health and Human Development.

Nicholson, T. & Ng, G. L. (2006). The case for teaching phonemic awareness and simple phonics to preschoolers. In R. M. Joshi & P. Aaron (eds.), *Handbook of orthography and literacy* (pp. 637–48). Mahwah, NJ: Lawrence Erlbaum.

Perfetti, C., Landi, N., & Oakhill, J. (2005). The acquisition of reading comprehension skill. In M. Snowling & C. Hulme (eds.), *The science of reading* (pp. 227–47). Malden, MA: Blackwell.

Perfetti, C. & Liu, Y. (2005). Orthography to phonology and meaning: Comparisons across and within writing systems. *Reading and Writing* 18, 193–210.

Pike, L. (1979). *An evaluation of alternative item formats for testing English as a second language*. TOEFL Research Reports, No. 2. Princeton, NJ: Educational Testing Service.

Pressley, M. (2006). *Reading instruction that works*, 3rd edn. New York: Guilford Press.

Proctor, C. P., Carlo, M., August, D., & Snow, C. (2005). Native Spanish-speaking children reading in English: Toward a model of comprehension. *Journal of Educational Psychology* 97, 246–56.

Qian, D. (2002). Investigating the relationship between vocabulary knowledge and academic reading performance: An assessment perspective. *Language Learning* 52, 513–36.

Rayner, K., Juhasz, B., & Pollatsek, A. (2005). Eye movements during reading. In M. Snowling & C. Hulme (eds.), *The science of reading* (pp. 79–97). Malden, MA: Blackwell.

Sabatini, J. (2002). Efficiency in word reading of adults: Ability group comparison. *Scientific Studies of Reading* 6, 267–98.

Samuels, S. (2006). Toward a model of reading fluency. In S. Samuels & A. Farstrup (eds.), *What research has to say about fluency instruction* (pp. 24–46). Newark, DE: International Reading Association.

Samuels & Farstrup (eds.) (2006). *What research has to say about fluency instruction*. Newark, DE: International Reading Association.

Sawaki, Y. & Sabatini, J. (2007). Reading efficiency and reading comprehension. Princeton, NJ: Educational Testing Service. Unpublished manuscript.

Schoonen, R., Hulstijn, J., & Bossers, B. (1998). Metacognitive and language-specific knowledge in native and foreign language reading comprehension: An empirical study among Dutch students in grades 6, 8, and 10. *Language Learning* 48, 71–106.

Sénéchal, M. (2006). Testing the home literacy model: Parent involvement is differentially related to grade 4 reading comprehension, fluency, spelling, and reading for pleasure. *Scientific Studies of Reading* 10, 59–88.

Silberstein, S., Dobson, B., & Clarke, M. (2002). *Reader's choice*, 4th edn. Ann Arbor, MI: University of Michigan Press.

Stahl, S. & Heubach, A. (2005). Fluency-oriented reading instruction. *Journal of Literacy Research* 37, 25–60.

Stahl, S. & Nagy, W. (2006). *Teaching word meanings*. Mahwah, NJ: Lawrence Erlbaum.

Stanovich, K. (2000). *Progress in understanding reading: Scientific foundations and new frontiers*. New York: Guilford Press.

Taguchi, E., Takayasu-Maass, M., & Gorsuch, G. (2004). Developing reading fluency in EFL: How assisted repeated reading and extensive reading affect fluency development. *Reading in a Foreign Language* 16, 2, 70–96.

Tan, A. & Nicholson, T. (1997). Flashcards revisited: Training poor readers to read words faster improves their comprehension of texts. *Journal of Educational Psychology* 89, 276–88.

Tang, G. (1992). The effect of graphic representation of knowledge structures on ESL reading comprehension. *Studies in Second Language Acquisition* 14, 177–95.

Tannenbaum, K., Torgesen, J., & Wagner, R. (2006). Relationships between word knowledge and reading comprehension in third-grade children. *Scientific Studies of Reading* 10, 381–98.

Taylor, A., Stevens, J., & Asher, J. W. (2006). The effects of explicit reading strategy training on L2 reading comprehension. In J. Norris & L. Ortega (eds.), *Synthesizing research on language learning and teaching* (pp. 213–44). Philadelphia: John Benjamins.

Trabasso, T. & Bouchard, E. (2002). Teaching readers how to comprehend texts strategically. In C. Block & M. Pressley (eds.), *Comprehension instruction: Research-based best practices* (pp. 176–200). New York: Guilford Press.

Tunmer, W. & Chapman, J. (2006). Beginning reading development. In R. M. Joshi & P. Aaron (eds.), *Handbook of orthography and literacy* (pp. 617–35). Mahwah, NJ: Lawrence Erlbaum.

Van Gelderen, A., Schoonen, R., de Glopper, K., et al. (2004). Linguistic knowledge, processing speed, and metacognitive knowledge in first- and second-language reading comprehension: A componential analysis. *Journal of Educational Psychology* 96, 19–30.

Wagner, R., Piasta, S., & Torgesen, J. (2006). Learning to read. In R. Traxler & M. Gernsbacher (eds.), *Handbook of psycholinguistics* (2nd edn., pp. 1111–42). San Diego, CA: Academic Press.

Walczyk, J., Kelly, K., Meche, S., & Braud, H. (1999). Time limitations enhance reading comprehension. *Contemporary Educational Psychology* 24, 156–65.

Weir, C. & Milanovich, M. (2003). *Continuity and innovation: Revising the Cambridge proficiency in English examination 1913–2002,* Studies in Language Testing 15. Cambridge: Cambridge University Press.

Weir, C., Huizhong, Y., & Yan, J. (2000). *An empirical investigation of the componentiality of L2 reading in English for academic purposes,* Studies in Language Testing 12. Cambridge: Cambridge University Press.

25 Learning to Read in New Writing Systems

KEIKO KODA

Reading development builds on spoken language competence. In all languages, learning to read inevitably requires learning to map graphic symbols onto the spoken language elements they represent. Understanding how one's writing system functions thus is vital in literacy learning and processing. In second-language reading, these mappings are more complex since they involve two sets of languages and writing systems. The complexity is further compounded by the diversity of second-language learners because literacy learning commences at different ages and under different circumstances. Hence, second-language learners' cognitive and linguistic resources vary considerably more than beginning first-language readers. In conceptualizing second-language reading development, such diversities – together with the dual-language involvement – must be incorporated. Consequently, the primary goals of this chapter are threefold: (1) to describe how knowledge of the writing system contributes to literacy learning; (2) to examine how this knowledge evolves; and (3) to explore how the knowledge acquired in one language affects learning to read in another. Since reading is a multi-faceted pursuit, consisting of a large number of operations and processing skills, clarifying the scope of the analysis is essential. The chapter, therefore, opens with brief descriptions of relevant terms and constructs.

Basic Concepts and Constructs

Learning to read

According to the Simple View of Reading (Gough & Tunmer, 1986; Hoover & Gough, 1990), learning to read entails the mastery of two basic operations – *decoding* and *comprehension*, which are acquired at disparate rates through separate channels. In this formulation, *decoding* refers to the extraction of phonological and morphological information from visual word displays, and *comprehension* to text meaning construction based on the extracted information. Obviously, *decoding* is unique to reading, while *comprehension* is shared, as a common element, in reading and listening. This implies that children amass comprehension skills through listening in the course of oral language development prior to formal literacy instruction. By the time they begin to read, their comprehension ability, in most instances, is already well developed. In principle, therefore, children should be able to utilize their comprehension ability acquired through listening, when learning to read. In reality, however, they rarely do so because they cannot connect graphic displays with their oral language vocabulary and other stored information. In order to exploit the previously acquired linguistic knowledge and comprehension skills in learning to read, they need to attain sufficient decoding competence. Unlike comprehension ability, however, decoding skills do not evolve as a corollary of oral language development. Their acquisition necessitates substantial print input and exposure. For these reasons, it is commonly accepted that learning to read essentially implies decoding skills development. Consequently, the current analysis focuses on the acquisition of decoding, or print information extraction, skills.

Writing system, orthography, and script

Following Coulmas (2003), the term *writing system* is used in this chapter in reference to both the writing system of a language and an abstract type of writing system. In the latter sense, writing systems can be classified into three types: alphabetic, syllabic, and logographic. In the alphabetic system, each symbol represents a phoneme, while, in the syllabary, individual symbols denote distinct syllables. In contrast, a logographic character corresponds holistically with the meaning and sound of an entire morpheme. Within each system, considerable variations exist in the specific details in which graphic symbols are physically placed in forming words. *Orthography* refers to these language-specific details, and has been defined as "the standardized variety of a given, language-specific, writing system" (Coulmas, 2003, p. 35). Finally, the term *script* refers to the graphic form of the symbols of a writing system. To illustrate, English and Russian writing systems are both alphabetic, but they differ in their scripts – the former employs the Roman script and the latter uses the Cyrillic. Further, English and Spanish are alphabetic, both employing the Roman script, but they differ orthographically in spelling conventions.

Inasmuch as learning to read entails uncovering how language elements correspond to graphic symbols, its learning process is directly affected by the *orthographic* properties of the writing system in which literacy is learned, and the resulting competencies reflect the precise way in which language elements are graphically encoded. As an illustration, Korean and Hebrew writing systems are both alphabetic, but their orthographic properties differ considerably from each other. The Korean Hangul, for example, consists of 24 basic symbols, each representing a single phoneme – either a vowel or a consonant. Unlike English, however, the Korean symbols do not appear individually; rather, they are always packaged into square blocks, representing distinct syllables. Reflecting this dual-level representation, Korean children exhibit strong sensitivity to both syllables and phonemes (Cho & McBride-Chang, 2005). In contrast, the Hebrew symbols represent only consonant phonemes (Frost & Bentin, 1992; Shimron, 2006). Hebrew vowels are shown in the form of dots and dashes, and placed below, above or to the left of symbols. In the consonantal Hebrew, consequently, children develop stronger sensitivity to consonants than vowels (Geva, 2008). It order to understand the long-term consequence of literacy experience in a particular language for learning to read in another, it is critical to clarify, through careful analysis, the *orthographic* properties of the writing systems involved.

Second-language readers

Second-language reading encompasses several distinct "reader" groups, because, unlike first-language reading, it commences at different ages and occurs under diverse circumstances. Several distinct "reader" groups, for example, include preschool children learning to read without prior literacy experience, school-age children at disparate stages of literacy development in their first language, and adult learners fully literate in their first language. Four factors are particularly pertinent to second-language reader categorizations: (1) age at which second-language literacy learning commences; (2) attainment level of first-language (or any prior) literacy; (3) second-language proficiency – vocabulary knowledge, in particular; and (4) amounts of second-language print input and exposure. These factors collectively determine the cognitive and linguistic resources available to a particular group of readers at the onset of second-language literacy learning. Each of the factors, moreover, interacts with contextual variations relating to "where," "how," and "why" second-language literacy is being pursued. For example, the learning experience of six-year old native Korean children acquiring reading skills in English as a second language in an American public school is strikingly different from that of native English-speaking students taking an elementary Chinese course to fulfill a foreign-language requirement in an American university. Hence, it is critical to take into account these and other variables when comparing and synthesizing empirical findings across studies involving diverse groups of second-language readers.

The Mechanism of Transfer

Second-language reading is unique in that it involves two languages in its operations. To understand its development, therefore, it is necessary to consider what "involving" two languages means; how the dual-language involvement affects learning to read in a second language; and how the aggregated impacts can be empirically examined. Cross-language transfer is central to the current analysis because it clarifies how performance variations among second-language readers relate to their first-language learning-to-read experiences. Although transfer has long been a major theoretical concept in second-language research, there is little consensus as to what constitutes transfer, how it occurs, and how it affects second-language learning.

Traditionally, transfer has been viewed as a learner's reliance on first-language knowledge. Krashen (1983), for example, regards transfer as the resultant state stemming from the learner's falling back on old knowledge, or first-language rules, when new knowledge is not yet sufficiently developed. Gass and Selinker (1983) offer a similar, but somewhat more refined, view: "the learner is transferring prior linguistic knowledge resulting in IL (interlanguage) forms which, when compared by the researchers to the target language norms, can be termed 'positive,' 'negative,' or 'neutral" (p. 6). Odlin (1989) reinforces the general thrust of this notion by stating, "transfer is the influence from similarities and differences between the target language and any other language that has been previously (and perhaps imperfectly) acquired" (p. 27). These views of transfer share two implicit assumptions. First, what is transferred is linguistic knowledge, conceived as a set of rules. Second, the reliance on first-language knowledge is, more or less, associated with an inadequate grasp of second-language rules. Consequently, these views further presume that transfer tends to cease when second-language linguistic knowledge has developed and, more critically, that once sufficient proficiency is attained, first-language knowledge plays no role in explaining individual differences in second-language linguistic knowledge.

These contentions, nonetheless, are no longer uniformly endorsed. As a case in point, in functionalist theories, language is viewed as a set of relations between forms and functions (Van Valin, 1991), and its acquisition as the process of internalizing form–function relationships through cumulative use of language in communication (MacWhinney & Bates, 1989). Hence, the functionalist view contends that language learning is driven by the functional contribution of linguistic forms in communication, and in so doing, explains why systematic variations occur in the internalized relationships across languages and learners within a single language. Under the functionalist suppositions, then, what is transferred should be the internalized form–function relationships and their mapping skills, rather than a set of fixed rules, as traditionally conceived.

The functionalist view alone, however, does not adequately explain how recurring patterns of form–function correspondences are detected, abstracted, and internalized. An additional theory is necessary to clarify how mapping patterns emerge through communicative use of language. Since learning to read involves establishing mapping patterns between language elements and graphic symbols, such clarification is equally useful in conceptualizing how orthographic knowledge develops in a particular language. By extension, moreover, second-language learning to read can also be regarded as the process of forming additional sets of sound–symbol, as well as morpheme–symbol, mappings in a new language. The clarification should also be vital in conceptualizing how previously established mapping patterns alter the formation of new mapping patterns.

Connectionism is one such theory, offering plausible explanations of how form–function relationships emerge. Its main contention is that the internalization of such relationships occurs through cumulative mappings experience. The more frequently particular patterns of mappings are experienced, the stronger the links holding the elements to be mapped together. As such, the theory describes knowledge acquisition as a gradual transition from deliberate efforts to automatic execution, rather than an all-or-nothing process. It also views knowledge as a dynamic, ever-changing state, rather than a static entity. Hence, in this theory, input frequency is a key determinant of "acquisition" because "rules of language, at all processing levels, are structural regularities evolving from learners' lifetime analysis of the distributional characteristics of the language input" (Ellis, 2002, p. 144). It should be underscored, moreover, that connectionism makes no distinction between language learning and other domains of learning, nor between knowledge acquisition and skills development. Consequently, the internalization of a particular form–function relationship can be recognized as such when the mapping becomes "automated" – that is, non-deliberate, non-volitional, activation initiated through input (Logan, 1988).

Building on these contentions, transfer is operationally defined as an automatic activation of well-established mapping skills in the first language, triggered by second-language input. Although this definition is restrictive in that it limits the scope to the operations wherein automaticity is attainable, such restriction is necessary in order to address a range of critical issues in a theoretically coherent fashion. This view of transfer makes several specific predictions. First, for transfer to occur, the competencies to be transferred must be well rehearsed – to the point of automaticity – in the first language. Second, transfer is not likely to cease at any given point in second-language development. Third, transferred competencies will continuously mature through processing experience with second-language input. Evidently, these predictions are distinct from those underlying the earlier views of transfer. Finally, the automatic activation implies that previously established first-language mapping patterns operate during second-language input processing – irrespective of a learner's intent, first-language background, and second-language proficiency. This, in turn, suggests that transferred first-language skills facilitate second-language reading acquisition to the extent that the two writing systems involved impose similar processing requirements. It is important, therefore, to be clear about differences and similarities in the learning-to-read requirements in diverse languages. In this regard, the notion of reading universals is essential, because it offers a conceptual base for identifying and comparing such requirements across languages and writing systems.

Reading Universals

According to the universal grammar of reading by Perfetti and associates (Perfetti, 2003; Perfetti & Dunlap, 2008; Perfetti & Liu, 2005), reading is a dynamic pursuit embedded in two interrelated systems: language and writing system. Inevitably, reading acquisition requires a linkage of the two, entailing mapping between spoken language elements and graphic symbols (e.g., Fowler & Liberman, 1995; Goswami & Bryant, 1990; Nagy & Anderson, 1999). In learning to read, therefore, children must first recognize which language elements are directly encoded in the writing system (the general mapping principle), and then deduce precisely how these elements are encoded (the mapping details). For example, children learning to read English must first understand that each letter represents a distinct sound (the alphabetic principle), and then gradually work out the details of sound–symbol correspondences (the mapping details) through repeated print decoding and encoding experience.

To successfully grasp general mapping principles, children in all languages must gain several basic insights: that print relates to speech; that speech can be segmented into a sequence of sounds; and, most critically, that these segmented sounds systematically relate to the graphic symbols in the writing system. Since these insights do not involve language-specific details, once they are developed in one language, they should be readily available and fully functional in subsequent literacy learning in another language. This, however, is not necessarily the case for mapping details, because their acquisition requires substantial print input and experience, and therefore, the acquired mapping details should vary systematically in diverse languages to the extent that their orthographic properties deviate. What is common across languages in the latter task lies only in the task itself. Prior experience fosters an explicit understanding of what is to be accomplished in the task, and this, in turn, can expedite the process by allowing learners to be more reflective and strategic.

The clear implication is that second-language learning to read is a repeated process to the extent that the literacy experiences in the two languages involved are similar. Such similarities should allow second-language learners to exploit the resources accumulated through prior literacy learning usefully, thereby accelerating second-language reading development. Thus, in essence, the concept of reading universals, properly incorporated, significantly contributes to theories of reading transfer by providing a basis for conceptualizing the specific facilitation stemming from prior literacy experience.

Metalinguistic Awareness

Of late, interest in metalinguistic awareness has risen sharply among reading researchers. Metalinguistic awareness is a multi-dimensional construct, and its facets can be defined in conjunction with various structural features of language (e.g., Adams, 1990; Stahl & Murray, 1994; Yopp, 1988). Bialystok (2001) describes metalinguistic awareness as an explicit representation of "the abstract structure that organizes sets of linguistic rules without being directly instantiated in any of them" (2001, p. 123). Although such insights evolve through the result of learning and using a particular language, metalinguistic awareness is distinct from linguistic knowledge in that it implies an understanding of language in its most fundamental and generalized properties, independent of surface form variations. For example, among English-speaking children, syntactic awareness reflects the realization that the order in which words are presented determines sentence meaning. An abstract notion of this sort contrasts with a more specific knowledge of the canonical word order (subject-verb-object) in English sentences. The logical question then is how metalinguistic awareness facilitates literacy learning and processing.

Roles of metalinguistic awareness in learning to read

As noted repeatedly, reading is embedded in spoken language and writing system, and its acquisition entails making links between the two. Accordingly, the present consensus is that learning to read is fundamentally metalinguistic because it necessitates an understanding of how spoken language elements are partitioned and mapped onto graphic symbols (e.g., Fowler & Liberman, 1995; Goswami & Bryant, 1990; Kuo & Anderson, in press; Nagy & Anderson, 1999). Since the primary unit of the mappings is either phonology or morphology, two specific facets are of vital significance for learning to read in any language: grapho-phonological (i.e., recognizing the relationship between graphic symbols and speech sounds), and grapho-morphological (i.e., recognizing the relationship between graphic symbols and morphological elements).

The role of metalinguistic awareness in literacy learning in English has been extensively studied over the past two decades. Evidence from research focusing on phonological awareness has led to the widely endorsed conviction that to master an alphabetic script, children must not only recognize that words can be divided into sequences of phonemes, but also acquire the ability to analyze a word's internal structure in order to identify its phonemic constituents. Early reading studies, in fact, show that children's sensitivity to the phonological structure of spoken words is directly related to their ability to read and spell words (e.g., Stahl & Murray, 1994; Stanovich, 2000; Stanovich, Cunningham, & Cramer, 1984; Yopp, 1988); phonological segmentation capability is a powerful predictor of reading success among early- and middle-grade students (e.g., Bryant, MacLean, & Bradley, 1990; Juel, Griffith, & Gough, 1986); and reading progress is significantly enhanced by phonological awareness training (e.g., Bradley & Bryant, 1991). Phonological deficits, moreover, are a common attribute of weak readers in typologically diverse languages, including Arabic (e.g., Abu Rabia, 1995), Portuguese (Da Fontoura & Siegel, 1995), Chinese (e.g., So & Siegel, 1997; Zhang & Perfetti, 1993), and Japanese (Kuhara-Kojima et al., 1996).

Contributions of morphological awareness to reading development have also been examined. It has been found that the ability to segment a word into its morphological constituents is a reliable predictor of reading achievement, independent of phonological awareness (e.g., Carlisle, 1995; Carlisle & Nomanbhoy, 1993; Fowler & Liberman, 1995); considerably more omissions of inflectional and derivational morphemes occur in the writing and speaking of less skilled readers (e.g., Duques, 1989; Henderson & Shores, 1982; Rubin, 1991); and ability to use morphological information during sentence comprehension distinguishes skilled from less-skilled high school readers (e.g., Tyler & Nagy, 1989, 1990). Reflecting its multidimensionality, morphological awareness evolves gradually over time, as its diverse facets mature according to their own timetables. As an illustration,

native English-speaking children are sensitized to inflectional morphemes in structurally transparent words well before schooling (Berko, 1958; Carlisle, 2003),
but the productive use of inflectional information does not occur until grade two
or three (Bear et al., 1996). The awareness of derivational morphemes is a late-
developing facet, emerging between Grades four and eight (Ku & Anderson, 2003;
Tyler & Nagy, 1989, 1990). Similar developmental disparities have been reported in
studies investigating morphological awareness among native Chinese-speaking
children (Ku & Anderson, 2003; Shu & Anderson, 1999). Viewed collectively,
findings from both phonological and morphological awareness studies make it
plain that metalinguistic insights facilitate the initial stages of literacy learning –
decoding development, in particular – in several distinct ways.

Cross-linguistic variations in metalinguistic awareness

Certain basic aspects of metalinguistic insights are prerequisites to reading acquisition, enabling children to initiate the critical task of linking spoken language
elements and graphic symbols. It is important to note, however, that the relationship between literacy and metalinguistic awareness is reciprocal, mutually
enhancing their development. Typically, children form sensitivity to structural
regularities of the language they are acquiring well before formal literacy instruction commences (MacWhinney, 1987; Slobin, 1985). While the early phases of
literacy acquisition are dependent on this rudimentary understanding, acquired
during oral language development, such sensitivity is progressively refined, and
gradually becomes explicit through print decoding and encoding experience (e.g.,
Bowey & Francis, 1991; Perfetti et al., 1987; Vellutino & Scanlon, 1987). Hence, the
ultimate form of metalinguistic awareness is an outcome of literacy, reflecting the
specific ways in which language elements are graphically encoded. Two implications arise from this developmental interface: (1) the facets of metalinguistic awareness underlying efficient print information extraction are closely allied with the
orthographic properties of the language in which literacy is learned; and (2)
lexical information – both phonological and morphological – is accessed through
orthographic knowledge, and so the information extraction skills are also shaped
to accommodate the language-specific orthographic properties. It seems reasonable to suggest, therefore, that literacy learning in diverse languages involves
distinct facets of metalinguistic awareness. In fact, reflecting the prominence of
grapheme–morpheme connections in Chinese characters, morphological awareness has been reported to be a stronger predictor than phonological awareness of
literacy acquisition in Chinese (Ku & Anderson, 2003; Li et al., 2002).

Conceptualizing Second Language Learning to Read: The Framework

The above analysis has demonstrated that (1) learning to read in all languages is
governed by the same set of universal principles, uniformly requiring a linkage

between a spoken language and the writing system; (2) metalinguistic awareness provides substantial facilitation in such linkage building; (3) metalinguistic awareness and subsequent decoding skills evolve gradually through print processing experience; and, most critically, (4) once developed, these literacy capabilities transfer across languages. Moreover, transfer is viewed as automatic activation of well-established first-language competencies triggered by second-language print input. As such, transfer is neither selective nor volitional, and occurs in all available competencies. Consequently, this view presumes that transfer does not cease at any given point in second-language reading development. Instead, transferred competencies continue to evolve through second-language print-processing experience, making incessant adjustments in accommodating the second-language orthographic properties. Thus, in short, three factors are critical in explaining possible variances in second-language reading development: (1) first-language competencies; (2) second-language print input, and (3) their interactions. The sections that follow provide brief explanations of how these factors jointly shape second-language reading sub-skills.

Universal underpinnings

In all languages, the initial learning-to-read task relies on non-language-specific metalinguistic insights shared across languages. When transferred, these insights should provide direct and equal facilitation for all learners regardless of their first-language background, guiding the process of learning the general mapping principle. Since underdeveloped capabilities are not likely to transfer, first-language literacy attainment, as a reliable indicator of the availability of the requisite metalinguistic capabilities, should serve as a strong predictor of initial reading development in a second language. It can be hypothesized, therefore, that first-language metalinguistic awareness – phonological awareness, in particular – systematically relates to second-language phonological awareness, as well as second-language decoding competence.

Shared metalinguistic foundations

Beyond the initial phase, however, learning the mapping details in a second language requires metalinguistic facets closely attuned to the second-language orthographic properties. First-language metalinguistic awarenesses are presumably available in this phase, as well. However, since they have been developed specifically in relation to the first language, they are not as serviceable as the non-language-specific facets underlying the general mapping principle. What is common across languages in this task lies only in the task itself. Prior experience fosters an explicit understanding of what is to be accomplished in the task, which, in turn, expedites the learning process by allowing learners to be more reflective and strategic. As such, the transferred awareness should offer useful top-down assistance by guiding the process of uncovering the specific ways in which language elements correspond with graphic symbols in the new writing system.

With such assistance, the task becomes more deductive in a second language, requiring less input for its completion than that required in the first language. Hence, it can also be hypothesized that first-language metalinguistic sophistication is a reliable predictor of the rapidity with which corresponding second-language metalinguistic awareness develops.

Orthographic distance

Since differences between the orthographic properties of the writing systems involved vary considerably among disparate learners (e.g., Spanish learners of English vs. Chinese learners of English), such variance also must be taken into consideration. When the method of representing specific linguistic information is similar across writing systems, information-extraction procedures are likely to be equally analogous, if not identical. Thus, transferred metalinguistic capabilities should provide substantial facilitation in second-language print-information extraction. The direct implication is that, when the two systems share similar orthographic properties, transferred competencies require minimal input and processing experience in a new language for fine-tuning. Consequently, a third hypothesis can be formulated: The orthographic distance between the two writing systems explains the differential rates at which second-language metalinguistic awareness and decoding skills develop among learners from diverse first-language backgrounds.

Second-language print input

Since the formation of language-specific awareness facets entails the detection of recurring grapheme–phoneme, and grapheme–morpheme, correspondences, it requires substantially more input than the non-language-specific facets underlying the general mapping principle. Therefore, amounts of second-language print input and experience are a dominant factor shaping second-language metalinguistic awareness and subsequent decoding skills. In particular, input frequency essentially determines the rate at which language-specific mapping patterns are internalized. Input regularity is also a key variable. Since linkage building is easier when the elements to be linked have regular, one-to-one, correspondences, regularity determines the ease with which mapping patterns are detected and abstracted. It can be hypothesized, therefore, that both quality and quantity of second-language print input are responsible, in large part, for determining ultimate attainment of second-language metalinguistic awareness and decoding competencies.

Cross-linguistic variation

To recapitulate, second-language competencies are shaped through continuous interaction between transferred first-language capabilities and second-language print input. Such cross-linguistic interplay typically induces sustained assimilation of processing experiences in both languages. Hence, the final hypothesis is that the resulting second-language metalinguistic awareness and decoding skills reflect both first- and second-language orthographic properties, and vary systematically across learners with diverse first-language backgrounds.

Although these hypotheses have yet to be tested empirically, preliminary evaluations of their predictive validity can be performed through systematic reviews of empirical findings from studies involving diverse groups of second-language readers. The subsequent section discusses relevant study findings and their collective implications.

Second-Language Learning to Read: Empirical Studies

Universal underpinnings

In view of the irrefutable contributions of phonological awareness in early reading development, the question is to what extent this awareness facilitates second-language learning to read, particularly among school-age learners. Phonological awareness is a by-product of a child's growing understanding of the segmental nature of spoken words. This fundamental realization precedes and supports reading acquisition, serving as a basis for symbol-to-sound mappings in typologically diverse languages, including logographic Chinese (Ho & Bryant, 1999; Li et al., 2002). Since the concept of word segmentation is not language specific, once developed in a language, it can facilitate learning to read in another, irrespective of their orthographic distance. Hence, in principle, the initial stage of second-language reading development among young learners, as in first-language literacy acquisition, relies heavily on phonological awareness.

Earlier studies of second-language phonological awareness focused on the extent to which this construct related to decoding ability among school-age learners. Cisero, Carlo, and Royer (1992), for example, contrasted English monolingual and Spanish-dominant, bilingual, first-grade, children in phoneme-detection performance, and concluded that in both groups, competent readers were superior in phonemic analysis to their less competent counterparts. In a subsequent study involving Spanish-dominant bilingual first graders, Durgunoglu, Nagy, and Hancin-Bhatt (1993) determined that first-language phonological awareness is a powerful predictor of word-recognition skills in both languages. These studies thus extended the widely accepted first-language research conclusions to bilingual populations. The Durgunoglu et al. study, moreover, highlights a strong possibility that phonological awareness developed in one language can enhance literacy learning in another.

More recent studies, employing a large battery of tasks in both first and second languages, concentrated on the inter-lingual connections in phonological awareness and decoding skills. Collectively, their findings suggest that significant relationships exist in phonological awareness; poor readers are uniformly weak in phonological skills in both languages; their deficiencies are usually "domain-specific" and not primarily attributable to non-phonological factors (e.g., Abu-Rabia, 1995; August, Calderon, & Carlo, 2001; Carlisle & Beeman, 2000; Cormier & Kelson, 2000; Gholamain & Geva, 1999; Verhoeven, 2000; Wade-Woolley & Geva, 2000). Given that phonological awarenesses in bilingual learners' two languages are closely related regardless of orthographic distance, one might question whether this awareness is shaped separately in each language or shared across languages as a general unitary ability. The question has been empirically addressed in a large-scale study involving 812 Spanish-English bilingual kindergarten children (Branum-Martin et al., 2006). The researchers measured phonological awareness using multiple tasks in the two languages. Their data demonstrated that task performances were strongly related across both tasks and languages, thus suggesting considerable overlap in this construct between the two Roman-alphabetic languages.

Viewed collectively, the currently available findings have shown that phonological awareness plays an equally vital role in first- and second-language learning to read among young learners. Even more significantly, phonological awarenesses in the children's two languages are closely interconnected. However, the extent to which such interconnections result from the commonalty of alphabetic scripts involved in most of the studies on record is not yet clear. On the one hand, we can speculate that cross-linguistic connections are reduced when learners deal with two orthographically unrelated languages, while, on the other, it seems equally plausible that strong inter-lingual connections remain – regardless of orthographic distance – because the basic facet of phonological awareness, prerequisite to literacy acquisition, does not vary from language to language. Seemingly, strong cross-linguistic relations in phonological awareness reported in recent studies involving bilingual children in two orthographically distant languages, Chinese and English (Bialystok, McBride-Chang, & Luk, 2005; Wang, Perfetti, & Liu, 2005) lend support for the emerging conviction that phonological awareness, at least its fundamental facet, is shared across languages. Further investigations, incorporating finely grained construct analyses, are needed to enhance our understanding of inter-lingual relationships in phonological awareness, and their contributions to biliteracy development among young bilingual learners.

Shared metalinguistic foundations

Beyond the initial phase, learning the mapping details entails the detection of recurring grapheme–phoneme, and grapheme–morpheme, correspondences, and thus necessitates the metalinguistic facets closely attuned to the orthographic properties specific to the language in which literacy is learned. These awareness facets, when transferred, are not likely to be fully functional in a new language. However, they likely promote reflections on what the task is about and how it can be best achieved because the ultimate goal of the task does not vary from one language to another. In this regard, adult second-language learners literate in their first language should benefit from their prior metalinguistic "training." Studies on adult learners of Japanese and Chinese offer some insights on the issue, generally suggesting that character-specific awareness evolves relatively early among these learners.

Ke (1998), for example, found that, after one year of Chinese study, his college-level participants became keenly aware of the utility of semantic radicals (i.e., character-internal graphic components which provide partial clues to character meaning) in building character knowledge, and, of even greater moment, that such awareness was a direct corollary of their character-recognition ability. Using a think-aloud protocol analysis, Everson and Ke (1997) determined that while intermediate learners depended on rote-memorization approaches to character identification, advanced learners were more analytical, invoking character segmentation and radical-information retrievals.

In a psycholinguistic experiment, Koda and Takahashi (2003) compared radical awareness among native and non-native kanji users through semantic category judgment. In the experiment, participants were asked to decide whether a presented character (e.g., "lake") belonged to a specific semantic category (e.g., "body of water"). Their findings demonstrated that the groups both benefited similarly from radicals – when extracting semantic information from single-character words. However, the groups' responses differed when the characters and radicals provided conflicting information, as in the case of the "water" radical used in a character whose meaning had no relevance to "water." Sophisticated readers should be able to detect the semantic conflict, but novices would not. Results clearly show this difference. While judgment speed among native kanji users declined considerably, their accuracy rate remained the same – presumably because they took time to make sure. Reaction times among non-native participants, in contrast, were minimally affected, but their error rates increased considerably – seemingly because they disregarded the incongruity. The findings thus indicate that second-language learners are sensitized to the basic function of semantic radicals and attentive to their information during Kanji processing. However, they still need to develop efficiency in detecting radical information validity, and selectivity in incorporating only valid information during kanji recognition.

In sum, studies involving adult second-language learners of Japanese and Chinese repeatedly suggest that these learners are progressively sensitized to the functional and structural properties of character components – and gradually rely on this sensitivity both in learning new characters and retrieving stored character information. Of greatest moment, however, such sensitivity readily develops with somewhat restricted character-learning experience (usually 250–400 characters) among metalinguistically adroit adult learners. This contrasts sharply with children – learning to read Chinese as their first language – who require knowledge of roughly 2,000 characters to develop similar metalinguistic insights (Shu & Anderson, 1999).

Orthographic distance

Once established in one language, metalinguistic and other literacy competencies transfer across languages, regardless of the orthographic distance between two writing systems. However, the degrees of facilitation brought about through transferred competencies vary because the distance determines amounts of modification necessary for fine-tuning the transferred skills. Therefore, orthographic distance should be responsible, in part, for processing efficiency at a given point in time among second-language learners with diverse first-language backgrounds. Empirical studies of ESL learners with different first-language backgrounds, in fact, demonstrate that more accurate and rapid performance occurs among those with alphabetic than non-alphabetic first-language backgrounds (e.g., Green & Meara, 1987; Koda, 2000; Muljani, Koda, & Moates, 1998). The critical question in this research is precisely how shared properties facilitate second-language processing through cross-language transfer.

Muljani and colleagues (1998) tested the distance effects on second-language intraword structural sensitivity. Comparing lexical-decision performance among proficiency-matched ESL learners with related (Indonesian; Roman-alphabetic) and unrelated (Chinese; logographic) first-language orthographic backgrounds, the study revealed that intraword structural congruity (i.e., spelling-pattern consistency) between the two alphabetic languages benefited lexical judgment among Indonesian, but not Chinese, participants. Indonesian superiority, however, was far less pronounced on the items whose spelling-patterns were unique to English. These findings clearly suggest that although congruous orthographic backgrounds induce general facilitation in lexical processing – accelerated efficiency only occurs precisely where the two languages share intra-word structural patterns – thereby posing identical processing requirements. Hence, orthographic distance not only explains overall performance differences among learners with related and unrelated first-language backgrounds, but it also highlights the ways in which first-language experience facilitates second-language lexical processing.

Second-language print input

Current psycholinguistic theories holds that both linguistic knowledge and language-processing skills evolve through input exposure and experience, underscoring the vital role of input in language learning and processing. Despite its obvious significance, we know little about the nature of input available to any particular group of second-language learners. As a result, impacts of input quality and quantity on second-language reading development have been largely unexplored. Only a few studies, to date, have directly investigated input characteristics and their relations to reading sub-skills development.

Wang, Perfetti, and Liu (2003), for example, examined how curriculum-based frequency affects character knowledge development among native English-speaking college students learning Chinese as a second language in the US.

Using a lexical judgment task, the researchers found that novice learners were capable of detecting structural violations, after studying Chinese only for one semester, without explicit instruction, and also that their performance was significantly faster and more accurate with high-frequency characters. The researchers interpreted these results as indicating that adult second-language learners are quickly sensitized to the major structural properties of the grapheme in a new writing system, and that input frequency strongly affects the formation of such sensitivity.

Impacts of print input and exposure have also been studied with school-age bilingual learners from a developmental perspective (Koda, Lu, & Zhang, 2007). Based on an in-depth analysis of input properties available to school-age Chinese heritage language (CHL) learners in the US, the researchers examined precisely how input properties affect the development of morphological awareness among grades three to five CHL learners. Their input analysis revealed that, during the six years in a weekend school, CHL students are introduced to 934 characters, roughly 30 percent of the characters explicitly taught to native Chinese-speaking children in China, and less than 20 percent of the morphological elements in common use. Despite the heavily limited input, proportions of the major character formation types and those of structurally regular, and functionally transparent, characters are similar between two text corpora – grades 1–6 textbooks for native Chinese-speaking children in China (Shu et al., 2003) and those for CHL students. These input characteristics were directly related to CHL students' morphological awareness. Although the input was limited, the students demonstrated a clear grasp of the characters' major structural properties and evolving sensitivity to the semantic constraints on character formation. Importantly, moreover, the three grade groups did not differ in either morphological awareness or character knowledge. Given that morphological awareness matures substantially between grades two and five both in English (Bear et al., 1996; Carlisle, 2003) and Chinese (Shu & Anderson, 1999; Ku & Anderson, 2003), this finding is astonishing. Further, no systematic relationship was found between morphological awareness and character knowledge. The researchers contend that although the basic awareness facets develop quickly among CHL students, their awareness remains basic without evolving into more refined capabilities. Moreover, their underdeveloped morphological awareness seemingly prohibits learners from incorporating additional characters newly introduced into their lexical memory each year, and thus, from expanding their character knowledge incrementally as they move up the grades.

Although still small in number, the two studies exploring second-language print input have yielded illuminating findings. It is important, therefore, that future studies invoke further in-depth analysis on print input to examine its specific impacts on reading sub-skills development systematically. A clearer understanding of the input available to a particular group of learners would allow us to make fairly accurate predictions of the extent and manner in which metalingusitic awareness and decoding skills are acquired by those learners in the given learning context.

Cross-linguistic variation

Within the current framework, it is presumed that first-language competencies, once transferred, continue evolving through second-language print input processing. The resulting second-language metalinguistic and decoding competencies reflect both first- and second-language orthographic properties and vary systematically across learners with diverse first-language orthographic backgrounds. Until recently, however, such cross-linguistic interplay has attracted limited attention in second-language reading research. Systematic investigations have just begun through comparisons of metalinguistic awareness and decoding skills among adult second-language learners from diverse first-language orthographic backgrounds.

In a series of studies, as a case in point, Koda and associates (Koda, 2000; Koda, Takahashi, & Fender, 1998) showed that variations in first-language morphological structure were directly related to efficiency in morphological structural analysis and information extraction among ESL learners with typologically similar (Korean: alphabetic, concatinative) and dissimilar (Chinese: logographic, non-concatinative) first-language backgrounds. Because of the typological congruity, Korean learners outperformed their Chinese counterparts in both tasks, but their superiority was far less pronounced in items representing linguistic features specific to English, the target language. Presumably, efficiency in extracting information from the second-language-specific features is gained only through processing experience with second-language print input, because it requires insights unavailable in either Korean or Chinese.

In related studies, Koda (1998, 1999) compared phonological awareness and orthographic sensitivity among proficiency-matched Korean and Chinese ESL learners. Since intraword segmentation is central to phonological processing in alphabetic systems, but not mandatory in logographic orthographies, it was hypothesized that alphabetic experience among Korean ESL learners would promote their acquisition of metalinguistic competencies in analyzing and manipulating segmental phonological information. It was further hypothesized that accelerated phonological awareness among Korean ESL learners would enhance their decoding development. Results complicated the already complex picture. Contrary to predictions, the groups differed neither in phonological awareness, nor in decoding. However, a clear contrast existed in the extent to which phonological awareness and decoding were related to reading comprehension. In the Korean data, the two variables were closely interconnected with reading performance, but no direct relationships were observed among the three variables in the Chinese data. The contrast was interpreted as suggesting that processing requirement congruity in the two languages seems to induce a strong preference for particular processing procedures. However, the study did not confirm the predicted advantage for second-language metalinguistic awareness formation among Korean ESL learners. Given that Korean employs a typologically congruent (alphabetic), yet unrelated (non-Roman), writing system, typological congruity alone did not achieve expected facilitation in second-language decoding development.

In more recent studies (Hamada & Koda, 2008; Wang, Koda, & Perfetti, 2003), first-language orthographic impacts on second-language decoding efficiency were examined. In the Wang et al. study (2003), participants were first presented with a category description, such as "flower," and then shown a target word. The task was to decide whether the word was a member of the shown category. Target words were either phonologically (e.g., "rows" for "rose") or graphically (e.g., "fees" for "feet") manipulated. The primary hypothesis was that the two ESL groups would respond differently to the two types of manipulation: Korean participants would be more likely to accept homophones as category members, whereas Chinese would make more false positive responses to graphically similar targets. The data showed, first, that both phonological and graphic manipulations significantly interfered with category judgment performance among ESL learners regardless of their first-language backgrounds. Importantly, however, the magnitude of interference stemming from each type varied noticeably between the groups. As predicted, Korean learners made more errors with homophonic (phonologically manipulated) items, while more serious interference occurred with similarly spelled (graphically manipulated) targets among Chinese learners. Here again, the results clearly suggest that the two groups rely upon different information during semantic processing of words, and, more critically, that these differences seem attributable to their first-language orthographic experiences.

In sum, cross-linguistic comparisons of second-language metalinguistic awareness and decoding collectively demonstrate that L1 orthographic experience has long-lasting effects on second-language reading development, further implying that L1 processing experience is a major source of performance variances among adult second-language learners. At the same time, the studies consistently show that second-language lexical processing was similarly affected, regardless of first-language background, by second-language input characteristics, including orthographic regularity (Hamada & Koda, 2008; Wang, Koda, & Perfetti, 2003), functional transparency (Koda & Takahashi, 2003) and word/morpheme frequency (Koda, 1999, 2000; Muljani et al., 1998). Of the greatest moment, however, in all studies, second-language input variables exerted stronger influence, overriding the variance attributable to first-language background. The emerging picture thus suggests that although processing experience in both first and second languages jointly affects second-language reading development, second-language inputappears to be a stronger force in shaping second-language processing skills.

Summary and Implications

The current review has demonstrated that learning to read in any language is constrained by both universal and language-specific properties of the writing system, and that second-language reading development is strongly affected by the properties of not one, but two writing systems. The major contentions can be summarized as follows:

- When transferred, previously acquired metalinguistic capabilities help establish a solid foundation for gaining basic insight into how language elements are graphically represented in a new writing system.
- Second-language print input is a dominant force shaping language-specific awareness facets and subsequent decoding skills in a second language.
- Amounts of second-language input and processing experience necessitated for the formation of second-language metalinguistic sensitivity and decoding skills vary among learners with similar, and dissimilar, first-language orthographic backgrounds.
- Since second-language metalinguistic awareness and decoding skills evolve through continuous interaction between transferred first-language competencies and second-language print input, the resulting competencies vary systematically across learners from diverse first-language backgrounds.

These insights have significant implications for second-language literacy instruction. To begin with, second-language learning to read is frequently a repeated process for those who are literate in their first language. They possess the metalinguistic and other foundational competencies underlying literacy development in all languages. Therefore, once transferred, these competencies provide substantial facilitation in learning to read in a new language. It is thus essential that what learners bring to the learning process be clearly understood. Although the notion of shared underlying competencies, in itself, is not new, recent advancements in reading research offer far more specific information regarding both universal and language-specific requisites for learning to read in diverse languages (Koda & Zheler, 2008). It seems sensible, therefore, to incorporate research-based insights in fine-tuning instructional approaches in order to meet the needs of students with greater accuracy.

Second, although a linkage between speech and print is universally required in learning to read, how they are linked varies considerably across languages. Therefore, when the mapping skills established in one language transfer to another, they are functional in the second language only to the extent that the two writing systems demand similar mapping patterns. This implies that learners from diverse first-language backgrounds face qualitatively different challenges when learning to read a particular second language. Although it is not reasonable to expect second-language teachers to know the orthographic properties of every writing system, it is important that they remain aware of such cross-linguistic variation, so as to be sensitive to the type and level of difficulty their students may encounter.

Similarly, orthographic distance directly affects second-language decoding efficiency. The clear implication is that students from similar and dissimilar first-language orthographic backgrounds acquire decoding efficiency at disparate rates. Since many of the comprehension operations depend on decoding competencies, delays in acquiring optimal efficiency are likely to create complications in subsequent comprehension sub-skills development. Early detection of decoding problems is thus vital. Moreover, in identifying potential sources of decoding problems, orthographic distance should be taken into account as a possible factor.

Finally, second-language input is a major force shaping literacy competencies. Input frequency clarifies why particular linguistic features are processed more rapidly and accurately than others, as well as why some learners acquire processing skills faster and more easily. Since learning to read demands detection of regularly co-occurring elements, input regularity also plays a prominent role in promoting reading skills development. Given its powerful impact, it is essential that the input available to a particular group of learners in a given instructional context be carefully analyzed and clearly understood. Although it is unrealistic to replicate real-life input features (both quantitatively and qualitatively) in a formal instructional context, rational input modifications of selective features are possible and potentially effective. Self-evidently, more research is needed to inform teachers and textbook writers of the specific input features that are facilitative, and therefore should be incorporated in instructional materials.

REFERENCES

Abu Rabia, S. (1995). Learning to read in Arabic: Reading, syntactic, orthographic and working memory skills in normally achieving and poor Arabic readers. *Reading Psychology* 16, 351–94.

Adams, M. J. (1990). *Beginning to read*. Cambridge, MA: MIT Press.

August, D., Calderon, M., & Carlo, M. (2001). Transfer of skills from Spanish to English: A study of young learners. Updated review of current literature relevant to the technical issues in the implementation of the study.

Bear, D. R., Invernizzi, M., Templeton, S., & Johnston, F. (1996). *Words their way: Word study for phonics vocabulary, and spelling instruction*. Upper Saddle River, NJ: Merrill.

Berko, J. (1958). The child's learning of English morphology. *Word* 14, 150–77.

Bialystock, E. (2001). *Bilingualism in development*. Cambridge: Cambridge University Press.

Bialystok, E., McBride-Chang, C., & Luk, G. (2005). Bilingualism, language proficiency, and learning to read in two writing systems. *Journal of Educational Psychology* 97, 580–90.

Bowey, J. A. & Francis, J. (1991). Phonological analysis as a function of age and exposure to reading instruction. *Applied Psycholinguistics* 12, 91–121.

Bradley, L. & Bryant, P. E. (1901). Phonological skills before and after learning to read. In S. A. Brady & D. P. Shankweiler (eds.), *Phonological processing in literacy* (pp. 37–45). Hillsdale, NJ: Lawrence Erlbaum.

Branum-Martin, L., Fletcher, J. M., Carlson, C. D., Ortiz, A., Carlo, M., & Francis, D. J. (2006). Bilingual phonological awareness: Multilevel construct validation among Spanish-speaking kindergarteners in transitional bilingual education classrooms. *Journal of Educational Psychology* 98, 170–81.

Bryant, P. E., MacLean, M., & Bradley, L. L. (1990). Rhyme, language, and children's reading. *Applied Psycholinguistics* 11, 237–51.

Carlisle, J. (1995). Morphological awareness and early reading achievement. In L. B. Feldman (ed.), *Morphological aspects of language processing* (pp. 189–209). Hillsdale, NJ: Lawrence Erlbaum.

Carlisle, J. (2003). Morphology matters in learning to read: A commentary. *Reading Psychology* 24, 291–322.

Carlisle, J. F. & Beeman, M. M. (2000). The effects of language of instruction on the reading and writing achievement of first-grade Hispanic children. *Scientific Studies of Reading* 4, 331–53.

Carlisle, J. F. & Nomanbhoy, D. (1993). Phonological and morphological development. *Applied Psycholinguistics* 14, 177–95.

Cho, J.-R. & McBride-Chang, C. (2005). Correlates of Korea Hangul acquisition among kindergarteners and second graders. *Scientific Studies of Reading* 9, 3–16.

Cisero, C. A., Carlo, M. S. & Royer, J. M. (1992). Can a child raised as English speaking be phonemically aware in another language? Paper presented at the annual meeting of the American Educational Research Association, San Francisco, CA.

Cormier, P. & Kelson, S. (2000). The roles of phonological and syntactic awareness in the use of plural morphemes among children in French immersion. *Scientific Studies of Reading* 4, 267–94.

Coulmas, F. (2003). *Writing systems*. New York: Cambridge University Press.

Da Fontoura, H. A. & Siegel, L. S. (1995). Reading syntactic and memory skills of Portuguese-English Canadian children. *Reading and Writing* 7, 139–53.

Duques, S. (1989). Grammatical deficiency in writing: An investigation of learning disabled colleges students. *Reading and Writing* 2, 1–17.

Durgunoglu, A. Y., Nagy, W. E., & Hancin-Bhatt, B. J. (1993). Cross-language transfer of phonemic awareness. *Journal of Educational Psychology* 85, 453–65.

Ellis, N. (2002). Frequency effects in language processing: A review with implications for theories of implicit and explicit language acquisition. *Studies in Second Language Acquisition* 24, 143–88.

Everson, M. E. & Ke, C. (1997). An inquiry into the reading strategies of intermediate and advanced learners of Chinese as a Foreign Language. *Journal of the Chinese Language Teachers Association* 32, 1–20.

Fowler, A. E. & Liberman, I. Y. (1995). The role of phonology and orthography in morphological awareness. In L. B. Feldman (ed.), *Morphological aspects of language processing* (pp. 157–88). Hillsdale, NJ: Lawrence Erlbaum.

Frost, R. & Bentin, S. (1992). Processing phonological and semantic ambiguity: Evidence from semantic priming at different SOAs. *Journal of Experimental Psychology: Learning, Memory, and Cognition* 18, 58–68.

Gass, S. & Selinker, L. (eds.) (1983). *Language transfer in language learning*. Rowley, MA: Newbury House.

Geva, E. (2008). Facets of metalinguistic awareness related to reading development in Hebrew: Evidence from monolingual and bilingual children. In K. Koda & A. M. Zehler (eds.), *Learning to read across languages: Cross-linguistic relationships in first and second language literacy development* (pp. 154–87). New York: Routledge.

Gholamain, M. & Geva, E. (1999). Orthographic and cognitive factors in the concurrent development of basic reading skills in English and Persian. *Language Learning* 49, 183–217.

Goswami, U. & Bryant, P. (1990). *Phonological skills and learning to read*. Hove, UK: Lawrence Erlbaum.

Gough, P. & Tunmer, W. (1986). Decoding, reading, and reading disability. *RASE: Remedial & Special Education* 7, 6–10.

Green, D. W. & Meara, P. (1987). The effects of script on visual search. *Second Language Research* 3, 102–17.

Hamada, M. & Koda, K. (2008). Second language vocabulary acquisition: Influence of first language orthographic experience on decoding and lexical memory. *Language Learning* 58, 1–31.

Henderson, A. J. & Shores, R. E. (1982). How learning disabled students' failure to attend to suffixes affects their oral reading performance. *Journal of Learning Disabilities* 15, 178–82.

Ho, C. S.-H. & Bryant, P. (1999). Different visual skills are important in learning to read English and Chinese. *Educational and Child Psychology* 16, 4–14.

Hoover, W. A. & Gough, P. B. (1990). The simple view of reading. *Reading and Writing* 2, 127–60.

Juel, C., Griffith, P. L., & Gough, P. B. (1986). Acquisition of literacy: A longitudinal study of children in first and second grade. *Journal of Educational Psychology* 78, 243–55.

Ke, C. (1998). Effects of language background on the learning of Chinese characters among foreign language students. *Foreign Language Annals* 31, 91–100.

Koda, K. (1998). The role of phonemic awareness in L2 reading. *Second Language Research* 14, 194–215.

Koda, K. (1999). Development of L2 intraword structural sensitivity and decoding skills. *Modern Language Journal* 83, 51–64.

Koda, K. (2000). Cross-linguistic variations in L2 morphological awareness. *Applied Psycholinguistics* 21, 297–320.

Koda, K., Lu, C., & Zhang, Y. (2007). Properties of characters in heritage Chinese textbooks and their implications for character knowledge development among Chinese heritage language learners. In A. W. He & Y. Xiao (eds.), *Chinese as a heritage language*. Hawai'i: University of Hawai'i Press.

Koda, K. & Takahashi, T. (2003). Role of radical awareness in lexical inference in Kanji. Manuscript submitted for publication.

Koda, K., Takahashi, E., & Fender, M. (1998). Effects of L1 processing experience on L2 morphological awareness. *Ilha do Desterro* 35, 59–87.

Koda, K. & Zheler, A. M. (eds.) (2008). *Learning to read across languages: Cross-linguistic relationships in first and second language literacy development*. New York: Routledge.

Krashen, S. (1983). Newmark's "Ignorance Hypothesis" and current second language acquisition theory. In In S. Gass & L. Selinker (eds.), *Language transfer in language learning* (pp. 135–56). Rowley, MA: Newbury House.

Ku, Y.-M. & Anderson, R. C. (2003). Development of morphological awareness in Chinese and English. *Reading and Writing* 16, 399–422.

Kuhara-Kojima, K., Hatano, G., Saito, H., & Haebara, T. (1996). Vocalization latencies of skilled and less skilled comprehenders for words written in hiragana and kanji. *Reading Research Quarterly* 31, 158–71.

Kuo, L. & Anderson, R. C. (in press). Conceptual and methodological issues in comparing metalinguistics awareness across languages. In K. Koda & A. M. Zehler (eds.), *Learning to read across languages: Cross-linguistic relationships in first and second language literacy development*. Mahwah, NJ: Lawrence Erlbaum.

Li, W., Anderson, R. C., Nagy, W., & Zhang, H. (2002). Facets of metalinguistic awareness that contribute to Chinese literacy. In W. Li, J. S. Gaffiney, & J. L. Packard (eds.), *Chinese children's reading acquisition: Theoretical and pedagogical issues* (pp. 87–106). Boston, MA: Kluwer Academic.

Logan, G. D. (1988). Toward an instance theory of automatization. *Psychological Review* 95, 492–527.

MacWhinney, B. (1987). The Competition model. In B. MacWhinney (ed.), *Mechanisms of language acquisition* (pp. 249–308). Hillsdale, NJ: Lawrence Erlbaum.

MacWhinney, B. & Bates, E. (eds.) (1989). *The crosslinguistic study of sentence processing.* New York: Cambridge University Press.

Muljani, M., Koda, K., & Moates, D. (1998). Development of L2 word recognition: A Connectionist approach. *Applied Psycholinguistics* 19, 99–114.

Nagy, W. E. & Anderson, R. C. (1999). Metalinguistic awareness and literacy acquisition in different languages. In D. Wagner, R. Venezky, & B. Street (eds.), *Literacy: An international handbook* (pp. 155–60). New York: Garland.

Odlin, T. (1989). *Language transfer.* New York: Cambridge University Press.

Perfetti, C. A. (2003). The universal grammar of reading. *Scientific Studies of Reading* 7, 3–24.

Perfetti, C. A., Beck, I., Bell, L. C., & Hughes, C. (1987). Phonemic knowledge and learning to read are reciprocal: A longitudinal study of first grade children. *Merrill-Palmer Quarterly* 33, 283–319.

Perfetti, C. A. & Dunlap, S. (2008). Learning to read: General principles and writing system variations. In K. Koda & A. M. Zehler (eds.), *Learning to read across languages: Cross-linguistic relationships in first and second language literacy development* (pp. 13–38). New York: Routledge.

Perfetti, C. A. & Liu, Y. (2005). Orthography to phonology and meaning: Comparisons across and within writing systems. *Reading and Writing* 18, 193–210.

Rubin, H. (1991). Morphological knowledge and writing ability. In R. M. Joshi (ed.), *Written language disorders* (pp. 43–69). Boston, MA: Kluwer Academic.

Shimron, J. (2006). *Reading Hebrew: The language and the psychology of reading it.* Mahwah, NJ: Lawrence Erlbaum.

Shu, H. & Anderson, R. C. (1999). Learning to read Chinese: The development of metalinguistic awareness. In A. Inhuff, J. Wang, & H. C. Chen (eds.), *Reading Chinese scripts: A cognitive analysis* (pp. 1–18). Mahwah, NJ: Lawrence Erlbaum.

Shu, H., Chen, X., Anderson, R. C., Wu, N., & Xuan, Y. (2003). Properties of school Chinese: Implications for learning to read. *Child Development* 74, 27–47.

Slobin, D. I. (ed.) (1985). *The crosslinguistic study of language acquisition, 2.* Hillsdale, NJ: Lawrence Erlbaum.

So, D. & Siegel, L. S. (1997). Learning to read Chinese: Semantic, syntactic, phonological and short-term memory skills in normally achieving and poor Chinese readers. *Reading and Writing* 9, 1–21.

Stahl, S. A. & Murray, B. A. (1994). Defining phonological awareness and its relationship to early reading. *Journal of Educational Psychology* 86, 221–34.

Stanovitch, K. E. (2000). *Progress in understanding reading: Scientific foundations and new frontiers.* New York: Guilford.

Stanovich, K. E., Cunningham, A. E., & Cramer, B. B. (1984). Assessing phonological awareness of kindergarten children: Issues of task comparability. *Journal of Experimental Psychology* 38, 175–90.

Tyler, A. & Nagy, W. (1989). The acquisition of English derivational morphology. *Journal of Memory and Language* 28, 649–67.

Tyler, A. & Nagy, W. (1990). Use of derivational morphology during reading. *Cognition* 36, 17–34.

Van Valin, R. D. (1991). Functionalist linguistic theory and language acquisition. *First Language* 11, 7–40.

Vellutino, F. R. & Scanlon, D. M. (1987). Phonological coding, phonological awareness, and reading ability: Evidence from a longitudinal and experimental study. *Merrill-Palmer Quarterly* 33, 321–63.

Verhoeven, L. (2000). Components in early second language reading and spelling. *Scientific Studies of Reading* 4, 313–30.

Wade-Woolley, L. & Geva, E. (2000). Processing novel phonemic contrasts in the acquisition of L2 word reading. *Scientific Studies of Reading* 4, 295–311.

Wang, M., Koda, K., & Perfetti, C. A. (2003). Alphabetic and non-alphabetic L1 effects in English semantic processing: A comparison of Korean and Chinese English L2 learners. *Cognition* 87, 129–49.

Wang, M., Perfetti, C. A., & Liu, Y. (2003). Alphabetic readers quickly acquire orthographic structure in learning to read Chinese. *Scientific Studies of Reading* 7, 183–208.

Wang, M., Perfetti, C. A., & Liu, Y. (2005). Chinese-English biliteracy acquisition: Cross-language and writing system transfer. *Cognition* 97, 67–88.

Yopp, H. K. (1988). The validity and reliability of phonemic awareness tests. *Reading Research Quarterly* 23, 159–77.

Zhang, S. & Perfetti, C. A. (1993). The tongue-twister effect in reading Chinese. *Journal of Experimental Psychology: Learning, Memory and Cognition* 19, 1–12.

26 Teaching and Testing Writing

CHARLENE POLIO AND JESSICA WILLIAMS

Theoretical and empirical research falling under the scope of second/foreign language (L2) writing covers a vast array of topics and epistemological traditions. Such variety is not undesirable, given that L2 writing is undeniably a complex process that involves both the cognitive processes of second language acquisition (SLA), as well as the genres, purposes, and values of the targeted L2 discourse community. Although it may be naïve to imagine that research on, for example, the role of working memory in text production and language socialization will ever intersect, we believe that the teaching of writing can be informed by a variety of perspectives, including, but not limited to, how learners process feedback (e.g., Sachs & Polio, 2007), and syntactic representations of writing (e.g., Cleland & Pickering, 2006), as well as what students bring to the writing task in terms of cultural identification and experience (e.g., Jarrett, Losh, & Puente, 2006; Liebowitz, 2006).

Scholars of L2 writing have lamented the lack of a coherent theory of writing (e.g., Hedgcock, 2005). Indeed there are few models of L2 writing, and none is comprehensive. Some focus on L2 writers' processes (Sasaki, 2000, 2002; Zimmerman, 2000), whereas others focus on the knowledge that writers bring to the writing task and what they share with readers in a discourse community (Matsuda, 1997). Wang and Wen (2002) emphasize both the writers' processes and writer knowledge, as well the role of both the first language (L1) and the L2 in the process. Hayes' (1996) model has brought together both cognitive and social factors. However, because the Hayes model pertains to L1 writers, it does not address issues of L2 language proficiency and the role of the L1. And, although this model has been expanded from an earlier cognitive model (Hayes & Flower, 1980) to include some social factors, its treatment of social factors remains minimal. It does not address social issues currently being explored in the L2 writing literature, such as race, class, and gender (Kubota, 2003) and voice (Helms-Park & Stapleton, 2003; Stapleton, 2002).

In the absence of a comprehensive model of L2 writing, we organize our discussion around some factors that are discussed in the current research and have influenced the teaching of L2 writing. We begin by exploring the relationship between SLA and writing with a focus on cognitive issues related to text production and language learning. Next, we turn to the writing process and examine the effect that research in this area has had on teaching. Although most of the academic scholarship on the teaching of writing has been conducted in North America, we offer a short exploration of L2 writing instruction in Europe and Asia. We then discuss more recent developments that reflect the social turn in writing pedagogy. Although research in these areas is distinct, each has had an important impact on the teaching of writing. It is essential to keep in mind that L2 writing requires (1) learning an L2, (2) creating a text, and (3) adapting it to a specific discourse community. Next we turn to a brief discussion of assessment issues.

Cognitive Factors in Learning to Write

An understanding of SLA is essential for those interested in teaching writing. Learners need to acquire and generate the L2 in order to write in it. However, this is not a one-way process: writing can facilitate general language proficiency and teachers can use writing to promote other skills. The impact of writing on oral skills has not been widely researched (see Weissberg, 2006; Williams, 2008). Weissberg (2000), in a study of adult L2 classroom learners, demonstrated that new forms emerged first in journal writing and only later were the learners willing or able to use those forms orally. Harklau (2002) also found earlier emergence in the writing of high school ESL students. In addition, she convincingly showed that these learners had greater access to written input, generated more written language than oral, and received more feedback on their writing than on speech. A complete overview of the relationship of writing and SLA is, however, beyond the scope of this chapter, and we have therefore chosen to limit our discussion to two specific areas: writing as focus on form and pushed output, and written error correction.

Writing as focus on form and pushed output

There has been extensive discussion in SLA research and language teaching regarding the role of form-focused instruction (for reviews, see Ellis, 2001; Norris & Ortega, 2000; Spada, 1997; Williams, 2005). Although form-focused instruction is often seen as a teacher's attempt to draw learners' attention to form, the simple act of writing can help learners pay attention to language form, even without any teacher intervention. Kim et al. (2001) showed that writing allowed elementary school ESL students to "make language 'stand still' so that it can be inspected closely, carefully, and deliberately" (p. 339). The modality provides learners with a record of their language that they can look at and monitor, which, in speaking, would result in reduced fluency. This was stated quite explicitly by Cumming (1990), drawing on Swain's (1985) work on output as a means of facilitating acquisition. He stated:

> Composition writing elicits an attention to form–meaning relations that may prompt learners to refine their linguistic expression – and hence their control over their linguistic knowledge – so that it is more accurately representative of their thoughts and of standard usage. (p. 483)

With regard to empirical research, recent studies suggest learners can and do pay attention to language form in written texts. Wong (2001) showed that learners can attend to form and meaning at the same time in the written, but not oral, modality. Studies have also shown that when students are provided with copies of their own writing, they can correct many of their own errors without any feedback or any specific instructions on how to edit their writing (Gass, 1983; Polio, Fleck, & Leder, 1998). Of course, with teacher intervention and strategy instruction, students may be able to correct more of their errors (Ferris, 2002).

There is also evidence that learners' attention to form increases in certain collaborative writing activities. Swain (1998) used a dictogloss, a task in which students reconstruct passages after listening to them, as a way to help them focus on form while expressing meaning. Students worked in pairs after taking notes on a passage and were able to reflect consciously on their own output. Storch (2005) studied students writing essays alone and in pairs. She found that the students working in pairs produced more grammatically accurate and syntactically complex essays. Thus, both the modality and the collaborative nature of the output activity enhanced the opportunities to focus on form.

Swain began this line of research in response to the disappointing level of grammatical accuracy of many learners in Canadian immersion programs. She argued, among other things, that learners were not producing enough language and that output helps learners notice problems and gaps in their language. Swain maintained that in order for learners to progress, they needed to complete tasks that would help them move beyond their current levels by producing what she called pushed output. In such tasks, learners try out new grammatical structures and/or vocabulary that they may not have mastered. Dictoglosses, in addition to increasing learners' attention to form, also pushed their output because they had to produce language that was not their own and was beyond their current level. In two other studies, Qi and Lapkin (2001) and Sachs and Polio (2007) used reformulation tasks, in which learners rewrote their drafts following reformulation by native speakers. In both studies, learners paid attention to language form as they tried to produce output beyond the level of their current knowledge. In addition, students in both studies noticed gaps in their language as they were trying to produce their original texts.

One key to the effectiveness of writing tasks in promoting focus on form and pushed output may be planning opportunities. Several studies of oral language (e.g., Foster & Skehan, 1996; Ortega, 1999) have shown that giving students time to plan before they speak improves their oral language production, specifically their fluency and syntactic complexity, although not their grammatical accuracy. Ellis and Yuan (2004) extended this line of research to writing. They examined the writing of learners when they were given time to plan what they were going to write and when they were not. They also included an online planning condition in which participants were not given time to plan but rather were given unlimited time to write. They found the same results as the studies of oral language: pre-task planning improved fluency and complexity but not accuracy. Accuracy did improve, however, in the online planning condition.

Grammar error correction

Error correction in writing is probably the most debated and controversial topic in the field. Yet despite many empirical studies and polemical discussions, and the fact that learners, and often teachers (I. Lee, 2004), prefer comprehensive feedback on language, the question of the effectiveness of written error correction remains unresolved. (For a comprehensive review of the research and issues see Ferris, 2002, 2004, 2006.) Truscott (1996) propelled the issue to the forefront of the field when he stated, "Grammar has no place in writing classes and should be abandoned" (p. 361). He correctly argued that no studies at that time had shown any long-term benefits for error correction. He also maintained that correction is harmful because it diverts teachers' time from other tasks that might be more helpful to their students. Furthermore, it may cause students to use simpler language and take fewer risks to avoid making errors.

One reason for the lack of consensus rests in the design of the studies. There are logistical problems in implementing carefully controlled studies. Establishing definitions and reliable measures of various constructs has also proven challenging. It is difficult to ensure that all factors but error correction are held constant, and for ethical reasons, it is even more difficult to include a control group that receives no error correction. In addition, the operationalization of error correction has varied and been extended to pedagogical techniques, such as underlining and coding errors. Ten years after Truscott's challenge, the issue has still not been resolved. Although several studies that have showed that teachers' error corrections on a draft result in more grammatically accurate revisions (Ashwell, 2000; Chandler, 2003; Fathman & Whalley, 1990; Ferris, 2006), none has convincingly shown any long-term effect on learners' writing. Polio et al. (1998) found no long-term effect when students' writing from an error correction group and a control group were compared over the course of a semester. The problem with this and other studies is that a lack of difference between the two groups can be attributed to a myriad of factors, including the lack of a sufficiently reliable measure of grammatical accuracy (Polio, 1997; Wolfe-Quintero, Inagaki, & Kim, 1998), lack of a control group, too short a treatment period, or study-external factors, such as other instruction that students were receiving at the time of the study.

In an attempt to show a long-term effect for error correction, Chandler (2003) compared two groups, one that received error correction and one that simply had their errors underlined by the teacher. At the end of 10 weeks, she compared the learners' accuracy on a new piece of writing. The error correction group did better than the group which had their errors underlined. However, there are two problems with the study: first the error correction group wrote twice as much as the underline group. Second, Chandler examined only grammatical accuracy. As Truscott (2004) correctly pointed out, it is possible that the error correction caused students to write more correct but less complex sentences in an effort to avoid making errors.

Bitchener, Young, and Cameron (2005) compared students who received no feedback, students who received direct explicit correction, and students who received direct explicit correction plus teacher–student conferences. They found no difference in the three groups' overall improvement over 12 weeks, but did find that the error correction-plus-conference group did better on certain grammatical features. Furthermore, learners did not progress in a linear manner. Despite flaws similar to those described for Chandler's study, the results underscore the complexity of learner response to error correction over time.

Although findings on the effectiveness of an explicit focus on form in L2 writing have been less than conclusive, in SLA more generally, two reviews of research (Ellis, 2001; Norris & Ortega, 2000) have argued that explicit focus on language form, which includes error correction, does facilitate acquisition. Others have argued for more implicit ways of drawing learner attention to forms, in particular, the use of recasts. Although the usefulness of oral recasts remains controversial (see, e.g., Lyster, 2004; Panova & Lyster, 2002), many studies have shown their effectiveness (Doughty & Varela, 1998; Leeman, 2003; Long, 2007; Mackey, 2006; Mackey & Goo, 2007; Mackey & Philp, 1998; Philp, 2003). If oral recasts are effective, written error corrections in the form of recasts should be especially effective (e.g., Ayoun, 2004), because, as we have noted, in writing, learners are more likely to perceive the correction and have more time to focus on their language during production, although unlike oral recasts, they are not offered during communication.

The Writing Process and Process Approach

Researchers began studying writers' processes in reaction to the current-traditional approach (or traditional paradigm). This approach to L1 writing instruction stressed reading literary texts and reproducing models of various rhetorical modes, with little attention to how writers write. Both the expressivist and the cognitive approaches developed in response to this long-entrenched pedagogy. The expressivists emphasized writing as a process of discovering meaning and personal voice. In the classroom, this approach was manifested as activities to generate and discover ideas and as a reduced focus on accuracy. The cognitive approach, in contrast, viewed writing as a problem-solving activity. Students were encouraged to brainstorm, plan, get feedback, and revise. After some debate (e.g., Hamp-Lyons, 1986; Horowitz, 1986), it became clear that the insights of the expressivist and cognitive approaches, and even a concern for formal accuracy, need not be mutually exclusive. Today, the term "process writing" has come to mean many things, but in general, it casts writing as an exploratory and recursive, rather than linear, pre-determined process. In the classroom, a process approach has come to mean that teachers, and often peers, intervene at one or several points in the writing process (Susser, 1994). Process writing in its various forms has dominated L1 and L2 writing classrooms for the past 20 years, and even most FL classrooms (Reichelt, 2001), at least in North America. We begin with a discussion of research on the general writing process and then discuss the ways that teachers can intervene, in particular, with the use of effective peer feedback.

Second language learners' composing processes

Krappels (1990) comprehensively reviewed research on L2 writing processes and concluded that although the quality of research had improved, the small scale of these studies made it difficult to generalize the results, which were often contradictory. Sixteen years later, research on the writing process continues, but is still somewhat difficult to interpret, particularly with regard to how it should inform classroom teaching. Several different techniques have been used to investigate the writing process. The most common is the think-aloud protocol, in which learners talk about what they are writing as they do it, but other techniques, including stimulated recall, have also been used. Each method carries its own set of problems (see Polio, 2003, for a review of the various methods), not the least of which is the time-consuming nature of the procedures, with the result that studies of the writing process rely on extremely small sample sizes. As such, it remains difficult to generalize about what L2 writers do as they write. Furthermore, data are collected in controlled settings, allowing researchers to maximize the reliability of their results. However, such settings bear little resemblance to real-life writing situations and, although this does not invalidate the studies, it does limit the generalizability of the findings.

Silva and Brice (2004) surveyed research on the writing process more recently and concluded that studies have become more focused, in that many have examined one specific aspect of the writing process. Studies of the general writing process of specific groups of students (e.g., Bosher, 1998; Roca de Larios, Murphy, & Manchon, 1999) can draw teachers' attention to possible problems that these learners encounter while writing. Studies that focus on one particular aspect of writing may be more informative. For example, Christianson (1997) studied how learners used dictionaries while writing, and was able to identify specific problems that cause learners to use inappropriate words. Roca de Larios, Manchon, and Murphy (2006) examined only formulation, that is, the point at which ideas were verbalized or written.

Probably of most use to writing teachers, however, are studies of the writing process after a specific kind of instruction. Several studies have investigated early stages of the writing process, for example, pedagogical techniques that encourage extended prewriting. Prewriting is an essential component of a process approach, and most textbooks devote a substantial amount of space to getting students to generate ideas, but surprisingly little research has examined prewriting techniques. Lally (2000) studied the effects of idea generation in students' L1 and L2, in this case English and French, respectively. Although she did not find a statistically significant difference in essay quality, she raised the issue of the use of the L1 in prewriting activities. In another important study, Shi (1998) studied prewriting under three different conditions: no discussion, teacher-led discussion, and peer discussion. Her results were complex, but she did not find a clear benefit in essay quality for any one condition.

Using both cross-sectional and longitudinal data, Sasaki (2000) studied the differences in the writing process of novices and experts before and after instruction. Using different methods to triangulate the data, she concluded, among other things, that after instruction, novice writers began to use some of the strategies of skilled writers, such as global planning and rereading. They did not, however, write more fluently. Effect-of-instruction studies such as this can shed light on what is teachable. In contrast, in studies that simply compare novice and expert (or skilled and unskilled) writers (e.g., Zamel, 1983), one cannot infer a cause–effect relationship between specific strategies and writing quality.

Teacher feedback

Intervention at various points in a students' writing process is one of the main features of the process approach. Teacher feedback that focuses on content and organization has received a huge amount of attention, and a complete summary is not possible here. (Comprehensive discussions can be found in Ferris, 2003; and Goldstein, 2005.) One of the issues related to written feedback is the difficulty students have with interpreting feedback and whether or not they actually respond to it. Although feedback can be confusing (Cohen & Cavalcanti, 1990), many students do respond to it when rewriting their papers (Ferris, 1997). Students and teachers need to communicate clearly about feedback. Goldstein (2005) gives suggestions for students to help their teachers in this respect. For example, she recommends that students complete cover sheets for their essays that direct the teacher to the students' perceived problems.

Other research has examined feedback in writing conferences. Goldstein and Conrad (1990) and Patthey-Chavez and Ferris (1997) found that topics that were negotiated were more likely to be revised than topics for which the teachers simply provided suggestions. Others have extended writing conference research to the context of writing centers. This is an important area of inquiry because of the proliferation of such centers, at least in North America, as well as the increase in number of L2 learners who use them. Writing centers were originally created for native-speaker peer tutoring using a nondirective approach (Williams & Severino, 2004). This approach differs from peer response, discussed below, because there is an implicit assumption, especially for L2 learners, that the peer tutor has more expertise in writing and in the L2. Williams (2004) studied L2 writers with their peer tutors and found, like Goldstein and Conrad (1990), that more revisions occurred when students participated, but also that more direct suggestions were more helpful. Jones et al. (2006) examined online vs. face-to-face tutoring in a writing center in Hong Kong. They found that more equal participation took place in the online sessions, and that participants in online sessions focused more on global issues, whereas those in the face-to-face sessions focused more on language issues.

Peer response

Peer response (also called peer review or peer feedback) is another intervention that is common in process writing classrooms. Over the last 15 years, there has been extensive research on the effectiveness of peer response in L2 writing instruction. (Peer response here refers to feedback on content and organization. We know of no studies in which peers were instructed to correct grammar.) The effects of peer response have been examined in the short term, from draft to revision, and in the long term. Research on peer review has also addressed the quality of writing, and students' attitudes as indicator of the benefits of peer review, as well as the types of revisions that students make in response to peer feedback. For comprehensive reviews, see Hyland and Hyland (2006), Liu and Hansen (2002), and Rollinson (2005).

With regard to attitudes, some studies have shown that learners prefer teacher feedback to learner feedback when given a choice (Zhang, 1995). Jacobs et al. (1998), however, surveyed Hong Kong and Taiwanese EFL students, almost all of whom said that they preferred to have both peer feedback and teacher feedback. McGroarty and Zhu (1997) found that students who were trained in peer review had a more positive attitude toward it than students who were not.

Other researchers have assessed the quality of learner feedback. Mendonça and Johnson (1994) studied learners' oral comments and found that responders initiated negotiations when they did not understand their peers' meaning, and gave suggestions to improve the writing, but interestingly, almost never corrected grammar. McGroarty and Zhu (1997) studied the effects of training on response quality. They compared two groups of university ESL students, one which had received extensive training on peer review and one which had not. They found that the students who received the training gave significantly more feedback, and more global and relevant feedback. In this sense, the training was successful, but a more important question is whether peer response results in more successful revision and, furthermore, whether it has any long-term effect.

McGroarty and Zhu (1997) examined the effects of peer response training on the quality of learners' writing. They compared the holistic writing scores of trained and untrained students and found that even though the trained group was giving more substantial comments, the essays revised on the basis of these comments did not receive higher ratings. To determine the long-term effects of peer review training, they compared the end-of-the-term writing portfolios of the two groups and found that the trained group performed only a little better. Berg (1999) also examined the effects of peer reviewing training on student writing. She examined effectiveness not by looking at the comments or the students' attitudes, but rather by studying the revisions the students made, and like McGroarty and Zhu, the overall quality of the writing. She found the learners who had received training made more meaning-based changes than those who had not received training. More important, the trained groups' essays were rated significantly higher on a holistic scale than those of the untrained group. These findings need to be interpreted cautiously because it is not known whether the meaning-based revisions and higher holistic scores were the results of comments received from trained peers or from the training the writers themselves received. In either case, however, the training was effective.

The conclusion from this research is that peer response instruction, not peer response itself, is beneficial. Even though the long-term effects have not been clearly shown, other benefits exists: learners spend more time speaking in the target language, the training or response may help the learners revise their own writing, and it may help reduce teachers' workload.

Writing Pedagogy outside of North America

Although process pedagogies have long dominated North American classrooms, this has not always been the case elsewhere. English is the dominant foreign language in most settings outside of North America and is certainly the only one in which there exists significant research on writing. We therefore limit our discussion to English. Most descriptions of ELT outside North America do not focus specifically on writing. In China, for example, writing instruction is viewed as part of the "holistic development of the students' English ability rather than a separate course" (You, 2004a, p. 256). At the university level, L2 writing instruction has been influenced by the globalization of Western writing pedagogies (Cahill, 1999; You, 2004b), but more powerfully by the tests that determine students' futures: The College English Test (CET) and the National Matriculation English Test (NMET). In spite of many teachers' awareness of more labor-intensive approaches to writing instruction, including genre and process pedagogies, the realities of large classes, students' relatively low proficiency, overworked and underpaid teachers, and lack of teacher preparation have forced most teachers to teach to these tests and utilize more traditional pedagogies involving models and memorization (You, 2004a, 2004b).

In both Japan and Korea, the situation is similar, even when this is at odds with national curricula that espouse more meaning-based and collaborative pedagogies (Butler & Iino, 2005; Chang, 2004; Gates, 2003; Gorsuch, 1998; Kubota, 2001). Most important are high-stakes tests, which may not assess writing directly, instead testing sentence-level knowledge and the ability to reproduce models (Kikuchi, 2006). Most writing instruction in both the L1 and the L2 at the secondary level in Japan is aimed at passing these examinations (Kobayashi & Rinnert, 2002). Chang (2004) compared the teaching of writing in Korean middle and high school to the Seventh National Curriculum, which called for a greater emphasis on communication. She found that the vast majority of writing activities were closed-ended and focused on grammatical accuracy. Textbooks included minimal open-ended writing activity, and 77 percent of the high school students in her sample reported never having written more than a paragraph in English. Gates (2003) reports similar findings for Japan, in that classroom practices and textbooks were at odds with the Ministry of Education's guidelines to give all language teaching, including writing instruction, a greater focus on the expression of meaning.

In Europe, although it is difficult to make generalizations across such a wide variety of contexts, instruction in FL writing has generally taken a back seat to instruction in oral communication in recent years. However, interest in improving written proficiency is increasing (Reichelt, 1997, 2005). In countries that have a tradition of explicit L1 writing instruction (e.g., Germany), explicit instruction in L2 writing is considered unnecessary because learners can draw on their knowledge of writing in their L1. In contexts without a tradition of formal or explicit teaching of L1 writing, such as Poland and Ukraine, instruction has either tended to focus on personal essays or become a pretext for formal practice of newly acquired vocabulary and grammar (Reichelt, 1997; Tarnopolsky, 2000).

In the past 20 years, the teaching and assessment (see Assessing Writing, below) of foreign languages in general, including writing, across Europe have been dominated by the development of the Common European Frame of Reference (CEFR) by the Council of Europe (Council of Europe, 2001). The CEFR is not aimed at creating uniformity of instruction across the continent; rather, it was developed to assist learners, teachers, materials and curriculum designers, and testers toward a common understanding of language proficiency and language use, including writing (Figueras et al., 2005; Heyworth, 2006). It does not explicitly state any specific pedagogy, but assumes a "communicative, action-based, learner-centred view of language learning" (Heyworth, p. 181). Perhaps more important, it provides "the most comprehensive and broad-based effort to create holistic and analytic scales of language use and language competence, and to employ sound empirical methods for deriving useful descriptors of the same" (Norris, 2005, p. 399).

The Frame of Reference consists of descriptors of language proficiency at six global levels. There are also self-assessment grids and rating scales that include a section on what the learner can do in writing. There are both general descriptors (e.g., *I can write simple connected text on topics which are familiar or of personal interest. I can write personal letters describing experiences and impressions*), more detailed breakdowns of writing competencies, and "Can do" descriptions in terms of particular contexts, such as tourism, work, and study (e.g., *CAN write to a hotel to ask about the availability of services, for example, facilities for the disabled*), which are designed to link the CEFR to assessment instruments, such as the ALTE Can Do Project (Council of Europe, 2001, Appendix D), the computer-based diagnostic test DIALANG (Alderson & Huhta, 2005), and the European Language Portfolio for learner self-assessment (Little, 2005).

Post-Process Approaches

A greater diversity of approaches has also begun to characterize L2 writing instruction in North America. In the last 10 years, there has been a growing trend away from process writing in the academy, although this is largely not the case in L2 writing classrooms. There are several reasons why writing scholars have questioned reliance on process approaches in L2 settings, not the least of which is that elements of this approach turned out to be ineffective in some contexts outside of the North American university classroom or with writers from disparate cultural backgrounds (Carson & Nelson, 1996; Holliday, 1994; Hu, 2005; Pennycook, 1996; Ramanathan & Atkinson, 1999; Shen, 1989). Writing instruction has taken a social turn, via various, sometimes overlapping, sometimes conflicting, routes. The major developments have been in the areas of genre-based and situated learning pedagogies, sociocultural approaches, and critical pedagogy.

Genre-based writing instruction

Probably the most influential of these approaches are genre-based pedagogies. One of the most potent objections to process writing instruction was to its early emphasis on individual voice and self-discovery (e.g., Horowitz, 1986). Some have objected that the dominant place for voice and the expression of meaning has been accompanied by a diminution in the importance of formal features of writing. This can create problems, particularly for non-mainstream learners, including L2 writers (Graff, 2003; Hinkel, 2002, 2004; Hyland, 2004; Scarcella, 2002). Delpit's (1999) objections to such pedagogy, although focused primarily on the struggles of African-American learners, might apply equally to L2 writers. Such an approach, she argues, disadvantages minority learners. The self-discovery process assumes a great deal of cultural knowledge that middle-class American students may well have. Yet, it is far less likely that L2 writers will have access to the same knowledge, and they are often left guessing as to what they are supposed to be learning or discovering. As result, there have been calls for more "visible pedagogy" (Bernstein, 1990, p. 90) in which what they are to learn is made clear to students.

One such visible pedagogy is the teaching of genres. Genre means different things to different scholars; however, it is generally considered to be recurring or characteristic textual (oral or written) responses to the requirements of the social context. Most genre scholars will agree that genres are socially constructed and goal-oriented (Martin, 1992). Written genres can only be understood within a specific context and they are produced for specific social purposes. Although specific approaches to genre differ, all agree that it essential that the language and functions of texts be viewed together, in both research and pedagogy.

Genre theorists differ, however, with respect to the extent that they emphasize language and rhetorical structures or the social contexts of writing (J. Flowerdew, 2002; Hyon, 1996; Pang, 2002). Scholars who focus on linguistic features are more frequently associated with the Sydney School and the work of Michael Halliday. This work has been highly influential, especially in Australia, where it has been used extensively to develop secondary school curricula. Studies within this functional-systemic approach have examined how registers are constructed from linguistic resources to achieve particular meanings within specific contexts, for example, the research article or the medical report. Writers need to master these registers to be successful within specific contexts. Genre-based writing instruction lays bare the linguistic and rhetorical bones of different registers in order to facilitate this mastery. This approach has been widely adopted in ESP pedagogy, in which learners receive explicit instruction on the complex linguistic and discourse demands of scientific and other discipline-specific forms of writing (e.g., Dudley-Evans, 1997; Jacoby, Leech, & Holten, 1995; Swales, 1990), as well as, to a lesser extent, in foreign language pedagogy (e.g., Byrnes & Sprang, 2003; Swaffer, 2003).

A second, more socially oriented approach, still focusing on genre, is usually associated with New Rhetoric, based on the writings of Bakhtin, but also drawing on the work of Lave and Wenger (1991) on situated learning. Bakhtin maintains that language is inherently dialogic, connecting the past to the present, new texts to previous texts, and speakers and writers to their social context, in particular, their audience. Language learning, too, is viewed as dialogic, taking place within social interaction, rather than within individuals (Johnson, 2004). Research applying these theories to L2 acquisition is relatively new, and applications to L2 writing instruction have been largely exploratory (e.g., Adam & Artemeva, 2002; Braxley, 2005; Orr, 2005). Finally, situated learning approaches view learning as a social process, embedded in relationships between experts and novices, rather than as the transfer of knowledge. There have been few attempts to incorporate situated learning into L2 writing instruction, perhaps because most institutional instruction in L2 writing does not lend itself to *legitimate peripheral participation,* the term Lave and Wenger use to describe the initial stages of situated learning. As Johns (1995b) has pointed out, most L2 writing classrooms provide instruction in school genres (e.g., the five-paragraph essay, the research paper), which differ considerably from authentic genres, making the sort of apprenticeship described in situated learning all the more difficult to achieve.

Genre-based writing pedagogy as a whole has arisen, in part, because of dissatisfaction with process instruction that often casts writing as a solitary process taking place inside the brains of individual learners, but also as result of a new understanding of literacy as not just a cognitive competence, but a purposeful social process, as well. Hyland (2004) describes some of the advantages of genre-based writing pedagogy over process approaches. Most important, it is explicit and systematic; it is clear from the outset what students are to learn and the path by which they are to arrive at this goal. In addition, the genres chosen for instruction are based on student needs. Genre theorists, such as Hyland (1990, 2004), Feez (2002), and Christie (1989), also claim that making genres explicit and offering a staged pedagogy for understanding them provides students with access to the discourses of power, which may be obscured in more implicit process pedagogies.

Genre theory in writing instruction has not been without detractors. (For reviews of these arguments, see Benesch, 2001; Johns, 1995a). Some feel that genres are embedded in their social contexts in ways that are too complex to divorce them from these contexts and teach them in the classroom (Adam & Artemeva, 2002; Freedman & Adam, 2000). They argue that genres must remain anchored to their original contexts in order to be learned successfully, suggesting the need for a more situated pedagogy. A second objection is that genres are merely recipes. Kay and Dudley-Evans (1998), in a survey of teacher attitudes toward genre, found that many teachers felt that genre instruction could easily become similar to the rhetorical modes instruction of earlier current-traditional approaches, in which learners were taught formulaic modes of writing with little attention paid to their communicative purpose. Genre theorists acknowledge that genres do constrain learners' choices, but counter that such limits are, in fact, important for them to learn. Instruction that is unconstrained may result in learners' failure to learn dominant discourse modes and would ultimately be a disservice to learners (Christie, 1989; Hyland, 2004). Finally, critical theorists argue that teaching students the genres of dominant discourses merely recapitulates current power structures and only gives the illusion of access to power (Benesch, 1995, 2001; Canagarajah, 2002; Luke, 1996). This may be particularly applicable to second language and second dialect speakers, most of whom are already in relatively less powerful positions in society.

Perhaps the most important criticism, however, is that there is very little research on the impact of genre-based approaches in L2 writing instruction (Hyon, 2002). Only a few preliminary studies have been published (e.g., Henry & Roseberry, 1998; Reppen, 1995). Most writing on the topic tends to lay out the case for genre pedagogy and offer careful linguistic, rhetorical, and sometimes social analyses of existing genres (e.g., Hyland, 1990; Schleppegrell, 2001, 2004). Others offer pedagogical suggestions for curriculum development and instruction (e.g., Bhatia, 1991; Hyland, 2004; Johns, 1997; Macken-Horarik, 2002; Schleppegrell & Achugar, 2003; Swales & Feak, 1994). At this point, however, it is difficult to do more than speculate on the effectiveness of genre-based pedagogies in promoting either L2 acquisition or L2 writing proficiency.

As noted, one of the strengths of genre analyses is their careful exploration of the linguistic and rhetorical features of texts. These efforts have been significantly aided by advances in corpus linguistics. Pioneered by Sinclair (1990), this work allows genre analysts to look for patterns in massive amounts of linguistic data, controlling for genre. It is possible to determine which words cluster together or how particular words function within specific genres (Biber, Conrad, & Reppen, 1998; Biber et al., 1999; Hunston & Francis, 2000). The insights of these analyses have been incorporated into proposals for writing instruction (Belcher, 2006; Biber et al., 2002; Burnard & McEnerny, 2000; L. Flowerdew, 2003; Gaskill & Cobb, 2004; Hinkel, 2002; O'Sullivan & Chambers, 2006; Partington, 1998; Starfield, 2004; Tribble, 2002), either in the development of learner corpora or in activities that allow learners to explore the meaning and use of words and phrases, detect and correct errors, and make more targetlike word choices through the use of concordances and other corpus tools.

Sociocultural approaches

Unlike genre-based approaches to L2 writing, sociocultural approaches have largely been confined to research studies. Sociocultural theory (SCT), based on the work of Lev Vygotsky, argues "that the most important forms of human cognitive activity develop through interaction within these social and material environments" (Lantolf & Thorne, 2006, pp. 197–8). Many of the central constructs of SCT lend themselves easily to the writing classroom. Vygotsky maintains that learning reflects a process of internalization, that is, "the process of making what was once external assistance a resource that is internally available to the individual" (Lantolf & Thorne, 2006, p. 200). Both researchers and educators have been captivated by the construct *zone of proximal development* (ZPD), that is, the distance between the level of actual development and the level of potential development when assisted by another, either a more capable actor or a peer. This notion of assistance, often called scaffolding, fits in with many of the activities that are familiar in process pedagogy (Weissberg, 2006). As noted above, current classroom practice often includes collaborative peer work. One rationale for this practice is that together, learners may be able to accomplish what they could not do alone, a notion very much in keeping with one of the tenets of SCT – that collaborative learning precedes and promotes individual development.

Although there are a considerable number of studies of L2 writing that have applied the insights of SCT to the analysis of learner data (de Guerrero & Villamil, 2000, Nassaji & Cumming, 2000; Parks et al., 2006; Swain & Lapkin, 2002; Villamil & de Guerrero, 2006), there have been fewer attempts to use the insights of SCT directly in the L2 classroom; Aljaafreh and Lantolf (1994) and a follow-up study by Nassaji and Swain (2000) are two important exceptions. They show how SCT can be used to guide the provision of feedback to L2 writers, in particular, to address their linguistic development. Aljaafreh and Lantolf document the performance of an L2 writer assisted by an expert tutor. They show how the ZPD can be operationalized to deliver effective feedback: Feedback must be graduated, contingent, and continuously negotiated between the expert and novice. In other words, assistance must be offered that "encourages the learner to function at his or her potential level of ability" (p. 468). Both the amount and nature of necessary feedback are likely to change as the learner appropriates the process; hence, the need for continuous dialogue and negotiation. Aljaafreh and Lantolf developed a scale to reflect this transition from the other-regulated stage (performance assisted by the tutor) to the self-regulated stage (unassisted performance). They matched the type of feedback to the learner's progress through these stages, resulting in a continuous negotiation of the ZPD. They claim that this type of feedback was an effective tool in facilitating the L2 writer's accurate use of English articles, and that the writer's development was revealed not only in production but also by the quality of the assistance required to perform the activity. In other words, the performance within the ZPD revealed not just performance but potential that shows the future direction of development. It is important to note, however, that development was operationalized as use during the tutoring session; long-term changes were not documented.

Nassaji and Swain (2000) followed up the Aljaafreh and Lantolf study with a more controlled, although still small, instructional study. They compared the effect of feedback on article use provided within the ZPD with random feedback.

The student who received negotiated assistance in response to her ZPD made greater and more consistent progress than the students who received non-negotiated feedback on errors. The dynamic nature of the ZPD makes its use in instruction both a challenge and an opportunity. Lantolf has suggested there may be future important applications of SCT, and specifically the ZPD construct, in assessment, because the ZPD allows researchers and testers to focus prospectively on learner development, as well as on current unassisted performance (Johnson, 2004; Poehner & Lantolf, 2005).

Critical pedagogy

Critical pedagogy spans far beyond the teaching of writing, or L2 instruction, and originates in the work of Freire, Foucault, Fairclough, and Kress. It comes into writing pedagogy in the form of *critical literacy.* Advocates of critical approaches argue that previous pedagogies reinforce power relationships and simply teach writers to adopt stances and genres that maintain their powerless positions (Benesch, 2001; Canagarajah, 2002; Leeman, 2005). Instead they advocate a pedagogy that will help learners become aware of those relationships, articulate them, and ideally, challenge them. In particular, critical pedagogy emphasizes the need to situate writing instruction within a social and political context that extends beyond the classroom, and to see the classroom itself as a social and political context with its own power relationships (Liebowitz, 2006; Wallace, 2001).

In contrast to genre-based pedagogies, there are few fully described examples of critical writing curricula. Wallace (2001) gives one of the more detailed descriptions of a course grounded in critical pedagogy. Much of it is engaged in developing critical awareness of texts within specific contexts. Yet, it is interesting to note that in addressing how writing is actually to be done, Wallace relies on the work of genre theorists and systemic functional linguistics. In other words, critical theory was the foundation for the students' exploration of literacy practices and power relationships. For instruction on how to write and on language choice, Wallace turns to Halliday.

Other descriptions of critical English for academic purposes (EAP) writing courses are less forthcoming, or perhaps they simply assume reliance on by-now-traditional process approaches (e.g., Benesch, 1998, 2001; Smoke, 2001). Instead, the course descriptions focus on raising awareness, with activities such as literacy journals and narratives, reflections on learning strategies, and ethnographic projects (Benesch, 2001; Canagarajah, 2002). They also stress thinking critically about topics that may be new to L2 learners, often with politically charged themes. Canagarajah suggests that an increased awareness of power relationships and the struggle against them may even extend to considerations of form, particularly as regards L2 writing instruction for World English users (2002, 2006). For example, he advocates a rethinking of errors as "choices," and of feedback on error as "negotiation" (2002, p. 52).

Morgan and Ramanathan (2005) describe activities in the critical literacy toolkit as it applies to L2 instruction in academic settings. They advocate the use of personal narratives that link the experience of individuals to power relationships in the larger sociopolitical context, encourage learners to question disciplinary texts, and promote reflection on individual participation in power structures, and especially, how the structures are evident in texts. Courses designed to encourage critical literacy may also include assignments that are immediately relevant to the learners, such as writing letters of protest to the university administration or articulating areas of conflict with a teacher, landlord, or community leader. Again, however, there is usually little mention of how writing is taught or practiced. This may mean that the critical pedagogy begins and ends with consideration and discussion of social and political contexts, and issues with instruction with nuts and bolts of writing, with ideas on issues of rhetorical and linguistics form drawn from other sources.

Critical approaches to L2 writing instruction have come under fire from two directions. First, many who favor genre pedagogy argue that critical literacy instruction, like the more expressivist strands of process instruction, are likely to disadvantage non-mainstream learners (Johns, 1995b, 2003; Swales, 1990). They argue that it is unfair to ask learners to question dominant discourses before they can use them. Instead, it is an educator's responsibility to give students access to these genres and help them toward mastery. Once they have gained access to these discourses, struggling against them should be left up to the learners and left out of the classroom. Another objection is that the focus on ideology is simply another form of hegemony, a misguided effort by intellectuals and ideologues to impose their own agenda on L2 learners (Allison, 1994; Santos, 1992, 2001) when learners' needs lie elsewhere.

All of these approaches that have taken the social turn share a deep appreciation for the social, and often political, context in which L2 writers must learn and live, and the belief that any effective writing instruction must take the context of writing into account, even as they advocate different ways for providing such instruction.

Assessing Writing

The purposes of L2 assessment are varied, and L2 writing assessment is no exception. Researchers have addressed ways to assess writing for research purposes, for large-scale testing (generally for gate-keeping and placement purposes), and for classroom feedback and grading. Assessing writing for research purposes generally involves measuring some aspect of a piece of writing to answer a research question, such as "Which type of error correction works best?" or "How does students' writing differ on two types of writing tasks?" Research studies generally use quantitative measures that can involve holistic measures of quality, analytic scales that break down writing into various components, or more objective measures, such as words per T-unit, errors per T-unit, or lexical type:token ratios. Objective measures have also been examined as possible measures of L2 writing development, in other words, how learners' writing changes over time (de Haan & van Esch, 2005; Ortega, 2003; Shaw & Liu, 1998; Wolfe-Quintero et al., 1998). Assessing writing for research purposes is beyond the scope of this paper; we focus here on assessment for such purposes as placement, gate-keeping, diagnostic, and achievement purposes. The majority of scholarly work on writing assessment focuses on large-scale assessment for a variety of reasons, including the availability of large samples of data. Furthermore, large educational and testing institutions are perhaps aware of the scrutiny that their practices may come under, and thus need to demonstrate the reliability and validity of their tests publicly. Therefore, what follows is a discussion of the issues and research in large-scale testing, and a relatively brief discussion of the classroom and alternative assessment.

Large-scale testing

As Hamp-Lyons states, ". . . few ESL professionals these days are prepared to believe that we can test writing by any means other than having students actually write" (2003, p. 165). Although in the past, some tests included indirect assessments of writing skills, today, most large-scale writing assessment requires students to write. This change came about as a concern for content validity and task authenticity, related to both the ethical issues behind assessing writing, and also the negative washback that can occur in classrooms if writing is assessed only through indirect tests. As noted in the discussion of L2 writing instruction, particularly in Asia, when national tests do not assess writing, teachers may not teach writing at all.

In order to develop a writing test, a test being a sample of behavior, one first needs to determine the purpose of the test and what skills a student is expected to have. Various frameworks for a variety of contexts have been developed, often with the goal of determining what skills should be assessed, such as in the European Common Framework. Another example is the Canadian Language Benchmarks (Nagy & Stewart, 2000), standards that can be used to assess language for work and study. For the writing component, descriptors range from "I can take a phone message with 5–7 details" to "I can write a complex formal research report of ten typed pages." Although the National Foreign Language Standards in the US (National Standards Foreign Language Project, 1996), used for K-12 contexts, are much less specific, the American Council on the Teaching of Foreign Languages guidelines (Breiner-Sanders, Swender, & Terry, 2001) do offer descriptors at various levels, and include tasks like "Can write all the symbols in an alphabetic or syllabic system or 50–100 characters or compounds in a character writing system" and "Can write most types of correspondence, such as memos, as well as social and business letters, and short research papers and statements of position in areas of special interest or in special fields." Although these guidelines can be somewhat useful for teachers and testers, it is not immediately clear how one might go about sampling writing behavior for assessment, particularly in a limited amount of time. In other words, what should serve as the writing task or prompt?

Weigle (2002) and Hamp-Lyons (2003) describe some of the variables that one needs to consider when constructing a writing prompt. Among them are topic, genre, number of tasks, whether or not students have a choice of prompts, and format. The choice of prompt is tied directly to a test's validity. To use the Test of English as a Foreign Language (TOEFL) as an example, the exam used to include a prompt that asked a general question, such as, "Do you agree or disagree with the following statement? Always telling the truth is the most important consideration in any relationship between people. Use specific reasons and examples to support your answer" (www.ets.org). The student had 30 minutes to answer the question. The new internet-based TOEFL includes the same type of general question, called an independent task, as well as an integrated writing task that requires students to read a short passage, listen to a related lecture, and then write a 20-minute essay relating the two. There is a wide variety of ways to determine the validity of such a writing test. One important consideration is content validity, the extent to which such writing tasks are representative of real tasks in the context that students are taking the test to enter, in this case, North American universities. For the new TOEFL, Cumming et al. (2004) interviewed experienced university ESL teachers as a means of assessing the tasks and determining ways to improve them. Determining task authenticity can, of course, encompass many more steps, however, as described by Wu and Stansfield (2001).

Single-item tests, such as the TOEFL independent tasks, have a variety of problems, as discussed in Weigle (2004), and the addition of a task in which students respond to some written or aural source text, such as the TOEFL, has been seen by many as a positive addition because it is more similar to actual university writing tasks (Cumming et al., 2000; Weigle, 2004). Weigle (2004) examined the implementation of an integrated university reading and writing ESL test and found it to be superior in terms of both reliability and validity to a test that simply had students respond to short prompts. Furthermore, the integrated test had the advantage of positive washback in the ESL classes. Cumming et al. (2005) found that the independent and integrated prompts did elicit writing that differed significantly on a variety of measures, the implication being that to assess students' writing, a variety of tasks, including those that integrate other skills, are necessary. In creating any writing prompt, it is essential to keep in mind the context for which one is eliciting written language samples. In the case of the TOEFL, there is the problem of coming up with one test to assess language proficiency for both undergraduate and graduate students in a wide range of academic fields. In the case of foreign language assessment in the US, the Educational Testing Service, in their Advanced Placement tests, has thus far maintained its use of a single-item prompt (www.ets.org), perhaps because the goals of the students taking the test are less clear.

The second major issue in large-scale testing is the grading of the texts produced by the prompts. A variety of scales or rubrics exist, both holistic and analytic, and primary and multitrait. Over the years, the advantages and disadvantages of each type regarding reliability, validity, practicality, and authenticity, have been debated (e.g., Cohen, 1994; Weigle, 2004), and the scale must certainly be appropriate to the context. Recently, attention has also been directed to the characteristics and training of the raters themselves. Weigle (1994, 1998) studied how experience affected raters' scores both before and after training, as well the interaction of experience, training, and prompt. Shi (2001) studied native and non-native EFL teachers' ratings of Chinese students' essays using a holistic scale, and found that although there were no significant quantitative differences in the scores, written comments revealed the Chinese teachers and the native English-speaking teachers were attending to different criteria. Lumley (2002) found that although a set of experienced raters were giving similar scores, they were placing different emphases on different components of the scale they were using, echoing the concerns of others who have claimed that rater training may lead to reliability at the expense of validity (Huot, 1993).

Classroom assessment and portfolios

Classroom teachers need to assess writing to assign grades by measuring student achievement, and to give feedback. Certainly, teachers want to assess writing in a way that is reliable and valid, just as in large-scale testing, but there are also concerns about providing students with feedback on their writing, something that is minimally a concern on most large-scale tests. To this end, it is unlikely that a classroom teacher would assign a holistic score, such as the one used for the TOEFL, because analytic scales generally provide learners with more information about where their strengths and weaknesses lie. Weigle (2004) provides an excellent summary of the relationship between concerns related to large-scale testing and classroom testing.

With regard to how teachers actually assess writing, little research has been conducted. One notable exception is Cumming (2001), who interviewed 48 experienced ESL and EFL teachers about their assessment practices. Although he expected to find differences in second and foreign language contexts, he did not. What he found were differences related to teaching writing for general versus specific purposes. For example, in specific-purpose courses, teachers defined their own standards, based on the syllabus and focused on a limited range of criteria. In the general purposes courses, teachers had a wide variety of ways to assess writing, focusing on a wide variety of goals.

Brindley (2001) reviewed research on teacher-constructed assessment tasks as a way to assess competencies outlined in the Australian Adult Migrant English Program. He stated that the tasks varied widely (Wigglesworth, 2002, as cited in Brindley), and in the case of writing, although teachers agreed on overall competency attainment, they did not agree as much on specific criteria (Smith, 2000, as cited in Brindley). He suggested that because of the time-consuming nature of developing assessment tasks, teachers should be given a task bank containing piloted tasks to ensure greater comparability across classrooms in which teachers are expected to assess their students' writing in relation to a set of outcomes. Arkoudis and O'Loughlin (2004) further explored the problems of teachers implementing top-down standards in an Australian context. In a qualitative study, they explored the teachers' perspectives and revealed the contradictions of using one particular outcomes-based assessment framework in the classroom.

Self-assessment may be used by classroom teachers as a way to make learners more aware of their strengths and weaknesses. As in peer review, learners can be given questions to answer or rubrics to evaluate their own writing. They can also be given guidelines and techniques for assessing their writing process (Brown, 2005; Sullivan & Lindgren, 2002). Luoma and Tarnanen (2003) reported on the construction of a self-assessment instrument for writers learning Finnish as a second language. The instrument was based on the DIALANG project (www.dialang.org) in which learners could assess their language skills in relation to the Common European Framework. Luoma and Tarnanen had students compare their writing to benchmark texts and assess their own work. The learners found the instrument to be helpful, but not to be a complete replacement for teacher feedback. Self-assessment is not intended to replace other means of assessment. Instead, as Luoma and Tarnanen stated (p. 461), "What self-rating systems can do is to provide another means for learners to practice writing and self-reflection."

Over the last 15 years, much has been written about the use of alternative forms of L2 assessment. Portfolios, which include some form of self-assessment, have been praised for their construct validity and authenticity. Concerns have been raised, however, about their lack of reliability and impracticality (e.g., Weigle, 2002). Empirical studies are necessary to determine how they can best be implemented. Hirvela and Sweetland (2005) completed a case study of two ESL writers in classes that required them to develop portfolios. By following the two students, they showed how they responded to the requirements and what they did and did not understand about the portfolio's purpose. Kraemer (2005) described in detail her implementation of the portfolio component of a German FL class at a US university. She gathered students' opinions on the procedure and found that they considred the portfolios an effective teaching tool, as well as a preferable form of assessment. Although portfolios are more commonly used in the class, they can be used at the program level, as well. Song and August (2002) described the use of portfolios as an alternative to traditional testing for an ESL exit test. They found that the portfolio system was preferable because it successfully identified students who proceeded to do well in the subsequent English composition course, but who had failed a traditional exam.

The effects of technology on assessment

Technology is changing the logistics of assessment. With regard to writing, students often type their essays instead of handwriting, and this has led researchers to examine how computers can affect the assessment of students' writing. Li (2006) studied ESL writers completing two comparable essays by hand and on a word processor. The students revised more and paid more attention to higher-order thinking skills while using the computer. However, although there were no significant differences on a variety of traits, including communicative quality, organization, and linguistic accuracy and appropriateness, the computer-written essays were better in terms of argumentation, presumably because of the ease of making higher-level revisions. Wolfe and Manalo (2004) also studied essays written by hand and on a word processor, but in their studies, students chose which medium to use. Controlling for demographic variables, they found that lower-proficiency students did slightly better on handwritten essays, whereas higher-proficiency students did not perform differently under the two conditions.

Wolfe and Manolo did not control for the medium in which raters graded the essays, meaning that they could have been influenced by how the content of the essay was presented, but they state that previous research suggests that such a problem is minimal. H. K. Lee (2004) did examine raters' scores on handwritten, researcher-transcribed typed essays, and student-written typed essays. He found that reliability was higher on the transcribed and typed essays when the raters used a holistic scale, probably because holistic scales assess overall judgment. Like Li, he looked at the quality of the essays in a repeated measures design, and found no differences with regard to holistic scores, but significantly higher scores on the typed essays when an analytic scale was used.

Ethics in L2 writing assessment

Discussions of ethical issues related to L2 assessment have increased in the literature within the last 10 years (e.g., Hamp-Lyons, 1997; Kunnan, 2000; Shohamy, 1997). Cumming (2002) points out that these issues are particularly acute in the assessment of writing because it often involves expressing personal views, resulting in a form for others to evaluate. One could argue that any study addressing the reliability and validity of writing assessment involves ethical concerns. If an assessment measure is not reliable and valid, it cannot be ethical. Furthermore, studies of how tests are used, including Weigle (2004), and Braine (2001), who studied problems with the implementation of an exit writing exam, deal with ethical issues related to the use of tests. The ethics of a test cannot be determined in a vacuum, only in relationship to its use, and a test that is ethical in one context may not be ethical in another. For example, Cumming (2002) discusses ethical dilemmas in the assessment of writing in high-stakes large-scale testing. He explains that tests often become a unique writing context, and that context "must on one hand represent the constructs to be assessed but on the other hand not be biased for or against any particular population or sub-population" (p. 80). High-stakes tests need to be consistent, thus making it difficult to use alternative forms of assessment, where many variables cannot be controlled. Furthermore, what they test needs to be clearly explained to potential test-takers.

One final important consideration in settings where English is not a mother tongue is the model of English on which assessment should be based. Of course, this issue is not limited to writing, and in fact, of all of the areas of instruction and assessment, writing is probably the least permeable to local variation. Nevertheless, some scholars have questioned the hegemony of dominant native-speaker models both inside and outside North America (Canagarajah, 2006; Horner &

Trimbur, 2002; Jenkins, 2006; Kubota, 2001), and some have urged that testing institutions reexamine the ways in which their instruments (e.g., TOEFL, TOEIC, IELTS) serve the entire international community (Brown, 2004; Davies, Hamp-Lyons, & Kemp, 2003; Hamp-Lyons & Zhang, 2001; Lowenberg, 2002).

REFERENCES

Adam, C. & Artemeva, N. (2002). Writing instruction for English for Academic Purposes (EAP) classes: Introducing second language learners to the academic community. In A. Johns (ed.), *Genre in the classroom: Multiple perspectives* (pp. 179–96). Mahwah, NJ: Lawrence Erlbaum.

Alderson, C. & Huhta, A. (2005). The development of a suite of computer-based diagnostic tests based on the Common European Framework. *Language Testing* 22, 301–20.

Aljaafreh, A. & Lantolf, J. (1994). Negative feedback as regulation and second language learning in the zone of proximal development. *Modern Language Journal* 78, 465–83.

Allison, D. (1994). Comments on Sarah Benesch's "ESL, ideology and the politics of pragmatism." *TESOL Quarterly* 28, 618–23.

Arkoudis, S. & O'Loughlin, K. (2004). Tensions between validity and outcomes: Teacher assessment of written work of recently arrived immigrant ESL students. *Language Testing* 21, 284–304.

Ashwell, T. (2000). Patterns of teacher response to student writing in a multiple-draft composition classroom. *Journal of Second Language Writing* 9, 227–49.

Ayoun, D. (2004). The effectiveness of written recasts in the second language acquisition of aspectual distinctions in French: A follow-up study. *Modern Language Journal* 88, 31–55.

Belcher, D. (2006). English for specific purposes: Teaching to perceived needs and imagined futures in worlds of work, study and everyday life. *TESOL Quarterly* 40, 133–56.

Benesch, S. (1995). Genres and processes in sociocultural context. *Journal of Second Language Writing* 4, 191–5.

Benesch, S. (1998). Anorexia: A feminist EAP curriculum. In T. Smoke (ed.), *Adult ESL: Politics, pedagogy and participation in classrooms and community programs* (pp. 101–14). Mahwah, NJ: Lawrence Erlbaum.

Benesch, S. (2001). *Critical English for academic purposes*. Mahwah, NJ: Lawrence Erlbaum.

Berg, E. C. (1999). The effects of trained peer response on ESL students' revision types and writing quality. *Journal of Second Language Writing* 8, 215–41.

Bernstein, B. (1990). *The structuring of pedagogical discourse. Vol. 4: Class, codes and control.* London: Routledge.

Bhatia, R. (1991). A genre-based approach to ESP development. *World Englishes* 10, 1–14.

Biber, D., Conrad, S., & Reppen, R. (1998). *Corpus linguistics.* Cambridge: Cambridge University Press.

Biber, D., Conrad, S., Reppen, R., Byrd, P., & Helt, M. (2002). Speaking and writing in the university: A multidimensional comparison. *TESOL Quarterly* 36, 9–48.

Biber, D., Johansson, S., Leech, G., Conrad, S., & Finegan, E. (1999). *Longman grammar of spoken and written English.* Harlow, UK: Pearson.

Bitchener, J., Young, S., & Cameron, D. (2005). The effect of different types of corrective feedback on ESL student writing. *Journal of Second Language Writing* 14, 191–205.

Bosher, S. (1998). The composing processes of three Southeast Asian writers at the post-secondary level: An exploratory study. *Journal of Second Language Writing 7*, 205–41.

Braine, G. (2001). When an exit test fails. *System 29*, 221–34.

Braxley, K. (2005). Mastering academic English: International graduate students' use of dialogue and speech genres to meet the writing demands of graduate school. In J. Hall, G. Vitanova, & L. Marchenkova (eds.), *Dialogue with Bakhtin on second and foreign language learning: New perspectives* (pp. 11–32). Mahwah, NJ: Lawrence Erlbaum.

Breiner-Sanders, K., Swender, E., & Terry, R. (2001). ACTFL proficiency guidelines: Writing. ACTFL: www.actfl.org.

Brindley, G. (2001). Outcomes-based assessment in practice: Some examples and emerging insights. *Language Testing 18*, 393–407.

Brown, A. (2005). Self-assessment of writing in independent language learning programs: The value of annotated samples. *Assessing Writing 10*, 174–91.

Brown, J. D. (2004). What do we mean by bias, Englishes, Englishes in testing, and English language proficiency? *World Englishes 23*, 317–19.

Burnard, L. & McEnerny, T. (2000). *Rethinking language pedagogy from a corpus perspective.* London: Longman.

Butler, Y. G., & Iino, M. (2005). Current Japanese reforms in English language education: The 2003 "action plan." *Language Policy 4*, 25–45.

Byrnes, H. & Sprang, K. (2003). Fostering advanced L2 literacy: A genre-based cognitive approach. In H. Byrnes & H. H. Maxim (eds.), *Advanced foreign language learning: A challenge to college programs* (pp. 47–85). Boston: Thomson/Heinle.

Cahill, D. (1999). Contrastive rhetoric, orientalism and the Chinese second language writer. Unpublished doctoral dissertation, University of Illinois at Chicago.

Canagarajah, A. S. (2002). *Critical academic writing and multilingual students.* Ann Arbor, MI: University of Michigan Press.

Canagarajah, A. S. (2006). The place of World Englishes in composition: Pluralization continued. *College Composition and Communication 57*, 586–617.

Carson, J. & Nelson, G. (1996). Chinese students' perceptions of ESL peer response group interaction. *Journal of Second Language Writing 5*, 1–19.

Chandler, J. (2003). The efficacy of various kinds of error feedback for improvement in the accuracy and fluency of L2 student writing. *Journal of Second Language Writing 12*, 267–96.

Chang, M. J. (2004). Analysis of writing activities in Korean English textbooks. Unpublished master's thesis, Michigan State University, East Lansing, MI.

Christianson, K. (1997). Dictionary use by EFL writers: What really happens. *Journal of Second Language Writing 6*, 23–44.

Christie, F. (1989). *Language and education.* Oxford: Oxford University Press.

Cleland, A. & Pickering, M. (2006). Do speaking and writing employ the same syntactic representations? *Journal of Memory and Language 54*, 185–98.

Cohen, A. (1994). *Assessing language ability in the classroom.* Boston: Heinle.

Cohen, A. & Cavalcanti, M. (1990). Feedback on written compositions: Teacher and student verbal reports. In B. Kroll (ed.), *Second language writing: Research insights for the classroom* (pp. 155–77). Cambridge: Cambridge University Press.

Council of Europe (2001). *Common European Framework of Reference for Languages: Learning, teaching, assessment.* Cambridge: Cambridge University Press.

Cumming, A. (1990). Metalinguistic and ideational thinking in second language composing. *Written Communication 7*, 482–511.

Cumming, A. (2001). ESL/EFL instructor's practices for writing assessment: Specific purposes or general purposes? *Language Testing* 18, 207–24.

Cumming, A. (2002). Assessing L2 writing: Alternative constructs and ethical dilemmas. *Assessing Writing* 8, 73–83.

Cumming, A., Grant, L., Mulcahy-Ernt, P., & Powers, D. (2004). A teacher-verification study of speaking and writing prototype tasks for a new TOEFL. *Language Testing* 21, 107–45.

Cumming, A., Kantor, R., Baba, K., Erdosy, U., Eousanzoui, K., & James, M. (2005). Differences in written discourse in independent and integrated prototype tasks for next generation TOEFL. *Assessing Writing* 10, 5–43.

Cumming, A., Kantor, R., Powers, D., Santos, T., & Taylor, C. (2000). TOEFL 2000 writing framework: A working paper (TOEFL monograph no. MS-18; ETS RM-00-05). Princeton: Educational Testing Service.

Davies, A., Hamp-Lyons, L., & Kemp, C. (2003). Whose norms? International proficiency tests in English. *World Englishes* 22, 571–84.

de Guerrero, M. & Villamil, O. (2000). Activating the ZPD: Scaffolding in L2 peer revision. *Modern Language Journal* 84, 484–96.

de Haan, P. & van Esch, K. (2005). The development of writing in English and Spanish as foreign languages. *Assessing Writing* 10, 100–16.

Delpit, L. (1999). The silenced dialogue: Power and pedagogy in educating other people's children. *Harvard Educational Review* 58, 280–98.

Doughty, C. & Varela, E. (1998). Communicative focus on form. In C. J. Doughty & J. Williams (eds.), *Focus on form in classroom second language acquisition* (pp. 114–38). Cambridge: Cambridge University Press.

Dudley-Evans, T. (1997). Genre models for the teaching of academic writing to second language speakers: Advantages and disadvantages. In T. Miller (ed.), *Functional approaches to written text: Classroom applications* (pp. 150–9). Washington DC: USIS.

Ellis, R. (2001). Introduction: Investigating form-focused instruction. *Language Learning* 51, SUPP/1, 1–46.

Ellis, R. & Yuan, F. (2004). The effects of planning on fluency, complexity, and accuracy in second language narrative writing. *Studies in Second Language Acquisition* 26, 59–84.

Fathman, A. & Whalley, E. (1990). Teacher response to student correction: Focus on form versus content. In B. Kroll (ed.), *Second language writing: Research insights for the classroom* (pp. 178–85). Cambridge: Cambridge University Press.

Feez, S. (2002). Heritage and innovation in second language education. In A. Johns (ed.), *Genre in the classroom: Multiple perspectives* (pp. 43–69). Mahwah, NJ: Lawrence Erlbaum.

Ferris, D. (1997). The influence of teacher commentary on student revision. *TESOL Quarterly* 29, 33–53.

Ferris, D. (2002). *Treatment of error in second language student writing*. Ann Arbor, MI: University of Michigan Press.

Ferris, D. (2003). *Response to student writing: Implications for second language students*. Mahwah, NJ: Lawrence Erlbaum.

Ferris, D. (2004). The "grammar correction" debate in L2 writing: Where are we, and where do we go from here? (and what do we do in the meantime . . . ?). *Journal of Second Language Writing* 13, 49–62.

Ferris, D. (2006). Does error feedback help student writers? New evidence on the short- and long-term effects of written error correction. In K. Hyland & F. Hyland (eds.), *Feedback in second language writing* (pp. 81–104). Cambridge: Cambridge University Press.

Figueras, N., North, B., Takala, S., Verhelst, N., & Van Avermaet, P. (2005). Relating examinations to the Common European Framework: A manual. *Language Testing* 22, 261–79.

Flowerdew, J. (2002). Genre in the classroom: A linguistic approach. In A. Johns (ed.), *Genre in the classroom: Multiple perspectives* (pp. 91–102). Mahwah, NJ: Lawrence Erlbaum.

Flowerdew, L. (2003). A combined corpus and systemic-functional analysis of the problem-solution pattern in a student and professional corpus of technical writing. *TESOL Quarterly* 37, 489–511.

Foster, P. & Skehan, P. (1996). The influence of planning and task type on second language performance. *Studies in Second Language Acquisition* 18, 299–324.

Freedman, A. & Adam, C. (2000). Write where you are: Situated learning to write in university and workplace settings. In P. Dias & A. Pare (eds.), *Transitions: Writing in workplace and academic settings* (pp. 31–60). Creskill, NJ: Hampton Press.

Gaskill, D. & Cobb, T. (2004). Can learners use concordance feedback for writing errors? *System* 32, 301–19.

Gass, S. (1983). The development of L2 intuitions. *TESOL Quarterly* 17, 273–91.

Gates, S. (2003). Inconsistencies in writing within the Japanese junior high school EFL education system. *JALT Journal* 25, 197–217.

Goldstein, L. (2005). *Teacher written commentary in second language writing classrooms.* Ann Arbor, MI: University of Michigan Press.

Goldstein, L. & Conrad, S. (1990). Input and negotiation of meaning in ESL writing conferences. *TESOL Quarterly* 24, 443–60.

Gorsuch, G. (1998). Yakudoku EFL instruction in two Japanese high school classrooms: An exploratory study. *JALT Journal* 20, 6–32.

Graff, G. (2003). *Clueless in academe: How schooling obscures the life of the mind.* New Haven, CT: Yale University Press.

Hamp-Lyons, L. (1986). No new lamps for old yet, please. *TESOL Quarterly* 20, 790–6.

Hamp-Lyons, L. (1997). Washback, impact and validity: Ethical concerns. *Language Testing* 14, 295–303.

Hamp-Lyons, L. (2003). Writing teachers as assessors of writing. In B. Kroll (ed.), *Exploring the dynamics of second language writing* (pp. 162–89). New York: Cambridge University Press.

Hamp-Lyons, L. & Zhang, B. (2001). World Englishes: Issues in and from academic writing. In J. Flowerdew & M. Peacock (eds.), *Research perspectives on English for academic purposes* (pp. 101–16). Cambridge: Cambridge University Press.

Harklau, L. (2002). The role of writing in classroom second language acquisition. *Journal of Second Language Writing* 11, 329–50.

Hayes, J. R. (1996). A new framework for understanding cognition and affect in writing. In C. Levy & S. Ransdell (eds.), *The science of writing* (pp. 1–27). Mahwah, NJ: Lawrence Erlbaum.

Hayes, J. R. & Flower, L. S. (1980). Identifying the organization of writing processes. In L. Gregg & E. R. Steinberg (eds.), *Cognitive processes in writing* (pp. 3–30). Hillsdale, NJ: Lawrence Erlbaum.

Hedgcock, J. (2005). Taking stock of research and pedagogy in L2 writing. In E. Hinkel (ed.), *Handbook of research in second language teaching and learning* (pp. 597–614). Mahwah, NJ: Lawrence Erlbaum.

Helms-Park, R. & Stapleton, P. (2003). Questioning the importance of individualized voice in undergraduate L2 argumentative writing: An empirical study with pedagogical implications. *Journal of Second Language Writing* 12, 245–65.

Henry, A. & Roseberry, R. (1998). An evaluation of genre-based approach to the teaching of EAP/ESP writing. *TESOL Quarterly* 32, 147–56.

Heyworth, F. (2006). The Common European Framework. *ELT Journal* 60, 181–3.

Hinkel, E. (2002). *Second language writers' text.* Mahwah, NJ: Lawrence Erlbaum.

Hinkel, E. (2004). *Teaching academic ESL writing.* Mahwah, NJ: Lawrence Erlbaum.

Hirvela, A. & Sweetland, Y. (2005). Two case studies of L2 writers' experiences across language-directed portfolio contexts. *Assessing Writing* 10, 192–213.

Holliday, A. (1994). *Appropriate methodology and social context.* Cambridge: Cambridge University Press.

Horner, B. & Trimbur, J. (2002). English Only and U.S. college composition. *College Composition and Communication* 53, 594–630.

Horowitz, D. (1986). Process not product: Less than meets the eye. *TESOL Quarterly* 20, 141–4.

Hu, G. (2005). English language education in China: Policies, progress, and problems. *Language Policy* 4, 5–24.

Hunston, S. & Francis, G. (2000). *Pattern grammar.* Amsterdam: John Benjamins.

Huot, B. A. (1993). The influence of holistic scoring procedures on reading and rating student essays. In M. Williamson & B. Huot (eds.), *Validating holistic scoring for writing assessment: Theoretical and empirical foundations* (pp. 206–36). Cresskill, NJ: Hampton Press.

Hyland, K. (1990). A genre description of the argumentative essay. *RELC Journal* 21, 66–78.

Hyland, K. (2003). *Second language writing.* Cambridge: Cambridge University Press.

Hyland, K. (2004). *Genre and second language writing.* Ann Arbor, MI: University of Michigan Press.

Hyland, K. & Hyland, F. (2006). Contexts and issues in feedback on L2 writing. In K. Hyland & F. Hyland (eds.), *Feedback in second language writing* (pp. 1–19). Cambridge: Cambridge University Press.

Hyon, S. (1996). Genres in three traditions: Implications for ESL. *TESOL Quarterly* 30, 693–722.

Hyon, S. (2002). Genre and ESL reading: A classroom study. In A. Johns (ed.), *Genre in the classroom: Multiple perspectives* (pp. 121–41). Mahwah, NJ: Lawrence Erlbaum.

Jacobs, G., Curtis, A., Braine, G., & Huang, S. Y. (1998). Feedback on student writing: Taking the middle path. *Journal of Second Language Writing* 7, 307–18.

Jacoby, S., Leech, D., & Holten, C. (1995). A genre-based approach developmental writing course for undergraduate science majors. In D. Belcher & G. Braine (eds.), *Academic writing in a second language* (pp. 351–73). Norwood, NJ: Ablex.

Jarrett, S., Losh, E., & Puente, D. (2006). Transnational identifications: Biliterate writers in a first-year humanities course. *Journal of Second Language Writing* 15, 24–48.

Jenkins, J. (2006). Current perspectives on teaching world Englishes and English as a lingua franca. *TESOL Quarterly* 40, 157–81.

Johns, A. (1995a). Genre and pedagogical purpose. *Journal of Second Language Writing* 4, 181–90.

Johns, A. (1995b). Teaching classroom and authentic genres. In D. Belcher & G. Braine (eds.), *Academic writing in a second language* (pp. 277–92). Norwood, NJ: Ablex.

Johns, A. (1997). *Text, role and context: Developing academic literacies.* Cambridge: Cambridge University Press.

Johns, A. (2003). Genre and ESL/EFL composition instruction. In B. Kroll (ed.), *Exploring the dynamics of second language writing* (pp. 195–217). Cambridge: Cambridge University Press.

Johnson, M. (2004). *A philosophy of second language acquisition*. New Haven, CT: Yale University Press.

Jones, R., Garralda, A., Li, D., & Loch, G. (2006). Dynamics in on-line and face-to-face peer-tutoring sessions for second language writers. *Journal of Second Language Writing* 15, 1–23.

Kay, H. & Dudley-Evans, T. (1998). Genre: What teachers think. *ELT Journal* 52, 308–14.

Kikuchi, K. (2006). Revisiting English entrance exams at Japanese universities after a decade. *JALT Journal* 28, 77–96.

Kim, Y., Lowenstein, K. L., Pearson, P. D., & McLellan, M. (2001). A framework for conceptualizing and evaluating the contributions of written language activity in oral language development for ESL students. In J. V. Hoffman, D. L. Schallert, C. M. Fairbanks, J. Worthy, & B. Maloch (eds.), *50th Yearbook of the National Reading Conference*. Chicago, IL: National Reading Conference.

Kobayashi, H. & Rinnert, C. (2002). High school student perceptions of first language literacy instruction: Implications for second language writing. *Journal of Second Language Writing* 11, 91–116.

Kraemer, A. N. (2005). Implementing portfolio assessment in second-year German language classrooms. Unpublished master's thesis, Michigan State University, East Lansing, MI.

Krappels, A. (1990). An overview of second language writing process research. In B. Kroll (ed.), *Second language writing: Research insights for the classroom* (pp. 37–56). Cambridge: Cambridge University Press.

Kubota, R. (2001). The impact of globalization on language teaching in Japan. In D. Block & D. Cameron (eds.), *Globalization and language teaching* (pp. 13–28). London: Routledge.

Kubota, R. (2003). New approaches to gender, class, and race in second language writing. *Journal of Second Language Writing* 12, 31–47.

Kunnan, A. (2000). Fairness and justice for all. In A. Kunnan (ed.), *Fairness and validation in language assessment* (pp. 1–14). Cambridge: Cambridge University Press.

Lally, C. (2000). First language influences in second language composition: The effect of pre-writing. *Foreign Language Annals* 33, 428–32.

Lantolf, J. & Thorne, S. (2006). Sociocultural theory and second language learning. In B. VanPatten & J. Williams (eds.), *Theories in second language acquisition: An introduction* (pp. 197–220). Mahwah, NJ: Lawrence Erlbaum.

Lave, J. & Wenger, E. (1991). *Situated learning: Legitimate peripheral participation*. Cambridge: Cambridge University Press.

Lee, H. K. (2004). A comparative study of ESL writers' performance in a paper-based and a computer-delivered writing test. *Assessing Writing* 9, 4–26.

Lee, I. (2004). Error correction in L2 secondary writing classrooms: The case of Hong Kong. *Journal of Second Language Writing* 13, 285–312.

Leeman, J. (2003). Recasts and second language development. *Studies in Second Language Acquisition* 25, 37–63

Leeman, J. (2005). Engaging critical pedagogy. Spanish for native speakers. *Foreign Language Annals* 38, 35–45.

Li, J. (2006). The mediation of technology in ESL writing and its implications for writing assessment. *Assessing Writing* 11, 5–21.

Liebowitz, B. (2006). Learning in an additional language in a multilingual society: A South African case study on university-level writing. *TESOL Quarterly* 39, 661–81.

Little, D. (2005). The Common European Framework and the European Language Portfolio: Involving learners and their judgements in the assessment process. *Language Testing* 22, 321–36.

Liu, J. & Hansen, J. (2002). *Peer response in second language writing classrooms.* Ann Arbor, MI: University of Michigan Press.

Long, M. H. (2007). Recasts in SLA: The story so far. In M. H. Long, *Problems in SLA* (pp. 75–116). Mahwah, NJ: Lawrence Erlbaum.

Lowenberg, P. (2002). Assessing English proficiency in the Expanding Circle. *World Englishes* 21, 431–35.

Luke, A. (1996). Genres of power? Literacy education and the production of capital. In R. Hasan & A. Williams (eds.), *Literacy in society* (pp. 308–38). London: Longman.

Lumley, T. (2002). Assessment criteria in a large-scale writing test: What do they really mean to the raters? *Language Testing* 19, 246–76.

Luoma, S. & Tarnanen, M. (2003). Creating a self-rating instrument for second language writing: From idea to implementation. *Language Testing* 20, 440–65.

Lyster, R. (2004). Differential effects of prompts and recasts in form-focused interaction. *Studies in Second Language Acquisition* 26, 399–432.

Macken-Horarik, M. (2002). "Something to shoot for": A systemic functional approach to teaching genre in secondary school science. In A. Johns (ed.), *Genre in the classroom: Multiple perspectives* (pp. 17–42). Mahwah, NJ: Lawrence Erlbaum.

Mackey, A. (2006). Feedback, noticing and second language development: An empirical study of L2 classroom interaction. *Applied Linguistics* 27, 405–30.

Mackey, A. & Goo, J. (2007). Interaction research in SLA: A meta-analysis and research synthesis. In A. Mackey (ed.), *Conversational interaction in second language acquisition* (pp. 407–52). Oxford: Oxford University Press.

Mackey, A. & Philp, J. (1998). Conversational interaction and second language development: Recasts, responses, and red herrings? *The Modern Language Journal* 82, 338–56.

Martin, J. (1992). *English text: System and structure.* Amsterdam: John Benjamins.

Matsuda, P. (1997). Contrastive rhetoric in context: A dynamic model of L2 writing. *Journal of Second Language Writing* 6, 45–60.

McGroarty, M. & Zhu, W. (1997). Triangulation in classroom research: A study of peer revision. *Language Learning* 47, 1–43.

Mendonça, C. & Johnson, K. (1994). Peer review negotiations: Revision activities in ESL writing instruction. *TESOL Quarterly* 28, 745–69.

Morgan, B. & Ramanathan, V. (2005). Critical literacies and language education: Global and local perspectives. *Annual Review of Applied Linguistics* 25, 151–69.

Nagy, P. & Stewart, G. (2000). *Canadian language benchmarks companion tables.* www.language.ca/display_page.asp?page_id=439.

Nassaji, H. & Cumming, A. (2000). What's in a ZPD? A case study of a young ESL student and teacher interacting through dialogue journals. *Language Teaching Research* 4, 95–121.

Nassaji, H. & Swain, M. (2000). A Vygotskian perspective on corrective feedback in L2: The effect of random versus negotiated help on the learning of English articles. *Language Awareness* 9, 34–51.

National Standards Foreign Language Project (1996). *Standards for foreign language learning: Preparing for the 21st century.* Yonkers, NY: National Standards in Foreign Language Education Project.

Norris, J. (2005). Book review: *Common European Framework of Reference for Languages: Learning, teaching, assessment. Language Testing* 22, 399–411.

Norris, J. & Ortega, L. (2000). Effectiveness of L2 instruction: A research synthesis and quantitative meta-analysis. *Language Learning* 50, 417–528.

Orr, J. (2005). Dialogic investigations: Cultural artifacts in ESL composition classes. In J. Hall, G. Vitanova, & L. Marchenkova (eds.), *Dialogue with Bakhtin on second and foreign language learning: New perspectives* (pp. 55–76). Mahwah, NJ: Lawrence Erlbaum.

Ortega, L. (1999). Planning and focus on form in L2 oral performance. *Studies in Second Language Acquisition* 21, 109–48

Ortega, L. (2003). Syntactic complexity measures and their relationship to L2 proficiency: A research synthesis of college-level L2 writing. *Applied Linguistics* 24, 492–518

O'Sullivan, I. & Chambers, E. (2006). Learners' writing skills in French: Corpus consultation and learner evaluation. *Journal of Second Language Writing* 15, 49–68.

Pang, T. (2002). Textual analysis and contextual awareness building: A comparison of two approaches to teaching genre. In A. Johns (ed.), *Genre in the classroom: Multiple perspectives* (pp. 145–61). Mahwah, NJ: Lawrence Erlbaum.

Panova, I. & Lyster, R. (2002). Patterns of corrective feedback and uptake in the adult ESL classroom. *TESOL Quarterly* 36, 573–95.

Parks, S., Huot, D., Hamers, J., & H-Lemonnier, F. (2006). "History of Theatre" websites: A brief history of the writing process in a high school ESL language arts class. *Journal of Second Language Writing* 14, 233–58.

Partington, A. (1998). *Patterns and meaning: Using corpora for English language research and teaching.* Amsterdam: John Benjamins.

Patthey-Chavez, G. & Ferris, D. (1997). Writing conferences and the weaving of multi-voiced texts in college composition. *Research in the Teaching of English* 31, 51–90.

Pennycook, A. (1996). Borrowing others' words: Text, ownership, memory and plagiarism. *TESOL Quarterly* 30, 201–30.

Philp, J. (2003). Constraints on "noticing the gap": Nonnative speakers' noticing of recasts in NS–NNS interaction. *Studies in Second Language Acquisition* 25, 99–126.

Poehner, M. & Lantolf, J. (2005). Dynamic assessment in the language classroom. *Language Teaching Research* 9, 233–65.

Polio, C. (1997). Measures of linguistic accuracy in second language writing research. *Language Learning* 47, 101–43.

Polio, C. (2003). An overview of approaches to second language writing research. In B. Kroll (ed.), *Exploring the dynamics of second language writing* (pp. 35–65). Cambridge: Cambridge University Press.

Polio, C., Fleck, C., & Leder, N. (1998). "If only I had more time:" ESL learners' changes in linguistic accuracy on essay revisions. *Journal of Second Language Writing* 7, 43–68.

Qi, D. S. & Lapkin, S. (2001). Exploring the role of noticing in a three-stage second language writing task. *Journal of Second Language Writing* 10, 277–303.

Ramanathan, V. & Atkinson, D. (1999). Individualism, academic writing and ESL writers. *Journal of Second Language Writing* 8, 45–75.

Reichelt, M. (1997). Writing instruction at the German Gymnasium: A 13th grade English class writes the Arbitur. *Journal of Second Language Writing* 6, 265–91.

Reichelt, M. (2001). A critical review of foreign language writing research on pedagogical practices. *Modern Language Journal* 85, 578–98.

Reichelt, M. (2005). English-language writing instruction in Poland. *Journal of Second Language Writing* 14, 215–32.

Reppen, R. (1995). A genre-based approach to content writing instruction. *TESOL Journal* 4, 32–5.

Roca de Larios, J., Manchon, R., & Murphy, L. (2006). Generating text in native and foreign language writing: A temporal analysis of problem-solving formulation processes. *Modern Language Journal* 90, 100–14.

Roca de Larios, J., Murphy, L., & Manchon, R. (1999). The use of restructuring strategies in EFL writing: A study of Spanish learners of English as a foreign language. *Journal of Second Language Writing* 8, 13–44.

Rollinson, P. (2005). Using peer feedback in the ESL writing class. *ELT Journal* 59, 23–30.

Sachs, R. & Polio, C. (2007). Learners' uses of two types of written feedback on an L2 writing revision task. *Studies in Second Language Acquisition* 29, 67–100.

Santos, T. (1992). Ideology in composition: L1 and ESL. *Journal of Second Language Writing* 1, 1–15.

Santos, T. (2001). The place of politics in second language writing. In T. Silva & P. Matsuda (eds.), *On second language writing* (pp. 173–90) Mahwah, NJ: Lawrence Erlbaum.

Sasaki, M. (2000). Toward an empirical model of EFL writing processes. *Journal of Second Language Writing* 9, 259–92.

Sasaki, M. (2002). Building an empirically-based model of EFL learners' writing processes. In S. Ransdell & M-L. Barbier (eds.), *New directions for research in L2 writing* (pp. 49–80). Amsterdam: Kluwer Academic.

Scarcella, R. (2002). Some key factors affecting English language learners' development of advanced literacy. In M. Schleppegrell & M. C. Colombi (eds.), *Developing advanced literacy in first and second languages* (pp. 209–26). Mahwah, NJ: Lawrence Erlbaum.

Schleppegrell, M. (2001). Linguistic features of the language of schooling. *Language and Education* 12, 431–59.

Schleppegrell, M. (2004). *The language of schooling: A functional linguistic perspective*. Mahwah, NJ: Lawrence Erlbaum.

Schleppegrell, M. & Achugar, M. (2003). Language learning and learning history: A functional linguistics approach. *TESOL Journal* 12, 21–7.

Shaw, P. & Liu, E. (1998). What develops in the development of second-language writing? *Applied Linguistics* 19, 225–54.

Shen, F. (1989). The classroom and the wider culture: Identity as a key to learning English composition. *College Composition and Communication* 40, 459–66.

Shi, L. (1998). Effects of prewriting discussions on adult ESL students' compositions. *Journal of Second Language Writing* 7, 319–45.

Shi, L. (2001). Native- and nonnative-speaking EFL teachers' evaluation of Chinese students' English writing. *Language Testing* 18, 303–25.

Shohamy, E. (1997). Testing methods, testing consequences: Are they ethical? Are they fair? *Language Testing* 14, 340–9.

Silva, T. & Brice, C. (2004). Research in teaching writing. *Annual Review of Applied Linguistics* 24, 70–106.

Sinclair, J. (1990). *Corpus, concordance, collocation*. Oxford: Oxford University Press.

Smoke, T. (2001). Instructional strategies for making ESL students integral to the university. In T. Silva & P. Matsuda (eds.), *On second language writing* (pp. 129–41) Mahwah, NJ: Lawrence Erlbaum.

Song, B. & August, B. (2002). Using portfolios to assess the writing of ESL students: A powerful alternative? *Journal of Second Language Writing* 11, 49–72.

Spada, N. (1997). Form-focused instruction and second language acquisition: A review of classroom and laboratory research. *Language Teaching* 30, 73–87.

Stapleton, P. (2002). Critiquing voice as a viable pedagogical tool in L2 writing: Returning the spotlight to ideas. *Journal of Second Language Writing* 11, 177–90.

Starfield, S. (2004). "Why does this feel empowering?": Thesis writing, concordancing and the *corporatizing university*. In B. Norton & K. Toohey (eds.), *Critical pedagogy and language learning* (pp. 138–57). Cambridge: Cambridge University Press.

Storch, N. (2005). Collaborative writing: Product, process, and students' reflections. *Journal of Second Language Writing* 14, 153–73.

Sullivan, K. & Lindgren, E. (2002). Self-assessment in autonomous computer-aided second language writing. *ELT Journal* 56, 258–66.

Susser, B. (1994). Process approaches in ESL/EFL writing instruction. *Journal of Second Language Writing* 3, 31–48.

Swaffer, J. (2003). A template for advanced learning tasks: Staging genre reading and cultural literacy through the précis. In H. Byrnes & H. H. Maxim (eds.), *Advanced foreign language learning: A challenge to college programs* (pp. 19–45). Boston, MA: Thomson/Heinle.

Swain, M. (1985). Communicative competence: Some roles of comprehensible input and comprehensible output in its development. In S. Gass & C. Madden (eds.), *Input and second language acquisition* (pp. 235–56). Rowley, MA: Newbury House.

Swain, M. (1998). Focus on form through conscious reflection. In C. J. Doughty & J. Williams (eds.), *Focus on form in classroom second language acquisition* (pp. 64–81). Cambridge: Cambridge University Press.

Swain, M. & Lapkin, S. (2002). Talking it through: Two French learners' response to reformulation. *International Journal of Educational Research* 37, 285–304.

Swales, J. (1990). *Genre analysis: English in academic and research settings*. Cambridge: Cambridge University Press.

Swales, J. & Feak, C. (1994). *Academic writing for graduate students*. Ann Arbor, MI: University of Michigan Press.

Tarnopolsky, O. (2000). Writing English as a foreign language: A report from the Ukraine. *Journal of Second Language Writing* 9, 209–26.

Tribble, C. (2002). Corpora and corpus analysis: New windows on academic writing. In J. Flowerdew (ed.), *Academic discourse* (pp. 131–49). London: Pearson.

Truscott, J. (1996). The case against grammar correction in L2 writing classes. *Language Learning* 46, 327–69.

Truscott, J. (2004). Evidence and conjecture on the effects of correction: A response to Chandler. *Journal of Second Language Writing* 13, 337–44.

Villamil, O. & de Guerrero, M. (2006). Sociocultural theory: A framework for understanding social–cognitive dimensions of peer feedback. In K. Hyland & F. Hyland (eds.), *Feedback in second language writing* (pp. 23–41). Cambridge: Cambridge University Press.

Wallace, C. (2001). Critical literacy in the second language classroom. Power and control. In B. Comber & A. Simpson (eds.), *Negotiating critical literacies in the classroom* (pp. 209–228). Mahwah, NJ: Lawrence Erlbaum.

Wang, W. & Wen, Q. (2002). L1 use in the L2 composing process: An exploratory study of 16 Chinese EFL writers. *Journal of Second Language Writing* 11, 225–46.

Weigle, S. (1994). Effects of training on raters of ESL compositions. *Language Testing* 11, 197–223.

Weigle, S. (1998). Using FACETS to model rater training effects. *Language Testing* 15, 263–87.

Weigle, S. (2002). *Assessing writing*. New York: Cambridge University Press.

Weigle, S. (2004). Integrating reading and writing in a competency test for non-native speakers of English. *Assessing Writing* 9, 27–55.

Weissberg, R. (2000). Developing relationships in the acquisition of English syntax: Writing versus speech. *Learning and Instruction* 10, 37–53.

Weissberg, R. (2006). *Connecting speaking and writing*. Ann Arbor, MI: University of Michigan Press.

Williams, J. (2004). Tutoring and revision: Second language writers in the writing center. *Journal of Second Language Writing* 13, 173–201.

Williams, J. (2005). Form-focused instruction. In E. Hinkel (ed.), *Handbook of research in second language teaching and learning* (pp. 671–92). Mahwah, NJ: Lawrence Erlbaum.

Williams, J. (2008). The speaking–writing connection in second language and academic literacy development. In D. Belcher & A. Hirvela (eds.), *The oral/literate connection: Perspectives on L2 speaking, writing, and other media interactions* (pp. 10–25). Ann Arbor, MI: University of Michigan Press.

Williams, J. & Severino, C. (2004). The writing center and second language writers. *Journal of Second Language Writing* 13, 165–72.

Wolfe, E. & Manalo, J. (2004). Composition medium comparability in a direct writing assessment of non-native English speakers. *Language Learning & Technology* 8, 53–65.

Wolfe-Quintero, K., Inagaki, S., & Kim, H. Y. (1998). Second language development in writing: Measures of fluency, accuracy, and complexity. (Technical Report No. 17). Honolulu: National Foreign Language Resource Center.

Wong, W. (2001). Modality and attention to meaning and form in the input. *Studies in Second Language Acquisition* 23, 345–68.

Wu, W. & Stansfield, C. (2001). Towards authenticity of task in test development. *Language Testing* 18, 187–206.

You, X. (2004a). New directions in EFL writing: A report from China. *Journal of Second Language Writing* 13, 253–6.

You, X. (2004b). "The choice made from no choice": English writing instruction in a Chinese university. *Journal of Second Language Writing* 13, 97–110.

Zamel, V. (1983). The composing processes of advanced ESL students: Six case studies. *TESOL Quarterly* 17, 165–90.

Zhang, S. (1995). Reexamining the affective advantage of peer feedback in the ESL writing class. *Journal of Second Language Writing* 4, 209–22.

Zimmermann, R. (2000). L2 writing: Subprocesses. A model of formulating and empirical findings. *Learning and Instruction* 10, 73–99.

27 Teaching and Testing Grammar

DIANE LARSEN-FREEMAN

Introduction

Perhaps no term in the language teaching field is as ambiguous as *grammar*. It has been used to mean:

1 an internal mental system that generates and interprets novel utterances (mental grammar)
2 a set of prescriptions and proscriptions about language forms and their use for a particular language (prescriptive grammar)
3 a description of language behavior by proficient users of a language (descriptive grammar)
4 the focus of a given linguistic theory (linguistic grammar)
5 a work that treats the major structures of a language (reference grammar)
6 the structures and rules compiled for instructional and assessment purposes (pedagogical grammar)
7 the structures and rules compiled for instructional purposes for teachers (usually a more comprehensive and detailed version of (6)) (teacher's grammar)

A reading of this list readily reveals why the use of the term "grammar" is fraught with ambiguity. It includes both implicit and explicit grammars, universal and language-specific grammars, the way that language "ought to be used" and the way it actually is used, theoretically exclusive grammars and more eclectic ones, etc. The ambiguity in the term "grammar" is magnified by the fact that every one of these seven definitions is multidimensional. For instance, (1) can be used to represent both learner grammars and proficient language speaker grammars. Descriptive grammars (3) can take as their starting point the form or structure of language (formal grammar), or conversely, can conceive of language as largely social interaction, seeking to explain why one linguistic form is more appropriate than another in satisfying a particular communicative purpose in a particular context (functional grammar). To cite a final example, linguistic grammars (4) adopt distinct theoretical units: structures (Structural Linguistics), rules (Traditional Grammar), principles and parameters (Generative Linguistics), constraints (Lexical Functional Grammar; Optimality Theory; Head-Driven Phrase Structure Grammar), texts (Systemic Functional Linguistics), constructions (Cognitive Linguistics; Construction Grammar), patterned sequences (Corpus Linguistics; Pattern Grammar), and so forth.

The lesson in all this is that it is important to be clear about what is meant when one is making claims about grammar. Thus, following this introduction, a definition of a pedagogical grammar (6) will be proposed, one that is broad enough to draw on many of these linguistic theories for their insights, yet sufficiently focused to fulfill its teaching and testing functions. Then, too, as with any subject, an understanding of grammar teaching and assessment is better served by knowing how the subject is learned or acquired. Indeed, it was this awareness that drew many language teachers to investigate the learning of grammar, which in turn led to the establishment of SLA as a separate area of inquiry in the early 1970s. Much work has been done since then, and many SLA researchers still take the explanandum to be a mental grammar (1). Obviously, though, a comprehensive review of SLA findings is beyond the scope of this chapter.

A Definition

Many pedagogical grammars are formal, comprising morphosyntactic rules from traditional and structural linguistics and, to a lesser extent, from Generative Linguistics. Formal grammarians assume a faculty of language must provide first, a structured inventory of possible lexical items (the core semantics of minimal meaning-bearing elements) and second, the grammatical rules or principles that allow infinite combinations of symbols, hierarchically organized. The grammatical principles provide the means to construct from these lexical items the infinite variety of internal structures that enter into thought, interpretation, planning, and other human mental acts (Chomsky, 2004).

Generative Linguistics' principles and parameters approach continues to be productive in accounting for similarities and differences across languages; however, its newer Minimalist Program has not had an impact on pedagogical grammars. This is because "the emphasis in Generative Linguistics has been on identifying ever larger regularities in grammar, to the point that the 'essence' of grammar has been distilled in the Minimalist Program to Merge and Move, or perhaps only to Internal and External Merge" (Culicover & Jackendoff, 2005, p. 534). Such minimalism may be useful for addressing its goal of accounting for language evolution or language acquisition under conditions of inadequate input, but it is not going to advance the quest to facilitate the teaching of second and foreign languages because of its level of abstraction (Larsen-Freeman, 2005, 2006a).

Functional grammarians start from a very different position. Although there are different models of functional grammar, functionalists share the conviction that it is the use that determines the form that is used for a particular purpose. Thus, functional grammarians see pragmatics and meaning as central, i.e., grammar is a resource for making and exchanging meaning (Halliday, 1994). In Halliday's Systemic-Functional theory, three types of meaning in grammatical structure can be identified: ideational meaning (how our experience and inner thoughts are represented), interpersonal meaning (how we interact with others through language), and textual meaning (how coherence is created in spoken and written texts).

By way of contrast with minimalism, newer functional and cognitive linguistic theories focus on language as it is actually used. The new theories, often referred to collectively as "usage-based," propose that grammatical rules do not precede, but rather, emerge from language use (Bybee, 1985, 2006; Croft, 1991; Givón, 1995; Goldberg, 1995; Hopper, 1988; Langacker, 1987, etc.). Such rules are probalistic, rather than deterministic. In this way, grammar is said not to be innate or the starting point of a faculty of language, but rather, is derivative. Moreover, in these theories, the traditional distinction between grammar and lexicon is not always observed. "As opposed to conceiving of linguistic rules as algebraic procedures for combining words and morphemes that do not themselves contribute to meaning, this approach conceives of linguistic constructions as themselves meaningful linguistic symbols" (Tomasello, 2003, p. 5). Constructions range from morphemes to syntactic structures such as verb–argument patterns, to meaningful phrasal and clausal sequences. Such a theoretical position finds support in corpus-based grammars (e.g., Biber et al., 1999; Carter & McCarthy, 2006; *Collins COBUILD*, 1990), which rely on computer-assisted research to show the patterned lexical/grammatical sequences in language usage. For example, there are relatively fixed English patterns with limited options for slot fillers to express time relationships as in *a ___ ago* (e.g., *a day ago, an hour ago, a short while ago*).

Although there have certainly been linguists who have advocated the consolidation of lexicon and grammar all along (e.g., Bolinger, 1968; Chafe, 1970; Nattinger & DeCarrico, 1992; Pawley & Syder, 1983), and the reconceptualization of grammar as "lexicogrammar" (Celce-Murcia & Larsen-Freeman, 1999; Halliday, 1985), the fact that usage-based theories occupy the forefront of linguistics today represents a major change in the way grammar is conceived. However, from a pedagogical grammar perspective, they bring with them the potential for a problem as well, one exactly opposite to that of the Minimalist Program's abstraction. If it is lexicogrammatical constructions that are the units of analysis, this can easily lead to a proliferation of mini-grammars, with every unique pattern (or even lexical item) requiring a grammar of its own. For example, the English lexical item *matter* is often preceded by an indefinite article and followed by the preposition *of* and a gerund beginning with *-ing* (e.g., *a matter of developing skills, a matter of learning a body of information, a matter of becoming able to*) (Hunston & Francis, 1999). There is, therefore, little point in treating *matter* as a single lexical item that can be slotted into a general grammar of English. Rather, the word *matter* comes with attendant phraseology. While this level of analysis may be warranted in a comprehensive reference grammar, such generalizations may be too narrow for a pedagogical grammar.

One final point to be made is that linguistic grammars, no matter what the unit of analysis, describe the abstract system underlying a language. Neither rules nor patterns contain directions for actually producing or comprehending language (Garrett, 1986). While attempts are underway to produce a real-time description of syntax, an account of how grammatical speech is produced in real time (Brazil, 1995), we still do not have a processing account of how speakers express and comprehend meaning.

Nevertheless, a description of the system is an essential starting point for proper pedagogy. A definition for a pedagogical grammar that is broad enough to accommodate both traditional and newer approaches, and one that can be applied to different languages, is that *grammar is a system of meaningful structures and patterns that are governed by particular pragmatic constraints.* Larsen-Freeman (2001) has referred to the three dimensions present in this definition of grammar as *form, meaning,* and *use.*

An example from English will have to suffice here. As cognitive linguists and construction grammarians have observed, the passive voice has the grammatical *meaning* of communicating something about/to which something happens/ed. Learners need to know this, and they need to know how to *form* the passive construction – in English, for example with some form of the *be* verb and the past participle. They also need to know when to *use* the passive. Such occasions include when the agent is unknown, should be concealed, is redundant, or when the use of the passive reflects the preferred word order for marking given and new information, etc. Not knowing when to use a structure appropriately results in overuse and underuse of the target structure, as for learners of Chinese having difficulty suppressing overt subjects (Odlin, 2003), or learners of Korean failing to choose correctly between the discursive patterns of *V-a/e pelita* versus *V-ko malta,* completive aspect markers (Strauss, Lee, & Ahn, 2006). In fact, learning to make a specific choice between two structures with approximately the same meaning in a context-appropriate way is *the* challenge in learning grammar, according to Rea Dickens and Woods (1988).

The *structures and patterns* in the above definition (with examples) include:

Morphemes
In Turkish, the roots of verbs each have thousands of different forms (Hankamer, 1989).

Function words
Indonesian auxiliaries (*sudah* and *siang*) are used as tense/aspect markers.

Phrases
Subcategorization constraints vary from language to language and produce different transitivity patterns. For example, in Chinese, (*fuk6 mou6 (serve)*) is intransitive (Chan, 2004, p. 60), whereas in English, *serve* must take an object.

Clauses

Canonical word order in English is S-V-DO-IO; in Japanese, it is S-IO-DO-V (Cann, Kempson, & Marten, 2005).

Clausal formulas/constructions/patterned sequences

French formulas (*je ne sais pas*; *des choses comme ca*; *c'est* _____ ; *il y a* _____) (from work by Raupach on German acquirers of French, cited in Weinert, 1995).

Discourse-level patterns

Chinese supra-sentential topic chaining or English theme–rheme organization.

Typological patterns

Patterns that arise from language typology, realized, for example, in the topic prominence of Korean, Chinese, and Japanese versus the subject prominence of Arabic, Farsi, Spanish, and English.

Grammar Pedagogy (in General)

Before discussing grammar teaching in any detail, several general points should be made. First, although linguists believe that languages are equally complex, *where* they are complex varies. For instance, teachers of Russian to speakers of English spend a great deal of time teaching inflected morphology and the complicated system of verbal aspect (Russian is classified by the United States Defense Language Institute as a challenging category 3 language in terms of the difficulties that it poses to learners who are native speakers of English), and teachers of German spend time on the form of function words, because, for example, German has six distinct forms of the definite article, inflected for case, number, and gender. Second, implicit in these claims is the assumption that to some extent the learning challenge the grammatical complexity presents will differ depending on the starting point, e.g., Portuguese speakers will have an easier time learning Spanish grammar than speakers of non-Romance languages, all other things being equal. Third, since learners build on earlier knowledge, it is also the case that knowledge of other languages can influence the acquisition of grammar. For example, in learning Italian, English and Spanish first-language speakers who knew some French were found to use significantly more subject insertion than speakers without knowledge of French (De Angelis, 2005). In addition to the learners' knowledge of other languages, there are many other factors known to affect the rate of acquisition of grammatical forms, e.g., their frequency, salience, and the consistency of their meaning (DeKeyser, 2005).

It should also be noted that the pedagogic approach to the teaching of grammar in various parts of the world differs, depending not only on different grammatical complexities, but also on the pedagogic traditions. For example, Sampson (1984) points out that both the teacher and the texts are seen as crucial models for learning in the Chinese educational system. Also, in a survey of teachers in

Colombia, Schulz (2001) found that Colombian students and teachers had stronger beliefs in the efficacy of explicit grammar instruction and error correction than did their US counterparts. Indeed, it is not uncommon to hear of teachers who are not particularly impressed with the benefit of grammar instruction, yet who are teaching grammar, nonetheless, because that is what students expect (see, e.g., Borg, 1999).

Approaches to Grammar Teaching

Four approaches to the teaching of grammar will be presented here: PPP, input-processing, focus on form, and grammaring, in addition to one non-interventionist approach to language teaching that calls for no explicit grammar instruction.

PPP

Across the various languages and subsystems of grammar, perhaps the most widely practiced traditional approach to grammatical instruction has been portrayed as the three Ps – present, practice, produce.

In the first stage, an understanding of the grammar point is provided; sometimes by pointing out the differences between the L1 and L2. In the second stage, students practice the grammar structure using oral drills and written exercises. In the third stage, students are given "frequent opportunities for communicative use of the grammar to promote automatic and accurate use" (Sheen, 2003, p. 226).

DeKeyser (1997) offers Anderson's skill-based approach to explain how grammar practice may work in the second stage. Once students are given a rule (declarative knowledge) in the first step, output practice aids students to proceduralize their knowledge. In other words, with practice, declarative knowledge takes the form of procedural knowledge, which encodes behavior. Continued practice automatizes the use of the rule so that students do not have to think consciously about the rule any longer. As Doughty and Williams (1998, p. 49) put it, "proceduralization is achieved by engaging in the target behavior – or procedure – while temporarily leaning on declarative crutches . . ."

Countless generations of students have been taught grammar in this way – and many have succeeded with this form of instruction. In support of this, following their meta-analysis of research on the effectiveness of instruction, Norris and Ortega (2000) conclude that "L2 instruction of particular language forms induces substantial target-oriented change . . ." (p. 500). However, it is also true that the traditional approach has had its detractors. One of most trenchant criticisms of this approach is that students fail to apply their knowledge of grammar when they are communicating. Appropriating Alfred North Whitehead's term, Larsen-Freeman (2003) has referred to this as the "inert knowledge problem." Students know the grammar – at least, they know the grammar rules explicitly – but they fail to apply them in communication. This problem has been discussed by others as the "non-interface problem," in that there is no apparent connection between explicit knowledge of the rules and implicit control of the system, and the "learnability problem," following from the observation that grammar is not learned in a linear and atomistic fashion (R. Ellis, 1993). Moreover, what learners do produce bears no resemblance to what has been presented to them or has been practiced.

Non-interventionist

Such observations led one influential researcher, Krashen (1981, 1982), to claim that explicit grammar instruction has very little impact on the natural acquisition process because, he argued, studying grammar rules can never lead to their unconscious deployment in fluent communication. According to Krashen, the only way for students to acquire grammar is to get exposure to comprehensible input in the target language in an affectively non-threatening situation, where the input is finely tuned to students' level of proficiency. Krashen believes that if the input is understood and there is enough of it, the necessary grammar will automatically be acquired. At best, students can use their grammar knowledge to monitor and revise their spoken and written products after they have been produced. Other non-interventionist positions have been adopted as well. "While differing considerably . . . each has claimed that the best way to learn a language . . . is not by treating it as an object of study, but by experiencing it as a medium of communication" (Long, 1991, p. 41).

Studies of French immersion programs in Canada, however, show that when language is only used as a medium of communication, with no explicit attention being paid to grammatical form, the interlanguages of naturalistic learners go through long periods of stability, in which non-native forms are used (Harley & Swain, 1984). White (1987) makes the point that the positive evidence that immersion students receive is not always sufficient for learners to analyze the complex grammatical features of French. In other words, ". . . while positive evidence contains information about what is possible in the target language, it does not contain information about what is *not* possible" (Spada, 1997, pp. 80–1). Thus, learners require the "negative evidence" that they get from instruction (e.g., corrective feedback) to help them sort out L1/L2 differences. Larsen-Freeman and Long (1991) have made the further point that the right kind of formal instruction should accelerate natural acquisition, not merely imitate it.

Input-processing

VanPatten (1990) argued that the problem is that L2 learners have difficulty attending simultaneously to meaning and form. To remedy this problem, VanPatten (2004) has proposed "input processing," whereby learners are guided to pay attention to a feature in the target language input that is likely to cause a problem. The following task from Cadierno (1992, as discussed in Doughty & Williams, 1998) illustrates input-processing. For this task, students are shown a picture and are asked to imagine that they are one of the characters in the picture. They then have to listen to a sentence in the target language and to select the picture that best matches it. For example, when the target language is Spanish and the students are English speakers, they hear:

Te busca el señor. ('The man is looking for you.')

Later when viewing two more pictures, the students hear:

Tú buscas al señor. ('You are looking for the man.')

English speakers use word order to determine subjects and objects. Presumably, however, with information about differences in Spanish and with enough of this input-processing practice, students will learn to discern the difference in meaning, and that distinguishing subjects from objects requires paying attention to the ends of words and to small differences in the function words themselves (e.g., *te* vs. *tú* and *el* vs. *al*).

Focus on form

Noting that some aspects of an L2 require awareness and/or attention to language form, and further, that implicit learning is not sufficient for SLA mastery, Long (1991) calls for a focus on form within a communicative or meaning-based approach to language teaching, such as task-based (e.g., R. Ellis, 2003; Pica, Kang, & Sauro, 2006) or content-based language teaching. Rodgers (2006), for example, has demonstrated that when third-semester students of Italian engaged in content-based instruction, in which they studied Italian geography, and at the same time, either through incidental or planned opportunities, attended to problematic grammatical features, the students increased not only in their knowledge of geography, but also in their form–function abilities. Since there is a limit on what learners can pay attention to, focusing on form may help learners to notice structures (Schmidt, 1990) that would otherwise escape their attention when they are engaged in communication or studying content. Long (1991, p. 47) hypothesizes that "a systematic, non-interfering focus on form produces a faster rate of learning and (probably) higher levels of ultimate SL attainment than instruction with no focus on form." Various means of non-intrusive focusing on form have been proposed and studied.

Input enhancement

Sharwood Smith (1993) suggests that visual enhancement (color-coding, underlining, boldfacing, enlarging the font) be made to written instructional texts in an attempt to make certain features of the input more salient. Input enhancement can also apply to speech. For instance, phonological manipulations such as oral repetition might help learners pay attention to grammar structures in the input. At this point, however, the contribution of visual input enhancement is not clear (Wong, 2003), though Jensen and Vinther did find a significant increase in grammatical accuracy of Danish learners of Spanish when input was enhanced through exact repetition and through speech rate reduction (2003).

Input flooding/Priming

A second means of calling attention to form is flooding meaningful input with the target form. For example, talking about historical events would give learners abundant opportunities to notice the past tense. One possible function of input flooding, besides making certain features in the input more frequent and thus more salient, is that it might prime the production of a particular structure. "Syntactic priming is a speaker's tendency to produce a previously spoken or heard structure" (Mackey & Gass, 2006, p. 173).

Output production

Believing comprehensible input alone to be inadequate for accomplishing successful second-language acquisition, Swain (1985) advocated the use of output production in language teaching (see also Morgan-Short & Wood Bowden, 2006; Shehadeh, 2003; Toth, 2006). "Comprehensible output," according to Swain, forces learners to move from semantic processing of input to syntactic processing, in order to produce target output. She also hypothesizes that comprehensible output serves to have learners notice features of the target language, especially "to notice what they do not know, or know only partially" (Swain, 1995, p. 129).

Long (1996) concurs about the importance of noticing. "[C]ommunicative trouble can lead learners to recognize that a linguistic problem exists, switch their attentional focus from message to form, identify the problem, and notice the needed item in the input" (p. 425). Indeed, helping students to notice their errors is an important function of focusing on form, a point to which I return later.

Not everyone is convinced by an input-processing or focus-on-form approach, however. While acknowledging the "carry-over" problem, i.e., the difficulty of achieving simultaneous fluent and accurate spontaneous production, Swan (2005) disputes the claim that the traditional PPP has failed. Further, he admonishes that it does not follow that the problem will be solved by eliminating the first two Ps.

Grammaring

Larsen-Freeman (2001, 2003) offers "grammaring" – the ability to use grammar structures accurately, meaningfully, and appropriately as the proper goal of grammar instruction. The addition of "-ing" to grammar is meant to suggest a dynamic process of grammar using. In order to realize this goal, it is not sufficient for students to notice or comprehend grammatical structures. Students must also practice *meaningful use of grammar* in a way that takes into account "transfer-appropriate" processing (Roediger & Guynn, 1996). This means that in order for students to overcome the inert knowledge problem and transfer what they can do in communicative practice to real communication outside of the classroom, there must be a psychological similarity between the conditions of learning and the conditions of use (Segalowitz, 2003). Bearing the need for psychological similarity in mind, Gatbonton and Segalowitz (1988) offer "creative automatization." Rather than automatizing knowledge of rules, as was suggested by DeKeyser,

Gabonton and Segalowitz call for practice that automates control of patterned sequences, ones that would naturally occur in given communicative contexts.

Of course, what is practiced and the way it is practiced will depend on the nature of the learning challenge. Some structures may need little, if any, pedagogical focus. With others, when the learning challenge is how to *form* the construction, it is important that learners get to practice the target item over and over again meaningfully, for example by using it in a task-essential way (Fotos, 2002; Loschky & Bley-Vroman, 1993; Samuda, 2001). When the challenge is *meaning*, students need practice in associating form and meaning, such as associating various spatial and temporal meanings with prepositions. Finally, when the challenge is *use*, students need to be given situations where they are forced to decide between the use of two or more different forms with roughly the same meaning, but which are not equally appropriate in a given context. Use would be a challenge for learners, for example, in choosing between the active and passive voices or between English present perfect and past tenses.

Larsen-Freeman (2003) underscores the importance of output practice in addition to consciousness-raising activities; however, she goes a step further in suggesting that output practice is not only useful for the purpose of rehearsal and automatizing, but that it also leads to restructuring of the underlying system (McLaughlin, 1990) and to linguistic innovation or morphogenesis. The fact that "the act of playing the game has a way of changing the rules" (Larsen-Freeman, 1997) blurs the distinction between the essence of a linguistic system and its use. This also means for Larsen-Freeman (2006b) that although there is stability in a grammatical system, there is no stasis.

As a consequence, Larsen-Freeman (2006a) calls for grammar teaching to help develop capacity within students, not formal grammatical competence (Widdowson, 1983). Capacity involves learners using lexicogrammatical resources for the creation of meaning. Doing so enables language learners to move beyond the memorized formulas and static rules they employ, especially at the beginning of instruction. This is what accounts for the fact that language changes all the time; it does so due to the cumulative innovations that language users make at the local level as they adapt their language resources to new communicative contexts (Larsen-Freeman & Cameron, 2008). In order to develop capacity, learners need to abstract from frequently occurring exemplars. Higher-level constructs, such as schemata, prototypes, and complex constructions, emerge from the interaction of lower-level forms. As learners master the system at an optimal level of abstraction, they are no longer learning only to conform to grammatical uniformity. They are acquiring a way to create and understand meaning.

Other benefits of grammar instruction have been proposed (R. Ellis, 1993, 1998, 2006). One is to help students "notice the gap" between new features in a structure and how they differ from the learners' interlanguages (Schmidt & Frota, 1986). Grammar instruction can also help students generalize their knowledge to new structures (Gass, 1982). Another contribution of grammar teaching may be to fill in the gaps in the input (Spada & Lightbown, 1993), since classroom language will not necessarily represent all grammatical structures that students need to acquire.

Other Topics

Several other topics related to the teaching and testing of grammar are implied or previewed in this chapter so far, but merit separate treatment.

Explicit versus implicit revisited

A great deal of the controversy in the teaching of grammar can be ascribed to the general issue of whether an explicit or implicit approach to teaching structure is best. Explicit instruction is where students are instructed in the rules or patterns (deductive) or guided to induce them, themselves (inductive). An implicit approach makes no reference to rules or patterns (see also a related, but somewhat different, distinction between incidental and intentional learning, Hulstijn, 2003).

Although Norris and Ortega (2000, p. 500) found evidence to support the value of explicit teaching (including inductive and deductive approaches), the outcomes of instruction that their meta-analysis included tended to be ones where learners had to demonstrate explicit knowledge or perform on discrete/ decontextualized test items, measures that would presumably favor explicit knowledge (Doughty, 2003; Norris & Ortega, 2000, p. 501).

Another issue is the source of the explicit rules. Instead of presenting students with rules, for instance, Fotos and Ellis (1991) give students linguistic data from which they could work out the rules inductively in their own way. An inductive approach may be very fitting for complex rules, which are difficult to articulate and internalize. In a modification of an inductive approach, Adair-Hauck, Donato, and Cumo-Johanssen (2005) recommend a guided-participatory approach to rule formation, rather than the teacher providing the learner with explanations, or the learners being left to analyze the grammar explanations implicitly for themselves.

On a slightly different note, Larsen-Freeman (2000, 2003) makes the case for guiding students to understand the *reason* why things are the way they are. To the extent that teachers can reduce the arbitrariness in grammatical rules (i.e., teaching meaning-based reasons rather than solely form-based rules), students' learning burden is eased. For instance, if students understand the theme–rheme pattern of discourse organization in English, they will understand a number of different grammatical phenomena, e.g., the form of predicative phrases in sentences with existential *there*, word order variation with direct and indirect objects, and word order variation with phrasal verbs and their particles. Thus, an additional value to reasons is that they are broader than rules, in that they can be applied to many different structures (see also, Rutherford, 1987).

Significantly, although the general assumption behind the non-interface stance, that explicit knowledge cannot become implicit knowledge, may be technically true, it may be overstated. While it is the case that implicit and explicit knowledge are different, it is claimed at the same time that explicit knowledge can influence implicit knowledge (N. Ellis, 2002, p. 164). This fact is significant for older learners who may no longer learn as well implicitly as they did as children learning their first language. N. Ellis (2005) and N. Ellis and Larsen-Freeman (2006) point out that it is especially in the area of grammatical morphology that conscious involvement may be necessary for successful learning. For without it, the low salience and low communicative value of the morphemes, in English at any rate, lead to L2 learners' continuing to process these aspects of language implicitly, following the habits and tunings laid down by the L1. "Consciousness is necessary to change behavior" (N. Ellis, 2005, p. 327). Changing the cues that learners focus on in their language processing changes what their implicit learning systems tune into. DeKeyser (2003) makes a similar point and adds that the reverse is also true – implicit knowledge can be made explicit when attempting to convey it verbally to someone else (as teachers have always done).

Clearly, at the level of debate, explicit versus implicit is too general to be resolved categorically. For instance, DeKeyser (2003) cautions that implicit learning is severely hampered when the learning task requires establishing a relationship between elements that are at some distance, separated by several other elements. There are also issues with regards to the intensity of grammar instruction (Collins et al., 1999). Perhaps all that can be said with certainty at this point is that students who receive a blend of implicit and explicit grammar instruction are likely to be well served (N. Ellis, 1995; MacWhinney, 1997).

Metalanguage

Closely related to teaching grammar explicitly is the role of metalanguage or grammatical terminology. Borg (1999) makes it clear that teachers have a wide range of views on whether metalanguage facilitates learning, and Sharwood Smith (1993) notes that whether or not to use grammatical terminology is still an empirical question. However, once again, general prescriptions are probably not in order because there are aspects of certain languages, e.g., in French, sometimes the masculine and feminine forms are homophones (*bleu*, masculine for *blue*, and *bleue* its feminine counterpart) (Patsy Lightbown, personal communication), such that the concept of gender and the way it is marked would seem to be needed to help learners understand why there are two forms in writing.

Swain and Lapkin (1998) track students' use of metalanguage in collaborative dialogues. For example, they report on an episode where two learners of French discuss the verb *sortir* and whether it does or does not take the reflexive form. The researchers assert that such "language-related episodes," where learners work together to use grammatical metalanguage and the reasoning of others to expand their knowledge of the language, helps learners at the same time to regulate their own cognitive functioning.

Syllabus design

Various principles (e.g., teaching simpler structures first, or more frequently occurring ones, or those with the most communicative utility) have been invoked over the years for the sequencing of structures in grammatical syllabi (Larsen-

Freeman, 1974). However, it has also been established that there are naturally occurring developmental sequences, and U-shaped learning curves, backsliding, and restructuring, which would seem to argue against any such overall principled sequencing of grammar structures in instruction. The concern for developmental readiness is further borne out in work by Pienemann (1984; 1998) and his associates, which has established that certain speech-processing strategies constrain development in the acquisition of German word order. For this reason, students' control of the strategies determines what is learnable, and, therefore, what is teachable at any given moment. These researchers also suggest the futility of attempting to teach word order beyond a learner's current processing ability. Indeed, R. Ellis (1989) found that students learning German word-order rules applied the rules in their interlanguage in the "natural" sequence, no matter how much instructional emphasis each was given (but, cf. Tarone & Liu, 1995).

While developmental sequences may indeed be impervious to instruction, it is likely the case that instruction accelerates the overall rate of acquisition. In support of this claim, Lightbown suggests that grammar instruction in advance of learners' readiness may prime their subsequent noticing (Lightbown, 1998), and Terrell offers a role for grammar instruction in providing students with advance organizers (1991). Acknowledging the constraints that developmental sequences may pose, but mindful of the accelerated learning that comes with grammatical instruction, Larsen-Freeman (2003) recommends that teachers adopt a "grammar checklist" rather than a sequence. In this way, teachers have an unordered set of grammar structures they need to teach, but they can do so locally in a way that attends to their students' readiness to learn. It also means that grammar structures can be worked on as they arise in content or during communicative activities, thus the contextualization that is facilitative of learning the grammar is already present. Finally, using a checklist also prompts teachers to work on certain structures that do not naturally arise during classroom activities, perhaps because students avoid them.

Individual differences

Teachers do not just teach grammar, of course; they teach grammar to particular students. Who the students are will also affect grammar instruction. This point was made earlier with regards to cultural expectations for grammar instruction, learners' language backgrounds, and the need to "localize" sequencing. In addition, the level of learners' target language proficiency should inform pedagogical decisions. For example, Zobl (1985) notes that at a certain point, learners need exposure to marked data if their interlanguage development is not to stagnate. Clearly, there are also individual style differences, which should be taken into account. For instance, Hatch (1974) distinguished between two different types of learners: rule formers and data gatherers, the former of an analytic mind and the latter more likely to memorize pattern sequences. Skehan's (1998) research demonstrating language aptitude differences, partially attributed to differing propensitities for language analysis, is also relevant in this regard (see also,

Robinson, 2002). More recently, work by Larsen-Freeman (2006c) has shown that the pressures for competing cognitive resources, e.g., the allocation of attention, lead learners to adopt either grammatical or more expressive orientations to the language-learning challenge.

Error correction/feedback

A huge issue in grammar teaching, but perhaps the most controversial one (Larsen-Freeman, 1991; Truscott, 1999), is the question of error correction. While some feel that correcting students' errors causes students to experience debilitating anxiety, most research supports the value of giving learners feedback on their non-targetlike performance in an affectively-supportive way. However, it is far from clear which error correction techniques are the most efficacious. For one thing, as with other aspects of grammar instruction, providing learners with feedback can be done explicitly or implicitly. The latter takes place through such means as clarification requests, confirmation checks, and recasts, as in the following exchange between a learner (L) and the teacher (T):

> L: I was in pub.
> T: In the pub?
> L: Yeah and I was drinking beer with my friend
> T: Which pub did you go to?
>
> (Loewen, 2005)

The teacher reformulates the learner's initial utterance to include the definite article. Recasts such as this one have great appeal as correction strategies because they are minimally intrusive and occur within meaning-focused activities (Doughty, 2001). Besides, teachers provide them quite naturally, and therefore, frequently.

One problem with recasts, however, is that they can be ambiguous (Lyster, 1998), limiting their acquisition potential. For instance, sometimes teachers repeat correct forms. It is also possible that learners respond to them differently. Some appear to ignore them – at least they do not immediately uptake the correct form (Lyster & Ranta, 1997) – although immediate successful uptake may not be a factor in acquisition (Mackey & Philp, 1998). Other learners who respond to recasts do so in private speech rather than social speech (Ohta, 2000). Indeed, the efficacy of recasts may be determined by a host of factors, such as learners' level of literacy (Tarone & Bigelow, 2005) or their proficiency (Ammar & Spada, 2006). It is also the case that recasts may have a differential effect depending on the linguistic target. For example, in one study of Spanish learners, recasts helped learners with adverb placement, but not with the use of clitic pronouns (Ortega & Long, 1997).

A more direct approach, but one that can still be applied while learners are engaged in communicative activities, is a teacher's use of prompts. For example, Lyster (2004) observes that prompts of varying sorts – such as repeating a student's error verbatim with rising intonation or providing metalinguistic comments – withhold approval and allow students to self-repair.

Then, too, when there is an L1–L2 contrast, the learner may need explicit negative feedback. For example, there is a contrast between English and German with regard to adverbial fronting. In German, one can front an adverbial, but must adhere to the word order of Adv + V + Sub + Obj when doing so:

Gestern sah ich den Film.
'Yesterday saw I the film.'

When learning German, an English speaker's original hypothesis might be that the order Adv + Sub + V + Obj is possible, as it is in English. Without negative feedback, learners may never receive evidence that the English word order is impossible in German. Indeed, Selinker and Lakshmanan (1992) hold that L1 language transfer is a privileged co-factor in fossilized forms, i.e., those non-targetlike forms that have become stable for long periods of time in learners' interlanguages (Han, 2004; Han & Odlin, 2006).

It is important to point out that the "error" does not have to be an error of form at all. For example, Negueruela et al. (2004) show that "even advanced language learners have problems appropriately indicating motion events when they have to cross typological boundaries between their target languages and their native languages. English speakers learning Spanish, for instance, tend to express manner in Spanish as they do in English, which does not result in an error of form but which leads them to mark manner very differently from Spanish speakers. The same is true for grammatical errors relating to pragmatics, when an accurate and meaningful form is used, but one that is inappropriate to the context.

Of course, no technique, even giving the learner the correct form, is effective unless the student can perceive the difference between the recast and what he or she has just said. It would seem necessary for the learners to notice the gap (Nicholas, Lightbown, & Spada, 2001). Long's comments (2007, pp. 114–15) about recasts likely apply to all error correction techniques: ". . . there is some evidence that recasts, like instruction in general, are differentially frequent and effective, depending on setting, learner age, proficiency, and type of L2 structure . . . as well as developmental stage and task." Indeed, it is unlikely that there is one feedback strategy that is better than others for all occasions. Thus, error correction ultimately comes down to adjusting feedback to individual learners. Adjustments cannot be determined *a priori*; rather they must be collaboratively negotiated online with the learner (Aljaafreh & Lantolf, 1994).

Spoken versus written grammar

With access to corpora of oral data, it has become increasingly apparent that there are differences in the grammar of the spoken versus written form (e.g., Biber, 1986; Carter & McCarthy, 1995); however, Leech (2000) contends that in English, at least, spoken and written forms utilize the same grammatical repertoires, but do so with different frequencies. Reinforcing this point for French, Waugh (1991) studied the distribution of the *passé simple* form and found that it was much more common in writing, presumably because it shows detachment. On the other hand, the differences between the two media may be more dramatic. For example, in Arabic, it has long been known that spoken regional dialects are markedly different from classical written Arabic. In any case, it is important to note the written bias in linguistics (Linell, 2005).

Grammatical Assessment

In the traditional approach to assessing grammar, grammatical knowledge is defined in terms of accurate production and comprehension, and then assessed through the four skills. Testing is typically done by means of decontextualized, discrete-point items such as sentence unscrambling, fill-in-the-blanks, error correction, sentence completion, sentence combining, picture description, elicited imitation, judging grammatical correctness, and modified cloze passages. Such formats test grammar knowledge, but they do not assess whether test takers can use grammar correctly in real-life speaking or writing. A significant contribution of the communicative or proficiency-based approach in the 1970s and 1980s was a shift from seeing language proficiency in terms of knowledge of structures, which could best be assessed using discrete-point items, to the ability to integrate and use the knowledge in performance, which could best be assessed through the production and comprehension of written texts and through face-to-face interaction under real-time processing conditions (McNamara & Roever, 2006, pp. 43–4).

In the latter, more integrative, approach to grammar assessment, grammatical performance is typically assessed by raters using scales that gauge grammatical accuracy, complexity, and the range of grammatical structures used. The judgments are subjective, and because the assessment formats are more open-ended, they are subject to possible inconsistencies. For this reason, certain factors, such as rater severity and prompt difficulty, must be examined, usually accomplished by means of generalizability theory or item-response theory (Purpura, 2006).

Because of the preference in recent years for measuring the use of grammar holistically through speaking and writing, some standardized examinations, e.g., the TOEFL, no longer have a separate section of the test that deals with structure explicitly. The decision to eliminate the explicit testing of grammar was made in at least two cases based on research showing that a separate subtest of grammatical knowledge could not be adequately differentiated from other sections of a test (Cushing Weigle & Lynch, 1995 and Alderson, 1993, cited in Purpura, 2004). A consequence of such decisions, however, is that it is difficult to separate out what in the ability to read or write the texts is due to the lack of knowledge concerning grammatical structures and what might be due to other factors. We also have no way of diagnosing grammatical difficulties learners may be experiencing or in providing them with feedback (Purpura, 2004). In sum, discrete-point and integrative tests represent different approaches to grammar assessment, each of which have a contribution to make.

Innovations in grammar assessment

There are a number of innovations underway, or at least proposed, in the way grammar is being assessed.

Redefining the construct

The first involves a definition of the grammar construct itself. Expanding beyond form to include grammatical meaning is one such move. For instance, Purpura (2004, p. 89) defines grammatical ability for assessment purposes as involving "the capacity to realize grammatical knowledge accurately and meaningfully in test-taking or other language-use contexts." Grammatical ability may (also) interact with pragmatic ability, which Purpura considers a different ability area.

Expanding the grammatical construct even further are researchers at the University of Michigan who are responsible for developing standard examinations of English proficiency (the ECCE and ECPE). They are going beyond the assessment of grammatical form and meaning and including grammatical use as well. Doing so necessitates assessing how grammar functions at the discourse level, where its use in cohesion, thematic continuity, anaphora, cataphora, grammatical focus, backgrounding and foregrounding, etc., are measured, as well as assessing students' knowledge of how sociolinguistic functions, such as constructing identity, conveying politeness, displaying power, etc., are realized grammatically. Speakers have a choice of which of their grammatical resources to deploy. Grammar is not a linguistic straitjacket (Larsen-Freeman, 2002; see also Batstone, 1994; Cullen, 2008).

Partial scoring

Discrete-point tests usually rely on dichotomous scoring of grammatical accuracy. Recently, it has been proposed that scoring grammatical items polytomously would yield information about learners who have an intermediary knowledge of grammar, rather than their being treated as if they have no knowledge at all (Purpura, 2006). To examine the extent to which answers on multiple-choice grammar items can be ordered along a path of progressive attainment, Purpura (2006) examined the grammar section of the University of Michigan ECPE, and found that many of the items did show what seemed to be a progressive attainment pattern in the response patterns of 1,000 candidates. If these items are indeed measuring developmental levels, dichotomous scoring raises several concerns. First, a considerable amount of developmental information is lost with students who have partial knowledge. More seriously, scoring dichotomously underestimates some students' true ability, and it makes it impossible for some students to receive feedback appropriate to their developmental level. While partial scoring is not a complete solution, it is one step in the long-hoped-for development of an interlanguage-sensitive approach to assessment (Larsen-Freeman & Long, 1991).

The social dimension

Language tests have ignored the social use dimension of language and have followed traditional psychometric methods in measuring isolated pieces of grammar and vocabulary knowledge; as a consequence, measuring test takers' ability to use language in social contexts has been overlooked (McNamara & Roever, 2006). Importantly, this awareness goes beyond extending the construct being measured. A social view of performance is incompatible with the traditional view of performance as a simple projection or display of individual competence. Increasingly, therefore, language testers are questioning whether it is possible to isolate the contributions of test takers from those of the test takers' interlocutors, say in oral proficiency interviews.

Along somewhat similar lines, Lantolf and Poehner (2004) call for "dynamic assessment," arguing against the assumption that the best sort of assessment is that of independent problem solving. Since higher order thinking emerges from our interactions with others, dynamic assessment involves testing the examinee before and after an intervention designed to teach the student how to perform better on the test. The student's final score represents the difference between pre-test (before learning) and post-test (after learning) scores.

The standard

Another issue that could be discussed under grammar teaching or testing is the issue of what the target standard is. For instance, some researchers have claimed that as English increasingly becomes the language of communication between non-native speakers, it is likely that "ungrammatical, but unproblematic" constructions, such as "he look very sad," "a picture who gives the impression" (Seidlhofer, 2001, p. 147), once they exist sufficiently frequently in non-native speaker discourse, would arguably become standardized and exist as a variety (English as a *lingua franca*) alongside English as a native language. Kachru and Nelson (1996, in Siegel, 2003) point out that considering the non-native features of indigenized varieties to be the result of L1 interference and fossilization would be wrong because learners may not wish to emulate a native standard, and standard models may not be available in the environment. Even for those who do wish to emulate a native standard, there is always the question concerning ultimate attainment in a classroom setting. For instance, in discussing the teaching of Russian as a foreign language, Rifkin (2005) advocates that students study abroad in a Russian-speaking environment because there is a ceiling effect as to what can be accomplished in a class where Russian is the target language.

The instruction and assessment of grammar will likely continue to foment a great deal of discussion as the field struggles with how to do both in harmony with students' natural learning processes. The effort is worth it for there is much at stake.

REFERENCES

Adair Hauck, B., Donato, R., & Cumo-Johanssen, P. (2005). Using a story-based approach to teach grammar. In J. Shrum & E. Glisan (eds.), *Teacher's handbook: Contextualized language instruction* (pp. 189–213). Boston, MA: Thomson/Heinle.

Aljaafreh, A. & Lantolf, J. (1994). Negative feedback as regulation and second language learning in the zone of proximal development. *Modern Language Journal* 78, 4, 465–83.

Ammar, A. & Spada, N. (2006). One size fits all? Recasts, prompts, and L2 learning. *Studies in Second Language Acquisition* 28, 4, 543–74.

Batstone, R. (1994). Product and process: Grammar in the second language classroom. In M. Bygate, A. Tonkyn, & E. Williams (eds.), *Grammar and the second language teacher* (pp. 224–36). Hemel Hempstead: Prentice-Hall International

Biber, D. (1986). Spoken and written textual dimensions in English: Resolving the contradictory findings. *Language* 62, 2, 384–414.

Biber, D., Johansson, S., Leech, G., Conrad, S., & Finegan, E. (1999). *Longman grammar of spoken and written English.* Harlow: Longman.

Bolinger, D. (1968). Entailment and the meaning of structures. *Glossa* 2, 2, 119–27.

Borg, S. (1999). The use of grammatical terminology in the second language classroom. *Applied Linguistics* 20, 1, 95–126.

Brazil, D. (1995). *A grammar of speech.* Oxford: Oxford University Press.

Bybee, J. (1985). *Morphology: A study of the relation between meaning and form.* Amsterdam/Philadelphia: John Benjamins.

Bybee, J. (2006). From usage to grammar: The mind's response to repetition. *Language* 82, 4, 711–33.

Cann, R., Kempson, R., & Marten, L. (2005). *The dynamics of language: An introduction.* Amsterdam: Elsevier Academic Press.

Carter, R. & McCarthy, M. (1995). Grammar and the spoken language. *Applied Linguistics* 16, 2, 141–58.

Carter, R. & McCarthy, M. (2006). *Cambridge grammar of English.* Cambridge: Cambridge University Press.

Celce-Murcia, M. & Larsen-Freeman, D. (1999). *The grammar book: An ESL/EFL teacher's course.* Boston: Heinle/Thomson.

Chafe, W. (1970). *Meaning and the structure of language.* Chicago: The University of Chicago Press.

Chan, A. (2004). Syntactic transfer: Evidence from the interlanguage of Hong Kong Chinese ESL learners. *Modern Language Journal* 88, 1, 56–74.

Chomsky, N. (2004). Three factors in language design. Unpublished manuscript.

Collins COBUILD English Grammar (1990). London: Collins ELT.

Collins, L., Halter, R., Lightbown, P., & Spada, N. (1999). Time and distribution of time in L2 instruction. *TESOL Quarterly* 33, 4, 655–80.

Croft, W. (1991). *Syntactic categories and grammatical relations: the cognitive organization of information.* Chicago: University of Chicago Press.

Culicover, P. & Jackendoff, R. (2005). *Simpler syntax.* Oxford: Oxford University Press.

Cullen, R. (2008). Teaching grammar as a liberating force. *ELT Journal* 62, 221–30.

De Angelis, G. (2005). Interlanguage transfer of function words. *Language Learning* 55, 3, 379–414.

DeKeyser, R. (1997). Beyond explicit rule learning: Automatizing second language morphosyntax. *Studies in Second Language Acquisition* 19, 2, 195–221.

DeKeyser, R. (2003). Implicit and explicit learning. In C. J. Doughty & M. H. Long (eds.), *The handbook of second language acquisition* (pp. 313–48). Malden, MA: Blackwell.

DeKeyser, R. (2005). What makes learning second-language grammar difficult? A review of issues. *Language Learning* 55, Supplement 1, 1–25.

Doughty, C. J. (2001). Cognitive underpinnings of focus on form. In P. Robinson (ed.), *Cognition and second language instruction* (pp. 206–57). Cambridge: Cambridge University Press.

Doughty, C. J. (2003). Instructed SLA: Constraints, compensation, and enhancement. In C. J. Doughty & M. H. Long (eds.), *The handbook of second language acquisition* (pp. 256–310). Malden, MA: Blackwell.

Doughty, C. J. & Williams, J. (eds.) (1998). *Focus on form in classroom second language acquisition.* New York: Cambridge University Press.

Ellis, N. (1995). Consciousness in second language acquisition: A review of field studies and laboratory experiments. *Language Awareness* 4, 3, 123–46.

Ellis, N. (2002). Frequency effects in language processing: A review with implications for theories of implicit and explicit language acquisition. *Studies in Second Language Acquisition* 24, 2, 143–88.

Ellis, N. (2005). At the interface: Dynamic interactions of explicit and implicit language knowledge. *Studies in Second Language Acquisition* 27, 2, 305–52.

Ellis, N. & Larsen-Freeman, D. (2006). Language emergence: Implications for applied linguistics – Introduction to this special issue. *Applied Linguistics* 27, 4, 558–89.

Ellis, R. (1989). Are classroom and naturalistic acquisition the same? A study of the classroom acquisition of German word order rules. *Studies in Second Language Acquisition* 11, 3, 305–28.

Ellis, R. (1993). The structural syllabus and second language acquisition. *TESOL Quarterly* 27, 1, 91–113.

Ellis, R. (1998). Teaching and research: Options in grammar teaching. *TESOL Quarterly* 32, 1, 38–60.

Ellis, R. (2003). *Task-based language learning and teaching.* Oxford: Oxford University Press.

Ellis, R. (2006). Current issues in the teaching of grammar: An SLA perspective. *TESOL Quarterly* 40, 1, 83–107.

Fotos, S. (2002). Structure-based interactive tasks for the EFL grammar learner. In E. Hinkel & S. Fotos (eds.), *New perspectives on grammar teaching in second language classrooms* (pp. 135–54). Mahwah, NJ: Lawrence Erlbaum.

Fotos, S. & Ellis, R. (1991). Communicating about grammar: A task-based approach. *TESOL Quarterly* 25, 4, 605–28.

Garrett, N. (1986). The problem with grammar: What kind can the language learner use? *Modern Language Journal* 70, 1, 133–48.

Gass, S. (1982). From theory to practice. In M. Hines & W. Rutherford (eds.), *On TESOL '81* (pp. 129–39). Washington, DC: TESOL.

Gatbonton, E. & Segalowitz, N. (1988). Creative automatization: Principles for promoting fluency within a communicative framework. *TESOL Quarterly* 22, 3, 473–92.

Givón, T. (1995). *Functionalism and grammar.* Amsterdam/Philadelphia: John Benjamins.

Goldberg, A. (1995). *Constructions: A construction grammar approach to argument structure.* Chicago: University of Chicago Press.

Halliday, M. A. K. (1985). *An introduction to functional grammar.* London: Edward Arnold.

Halliday, M. A. K. (1994). *An introduction to functional grammar*, 2nd edn. London: Edward Arnold.

Han, Z.-H. (2004). *Fossilization in adult second language acquisition*. Clevedon, UK: Multilingual Matters.

Han, Z.-H. & Odlin, T. (eds.) (2006). *Studies of fossilization in second language acquisition*. Clevedon, UK: Multilingual Matters.

Hankamer, J. (1989). Morphological parsing and the lexicon. In W. Marslen-Wilson (ed.), *Lexical representation and process* (pp. 392–408). Cambridge, MA: MIT Press.

Harley, B. & Swain, M. (1984). The interlanguage of immersion students and its implications for second language teaching. In A. Davies, C. Criper, & A. Howatt (eds.), *Interlanguage* (pp. 291–311). Edinburgh: Edinburgh University Press.

Hatch, E. (1974). Second language learning – universals? *Working Papers on Bilingualism* 3, 1–17.

Hopper, P. (1988). Emergent grammar and the *a priori* grammar postulate. In D. Tannen (ed.), *Linguistics in context* (pp. 117–34). Norwood, NJ: Ablex.

Hulstijn, J. (2003). Incidental and intentional learning. In C. J. Doughty & M. H. Long (eds.), *The handbook of second language acquisition* (pp. 349–81). Malden, MA: Blackwell.

Hunston, S. & Francis, G. (1999). *Pattern grammar: A corpus-driven approach to the lexical grammar of English*. Amsterdam/Philadelphia: John Benjamins.

Jensen, E. & Vinther, T. (2003). Exact repetition as input enhancement in second language acquisition. *Language Learning* 53, 3, 373–428.

Krashen, S. (1981). *Second language acquisition and second language learning*. Oxford: Pergamon.

Krashen, S. (1982). *Principles and practice in second language acquisition*. Englewood Cliffs, NJ: Prentice-Hall.

Langacker, R. (1987). *Foundations of cognitive grammar*, vol. 1. Stanford, CA: Stanford University Press.

Lantolf, J. & Poehner, M. (2004). Dynamic assessment of L2 development: Managing the past into the future. *Journal of Applied Linguistics* 1, 1, 49–72.

Larsen-Freeman, D. (1974). A re-examination of grammatical structure sequencing. In R. Crymes & W. Norrris (eds.), *On TESOL '74* (pp. 83–93). Washington, DC: TESOL.

Larsen-Freeman, D. (1991). Consensus and divergence on the content, role, and process of teaching grammar. In J. Alatis (ed.), *Georgetown University Round Table on Languages and Linguistics 1991: Linguistics and language pedagogy: The state of the art* (pp. 260–72). Washington, DC: Georgetown University Press.

Larsen-Freeman, D. (1997). Chaos/complexity science and second language acquisition. *Applied Linguistics* 18, 2, 141–65.

Larsen-Freeman, D. (2000). Grammar: Rules and reasons working together. *ESL/EFL Magazine*, January/February, 10–12.

Larsen-Freeman, D. (2001). Teaching grammar. In M. Celce-Murcia (ed.), *Teaching English as a second or foreign language* (3rd edn., pp. 251–66). Boston, MA: Thomson/Heinle.

Larsen-Freeman, D. (2002). The grammar of choice. In E. Hinkel & S. Fotos (eds.), *New perspectives on grammar teaching in second language classrooms* (pp. 103–18). Mahwah, NJ: Lawrence Erlbaum.

Larsen-Freeman, D. (2003). *Teaching language: From grammar to grammaring*. Boston, MA: Thomson/Heinle.

Larsen-Freeman, D. (2005). Functional grammar: On the value and limitations of dependability, inference, and generalizability. In M. Chalhoub-Deville, C. Chapelle, & P. Duff (eds.), *Inference and generalizability in applied linguistics* (pp. 115–33). Amsterdam/Philadelphia: John Benjamins.

Larsen-Freeman, D. (2006a). On dynamism of grammar in contextualizing communicative competence. *Review of Applied Linguistics in China* 2, 51–63.

Larsen-Freeman, D. (2006b). Second language acquisition and the issue of fossilization: There is no end, and there is no state. In Z.-H. Han & T. Odlin (eds.), *Studies of fossilization in second language acquisition* (pp. 189–200). Clevedon, UK: Multilingual Matters.

Larsen-Freeman, D. (2006c). The emergence of complexity, fluency, and accuracy in the oral and written production of five Chinese learners of English. *Applied Linguistics* 27, 4, 590–619.

Larsen-Freeman, D. & Cameron, L. (2008). *Complex systems and applied linguistics.* Oxford: Oxford University Press.

Larsen-Freeman, D. & Long, M. H. (1991). *An introduction to second language acquisition research.* London: Longman.

Leech, G. (2000). Grammars of spoken English: New outcomes of corpus-oriented research. *Language Learning* 50, 4, 675–724.

Lightbown, P. (1998). The importance of timing in focus on form. In C. J. Doughty & J. Williams (eds.), *Focus on form in classroom second language acquisition* (pp. 177–96). Cambridge: Cambridge University Press.

Linell, P. (2005). *The written language bias in linguistics.* London: Routledge.

Loewen, S. (2005). Incidental focus on form and second language learning. *Studies in Second Language Acquisition* 27, 3, 361–86.

Long, M. H. (1991). Focus on form: A design feature in language teaching methodology. In K. de Bot, R. Ginsberg, & C. Kramsch (eds.), *Foreign language research in cross-cultural perspective* (pp. 39–52). Amsterdam: John Benjamins.

Long, M. H. (1996). The role of the linguistic environment in second language acquisition. In W. Ritchie & T. Bhatia (eds.), *Handbook of research on second language acquisition*, vol. 2 (pp. 413–68). San Diego, CA: Academic Press.

Long, M. H. (2007). *Problems in SLA.* Mahwah, NJ: Lawrence Erlbaum.

Loschky, L. & Bley-Vroman, R. (1993). Grammar and task-based methodology. In G. Crookes & S. Gass (eds.), *Tasks and language learning: Integrating theory and practice* (pp. 123–67). Clevedon, UK: Multilingual Matters.

Lyster, R. (1998). Recasts, repetition and ambiguity in L2 classroom discourse. *Studies in Second Language Acquisition* 20, 1, 51–81.

Lyster, R. (2004). Differential effects of prompts and recasts in form-focused instruction. *Studies in Second Language Acquisition* 26, 3, 399–432.

Lyster, R. & Ranta, L. (1997). Corrective feedback and learner uptake: Negotiation of form in communicative classrooms. *Studies in Second Language Acquisition* 19, 1, 37–66.

Mackey, A. & Gass, S. (2006). Introduction to special issue. *Studies in Second Language Acquisition* 28, 2, 169–78.

Mackey, A. & Philp, J. (1998). Conversational interaction and second language development. *Modern Language Journal* 82, 3, 338–56.

MacWhinney, B. (1997). Implicit and explicit processes: Commentary. *Studies in Second Language Acquisition* 19, 2, 277–81.

McLaughlin, B. (1990). Restructuring. *Applied Linguistics* 11, 2, 113–28.

McNamara, T. & Roever, C. (2006). Language testing: The social dimension. *Language Learning* 56, Supplement 2.

Morgan-Short, K. & Wood Bowden, H. (2006). Processing instruction and meaningful output-based instruction: Effects on second language development. *Studies in Second Language Acquisition* 28, 1, 31–65.

Nattinger, J. & DeCarrico, J. (1992). *Lexical phrases and language teaching.* Oxford: Oxford University Press.

Negueruela, E., Lantolf, J., Jordan, S., & Gelabert, J. (2004). "The private function" of gesture in second language speaking activity: A study of motion verbs and gesturing in English and Spanish. *International Journal of Applied Linguistics* 14, 1, 113–47.

Nicholas, H., Lightbown, P., & Spada, N. (2001). Recasts as feedback to language learners. *Language Learning* 51, 4, 719–58.

Norris, J. & Ortega, N. (2000). Does type of instruction make a difference? Substantive findings from a meta-analytic review. *Language Learning* 51, Supplement 1, 157–213.

Odlin, T. (2003). Cross-linguistic influence. In C. J. Doughty & M. H. Long (eds.), *The handbook of second language acquisition* (pp. 436–86). Malden, MA: Blackwell.

Ohta, A. (2000). Rethinking recasts: A learner-centered examination of corrective feedback in the Japanese language classroom. In J. Kelly Hall & L. Stoops Verplaetz (eds.), *Second and foreign language learning through classroom interaction* (pp. 47–71). Mahwah, NJ: Lawrence Erlbaum.

Ortega, L. & Long, M. H. (1997). The effects of models and recasts on the acquisition of object topicalization and adverb placement in L2 Spanish. *Spanish Applied Linguistics* 1, 65–86.

Pawley, A. & Syder, F. (1983). Two puzzles for linguistic theory: Nativelike selection and nativelike fluency. In J. Richards & R. Schmidt (eds.), *Language and communication* (pp. 191–226). London: Longman.

Pica, T., Kang, H., & Sauro, S. (2006). Information gap tasks: Their multiple roles/contributions to interaction research methodology. *Studies in Second Language Acquisition* 28, 301–38.

Pienemann, M. (1984). Psychological constraints on the teachability of languages. *Studies in Second Language Acquisition* 6, 186–214.

Pienemann, M. (1998). *Language processing and second language development: Processability theory.* Amsterdam/Philadelphia: John Benjamins.

Purpura, J. (2004). *Assessing grammar.* Cambridge: Cambridge University Press.

Purpura, J. (2006). Issues and challenges in measuring SLA. Paper presesented at the American Association for Applied Linguistics Conference, June, Montreal.

Rea Dickens, P. & Woods, E. (1988). Some criteria for the development of communicative grammar tasks. *TESOL Quarterly* 22, 4, 623–46.

Rifkin, B. (2005). A ceiling effect in traditional classroom foreign language instruction: Data from Russian. *Modern Language Journal* 89, 1, 3–18.

Robinson, P. (2002). Effects of individual differences in intelligence, aptitude and working memory on adult incidental language acquisition. In P. Robinson (ed.), *Individual differences and instructed language learning* (pp. 211–65). Amsterdam/Philadelphia: John Benjamins.

Rodgers, D. (2006). Developing content and form: Encouraging evidence from Italian content-based instruction. *Modern Language Journal* 90, 3, 373–86.

Roediger, I. & Guynn, M. (1996). Retrieval processes. In E. Bork & R. Bork (eds.), *Memory* (pp. 197–236). New York: Academic Press.

Rutherford, W. (1987). *Second language grammar: Learning and teaching.* London: Longman.

Sampson, G. (1984). Exporting language teaching methods from Canada to China. *TESL Canada Journal* 1, 1, 19–31.

Samuda, V. (2001). Getting relationship between form and meaning in task performance: The role of the teacher. In M. Bygate, P. Skehan, & M. Swain (eds.), *Task-based learning: Language teaching, learning and assessment* (pp. 119–40). Harlow: Pearson.

Schmidt, R. (1990). The role of consciousness in second language learning. *Applied Linguistics* 11, 2, 129–58.

Schmidt, R. & Frota, S. (1986). Developing basic conversational ability in a second language. In R. Day (ed.), *Talking to learn* (pp. 237–326). Rowley, MA: Newbury House.

Schulz, R. (2001). Cultural differences in student and teacher perceptions concerning the role of grammar instruction and corrective feedback: USA and Colombia. *Modern Language Journal* 85, 2, 244–57.

Segalowitz, N. (2003). Automaticity and second languages. In C. J. Doughty & M. H. Long (eds.), *The handbook of second language acquisition* (pp. 382–408). Malden, MA: Blackwell.

Seidlhofer, B. (2001). Closing a conceptual gap: The case for a description of English as a lingua franca. *International Journal of Applied Linguistics* 11, 2, 133–58.

Selinker, L. & Lakshmanan, U. (1992). Language transfer and fossilization: The "multiple effects principle." In S. Gass & L. Selinker (eds.), *Language transfer in language learning* (pp. 197–216). Amsterdam/Philadelphia: John Benjamins.

Sharwood Smith, M. (1993). Input enhancement in instructed SLA: Theoretical bases. *Studies in Second Language Acquisition* 15, 2, 165–79.

Sheen, R. (2003). Focus on form: A myth in the making? *ELT Journal* 57, 3, 225–33.

Shehadeh, A. (2003). Learner output, hypothesis testing, and internalizing linguistic-knowledge. *Systems* 32, 155–71.

Siegel, J. (2003). Social context. In C. J. Doughty & M. H. Long (eds.), *The handbook of second language acquisition* (pp. 178–223). Malden, MA: Blackwell.

Skehan, P. (1998). *A cognitive approach to language learning.* Oxford: Oxford University Press.

Spada, N. (1997). State of the art: A review of classroom and laboratory research. *Language Teaching* 30, 73–87.

Spada, N. & Lightbown, P. (1993). Instruction and the development of questions in the L2 classroom. *Studies in Second Language Acquisition* 15, 2, 205–21.

Strauss, S., Lee, J., & Ahn, K. (2006). Applying conceptual grammar to advanced-level completive constructions in Korean. *Modern Language Journal* 90, 2, 185–209.

Swain, M. (1985). Communicative competence: Some roles of comprehensible input and comprehensible output in its development. In S. Gass & C. Madden (eds.), *Input in second language acquisition* (pp. 235–53). Rowley, MA: Newbury House.

Swain, M. (1995). Three functions of output in second language learning. In G. Cook & B. Seidlhofer (eds.), *Principle and practice in applied linguistics* (pp. 125–44). Oxford: Oxford University Press.

Swain, M. & Lapkin, S. (1998). Interaction and second language learning: Two adolescent French immersion students working together. *Modern Language Journal* 82, 3, 320–37.

Swan, M. (2005). Legislation by hypothesis: The case of task-based instruction. *Applied Linguistics* 26, 3, 376–401.

Tarone, E. & Bigelow, M. (2005). Impact of literacy on oral language processing: Implications for second language acquisition research. *Annual Review of Applied Linguistics* 77–97. Cambridge: Cambridge University Press.

Tarone, E. & Liu, G.-Q. (1995). Situational context, variation, and second language acquisition theory. In G. Cook & B. Seidlhofer (eds.), *Principle and practice in applied linguistics* (pp. 107–24). Oxford: Oxford University Press.

Terrell, T. (1991). The role of grammar in a communicative approach. *Modern Language Journal* 75, 1, 52–63.

Tomasello, M. (2003). *Constructing a language.* Cambridge, MA: Harvard University Press.

Toth, P. (2006). Processing instruction and the role for output in second language acquisition. *Language Learning* 56, 2, 319–95.

Truscott (1999). What's wrong with oral grammar correction. *The Canadian Modern Language Review* 55, 4, 437–55.

VanPatten, B. (1990). Attending to form and content in the input. *Studies in Second Language Acquisition* 12, 2, 287–301.

VanPatten, B. (2004). Input processing in second language acquisition. In B. VanPatten (ed.), *Processing instruction: Theory, research, and commentary* (pp. 5–31). Mahwah, NJ: Lawrence Erlbaum.

Waugh, L. (1991). Tense-aspect and hierarchy of meanings. In L. Waugh & S. Rudy (eds.), *Grammar invariance and variation* (pp. 241–60). Amsterdam/Philadelphia: John Benjamins.

Weinert, R. (1995). The role of formulaic language in second language acquisition: A review. *Applied Linguistics* 16, 2, 180–205.

White, L. (1987). Against comprehensible input: The input hypothesis and the development of second-language competence. *Applied Linguistics* 8, 2, 95–110.

Widdowson, H. (1983). *Learning purpose and language use.* Oxford: Oxford University Press.

Wong, W. (2003). The effects of textual enhancement and simplified input on L2 comprehension and acquisition of non-meaningful grammatical form. *Applied Language Learning* 14, 2, 109–32.

Zobl, H. (1985). Grammars in search of input and intake. In S. Gass & C. Madden (eds.), *Input in second language acquisition* (pp. 329–44). Rowley, MA: Newbury House.

28   Teaching and Testing Vocabulary

PAUL NATION AND TERESA CHUNG

A well-planned vocabulary component of a language course has the following features: it focuses on the appropriate level of vocabulary, it provides a balanced range of opportunities for learning, and it monitors and assesses the learners' vocabulary knowledge in useful ways. Put another way, a well-planned program answers these questions: What vocabulary? How should vocabulary be taught and learned? How should vocabulary knowledge and growth be assessed?

What Vocabulary?

An important step in planning the vocabulary component of a language course is deciding what vocabulary goals to set. A useful way of doing this is to find out how much vocabulary is needed to do certain tasks without assistance, like read a newspaper, take part in a conversation, or watch a movie. Research with second language learners by Hu and Nation (2000) and with first-language learners by Carver (1994) indicates that at least 98 percent coverage of the running words (tokens) is needed for unassisted reading. This means that there should not be more than one unknown word in every 50 running words.

In earlier studies there was a lot of guesswork and extrapolation involved in making such calculations (Hirsh & Nation, 1992; Sutarsyah, Nation, & Kennedy, 1994). However, there are now lists of the most frequent 14,000 words of English that can be used with the RANGE program (http://www.vuw.ac.nz/lals/staff/paul-nation/nation.aspx), and that are also incorporated into a web-based text analysis program (http://www.lextutor.ca/vp/). These programs can be used to determine the amount of vocabulary needed to reach 98 percent coverage (see Table 28.1, based on Nation, 2006).

The figures in Table 28.1 assume that proper nouns are known or that not knowing them does not hinder the comprehension of a text. The figures indicate that a vocabulary size of around 8,000–9,000 words is needed to deal successfully with a range of language uses (Adolphs & Schmitt, 2004; Nation, 2006). Even the

Table 28.1 Vocabulary size needed to reach 98 percent coverage in a variety of texts

Type of text	Vocabulary size
Children's movies	6,000 words
Conversation	7,000 words
Newspapers	8,000 words
Novels	9,000 words

Table 28.2 Percentage coverage by fourteen 1,000-word family lists of three newspaper corpora

Vocabulary level	Independent (UK)	New York Times	Dominion Post (NZ)
1st 1,000	76.59	75.72	75.11
2nd 1,000	8.68	8.38	8.96
3rd 1,000	2.86	2.66	3.23
4th 1,000	2.21	2.64	2.47
5th 1,000	1.27	1.24	1.38
6th 1,000	0.82	0.86	0.89
7th 1,000	0.55	0.66	0.56
8th 1,000	0.42	0.49	0.53
9th 1,000	0.31	0.35	0.31
10th 1,000	0.21	0.30	0.30
11th 1,000	0.27	0.20	0.23
12th 1,000	0.12	0.16	0.13
13th 1,000	0.13	0.13	0.09
14th 1,000	0.11	0.11	0.10
Proper nouns	4.29	4.62	4.15

most optimistic measures of the vocabulary growth of foreign or second language learners indicate that it takes at least a year, and usually much longer, to increase vocabulary size by a thousand words (Laufer & Paribakht, 1998; Nurweni & Read, 1999). It is thus necessary to be very strategic about what vocabulary is learned first, and what next, when trying to reach this goal. Table 28.2 provides data to reinforce this idea, by showing the vocabulary coverage of each successive 1,000 frequency and range-related words for various collections of newspaper texts.

   The three newspaper corpora consist of roughly equal amounts of text from *The Independent* (a British newspaper), *The New York Times*, and *The Dominion Post* (a New Zealand newspaper) within a three-month period. Each of the three corpora contains around 194,000 words.

The figures in Table 28.2 show that by far the largest amount of text coverage comes from the first 1,000 words, and that the coverage figures drop rapidly, so that on average, the fifth 1,000 words cover less than 1.4% of the tokens, and the ninth 1,000 0.35% or less of the tokens. For the *Independent*, a 5,000-word family vocabulary plus proper nouns provides 96% coverage. A 9,000-word vocabulary plus proper nouns is needed to reach 98% coverage.

There are two important conclusions to be drawn from these figures. First, it makes sense in terms of cost–benefit analysis to learn the vocabulary of English roughly in order of its frequency of occurrence. There is much more value to be gained from learning the second 1,000 words than the fourth 1,000 words. Secondly, the very high coverage provided by the first and second 1,000 words suggests that these words deserve a great deal of intensive attention of various kinds. Most of these 2,000 words occur with high frequency, no matter what kind of text is being focused on.

Vocabulary levels

A way to increase the efficiency of the vocabulary focus is to make use of specially designed vocabulary lists. A common way to do this is to distinguish four vocabulary levels: high-frequency, academic, technical, and low-frequency words.

(1) *High-frequency words*. These make up a group of around 2,000 word families. The classic list is Michael West's *A General Service List of English Words* (1953). This list needs updating (it does not contain words like *computer, email, internet*), but it still works reasonably well, and was made with young learners of English in mind. The first 2,000 words from the British National Corpus have a more adult and more formal flavor because of the nature of the British National Corpus (Nation, 2004a). Typically, the first 2,000 words of English cover between 80% and 90% of the running words in a text, depending on the type of text.

(2) *Academic words*. For learners who wish to do academic study through the medium of English in senior high school or in tertiary education, the next step after the high-frequency words is Coxhead's (2000) Academic Word List. This is a list of 570 word families that are very common across a wide range of academic disciplines. It covers around 10% of the running words in academic text, around 4% of the running words in newspapers, and less than 2% of the running words in novels. It is clearly a somewhat specialized vocabulary. There have been several textbooks produced to teach the Academic Word List; see, for example, Schmitt and Schmitt (2005) and Huntley (2006).

(3) *Technical words*. For learners who have very specific study or work purposes, the next level of vocabulary consists of technical words. These are words that are very closely associated with a specialist area, in the way the words *dwang, truss, nog, eaves* are associated with building, or that the words *negotiation, interaction, phoneme, token* are associated with applied linguistics.

Research on technical vocabulary (Chung & Nation, 2003, 2004) shows that the amount of technical vocabulary in specialized texts has generally been underestimated. Chung found that around 30% of the running words in an anatomy text were technical words, and around 20% of the words in an applied linguistics text were technical. Technical vocabulary can be found with around 90% accuracy by comparing the frequency of vocabulary in a technical text with the frequency of the same vocabulary in a large mixed corpus that does not contain any texts from the technical area being studied. Vocabulary that only occurs in the technical text and vocabulary that is over 50 times more frequent in the technical text is likely to be technical vocabulary. Technical vocabulary can come from high-frequency vocabulary, academic vocabulary, or low-frequency vocabulary.

(4) *Low-frequency words.* The remaining words of the language are low-frequency words. There are thousands of these of varying frequency, and as we have seen by looking at the coverage of the British National Corpus lists, many need to be learned, so that learners can reach the 98% coverage of text required for unassisted language use.

Multi-word units

Focusing on individual words has been criticized in course design because words often do not make much sense unless they are in phrases or larger units. Also, learning words in multi-word units means that they are learned with the collocations and grammar with which they need to be used.

There are four major productive effects of learning multi-word units.

1   Learners will be able to produce grammatically correct utterances.
2   Learners will be able to produce utterances that are nativelike.
3   Learners will be able to produce utterances fluently.
4   Learners will be able to communicate very early in their language learning.

Behind all these effects is the idea that learners will be able to make use of instances of grammatical features without having to have control of the system that might be needed to make creative use of the features. These effects also have their receptive equivalents.

The effects have been pointed out by writers like Palmer (1925): "What is then the fundamental guiding principle of . . . those who are anxious to become proficient in foreign conversation? – *Memorize perfectly the largest number of common and useful word groups!*" This idea is also supported by Pawley and Syder (1983), and was popularized by Lewis (1993, 1997) in his lexical approach, which advocates the learning of multi-word units as one of the major focuses of language learning.

A fundamental problem with discussion about multi-word units has been the proliferation of terminology that has been very poorly defined. Without good definitions, it is not possible to have replicable corpus searches. Where clear and consistent criteria were set up to classify multi-word units, the criteria tended to be ones of convenience to meet the needs of computer searches. More recently, however, there have been attempts to establish clear criteria and to apply them in a systematic way.

Grant and Bauer (2004) used the two criteria of compositionality (Can the meaning of the whole be related to the meaning of the parts?) and figurativeness to classify three major kinds of multi-word units: core idioms, figuratives, and literals. The two criteria are applied following the steps in Figure 28.1. First, the item is checked to see if it is compositional, that is, do the meanings of the parts make up the meaning of the whole? If they do, it is classified as a literal, for example, *at six o'clock*. Literals are thus compositional and non-figurative. The meaning of the whole can be understood from the meaning of the parts. There are thousands of these in English, and further criteria like frequency and grammatical well-formedness, are needed to distinguish them from items that are not usefully regarded as multi-word units.

If the item is non-compositional, it is then checked to see if it is a figurative. A figurative is a multi-word unit where the meanings of the parts do not give you the actual meaning of the whole. When a learner meets the clause, "We decided to kill two birds with one stone," in context, this may be initially confusing because the text so far has had nothing to do with birds, stones, or killing. So a figurative is non-compositional. However, by applying a strategy of interpretation, it is possible to see how the literal meaning of *kill two birds with one stone* reflects its figurative meaning "to do two jobs at once." Some figuratives are quite easy to interpret, e.g., *We want to make sure we are singing from the same hymn sheet*, while others require considerable background knowledge, e.g., *You have to take it with a grain of salt*. There are a lot of figuratives in English, and new ones are created every day.

If the item is not a figurative, it is classified as a core idiom. A core idiom is a multi-word unit where the meaning of the parts does not make up the meaning

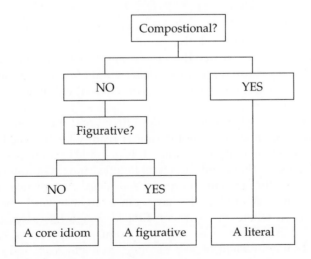

Figure 28.1 Classification of multi-word units

of the whole. In addition, the meaning of the whole cannot be arrived at by applying a figurative interpretation to the unit. So, if we meet the phrase *as well as*, as in *you as well as me*, knowing the meanings of *as*, and *well* does not help us understand the phrase. The term *core idiom* is used to separate it from the many looser uses of the word *idiom*. When the criteria of compositionality and figurativeness are carefully applied, there turn out to be just over 100 core idioms in English (Grant & Nation, 2006).

The researcher who has done the most to investigate the teaching and learning of figuratives is Frank Boers. The research of Boers and his colleagues has provided very useful guidelines that not only apply to figuratives but also to core idioms and literals.

1   The use of figurative sequences in speaking results in higher oral proficiency scores (Boers et al., 2006).
2   The source domains of idioms and figuratives differ from one language to another and reflect the culture and history of the speakers of that language (Boers, Demecheleer, & Eyckmans, 2004).
3   Figuratives vary considerably in the transparency of the expression (for example, *rock the boat* compared with *out for a duck*) (Boers, Eyckmans, & Stengers, in press).
4   Giving deliberate attention to figurative sequences can help their learning (Boers et al., 2006).
5   Associating a figurative with its source domain (sailing, cricket, war, etc.) and its etymology helps in understanding the expression and helps learning (Boers, Eyckmans, & Stengers, 2006).
6   Around 20 percent of figurative expressions make use of alliteration (*through thick and thin*) and assonance (*high and dry*) to some degree, and focusing on this helps learning.

The research of Boers and his colleagues challenges some of the conventional wisdom. It is often suggested that multi-word units should be learned as unanalyzed wholes. The research does not support this. Etymological elaboration helps learning. It is also suggested that items should be learned through a meaning focus. The research shows that giving conscious attention to form (alliteration and assonance) also helps learning.

The different nature of core idioms, figuratives, and literals suggests different learning focuses. Because core idioms cannot readily be analyzed, they need to be learned as largely unanalyzed wholes. It is possible in some cases, however, to create etymologies for them and these will help learning. Figuratives can be very effectively learned through an interpretive strategy that relates the literal and figurative meanings. While literals may seem straightforward, they can be subdivided into those where the learners' first language has a parallel word-for-word expression and those where the first-language expression is different. For example, the Thai equivalent of *good morning, good afternoon,* and *good evening* is one word *sawasdee*. Thus, for Thai learners, these three literals require a bit more learning effort than the expression *next week* which has a word-for-word equivalent in Thai, *athit na*, although with Thai word order. Shin and Nation (2006) found that about one third of the high-frequency, grammatically well-formed English multi-word units did not have word-for-word equivalents in Korean.

Boers and his colleagues developed three computer-based activities to help the learning of figurative sequences and to use in their studies. These three activities make up their *Idiom teacher*. The first two activities are multiple-choice with feedback. Once the item is answered, the correct answer is given or the learner keeps choosing until the correct answer is chosen. Activity one is *Identify the source*, where learners have to choose from four choices the domain that the phrase comes from, for example, that *close to the wind* comes from sailing. The second activity focuses on comprehension; learners have to choose which of four meanings describes the meaning of the multi-word unit. The third activity provides the expression in a defining context, but with a word missing from the expression which learners have to complete. These test/teach activities proved very effective in getting learners to think about and learn figuratives.

Biber, Conrad, and Cortes (2004) used frequency and range to identify "lexical bundles," and found in the total corpus of over 14 million tokens, 138 four-word sequences occurring at least 40 times per million words. The bundles did not have to be complete structural units (grammatically well-formed). Biber et al. say that "only 15 percent of the lexical bundles in conversation can be regarded as complete phrases or clauses, while less than five percent of the lexical bundles in academic prose represent complete structural units" (p. 377). Well-conducted research like this is providing a good basis for the systematic incorporation of multi-word units into language syllabus design.

How Should Vocabulary Be Taught and Learned?

One way to make sure that opportunities for vocabulary learning are properly balanced in a course is to see that there is a roughly even allocation of learning activities to each of the four strands of meaning-focused input, meaning-focused output, language-focused learning, and fluency development (Nation, 2007). Each strand should receive about the same amount of time in a well-balanced course. This includes what happens both inside and outside the classroom.

Meaning-focused input

Meaning-focused input involves learning via comprehensible input obtained through listening and reading. A very important part of the meaning-focused input strand is an extensive reading program, where learners read large amounts of interesting texts. There has been continued and growing interest in extensive reading. Day and Bamford's (1998) book was followed by a very substantial collection of activities (Bamford & Day, 2004) aimed at encouraging, organizing and monitoring extensive reading. Along with these publications, the Extensive

Reading Foundation has been established (www.erfoundation.org/), with the goal of promoting extensive reading and encouraging the production of high-quality graded readers. The foundation has set up a process for judging and giving awards to various levels of graded readers each year.

This promotion of extensive reading has been accompanied by high-quality research on vocabulary learning from extensive reading. Waring and Takaki's (2003) study of vocabulary learning from one graded reader showed that there are various kinds of levels of vocabulary learning, which, if viewed together, represent a significant increase in learning. Waring and Takaki used three vocabulary tests of differing difficulty to measure incidental vocabulary learning. One was a word-form recognition test, where learners chose words they had seen in the text from those that did not occur in the text. Learners scored about 16 out of 25 on this rather easy test. Another test was a receptive multiple-choice test, where learners were provided with words from the text with four-item first-language choices. Learners scored about 12 out of 25 on this test. The most difficult was a translation test, where learners saw words from the text and had to provide first-language translations for them. Learners scored about 4 out of 25 on this test. Taken together, this means that of the words tested, four were known reasonably well, an additional eight were partly known, and an additional four were on the first step towards being known. This is a very reasonable outcome from a piece of incidental learning that took around 56 minutes and undoubtedly resulted in other kinds of learning and skill improvement, as well. In a very detailed case study, Pigada and Schmitt (2006) found large amounts of incidental vocabulary learning of various strengths from sustained extensive reading. Horst (2005) also found evidence of substantial amounts of learning.

One way of helping reading and encouraging vocabulary learning from reading is to provide glosses of words that are likely to be unknown. A gloss is a short note on the meaning of a word provided after the text or in the margin near where the word occurs. There has been a renewed interest in glossing as a result of the growth of computer-assisted language learning. Reading texts presented on the computer provide opportunities for hypertext links and even direct links to dictionaries. In this way, glossing and dictionary use have moved closer to each other.

In many ways, research on glossing deals with issues that are very important in the wider teaching and learning of vocabulary. These include:

1   The relative advantages of the first language compared with the second language in communicating meaning. Research on first-language learners' understanding of definitions indicates that short, clear definitions are the best (McKeown, 1993). Second language translations are likely to meet this condition for second language readers, particularly lower-proficiency readers. Taylor (2006) suggests that the effectiveness of the language of the gloss may be dependent on the language used to test comprehension of the text, with L2 glosses being more effective if comprehension of the text is tested in L2.

2   The role of deep processing in vocabulary learning. In a very detailed qualitative study, Rott (2005) compared three-item multiple-choice translation glosses

with single translation glosses. Each target item occurred four times in the text, so the effect of repeated encounters was also examined. Multiple-choice glosses led to better long-term retention and more complete comprehension. Rott's study allowed her to explain this advantage which seemed to occur through the use of multiple information sources and multiple processing strategies. Rott's study thus made a major contribution to understanding not only how glossing should be carried out, but also the processes that underlie effective vocabulary learning.

3   The giving of deliberate attention to language features in the context of a message-focused task. Glossing tends to increase vocabulary learning.
4   The effect of multiple encounters with a word. Generally, repetition helps learning, but its effects are not guaranteed.
5   The role of textual enhancement (highlighting, bolding) in learning. Such enhancement tends to improve learning of the form rather than the meaning.
6   The length of retention after the first encounters. Rott, Williams, and Cameron (2002) found that five weeks' delay was too long between encounter and testing.

The activities that encourage vocabulary learning through meaning-focused input include listening to stories where the teacher notes unfamiliar words on the board or quickly explains their meaning, extensive reading, and taking part in interactive speaking and reading activities.

Meaning-focused output

Meaning-focused output involves learning through speaking and writing. If vocabulary is used in generative or creative ways, then memory for these words is strengthened (Joe, 1998). Activities like retelling, role plays, rewriting for a different purpose, and group and pair work involving negotiation can be very effective sources of vocabulary learning (Joe, Nation, & Newton, 1996).

Language-focused learning

Language-focused learning involves the deliberate learning and the deliberate study of vocabulary and vocabulary-learning strategies. In terms of efficiency, the most effective deliberate learning of vocabulary involves the use of small word cards with the target word or phrase on one side and the first-language translation on the other. Nation (2001, pp. 296–316) describes this learning strategy in detail. Strategy training is also a very efficient use of the language-focused learning strand in the classroom. Learners can benefit from training in guessing from context (Walters, 2004, 2006), dictionary use, using word cards, and using word parts.

The direct teaching of vocabulary is not a particularly efficient use of class time, but can be usefully done during intensive reading (Nation, 2004b) and as unknown words occur in the range of classroom activities. Nation (2008) suggests a variety of vocabulary-teaching activities that require various levels of preparation.

Computer-assisted vocabulary learning can be an effective way of getting help with vocabulary. Computer-assisted vocabulary learning covers a wide range of possibilities. First, it can include computer-based analysis of vocabulary, which has resulted in the creation of frequency-based word lists (Nation, 2006), the Academic Word List (Coxhead, 2000), and procedures for determining technical vocabulary (Chung & Nation, 2003; Chujo & Utiyama, 2006). Second, it can include the analysis of texts to determine their suitability for particular learners or to indicate how they should be adapted or sequenced (www.lextutor.ca/vp/). Such analysis can also be used as a way of monitoring the lexical richness of texts produced by learners for research and assessment purposes (Laufer & Nation, 1995; Morris & Cobb, 2004). Third, it can include programs designed for the deliberate learning of vocabulary (Cobb, 1999; Horst, Cobb, & Nicolae, 2005; Mondria & Mondria-de-Vries, 1994). Fourth, it can include the use of text-linked aids, such as spoken support, hypertext, glosses, concordances, dictionary look-ups, and electronic dictionaries, which support reading (Cobb, 1997; Cobb, Greaves, & Horst, 2001). Fifth, it can include the use of word-processing tools, such as highlighting, track changes, comments and hypertext links, to provide feedback on electronically submitted written work (Gaskell & Cobb, 2004). Not surprisingly, there has been an increasing amount of research and the development of applications in each of these areas as computer technology has developed. In this review we will focus on the use of text-linked aids because this is closest to what is commonly considered computer-assisted vocabulary learning, and because there has been useful innovation and research in the area, much of it involving the research of Tom Cobb and his colleagues.

Cobb's website (www.lextutor.ca) has an ever-increasing variety of research tools, resources and learning programs that are freely available to those who want to use them. Let us look at one set of programs before focusing on concordancing, which has interested both researchers and teachers since electronic concordancers first became available. The Hypertext program (www.lextutor.ca/hypertext/) on Cobb's website involves the learner working with an electronic text that can be pasted into the program. The program then provides the following support for reading.

1 *Spoken form.* Clicking once on any word provides the spoken form of the word. In a separate program under the Text-to-Speech heading on Cobb's web page, it is possible to link written texts to their spoken form where these exist. Useful sites for texts available in both spoken and written form can also be found from the Compleat Lexical Tutor website.

2 *Examples in context.* Clicking twice on a word brings up several instances of the word in context (a concordance).

> of the Arkansas. It was hoped that to this post would <u>flow</u> a large quantity of furs from the west, principally do
>
> among Mr. Coward's more memorable works. The melodies <u>flow</u> along pleasantly, as Mr. Coward's songs usually do,
>
> be if it was made by a rusty tool; this would stop the <u>flow</u> and also prevent infection. My lawyer told me that his

These extra contexts can be used to help guess the meaning of the unknown word, to gain information about the use of the word (grammar and collocates), and to gain information about the range of senses of the word.

3   *Meaning.* Clicking on a link brings up a substantial dictionary entry for a word from a range of possible dictionaries, including learner dictionaries.

4   *Revision.* Holding down the Alt-key and clicking puts the word in a box at the top of the screen for later revision. These revision activities can include (a) a dictation test, where the word is heard and the learner has to write the word; (b) a meaning test, where a concordance appears but the pivot word is missing and must be chosen from the list in the box.

The concordancer and dictator are also available as stand-alone programs not linked to a text.

Concordancers have long been suggested as tools for vocabulary learning. Study of concordances can provide a range of information about a word, including its meaning, the range of forms it can have, its grammar, its collocates, its frequency and the relative frequency of its various forms, uses and meanings. Seeing a concordance of a word is in some ways similar to meeting examples of the word while reading. The advantage of the concordance is that all these examples can be readily compared with one another and more deliberate generalizations made from them. It also means that a guess at the meaning of a word is more likely to be successful, as there is much more data available. The disadvantages are that the encounters are not spaced (spaced repetition is better for retention than massed repetition), and the study of concordances is time-consuming. Cobb (1997) compared learners using concordances with those doing the same kinds of activities without concordances and found a 12 percent vocabulary-learning advantage for concordance users. There is evidence that students generally enjoy using concordances, but concordance use is still a largely under-researched area.

Fluency development

The fourth strand of a well-balanced course is the strand of fluency development. Fluency development needs to occur in each of the four skills of listening, speaking, reading, and writing. Speaking fluency activities include 4/3/2, where learners deliver the same talk to three successive listeners in a four-minute, then a three-minute, and then a two-minute time frame, and pyramid-ranking activities, where learners deal with the same items to rank in pairs, and then groups, and then as a whole class. Reading fluency activities include timed texts with questions, and repeated reading. Writing activities include ten-minute writing, where learners get positive feedback on quantity and content, but not on form, and writing about things that have already been read about and talked about. Fluency development tends to be a neglected strand in most courses, but it is important that learners not only learn new language items but also are able to access and use them fluently.

How Should Vocabulary Knowledge Be Monitored and Assessed?

Vocabulary testing can be used to see what level of vocabulary learners should be focusing on (a diagnostic goal), to see how much vocabulary learners know and how well they know it (a proficiency goal), and to see what vocabulary they have recently learned and how well they have learned it (an achievement goal).

Diagnostic testing

The *Vocabulary Levels Test* (Read, 2000, pp. 118–26; Schmitt, Schmitt, & Clapham, 2001) was designed to look at high-frequency, academic, and low-frequency vocabulary. Although it has been used to measure vocabulary size, it was not designed to do that. Because the Vocabulary Levels Test is a monolingual test, there is no section testing the first 1,000 words, as the meanings of these words cannot be represented using more frequent vocabulary than the tested words. The first 1,000 words is an extremely important group of words of which many learners may have poor knowledge. Because of this, some bilingual tests of the first 1,000 and the second 1,000 words have been developed, where the meanings of the tested words are given in the first language of the test takers. The Vocabulary Levels Test is also available online at www.lextutor.ca.

Proficiency testing

Vocabulary proficiency testing has typically involved the measurement of vocabulary size, but there are now innovative approaches to measuring how well vocabulary is known and how diverse a vocabulary learners actually use. The distinction between how many words are known and how well they are known has been described as the distinction between breadth of vocabulary knowledge and depth of vocabulary knowledge. Read (2004) has usefully distinguished between several meanings of depth – precision of meaning, comprehensive word knowledge, and network knowledge.

Read's (1993, 2000, pp. 180–6) Vocabulary Associates Test is a well-researched example of a network knowledge measure. It involves items like the following, where learners need to choose elements of meaning and collocates of the test item. Each item involves choosing four words out of the eight provided.

sound
(A) logical (B) healthy (C) bold (D) solid (E) snow (F) temperature (G) sleep (H) dance

The test and variants of it have been found to be reliable and results to correlate well with a measure of reading comprehension (Qian & Schedl, 2004).

There has been a range of innovative attempts to measure the diversity of vocabulary used in learners' writing and speech. One approach is to calculate the number of different words (types or lemmas) used in relation to the number of running words (tokens) used. An early measure of this was the type–token ratio, but this has been found to be strongly related to text length. Malvern and Richards (1997; Duran et al., 2004) have developed a much more sophisticated measure, D, that avoids the weaknesses of the type–token ratio. This measure has fuelled a resurgence of research in this area (Daller, van Hout, & Treffers-Daller, 2003). Software using D (vocd) is available at http://childes.psy.cmu.edu as a part of the CLAN suite of programs for the analysis of children's language. D measures "the extent to which the active vocabulary is employed and how richly it is deployed" (Duran et al., 2004). See Jarvis (2002) for a positive critique of D.

The lexical frequency Profile (Laufer & Nation, 1995) attempts to relate vocabulary diversity to word frequency levels. In this way it may have diagnostic value as well as being a proficiency measure. There has been debate about the relative merits of this kind of measure and those based on modeling (Laufer, 2005; Meara, 2005). Meara has also suggested other innovative methods for measuring productive vocabulary (Meara & Bell, 2001; Meara & Fitzpatrick, 2000).

Achievement testing

Laufer and her colleagues (Laufer & Goldstein, 2004; Laufer et al., 2004) examined four kinds of tests that can be used in both monolingual and bilingual versions. In the examples below, the monolingual example is given first. Laufer and Goldstein used a bilingual test, Laufer et al. monolingual tests.

1   Active recall (supplying a form for a given meaning; the first letter of the tested word is given to prevent learners from supplying non-target words)

> Turn into water *m*_____ (monolingual)
> *m*_____   mencairkan (bilingual)

2   Passive recall (supplying the meaning for a given form; the first letter of the translation is given)

> When something *melts it turns into* _____.
> Translate the following words into Indonesian.
> *melt*

3   Active recognition (choosing the target word form from four options)

> *Turn into water*   a. elect b. blame c. melt d. threaten
> Select the correct translation for the following words.
> mencairkan   a. elect b. blame c. melt d. threaten

4   Passive recognition (choosing the meaning of the target word from four
    options)

> *Melt* a. choose b. accuse c. make threats d. turn into water
> *Melt* a. menolong b. mencairkan c. memeriksa d. memandang

In the two studies, Laufer et al. found:

1   There was a hierarchy of difficulty in the order given above from the most
    difficult, active recall, to the least difficult, passive recognition.
2   The four formats were significantly different from each other. Active recall
    was very difficult compared with the other formats; the difference between
    active and passive recognition was much smaller.
3   Knowledge did not seem to grow at an even pace in the four strength meas-
    ures. The more difficult recall formats seemed to take much longer to show
    growth.
4   Vocabulary knowledge is not an all-or-nothing phenomenon. Knowledge of
    words develops cumulatively and there is value in having tests that show this
    change in strength of knowledge.

An important message from this research for achievement testing is that there
is a variety of test formats that could be used and which differ from each other in
difficulty. It is thus very important to consider the level of knowledge that learners are likely to have when choosing a format to measure this knowledge. Choosing a very difficult format, such as active recall, could underestimate learning.
Choosing a format that is too easy may not give credit for additional knowledge
that learners have. When considering the type of item to choose, the following
factors are important.

1   How large is the learners' vocabulary? If their vocabulary size is small, bi-
    lingual items would be better than monolingual items.
2   What kind of learning did the learners do? If the learning was through
    reading or listening, then passive measures are more suitable. If substantial
    attention was given to the learning and active retrieval was used, then active
    measures are more suitable.
3   How long ago did the learning occur? The longer the time gap, the easier the
    item format needs to be.
4   How difficult does the teacher want the test to be?

This review of teaching, learning and testing vocabulary has shown the increasing effect of computing technology on vocabulary research and teaching. This
effect is apparent in corpus-based research, in providing aids to assist reading
and learning vocabulary from reading, and in the deliberate learning of vocabulary. Undoubtedly, this effect will increase as ways of dealing with multi-word
units become more sophisticated.

REFERENCES

Adolphs, S. & Schmitt, N. (2003). Lexical coverage of spoken discourse. *Applied Linguistics* 24, 4, 425–38.

Bamford, J. & Day, R. R. (eds.) (2004). *Extensive reading activities for teaching language.* Cambridge: Cambridge University Press.

Biber, D., Conrad, S., & Cortes, V. (2004). "If you look at . . .": Lexical bundles in university teaching and textbooks. *Applied Linguistics* 25, 3, 371–405.

Boers, F., Demechleer, M., & Eyckmans, J. (2004). Cross-cultural variation as a variable in comprehending and remembering figurative idioms. *European Journal of English Studies* 8, 3, 375–88.

Boers, F., Eyckmans, J., Kappel, J., Stengers, H., & Demecheleer, M. (2006). Formulaic sequences and perceived oral proficiency: Putting the Lexical Approach to the test. *Language Teaching Research* 10, 3, 245–61.

Boers, F., Eyckmans, J., & Stengers, H. (2006). Presenting figurative idioms with a touch of etymology: More than mere mnemonics. *Language Teaching Research* 11, 43–62.

Carver, R. P. (1994). Percentage of unknown vocabulary words in text as a function of the relative difficulty of the text: Implications for instruction. *Journal of Reading Behavior* 26, 4, 413–37.

Chujo, K. & Utiyama, M. (2006). Selecting level-specific specialized vocabulary using statistical measures. *System* 34, 255–69.

Chung, T. M. & Nation, P. (2003). Technical vocabulary in specialised texts. *Reading in a Foreign Language* 15, 2, 103–16.

Chung, T. M. & Nation, P. (2004). Identifying technical vocabulary. *System* 32, 2, 251–63.

Cobb, T. (1997). Is there any measurable learning from hands-on concordancing? *System* 25, 3, 301–15.

Cobb, T. (1999). Breadth and depth of vocabulary acquisition with hands-on concordancing. *Computer Assisted Language Learning* 12, 4, 345–60.

Cobb, T., Greaves, C., & Horst, M. (2001). Can the rate of lexical acquisition from reading be increased? An experiment in reading French with a suite of on-line resources. In P. Raymond & C. Cornaire, *Regards sur la didactique des langues secondes* (pp. 133–53). Montréal: Éditions logique.

Coxhead, A. (2000). A new academic word list. *TESOL Quarterly* 34, 2, 213–38.

Daller, H., van Hout, R., & Treffers-Daller, J. (2003). Lexical richness in the spontaneous speech of bilinguals. *Applied Linguistics* 24, 2, 197–222.

Day, R. R. & Bamford, J. (1998). *Extensive reading in the second language classroom.* Cambridge: Cambridge University Press.

Duran, P., Malvern, D., Richards, B., & Chipere, N. (2004). Developmental trends in lexical diversity. *Applied Linguistics* 25, 2, 220–42.

Gaskell, D. & Cobb, T. (2004). Can learners use concordance feedback for writing errors? *System* 32, 3, 301–19.

Grant, L. & Bauer, L. (2004). Criteria for redefining idioms: Are we barking up the wrong tree? *Applied Linguistics* 25, 1, 38–61.

Grant, L. & Nation, I. S. P. (2006). How many idioms are there in English? *ITL – International Journal of Applied Linguistics* 151, 1–14.

Hirsh, D. & Nation, P. (1992). What vocabulary size is needed to read unsimplified texts for pleasure? *Reading in a Foreign Language* 8, 2, 689–96.

Horst, M. (2005). Learning L2 vocabulary through extensive reading: A measurement study. *Canadian Modern Language Review* 61, 3, 355–82 .

Horst, M., Cobb, T., & Nicolae, I. (2005). Expanding academic vocabulary with an interactive on-line database. *Language Learning and Technology* 9, 2, 90–110.

Hu, M. & Nation, I. S. P. (2000). Vocabulary density and reading comprehension. *Reading in a Foreign Language* 13, 1, 403–30.

Huntley, H. (2006). *Essential academic vocabulary*. Boston: Houghton Mifflin.

Jarvis, S. (2002). Short texts, best-fitting curves and new measures of lexical diversity. *Language Testing* 19, 1, 57–84.

Joe, A. (1998). What effects do text-based tasks promoting generation have on incidental vocabulary acquisition? *Applied Linguistics* 19, 3, 357–77.

Joe, A., Nation, P., & Newton, J. (1996). Vocabulary learning and speaking activities. *English Teaching Forum* 34, 1, 2–7.

Laufer, B. (2005). Lexical frequency profiles: From Monte Carlo to the real world. A response to Meara (2005). *Applied Linguistics* 26, 4, 582–8.

Laufer, B., Elder, C., Hill, K., & Congdon, P. (2004). Size and strength: Do we need both to measure vocabulary knowledge? *Language Testing* 21, 2, 202–26.

Laufer, B. & Goldstein, Z. (2004). Testing vocabulary knowledge: Size, strength, and computer adaptiveness. *Language Learning* 54, 3, 399–436.

Laufer, B. & Nation, P. (1995). Vocabulary size and use: Lexical richness in L2 written production. *Applied Linguistics* 16, 3, 307–22.

Laufer, B. & Paribakht, T. S. (1998). The relationship between passive and active vocabularies: Effects of language learning context. *Language Learning* 48, 3, 365–91.

Lewis, M. (1993). *The lexical approach*. Hove, UK: Language Teaching Publications.

Lewis, M. (1997). *Implementing the lexical approach*. Hove, UK: Language Teaching Publications.

Malvern, D. & Richards, B. (1997). A new measure of lexical diversity. In A. Ryan & A. Wray (eds.), *Evolving models of language* (pp. 58–71). Clevedon, UK: Multilingual Matters.

McKeown, M. G. (1993). Creating effective definitions for young word learners. *Reading Research Quarterly* 28, 1, 17–31.

Meara, P. (2005). Lexical frequency profiles: A Monte Carlo analysis. *Applied Linguistics* 26, 1, 32–47.

Meara, P. & Bell, H. (2001). P_Lex: A simple and effective way of describing the lexical characteristics of short texts. *Prospect* 16, 3, 5–19.

Meara, P. & Fitzpatrick, T. (2000). An improved method of assessing productive vocabulary in L2. *System* 28, 19–30.

Mondria, J.-A. & Mondria-de Vries, S. (1994). Efficiently memorizing words with the help of word cards and "hand computer": Theory and applications. *System* 22, 1, 47–57.

Morris, L. & Cobb, T. (2004). Vocabulary profiles as predictors of the academic performance of Teaching English as a Second Language trainees. *System* 32, 75–87.

Nation, I. S. P. (2001). *Learning vocabulary in another language*. Cambridge: Cambridge University Press.

Nation, I. S. P. (2004a). A study of the most frequent word families in the British National Corpus. In P. Bogaards & B. Laufer (eds.), *Vocabulary in a second language: Selection, acquisition, and testing* (pp. 3–13). John Benjamins, Amsterdam.

Nation, I. S. P. (2004b). Vocabulary learning and intensive reading. *EA Journal* 21, 2, 20–9.

Nation, I. S. P. (2006). How large a vocabulary is needed for reading and listening? *Canadian Modern Language Review* 63, 1, 59–82.

Nation, I. S. P. (2007). The four strands. *Innovation in Language Learning and Teaching* 1, 1, 1–12.

Nation, I. S. P. (2008). *Teaching vocabulary: Strategies and techniques.* New York: Thomson Heinle.

Nurweni, A. & Read, J. (1999). The English vocabulary knowledge of Indonesian university students. *English for Specific Purposes* 18, 2, 161–75.

Palmer, H. E. (1925). Conversation. In R. C. Smith (1999) *The Writings of Harold E. Palmer: An Overview* (pp. 185–91). Tokyo: Hon-no-Tomosha.

Pawley, A. & Syder, F. H. (1983). Two puzzles for linguistic theory: Nativelike selection and nativelike fluency. In J. C. Richards & R. W. Schmidt (eds.), *Language and communication* (pp. 191–225). Longman, London.

Pigada, M. & Schmitt, N. (2006). Vocabulary acquisition from extensive reading: A case study. *Reading in a Foreign Language* 18, 1, 1–28.

Qian, D. & Schedl, M. (2004). Evaluation of an in-depth vocabulary knowledge measure for assessing reading performance. *Language Testing* 21, 1, 28–52.

Read, J. (1993). The development of a new measure of L2 vocabulary knowledge. *Language Testing* 10, 3, 355–71.

Read, J. (2000). *Assessing vocabulary.* Cambridge : Cambridge University Press.

Read, J. (2004). Plumbing the depths: How should the construct of vocabulary knowledge be defined? In P. Bogaards & B. Laufer (eds.), *Vocabulary in a second language: Selection, acquisition and testing* (pp. 209–27). Amsterdam: John Benjamins.

Rott, S. (2005). Processing glosses: A qualitative exploration of how form–meaning connections are established and strengthened. *Reading in a Foreign Language* 17, 2, 95–124.

Rott, S., Williams, J., & Cameron, R. (2002). The effect of multiple-choice glosses and input-output cycles on lexical acquisition and retention. *Language Teaching Research* 6, 3, 183–222.

Schmitt, D. & Schmitt, N. (2005). *Focus on vocabulary.* White Plains, NY: Longman Pearson Education.

Schmitt, N., Schmitt, D., & Clapham, C. (2001). Developing and exploring the behaviour of two new versions of the Vocabulary Levels Test. *Language Testing* 18, 1, 55–88.

Shin, D. & Nation, I. S. P. (2006). Beyond single words: The most frequent collocations in spoken English. *ELT Journal* 62, 4, 339–48.

Sutarsyah, C., Nation, P., & Kennedy, G. (1994). How useful is EAP vocabulary for ESP? A corpus based study. *RELC Journal* 25, 2, 34–50.

Taylor, A. (2006). Factors associated with glossing: Comments on Ko (2005). *Reading in a Foreign Language* 18, 1, 72–3.

Walters, J. (2004). Teaching the use of context to infer meaning: A longitudinal survey of L1 and L2 vocabulary research. *Language Teaching* 37, 243–52.

Walters, J. (2006). Methods of teaching inferring meaning from context. *RELC Journal* 37, 2, 176–90.

Waring, R. & Takaki, M. (2003). At what rate do learners learn and retain new vocabulary from reading a graded reader? *Reading in a Foreign Language* 15, 2, 130–63.

West, M. (1953). *A general service list of English words.* London: Longman, Green & Co.

29 Teaching and Testing Pragmatics

CARSTEN ROEVER

Pragmatics

Pragmatics is commonly viewed as the study of language in use (Crystal, 1997; Mey, 2001), topicalizing the incorporation of context factors in discourse (Levinson, 1983). Such context factors can include, for example, the physical setting in which the discourse takes place, the relationship between the participants in terms of Brown and Levinson's (1987) relationship factors (relative power, degree of imposition, social distance), and the participants' shared knowledge about the topic of the discourse and social rules and norms. Pragmatics therefore contributes a social and contextual dimension to the study of language, extending analyses beyond deliberations on linguistic form, and concerns itself with situated language function.

Pragmatics as a field incorporates the study of a range of research areas. Most research has probably been undertaken on speech acts, such as requests, apologies, and refusals, but there is also a significant amount of work on discourse topics, including the structuring of spoken and written discourse. Smaller areas include implicature, routine formulae, and deixis.

With regard to language users' pragmatic knowledge, Leech (1983) distinguishes between knowledge of sociopragmatics and pragmalinguistics. Sociopragmatic knowledge encompasses knowledge of the social rules of language use, including knowledge of appropriateness, the meaning of situational and interlocutor factors, and social conventions and taboos. Pragmalinguistic knowledge incorporates the linguistic tools necessary for implementing speech intentions, and relies crucially on general target language knowledge. It is essential that both aspects of pragmatic knowledge are developed and accurately mapped onto one another. If a language user has the sociopragmatic knowledge to understand that a polite request is necessary in a given situation but lacks the pragmalinguistic knowledge of modals, interrogatives, and conventionalized formulae to utter it, pragmatic failure will likely result. Conversely, if a language user has control of pragmalinguistic tools without awareness of sociopragmatic rules of usage, she or he might produce well-formed sentences which are so non-conventional that they are incomprehensible or have disastrous consequences at the relationship level.

Pragmatic competence is represented in all major models of communicative competence. In Canale and Swain's (1980) original model, "sociocultural rules of use" and "discourse rules" are part of sociolinguistic competence. The former are mostly concerned with appropriateness, whereas the latter refer to coherence and cohesion in discourse. Canale's revision (1983) of the original model makes discourse competence its own category and limits sociolinguistic competence to appropriateness. Bachman (1990) offers a more radical revision, subsuming "illocutionary competence" under general language competence, and distinct from "textual competence" (akin to Canale's "discourse competence") and sociolinguistic competence, which describes a sensitivity to register, dialect, and nativelike use. Pragmatic competence is not wholly confined to the language dimension of Bachman's model, as one part of the assessment component in his strategic competence category is the evaluation of the interlocutor, the speaker-hearer's relationship to the interlocutor, and the situation. These strategic abilities draw on sociopragmatic competence, and also on pragmalinguistic competence to the extent that a hearer's evaluation of the interlocutor is influenced by the interlocutor's stance toward the hearer, which is encoded linguistically.

The important role played by pragmatic competence as a part of communicative competence should translate into pragmatics receiving pedagogical attention equal to grammar or vocabulary. While there is increasing research on teaching pragmatics, this area still lags far behind other aspects of language competence in its integration in language teaching methodology and research on pedagogical interventions.

Learning Pragmatics and the Structure of Pragmatic Competence

Learning pragmatics has essentially the same conditions and follows the same steps as second language learning in general, but is complicated by the need to learn non-linguistic rules of social conduct and social relationships. While such rules are frequently linguistically indexed (through address terms or morphology), using linguistic data to build sociopragmatic knowledge is difficult for low-proficiency learners, who may not notice salient features in the input. At the same time, even low-proficiency learners have access to non-linguistic input about interactional norms (physical proximity, touch, bowing), and are familiar with basic, universally applicable pragmatic concepts (see Kasper & Rose, 2002, for a comprehensive discussion) as well as L1-specific rules and norms, which they can transfer more or less profitably.

Figure 29.1 shows a model of pragmatics learning. Both, sociopragmatic input and general linguistic input are necessary, and need to involve language use in interaction and the modeling of language use associated with relevant social roles. On the sociopragmatic side, learners need to attend to sociopragmatic features of the input, i.e., to expressions of interlocutor relationships and context influences. Noticing these features and processing them leads to intake, and allows learners to construct theories and consequently knowledge about what interlocutor characteristics are sociopragmatically relevant and how context influences language use. To build up pragmalinguistic knowledge, learners need to attend to the pragmatic aspects of general linguistic input, e.g., the use of modals and questions to express conventional indirectness in requests and not just to hedge declarative statements. The ability to identify what aspects of the input constitute pragmalinguistic tools increases with greater sociopragmatic knowledge: if learners know that age difference is a relevant context feature in a given setting, it is likely that it will be linguistically encoded, and they then just need to identify how it is encoded in the language input. Input that is identified as pragmalinguistically relevant can become intake and part of pragmalinguistic knowledge. That knowledge then needs to be connected to sociopragmatic knowledge, but this probably occurs throughout the acquisition process. L1 transfer is operative at all times and influences the learners' developing sociopragmatic, pragmalinguistic, and general L2 knowledge.

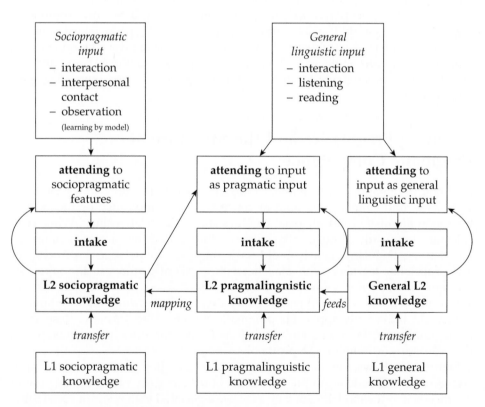

Figure 29.1   Model of pragmatics learning

Instructed Learning of Pragmatics

While acquisitional processes are likely to run in similar ways in natural or instructed learning of pragmatics, there are clear differences between the circumstances of acquisition in natural contexts and in classrooms. The former tend to provide more input and exposure to a much wider range of social roles but are likely to lead to slower learning, as learners do not receive any help in structuring input for easier processing. The latter have a much narrower range of input and interaction opportunities but have the potential to help accelerate learning by targeting instruction at learners' needs and developmental readiness. The first question that arises in instructed learning of pragmatics is whether pragmatics is in principle teachable.

Teachability

The teachability of pragmatics has been established beyond a reasonable doubt, as a considerable number of studies have demonstrated instructional effects in a variety of areas. For example, Yoshimi (2001) showed that an instructed group of Japanese as a foreign language (JFL) learners used interactional markers with much higher frequency than an uninstructed group. Billmyer (1990) obtained a similar finding for compliments, Lyster (1994) showed an advantage of an instructed over an uninstructed group in distinguishing *tu/vous* in French, and Wishnoff (2000) found much greater use of hedges in formal and informal written production among instructed than uninstructed learners. Ohta (2001), as well as Kanagy (1999) and Kanagy and Igarashi (1997), found that teacher modeling of pragmatic routines was effective in a foreign language (JFL) setting. Further studies are discussed throughout this section.

It is worth noting that not all studies have documented an unqualified success in instructed learning. In studies by Yoshimi (2001), Liddicoat and Crozet (2001), and Olshtain and Cohen (1990), learners improved some aspect of their L2 pragmatic performance, but not all targeted aspects. Studies by Fukuya and Clark (2001) on mitigators, and LoCastro (1997) on sociopragmatic awareness, did not show any teaching effects, which Rose (2005) suspects may be due to the measurement in LoCastro's case and the brevity of treatment in Fukuya and Clark's.

Instructional considerations

While it is comforting that pragmatics is generally amenable to instructional interventions, the more interesting overarching question is in fact the three-way interaction between target features, types of interventions, and learners: What kinds of target features (e.g., speech acts, interactional abilities, formulae, implicature comprehension) should be taught to what kinds of learners (in terms of proficiency or developmental level) using what kinds of methods (implicit or explicit)? Understanding this three-way interaction will also go a long way toward explaining partial success or lack of success in instructed pragmatics studies.

This somewhat daunting question can be split into three parts. The first sub-question concerns the necessity for instructional intervention: Which features require targeted instruction because they would otherwise not be learned or learned only slowly or incompletely?

The second consideration is the learner's developmental readiness to acquire a given feature. Just as complex relative clauses could not profitably be taught to beginning learners, different pragmatic features may require the learner already to have acquired certain other features. Not much work has been done in this area for pragmatics, but some findings from developmental studies allow an outline of possible directions in this area.

Finally, the question arises of how to profitably teach a feature. Recent studies have investigated this in relation to implicit and explicit instruction, which has also been thoroughly investigated in general language teaching research (see Norris & Ortega, 2000, for a meta-analysis).

What to teach?

SLA research has shown that certain L2 features are difficult for learners to acquire without instruction, e.g., adverb placement (White, 1991) or interrogatives for L1 French-speaking learners of English (White et al., 1991). Such features can become evident through longitudinal studies that show certain errors or infelicities persisting over extended periods, or studies of high-ability learners who still show deficits in some areas. In pragmatics research, very few studies of advanced learners exist, and there is also only a limited number of longitudinal studies. However, some candidate areas for instruction can be identified.

One possible feature is formulaic implicature. Bouton (1994, 1999) showed that learners' comprehension of formulaic implicature does not develop over time through increases in world knowledge and L2 proficiency, unlike their comprehension of idiosyncratic implicature. These findings are supported by Roever (2005), who found some positive effect of proficiency on comprehension of formulaic implicature, but this tendency was not as pronounced as in the case of idiosyncratic implicature, and learners' scores on formulaic implicature items remained below scores on idiosyncratic implicature items at nearly all proficiency levels. When Bouton (1994) taught learners how to interpret and decode formulaic implicature, their scores jumped to near perfect levels. Interestingly, idiosyncratic implicature proved impervious to instruction.

Another area where even quite advanced learners have shown persistent deficits is sociopragmatic knowledge in foreign language settings. In Bardovi-Harlig and Dörnyei's study (1998), their Hungarian group showed less awareness of pragmatic infelicities than grammatical errors. In Niezgoda's and Roever's (2001) replication with a highly select sample, severity ratings for pragmatic errors were similar to ratings for grammatical errors, but the higher-proficiency group found significantly fewer pragmatic than grammatical errors. Rose (2000) found that his L1 Cantonese-speaking learners of English in Hong Kong developed pragmalinguistically, but not sociopragmatically, producing more complex requests and apologies but with little contextual sensitivity. Matsumura (2001) showed that Japanese ESL learners had distinctly more nativelike judgments of the appropriateness of advice after one year of study abroad in Canada than a comparable group of Japanese EFL learners. Similarly, Cook (2001) found that JFL learners had great difficulty judging speech styles in Japanese, and rated speech as acceptable that was glaringly inappropriate to native speakers.

It seems that learning of sociopragmatic rules is more difficult outside the target language setting, which in itself is not surprising: learners living in the target language setting have much more opportunity to observe models and are exposed to a far greater range of social roles and situations than in the foreign language learning context. In the foreign language context, pragmatically relevant input is limited (Kasper, 1989; Lörscher, 1986), teachers are often the only models of appropriate behavior (but even they may not have high sociopragmatic competence), and learners are often not exposed to social situations and social roles other than those of being students in a classroom.

But simple exposure to situated language use in the target speech community has also been shown not always to be sufficient. In Bardovi-Harlig and Hartford's (1993) longitudinal study of advising sessions, their participants learned the sociopragmatic rules of being expected to initiate suggestions rather than being asked for them or relying on rejections, but they never approached native-speaker levels in using mitigators and avoiding aggravators. Due to the status incongruence between students and advisers, the use of mitigators was never modeled for them, so instruction may be necessary in cases where learners are unlikely to receive input that allows them to develop status-appropriate pragmalinguistic abilities.

A final area that may benefit from instruction concerns discourse structuring and embedding, which can lead to misunderstanding and mistaken impressions. Even highly proficient L2 speakers often follow their L1's rules in structuring a discourse contribution, and thereby become unclear and difficult for interlocutors to understand (Holmes, 2003; Young, 1994). Hearers in turn may attribute these communication problems to the speaker "not thinking clearly" and develop an unjustified negative impression. Little developmental research exists on the structuring of larger discourse contributions, so this area requires further investigation.

When to teach?

While there is little work on developmental stages in pragmatic comprehension or sociopragmatics, studies on pragmalinguistic development indicate a move from reliance on unanalyzed routine formulae to a greater range of features, more complexity, and more targetlike constructions. This may be (but is not always) accompanied by sociopragmatic adjustments to adapt politeness levels and sociopragmatic markers to a specific interlocutor. Pragmalinguistic development goes hand in hand with an increase in general L2 proficiency, in terms of greater control, analysis, and automatization, which allows learners to produce more language with less effort. Untutored sociopragmatic development, as argued above, is greatly dependent on the availability of status-appropriate modeling.

The only stage sequence identified in pragmatics so far is Kasper and Rose's (2002) five-stage sequence for the development of requests, based on studies by Ellis (1992) and Achiba (2002). The sequence begins with a pre-formulaic stage, where even routine formulae are not yet present, followed by a formulaic stage with routine formulae, an "unpacking" stage with increasing use of conventional indirectness, an "expansion" stage with more mitigation and complex syntax, and a "fine-tuning" stage with adjustment of the nuances of requests to inter-locutor and context factors. It is likely (but has yet to be shown empirically) that targeted instruction would accelerate learners' development through these stages.

Another interesting finding with possible instructional implications is that prag-matic and grammatical development can be disjointed: Salsbury and Bardovi-Harlig (2000, 2001) found learners not necessarily using modals for pragmatic purposes, although these modals were already present in their interlanguage. Rost-Roth (1999) reports similar findings for modal particles in German, and Eisenstein and Bodman (1993) show how advanced L2 proficiency enables trans-fer and leads to pragmalinguistically incorrect usage. Learners, therefore, may benefit from having their attention drawn to the pragmalinguistic functions of general L2 grammatical features.

With regard to discourse abilities, Yoshimi's (2001) instructed learners were able to use interactional markers for some purposes (to structure event sequences, to introduce background information), but not others (to mark shifts in perspective, or highlight the point of a story). Yoshimi explains that the establishment of a coherent narrative was already challenging for learners, which suggests that they may not have been developmentally ready for other uses of interactional markers.

Similarly, Liddicoat and Crozet (2001) found that it was easier for learners to adjust the content of their interactional contributions in small-talk exchanges than to integrate features that signal engagement and interest, like repetition and overlap. Liddicoat and Crozet suggest that content modifications are more sub-ject to conscious control than affiliative devices, which require a greater degree of automaticity to implement.

How to teach?

Studies that have investigated the effect of different types of interventions invari-ably compare more explicit with more implicit instruction (Rose, 2005), and have generally found an advantage for more explicit teaching. Jeon and Kaya (2006) conducted a small-scale meta-analysis of 13 instructional pragmatics studies. They found a clear advantage for explicit over implicit instruction, although the small number of studies meant that generalizations should only be made with caution. Detecting instructional effects is also complicated by the insufficiency of many testing instruments that have been designed ad hoc. This can lead to Type I error, when the instrument underrepresents the construct and only tests the very nar-row range of exemplars that have been taught. Conversely, there is a risk of Type II error when the instrument is not sensitive enough to detect small changes in learners' pragmatic competence. Of course, most studies that do not find "significant" effects are never published, so among the published ones, Type I error is likely to be more prevalent than Type II.

In general, explicit instruction means metapragmatic explanation being provided as rules of use, sometimes combined with examples. Implicit instruction generally means that examples of the use of the target feature are provided, but without metapragmatic explanation and often without telling the learners what the target feature is. The advantage found for more explicit instruction can be explained in terms of the noticing hypothesis (Schmidt, 1995, 2001), and is most likely due to explicit instruction's greater efficiency in drawing students' attention to the target feature and thereby allowing them to focus on input containing it. This leads to more processing space being allocated to the exclusive processing of the target feature (possibly to the detriment of other aspects of the input), whereas implicit teaching does not direct attention as efficiently to the feature under investigation.

The advantages of more, rather than less, explicit teaching have been shown across a range of pragmatic features. In teaching routine formulae, Wildner-Bassett (1986) and House (1996) both found advantages for their more explicitly taught group, with Wildner-Bassett's learners showing greater fluency in the use of agreement/disagreement gambits, and House's more explicitly taught learners also deploying their discourse routines in a more targetlike manner. Tateyama et al. (1997) found that students who had been taught the Japanese apology routine "sumimasen" explicitly, outperformed an implicit group on DCTs and role-plays after only 25 minutes of instruction.[1] Curiously, in a follow-up study that involved four 20-minute instructional episodes over eight weeks, Tateyama (2001) found no statistically significant differences between implicit and explicit groups, with the DCT measure showing an increase in the explicit group's scores, and a decrease in the implicit group's, while the role-play measure showed the opposite tendency. Tateyama accounts for this finding by noting the greater language contact and overall stronger academic performance of the implicit group, which may have balanced out the facilitative effect of explicit instruction. This explanation highlights the fact that instruction interacts with learner background variables and that high-aptitude and motivated learners can profit from any kind of instruction (as Niezgoda & Roever, 2001, also found).

In the area of speech acts, Rose and Ng (2001) found more nativelike compliment responses for their explicit instruction group, but no difference in syntactic formulae between implicitly and explicitly taught learners. However, both groups outperformed a control group, showing that implicit teaching does have an effect, but possibly not as much of an effect as more explicit teaching. Koike and Pearson (2005) compared explicit and implicit instruction coupled with explicit or implicit feedback for suggestions in Spanish. They found that learners who received explicit instruction and explicit feedback outperformed all other groups on a multiple-choice test administered one week after instruction, and they managed to maintain their gains on a delayed post-test five weeks after instruction. The findings of an open-ended dialogue test were more mixed, showing no maintenance of gains on the delayed post-test, but noticeable increases on the regular post-test by the "explicit instruction coupled with explicit feedback" group and the "implicit instruction coupled with implicit feedback" group. In another study of suggestions, Martínez-Flor and Fukuya (2005) administered a treatment of six

2-hour sessions over sixteen weeks for L1 Spanish-speaking EFL learners. They found strong treatment effects for both the explicit and the implicit group, compared to a control group, with the explicit group consistently performing best. No delayed post-test was administered. Alcón Soler (2005) reports very similar findings on the learning of request strategies from an instructional sequence encompassing 15 self-study episodes. Also working on requests, Takahashi (2001) taught bi-clausal requests in four 90-minute sessions over four weeks, and compared an explicit teaching condition with three implicit conditions. She found that the explicitly taught group outperformed the implicit groups, and among the implicit groups, highest scores were obtained by the form comparison group, which had compared its own performance on a DCT with native-speaker models from role-play data. In a follow-up study, Takahashi (2005) provided a qualitative analysis showing that the comparison condition led to greater noticing than the form-search condition.

Problems with Teaching Pragmatics

The main problem with discussing the teaching of pragmatics in general is that it is not widely taught in any systematic way. This is probably due to pragmatics not being well integrated in large methodological approaches, which tend to focus on grammar, vocabulary, and the four skills. Pragmatics does not play any significant role in traditional grammar-translation language teaching, whereas in courses following a notional-functional syllabus, routine formulae would certainly be taught, but there would be little consideration of learners' readiness to learn pragmatic features and equally little help in mapping sociopragmatic rules and pragmalinguistic tools onto one another. In most more or less communicatively oriented language-teaching settings, pragmatic content would probably be addressed incidentally, but there has not been any systematic attempt at designing a "pragmatic syllabus." Of course, any such syllabus would have to be integrated with a general language teaching syllabus, but research has shown clearly enough that certain aspects of pragmatics warrant instructional attention. The most promising type of syllabus that would fully integrate pragmatics is a syllabus designed around tasks (Long & Crookes, 1992, 1993), as such a task-based syllabus would have as its goal that learners should be able do target tasks successfully in a way that is considered acceptable in real-world settings.[2] Pragmatics would necessarily be a part of such a task-based syllabus because it is necessarily part of real-world language use. In addition, the psycholinguistic orientation of task-based syllabi, which require the sequencing of pedagogic tasks according to learners' readiness, would ensure a close link between development of the learners' general L2 competence and pragmatic competence.

Teaching techniques and materials design

Once a decision is made to teach pragmatics as part of a regular curriculum, the issue of teaching techniques and materials design demands immediate attention.

A small number of studies have investigated these areas, mostly focusing on consciousness-raising and materials design based on data from natural interaction.

With regard to materials design, Boxer and Pickering (1995) show that many existing materials are not accurate reflections of real-world discourse. In a move to ameliorate this problem, Huth and Taleghani-Nikazm (2006) show how materials to teach German phone conversation openings can be developed based on findings from conversation analysis (CA). From the CA literature, Huth and Taleghani-Nikazm drew examples of opening sequences for telephone conversations from American English and German (e.g., Pavlidou, 1994; Schegloff, 1979; Schegloff & Sacks, 1973; Taleghani-Nikazm, 2002), and used them for activities that raised learners' awareness of cross-cultural differences. Coupled with metapragmatic reflection, these materials and activities served to improve learners' performance noticeably.

It is of course possible to employ techniques and materials similar to the ones used in the empirical studies mentioned above. For example, Crandall and Basturkmen (2004) developed an instructional sequence of 5–6 hours for teaching requests in a status-unequal setting (international students to professors). Similarly to Takahashi (2001, 2005), Crandall and Basturkmen relied essentially on form comparison, but added explicit metapragmatic reflection. They had students role-play requests, engage in metapragmatic reflection on requests, analyze their own role-plays, and compare their own production with authentic NS data. Students evaluated the instruction as being useful and not too challenging, and they showed clear convergence toward the NS norm. Lee and McChesney (1999) give an example of a discourse-rating task, used in an instructional sequence to increase students' awareness of sociopragmatic appropriateness. Meier (1997) advocates an awareness-raising approach that involves metapragmatic reflection on the nature of appropriateness in communication, learners' own experiences in "critical incidents," and example dialogues and role-plays. Clennell (1999) relied even more heavily on learners' experiences by having learners interview native speakers, transcribe their interviews, and then discuss them in class with a focus on discourse conventions.

While all these instructional activities involve awareness raising and practice, it is noteworthy that they are not embedded in a larger curricular sequence, and not motivated by psycholinguistic findings on development. Also, many of the materials used require time-intensive development effort. As argued above, the teaching of pragmatics has yet to be integrated well in curricula and go beyond occasional projects on isolated features.

Testing of Pragmatics

As pragmatic competence is represented in all models of communicative competence, the assessment of learners' L2 pragmatic competence could reasonably be expected to be a large area of second language testing research. However, there are only few tests which explicitly assess pragmatic abilities, and none of them have had the impact of large-scale test batteries like TOEFL or IELTS. Some aspects of pragmatic competence can be included in scales for rating speaking performance in oral proficiency interviews, but pragmatics does not usually constitute a focus of the rating.

Studies of testing pragmatics can be classified according to their emphasis on testing sociopragmatics versus pragmalinguistics. On the sociopragmatic side, Hudson, Detmer, and Brown's (1995) study and its replications by Yamashita (1996), Yoshitake (1997), and Ahn (2005) constitute the largest test development and validation project, focusing on appropriateness for the speech acts apology, request, and refusal. Cook (2001) reports a small-scale study investigating learners' recognition of appropriate speech styles in Japanese, and Liu (2006) undertook a test development and validation project to design the elusive multiple-choice discourse completion test.

On the pragmalinguistic side, Bouton (1988, 1994, 1999) assessed comprehension of conversational implicature, and Roever (2005, 2006, 2007) designed and validated a web-based test battery of ESL pragmalinguistics, covering implicature, routines, and speech acts.

Tests of sociopragmatics

Hudson et al. (1995) compared various measures of sociopragmatic appropriateness. Their original test was focused on L1 Japanese-speaking ESL learners and covered the speech acts apology, request, and refusal. Yamashita (1996) adapted the test for L1 English-speaking learners of Japanese in Japan, Ahn (2005) for learners of Korean in the US, and Yoshitake (1997) used it for Japanese learners of English in an EFL situation. Hudson et al. included three types of DCTs (written, oral, and multiple-choice), a role-play task, and two self-assessment measures. While Hudson et al. (1995) describe the test development process, Brown (2001, 2008) discusses operational test findings from Yamashita's and Yoshitake's administrations. Possibly due to the small size and homogeneity of Yoshitake's population, the reliability of all the measures except the self-assessments is fairly low (in the 0.5–0.7 range). In Yamashita's and Ahn's studies, which employed larger populations with a greater range of proficiency levels, all measures have much higher reliability except the multiple-choice DCT in Yamashita's study, which proved highly unreliable (Ahn did not use a multiple-choice DCT). This is unfortunate, as multiple-choice DCTs are far more practical than the other DCT versions and the role-plays, all of which are resource-intensive in their administration, their scoring, or both. Self-assessments are practical and reliable, but not suitable for assessments that involve stakes. So the search for reliable multiple-choice DCTs has become somewhat of a "holy grail" in pragmatics assessment research.

In the most comprehensive study of this issue to date, Liu (2006) developed a multiple-choice DCT with requests and apologies for L1 Mandarin-speaking learners of English. He generated items empirically, asking learners to remember a situation where they made a request or apologized. He used these situations as a traditional written DCT and collected a corpus of responses from learners and native speakers, using some of the learner responses as distractors in the final version, and the native-speaker responses as correct answers. He administered his test to 200 Chinese EFL learners and found satisfactory reliability in the 0.8 range for his multiple-choice DCT. In a Rasch analysis of the results, he found no misfitting items, but a factor analysis showed independent request and apology factors, i.e., learners' ability to judge requests for their appropriateness was apparently unrelated to their ability to judge apologies, a finding which Liu does not explain. McNamara and Roever (2006) express surprise at the finding of separate factors for requests and apologies, and they also question Liu's construction of his items, suggesting that the suppliance of distractors by non-native speakers and correct answers by native speakers might have led to learners judging idiomaticity rather than appropriateness.

In a study not based on speech acts, Cook (2001) asked L1 English-speaking learners of Japanese at a US university to judge the appropriateness of three pieces of coherent monologic discourse, playing tape-recorded self-introductions of applicants for a bilingual sales clerk position. Test takers were familiar with the selection criteria for the position, which required a great deal of interaction with Japanese-speaking customers. One of the samples fit the criteria slightly better than the other two, but exhibited a speech style that was not humble enough and far too informal, which would immediately disqualify the applicant from any further consideration. However, over 80 percent of test takers chose this applicant as the most suitable, not recognizing the glaring inappropriateness of the applicant's speech. Cook's study is interesting in that it goes beyond judgments of isolated utterances and asks test takers to engage with more complex, extended discourse. It opens up possibilities for more discourse-oriented work in assessing knowledge of sociopragmatic appropriateness, and it demonstrates that testing of sociopragmatics does not necessarily have to be L1-specific: all other sociopragmatic instruments were designed for learners of a specific L1–L2 combination, thereby greatly limiting their applicability.

Tests of pragmalinguistics

Bouton (1988, 1994) developed a multiple-choice test of ESL implicature, assessing test takers' ability to comprehend general conversational implicature and some types of formulaic implicature, including indirect criticism and the Pope Q ("Is the Pope Catholic?"). He administered the instrument to several hundred international students at a US university, and found that conversational implicature was generally easier than formulaic implicature, and that comprehension ability improved over time, whereas comprehension of formulaic implicature did not develop without instruction (as discussed above).

Roever (2005, 2006b) developed a comprehensive web-based test battery assessing knowledge of implicature, routines, and speech acts, and validated it following Messick (1989). He based his implicature items on Bouton's work, adapting 12 multiple-choice items of conversational and formulaic implicature. The 12 multiple-choice routine items covered a variety of settings and situations (e.g., invitation, introduction, restaurant), and measured test takers' ability to recognize the correct routine formulae to be used in the situation. The speech act section comprised the speech acts request, apology, and refusal, with degree of imposition varied as high or low. The format of the 12 speech act items was a DCT with a rejoinder, i.e., a response by the imaginary interlocutor following the gap. Since the focus of the speech act section was the assessment of participants' knowledge of pragmatic strategies and their linguistic implementation, rather than appropriateness of language use, the situations and the rejoinders were designed to elicit two pragmatic strategies, e.g., an apology formula like "I'm sorry" and an offer of repair like "I'll buy you a new one." Roever administered his instrument to 267 ESL and EFL learners in the United States, Germany, and Japan, and found reliabilities in the 0.8 range for the speech acts and implicature section, slightly lower reliability for routines, and a total reliability of 0.9. Roever argues that the test is highly practical because the two multiple-choice sections are self-scoring, and the scoring of the speech act section is simplified by the rejoinder constraining the range of possible responses.

As pragmalinguistic instruments are usually not L1-specific, they tend to be widely usable, but issues of possible L1-induced bias need to be examined (Roever, 2007).

Problems and Prospects in Testing Pragmatics

A long-standing problem in any assessments of pragmatics is the issue of context. Since pragmatic knowledge is about language use in context, test instruments must establish this context, which is notoriously difficult. No testing situation can perfectly emulate the real world, except where real-world performance itself is the test, and options for recreating authentic conditions are limited because the more a test simulates complex language use situations, the more resource-intensive and impractical it becomes.

But even in more traditional paper-and-pencil (or computer-based) testing settings, practicality looms large as an issue for testing pragmatics. Since pragmatics is concerned with language use, the applicability of judgment or multiple-choice items is limited. They may be sufficient to test recognition of conventional routine formulae or judgments of appropriateness, but they will not be able to capture whether learners have control of strategies to produce complex speech acts or can open and close conversations. Learners will need to demonstrate their knowledge of L2 pragmatics by using it in productive test tasks, though this use can be offline (without the pressure of a real-world communicative situation), unless a performance test is called for. Such productive tasks commonly include discourse completion tasks (DCTs) and role-plays, both of which require ratings, with role-plays also requiring one-on-one administration. DCTs are not suitable for testing any aspect of pragmatics that requires extended negotiation, but they are useful to elicit semantic formulae learners may know (McNamara & Roever, 2006), or to test aspects of pragmatic knowledge that do not require much negotiation, e.g., address terms.

The content validity of pragmatics assessment is equally problematic. Given the larger domains of routine formulae, implicatures, or speech acts, how does one test a representative subset of each? This problem can be easily circumvented in task-based assessment, which is informed by a detailed analysis of the language requirements of the target situation, but for general tests of pragmatics, content coverage is a problem and limits conclusions that can be drawn from scores.

Conclusion

The challenge in teaching pragmatics is no longer to ascertain that it can be done (it can), or whether explicit or implicit techniques are generally more effective (explicit ones are). Rather, the challenge is to achieve curricular integration of pragmatic instruction in syllabi and textbooks at every level, and across teaching settings. This will not occur unless second language teachers are routinely trained in interlanguage pragmatics as part of their SLA training, and teaching materials systematically integrate pragmatics. At the same time, major testing instruments need to include assessment of pragmatic knowledge as a full component and thereby create positive washback.

Interlanguage pragmatics research needs to pay more attention to developmental stages and the impact of different learning settings and learning opportunities on acquisition. Such knowledge can be used to accelerate learning through instruction and fill gaps where the learning environment alone does not provide sufficient input, or learners are unable to process the input effectively. Overall, instruction and assessment in pragmatics is a growing field with wide scope for further research.

NOTES

1 A discourse completion test (DCT) is a common research tool in pragmatics research, consisting minimally of a situation description and a space for respondents to enter what they would say in that situation.
2 Note that tasks here are understood as units of syllabus design (Long & Crookes, 1993). This requires a needs analysis, an analysis of the target discourse domain, and sequencing of pedagogic tasks in an analytic syllabus. Simply using tasks as classroom language teaching activities to "dress up" a traditional synthetic syllabus is not sufficient.

REFERENCES

Achiba, M. (2002). *Learning to request in a second language: Child interlanguage pragmatics.* Clevedon, UK: Multilingual Matters.

Ahn, R. C. (2005). Five measures of interlanguage pragmatics in KFL (Korean as a foreign language) learners. Unpublished doctoral thesis, University of Hawai'i at Manoa.

Alcón Soler, E. (2005). Does instruction work for learning pragmatics in the EFL context? *System* 33, 3, 417–35.

Bachman, L. F. (1990). *Fundamental considerations in language testing.* Oxford: Oxford University Press.

Bardovi-Harlig, K. & Dörnyei, Z. (1998). Do language learners recognize pragmatic violations? Pragmatic versus grammatical awareness in instructed L2 learning. *TESOL Quarterly* 32, 233–62.

Bardovi-Harlig, K. & Hartford, B. S. (1993). Learning the rules of academic talk: A longitudinal study of pragmatic development. *Studies in Second Language Acquisition* 15, 279–304.

Billmyer, K. (1990). I really like your lifestyle: ESL learners learning how to compliment. *Penn Working Papers in Educational Linguistics* 6, 2, 31–48.

Bouton, L. (1988). A cross-cultural study of ability to interpret implicatures in English. *World Englishes* 17, 183–96.

Bouton, L. (1994). Conversational implicature in the second language: Learned slowly when not deliberately taught. *Journal of Pragmatics* 22, 157–67.

Bouton, L. (1999). The amenability of implicature to focused classroom instruction. Paper presented at TESOL 1999, New York, March.

Boxer, D. & Pickering, L. (1995). Problems in the presentation of speech acts in ELT materials: The case of complaints. *ELT Journal* 49, 1, 44–58.

Brown, J. D. (2001). Six types of pragmatics tests in two different contexts. In K. Rose & G. Kasper (eds.), *Pragmatics in language teaching* (pp. 301–25). Cambridge: Cambridge University Press.

Brown, J. D. (2008). Raters, functions, item types and the dependability of L2 pragmatics tests. In E. Alcón Soler & A. Martínez-Flor (eds.), *Investigating pragmatics in foreign language learning, teaching and testing* (pp. 224–48). Clevedon, UK: Multilingual Matters.

Brown, P. & Levinson, S. D. (1987). *Politeness: Some universals in language usage.* Cambridge: Cambridge University Press.

Canale, M. (1983). From communicative competence to communicative language pedagogy. In J. Richards & R. Schmidt (eds.), *Language and Communication* (pp. 2–27). London: Longman.

Canale, M. & Swain, M. (1980). Theoretical bases of communicative approaches to second language teaching and testing. *Applied Linguistics* 1, 1–47.

Clennell, C. (1999). Promoting pragmatic awareness and spoken discourse skills with EAP classes. *ELT Journal* 53, 2, 82–91.

Cook, H. M. (2001). Why can't learners of JFL distinguish polite from impolite speech styles? In K. Rose & G. Kasper (eds.), *Pragmatics in language teaching* (pp. 80–102). Cambridge: Cambridge University Press.

Crandall, E. & Basturkmen, H. (2004). Evaluating pragmatics-focused materials. *ELT Journal* 58, 1, 38–49.

Crystal, D. (1997). *The Cambridge encyclopedia of language.* New York: Cambridge University Press.

Eisenstein, M. & Bodman, J. (1993). Expressing gratitude in American English. In G. Kasper & S. Blum-Kulka (eds.), *Interlanguage pragmatics* (pp. 64–81). Oxford: Oxford University Press.

Ellis, R. (1992). Learning to communicate in the classroom: A study of two learner's requests. *Studies in Second Language Acquisition* 14, 1–23.

Fukuya, Y. & Clark, M. (2001). A comparison of input enhancement and explicit instruction of mitigators. In L. F. Bouton (ed.), *Pragmatics and language learning* (Monograph Series, vol. 10, pp. 111–30). Urbana-Champaign, IL: DEIL.

Holmes, J. (2003). "I couldn't follow her story . . .": Ethnic differences in New Zealand narratives. In J. House, G. Kasper, & S. Ross (eds.), *Misunderstanding in social life* (pp. 173–98). Harlow, UK: Pearson Education.

House, J. (1996). Developing pragmatic fluency in English as a foreign language: Routines and metapragmatic awareness. *Studies in Second Language Acquisition* 18, 225–52.

Hudson, T., Detmer, E., & Brown, J. D. (1995). *Developing prototypic measures of cross-cultural pragmatics* (Technical Report #7). Honolulu: University of Hawai'i, Second Language Teaching and Curriculum Center.

Huth, T. & Taleghani-Nikazm, C. (2006). How can insights from conversation analysis be directly applied to teaching L2 pragmatics? *Language Teaching Research* 10, 1, 53–79.

Jeon, E. H. & Kaya, T. (2006). Effects of L2 instruction on interlanguage pragmatic development: A meta-analysis. In J. M. Norris & L. Ortega (eds.), *Synthesizing research on language learning and teaching* (pp. 165–212). Amsterdam: John Benjamins.

Kanagy, R. (1999). Interactional routines as a mechanism for L2 acquisition and socialization in an immersion context. *Journal of Pragmatics* 31, 1467–92.

Kanagy, R. & Igarashi, K. (1997). Acquisition of pragmatics competence in a Japanese immersion kindergarten. In L. F. Bouton (ed.), *Pragmatics and language learning* (Monograph Series, vol. 8, pp. 243–65). Urbana-Champaign, IL: DEIL.

Kasper, G. (1989). Interactive procedures in interlanguage discourse. In W. Olesky (ed.), *Contrastive pragmatics* (pp. 189–229). Amsterdam: John Benjamins

Kasper, G. & Rose, K. R. (2002). *Pragmatic development in a second language.* Malden, MA: Blackwell.

Koike, D. A. & Pearson, L. (2005). The effect of instruction and feedback in the development of pragmatic competence. *System* 33, 3, 481–501.

Lee, J. S. & McChesney, B. (1999). Discourse rating tasks: A teaching tool for developing sociocultural competence. *ELT Journal* 54, 2, 161–8.

Leech, G. (1983). *Principles of pragmatics.* London: Longman.

Levinson, S. (1983). *Pragmatics.* New York: Cambridge University Press.

Liddicoat, A. & Crozet, C. (2001). Acquiring French interactional norms through instruction. In K. Rose & G. Kasper (eds.), *Pragmatics in language teaching* (pp. 125–44). Cambridge: Cambridge University Press.

Liu, J. (2006). *Measuring interlanguage pragmatic knowledge of EFL learners.* Frankfurt: Peter Lang.

LoCastro, V. (1997). Pedagogical intervention and pragmatic competence development. *Applied Language Learning* 8, 75–109.

Long, M. H. & Crookes, G. (1992). Three approaches to task-based syllabus design. *TESOL Quarterly* 26, 1, 27–56.

Long, M. H. & Crookes, G. (1993). Units of analysis in syllabus design: The case for task. In G. Crookes & S. Gass (eds.), *Tasks in pedagogical context: Integrating theory and practice* (pp. 9–56). Clevedon, UK: Multilingual Matters.

Lörscher, W. (1986). Conversational structures in the foreign language classroom. In G. Kasper (ed.), *Learning, teaching and communication in the foreign language classroom* (pp. 183–99). Århus: Århus University Press.

Lyster, R. (1994). The effect of functional-analytic teaching on aspects of French immersion students sociolinguistic competence. *Applied Linguistics* 15, 263–87.

Martínez-Flor, A. & Fukuya, Y. J. (2005). The effects of instruction on learners' production of appropriate and accurate suggestions. *System* 33, 3, 463–80.

Matsumura, S. (2001). Learning the rules for offering advice: A quantitative approach to second language socialization. *Language Learning* 51, 635–79.

McNamara, T. F. & Roever, C. (2006). *Language testing: The social dimension*. Oxford: Blackwell.

Meier, A. J. (1997). Teaching the universals of politeness. *ELT Journal* 51, 1, 21–8.

Messick, S. (1989). Validity. In R. L. Linn (ed.), *Educational measurement* (pp. 13–103). New York: Macmillan.

Mey, J. (2001). *Pragmatics*. Oxford: Blackwell.

Niezgoda, K. & Roever, C. (2001). Grammatical and pragmatic awareness: A function of the learning environment? In K. Rose & G. Kasper (eds.), *Pragmatics in language teaching* (pp. 63–79). Cambridge: Cambridge University Press.

Norris, J. & Ortega, L. (2000). Effectiveness of L2 instruction: A research synthesis and quantitative meta-analysis. *Language Learning* 50, 417–528.

Ohta, A. S. (2001). *Second language acquisition processes in the classroom: Learning Japanese*. Mahwah, NJ: Lawrence Earlbaum.

Olshtain, E. & Cohen, A. (1990). The learning of complex speech act behavior. *TESL Canada Journal* 7, 45–65.

Pavlidou, T. (1994). Contrasting German-Greek politeness and the consequences. *Journal of Pragmatics* 21, 487–511.

Roever, C. (2005). *Testing ESL pragmatics*. Frankfurt: Peter Lang.

Roever, C. (2006). Validation of a web-based test of ESL pragmalinguistics. *Language Testing* 23, 2, 229–56.

Roever, C. (2007). DIF in the assessment of second language pragmatics. *Language Assessment Quarterly* 4, 2, 165–89.

Rose, K. R. (2000). An exploratory cross-sectional study of interlanguage pragmatic development. *Studies in Second Language Acquisition* 22, 27–67.

Rose, K. R. (2005). On the effects of instruction in second language pragmatics. *System* 33, 3, 385–99.

Rose, K. R. & Ng, C. (2001). Inductive and deductive teaching of compliments and compliment responses. In K. R. Rose & G. Kasper (eds.), *Pragmatics in language teaching* (pp. 145–70). Cambridge: Cambridge University Press.

Rost-Roth, M. (1999). Der Erwerb der Modalpartikeln. In N. Dittmar & A. Giacalone Ramat (eds.), *Grammatik und Diskurs* (pp. 165–209). Tübingen: Stauffenburg.

Salsbury, T. & Bardovi-Harlig, K. (2000). Oppositional talk and the acquisition of modality in L2 English. In B. Swierzbin, F. Morris, M. Anderson, C. A. Klee, & E. Tarone (eds.), *Social and cognitive factors in second language acquisition* (pp. 56–76). Somerville, MA: Cascadilla Press.

Salsbury, T. & Bardovi-Harlig, K. (2001). "I know your mean but I don't think so": Disagreements in L2 English. In L. F. Bouton (ed.), *Pragmatics and language learning* (Monograph Series vol. 10, pp. 131–51). Urbana, IL: DEIL.

Schegloff, E. A. (1979). Identification and recognition in telephone conversation openings. In G. Psathas (ed.), *Everyday language: Studies in ethnomethodology* (pp. 23–78). New York: Irvington Press.

Schegloff, E. A. & Sacks, H. (1973). Opening up closing. *Semiotica* 8, 4, 289–327.

Schmidt, R. (1995). Consciousness and foreign language learning: A tutorial on the role of attention and awareness in learning. In R. Schmidt (ed.), *Attention and awareness in foreign language learning* (Technical Report #9, pp. 1–63). Honolulu: University of Hawai'i, Second Language Teaching and Curriculum Center.

Schmidt, R. (2001). Attention. In P. Robinson (ed.), *Cognition and second language instruction* (pp. 3–32). Cambridge: Cambridge University Press.

Takahashi, S. (2001). The role of input enhancement in developing pragmatic competence. In K. R. Rose & G. Kasper (eds.), *Pragmatics in language teaching* (pp. 200–22). Cambridge: Cambridge University Press.

Takahashi, S. (2005). Noticing in task performance and learning outcomes: A qualitative analysis of instructional effects in interlanguage pragmatics. *System* 33, 3, 437–61.

Taleghani-Nikazm, C. (2002). A conversation analytical study of telephone conversation openings between native and non-native speakers. *Journal of Pragmatics* 34, 1807–32.

Tateyama, Y. (2001). Explicit and implicit teaching of pragmatics routines: Japanese sumimasen. In K. R. Rose & G. Kasper (eds.), *Pragmatics in language teaching* (pp. 145–70). Cambridge: Cambridge University Press.

Tateyama, Y., Kasper, G., Mui, L., Tay, H.-M., & Thananart, O. (1997). Explicit and implicit teaching of pragmatic routines. In L. Bouton (ed.), *Pragmatics and language learning*, vol. 8 (pp. 163–77). Urbana, IL: University of Illinois at Urbana-Champaign.

White, L. (1991). Adverb placement in second language acquisition: Some positive and negative evidence in the classroom. *Second Language Research* 7, 2, 133–61.

White, L., Spada, N., Lightbown, P., & Ranta, L. (1991). Input enhancement and L2 question formation. *Applied Linguistics* 12, 4, 416–32.

Wildner-Bassett, M. (1986). Teaching and learning "polite noises": Improving pragmatic aspects of advanced adult learners' interlanguage. In G. Kasper (ed.), *Learning, teaching and communication in the foreign language classroom* (pp. 163–78). Århus: Århus University Press.

Wishnoff, J. (2000). Hedging your bets: L2 learners' acquisition of pragmatic devices in academic writing and computer-mediated discourse. *Second Language Studies, Working Papers of the Department of Second Language Studies, University of Hawai'i* 19, 119–57.

Yamashita, S. O. (1996). *Six measures of JSL pragmatics* (Technical Report #14). Honolulu: University of Hawai'i, Second Language Teaching and Curriculum Center.

Yoshimi, D. (2001). Explicit instruction and JFL learners' use of interactional discourse markers. In K. R. Rose & G. Kasper (eds.), *Pragmatics in language teaching* (pp. 223–44). Cambridge: Cambridge University Press.

Yoshitake, S. S. (1997). Measuring interlanguage pragmatic competence of Japanese students of English as a foreign language: A multi-test framework evaluation. Unpublished doctoral dissertation, Columbia Pacific University, Novata, CA.

Young, L. W. L. (1994). *Crosstalk and culture in Sino-American communication*. Cambridge: Cambridge University Press.

30 Task-Based Teaching and Testing

JOHN M. NORRIS

Introduction

Task-based language teaching (TBLT) is an approach to second or foreign language education that integrates theoretical and empirical foundations for good pedagogy with a focus on tangible learning outcomes in the form of "tasks" – that is, what learners are able to *do* with the language. Task-based practice draws on diverse sources, including philosophy of education, theories of second language acquisition, and research-based evidence about effective instruction. Equally important, TBLT acts on the exigencies of language learning in human endeavors, and the often ineffectual responses of language education to date, by providing a framework within which educators can construct effective programs that meet the language use needs of learners and society.

Though there is global interest in the value of TBLT to foster worthwhile language learning, there is also diversity in the educational scope, practical applications, and research associated with the name. Certainly, TBLT remains a contested domain of inquiry and practice, though much of the debate surrounding TBLT results from incomplete understandings of precisely what this educational approach comprises. In the following, I review key underpinnings of task-based instruction, its emergence within language education, and its component parts. I then highlight the fundamental processes of teaching and testing, outlining a task-based approach to each and posing questions in need of inquiry. I conclude by forecasting several challenges that will condition the ultimate contribution of TBLT to language education.

Task-Based Language Education

At its most basic, task-based instruction rejects the notion that knowledge can be learned independently of its application and embraces instead the value of learning by doing, or "experiential learning" (Dewey, 1933). In Dewey's terms, principal elements around which instruction should be built are "activities worthwhile for their own sake" (p. 87), and it is by engaging learners in doing valued activities that relevant declarative and procedural knowledge is developed, learners are motivated to engage with instructional content, and learners develop deep linkages between what they learn and how that learning can be put to use beyond the classroom. Crucial cognitive and emotional mechanisms are triggered through learning by doing things holistically, including in particular the essential feedback loop (James, 1899) whereby "we receive sensible news of our behavior and its results" (p. 41) in the context of, and relatable to, the activity that we are immediately focused on doing. Furthermore, holistic activities provide learners the opportunity to analyze what they do, what works, and what doesn't, thereby constructing their own explanations (Dewey, 1938) and rendering such understandings "available under actual conditions of life" (p. 48).

These and related tenets of experiential learning have grown into diverse models of practice, including cognitive psychological learning theories (e.g., Sternberg, 2003), apprenticeship and socialization frameworks (e.g., Lave & Wenger, 1991), and others (e.g., Kolb, 1984). Key is the idea that holistic activity structures, such as tasks, offer an ideal frame within which knowledge use can be experienced and understood, and from which learning opportunities should be developed. For example, Sternberg (2003) advocated:

> For starters, this means having students do tasks, or at least meaningful simulations, that experts do in the various disciplines. Second, it means teaching them to think in ways that experts do when they perform these tasks. (p. 5)

Following these models, "task" has proved to be an effective organizing principle for the implementation of experiential learning across diverse disciplines, including medicine (e.g., Virjo, Holmberg-Mattila, & Mattila, 2001), environmental studies (e.g., Wright, 2000), and social work (e.g., Reid, 1997). In language education, too, "task" has emerged as a heuristic for encapsulating the many benefits of experiential learning, as summarized in Samuda and Bygate (2008): "What we are calling 'tasks' can thus be seen as a means of creating experience-based opportunities for language learning" (p. 36).

In the recent history of language teaching (cf. Musumeci, this volume), the need for an organizing principle like "task" materialized in the 1980s, responding to dissatisfaction with dominant traditions and in consonance with findings from research into how second language acquisition occurs in instructed and naturalistic settings (Long, 1985). Prevailing language teaching methods of the post-war era were found lacking on several scores: (1) they presented language forms (grammatical rules, vocabulary words, etc.) in an arbitrary order and disarticulated from their communicative functions; (2) they posited rapid and complete development of accuracy in response to rule- or pattern-based learning; and (3) they presumed the transfer of accumulated bits of discrete knowledge about the language into the ability to utilize the language for communication. By adopting a synthetic approach to syllabus design (i.e., where learners synthesize discrete

facts into holistic understandings; Wilkins, 1976) and a focus-on-forms methodology (i.e., teaching language forms disconnected from their functional uses; Long
& Robinson, 1998), these approaches ran counter to how, and how quickly, language is actually acquired, and they generally met with disappointing outcomes
and disenchanted learners (Widdowson, 1978).

Communicative language teaching (CLT) represented the opposite swing of
the pendulum, countering that language learning in the classroom must mimic the
naturalistic acquisition of communicative abilities outside of the classroom. The
natural approach (Krashen & Terrell, 1983), immersion education, and other
strong forms of CLT adopted an analytic syllabus (whereby learners experience
language in holistic chunks and analyze the parts as needed) and a focus-
on-meaning methodology (stressing comprehensible input, communication, and
respect for interlanguage development). However, while communicative classrooms proved more interesting and motivating than their predecessors, CLT fell
short in several regards: (1) learners achieved high levels of communicative success without concomitant levels of grammatical accuracy (accuracy not necessary
for meaningful communication); (2) even very long periods of exposure to rich
input in the target language, as in immersion settings, were insufficient for achieving nativelike ultimate attainment (Swain & Lapkin, 1982); and (3) most formal
language education contexts could ill afford the substantial time and resources
for learners to benefit maximally from learning through naturalistic processes.
Simultaneously, research had begun to identify clear benefits of planned exposure to acquisitional processes including input, interaction, and output; that is, it
did seem that learning experiences could be manipulated intentionally to bring
about the acquisition of language forms through a variety of instructional techniques (Norris & Ortega, 2000).

The concept of "task" presented an opportunity to consolidate these ideas into
an integrated approach which might accomplish a variety of instructional ends.
Early recourse to tasks in language teaching focused on ways of bringing "real"
communication and learner-centered processes into the classroom, by respecting
learners' interests and attending to interlanguage development as it unfolded in
the use of language (Breen, 1987; Long, 1985; Prabhu, 1987). Tasks provided
motivating communication activities that bore some relevance to language use
beyond the classroom. Tasks also had the advantage of offering learners some
reason for communicating, beyond practicing to do so, in that they came replete
with actual outcomes, criteria for success or failure, even tangible results (getting
what you ordered at the restaurant, winning the debate, etc.). In the classroom,
tasks enabled teachers and learners to see language development as it unfolded
in communication trial and error, thereby establishing a linkage between functions, the language forms that realized them, and the meaning-bearing uses to
which they were put.

Building upon these first principles, subsequent attention to tasks incorporated
available research findings and extended the scope of considerations (Crookes &
Gass, 1993a, 1993b; Skehan, 1996, 1998). It became apparent that certain tasks
behaved in more or less predictable ways that could direct learners' attention at

particular aspects of the language in use. Task features (amount of information, interlocutor relationships, etc.), conditions (planning time, stress, etc.), and other characteristics could be designed such that the likelihood of certain kinds of language development was enhanced. Similarly, by challenging learners to use the target language – to negotiate for meaning – teachers were afforded the opportunity to apply a variety of feedback techniques for increasing learners' noticing and awareness of how the target language might realize communicative functions. Critically, this "focus-on-form" methodology (Long, 1991; Long & Robinson, 1998) was intended to occur within the otherwise task-driven communication that was taking place, through brief attention to aspects of communicative need, thereby enhancing the probability that learners would associate the form-focus with the meaning to which it was related.

Ultimately, drawing on several decades of discussion and research, TBLT emerged as much more than a language teaching "method," fun communicative techniques, or the kinds of clever activities that good teachers have always done. At its most complete, TBLT applies available understandings and evidence to the comprehensive design of entire language education programs. Though several task-based architectures have been proposed (e.g., Ellis, 2003; Skehan, 1998; Prabhu, 1987; Willis, 1996), most subscribe to the following elements (Long & Crookes, 1993; Long & Norris, 2000):

- *Needs analysis*: Following fundamental principles of program design (Patton, 1997), the needs that an L2 educational program will meet are first specified, ideally on the basis of a thorough-going analysis of the kinds of language use tasks that learners should be able to accomplish upon completion of a program (Long, 2005b). Needs analysis (Brown, this volume) integrates multiple sources of information from multiple methodological perspectives – including, but not limited to, learners' goals, the values of program constituents, occupational or societal demands, observations of language use situations, etc. – in identifying exactly what learning outcomes will be targeted by the program.
- *Task selection and sequencing*: Based on needs, relevant target tasks and/or task types are articulated to unit, course, and syllabus sequences as befits the program's theory of learner development. Several possible frames may be adopted (e.g., Estaire & Zanón, 1994; Robinson, 2001; Skehan, 1998), though most task-based approaches incorporate both a content rationale (i.e., grouping of tasks by thematic relationships) and a complexity rationale (i.e., locating tasks along a progression from least to most complex). At their most effective, sequencing decisions draw upon intimate knowledge of the learner population, as well as understanding of the communication demands and acquisition opportunities comprised by diverse language use tasks.
- *Materials and instruction development*: Once sequenced, tasks are didacticized through learning experiences that maintain a vision of the target task throughout while incorporating language, procedural, and content knowledge via learners' engagement with pedagogic activities (Chaudron et al., 2005). Materials and instruction minimally provide: (1) substantial language/content

input through examples of authentic tasks; (2) sustained analytic work on portions of tasks that have been elaborated to facilitate a focus on form; (3) interactive activities, structured and scaffolded in ways that maximize noticing and awareness of form–function–meaning relationships; and (4) target-task performances, emphasizing the transfer of learning to non-instructional settings and providing opportunities for feedback.

- *Teaching*: Teachers facilitate the essential link between instructional materials and their use with learners in classrooms. In task-based teaching, learners must be schematized to the expected procedures and outcomes of tasks, monitored in their performance of tasks, and offered opportunities for enhanced understandings of language use throughout. It is up to the teacher to initiate these task processes flexibly and adjust them as necessary, such that maximal learning may be realized with sensitivity to the ways in which learners actually engage with tasks (Samuda, 2001).
- *Assessment*: Regular assessment of students' task-based learning takes place throughout the delivery of courses and programs to meet diverse purposes (Norris, 2002). Though a variety of instruments and procedures may be necessary, assessment within task-based programs emphasizes the performance of target tasks (as opposed to the demonstration of knowledge about the language), primarily as a mechanism for providing meaningful feedback to learners and teachers, for determining students' abilities with target tasks, and for ensuring an overall focus on target-task learning throughout the program.
- *Program evaluation*: Essential to the ultimate effectiveness of task-based education, and drawing on assessment, as well as other sources of evidence, evaluation enables language educators to understand, improve, judge, and otherwise ascertain that all of the above elements are functioning conjointly in support of targeted outcomes. In task-based programs, evaluation focuses on the relevance of target tasks for learners, the appropriateness of sequencing decisions and L2 acquisition expectations, the effectiveness of materials, the preparation and support of teachers, and the validity of assessments vis-à-vis the interpretations and uses to which they are put. Evaluation also provides a programmatic frame of reference within which observations about task-based teaching and learning may be thoroughly understood.

While introducing tasks in existing language education programs may offer some benefits (see notions of "task-supported" teaching in Samuda & Bygate, 2008; Ellis, 2003), the full advantages of task-based learning are not likely to be realized outside of a programmatic commitment to task as the basis for educational design. Where any one of the elements above occurs in the absence of the others the ultimate effectiveness of task-based learning will likely break down, a consideration often missed by TBLT critics. However, where a long-term commitment is made to the development of task-based language teaching *programs* that incorporate these elements (e.g., Van den Branden, 2006), evidence suggests that language and task abilities advance in tandem, learners achieve expectations, and language teaching evolves into a potentially more meaningful endeavor.

Task-Based Teaching

While vital planning and deployment of resources occur during curriculum design, the actual implementation of language learning occurs during task-based teaching, that is, what teachers and learners do with tasks in the classroom (or other venue). Highly structured approaches (e.g., Willis, 1996) may provide immediately useful ways of framing some classroom work, but task-based teaching calls upon more than just pre-, during-, and post-task activities or other formulae. With respect to the actual range of tasks that may be targeted for instruction, it is likely that flexible implementation of general methodological principles (Long, this volume) will be required to meet the needs of diverse contexts and learners. In general, though, several phases of classroom work highlight what teachers and learners do during task-based teaching (see the complete example in Chaudron et al., 2005).

A *task input* phase typically initiates the teaching sequence, preceding any pedagogic activities. Building from the idea that exposure to language in use can facilitate considerable amounts of L2 acquisition, the input phase introduces the target task as it is realized in actual communication. Repeated viewing of video segments, observing live performances, reading texts, and other techniques enable the presentation of a full-fledged target task without manipulation. By seeing what they will do in its entirety, learners become motivated and begin to establish essential linkages to the contexts in which the target task occurs. By engaging receptively with the task, learners begin to focus their attention on trying to understand what is being said or written, thereby initiating their noticing of what forms are used in what ways. In addition to the incidental acquisition of some forms, through association with the physical and linguistic context of the task, learners also begin to identify gaps in their individual L2 repertoires. During this input phase, the teacher acts as provider of input, either by performing tasks or by presenting various recorded task exemplars (and teachers play an important role in making sure the tasks are appropriate to the learners). Teachers avoid didactic treatment of the tasks at this point, however, so that learners are afforded maximal opportunity to attend to the contextual, content, linguistic, functional, and other features that combine to form the holistic target task.

Building from thorough exposure to the target task, *pedagogic task work* ensues. It is during this phase that tasks are segmented, elaborated, and otherwise manipulated by the teacher, with the objective of raising learners' awareness of new language forms and their use for particular functions. Typically, this phase features multiple iterations of work on increasingly complete versions of the target task, often moving from comprehension to production. Early stages of task work emphasize important form–function relationships, through input enhancement (e.g., textual or oral emphasis, focused listening) or through learner analysis of task discourse (e.g., identification of known and unknown vocabulary). Interactive tasks in pairs or small groups then require learners to utilize existing and new language. Such tasks present learners with information gaps to be overcome, problems to be solved, decisions to be made, or otherwise meaningful reasons to interact with each other, that negotiation of meaning often leading to communication breakdown and the opportunity for self-, other-, or teacher-initiated feedback. Feedback episodes, then, play a key role during this phase, as a primary mechanism for focus-on-form. Different kinds of feedback, such as recasts, models, brief grammatical explanations, and others can be deployed as a way of fostering greater awareness and incorporation of language forms where they are particularly needed. Subsequent introduction of distinct task types or conditions also may help learners to focus differentially on features of their language use (e.g., accuracy, complexity, fluency; Skehan, 1998). For example, the introduction of planning time prior to a story-telling task (Ortega, 2005) may allow learners the cognitive space to incorporate newly acquired forms into a syntactically more complex narration.

The didactic possibilities available for this phase are considerable (Ellis, 2003), as are the language forms to which they may be directed (vocabulary, syntax, pronunciation, pragmatics, discourse structure, etc.). A key responsibility of teachers is to select a variety of pedagogic tasks that respond to potentially diverse learner types (e.g., with different aptitudes or motivational complexes, see Robinson, 2001). Furthermore, teachers must ensure that learners understand the purposive, procedural, and goal-oriented nature of pedagogic tasks; teacher framing and scaffolding is essential in this regard, and without it, learners will do unrelated things. In addition, perhaps most critically, teachers monitor both task processes and learner language use, and they must ultimately arbitrate the appropriate occasions for feedback interventions.

Following what may be multiple iterations of pedagogic task work, *target task performance* calls upon learners to deploy what they have learned in doing the target task. Depending on learners and curriculum, of course, this doing may involve anything from a brief communicative transaction (e.g., ordering a meal, writing an e-mail message, following directions on a map) to longer pieces of work (e.g., taking accurate lecture notes, following a manual to repair an engine part) to extended performances (e.g., participating in a debate, teaching a class). The target task performance also may be staged to facilitate learner attention to outcomes that aggregate along the way to accomplishing complex tasks. For example, in preparing for an academic presentation, students may engage in title and abstract writing, assembling a handout, preparing audiovisual materials, drafting presentation notes, and then putting the elements together into the full presentation. The teacher's job at this point is to replicate the conditions under which the target task will be performed, providing an audience (simulated or real), reproducing constraints (physical surroundings, available resources), introducing authentic complications (interlocutor questions, disturbances, criteria to be met), and so on. By "going it alone" with a target task *in situ*, learners practice the use of language for meaningful purposes, thereby engaging their developing cognitive, motivational, linguistic, content-knowledge, and other resources under conditions that vary from the safety of structured pedagogic tasks. In doing so, they also come to understand the range of competing factors (stress, interlocutor reactions, unexpected interruptions) that constitute purposeful language use, and they extend their language and content learning to incorporate strategies for dealing with actual communication (e.g., circumlocution, questioning, repetition).

Often, a *task follow-up* phase can enhance the learning that has taken place over previous phases of the task-based cycle. Thus, the target task performance establishes a key watershed point at which teachers and learners can reflect on task success or failure, performance strengths, gaps that remain in language/content/ task knowledge, and related concerns, all leading to instructional decisions regarding what features are in need of subsequent repetition or expansion. Here, teacher guidance is again essential for identifying salient gaps and providing relevant feedback; follow-up activities offer another chance for focus-on-form to take place with the added cognitive consonance provided by doing the full task. The principle to keep in mind is that focus-on-form works best when there is a "focus"; an essay covered in red ink identifying all "errors" may not prove as effective as the careful highlighting of selected form–function issues that bear relevance to communicative success and the features targeted during preceding pedagogic task phases. Procedurally, the follow-up phase may involve a variety of activities, such as teacher presentation of common patterns that emerged across students, learner analysis of their own and others' performances (e.g., in video-taped or written format), and individual or group work on refining and repeating task performances.

Several aspects of this task-based teaching cycle are in need of inquiry. As TBLT is applied across diverse learner populations, it will be important to investigate what among the available task-based techniques prove the most effective with particular learner types, including, for example, young learners, learners with differing motivations, learners with little or no literacy, and learners at differing L2 proficiency levels. At a minimum, researchers will need to describe or measure learner types to enable accurate generalizations/limitations regarding their findings (Norris & Ortega, 2003). Additionally, along with diverse learners come diverse tasks, and it is as yet uncertain to what extent available techniques enable acquisition of abilities that underlie a variety of potential target tasks. For example, many of the researched pedagogic tasks involve spoken interaction, but whether this mode of teaching leads to efficient learning of highly literate target L2 uses remains little understood. Finally, it should be clear that much more goes on in the task-based classroom than simply turning learners loose on tasks (or vice versa). Teachers play an essential role throughout the task lesson cycle, motivating, schematizing, scaffolding, monitoring, intervening, and so on. It is critical that research examine exactly what training, resources, and support teachers need in order to meet this array of expectations.

Task-Based Testing

Though often narrowly construed as "testing," task-based assessment incorporates a variety of instruments and procedures (not just tests) for gathering data about student learning, in order to provide an empirical basis for decisions and actions that must occur in education. Tasks have captured the attention of testers for some time (e.g., Cureton, 1951), because they present goal-oriented, contextualized challenges that prompt examinees to deploy cognitive skills and domain-related knowledge in authentic performance rather than merely displaying what they know in selected-response and other discrete forms of tests (Kane, 2001; Wiggins, 1998). For language testing, in particular, recent interest in task reflects the need to incorporate language use into assessments, such that interpretations about learners' abilities to communicate are warranted (Brindley, 1994; Norris et al., 1998). While language testers have concerned themselves primarily with psychometric issues of what gets tested in task-based performance, much less attention has been afforded more fundamental questions regarding why and how task-based assessments are being used in language education settings (Norris, 2002). At stake for educators is not whether task-based assessments accurately represent theoretical language ability constructs; rather, as Cureton (1951) pointed out, it is "how well a test does the job it was employed to do" (p. 621).

How are assessments used in task-based programs and related settings? While intended uses vary in the details, as befits the distinct users of assessment information, several common purposes for assessment have emerged over the past decade or so of experiences with TBLT. On the one hand, *summative* assessments incorporate specific target tasks or task types for making often high-stakes judgments about learners and the programs that educate them (e.g., Gysen & Van Avermaet, 2005). For example, certification of learners' task abilities is essential for jobs that require extensive communication, such as air traffic controllers, interpreters/translators, or international teaching assistants. Additionally, certification of task abilities may play a broader role in providing learners and the public with information on the basic social domains within which a language user can function. Judgments regarding whether learners can meet minimum task requirements also are used for making program acceptance or placement decisions, as in second language vocational training settings. Finally, tasks may be incorporated into assessments for the purpose of holding programs accountable to educational standards or for washing back onto the ways in which language teaching is occurring. Common to these summative uses for tasks-based assessment are particular qualities: (1) dependence on representative tasks that can be trusted to reflect language use in actual targeted domains (general or specific); (2) replication of authentic task performance conditions and criteria; and (3) consistency in administration and reliability in rating, scoring, or otherwise judging task performances.

Assessment may also provide constituents in task-based classrooms and programs with the kinds of rich information needed to support experiential learning and foster students' abilities to do things with language. These *formative* uses for assessment call upon tasks to enable a close understanding of learner development and facilitate the provision of relevant feedback to teachers, learners, curriculum developers, and others (e.g., Byrnes, 2002). Thus, performance of curriculum- and lesson-embedded tasks throughout teaching sequences provide learners the opportunity to demonstrate what language and content features they are acquiring and how well they can put that knowledge to use. These assessments serve an important motivational and awareness-raising function, giving learners a clear target for learning and pushing them to do so. They also offer a frame of reference within which teachers and learners can observe, reflect on, judge, and otherwise understand the effectiveness of pedagogic activities and learning processes. Within the task frame, specific feedback can be provided to individual learners about particular aspects of task performance and L2 learning, thereby helping them to help themselves, and patterns of performance across students offer important feedback to teachers for the adaptation of materials and instruction. Furthermore, the accumulation of task-based assessment data over longer term instructional sequences offers an invaluable basis for illuminating actual patterns of learner language development in comparison with curricular expectations. It is this combination of process (L2 development) and product (task performance) data that most distinguishes formative from summative task-based assessments. Formative uses for assessment prioritize certain characteristics: (1) close articulation of tasks to curricular sequences and learning expectations; (2) thorough and accessible guidelines for task performance expectations and assessment criteria; (3) the use of language profiles, analytic rating scales, and other information-rich mechanisms for providing meaningful feedback about diverse L2 and task features; (4) multiple iterations of teacher (and potentially learner self-) assessment at different stages of task completion; and (5) frameworks for tracking and interpreting important aspects of learner development over time.

Several concerns at the interface of tasks, TBLT, and assessment would benefit from further empirical attention. To date, related inquiry has been driven largely by the question of "what constitutes a task-based language assessment?", adhering to a monolithic model of testing that seeks primarily to inform interpretations about theorized language proficiency constructs. A more educationally relevant approach might be to adopt a "validity evaluation" model (Norris, 2008), which derives research priorities from the actual uses to which assessments are put, the contexts in which they are used, and the individuals or groups who are using them. In conjunction with summative uses for assessment, key areas in need of attention include the extent to which performance on assessment tasks can be assumed to extrapolate to other tasks beyond the test setting, the relevance of rating scales and criteria for the kinds of high-stakes interpretations that are being made about learners, and the impact that introduction of tasks into summative tests may be having on educational systems (including learner, teacher, and public attitudes toward language education). With more formative uses of assessment, inquiry will illuminate which tasks help reveal learners' emerging accuracy, complexity, and fluency with various language forms, and it will disentangle a variety of task-setting and learner individual-differences factors from language features of interest. Research is also much needed into classroom diagnostic and feedback frameworks that can help teachers to efficiently analyze task performances, turn those analyses into maximally useful understandings of learner development, and communicate with students in terms that help them to learn.

Challenges and Opportunities for Task-Based Language Teaching

Though contested at times, task-based principles have begun to gain purchase in a variety of educational settings, and TBLT shows signs of crystallizing into a robust domain of inquiry, with an international conference series (www.tblt.org), a book series (*Task-based language teaching: Issues, research, and practice*), and a healthy literature. However, the extent to which TBLT offers sustainable solutions – in an increasingly volatile policy and practice environment – will be conditioned by the ways in which researchers, educationalists, and practitioners meet several critical challenges to the application of task-based ideas.

A top priority must be the transformation of task-based research into an educationally relevant endeavor. While indirect value may be gained from research that focuses on the generation or testing of theories about instruction and acquisition, it is not the case that primary studies of a few task features or learner conversations will, on their own, provide much in the way of warranted implications for task-based teaching in practice. To be sure, theory-driven primary studies can contribute isolated bits of information which, once sufficient studies have accumulated (Norris & Ortega, 2006), may shed light on fundamental questions about tasks and instructed L2 acquisition (e.g., the effectiveness of certain task design features; see Keck et al., 2006). However, alternative epistemologies are required where research seeks to illuminate organic questions of interest to those who are responsible for making language learning happen (teachers, administrators, curriculum developers). Language education in practice, rather than theory, is an extremely complex and multivariate undertaking, and research that informs education must adopt methodologies that reflect the full scope of what is going on; to do otherwise is to sell short the task-based proposal from the outset by focusing on only selected parts of what is intended to be a holistic enterprise.

What methods might work? Certainly, mixed-methods designs (Cresswell & Clark, 2007) will prove more effective than methodologically constrained designs (e.g., conversation analysis, which only derives evidence from observable discourse), in that they account for a complex array of factors that interact in any task-based episode (e.g., teacher, learner, task, and setting variables). Similarly, longitudinal studies (Ortega & Iberri-Shea, 2005) of task-based instruction will be essential for capturing just how teaching and learning happen; given that task-based proposals are intended for the level of multiple lessons, units, full courses, and cross-curricular sequences, it seems clear that *only* longitudinal studies looking across these periods of instruction will illuminate task-based development. Finally, most directly relevant for educational decision-making will be the application of program evaluation to the pragmatic resolution of questions as they arise in the delivery of full TBLT programs. While theoretical research informs *conclusion*-oriented inquiry, evaluation operationalizes *decision*-oriented inquiry (Cronbach & Suppes, 1969). Adopting ongoing evaluation will enable decision-makers to address priority questions about elements of task-based programs, gather information that is immediately relevant, turn that information into decisions and actions, and then pose new questions. An excellent example of this iterative approach can be found in ten years of evaluative work on task-based teacher development programs in Dutch language education throughout Belgium (Van den Branden, 2006).

A second major challenge is identifying meaningful starting and ending points to language education classes and programs. From a task-based perspective, needs analysis provides an empirical response, offering triangulated understandings of what target tasks are most relevant for particular groups of learners and what the associated language/content expectations may be. Unfortunately, task-based needs analysis has suffered frequent mis-understanding among practitioners and mis-representation in the literature. Common reactions include claims that learners cannot be expected to know their own needs, learners do not have any apparent uses for the language, the instrumental focus of needs undermines the broad value of language education, and similar.

To rectify these debilitating perceptions, it behooves the TBLT community to encourage greater consistency vis-à-vis the nature of needs analysis and the language tasks that may ensue. First, it is absolutely critical to clarify that needs are what educational and social programs are designed to meet; without needs of some sort, programs are essentially pointless. Second, needs analysis does not rely on learners to identify their own language use situations and tasks, though there is a didactic role to be played by learners thinking about how they might use language. Good educational needs analysis does take the learners as the point of embarkation, but it incorporates multiple sources of information and methodologies of data collection to elicit insights into the kinds of language use that learners will confront (Long, 2005a). Third, needs might issue equally from the target tasks that a group of language educators hold valuable for their program and from analysis of how those tasks are accomplished in language use situations. The point is that some effort is made to justify what the language program is targeting – where ability to do things with the language is a major expectation (as it surely must be in language education), then it is essential to establish just what those things are. Fourth, it must be clear that *any* of the valued things that people do with language can be identified as the needs addressed by a language program, including survival tasks, mundane job tasks, tasks that enable access to education, and creative artistic tasks, to name a few (see diverse needs in Van Avermaet & Gysen, 2006). It will be particularly important to help the language teaching community understand this last point, as it is these truly valued, yet varied, goals of doing things with language that serve to define the potential contribution of task-based programs. In the end, just as TBLT polices its own discourse, it also will be worth posing the same question to all language programs: What are the needs to which your efforts are targeted, and to what extent do they offer defensible goals for language education?

A third challenge issues from the simple fact that innovation – planned and executed change – will be required if the purported benefits of TBLT are to be realized. Of particular salience is how TBLT can be implemented in light of both the cultural traditions and the teaching practice dimensions of innovation (Carless, 2004; Markee, 1996). Though little researched, much has been asserted about the incongruence of task-based ideas with non-Western societies, foreign language instruction, and other educational "cultures." Large class sizes, novice or young learners, minimal contact hours, classroom power hierarchies, non-interactiveness of students, exam-driven learning, teacher intransigence or apathy, and other impediments are regularly cited as justification for not engaging in TBLT. Certainly, cultural values, institutional constraints, and histories of practice will shape the possibilities that any approach to language teaching may realize, and it is important to enter into innovation gradually and with sensitivity to what is possible and what is not (Carless, 2007). Nevertheless, several countervailing realities speak to the viability, even the necessity, of TBLT-oriented innovation.

For one, recent educational policies imply that innovation will be necessary if the value of language learning is to be realized. For example, countries in East Asia and the European Union have witnessed the rise of policies emphasizing the need for learners to develop communicative abilities that enable them to do things with language, and "task" has figured explicitly into related documents (e.g., Council of Europe, 2001; Curriculum Development Council, 2002). Likewise, in re-structuring language curriculum to target communicative abilities in these contexts, it has become apparent to educationalists that L2 acquisition does generally call upon predictable cognitive processes and that these may be maximized through a context that features rich input, purposeful interaction, pushed output, and related techniques characteristic of task-based instruction (e.g., Izumi, 2003). Furthermore, for a variety of reasons, language teachers in supposedly unlikely contexts are incorporating tasks to bring about change. For example, teachers in Hong Kong and Japan (e.g., Flowerdew, 2005; Watanabe, Konoeda, & Mochizuki, 2007) have introduced tasks into the language classroom to raise learners' critical awareness of their own language needs in spite of institutionalized traditions. In foreign language education (e.g., Byrnes et al., 2006; González-Lloret, 2003; Leaver & Willis, 2004) teachers have turned to tasks as a way of operationalizing language acquisition in tertiary classes that both respect adult learners and push them to advanced abilities. Even with young learners (e.g., Van Gorp & Bogaert, 2006), teachers have found tasks to be effective ways of developing learners' language and cognitive abilities while maintaining interesting and motivating classroom environments.

While these examples testify to the viability of task-based innovation, it remains an empirical question as to why and how innovation occurs and the requirements for educational systems and actors. Large-scale inquiry (e.g., policy analysis, program evaluation) should address the interrelationships between educational policy, resource demands, institutional structures, and cultural patterns that encourage or constrain innovation. Smaller-scale teacher-driven inquiry (e.g., action research) will shed needed light on the central role played by teachers in the success or failure of any innovation, providing grounded evidence regarding how teachers continue to learn, professional demands for doing so, values that motivate teachers, and processes that facilitate change.

As we consider the possibilities and limitations of task-based innovation, and as we move ahead with the evolution of language teaching in response to an ever-changing social and educational environment, it will pay to keep a few basics in mind. Communicating is a fundamental fact of human cultures, and learning to communicate – learning to use language to do things – in another language offers considerable value from instrumental, aesthetic, moral, cognitive, and other perspectives. A basic question that must be answered by all language educators, then, is "what do our learners learn how to do, and how do they learn to do it"? Task offers a helpful way of encapsulating the things humans tend to do with language, in particular because it emphasizes the functional sense of language use. Without that impetus toward use, language reverts to a body of knowledge to be apprehended, a canon of great words, but not a particularly functional (or essential?) ability. Task also provides a useful frame of reference, directing teachers and learners toward a purpose for communicating, affording contextualized meaning to language forms, and indicating starting and ending points to the communicative effort. It is within this frame that task also helps to operationalize the fundamental point at which language learning occurs, as learners become aware of the language forms that provide particular meanings appropriate for achieving particular functions.

At the same time, task comes with a price. It counters our traditions of practice, requires rethinking the outcomes of our programs, and implies an overhaul of the teaching and testing that is going on in many language classrooms. Task challenges us to respect (and investigate) the actual uses to which language is put in diverse cultures and discourse domains, rather than adopting a one-size-fits-all approach to language. Task also demands that we think about language use and language learning in holistic terms. To achieve the benefits of task-based practice, we must first accept that language develops not as accretion of discrete bits of knowledge but through a series of holistic experiences. That holism also translates into the development of language education programs. Thus, just as task instantiates and facilitates the organic interaction of form, meaning, and function, so too do task-based programs enable learning on the basis of a holistic educational ecology wherein curriculum, instruction, assessment, and other processes interact to bring about learning. Though challenging, this vision of task-based language learning offers one comprehensive alternative to the status quo. That alternative may help us realize a language education practice that is valuable to a variety of discourse communities, the language learners who need and want to interact with them, and the language teaching profession whose job it is to facilitate their doing so.

REFERENCES

Breen, M. (1987). Learner contributions to task design. In C. Candlin & D. Murphy (eds.), *Language learning tasks* (pp. 23–46). Englewood Cliffs, NJ: Prentice-Hall.

Brindley, G. (1994). Task-centred assessment in language learning: The promise and the challenge. In N. Bird et al. (eds.), *Language and learning: Papers presented at the Annual International Language in Education Conference* (Hong Kong, 1993) (pp. 73–94). Hong Kong: Hong Kong Education Department.

Byrnes, H. (2002). The role of task and task-based assessment in a content-oriented collegiate foreign language curriculum. *Language Testing* 19, 419–37.

Byrnes, H., Crane, C., Maxim, H., & Sprang, K. (2006). Taking text to task: Issues and choices in curriculum construction. *ITL – International Journal of Applied Linguistics* 152, 85–109.

Carless, D. (2004). Issues in teachers' re-interpretation of a task-based innovation in primary schools. *TESOL Quarterly* 38, 639–62.

Carless, D. (2007). The suitability of task-based approaches for secondary schools: Perspectives from Hong Kong. *System* 35, 4, 595–608.

Chaudron, C., Doughty, C., Kim, Y., et al. (2005). A task-based needs analysis of a tertiary Korean as a foreign language program. In M. H. Long (ed.), *Second language needs analysis* (pp. 225–61). Cambridge: Cambridge University Press.

Council of Europe (2001). *Common European Framework of Reference for languages: Learning, teaching, assessment.* Cambridge: Cambridge University Press.

Cresswell, J. & Clark, V. (2007). *Designing and conducting mixed methods research.* Thousand Oaks, CA: Sage.

Cronbach, L. & Suppes, P. (eds.) (1969). *Research for tomorrow's schools: Disciplined inquiry of education.* New York: Macmillan.

Crookes, G. & Gass, S. (eds.) (1993a). *Tasks and language learning: Integrating theory and practice.* Clevedon, UK: Multilingual Matters.

Crookes, G. & Gass, S. (eds.) (1993b). *Tasks in a pedagogical context: Integrating theory and practice.* Clevedon, UK: Multilingual Matters.

Cureton, E. E. (1951). Validity. In E. F. Lingquist (ed.), *Educational measurement* (pp. 621–94). Washington, DC: American Council on Education.

Curriculum Development Council (2002). *English language education: Key learning area curriculum guide (primary 1–secondary 3).* Hong Kong SAR, China: Government Printer.

Dewey, J. (1933). *How we think: A restatement of the relation of reflective thinking to the educative process.* Boston: Henry Holt.

Dewey, J. (1938). *Experience and education.* New York: Macmillan/Collier.

Ellis, R. (2003). *Task-based language learning and teaching.* Oxford: Oxford University Press.

Estaire, S. & Zanón, J. (1994). *Planning classwork: A task-based approach.* Oxford: Oxford University Press.

Flowerdew, L. (2005). Integrating traditional and critical approaches to syllabus design: The "what", the "how", and the "why?". *Journal of English for Academic Purposes* 4, 135–47.

González-Lloret, M. (2003). Designing task-based call to promote interaction: En busca de esmeraldas. *Language Learning & Technology* 7, 86–104.

Gysen, S. & Van Avermaet, P. (2005). Issues in functional language performance assessment: The case of the Certificate Dutch as a Foreign Language. *Language Assessment Quarterly* 2, 51–68.

Izumi, S. (2003). EFL education in Japan from the perspective of second language acquisition research. *Sophia Linguistica* 50, 3–14.

James, W. (1899/1958). *Talks to teachers.* New York: W. W. Norton and Company.

Kane, M. T. (2001). Current concerns in validity theory. *Journal of Educational Measurement* 38, 319–42.

Keck, C., Iberri-Shea, G., Tracy-Ventura, N., & Wa-Mbaleka, S. (2006). Investigating the empirical link between task-based interaction and acquisition: A meta-analysis. In J. M. Norris & L. Ortega (eds.), *Synthesizing research on language learning and teaching* (pp. 91–131). Philadelphia: John Benjamins.

Kolb, D. (1984). *Experiential learning: Experience as the source of learning and development.* Englewood Cliffs, NJ: Prentice-Hall.

Krashen, S. & Terrell, T. (1983). *The natural approach: Language acquisition in the classroom.* Oxford: Pergamon.

Lave, J. & Wenger, E. (1991). *Situated learning: Legitimate peripheral participation.* Cambridge: Cambridge University Press.

Leaver, B. L. & Willis, J. R. (eds.) (2004). *Task-based instruction in foreign language education: Practices and programs.* Washington, DC: Georgetown University Press.

Long, M. H. (1985). A role for instruction in second language acquisition: Task-based language training. In K. Hyltenstam & M. Pienemann (eds.), *Modelling and assessing second language acquisition* (pp. 77–99). Clevedon, UK: Multilingual Matters.

Long, M. H. (1991). Focus on form: A design feature in language teaching methodology. In K. de Bot, R. B. Ginsberg, & C. Kramsch (eds.), *Foreign language research in cross-cultural perspective* (pp. 39–52). Amsterdam: John Benjamins.

Long, M. H. (2005a). Methodological issues in learner needs analysis. In M. H. Long (ed.), *Second language needs analysis* (pp. 19–76). Cambridge: Cambridge University Press.

Long, M. H. (ed.) (2005b). *Second language needs analysis.* Cambridge: Cambridge University Press.

Long, M. H. & Crookes, G. (1993). Units of analysis in syllabus design: The case for task. In G. Crookes & S. Gass (eds.), *Tasks in a pedagogical context: Integrating theory and practice* (pp. 9–54). Clevedon, UK: Multilingual Matters.

Long, M. H. & Norris, J. M. (2000). Task-based teaching and assessment. In M. Byram (ed.), *Encyclopedia of language teaching* (pp. 597–603). London: Routledge.

Long, M. H. & Robinson, P. (1998). Focus on form: Theory, research, and practice. In C. J. Doughty & J. Williams (eds.), *Focus on form in classroom second language acquisition* (pp. 15–41). Cambridge: Cambridge University Press.

Markee, N. (1996). *Managing curricular innovation.* Cambridge: Cambridge University Press.

Norris, J. M. (2002). Interpretations, intended uses and designs in task-based language assessment. *Language Testing* 19, 4, 337–46.

Norris, J. M. (2008). *Validity evaluation in language assessment.* New York: Peter Lang.

Norris, J. M., Brown, J. D., Hudson, T. D., & Yoshioka, J. (1998). *Designing second language performance assessment.* Honolulu: University of Hawai'i Press.

Norris, J. M. & Ortega, L. (2000). Effectiveness of L2 instruction: A research synthesis and quantitative meta-analysis. *Language Learning* 50, 417–528.

Norris, J. M. & Ortega, L. (2003). Defining and measuring SLA. In C. J. Doughty & M. H. Long (eds.), *Handbook of second language acquisition* (pp. 716–61). Oxford: Blackwell.

Norris, J. M. & Ortega, L. (eds.) (2006). *Synthesizing research on language learning and teaching.* Philadelphia: John Benjamins.

Ortega, L. (2005). What do learners plan? Learner-driven attention to form during pre-task planning. In R. Ellis (ed.), *Planning and task performance in a second language* (pp. 77–109). Philadelphia: John Benjamins.

Ortega, L. & Iberri-Shea, G. (2005). Longitudinal research in SLA: Recent trends and future directions. *Annual Review of Applied Linguistics* 25, 26–45.

Patton, M. Q. (1997). *Utilization-focused evaluation: The new century text* (3rd ed.). Thousand Oaks, CA: Sage.

Prabhu, N. S. (1987). *Second language pedagogy*. Oxford: Oxford University Press.

Reid, W. J. (1997). Research on task-centered practice. *Social Work Research* 21, 3, 132–7.

Robinson, P. (2001). Task complexity, cognition and second language syllabus design: A triadic framework for examining task influences on SLA. In P. Robinson (ed.), *Cognition and second language instruction* (pp. 287–318). Cambridge: Cambridge University Press.

Samuda, V. (2001). Guiding relationships between form and meaning during task performance: The role of the teacher. In M. Bygate, P. Skehan, & M. Swain (eds.), *Researching pedagogic tasks: Second language learning, teaching, and testing* (pp. 119–34). Harlow, UK: Longman.

Samuda, V. & Bygate, M. (2008). *Tasks in second language learning*. New York: Palgrave Macmillan.

Skehan, P. (1996). A framework for the implementation of task-based instruction. *Applied Linguistics* 17, 38–62.

Skehan, P. (1998). *A cognitive approach to language learning*. Oxford: Oxford University Press.

Sternberg, R. J. (2003). What is an "expert student?". *Educational Researcher* 32, 8, 5–9.

Swain, M. & Lapkin, S. (1982). *Evaluating bilingual education: A Canadian case study*. Clevedon, UK: Multilingual Matters.

Van Avermaet, P. & Gysen, S. (2006). From needs to tasks: Language learning needs in a task-based approach. In K. Van den Branden (ed.), *Task-based language education: From theory to practice* (pp. 17–46). Cambridge: Cambridge University Press.

Van den Branden, K. (2006). Training teachers: Task-based as well? In K. Van den Branden (ed.), *Task-based language education: From theory to practice* (pp. 217–73). Cambridge: Cambridge University Press.

Van Gorp, K. & Bogaert, N. (2006). Developing language tasks for primary and secondary education. In K. Van den Branden (ed.), *Task-based language education: From theory to practice* (pp. 76–105). Cambridge: Cambridge University Press.

Virjo, I., Holmberg-Mattila, D., & Mattila, K. (2001). Task-based learning (TBL) in undergraduate medical education. *Medical Teacher* 23, 1, 55–8.

Watanabe, Y., Konoeda, K., & Mochizuki, N. (2007). Task-based critical pedagogy in JHS EFL. Paper presented at the JALT International Conference on Language Teaching and Learning, Tokyo, Japan.

Widdowson, H. (1978). *Teaching language as communication*. Oxford: Oxford University Press.

Wiggins, G. (1998). *Educative assessment: Designing assessments to inform and improve student performance*. San Francisco: Jossey-Bass.

Wilkins, D. (1976). *Notional syllabuses. A taxonomy and its relevance to foreign language curriculum development*. Oxford: Oxford University Press.

Willis, J. (1996). *A framework for task-based learning*. Harlow, UK: Longman.

Wright, T. (2000). No more pencils. No more books? Arguing for the use of experiential learning in post secondary environmental studies classrooms. *Electronic Green Journal*, Dec 2000, n.p.

31 Radical Language Teaching

GRAHAM CROOKES

Introduction

Over the centuries and across numerous civilizations, language teaching and learning has often had associations with concentrations of power. Structures and systems for the teaching of languages have often worked to distribute resources under conditions of scarcity and to extend the reach of sets of ideas; people have sought to learn languages to gain access to power and to resist oppression, and people have tried to teach languages so as to gain control or extend influence over others. In these guises language teaching is as political as any other domain of education – and possibly more so because of the role of language in the formation of identities and its implication in ideologies. In this chapter I review understandings of language teaching that emphasize this perspective and concern themselves with values opposed to those of a supposed "mainstream."

The idea of a particular kind of language teaching being associated with values (anti-imperial, anti-feudal, anti-patriarchal, anti-capitalist, anti-racist, anti-heterosexist, etc.), opposed to those promoted by elites as "mainstream," is mainly possible only in association with the rise of language teaching as an identifiable enterprise both within mass education but also somewhat distinct from it, i.e., capable of being carried out in proprietary schools in which no other subject is taught, within independent alternative schools, or within structures of specialized semi-autonomous adult education, such as refugee camps and literacy campaigns. So generally speaking, it was not until the latter part of the twentieth century that language teaching was sufficiently self-aware to conceive of itself, as a professional field, as having political agendas, and within them, to conceive of the possibility of some of this work as having a radical orientation.

I will use the word "radical" to gather together various strands of thought, primarily opposed to oppressive forces in societies, which a few language teaching specialists have drawn upon in developing curriculum theory and instructional practice. The most prominent line within this area of our field is associated with the popular term "critical," but following Gore (1998), and with particular reference to the second most prominent subdomain within the area under consideration here, namely feminist approaches to learning and teaching, the term "radical" allows these two trends to be encompassed under a heading which reflects their association, without privileging either of them. In addition, since "critical" has often been associated with one prominent political analysis tradition deriving from Marxist ideas, even though there are others that should also be considered, a broader term is obviously helpful.[1] In order to encompass the full range of perspectives deserving treatment here, I begin the body of this chapter by way of some extended historical background pertaining to radical education overall, before narrowing down to language-related aspects of the topic.

Historical Background to Radical Education

The French revolution (1789) brought about the first large-scale modern initiatives in state education intended to foster a radical social consciousness, with many of the distinctive characteristics that were to manifest themselves in subsequent radical educational initiatives. As with the Revolution, these initiatives were not long-lasting. During the nineteenth century, as Europe continued to move through a period of upheaval, forces further to the left than the liberal movement began to gain strength as a growing working class and a rural peasantry were increasingly radicalized. The most prominent international organization with a radical agenda split between followers of Marx and of Bakunin, with regard to the emphasis on control or freedom that was to characterize the subsequent distinction between communists and anarchists. But at this time, these prominent radicals agreed on one thing: an opposition to existing incipient forms of state education. Both early Marxists and libertarian socialists assumed that any existing state would control education to the disadvantage of emancipatory forces. At a time when state education was not yet widespread and all-encompassing, and state bureaucracies not so powerful, calls for independent radical schools were not impractical.

By the middle of the nineteenth century, some schools, notably in France, made use of or allied themselves with the anti-authoritarian tendencies I have just alluded to, which at this time were going under the heading "libertarian" (even though previously they might have used a term such as "anarchist," associated with the theorist and activist Proudhon). They drew on the concept of "integral education" – education for both mind and body, with a vocational character, and sympathetic to the position of working people.[2] It was intended to be anti-individualist, de-centralized, and cooperative; and involved adult as well as child education. These ideas about the content and structure of schools were taken to Spain by Francisco Ferrer, who was successful in popularizing them during the first decade of the twentieth century (Avrich, 1980, p. 26, in Smith, 1983). Ferrer also established an associated international organization, and journals and periodicals spread the ideas. In 1909, Ferrer was tried on false charges by the Spanish authorities for political reasons and executed, which served to spread his ideas further. Ferrer schools were started all over Europe, and in South America, China, and Japan. "The most vigorous response of all came from the United States" (Smith, 1983, p. 6). According to Smith, during this period the growth of radical ideas and "syndicalism" (i.e., trade union activity) among teachers in state schools led to "the argument that state schools could be reformed along libertarian lines from within" (p. 13). In theorizing the Modern School, Ferrer (e.g., 1913) pulled together many ideas that were radical at their time but are commonplace nowadays: coeducation, active learning, a scientific approach (inquiry and data analysis) applied throughout the curriculum, the same emphasis on the practical as well as the theoretical, and the use of the actual environment as a learning medium (resource centers, school trips, and the like).

Smith (1983) sees a gradual move away from the vocational emphasis of early integral education toward the theoretical development of a general core curriculum that would be consistent with anarchist or libertarian principles. This he finds in the educational writings of Kropotkin (e.g., 1974/1899) and also of Tolstoy (1967), who was actively involved in running an experimental school for several years. These two authors emphasized intrinsic motivation, and positive conditions in schools leading naturally to learning, without much needed in the way of direct instruction or external (punishment or reward) motivation. These positive conditions related to (1) the "love, support and emotional encouragement" of students, and (2) freedom – an absence of coercion, an "approach to the freer conditions in which cultural learning took place" and a redefinition of the teacher–student relationship to one more egalitarian, in light of that concern with freedom (Smith, 1983, p. 72). Particularly important for language teaching specialists, theorists in this line, whether of the nineteenth century or the twentieth (e.g., Holt, 1976; Neill, 1960), recognize a natural inclination on the part of children (at least) to learn, and believe that that students can "naturally" organize their learning experiences, and will indeed learn in a somewhat unconscious and natural way if placed in the right educational environment. For example, Paul Goodman (1974) was one of a number of such theorists to hold up L1 acquisition as characteristic of the kind of natural learning that he and other radical educators in this line wanted to see generalized to all kinds of learning. Holt in particular looked to the "natural" characteristics of child development, and to children's natural and persistent behavior to explore and thereby learn the world around them (including the language around them) as a basic model for the kind of learning they wanted to see in schools.

The emphasis on egalitarian and supportive relations between teacher and student, on a group orientation, and on non-directive pedagogical techniques were certainly radical when they first manifested themselves in free schools and the Modern School movement of the late nineteenth century. But with the considerable social changes that took place during the twentieth century and accelerated during the 1960s, by 1976 Holt was able to find what he regarded as an excellent example of a pedagogy that respected the natural processes of learning (exemplified in L1 acquisition) in some state elementary schools (he refers to those of Denmark).[3] Smith's further theorizing of this places the emphasis on shifting the function of teaching from direct instruction to the provision of feedback. Using the terms of psycholinguist Ken Goodman (1967; later incorporated into such developments as the Whole Language Approach), he notes that for the teacher, "the problem is how to fit in with the psycholinguistic guessing game" involved in learning to read. "Teaching functions take on the character of feedback . . . designed to help a learner improve on an already existing performance. The learner makes his move first and only then can the teacher offer advice . . ." The teacher should not talk too much, and must respond to the developmental needs of the learner (Smith, 1983, p. 84). Learner initiative and choice are to be emphasized, as means of developing and nurturing the free will that is crucial for individual freedom.[4]

I have mentioned the divergence between the two early traditions of radicalism. The concepts of sociopolitical critique and anti-authoritarianism were unified for one part of the old left (anarchism) but not for the other (communism). Considering the latter during the historical period just reviewed, studies of education in the Soviet Union comment that despite early attempts in the 1920s which reformed education in progressive and Montessori-like directions (along with the abolition of uniforms, examinations, grades, etc.), subsequently under Stalinist influence and with the desire to build a strong state through state education, political critique ceased to manifest interest in freedom at the classroom level or within the organization of schools.[5]

The existence of authoritarian state socialism ensured that even outside of communist countries, the availability of Marxist lines of sociopolitical critique was much greater than of those inspired by Proudhon or Bakunin; and relatedly, they manifested a greater degree of academic development. So despite the non-existence of radical education in communist countries, educational philosophy of the twentieth century that drew on alternative social theories, and on critiques of existing political systems, tended to draw on developments of Marxist theories (to which I now turn).

Developments under the Heading "Critical"

Contrary to the expectations of Marxist-inspired actors and analysts, elements of socialist forms of political organization flickered in and out of existence but were not long-lasting, and by the middle of the twentieth century, theorists who continued to develop this theoretical position revised pre-existing Marxist social theory in a variety of directions. Among these, a prominent group of alternative social theorists adopted the label "critical theory." Influenced by them and by progressive and radical educational practices available by mid-century, a theory and practice of curriculum and instruction intended to be in accord with radical efforts for social change was developed, in Brazil in the 1960s, by Paulo Freire – "critical pedagogy." For some specialists (e.g., Shotton, 1992; Smith, 1983; Spring, 1975, 1994) this, in its opposition to oppression of all kinds, was sufficiently akin to the libertarian traditions mentioned earlier to be discussed alongside them.[6] It is this educational tradition that has become most popular among language teaching specialists drawing on radical social philosophy. It is not surprising that it has had considerable influence within language teaching, because unlike other non-mainstream educational traditions, it begins with and is directly concerned with language, specifically literacy; not only that, but it takes culture as its central focus; and it was initially located outside the main state sector in an area hospitable to alternatives – adult education.

Low literacy rates and poverty have tended to go hand in hand, and throughout the latter half of the twentieth century, many agencies in poorer countries have worked within adult education systems to try to foster greater literacy. In understanding the development of the critical pedagogy movement, the early pedagogy of adult literacy is an intriguing precursor. In South America, after World War II, elements within the Catholic Church became radicalized, and began more strongly to articulate the critique of material society that is implicit in some Christian teachings (liberation theology). Various strands of influence, including both Christian and socialist, were taken up and developed in literacy education and practice by Freire. In Brazil, citizens had to pass a literacy test in order to have a vote; typically the poor were thus disenfranchised, so literacy education became an important means of fostering peaceful social and political change there. Unfortunately, as some say, if voting led to radical social change it would be made illegal, and so it more or less proved in this case. Following a right-wing coup, Freire was first imprisoned and then exiled. As a result, circulating in the English-speaking world from the late 1960s on (to an extent that they did not, at first, in Brazilian Portuguese- or Spanish-using areas), Freire's ideas entered foreign language education and ESL education from the mid 1970s on. Taylor (1993, pp. 73–4) provides the following comments[7] concerning some of Freire's sources:

> The genius of Freire was to bring together a range of pedagogies and learning/teaching techniques to create a method of teaching which is now known throughout the world as the "Método Paulo Freire," a method which is both a process of literacy acquisition and a process of conscientization. It is based on the simple but fundamental technique of *problematizing* or "problem posing," and is therefore the antithesis of Banking Education which seeks solutions or gives answers. It consists of daring to interrogate what is given, bringing into question known structures, and examining conventional or taken-for-granted "explanations" of reality. It discovers and then reacts to possibility of "contradiction," identifying ways in which things can be said, done, or exist differently.
>
> In *Education: The Practice of Freedom*, [1974/1967] Freire explains the details of his method which has changed very little over the years. It is a three-stage investigation, which poses three fundamentally different questions. First, there is a NAMING stage where one asks the question: what is the problem, what is the question under discussion? Second, there is a REFLECTION stage: why is this the case? How do we explain this situation? Finally, there is the ACTION stage: what can be done to change this situation? What options do we have?
>
> . . .

"It is a permanent, critical approach to reality in order to discover it and discover the myths that deceive us and help us to maintain the oppressive, dehumanizing structures. It leaves nobody inactive. It implies that people take the role of agents, makers and remakers of the world." (Freire, 1971, p. 24)

The three-stage structure of the method, however, was not Freire's creation. It parallels a process popular in the 1960s within the Basic Ecclesiastic Communities (*Comunidades Eclesiales de Base: CEB*) in Brazil. As the basis of the social education programme, especially in the literacy campaign broadcast nationwide by the Church's Basic Education Movement (MEB), they used a method known widely as *See-Judge-Act*: what is the case, why is it so, and what can be done about it?

Critical Pedagogy in Second and Foreign Language Areas

Although Freire complained about formulations (and critiques) of his ideas that implied some fixed "Freire Method," an initial understanding of what his ideas imply for practice can clearly be obtained from a sketch of the typical procedures he instituted in literacy classes. For him, it was very important that the curriculum begin with the concerns and issues of the students. For beginning literacy, the core words should relate to the issues of the students' life and the things in their life that were problematic, which they might be able to change and improve through the tool of literacy and the changed consciousness that would come from that. When literacy courses were delivered within the students' home communities, the instructional team spent time living in the community, to develop an ethnographically grounded basis for the curriculum. A characteristic feature is the use of visual images (pictures or later, photos) of certain aspects of the students' life. But in addition, since one underlying goal of the approach is to foster the freedom of the students, the students themselves play a substantial role in the development of curriculum content and even materials. The pictures, for example, are used as projective devices; through commenting on them and discussing them, students develop or articulate some aspects of the topics or language content they wish to learn, that they wish to be able to command.

One of the first S/FL specialists to research and develop the application of these ideas to FL language teaching was Crawford, in her 1978 dissertation. There she identified 20 key principles, from which I excerpt the following as illustrative:

1 The purpose of education is to develop critical thinking by presenting [the students'] situation to them as a problem so that they can perceive, reflect and act on it.
2 The content of curriculum derives from the life situation of the learners as expressed in the themes of their reality.
3 The learners produce their own learning materials.

4 The task of planning is first to organize generative themes and second to organize subject matter as it relates to those themes.
5 The teacher participates as a learner among learners.
6 The teacher contributes his/her ideas, experiences, opinions, and perceptions to the dialogical process.
7 The teacher's function is one of posing problems.
8 The students possess the right to and power of decision making.

At the same time, the first manifestations of this line of curriculum theory began to appear in the ESL literature (Moriarty & Wallerstein, 1979, 1980; Wallerstein, 1983a, 1983b, 1983c).

From these early beginnings, the literature of critical pedagogy in our field has gone on to develop two main strands, which parallel developments in mainstream critical pedagogy. There are the more abstract sociopolitical critiques: in the mainstream area, of Giroux (e.g., 1983) and McLaren (e.g., 1994) – in language teaching, in for example the work of Pennycook (e.g., 2001). And then there are more practical discussions of classrooms, instructional practices, and materials. In mainstream critical pedagogy these descend fairly directly from Freire's own work and also of his sometime co-author Shor (e.g., Shor & Freire, 1987; Shor, 1992). In language teaching this sort of discussion and accounts of practice are most obviously prominent in the work of Auerbach (e.g., 1992), Benesch (e.g., 1996), and Morgan (e.g., 1998). And as Freire was from the third world and advised anticolonial governments in Africa, it is noteworthy that critical S/FL pedagogy has its own anti- or postcolonial wing (e.g., Canagarajah, 2002).

Feminist Pedagogy and Language Teaching

Feminism, as a movement for radical social change, is based on "the central premise" (Lather, 1987/1994, p. 242) "that gender is a basic organizing principle of all known societies and that, along with race, class, and the sheer specificity of historical circumstance, it profoundly shapes/mediates the concrete conditions of our lives." It includes the position that most cultures in history, including to a substantial extent present Western culture, are or have been patriarchal, in the sense that concerns "men in positions of power and influence in society, with cultural values and norms being seen as favouring men" (*Oxford English Dictionary*, 2008).

In the 1960s, feminism developed a "second wave" (the first having been active particularly from the late 1800s on and having obtained suffrage through direct action and a range of engagements with organized institutional political structures). Second-wave feminism made substantial use of "consciousness-raising groups," themselves presumably taking off from the encounter group movement (based in humanist psychology and existential philosophy); these small groups were places for women to review their thinking and develop a revised self-concept, as well as, often, a program of action. They were in a sense educational; they were certainly sites for self-education. This experience seems to have come into contact with the critical pedagogy tradition, and led to a development of a feminist pedagogy which drew from Freirean ideas while fairly quickly presenting a substantial critique of them (as patriarchal, notably through their failure to recognize gender as a site of oppression). Within this overall framework, curriculum occupies (as ever) a central place. Noted feminist scholar Tetrault (2004; see also Maher & Tetrault, 2001) identifies four phases of curriculum development that might be passed through on the way to a feminist pedagogy. In the first, male-defined curriculum, it is assumed that male experience is universal. In the second, a "contribution curriculum," women are token figures, tossed in as indicative of women's "contribution." Tetrault's third variant is the "bifocal" curriculum. This is "open to the possibility of seeing the world through women's eyes," but "thinking about women and men is dualistic and dichotomized" (p. 167). Fourth, in "women's curriculum" it is "women's activities, not men's, [that] are the measure of significance." Within this most recent area of development, a "pluralistic conceptualization of women" is called for . . . Historians ask how the particulars of race, ethnicity, social class, marital status, and sexual orientation challenge the homogeneity of women's experiences. Third World feminists critique hegemonic 'Western' feminisms and formulate [alternatives]. . . ." The fifth and final phase is "gender-balanced curriculum." This is "conscious of the limitations of seeing women in isolation and aware of the relational character of gender," and in it, the "pluralistic and multifocal conception of women that emerged" in the previous phase "is extended to [all] human beings." In this sense, it reflects an inclusive feminism (Hooks, 1989; cf. Zack, 2005), in which what is good for women is most likely good for men too.

Narrowing now to the realm of ESL, the work of Vandrick (1994, 1998, 2003) is the primary source for S/FL feminist pedagogy. In her 1994 article, she provides a useful summary of ESL feminist pedagogy developments up to that point in time. In Vandrick's view of feminist pedagogy, the classroom ideally functions as a "liberatory environment" (p. 76) in which students also teach, and are subjects not objects, and through which consciousness could be changed. Vandrick follows Shrewsbury (1993) to refer to how students in such classrooms develop "enhanced autonomy but at the same time, mutuality; discovery of own voice . . . authenticity" (pp. 76–7) and also speaks hopefully of establishing "community" in such classrooms. Within such a classroom, leadership would be liberatory, acting on feminist beliefs. The practical implications of this require teachers to (among other things) alter the curriculum and utilize feminist process skills. And though there cannot be one "specific set of practices" (Vandrick, 1994, p. 84), nevertheless the feminist ESL teacher should have a curriculum that is bias-free and have materials that avoid stereotyping; raise consciousness concerning the gendered nature of English; be aware of gender-related differences in learning styles; give female students equal time and treatment in class; provide help for male students who are incompetent in this domain; explore cultural differences in this area; be a role model; not tolerate sexist behavior among colleagues; "put the feminine at the center of your teaching" and "practice affirmative action in the classroom" (Carson, 1993, p. 36).

Some Additional and Some Missing Pieces of Radical Language Teaching

In recent years, some additional areas of development have appeared in radical language teaching. Language teaching and/or applied linguistics has been very slow, compared with the field of education, to consider the implications of race as a form or site of oppression. A recent special issue of the flagship journal *TESOL Quarterly* was devoted to it (2006), but this is indicative of the previous neglect of the topic. Oppression based on societal insistence on a particular sexual orientation and oppression of those not conforming (heterosexism) has been recognized by radical educational practitioners, and has become apparent in some theoretical literature (e.g., Pinar, 1998), producing a handful of articles in language teaching marked generally by a practical orientation (Nelson, 1999).[8]

Radical language teaching of the Freirean variety was from the beginning associated with languages other than English. Freirean L1 literacy instruction continues to be documented under conditions somewhat similar to those in which it originally emerged (e.g., Purcell-Gates & Waterman, 2000). The FL field within English-speaking countries has been less active in taking up these ideas despite their early development by Crawford (1978, and her subsequent publications in FL sources: Crawford-Lange, 1981, 1982). Newer proponents (notably Osborn, 2000; Reagan & Osborn, 1998, 2002) have provided useful analyses and advocacy but have few actual instances of radical FL pedagogy to report on. Over the last 10 years, the teaching of Japanese as a foreign language (in the US) has produced some reports and discussion (Kubota, e.g., 1996; Siegel & Okamoto, 2003) containing advice, critique, and occasional accounts of actual short pedagogical initiatives (e.g., Ohara, Saft, & Crookes, 2001).[9]

Along with other non-mainstream approaches that favor an activity-based curriculum and an active role for the student, radical pedagogies have been seen by some as culturally inappropriate for use in some areas. While this position is based on a fallacious generalization of the characteristics of "small cultures" (Holliday, 1994, 1999), or temporary historical-cultural conditions (Shin & Crookes, 2005a), to countries or cultures as a whole (cf. Kubota, 1999), it is true that there are few reports of radical language pedagogy outside of nominally liberal, pluralistic societies. However, a handful of small-scale trials have been reported (e.g., Shin & Crookes, 2005b) which (not surprisingly) concern the teaching of English – however in EFL, rather than ESL contexts.

Distinctiveness of Radical Language Teaching?

Radical approaches in language teaching are clearly different from other language teaching approaches at some level, since they hold a particular perspective on society, espouse and advocate particular values and conceptions of society and of the individual, and above all have an activist perspective – that is, set themselves against the status quo and assume that students have a degree of agency in and on society which it is the role of curriculum and pedagogical practice to reflect and support. Are they distinctive in other ways?

Gore (1998) pulls together both critical and feminist mainstream education discussions to suggest that it is unlikely, given the basic constraints of classrooms and of formal education as a set of social practices within modernity, that entirely new ways of teaching could actually be developed. It is more likely, she contends, that teachers with radical perspectives draw selectively from mainly pre-existing pedagogical options, and implement them naturally with a heightened attention to the morality of their teaching practices and their congruence with their activist educational aims.

Critical and feminist pedagogy clearly were and are in line with broadly progressive understandings of educational practice. It is not surprising to find that critical language classrooms tend to have features that we would recognize as typical of many "communicative" language classrooms, since there is a shared progressive inheritance (Lin & Luk, 2002). A great deal can be encompassed under the heading "communicative," of course. Adult ESL classes with a critical orientation, as described by Auerbach and colleagues, are distinctly oriented to the real-world tasks that their students need to engage in (not necessarily deriving merely from their employment, of course, as opposed to their lives). At the same time they may give extended and systematic attention to the forms of language, to an extent well beyond a "strong" communicative orientation (and similarly beyond the position of many emphasizing focus on form within a task-based perspective). This follows from a strong interest in learner input into, even determination of, not only content to be learned but also ways of learning it. At the same time, a central area of similarity between this line and both older communicative and more recent task-based lines is the great importance placed on deriving the content to be taught from, as far as possible, identifiable needs of the students, and with a definite orientation to the kind of things they will need to do with the target language, in their life in the real world. In practice (and in published materials), communicative approaches often seem to concern themselves with basically a middle-class, potentially internationally mobile individual; the critical tradition begins with a conception of the typical student as possibly poor or working class, perhaps needing a second or foreign language capacity because they are refugees, forced by circumstances to relocate, and probably faced with difficult living circumstances in which survival English is the first step to an English capacity that can actually improve their circumstances. It (optimistically) hopes for an activist orientation in its students. In practice, I think the visitor to one of the rare classrooms with an explicitly radical orientation would find quite a bit of overlap between that and many other language classrooms, although phrases on the board are more likely to be those of protest or resistance, rather than polite requests to book a room in a hotel or a vacation on the French Riviera.

I do not think there is anything completely different in classroom practices, curriculum, or learning theory that sets off radical language teaching absolutely from other approaches to language teaching; it is the values of the curriculum, the philosophy of the teachers and students, and the long-term aims of programs of this kind which are different. Some language teaching specialists who are interested in this topic wonder whether its practices can be justified, given the apparent lack of attention, indeed lack of concern, with an underlying theory of language learning. Perhaps the beliefs about language learning of radical language teachers are as diverse as those of other groups of language teachers and the worry is one mainly confined to specialists.[10] In any case, radical language teachers have far more important things to worry about. Just getting any program that even covertly espouses any of the main values of a radical position up and running is extremely difficult. To clearly advocate a radical position eliminates many funding sources ahead of time, and courts being closed down subsequently. Educational initiatives of this kind tend to have a short life and find it difficult to self-finance, except under exceptional circumstances. To the extent that this is true, even straightforward descriptions of practice are likely to be few; instead the interested and inquiring reader is faced with many largely data-free theoretical expositions that keep a few dissident academics in work (and maintain their grip on a handful of tenured positions); these are intended to encourage the troops but may frustrate those seeking formal program evaluation reports, let alone a learning theory basis for radical language teaching. There are many broader accounts of radical educational practice, particularly case studies, but they typically relate to schools as a whole, not language teaching programs. What we really need are manuals of advice and practice concerning fundraising, organization, administration, public relations, and community support, if radical language teaching is to survive and prosper (see Crookes & Talmy, 2004).[11] In particular, more published textbooks (along the lines of Auerbach & Wallerstein, 1987) would be extremely helpful to teachers wishing to develop themselves in this area, and to teacher educators searching for examples to show of radical language teaching practices. The potential for growth in this domain of language teaching is considerable; more to the point, the work will always be needed, so long as language is a tool of oppression, a site of struggle, and weapon for social improvement and change.

NOTES

1 The term is fairly widely, and loosely used in education. See journals such as *Radical Pedagogy* (http://radicalpedagogy.icaap.org/) and *Radical Teacher* (www.radicalteacher.org), or cf. Buckingham (1998).
2 See Doughty and Long (2003), who draw on the concepts of integral education in developing task-based language teaching.
3 Danish schools continued to provide a home for non-coercive pedagogy: see Dam (1995).
4 This tradition, then, was active in a number of geographical areas, both inside and outside the state system. It even penetrated, for example, the US state education system in the late 1960s, with a small number of state schools finding conditions allowing them to adopt more radical practices (Miller, 2002; Neumann, 2003). Although greatly diminished in number, a handful have persisted (e.g., Basile, 2004) and this work has probably fed into the uptake of the US "charter school" concept by

those seeking radical school alternatives that can benefit from state support (Rofes & Stulberg, 2005). Whether such a strategy is still feasible in the era of No Child Left Behind is obviously a matter of debate, in which proponents of the two lines mentioned here are respectively optimistic and pessimistic concerning the outcomes for radical educators who engage with the state system.

5   "Educational liberalism had some effect on Soviet education in the period immediately following the 1917 revolution. Since the Stalin era, however, most educational decrees have advanced the cause of educational conservatism." (Dupuis, 1966, p. 203; see also Huxley, 1946). "Some Soviet educators advocated a revolutionary reassessment of schooling itself, [e.g.,] Shulgin, director of the . . . Institute of Pedagogy in Moscow from 1922 onward. In many ways, Shulgin's ideas on education resembled those of the progressive movement . . . At the end of the 1920s, the climate of education began to change . . . Soviet education returned to a traditional model, with the reassertion of teacher authority, a traditional curriculum and an elimination of democratic organization" (Small, 2005, p. 160–1).

6   The connection between Freire's earliest work and critical theory is less clear than the names might suggest, according to Taylor (1993). Smith (1983) comments, "Freire does not follow Marx in important respects . . . [but] Freire cannot be said in any general sense to be an anarchist. Nevertheless, when we look at his educational position we shall find that it bears a distinct resemblance . . ." (pp. 107–8).

7   Cf. Fernandes (1985); see Mayo (2004) for a well-informed appraisal of Taylor's analysis.

8   Of course, to refer to a singular identity (gay, black, woman) is not particularly up-to-date. We are well-advised to be wary of essentialism (although most of the older radical traditions I have been discussing have no hesitation about it, indeed, had no idea that there was an alternative). More recent theoretical discussions of radical language teaching are quite familiar with poststructuralist views on learning (and identity); space does not permit discussion of whether these have distinctive practical manifestations in radical language teaching.

9   However, there is very little evidence of what is admittedly very much a minority view within other domains of FL instruction, or appearing in the literatures of language teaching outside the US. Searches (in *Linguistics and Language Behavior Abstracts*) coupling critical or radical pedagogy with languages taught (excluding English) produce only Japanese-oriented references emanating from US-based scholars; one finds little suggestion that teachers of e.g., Arabic, Chinese, etc., in the US have published in this domain. EFL specialists are the primary consumers of this discourse among language teachers outside the US, as a handful of publications referencing Taiwan and Korea indicate.

10 But it deserves attention from specialists, though space does not permit a discussion of the topic here.

11 Comparable with the advice available concerning the broader area of "democratic" education gathered by AERO (Alternative Education Resource Organization) (www.educationrevolution.org).

REFERENCES

Auerbach, E. R. (1992). *Making meaning, making change: A guide to participatory curriculum development for adult ESL and family literacy.* Washington, DC: Center for Applied Linguistics.

Auerbach, E. R. & Wallerstein, N. (1987). *ESL for action: Problem-posing at work* (Students' book and Teachers book). Reading, MA: Addison-Wesley.

Avrich, P. (1980). *The Modern School movement.* Princeton, NJ: Princeton University Press.

Basile, C. G. (2004). *A good little school.* Albany, NY: State University of New York Press.

Benesch, S. (1996). Needs analysis and curriculum development in EAP: An example of a critical approach. *TESOL Quarterly* 30, 4, 723–38.

Buckingham, D. (1998). *Teaching popular culture: Beyond radical pedagogy.* London: UCL Press.

Canagarajah, A. S. (2000). *A geopolitics of academic writing.* Pittsburgh, PA: University of Pittsburgh Press.

Carson, C. J. (1993). Attacking a legacy of sexist grammar in the French class: A modest beginning. *Feminist Teacher* 7, 2, 34–6.

Crawford, L. M. (1978). Paulo Freire's philosophy: Derivation of curricular principles and their application to second language curriculum design. PhD dissertation, University of Minnesota.

Crawford-Lange, L. M. (1981). Redirecting foreign language curricula: Paulo Freire's contribution. *Foreign Language Annals* 14, 257–73.

Crawford-Lange, L. M. (1982). Curricular alternatives for second language learning. In T. V. Higgs (ed.), *Curriculum competence, and the foreign language teacher* (pp. 81–113). Skokie, IL: National Textbook Co. Reprinted in M. H. Long & J. C. Richards (eds.) (1987), *Methodology in TESOL: A book of readings* (pp. 120–44). Rowley, MA: Newbury House.

Crookes, G. & Talmy, S. (2004). Second/Foreign Language program preservation and advancement: Literatures and lessons for teachers and teacher education. *Critical Inquiry in Language Studies* 1, 4, 219–36.

Dam, L. (1995). *Learner autonomy 3: From theory to classroom practice.* Dublin: Authentik Language Learning Resources.

Doughty, C. J. & Long, M. H. (2003). Optimal psycholinguistic environments for distance foreign language learning. *Language Learning & Technology* 7, 3, 50–80.

Dupuis, A. M. (1966). *Philosophy of education in historical perspective.* Chicago, IL: Rand McNally.

Ferrer, F. (1913). *The origins and ideas of the Modern School.* London: Watts.

Fernandes, L. (1985). Basic Ecclesiastic communities in Brazil. *Harvard Educational Review* 55, 1, 76–85.

Freire, P. (1974/1967). Education: The practice of freedom. In P. Freire, *Education for critical consciousness.* London: Sheed & Ward. Originally published in 1967 as *Educação ecomo práctica de liberdade*, Rio de Janeiro: Paz e Terra.

Freire, P. (1971). A few notions about the word conscientization. *Hard Cheese* 1, 23–8.

Giroux, H. (1983). *Theory and resistance in education.* South Hadley, MA: Bergin & Garvey.

Goodman, K. (1967). Reading: A psycholinguistic guess game. *Journal of the Reading Specialist* 6, 1, 126–35.

Goodman, K. (1974). Mini-schools: A prescription for the reading problem. In I. Lister (ed.), *Deschooling: A reader* (pp. 34–6). Cambridge: Cambridge University Press.

Gore, J. (1998). On the limits to empowerment through critical and feminist pedagogies. In D. Carlson & M. Apple (eds.), *Power/Knowledge/Pedagogy* (pp. 271–88). Boulder, CO: Westview Press.

Holliday, A. (1994). Student culture and English language education: An international perspective. *Language, Culture, and Curriculum* 7, 2, 125–43.

Holliday, A. (1999). Small cultures. *Applied Linguistics* 20, 2, 237–64.

Holt, J. (1976). *Instead of education.* New York: Dutton.

Hooks, B. (1989). *Talking back, thinking feminism, thinking black*. Boston, MA: South End Press.

Huxley, A. (1946). *Ends and means*. London: Chatto & Windus.

Kropotkin, P. (1974/1899). *Fields, factories and workshops tomorrow*, edited by C. Ward. London: Allen & Unwin.

Kubota, R. (1996). Critical pedagogy and critical literacy in teaching Japanese [in Japanese]. *Japanese-Language Education around the Globe* 6, 35–48. The Japan Foundation Japanese Language Institute.

Kubota, R. (1999). Japanese culture constructed by discourses: Implications for applied linguistics research and ELT. *TESOL Quarterly* 33, 9–35.

Lather, P. (1987). The absent presence: Patriarchy, capitalism, and the nature of teacher work. *Teacher Education Quarterly* 14, 2, 25–38. Reprinted in L. Stone (ed.) (1994), *The education feminism reader* (pp. 242–51). New York: Routledge.

Lin, A. & Luk, J. (2002). Beyond progressive liberalism and cultural relativism: Towards critical postmodernist, sociohistorically situated perspectives in classroom studies. *Canadian Modern Language Review* 59, 1, 97–124.

Maher, F. & Tetrault, M. K. (2001). *The feminist classroom*, 2nd edn. New York: Rowman & Littlefield.

Mayo, P. (2004). *Liberating praxis: Paulo Freire's legacy for radical education and politics*. New York: Praeger.

McLaren, P. (1994). *Life in schools: An introduction to critical pedagogy in the foundations of education*, 2nd edn. New York: Longman.

McMahill, C. (1997). Communities of resistance: A case study of two feminist English classes in Japan. *TESOL Quarterly* 31, 3, 612–21.

Miller, R. (2002). *Free schools, free people*. Albany, NY: SUNY Press.

Morgan, B. (1998). *The ESL classroom: Teaching, critical practice and community development*. Toronto: University of Toronto Press.

Moriarty, P. & Wallerstein, N. (1979). Student/teacher/learner, a Freire approach to ABE/ESL. *Adult Literacy and Basic Education* 3, 3, 193–200.

Moriarty, P. & Wallerstein, N. (1980). By teaching we can learn, a Freire process for teachers. *California Journal of Teacher Education* 7, 1, 39–46.

Neill, A. S. (1960/1993). *Summerhill School: a new view of childhood* . New York: St. Martin's Press.

Nelson, C. (1999). Sexual identities in ESL: Queer theory and classroom inquiry. *TESOL Quarterly* 33, 3, 371–91.

Neumann, R. (2003). *Sixties legacy: A history of the public alternative schools movement, 1967–2001*. New York: Peter Lang.

Ohara, Y., Saft, S., & Crookes, G. (2001). Towards feminist critical pedagogy in a beginning Japanese as a foreign language class. *Japanese Language and Literature* 35, 2, 105–33.

Osborn, T. (2000). *Critical reflection and the foreign language classroom*. Westport, CT: Bergin & Garvey.

Pennycook, A. (2001). *Critical applied linguistics: A critical introduction*. Mahwah, NJ: Lawrence Erlbaum.

Pinar, W. (ed.) (1998). *Queer theory in education*. Mahwah, NJ: Lawrence Erlbaum.

Purcell-Gates, V. & Waterman, R. (2000). *Now we read, we see, we speak: Portrait of literacy development in an adult Freirean-based class*. Mahwah, NJ: Lawrence Erlbaum.

Reagan, T. G. & Osborn, T. A. (1998). Power, authority, and domination in foreign language education. *Educational Foundations* 12, 45–62

Reagan, T. G. & Osborn, T. A. (2002). *The foreign language educator in society: Toward a critical pedagogy*. Mahwah, NJ: Lawrence Erlbaum.

Rofes, E. & Stulberg, L. M. (eds.) (2005). *The emancipatory promise of charter schools: Toward a progressive politics of school choice.* Albany, NY: SUNY Press.

Shin, H. & Crookes, G. (2005a). Indigenous critical traditions for TEFL? A historical and comparative perspective in the case of Korea. *Critical Inquiry in Language Studies* 2, 2, 95–112.

Shin, H. & Crookes, G. (2005b). Exploring the possibilities for EFL critical pedagogy in Korea: A two-part case study. *Critical Inquiry in Language Studies* 2, 2, 112–38.

Shor, I. (1992). *Empowering education: Critical teaching for social change.* Chicago, IL: University of Chicago Press.

Shor, I. & Freire, P. (1987). *A pedagogy for liberation: Dialogues on transforming education.* South Hadley, MA: Bergin & Garvey.

Shotton, J. (1992). Libertarian education and state schooling in England, 1918–90. *Educational Review* 44, 1, 81–91.

Shrewsbury, C. (1993). What is feminist pedagogy? *Womens' Studies Quarterly* 21, 8–16.

Siegel, M. & Okamoto, S. (2003). Towards reconceptualizing the teaching and learning of gendered speech styles in Japanese as a Foreign Language. *Japanese Language and Literature* 37, 1, 49–66.

Small, R. (2005). *Marx and education.* Aldershot, UK: Ashgate.

Smith, M. P. (1983). *The libertarians and education.* London: George Allen & Unwin.

Spring, J. (1975). *A primer of libertarian education.* New York: Free Life Editions.

Spring, J. (1994). *Wheels in the head: Educational philosophies of authority, freedom, and culture from Socrates to Paulo Freire.* NewYork: McGraw-Hill.

Taylor, P. V. (1993). *The texts of Paulo Freire.* Buckingham, UK: Open University Press.

Tetrault, M. K. (2004). Classrooms for diversity: Rethinking curriculum and pedagogy. In J. A. Banks & C. A. McGee Banks (eds.), *Multicultural education: Issues and perspectives* (5th edn., pp. 164–85). New York: John Wiley/Jossey-Bass.

Tolstoy, L. (1967). *Tolstoy on education*, translated by L. Wiener. Chicago: University of Chicago Press.

Vandrick, S. (1994). Feminist pedagogy and ESL. *College English* 4, 2, 69–92.

Vandrick, S. (1998). In T. Smoke (ed.), *Adult ESL: Politics, pedagogy, and participation in classroom and community programs* (pp. 73–88). Mahwah, NJ: Lawrence Erlbaum.

Wallerstein, N. (1983a). *Language and culture in conflict: Problem-posing in the ESL classroom.* Reading, MA: Addison-Wesley.

Wallerstein, N. (1983b). Problem posing can help students learn: from refugee camps to resettlement country classrooms. *TESOL Newsletter* 17, 5, 1–2, 5.

Wallerstein, N. (1983c). Teaching approach of Paulo Freire. In J. Oller & R. Amato (eds.), *Methods that work* (pp. 190–204). Rowley, MA: Newbury Press.

Zack, N. (2005). *Inclusive feminism: A third wave theory of women's commonality.* New York: Rowman & Littlefield.

FURTHER READING

Norton, B. & Toohey, K. (2004). *Critical pedagogies and language learning.* Cambridge: Cambridge University Press.

32 Diagnostic Feedback in Language Assessment

ANTONY JOHN KUNNAN AND EUNICE EUNHEE JANG

Introduction

In this chapter, we discuss the role of diagnostic feedback in language assessments. In the traditional way of examining diagnostic feedback, a narrow scope test specifically designed for diagnosis was considered necessary to provide such feedback. Such tests are rare because the attention of most language test development and research has been on proficiency and achievement testing and, as a result, the concept of diagnostic feedback has not been developed sufficiently. In a forward-looking approach, it is argued that diagnostic feedback can be incorporated into achievement and proficiency testing. Although this has happened somewhat unsystematically in the last decade, language testing researchers have recently shown that it is a feasible approach. The chapter provides examples of this approach and then concludes with the challenges that face researchers interested in diagnostic feedback.

Definitions and Scope

Over forty years ago, Davies (1968) presented traditional definitions of the purposes of tests as follows:

> we speak of Proficiency (Aptitude) *for* or *in* something to do something else; we speak of Achievement (Attainment) *in* something by itself; and we speak of Diagnosis *of* something. Thus in this usage Proficiency (Aptitude) tests the student's present ability for future learning. Achievement (Attainment) tests his present knowledge as indicative of past learning, and Diagnosis is the teacher's concern of what has gone wrong. (pp. 6–7)

Davies' own usage was slightly different: "it distinguishes four uses combining Achievement and Attainment, in terms of time and subject matter symbolized by X (p. 7). He showed the purposes of tests as follows:

Achievement: $\leftarrow X$
Proficiency: $\leftarrow X \rightarrow Y$
Aptitude: $(X) \rightarrow X$
Diagnosis: $\leftarrow X \rightarrow$

In this view, achievement tests are concerned with the past, proficiency tests are concerned with past and the future, and aptitude tests look forward. Diagnostic tests, on the other hand, are concerned with the past in terms of performance and the future in terms of providing information to instructors, students, and parents regarding the strengths and weaknesses of the students' performance.

In contrast, Bachman (1990) argued that language tests can be classified according to the type of decision to be made. He stated "we can speak of *selection*, *entrance*, and *readiness* tests with regard to admission decisions, *placement* and *diagnostic* tests with regard to identifying the appropriate instructional level or specific areas in which instruction is needed, and *progress*, *achievement*, *attainment*, or *mastery* tests with respect to decisions about how individuals should proceed through the program, or how well they are attaining the program's objectives" (p. 70). Bachman further argued that

> Virtually any language test has some potential for providing diagnostic information. A placement test can be regarded as a broad-band diagnostic test in that it distinguishes relatively weak from relatively strong students so that they can provide learning activities at the appropriate level. Similarly, a readiness test differentiates students who are ready for instruction from those who are not . . . When we speak of a diagnostic test, however, we are generally referring to a test that has been designed and developed specifically to provide detailed information about the specific content domains that are covered in a given program . . . Thus, diagnostic tests may be either theory or syllabus-based. (p. 60)

Alderson, Clapham, and Wall (1995) stated their position as follows:

> Diagnostic tests seek to identify those areas in which a student needs further help. These tests can be fairly general, and show, for example, whether a student needs particular help with one of the four main language skills; or they can be more specific, seeking perhaps to identify weaknesses in a student's use of grammar . . . However, achievement and proficiency tests are themselves frequently used, albeit unsystematically, for diagnostic purposes. (p. 12)

More than a decade has passed since these statements, but they are arguably still accurate, as there are very few specifically created diagnostic tests in second or foreign language testing. However, recently there have been a few attempts to provide some diagnostic information from achievement and proficiency tests.

Large-Scale Assessment Context

A large-scale assessment context is typically aimed at serving summative purposes, for example, evaluating what students have learned and whether they are ready to move to the next level of education. When assessment is used for this particular purpose, assessors concentrate on the linkage between the curricular detail in the target domain being taught and tested items in a test. This approach also conforms to the *Standards for educational and psychological testing* (AERA, APA, & NCME, 1999) guidelines:

> When a test is used as an indicator of achievement in an instructional domain or with respect to specified curriculum standards, evidence of the extent to which the test samples the range of knowledge and elicits the processes reflected in the target domain should be provided. Both tested and target domain should be described in sufficient detail so their relationship can be evaluated. The analyses should make explicit those aspects of the target domain that the test represents as well as those aspects that it fails to represent. (p. 145)

In practice, however, achievement and proficiency tests have been used for many purposes; and hence, the linkage between test items and curriculum standards is often unclear. For example, in the school context, achievement tests are used to monitor student progress through standardized test administration, scoring, and reporting, to collect uniform baseline information from a large group of students across geographical areas, and to provide rough diagnostic information to all stakeholders (teachers, students, parents, school administrators). Proficiency tests are used in different ways, such as in college and university level entrance examinations to provide a ranking among students (as only the high-scoring are rewarded with admission to colleges and universities). Often, these same tests are used to measure student achievement across geographical regions and to evaluate language programs for government or private accountability purposes. As these purposes are varied, the links between test items and curriculum standards is achieved by focusing on test reliability and validity of test score interpretations, in addition to uniformity of testing practice (including test administration, test time, test forms, test raters, scoring, reporting, and score interpretation) across geographical regions. While this focus on reliability, validity, and uniformity has served large-scale achievement testing reasonably well, there have been criticisms regarding the lack of useful diagnostic feedback to test takers and test score users (including teachers, parents and others) (Kunnan, 2004, 2008).

This approach to traditional testing has also resulted in focusing on quantitative assessments of an individual student's general language ability relative to other students in the normative group (Brown & Hudson, 2002; Glaser, 1994). Such norm-referenced interpretations of test results have been criticized for their lack of pedagogically meaningful information with which teachers and students can better understand the meaning of test scores and students' strengths and weaknesses in a specific academic domain, and for the lack of constructive guidance for instructional remediation. Further, while considerable theoretical and practical efforts have been made in advancing the concept of communicative language, authentic materials, and improved scoring into assessments (for example, Bachman & Palmer, 1996; Purpura, 2004), the use of aggregated test scores as an overall measure of language proficiency or achievement levels, with little or no diagnostic feedback, has made such efforts less profitable to test score users, such as principals, teachers, parents, and students.

There have been a number of exhortations and suggestions to increase the usefulness of test results from researchers. Spolsky (1990) argued that it is the tester's moral responsibility to ensure interpretability of test information, as well as accuracy. He suggested the creation of "profiles" that show multiple skills tested in more than one way as a more valuable scoring reporting method. Shohamy (1992) proposed a collaborative diagnostic feedback model in which tests provide useful information for teaching and learning advancement. Alderson, Clapham, and Wall (1995) provided extensive discussions about various practical issues concerning how to prepare instructionally useful score reports.

In practice, however, the most common and limited diagnostic feedback, if it can be called that, is still the total score for the test, and in some cases, section or paper subscores (such as scores for different skill areas, like listening, speaking, reading, or writing, and/or language components, such as grammar or vocabulary). But large-scale language proficiency tests used for admission to English-medium universities in Australia, Canada, the UK, and the US have recently begun to provide some limited diagnostic feedback, in addition to total and section or paper scores.[1] A brief description of the diagnostic feedback from three well-known tests is provided.

The Test of English as a Foreign Language (TOEFL)

The current TOEFL provides the following information, according to its website:

> Your scores are based on your performance on the questions in the test. You must answer at least one question in each Reading and Listening section, write at least one essay, and complete at least one Speaking task to receive an official score report. For the Internet based test, you will receive four section scores and a total score: Reading (0–30), Listening (0–30), Speaking (0–30), Writing (0–30), and Total Score (0–120). In addition to numeric scores, your examinee score record also includes performance feedback that indicates your performance level and a description of the kinds of tasks that test takers within the reported score range can typically do.

A sample TOEFL Internet-based Test Examinee Score Report (available on the TOEFL website) illustrates how the enhanced performance feedback is provided. In the sample, "typical" performance feedback is provided based on the test taker's scaled scores, which are 17 points for reading, listening, and writing each, and 14 for speaking. The feedback for the reading and listening skills is more general and speaking and writing skills feedback is more detailed, as these are related to task types. Here is an example of a performance descriptor for reading and listening:

> Test takers who score at the low level *typically* "have difficulty identifying the author's purpose, except when that purpose is explicitly stated in the text or easy to infer from the text."

Such reading and listening proficiency descriptors were developed based on a scale-anchoring study (Y. Sawaki, personal communication, April 2007). The scale-anchoring steps included the following: determining several cut points on a scale, mapping items on the scale in terms of difficulty, identifying items that define each ability level, and specifying the abilities and other characteristics of the items that define each level. Proficiency descriptors for speaking and writing skills were developed based on the rubrics and advice from a teacher panel with the help of categories (for example, speaking about familiar topics, about campus situations, and about academic course content) and levels of performance (good, fair, limited, and weak).

The International English Language Testing System (IELTS)

IELTS test takers receive scores on a band scale from 1 to 9 based on their performance on each of the four individual modules (listening, reading, speaking, and writing) which are equally weighted. The overall band score is calculated by taking the mean of the total of the four individual module scores. Band descriptors for writing and speaking have been developed to help stakeholders better understand the level of performance required to attain a particular band score in each of the criterion areas. Samples of a writing task descriptor and a speaking descriptor (available on the IELTS website) illustrate the type of feedback that is provided at each of the band levels.

The Michigan English Language Assessment Battery (MELAB)

MELAB test takers receive score reports based on their performance on composition, listening, grammar, cloze, vocabulary, reading, and an optional speaking test. Reports include scores of performance on the different parts of the MELAB, and these are averaged to produce a final MELAB score. Samples of composition descriptors according to score level and a speaking descriptor (available on the MELAB website) illustrate the type of feedback provided at each of the score levels.

While these examples of diagnostic feedback provide the necessary link between previous instruction and the test, and help test takers interpret their scores and performance, scale-anchoring with descriptors based on group performance at a score level cannot provide specific individualized feedback. Therefore, while this is a major step toward providing feedback to test takers and other stakeholders, the feedback is so "typical" for a group of test takers in a particular score range that its usefulness to individuals is limited. Another approach is to provide a profile score on a scale based on percentile ranks, as determined by positioning an individual score against the norm. But profiling a students' proficiency in this way provides little diagnostic information other than his or her relative position with respect to other test takers on the standardized scale.

Classroom Assessment Context

Classroom-based assessment is aimed at providing teachers with information needed to evaluate students' level of achievement with reference to curricular goals or standards and students with diagnostic feedback regarding their performance. This type of assessment is generally referred to as formative assessment. Teachers can use this information to inform their instruction, evaluate resources, and provide feedback to students to promote their learning; students can use this type of information to understand their strengths and weaknesses. Many formal and informal techniques are used in this type of assessment. A range of test response formats, such as short answer, fill-in-the-blanks, multiple-choice, and alternative performance-based, are widely used to assess student achievement. While traditional multiple-choice response format tests are time-efficient and objective in scoring, they are limited to measuring the knowledge state and comprehension abilities in a discrete manner. Extended production and performance-based assessments are considered to serve our needs to assess students' achievement in the context of language use better, particularly because of the complex nature of second and foreign language processing and production. Examples of performance-based achievement assessment include both oral and written tasks, such as speeches and essays, portfolios, and performance tasks, like drama and role-play. Other observational techniques that are increasingly used to assess learning outcomes in the classroom include teacher's direct observation. This technique could provide information not only about achievement in the cognitive domain, but also about non-cognitive outcomes or changes, such as students' motivation, attitudes, and personal/social development. For example, a teacher's anecdotal records can provide a systematic source of information on second and foreign language development.

Edelenbos and Kubanek-German (2004) provided an argument for language teachers to be equipped with a new concept, "diagnostic competence." Diagnostic competence is "the ability to interpret students' foreign language growth, to skillfully deal with assessment material and to provide students with appropriate help in response to this competence" (2004, p. 260). Based on their research in Germany and the Netherlands, they provided a working definition of a teacher's diagnostic competence in three parts:

(1) diagnostic competence is an attribute of teachers who aim to improve the quality of foreign language growth of their pupils; (2) diagnostic competence can be seen as a combination of pedagogical attitude towards the learner, hermeneutic abilities: seeing, observing, comparing, interpreting, evoking, self-distance, openness; scaffolding learning: as an application of the 'diagnosis'; (3) diagnostic competence precedes assessment. It is what teachers need in order to assess. (p. 277)

Unfortunately, until traditional teacher training programs train new teachers with these capabilities, diagnostic competence will remain a distant goal.

In a related move, the concept of "dynamic assessment" reconfigures the role of teachers to include assessment as part of their responsibilities (Lantolf & Poehner, 2004). Leung (2007) presents the concept of dynamic assessment (DA) as assessment *for* learning (AfL), in contrast to static assessment, which could be characterized mainly as assessment *of* learning:

> In conceptual terms, one of the fundamental differences between static assessment and DA is that the former would seek to measure pre-defined abilities with instruments and activities (tests and tasks) that would require unassisted, and in the main, solo performance, while DA is built on the dynamic interaction between the examiner and the examinee in which the examiner responds to the examinee's difficulties with appropriate support in the form of leading questions, meta-cognitive prompts and other forms of feedback. (p. 260)

Of course, such a move by teachers would need a rethinking of how they would operate in the classroom context. Leung lists four of the ten principles of AfL that are relevant for the reconceptualization of teachers' assessment role (Assessment Reform Group, 2002):

(1) Assessment for learning should be part of effective planning of teaching and learning . . .
(2) Assessment for learning should focus on students' learning . . .
(3) Assessment for learning should be recognised as central to classroom practice . . .
(4) Learners should receive constructive guidance about how to improve . . .

(Leung, 2007, p. 266)

In addition to informal teacher observational techniques, self-assessments are recognized as important tools for assessing student achievement and receiving diagnostic feedback. Self-assessment is aimed at encouraging students to develop critical thinking and meta-awareness of their own language development. In this view, students are acknowledged as the primary critical assessor of their own learning. They are actively engaged in critically assessing their own learning by making sense of information, relating it to their prior knowledge and experience, and using it for planning for new learning. Assessment is not done to or for them, but with and by them (Afflerbach, 2002; Earl & Katz, 2006). Although the merits of self-assessment are obvious, it is not widely used as part of achievement testing in the school context partly because of the difficulties with student underestimation and overestimation of their abilities and partly because school districts have not begun to see these tools as valuable. Therefore, standardized achievement tests designed and developed by testing agencies (most often with no assistance from teachers) continue to be used in the school context.

A new approach that is being used in school contexts is to construct proficiency profiles. This approach determines whether or not a student has performed at "proficient" or non-proficient levels in his/her tests using a cut-off point based on content experts' judgments. Although this method allows for input from teachers and content experts, the standards-setting procedure has been heatedly debated because of its uncertainty in determining cut-off points distinguishing students' mastery levels. Researchers often call this feature of the standard-setting procedure its *Achilles' heel* (Jang & Ryan, 2003; Kane, 2001). As has been well documented, standards-setting involves interpretations of test results and use (Brennan, 2001; Cizek, 2001) and is a value-laden and judgmental activity that inevitably faces problems, such as subjectivity, human biases, and ambiguity. These concerns have reduced the value of diagnostic feedback and have led educational measurement professionals to pay considerable attention to technical procedures for creating defensible standards.

New Approaches

Over the past decade, cognitive skills diagnostic assessment has drawn much attention among educational researchers and practitioners who have faced increasing demands for formative diagnostic feedback through a more fine-grained reporting of examinees' skill mastery profiles (Alderson, 2005; Buck & Tatsuoka, 1998; DiBello, Stout, & Roussos, 1995; Frederiksen et al., 1990; Hartz, 2002; Shohamy, 1992; Tatsuoka, 1983). As there is a growing body of research into the impact of testing on teachers, learners, educational curriculum, and society (Cheng, Watanabe, & Curtis, 2005; Schwandt & Jang, 2004; Shohamy, 2001), testing consumers have been calling for more descriptive test information that allows meaningful interpretations and fair use of test results for improving instructional design and guiding students' learning.

While it may be ideal to design a diagnostic assessment instrument to be used specifically for the purpose of diagnosis, many researchers working in large-scale educational assessments originally designed for purposes other than diagnosis are interested in examining whether large-scale assessments can provide useful diagnostic feedback for test takers and test-score users. In addition, the quality of the feedback is important. If diagnostic feedback provided to students is not dependable; its practical usefulness is cast into question. Further, students' perception and the actions taken to close the gap between test scores and their abilities and their desired learning goals must be meaningful. Therefore, feedback provided to students needs to be sufficiently diagnostic in order to allow learners to reset their own learning goals by breaking down goals into manageable tasks (Black & Wiliam, 1998; Stiggins, 2001). But, in planning to make feedback more diagnostic and dependable, we need to be aware that not all feedback has positive effects on learning and self-esteem (Dweck, 1986). Differential effects of diagnostic feedback can be caused by students' different ability levels, their learning attitudes, goal orientation, or learning contexts. Usefulness of feedback can also vary depending on focus on either strengths or shortcomings or both and either evaluative or descriptive purpose (Tunstall & Gipps, 1996). Thus, diagnostic feedback needs to consider learners' beliefs about learning goals, about their own ability, and cognitive and metacognitive learning styles (Kunnan, 1995). It needs to further consider the link between assessment tasks and learners' cognitive skills in light of the kinds of inferences made for diagnosing learners' current knowledge/skill mastery state and actions taken for facilitating the learning progress.

In the field of educational measurement, various cognitive models have been proposed to measure a test taker's mastery level of a set of skills from an administered test (see DiBello, Roussos, & Stout, 2007; Embretson, 1991; Hartz & Roussos, 2005; Leighton & Gierl, 2007; Tatsuoka, 1983, for details). Several of these models have been applied to second language assessment in reading and listening. For example, the Rule Space Model was applied to a short-answer listening comprehension test administered to Japanese college students (Buck & Tatsuoka, 1998), to TOEFL reading subtests (Kasai, 1997), and was recently used to provide *"Score Report Plus"* to students who took the Preliminary SAT and National Merit Scholarship Qualifying Test.

Jang's (2005) diagnosis report card called *DiagnOsis* is another example of the cognitive diagnostic assessment approach. Diagnostic feedback contained in *DiagnOsis* consists of four major components: Review your answers; Improve your skills; How to interpret skill mastery; and Skill descriptors (see Appendix). The most interesting component of *DiagnOsis* is skill mastery standing expressed in a bar graph. It shows an individual student's strengths and weaknesses in assessed subskills. Figure 32.1 shows Yoshi's (pseudonym) skill mastery probabilities in nine reading skills which were estimated through application of the Fusion Model (Hartz & Roussos, 2005) to large-scale L2 reading comprehension test data. Skill mastery probability for each skill ranges from 0 to 1, and the gray area in the graph is an indifference region. When a learner's skill mastery probability falls in the indifference region, mastery standing is undetermined. Otherwise, skill mastery status is determined as either a master or a non-master

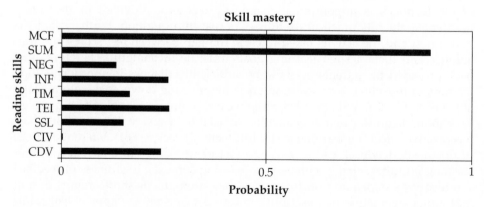

Figure 32.1   Skill mastery probabilities in nine reading skills

of a specific skill. Detailed descriptions of the subskills are presented with test items rank-ordered by the magnitude of diagnostic information in the full report.

Jang (2005) also shows how self-assessment can be combined with psychometric diagnostic information for student skill profiling through a study of five cases selected from 1,372 test takers. The five cases shared similar observed scores ranging from 24 to 26 out of a total of 41 points. However, their estimated skill mastery probabilities varied to great extent. She also considered test takers' background information, such as gender, first language, reason for taking the test, and self-ratings of reading comprehension skills. Table 32.1 shows a summary of the information collected for skill profiling. The analysis of the five cases clearly shows that learners' self-assessment is in agreement with statistically estimated skill mastery probabilities, although Case 3 shows disagreement.

Other examples of self-assessment as learning and assessment tools include DIALANG, which is a computer-delivered diagnostic language assessment system (Alderson & Huhta, 2005). Users can take tests of reading, listening, writing, vocabulary, and structures in 14 different European languages. Test results are reported on the six levels of descriptors of communicative activities included in the Common European Framework of Reference (CEFR; Council of Europe, 2001). Alderson and Huhta (2005) claim that DIALANG is the first large-scale language assessment system that aims at diagnosing rather than selecting or certifying language proficiency. Notable is its capacity to provide learners with responsibility for the assessment process through self-assessment. Descriptors of communicative activities from the CEFR are used for self-assessment using "can-do" statements, as well as for diagnostic reporting scales. Learners are provided with the opportunity to review any mismatch between their test results and their self-assessed CEFR levels. DIALANG offers a variety of feedback. It reports users' performance levels, along with advice and awareness-raising information aimed at helping them to take action for further language learning. For example, feedback in "Check your answers" can be used to review a user's answers at both the item and subskill levels (see, Alderson & Huhta, 2005, for a more comprehensive description of DIALANG).

Another instance of the use of self-assessment is found in the European Language Portfolio (ELP). A portfolio is a collection of a student's work, usually selected by the student from a larger corpus and often with a reflective note on the selected work. Self-assessment is an essential component of the ELP, which consists of three components: Language Passport, Language Biography, and Dossier (Little, 2005). The Language Passport provides an overview of the learner's language proficiency in terms of CEF-referenced skills and any significant language learning experiences. The Language Biography emphasizes the learner's involvement in planning, self-assessing and monitoring his or her own learning process. Learners are encouraged to state what they can do in one or more than one language. The Dossier allows learners to document all materials related to achievement and experiences appearing in the Language Biography or Language Passport. The overarching goal of the ELP is to make the language learning process more transparent to students and help them develop the ability to self-assess and monitor their own learning.

Table 32.1 Summary of skill profiles (from Jang 2005)

Cases	Reason	Self-assessment of reading	Mastered skills
1 (Female, Venezuela)	To study abroad (undergraduate)	"Reading is not as good as other skills." "I have some difficulty taking courses taught in English due to problems with reading."	None
2 (Male, Indonesia)	To study abroad (graduate)	"Reading is not as good as other skills." "I am very good at understanding graphs and charts in academic text."	1 skill (Summarizing)
3 (Female, Columbia)	To study abroad (undergraduate)	"I have no difficulty with reading in English." "Reading is my best skill."	2 skills (Vocabulary, Summarizing)
4 (Female, Vietnam)	To demonstrate English proficiency to company	"Reading is my best skill." "My weak areas are understanding charts and graphs in academic text and how to relate different ideas to each other."	7 skills (Vocabulary; Comprehension of explicit and implicit textual information; Summarizing; Contrasting ideas, etc.)
5 (Female, Lebanon)	To demonstrate English proficiency to company	"Reading is my best skill." "I am good at vocabulary and understanding relative importance of ideas."	8 skills (Comprehension of explicit and implicit textual information; Negation; Inferencing; Summarizing; Contrasting ideas, etc.)

Challenges

Skills diagnosis and feedback raise some critical challenges concerning pedagogical, ideological, and technological barriers (Linn, 1986, 1990). From the pedagogical perspective, while the behaviorist view of learning is still widely held in much of current large-scale assessment practice, contemporary perspectives on learning and knowledge acquisition agree that learning takes place through interaction of an individual's mind with physical, social, and cultural contexts (Greeno, Collins, & Resnick, 1996). Considering different beliefs about how learning takes place and which instructional approach best suits learning, cognitive skills diagnostic assessment needs to be discussed in terms of its theoretical/philosophical assumptions about the learning process and the roles of assessment in broader educational contexts.

From the point of view of language assessment, there are specific substantive challenges. Alderson (2006) argued, based on his experience with the "Can-do" statements used in the Common European Framework of Reference for Languages, (CEFR or CEF) and the DIALANG project, that there "are virtually no significant differences across CEFR levels in terms of difficulty of the diagnostic subskills that DIALANG endeavoured to test" (p. 4). He elaborated further

> Learners who achieved scores indicating they were at higher CEF levels showed weaknesses in all three sub-skills. It appears not to be the case that as one's reading ability develops, this is associated with an increasing ability to make inferences, for example, rather than to understand the main idea . . . Similar conclusions were reached with respect to listening. Even low-level learners are able to answer some questions that test inferencing abilities, as well as items testing the ability to understand main ideas. (p. 4)

Alderson (2006) concluded that in order to diagnose language development,

> we will need to have a much better understanding of foreign language ability. If we can then incorporate such understandings into assessment and make them useful to learners through the provision of meaningful and useful feedback and follow-up, then diagnosis will truly have become the interface between learning and assessment. (p. 15)

Further, while cognitive diagnostic assessment is aimed at providing formative diagnostic feedback for advancing teaching and learning, we need to be aware of any unintended consequences of the use of skills diagnostic information. Collins (1990) warns us that unintended menacing side-effects might occur in the use of skills diagnostic information in a high-stakes testing situation. There is ample evidence that assessment merely serving as an accountability system makes teachers teach to tests and makes students pay attention to tested subjects or topics.

In addition, most currently available diagnosis models do not have much capacity to allow for various test formats, such as constructed response items. As testing technology drives education, the use of skills diagnostic information in standardized high-stakes testing situations might limit current educational measurement to a narrow behaviorist array of discrete skills. Thus, the use of standardized tests for diagnostic purposes without a strong alignment with the curriculum may create psychometric challenges and concerns about different principles guiding the construction of tests and, also, concerns regarding test washback.

Conclusion

The main vision in using diagnostic assessment in large-scale and classroom assessment contexts is to help assess students' abilities and understanding with feedback not only about what students know, but about how they think and learn in content domains, to help teachers have resources of a variety of research-based classroom assessment tools, to help recognize and support students' strengths and create more optimal learning environments, and to help students become critical evaluators of their own learning (Pellegrino, Chudowsky, & Glaser, 2001). In order to bring diagnostic assessment to full fruition, it is hoped that the integration of technology into assessment will enable teachers and students to share learning goals, design individualized assessments, and engage in real-life problem-solving tasks. Also, it is hoped that the reconceptualization of educational assessment and measurement may encourage students to show evidence of their understanding in many different ways, not only by performing on traditional tests, but also by writing essays, presenting projects, transforming their new knowledge into alternative expressions such as drama, poetry, or visual arts. Thus, collaboration among the various educational constituencies by informing each other using their own expertise and experience and sharing responsibilities is the key to successful integration of three essential components: curriculum, instruction, and assessment.

The main limitations that need to be overcome so that diagnostic feedback is routinely possible include the following: continued use of the traditional reliability-obsessed, deficiency-oriented approach to diagnosis instead of broadening assessment into performance assessment; better understanding of language ability and language development to be incorporated into a diagnostic feedback model; and the critical need to expand the total and subscore-based reporting with meaningful diagnostic feedback. When these limitations are fully overcome, diagnostic feedback can routinely be offered in all assessments, not just in so called diagnostic tests, and diagnostic feedback can reach its full potential of integrating assessment with teaching, learning, and the curriculum.

NOTE

1   Scale points and score descriptors for holistic and analytical scales were available for extended discourse tests such as writing and speaking (examples, the Test of Written English and the Test of Spoken English) in the 1980s and 1990s.

REFERENCES

Afflerbach, P. (2002). Teaching reading self-assessment strategies. In C. C. Block & M. Pressley (eds.), *Comprehension instruction: Research-based best practices* (pp. 96–111). New York: Guilford.

Alderson, J. C. (2005). *Diagnosing foreign language proficiency: The interface between learning and assessment*. London: Continuum.

Alderson, J. C. (2006). The challenge of (diagnostic) testing: Do we know what we are measuring? Paper presented at the Language Testing Research Colloquium, Ottawa.

Alderson, J. C., Clapham, C., & Wall, D. (1995). *Language testing construction and evaluation*. Cambridge: Cambridge University Press.

Alderson, J. C. & Huhta, A. (2005). The development of a suite of computer-based diagnostic tests based on the Common European Framework. *Language Testing* 22, 301–20.

AERA, APA, & NCME (1999). *Standards for educational and psychological testing*. Washington, DC: American Educational Research Association, American Psychological Asssociation, National Council on Measurement in Education.

Assessment Reform Group (2002). *Testing, motivation and learning*. School of Education: University of Cambridge.

Bachman, L. (1990). *Fundamental considerations in language testing*. Oxford: Oxford University Press.

Bachman, L. & Palmer, A. (1996). *Language assessment in practice*. Oxford: Oxford University Press.

Black, P. J. & Wiliam, D. (1998). Assessment and classroom learning. *Assessment in Education* 5, 7–74.

Brennan, R. L. (2001). Some problems, pitfalls, and paradoxes in educational measurement. *Educational Measurement: Issues and Practice* 20, 4, 6–18.

Brown, J. D. & Hudson, T. (2002). *Criterion-referenced language testing*. Cambridge: Cambridge University Press.

Buck, G. & Tatsuoka, K. (1998). Application of the rule-space procedure to language testing: Examining attributes of a free response listening test. *Language Testing* 15, 119–57.

Cheng, L., Watanabe, Y., & Curtis, A. (eds.) (2005). *Washback in language testing: Research contexts and methods*. Mahwah, NJ: Lawrence Erlbaum.

Cizek, G. (ed.) (2001). *Setting performance standards*. Mahwah, NJ: Lawrence Erlbaum.

Collins, A. (1990). Reformulating testing to measure learning and thinking. In N. Frederiksen, R. Glaser, A. Lesgold, & M. Shafto (eds.), *Diagnostic monitoring of skill and knowledge acquisition* (pp. 75–88). Mahwah, NJ: Lawrence Erlbaum.

Council of Europe (2001). *Common European Framework of Reference for languages: Learning, teaching, assessment*. Cambridge: Cambridge University Press.

Davidson, F. & Henning, G. (1985). A self-rating scale of English difficulty. *Language Testing* 2, 164–78.

Davies, A. (1968). *Language testing symposium: A psycholinguistic perspective.* London: Oxford University Press.

DiBello, L. V., Roussos, L. A., & Stout, W. (2007). Review of cognitive diagnostic assessment and a summary of psychometric models. In C. R. Rao & S. Sinharay (eds.), *Handbook of statistics, Vol. 26: Psychometrics* (pp. 45–79). Amsterdam: Elsevier Science.

DiBello, L. V., Stout, W. F., & Roussos, L. A. (1995). Unified cognitive/psychometric diagnostic assessment likelihood-based classification techniques. In N. Frederiksen, R. Glaser, A. Lesgold, & M. Shafto (eds.), *Diagnostic monitoring of skill and knowledge acquisition* (pp. 361–90). Mahwah, NJ: Lawrence Erlbaum.

Dweck, C. S. (1986). Motivational processes affecting learning. *American Psychologist* 41, 1040–8.

Earl, L. & Katz, S. (2006). *Rethinking classroom assessment with purpose in mind.* Winnipeg, Manitoba: Western Northern Canadian Protocol.

Edelenbos, P. & Kubanek-German, A. (2004). Teacher assessment: the concept of "diagnostic competence." *Language Testing* 21, 259–83.

Embretson, S. (1991). A multidimensional latent trait model for measuring learning and change. *Psychometrika* 37, 359–74.

Frederiksen, N., Glaser, R., Lesgold, A., & Shafto, M. (eds.) (1990). *Diagnostic monitoring of skill and knowledge acquisition.* Mahwah, NJ: Lawrence Erlbaum.

Glaser, R. (1994). Instructional technology and the measurement of learning outcomes: Some questions. *Educational Measurement: Issues and Practice* 13, 6–8.

Greeno, J. G., Collins, A. M., & Resnick, L. B. (1996). Cognition and learning. In D. C. Berliner & R. C. Calfee (eds.), *Handbook of educational psychology* (pp. 15–45). New York: Macmillan.

Hartz, S. M. (2002). A Bayesian framework for the unified model for assessing cognitive abilities: Blending theory with practicality. Unpublished doctoral dissertation, University of Illinois at Urbana-Champaign.

Hartz, S. M. & Roussos, L. A. (2005). *The Fusion Model for skills diagnosis: Blending theory with practice,* ETS Research Report. Princeton, NJ: Educational Testing Service.

Jang, E. E. (2005). A validity narrative: Effects of reading skills diagnosis on teaching and learning in the context of NG TOEFL. Unpublished doctoral dissertation, University of Illinois at Urbana-Champaign.

Jang, E. E. & Ryan, K. (2003). Bridging gaps among curriculum, teaching and learning, and assessment [Review of the book *Large-scale assessment: Dimensions, dilemmas, and policy,* E. Kifer, 2001]. *Journal of Curriculum Studies* 35, 499–512.

Kane, M. J. (1992). An argument-based approach to validity. *Psychological Bulletin* 112, 527–35.

Kane, M. J. (2001). So much remains the same: Conception and status of validation in setting standards. In G. J. Cizek (ed.), *Setting performance standards* (pp. 53–88). London: Lawrence Erlbaum.

Kasai, M. (1997). Application of the rule space model to the reading comprehension section of the test of English as a foreign language (TOEFL). Unpublished doctoral dissertation. University of Illinois, Urbana Champaign.

Kunnan, A. J. (1995). *Test taker characteristics and test performance: A structural modeling study.* Cambridge: Cambridge University Press.

Kunnan, A. J. (2004). Test fairness. In M. Milanovic & C. Weir (eds.), *European Year of Languages Conference Papers, Barcelona* (pp. 27–48). Cambridge: Cambridge University Press.

Kunnan, A. J. (2008). Towards a model of test evaluation: Using the Test Fairness and Wider Context frameworks. In L. Taylor & C. Weir (eds.), *Multilingualism and Assessment: Achieving transparency, assuring quality, sustaining diversity*, (papers from the ALTE Berlin Conference, May 2005, pp. 229–51). Cambridge: Cambridge University Press.

Lantolf, J. P. & Poehner, M. E. (2004). Dynamic assessment: Bringing the past into the future, *Journal of Applied Linguistics* 1, 49–74.

Leighton, J. P. & Gierl, M. J. (eds.) (2007). *Cognitive diagnostic assessment for education: Theory and practices.* Cambridge: Cambridge University Press.

Leung, C. (2007). Dynamic Assessment: Assessment as teaching? *Language Assessment Quarterly* 4, 257–78.

Linn, R. L. (1986). Barriers to new test design. In E. E. Freeman (ed.), *Proceedings of the 1985 ETS Invitational Conference* (pp. 69–79). Princeton, NJ: Educational Testing Service.

Linn, R. L. (1990). Diagnostic testing. In N. Frederiksen, R. Glaser, A. Lesgold, & M. Shafto (eds.), *Diagnostic monitoring of skill and knowledge acquisition* (pp. 489–98). Mahwah, NJ: Lawrence Erlbaum.

Little, D. (2005). The Common European Framework and the European Language Portfolio: Involving learners and their judgements in the assessment process. *Language Testing* 22, 321–36.

McMillan, J. H. (2003). Understanding and improving teachers' classroom assessment decision-making: Implications for theory and practice. *Educational Measurement: Issues and Practice* 22, 34–43.

Nicols, P. D., Chipman, S. F., & Brennan, R. L. (eds.) (1995). *Cognitively diagnostic assessment.* Mahwah, NJ: Lawrence Erlbaum.

Oscarson, M. (1989). Self-assessment of language proficiency: Rationale and applications. *Language Testing* 6, 1–13.

Pellegrino, J. W., Chudowsky, N., & Glaser, R. (2001). *Knowing what students know: The science and design of educational assessment.* Washington, DC: National Academy Press.

Purpura, J. (2004). *Assessing grammar.* Cambridge: Cambridge University Press.

Ross, S. (1998). Self-assessment in second language testing: A meta-analysis and analysis of experiential factors. *Language Testing* 15, 1–20.

Schwandt, T. & Jang, E. E. (2004). Linking validity and ethics in language testing: Insights from the hermeneutic turn in social science. *Studies in Educational Evaluation* 30, 265–80.

Sheehan, K. M. (1997). A tree-based approach to proficiency scaling and diagnostic assessment. *Journal of Educational Measurement* 34, 333–52.

Shohamy, E. (1992). Beyond performance testing: A diagnostic feedback testing model for assessing foreign language learning. *Modern Language Journal* 76, 513–21.

Shohamy, E. (2001). *The power of tests: A critical perspective of the uses of language tests.* London: Longman/Pearson Education.

Spolsky, B. (1990). Social aspects of individual assessment. In J. de Jong & D. K. Stevenson (eds.), *Individualizing the assessment of language abilities* (pp. 3–15). Clevedon, UK: Multilingual Matters.

Stiggins, R. (2001). The unfulfilled promise of classroom assessment. *Educational Measurement: Issues and Practice* 20, 5–15.

Tatsuoka, K. (1983). Rule space: An approach for dealing with misconceptions based on item response theory. *Journal of Educational Measurement* 20, 345–54.

Tunstall, P. & Gipps, C. (1996). Teacher feedback to young children in formative assessment: A typology. *British Educational Research Journal* 22, 389–404.

DiagnOsis scoring report

Review Your Answers

Question	1	2	3	4	5	6	7	8	9	10	11	12	13	14	15	16	17	18	19	20	21	22	23	24	25	26	27	28	29	30	31	32	33	34	35	36	37
Your Answer	√	√	√	2	√	1	3	2	√	1	√	1	+1	√	2	√	√	√	√	2	√	1	1	4	4,6	3	√	4	√	√	√	√	4	1	3		1,3,6 / 2,5
Correct Answer	2	3	2	3	3	3	1	1	1	4	4	3	2,4,6	2	3	2	1	3	2	3	4	2	4	1	1,5,6	4	2	2	3	3	1	2	2	2	4	1	1,5,6 / 3,7
Difficulty	e	m	e	h	m	m	h	h	m	m	h	h	m	m	e	m	m	m	e	e	e	h	h	m	m	m	e	h	m	e	e	e	m	h	h	m	h

Key
√ Correct
o Omitted
+ Partial points
e = Easy, m = Medium, h = Hard
(Difficulty is based on 1372 students' performance on this test)

Scoring
Correct answers to questions with 4 choices = Plus 1 point
Wrong or omitted answer = No point
Q13 & 25: 3 correct = 2 points, 2 correct = 1 point
Q37: 5 correct = 3 points, 4 correct = 2 points, 3 correct = 1 point

Score
You earned **20** out of maximum **41** points.

10 points from	12	easy questions
8 points from	17	medium questions
2 points from	8	hard questions

How to Interpret Skill Mastery

- Nine primary reading skills are assessed in this reading comprehension test. Please review skill descriptions and example questions attached to this scoring report.
- The graph on the left side shows your probable mastery standing of each skill.
- The grey region indicates that your probable mastery standing cannot be determined.
- There may be some measurement error associated with the classification.
- This diagnostic information can be more useful when used in combination with your teacher's and your own evaluation of your reading skills.

Improve Your Skills

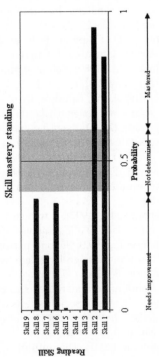

Skill mastery standing

Reading Skill: Skill 9, Skill 8, Skill 7, Skill 6, Skill 5, Skill 4, Skill 3, Skill 2, Skill 1

Probability: 0 — 0.5 — 1

Needs improvement ◄► Not determined ◄► Mastered

Figure 32.2a   *DiagnOsis* scoring report card

Primary Skill Descriptions and Example Questions

	Skill Descriptions	Example Questions
	Skill 1: Deduce word meaning from context Deducing the meaning of a word or a phrase by searching and analyzing text and by using contextual clues in the text.	33, 14, 32, 4, 3, 11
	Skill 2: Determine word meaning out of context Determine word meaning out of context with recourse to background knowledge	9, 27, 10, 29, 19, 21, 7
	Skill 3: Comprehend text through syntactic and semantic links Comprehend relations between s parts of text through lexical and grammatical cohesion devices within and across successive sentences without logical problems	3, 26, 12, 36, 4, 2, 22, 33, 24
	Skill 4: Comprehension of text-explicit information Read quickly across sentences within a paragraph and comprehend literal meaning of explicitly stated information.	22, 18, 30, 17, 8, 24, 36, 20, 12, 25, 14
	Skill 5: Comprehend text-implicit information at global level Read selectively a paragraph or across paragraphs to recognize salient ideas paraphrased based on implicit information in text.	6, 34, 26, 4, 5, 35
	Skill 6: Infer major arguments or a writer's purpose Skim through paragraphs and make propositional inferences about arguments or a writer's purpose with recourse to implicitly stated information or prior knowledge	31, 16, 23, 15, 28, 2, 11, 7, 32
	Skill 7: Comprehend negatively stated information Read carefully or expeditiously to locate relevant information in text and to determine which information is true or not true.	22, 7, 28, 5
	Skill 8: Summarize major ideas from minor details Analyze and evaluate relative importance of information in the text by distinguishing major ideas from supporting details.	13, 5, 17, 25, 20
	Skill 9: Determine contrasting ideas through diagrammatic display Recognize major contrasts and arguments in the text whose rhetorical structure contains the relationships such as compare/contrast, cause/effect or alternative arguments and map them into mental framework	37, 23, 35

Not all example questions are equally informative in assessing related skills. Questions are listed in the order from most informative to least informative.
indicates that these skills are weak areas you need to improve. '?' indicates that your mastery is not determined.

Figure 32.2b *DiagnOsis* scoring report card (cont.)

33 Computer-Assisted Teaching and Testing

CAROL A. CHAPELLE

Introduction

Changes in second and foreign language teaching and testing prompted by computer technology cut across domains of language education, including materials development, teaching methodology, classroom research, program evaluation, diffusion of innovation, and teacher education. The fact that many chapters in this handbook touch on technology-related issues reflects the integration of computer technology, which is used for construction of innovative learning and assessment tasks that provide opportunities for learners to engage with the target language and target language speakers within and beyond the classroom. Such tasks are varied and complex, and, therefore, a distinct area of applied linguistics is concerned with computer-assisted second language acquisition (CASLA), including computer-assisted language learning (CALL) and computer-assisted language testing (CALT). Foreign language educators in the United States assert that CALL has not entered the mainstream of practice, but it is a regular topic of professional discussion (Arnold & Ducate, 2006). Moreover, computer technology continues to increase in everyday utility among language learners as uses of communication devices such as blogs, wikies, and iPods are cultural practices that students engage in outside of class (Kern, 2006; Thorne & Payne, 2005), as are technology-delivered high-stakes tests.

If technology is integrated into language education, what remains to be said about computer-assisted teaching and testing? One response is that the complexity of computer applications, communication tools, databases, and hardware requires focused study. In other words, professionals hoping to improve language learning and assessment through technology need to know the options for how, when, and where computer technology is used, as shown in Flowerdew and Brett & Gonzalez-Lloret (both this volume). A second response is that technology creates opportunities for reflection on the development and evaluation of innovation in the profession as a whole. Technology seems to prompt the complacent language educator to become a critical evaluator. Perhaps the attention of the critic has fostered research assessing the difference that technology makes. Such research, in turn, prompts reflection on what the difference entails, and how it can be documented and demonstrated to others in the field. The technology difference is, therefore, a good point of departure for discussion of CALL and CALT. In both areas, quantifying difference has been seen as limiting by those attempting to develop innovative technologies, and, therefore, both the sections on teaching and testing describe other perspectives that have helped researchers in applied linguistics and technology to explore the potentials of technology.

Language Teaching

The journals publishing on technology and language learning reveal a variety of types of papers with a range of objectives (Levy & Stockwell, 2006), but readers who are not working in CALL are typically most interested in research that demonstrates what CALL can do for language learning. In fact, many readers interested in CALL ask this question: What are the substantive, measurable differences in how well language is taught or assessed when computer technology is used relative to classroom learning?

Quantifying the technology difference

A number of experimental and quasi-experimental studies have been conducted to attempt to demonstrate quantitative effects of the use of technology relative to learning through classroom instruction (Dunkel, 1991). A recent meta-analysis of this work (Zhao, 2003) concluded that it is possible to use and evaluate technology in a manner that produces measurable positive results, but equally important are the caveats that Zhao provides. First, technology refers to a wide variety of tools and practices which are configured in many different ways across classrooms, as shown in Brett & Gonzales-Lloret and Long (both this volume). When technology can refer to everything from inclusion of a Web tutor for vocabulary to the interface for a completely online course, what does it mean to say that *technology use* results in measurable gains? Second, the effects identified from technology studies need to be interpreted as effects of technology use rather than effects of technology itself. For example, an evaluation of the effects of a French grammar-checking program must actually be interpreted as effects from the use of that program within an overall pedagogy for teaching writing (Burston, 2001). Third, the effects that are measured in any study are the result of more learning and practice than what is done on the computer. Language learning is a complex process requiring multiple instances of exposure, negotiation, and practice. In such a dynamic and multifaceted process, it is difficult to attribute effects of learning something to a specific instructional factor.

These points have been made by those attempting to evaluate CALL for many years (e.g., Pederson, 1987), yet showing effects of instructional treatments is a legitimate challenge of educational research, which devises research designs to do just that. Accordingly, some researchers argue for the value of comparisons between technology and face-to-face classrooms. Comparative studies investigating the outcomes of two real options for teaching, such as how a particular unit will be covered (Allum, 2002) or how a curriculum will be delivered (Chenoweth & Murday, 2003; Scida & Saury, 2006), appear regularly in the technology journals. In these cases it is the real pedagogical options that are of interest, rather than computer technology. In other words, research provides pragmatically useful, context-specific data, rather than attempting to isolate general computer technology effects. In contrast, a meta-analysis attempts to identify effects that can be generalized across a defined set of situations; therefore, it seems that a meta-analysis needs to identify some finer-grained aspects of technology-pedagogy to serve as points of comparison. Norris and Ortega (2006) offer principles and examples of how research synthesis (including meta-analysis) might fruitfully be considered, but ultimately, moving in this direction requires a closer look at motivations for comparisons in technology research. Such comparisons often do not attempt to contrast technology with the classroom.

Comparisons focused on aspects of technology-pedagogy

Because of increased enrollment in Spanish courses in the US, some universities have designed hybrid courses, which would require less instructor time, and, therefore, would potentially save on human resources. Scida and Saury (2006) report on a study in which they compared a hybrid and classroom course in order to convince their colleagues that students would not suffer from less class time if, in addition, they engaged in rote exercises and drills on the computer. The descriptive data of course grades show that the students in the hybrid course performed at least as well or better than those in the face-to-face class. Another study investigated the effect of video on foreign language learning, based on the beliefs that because video offers language learners opportunities to see the dynamics of communication, and because such materials were widely available, it may offer a better and feasible option for listening comprehension (Secules, Herron, & Tomasello, 1992). Nagata (1993, 1995) introduced her studies comparing the effectiveness of different types of feedback as seeking empirical verification for a commonsense assumption: "It seems reasonable to suppose that intelligent CALI [computer-assisted language instruction] is better" (Nagata, 1995, p. 47). In these three cases comparisons were made because of pragmatic concerns or to test commonsense or belief-based practices. In the two latter cases, the hypothesized effects were observed, and in the former, the researchers found what they considered convincing data.

Another motivation for comparisons comes from prior research results. Borrás and Lafayette (1994) begin their report of comparisons between the effects of video with and without subtitles by citing research. Guillory (1998) cited opinions and rationales suggesting the value of textual support for listening, as well as prior research supporting its use. Chun and Plass (1996) introduced their study of the effects of multimedia annotations on vocabulary acquisition by discussing research that had investigated incidental learning of vocabulary, effects of online dictionaries, and look-up behavior. Their subsequent research adopted a cognitive theory of why and how pictorial and written verbal support help (Plass et al., 1998; Jones & Plass, 2002). Results provided evidence for the hypothesized value of multimodal input. Yoshii and Flaitz (2002) continued this line of research, using an experimental design with 150 ESL learners. This quantitative study, with a pre-test, random assignment into groups, and multiple forms of immediate and delayed assessments, provided strong evidence for the superior effects of a combination of input over a single form.

Grace (1998) drew on another cognitive learning theory, depth of processing theory, to explain how and why sentence-level translations might be expected to support acquisition. Theoretically, the value of the mental energy required to map the L1 to the L2 is hypothesized to be valuable for learning on the basis of work in psychology on the relationship between mental energy and "deep processing." Operationally, the sentence-level translation of input is intended to require mental energy as the reader attempts to map the unknown L2 forms to the L1 help.

These examples of comparison studies in CALL show how researchers have moved beyond *technology* as an explanatory variable. Results can be further interpreted from the perspective of constructs and hypotheses from second language acquisition (Gass, 1997; Long, 1996; Pica, 1994). In studies by Borrás and Lafayette (1994) and by Guillory (1998) the software provided L2 subtitles and key word support which offered learners some input modification through the presentation of input in two modes. In such cases, if learners attempt to comprehend the message of the aural input through listening, and refer to the written text only as needed, this support should modify the aural input and aid comprehension. In the study by Grace (1998), L1 translation and multiple forms of annotations for vocabulary would also be expected to provide modified input, resolve miscomprehension, and prompt noticing. In studies by Chun and Plass (1996), Jones and Plass (2002), and Plass et al. (1998), learners were provided multiple forms of modified input in the form of aural input, translations, images, and video, all of which provide valuable modified input and resolve miscomprehension, as well as prompt noticing and deep processing of input. In the study by Nagata (1995), learners were provided informative feedback that would be expected to prompt their noticing of gaps in their linguistic knowledge and help them to correct their production.

In short, these aspects of instructional design in CALL can be construed as creating opportunities for beneficial interactions, and even a highly structured form of negotiation of meaning, as learners control the input and its various modified forms (Chapelle, 2003). In other words, it is productive to interpret CALL research results in view of how specific technology-pedagogic practices operationalize methodological principles (Doughty & Long, 2003), such as those described in Long (this volume).

Comparison research and SLA

Research motivated by questions about methodological principles has investigated the use of the computer to present conditions for learning in controlled settings (e.g., deGraaff, 1997; DeKeyser, 1995; Doughty, 1991; Robinson, 1996), but recent research appearing in pedagogically oriented journals investigates more open-ended tasks. Frames of reference from second language studies, primarily from cognitive interactionist theory and sociocultural theory, are used for designing studies. Table 33.1 summarizes examples, which compare different forms of computer-mediated communication (CMC) and face-to-face conversations. For the most part, this research uses focused discourse analysis to study communication breakdowns and repair moves which may be indicative of instances when learners' attention is directed to language.

The first three studies in Table 33.1 compared conditions for vocabulary learning. De la Fuente (2003) compared oral face-to-face communication with written synchronous CMC, hypothesizing that communication through interactive text would provide opportunities for noticing language and for self-correction not present in oral communication, and accordingly, students engaging in written communication would best learn the vocabulary in the tasks. Smith (2004) compared retention of vocabulary that ESL learners were exposed to in two different conditions of written CMC. In one condition, preemptive input was given, and in the other, learners were exposed to the new vocabulary through negotiated interaction. He found that lexical items that were negotiated were more likely to be retained. Chen, Belkada, and Okamoto (2004) compared the effectiveness of CALL tasks consisting of learner–computer interaction through a computer-delivered dictation and note-taking task and CALL tasks with CMC prompted by the same task content. Overall, results suggest that the written interactions with human interlocutors or the computer are both good for vocabulary learning.

Fernández-Garciá and Martínez-Arbelaiz (2003) compared the amount of negotiation of meaning that took place in oral conversation and through text-based synchronous CMC. Because of learners' familiarity with the topics and the open-endedness of the tasks, communication breakdowns were rare, and, therefore, so was negotiation of meaning, particularly among learners. In communication with native speakers of Spanish, the communication breakdowns and negotiation that occurred were primarily during the oral communication. Jepson (2005) compared L2 learners' repair moves in synchronous text chat rooms and in voice chat rooms on the Internet with no specific task set for them. Under these circumstances, voice chat generated more repair moves and moves associated with negative feedback consisting of recasts, explicit feedback, and questions, as well as uptake consisting of incorporations of feedback and self-corrections.

Pellettieri's (2000) ground-breaking study of Spanish learners' text chat conversations found that learners negotiated both form and meaning, that learners self corrected and corrected each other, and that task type affected the quality of negotiation. Following from this work, Fernández-Garciá and Martínez-Arbelaiz (2002) investigated whether or not negotiation of meaning would take place in text chat discussion among third-year university students studying Spanish. They found some instances of L2 negotiation as learners discussed questions about readings, but also found many instances of resolution of communication

Table 33.1 Comparison studies of computer-mediated communication focused on SLA constructs

Research focus	Point of comparison	Results
1 Negotiation of meaning (De la Fuente, 2003)	Synchronous text-based CMC and oral face-to-face conversation for acquisition of vocabulary from communication tasks	CMC and oral face-to-face interaction were equally effective for vocabulary learning, except for oral production of words for which oral face-to-face was better.
2 Negotiated interaction (Smith, 2004)	Negotiated interaction and preemptive input for retention of new vocabulary in written CMC	Lexical items that were negotiated were more likely to be retained.
3 Two types of interaction (Chen, Belkada, & Okamoto, 2004)	Intra-personal and interpersonal negotiation online for vocabulary acquisition	Both were equally successful for vocabulary acquisition.
4 Negotiation of meaning (Fernández-Garciá & Martínez-Arbelaiz, 2003)	Oral face-to-face conversation and text chat for promoting negotiation of meaning	Oral communication with native speakers resulted in more communication breakdowns and negotiation, but communication among non-native speakers was relatively free of breakdowns.
5 Repair moves (Jepson, 2005)	Synchronous text chat rooms and in-voice chat rooms for L2 learners' repair moves	Voice chat generated more repair moves than text chat; clarification requests were the most frequent.

Table 33.1 *(cont'd)*

Research focus	Point of comparison	Results
6 Negotiation of meaning and form-focused interaction (Pellettieri, 2000)	Types of communication tasks in written chat for negotiation strategies	Negotiation of both form and meaning; learners self-corrected and corrected each other; task affected the quality of negotiation.
7 Negotiation of meaning (Fernández-Garciá & Martínez-Arbelaiz, 2002)	Text-based CMC relative to findings in face-to-face communication for negotiation of meaning	Negotiation of meaning does occur, but indictors of misunderstanding are more frequently explicit than in oral conversation.
8 Negotiation of meaning (Blake, 2000)	Task types in written chat for amount of negotiation	Similar to face-to-face communication tasks, the jigsaw tasks produced more negotiation of meaning.
9 Form-focused and meaning-focused communication tasks (Fiori, 2005)	CMC tasks with form and meaning vs. meaning only focus for grammar learning	Form and meaning tasks are better for serious conversations and for grammar learning.
10 Oral proficiency development (Payne & Whitney, 2002)	Oral face-to-face and written chat for developing speaking ability	Groups engaged in written chat increased oral proficiency more than all oral face-to-face discussion groups.
11 Refusal strategies (Sykes, 2005)	Oral face-to-face, oral chat, and written chat for development of refusal strategies	Refusal strategies were best developed through written chat tasks.

breakdown through the use of the L1. Also, looking for negotiation, Blake (2000) compared types of communication tasks constructed in accordance with those designed by researchers investigating face-to-face communication. He found that the jigsaw tasks in written synchronous CMC, like those in face-to-face communication, seem to prompt negotiation of meaning best. He characterized the process of completing the CMC tasks as an opportunity for the learners to heighten metalinguistic awareness of their vocabulary knowledge.

Other studies comparing task types have found differences in the learners' discourse (e.g., Lamy & Goodfellow, 1999); therefore, the role of the teacher in planning and carrying out CMC activities is worthy of investigation. One study of systematic chat use in the classroom of third-year university Spanish learners demonstrated the impact of how the teacher plans for CMC tasks (Fiori, 2005). Learners in two groups, a meaning- and form-focused group, and a meaning-focused group, participated in regular communication activities over a several-week period for a total of approximately 350 minutes each. The form- and meaning-focused group was given consciousness raising activities to accompany the chat sessions, including preparation of pre-task questions, access to a dictionary during the chat, and interventions from the teacher on particular grammatical points. The form- and meaning-focused group outperformed the meaning-focused group on the relevant grammatical points. The chat scripts also revealed how the form- and meaning-focused group remained in a serious, academic frame of mind, whereas in the meaning-focused group students were prone to joke around, bully each other, use English, and fail to collaborate (Fiori, 2005).

Other studies have compared oral vs. written chat for development of aspects of language ability. Payne and Whitney (2002) found that a combination of oral and written interactive communication was better for improvement in oral proficiency in intermediate Spanish than oral CMC alone. Similarly, Sykes (2005) found that third-year Spanish learners who engaged in written chat increased their oral proficiency more than oral CMC or face-to-face discussion groups in a controlled classroom study in which learners role-played refusals in one of three conditions. All three groups watched and completed reflection questions on model native-speaker dialogues including refusals. The group that practiced using written chat outperformed the other two groups in the complexity and variety of the strategies they used – a finding the researcher attributes to the characteristics of written CMC, which include a setting with lower communication stress, time to plan, and a written record for reflection. Added to prior findings of more equal participation in written CMC than in oral face-to-face communication (Warschauer, 1995/1996), these studies show an important role for written synchronous CMC.

The research shows the value of both oral and written CMC in classroom instruction, as well as the critical role of the teacher in designating task conditions. These findings have been made through selection of points of comparison that are constructed through technology and that are pertinent to second language learning. Findings shed some light on the use and usefulness of specific aspects of technology-pedagogy.

Beyond comparisons: SLS-based description

Descriptive research, which examines computer-mediated learner interactions without the face-to-face classroom as a point of comparison, has been important in the study of educational technology (Knupfer & McLellen, 1996), and second language education is no different. A range of phenomena from second language studies (SLS) have been investigated in research, including grammatical performance, negotiation strategies, pragmatic development, and technology-communication choices that learners make.

Belz (2004) documented the process of microgenesis of a grammatical marker in German (the *da*-compound) from a 100,000-word corpus of data from CMC gathered over a two-week period, finding a change in the range and complexity of learners' uses of this grammatical particle. Stockwell and Harrington (2003) documented measurable improvement in syntactic performance in the email messages of Japanese learners over five weeks of email contact with native speakers of Japanese. Chun (1994) investigated the functions used by first-year German learners in written synchronous CMC in the classroom, finding a number of speech acts, such as asking questions and requesting clarifications. In each of these studies, the researchers speculate that the electronic communication in which the language appears may be instrumental in its development.

Descriptions of strategic communication in CMC have documented how negotiation takes place and reveal some evidence of intercultural competence. Investigating intermediate Spanish learners' use of negotiation in synchronous text CMC, Lee (2001) found that overall, the learners used negotiation effectively for meaning-focused communication, but negotiations did not help them to use grammatically correct language because of their primary focus on meaning. Blake and Zyzik (2003) found that heritage learner–L2 learner pairs engaged in the same types of negotiation routines (e.g., "clarification requests, expansions, recasts, self corrections") as L2 learner pairs (p. 538), and that these focused on lexical items for the most part, with many syntactic errors going unnoticed. Belz (2003) examined the specific linguistic features that may reveal the learners' level of intercultural competence (IC) in the CMC of learners of English and German. Focusing on language which revealed suspension of disbelief about the other person and their culture, she found some evidence of intercultural competence through a discourse/content analysis of the appraisals that appeared in the learners' language.

From a longitudinal ethnographic study of English learners of German and French, Belz (2001, 2003) and Belz and Kinginger (2003) reported on several aspects of learning from a sociocultural perspective (Lantolf, 2000). The English speakers in the United States were assigned joint projects with their German-speaking or French-speaking counterparts in Europe. Based on analysis of the development of the distinction between the formal and informal second person pronouns, Belz and Kinginger point out that pragmatic competence is better developed through opportunities to interact with a variety of interlocutors outside the classroom. Findings from the study of this project-based communication indicated that factors such as access to technology and attitudes affected critical aspects of the language practice in which the learners were intended to engage (Belz, 2001).

Other studies have looked at situational and cultural factors affecting collaboration and language use. Jeon-Ellis, Debski, and Wigglesworth (2005) investigated the "impact of collaborative relationships on generating learning opportunities for students and the role of computers in creating learning opportunities" for first-year French students in Australia who engaged in oral communication to create multimedia projects. Findings included relationships between beneficial language-related episodes and the learners' social inclusion with the group. Thorne's (2003) broader perspective included the learners' choice of tools for telecollaborative communication. American learners of French chose email, instant messenger, and other forms of Internet communication based on their past experience. This analysis of the learners' communications showed how learners' prior knowledge was a basis for habits of technologically mediated communication in their second language, and ethnographic studies of learners' technology use suggest the significance of this medium for language development (e.g., Lam, 2000).

Overall, these descriptive studies reveal expanded means for learners to engage in second language conversation, which, if chosen, may prove beneficial for language development, and particularly, for development of ability to communicate through technology, which "presents us with a channel which facilitates and constrains our ability to communicate in ways that are fundamentally different from those found in other semiotic situations" (Crystal, 2001, p. 5). Descriptive work reveals the patterns of discourse occurring in these unfamiliar contexts (e.g., Herring, 1996; Negretti, 1999).

The Technology Difference in Language Testing

Although technology intersects with many facets of language testing (Burstein et al., 1996), the language-testing enterprise operates in a corporate culture where questions about computer-assisted test delivery are addressed based on such considerations as the actions of other parts of the company, the competition, and the test users. In this setting, one might argue that the technology difference for language testing should be investigated to assess how technology affects the measurement of language ability (Sawaki, 2001). In fact, only a few studies have looked at comparisons, whereas others have focused on specific threats to validity. Both types of research have been conducted under a presumption that the technology, although efficient, is suspect in terms of the negative effects it might have on testing (Stansfield, 1986), but a more innovative agenda appears to be on the horizon.

Comparison studies

A number of potential technology effects on test methods might influence test takers and test taking (Chapelle & Douglas, 2006). For example, multimedia allows for a variety of input and response types, enhancing contextualization of language. Input can be adapted in response to test takers' responses and actions, allowing for computer-adaptive tests and rapid feedback. Natural language processing allows for automated scoring of complex linguistic responses, affecting the resulting scores. Comparison research is conducted on the assumption that an existing paper-and-pencil or face-to-face testing procedure produces a score whose meaning and use have been adequately argued and that, therefore, the computer-assisted test can be measured against an existing one to identify the effects of the technology.

Research assessing differences between a paper-and-pencil test and a proposed computer-assisted replacement was reported by Choi, Kim, and Boo (2003), who investigated the computer version of the Test of English Proficiency developed by Seoul National University. They used a range of empirical methods that offered complementary perspectives about score meaning of the two versions of the test: content analysis, correlational analyses, ANOVA, and confirmatory factor analysis. Findings indicated similarities between the two versions of each of the different parts of the test, but the degree of similarity across sections differed somewhat. Research was also conducted on the TOEFL to investigate the similarity between the paper-and-pencil version and the test tasks to be used on the computer-based TOEFL introduced in 1998 (Taylor et al., 1999). A correlation of 0.84 was calculated between the scores that students received on the two tests, the computer-delivered and paper-and-pencil TOEFL, but the main purpose of this study was to assess the extent to which examinees' scores could be made comparable by giving all examinees a tutorial that would help to familiarize them with the computer. The analysis of interest to the researchers showed no practical effect of computer familiarity on scores obtained on the computer-based test.

Beyond comparisons

The majority of research on CALT focuses on aspects of the test suspected of affecting test scores in unknown ways, in other words, factors that threaten validity (Messick, 1989). For example, the fact that an interactive computer interface makes new task types possible suggests the need to study the new tasks and what they measure. This type of research is typically conducted by test developers for their own information, and, therefore, not reported in journals, but such studies of prototyping new assessment tasks for the TOEFL were reported by Enright et al. (forthcoming). Concerns have been raised that adaptive selection of items may not appropriately sample test content, causing test takers anxiety, and some research has explored this issue (e.g., Vispoel, Hendrickson, & Bleiler, 2000). Concerns about the scores given by a natural language processing system prompt research investigating the scores (Powers et al., 2001).

These focal areas for research are evident in guidelines for CALT design and evaluation as researchers have attempted to identify interface issues that affect the quality of the test-taking process (Noijons, 1994; Fulcher, 2003). Such guidelines concerning technical quality are also intended to mitigate problems of test anxiety that might be heightened if a test taker encounters a confusing interface, as well as possibilities of breaches in test security. Despite the need for research and guidelines intended to identify and minimize threats to test validity, the basic approach of treating technology itself as a threat to the real business of language assessment fails to realize the potential that some researchers see for technology in testing, i.e., the development of innovative assessments that combine the rigor of assessment practices with the capabilities of technology to help students learn (Roever, 2001).

An innovative agenda

Contrary to the assumption that technology should be treated as suspect, one might hope that technology would be instrumental in expansion and innovation in language testing (Alderson, 1988; Corbel, 1993). For example, to test constructs of literacy through technology, or electronic literacy, technology would be essential in test delivery, and one would not seek equivalent scores on a corresponding paper-and-pencil version to argue for validity. Instead, the construct itself would require the use of technology for developing an assessment for making inferences about learners' ability to work with electronic information. Educational Testing Service's ICT Literacy Assessment measures the ability to use language and critical-thinking skills for problem solving within a technological environment. Test takers are aided by technology as they perform the required tasks, such as extracting information from a database, or composing an email message based on findings from electronic sources. For such a test, a critical aspect of the validation argument would be demonstration that test scores could be extrapolated to performance in context.

A second example of an innovative technology-based assessment is one that is available for free on the Web for students to get an assessment of their level of language ability for their own information and enjoyment. Such an example was developed as a European Union project, DIALANG, for assessing ability in many of the EU languages. Such a project demonstrates the need to better understand, and in fact to develop theory and practice associated with, diagnostic assessment (Alderson, 2005; Clark, 1989). Future generations of such assessments promise to offer even greater challenges as test developers attempt to make use of the results of language-recognition technologies, which extend beyond what human raters can do. The challenge of designing and making use of tests intended to provide learners with specific diagnostic information has only begun to be explored (e.g., Coniam, 1996).

A third example of innovation appears as the assessments that are built into CALL programs for informing learners about their achievement on the objectives of a unit of study (Marty, 1981; Rost, 2003). Such tests need to be evaluated in terms of the adequacy of their content coverage, learners' performance, and the extent to which learners enjoy the test and find the feedback useful and motivating. In all of these examples, the comparison of performance on an equivalent paper-and-pencil test would not be key in an argument supporting score interpretation and use.

The need for a useful way of evaluating such tests is evident from these examples as well as from reports of evaluation of innovative CALT projects (e.g., Chapelle, Jamieson, & Hegelheimer, 2003; Hémard & Cushion, 2003). In innovative CALT, the test use alone cannot be the starting point for development of the validation argument. If innovative test uses are to be pursued, test developers' assumptions about the role of technology in assessment need to be revealed, reflected upon, and perhaps changed. Assumptions about technology are critically tied to knowledge about technology and the capabilities of technology that are relevant for expanding test uses.

Conclusion

In a special issue of *CALICO Journal* focusing on what it takes to teach online, Hauck and Stickler (2006) point to the need to develop professional knowledge in this area if teaching, and I could add, testing, online is ever going to be appreciated for its value, rather than appearing to be a weak alternative to classroom teaching and assessment. Research discussed in this chapter provides at least a start to such professional knowledge. Through examination of specific aspects of pedagogy that are operationalized through technology, research is beginning to show some of the unique benefits of online learning for language study. The research fruitfully draws on a combination of technology and second language studies to design materials and research that illuminate how learners can engage in communication and language learning through technology. Such research does not attempt to isolate effects of technology, but rather focuses on the design, use and effects of specific technology-based pedagogic practices. Interactionist and sociocultural theory offer constructs that have been useful for studying language learning experiences online. These constructs, in turn, require researchers to expand beyond research methods that compare learning outcomes on language measures, because such constructs provide both the opportunity and the need for researchers to examine the language and interaction that learners engage in as they work on CALL tasks.

REFERENCES

Alderson, J. C. (1988). *Innovations in language testing: Can the microcomputer help?* Special Report No. 1 Language Testing Update. Lancaster, UK: University of Lancaster.

Alderson, J. C. (2005). *Diagnosing foreign language proficiency: The interface between learning and assessment.* London: Continuum.

Allum, P. (2002). CALL in the classroom: The case for comparative research. *ReCALL* 14, 1, 146–66.

Arnold, N. & Ducate, L. (2006). CALL: Where are we and where do we go from here? In L. Ducate & N. Arnold (eds.), *Calling on CALL: From theory and research to new directions in foreign language teaching*, (pp. 1–20). San Marcos, TX: CALICO.

Belz, J. A. (2001). Institutional and individual dimensions of transatlantic group work in network-based language teaching. *ReCALL* 13, 2, 213–31.

Belz, J. A. (2003). Linguistic perspectives on the development of intercultural competence in telecollaboration. *Language Learning & Technology* 7, 2, 68–117.

Belz, J. A. (2004). Learner corpus analysis and the development of foreign language proficiency. *System* 32, 4, 577–91.

Belz, J. A. & Kinginger, C. (2003). Discourse options and the development of pragmatic competence by classroom learners of German: The case of address forms. *Language Learning* 53, 4, 591–648.

Blake, R. J. (2000). Computer-mediated communication: A window on L2 Spanish interlanguage. *Language Learning & Technology* 4, 1, 120–36.

Blake, R. J. & Zyzik, E. C. (2003). Who's helping whom?: Learner/heritage-speakers' networked discussions in Spanish. *Applied Linguistics* 24, 4, 519–44.

Borrás, I. & Lafayette, R. C. (1994). Effects of multimedia courseware subtitling on the speaking performance of college students of French. *The Modern Language Journal* 78, 61–75.

Burstein, J., Frase, L., Ginther, A., & Grant, L. (1996). Technologies for language assessment. *Annual Review of Applied Linguistics*, 16, 240–60.

Burston, J. (2001). Computer-based grammar checker and self-monitoring. *CALICO Journal* 18, 3, 499–515.

Chapelle, C. A. (2003). *English language learning and technology: Lectures on applied linguistics in the age of information and communication technology*. Amsterdam: John Benjamins.

Chapelle, C. A. & Douglas, D. (2006). *Assessing language through computer technology*. Cambridge: Cambridge University Press.

Chapelle, C., Jamieson, J., & Hegelheimer, V. (2003). Validation of a web-based ESL test. *Language Testing* 20, 4, 409–39.

Chen, J., Belkada, S., & Okamoto, T. (2004). How a web-based course facilitates acquisition of English for Academic Purposes. *Language Learning & Technology* 8, 2, 33–49.

Chenoweth, N. A. & Murday, K. (2003). Measuring student learning in an online French course. *CALICO Journal* 20, 2, 285–314.

Choi, I.-C., Kim, K. S., & Boo, J. (2003). Comparability of a paper-based language test and a computer-based language test. *Language Testing* 20, 3, 295–320.

Chun, D. M. (1994). Using computer networking to facilitate the acquisition of interactive competence. *System* 22, 1, 17–31.

Chun, D. M. & Plass, J. L. (1996). Effects of multimedia annotations on vocabulary acquisition. *The Modern Language Journal* 80, 183–98.

Clark, J. L. D. (1989). Multipurpose language tests: Is a conceptual and operational synthesis possible? In J. E. Alatis (ed.), *Georgetown University Round Table on Language and Linguistics. Language teaching, testing, and technology: Lessons from the past with a view toward the future* (pp. 206–15). Washington, DC: Georgetown University Press.

Coniam, D. (1996). Computerized dictation for assessing listening proficiency. *CALICO Journal*, 13, 2&3, 73–85.

Corbel, C. (1993). *Computer-enhanced language assessment*, Research Report Series 2. Sydney, Australia: National Centre for English Language Teaching and Research, Maquarie University.

Crystal, D. (2001). *Language and the Internet*. Cambridge: Cambridge University Press.

de Graaff, R. (1997). The experanto experiment: Effects of explicit instruction on second language acquisition. *Studies in Second Language Acquisition* 19, 249–76.

DeKeyser, R. M. (1995). Learning second language grammar rules: An experiment with a miniature linguistic system. *Studies in Second Language Acquisition* 17, 379–410.

De la Fuente, M. J. (2003). Is SLA interactionist theory relavant to CALL? A study of the effects of computer-mediated interaction in L2 vocabulary acquisition. *Computer Assisted Language Learning* 16, 1, 47–81.

Doughty, C. J. (1991). Second language instruction does make a difference: Evidence from an empirical study of SL relativization. *Studies in Second Language Acquisition* 13, 431–69.

Doughty, C. J. & Long, M. H. (2003). Optimal psycholinguistic environments for distance foreign language learning. *Language Learning & Technology* 7, 3, 50–80.

Dunkel, P. (1991). The effectiveness research on computer-assisted instruction and computer-assisted language learning. In P. Dunkel (ed.), *Computer-assisted language learning and testing: Research issues and practice* (pp. 5–36). New York: Newbury House.

Enright, M., Bridgeman, B., Eignor, D., et al. (2008). Prototyping new assessment tasks. In C. A. Chapelle, M. Enright, & J. Jamieson (eds.), *Building a validity argument for the Test of English as a Foreign Language* (pp. 97–143). Mahwah, NJ: Lawrence Erlbaum.

Fernández-Garciá, M. & Martínez-Arbelaiz, A. (2002). Negotiation of meaning in nonnative speaker–nonnative speaker synchronous discussions. *CALICO Journal* 19, 2, 279–94.

Fernández-Garciá, M. & Martínez-Arbelaiz, A. (2003). Learners' interactions: A comparison of oral and computer-assisted written conversation. *ReCALL* 15, 1, 113–36.

Fiori, M. L. (2005). The development of grammatical competence through synchronous computer-mediated communication. *CALICO Journal* 2, 3, 567–602.

Fulcher, G. (2003). Interface design in computer based language testing. *Language Testing* 20, 4, 384–408.

Gass, S. (1997). *Input, interaction, and the second language learner*. Mahwah, NJ: Lawrence Erlbaum.

Grace, C. A. (1998). Retention of word meanings inferred from context and sentence-level translations: Implications for the design of beginning-level CALL software. *The Modern Language Journal* 82, 533–44.

Guillory, H. G. (1998). The effects of keyword captions to authentic French video on learner comprehension. *CALICO Journal* 15, 1–3, 89–108.

Hauck, M. & Stickler, U. (2006). What does it take to teach online? *CALICO Journal* 23, 3, 463–75.

Hémard, D. & Cushion, S. (2003). Design and evaluation of an online test: Assessment conceived as a complementary CALL too. *Computer Assisted Language Learning* 16, 2–3, 119–39.

Herring, S. C. (ed.) (1996). *Computer-mediated communication: Linguistic, social, and cross-cultural perspectives*. Amsterdam: John Benjamins.

Jeon-Ellis, G., Debski, R., & Wigglesworth, G. (2005). Oral interaction around computers in the project-oriented CALL classroom. *Language Learning & Technology* 9, 3, 121–45.

Jepson, K. (2005). Conversations – and negotiated interaction – in text and voice chat rooms. *Language Learning & Technology* 9, 3, 79–98.

Jones, L. C. & Plass, J. L. (2002). Supporting listening comprehension and vocabulary acquisition in French with multimedia annotations. *Modern Language Journal* 86, 546–61.

Kern, R. (2006). Perspectives on technology in learning and teaching languages. *TESOL Quarterly* 40, 1, 183–210.

Knupfer, N. N. & McLellen, H. (1996). Descriptive research methodologies. In D. H. Jonassen (ed.), *Handbook of research for educational communications and technology* (pp. 1196–212). New York: Simon & Schuster Macmillan.

Lam, W. S. E. (2000). Second language literacy and the design of the self: A case study of a teenager writing on the internet. *TESOL Quarterly* 34, 3, 457–82.

Lamy, M-N. & Goodfellow, R. (1999). "Reflective conversation" in the virtual language classroom. *Language Learning & Technology* 2, 2, 43–61.

Lantolf, J. (ed.) (2000). *Sociocultural theory and second language learning.* Oxford: Oxford University Press.

Lee, L. (2001). Online interaction: Negotiation of meaning and strategies used among learners of Spanish. *ReCALL* 13, 2, 232–44.

Levy, M. & Stockwell, G. (2006). *CALL dimensions: Options and issues in computer-assisted language learning.* Mahwah, NJ: Lawrence Erlbaum.

Long, M. H. (1996). The role of linguistic environment in second language acquisition. In W. C. Ritchie & T. K. Bhatia (eds.), *Handbook of second language acquisition* (pp. 413–68). San Diego: Academic Press.

Marty, F. (1981). Reflections on the use of computers in second language acquisition. *Studies in Language Learning* 3, 1, 25–53.

Messick, S. (1989). Validity. In R. L. Linn (ed.), *Educational measurement* (3rd edn., pp. 13–103). New York: Macmillan.

Nagata, N. (1995). An effective application of natural language processing in second language processing in second language instruction. *CALICO Journal* 13, 1, 47–67.

Nagata, N. (1993). Intelligent computer feedback for second language instruction. *The Modern Language Journal* 77(3), 330–9.

Negretti, R. (1999). Web-based activities and SLA: A conversation analysis research approach. *Language Learning & Technology* 3(1), 75–87.

Noijons, J. (1994). Testing computer assisted language tests: Towards a checklist for CALT. *CALICO Journal* 12, 37–58.

Norris, J. & Ortega, L. (eds.) (2006). *Synthesizing research on language learning and teaching.* Amsterdam: John Benjamins.

Payne, S. & Whitney, P. J. (2002). Developing L2 oral proficiency through synchronous CMC: Output, working memory, and interlanguage development. *CALICO Journal* 20, 1, 7–32.

Pederson, K. M. (1987). Research on CALL. In W. F. Smith (ed.), *Modern media in foreign language education: Theory and implementation* (pp. 99–132). Lincolnwood, IL: National Textbook Company.

Pellettieri, J. (2000). Negotiation in cyberspace: The role of *chatting* in the development of grammatical competence in the virtual foreign language classroom. In M. Warschauer & R. Kern (eds.), *Network-based language teaching: Concepts and practice* (pp. 59–86). Cambridge: Cambridge University Press.

Pica, T. (1994). Research on negotiation: What does it reveal about second-language learning conditions, processes, and outcomes? *Language Learning* 44, 3, 493–527.

Plass, J. L., Chun, D. M., Mayer, R. E., & Leutner, D. (1998). Supporting visual and verbal learning preferences in a second-language multimedia learning environment. *Journal of Educational Psychology* 90, 1, 25–36.

Powers, D. E., Burstein, E., Chodorow, M., Fowles, M. E., & Kukich, K. (2001). Stumping E-Rater: Challenging the validity of automated essay scoring. Educational Testing Service research report 01-03.

Robinson, P. (1996). Learning simple and complex second language rules under implicit, incidental, rule-search, and instructed conditions. *Studies in Second Language Acquisition* 18, 27–67.

Roever, C. (2001). Web-based language testing. *Language Learning & Technology* 5, 2, 84–94.

Rost, M. (2003). Longman English Interactive [computer software]. New York: Pearson Education.

Sawaki, Y. (2001). Comparability of conventional and computerized tests of reading in a second language. *Language Learning & Technology* 5, 2, 38–59.

Scida, E. E. & Saury, R. E. (2006). Hybrid courses and their impact on student and classroom performance: A case study at the University of Virginia. *CALICO Journal* 23, 3, 517–32.

Secules, T., Herron, C., & Tomasello, M. (1992). The effect of video context on foreign language learning. *Modern Language Journal* 76, 480–9.

Smith, B. (2004). Computer-mediated negotiated interaction and lexical acquisition. *Studies in Second Language Acquisition* 26, 365–98.

Stansfield, C. (ed.) (1986). *Technology and language testing*. Washington, DC: TESOL Publications.

Stockwell, G. & Harrington, M. (2003). The incidental development of L2 proficiency in NS–NNS email interactions. *CALICO Journal* 20, 2, 337–59.

Sykes, J. M. (2005). Synchronous CMC and pragmatic development: Effects of oral and written chat. *CALICO Journal* 22, 3, 399–431.

Taylor, C., Kirsch, I., Eignor, D., & Jamieson, J. (1999). Examining the relationship between computer familiarity and performance on computer-based language tasks. *Language Learning* 49, 2, 219–74.

Thorne, S. L. (2003). Artifacts and cultures-of-use in intercultural communication. *Language Learning, & Technology* 7, 2, 38–67.

Thorne, S. L. & Payne, S. (2005). Evolutionary trajectories, Internet-mediated expression, and language education. *CALICO Journal* 22, 3, 371–98.

Vispoel, W. P., Hendrickson, A. B., & Bleiler, T. (2000). Limiting answer review and change on computerized adaptive vocabulary tests: Psychometric and attitudinal results. *Journal of Educational Measurement* 37, 1, 21–38.

Warschauer, M. (1995/1996). Comparing face-to-face and electronic discussion in the second language classroom. *CALICO Journal* 13, 2&3, 7–25.

Yoshii, M. & Flaitz, J. (2002). Second language incidental vocabulary retention: The effect of text and picture annotation types. *CALICO Journal* 20, 1, 33–58.

Zhao, Y. (2003). Recent developments in technology and language learning: A literature review and meta-analysis. *CALICO Journal* 21, 1, 7–27.

Part VII   Teacher Education

34 Language Teacher Education

RENÉE JOURDENAIS

Language teacher education – of what should it consist? Some would argue that it is largely an issue of providing teachers with successful classroom activities. Others may identify it as more of an academic endeavor with a course of study to pursue. Are these, in fact, two different perspectives? Or can these views of teacher education coexist? This chapter will provide an overview of such views and debates related to language teacher education, closing with perspectives as to how we might best prepare teachers for their role as language educators.

First, let's begin by asking if teachers need to be formally educated in order to teach language? Certainly, we have all seen job announcements for teaching positions in which being a "native speaker" seems to be the only qualification required. Is it possible that simply being a successful user of the language is sufficient for translation into a successful teaching career? Undoubtedly, there are some very successful language teachers out there who began their careers with such qualifications. However, we also frequently see these teachers, some time later, seeking workshops or enrolling in teacher education programs which suggests that, in some way, some level of further preparation is needed in order for teachers to be successful in their classrooms and in their professions. But what should this education consist of? Is it enough to have novice teachers work with mentor teachers in the classroom? Or do teachers need academic instruction in certain theoretical areas?

What Is "Teaching"?

Pennington (1999) presents a continuum of perspectives on teaching, ranging from the view of teaching as "magic" to a view of teaching as "science" (p. 100). In the former, teaching is perceived as something "mysterious . . . dependent on personal and individual factors that can never be fully known or described" (p. 101) and thus may not require or be conducive to formal training. We have all heard of those who are "naturals" in the classroom, for whom teaching seems to be part of their very being. In the latter view, however, teaching-as-science, teaching is viewed as something that can be clearly delineated, defined, and presented – a body of knowledge to be learned, courses to be taken. As an alternative to these two ends of the continuum, Pennington (1999) proposes that we view "teaching-as-profession" in which "the aim of teacher education can be characterized as helping teachers to synthesize and consolidate personal and shared knowledge in a professional persona which bridges the subjective and the intersubjective, the 'art' and the 'craft' – or the 'magic' and the 'science' – of teaching" (p. 106).

Wallace (1991) shares a similar perspective. He first outlines a distinction between teaching as a "craft" and teaching as "applied science." In the "craft" model, teachers learn their skills through the observation and imitation of more experienced teachers. The "applied science" model, on the other hand, views teaching expertise as being gained through study of scientific findings in the field. He notes that both models have their strengths and weaknesses. The former, the "craft" model, acknowledges the role of what Wallace terms "experiential knowledge" in successful pedagogy. However, this model may lead to imitative, non-reflective teaching, as novice teachers may simply "do-as-they-see" without necessarily reflecting upon whether or not their observations were of sound practices. The "applied science" model, on the other hand, allows for continued input and development of teachers based on a growing body of research and knowledge, but may simplify (or sometimes even ignore) the teaching context. Freeman and Johnson (1998) have criticized this "applied science" perspective of teacher training, pointing out that

> [T]eachers are not empty vessels waiting to be filled with theoretical and pedagogical skills; they are individuals who enter teacher education programs with prior experiences, personal values, and beliefs that inform their knowledge about teaching and shape that they do in their classrooms . . . [L]earning to teach is affected by the sum of a person's experiences, some figuring more prominently than others, and . . . it requires the acquisition and interaction of knowledge and beliefs about oneself as a teacher, of the content to be taught, of one's students, and of classroom life. (Freeman & Johnson, 1998, p. 401)

Bartels (1999), too, criticizes the "applied science" view of teacher education, stating that too much emphasis is placed on "apprenticing" teachers into academics and that more attention should be placed on how "abstract principles are manifested in instruction in specific classrooms" (p. 56). Freeman and Johnson (1998) argue that instead the focus of teacher education should be on teachers as learners themselves, schooling as a sociocultural context, and the activity of teaching as it relates to the teacher-as-learner and the context in which the schooling takes place (pp. 409–10). That is, teaching cannot be seen as "magic" that happens within an individual, a "craft" developed between teachers and their classrooms, nor is it a pre-determined body of knowledge to be imparted through academic coursework. Rather, teaching must be explored within the complexity of its social, intrapersonal, and interpersonal contexts.

The Training of Teachers

Wallace (1991) proposes a "reflective" model of teacher education which incorporates teachers more actively into the education process. In this model, teachers draw from both the received knowledge of the field and the experiential knowledge of the classroom practitioner, as represented in Figure 34.1. This figure suggests that as teachers utilize experiential and received knowledge in their practice, they engage in reflection which allows them to re-examine their practice in light of their decisions, concerns, experiences, and knowledge. This reflection feeds back into their practices. In this model then, what teachers bring to their practice in the form of reflective behavior plays a role equal to that of the received and experiential knowledge gained from more traditional perspectives of teacher education. In fact, Freeman and Johnson (1998, 2005a, 2005b) and Freeman and Graves (2004) feel that what teachers think and believe about their practices comprise key components in determining what their students do or do not learn.

Hedgcock (2002), too, is interested in the teacher-as-learner. However, he raises concerns about teacher education models which may focus heavily on teacher reflection. He emphasizes the importance of maintaining a balance between the more theoretical and the more experiential forms of teacher education in his call for a "socioliterate approach" to teacher education:

> FL and L2 language teacher education should value declarative, critical knowledge as necessary for, and complementary to, the growth of procedural and tactical classroom skills. Excessive emphasis on procedures, techniques, and self-awareness can compromise novices' prospects for transcending their regrettably unprestigious status as practitioners (Johnson, 1997, p. 300). (Hedgcock, 2002)

Here Hedgcock highlights a tension in the field, a separation – in perspective, if not actually in fact – between practice and theory in language education. As

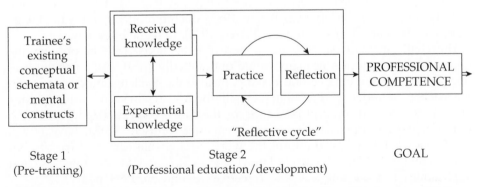

Figure 34.1 Reflective practice model of professional education/development (Wallace, 1991)

Johnson (1997) states, "those who construct theory are . . . generally held in higher esteem than and hold positions of power over those who construct practice" (p. 779). Hedgcock (2002) says that such beliefs lead to "a particularly damaging dichotomy" set up between theory and practice (p. 308) which leads many novice teachers to see theory as something "authoritarian and prescriptive" (Clarke, 1994, p. 9). In fact, Clarke (1994) has argued that the "distinction between theory and practice . . . is generally dysfunctional for teachers" (p. 9).

The Great Debate

One such articulation of this theory/practice divide has occurred in the debate regarding the role of second language acquisition theory in teacher education. In 1989, Freeman wrote that applied linguistics research and research in SLA were "ancillary" to language teaching and "should not be the primary subject of language teacher education" (p. 29). This remark has evoked numerous contra-dictory responses from researchers and teacher educators in the field who, in fact, feel that such research is at the core of what teachers need to understand in order to be successful in their classrooms and with their learners (e.g., Hedgcock, 2002; Jourdenais, 2004; Tarone & Allwright, 2005; Yates & Muchisky, 2003). Tarone and Allwright (2005), for example, emphasize that "there is a great deal of SLA research that is directly relevant to classroom processes of SLA and that should be familiar to classroom teachers because it can directly affect choices they make in their classrooms, which can affect the success or failure of their students" (p. 20). Such research may include (but is by no means limited to) research done on classroom interactions (e.g., Gass, Mackey, & Pica, 1998; Swain, 2000), the effects of various types of error correction (e.g., Lyster, 2001; Mackey, Gass, & McDonough, 2000) and grammatical presentation (e.g., Doughty & Varela, 1998; Ellis, 2002; Hinkel & Fotos, 2002), information gleaned on developmental pro-cesses and orders (e.g., Kasper & Schmidt, 1996; Pienemann, 1999), the processes involved in scaffolding learning (e.g., Gibbons, 2003; Lantolf & Pavlenko, 1995; van Lier, 2000), as well as research on strategy use (e.g., O'Malley & Chamot, 1990; Oxford, 1996), anxiety (e.g., Bailey, 1983; MacIntyre, 1997), motivation (e.g., Gardner, 2001) and investment (e.g., Peirce, 1995), to name but a few.

The challenge with such research may not be necessarily in proving the relevance of these topics, as many would undoubtedly see at least a few implica-tions here for classroom decision-making. Instead the challenge may lie in assist-ing teachers to understand and interact with the research in such a way that they are able to assess theoretical relevance for their own contexts (Hedgcock, 2002; Johnson, 1997; Jourdenais, 2004). As Freeman & Johnson (2005a) have noted, "such knowledge needs to inform the work of language teachers" (p. 30), but they maintain that "much current knowledge in SLA may be of limited use and applicability to practicing teachers" (Freeman & Johnson, 1998, p. 412).

Similar arguments have been made regarding the practicality of language aware-ness in teacher education programs. How much linguistic knowledge does a language teacher need in order to be successful in the classroom? Many have argued that there is little need for teachers to have explicit knowledge about language (e.g., Bartels, 1999, 2005; Freeman & Johnson, 1998). Others, however, are concerned about the level of awareness language teachers have about their target language and how well they are able to instruct learners as a result of that knowledge (e.g., Hedgcock, 2002; Trappes-Lomax, 2002; Widdowson, 2002).

Whatever level of language awareness may be desirable, there is evidence that some teachers may not be being adequately prepared in teacher education programs to address their learners' linguistic needs. After a recent review of studies which examined teachers' content knowledge, the American Educational Research Association (AERA) Panel on Research and Teacher Education (Cochran-Smith & Zeichner, 2005) reported that although teachers had basic information about their subject matter, few had a deeper understanding that allowed them "to move beyond simple statement of the principles as rules" (p. 271). They went on to say that "[t]eacher candidates had limited and often inaccurate, knowledge of the principles of grammar needed to explain problematic cases. Subject matter courses had left many of them with gaps in the content knowledge needed to teach grammar on the basis of principles" (p. 273). Hedgcock (2002) also notes that "[l]anguage teachers are often underprepared to provide the descriptive and explanatory information that so many language learners expect to gain from classroom instruction" (p. 306).

The Need for Awareness

Many fear that attention to language has waned in teacher education programs: "We are coming out of a period in which the traditional centrality of language – and in particular the conception of it as a system of knowledge capturable, teachable and learnable as 'grammar' – has been downplayed" (Trappes-Lomax, 2002, p. 2). Arguably, this lack of focus on "grammar" has been impacted by trends in teaching. For example, the communicative approach to language teaching placed little (if any) emphasis on explicit instruction of grammar. Thus teachers coming into the profession during the communicative era may have been less likely to receive "language" training than those who were trained during the days of grammar-translation techniques. Trappes-Lomax (2002) argues that "our task is to reintegrate language more fully into LTE [language teacher education], in a form compatible with the evolved view of language teaching as involving *both* communicative proficiency and consciousness of language" (p. 3, original emphasis). Widdowson (2002) supports this perspective, emphasizing that teachers are teaching language as a subject – more specifically, a particular language as a foreign language – and they must understand the various components of this language in such a way that they can determine what is most important for learners to know, how to make this knowledge accessible to learners, how to make it learnable, and how to make it useful and real for learners' particular sociocultural contexts. Reflecting these types of understanding, Wright (2002) identifies three domains of language awareness that teachers should have: the *user* domain, the *analyst* domain, and the *teacher* domain. The first, the *user* domain,

> involves not only the ability to use the language appropriately in a variety of situations but also an awareness of the social and pragmatic norms which underlie such appropriate use. The *analyst* domain covers knowledge of language – knowledge of how language in general and the target language in particular work . . . It includes understanding of the forms and the functions of language systems – grammar, vocabulary and phonology. The *teacher* domain involves an awareness of how to create and exploit language learning opportunities, the significance of classroom interaction and of learner output. (p. 118, original emphasis)

Language teacher education must, therefore, focus on ways of assisting teachers with each of these three domains. It is not enough that teachers be successful users of the target language; nor is it sufficient that they understand how the language itself works. They must have a level of awareness of language that enables them to assess, analyze, and present it to learners in ways that will enhance acquisition.

Bridging the Divide

Looking at both the debate about the role of SLA theory and the debate regarding the role of linguistic knowledge, it appears that the argument revolves less around content than it does about the manner in which teachers are educated. There seems to be little disagreement that teachers must know about language and language learning in order to be successful in their classrooms. By focusing so intently on a theory/practice divide, we are indeed doing a disservice to teachers if our attention – and theirs – is directed away from helping them to gain the knowledge and expertise they need. In fact, Williams (1999, citing Griffiths & Tann, 1992) argues that "the problem lies in actually perceiving a dichotomy between theory and practice" (p. 14). She, instead, prefers to see theory and practice as "two sides of the same coin, as inextricably linked: what could be called '*theory with practice*'" (p. 14, original emphasis). She notes that Eraut (1994) "makes the helpful distinction between public and private theories" (Williams, 1999, p. 14). Public theories are those often held as a component of the "received knowledge" of a field, articulated in published literature and research. Private theories, on the other hand, are those that individuals espouse which are, perhaps, reflected in their beliefs and actions. Griffiths and Tann (1992) claim that the distinction made between theory and practice "is, in effect, a divide between personal and public theories," as all practice is based on some type of personal theory (p. 76). Williams (1999) thus proposes a model (see Figure 34.2) in which personal and public theories interact with each other and each interacts with practice:

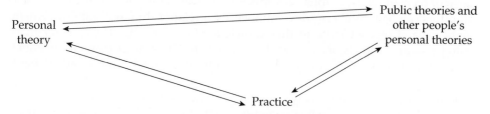

Figure 34.2   Relationships between public and private theories

Personal theories are those that inform and give rise to practice, whether they are explicitly stated or not. Reflection on practice enables personal theories to be constructed. Personal theories can be made public by writing them down for publication or delivering them at conferences. Public theories can become incorporated into personal theories by being reconstructed. Public theories can be put into practice, but they are necessarily reconstructed in the light of their particular context and participants. Practice can become public through communication. (p. 15)

It is, in essence, this idea of public theories becoming "incorporated into personal theories" that drives Hedgcock's (2002) sociocognitive approach to teacher education. Hedgcock (2002) argues that novice teachers need to develop skills which enable them to question, critique, and challenge the received knowledge of the field so that they might see these works "not as definitive or authoritative but as resources for constructing their own operational theories of classroom practice" (p. 309). Larsen-Freeman (2004) supports this perspective, claiming that "teachers need to cultivate a consumer mentality. We need not be dictated to by others" (p. 69). It is this authoritative view of knowledge that has been problematic in many teacher education programs:

L2 teacher education programs tend to present teachers with a quantifiable amount of knowledge, usually in the form of general theories and methods that are characterized as being applicable to any language learning or teaching context. In addition, this knowledge tends to be oversimplified, decontextualized, compartmentalized into separate course offerings, and transmitted through passive instructional strategies such as course readings, lectures, exams, and term papers. (Johnson, 1997, p. 780)

Johnson (1997) argues that knowledge gained in this way remains disconnected from teachers' classroom realities:

If teachers do not examine the theoretical knowledge they master in their education programs within the familiar context of their own learning and teaching experiences, if that knowledge is not situated within the social context where it is to be used, if the interconnectedness of that knowledge is not made obvious, and if teachers have few opportunities to use that knowledge in situated and interpretative ways, then theory will continue to have little relevance for practice. (p. 781)

Larsen-Freeman (2004) emphasizes this fact, as well, and points out that teacher educators can help teachers "develop their own relationship to disciplines which might expand or contribute to this knowledge base" (p. 71). Thus, rather than seeing research and theory as pre-determined, teachers must come to examine such contributions in the field as components of their education and of their developing belief systems.

Hedgcock (2002) outlines ways in which teachers can be encouraged to examine and situate this knowledge, beginning first with an introduction of teachers to the discourses, texts, and genres that are prevalent in the applied linguistics field. As teachers gain the ability to read, understand, and critically evaluate what is being researched and discussed in the field, they are encouraged to systematically reflect – both retrospectively and prospectively – on their own practice as it relates to these theories. This awareness "can lead to a balanced integration of public and personal theory in the individual's professional value system" (Hedgcock, 2002, p. 312).

One manner in which teachers can be encouraged to participate in public theory is by contributing to research in the field. Markee (1997) points out a number of constraints which have traditionally hampered teachers' involvement in the research community: (1) research is written by researchers for researchers, and thus it may not be readily accessible to teachers; (2) topics addressed in research studies may not be directly applicable to language classrooms; (3) the hierarchical relationship between researchers and teachers may lead to teachers' voices being less heard; (4) research that teachers do may not be "rigorous" enough for publication in the prevailing research journals; and (5) teachers may not want to and/or have time to publish and/or conduct research (pp. 88–9). Markee looks, however, toward *action research* as a possible means for bridging these constraints.

As Richards (1998) reminds us, action research "takes its name from two processes that are central to it: a data-gathering component (the research element) and a focus on bringing about change (the action component)" (p. 28). It thus seems a likely candidate for bridging the theory/practice divide. Van Lier (1994a) defines action research

> as a way of working in which certain activities occur in cycles: we *plan* some kind of action (based, perhaps on some problem we have defined, or an idea based on reading or research), we *carry it out*, we *observe* the process (preferably with a partner), we *reflect* (and converse, if possible, with our collaborator), and in the light of our reflections we revise the plan and continue with the process. (p. 8)

He emphasizes that "practice must be seen as an opportunity to do research, and as a source of theory" (van Lier, 1994b, p. 7). Citing Feyerabend (1987, p. 284), van Lier (1994b) reminds us that "The knowledge we need to understand and to advance the sciences does not come from theories, it comes from participation" (p. 7). Thus, by encouraging teachers to participate in the research community as investigators of their own teaching practices, we can assist them not only in enhancing their own classroom practices, but also in expanding the domain of language education research to include more classroom-oriented foci, thereby, perhaps, expanding the relevance of applied linguistics research to a wider community of practitioners. As Bailey (1999) notes:

> To teach well is to take a research stance to our work – to question, to hypothesize, to be open to puzzles, to seek out data – not only to support our positions, but also to be open to data which may say things we don't want to hear ... It is by carefully examining the work of language learners and teachers that we improve the profession and create better learning environments for our students and ourselves. Thus, it is by encouraging teachers to examine what they do, to reflect critically upon it, and to act upon those findings, we, as teacher educators can assist teachers in participating in a broader professional community. (p. 38)

It is with this thought in mind that this chapter comes to a close. By examining various perspectives on language teacher education, I hope to have highlighted that these diverse – and sometimes contentious – viewpoints share a common focal purpose, to best prepare teachers with the knowledge and skills needed to enhance both learners' language learning experiences and teachers' own opportunities for professional growth and development.

NOTE

I am grateful to Cambridge University Press for permission to reproduce Figure 34.1.

REFERENCES

Bailey, K. (1983). Competitiveness and anxiety in adult second language learning: Looking *at* and *through* the diary studies. In H. Seliger & M. H. Long (ed.), *Classroom-oriented research in second language acquisition* (pp. 67–102). Rowley, MA: Newbury House.

Bailey, K. (1999). Looking back down the road: Twenty-five years of language classroom research. Plenary address given at the TESOL Convention. New York.

Bartels, N. (1999). How teachers use their knowledge of English. In H. Trappes-Lomax & I. McGrath (eds.), *Theory in language teacher education* (pp. 46–56). Harlow, UK: Longman.

Bartels, N. (2005). Applied linguistics and language teacher education: What we know. In N. Bartels (ed.), *Applied linguistics and language teacher education* (pp. 405–24). New York: Springer/Kluwer.

Borg, S. (2005). Teacher cognition in language teaching. In K. Johnson (ed.), *Expertise in second language learning and teaching* (pp. 190–209). Basingstoke, UK: Palgrave Macmillan.

Clarke, M. (1994). The dysfunctions of the theory/practice discourse. *TESOL Quarterly* 28, 9–26.

Cochran-Smith, M. & Zeichner, K. (2005). *Studying teacher education: The report of the AERA Panel on Research and Teacher Education.* Mahwah, NJ: Lawrence Erlbaum.

Doughty, C. & Varela, E. (1998). Communicative focus on form. In C. J. Doughty & J. Williams (eds.), *Focus on form in classroom second language acquisition.* (pp. 114–38). New York: Cambridge University Press.

Ellis, R. (2002). The place of grammar instruction in the second/foreign language curriculum. In E. Hinkel & S. Fotos (eds.), *New perspectives on grammar teaching in second language classrooms.* (pp. 17–34). Mahwah, NJ: Lawrence Erlbaum.

Eraut, M. (1994). The acquisition and use of educational theory by beginning teachers. In G. Harvard & P. Hodkinson (eds.), *Action and reflection in teacher education* (pp. 69–88). Norwood, NJ: Ablex.

Feyerabend, P. (1987). *Farewell to reason.* London: Verso.

Freeman, D. (1989). Teacher training, development, and decision-making: A model of teaching and related strategies in language teacher education. *TESOL Quarterly* 28, 27–47.

Freeman, D. & Graves, K. (2004). Examining language teachers' teaching knowledge. In M. Hawkins & S. Irujo (eds.), *Collaborative conversations among language teacher educators* (pp. 87–104). Alexandria, VA: TESOL.

Freeman, D. & Johnson, K. (1998). Reconceptualizing the knowledge-base of language teacher education. *TESOL Quarterly* 32, 397–417.

Freeman, D. & Johnson, K. (2004). Comments on Robert Yates and Dennis Muchisky's "On reconceptualizing teacher education": Readers react . . . Common misconceptions about the quiet revolution. *TESOL Quarterly* 38, 119–27.

Freeman, D. & Johnson, K. (2005a). A response to Tarone and Allwright. In D. Tedick (ed.), *Second language teacher education: International perspectives* (pp. 25–32). Mahwah, NJ: Lawrence Erlbaum.

Freeman, D. & Johnson, K. (2005b). Toward linking teacher knowledge and student learning. In D. Tedick (ed.), *Second language teacher education: International perspectives* (pp. 73–95). Mahwah, NJ: Lawrence Erlbaum.

Gardner, R. C. (2001). Integrative motivation and second language acquisition. In Z. Dornyei & R. Schmidt (eds.), *Motivation and second language acquisition* (Technical Report No. 23, pp. 1–19). Honolulu: University of Hawai'i.

Gass, S., Mackey, A., & Pica, T. (1998). The role of input and interaction in second language acquisition: Introduction to the special issue. *The Modern Language Journal* 82, 299–307.

Gibbons, P. (2003). Mediating language learning: Teacher interaction with ESL students in a content-based classroom. *TESOL Quarterly* 37, 247–72.

Griffiths, M. & Tann, S. (1992). Using reflective practice to link personal and public theories. *Journal of Education for Teaching* 18, 69–84.

Hedgcock, J. (2002). Toward a socioliterate approach to second language teacher education. *Modern Language Journal* 86, 299–317.

Hinkel, E. & Fotos, S. (2002). *New perspectives on grammar teaching in second language classrooms.* Mahwah, NJ: Lawrence Erlbaum.

Johnson, K. (1996). The vision versus the reality: The tensions of the TESOL practicum. In D. Freeman & J. Richards (eds.), *Teacher learning in language teaching* (pp. 30–49). New York: Cambridge University Press.

Johnson, K. (1997). The author responds . . . *TESOL Quarterly* 31, 779–80.

Jourdenais, R. (2004). Finding membership in the discourse community of language educators. Paper presented at AAAL. Portand, OR.

Kasper, G. & Schmidt, R. (1996). Developmental issues in interlanguage pragmatics. *Studies in Second Language Acquisition* 18, 149–69.

Kumaravadivelu, B. (1999). Theorising practice, practicing theory: The role of critical class-room observation. In H. Trappes-Lomax & I. McGrath (eds.), *Theory in language teacher education* (pp. 33–45). Harlow, UK: Longman.

Lantolf, J. P. & Pavlenko, A. (1995). Sociocultural theory and second language acquisition. *Annual Review of Applied Linguistics* 15, 108–24.

Larsen-Freeman, D. (2004). The nature of linguistics in a language teacher education pro-gram. In M. Hawkins & S. Irujo (eds.), *Collaborative conversations among language teacher educators* (pp. 69–86). Alexandria, VA: TESOL.

Lyster, R. (2001). Negotiation of form, recasts, and explicit correction in relation to error types and learner repair in immersion classrooms. *Language Learning* 51, Supplement 1, 265–301.

Mackey, A., Gass, S., & McDonough, K. (2000). How do learners perceive interactional feedback? *Studies in Second Language Acquisition* 22, 471–97.

MacIntyre, P. (1997). Language anxiety: A review of the research for language teachers. In D. J. Young (ed.), *Affect in foreign language and second language learning: A practical guide to creating low-anxiety classroom atmosphere* (pp. 24–45). Boston, MA: McGraw-Hill.

Markee, N. (1997). Second language acquisition research: A resource for changing teachers' professional cultures? *Modern Language Journal* 81, 80–93.

O'Malley, J. M. & Chamot, A. (1999). *Learning strategies in second language acquisition.* New York: Cambridge University Press.

Oxford, R. (ed.) (1996). *Language learning strategies around the world: Cross-cultural perspect-ives.* Manoa: University of Hawai'i Press.

Peirce, B. N. (1995). Social identity, investment, and language learning. *TESOL Quarterly* 29, 9–31.

Pennington, M. (1999). Rules to break and rules to play by: Implications of different conceptions of teaching for language teacher development. In H. Trappes-Lomax & I. McGrath (eds.), *Theory in language teacher education* (pp. 99–108). Harlow, UK: Longman.

Pienemann, M. (1999). *Language processing and second language development: Processability Theory.* Amsterdam: John Benjamins.

Richards, J. (1998). *Beyond training: Perspectives on language teacher education.* Cambridge: Cambridge University Press.

Richards, J. & Farrell, T. (2005). *Professional development for language teachers: Strategies for teacher learning.* New York: Cambridge University Press.

Swain, M. (2000). The output hypothesis and beyond: Mediating acquisition through collaborative dialogue. In J. P. Lantolf (ed.), *Sociocultural theory and second language learning* (pp. 97–114). Oxford: Oxford University Press.

Tarone, E. & Allwright, D. (2005). Second language teacher learning and student second language learning: Shaping the knowledge base. In D. Tedick (ed.), *Second language teacher education: International perspectives* (pp. 5–23). Mahwah, NJ: Lawrence Erlbaum.

Trappes-Lomax, H. (ed.) (2002). *Language in language teacher education.* Amsterdam: John Benjamins.

Tsui, A. (2005). Expertise in teaching: Perspectives and issues. In K. Johnson (ed.), *Expertise in second language learning and teaching* (pp. 167–89). Basingstoke, UK: Palgrave Macmillan.

van Lier, L. (1994a). Action research. *Sintagma* 6, 31–7.

van Lier, L. (1994b). Some features of a theory of practice. *TESOL Journal* 4, 6–10.

van Lier, L. (2000). From input to affordance: Social-interactive learning from an ecological perspective. In J. P. Lantolf (ed.), *Sociocultural theory and second language learning* (pp. 245–59). Oxford: Oxford University Press.

Wallace, M. (1991). *Training foreign language teachers: A reflective approach*. Cambridge: Cambridge University Press.

Waters, A. (2005). Expertise in teacher education: Helping teachers to learn. In K. Johnson (ed.), *Expertise in second language learning and teaching* (pp. 210–29). Basingstoke, UK: Palgrave Macmillan.

Widdowson, H. (2002). Language teaching: Defining the subject. In H. Trappes-Lomax (ed.), *Language in language teacher education* (pp. 67–81). Amsterdam: John Benjamins.

Williams, M. (1999). Learning teaching: A social constructivist approach – theory and practice or theory with practice? In H. Trappes-Lomax & I. McGrath (eds.), *Theory in language teacher education* (pp. 11–20). Harlow, UK: Longman.

Wright, T. (2002). Doing language awareness: Issues for language study in language teacher education. In H. Trappes-Lomax (ed.), *Language in language teacher education* (pp. 115–30). Amsterdam: John Benjamins.

Yates, R. & Muchisky, D. (2003). On reconceptualizing teacher education. *TESOL Quarterly* 37, 135–47.

35 Diffusion and Implementation of Innovations

KRIS VAN DEN BRANDEN

Introduction

Although past decades have been characterized by strong social, political, economic, and technological evolutions, education has not radically changed its basic organizational structure. The outside world has witnessed vast changes accompanying the turn from an industrial to a technology-based information society, yet in many classrooms around the world, teachers are still standing in front of a group of students with a piece of chalk in their hand.

This observation becomes particularly fascinating in light of the multitude of new ideas, tools, and practices that teachers have been confronted with during recent years. Many teachers around the world today share the feeling that their practices are constantly being challenged and questioned by experts, technicians, policy makers, and scientists, each of whom appears to be particularly eager to introduce their newest innovation, which is claimed to raise the efficiency of education in terms of the learning it stimulates. Many of these innovations have been met with interest among teachers and quick adoption in a first (enthusiastic) phase, yet few of them have been completely institutionalized in daily classroom practice.

Basically, second and foreign language education are no exceptions to this rule. There is hardly a single aspect of second or foreign language education that has not been the subject of an educational innovation during recent years. Among the multitude of innovations that have swept over the field since the 1980s, three broad movements have been particularly prominent:

1 Innovations aiming for the implementation of more communicative, functional language teaching methods: A wide variety of innovative approaches and tools, using many different names (e.g., Communicative Language Teaching, Task-based Language Teaching, the Natural Approach) share a concern for introducing more meaning-based communication and authentic interaction in the classroom, in response to the one-sided emphasis on the teaching and practicing of isolated forms in more "traditional" language classrooms. Many of

these innovations have been accompanied by a call for greater learner initiative, activity, and autonomy (e.g., the learner-centered curriculum, the negotiated syllabus) and more interaction among learners (e.g., cooperative learning).

2   Innovations aiming for the introduction of modern technology in second/ foreign language education: Spurred by the extreme rate at which modern technology has permeated society, many educational innovations (often subsumed under the heading of "computer-assisted language learning") have attempted to support teachers in introducing multimedia (e.g., video, television, computers, the Internet) into the classroom and to implement new forms of education, including distance learning, that exploit the opportunities and new conditions for learning that technology allows today.

3   Innovations emphasizing the importance of measuring learner growth and assessing the output of language education: Very often driven by national and supranational educational policy, many schools and educational systems around the world have been confronted with increasingly strong demands to demonstrate the effect of language education in terms of student output. Language test development has proliferated and, especially with regard to the languages that are most spoken in the world, has become big business. At the same time, conceptual innovations in the domain of language assessment have attempted to link assessment practices with the two above-mentioned innovations by focusing on meaningful communication in real-life situations (e.g., performance-based language assessment) and learner autonomy and initiative (e.g., self-assessment, portfolio, alternative testing) and by exploring the use of multimedia to organize more valid and reliable test administration.

Specialized tools, inservice training and preservice training programs, pedagogical handbooks and articles, second/foreign language research, conferences, and Internet communication have all been mobilized in the diffusion and the implementation of these, and other, innovations in the language classroom, with varying effects.

This chapter aims to investigate under what conditions language teachers gain knowledge about innovations, decide to adopt them and, ultimately, integrate them in their daily classroom practice. As I will make clear, a multitude of variables should be considered in this respect, including features of the innovation itself and the way it is communicated and implemented, as well as features of all the stakeholders involved, of the teachers who are the clients of the innovation, and of the contextual conditions under which the latter have to operate. In other words, the answer to Markee's (1997, p. 82) central question "Who adopts what, where, when, why, and how?" is, to put it mildly, quite complicated.

What Is an Innovation?

According to Rogers (2003, p. 12), an innovation is "an idea, practice, or object that is perceived as new by an individual or other unit of adoption." Whether something is new should not so much be objectively proven, but rather is determined by how teachers, headmasters, and other parties involved in the organization of language education perceive certain ideas, practices, or objects. Rogers' definition also implies that the term "innovation" may apply to a wide variety of aspects of educational activity. As the introduction already made clear, some recent innovations have to do with broad pedagogical views and principles concerning how second language education should be organized, while other innovations have to do with infrastructural and contextual variables in education, with testing and evaluation, with the design of a curriculum or methodological options, as well as with aspects of teamwork and school language policy.

Rogers (2003, p. 35) uses the term "diffusion" to denote the process "in which an innovation is communicated through certain channels over time among the members of a social system." Through diffusion, teachers gain knowledge about an innovation. In practice, communication about innovations tends to be messy and chaotic rather than univocal and tightly organized. Innovations that are mandated from above, for instance by educational policy makers or second language researchers, often have to pass through many stages before eventually being communicated to the teacher in the classroom. With each link in the communication chain, the innovation tends to be re-interpreted and re-created by the change agents and clients involved. Change agents (researchers, syllabus developers, teacher trainers, pedagogical counsellors, school administrators, teacher colleagues, etc.) will often have their own reasons to add their personal touch to the description of the innovation. For instance, the innovation may be at odds with their personal (or their unit's) view on language education, the implementation of the innovation may, in their view, have too great financial or organizational consequences, or it may cause too much uncertainty and discontent among teachers. As a result, teachers who are learning about an innovation from different sources may be confronted with widely differing versions of the same story. One striking effect of the fact that innovations have to find their way through the communication channels of the educational system is that key concepts of innovations typically become loaded with a multitude of meanings after a while, many of which will strongly deviate from the way those concepts were originally conceived. What, after all these years, does the term "communicative" in communicative language teaching stand for? And how many different definitions of "task" (as in task-based language learning) or "computer-assisted language learning" are currently available?

The diffusion of innovations is successful to the extent that the targeted clients are reached and informed. Success of diffusion efforts is only partly dependent on the strength of the communication networks that are set up. Equally important are the "clients" of the innovation themselves. Not all second language teachers are equally ready to be informed about yet another innovation or have equal access to the communication channels that are used. For many second and foreign language teachers, not so much external change agents or the available literature, but fellow teachers (in their own school) will constitute the primary source through which they gain knowledge about innovations (see below).

Gaining knowledge about an innovation constitutes the crucial first step in a process that may ultimately lead to the implementation of the innovation in the language classroom. This "innovation-decision process," as Rogers (2003) calls it, is the process through which an individual (or other decision-making unit) passes from first knowledge of an innovation to forming an attitude toward the innovation (persuasion), to a decision to adopt or reject (decision), to implementation of the new idea (implementation), and to confirmation of this decision (confirmation). Fullan and Park (1981, p. 10) define the actual implementation of an innovation as "alterations from existing practice to some new or revised practice (potentially involving materials, teaching, and beliefs) in order to achieve certain desired student learning outcomes." According to Fullan (2001), three phases of implementation can be distinguished. The first is *initiation*, during which a change begins (through inservice training, setting school policy, etc.) and teachers pass through Rogers' first phases of knowledge and persuasion. The second is the *actual implementation*, when teachers begin to use the innovation in the classroom. The third, *institutionalization*, occurs when the innovation becomes fully incorporated in everyday classroom practice. Initiation, implementation, and institutionalization should not be seen as stages that automatically follow one another. During each of these stages, the innovation may be discarded by the teacher. During the initial phase, when teachers are first confronted with the innovation and gain more knowledge about it, much will depend on whether they are persuaded of its value. This first evaluation may result in preliminary decisions to reject or adopt and implement the innovation. In a next phase, while implementing teachers build up more experience with the innovation, they may decide to disconfirm or confirm their previous decisions. The latter stage appears to be particularly crucial: as many as 75 percent of all innovations fail in the long term because adopters either reject them during the implementation stage, or modify their opinions about their utility or validity before the innovation becomes institutionalized (Markee, 1997; Adams & Chen, 1981).

The time aspect of innovation-decision processes can also be formulated in terms of who is adopting at what stage in the innovative process. Rogers (2003) distinguishes five categories of adopters according to the time it takes for the innovation to be adopted in the classroom. Very often, the adoption of an innovation takes a slow start as a small minority, the *innovators*, explore the advantages of implementation and try it out in the classroom. Many innovations never pass beyond this stage (Markee, 1997). In successful cases, however, this cautious start is followed by a burst of activity and enthusiasm, during which three categories of adopters (*early adopters, early majority adopters, later majority adopters*) jump on the bandwagon. In a final phase, the adoption rate levels off as the *laggards* decide to implement the innovation. The rate of adoption that these five categories of adopters display is typically represented in an S-shaped curve. The leveling phase of the S usually indicates that the innovation has been institutionalized within the educational system.

The Central Role of Teachers' Concerns

Ultimately, it is the second/foreign language teacher who decides what innovations will find their way into the second/foreign language classroom. Innovative practices can be facilitated, communicated and supported from above, but they cannot be mandated by force, as some policy makers, researchers, or principals would like to believe. Mandated innovations may sometimes be successful in the short term, but as long as teachers have not fully endorsed the innovation at both a conceptual and practical level, the implementation will often be restricted to superficial change, doomed to die out in the long term. Language teachers, then, have to build up a sense of ownership with regard to the innovation (Bailey, 1992); they have to be able to assign personal meaning to the innovation and build confidence that their daily classroom practice will become better for themselves and for their students as a result of adopting it. In this respect, innovation fundamentally differs from mere change, in that it is goal-directed and deliberately aims for improvement; in the eyes of teachers, innovation will only be worthwhile if it yields better learning results for their students, and more comfortable, efficient or pleasant classroom practice for themselves.

As for the latter, most language teachers' principal aim is to create powerful language-learning environments for all their students. With this aim in mind, language teachers try to take appropriate actions in the classroom. In a review article on teacher cognition in language teaching, Borg (2003, p. 81) describes teachers as "active, thinking decision-makers who make instructional choices by drawing on complex, practically-oriented, personalized, and context-sensitive networks of knowledge, thoughts and beliefs." What language teachers do in the classroom is inspired by what they know, believe, and think about the different aspects of their profession. These include ideas about education in general, and language education in particular, ideas about their students, about the school context in which they have to operate, and about the broader socio-cultural and political context in which their educational practice is embedded. The relationship between teacher cognitions and teacher actions is not unidirectional, but interactive. Teacher cognitions not only feed and inspire actions in the classroom, but actions taken in the classroom also feed perceptions: each will influence the other as the teacher works from day to day (Van den Branden, 2006).

Research into the exact relationship between teacher cognitions and teacher actions aims to yield deeper insights into what "drives" teachers to act in a particular way in the classroom. Obviously, this kind of research is highly relevant for the diffusion and implementation of innovations. Innovations that fail to tune into what drives teacher actions will probably stand a smaller chance of success than programs that take into account the many variables that have an impact on the decisions that teachers make and the resulting actions they take. In this respect, a number of features of innovations have been identified as promoting or inhibiting their acceptance and implementation by (language) teachers (Borg, 2006; R. Ellis, 2003; Markee, 1997; Rogers, 2003):

1 The *relative advantages* of adopting the innovation: for language teachers, advantages may be of diverse kinds, including gains in terms of workload or time management, gains in terms of educational effectiveness, and personal gain and prestige. As mentioned above, teachers should, ideally, perceive innovations as advantageous for their students and for themselves.

2 The extent to which the innovation is *compatible* with the teachers' previous practice and contextual conditions: Innovations should not be too different from teachers' current beliefs and practices, nor deviate too strongly from the local/regional educational philosophy and broader socio-cultural context. In other words, innovations should be new, but not too new. Teachers, in general, prefer smooth transitions over sudden landslides.

3 The *complexity* of the innovation: Innovations that are easy to understand are more likely to be adopted. Teachers should be able to get a conceptual and practical grip on the new ideas or tools easily.

4 Its *trialability*: This refers to the extent to which the teacher is allowed time and space to try out the innovation and give personal meaning to it. Markee (1997) adds to this that innovations that can be cut into smaller parts, each of which can be tried out separately, often will score better than innovations that have to be accepted and implemented all at once.

5 Its *observability*: Implementation may be enhanced if teachers are able to observe colleagues while trying out the innovation. For many teachers, this will provide a safe entry into the implementation stage, as it provides them with valuable information on what will happen in the classroom, and how students will react if the innovation is put to practice. In addition, an innovation will also be accepted more easily by teachers if its effects at the level of student learning are observable.

6 Its *feasibility*: The implementation of innovations should be perceived by teachers as practically doable and compatible with practical constraints, such as timetables, class sizes, and available teaching aids.

7 Its *concreteness*: Teachers have to be able to translate the theory or philosophy behind the innovation into concrete actions in the classroom. Teachers need to have a clear picture of what they, and their students, are supposed to do, and what the practical consequences of these actions will be.

8 Its *problem-orientedness*: Innovations that provide an answer or potential solution to problems and needs that teachers experience themselves stand a better chance of being adopted than innovations that do not.

All these features together strongly suggest that innovations in the field of second and foreign language education are more likely to fail, or not reach the stage of institutionalization, if they fail to pay sufficient attention to the practitioners' context. For instance, the many attempts at introducing communicative and task-based approaches in the Asia Pacific region (among other countries, in Hong Kong, South Korea, Japan, China, Vietnam, and Indonesia) during the past decades have proven problematic for exactly this reason (e.g., Carless, 2003; G. Ellis, 1996; Li, 1998; Zhang, 2007). Research into these Asian innovation projects reveals that in many cases insufficient attention was paid to setting up strong communication and support networks, to providing teachers with sufficient teaching aids in order to make the implementation concrete, and to creating favorable conditions in terms of class size and professional development for making the innovation feasible. Moreover, in many cases, tensions arising between deeply entrenched social traditions and firmly established teacher–student relations in the classroom, on the one hand, and the interactive patterns promoted and pushed by change agents, on the other, were not always acknowledged, let alone discussed and worked through with the teachers. As Li (1998, p. 677) puts it in the title of her research article, commenting on the implementation of the communicative language approach in South Korea: "It's always more difficult than you plan and imagine."

Supporting Teachers throughout the Implementation Process

From the above, it can be inferred that in order for an innovation to be integrated in classroom practice, it is not enough to inform teachers about the innovation and then leave them to their own devices. This, in fact, is an almost sure road to perdition. Evidently, building and sustaining strong and dense communication networks that help teachers to build up a concrete, correct, and coherent picture of what the innovation is about is essential, but it is not sufficient. Teachers should not only be informed about what the innovation stands for, they should be supported throughout all the following phases of the innovation-decision process, especially when they introduce the innovation into the classroom. Change in language teachers' beliefs and practices, then, should be seen as a process rather than an event; it entails an unfolding of experience and a gradual development of skill and sophistication in using the innovation (Dooley, 1999). As a result, it calls for sustained effort and support.

One crucial aspect of this support structure has to do with teaching aids and tools. Many innovations have proven problematic because teachers were not provided with tools that can be readily used in the classroom. For instance, language teachers are often told by teacher trainers, second language researchers, or educational experts that it is wise to focus on form in their classrooms, to confront their students with cooperative learning or information-gap tasks, or to assess their learners' growth by using performance-based tests, but then face the challenge of translating this wisdom into daily classroom practice. Workshops in which teachers themselves develop activities and tools that make the innovation concrete have been claimed to enhance teachers' understanding of the innovation and create a sense of ownership, yet, on the other hand, language teachers often lack the time and space to develop tools that are consistent with the basic philosophy behind the innovation. In addition, having to develop new tools themselves may add to teachers' perceptions of the innovation as creating a greater workload and a sense of being mandated from above to do things the teachers themselves did not ask for. Moreover, for some innovations, such as the development of multimedia tools or valid and reliable language assessment measures, specific expertise may be needed. For all these reasons, Ellis (2003) suggests that teachers should not devote their precious time to developing materials, but instead should focus on the essence of their job: setting up the kind of interaction in the classroom with their learners that stimulates language acquisition. Rather than developing tasks or tests, they should use them.

The impact of providing teachers with suitable teaching aids may be considerable, but should not be overestimated, either. Even if the new teaching aids are used by adopting teachers in the classroom, this does not automatically mean that these teachers' classroom practices change drastically, or move in the direction intended by the change agents. Very often, teachers adapt the teaching aids to their own common practice instead of changing their own behavior:

> Adoption and diffusion efforts do not automatically ensure the best interest of the (educational) system. Installation efforts are often little more than attempts to promote painless infusion, to install without really changing, and to accommodate but not to improve. (Hannafin, Dalton, & Hooper, 1987, p. 7)

The greatest single educational system barrier for an innovation may, then, be the system itself (Dooley, 1999). Teachers teach in the way they themselves were taught, and show strong resistance toward radically modifying the teaching behavior that they are so familiar with. For teachers, sticking to what is well known is a powerful strategy to reduce uncertainty and vulnerability. No matter what researchers, teacher trainers, educationalists, or innovation stakeholders may claim, there is no perfect match between teaching and learning. Education offers no guarantees. In order to cope with this unsettling truth, teachers must create for themselves a feeling of being able to control, and direct, learning, at least to a certain extent. Innovations, then, can be seen as a variable adding to, or creating new, uncertainty, rather than taking some of it away.

Region-wide studies of the implementation of task-based language syllabi in Flanders (Van den Branden, 2006) vividly illustrate this phenomenon. Many teachers in these studies were observed to be modifying the task-based activities they were offered to better suit their prevailing classroom practices on a large scale. Teachers, for instance, who attached great importance to tightly controlling what was going on in the classroom, often felt uncomfortable with the high degree of learner autonomy and learner initative that the task-based syllabus aimed for. In response, these teachers did not strictly follow the syllabus guidelines, but instead, changed the activities so as to allow them the degree of control they were used to having. For instance, some teachers were found to turn group work into lockstep-type activities, to read texts aloud to their students that the latter were supposed to read for comprehension in silence, and to monitor class discussions themselves while the syllabus suggested that one of the students would act as chair.

Similar conflicts between the degree of control the teacher perceives to be necessary or desirable and the degree of control that the innovation ascribes to the learners have also been at the heart of the implementation of new technologies in language education. The educational literature describing the great potential of computer-assisted language learning in terms of enhancing language development (e.g., Beatty, 2003; Chapelle, 1998) strongly emphasizes that working with ICT in the classroom elicits high degrees of learner motivation and involvement because it allows learners to design their own learning paths by deciding for themselves which activities from the syllabus they will perform in which particular order. As much as this complies with the basic insight that language learning is a highly individual process that learners construct for themselves, for teachers, this calls up nightmares of unmanageable classrooms and teacher-free education.

The need to maintain control over what happens in the classroom is only one example of the clashes that may arise between the innovations dominating the current domain of second/foreign language education and teachers' firm beliefs and deeply entrenched classroom traditions. It is a concern typically arising in the first phases of implementation when according to *Concerns Theory* (Hall & Hord, 1987), teachers will have many self concerns, having to do with how the innovation will affect them personally. When these concerns are taken into account and catered for, and teachers keep investing energy and time in implementing the innovation, teachers' concerns will gradually become more preoccupied with the area of management (task concerns). As the teacher becomes more familiar, experienced, and skilled, concerns will shift to such matters as the effect of the new practices on learners' growth. Many teachers will need practical and moral support to persist with experimenting. Communication and interaction are keys to guiding and supporting teachers through these different implementation stages, and diminishing teachers' resistance and uncertainty.

Communication and interaction with colleagues and principals

However much expertise second language researchers, syllabus developers, and inservice trainers may show while advocating an innovation, for many teachers, these change agents will be, and will always remain, outsiders. In fact, this is probably one of the main reasons why innovations that are mandated from above often fail: they do not speak the language of the teacher. Fellow teachers on the other hand, especially those who operate in the same school or in a similar educational context, will often share the same doubts and worries, and experience on a day-to-day basis what it means to be teaching a second/foreign language to a particular group of students. Innovations that are taken up by school teams rather than by individual enthusiasts, and that create ample space for staff development and shared teacher experience, will therefore stand a better chance of success.

Language teachers may support their colleagues in many different ways while implementing an innovation. When gaining knowledge about the innovation, they may discuss it from a theoretical point of view, exchange views on how it will affect their practices, and assess what particular advantages it may yield. When implementing the innovation, teachers may prepare lessons together, anticipating possible problems or obstacles, while afterwards, teachers may share their experiences, discuss the problems that actually arose, and look for ways of coping with them in the future. Besides discussing the innovation, teachers may also share actual classroom practice, for instance by observing one another, or by team-teaching certain lessons.

Principals can play a crucial role in encouraging teachers to try out the new ideas and to persist while doing so, in creating an atmosphere that allows for experimentation, in creating favorable conditions in terms of staff development and inservice training, and in monitoring the innovation process at team level. Principals should create time for the teachers to go through the change process: this should include planning time, time to experiment in the classroom, and time to reflect on classroom experiences, preferably during normal working hours. They should take care that teachers not only go through the motions, introducing some new techniques or new tools in the classroom, but also assign personal meaning to the educational philosophy behind the innovation (Fullan, 2001). Ultimately, principals should work toward visions and practices that are shared by the whole school team. This calls for a climate in which informal and formal meetings are encouraged, links between the innovation and the overall school language policy are discussed together, and all team members become committed to working out solutions to the problems and challenges the school faces.

Interaction with inservice trainers and coaches

In many cases, external coaches can make the implementation of an innovation a more worthwhile experience for teachers. Even though they may be perceived as outsiders, external coaches can still perform tasks for which specific expertise is needed (such as developing syllabi or tests), provide teachers with more insight into the innovation's basic philosophy, exchange information about how other schools are coping with typical implementation problems, and coach teachers in building up professional skills and expertise. In line with the above, however, the support offered to teachers should strive to be as practice-based as possible and take into account the different kinds of worries (practical, theoretical, socio-emotional) that teachers are bound to have during the implementation process.

For inservice trainers and coaches, then, it is important to follow the lead and the pace of the teacher. In other words, the specific route that the implementation process follows should be dictated far more by teachers' personal interpretations of the innovation, and the questions and problems they are confronted with while trying it out, than by a fixed scenario, describing the ideal way of implementing the innovation (step by step) into an abstract classroom. In the above-mentioned research into the implementation of task-based language teaching in Flanders (Van den Branden, 2006), teachers' adoption process appeared to be positively influenced by the extent to which they were able to discuss concrete classroom activities with an external coach. The questions raised during these coaching sessions ranged from very fundamental questions about the basic rationale behind task-based language teaching to very concrete, almost trivial, questions on practical issues (such as the time that certain phases of a task-based lesson should take, or how to rearrange the classroom, or clever ways to distribute pictures quickly). These practical issues and contextual constraints occupied teachers' minds very strongly, to such an extent that, if they were not solved, some teachers refrained from implementing the new task-based syllabus altogether, because they found it "too much trouble." Coaching sessions that started from concrete classroom actions were appreciated so much by teachers because they stood close to their own classroom practice: high-sounding principles such as stimulating students' initiative, differentiating between students, working with challenging and motivating tasks, and negotiating meaning, could be translated to a very concrete, almost tactile, level and become "real." In addition, specific problems that the individual teacher faced and that differed to a great extent from the questions and worries that other teachers had, were not ignored. All this gave the teachers a feeling of being taken seriously, and provided them with a sense of ownership as the innovation was handed over to them. Coaches proved to be an immense support to teachers when looking for alternatives for things that turned out to be problematic in their personal practice. Furthermore, in feedback sessions following classroom observations conducted by the coach, teachers were inspired to make explicit why they had taken particular decisions in the classroom, in this way making their own pedagogical views explicit, not only to the coach, but to themselves. This often paved the way for them to gain much better insight into their own drives and beliefs and opened up options for considering alternatives. In a number of cases, these classroom observation and feedback sessions appeared to have direct effects on teacher actions. Furthermore, many of the teachers who were involved in these sessions expressed their strong appreciation for this type of coaching.

Innovation and Language Assessment

Innovations are not goals in their own right. Whether they are mandated from above or develop "bottom-up" from language teachers' efforts to cope with the problems they face, their main goal is to enhance learner development. Ultimately, the power of innovations should be measured by whether learners are making more progress than before the innovation was implemented.

Individual teachers and school teams, then, should have a clear view of the language-learning goals they aim to reach with their students. In addition, before embarking on the implementation process of a particular innovation, school team members should make clear, and agree upon, what language learning goals will be pursued, and what progress should be made by the learners as a result of the innovation. School team members should be able to make explicit for themselves in what ways the innovation is believed to enhance language learning more than current school practice, and what particular actions need to be taken by the different school team members in order to make the innovation work. As mentioned above, innovations in the field of second/foreign language learning should be part of an overall (school) language policy. Quite often, innovations slowly but surely die out because goals and objectives were not made clear from the very beginning, and as a result, a solid basis for evaluating the impact of the innovation on a permanent basis is totally lacking.

In order to be able to assess effects at the level of students' language learning, the school should have reliable and valid assessment tools at its disposal. Innovations may focus on any aspect of second/foreign language learning, yet, almost inevitably, they will always include an aspect of language assessment. In fact, many of the innovations discussed in this chapter so far have proven problematic because certain aspects of the innovation conflicted with teachers' assessment practices. For instance, efforts taken to introduce communicative language teaching practices are often undone because they do not match established assessment practices or official exam procedures. Group work and cooperative learning often confront teachers with the challenge of developing or finding new assessment methods, and leave teachers wondering exactly what was learnt in the student groups. Many multimedia tools for language learning available on the market do not include tests.

On the whole, the domain of language assessment itself has undergone vast changes during recent years, and has witnessed its own share of innovations, yet, in many countries, its pace has been somewhat slower than innovations with regard to pedagogical aspects of language education. While innovative pedagogical approaches stress the importance of using language for real-world purposes, and an increasing number of teachers are moving in this direction at their own steady pace, many tests and exams administered at nationwide, regional, or school level still focus strongly on morpho-grammatical accuracy. As a result, many language teachers feel caught between opposing forces. With all the moral support they receive from parents, policy makers and the inspectorate, and the power they exert upon learners' school careers, testing and assessment practices have a very strong impact on what teachers do and think, so much so that the tail will very often wag the dog:

> a communicative approach to language teaching is more likely to be adopted when the test at the end of a course is itself communicative. A test can be a very powerful instrument for effecting change in the language curriculum . . . (Weir, 1990, p. 27)

Therefore, teachers and school teams, as much as external change agents and innovation stakeholders, should carefully consider the links between the innovation and language assessment practices, and try to synchronize teaching innovation programs as much as possible with attempts to innovate assessment practices.

Conclusions

Innovations in the field of second and foreign language education do not differ from innovations in many other educational domains, in that they require sustained effort and sustained support of teachers as they move through the different phases of the innovation-decision process. Since the teacher ultimately decides what will happen to innovations in the field of second and foreign language education, it is imperative that teachers' concerns and beliefs, as well as the characteristics and constraints of the local conditions in which they operate, are taken into account; otherwise, innovations are bound to cause only superficial change.

REFERENCES

Adams, R. & Chen, D. (1981). *The process of educational innovation: An international perspective.* London: Koran Page in association with Unesco Press.

Bailey, K. (1992). The process of innovation in language teacher development: What, why and how teachers change. In J. Flowerdew, M. Brock, & S. Hsia (eds.), *Perspectives on second language teacher education* (pp. 253–82). Hong Kong: City Polytechnic of Hong Kong.

Beatty, K. (2003). *Teaching and researching computer-assisted language learning.* London: Pearson Educational.

Borg, S. (2003). Teacher cognition in language teaching: A review of research on what language teachers think, know, believe, and do. *Language Teaching* 36, 81–109.

Borg, S. (2006). *Teacher cognition and language education: Research and practice.* London: Continuum.

Carless, D. R. (2003). Factors in the implementation of task-based teaching in primary schools. *System* 31, 485–500.

Chapelle, C. (1998). *Computer applications in second language acquisition: Foundations for teaching, testing and research.* Cambridge: Cambridge University Press.

Dooley, K. (1999). Towards a holistic model for the diffusion of educational technologies: An integrative review of educational innovation studies. *Educational Technology & Society* 2, 4, 1–12.

Ellis, G. (1996). How culturally appropriate is the Communicative Approach? *English Language Teaching Journal* 50, 3, 213–18.

Ellis, R. (2003). *Task-based language learning and teaching.* Oxford: Oxford University Press.

Fullan, M. (2001). *The new meaning of educational change.* New York: Teachers College Press.

Fullan, M. & Park, P. (1981). *Curriculum implementation: A resource booklet.* Toronto: Ontario Ministry of Education.

Hall, G. & Hord, S. (1987). *Change in schools.* Albany, NY: State University of New York Press.

Hannafin, M., Dalton, D., & Hooper, S. (1987). Computers in education. In E. Miller & M. Mosley (eds.), *Educational media and technology yearbook* (pp. 5–20). Littleton, CO: Libraries Unlimited.

Li, D. (1998). "It's always more difficult than you plan and imagine": Teachers' perceived difficulties in introducing the communicative approach in South Korea. *TESOL Quarterly* 32, 677–97.

Markee, N. (1997). Second language acquisition research: A resource for changing teachers' professional cultures? *The Modern Language Journal* 81, 1, 80–93.

Rogers, E. M. (2003). *Diffusion of innovations*, 5th edn. New York: Free Press.

Van den Branden, K. (2006). Teacher-training: Task-based as well? In K. Van den Branden (ed.), *Task-based language education: From theory to practice* (217–48). Cambridge: Cambridge University Press.

Weir, C. (1990). *Communicative language testing*. London: Prentice-Hall.

Zhang, E. (2007). TBLT-innovation in primary school English language teaching in mainland China. In K. Van den Branden, K. Van Gorp, & M. Verhelst (eds.), *Tasks in action: Task-based language education from a classroom-based perspective* (pp. 68–91). Cambridge: Cambridge Scholars Publishing.

Part VIII Assessing and Evaluating Instruction

36 Current Trends in Classroom Research

ROSAMOND F. MITCHELL

Introduction

This chapter deals with the current main trends in research into L2 classroom processes, i.e., interactions involving teachers and students with language learning as at least one intended outcome. L2 classrooms have been a meaningful site for applied linguistic research since at least the 1960s, but with gathering momentum in the 1970s and 1980s (Allwright & Bailey, 1991; Chaudron, 1988; Long, 1980a; Mitchell, 1985). The chapter begins with a brief historical overview of the origins of classroom research, and its principal concerns and methods up to the 1980s. Following sections deal with the most popular themes and theoretical frameworks that have driven classroom research since 1990 or so, and with the research methods used to explore those themes. The second, third, and fourth sections deal with the emergence of a greater concern from the 1980s onwards with different forms of language learning theory as drivers for classroom research: first of all, with interactionist SLA theory (Long, 1996), and more recently, also, with sociocultural theory of second language development (Lantolf, 2006; Lantolf & Thorne, 2006). The fifth section deals with the rise of qualitative research into the social relations obtaining within the L2 classroom, between teacher and students, and among the students themselves, which is a strong feature of classroom research in the 1990s and 2000s. This section reviews classic ethnographies and studies of the classroom as a community of practice, as well as more self-consciously "critical" and poststructuralist analyses. The sixth section deals with recent trends in practitioner research (developments in L2 classroom action research, exploratory practice). Finally, a concluding section evaluates the present strengths and weaknesses of classroom process research, its relations with other types of research relevant to L2 pedagogy, and likely future research directions.

Historical Background

Current traditions of research into L2 classrooms can be traced back to diverse roots in the second half of the twentieth century (see, e.g., ch. 1 of Allwright & Bailey, 1991). Following World War II, a behaviorist trend in teacher education was concerned to identify the classroom behaviors of effective teachers, so that novice teachers could be trained to copy and master these behaviors. This led to a strong focus among educational researchers on classroom interaction and the development of systematic classroom observation techniques, to be used both for the study and analysis of expert pedagogy, and also for the analysis of learner teachers' actions during training activities such as microteaching (see the survey in Dunkin & Biddle, 1974). The Flanders Interaction Analysis coding scheme (FIAC), with its concern to train novices to utilize more "democratic" classroom behaviors ("open" teacher questioning, student initiations, etc.), was the best known of many systematic observation schemes developed in the 1960s and 1970s (Flanders, 1970).

Following in this tradition, second language teacher educators were quick to propose their own systematic observation schemes which supposedly captured the behaviors of effective teachers in the special conditions of the L2 classroom, where language is an object of study and of practice, not only a means of communication. Some of the best known were the skills-focused scheme proposed by Jarvis (1968) and the FIAC-derived FLint scheme proposed by Moskowitz (1976). (See the fuller discussion in ch. 2 of Chaudron, 1988.)

A second boost to research on L2 classroom processes came from technological and associated methodological developments in L2 education in the 1960s and 1970s: it was of concern to discover whether the new audiolingual methods and associated language laboratories were actually more effective than traditional textbook-based instruction. Major classroom experiments designed to answer such questions, e.g., the Pennsylvania Project (Smith, 1970), produced inconclusive results; subsequent commentators suggested as one possible reason the "merging" in actual classroom practice of supposedly distinct teaching methods, and the failure of the project's observational methods to detect this (Clark, 1969). The basic lesson was drawn that future attempts to relate "inputs" to the L2 classroom, such as method choices, to "outputs" in the form of language learning gains, must record and analyze the intermediate processes and experiences, which could not be taken for granted. The classroom "black box" (Long, 1980b) must be opened and its workings documented. As successive methodological and technological innovations have followed (e.g., communicative language teaching, immersion education, content-based language learning, task-based learning, and computer-assisted language learning), efforts have been made to document classroom process more systematically in studies seeking to explore the relative effectiveness of these successive movements. (For studies of communicative language teaching, see, e.g., Frohlich, Spada, & Allen, 1985; Spada & Frohlich, 1995.)

A third, methodological impetus for language classroom research came from theoretical developments that conceived conversational interaction as the performance of speech acts carrying illocutionary force (Austen, 1962; Searle, 1969). In foreign language education, these ideas had their most immediate impact on syllabus design, with the emergence of so-called "functional" syllabi (Wilkins, 1976). However they were soon applied to the analysis of interaction in content classrooms (Bellack, Kliebard et al., 1966; Sinclair & Coulthard, 1975). The work of Sinclair and Coulthard, in particular, attracted the attention of L2 classroom researchers, with its new sets of labels and concepts for discussing classroom speech acts and sequences, such as the well-known "initiation-response-feedback" (IRF) exchange. Classroom "discourse analysis" was born.

By 1980, there was sufficient activity for Long to publish a general overview of classroom research (incidentally popularizing the metaphor of the classroom as a "black box"). The survey identified two main methodological trends. The first was "interaction analysis," where Long reviewed 22 different schemes for coding L2 classroom interaction. He pointed out a number of problems with this approach: the tendency for instruments to imitate those devised for content classrooms, ignoring L2-specific concerns and lacking theoretical foundations in language learning theory; the lack of empirical validation of the proposed sets of categories; a bias toward observation of the teacher rather than the students; and the problems of applying instruments designed for analysis of whole class instruction to small group activities. The second was anthropological inquiry into the social relations of the L2 classroom, described by Long (1980b) as still in its infancy. Long argued nonetheless for a research cycle in which qualitative/ ethnographic research techniques could be used to generate hypotheses about classroom learning, to be tested more formally and empirically validated (or not) through quantitative/psychometric techniques.

In 1988, Chaudron published another major overview of classroom research, this time of book length. In a methodological chapter (ch. 2), he illustrated and evaluated four research "traditions": "psychometric, interaction analysis, discourse analysis and ethnographic" (p. 13). As in Long's earlier survey paper, systematic observation instruments are discussed at length, and interaction analysis is presented as the most developed tradition, although its shortcomings are again rehearsed, and somewhat more examples are identified of discourse analysis and ethnographic research.

It is instructive to compare the 1980s pictures described by Long and Chaudron (and other contemporary reviewers such as Mitchell (1985)) with the position today. Systematic observation schemes supporting classic behavioral "interaction analysis" are less popular. Classroom researchers are much more conscious of a need to refer to SLA theory in some form, to support their a priori claims and hypotheses about the possible significance of different types of classroom event. This is true of classroom experiments or quasi-experiments, e.g., on the effectiveness of "focus on form," "enhanced input," "processing instruction," or different types of corrective feedback ("recasts," etc.). It is also true of more interpretive, non-experimental studies, which apply different types of discourse analysis techniques to study, e.g., peer metalinguistic talk or L2 scaffolding. Such interpretive studies have also increasingly been enhanced ("triangulated") by introspective techniques, like stimulated recall or think-aloud, or the study of learner private speech. The other major changes from the 1980s scene are the very strong emergence of anthropological/ethnographic research into social and cultural dimensions of the L2 classroom (below, "Researching Classrooms as Social Communities"), increased attention to the relations between researchers and classroom practitioners, and the possibility of the direct engagement by practitioners themselves in research (see below, "Practitioner Research").

Interactionist Classroom Research

Common sense tells us that in order to learn a particular language, it is necessary to be exposed to it and to use it. The L2 classroom is an environment created expressly to promote effective language learning, and consequently, the quality and nature of L2 experience available to classroom learners has been a central issue since classroom processes were first problematized. The 1960s and 1970s "interaction analysis" phase of L2 classroom research was driven by notions of effectiveness deriving from general learning theories. However, with the emergence of more specific theories of second language acquisition in the 1970s and 1980s, classroom researchers were quick to espouse them as frameworks that could generate more specific claims about the kinds of classroom L2 experience that should promote effective L2 learning.

A series of psycholinguistic claims about the role of environmental language in L2 learning that have proved of continuing interest to L2 classroom researchers are the *input hypothesis*, the *interaction hypothesis*, and the *output hypothesis*. (For a detailed recent treatment, see, e.g., Gass, 2003). In this section we introduce these hypotheses briefly and explore the strands of classroom research that have been inspired by them.

The *input hypothesis* proposed by Stephen Krashen from the late 1970s (see, e.g., Krashen, 1985) claims that for language acquisition to take place, all that is required is that the learner should be provided with, and pay attention to, L2 input that is comprehensible yet a little beyond his/her developmental stage. A psycholinguistic "Language Acquisition Device" (LAD) is posited that will process and assimilate new linguistic forms contained in "comprehensible input," without conscious explicit analysis on the learner's part. Krashen suggested that immersion programs, for example, where classroom learners are taught content subjects through a target L2, should prove an excellent environment for L2 acquisition, as a by-product of extensive and appropriately graded exposure to comprehensible input. However, his LAD remained essentially a "black box," without any sustained attempt to model the processes by which new environmental language might be processed, interpreted, and turned from input into "intake," i.e., integrated into the learner's growing L2 system.

The *output hypothesis* was proposed by Swain (1985, 1995, 2005) as an explicit alternative to the input hypothesis. Experience with French L2 immersion learners in Canada shows that while they typically develop near-native-speaker competence in receptive skills (listening and reading), they do not typically achieve native-speaker levels in productive skills (speaking and writing). Swain argues that reliance on L2 comprehensible input allows students to bypass syntactic processing and to rely on semantic processing to make sense of L2 material. Only the requirement that students produce the L2 for communicative purposes will force them to make hypotheses about the syntactic structure of the target language, and test these in interaction. For example:

> Learner: last weekend, a man painting, painting "beware of the dog"
> Teacher: sorry?
> Learner: a man painted, painted, painted on the wall "beware of the dog"
>
> (Nobuyoshi & Ellis, 1993)

The *interaction hypothesis* was first proposed by Long in the early 1980s (e.g., Long, 1980a, 1981, 1983b), and then in a revised version in Long (1996). Long's original argument was a straightforward development of Krashen's input hypothesis. His basic claim was that for learners to receive optimal input, which was both comprehensible but also a little beyond their current level in terms of grammatical structure, they needed to be able to control the input through a process of negotiation, i.e., through conversational interaction that included opportunities for repair and clarification of meaning. The 1996 revised version of the hypothesis reads:

> It is proposed that environmental contributions to acquisition are mediated by selective attention and the learner's developing L2 processing capacity, and that these resources are brought together most usefully, though not exclusively, during *negotiation for meaning*. Negative feedback obtained during negotiation work or else-where may be facilitative of L2 development, at least for vocabulary, morphology and language-specific syntax, and essential for learning certain specifiable L1–L2 contrasts. (Long, 1996, p. 414)

This definition includes a number of claims about the psycholinguistic processes that may be taking place inside the LAD during interaction and negotiation for meaning, in particular the role being played by learner attention to form (or "noticing"), and the potential significance of negative feedback for (1) informing learners that a certain usage is not possible, and (2) offering them an alternative usage at a time when they are likely to be attending and in a position to make use of the information. For example:

> Teacher: What did you do in the garden?
> NNS student (child): Mm, cut the tree
> Teacher: You cut the trees. Were they big trees or were they little bushes?
> NNS student (child): Big trees
>
> (Oliver, 2000)

Together, these three hypotheses (input, output, and interaction) have given a theoretical impulse to large numbers of classroom-related research studies with an SLA orientation. The studies take three basic forms: (1) descriptive studies, which seek to analyze regular classroom talk between teachers and students, or among students, in terms of the opportunities afforded for meaning negotiation, corrective feedback provided, and apparent learning outcomes in the form of "uptake"; (2) more focused "laboratory" studies, which require learners to undertake specially devised activities, such as "information gap"-type tasks with native speakers and/or with each other (Iwashita, 2003; Mackey, Oliver, & Leeman, 2003; Philp, 2003; Pica, Kang, & Sauro, 2006); and (3) experimental studies, which seek to test the various hypotheses in a controlled way by providing classroom learners with different forms of L2 input, interactive experience, and/or output (e.g., Ellis, Loewen, & Erlam, 2006; Leeman, 2003; Mackey, 1999; Mackey & Philp, 1998; Morgan-Short & Wood Bowden, 2006). Increasing numbers of studies show specific L2 learning gains as a result of negotiation of form and/or meaning, the provision of recasts and other forms of corrective feedback, and various kinds of salient L2 input; however, the picture is complex and variable, depending on the type of learners involved, the nature of the language forms being learned, etc. Recent reviews of aspects of this work can be found in Braidi (2002), Gass, Mackey, and Ross-Feldman (2005), Long (2007), Mackey & Goo (2007), and Nicholas, Lightbown, and Spada (2001). A recent issue of *Studies in Second Language Acquisition* (2006, 28, 2) edited by Gass and Mackey, provides an update on related methodological approaches.

In the remainder of this section we draw attention to examples of work of type (1), which has explored the regular interaction of the L2 classroom, and assess its contribution to the development of interactionist theory in its various forms.

Negotiation of meaning

The best-known early empirical work on L2 interaction which claimed that negotiation of meaning was significant for comprehension and, therefore, for learning was of type (2) above, i.e., conducted using specially set-up dyadic tasks (see, e.g., Long, 1980a, 1981, 1983b). Some classroom researchers carrying out type (1) research on classroom talk have questioned whether negotiation of meaning occurs frequently enough in task-based adult ESL classroom interaction to be significant for classroom learning (Foster, 1998). Researchers working in a Canadian French immersion context have claimed that classroom learner–teacher interaction is characterized by "negotiation of form" rather than negotiation of meaning (Lyster, 1998; Lyster & Ranta, 1997). However, a recent study by Gass et al. (2005) that compares the frequency of L2 meaning negotiation in task-based classroom and laboratory activity reports very similar frequencies, at least when information-gap and problem-solving activities are carried out.

Oliver has developed a particular interest in classroom interaction involving younger children. For example, in the study reported as Oliver (2000), she video-recorded teachers working in two different sets of ESL classrooms, with adults and with children, and transcribed and coded extracts from the recorded classroom talk. She shows that the adult learners were more likely to initiate non-targetlike utterances, probably because their teachers controlled their contributions less than those of children. Similarly the adult learners were significantly more likely than the children to experience regular negotiation of meaning during interaction with their teacher (in addition to more feedback of other kinds, i.e., recasts, or corrective feedback). Although the amount of negotiation was different, both children and adults were observed to make use of whatever new language forms were highlighted for them, at similar rates. As Oliver points out, the long-term consequences of these differing experiences for L2 classroom learning are still poorly understood.

Corrective feedback, recasts, and negative evidence

Corrective feedback is one of the most long-standing foci of research into teacher–student interaction, with mixed results (see, e.g., Chaudron, 1988; Mitchell, 1985). However, more recent versions of the interaction hypothesis have given increased theoretical importance to the provision of negative evidence about L2 structure for classroom learners, as noted above (Long, 1996). There is now a large body of research on the provision of implicit negative feedback, in particular, in the form of recasts (where the teacher repairs a faulty utterance produced by the learner). Recasts are viewed as a means of providing an element of "focus on form" in primarily communicative/content-oriented L2 classrooms (Doughty & Varela, 1998). There is ongoing definitional debate over whether such utterances constitute negative or positive evidence about the nature of the L2 target system (Leeman, 2003); there is also debate over the extent to which classroom learners actually "notice" them, an issue now being explored through use of such research techniques as stimulated recall (Carpenter et al., 2006; Mackey & Gass, 2005; Mackey, Gass et al., 2000). Finally, there is debate over whether learners learn from them. The most usual evidence offered is more or less immediate "uptake" of forms in learner speech (Long, 2007; Mackey & Goo, 2007; Nicholas et al., 2001).

While the extent of negotiation for meaning provided in L2 classrooms has been queried (Foster, 1998), many studies show that recasts are an extremely common teacher reaction to faulty learner utterances in classrooms of many different types. Doughty (1993) showed that her case study teacher of French L2 responded very consistently to correct student utterances with exact repetition, but to incorrect ones with recasts. In the French immersion study of Lyster and Ranta (1997), teachers responded to 55 percent of learners' errors with recasts, and Sheen (2004) found even higher proportions in a comparative study of New Zealand and Korean L2 classrooms. Lyster (1998) found that grammatical and phonological errors were typically responded to with recasts, whereas lexical errors were met with negotiation. Oliver (2000) found that around half of the errors produced by both adult and child learners were met with recasts in Australian ESL settings. "Uptake" of recasts, defined as learner self-repair and more or less immediate use of the correct L2 form, followed only about 30 percent of teacher recasts in the classrooms studied by Lyster and Ranta (1997) and by Lyster (1998). However, there are experimental teaching studies (Doughty & Varela, 1998; Mackey & Philp, 1998) that show that interaction, including systematic recasting of errors relating to a target L2 feature, can produce enhanced learning, by comparison with interaction patterns which exclude recasting. Doughty and Varela showed learning gains for French past tense forms in this way, while Mackey and Philp showed gains for English question forms.

Input and output

A number of descriptive studies have pursued the claim of the output hypothesis that learners' active production of L2 utterances is required for restructuring of L2 grammar systems. We have seen that the studies by Lyster and Ranta (1997) and Lyster (1998) noted that recasts were the commonest form of teacher response by French immersion teachers to L2 errors, yet only a minority of these were followed by learner utterances, including uptake of the new/corrected forms. (See Long, 2007, for a reanalysis of Lyster's results.) In a recent discussion (Lyster, 2004) recapitulates the view that recasts have an ambiguous status and may not be interpreted as negative feedback by immersion learners:

> Recasts . . . compete with many other demands on attention during content-based instruction and appear to be ambiguous, because they share discourse functions with a similar proportion of teacher repetitions of well-formed utterances (Lyster, 1998); that is, recasts of ill-formed utterances and repetitions of well-formed utterances together appear to confirm or disconfirm the meaning of a learner's utterance, not its form. (Lyster, 2004, p. 404)

Instead Lyster interprets his recent research as showing that feedback of the type he calls "negotiation of form" or "prompts" is "less ambiguous and more cognitively engaging" (p. 404). This type of feedback includes clarification requests, repetition of ill-formed utterances, and metalinguistic comment; what these tactics have in common is that they do not provide a well-formed model, but instead supposedly stimulate the learner to produce an improved version of their utterance, as suggested by Swain (1985) with her concept of "pushed" output. Citing de Bot (1996) in support, Lyster suggests that the act of retrieving target forms from long-term memory will strengthen knowledge representations, stimulate memory connections, and promote the restructuring of interlanguage representations (p. 407). In a number of descriptive studies in immersion and ESL classrooms, Lyster and colleagues have shown that while prompts may be relatively rare compared with recasts, they are much more likely to lead to student self-repair (Lyster, 1998; Panova & Lyster, 2002). In addition, Lyster (2004) conducted a classroom experiment comparing the impact of different types of negative feedback on immersion students' learning of French gender concord; the results partly confirmed his claims, showing that students who had experienced regular prompts with consequent increased opportunities for "pushed output" performed better on some post-tests than students who had received regular recasts. A further classroom experiment conducted by McDonough (2005) with Thai EFL learners produced similar results. However in a recent observational study comparing different teaching styles in immersion settings, Lyster and Mori (2006) present a more nuanced view, arguing that negative feedback which contrasts with the prevailing teaching style, whatever that may be (e.g., use of prompts/negotiation of form in "communicative" contexts), is most effective in promoting learner uptake and repair.

Another active strand of classroom research relevant to the original input and output hypotheses is a continuing tradition of classroom experiments comparing the effectiveness of various forms of input-based L2 instruction with instruction promoting student L2 output. Many of these experiments relate to so-called "processing instruction" (VanPatten, 1996, 2002). VanPatten and his associates have made the psycholinguistic argument that L2 learners will bypass the syntactic analysis of new L2 material that they encounter as input if they possibly can, as they have a preference for semantic processing, and can often rely on semantic processing alone to extract meanings from L2 utterances because of the redundancy and variety of meaning-carrying forms in natural language. For example, if a learner hears "Yesterday, I travelled by bus," the past time reference can be extracted from the temporal adverb "yesterday" and the learner is not obliged to notice or to process the verb inflection in order to decode an adequate overall meaning for the sentence. So far, this argument resembles Swain's claims concerning the inadequacy of Krashen's input hypothesis, which led her to formulate the output hypothesis. However, VanPatten takes an alternative position that conserves a key role for input in L2 learning, arguing that classroom learners should be forced systematically to process grammatical forms in L2 input through exercises and activities with reduced redundancy, and some studies have shown that students can indeed learn effectively through processing instruction (VanPatten & Cadierno, 1993). This view has been challenged, however, in other classroom experimental studies, which have generally concluded that output opportunities make an independent beneficial contribution to L2 development (Morgan-Short & Wood Bowden, 2006; Toth, 2006).

Explicit Instruction and "Focus on Form"

There is a general consensus among SLA researchers that, at least for older learners, instruction "makes a difference" (Long, 1983a), i.e., attending class boosts learning beyond what might be achieved by learning the target L2 entirely informally in the community. There is also a general consensus supported by a range of research that instruction that includes some form of attention to target language form boosts achievement among classroom learners (Ellis, 2001; Norris & Ortega, 2000). There is a considerable amount of research exploring the benefits of implicit versus explicit grammar instruction, and also comparing a "focus on form" approach with more traditional "focus on forms." While "focus on forms" is effectively a new label for traditional grammar instruction, implicit or explicit, "focus on form" (FonF) has been defined by Long (1991) as an incidental attempt to draw learners' attention to a linguistic element in context, while maintaining a primary focus on meaning.

Much of this research takes the form of instructional experiments (see DeGraaff & Housen, this volume). Here we touch on descriptive research that has explored the extent to which "focus on form" of various kinds is salient in regular class-room activity, and the extent to which it is associated with uptake of new L2 material. This involves some overlap with the discussion above of corrective feedback and its relationship with uptake.

In discussing a range of possible teaching techniques, Ellis (2001) has distin-guished among "planned" and "incidental" focus on form, and also between "pre-emptive" and "reactive" focus on form. A number of empirical studies have investigated the frequency of these different practices, and their association with learner uptake. Ellis, Basturkmen, & Loewen (2001) analyzed 12 hours of instruction and found that pre-emptive FonF was as common as reactive FonF, and was especially likely to be initiated by students; new language encountered in this way was more likely to be taken up and used by them in subsequent classroom talk. Loewen (2003) analyzed 32 hours of instruction in 12 ESL classes, and found great variability both in the frequency of FonF episodes, and also in the extent to which individual students took part in these. (He did not track uptake.) Similarly, Mackey, Polio, & McDonough (2004) compared the classroom talk of 18 novice and expert teachers, working from similar lesson plans, and found that the experienced teachers used significantly more of preemptive FonF, recasts and explicit negative feedback, than the novices, i.e., "the inexperienced teachers did not exploit opportunities to draw learners' attention to linguistic form as often as the experienced teachers" (p. 314). Given the inconsistent use of FonF which emerges across these and similar studies, and the need for more behavioral evidence regarding its impact on learning (but see Mackey & Goo, 2007; Norris & Ortega, 2000), more focused experimental work of the kind found in, for example, Ellis et al. (2006) is required to yield trustworthy conclusions about the significance for learning of high or low classroom usages of FonF.

Sociocultural Classroom Research

In this section, we review L2 classroom research inspired by sociocultural theory, i.e., by the body of theory inspired by the writings of the early twentieth-century Russian thinker Lev Semeonovitch Vygotsky. This theoretical perspective has been promoted among second language researchers primarily through the longstanding commitment of Lantolf and his associates, including most notably Lantolf (2000, 2006), Lantolf and Appel (1994), Lantolf and Thorne (2006). As Lantolf and Thorne point out (2006, pp. 2–3), the term "sociocultural" is poten-tially ambiguous, and is used by other SLA researchers, such as Norton (2000) or

Hall and Verplaetse (2000), with wider reference to language socialization, dialogue and the construction of L2 identity. Vygotskian sociocultural theory (SCT) has as its goal "to understand the relationship between human mental functioning, on the one hand, and cultural, historical and institutional setting, on the other" (Wertsch, 1995, in Lantolf & Thorne, 2006, p. 3). This relationship is seen as mediated by evolving cultural tools or artifacts, chief among which is language, itself the prime "tool for thought."

As outlined by Lantolf and Thorne (2006, pp. 29–52), sociocultural theory concerns itself with the development of human mental functions over different cultural-historical timescales. *Phylogenesis* is concerned with the emergence of the human race; *sociocultural history* is concerned with the development of human culture and its cognitive consequences (e.g., the impact of literacy and schooling on cognition, studied by Luria in Siberia and by Scribner and Cole (1981) among the Vai people in Liberia); *ontogenesis* is concerned with the development of the individual human being, from infancy to maturity; and *microgenesis* is concerned with short-term development (such as that which could take place within, e.g., a single language lesson).

Of these four domains, the last two have unsurprisingly attracted much the greatest attention from SCT researchers concerned with L2 development. Lantolf and Thorne (2006) cite Collignon (1994) as an example of a study in the sociocultural domain. This researcher studied Hmong migrant women acquiring ESL literacy in an adult classroom, and documented how they adapted Hmong gendered norms for learning the skill of sewing to the process of language learning. Thorne (2003) is another example. This paper is an application of SCT to classroom L2 learning that is primarily concerned with changing perceptions of cultural artifacts and their uses. Thorne reviews a number of small-scale studies of computer-mediated classroom communication (CMC) between learners of English and French as foreign languages, documented through capture of the actual electronic exchanges, supplemented by retrospective student interviews. He argues that CMC can be interpreted as an artifact with differing cultural meanings for students of different ages and levels of experience of Internet use. In the first study discussed by Thorne, the classroom promoted email exchanges between high school students in the USA and in France, but clashing cultural meanings of CMC blocked learning opportunities. In another college-level study, students were offered email and net-meeting opportunities for French–English exchanges as part of their L2 course requirements. In this case, the intercultural links were more successful and led to extensive code-switching interaction and target language-learning opportunities, but only after the students had rejected the officially sanctioned artifacts (email and net-meeting) in favor of instant messaging, which they perceived as more appropriate for peer communication.

Concerning the research methodology considered appropriate to study development in these different domains, SCT favors the application of the so-called "genetic method." The underlying principles are discussed at some length by Lantolf and Thorne (2006, pp. 25–58). The prime concern of the genetic method is to study some form of development of mental functions, as this unfolds in a social context, mediated by cultural artifacts or tools (such as language). The development may be intensified by providing the participants with some kind of task or problem to address, either alone or in concert with others. However, the genetic method is committed to studying "mediated mind" through observation and interpretation of activity in normal everyday circumstances:

> it undertakes to maintain the richness and complexity of "living reality" rather than distilling it "into its elementary components" for the purpose of constructing "abstract models that lose the properties of the phenomena themselves." (Lantolf, 2000, p. 18, with quotes from Luria, 1979)

In practice, this has meant that L2 classroom researchers operating within an SCT paradigm have typically worked intensively with fairly small numbers of learners. In some studies, ongoing regular classroom interactions between teacher and students or among students have been recorded, transcribed and closely analyzed, as in, for example, Ohta's longitudinal study of college level learners of L2 Japanese (Ohta, 2001). In others, students have undertaken specially selected L2 tasks, such as dictogloss (Swain & Lapkin, 2001), information gap (Platt & Brooks, 2002) or reformulation (Swain & Lapkin, 2003). Their spoken (and sometimes gestural) interaction while working through these tasks has been recorded and analyzed. Researchers using a genetic approach in this way to study the microgenesis of L2 may also invite learners to reflect on and talk about the activity they have undertaken, in a form of stimulated recall, but they expect that process itself to contribute to development, and to require study in a reflexive way (Swain & Lapkin, 2007). Finally, Lantolf and Thorne review a number of larger-scale pedagogical innovations grounded in sociocultural principles, some involving explicit deductive L2 instruction, "systemic-theoretical instruction" (e.g., Negueruela, 2003), others involving "dynamic assessment," a procedure where assessment is systematically integrated with instruction and aims to modify the learner's performance (e.g., Poehner & Lantolf, 2005). Again, the effects of these innovations are researched through the genetic approach by tracking, documenting, and interpreting ongoing instructional exchanges, rather than by formal experimental means including comparison and control groups.

Empirical L2 classroom studies in an SCT framework can be related to a number of key concepts associated with the framework: activity theory, private speech, and internalization, the Zone of Proximal Development (ZPD), "scaffolding," and collaborative dialogue. The following paragraphs will give a flavor of this work.

Activity theory

The general evolution of this ambitious, yet somewhat elusive, concept is described in detail by Lantolf and Thorne (2006). They explain "third generation" (i.e., current) activity theory as follows:

Constructing an activity system as a research object involves defining the roles that people, institutions, and artefacts play in moment-to-moment practice . . . This framework privileges human agency while also understanding it as mediated and constrained by technologies (for example, computers, books and writing instruments), semiotic tools such as languages and literacies, pedagogical frameworks and conceptions of learning, by the relevant communities, and by the historical and emergent rules and divisions of labour that structure the ongoing activity . . . (p. 224)

That is to say, the theory aims to unite an array of individual and social factors around the notion of goal-directed activity, and explain its evolution. In L2 classroom research, activity theory has been tapped to a fairly limited extent. A number of researchers have appealed to the concept when demonstrating how learners may bring their own agency to bear and interpret a given classroom task very differently from the intentions of their teacher (and learn diverse things from carrying it out). This was shown, for example, by Coughlan and Duff (1994) with reference to L2 story re-telling, and by others (Donato, 2000; Roebuck, 2000) with reference to L2 writing tasks. As we have seen above, (Thorne, 2003) deals with FL intercultural interaction among high school and college students, instigated by their institutions and mediated by a range of Internet tools (email, net-meeting, instant messaging). He shows that past experience of using these cultural artifacts (both individual and collective) affects the ways in which students engage in CMC, and that this in turn affects both the processes and outcomes of target language use and development.

Private speech, imitation, and L2 internalization

As we have seen, SCT views language as the prime cultural artifact that mediates the development of higher mental functions (memory, attention, etc.). For this reason, SCT researchers are not only interested in social uses of language for interaction and interpersonal communication, but also in the nature and uses of "private speech" and "inner speech" as means for individual self-regulation and the management of cognition. L2 classroom researchers have paid some attention to the way students manage their activities in class, noting that L1 is often used for self-regulatory purposes even during L2 activity (Centeno-Cortes & Jimenez-Jimenez, 2004).

Another important function of private speech for SCT, however, involves its role in the "internalization" of new language, where imitation is seen as central to the process, both for L1 and for L2 (Lantolf & Thorne, 2006, pp. 166–76). Capturing private speech presents methodological challenges for L2 classroom researchers, and the number of studies which have done this directly is small. However, Ohta (2001) presents extensive evidence of the use of L2 private speech by college learners of Japanese as a foreign language. In this study, seven volunteer students wore individual microphones and were recorded at intervals during normal class time over a full academic session. Ohta has transcribed

Table 36.1   Types of private speech (Ohta, 2001, p. 40)

Vicarious response	Learner covertly answers a question addressed to another student . . . completes the utterance of another, or repairs another's error.
Repetition	Learner [privately] repeats words, phrases and sentences . . . Material repeated may or may not be in the immediately preceding context.
Manipulation	Learner manipulates sentence structure, morphology or sounds.

and analyzed in detail 34 hours of talk collected in this way, and amassed a considerable corpus of learner private speech in Japanese. The L2 private speech was of various types, shown in Table 36.1. Reviewing this and a small number of other studies, Lantolf and Thorne (2006) conclude that learners pay more attention to recasts and corrective feedback than has been shown in other styles of research. Both children and adults imitate and experiment privately with the linguistic models available in their environment, selectively attending to specific features which may be other than the ones in focus for their teachers (pp. 204–6).

Zone of Proximal Development (ZPD)

Vygotsky's often-quoted definition for the ZPD reads as follows:

> The zone of proximal development . . . is the distance between the actual developmental level as determined by independent problem-solving and the level of potential development as determined by problem-solving under adult guidance or in collaboration with more capable peers. (Vygotsky, 1978, p. 86)

It can be related to Vygotsky's general law of cognitive development:

> Every function in the child's cultural development appears twice: first, on the social level, and later, on the individual level: first, between people (interpsychological) and then inside the child (intra psychological). This applies equally to voluntary attention, to logical memory, and to the formation of concepts. All the higher functions originate as actual relations between human individuals. (Vygotsky, 1978, p. 57)

As shown in detail by Kinginger (2002) and Lantolf and Thorne (2006, pp. 263–90), however, the ZPD concept was not fully developed in Vygotsky's own writings and has been subject to multiple educational interpretations. Kinginger points out that the ZPD may be isolated from a more general SCT framework and interpreted in a conservative way to mean the drilling of learners toward fixed curriculum objectives through traditional IRF sequences; alternatively, it may be interpreted in much more progressive and open-ended ways, where it is the site of open-ended development and the creation of new knowledge, as argued, e.g., in the work of Newman and Holzman (1993).

As far as L2 classroom research is concerned, the ZPD concept has provided a stimulus and theoretical backdrop for explorations of instructional and collaborative dialogue as sites of L2 development. The metaphor of "scaffolding" first proposed by Wood, Bruner, and Ross (1976) is not part of Vygotsky's original ZPD framework, as Lantolf and Thorne (2006, pp. 274–6) point out, and there are some problems with the reconciliation of the two concepts; however, this metaphor has also proved attractive to L2 classroom researchers.

For example, instructional dialogues between teacher and student around L2 student texts have been studied by Aljaafreh & Lantolf (1994) and Nassaji and Swain (2000). The first of these two studies tracked interactions between a tutor and his students over time, and showed the graduated nature of the support provided by the tutor, and progressive handover of responsibility for corrective feedback to the students themselves as they internalized the language forms encountered and discussed. The second study explored the relative effectiveness of graduated versus random feedback, and showed that usable feedback is highly contextualized and related to the learner's current developmental stage. In some further examples, McCormick and Donato (2000) interpreted teacher questioning in whole class dialogic interaction in terms of scaffolded assistance, and Ohta (2001) studied corrective feedback and recasts in both teacher-fronted and peer collaborative settings, as an "affordance" available to learners in the ZPD that may be an interpsychological bridge to the internalization of new forms (p. 128).

However, the most popular application of SCT theory in L2 classroom research to date has been work on classroom dialogue among student peers, and its potential contribution to student learning, using notions of scaffolding, mediation, and interpsychological activity. A brief review and discussion can be found in Donato (2004). Among others, Swain, Lapkin and colleagues have been prominent in running an extended series of studies of collaboration among students in French immersion contexts undertaking a variety of tasks, and documenting scaffolding and intermental activity around the development of both L2 forms and metalinguistic knowledge (Swain & Lapkin, 2001, 2003; Lapkin, Swain, & Smith, 2002). A major part of Ohta's longitudinal study of college learners of Japanese is devoted to the analysis of "peer learning." In this study, student talk was recorded individually and transcribed using conversation analysis conventions, and analyzed in detail on a number of dimensions. Ohta documented regular and sustained peer assistance throughout the sessions. This included "waiting," "prompting," "co-construction," and "explaining in L1" when a peer interlocutor was struggling to produce an L2 utterance, and in addition, indicating the need for repair and/or providing repair, when the interlocutor made an error. She argues that students can notice and correct errors more easily in others' speech than in their own, for reasons to do with differences in the required memory load and capacity for attention during speech production and reception. Overall, Ohta

Table 36.2   Benefits of peer L2 interactive tasks (Ohta, 2001, p. 126)

General development	Giving and receiving assistance . . . promotes development as learners work on a common interactive task. Learners draw on their strengths to help one another, and use the L2 for a wider range of functions and activities than they do in teacher-fronted practice.
Vocabulary	Learners use vocabulary being learned and help each other to recall and use L2 vocabulary. Learners help each other with "word searches" and actively suggest alternative vocabulary to each other.
Pronunciation	The opportunity to use L2 in interactive tasks helps learners . . . both via self-correction and . . . when their partners notice their pronunciation problems.
Grammar	Learners cooperatively build utterances they cannot yet individually produce, working toward independence. Learners notice their own grammatical errors, as well as the errors of others, with peer interlocutors benefiting from this process.
Interactional style	Working together allows learners to try different types of utterances they notice the teacher using, and to learn from each other how to interact appropriately.

argues that her data demonstrate the developmental benefits of peer L2 inter-active tasks shown in Table 36.2.

Researching Classrooms as Social Communities

As we saw earlier, 1980s reviews of classroom research acknowledged the exist-ence of a tradition of qualitative/ethnographic classroom research, but found few L2 classroom studies of this type. From the 1990s, the range and numbers of research studies focusing on the social relations prevailing within the L2 class-room has greatly increased; for example, the journal *TESOL Quarterly* has been particularly active in promoting "qualitative" research, publishing methodological guidance, as well as increasing numbers of substantive papers in this tradition (e.g., Davis, 1995; Lazaraton, 1995, 2003). Other related methodological discus-sions include a 2002 special issue of *Applied Linguistics* (23, 3) edited by Zuengler and Mori, and methods textbooks which pay substantial attention to qualitative classroom research, such as McKay (2005), Richards (2003). Qualitative class-room studies now range from "classic" ethnographies on different scales, to the application of conversation analysis to the study of classroom talk (e.g., Markee & Kasper, 2004; Seedhouse, 2004, 2005), and the "critical" interpretation of identity formation, gender, ethnic and power relationships in the L2 classroom (e.g., Norton & Toohey, 2004; Sunderland, 2000).

Ethnographies of communication conducted in L2 classroom settings have given rich insights into L2 student identities and how they are constructed. The book-length study by Heller (1999) investigates a high school with a historical commitment to the maintenance of French cultural heritage and French-medium instruction, in the wider anglophone environment of Toronto, Canada. Yet only a minority of the students are of francophone Ontarian origin; there are also tensions between the French-medium environment of formal classroom interaction and the dominance of English in student leisure time; Heller shows how many immigrant students from a French-speaking diaspora who attend the school do not identify with its "heritage" philosophy and have primarily instrumental reasons for developing and sustaining their personal bilingualism. Duff has also conducted a number of ethnographic classroom studies (Duff, 1994, 2002a, 2002b), including a recent study of relations between adolescent Asian ESL students, white anglophone students, and their "Canadian Studies" teacher in another Canadian high school (Duff, 2002a). She comments that "Chinese-background students in my study seemed relegated interactionally to a second-class 'other(ed)' existence in the midst of a group of highly vocal local students" (p. 310); over a school year this pattern did not change. However, the Chinese-background students had complex identities to negotiate, and Duff comments that even those who had been resident in Canada for 10 years or more "didn't seem to need to" participate actively in class; "they had other multilingual repertoires, literacies and expertise to draw on and use in the multiple discourse communities they belonged to locally and internationally" (p. 314). Similar studies have shed light on how younger and older L2 learners construct for themselves the identities of "good students" or alternatively of "popular students" (McKay & Wong, 1996; Willett, 1995).

Ethnographies of the kinds just discussed typically combine analyses of classroom interaction with other types of data, such as interviews or documents. However, there has been a recent rise in interest among applied linguists in conversation analysis (CA), an approach which relies strictly on close analysis of "talk-in-interaction" to uncover participants' perspectives, and describe how they achieve order and organization of social interaction through their talk (Markee & Kasper, 2004; Schegloff et al., 2002; Seedhouse, 2005, p. 166). Seedhouse (2005) reviews the contributions of CA to the analysis of classroom processes to date. He draws attention to studies that document in detail the communicative resources available to L2 learners, including gesture, interactional tactics, and phonology, and demonstrate their skill in exploiting these in classroom communication (Carroll, 2004, 2005; Olsher, 2004). Markee (2004) uses CA to document learners' skill in switching between on- and off-task talk, and (Mori, 2004) shows how Japanese L2 learners use "side sequences" to negotiate individual learning goals. Seedhouse himself has conducted one of the most extensive CA based studies (Seedhouse, 2004), analyzing talk in four different L2 classroom contexts in terms of turn-taking, repair and overall "interactional architecture." Seedhouse draws on these analyses to stress that the L2 classroom is a dynamic and fluid interactional environment, which is "talked in and out of being" by participants (2004, p. 199). The potential contribution of CA methodology to SLA research is considered by both Markee (2005) and Seedhouse (2005). Seedhouse points out its affinity with sociocultural theory, and notes that CA methods have been used extensively by classroom researchers interested in second language development from an SCT perspective, such as Ohta (2001).

The final current strand in qualitative L2 classroom research discussed here is that associated with "critical" approaches to applied linguistics and to language education (Luke, 2004). Practitioners of this approach are typically adherents of "critical," feminist and/or poststructuralist theory, and are "interested in relationships between language learning and social change" (Norton & Toohey, 2004, p. 1). They question "liberal multiculturalism" and the essentializing of the L2 learner as the "other" (Kubota, 2001, 2004). Consequently, this classroom research tradition is concerned to illuminate and critique classroom practices "in terms of the social visions such practices support" (Norton & Toohey, 2004, p. 1).

Ethnicity, minorities, and racism

Toohey herself (2000, 2001) has conducted an extended study of an anglophone elementary school classroom, tracing the degree of success of different ESL children in joining the classroom "community of practice" as it operated among the child peer group. She shows in detail how an Asian ESL child was marginalized, and her learning opportunities reduced, through disputational talk with other monolingual white children, while a white European ESL child was much more successful in gaining membership of the English-speaking classroom community. Kubota, Austin, and Saito-Abbot (2003) conducted an exploratory study of ethnic diversity in university L2 classrooms in the USA, finding that student groups for, e.g., L2 Spanish became less diverse as classes became more advanced; minority students in these classes reported some negative experiences and feelings of detachment from ethnic identity.

Gender and sexuality

L2 classroom research on gender is surveyed by Sunderland (2000) and Pavlenko (2004). Gendered patterns of participation in classroom talk are a common focus of such research, with, e.g., Sunderland (2004) showing girls as assertive and dominant in foreign language classroom discourse in a UK secondary school. In contrast, Poole (1992) documents a gendered hierarchy in an adult literacy classroom, with female minority students having the most limited participation opportunities. Using a "community of practice" perspective, Morita (2004) documents and interprets the "silences" of Asian female college students studying in an L2 environment. She shows that behind their reticence, the students were "actively negotiating their multiple roles and identities in the classroom" (p. 587), arguing against an "essentializing" view of Asian women as "quiet, passive, timid or indirect" (p. 597). Both these writers show how gender is just one of multiple identities in play for members of classroom communities of practice. Sunderland even argues that classroom talk may not be the most relevant site for "identification of injustice, inequality and opportunity in FL education" (2004, p. 233).

Resistance and agency

The study by Morita (2004) includes evidence of female students' resistance to being stereotyped by their teachers in various ways, e.g., as having a "'language problem." Resistance among students to conventional and conformist classroom discourse practices is also documented by Canagarajah (2004), who shows how students' intimate exchanges via email, net meetings and informal talk provided what he calls "safe houses" for alternative values and voices. Rampton (2002) shows how adolescents in UK secondary school used management phrases borrowed from their FL German lessons to challenge the authority of teachers in ritual ways in other school contexts.

Practitioner Research

Research into classroom processes, like other forms of applied linguistic research, has largely been led and directed by university-based academics with a professional commitment to research and publication. However, many of these applied linguistics researchers have been L2 instructors at some point in their personal careers, and many are in active contact with teachers through involvement with programs of L2 teacher education. As in other areas of education, the 1980s and 1990s saw increasing interest in the involvement of practitioners as active partners in the research process, with the appearance of a range of research methods publications targeting language teachers as a substantial component of their audience (Allwright & Bailey, 1991; Brumfit & Mitchell, 1989; Burns, 1999; Freeman, 1998; Nunan, 1989; Wallace, 1998). A large part of the audience for such publications has been teachers in preservice or inservice training, meeting requirements for classroom-based research projects and dissertations. An alternative model not dependent on the award of teacher qualifications involves the establishment of collaborative networks linking university-based researchers with groups of local teachers. (See Allwright (2003) and Edge (2001) for examples from Brazil, Egypt, and elsewhere, and other examples cited in Burns (2005), including the work of Mathew (1997) with secondary school English teachers in India, and that of Tinker Sachs (2002) with primary and secondary school English teachers in Hong Kong.) Some professional bodies promote looser supportive networks for practitioner research (e.g., the Research Special Interest Group within IATEFL: see www.btinternet.com/~simon.borg/ReSIG). Finally, classroom research may

Table 36.3   Characteristics of action research (Burns, 2005, p. 61)

Philosophical assumptions	People within social situations can solve problems through self-study and intervention
Purpose	To develop solutions to problems identified within one's own social environment
Main methods	Mainly qualitative, interpretive, cases studied reflectively through cyclical observational and non-observational means
Outcomes	Action to effect change and improvement, and deeper understanding in one's own social situation
Criteria for judgments	Subjectivity, feasibility, trustworthiness, and resonance of research outcomes with those in the same or similar social situation

be conducted independently by more experienced and confident practitioners, although such research is typically published in local professional journals or on professional Internet sites, and its extent may, therefore, be underestimated. (In the United Kingdom for example, such research is typically published in the *Language Learning Journal* of the Association for Language Learning, or more recently through the government-sponsored website www.teachernet.gov.uk.)

There has been a strong historical expectation that practitioner research in L2 classrooms will take the form of "action research" (AR). (To illustrate, the September 2006 conference of the IATEFL Research SIG was titled "Action Research: Rewards and challenges.") In a recent review, Burns (2005) traces the origins of AR back to the early twentieth century rejection by John Dewey of a separation between research and practice, and more particularly, to the post-war work of Kurt Lewin, with his vision of socially motivated enquiry leading directly to social action (Lewin, 1948). Burns identifies the distinctive characteristics of AR as shown in Table 36.3.

A commonly cited model for the AR process is that offered by Kemmis and McTaggart (1988), involving the four stages of planning, action, observation, and reflection. However, this model has been seen as artificially rigid, and Burns herself argues that the L2 teachers who have been her AR collaborators have worked through a more complex set of experiences:

1   Exploring: feeling one's way into research topics
2   Identifying: fact-finding to begin refining the topic
3   Planning: developing an action plan for gathering data
4   Collecting data: using initial data-gathering techniques related to the action

  5   Analyzing/reflecting: analyzing data to stimulate early reflection
  6   Hypothesizing/speculating: predicting based on analysis/reflection
  7   Intervening: changing and modifying teaching approaches
  8   Observing: noticing and reflecting on the outcomes of the changes
  9   Reporting: verbalizing and theorizing the processes and outcomes
10   Writing: documenting accounts of the research
11   Presenting: giving reports/presentations on the research.

(Burns, 2005, p. 59)

The concept of educational AR has inbuilt tensions and has been subject to a range of criticisms, again reviewed usefully by Burns (2005, pp. 67–70). There has been debate about the scope and ambitions appropriate for action research: are these to provide technical fixes to local classroom problems (Edge, 2001; Wallace, 1998), to provide personal growth and career development opportunities for teachers (Freeman, 1998), to contribute to the production of more generalized knowledge about pedagogy (Stenhouse, 1975), and/or to contribute to wider educational change through critical/emancipatory activity (Carr & Kemmis, 1986; Elliott, 1991)? Various commentators are agreed that the first two of these objectives have had some success, while the latter two are much more problematic. Burns concludes, "An examination of the current forms and purposes of AR . . . confirms that to date it is portrayed predominantly as a means of enhancing teacher professional development. The current goals and outcomes tend to be in the realms of personal and/or professional action and teacher growth rather than in the production of knowledge about curriculum, pedagogy or educational systems" (2005, p. 63).

The barriers which face classroom AR as a means of advancing our general understanding of language pedagogy significantly arise from several stages in the AR process, and thus may be fairly intractable. The theoretical needs of AR projects, which are essentially problem-solving in nature, may be satisfied by practitioners' rediscovery of already established theoretical perspectives on pedagogy (e.g., action research familiar to this writer from a range of teacher projects, which essentially rediscovered the benefits of communicative target language use, of group work, or of task-based learning); reporting of AR projects for a wider public is often restricted by practitioners' perception of this step as redundant, and/or by difficulty in maintaining commitment to the norms and timescales of research publication (Toohey & Waterstone, 2004); and the cumulation of AR findings beyond local and individual contexts is normally beyond the resources of individual practitioners.

While action research remains the dominant paradigm associated with L2 practitioner research, an alternative, "exploratory practice," has achieved recognition recently, with the publication of a special issue of the journal *Language Teaching Research* (7, 2, 2003), a contribution by Allwright to another special issue of *Modern Language Journal* (89, 3, Allwright, 2005), and a sequence of linked papers in subsequent issues of *Language Teaching Research*. In his 2005 paper, Allwright outlines the origins of exploratory practice in his growing dissatisfaction with both "academic research" and "action research" as styles of practitioner research. He regards even action research as overly respectful of academic research norms and traditions, and too narrowly preoccupied with problem-solving and the achievement of efficiency in the delivery of language learning gains. Allwright argues that action research is overly demanding of teachers' energy and commitment, and can therefore lead to burn-out and alienation from research. Instead, Allwright (2003, 2005) advocates a form of classroom research that concentrates on the development of participants' understanding of classroom processes and improvement of their "quality of life" within the classroom. In this framework, there is a deliberate attempt to change the discourse of research; thus, for example, the problems to be researched are referred to as "puzzles" rather than as "research questions" (Lyra, Fish, & Braga, 2003; Nobrega Kuschnir, & dos Santos Machado, 2003). Another distinctive feature of exploratory practice is the insistence that learners, as well as teachers, should be research partners, and that the procedures used for data collection should be closely allied to "normal" pedagogic activities, rather than any special/additional research activities. He sums up the underlying principles of exploratory practice as shown in Table 36.4 (with some accompanying "suggestions").

The remainder of the *Language Teaching Research* special issue (7, 2, 2003), plus the "Practitioner Research" section in subsequent issues of the journal, presents a number of specific examples of the use of exploratory practice in different L2 classroom contexts. The papers of Zhang (2004) and Gunn (2005) may be taken as examples. Zhang is a teacher of intensive English reading in a Chinese higher education setting. She first of all reports different unsuccessful attempts to improve students' sense of achievement in her class through varying approaches to the management of whole-class interaction (changing from a strongly teacher-directed style to a more dialogic approach). She is critical of these "action research"-style initiatives, which homed in directly on achievement, and then describes a more fundamental change in class organization, toward a group work approach in which students took much more (shared) responsibility for research-

Table 36.4   Principles of exploratory practice (Allwright, 2005, p. 360)

Principle 1	Put 'quality of life' first
Principle 2	Work primarily to understand language classroom life
Principle 3	Involve everybody
Principle 4	Work to bring people together
Principle 5	Work also for mutual development
Principle 6	Make the work a continuous enterprise
Suggestion 1	Minimize the extra effort of all sorts for all concerned
Suggestion 2	Integrate the "work for understanding" into the existing working life of the classroom

ing and leading group activities. Zhang argues that this initiative illustrates exploratory practice principles, because (1) it aimed at improving learners' enjoyment of the class (i.e., their "quality of life"), rather than aiming directly at enhancing achievement; and (2) it was highly involving and personally developmental for the students (they learned collaboration and library research skills, as well as working for the narrower L2 reading skill objectives of the course). Similarly, Gunn (2005) argues that following EP principles allowed her to develop an effective learning community in her English writing classroom in Sharjah, through very consistent consultation with students and use of feedback dialogues to develop an understanding of their needs.

These studies reflect high practitioner commitment and provide very good insights into how, in particular contexts, students' involvement and enjoyment of classroom activities can be increased, with perceived positive benefits for their learning experience. As with the action research examples, however, it would seem that their main contribution is to teachers' professional development (both direct and indirect), rather than, for example, to the theory of group work or of L2 writing instruction. Indeed, given the explicit principles of EP, this is quite clearly the main intended benefit, and because it is more modest, it seems more realizable than some claims created for teacher action research.

Conclusion

This chapter has defined L2 classroom research as essentially concerned with relations and processes operating between teachers and students, and/or among students, engaged on the officially declared enterprise of second language learning in an organized environment. It is clear that conceived in this way, classroom research is a highly active field, with multiple theoretical, social and practical aspirations, and diversity of scale and methods. The chapter has concentrated on a particular selection of themes, but almost any theme of interest to L2 learning and teaching has its reflex in classroom research. Thus, sections could have been included on classroom research relating to learning strategies, language learning motivation, intercultural communication, teacher beliefs, virtual learning environments, and a range of other themes.

This diversity stems from the underlying lack of unity in applied linguistics regarding both learning theories and theories of knowledge; the "merger" of classroom research into a more unified enterprise is unlikely to happen any time soon. However, within the different identifiable traditions of classroom research, a number of developments are apparent that show its increasing sophistication. Technological development is allowing capture of vastly increased amounts of classroom material, on an increased number of dimensions (video as well as audio, CMC as well as face-to-face communication): a practical example is the *Multimedia Adult English Learner Corpus* being created at Portland State University, Oregon. Within classroom research inspired by "interactionist" theory, the kind of cycle envisaged by Long (1980a), where there is interaction between descriptive classroom studies and more focused experimental work, is clearly apparent. Here also, the range of research techniques is widening productively, with the increasing use of introspective techniques to get closer to learners' input processing in real time. Within work inspired by SCT theory, larger-scale empirical studies are appearing and CA techniques are proving useful to trace the fine detail of "microgenetic processes." Sociolinguistic work and "critical" research inspired by social justice commitments have made very great progress over the past 15 years or so in illuminating the great variety of social contexts and educational cultures within which L2 classrooms are set, the resulting variety of "classroom cultures" themselves, and also the structured inequalities which continue to beset the classroom language-learning process.

Discernible across all of these traditions, however, is a fundamental concern with illuminating the learner's inner mental processes and state of being (whether conceived in terms of "attention" and "memory," of "activity theory," "identity," and/or "agency") and joining these up somehow with their social L2 experiences. To gain a fuller understanding of these relationships, and make a consistent contribution to the different research traditions we have acknowledged, it is probably necessary for classroom researchers – paradoxically – to become somewhat less classroom-focused, and to track learners' L2 experiences in a more unified and consistent fashion, both inside and outside the classroom (as only a small number of ethnographic studies and diary-based studies have previously done). This is starting to happen within some of the other traditions, at least where new technology now makes it easiest – in studies of language students' use of various forms of computer-mediated communication. Classroom research will never become a unified phenomenon, but within the different traditions, more systematic recognition that classrooms are just one of many learning sites between which learners move, is timely, increasingly practical, and likely to prove productive.

NOTE

I am grateful to Lawrence Erlbaum for permission to reproduce Tables 36.1 and 36.2 and to Cambridge University Press for permission to reproduce Table 36.3.

REFERENCES

Aljaafreh, A. & Lantolf, J. P. (1994). Negative feedback as regulation and second language learning in the Zone of Proximal Development. *Modern Language Journal* 78, 465–83.

Allwright, D. (2003). Exploratory practice: Rethinking practitioner research in language teaching. *Language Teaching Research* 7, 2, 113–31.

Allwright, D. (2005). Developing principles for practitioner research: The case of exploratory practice. *Modern Language Journal* 89, 3, 353–66.

Allwright, D. & Bailey, K. M. (1991). *Focus on the language classroom: An introduction to classroom research for language teachers*. Cambridge: Cambridge University Press.

Austen, J. L. (1962). *How to do things with words*. Oxford: Oxford University Press.

Bellack, A. A., Kliebard, H. M. et al. (1966). *The language of the classroom*. New York: Teachers College Press.

Braidi, S. (2002). Reexamining the role of recasts in native-speaker/nonnative-speaker interactions. *Language Learning* 52, 1–42.

Brumfit, C. J. & Mitchell, R. (eds.) (1989). *Research in the language classroom*, ELT Documents. London: Modern English Publications and the British Council.

Burns, A. (1999). *Collaborative action research for language teachers*. Cambridge: Cambridge University Press.

Burns, A. (2005). Action research: An evolving paradigm? *Language Teaching* 38, 57–74.

Canagarajah, S. (2004). Subversive identities, pedagogical safe houses, and critical learning. In B. Norton & K. Toohey (eds.), *Critical pedagogies and language learning* (pp. 116–37). Cambridge: Cambridge University Press.

Carpenter, H., Jeon, K. S., MacGregor, D., & Mackey, A. (2006). Learners' interpretations of recasts. *Studies in Second Language Acquisition* 28, 2, 209–36.

Carr, W. & Kemmis, S. (1986). *Becoming critical: Knowing through action research*. London: Falmer Press.

Carroll, D. (2004). Restarts in novice turn-beginnings: Disfluencies or interactional achievements? In R. Gardner & J. Wagner (eds.), *Second language talk* (pp. 318–45). London: Continuum.

Carroll, D. (2005). Vowel-marking as an interactional resource in Japanese novice ESL conversation. In K. Richards & P. Seedhouse (eds.), *Applying conversation analysis* (pp. 214–134). Basingstoke, UK: Palgrave Macmillan.

Centeno-Cortes, B. & Jimenez-Jimenez, A. (2004). Problem-solving tasks in a foreign language: The importance of the L1 in private verbal thinking. *International Journal of Applied Linguistics* 14, 7–35.

Chaudron, C. (1988). *Second language classrooms: Research on teaching and learning*. Cambridge: Cambridge University Press.

Clark, J. L. D. (1969). The Pennsylvania Project and the "audiolingual vs traditional" question. *Modern Language Journal* 53, 6, 388–96.

Collignon, F. F. (1994). From "Paj Ntaub" to paragraphs: perspectives on Hmong processes of composing. In V. John-Steiner, C. P. Panofsky & L. W. Smith (eds.), *Sociocultural approaches to language and literacy: An interactionist perspective* (pp. 331–46). Cambridge: Cambridge University Press.

Coughlan, P. & Duff, P. A. (1994). Same task, different activities: Analysis of a second language acquisition task from an activity theory perspective. In J. P. Lantolf & G. Appel (eds.), *Vygotskian approaches to second language research* (pp. 173–94). Norwood, NJ: Ablex.

Davis, K. A. (1995). Qualitative theory and methods in appied linguistics research. *TESOL Quarterly* 29, 3, 427–54.

Donato, R. (2000). Sociocultural contributions to understanding the foreign and second language classroom. In J. P. Lantolf (ed.), *Sociocultural theory and second language learning* (pp. 27–50). Oxford: Oxford University Press.

Donato, R. (2004). Aspects of collaboration in pedagogical discourse. *Annual Review of Applied Linguistics* 24, 284–302.

Doughty, C. J. (1993). Fine-tuning of feedback by competent speakers to language learners. In J. Alatis (ed.), *Strategic interaction and language acquisition: Theory, practice and research. Georgetown Round Table on Language and Linguistics* (pp. 96–108). Washington, DC: Georgetown University Press.

Doughty, C. J. & Varela, E. (1998). Communicative focus on form. In C. J. Doughty & J. Williams (eds.), *Focus on form in classroom second language acquisition* (pp. 114–38). Cambridge: Cambridge University Press.

Duff, P. A. (1994). An ethnography of communication in immersion classes in Hungary. *TESOL Quarterly* 29, 505–37.

Duff, P. A. (2002a). The discursive co-construction of knowledge, identity, and difference: An ethnography of communication in the high school mainstream. *Applied Linguistics* 23, 3, 289–322.

Duff, P. A. (2002b). Pop culture and ESL students: Intertextuality, identity and participation in classroom discussions. *Journal of Adolescent and Adult Literacy* 45, 6, 482–7.

Dunkin, M. J. & Biddle, B. J. (1974). *The study of teaching.* New York: Holt, Rinehart and Winston.

Edge, J. (ed.) (2001). *Action research: Case studies in TESOL practice.* Alexandria: TESOL.

Elliott, J. (1991). *Action research for educational change.* Milton Keynes: Open University Press.

Ellis, R. (2001). Introduction: investigating form-focussed instruction. *Language Learning* 51, Supplement 1, 1–46.

Ellis, R., Basturkmen, H., & Loewen, S. (2001). Preemptive focus on form in the ESL classroom. *TESOL Quarterly* 35, 3, 407–32.

Ellis, R., Loewen, S., & Erlam, R. (2006). Implicit and explicit corrective feedback and the acquisition of L2 grammar. *Studies in Second Language Acquisition* 28, 2, 339–68.

Flanders, N. A. (1970). *Analysing teaching behaviour.* Reading, MA: Addison Wesley.

Foster, P. (1998). A classroom perspective on the negotiation of meaning. *Applied Linguistics* 19, 1–23.

Freeman, D. (1998). *Doing teacher research: From inquiry to understanding.* Boston, MA: Heinle and Heinle.

Frohlich, M., Spada, N., & Allen, P. (1985). Differences in the communicative orientation of L2 classrooms. *TESOL Quarterly* 19, 27–57.

Gass, S. M. (2003). Input and interaction. In C. J. Doughty & M. H. Long (eds.), *The handbook of second language acquisition* (pp. 224–55). Oxford: Blackwell.

Gass, S., Mackey, A., & Ross-Feldman, L. (2005). Task based interactions in classroom and laboratory settings. *Language Learning* 55, 4, 575–611.

Gunn, C. (2005). Prioritizing practitioner research: An example from the field. *Language Teaching Research* 9, 1, 97–112.

Hall, J. K. & Verplaetse, L. S. (2000). Second and foreign language learning through classroom interaction. In J. K. Hall & L. S. Verplaetse (eds.), *Second and foreign language learning through classroom interaction* (pp. 1–22). Mahwah, NJ: Lawrence Erlbaum.

Heller, M. (1999). *Linguistic minorities and modernity.* Harlow, UK: Longman.

Iwashita, N. (2003). Negative feedback and positive evidence in task-based interaction: Differential effects on L2 development. *Studies in Second Language Acquisition* 25, 1, 1–36.

Jarvis, G. A. (1968). A behavioral observation system for classroom foreign language skill acquisition activities. *Modern Language Journal* 52, 6, 335–41.

Kemmis, S. & McTaggart, R. (1988). *The action research planner.* Geelong, Australia: Deakin University Press.

Kinginger, C. (2002). Defining the zone of proximal development in US foreign language education. *Applied Linguistics* 23, 2, 240–61.

Krashen, S. D. (1985). *The input hypothesis.* London: Longman.

Kubota, R. (2001). Discursive construction of the images of U.S. classrooms. *TESOL Quarterly* 35, 1, 9–38.

Kubota, R. (2004). Critical multiculturalism and second language education. In B. Norton & K. Toohey (eds.), *Critical pedagogies and language education* (pp. 30–52). Cambridge: Cambridge University Press.

Kubota, R., Austin, T., & Saito-Abbot, Y. (2003). Diversity and inclusion of sociopolitical issues in foreign language classrooms: An exploratory survey. *Foreign Language Annals* 36, 1, 12–24.

Lantolf, J. P. (ed.) (2000). *Sociocultural theory and second language learning*. Oxford: Oxford University Press.

Lantolf, J. P. (2006). Sociocultural theory and L2: State of the art. *Studies in Second Language Acquisition* 28, 1, 67–110.

Lantolf, J. P. & Appel, G. (eds.) (1994). *Vygotskian approaches to second language acquisition*. Norwood, NJ: Ablex.

Lantolf, J. P. & Thorne, S. L. (2006). *Sociocultural theory and the genesis of second language development*. Oxford: Oxford University Press.

Lapkin, S., Swain, M., & Smith, M. (2002). Reformulation and the learning of French pronominal verbs in a Canadian French immersion context. *Modern Language Journal* 86, 4, 485–507.

Lazaraton, A. (1995). Qualitative research in applied linguistics: A progress report. *TESOL Quarterly* 29, 3, 455–72.

Lazaraton, A. (2003). Evaluative criteria for qualitative research in applied linguistics: Whose criteria and whose research? *Modern Language Journal* 87, 1, 1–12.

Leeman, J. (2003). Recasts and second language development: Beyond negative evidence. *Studies in Second Language Acquisition* 25, 1, 37–64.

Lewin, K. (1948). *Resolving social conflicts: Selected papers on group dynamics*. New York: Harper and Row.

Loewen, S. (2003). Variation in the frequency and characteristics of incidental focus on form. *Language Teaching Research* 7, 3, 315–46.

Long, M. H. (1980a). *Input, interaction and second language acquisition*. Los Angeles: University of California.

Long, M. H. (1980b). Inside the "black box": Methodological issues in classroom research on language learning. *Language Learning* 30, 1, 1–42.

Long, M. H. (1981). Input, interaction and second language acquisition. *Annals of the New York Academy of Sciences* 379, 159–78.

Long, M. H. (1983a). Does instruction make a difference? A review of research. *TESOL Quarterly* 17, 3, 359–82.

Long, M. H. (1983b). Native speaker/non-native speaker conversation and the negotiation of comprehensible input. *Applied Linguistics* 4, 2, 126–41.

Long, M. H. (1991). Focus on form: A design feature in language teaching methodology. In K. de Bot, R. Ginsberg, & C. Kramsch (eds.), *Foreign language research in cross-cultural perspective* (pp. 39–52). Amsterdam: John Benjamins.

Long, M. H. (1996). The role of the linguistic environment in second language acquisition. In W. C. Ritchie & T. K. Bhatia (eds.), *Handbook of second language acquisition* (pp. 413–68). San Diego: Academic Press.

Long, M. H. (2007). Recasts in SLA: The story so far. In M. H. Long (ed.), *Problems in SLA* (pp. 75–116). Mahwah, NJ: Lawrence Erlbaum.

Luke, A. (2004). Two takes on the critical. In B. Norton & K. Toohey (eds.), *Critical pedagogies and language learning* (pp. 21–9). Cambridge: Cambridge University Press.

Lyra, I., Fish, S., & Braga, W. (2003). What puzzles teachers in Rio de Janeiro, and what keeps them going? *Language Teaching Research* 7, 2, 143–62.

Lyster, R. (1998). Negotiation of form, recasts, and explicit correction in relation to error types and learner repair in immersion classrooms. *Language Learning* 48, 183–218.

Lyster, R. (2004). Differential effects of prompts and recasts in form-focused instruction. *Studies in Second Language Acquisition* 26, 3, 399–432.

Lyster, R. & Mori, H. (2006). Interactional feedback and instructional counterbalance. *Studies in Second Language Acquisition* 28, 269–300.

Lyster, R. & Ranta, E. (1997). Corrective feedback and learner uptake: Negotiation of form in communicative classrooms. *Studies in Second Language Acquisition* 19, 37–61.

Mackey, A. (1999). Input, interaction and second language development. *Studies in Second Language Acquisition* 21, 557–87.

Mackey, A. & Gass, S. M. (2005). *Second language research: Methodology and design*. Mahwah, NJ: Lawrence Erlbaum.

Mackey, A., Gass, S. M., et al. (2000). How do learners perceive implicit negative feedback? *Studies in Second Language Acquisition* 19, 37–66.

Mackey, A. & Goo, J. (2007). Interaction research in SLA: A meta-analysis and research synthesis. In A. Mackey (ed.), *Conversational interaction in second language acquisition* (pp. 407–52). Oxford: Oxford University Press.

Mackey, A., Oliver, R., & Leeman, J. (2003). Interactional input and the incorporation of feedback: An exploration of NS–NNS and NNS–NNS adult and child dyads. *Language Learning* 53, 1, 35–66.

Mackey, A. & Philp, J. (1998). Conversational interaction and second language development: Recasts, responses and red herrings? *Modern Language Journal* 82, 338–56.

Mackey, A., C. Polio, & McDonough, K. (2004). The relationship between experience, education and teachers' use of incidental focus-on-form techniques. *Language Teaching Research* 8, 3, 301–28.

Markee, N. (2004). Zones of interactional transition in ESL classes. *Modern Language Journal* 88, 4, 583–96.

Markee, N. (2005). Conversation analysis for second language acquisition. In E. Hinkel (ed.), *Handbook of research in second language teaching and learning* (pp. 355–74). Mahwah, NJ: Lawrence Erlbaum.

Markee, N. & Kasper, G. (2004). Classroom talks: An introduction. *Modern Language Journal* 88, 4, 491–500.

Mathew, R. (1997). *CBSE-ELT curriculum implementation study: Final report*. Hyderabad, Department of Evaluation, Central Institute of English and Foreign Languages.

McCormick, D. & Donato, R. (2000). Teacher questions as scaffolded assistance in an ESLclassroom. In J. K. Hall & L. S. Verplaetse (eds.), *Second and foreign language learning through classroom interaction* (pp. 182–201). Mahwah, NJ: Lawrence Erlbaum.

McDonough, K. (2005). Identifying the impact of negative feedback and learners' responses on ESL question development. *Studies in Second Language Acquisition* 27, 1, 79–103.

McKay, S. (2005). *Researching second language classrooms*. Mahwah, NJ: Lawrence Erlbaum.

McKay, S. & Wong, S.-L. C. (1996). Multiple discourses, multiple identities: Investment and agency in second-language learning among Chinese adolescent immigrant students. *Harvard Educational Review* 66, 577–608.

Mitchell, R. (1985). Process research in second-language classrooms. *Language Teaching* 18, 4, 483–628.

Morgan-Short, K. & Wood Bowden, H. (2006). Processing instruction and meaningful output-based instruction: Effects on second language development. *Studies in Second Language Acquisition* 28, 1, 31–66.

Mori, J. (2004). Negotiating sequential boundaries and learning opportunities: A case from a Japanese language classroom. *Modern Language Journal* 88, 4, 536–50.

Morita, N. (2004). Negotiating participation and identity in second language academic communities. *TESOL Quarterly* 38, 4, 573–603.

Moskowitz, G. (1976). The classroom interaction of outstanding foreign language teachers. *Foreign Language Annals* 9, 2, 135–57.

Nassaji, H. & Swain, M. (2000). A Vygotskian perspective on corrective feedback in L2: The effect of random versus negotiated help on the learning of English articles. *Language Awareness* 9, 34–51.

Negueruela, E. (2003). A sociocultural approach to the teaching and learning of second languages: Systemic-theoretical instruction and L2 development. Doctoral dissertation Pennsylvania State University.

Newman, F. & Holzman, L. (1993). *Lev Vygotsky: Revolutionary scientist*. London: Routledge.

Nicholas, H., Lightbown, P. M., & Spada, N. (2001). Recasts as feedback to language learners. *Language Learning* 51, 719–58.

Nobrega Kuschnir, A. & dos Santos Machado, B. (2003). Puzzling, and puzzling about puzzle development. *Language Teaching Research* 7, 2, 163–80.

Nobuyoshi, J. & Ellis, R. (1993). Focused communication tasks and second language acquisition. *ELT Journal* 47, 203–10.

Norris, J. M. & Ortega, L. (2000). Effectiveness of L2 instruction: A research synthesis and quantitative meta-analysis. *Language Learning* 50, 3, 417–528.

Norton, B. (2000). *Identity and language learning: Gender, ethnicity and educational change*. Harlow, UK: Longman.

Norton, B. & Toohey, K. (eds.) (2004). *Critical pedagogies and language learning*. Cambridge: Cambridge University Press.

Nunan, D. (1989). *Understanding language classrooms: A guide for teacher-initiated action*. New York: Prentice-Hall.

Ohta, A. S. (2001). *Second language acquisition processes in the classroom: Learning Japanese*. Mahwah, NJ: Lawrence Erlbaum.

Oliver, R. (2000). Age differences in negotiation and feedback in classroom and pairwork. *Language Learning* 50, 1, 119–51.

Olsher, D. (2004). Talk and gesture: The embodied completion of sequential actions in spoken interaction. In R. Gardner & J. Wagner (eds.), *Second language talk* (pp. 346–80). London: Continuum.

Panova, I. & Lyster, R. (2002). Patterns of corrective feedback and uptake in an adult ESL classroom. *TESOL Quarterly* 36, 4, 573–95.

Pavlenko, A. (2004). Gender and sexuality in foreign and second language education: Critical and feminist approaches. In B. Norton & K. Toohey (eds.), *Critical pedagogies and language learning* (pp. 53–72). Cambridge: Cambridge University Press.

Philp, J. (2003). Constraints on "noticing the gap": Nonnative speakers' noticing of recasts in NS–NNS interaction. *Studies in Second Language Acquisition* 25, 99–126.

Pica, T., Kang, H.-S., & Sauro, S. (2006). Information gap tasks: Their multiple roles and contributions to interaction research methodology. *Studies in Second Language Acquisition* 28, 301–38.

Platt, E. & Brooks, F. B. (2002). Task engagement: A turning point in foreign language development. *Language Learning* 52, 365–400.

Poehner, M. E. & Lantolf, J. P. (2005). Dynamic assessment in the language classroom. *Language Teaching Research* 9, 233–65.

Poole, D. (1992). Language socialisation in the second language classroom. *Language Learning* 42, 593–616.

Rampton, B. (2002). Ritual and foreign language practices at school. *Language in Society* 31, 4, 491–525.

Richards, K. (2003). *Qualitative inquiry in TESOL*. Basingstoke, UK: Palgrave Macmillan.

Roebuck, R. (2000). Subjects speak out: How learners position themselves in a psycholinguistic task. In J. P. Lantolf (ed.), *Sociocultural theory and second language learning* (pp. 79–96). Oxford: Oxford University Press.

Schegloff, E. A., Koshik, I., Jacoby, S., & Olsher, D. (2002). Conversation analysis and applied linguistics. *Annual Review of Applied Linguistics* 22, 3–31.

Scribner, S. & Cole, M. (1981). *The psychology of literacy*. Cambridge, MA: Harvard University Press.

Searle, J. R. (1969). *Speech acts*. Cambridge: Cambridge University Press.

Seedhouse, P. (2004). *The interactional architecture of the language classroom: A conversation analysis perspective*. Oxford: Blackwell.

Seedhouse, P. (2005). Conversation analysis and language learning. *Language Teaching* 38, 4. 165–87.

Sheen, Y. (2004). Corrective feedback and learner uptake in communicative classrooms across instructional settings. *Language Teaching Research* 8, 3, 263–300.

Sinclair, J. M. & Coulthard, M. (1975). *Towards an analysis of discourse*. Oxford: Oxford University Press.

Smith, P. D. (1970). *A comparison of the cognitive and audiolingual approaches to foreign language instruction: The Pennsylvania Foreign Language Project*. Philadelphia: Center for Curriculum Development.

Spada, N. & Frohlich, M. (eds.) (1995). *Communicative orientation of language teaching: Coding conventions and applications*. Sydney: NCELTR.

Stenhouse, L. (1975). *An introduction to curriculum research and development*. London: Heinemann.

Sunderland, J. (2000). New understandings of gender and language classroom research: Texts, teacher talk and student talk. *Language Teaching Research* 4, 2, 149–73.

Sunderland, J. (2004). Classroom interaction, gender, and foreign language learning. In B. Norton & K. Toohey (eds.), *Critical pedagogies and language learning* (pp. 222–41). Cambridge: Cambridge University Press.

Swain, M. (1985). Communicative competence: Some roles of comprehensible input and comprehensible output in its development. In S. Gass & C. Madden (eds.), *Input in second language acquisition* (pp. 235–53). Rowley, MA: Newbury House.

Swain, M. (1995). Three functions of output in second language learning. In G. Cook & B. Seidlhofer (eds.), *Principle and practice in applied linguistics: Studies in honour of H. G. Widdowson* (pp. 125–44). Oxford: Oxford University Press.

Swain, M. (2005). The Output Hypothesis: Theory and research. In E. Hinkel (ed.), *Handbook of research in second language teaching and learning* (pp. 471–84). Mahwah, NJ: Lawrence Erlbaum.

Swain, M. & Lapkin, S. (2001). Focus on form through collaborative dialogue: Exploring task effects. In M. Bygate, P. Skehan, & M. Swain (eds.), *Researching pedagogic tasks: Second language learning, teaching and testing* (pp. 99–118). Harlow, UK: Longman.

Swain, M. & Lapkin, S. (2003). Talking it through: Two French immersion learners' response to reformulation. *International Journal of Educational Research* 37, 285–304.

Swain, M. & Lapkin, S. (2007). "Oh, I get it now!" From production to comprehension in second language learning. In D. M. Brinton, O. Kagan, & S. Bauckus (eds.), *Heritage language education: A new field emerging* (pp. 301–20). London: Routledge.

Thorne, S. L. (2003). Artifacts and cultures-of-use in intercultural communication. *Language Learning & Technology* 7, 38–67.

Tinker Sachs, G. (2002). Teacher and researcher autonomy in action research. *Prospect: A Journal of Australian TESOL* 15, 3, 35–51.

Toohey, K. (2000). *Learning English at school: Identity, social relations and classroom practice.* Clevedon, UK: Multilingual Matters.

Toohey, K. (2001). Disputes in child L2 learning. *TESOL Quarterly* 35, 2, 257–78.

Toohey, K. & Waterstone, B. (2004). Negotiating expertise in an action research community. In B. Norton & K. Toohey (eds.), *Critical pedagogies and language learning* (pp. 219–310). Cambridge: Cambridge University Press.

Toth, P. D. (2006). Processing instruction and a role for output in second language acquisition. *Language Learning* 56, 2, 319–85.

VanPatten, B. (1996). *Input processing and grammar instruction: Theory and research.* Westport CT: Ablex.

VanPatten, B. (2002). Processing instruction: An update. *Language Learning* 52, 755–803.

VanPatten, B. & Cadierno, T. (1993). Input processing and second language acquisition: A role for instruction. *Modern Language Journal* 77, 45–57.

Vygotsky, L. S. (1978). *Mind in society: The development of higher psychological processes.* Cambridge, MA: Harvard University Press.

Wallace, M. (1998). *Action research for language teachers.* Cambridge: Cambridge University Press.

Wilkins, D. A. (1976). *Notional syllabuses.* Oxford: Oxford University Press.

Willett, J. (1995). Becoming first graders in an L2: An ethnographic study of L2 socialisation. *TESOL Quarterly* 29, 3, 473–503.

Wood, D., Bruner, J., & Ross, G. (1976). The role of tutoring in problem-solving. *Journal of Child Psychology and Psychiatry* 17, 89–100.

Zhang, R. (2004). Using the principles of exploratory practice to guide group work in an extensive reading class in China. *Language Teaching Research* 8, 3, 331–46.

37 Issues in Language Teacher Evaluation

KATHLEEN M. BAILEY

This chapter examines current issues in the evaluation of language teachers, a complex and contentious topic. Writing in the field of general education, Brazer (1991, p. 82) has dubbed teacher evaluation "a theater of the absurd." Popham (1988) says that it is "with few exceptions, an anemic and impotent enterprise – promising much but producing little" (p. 269). Nunan and Lamb (1996) say that for many teachers, supervision and evaluation

> are mandatory aspects of their terms of employment. Others are never evaluated (not in a formal sense at least). External evaluation, particularly when it is for purposes of certification or continued employment, can be extremely threatening [and may be] the most anxiety-creating situation the teacher is ever likely to face. (pp. 238–9)

Teacher evaluation is a major component of teacher supervision, a profession which has been called "managing messes" (Schön, 1983, p. 14) and the "reluctant professions" (Mosher & Purpel, 1972). It seems then, from several points of view, that teacher evaluation is fraught with difficulty.

This chapter will address the following questions about teacher evaluation, focusing in some regards specifically on language teacher evaluation:

1 What are the main purposes of teacher evaluation?
2 What do we know about effective teaching?
3 What criteria are used for teacher evaluation?
4 Who is involved in the teacher evaluation process?
5 What types of data can be used to inform teacher evaluation?

The chapter will conclude with a discussion of some principles that can be used to inform language teacher evaluation.

What Are the Main Purposes of Language Teacher Evaluation?

Three basic types of evaluation are identified in the program evaluation literature. The two most frequently discussed are *formative evaluation* and *summative evaluation*. The former provides feedback for program improvement. The latter typically occurs at the end of a program or a funding period for a program. Summative evaluations are often used to decide if a program will be sustained or canceled, or if funding will cease.

These two terms apply to teacher evaluation, as well. Formative evaluation is used "to gain intermittent feedback concerning the nature of some activity or practice while it is in progress" (Daresh, 2001, p. 282). While formative evaluation of teachers is related to promoting professional development and helping teachers improve, summative evaluation of teachers is associated with tenure, promotion, or "terminating" (Hazi, 1994, p. 200).

Formative and summative evaluation both serve individual goals and organizational goals (Darling-Hammond, Wise, & Pease, 1983, p. 302; see Table 37.1). The individual goal of formative evaluation is staff development, while school improvement is its organizational goal. The individual goal of summative evaluation is to make job status decisions (in our case, for language teachers). Its organizational goal revolves around school status decisions, such as whether or not a program should be accredited. Thus, Formative and summative evaluation are macro-concepts. Acheson and Gall (1997) discuss the specific steps that should be followed in planning formative and summative evaluations. (These authors were writing about teachers in US primary and secondary schools in general education.) First, standards should be set which define the criteria for judging effective teaching. Second, job descriptions must be written which spell out the performance expected of teachers in particular teaching situations. Then, based on these standards and the job descriptions, goals can be set. These three steps provide the context for both formative and summative evaluation.

Table 37.1   Individual and institutional goals in formative and summative evaluation (following Darling-Hammond et al., 1983, p. 302)

	Formative evaluation	*Summative evaluation*
Individual goal	Staff development (e.g., improvement of individual teachers' skills and knowledge)	Job status decisions (e.g., retention or promotion of a particular teacher)
Institutional goal	School improvement (e.g., an increase in students' achievement test scores)	School status decisions (e.g., accreditation or probation)

The specific processes of formative evaluation, in Acheson and Gall's (1997) terms, should involve planning classroom observations and then collecting data during the observations. Afterwards, the feedback discussion between the teacher and the supervisor should be based on those data. Where improvement is called for, a plan for assistance should be negotiated between the teacher and the supervisor. In cases of summative evaluation, according to Acheson and Gall, a formal evaluation report should be filed, and a post-evaluation interview should be conducted with the teacher. If the teacher's work does not improve, a dismissal procedure can be initiated.

A third basic type, *diagnostic evaluation*, has been described by Daresh (2001). Diagnostic evaluation yields baseline data about a situation prior to any attempted change. It is used "to determine the beginning status or condition of something . . . prior to the application or intervention or treatment" (2001, p. 281). It follows, therefore, that diagnostic evaluation should be conducted before formative evaluations. Diagnostic evaluations might be used, for instance, in a mentoring program for novice teachers, in which a mentor would first observe the new teacher a few times before suggesting any changes in the teacher's practice. Later, after there have been ample opportunities for the feedback from the formative evaluations to be incorporated, a summative evaluation would be conducted.

The sequence above is somewhat idealized. In teacher evaluation, it is not always clear whether any given interim evaluation process is purely formative, or whether it contributes in some way to a summative evaluation. Teachers may not be willing to share their concerns with principals, department heads, or supervisors during formative evaluations if they (the teachers) fear that their shortcomings will be used against them in a more formal summative evaluation process later. In fact, writing in general education, Popham (1988) has referred to the "dysfunctional marriage of formative and summative teacher evaluation" (p. 269).

What Do We Know about Effective Teaching?

Teacher evaluation depends on some understanding of effective teaching, but over the years there has been a great deal of debate about how to define and measure teacher effectiveness. As Stodolsky (1984) noted, "Evaluation of teachers rests on the assumption that the characteristics of good or effective teachers are known and recognizable" (p. 11).

Effective teaching is a complex construct, which is influenced by many variables, including the subject matter, students' ages and proficiency levels, institutional resources and constraints, and the cultural values of the educational system. Teachers have often been evaluated in terms of "how they matched profiles of good teachers derived from the opinions of experts, despite the fact that there was no evidence that teachers having these characteristics were actually successful in bringing about higher levels of learning in their pupils" (Richards, 1990, pp. 4–5). As Gebhard notes, "The search for effective teaching goes on. For these reasons, since we do not know much about the effects of our teaching behaviors on learning it is difficult to justify what teachers should do in the classroom" (1984, p. 503). These factors also make it difficult to justify telling teachers to change their behavior during the evaluation process. For this reason, alternatives to traditional directive supervision have arisen (see Freeman, 1982, 1989; and Gebhard, 1984).

Much of the research on effective teaching was conducted from the 1960s to the 1980s, using the *process-product approach* to educational research (Long, 1984) (i.e., documenting classroom processes in order to connect them empirically to learning outcomes). Definitions of effective teaching have changed somewhat over time. During the 1960s Rosencranz and Biddle defined teacher competence as "the ability of a teacher to behave in specified ways within a social situation in order to produce empirically demonstrated effects approved by those in the environment in which he functions" (1964, p. 241). Unfortunately, there are few language teaching situations where clear "empirically demonstrated effects" of teaching can inform teacher evaluations. Biddle also defined teacher effectiveness as "the ability of a teacher to produce agreed-upon educational effects in a given situation or context" (1964, p. 20). This definition hinges on stated goals – the "agreed-upon educational effects" that the teaching is supposed to produce – but it does not specify *how* teachers achieve those effects. One approach to measuring teacher effectiveness is to compare the teaching to an established standard of performance. In this model, the agreed-upon standards are usually presented as clear behavioral statements, rather than in theoretical terms, so that evaluative observation data can be compared to those standards.

Acheson and Gall also relate teacher effectiveness to the curriculum: "a teacher is more or less effective depending on how much of the academic curriculum is mastered by his or her students" (1997, p. 25). This definition does not address differences in students' abilities, prior learning, study habits, or motivation, or the impact of situational variables on the school or program. Such definitions may be useful, since "they can be applied in any context, but they often sidestep the very situational factors that influence the teacher's impact on the students' learning" (Bailey, 2006, p. 214).

Language teachers can be evaluated, in part, based on their students' achievement. Strevens views teaching excellence as "the repeated association of a particular sort of teaching with high rates of success on the part of the learners . . . Indeed, excellence in teaching has no meaning unless it is in relation to superior achievement in learning" (1989, p. 74). However, if teaching effectiveness is to be determined by students' learning, then we need to document that learning to provide data for evaluating teachers.

Measuring student achievement is an entire field of study, and reviewing that body of literature is beyond the scope of this chapter. Here we will just note that in order to determine what students have learned in a particular course, one must ascertain what they knew or could do at the beginning and at the end of that course, and then identify any differences in their pre-course and post-course knowledge and skills. This approach to evaluation is only useful if the before and after measures are appropriate, reliable, valid, and not identical to one another.

Defining good teaching on the basis of learning outcomes "would require that that teacher's classroom acts caused the learning" (Zahorik, 1992, p. 394). To attribute students' learning to teachers' teaching one must

> discount students' prior knowledge, aptitude for the particular task, interest, and many other possible causes, such as conditions of the learning environment, the mix of students in the classroom, instructional materials, administrative policies, and involvement of parents. (Zahorik, 1992, p. 394)

Zahorik concludes that "using student learning to measure teaching quality is fraught with conceptual problems" (p. 394).

We must consider student achievement data in light of other factors. Language learners, even in homogeneous classes, may differ on several variables that could influence such outcomes: aptitude, motivation, learning styles, study habits, test-taking skills, and so on. Pennington (1989) says that student achievement is "an unstable measure" and that "there is a great deal of unpredictable individual variation in test scores produced in a specific course or courses as taught by a particular teacher" (p. 171). For these reasons, although students' progress is a central concept in teacher effectiveness and, therefore, in teacher evaluation, teachers should never be evaluated solely on learning gains (or the lack thereof).

There are some findings about effective teaching, however, in both general education and language education, which can inform the teacher evaluation process. Over the years, research in general education has found that teachers whose students learn more than other teachers' students display certain behaviors, attitudes, and skills in common. Citing an early synthesis by Rosenshine and Furst (1973), Acheson and Gall (1997, pp. 25–6) identify the following characteristics of successful teachers:

1   clarity
2   use of varied materials and methods
3   enthusiasm
4   a task-oriented, businesslike approach to teaching
5   avoidance of harsh criticism
6   an indirect teaching style
7   emphasizing content covered on achievement tests
8   using structuring statements to provide an overview for what is about to happen or has happened, and
9   use of questions at many cognitive levels.

These authors conclude that studies published after 1970 "have continued to demonstrate the effectiveness of these teacher characteristics in promoting student learning" (1997, p. 26).

Four key patterns in effective teaching research were identified by Glickman, Gordon, and Ross-Gordon (1998, p. 91):

1 Effective teachers have a sense of being in charge, a "can do" attitude. Although effective teachers face the same kinds of problems as ineffective teachers, they see them as challenges to be met, not suffering to be endured.
2 Effective teachers spend whatever time and effort is necessary to assure that all students learn. They give special attention . . . to slower students.
3 Effective teachers have realistic professional attitudes toward students. They possess neither romantic nor cynical views of their students. They see themselves as "diagnosticians and problem solvers," rather than as "mother substitutes" or "disciplinarians" (Brophy & Evertson, 1976, p. 45).
4 Effective teachers expect their students to achieve. They believe that all students can learn essential knowledge and skills.

While Glickman et al. (1998) were reviewing research in general education, the statements above can also be applied to the evaluation of language teachers.

Identifying teacher effectiveness is not a simple process, perhaps especially in cross-cultural contexts. Medgyes notes that "outstanding teachers cannot be squeezed into any pigeonhole: all outstanding teachers are ideal in their own ways, and as such, are different from each other. The concept of the ideal teacher resists clear-cut definitions, because there are too many variables to consider" (2001, p. 440). A teacher who is outstanding at one school or with a certain age of learners might be merely average in another context. As Strevens points out, "informed teaching in the primary school calls for many differences in practice as compared with, for example, teaching English for specific purposes to mature adults" (1989, p. 84).

Strevens (1989) discussed constraints on excellence in language teaching. These include institutional conditions and the students' intention to learn. He says institutional conditions (which include available materials and equipment, typical class size, hours of instruction, and teacher preparation) must at least be adequate. Second, the "learners' 'intention to learn' needs to be raised and maintenanced" (1989, p. 81). He defined *intention to learn* as "the commitment, usually unconscious, on the part of a learner to give his or her attention and effort to learning" (pp. 81–2). In this view, effective teaching promotes both language learning and students' desire to continue learning.

Strevens added that "a set of regularly co-occurring features can be identified, so that one may refer to 'informed teaching' as the type of instruction and learning/teaching conditions that commonly produce effective learning" (1989:73). He identified six features of informed teaching: (1) the teacher has specialized training and experience; (2) the methodology and materials employed are varied, interesting, and perceived by the learners as relevant; (3) the teacher maintains a high "intention to learn" on the part of the learners; (4) the teacher promotes good relations with the learners and makes special efforts specifically for them; (5) there are ample opportunities for practicing the target language, in learner-centered and communicative ways; and, whenever possible, (6) teaching and learning are conducted at a high rate of intensity (20–25 hours per week).

Strevens concludes, "the informed teacher is an active, reactive, and interactive participant in a two-part learning/teaching process, the other part of which is actively supplied by the learner" (p. 82). Therefore, teacher evaluation processes must acknowledge that students are essential parts of the equation. No teacher's effectiveness can be assessed in a vacuum.

Some research in language teaching has used student achievement as the criterion variable. In a very early classroom study, Politzer (1970) investigated the relationship of students' achievement on several different French tests and the teaching behaviors of 17 secondary school French teachers. Theoretically, a strong positive correlation between a given teaching behavior and student achievement would indicate that the particular teaching behavior was "good" or "effective." Some correlations were found, but Politzer's interpretation of the results is more interesting than the statistical findings. He points out that there is no simple linear relationship between teaching behavior and student achievement: "With most teaching behaviors measured it is quite obvious that the correlations cannot possibly indicate 'the more the better,' 'the more the worse'" (1970, p. 38).

Instead, Politzer suggests that there is an optimum range for the use of various teaching behaviors, so what different teachers do in classrooms cannot be easily characterized as "good" or "bad" teaching (p. 41). He says there are

> probably very few teaching behaviors or devices which can be classified as intrinsically "bad" or "good." Ultimately, most teaching activities . . . have probably some value, but each activity is subject to what might be called a principle of economics. Each activity consumes a limited resource – namely time. Thus the value of each activity depends on the value of other activities which might be substituted for it at a given moment.

Politzer notes that effective teaching is partly a function of individual student differences and the particular teaching context. Therefore, "the 'good' teacher is the one who can make the right judgement as to what teaching device is the most valuable at any given moment" (p. 43).

Politzer's "principle of economics" leads to an interesting problem: Teaching behaviors are observable, but teachers' decision-making typically is not. People who observe and evaluate teachers do not have direct access to the mental processes teachers use in taking one course of action over another. In recent years, research has demonstrated that skilled teachers are able to interpret cues from students and change the course of their lesson plans as needed (Bailey, 1996; Johnson, 1992a, 1992b; Nunan, 1996). Ironically, observation instruments sometimes include rating categories that evaluate teachers on their ability to adhere to and complete the lesson plan, when in fact sometimes the better course of action is to depart from or abandon the lesson plan.

Nerenz and Knop reviewed the literature on the use of classroom time in general education, as well as the few studies on this topic that have been conducted on second and foreign language learning. They concluded that teachers influence achievement

> only inasmuch as they have an effect on the student's *active involvement* with the material to be learned. Simply put, the things teachers do determine the activities available to students; students' involvement in these activities determines, in large part, the learning outcomes. (1982, p. 244)

Nerenz and Knop define two key variables in their own research: The first was *allocated time*, "the amount of time which teachers set aside for particular aspects of the curriculum program" (p. 245). Allocated time is directly related to student achievement. Another key construct, *engaged time*, is "the amount of time in which a student was actively working on appropriate curriculum content" (p. 244). (Elsewhere *engaged time* is called *time on task*.)

Nerenz and Knop hypothesized that engaged time would predict success in foreign language learning: "The effective teacher is one who provides students with opportunities to learn the requisite curriculum content *and* who structures instruction so that students are actually involved – not merely 'busy' – with that content" (p. 245). It follows that good teaching "provides students with a maximal amount of exposure to the material within the construct of the school-wide program" (p. 246).

It appears that the ability to personalize language lessons may influence perceptions of teacher effectiveness. *Personalization* is defined as "any verbal exchange that involves (1) requesting or sharing facts about oneself or one's acquaintances; (2) requesting or expressing personal concerns; (3) sharing or eliciting private knowledge; [and] (4) remembering or restating the personalized content contributed by others" (Omaggio, 1982, p. 257).

Omaggio (1982) reported on parallel studies involving French as a foreign language classes at two US universities. Measures of French teachers' effectiveness were correlated with the personalization moves in their language lessons. At one university, two supervisors ranked the French instructors on their overall effectiveness as teachers. At the second university, students' evaluations of teachers were correlated with the measures of personalization. Statistically significant correlations were found between those teaching effectiveness measures and four measures of personalization. These were the percentage (1) of personalized teacher talk; (2) of personalized student talk; (3) of personalized student talk within the whole class hour; and (4) of time the teacher prompted or facilitated student responses. The findings were summarized as follows:

> When teacher effectiveness, as measured by subjective supervisory ratings and by end-of-semester student evaluation, was compared to in-class variables relating to degree of personalization . . . there was a high positive correlation between those measures. (Omaggio, 1982, p. 265)

Omaggio concluded that "the more effective teacher . . . is one who tries to incorporate such personalized language practice into daily lesson plans" (p. 266).

However, we should remember that these were findings from a correlational design. We cannot infer that a poor teacher who incorporates personalization behaviors will automatically become a better teacher. It is more likely that teachers who use personalization behaviors are those who are in tune with and concerned about their students' needs, welfare and personal lives.

What Criteria Are Used for Language Teacher Evaluation?

It used to be the case that the supervisor's opinion was the main criterion in teacher evaluation. Nowadays, however, many critieria are used in language teacher evaluation. Evaluation involves "the necessary existence and use of a *criterion* or standard to which the 'something' being evaluated may be compared to determine *relative worth*" (Daresh, 2001, p. 281, original italics). The main difficulty lies in determining the standards against which teachers' work will be compared. As McGreal (1988) notes, "an essential element of any effective evaluation system is a clear, visible, and appropriate set of evaluation criteria" (p. 13).

Sometimes, the criterion used to evaluate teachers is either individual opinion or the consensus of a group of evaluators. Historically, the most common evaluative criterion has been the individual supervisor's judgment or opinion. Sometimes an evaluation is carried out by a group of people (supervisors, peers, etc.) acting by consensus, rather than by one person, but the criterion here is still opinion – albeit the collective opinion of a group.

Teaching method is sometimes used in judging teacher effectiveness. If one method rather than another serves as a criterion for evaluation, then differing beliefs about appropriate methods can be a serious source of disagreement if teachers and their evaluators hold divergent views on what constitutes the "best" method(s) for teaching a language. If a program espouses a particular method, the issue is apparently a bit simpler, because teachers can be evaluated on how well they enact that method. For instance, if courses are to be based on a certain method, the teachers' contracts can specify that they will use that method. And if the method's behavioral manifestations are clear, then teachers can be evaluated on how well they implement the method. However, "this sort of methodological monism is rare" (Bailey, 2006, p. 209), and the concept of method is rather vague, and has been discredited of late (see, e.g., Kumaravadivelu, 2001). In addition, it cannot be assumed that teachers follow prescribed methods faithfully.

In addition, "the achievement of excellence is not a question of selecting this or that method. Methodology is sometimes an important factor, but it is virtually never the overriding reason for the achievement of excellence" (Strevens, 1989, p. 81). Professionally prepared teachers who work directly with learners are the people who really know those students' needs, abilities, and learning styles. Well-educated teachers are prepared to make good judgments about alternatives. Therefore, judging teachers on how well they adhere to a prescribed method is a shaky proposition. Smith, Stenson, and Winkler (1980, p. 9) state that requiring the use of any given teaching method may reveal that "some teachers are unwilling to adopt the method in question because they do not believe in it, while others, though willing, may be unable to comply." Furthermore, we do not have convincing evidence that any one method is superior to another. In the absence of clear data supporting any given teaching method, it is risky to use methodological criteria for judging teachers' performance. And given the frequent swing of the methodological pendulum in our field, different generations of teachers and supervisors may have been prepared to work with widely divergent teaching methods. In fact, "with the plethora of teaching methods and the lack of evidence as to the superiority of one method over another, method is seldom a viable criterion for language teacher evaluation" (Bailey, 2006, p. 210).

Teacher competencies are statements about what novice teachers are supposed to know and be able to do. Rhodes and Heining-Boynton (1993, p. 167) listed the following competencies for elementary school foreign language teachers in North Carolina:

1   An understanding of second language acquisition in childhood and its relation to first language development
2   Knowledge of instructional methods appropriate to foreign language instruction in the elementary school
3   Knowledge of instructional resources appropriate to foreign language instruction in the elementary school
4   Knowledge of appropriate assessment and evaluation for foreign language instruction in the elementary school
5   Ability to develop reading and writing skills in learners who are simultaneously acquiring literacy skills in their first language
6   Ability to teach aspects of the target culture appropriate to the development needs and interests of students, including children's literature appropriate to the target culture
7   Knowledge of K-12 foreign language curriculum and the elementary curriculum, the relationship among the content areas, and ability to teach, integrate, or reinforce the elementary school curriculum through or in a foreign language
8   Knowledge of elementary school principles and practices, effective classroom management techniques, and the ability to apply such knowledge to create an affective and physical environment conducive to foreign language learning
9   Proficiency in the foreign language
10   Knowledge of child development
11   Knowledge of the history of foreign language education in the United States and the rationale for various program models in the elementary school
12   Awareness of the need for personal and professional growth
13   An understanding of the need for cooperation among foreign language teachers, other classroom teachers, counselors, school administrators, university personnel, and community members
14   Awareness of skills for program

In evaluating novice teachers, competency statements may be helpful, but some competencies (e.g., proficiency in the foreign language) are more directly observable and assessable than others (e.g., awareness of the need for professional growth).

Evaluators may judge teachers' work against specified standards, which can be stated as performance goals or embedded in an observation instrument. When the desired behavior is described in objective terms, teachers are able to see what is expected, because the descriptive language provides a common frame of reference for teachers and supervisors. An explicit statement of objectives works to the supervisors' advantage as well, because it provides criteria for evaluating teachers' performance. Teachers are more likely to teach to performance standards and give them credence as evaluative criteria if they have helped develop those criteria.

There are three basic types of performance reviews. Although there are variations among them, these three main approaches are comparative reviews, absolute methods, and results-oriented methods (White et al., 1991).

In *comparative reviews*, as the name suggests, teachers are compared to one another and then rank-ordered in terms of their worth to the program. Such comparisons can be highly subjective. In the absence of clear, articulated, public ranking criteria, tremendous power and responsibility are accorded to the person(s) doing the ranking. In addition, professional development, team-building, and collegiality can be undermined in comparative reviews because "it is very difficult to give individual feedback and encourage development with such a system" (White et al., p. 69). Comparative reviews follow the same logic as norm-referenced tests: The value of one person's performance is interpreted relative to that of another person.

A second approach is *absolute methods* (p. 65), in which supervisors evaluate "the performance of an individual by reference to objectively defined standards of performance and not by comparison of others" (p. 69). This approach is similar to criterion-referenced assessment.

The third type of performance review is the category of *results-oriented methods*. In this approach, "performance is viewed as a series of expected results which can be compared to actual performance results" (p. 72). Here, there is an assumption that "shared goal setting will gain individual commitment and that managers will also support and provide resources to jointly agreed plans" (p. 74).

Who Is Involved in the Language Teacher Evaluation Process?

Language teachers are evaluated by any number of individuals in positions of authority, including principals, program administrators, chairpersons, and senior teachers. Language teachers are also evaluated by students and by students' parents, or by adult students' employers. In some countries, perhaps especially those that have a central ministry of education, regional inspectors evaluate teachers throughout large parts of the country.

The regional inspector system of Cyprus was discussed by Mansour (1993, p. 49), who asserts that even a dedicated inspector may be overwhelmed by the workload:

> Let us consider as an example a newly appointed supervisor in a Ministry of Education in a country with limited resources: Our new supervisor has gone through a brief training programme – something like two days – where he has been lectured about the golden rules of supervision; he now wants to expunge his disbelief in supervision, a reminiscence of his days as a teacher. He has envisaged that he will get to know each of his teachers individually and allocate several hours a week for each teacher. When he starts working, our supervisor is disheartened to find that he has 80–110 teachers to supervise in 100–110 days of actual teaching in a semester.

Unfortunately, this inspector eventually "realises that the best he can do is to visit each teacher twice in a semester – just as it is stated in the regulations".

Similar workloads were described in the regional inspector system in Slovenia (Gaies & Bowers, 1990). At the time their report was published, Gaies and Bowers said that one inspector usually supervised "50 English teachers and 15 German teachers in 28 primary schools, and a total of 48 language teachers (30 English, 10 German, 5 French, and 3 Russian) in 14 secondary schools" (p. 172). Due to these responsibilities and given the time constraints, inspectors often remain outsiders to, and perhaps unwelcome visitors in, teachers' professional lives.

The value of the external inspector system has been questioned, but there are probably some benefits of this approach (Bailey, 2006). First, it may be positive for teachers to receive feedback on their teaching from someone who is not a regular colleague. This practice may help to save face and maintain collegial relations within a school. External inspectors may offer some helpful cross-fertilization of ideas within a region, by sharing teaching ideas generated in one area with teachers in another area. Regional inspectors may have been chosen because they are well educated and experienced, and actually have useful advice to offer. Finally, the inspector's status as an outsider may lend credibility to the suggestions or recognition they offer teachers.

There are at least two difficulties with the regional inspector system, however (Bailey, 2006, p. 187): "(1) The supervisors may not be familiar with the students and the local conditions, and (2) time constraints and geography work against inspectors' having any real positive impact on the teachers."

Parents of elementary and secondary school pupils sometimes evaluate language teachers. While parents' input is often not formally solicited (e.g., with an evaluation form), in many school systems, they are encouraged to be involved with their children's education and to provide feedback. However, the extent to which parents give feedback on their children's education may vary from one culture to another (Bailey, 2006).

If teachers are working in a culture other than their own, the patterns of parental interaction with teachers and other school officials may differ from those in their home cultures. Even if a teacher is working in his or her home culture, if the students are second language learners and the parents are refugees or recent immigrants, they may not understand what constitutes acceptable communication with teachers. In addition, they may lack the language proficiency to deal with school officials. For example, migrant farmworkers in California may not be literate in either their first language or in English, and they may not speak English confidently enough to communicate with monolingual English-speaking teachers and other school personnel.

In tertiary, professional, and workplace contexts, teachers are sometimes evaluated by students' employers and sponsoring organizations. These groups are referred to as "user agencies." The evaluations they provide can be quite anecdotal and indirect, or they can be regularly solicited from the graduates' employers or sponsors in a more systematic process (Bailey, 2006).

In some areas, teacher evaluation is conducted by supervisors based within a particular school. For example, at the University of the United Arab Emirates (UAE), a supervisor is responsible for evaluating 12 EFL teachers per team (Murdoch, 2000). This procedure entails "a series of instruments and processes which are implemented sequentially during each 16-week teaching semester" (p. 57). The materials used in the evaluation process include a teacher-generated questionnaire, the observation(s) and follow-up conference(s), the students' evaluation, an action plan from the teacher being evaluated, and the supervisor's report (p. 57).

There are several advantages to having supervisors working in the same program as the teachers they supervise (Bailey, 2006). First, they are presumably quite familiar with the students, the curriculum, and the constraints of the program. Second, their physical location within the school is an advantage over regional inspectors, who often travel quite far to observe teachers. This proximity may make local supervisors more familiar and more available to teachers. As a result, the opinions of local supervisors may be more credible to teachers than those of outsiders (Bailey, 2006). On the other hand, a possible disadvantage is that – depending on how the school-based supervisors conduct evaluations – their presence may generate tension within a school or program. In cases where supervisors provide primarily critical feedback to teachers, a climate of mistrust and unease may be fostered by their regular presence.

Sometimes language teachers are evaluated by their peers, but there seems to be little published research on this topic in language education. In some professions, peer evaluation is "part of the professional's ethical responsibility to clients and to the profession itself, because it furthers the continual development, transmittal, and enforcement of standards of practice" (Darling-Hammond, 1986, p. 558).

Student Evaluation of Teaching (SET) is used in both language and general education. This procedure is often viewed as suspect, with critics claiming it is little more than a popularity contest. There are additional potential problems, however, in multicultural classrooms. Where teachers do not share the students' home culture(s), the teachers' and students' ideas of effective teaching may differ widely. And, as Nunan and Lamb point out, "being evaluated by students can be a frightening prospect for some teachers. It can also be considered culturally inappropriate in many contexts and situations" (1996, p. 244). If this is the case, then the evaluations students provide may not be valid. For example, if students feel it is not their place to evaluate their teachers, they may give overly positive ratings of the teachers and avoid offering criticism.

In the UAE student evaluation of teaching process, at least one of a teacher's classes is given a questionnaire to complete.

> The purpose of this questionnaire is to get feedback directly from students on aspects of the teacher's performance which they can usefully comment on. The questionnaire covers such basic areas as a teacher's speed of speech; the clarity of his/her explanations; the effective use of groups; the ability to establish a rapport with students; the teacher's ability to give attention to all the students, and to make learning interesting. . . . (Murdoch, 2000, pp. 59–60)

In this system, the students evaluate teachers on a five-point scale. They may also write open-ended comments. The supervisor then uses the teachers' average ratings and analyzes the students' comments to determine if any issues should be discussed with the teacher.

Language teachers themselves can also provide information for the evaluation process (Bailey, 2006). Wajnryb notes that "few would dispute the place of self-evaluation in the process of learning teaching" (1986, p. 69). Glickman et al. (1998, pp. 315–16) list six ways that self-evaluation can help teachers' professional development:

1 Visits to the classrooms of several expert teachers for the purpose of comparing expert teaching to one's own teaching and identifying self-improvement goals based on such comparisons
2 Videotaping one's own teaching, then analyzing teaching performance while reviewing the videotape
3 Designing and selecting or analyzing results of surveys or questionnaires administered to students or parents
4 Interviewing supervisors, peers, students, or parents about effective teaching and learning or about one's own instructional performance
5 Keeping a journal of teaching experiences, problems, and successes, accompanied by critical reflection for the purpose of . . . improvement
6 The development of a teaching portfolio for . . . self-reflection and analysis

(We will return to the issue of teaching portfolios below.)

Figure 37.1 depicts the people who can be involved in the teacher-evaluation process arrayed along a continuum from those who are totally external to the reality of teachers' lives in their classrooms to those who are quite centrally involved with that reality. Of course, there can be some variation in this ranking. For instance, if an oil company in Canada sent a group of engineers to Kuwait to learn Arabic for the purposes of working in the petroleum industry, that company – as user agency – would be more distant from the classroom context than would Kuwaiti regional inspectors.

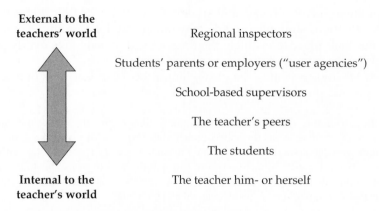

**External to the
teachers' world**

Regional inspectors

Students' parents or employers ("user agencies")

School-based supervisors

The teacher's peers

The students

**Internal to the
teacher's world**

The teacher him- or herself

Figure 37.1   People involved in the teacher evaluation process

What Types of Data Can Be Used to Inform Teacher Evaluation?

Murdoch (1998, Multiple Data Sources section, para. 1) notes that there is a "trend towards gathering data from different users' perspectives: teachers, students, testing experts, course coordinators, teacher trainers, outside experts, etc." Just as it is possible to solicit evaluative data from various people, is also possible to include multiple types of data in the evaluation of language teachers.

Pennington (1989) categorizes language teacher evaluation tools as being either *fluid-response instruments* or *fixed-response instruments*. The fluid response instruments include "conversations, letters, and open-ended questionnaires" (p. 168). The fixed response instruments consist of "limited response questionnaires, rating scales, tests, and different kinds of summative descriptive data" (p. 168).

There are pros and cons of both types of data. Fluid-response instruments allow individuals to comment on teachers' work, but they are "difficult to interpret, to tally, and to score in any reliable manner" (Pennington, 1989, p. 169). Fixed response instruments are efficient in terms of the initial ratings and subsequent tabulations, but they "discourage reflective, thoughtful responses and do not allow respondents to convey detailed, specific information" (p. 169). Pennington feels that these two types of instruments provide complementary information and, therefore, both should be used in teacher evaluation.

Using multiple sources of information in teacher evaluation can be beneficial in at least three ways (Bailey, 2006). First, more information from knowledgeable sources will provide a more valid and reliable basis for evaluating teachers' work. Second, evaluations will be on more solid ethical and legal grounds if more than one kind of data influences any decisions resulting from the evaluation process. Third, everyone involved will have more confidence in the outcomes of an evaluation process if a range of data and evaluative methods are used.

An interesting recent development in teacher evaluations is the use of teaching portfolios compiled by the teachers themselves. Teaching portfolios can be valuable components of an evaluation process because "the best assessment is self-assessment. Teachers are more likely to act on what they find out about themselves" (Green & Smyser, 1996, p. x). A teaching portfolio is defined as "a purposeful collection of any aspect of a teacher's work that tells the story of a teacher's efforts, skills, abilities, achievements, and contributions to his/her colleagues, institution, academic discipline or community" (Brown & Wolfe-Quintero, 1997, p. 28). These authors say that "because of the reflective nature of portfolios, developing one inevitably enlarges one's view of what teaching is" (p. 28). In this sense, creating a teaching portfolio is a professional development activity.

Recently, preservice language teacher education programs have begun to use teaching portfolios in teacher evaluation. For example, portfolios have been used to evaluate pre-service language teachers in the practicum context. Liu (2000, p. 21) says it is helpful for each practicum student's portfolio to include

the student's lesson plans, journals, observation reports, and the instructor's written feedback on the student's work, including teaching ... The various forms of information that come from the practicum students' experiences at different sites and in different contexts also make it easier for the university course instructor to conduct multiple-index evaluations of the practicum students.

Liu concludes that "using multiple indexes to assess practicum students' performance enhances the validity of the student evaluation" (p. 21).

Working in Italy, Calzoni (2001) lists three key ways that teaching portfolios might be used in a teacher evaluation process: "to find out the teacher's level of performance; to find out what level of performance the teacher is capable of at a certain time; and to find out whether, after a given period, the educational goals identified at the beginning of the assessment process have been reached" (p. 15). She cautions that teachers must be informed in advance about the objectives and the criteria with which they will be evaluated.

Calzoni notes that the portfolio's sequence and contents could be based on uniform requirements, but how teachers meet those requirements could be personal and individualized. For these reasons, using portfolios in teaching evaluations can combat the top-down imbalance of traditional evaluation, because the teachers themselves have some degree of control over what is included in the portfolio.

Teaching portfolios can be particularly helpful to both the teachers undergoing evaluation and the person(s) responsible for that evaluation because

(1) The act of creating and maintaining a portfolio may motivate teachers to improve their performance and develop themselves professionally ... [and] (2) the information included in a portfolio can assist administrators, as current or prospective employers, in evaluating the teachers' qualifications. (Wolfe-Quintero & Brown, 1998, p. 24)

Portfolios are used in some inservice contexts, as well. In the Hawai'i English Language Program, full-time teachers are evaluated annually by a committee. Brown and Wolfe-Quintero report that "The evaluation committee found that the portfolios added an important dimension to the annual review because they intersected with student evaluations and administrators' observations to reveal a deeper picture of instructors' strengths as well as areas of recommended growth" (p. 26).

Concluding Comments

There are many problems in language teacher evaluation, partly due to the fact that myriad complex social variables influence language teaching (e.g., class size, student motivation, availability of well-prepared teachers, access to appropriate materials), and these variables differ widely from one context to another. Consequently, it is virtually impossible to identify universal criteria for language teacher evaluation.

In spite of its importance (both to programs and to the individuals involved), language teacher evaluation is sometimes not given enough time, attention, or resources, compared to other initiatives (Bailey, 2006). Murdoch laments that "teacher evaluation matters are often perceived to be of secondary importance, and as a result, tend to be poorly developed in many institutions" (2000, p. 5). In many teaching contexts, performance reviews are based on infrequent observations by a supervisor who has little time for observations and conferencing. As a result, Murdoch says, these ad-hoc evaluation procedures "can only produce universal teacher anxiety, a lack of belief in the validity of observation, and a subtle undermining of other institutional initiatives to support teachers' efforts to deliver courses effectively" (p. 5).

Teacher evaluation processes can also be developed through the use of fair and effective principles, however. A discussion of such principles is provided by Murdoch (2000, pp. 55–6), who states that "a progressive teacher-performance review system needs to be founded on five key principles or aims": (1) to encourage reflective practice; (2) to empower and motivate teachers; (3) to assess all aspects of a teacher's professional activity; (4) to take account of students' views; and (5) to promote collaboration.

The first principle, *to encourage reflective practice*, is related to formative evaluation. Practicing reflective teaching involves systematically gathering data about one's own teaching, reviewing those data, and using those reflections to bring about improvement (Richards & Lockhart, 1994). If teachers are expected to continue their own professional development, teacher evaluation should encourage reflective teaching.

Murdoch's second principle is *to empower and motivate teachers*. Effective performance reviews provide teachers with central roles in developing the instruments and procedures used in evaluating their work (Murdoch, 2000, p. 55). He feels teachers can be empowered by setting their own objectives based on the activities they do most often.

The third principle of effective evaluation is that it will *assess all aspects of a teacher's professional activity*. Murdoch notes that "a common failing of many teacher-performance reviews is that they make judgements about teachers based on unrepresentative samples – usually isolated observations – of a teacher's work" (p. 56).

Fourth, an evaluation system should *take account of students' views*. Ideally, in a student-centered curriculum, evaluation should recognize the value of "collecting students' views about their teacher and the classroom environment. This also makes practical sense, since they are the ones who spend the most time interacting with a teacher" (p. 56).

Regarding the fifth principle, to promote collaboration, Murdoch says "the relations between a supervisor, senior teacher, or director of studies with the teachers whom he/she evaluates must be built on dialogue . . . In order to tune in on the teacher's perspective, a non-dogmatic approach to teaching issues is essential" (p. 56).

In this chapter we considered three primary purposes for language teacher evaluation: formative, summative, and diagnostic. We looked at some research on effective teaching and considered the various criteria that can be used in language teacher evaluation. We saw that many different people can be involved in teacher evaluation and that there are several potential types of information for language teacher evaluation, including teachers' portfolios. In closing, we examined Murdoch's (2000) principles for developing a performance review system. Applying such principles systematically and fairly can help alleviate some of the problems and anxiety normally associated with language teacher evaluation.

REFERENCES

Acheson, K. A. & Gall, M. D. (1997). *Techniques in the clinical supervision of teachers: Preservice and inservice applications*, 4th edn. New York: Longman.

Bailey, K. M. (1996). The best laid plans: Teachers' in-class decisions to depart from their lesson plans. In K. M. Bailey & D. Nunan (eds.), *Voices from the language classroom* (pp. 15–40). Cambridge: Cambridge University Press.

Bailey, K. M. (2006). *Language teacher supervision: A case-based approach*. New York: Cambridge University Press.

Biddle, B. J. (1964). The integration of teacher effectiveness research. In B. J. Biddle & W. J. Ellena (eds.), *Contemporary research on teacher effectiveness* (pp. 1–40). New York: Holt, Rinehart and Winston.

Brazer, S. D. (1991). The assistant principal: The search for meaning in teacher evaluation. *Educational Leadership* 48, 6, 82.

Brophy, J. E. & Everston, C. M. (1976). *Learning from teaching: A developmental perspective*. Boston, MA: Allyn and Bacon.

Brown, J. D. & Wolfe-Quintero, K. (1997). Teacher portfolios for evaluation: A great idea or a waste of time? *Language Teacher* 21, 1, 28–30.

Calzoni, D. (2001). Teacher portfolios. *IATEFL Teacher Development SIG Newsletter* 1, 1, 13–16.

Daresh, J. C. (2001). *Supervision as proactive leadership*, 3rd edn. Prospect Heights, IL: Waveland Press.

Darling-Hammond, L. (1986). A proposal for evaluation in the teaching profession. *Elementary School Journal* 86, 4, 531–51.

Darling-Hammond, L., Wise, A. E., & Pease, S. R. (1983). Teacher evaluation in the organizational context: A review of the literature. *Review of Educational Research* 53, 3, 285–328.

Freeman, D. (1982). Observing teachers: Three approaches to inservice training and development. *TESOL Quarterly* 16, 1, 21–8.

Freeman, D. (1989). Teacher training, development and decision making: A model of teaching and related strategies for language teacher education. *TESOL Quarterly* 23, 1, 27–45.

Gaies, S. & Bowers, R. (1990). Clinical supervision of language teaching: The supervisor as trainer and educator. In J. C. Richards & D. Nunan (eds.), *Second language teacher education* (pp. 167–81). New York: Cambridge University Press.

Gebhard, J. G. (1984). Models of supervision: Choices. *TESOL Quarterly* 18, 3, 501–14. Reprinted in J. C. Richards & D. Nunan (eds.) (1990), *Second language teacher education* (pp. 156–66). New York: Cambridge University Press.

Glickman, C. D., Gordon, S. P., & Ross-Gordon, J. M. (1998). *Supervision of instruction: A developmental approach*, 4th edn. Boston, MA: Allyn and Bacon.

Green, J. E. & Smyser, S. O. (1996). *The teacher portfolio: A strategy for professional development and evaluation*. Lancaster, PA: Technomic Publishing.

Hazi, H. M. (1994). The teacher evaluation-supervision dilemma: A case of entanglements and irreconcilable differences. *Journal of Curriculum and Supervision* 9, 2, 195–216.

Johnson, K. E. (1992a). The instructional decisions of pre-service English as a second language teachers: New directions for teacher preparation programs. In J. Flowerdew, M. N. Brock, & S. Hsia (eds.), *Perspectives on second language teacher development* (pp. 115–34). Hong Kong: City Polytechnic of Hong Kong.

Johnson, K. E. (1992b). Learning to teach: Instructional actions and decisions of preservice ESL teachers. *TESOL Quarterly* 26, 3, 507–35.

Kumaravadivelu, B. (2001). Toward a postmethod pedagogy. *TESOL Quarterly* 35, 4, 537–60.

Liu, D. (2000). Multiple-site practicum: Opportunities for diverse learning and teaching experiences. *TESOL Journal* 9, 1, 18–22.

Long, M. H. (1984). Process and product in ESL program evaluation. *TESOL Quarterly* 18, 3, 409–25.

Mansour, W. (1993). Towards developmental ELT supervision. *English Teacher Forum* 31, 3, 48–50.

McGreal, T. L. (1988). Evaluation for enhancing instruction: Linking teacher evaluation and staff development. In S. J. Stanley & J. W. Popham (eds.), *Teacher evaluation: Six prescriptions for success* (pp. 1–29). Alexandria, VA: ASCD.

Medgyes, P. (2001). When the teacher is a non-native speaker. In M. Celce-Murcia (ed.), *Teaching English as a second or foreign language* (3rd edn., pp. 415–27). Boston: Heinle and Heinle.

Mosher, R. L. & Purpel, D. E. (1972). *Supervision: The reluctant profession*. New York: Houghton Mifflin.

Murdoch, G. (1998). A progressive teacher evaluation system [Electronic version]. *The English Teaching Forum* 36, 3, 2–11.

Murdoch, G. (2000). Introducing a teacher-supportive evaluation system. *English Language Teaching Journal* 54, 1, 54–64.

Nerenz, A. G. & Knop, C. (1982). A time-based approach to the study of teacher effectiveness. *Modern Language Journal* 66, 3, 243–54.

Nunan, D. (1996). Hidden voices: Insider's perspectives on classroom interaction. In K. M. Bailey & D. Nunan (eds.), *Voices from the language classroom* (pp. 41–56). Cambridge: Cambridge University Press.

Nunan, D. & Lamb, C. (1996). *The self-directed teacher: Managing the learning process.* Cambridge: Cambridge University Press.

Omaggio, A. C. (1982). The relationship between personalized classroom talk and teacher effectiveness ratings: Some research results. *Foreign Language Annals* 14, 4, 255–69.

Pennington, M. C. (1989). Directions for faculty evaluation in language education. *Language, Culture and Curriculum* 2, 3, 167–93.

Politzer, R. L. (1970). Some reflections on "good" and "bad" language teaching behaviors. *Language Learning* 20, 31–43.

Popham, W. J. (1988). The dysfunctional marriage of formative and summative teacher evaluation. *Journal of Personnel Evaluation in Education* 1, 269–73.

Rhodes, N. C. & Heining-Boynton, A. L. (1993). Teacher training with a twist: A collaborative project in North Carolina. *Foreign Language Annals* 26, 2, 155–70.

Richards, J. C. (1990). The dilemma of teacher education in second language teaching. In J. C. Richards & D. Nunan (eds.), *Second language teacher education* (pp. 3–15). Cambridge: Cambridge University Press.

Richards, J. C. & Lockhart, C. (1994). *Reflective teaching in second language classrooms.* Cambridge: Cambridge University Press.

Rosencranz, H. A. & Biddle, B. J. (1964). The role approach to teacher competence. In B. J. Biddle & W. J. Ellena (eds.), *Contemporary research on teacher effectiveness* (pp. 232–63). New York: Holt, Rinehart and Winston.

Rosenshine, B. V. & Furst, N. (1973). The use of direct observation to study teaching. In R. M. W. Travers (ed.), *Handbook of research on teaching* (2nd edn., pp. 122–83). Chicago: Rand McNally.

Schön, D. A. (1983). *The reflective practitioner: How professionals think in action.* New York: Basic Books.

Smith, J., Stenson, N., & Winkler, K. A. (1980). Toward more effective teacher observation and evaluation. Paper presented at the 1980 TESOL Convention, San Francisco.

Stodolsky, S. S. (1984). Teacher evaluation: The limits of looking. *Educational Researcher* 13, 11–22.

Strevens, P. (1989). The achievement of excellence in language teaching. In J. H. Esling (ed.), *Multicultural education and policy: ESL in the 1990's* (pp. 73–87). Toronto: Ontario Institute for Studies in Education.

Wajnryb, R. (1986). Learning to teach: The place of self-evaluation. *TESL Reporter* 19, 4, 69–73.

White, R., Martin, M., Stimpson, M., & Hodge, R. (1991). *Management in English language teaching.* New York: Cambridge University Press.

Wolfe-Quintero, K. & Brown, J. D. (1998). Teacher portfolios. *TESOL Journal* 7, 6, 24–7.

Zahorik, J. A. (1992). Perspectives and imperatives: Good teaching and supervision. *Journal of Curriculum and Supervision* 7, 4, 393–404.

38 Investigating the Effects and Effectiveness of L2 Instruction

RICK DE GRAAFF AND
ALEX HOUSEN

Introduction

For the purposes of this chapter, we define second language (L2)[1] instruction as any deliberate attempt to promote language learning by manipulating the mechanisms of learning and/or the conditions under which these operate.[2] This deliberately broad definition covers a wide range of pedagogic and didactic approaches, methods, strategies, techniques, practices, and activities, all of which can be applied in a wide range of settings (although most typically in a classroom). Different types of instruction will be considered later.

The role and effectiveness of instruction in second language acquisition (SLA) have been controversial since antiquity (see Richards & Rodgers, 2001, for an overview). Does instruction really enable the learning of a second or foreign language, or at least facilitate it? Most language teachers have, for obvious reasons perhaps, assumed that it does, but SLA researchers have been more divided. Those who adhere to what Long and Robinson (1998) have called a non-interventionist view see no, or at best a nugatory, role for instruction, on the assumption that L2 learning, like L1 acquisition, is essentially an incidental process guided by universal mechanisms that are largely impervious to intervention (Breen & Candlin, 1980; Krashen, 1985, 1994; Krashen & Terrell, 1983; Prabhu, 1987; Schwartz, 1993).

Proponents of an interventionist position consider this view to be misguided, extreme, or at least premature (e.g., Rutherford & Sharwood-Smith, 1985; R. Ellis, 1991, 1997b, 2005; Long, 1983, 1988). They believe that L2 instruction can make a difference in how (well) learners acquire a second language: "while it may not be necessary to achieve competence in the L2, it undoubtedly helps" (R. Ellis, 2005, p. 725). This assumption is supported by cumulative evidence from different types of research. These include studies that compare L2 instruction with naturalistic exposure or meaning-driven communication in both second and foreign language contexts (see reviews in R. Ellis, 1994, 1997b; Larsen-Freeman

& Long, 1991; Long, 1983, 1988), and studies that compare different types of L2 instruction relative to control conditions (see the review in Norris & Ortega, 2000; see also R. Ellis, 2001, 2002). This research has involved a wide variety of learners (children and adults; beginners, intermediate and advanced learners). Norris and Ortega's (2000) meta-analysis of the experimental research further suggests that not only does instruction have an effect on learning outcome, but the net effect of L2 instruction is substantial, so that "L2 instruction can be characterized as effective in its own right" (Norris & Ortega, 2000, p. 480). There are even theoretical arguments that L2 instruction may be indispensable for successful SLA, at least for some types of learners (e.g., adult learners, or foreign language learners, who may have little contact with the L2 outside the instructional setting), or for some aspects of the L2 system (e.g., non-salient aspects of grammar) and L2 proficiency (e.g., high levels of grammatical accuracy) (DeKeyser, 2000; Doughty, 2003). Whatever the case may be, the position taken by most researchers today, including the authors of this chapter, is that SLA is a process which can be influenced by instruction, though not necessarily *ad libitum*, and it is exactly this relative openness of SLA to instruction which has to be explored, so that it can be exploited for both theoretical and practical purposes.

The study of L2 instruction has practical and theoretical significance. Its practical significance arises from the assumption that a better understanding of how instruction affects L2 learning may lead to more effective L2 teaching; its theoretical importance is related to the understanding of how the brain processes linguistic input of various kinds to arrive at linguistic representations in the mind (Spada & Lightbown, 2002). This twofold significance may explain why the past 25 years, in particular, have seen such an explosion of research on the effects and effectiveness of L2 instruction. Comprehensive surveys of this research can be found in, inter alia, R. Ellis (1994, 1997b, 2001, 2002, 2005, 2006b), Doughty (2003), Norris & Ortega (2000, 2001), Spada (1997), and Williams (2005). This chapter will not seek to add to these surveys. Rather we will present a framework for investigating the role of instruction in SLA and identify major research issues in terms of this framework. Next we will consider these issues in the light of the research methods that have been employed in the investigation of L2 instruction. We will conclude by formulating recommendations for future research on the role of instruction for second and foreign language learning and teaching, focusing on usefulness and applicability for teaching practice.

A Conceptual Framework for Investigating L2 Instruction

In order to consider the effects and effectiveness of L2 instruction, we must first be clear about what we mean by these two terms. The term *effect* refers to any observable change in learner outcome (knowledge, disposition or behavior) that can be attributed to an instructional intervention (possibly in interaction with other, contextual variables). *Effectiveness* (or *efficacy*, *usefulness*) refers to the extent to which the actual outcomes of instruction match the intended or desired effects (within the practical constraints imposed by the larger instructional context). Effective instruction, then, is context-appropriate instruction, that is, goal-appropriate, learner-appropriate, and resources-appropriate.

In the following two sections, we present a framework that identifies major dimensions along which the effects of L2 instruction may be fruitfully investigated. This framework includes both (1) the nature of the effects of instruction on SLA, and (2) the factors that moderate these effects and, hence, the effectiveness of instruction.

Potential effects of instruction

The variegated effects of instruction on SLA can be envisaged in terms of (1) the basic dimensions of SLA, (2) the basic components of SLA, and (3) the different types of L2 knowledge that instruction yields. These three sets of factors are elucidated below.

Effects on the basic dimensions of SLA

Instruction can, at least in principle, affect any one of the three basic dimensions of the L2 learning process, as described by, inter alia, Klein (1986) and R. Ellis (1994):

1   it may affect the *route* of L2 acquisition, i.e., lead learners to acquire the various features of the L2 in a different order from, for example, non-instructed learners;
2   it may affect the *rate* of L2 acquisition, i.e., accelerate it or slow it down;
3   it may affect *ultimate levels of attainment* and the *end-state* of L2 learning; i.e., instructed language learners may reach either a higher or lower ultimate stage of interlanguage development and level of L2 proficiency than non-instructed learners.

These three dimensions of SLA provided the broad framework for a series of studies conducted in the 1980s to examine specific effects of instruction (e.g., Eckman, Bell, & Nelson, 1988; R. Ellis, 1989; Pavesi, 1986; Pica, 1983; Pienemann, 1989; see surveys in R. Ellis, 1994; Larsen-Freeman & Long, 1991; Long, 1983, 1988). Collectively, these studies have led to the following claims:

1   For those (grammatical) aspects of language which are developmentally constrained by natural processing mechanisms or by universal principles of language, instruction seems incapable of overriding the "natural" route of acquisition. Both instructed and naturalistic (non-instructed) learners follow the same orders and proceed through the same sequences of acquisition, at least when measured by spontaneous production tasks.
2   When appropriately timed (i.e., when it targets structures within the learner's "developmental reach"), instruction can assist learners to move faster along the natural route of development, so that their rate of acquisition is accelerated when compared to non-instructed learners.

3 (a) Overall, instructed learners ultimately reach higher stages of inter-language development and higher levels of proficiency than uninstructed L2 learners.

   (b) In particular, instructed learners attain higher levels of grammatical accuracy than non-instructed learners, although not necessarily higher levels of communicative fluency.

   (c) Instruction may even be necessary to overcome premature fossilization of specific grammatical subsystems, in particular, aspects of the L2 that cannot be learned on the basis of mere exposure or that go by unnoticed or seem communicatively redundant to the learner.

The observation of natural orders and sequences of acquisition seems to limit the potential effectiveness of instruction (cf. claim 1). The second claim implies that instruction would only be effective when it is targeted at an L2 structure within the learner's developmental reach. The logical and practical corollary of these two claims is that, firstly, for instruction to be effective, it must be continuously adapted to learners' changing developmental needs as they move along the natural route of acquisition; and, secondly, that the effectiveness of instruction crucially depends on knowing when to instruct which aspect of the language, and in which order (R. Ellis, 1994, 1997b). Putting these principles into practice would be problematic, however, if for no other reason than that our knowledge about which aspects of language develop in a fixed order and why they do so is still too limited to make reliable pedagogical decisions (DeKeyser, 1998; R. Ellis, 1997b; Lightbown, 1998, 2000). But the effectiveness of instruction need not be as limited as the claims above suggest. Recent research indicates that, contrary to the long-held belief that developmental orders are primarily driven by universal processing constraints, which may indeed be impervious to instructional intervention, the orders are primarily caused by "learner-external" features, such as the perceptual saliency of linguistic features in the input or their communicative value (Goldschneider & DeKeyser, 2001). If so, the notion of developmental readiness is downplayed, and there may still be a stronger role for instruction if it succeeds in manipulating either the amount and saliency of exposure or the learner's input processing strategies in such a way that acquisition is facilitated. We will return to this possibility shortly.

Essential components of SLA

As Klein (1986) points out, successful SLA depends on three basic conditions: first, the learner must have sufficient exposure to the L2 (i.e., have sufficient input and output opportunities); second, he or she must (still) possess a functional language faculty, which comprises mental resources used for processing and internalizing linguistic material; and, third, he or she must have the appropriate propensity (e.g., motivation) to put his or her language faculty to actual use. Thus, in terms of the essential components of SLA, instruction can be viewed as doing one, or several, of the following:

- provide learners with exposure to the L2 (i.e., input and output opportunities), which is otherwise insufficiently available;
- influence learners' propensity to use and learn the target language (e.g., by stimulating their motivation);
- trigger or enhance acquisition processes and processing mechanisms, which are otherwise insufficiently activated (e.g., noticing, automatization processes, restructuring of linguistic representations).

The observation that instruction is effective for L2 learners for whom classroom instruction is the only significant source of and context for exposure to the L2, as is often the case in foreign language learning contexts, is probably as trite as it is true. More instructive are the findings of studies conducted in second language and study-abroad contexts, where learners have access to both instruction and naturalistic exposure (e.g., Howard, 2005; Spada, 1986; for reviews, see R. Ellis, 1994; Freed, 1998; Larsen-Freeman & Long, 1991; Long, 1983, 1988). These studies indicate that when either type and amount of naturalistic exposure or type and amount of instruction are held constant, the advantages of instruction are supported (Doughty, 2003; Long, 1983). All other things being equal, then, classroom instruction seems more effective for SLA than mere communicative exposure, although a combination of the two probably constitutes the optimal mix.

Research on how instruction may affect learners' propensity to acquire an L2 is particularly thin on the ground. Propensity factors are dependent on the learners' socio-affective disposition, that is, on their needs, attitudes, and, particularly, motivations. Researchers (and L2 teachers) have long recognized the crucial role of L2 motivation in SLA and agree that "motivating students should be seen as central in teaching effectiveness" (Dörnyei, 1998, p. 130). It is therefore surprising that researchers have only recently started to consider how instruction can shape L2 motivation or otherwise create a socio-affective disposition conducive to SLA.[3] A central focus in this line of research is the concept of intrinsic motivation, the motivation that is generated through, for example, the use of authentic, goal-oriented, high interest instructional activities. Interest in how instructional variables can affect motivation is further fuelled by the growing interest in task-based instruction, which stresses the importance of learners' "engagement": instructional tasks must be "challenging" so that they will be cognitively involving and intrinsically motivating (see R. Ellis, 2003, 2005; Long, 1985; Platt & Brooks, 2002). Examples of such task-based studies include Peacock (1997), who examined the use of authentic teaching materials to promote motivation, and Green (1993), who looked at the relationship between task variables and motivation, task enjoyment and task effectiveness.

In contrast to the exposure and propensity components, much research has considered the effects of instruction within the domain of SLA processes. As Long pointed out in his 1988 review, "the SLA literature contains a dazzling array of putative acquisition processes" (p. 119). In the last 15 years, SLA researchers have increasingly adopted an information-processing approach (cf. McLaughlin & Heredia, 1996) to investigate how instruction can influence those processes. The effectiveness of instruction is operationalized psycholinguistically, in terms of input-processing enhancements that help learners extract relevant linguistic structures from the L2 input and store them as linguistic representations in memory, and in terms of knowledge retrieval enhancements that help learners maximize access to their L2 knowledge for language performance. Drawing on processing models of SLA (e.g., Robinson, 2001; Skehan, 1998, 2002), Housen and Pierrard (2005) have proposed that, for the purpose of investigating the role and effects of instruction, SLA may be envisaged as comprising three broad types of processes: knowledge internalization, knowledge modification, and knowledge consolidation. Accordingly, the goals and results of instruction may enable learners to:

- internalize new L2 features – internalization involves noticing, analyzing, and eventually integrating, L2 features into memory as knowledge, so that learners become more elaborate and sophisticated L2 users with, for example, a richer and deeper lexical, grammatical or phonological repertoire;
- modify (i.e., restructure, extend, fine-tune) their L2 knowledge, including the deviant, non-targetlike aspects of their interlanguage, so that they become not only more complex but also more accurate L2 users;
- consolidate their L2 knowledge, for example, through deeper processing and automatization, so that they can use their L2 with greater ease and for a wider range of tasks and functions, in short, so that they become more fluent and more stable L2 users.

This threefold taxonomy characterizes SLA processes in terms of measurable performance manifestations of the knowledge and skills that the respective processes are supposed to yield, that is, learners' linguistic richness, complexity, accuracy, fluency and variability. As such, it enables global yet researchable claims about the effects of instruction.

Most instruction research to date has investigated whether instruction can influence learners' allocation of attentional resources to the point of *noticing*, i.e., the critical level of awareness, at which selected language features are extracted from the input and registered in short-term memory as intake before being further processed and integrated in long-term memory – or not, as the case may be (cf. Schmidt, 1995, 2001; see also, Robinson, 1996a, 1996b, 2003; Tomlin & Villa, 1994). The literature discusses several instructional procedures that may promote noticing, although it is often not exactly clear why these procedures are effective, or, rather, are sometimes effective and sometimes not (see Doughty & Williams, 1998a; R. Ellis, 2001, 2002, 2005; Williams, 2005). We will return to this issue below.

Noticing relevant L2 features in the input and converting them to intake is a necessary, but only a first, stage in the acquisition process. Once noticed, these features will have to be further processed and integrated into the learner's developing L2 system, proceduralized, and eventually automatized to enable accurate and fluent spontaneous language use (McLaughlin & Heredia, 1996; Segalowitz, 2003; Skehan, 1998, 2002). There is some empirical evidence to suggest that instruction can also assist these other learning processes that operate at later stages in the acquisition process. For instance, hole- and gap-noticing activities, which make learners aware of, respectively, the holes in their L2 knowledge and the discrepancy between their own L2 output and the target input, are said not only to promote noticing but also to lead the learner to restructure or otherwise modify his or her interlanguage knowledge toward the target norm (Swain, 1995, 1998, 2005; Swain & Lapkin, 1998; Williams, 2005). A similar role is attributed to corrective feedback activities on learner errors, such as recasts and overt corrections (for a discussion of the effectiveness of the various feedback options, see Russell & Spada, 2006).

Some studies also suggest that instruction can increase learners' control over their developing L2 knowledge, and the speed and efficiency with which they can access their knowledge in L2 production and comprehension tasks (e.g., Gass et al., 1999; VanPatten & Cadierno, 1993; VanPatten & Sanz, 1995), although the degree of automatization needed for spontaneous, fluent language use is probably a lengthy process that can only be obtained with substantial and appropriate practice in meaningful interaction (DeKeyser & Juffs, 2005; Segalowitz, 2003; see Gatbonton & Segalowitz, 1988, and Robinson, 2001, for concrete examples of how instructional activities can promote automatization; see N. Ellis & Laporte, 1997, for a critical discussion of the effectiveness of various types of practice for automatization and other aspects of SLA). Other studies suggest that certain instructional activities, such as those that require learners to creatively produce their own output, can trigger deeper and more elaborate processing of L2 forms, resulting in more solid and durable L2 knowledge (Izumi, 2002; Swain, 2005).

SLA processes are often discussed in terms of the implicit–explicit distinction. This distinction, which originated in research in experimental psychology (e.g., Reber, 1993), was introduced in SLA research by Krashen (1981, 1985), who considered the *implicit* process of L2 *acquisition* to be qualitatively different from the *explicit* process of L2 *learning*, with acquisition being impervious to instruction, while learning hinged on instruction. Over the years, the terms implicit and explicit learning have come to mean different things to different researchers. DeKeyser (2003) defines implicit learning as "learning without awareness of what is being learned" (p. 314). For Hulstijn (2002), implicit learning requires substantial exposure to L2 material, and is a largely subconscious and unintentional computational process leading to knowledge represented in the form of "networks with layers of hidden units representing knowledge in a distributed, subsymbolic way" (Hulstijn, 2002, p. 193). In contrast, explicit learning is "a conscious, deliberative process of concept formation and concept linking" (Hulstijn, 2002, p. 206). In this view, explicit learning is seen as a willfully controlled process, and therefore as more amenable to instruction than implicit learning.

Other researchers stress that implicit and explicit learning both involve the allocation of attentional resources to input – albeit to different degrees of awareness – and both result in memorial representations of input features (de Graaff, 1997a, 1997b; Robinson, 1996a, 1996b, 1997a). In this view, the distinction is best defined in terms of the conditions under which the learning takes place, or in terms of the different types of knowledge that result from the learning.

Some authors doubt whether truly implicit learning processes, at least of the type that operate in first language acquisition, are effective in classroom contexts (as implicit learning often leads to incomplete knowledge with classroom learners), or feasible (given the massive amounts of exposure and time that these processes demand), or are even at all possible for post-childhood learners, due to maturational changes in cognition (DeKeyser, 1994, 2003; DeKeyser & Juffs, 2005; Doughty, 2003; R. Ellis, 2002). The implication, then, is that explicit learning is the only viable option for adult L2 learners, and that instruction is "necessary to compensate for developmental changes that put adults at a cognitive disadvantage" (Doughty, 2003, p. 257).

Whatever the case may be, the evidence from studies that compare the effectiveness of implicit and explicit types of learning with adult learners (e.g., Alanen, 1995; de Graaff, 1997b; DeKeyser, 1995; Robinson, 1996b, 1997b) speaks clearly in favor of explicit learning, at least, in the case of simple rules (DeKeyser, 2003; Norris & Ortega, 2000, 2001). However, few studies have directly compared implicit and explicit learning, and there are doubts about the usefulness of the kind of knowledge that explicit learning yields. This last remark brings us to the third way in which the effects of instruction can be envisaged, namely in terms of the types of knowledge it promotes.

Types of L2 knowledge

For about 30 years now, the potential role and effects of L2 instruction have been discussed in terms of possible interfaces between different types of knowledge that L2 learners may develop as a result of the operation of SLA processes. The most common distinction in SLA research is between implicit and explicit knowledge (see also DeKeyser, this volume).[4] *Implicit* knowledge is characterized as intuitive and abstract knowledge *of* language that is subconsciously and incidentally "acquired" (to use Krashen's terminology), usually as a "by-product" of engaging in authentic communication. In contrast, *explicit* knowledge is broadly defined as knowledge *about* language, a more conscious type of knowledge that is "learned" intentionally. Explicit knowledge can be further broken down into *analyzed* knowledge and *metalinguistic* knowledge (Bialystok, 1994). Analyzed knowledge refers to the extent to which learners are able to form a propositional mental representation of language features, and it involves a higher form of awareness or consciousness than implicit knowledge. Metalinguistic knowledge is verbalized (or verbalizable) knowledge about the structure and functions of language and may involve knowledge of the theoretical constructs and technical terminology for describing language (*metalingual* knowledge).

Although in language performance, the L2 learner can call on each knowledge store separately or simultaneously, implicit knowledge is generally considered the primary type of knowledge for L2 learners to develop because it is the default knowledge store for generating utterances in most instances of language performance. Implicit knowledge manifests itself most typically as the ability to use the L2 system (sounds, words, grammar) fluently and accurately in spontaneous language use. In contrast, the primary manifestation of explicit knowledge is in controlled, problem-solving language tasks that demand learners to pay focal attention to the choice of linguistic forms (e.g., in a cloze task or grammaticality judgment task). Explicit knowledge, then, seems to have little value in and of itself outside its use in typical classroom tasks, though it is also claimed to manifest itself intermittently in more spontaneous language behavior (DeKeyser, 2003, this volume; DeKeyser & Juffs, 2005; R. Ellis, 1997a, 2004).

Regardless of whether explicit knowledge has any usefulness in and of itself, there is also the question whether it can play a role in the development of implicit knowledge. Three theoretical positions can be distinguished here, each claiming a different role for explicit knowledge and for instruction in the course of SLA: the no interface, weak interface and strong interface hypotheses.

The no interface hypothesis holds that implicit and explicit knowledge result from two different types of learning processes (acquisition vs. learning) and are completely separate from each other (Krashen, 1985; see also Hulstijn, 2002). Important to the discussion here are the claims that implicit knowledge cannot be directly taught, that the explicit knowledge which results from instruction plays only a very limited role in L2 use, and that the development of L2 proficiency, and, therefore, the role of L2 instruction, is largely confined to providing adequate exposure and creating an appropriate affective climate for the operation of implicit acquisition processes.

The weak interface hypothesis (R. Ellis, 1990, 1994, 1997b) also claims that implicit and explicit knowledge are two separately coexisting knowledge systems. L2 knowledge ideally starts out as implicit knowledge, for example through the use of instructional tasks that facilitate noticing (e.g., interpretation tasks). Explicit knowledge can be promoted by means of awareness-raising tasks that lead learners to discover their own explicit grammar rules. This explicit knowledge cannot become implicit (although it can be automatized), but it may still create opportunities for developing implicit knowledge by priming learners to notice non-salient features in the input or discrepancies between the input and their own output.

Finally, the strong interface hypothesis holds that explicit and implicit knowledge are not fundamentally distinct but, rather, extremes on one continuum. The implication is that the nature of L2 knowledge can change in the course of acquisition. Instructed L2 learners start out with developing explicit knowledge through instruction (e.g., through explicit rule presentation and focused practice) which they may then proceduralize and automatize (e.g., through communicative practice) to the point that it becomes virtually implicit (DeKeyser, 1997, 1998, 2001, 2003; O'Malley, Chamot, & Walker, 1987; Sharwood-Smith, 1988).

Differences in theoretical argumentation aside, the cumulative empirical evidence from studies in the laboratory, the L2 classroom as well as in the naturalistic L2 environment, indicates that L2 instruction is most effective for developing explicit knowledge (DeKeyser, 1997, 1998, 2003; N. Ellis, 2002; R. Ellis, 1993,

1997a, 2002). However, this type of knowledge is generally considered to be of limited value for L2 communication, at least without the elaborate proceduralization and automatization processes through which this explicit knowledge may eventually become "functionally equivalent to implicitly acquired knowledge" (DeKeyser & Juffs, 2005, p. 41). The reverse is true for implicit knowledge: while no one doubts its value, many remain skeptical about whether it can effectively be developed through instruction. Some scholars, therefore, suggest that "[p]erhaps we do not have to bother with trying to teach implicit knowledge directly" (R. Ellis, 2002, p. 234), but instead focus on "ways to maximize explicit learning and the automatization of its product" (DeKeyser & Juffs, 2005, p. 445).

Factors moderating the effectiveness of L2 instruction

Whatever the exact nature of the effects and effectiveness of instruction for SLA, it seems reasonable to assume that they will be moderated by at least three sets of factors, pertaining to the *how*, the *what*, and the *who* of L2 instruction: (1) the type of instruction, (2) the type of language features targeted for instruction, and (3) the type of learner who receives the instruction (the instructee). Each of these factors will be briefly considered in turn.

The relative effectiveness of different types of L2 instruction

Are some forms of instruction more effective for SLA than others? In order to answer this important question, it is first necessary to identify what the relevant different forms of instruction are. Comparative research in the 1960s and 1970s defined different types of instruction in terms of global pedagogical methods (e.g., the Grammar-Translation versus Audio-Lingual method). Current SLA research operationalizes type of instruction mainly in psycholinguistic terms derived from computational models of learning. Recent instruction taxonomies make a first broad distinction in terms of the direction of the learner's focal attention between form-focused instruction and meaning-focused instruction (R. Ellis, 1999, 2001; Norris & Ortega, 2000; Spada, 1997; Williams, 2005).

In meaning-focused instruction (MFI), the learner's focal attention is predominantly on the communication of relevant meanings and authentic messages (R. Ellis, 1999, 2001). Examples of MFI can be found in the Natural Approach to L2 teaching (Krashen & Terrell, 1983) and other forms of communicative language teaching (CLT) (Nunan, 1989; Prabhu, 1987), immersion programs (Johnson & Swain, 1997; Johnstone, 2002), in some content-based second language programs (or content and language integrated learning (CLIL) as it is called in Europe; cf. Baker, 2006; Wesche & Skehan, 2002; see also www.clilcompendium.com), and also in proposals for task-based instruction (cf. Crookes & Gass, 1993; R. Ellis, 2003, 2005).

Empirical evidence for the effectiveness of strong forms of MFI is somewhat mixed. Evaluations of immersion programs have indicated that while immersion pupils attain high levels of receptive skills in their L2, their productive skills are much more limited, especially their ability to produce grammatically accurate, lexically precise and sociolinguistically appropriate extended discourse. One of the reasons for this incomplete learning is that immersion students are too focused on communicating message content and fail to notice and acquire less salient or communicatively redundant lexical and grammatical forms; that is, they focus on fluency while neglecting accuracy. For this reason many immersion and other content-based L2 programs now also include a "focus on form" component (R. Ellis, 2005; Lightbown & Spada, 1990, 1994), and most SLA researchers now believe with Long (1988) that "a focus on form is probably a key feature of SL instruction" (p. 136).

The term "form-focused instruction" (FFI) here refers to any instructional activity which aims at drawing learners' attention to language form, where "form" stands for grammatical structures, lexical items, phonological features and even sociolinguistic and pragmatic features of language.[5] FFI can take many forms, and several taxonomies have been proposed that can help researchers identify exactly what aspect(s) of a particular form-focused activity determines its effectiveness (e.g., Doughty & Williams, 1998b; R. Ellis, 2001, 2002, 2006b; Long & Robinson, 1998; Williams, 2005). For instance, Doughty and Williams (1998b) propose a taxonomy based on the scalar criterion of "obtrusiveness," i.e., whether the instructional intervention interrupts processing and communication. R. Ellis' (2001) taxonomy of FFI makes a primary distinction in terms of two criteria: where the primary focus is placed (whether on form or on meaning), and how the focus is distributed in the instruction (whether intensively (narrow focus) or extensively (wide focus)). One of the most elaborate taxonomies of FFI is Williams' (2005), which is based on five criteria: in addition to "obtrusiveness," Williams includes "problematicity" (whether or not the instructional intervention is motivated by a communicative problem), "planning" (whether the instruction is proactive or reactive), "targetedness" (whether targeted or general; cf. R. Ellis' (2001) notions of intensive versus extensive distribution), and "locus of responsibility" (whether the responsibility for initiating the instructional intervention lies with the instructor or with the learner).

The psycholinguistic and practical validity of these taxonomies have yet to be demonstrated. Consequently, much research comparing the relative effectiveness of different FFI types has classified the different instructional options in terms of a more general criterion, namely degree of "explicitness": from implicit instructional techniques, such as input flooding, input enhancement techniques and recasts, to increasingly more explicit techniques and activities, such as consciousness-raising tasks, cloze tasks, dictogloss tasks, overt error correction, garden path techniques, and the presentation and practice of metalinguistic rules. Table 38.1 lists a number of features that have been variably associated with implicit and explicit forms of FFI (cf. DeKeyser, 1995; Doughty, 2003; R. Ellis, 2001, 2002; Norris & Ortega, 2000; Spada, 1997). The two columns in Table 38.1 should be seen as the extremes of a continuum.

The distinction between implicit and explicit FFI covers Long's well-known distinction between Focus-on-Form instruction (FonF) and Focus-on-FormS

Table 38.1 Implicit and explicit forms of form-focused instruction

Implicit FFI	*Explicit FFI*
• attracts attention to language form	• directs attention to language form
• language serves primarily as a tool for communication	• language serves as an object of study
• delivered spontaneously and incidentally (e.g., in an otherwise communication-oriented activity)	• predetermined and planned (e.g., as the main focus and goal of a teaching activity)
• unobtrusive (minimal interruption of communication of meaning)	• obtrusive (interruption of communication of meaning)
• presents target forms in context	• presents target forms in isolation
• no rule explanation or directions to attend to forms to discover rules; no use of metalanguage	• use of rule explanation or directions to attend to forms to discover rules; use of metalinguistic terminology
• encourages free use of target form	• involves controlled practice of target form

instruction (FonFss). FonF instruction "overtly draws students' attention to linguistic elements as they arise incidentally in lessons whose overriding focus is on meaning or communication" (Long, 1991, pp. 45–6), whereas FonFs "always entails isolation or extraction of linguistic features from context or from communicative activity" (Doughty & Williams, 1998a, p. 3). There are other dimensions along which FFI can vary that cut across the implicit–explicit distinction, such as whether the instruction proceeds deductively or inductively (DeCoo, 1996; Fotos, 1993; Fotos & Ellis, 1991; Hendrix, Housen, & Pierrard, 2002), or whether it is oriented toward the input or toward the learners' own output (VanPatten, 1996).

Several studies have compared the relative effectiveness of implicit and explicit types of instruction. Forty-nine of these were included in Norris and Ortega's (2000) meta-analysis, representing 98 unique instructional treatments. Norris and Ortega classified these instructional treatments as "explicit" when metalinguistic rules were explained to learners, or when learners were directed to discover rules by attending to forms, and as "implicit" when "neither rule presentation nor directions to attend to particular forms were part of a treatment" (Norris & Ortega, 2000, p. 437). Explicit types of instruction proved to be significantly more effective than implicit types. However, Norris and Ortega discuss a number of important biases in their sample that warrant caution in drawing firm conclusions about the relative effectiveness of implicit versus explicit types of instruction (for an extensive discussion, see also Doughty, 2003, and below).

The relative effectiveness of L2 instruction for different types of learners

Different instructional procedures are often presented as "effective" without speci-fication of for whom and for what they might be most effective. Starting with the former, it is generally believed that L2 instruction will be maximally effective if it is matched to the way individual learners learn (Cronbach & Snow, 1977; R. Ellis, 1994; Sternberg, 2002). The way learners learn an L2 is likely to be influenced by a host of factors, including age and cognitive maturity, cognitive learning style (e.g., holistic versus analytic), language learning aptitude, motivation, attitudes, personality (e.g., degree of extraversion and anxiety), and level of L2 proficiency at the time of instruction. Researchers have rarely investigated these factors in relation to different types of L2 instruction. R. Ellis (1994, ch. 14) and Skehan (1989) provide reviews of relevant research in this domain (see also Sawyer & Ranta, 2001; Skehan, 1998, 2002; and contributions to Robinson, 2002a).

Most research in this area has focused on the interaction of instruction and cognitive factors (especially aptitude and learning style) and is generally known as "aptitude-treatment interaction" research, after Cronbach and Snow (1977). The findings of these investigations tentatively suggest that instructional effective-ness can indeed be enhanced by adapting the type of instructional approach (e.g., explicit-deductive versus implicit-inductive) to individual differences in learning styles and aptitude (e.g., Sein & Robey, 1991; Wesche, 1981; see also contributions to Reid, 1995, and Robinson, 2002a).

There are a number of theoretical arguments to motivate the hypothesis that also age will have an impact on the relative effectiveness of different types of instruction. For instance, the process of maturation is known to affect cognitive functioning radically, resulting either in decreased ability to learn implicitly or to increased reliance on explicit learning abilities, or both (Doughty, 2003; Bialystok, 1997; Birdsong & Molis, 2001). One implication of this would be that for adult L2 learners, but not for child L2 learners, implicit and explicit knowledge interact (DeKeyser, 2000), which in turn would imply that adult and child learners will react differently to different instructional treatments. Such compelling arguments notwithstanding, there has been no research that directly addresses the interac-tion between age and the effectiveness of different types of instruction.[6] Some studies are suggestive of a possible relationship between learners' age and instruc-tional effectiveness, but the results cannot be unequivocally assigned to age since the variable is usually confounded with other potential moderating variables, such as proficiency level, type of target form or type of instruction (R. Ellis, 2002). There is a need, then, for controlled studies comparing the effectiveness of vari-ous types of L2 instruction for young versus older (i.e., post-puberty) learners.

Another potential constraining learner factor for effective instruction is the learner's developmental stage or proficiency level. It was already mentioned that instruction has been found to be advantageous for beginning, intermediate and advanced L2 learners (see R. Ellis, 1994; Larsen-Freeman & Long, 1991; Long,

1983). What is not yet clear, however, is whether different forms of instruction are more effective for some proficiency levels or at some developmental stages than at others. Suggestions of such a relationship can be found, for example, in the recommendations by the Council of Europe's "Common European Framework of Reference for Languages" (2001), which imply that form-focused instruction aimed at developing grammatical control may be effective only from the B1 to B2 proficiency level (independent language users) onward. There are also theoretical arguments for such a limited utility of FFI. According to computational accounts of implicit knowledge development, early L2 development is primarily a matter of extracting chunks and low-scope patterns from the input (N. Ellis, 2002, 2003; Pienemann, 1998; Pienemann & Johnston, 1987), the implication being that form-focused grammar instruction may be less effective for beginners (R. Ellis, 2002). Another argument that form-focused instruction would be more effective at later than at early stages of L2 development, made by VanPatten (1996) and Williams (1999), is that in the early stages, learners would focus entirely on decoding and expressing meaning, not form. Empirical evidence for these theoretical arguments, however, is still lacking. Some studies suggest that form-focused instruction can indeed facilitate the development of implicit knowledge with intermediate and advanced learners, but whether it also works for beginners has not yet been investigated (R. Ellis, 2002).

In sum, although individual learner factors are commonly believed to affect the success of instruction, research to date on the interaction between individual learner variables and instruction has been too restricted to draw any firm conclusions, restricted in terms of both the individual learner variables and the instructional conditions investigated. In particular, there is a need for SLA research to investigate how the different types of instruction discussed in the previous subsection affect different kinds of learners.

The relative effectiveness of L2 instruction for different types of language features

The effectiveness of instruction, and of different types of instruction, has also been related to the nature of the linguistic structure or rule to be taught. Many teachers and researchers assume that instruction is more effective for some language structures than for others. Statements to this effect were made by Krashen (1981), who claimed that only simple structures can be successfully taught, while complex structures can only be acquired implicitly, not taught. Although the implication may be clear, the problem remains: exactly what makes a given structure simple or complex, and hence, more or less "teachable"?

To date, no generally agreed definition or metric of structural complexity exists. Instead, different studies have variably defined complexity in terms of such factors as the perceptual salience and frequency of a structure in the input, its communicative value (or redundancy), the linguistic domain to which it pertains (syntax, morphology, lexis, phonology), the degree of contrast with the corresponding structure in the L1, the scope and reliability of a linguistic rule, the type of processing mechanisms involved in the learning of a feature (i.e., item vs. rule-based learning), the transparency of the mapping between a structure's form and function, its compositional nature, its markedness, and so forth (DeKeyser, 1998; Doughty & Williams, 1998b; R. Ellis, 1994, 1997a; Harley, 1994; Housen, Pierrard, & Van Daele, 2005; Hulstijn & de Graaff, 1994; Williams & Evans, 1998). With so many definitions and operationalizations of complexity, comparing the findings of different studies is problematic. Moreover, empirical evidence for an influence of the nature of the target structure on instructional effectiveness has been equivocal, with some studies finding clear differential results of instruction depending on the nature of the target structure taught (e.g., DeKeyser, 1995; Robinson, 1996a, 1996b), and other studies reporting few or no significant effects (e.g., de Graaff, 1997a; Housen et al., 2005). Also the direction of the relationship between type of structure and instruction remains unclear. For instance, DeKeyser (1995) and Robinson (1996a, 1996b) found explicit instruction to be most effective with simple structures, while de Graaff (1997b) and Housen et al. (2005) reported more advantages of explicit instruction with the complex structures in their studies. Clearly, there is a need for a more fine-grained analysis of what is meant by type of structure and structural complexity in order to select truly contrastive structures in experimental designs.

Summary

It is clear that the effectiveness of instruction depends on a wide range of factors. Three sets have been considered in this subsection: type of instruction, type of learner, and type of target structure. Their impact on instructional effectiveness has been hypothesized for a number of reasons, but for none of them compellingly. And while some empirical studies report differentiated instructional effects according to these factors, a review of findings does not provide a clear-cut picture, and identifying the exact variables that cause differentiation remains problematic. Obviously, other moderating factors also exist, including the intensity, frequency and duration of the instructional intervention, and the nature of the procedures used to assess instructional outcomes. These and other methodological factors will be addressed below.

Evaluating Research and Empirical Findings on the Effects of Instruction

The conclusion drawn from the discussion above is that the available evidence for all but the most general claim, that instruction may have an effect of some kind, is inconclusive, owing in part to lack of conceptual clarity and theoretical limitations, but also owing to methodological limitations and inadequacies. Norris and Ortega (2000, 2003, 2006) have stressed the weakness of much research on the effectiveness of instruction in SLA, which does not sufficiently control the student model ("what are we measuring"?) or make it explicit, the task model ("where do we measure it?"), or the evidence model ("how do we measure it?"). As both SLA theory and instructional contexts are involved in instructed SLA, explicitly justifying educational context, linguistic target, theory of learning, and instructional technique is essential.

It is to a discussion of these issues that we turn now. We do so by addressing the following questions:

1 Which effects of instruction have been empirically investigated, and by which methodology? What are the major research findings and discussions to date concerning the effects and effectiveness of instruction? What are the relevant factors that determine those effects and, hence, the effectiveness of instruction?
2 What is the relevance for language teaching of the available findings and conclusions? What are the limitations? What recommendations can be made for future research on the role of instruction for F/SLL?

Overview of research methods

As befits the complexity of the phenomenon under investigation, studies of the effects of L2 instruction have adopted a variety of research approaches. R. Ellis (2005, p. 9) lists the following:

- descriptive studies of language use in classroom contexts;
- experimental studies of learning outcomes in relation to instructional treatment;
- ethnographic studies, by means of classroom observations and teacher and learner reports;
- correlational studies of different sets of learning and learner variables.

In particular, experimental studies seek to measure the magnitude of the effect of instruction on language proficiency. As discussed in the previous section, experimental studies conducted over the past two decades have investigated effects of instruction in relation to a variety of mediating factors, including:

- Type of instruction: this variable figures most often as the prime independent variable in experimental studies. Type of instruction has been operationalized in terms of such contrasts as form-focused versus meaning-focused, focus on form versus focus on forms, input processing versus output-based, focused or open-ended tasks in task-based instruction, implicit versus explicit, inductive versus deductive, feedback types (recasts, confirmation checks, correction, explanation, etc.).
- Type of learner, referring to age, proficiency level, second language or foreign language context, language background (type of L1, experience in learning L2s), motivation, aptitude, etc.

- Type of target or language feature, in terms of linguistic domain, most research having focused on the effects of instruction on the acquisition of morphosyntax, in relation to, for example, the regularity, scope, complexity, lexicality, frequency, and saliency of the target structure (see Hulstijn, 2005, and Hulstijn & de Graaff, 1994, for further elaboration). Other domains of language have received far less attention. (For examples of instruction studies in the domain of phonology, see Derwing, Murray, & Wiebe, 1998; Díaz-Campos, 2004; Elliott, 1997; N. Ellis, 1993; Gorsuch, 2001; Hardison, 2003; Mennim, 2003. For vocabulary, see Laufer, 2005. For socio-pragmatics, see Bouton, 1994; Lyster, 1994; and other contributions to Bouton & Kachru, 1994; Kasper, 2001; Rose & Kasper, 2001; and Rose, 2005).

It might further be relevant with respect to implications for language teaching practice to distinguish between different types of educational context, such as primary, secondary, higher or adult education; classroom or study abroad; learners (and teachers) with the same L1 or with different L1s.

Effect-of-instruction research has used a wide variety of research designs, including both cross-sectional and longitudinal studies, process- and product-oriented studies, qualitative and quantitative studies, post-test only, pre-test–post-test and post-test–delayed post-test designs. These designs have been implemented in both naturalistic (classroom) and more controlled (laboratory) settings. Sample sizes have ranged from individual students to entire classes and larger (both intact classes and randomly selected groups).

Treatments in experimental instruction studies include oral as well as written tasks; oral as well as written instructions, planned as well as unplanned corrective feedback; focused as well as unfocused tasks; tasks directed at the acquisition of new linguistic items, as well as tasks directed at further development of fluency, accuracy or complexity; meaning- as well as form-oriented tasks; and individual as well as group-based tasks.

Dependent variables in studies of the effect of instruction include the same variety of test tasks as treatment tasks. Norris and Ortega (2000) distinguished studies using metalinguistic judgment, selected response, constrained constructed response, and free constructed response. Both oral and written test tasks are used. Tests may focus on (but without always explicitly distinguishing and specifying) learning in terms of language internalization, language modification or language consolidation.

Conclusions from research findings

Given the multitude of mediating factors and the variety of research methods used, it is hard to formulate generalizable conclusions, and even more difficult to formulate implications or recommendations that are relevant to, and useful for, teaching practice. In the SLA literature, several meta-studies and review studies of the effect of instruction on second language learning have been published in recent years. We have already mentioned Norris and Ortega's (2000) meta-analysis of studies comparing the effects of implicit versus explicit types of instruction. R. Ellis (2002) reviewed 11 studies that examined the effect of form-focused instruction on learners' free production (taken to be a measure of implicit knowledge). Russell and Spada (2006) collected 56 studies on the effectiveness of corrective feedback and conducted a meta-analysis of 31 of those. Spada and Tomita (2007) conducted a meta-analysis of 30 studies to investigate the effects of different types of instruction on complex and simple features of language. Other reviews have been carried out by Doughty and Williams (1998b), Long and Robinson (1998), and Spada (1997), examining experimental research on the role of noticing and focus on form in language learning.

Evidently, the body of research on the effect of instruction on SLA is still growing. An inventory of recent empirical classroom-based research on explicit form-focused instruction includes studies by Allen (2000), Izumi (2002), Erlam (2003a, 2003b), Sanz and Morgan-Short (2004), Radwan (2005) and Morgan-Short and Bowden (2006). An inventory of recent classroom-based research on incidental form-focused instruction as part of corrective feedback includes Han (2002), Iwashita (2003), Lyster (2004), Loewen (2005) and Ellis, Loewen, and Erlam (2006). Overall, the results of these studies concur with Norris and Ortega's (2000) meta-analysis, in which explicit instruction was shown to have the strongest effect on language learning, especially when form–meaning connections are stressed. This finding has been taken to suggest that, other things being equal, explicit forms of instruction are superior to more implicit types of instruction. However, some researchers have indicated validity problems in relation to research design and measurement of learning outcomes, detracting from the reliability of the previous conclusion (see, e.g., Doughty, 2003). Ellis (2001, p. 25) argues for the desirability of isolating different options in researching the effects of form-focused instruction, in order to evaluate their specific contribution to learning. However, Norris and Ortega's statistical meta-analysis (2000) has shown that it is difficult to compare studies in this respect, as researchers have proceeded in many different ways. With respect to the relation between complexity and language learning, for example, different conceptualizations are used, as well as different definitions, different operationalizations, and different measures. As a result, no common agreement or practice exists as to which tests measure which type of knowledge, or what knowledge is responsible for what type of performance. DeKeyser (2003, p. 320) points out that no perfect tests or procedures exist for distinguishing the results of implicit and explicit learning or the availability of implicit or explicit knowledge.

Other researchers discuss the uncertainty of the stability of the effects found, and, therefore, of the generalizabiliy of research findings to different levels of acquisition attained by learners. Doughty (2003, p. 269) argues that in many cases, it remains unclear whether observed effects of instruction are durable beyond the typical post-test or delayed post-test period. Ellis (1997b) stresses that some instructional effects may remain unnoticed, as they may only manifest themselves at later stages of development. For that matter, inclusion of a delayed post-test in a research design is usually recommended, but it does not guarantee that such differential effects will be revealed. As R. Ellis (2001, p. 34) further argues, it is important to realize that different measures can produce different results; therefore, it is essential to report and discuss the reliability and validity of tests that are used. R. Ellis (2001), as well as Norris and Ortega (2000, 2001), stress the importance of a multiple measures research design, using a combination of test types measuring different aspects of L2 acquisition.

As the extent to which the different measurement types can reveal the outcomes of the acquisition process investigated remains uncertain, the use of additional, process-oriented tests is of particular importance. Studies that make use of intro- and retrospective procedures, such as think-aloud protocols, sometimes reveal aspects of language use that may indicate differential effects on acquisition that remain unnoticed by outcome-oriented tests, as discussed by Faerch and Kasper (1987), Leow and Morgan-Short (2004), and Moonen, de Graaff, and Westhoff (2006). Further, process-oriented research may reveal the effect of instruction not only on the amount of learning, but also on different ways in which learning effects are realized in individual learners. Ellis (2001) indicates that hybrid research, using both process-oriented, interpretative measures and product-oriented, experimental measures, is becoming increasingly common.

In conclusion, most research has found at least some effect of instruction on some aspects of L2 acquisition. We have attempted to indicate the kinds of research methods that have been used to answer different kinds of research questions, and the kinds of issues that remain problematic or controversial. Clearly, in order to be relevant, useful, and applicable to language teaching practice, knowledge and information about the effectiveness of specific types of instruction, on individual learner characteristics, and on the practical circumstances under which instruction can be applied in language teaching, has to be available. Effective instruction, in other words, is context-appropriate, that is, its effect, relevance and usefulness depend on goals, learners, resources, and the environment. In the next section, we will discuss the findings about the effectiveness of instruction that might be helpful for language teaching practice.

Conclusions and Implications for Teaching Practice

The potential effects of instruction on SLA are multiple, varied and variable, and a large number of factors have been both hypothesized and found to bear on the effects and effectiveness of instruction. In this chapter we have discussed two sets of key issues that are commanding the attention of researchers:

1   How does instruction affect (a) the basic dimensions of SLA (its route, rate and end-state), (b) the basic components of SLA (exposure, learning propensity, internal processes and mechanisms), and (c) the different types of knowledge and skills that L2 learners develop (implicit versus explicit; declarative versus procedural)?

2   How are the effects and effectiveness of instruction affected by (a) the type of instruction used, (b) the type of learner, and (c) the type of structure taught?

These are, first and foremost, empirical questions for L2 instruction research to answer. As we have seen in the previous section, SLA researchers have addressed aspects of these key issues from different perspectives, resulting in relevant findings for a more comprehensive theory of instructed SLA. What, however, is the relevance of the available findings and conclusions for language teaching? What are the limitations? And what recommendations can be made for future research on the role of instruction with respect to language teaching?

Several researchers have tried to draw general conclusions from SLA research for language teaching practice. R. Ellis (2005) formulates ten general principles for successful instructed learning, including a need for both a repertoire of formulaic expressions and rule-based competence, a focus on meaning as well as on form, development of implicit knowledge (while not neglecting the relevance of explicit knowledge), taking the learners' "built-in syllabus" and individual differences into account, and providing extensive L2 input as well as opportunities for output and interaction. R. Ellis (2006a) considers eight key questions relating to grammar pedagogy in the light of findings from SLA research. Westhoff (2004) has worked out five basic components for successful language teaching in a report to the European Commission. Those include availability of extensive authentic comprehensible input, opportunities for, and guiding of, both content-oriented and form-oriented processing, opportunities for output production in meaningful interaction, and paying attention to individual needs for language-learning strategies. (See Driessen et al., 2008, for further elaboration of these components.)

With respect to the much-debated effectiveness of instruction for L2 proficiency as based on implicit knowledge, the overall results of meta-analyses and other research findings discussed in this chapter tend to indicate a preference for a rule-based perspective in the learner. Types of instruction that focus on form or promote a rule-based perspective show a development of learner proficiency in terms of accuracy and complexity. No strong claims can be made for the area of fluency, because production assessment activities in most studies are controlled in some way. Still, some results suggest that knowledge elements induced by explicit instruction may still be applied in or facilitate the production of spontaneous speech.

One could remark critically that many conclusions from L2 instructional research are already common practice for many teachers, which could be interpreted as diminishing the relevance of this research for teaching practice. However, one can also consider it important that the apparent success of much common practice based on actual experience is borne out by experimental research. Teachers, then, can find justifications for their pedagogic repertoire in the findings in SLA research on the effect, relevance and relativity of instruction. Gass (1995) stresses the relevance of SLA research for the evaluation of whether what is being done in a language classroom is appropriate for language learning, and for the prediction of whether particular phenomena in (individual) language acquisition processes will take place. She advocates that teachers and researchers should work in tandem ". . . to determine how SLA findings can be evaluated and made applicable to a classroom situation, and to determine which SLA findings to use." (p. 16). Lightbown (2000) for her part argues that ". . . there is now a rich literature of SLA research which can help shape teachers' expectations for themselves and their students, and provide valuable clues to effective peda-gogical practice" (p. 452).

Evidently, many teacher concerns with respect to pedagogical issues remain inconclusive, unsolved, or unaddressed by SLA research. It is clear that SLA research and language pedagogy in many respects have their own concerns and agendas. However, speaking each other's languages and being able and willing to listen to each other helps us not to neglect the issues, findings, and solutions that matter to both. One way to do so is by carrying out collaborative action research, i.e., action research conducted by teachers and researchers together, in order to try out the conclusions from well-controlled empirical research in concrete but fuzzy classroom settings with heterogeneous student populations (Gass, 1995; Haley & Rentz, 2002; Lightbown, 2000). Instruction that proves to be somehow effective, not only in empirical research but also in daily teaching practice, should find its way into both teacher training programs and curriculum, syllabus and textbook design.

NOTES

The authors wish to thank the editors of this handbook, the reviewers, and Nina Spada, for their valuable feedback on this chapter. We also wish to thank Nico Schipper and Gert Sollie, graudate students at Utrecht University, for their much appreciated aid in retriev-ing and annotating recent publications on the main topics of this chapter.

1   Unless explicitly stated otherwise, the term "second language," its derivations (e.g., second language acquisition, second language teaching) and abbreviations (e.g., L2, SLA) will be used in this chapter as a cover term to include "foreign language."

2   "Instruction" is thus a narrower concept than "teaching," which refers to any teacher-related behavior in an educational setting. Note also that the intentionality of the instruction or instructor implied in this definition does not necessarily imply any intentionality on the part of the learning or learner.

3   There exists, of course, an extensive body of research on socio-affective factors in second and foreign language learning, but this research has been concerned either with conceptualizing the construct of L2 motivation and other related socio-affective variables, such as anxiety and self-confidence, or with describing the socio-affective profile of L2 learners in specific sociocultural and educational contexts, and its relationship with general measures of L2 achievement or proficiency. Dörnyei (1998) provides a survey of both lines of research.

4   Another common distinction in SLA research is between *declarative* and *procedural* knowledge (e.g., DeKeyser, 1998; Towell & Hawkins, 1994). The explicit–implicit and declarative–procedural knowledge distinctions are sometimes conflated (e.g., DeKeyser,

1998; DeKeyser & Juffs, 2005; R. Ellis, 2004), but the two are not necessarily the same (see R. Ellis, 2008, pp. 429–31 for a discussion).

5   For a discussion of terminological issues connected with the use of "form-focused instruction" and related terms, such as "forms-focused instruction" and "focus-on-form instruction," see R. Ellis (2001), Spada (1997), and Doughty & Williams (1998a).

6   There is, of course, a voluminous literature on the effect of age of onset of learning and the critical age period on the rate and ultimate attainment of SLA (see Harley & Wang, 1997; Johnson & Newport, 1989; Singleton & Ryan, 2004), but this research does not address the impact of age on the relative effectiveness of different types of instruction.

REFERENCES

Alanen, R. (1995). Input enhancement and rule presentation in second language acquisition. In R. Schmidt (ed.), *Attention and awareness in foreign language learning and teaching* (pp. 259–302). Honolulu: University of Hawai'i Press.

Allen, L. Q. (2000). Form–meaning connections and the French causative. *Studies in Second Language Acquisition* 22, 1, 69–84.

Baker, C. (2006). *Foundations of bilingual education and bilingualism*, 4th edn. Clevedon, UK: Multilingual Matters.

Bialystok, E. (1994). Analysis and control in the development of second language proficiency. *Studies in Second Language Acquisition* 16, 2, 157–68.

Bialystok, E. (1997). The structure of age: In search of barriers to SLA. *Second Language Research* 13, 2, 116–37.

Birdsong, D. & Molis, M. (2001). On the evidence for maturational constraints in second language acquisition. *Journal of Memory and Language* 44, 2, 235–49.

Bouton, L. F. (1994). Can NNS skill in interpreting implicatures in American English be improved through explicit instruction? A pilot study. In L. F. Bouton & Y. Kachru (eds.), *Pragmatics and language learning*, (vol. 5, pp. 88–109). University of Illinois, Urbana-Champaign: Division of English as an International Language.

Bouton, L. F. & Kachru, Y. (eds.) (1994). *Pragmatics and language learning* (vol. 5). University of Illinois, Urbana-Champaign: Division of English as an International Language.

Breen, M. P. & Candlin, C. (1980). The essentials of a communicative curriculum in language teaching. *Applied linguistics*, 1, 2, 89–112.

Council of Europe (2001). *Common European Framework of Reference for Languages: Learning, teaching, assessment*. Cambridge: Cambridge University Press.

Cronbach, L. & Snow, R. (1977). *Aptitudes and instructional methods*. New York: Irvington.

Crookes, G. & Gass, S. (eds.) (1993). *Tasks and language learning: Integrating theory and practice*. Clevedon, UK: Multilingual Matters.

DeCoo, W. (1996). The induction-deduction opposition: Ambiguities and complexities of the didactic reality. *International Review of Applied Linguistics*, 34, 1, 95–118.

DeKeyser, R. M. (1994). How implicit can adult second language learning be? *AILA Review* 11, 83–96.

DeKeyser, R. M. (1995). Learning second language grammar rules: An experiment with a miniature linguistic system. *Studies in Second Language Acquisition* 17, 3, 379–410.

DeKeyser, R. M. (1997). Beyond explicit rule learning: automatizing second language morphosyntax. *Studies in Second Language Acquisition*, 19, 2, 195–221.

DeKeyser, R. M. (1998). Beyond focus on form: Cognitive perspectives on learning and practicing second language grammar. In C. J. Doughty & J. Williams (eds.), *Focus on form in classroom second language acquisition* (pp. 42–63). New York: Cambridge University Press.

DeKeyser, R. M. (2000). The robustness of critical period effects in second language acquisition. *Studies in Second Language Acquisition* 22, 4, 499–533.

DeKeyser, R. M. (2001). Automaticity and automatization. In P. Robinson (ed.), *Cognition and second language instruction* (pp. 125–51). New York: Cambridge University Press.

DeKeyser, R. M. (2003). Implicit and explicit learning. In C. J. Doughty & M. H. Long (eds.), *The handbook of second language acquisition* (pp. 313–49). Oxford: Blackwell.

DeKeyser, R. M. & Juffs, A. (2005). Cognitive considerations in L2 learning. In E. Hinkel (ed.), *Handbook of research in second language teaching and learning* (pp. 437–54). Mahwah, NJ: Lawrence Erlbaum.

Derwing, M., Murray, M., & Wiebe, G. (1998). Evidence in favor of a broad framework for pronunciation instruction. *Language Learning* 48, 3, 393–410.

Díaz-Campos, M. (2004). Context of learning in the acquisition of Spanish second language phonology. *Studies in Second Language Acquisition* 26, 2, 249–73.

Dörnyei, Z. (1998). Motivation in second and foreign language learning. *Language Teaching* 31, 117–35.

Doughty, C. J. (2003). Instructed SLA: Constraints, compensation, and enhancement. In C. J. Doughty & M. H. Long (eds.), *The handbook of second language acquisition* (pp. 256–310). Oxford: Blackwell.

Doughty, C. J. & Long, M. H. (eds.) (2003). *The handbook of second language acquisition.* Oxford: Blackwell.

Doughty, C. J. & Williams, J. (1998a). Issues and terminology. In C. J. Doughty & J. Williams (eds.), *Focus on form in classroom second language acquisition* (pp. 1–11). Cambridge: Cambridge University Press.

Doughty, C. J. & Williams, J. (1998b). Pedagogical choices in focus on form acquisition. In C. J. Doughty & J. Williams (eds.), *Focus on form in classroom second language acquisition* (pp. 197–262). Cambridge: Cambridge University Press.

Driessen, C., Westhoff, G. J., Haenen, J., & Brekelmans, M. (2008). A qualitative analysis of language learning tasks: The design of a tool. *Journal of Curriculum Studies* 40, 1–18.

Eckman, F. R., Bell, L., & Nelson, D. (1988). On the generalization of relative clause instruction in the acquisition of English as a second language. *Applied Linguistics* 9, 1, 1–20.

Elliott, A. R. (1997). On the teaching and acquisition of pronunciation within a communicative approach. *Hispania* 80, 1, 95–108.

Ellis, N. (1993). Rules and instances in foreign language learning: Interactions of explicit and implicit knowledge. *European Journal of Cognitive Psychology* 5, 3, 289–318.

Ellis, N. (2002a). Frequency effects in language processing: A review with implications for theories of implicit and explicit language acquisition. *Studies in Second Language Acquisition* 24, 2, 141–88.

Ellis, N. (2002b). Reflections on frequency effects in language processing. *Studies in Second Language Acquisition* 24, 2, 297–339.

Ellis, N. (2003). Constructions, chunking and connectionism. In C. J. Doughty & M. H. Long (eds.), *The handbook of second language acquisition* (pp. 63–103). Oxford: Blackwell.

Ellis, N. & Laporte, N. (1997). Contexts of acquisition: Effects of formal instruction and naturalistic exposure on second language acquisition. In A. M. B. de Groot & J. F. Kroll (eds.), *Tutorials in bilingualism: Psycholinguistic perspectives* (pp. 53–83). Mahwah, NJ: Lawrence Erlbaum.

Ellis, R. (1989). Are classroom and naturalistic acquisition the same? A study of the classroom acquisition of German word order rules. *Studies in Second Language Acquisition*, 11, 3, 305–28.

Ellis, R. (1990). *Instructed second language acquisition*. Oxford: Basil Blackwell.

Ellis, R. (1991). *Second language acquisition and language pedagogy*. Clevedon, UK: Multilingual Matters.

Ellis, R. (1993). The structural syllabus and second language acquisition. *TESOL Quarterly* 27, 1, 91–113.

Ellis, R. (1994). *The study of second language acquisition*. Oxford: Oxford University Press.

Ellis, R. (1997a). Explicit knowledge and second language pedagogy. In L. van Lier & D. Corson (eds.), *Encyclopedia of language and education*, vol. 6: *Knowledge about Language* (pp. 109–18). Amsterdam: Kluwer Academic.

Ellis, R. (1997b). *Second language acquisition*. Oxford: Oxford University Press.

Ellis, R. (ed.) (1999). *Learning a second language through interaction*. Amsterdam: John Benjamins.

Ellis, R. (2001). Introduction: Investigating form-focused instruction. *Language Learning* 51, supplement 1, 1–46.

Ellis, R. (2002). Does form-focused instruction affect the acquisition of implicit knowledge? A review of the research. *Studies in Second Language Acquisition* 24, 2, 223–36.

Ellis, R. (2003). *Task-based language learning and teaching*. Oxford: Oxford University Press.

Ellis, R. (2004). The definition and measurement of explicit knowledge, *Language Learning* 54, 2, 227–75.

Ellis, R. (2005). *Instructed second language acquisition: A literature review*. Wellington, New Zealand: Ministry of Education.

Ellis, R. (2006a). Current issues in the teaching of grammar: An SLA perspective. *TESOL Quarterly* 40, 1, 83–107.

Ellis, R. (2006b). Researching the effects of form-focussed instruction on L2 acquisition. *AILA Review*, 19, 1, 18–41.

Ellis, R. (2008). *The study of second language acquisition*, 2nd edn. Oxford: Oxford University Press.

Ellis, R., Loewen, S., & Erlam, R. (2006). Implicit and explicit corrective feedback and the acquisition of L2 grammar. *Studies in Second Language Acquisition* 28, 2, 339–68.

Erlam, R. (2003a). Evaluating the relative effectiveness of structured-input and output-based instruction in foreign language learning: Results from an experimental study. *Studies in Second Language Acquisition* 25, 4, 559–82.

Erlam, R. (2003b). The effects of deductive and inductive instruction on the acquisition of direct object pronouns in French as a second language. *The Modern Language Journal* 87, 2, 242–60.

Faerch, C. & Kasper, G. (1987). From product to process: Introspective methods in second language research. In C. Faerch & G. Kasper (eds.), *Introspection in second language research* (pp. 5–23). Clevedon, UK: Multilingual Matters.

Fotos, S. (1993). Consciousness-raising and noticing through focus on form: Grammar task performance vs. formal instruction. *Applied Linguistics* 14, 4, 385–407.

Fotos, S. & Ellis, R. (1991). Communicating about grammar: A task-based approach. *TESOL Quarterly* 25, 4, 605–28.

Freed, B. (1998). An overview of issues and research in language learning in a study abroad setting. *Frontiers: The Interdisciplinary Journal of Study Abroad* 4, 31–60.

Gass, S. (1995). Learning and teaching: The necessary intersection. In F. Eckman, D. Highland, P. Lee, J. Mileham, & R. Rutkowski Weber (eds.), *Second language acquisition: Theory and pedagogy* (pp. 3–21). Mahwah, NJ: Lawrence Erlbaum.

Gass, S., Mackey, A., Alvarez, M., & Fernandez, M. (1999). The effects of task repetition on linguistic output. *Language Learning* 49, 4, 549–81.

Gatbonton, E. & Segalowitz, N. (1988). Creative automatization: Principles for promoting fluency within a communicative framework. *TESOL Quarterly* 22, 3, 473–92.

Goldschneider, J. & DeKeyser, R. M. (2001). Explaining the "natural order of L2 morpheme acquisition" in English: A meta-analysis of multiple determinants. *Language Learning* 51, 1, 1–50.

Gorsuch, F. (2001). Testing textbook theories and tests: The case of suprasegmentals in a pronunciation textbook. *System* 29, 1, 119–36.

Graaff, R. de (1997a). *Differential effects of explicit instruction on second language acquisition*, HIL dissertation series 35. The Hague: Holland Academic Graphics.

Graaff, R. de (1997b). The experanto experiment: Effects of explicit instruction on second language acquistion. *Studies in Second Language Acquisition* 19, 2, 249–76.

Green, J. M. (1993). Student attitudes toward communicative and non-communicative activities: Do enjoyment and effectiveness go together? *Modern Language Journal* 77, 1, 1–10.

Haley, M. & Rentz, P. (2002). Applying SLA research and theory to practice: What can a teacher do? *TESL-EJ* 5, 4, 1–9.

Han, Z. (2002). A study of the impact of recasts on tense consistency in L2 output. *TESOL Quarterly* 36, 4, 543–72.

Hardison, D. M. (2003). Acquisition of second-language speech: Effects of visual clues, context and talker variability. *Applied Psycholinguistics* 24, 4, 495–522.

Harley, B. (1994). Appealing to consciousness in the second language classroom. *AILA Review* 11, 57–68.

Harley, B. & Wang, W. (1997). The critical period hypothesis: Where are we now? In A. M. B. de Groot & J. F. Kroll (eds.), *Tutorials in bilingualism: Psycholinguistic perspectives* (pp. 19–51). Mahwah, NJ: Lawrence Erlbaum.

Hendrix, L., Housen, A., & Pierrard, M. (2002). Mode d'implémentation de l'instruction grammaticale explicite et appropriation de langues étrangères. *Acquisition et Interaction en Langue Etrangère* 16, 73–96.

Housen, A. & Pierrard, M. (2005a). Instructed second language acquisition: Introduction. In A. Housen & M. Pierrard (eds.), *Investigations in instructed second language acquisition* (pp. 1–26). Berlin: Mouton de Gruyter.

Housen, A. & Pierrard, M. (eds.) (2005b). *Investigations in instructed second language acquisition*. Berlin: Mouton de Gruyter.

Housen, A., Pierrard, M., & Van Daele, S. (2005). Rule complexity and the effectiveness of explicit grammar instruction. In A. Housen & M. Pierrard (eds.), *Investigations in instructed second language acquisition* (pp. 207–41). Berlin: Mouton de Gruyter.

Howard, M. (2005). On the role of context in the development of learner language: Insights from study abroad research. *International Journal of Applied Linguistics* 148, 1–20.

Hulstijn, J. (2002). Towards a unified account of the representation, processing and acquisition of second language knowledge. *Second Language Research* 18, 3, 193–223.

Hulstijn, J. (2005). Theoretical and empirical issues in the study of implicit and explicit second-language learning. *Studies in Second Language Acquisition* 27, 2, 129–40.

Hulstijn, J. & Graaff, R. de (1994). Under what conditions does explicit knowledge of a second language facilitate the acquisition of implicit knowledge? A research proposal. In J. Hulstijn & R. Schmidt (eds.), Consciousness in Second Language Learning, *AILA Review* 11, 97–109.

Iwashita, N. (2003). Negative feedback and positive evidence in task-based interaction: Differential effects on L2 development. *Studies in Second Language Acquisition* 25, 1, 1–36.

Izumi, S. (2002). Output, input enhancement, and the noticing hypothesis. *Studies in Second Language Acquistion* 24, 4, 541–77.

Johnson, J. S. & Newport, E. L. (1989). Critical period effects in second language learning: The influence of maturational state on the acquisition of English as a second language. *Cognitive Psychology* 21, 1, 60–99.

Johnson, R. K. & Swain, M. (1997). *Immersion education: International perspectives.* Cambridge: Cambridge University Press.

Johnstone, R. (2002). *Immersion in a second or additional language at school: A review of the international research.* Stirling: Scottish Centre for Information on Language Teaching, www.scilt.stir.ac.uk/pubs.htm.

Kasper, G. (2001). Four perspectives on L2 pragmatic development. *Applied Linguistics* 22, 4, 502–30.

Klein, W. (1986). *Second language acquisition.* Cambridge: Cambridge University Press.

Krashen, S. (1981). *Second language acquisition and second language learning.* Oxford: Pergamon.

Krashen, S. (1985). *The input hypothesis: Issues and implications.* London: Longman.

Krashen, S. (1994). The input hypothesis and its rivals. In N. Ellis (ed.), *Implicit and explicit learning of languages* (pp. 45–77). London: Academic Press.

Krashen, S. & Terrell, T. (1983). *The naturalistic approach: Language acquisition in the classroom.* Oxford: Pergamon.

Larsen-Freeman, D. & Long, M. H. (1991). *An introduction to second language acquisition research.* Londen/New York: Longman.

Laufer, B. (2005). Instructed second language vocabulary learning: The fault in the "default hypothesis." In A. Housen & M. Pierrard (eds.), *Investigations in instructed second language acquisition* (pp. 311–29). Berlin: Mouton de Gruyter.

Leow, R. P. & Morgan-Short, K. (2004). To think aloud or not to think aloud: The issue of reactivity in SLA research methodology. *Studies in Second Language Acquisition* 26, 1, 35–57.

Lightbown, P. (1998). The importance of timing in focus on form. In C. J. Doughty & J. Williams (eds.), *Focus on form in classroom second language acquisition* (pp. 177–96). Cambridge: Cambridge University Press.

Lightbown, P. (2000). Anniversary article: Classroom SLA research and second language teaching. *Applied Linguistics* 21, 4, 431–62.

Lightbown, P. & Spada, N. (1990). Focus-on-form and corrective feedback in communicative language teaching: Effects on second language learning. *Studies in Second Language Acquisition* 12, 4, 429–48.

Lightbown, P. & Spada, N. (1994). An innovative program for primary ESL in Quebec. *TESOL Quarterly* 28, 3, 563–79.

Loewen, S. (2005). Incidental focus on form and second language learning. *Studies in Second Language Acquisition* 27, 3, 361–86.

Long, M. H. (1983). Does second language instruction make a difference? A review of research. *TESOL Quarterly* 17, 3, 359–82.

Long, M. H. (1985). A role for instruction in second language acquisition: Task-based language teaching. In K. Hyltenstam & M. Pienemann (eds.), *Modelling and assessing second language acquisition* (pp. 77–99). Clevedon, UK: Multilingual Matters.

Long, M. H. (1988). Instructed interlanguage development. In L. Beebe (ed.), *Issues in second language acquisition: Multiple perspectives* (pp. 115–41). Rowley, MA: Newbury House.

Long, M. H. (1991). Focus on form: A design feature in language teaching methodology. In K. de Bot, R. Ginsberg, & C. Kramsch (eds.), *Foreign language research in cross–cultural perspective* (pp. 39–52). Amsterdam: John Benjamins.

Long, M. H. & Robinson, P. (1998). Focus on form: Theory, research and practice. In C. J. Doughty & J. Williams (eds.), *Focus on form in classroom language acquisition* (pp. 15–41). Cambridge: Cambridge University Press.

Lyster, R. (1994). The effect of functional-analytic teaching on aspects of French immersion students' sociolinguistic competence. *Applied Linguistics,*15, 3, 263–87.

Lyster, R. (2004). Differential effects of prompts and recasts in form-focussed instruction. *Studies in Second Language Acquisition* 26, 3, 399–432.

McLaughlin, B. & Heredia, R. (1996). Information processing approaches to research on second language acquisition and use. In R. Ritchie & T. Bhatia (eds.), *A handbook of second language acquisition* (pp. 213–28). San Diego: Academic Press.

Mennim, P. (2003). Rehearsed oral output and reactive focus on form. *ELT Journal* 57, 2, 130–8.

Moonen, M. L. I., Graaff, R. de, & Westhoff, G. J. (2006). Focused tasks, mental actions and second language learning: Cognitive and connectionist accounts of task effectiveness. *ITL – International Journal of Applied Linguistics* 152, 35–53.

Morgan-Short, K. & Bowden, H. W. (2006). Processing instruction and meaningful output-based instruction. *Studies in Second Language Acquisition* 28, 1, 31–65.

Norris, J. & Ortega, L. (2000). Effectiveness of L2 Instruction: A research synthesis and quantitative meta-analysis. *Language Learning* 50, 3, 417–528.

Norris, J. & Ortega, L. (2001). Does type of instruction make a difference? Substansive findings from a meta-analytic review. *Language Learning* 51, supplement 1, 157–213.

Norris, J. & Ortega, L. (2003). Defining and measuring SLA. In C. J. Doughty & M. H. Long (eds.), *The handbook of second language acquisition* (pp. 717–61). Malden, MA: Blackwell.

Norris, J. & Ortega, L. (eds.) (2006). *Synthesizing research on language learning and teaching.* Amsterdam/Philadelphia: John Benjamins.

Nunan, D. (1989). *Designing tasks for the communicative classroom.* Cambridge: Cambridge University Press.

O'Malley, J. M., Chamot, A. U., & Walker, C. (1987). Some applications of cognitive theory to second language acquisition. *Studies in Second Language Acquisition* 9, 3, 287–306.

Pavesi, M. (1986). Markedness, discoursal modes, and relative clause formation in a formal and an informal context. *Studies in Second Language Acquisition* 8, 1, 38–55.

Peacock, M. (1997). Comparing learner and teacher views on the usefulness and enjoyableness of materials. *International Journal of Applied Linguistics* 7, 2, 183–96.

Pica, T. (1983). Adult acquisition of English as a second language under different conditions of exposure. *Language Learning* 33, 4, 465–97.

Pienemann, M. (1989). Is language teachable? *Applied Linguistics* 10, 1, 52–79.

Pienemann, M. (1998). *Language processing and second language development: Processability theory.* Amsterdam: John Benjamins.

Pienemann, M. & Johnston, M. (1987). Factors influencing the development of language proficiency. In D. Nunan (ed.), *Applying second language acquisition research* (pp. 45–141). Adelaide, Australia: National Curriculum Resource Centre, AMEP.

Platt, E. & Brooks, F. B. (2002). Task engagement: A turning point in foreign language development. *Language Learning* 52, 2, 365–400.

Prabhu, N. S. (1987). *Second language pedagogy.* Oxford: Oxford University Press.

Radwan, A. (2005). The effectiveness of explicit attention to form in language learning. *System* 33, 1, 69–87.

Reber, A. (1993). *Implicit learning and tacit knowledge.* Oxford: Claredon Press.

Reid, J. (ed.) (1995). *Learning styles in the ESL/EFL classroom.* Boston, MA: Heinle and Heinle.

Richards, J. & Rodgers, T. (2001). *Approaches and methods in language teaching*, 2nd edn. Cambridge: Cambridge University Press.

Robinson, P. (1996a). *Consciousness, rules, and instructed second language acquisition*. Frankfurt: Peter Lang.

Robinson, P. (1996b). Learning simple and complex second language rules under implicit, incidental, rule-search and instructed conditions. *Studies in Second Language Acquisition* 18, 1, 27–68.

Robinson, P. (1997a). Generalizability and automaticity of second language learning under implicit, incidental, enhanced and instructed conditions. *Studies in Second Language Acquisition* 19, 2, 223–47.

Robinson, P. (1997b). Individual differences and the fundamental similarity of implicit and explicit second language learning. *Language Learning* 47, 1, 45–99.

Robinson, P. (ed.) (2001a). *Cognition and second language instruction*. Cambridge: Cambridge University Press.

Robinson, P. (2001b). Task complexity, cognitive resources, and syllabus design: A triadic framework for examining task influences on SLA. In P. Robinson (ed.), *Cognition and second language instruction* (pp. 287–318). Cambridge: Cambridge University Press.

Robinson, P. (ed.) (2002a). *Individual differences and instructed language learning*. Amsterdam: John Benjamins.

Robinson, P. (2002b). Learning conditions, aptitude complexes, and SLA: A framework for research and pedagogy. In P. Robinson (ed.), *Individual differences and instructed language learning* (pp. 113–33). Amsterdam: John Benjamins.

Robinson, P. (2003). Attention and memory during SLA. In C. J. Doughty & M. H. Long (eds.), *Handbook of second language acquisition* (pp. 631–78). Oxford: Blackwell.

Rose, K. (2005). On the effects of instruction in second language pragmatics. *System* 33, 3, 358–99.

Rose, K. & Kasper, G. (eds.) (2001). *Pragmatics and language teaching*. Cambridge: Cambridge University Press.

Russell, J. & Spada, N. (2006). The effectiveness of corrective feedback for the acquisition of L2 grammar. In J. Norris & L. Ortega (eds.), *Synthesizing research on language learning and teaching* (pp. 133–64). Philadelphia: John Benjamins.

Rutherford, W. & Sharwood Smith, M. (eds.) (1985). *Grammar and second language teaching: A book of readings*. Rowley, MA: Newbury House.

Sanz, C. & Morgan-Short, K. (2004). Positive evidence versus explicit rule presentation and explicit negative feedback: A computer assisted study. *Language Learning* 54, 1, 35–78.

Sawyer, M. & Ranta, L. (2001). Aptitude, individual differences and L2 instruction. In P. Robinson (ed.), *Cognition and second language instruction* (pp. 319–53). Cambridge: Cambridge University Press.

Schmidt, R. (1995). Consciousness and foreign language learning: A tutorial on the role of attention and awareness in learning. In R. Schmidt (ed.), *Attention and awareness in foreign language learning* (pp. 1–63). Honolulu: University of Hawai'i Press.

Schmidt, R. (2001). Attention. In P. Robinson (ed.), *Cognition and second language instruction* (pp. 3–32). Cambridge: Cambridge University Press.

Schwartz, B. (1993). On explicit and negative data effecting and affecting competence and linguistic behavior. *Studies in Second Language Acquisition* 15, 2, 147–62.

Segalowitz, N. (2003). Automaticity and second language acquisition. In C. J. Doughty & M. H. Long (eds.), *Handbook of second language acquisition* (pp. 382–408). Oxford: Blackwell.

Sein, M. & Robey, D. (1991). Learning style and the efficacy of computer training methods. *Perceptual and Motor Skills* 72, 1, 243–8.

Sharwood-Smith, M. (1988). Consciousness raising and the second language learner. In W. Rutherford & M. Sharwood-Smith (eds.), *Grammar and second language teaching* (pp. 51–60). Boston, MA: Heinle and Heinle.

Singleton, D. & Ryan, L. (2004). *Language acquisition: The age factor*. Clevedon, UK: Multilingual Matters.

Skehan, P. (1989). *Individual differences in second language learning*. London: Edward Arnold.

Skehan, P. (1998). *A cognitive approach to language learning*. Oxford: Oxford University Press.

Skehan, P. (2002). Theorizing and unpdating aptitude. In P. Robinson (ed.), *Individual differences and instructed language learning* (pp. 69–93). Philadelphia: John Benjamins.

Spada, N. (1986). The interaction between type of contact and type of instruction: Some effects on the L2 proficiency of adult learners. *Studies in Second Language Acquisition* 8, 2, 181–99.

Spada, N. (1997). Form-focused instruction and second language acquisition: A review of classroom and laboratory research. *Language Teaching* 30, 73–87.

Spada, N. & Lightbown, P. M. (2002). L1 and L2 in the education of Inuit children in northern Quebec: Abilities and perceptions. *Language and Education* 16, 3, 212–40.

Spada, N. & Tomita, Y. (2007). The complexities of selecting complex (and simple) forms in instructed SLA research. In S. Van Daele, A. Housen, F. Kuiken, M. Pierrard, & I. Vedder (eds.), *Complexity, accuracy and fluency in second language use, learning & teaching* (pp. 227–54). Wetteren: Universa Press.

Sternberg, R. (2002). The theory of successful intelligence and its implications for language aptitude testing. In P. Robinson (ed.), *Individual differences and instructed language learning* (pp. 13–43). Amsterdam: John Benjamins.

Swain, M. (1995). Three functions of output in second language learning. In G. Cook & B. Seidlehofer (eds.), *Principle and practice in applied linguistics* (pp. 245–56). Oxford: Oxford University Press.

Swain, M. (1998). Focus on form through conscious reflection. In C. J. Doughty & J. Williams (eds.), *Focus on form in classroom second language acquisition* (pp. 64–81). New York: Cambridge University Press.

Swain, M. (2005). The output hypothesis: Theory and research. In E. Hinkel (ed.), *Handbook of research in second language teaching and learning* (pp. 471–83). Mahwah, NJ: Lawrence Erlbaum.

Swain, M. & Lapkin, S. (1998). Interaction and second language learning: Two adolescent French immersion students working together. *Modern Language Journal* 82, 3, 320–37.

Tomlin, R. & Villa, V. (1994). Attention in cognitive science and second language acquisition. *Studies in Second Language Acquisition* 16, 2, 183–203.

Towell, R. & Hawkins, R. (1994). *Approaches to second language acquisition*. Clevedon, UK: Multilingual Matters.

VanPatten, W. (1996). *Input processing and grammar instruction in second language acquisition*. Norwood, NJ: Ablex.

VanPatten, B. & Cadierno, T. (1993). Explicit instruction and input processing. *Studies in Second Language Acquisition* 15, 2, 225–43.

VanPatten, B. & Sanz, C. (1995). From input to output: Processing instruction and communicative task. In F. Eckman, D. Highland, P. Lee, J. Mileham, & R. Weber (eds.), *SLA theory and pedagogy* (pp. 169–85). Hillsdale, NJ: Lawrence Erlbaum.

Wesche, M. (1981). Language aptitude measures in streaming, matching students with methods, and diagnosis of learning problems. In K. Diller (ed.), *Individual differences and universals in language aptitude* (pp. 119–54). Rowley, MA: Newbury House.

Wesche, M. & Skehan, P. (2002). Communicative, task-based and content-based language instruction. In R. Kaplan (ed.), *Oxford handbook of applied linguistics* (pp. 207–28). Oxford: Oxford University Press.

Westhoff, G. J. (2004). The art of playing a pinball machine: Characteristics of effective SLA-tasks. *Babylonia* 3, 58–62.

Williams, J. (1999). Memory, attention and inductive learning. *Studies in Second Language Acquisition* 21, 1, 1–48.

Williams, J. & Evans, J. (1998). What kind of focus and on which forms? In C. J. Doughty & J. Williams (eds.), *Focus on form in classroom second language acquisition* (pp. 139–51). Cambridge: Cambridge University Press.

Williams, J. (2005). Form-focused instruction. In E. Hinkel (ed.), *Handbook of research in second language teaching and learning* (pp. 671–92). Mahwah, NJ: Lawrence Erlbaum.

39 Program Evaluation

STEVEN J. ROSS

The major events of the twentieth century, two world wars, the Cold War, mass migration, and market globalization, have led to an exponential growth in modern foreign and second language instruction for strategic, settlement, and economic purposes. In parallel with this growth, the 1960s and 1970s saw an explosion of dramatically different options in language pedagogy, many of which were predicated on strikingly contrastive models of second language acquisition. The early days of language program evaluation in applied linguistics can be seen as an effort to reduce the field of competing models to arrive at an optimal model of language learning. The focus of evaluation in the era of methodology studies was set on the task of examining differential outcome evidence that would justify educational policy to adapt the "best" method. As Beretta (1986, 1992) pointed out, most methodology cum evaluation studies suffered from a lack of sufficient description of the processes that could define the putatively unique methods. The quest for differences between methodological options often confused evaluation with applied research goals (Alderson, 1992), which did little to provide information about optimal instructional systems, or even about what actually went on inside language classrooms. Language program evaluation was by then considered overly focused on differences in products, without any theory of SLA to offer a coherent explanation for why any particular outcomes would be expected. As applied linguistics matured as a discipline, language program evaluation began to look beyond the search for the universal Best Method and started sharpening the focus on the processes that contrastive methods offer in facilitating language learning. The new focus shifted to defining the processes of language programs (Cumming, 1987; Long, 1984; Ullman, 1990), with special emphasis on observation of what actually happened in language instruction. The novel process orientation offered an advantage over the outcomes-centered approaches of previous decades; it could provide a basis for ongoing feedback to practitioners. The process approach thus converged with conventional program evaluation in other social science disciplines, since it could offer an interim feedback function consonant with the two broad forms of evaluative results corresponding to Scriven's (1967) distinction between formative and summative goals.

In language program evaluation since the 1990s, a strong trend has been to utilize qualitative research methods for the purposes of formative assessment. Lynch (1990, 1992, 1996), for instance, relied on a "context adaptive" approach which featured continuous negotiation with stakeholders as to what outcomes they sought to achieve in their program. Working with similar assumptions about the formative potential for language program evaluation, Rea-Dickens (1999) endorsed a fluid and adaptive approach to evaluation, one that would be most likely to raise participants' awareness of their own practices and how current processes may not be in alignment with program goals. McKay (1991) and Richards (1997) had earlier endorsed approaches to evaluation that relied on involving program participants as active contributors to the definition of those goals.

While a typical language program evaluation could still be expected to feature some form of outcome analysis, by the 1990s a mixed mode of qualitative and quantitative approaches became more common. A number of papers in Alderson and Beretta (1992) sought to redress the problem of overemphasis on measured outcomes by adding substantive observational components to program evaluation designs employing the conventional quasi-experimental approach. Lynch (1992), for instance, included an observational component in an English for academic purposes program evaluation comparing an intervention group with an uninstructed control. Lynch noted the asymmetry between the qualitative component and the design, due to the fact that the control group went unobserved in the study. In a direct methodological study harking back to the early days of program efficacy research, Ross (1992) combined quasi-experimental design with multiple outcomes and extensive classroom observation. Differences in classroom processes, however, did not seamlessly lead to accurate predictions of differential outcomes, suggesting that observational data alone might not be sufficient for formulating exhaustively accurate hypotheses about program impacts.

Recently, the focus has gradually shifted from comparative designs focused on effect size estimation to process-oriented studies. Lynch (1996) has carried the mixed-mode language program evaluation torch furthest with approximately equal emphasis given to quantitative "positivist" analysis and qualitative "interpretivist" data gathering and analysis. Lynch (2003) moved beyond the evaluation methodology focus of contrastive paradigms to include the importance of values and ethical concerns in program evaluation approaches, with an emphasis on expanding the range of program stakeholders in the evaluation process.

A key element in the ethical dimension of language program evaluation is the extent to which different stakeholder groups are invited to participate in program evaluation design. Often, evaluation is motivated by a concern to justify funding for the program, or what Alderson (1992) referred to as the "value for money" motive. In such cases, an evaluation may be conducted by an external evaluator who may utilize criteria for evaluation that program participants might not have included in their own conceptualization of the program's goals. In such cases, issues of fairness to the program's participants come to the fore (Beretta,

1986) if evaluation criteria and comparative benchmarks are not first ratified by them. A delicate evaluation validity issue is often at stake, and a balance needs to be struck between competing views about evaluation criteria and methods. Some stakeholders may prioritize the formative aspect of an evaluation, while others may aim to optimize external validity by eliminating potential biases. In comparative designs, the potential for selection bias is well known (Shadish, Cook, & Campbell, 2002), further complicating intervention versus counterfactual designs aiming to provide such comparisons. Selection bias (Mohr, 1992) occurs when subtle differences exist between the program participants and members of a counterfactual group with whom the program recipients are to be compared. Without vigilant monitoring of program delivery and careful elimination of selection biases, misleading outcomes can result. Modern program evaluators are keen to avoid claims of unfairness, and now typically design evaluation projects to be as inclusive as possible, even if a summative warrant is given to the evaluation by the program's funding agency.

Stakeholders

A key step in planning an evaluation project is to identify different constituencies with an interest in the processes and outcomes of a program. In real-world language education, the most likely stakeholders will be the funding agencies, the participants, administrators, and any special interest groups in the wider community. An example of community interest is in migrant second language learning. In business or in the military (e.g., Lett, 2005), the interest in a language learning program may coincide with perceived long-term economic or strategic advantages. Different stakeholder constituencies may begin with highly divergent conceptual starting points concerning the processes that propel language learning, awareness of constraints that may impede it, and about the kinds of outcomes to be expected. Lynch (2003) distinguishes three levels of potential stakeholders, ranging from day-to-day participants, to those who might have a limited interest in long-term program outcomes. The level of involvement by different kinds of real and potential stakeholders in program evaluation planning can be expected to vary, depending on program goals and size. Kiely and Rea-Dickins (2005) acknowledge that different stakeholder constituencies may prioritize evaluation criteria in conflicting orders of importance, and may value various possible outcomes differently. Management-led evaluation, for instance, may prioritize tangible and quantitative outcomes, with the status quo ante or with comparison groups serving as controls, while teacher-led evaluations may aim to discover processes that have the potential for formative, ongoing betterment of the program over time. As Chen (2005) notes, the difference between the scientific view of how a program works and how other stakeholders may assess its value can lead to problems in accepting the results of an evaluation. Scriven (1998), for instance, contends that if confirming the merit of a program is the object of the evaluation, the actual processes by which the outcomes are achieved are not directly relevant to that evaluation goal. In this sense, the "black box" approach to confirming that goals have been achieved will be considered by some stakeholders as a sufficient evaluation strategy.

Evaluation Planning

Language program evaluation planning can be situated in the larger context of program needs analysis (Long, 2005). Just as different constituencies may hold different views on different possible needs language learners may have, there may be divergent views about the content, timing, and focus of the evaluation. Bachman (1981) for instance noted that a basic issue in planning an evaluation is whether the goal will be to gather evidence of outcomes for the purpose of program accountability, or to provide interim feedback to participants about strengths and weaknesses. Chen (2005) suggests that evaluation planners may need to offer different facets of evaluation to various stakeholders if there are differences in expectations as to the need for hard evidence of program impact versus a desire to have feedback that can steer the program towards more efficacious processes.

Program Theory and Logic

An essential component of program evaluation planning is a unified understanding among stakeholders of the program theory. A program theory is a set of prescriptive and descriptive assumptions about how a program is supposed to work in achieving its goals. It provides an explicit model of how a planned intervention will influence a desired outcome. Chen (2005) asserts that a program theory differs from a logic model (McLaughlin & Jordan, 2004; Wholey, 1979), in that the latter involves explicit and graphical models of how inputs interact with moderating variables to produce the desired outcomes. Logic models are often essential for getting stakeholders to recognize required inputs and processes in light of the program theory. A logic model needs to be visual and easily modifiable for stakeholders to develop a realistic idea of the overall program theory prior to the launching of a program of intervention. Logic models also lend themselves to simulation, which can be a useful pre-program step to facilitate understanding among stakeholder constituencies about program processes and constraints.

Program Planning and Design

An early phase in program planning is analysis of program feasibility. Policy makers or funding agencies in some cases may have unrealistic presuppositions about the processes that underlie a language program delivery, and even harbor misconceptions about plausible program outcomes. As an important proactive program-planning step, a feasibility analysis is often needed. The feasibility of

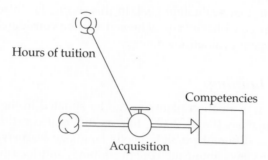

Figure 39.1   Initial logic model

executing a program may require numerous revisions of a program theory and logic model if different stakeholders begin with different expectations about program inputs, processes, outputs, and outcomes.

Program planning can begin with a draft of a program logic model shown to different constituencies or to focus group members representing stakeholders. A key element of a logic model is its adaptability and ability to show graphic or visual representations of program processes and outcomes. One tool for logic modeling is a dynamic systems simulator (Bruce & Matthias, 2001; Huckfeldt, Kohfeld, & Gikens, 1982). An example of how a dynamic system can be used for program planning through logic modeling follows with the use of STELLA (Richmond, 2001). As an illustration of the use of a logic model represented as a dynamic system simulation, a STELLA model is constructed here to show a logic model of an English language program for migrants.

Program planning meetings with the funding agency in the project could reveal that the initial assumption is an input–output model predicated directly on per capita funded hours of tuition. Hours of tuition funded by the program sponsors would lead to an accumulation of "competencies" until a client, a landed migrant or a refugee, reached a certification threshold, or until the number of funded hours of tuition expired. As a dynamic system, the basic logic model is represented in Figure 39.1.

The starting logic model does not have any moderating variables in it. Acquisition is hypothesized to be the direct linear function of hours of tuition used. Although the basic logic model is simple and intuitive to some stakeholders, it is likely to be incorrect. In a large-scale study of task-based learning by adult migrants, Ross (2000) identified two other individual difference variables directly affecting learning rates. Though individual difference variables are well known in the domain of second language acquisition (Robinson, 2002; Singleton & Ryan, 2004), their relevance to the initial logic model might not be initially apparent to some key stakeholders in the program. Once these stakeholders are made aware of the potential simulated impact of individual differences, the logic model can be redesigned. The simple input–output model would for instance be revised to

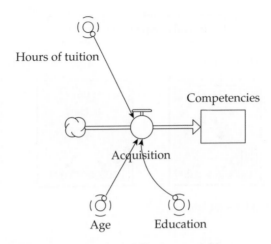

Hours of tuition

Competencies

Acquisition

Age   Education

Figure 39.2   Logic model with individual difference variables

include two new variables empirically established to influence the rate of competency acquisition. The revised model is shown in Figure 39.2.

The new logic model would give stakeholders a more realistic understanding of how the two added individual difference variables would promote or constrain language acquisition in the adult migrant population of program clients. A useful feature of some dynamic systems simulators is the possibility of creating a "what if" interface, so that stakeholders can modify key variables to get a feel for how much variation in outcomes could be expected. Figure 39.3 provides a snapshot of a dynamic system simulator designed to allow hypothetical manipulation of variables known to affect the outcomes of interest. The simulator software can be distributed to different stakeholders so as to facilitate experimentation with the logic model. The model itself can be redesigned as variables considered essential to the program theory are identified. The simulator in Figure 39.3 permits a "hands on" demonstration to program stakeholders of how successfully a 38-year-old client with 204 hours of instruction and 11.5 years of education would do in the program.

The impact of sample simulations may serve to dissuade some stakeholders from assuming that program impacts will necessarily be uniform and linear. Indeed, different hypothetical clients can be modeled with a logic model simulator by changing the settings on the simulation dials. A program simulation result can then be presented as a plausible time series or growth curve model for different hypothetical client profiles. Figure 39.4, for instance, shows growth curves over a five-year time frame, and assumes that 20 competencies would be needed to reach a survival level certification threshold. The simulator settings are manipulated to different projected outcomes for three different clients with exactly the same number of classroom contact hours. Client 1 at age 35 and a high school education would be projected to reach certification in 2 years. Client

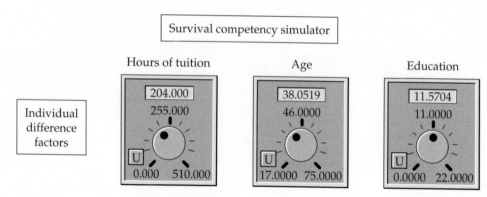

Figure 39.3   Logic model simulator I

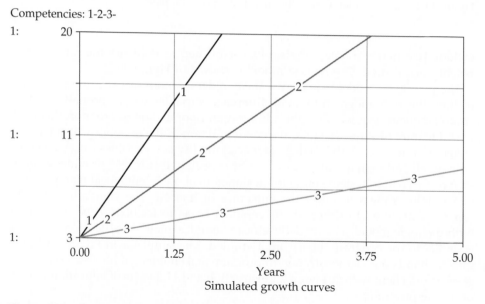

Figure 39.4   Comparative growth curves

2, aged 50, and with 4 years of home country education, would take 3.8 years to accumulate 20 competency tasks. Hypothetical Client 3, aged 65, with no prior education at all, would not complete a certificate under the current program design.

The impact of simulation of the program's logic model is in making potential causal variables visual. Stakeholders can thus better appreciate how a program's implementation may be more complex than they had originally envisaged.

Realistic Moderating Variables

A key feature of program success is to be found in the fidelity of its implementation. In a large language program for migrants, reaching achievement targets can realistically be expected only if the program is delivered as planned. Part of program planning thus needs to include estimations of moderating variables that could interfere with the planned program processes. Often, designers and managers of pedagogical interventions might not anticipate the kinds of factors that may impinge on program delivery. It is therefore prudent at the program planning stage to expand the list of stakeholders to include focus groups comprised of service providers, teachers, and the clients themselves (Alderson, 1992; Chen, 2005; Goldenkoff, 2004).

A benefit of expanding the stakeholder radius is in detecting non-pedagogical factors that may influence program implementation quality and, therefore, program impact. For instance, interviews and surveys on language use among adult migrant program clients could uncover a reduced need to use the target language within certain clients' communities. This information could be used to update the logic model to show a possible constraint on the learning of new competencies taught within the confines of the language classroom. Specifically, if certain transactional competencies are not in fact needed for survival within some clients' communities, there may be an attrition factor missing from the logic model. The attrition model may be based on accounts of adult learners forgetting the content of language lessons through non-use in the wider community.

Interviews with program administrators and teachers at the local level may indicate that in addition to varying needs and opportunities to use the taught competencies, there may be economic factors that reduce the number of exposure hours in the classroom. These economic factors may be directly relatable to macro-economic phenomena, e.g., inflation, or to local micro-economic influences, such as casual job opportunities for program clients. With this expanded set of factors, the logic model can be redesigned to include the social and economic influences on both the input frequency the program ideally would provide, and on outflows that may attenuate the assumed accumulation of program outcomes.

In the present example of the migrant language program logic model, the individual differences factors and hours of tuition model in the first simulation would require further modification. Figure 39.5 provides the revised logic model with a hypothesized linguistic enclosure factor, and an economic factor scaled as a percentage of influence. Both of these components are considered constraints on program implementation and outcomes.

In the revised logic model, a new factor "enclosure" is added to model the rate of attrition. If a client experienced, for instance, no enclosure and had no opportunity to use his or her native language, the influence of enclosure on the rate of attrition would be hypothesized to be zero. Conversely, if an adult client was residing in a community with complete linguistic autonomy from the host community, most transactions and virtually all interaction would be in the client's

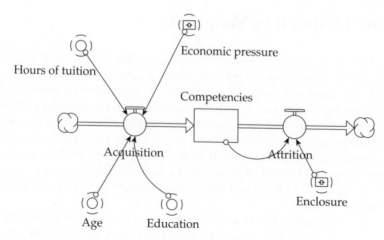

Figure 39.5   Logic model with social and economic factors

native language. The instructional program would be comparable to a foreign language within the larger community where the target language is used.

The economic factor "economic pressure" is also scalar, and shows how the need to work may for some clients compete with their availability to attend classes provided by the language program. Put together, the two new factors can be added to the revised simulator to show key stakeholders how these different moderating variables can be expected to influence the delivery of the program and expected outcomes (Figure 39.6). The redesigned simulator could then be used to allow stakeholders to conduct simulations for themselves with "typical" clients in more or less enclosed communities who might also experience varying levels of economic pressure – the need to trade off language-learning opportunities offered by the program to make ends meet financially. The resulting time series and growth curves would be expected to become non-linear and in some cases reach a plateau in the growth pattern. Figure 39.7 shows the growth curves for hypothetical cases of the first profile (curve 1) when there is 50 percent community enclosure and zero economic pressure. Another hypothetical program client would not reach the certification criterion in 5 years, owing to hypothesized attrition of the unutilized competencies (curve 4). With enclosure set to zero and economic pressure set to 50 percent, the same profile of client (200 hours, 36 years of age, and 12 years of education) would be projected to take 3 years to reach the certification level (curve 5).

The main advantage of dynamic model simulation of a program's logic model is that it can allow stakeholders to gain an understanding of the program's complexity even before the actual program begins. It can help dispel naïve assumptions about linear input-to-output correlations, and give program funders and other stakeholders a deeper appreciation of the possible factors that can come into play in the implementation phase of the real-world program.

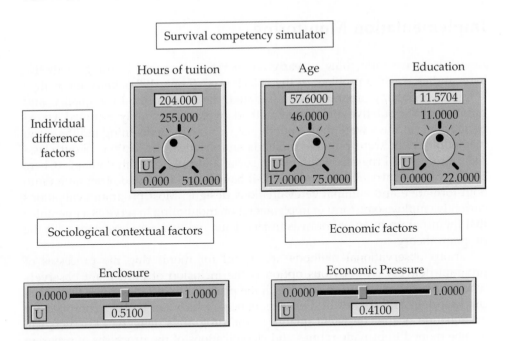

Figure 39.6 Logic model simulator II

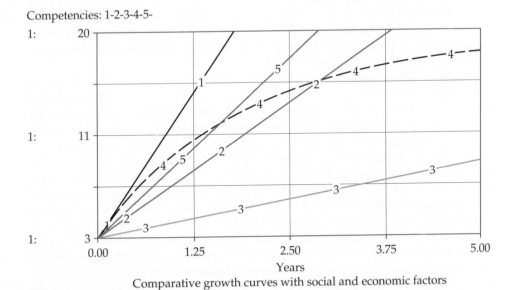

Comparative growth curves with social and economic factors

Figure 39.7 Comparative growth curves mediated by social and economic factors

Implementation Monitoring

A well-known shortcoming of early comparative language-learning methodology studies was the problem of the "black box" (Long, 1984). Once innovative
language pedagogy programs were initiated, the actual orthodoxy, quality, and
duration of the putative differential methods were often simply assumed. Unexpected null findings were thus ambiguous: was language learning indifferent to
methodology, or were putative methods simply idealized fictions about classroom processes? Program evaluators in social and public health domains (Chen,
2005; Wholey, Hatry, & Newcomer, 2004) have learned to build observation into
both formative and summative evaluations designs. Most program evaluations
currently employ some form of implementation monitoring to serve as a guarantee
that the program intervention was in fact delivered in ways consonant with the
program theory.

Various observational methods are useful for monitoring the processes of
program delivery. An obvious option is the inclusion of participant observers
who in some capacity are engaged with the program in different roles. Observers
can keep logs and diaries of their experiences, which can be later compiled for
examination of the consistent quality of the program's delivery. Observers can
also be trained to provide ratings and classifications of the processes of program
delivery (Lynch, 1996; Spada & Frolich, 1995). Focus groups (Goldenkoff, 2004)
comprising different constituency group members can be convened to provide
perspectives on how the program serves the needs of the clients. The focus group
membership selection criteria can be random, or stratified to include those who
are active program participants, while in other focus groups, the perspectives of
those who are at the fringe of the program may be deemed important to diagnose
problems in adequate delivery.

Another goal of implementation monitoring is to examine the fidelity of
the program's delivery according to the program's logic model. The design of
the program may make assumptions about who the participants are and how the
content of the syllabus matches prospective client needs. For instance, in the
above dynamic model featuring the putative effect of economic pressure, a survival syllabus design may be predicated on an analysis of the needs of adult
migrants to use language in particular workplace contexts. Implementation monitoring may reveal that unanticipated changes in economic pressure have caused
a large number of male clients to forego language tuition and instead engage in
opportunistic itinerant work activities that do not require the same language as
that featured in the original workplace language syllabus. The actual participants
in the program may be mothers with small children, whose linguistic needs
may differ dramatically from those of their spouses in the workplace scenarios.
In the event such unforeseen economic factors come to influence program delivery, fidelity analyses, if done early and often in a program, may provide
formative information sufficient for syllabus modification while the program is
in progress.

Evaluability

Program implementation monitoring and fidelity analyses address the key issue in program evaluability (Chen, 2005; Wholey, 2004). Often, evaluation schedules are timed to coincide with the fiscal year cycles when funding for the program needs to be renegotiated. Unless program evaluators and the program's funders are cognizant of the amount of time required for a program to "spool up", and are wary of possible problems of implementation, efforts to conduct a full evaluation may be premature and likely to provide discouraging results about program impacts. Instead of preset evaluation deadlines, program evaluation can utilize negotiated timelines in order to avoid invalid premature evaluations which may waste effort and resources. The concept of evaluability readiness (Chen, 2005) provides a method for assessing whether the various stakeholder constituencies are in agreement about the timing of the evaluation project. An evaluability assessment can thus serve as a precursor to the main evaluation effort. Program evaluations tend to go smoothly when a set of conditions are met: (1) if all key stakeholders are involved in the evaluability assessment; (2) if there is agreement about the fidelity of the program's implementation; (3) if there has been time to adjust the program delivery in light of needed changes; (4) if stakeholders can agree on the goals of the evaluation effort. The fourth condition may be difficult to negotiate when one constituency requires summative outcome evaluation, and another prefers a formative evaluation focus.

Outcomes Assessment

In the main, funding agencies tend to prefer "hard" evidence to justify funding for social intervention programs. There is a strong preference for program evaluations that involve direct "before and after" comparisons of program participants (Bonate, 2000). Chen (2005) notes that impact analyses can be categorized into two general approaches. Efficacy evaluations best demonstrate the potential impact of a program under ideal conditions, and often employ the fully randomized experimental design to do so. Efficacy analysis is thus related to the program theory by demonstrating that the hypothesized causal relation between the intervention and outcome is a strong one, without the ambiguity of potential threats to internal validity. Effectiveness evaluation, in contrast, aims to assess how a program functions under realistic circumstances, where true randomization might not be feasible. Here, the design options may be more akin to quasi-experimental research, where the effort is made to make design controls over selection bias and moderating variables. Both efficacy and effectiveness evaluation approaches involve mainly quantitative data collection and analysis, but do not rule out other forms of evidence to augment the quantitative data.

Evaluation trends in education have in general moved more to a "mixed mode" of evaluation focus, though there is a trend in language education to prefer formative assessment exclusively. Some language education evaluation authors (e.g., Kiely & Rea-Dickins, 2005) express a strong dispreference for quantitatively-oriented designs, endorsing instead various interpretivist designs (see Lynch, 2003). The decision to employ an outcome assessment may, however, depend on the conditions set down by key stakeholders, usually those who are paying for it. Many funding agencies provide continued funding of programs predicated on evidence that there has been tangible evidence of improvement. Since quantitative methods have evolved over many decades to measure change, they are arguably the best tools to indicate that there has been change. Other than in the efficacy framework using bona fide experimental conditions, most quantitative evaluations employing quasi-experimental designs do not yield unequivocal answers about program processes causing the observed outcomes. Their greatest shortcoming is in providing explanatory accounts as to why there has been change. Cook (2000) lists various reasons why educational evaluations have moved away from empirical causal models, and have increasingly opted for formative research, even without firm evidence of impacts consistent with program theory having transpired. Cook contends that experimental designs are still most likely to provide the best causal evidence of program impact, and are still the best approach if program funding is contingent on firm evidence that there has been the desired program impact. Experimental and quasi-experimental evaluation designs remain the norm when the results of impact studies are to be used to guide macro-level policy decisions.

The choice of research design can thus be expected to depend on the reporting requirements. If the evaluation is meant to be formative and process-oriented, evaluation designers may opt to employ qualitative research methods, such as diary studies, focus groups, intensive interviews, and ethnography. The result of a formative evaluation would be expected to inform program users about how the program works, and may indicate ways to make program processes more efficacious. If summative requirements are mandated, evaluators may be more inclined to use different forms of quantitative designs, such as experimental versus counterfactual conditions after randomization, quasi-experimental designs with methods of estimating selection bias (Mohr, 1992), regression discontinuity designs (Shadish, Cook, & Campbell, 2002), and regression point displacement designs (Trochim, 2002). An outline of these and other designs useful in program evaluation is provided in the following sections.

Quantitative Program Evaluation Designs

In efficacy designs devised to test the theoretical accuracy of a program theory under ideal laboratory conditions, the conventional preference is for a "clinical trials" model employing complete randomization. The effect of randomization of the program of intervention to schools, instructors, and students, is to neutralize any selection bias and thus isolate any differential causal effect of the intervention. The mandate to conduct the randomization is usually given to a central

Figure 39.8   Randomized intervention design

authority in collaboration with the program evaluation designers. Figure 39.8 sketches the components of randomized design. Authority to assign participants to the intervention condition (T) or the counterfactual condition (C) rests with program evaluation designers (D → R). The outcome (Y) must be a reliable and valid indicator of what the program theory defines as the consequence of the intervention. While this model has been the gold standard for clinical trials in medicine, it is comparatively rare in applied linguistics or in education in general because of logistical problems associated with total randomization to eliminate selection bias. Few educational evaluators have the authority to make participation an imperative, which is a key reason for its current rarity in education (Cook, 2000).

The analysis of outcomes in a randomized design is relatively straightforward. Since sources of pre-intervention differences are assumed to be neutralized through the randomization process, the conventional null hypothesis is that the means and variances of the T and C groups are equal. Analysis of variance models for testing the fixed and random effects of the intervention can be straightforwardly applied.

A more common situation in applied settings is when full randomization is not deemed feasible. In such cases, partial randomization may still be possible, leaving the possibility of selection bias affecting some facets of the design. In such cases, the quasi-experimental design strategy is to gather more data prior to the start of the intervention so as to make adjustments possible in the event there are pre-existing differences between the intervention and counterfactual conditions. The design thus requires one or more measures of the status quo ante on variables most likely to account for any pre-existing group differences. Figure 39.9 provides a sketch of a quasi-experimental design.

In the quasi-experimental design, measures of potential differences between the intervention and counterfactual groups pre-exist the program of intervention (Cook & Campbell, 1979; Shadish, Cook, & Campbell, 2002). X1 could, for instance, be a measure of language learning aptitude given to all participants. Y1 would be a pre-intervention parallel form measure of the outcome variable Y2. The

$$
\begin{array}{llll}
\text{X1 Y1 D} \rightarrow \text{[R]} & \text{T} & & \text{Y2} \\
\text{X1 Y1 D} \rightarrow \text{[R]} & \text{C} & & \text{Y2}
\end{array}
$$

Figure 39.9   Quasi-experimental design

program evaluation designers would strive to reduce as much bias as possible by partial randomization ($D \rightarrow [R]$), such as by randomly assigning the intervention to intact classes. In a quasi-experimental design, the analysis is typically more laborious and contingent on a number of assumptions. Pre-intervention equivalence in aptitude, for instance, would require that the language learning aptitude means are equivalent before the intervention. Likewise, pre-existing differences between the intact groups would assume equivalent means on the pretest. In the event that the null hypothesis is not rejected for the pre-intervention measures, the analysis can proceed, as in the experimental design, with a direct comparison between the T and C groups on the post-intervention measure of the outcome (Y2). The usual situation is that the pre-program group equivalences are non-random. In such cases, an analysis of covariance (ANCOVA) is required using the pre-intervention measures as covariates (Huitema, 1980). ANCOVA can be used to estimate the differential effect of T versus C on Y2, controlling for the pre-existing differences between T and C on the covariates. Interactions between the pre-intervention measures (e.g., aptitude and proficiency) and the intervention need also be examined to eliminate conditional effects of the intervention. Although ANCOVAs performed on quasi-experimental designs can often yield causal inferences, they are not nearly as powerful as fully randomized designs (Mohr, 1992; Rubin, Stuart, & Zanutto, 2004).

A recent innovation in quasi-experimental design involves the use of a set of covariates predicting a propensity score (Rubin & Thomas, 1996; Shadish, Cook, & Campbell, 2002). The propensity score is the probability of membership in a program intervention group versus membership in a counterfactual group. The propensity score permits case-control matched pairs along a scale representing the covariates. The propensity scores themselves can be employed as strata in an analysis of variance, or as covariates in an ANCOVA, to assess the effect of a program of intervention, and thus reduce the complexity of using a large set of covariates and their interactions with the intervention.

Less widely known in language program evaluation is the regression discontinuity design shown in Figure 39.10 (Trochim, 2002). It is a form of quasi-experiment, but does not require any randomization. Instead, the intervention is assigned only to program participants who are deemed to have the most need. It is thus considered more economical and potentially more ethical, since the intervention resources are applied where there is the largest potential for benefit. A pre-intervention measure (Y1) is made of the outcome using a parallel form, so that the difficulty of the pretest, Y1, is equivalent to that of the posttest, Y2. Depending on the resources available, a cut score is determined from the distribution of scores on the Y1 measures. In the case of a remedial intervention, participants below the cut score are assigned by the program designers ($D \rightarrow A$) to the intervention condition (T), while all participants scoring above the cut score are assigned to the counterfactual condition, and thus do not receive the intervention. Assuming the cut is at the mean, all scores below the mean become members of T, while all scores above are members of C. The outcome (Y2) is measured after the program is considered mature enough for the evaluation.

| Y1 | D → A | T | Y2 |
| Y1 | D → A | C | Y2 |

Figure 39.10   Regression discontinuity design

The main effects test of the program impact seeks to determine if there is a discontinuity or break in the regression slopes separating T and C. The regression discontinuity can be inspected graphically, as well. Figure 39.11 shows that there is a clear break in the regression line at the zero point on the centered

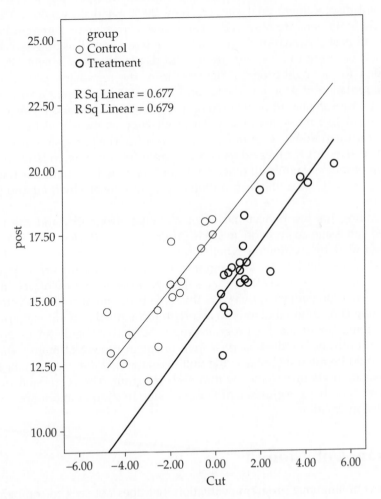

Figure 39.11   Regression discontinuity scatterplot

preintervention measure. The post-intervention scores of the T group have been lifted above what would have been a continuous regression line had the null hypothesis been upheld.

Like other quasi-experimental designs, the regression discontinuity has a few strong assumptions. One is that the membership assignment to the T or C conditions can only be made according to the pre-intervention measure Y1. No migration from C to T or vice versa is allowable. Another is that the effect of the intervention is linear across all ranges of T and C scores on Y2.

In some evaluations, counterfactual groups might not be available for direct comparison. There may be, as in meta-analysis data sets, mean scores from comparable programs reported in the literature, as well as other indicators, such as average hours of tuition and pre-test score means. When such data is available for comparison, another kind of quasi-experimental design is possible, the regression point-displacement analysis (Trochim, 2002; Shadish, Cook, & Campbell, 2002). The data here are observed mean scores across many different programs on pre-and-post test measures of a variable of interest as well as time as a covariate. The object of interest in the regression point displacement is whether the regression point for a single program deviates from the regression points seen in a larger population of programs. Boldt and Ross (1998) examined instruction time in hours across 38 institutional language programs in Korea and Japan, each with pre-and-post test measures of English proficiency as measured by the Test of English for International Communication – TOEIC. The regression model for the point displacement for these data contains an effect dummy code for the single program of interest, while all other programs are coded as counterfactual conditions. Figure 39.12 plots the distribution of program means by hour and pre-post test scores.

Controlling for the pretest means of all other programs, and the hours of reported language instruction in each program, the effect on the program in focus is tested by examining whether its regression point separates from the expected regression line for all programs. In Figure 39.12, the arrow points to a program mean on the posttest that suggests an outcome displaced from the overall regression pattern. If this were the focus program, it could be tested for its effect using conventional criteria to ascertain if the displacement is non-random. The inference about such a program might be that it yields an exceptionally beneficial outcome for the observed investment in time. Not many other inferences would be possible because the unit of analysis is the program mean, with no information about variance within each program. The regression point displacement is perhaps useful as a preliminary step to a larger and more rigorously controlled evaluation.

Program Cohesion

An aspect of language program evaluation that does not seek to compare a program with any particular counterfactual condition involves evaluation of internal

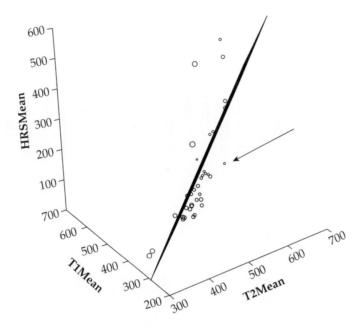

Figure 39.12   Regression point displacement scatterplot

program coherence. The notion of coherence is a quantitative analog to the earlier-mentioned idea of program fidelity, which is normally inferred from qualitative analyses (Miles & Huberman, 1994). Coherence analysis seeks to examine how instructional and assessments practices internal to the program co-vary with each other to produce an emergent property, such as proficiency change (Newmann, et al., 2001). In many language programs, the homogeneity of assessment practices may be incoherent to the extent that variation in achievement may not systematically co-vary with growth in proficiency. Diagnostics for program coherence over time may involve time-ordered analyses of achievement carry-over effects and their cumulative impact on proficiency gains through path analysis (Ross, 2003). A coherent program can be expected to show many non-random paths, while a fragmented one should show relatively few.

Another diagnostic approach to cohesion analysis may involve the examination of residual differences between predicted achievements relative to those actually observed. In this approach, reported achievements are tested for homogeneity across levels of a program. "Level" may refer to streams of proficiency determined by placement practices, or as individual class sections of a course assumed to be employing the same assessment criteria. A linear model can be used to generate expected scores from observed scores. For instance, if grades awarded by program instructors are the object of interest, pre-existing measures of student proficiency, as well as the earlier achievements of the same individual students, can be used to generate an expected score. The residual score

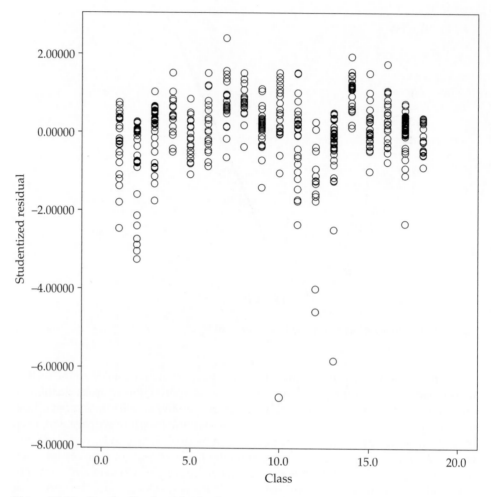

Figure 39.13   Standardized residuals plot

is defined as the difference between model prediction of each student's grade and that actually reported. These residuals for each program student can then be standardized to a convenient metric corresponding to the *t*-distribution, and then plotted by each section or class of the course. Figure 39.13 shows a scatterplot of standardized residuals by class sections. Homogeneous assessment practices within the program would be indicated by a rectangularshaped cluster of residuals, and no class section jutting above or below the rectangle.

As the standardized residuals are expected to have a mean of zero, class sections with substantive numbers of individual students above +/−2.0 may have used assessment criteria that differed from that mandated by program policy. Classes 2 and 12 for instance, appear to have used harsher than normal assessment criteria, as the majority of the students in these sections fell systematically below the zero point in the residuals. Class 14, in contrast, produced grades awarded by the instructor that were well beyond what was predicted by the students' own prior proficiency and earlier course achievements. The residuals analysis in this example suggests that there may be some lack of coherence among the instructors in their adherence to the program's mandated grading standards. After such diagnostics are performed, it is important to employ follow-up qualitative analysis (see Keily & Rea-Dickins, 2005), in order to pursue reasons why there is apparent incoherence. Follow-up interviews and surveys may reveal poor affective relations between instructors and students in some classes, and in others, exceptionally successful instructional strategies.

Value-Added Interventions

Programs may be designed to bring clients to a prescribed level. Evaluation efforts may therefore be focused on determining whether a program has reached the mandated target levels. A vexing problem in such criterion-referenced evaluations not only affects the fair setting of standards or benchmarks, but also can lead to misleading evaluation results. Linn (2000, 2003), for instance, sees as problematic the use of absolute benchmarks, such as those proposed for the No Child Left Behind Act of 2001. Instructional programs that would show strong trends toward improvement, but still fall short of the prescribed benchmark, would be considered by funding agencies as unsuccessful, and thus face sanctions. Programs that in fact have achieved comparably less improvement, but were actually near or above the benchmark at the outset of the evaluation, would be considered successful. The use of absolute standards may lead to issues of program evaluation unfairness (Beretta, 1986) when contextual effects, social capital, and economic factors are not factored into the program theory and logic model.

In reaction to absolute standards in program evaluation, a recent trend has been to develop models that assess the valued-added impacts of a program of intervention (Tekwe, et al., 2004). Such models typically aim to capture the contextual effects and normative environment inherent in clustered data – when program clients are nested in communities that are socio-economically unequal at the outset of the program. Value-added analyses of program impacts aim to assess long-term growth trajectories, employing multi-level models (Hox, 2002; Raudenbush & Bryk, 2002). Such models can assess the moderating effects of contextual covariates on growth over time, and thus focus on the observed trajectories of learning growth, instead of absolute summative outcomes reported as percentages of students who meet the criterion or standard. Although there is no single research method that can solve all of the complexities of real-world applied research, it now appears that value-added approaches are more likely to yield program-fair results than absolute standard evaluation designs (Raudenbush, 2004).

Conclusions

Approaches to language program evaluation depend on the factors that lead a program to the evaluation process. The methodology of evaluation needs to match program needs. If the evaluation effort is endogenous, with the goal of improving practice, qualitative methods have evolved to provide ample evidence of program processes leading to information to improve practice. If the evaluation mandate is exogenous, propelled by an accountability requirement, a wide array of quantitative methods are available to assess whether the desired effects have taken place. Language program evaluation may be best served by moving toward a "mixed method" approach (Chatterji, 2005), employing both hermeneutic and hypothetical-deductive research methods. As Chen (2005) suggests, an evaluation effort starting with a program theory and a logic model can lay the groundwork for providing evidence to satisfy stakeholders interested in outcomes, as well as yielding explanatory evidence about why the program succeeded or failed. Applied linguistics research focused on language program processes and outcomes can benefit from methodological pluralism. A mixed mode approach is more likely to provide evidence that there has been a program effect through quantitative methods, and can yield insights as to how such effects have occurred through qualitative methods. Language programs are likely to be best evaluated with evidence addressing both of these issues.

REFERENCES

Alderson, J. C. (1992). Guidelines for the evaluation of language education. In C. Alderson & A. Beretta (eds.), *Evaluating second language education* (pp. 274–304). Cambridge: Cambridge University Press.

Alderson, J. C. & Beretta, A. (1992). *Evaluating second language education*. Cambridge: Cambridge University Press.

Bachman, L. (1981). Formative evaluation in specific purpose program development. In R. Mackay & J. Palmer (eds.), *Languages for specific purposes: Program design and evaluation* (pp. 101–16). Rowley, MA: Newbury House.

Beretta, A. (1986). Program-fair language teaching evaluation. *TESOL Quarterly* 20, 3, 431–45.

Beretta, A. (1992). Evaluation of language education: An overview. In C. Alderson & A. Beretta (eds.), *Evaluating second language education* (pp. 5–24). Cambridge: Cambridge University Press.

Boldt, R. F. & Ross, S. J. (1998). Scores on the Test of English for International Communication as a function of training time and type. *TOEIC Technical Report* 3. Princeton, NJ: CGI.

Bonate, P. L. (2000). *Analysis of pretest-posttest designs*. Boca Raton: CRC Press.

Bruce, H. & Matthias, R. (2001). *Dynamic modeling*, 2nd edn. Berlin: Springer.

Chatterji, M. (2005). Evidence on "what works": An argument for extended-term mixed method (ETMM) evaluation designs. *Educational Researcher* 34, 14–24.

Chen, H. (2005). *Practical program evaluation*. Thousand Oaks, CA: Sage.

Cook, T. D. (2000). Randomized experiments in education: Why are they so rare? *Educational Evaluation and Policy Analysis* 24, 175–99.

Cook, T. D. & Campbell, D. (1979). *Quasi-experimentation: Design and analysis issues in field settings*. Chicago: Rand-McNally.

Cumming, A. (1987). What is a second-language program evaluation? *The Canadian Modern Language Review/La Revue Canadienne des Langues Vivantes* 43, 678–700.

Goldenkoff, R. (2004). Using focus groups. In J. Wholey, H. Hatry, & K. Newcomer (eds.), *Handbook of practical program evaluation* (2nd edn., pp. 340–62). New York: John Wiley & Sons.

Hox, J. (2002). *Multilevel analysis*. Mahwah, NJ: Lawrence Erlbaum.

Huckfeldt, R., Kohfeld, C., & Gikens, T. (1982). Dynamic modeling: An introduction. Sage University Paper Series, Quantitative Applications in the Social Sciences series No. 07-027.

Huitema, B. (1980). *Analysis of covariance and alternatives*. New York: John Wiley & Sons.

Kiely, R. & Rea-Dickins, P. (2005). *Program evaluation in language education*. Basingstoke, UK: Palgrave.

Lett, J. (2005). Foreign language needs assessment in the US military. In M. H. Long (ed.), *Second language needs analysis* (pp. 105–24). Cambridge: Cambridge University Press.

Linn, R. (2000). Assessments and accountability. *Educational Researcher* 29, 4–14.

Linn, R. (2003). Accountability: Responsibility and reasonable expectations. *Educational Researcher* 32, 3–13.

Long, M. H. (1984). Process and product in ESL program evaluation. *TESOL Quarterly* 18, 409–25.

Long, M. H. (2005). Methodological issues in learner needs analysis. In M. H. Long (ed.), *Second language needs analysis* (pp. 19–76). Cambridge: Cambridge University Press.

Lynch, B. (1990). A context-adaptive model for program evaluation. *TESOL Quarterly* 24, 23–42.

Lynch, B. (1992). Evaluating a program inside and out. In C. Alderson & A. Beretta (eds.), *Evaluating second language education* (pp. 61–95). Cambridge: Cambridge University Press.

Lynch, B. (1996). *Language program evaluation: Theory and practice*. Cambridge: Cambridge University Press.

Lynch, B. (2003). *Language assessment and programme evaluation*. Edinburgh: Edinburgh University Press.

Mackay, R. (1991). How program personnel can help maximize the utility of language program evaluations. In A. Sarinee (ed.), *Issues in language programme evaluation in the 1990's* (pp. 60–71), Anthology Series 27. Singapore: SEAMEO.

McLaughlin, J. A. & Jordan, G. B. (2004). Using logic models. In J. Wholey, H. Hatry, & K. Newcomer (eds.), *Handbook of practical program evaluation* (2nd edn., pp. 7–32). New York: John Wiley & Sons.

Miles, M. B. & Huberman, A. M. (1994). *Qualitative data analysis*, 2nd edn. Thousand Oaks, CA: Sage.

Mohr, L. (1992). *Impact analysis for program evaluation*, 2nd edn. Thousand Oaks, CA: Sage.

Newmann, F., Smith, B., Allensworth, E., & Bryk, A. (2001). Instructional program coherence: What it is and why it is should guide school improvement policy. *Educational Evaluation and Policy Analysis* 23, 297–321.

Raudenbush, S. (2004). Schooling, statistics, and poverty: Can we measure school improvement? William H. Angoff Memorial Lecture No. 9. Princeton, NJ: Educational Testing Service.

Raudenbush, S. & Bryk, A. (2002). *Hierarchical linear modeling: Applications and data analysis*, 2nd edn. Newbury Park, CA: Sage.

Rea-Dickins, P. (1999). Some shifts, twists, turns and tactics in language programme evaluation. *Les Cahiers de l'Apliut* 18, 3, 7–22.

Richards, D. (1997). Program evaluation in TESOL. *Prospect* 12, 1, 4–19.

Richmond, B. (2001). *Introduction to systems thinking: STELLA software*. Hanover, NH: High Performance Systems.

Robinson, P. (ed.) (2002). *Individual differences in instructed second language acquisition*. Amsterdam: John Benjamins.

Ross, S. J. (1992). Program-defining evaluation in a decade of eclecticism. In C. Alderson & A. Beretta (eds.), *Evaluating second language education*. Cambridge: Cambridge University Press.

Ross, S. J. (2000). Individual differences and learning outcomes in the Certificates in Spoken and Written English. In G. Brindley (ed.), *Studies in immigrant english language assessment*, vol. 1. Sydney: NCELTR.

Ross, S. J. (2003). A diachronic coherence model for language program evaluation. *Language Learning* 53, 1, 1–33.

Rubin, D., Stuart, E., & Zanutto, E. (2004). A potential outcomes view in value-added assessment in education. *Journal of Educational and Behavioral Statistics* 29, 103–16.

Rubin, D. & Thomas, N. (1996). Matching Using estimated propensity scores, relating theory to practice. *Biometrics* 52, 1, 249–64.

Scriven, M. (1967). The methodology of evaluation. In R. W. Tyler, R. M. Gagne, & M. Scriven (eds.), *Perspectives on curriculum evaluation* (pp. 39–83). Chicago: Rand McNally.

Scriven, M. (1998). Minimalist theory: The least theory that practice requires. *American Journal of Evaluation* 19, 57–78.

Shadish, W., Cook, T., & Campbell, D. (2002). *Experimental and quasi-experimental designs for generalized causal inference*. Boston, MA: Houghton Mifflin.

Singleton, D. & Ryan, L. (2004). *Language acquisition: The age factor*, 2nd edn. Clevedon, UK: Multilingual Matters.

Spada, N. & Frolich, M. (1995). *Communicative orientation to language teaching: Coding conventions and applications*. Sydney: NCELTR.

Tekwe, C., Carter, R., Ma, C., et al. (2004). An empirical comparison of statistical models for value-added assessment of school performance. *Journal of Educational and Behavioral Statistics* 29, 11–36.

Trochim, W. (2002). *The research methods knowledge base*, 2nd edn. Cincinnati, OH: Atomic Dog Publishers.

Ullmann, R. (1990). Using complementary approaches to evaluate second language programmes. *Language Culture and Curriculum* 3, 1, 19–38.

Wholey, J. (1979). *Evaluation: Promise and performance*. Washington, DC: Urban Institute.

Wholey, J. (2004). Evaluability assessment. In J. Wholey, H. Hatry, & K. Newcomer (eds.), *Handbook of practical program evaluation* (2nd edn., pp. 33–62). New York: John Wiley & Sons.

Wholey, J., Hatry, H., & Newcomer, K. (2004). *Handbook of practical program evaluation*, 2nd edn. New York: John Wiley & Sons.

Author Index

Subject Index

Page numbers in **bold** show an entire chapter about that subject